T

China

This seventh edition updated by

Andrew Commins, Simon Foster, Joanna James,
David Leffman, Simon Lewis, Phil
Charles Young

ROUGH
GUIDES

roughguides.com

Contents

OPPOSITE YUANYANG RICE TERRACES, YUNNAN **PREVIOUS PAGE** BEIJING SKYLINE

Introduction to
China

Splendidly diverse in its geographic, ethnic, culinary and social make-up, China is a nation on the march. Developing at a rate unmatched in human history, already huge cities are adding sprawling suburbs and cutting-edge architecture on a day-by-day basis, even as an ever-expanding web of high-speed rail ties the country together. Nevertheless, this apparent modernity is based on a civilization that has remained intact, continually recycling itself, for over four millennia. Chinese script reached perfection during the Han dynasty (220 BC–220 AD), and those stone lions standing sentinel outside sleek new skyscrapers first appeared as temple guardians over three thousand years ago. Indeed, it is the tension and contrasts between change and continuity that make modern China so fascinating.

The first thing that strikes visitors to the country is the extraordinary density of its population. In much of China, villages, towns and cities seem to sprawl endlessly into one another along the grey arteries of busy expressways. Move to the far south or west of the country, however, and the population thins out as it begins to vary: indeed, large areas are inhabited not by the "Chinese", but by scores of distinct ethnic minorities, ranging from animist hill tribes to urban Muslims. Here, the landscape begins to dominate: green paddy fields and misty hilltops in the southwest, the scorched, epic vistas of the old Silk Road in the northwest, and the magisterial mountains of Tibet.

While travel around the country itself is the easiest it has ever been, it would be wrong to pretend that it is an entirely simple matter to penetrate modern China. The main tourist highlights – the Great Wall, the Forbidden City, the Terracotta Army and the Yangzi gorges – are relatively few considering the vast size of the country, and much of China's historic architecture has been deliberately destroyed in the rush to modernize. Added to this are the frustrations of travelling in a land where few people speak English,

ABOVE GOLDEN STUPA, TAGONG, SICHUAN **OPPOSITE FROM TOP** HONG KONG; GIANT PANDAS, SICHUAN

the writing system is alien and foreigners are sometimes viewed as exotic objects of intense curiosity – though overall you'll find that the Chinese, despite a reputation for curtness, are generally hospitable and friendly.

Where to go

As China has opened up in recent years, so the emphasis on tourism has changed. Many well-known cities and sights have become so developed that their charm has vanished, while in remoter regions – particularly Tibet, Yunnan and the northwest – previously restricted or "undiscovered" places have become newly accessible. The following outline is a selection of both "classic" China sights and less-known attractions, which should come in handy when planning a schedule.

Inevitably, **Beijing** is on everyone's itinerary, and the Great Wall and the splendour of the Forbidden City are certainly not to be missed; the capital also offers some of the country's best food and nightlife. Chengde, too, just north of Beijing, has some stunning imperial buildings, constructed by emperors when this was their favoured retreat for the summer.

South of the capital, the **Yellow River** valley is the cradle of Chinese civilization, where remnants of the dynastic age lie scattered in a unique landscape of loess terraces. The cave temples at Datong and Luoyang are magnificent, with huge Buddhist sculptures staring out impassively across their now industrialized settings. Of the historic capitals, **Xi'an** is the most obvious destination, where the celebrated

0 | 600
kilometres

N

KAZAKHSTAN

Lake Balkhash

RUSSIA

MONGOLIA

ALTAI MOUNTAINS

Altay

Almaty

BISHKEK
KYRGYZSTAN

Torugart Pass

Yining

Ürümqi

Turpan

Hami

TIAN SHAN MOUNTAINS

Kashgar

Korla

XINJIANG

PAMIR MOUNTAINS

Khunjerab
Pass

Khotan

TAKLAMAKAN DESERT

Mogao
Caves

Dunhuang

Jiayuguan

KUNLUN MOUNTAINS

Golmud

Qinghai Lake

DISPUTED BOUNDARY

Ali

Mount
Kailash

TIBET

QINGHAI

Yangtze River

Yellow River

DISPUTED BOUNDARY

DELHI

NEPAL

Shigatse

Lhasa

SICHUAN

HIMALAYAS

Zhangmu

KATHMANDU

Mount
Everest

THIMPHU

BHUTAN

DISPUTED
BOUNDARY

Mekong River (Lancang)

Salween River (Nu Jiang)

INDIA

Tiger
Leaping
Gorge

Lijiang

Xiagua

BANGLADESH

DHAKA

Kolkata
(Calcutta)

BURMA
(MYANMAR)

BAY OF
BENGAL

XISHUANGBANNA

Jinghong

Mo Han

Kunming

THAILAND

ANHUI	安徽	JIANGXI	江西
BEIJING SHI (BJS)	北京市	JILIN	吉林
CHONGQING SHI	重庆市	LIAONING	辽宁
FUJIAN	福建	MACAU	澳门
GANSU	甘肃	NINGXIA	宁夏
GUANGDONG	广东	QINGHAI	青海
GUANGXI	广西	SHAANXI	陕西
GUIZHOU	贵州	SHANDONG	山东
HEBEI	河北	SHANGHAI SHI	上海市
HEILONGJIANG	黑龙江	SHANXI	山西
HENAN	河南	SICHUAN	四川
HONG KONG	香港	TIANJIN SHI (TJS)	天津市
HUBEI	湖北	TIBET	西藏
HUNAN	湖南	XINJIANG	新疆
INNER MONGOLIA	内蒙古	YUNNAN	云南
JIANGSU	江苏	ZHEJIANG	浙江

MARTIAL ARTS

Thousands of **martial arts** have evolved in China, usually in isolated communities that had to defend themselves, such as temples and clan villages. All, though, can be classed into two basic types: external, or hard, styles concentrate on building up physical strength to overpower opponents; the trickier internal, or soft, styles concentrate on developing and focusing the internal energy known as *qi*. Both styles use forms – prearranged sets of movements – to develop the necessary speed, power and timing; as well as kicks, punches and open palm strikes, they also incorporate movements inspired by animals.

The most famous external style is **Shaolin kung fu**, developed in the Shaolin Temple in Henan province (see p.266) and known for powerful kicks and animal styles – notably eagle, mantis and monkey. The classic Shaolin weapon is the staff, and there's even a drunken form, where the practitioner sways and lurches as if inebriated.

But the style that you're most likely to see – it's practised in the open air all over the country – is the internal **tai ji quan**. The body is held in a state of minimal tension to create the art's characteristic "soft" appearance. Its emphasis on slow movements and increasing *qi* flow means it is excellent for health, and it's a popular workout for the elderly.

Terracotta Army still stands guard over the tomb of Emperor Qin Shi Huang. Other ancient towns include sleepy Kaifeng in Henan, and Qufu, the birthplace of Confucius, in Shandong, both offering architectural treasures and an intimate, human scale that's missing in the large cities. The area is also well supplied with **holy mountains**, providing both beautiful scenery and a rare continuity with the past: Tai Shan is perhaps the grandest and most imperial of the country's pilgrimage sites; Song Shan in Henan sees followers of the contemporary kung fu craze making the trek to the Shaolin Temple, where the art originated; and Wutai Shan in Shanxi features some of the best-preserved religious sites in the country.

Dominating China's east coast near the mouth of the Yangzi, **Shanghai** is the mainland's most Westernized city, a booming port where the Art Deco monuments of the old European-built Bund – the riverside business centre – rub shoulders with a hyper-modern metropolis, crowned with two of the world's tallest skyscrapers. It's interesting to contrast Shanghai's cityscape with that of rival business hub **Hong Kong**, off China's south coast. With its colonial heritage and refreshingly cosmopolitan outlook, there's almost nothing Hong Kong cannot offer in the way of tourist facilities, from fine beaches to great eating, drinking and nightlife. Nearby **Macau** is also worth a visit, if not for its casinos then for its Baroque churches and Portuguese cuisine.

In the southwest of the country, Sichuan's **Chengdu** and Yunnan's **Kunming** remain two of China's most easy-going provincial capitals, and the entire region is, by any standards, exceptionally diverse, with landscapes encompassing everything from snowbound summits and alpine lakes to steamy tropical jungles. The karst (limestone peak) scenery is particularly renowned, especially along the Li River between **Yangshuo** and **Guilin** in Guangxi. In Sichuan, pilgrims flock to see the colossal Great Buddha at **Leshan**, and to ascend the holy mountain of **Emei Shan**; to the east, the city of **Chongqing** marks the start of river trips down the **Yangzi**, Asia's longest river, through the **Three Gorges**. As Yunnan and Guangxi share borders with Vietnam, Laos

FACT FILE

• With an **area** of 9.6 million square kilometres, China is the fourth-largest country in the world and the most populous nation on earth, with around 1.35 billion people. Of these, 92 percent are of the **Han** ethnic group, with the remainder comprising about sixty minorities such as Mongols, Uyghurs and Tibetans.

• The main **religions** are Buddhism, Taoism and Christianity, though the country is officially atheist.

• China's longest river is the **Yangzi** (6275km) and the highest peak is **Qomolongma** – Mount Everest (8850m) – on the Nepalese border.

• The **Chinese Communist Party** is the sole political organization, and is divided into Executive, Legislative and Judicial branches. The chief of state (President) and the head of government (Premier) are elected for five-year terms at the National People's Congress.

• After decades of state planning, the **economy** is now mixed, with nationally owned enterprises on the decline and free-market principles ubiquitous.

and Burma, while Sichuan rubs up against Tibet, it's not surprising to find that the region is home to near-extinct wildlife and dozens of ethnic autonomous regions. The attractions of the latter range from the traditional Bai town of **Dali**, the Naxi town of **Lijiang** and the Dai villages of **Xishuangbanna** in Yunnan, to the Khampa heartlands of western Sichuan, the exuberant festivals and textiles of Guizhou's Miao and the wooden architecture of Dong settlements in Guangxi's north.

The huge area of China referred to as the Northwest is where the people thin out and real wilderness begins. Inner Mongolia, just hours from Beijing, is already at the frontiers of Central Asia; here you can follow in the footsteps of Genghis Khan by going horseriding on the endless grasslands of the steppe. To the south and west, the old **Silk Road** heads out of Xi'an right to and through China's western borders, via **Jiayuguan**, terminus of the Great Wall of China, and the lavish Buddhist cave art in the sandy deserts of **Dunhuang**.

West of here lie the mountains and deserts of vast Xinjiang, where China blends into old Turkestan and where simple journeys between towns become modern travel epics. The oasis cities of **Turpan** and **Kashgar**, with their bazaars and Muslim heritage, are the main attractions, though the blue waters of **Tian Chi**, offering alpine scenery in the midst of searing desert, are deservedly popular. Beyond Kashgar, travellers face some of the most adventurous routes of all, over the Khunjerab and Torugut passes to Pakistan and Kyrgyzstan respectively.

Tibet remains an exotic destination, especially if you come across the border from Nepal or brave the long road in from Golmud in Qinghai province. Despite fifty years of Chinese rule, coupled with a mass migration of Han Chinese into the region, the manifestations of Tibetan culture remain intact – the Potala Palace in **Lhasa**, red-robed monks, lines of pilgrims turning prayer wheels, butter sculptures and gory frescoes decorating monastery halls. And Tibet's mountain scenery, which includes **Mount Everest**, is worth the trip in itself, even if opportunities for independent travel are more restricted than elsewhere in China.

Author picks

Our authors spent eight months researching every corner of China, from sprawling Mongolian grasslands to city nightclubs, Tibet's awe-inspiring mountains and Beijing's maze of *hutongs*. These destinations are some of their personal favourites.

High-tech cityscapes: For superlative views of electrifying urban architecture, head to the Peak in Hong Kong (p.543) or Shanghai's Financial Centre (p.366) – preferably at night – and gaze down across forests of luminous, futuristic towers.

Ethnic minorities: Experience China's cultural diversity among Miao hamlets (pp.630–633), Tibetan monastery towns (pp.881–909), Dai and Bai villages (p.669), Uyghur mosques (p.838) and Mongolian nomad tents (p.230).

Epic scenery: Drink in dramatic landscapes at Lake Karakul, its fridgid shores grazed by bactrian camels (p.849); Zhangjiajie's spectacular forest of splintered stone pinnacles, wreathed in cloud (p.435); and the grandeur of Meili Xue Shan's frosted summit (p.689).

Chinese cuisine: Indulge yourself with a crispy, calorie-laden Peking duck in Beijing (p.108), a simple bowl of beef noodles in Lanzhou (p.785), a bright and noisy *dim sum* breakfast in Hong Kong (p.568), or one of Sichuan's scorching, chilli-laden hotpots (p.724).

Top hikes: Wear out your hiking shoes on a two-day trail through Tiger Leaping Gorge (p.681); the 65km-long staircase to the summit of Emei Shan (p.735); or a two-hour leg stretch along Hong Kong's Dragon's Back path.

Traditional architecture: Explore the medieval walled town of Pingyao (p.252), Jokhang Tibetan temple (p.872), domestic buildings at Yixian (p.403), Dong drum towers at Zhaoxing (p.612), and Zigong's merchant guildhalls (p.740).

Vanished cultures: The country's inhospitable, far western fringes hide remains of long-forgotten civilizations: Tibet's all-but-unheard-of Guge Kingdom (p.908); and the haystack-shaped mausoleums of Ningxia's Western Xia rulers (p.225).

> Our author recommendations don't end here. We've flagged up our favourite places – a perfectly sited hotel, an atmospheric café, a special restaurant – throughout the guide, highlighted with the ★ symbol.

FROM TOP FINANCIAL CENTRE OBSERVATION DECK, SHANGHAI; THE JOKHANG, LHASA; DESERT DUNES, DUNHUANG

When to go

China's climate is extremely diverse. The **south** is subtropical, with wet, humid summers (April–Sept), when temperatures can approach 40°C, and a typhoon season on the southeast coast between July and September. Though it is often still hot enough to swim in the sea in December, the short winters (Jan–March) can be surprisingly chilly.

Central China has brief, cold winters, with temperatures dipping below zero, and long, hot, humid summers: the three Yangzi cities – Chongqing, Wuhan and Nanjing – are proverbially referred to as China's three "furnaces". Rainfall here is high all year round. The **Yellow River basin** marks a rough boundary beyond which central heating is fitted as standard in buildings, helping to make the region's harsh winters a little more tolerable. Winter temperatures in Beijing rarely rise above freezing from December to March, and biting winds off the Mongolian plains add a vicious wind-chill factor, yet summers can be well over 30°C. In **Inner Mongolia** and **Dongbei**, winters are at least clear and dry, but temperatures remain way below zero, while summers can be uncomfortably warm. **Xinjiang** gets fiercely hot in summer, though without the humidity of the rest of the country, and winters are as bitter as anywhere else in northern China. **Tibet** is ideal in midsummer, when its mountain plateaus are pleasantly warm and dry; in winter, however, temperatures in the capital, Lhasa, frequently fall below freezing.

Overall, the **best time to visit** China is spring or autumn, when the weather is at its most temperate.

AVERAGE TEMPERATURES AND RAINFALL

	Jan	Feb	Mar	Apr	May	Jun	Jul	Aug	Sep	Oct	Nov	Dec
BEIJING												
Max/min (°C)	1/-10	4/-8	11/-1	21/7	27/13	31/18	31/21	30/20	26/14	20/6	9/-2	3/-8
Max/min (°F)	34/14	39/18	52/30	70/45	81/55	88/64	88/70	86/68	79/57	68/43	48/28	37/18
rainfall (mm)	4	5	8	17	35	78	243	141	58	16	11	3
CHONGQING												
Max/min (°C)	9/5	13/7	18/11	23/16	27/19	29/22	34/24	35/25	28/22	22/16	16/12	3/-8
Max/min (°F)	48/41	55/45	64/52	73/61	81/66	84/72	93/75	95/77	82/72	72/61	61/54	37/18
rainfall (mm)	15	20	38	99	142	180	142	122	150	112	48	20
HONG KONG												
Max/min (°C)	18/13	17/13	19/16	24/19	28/23	29/26	31/26	31/26	29/25	27/23	23/18	20/15
Max/min (°F)	64/55	63/55	66/61	75/66	82/73	84/79	88/79	88/79	84/77	81/73	73/64	68/59
rainfall (mm)	33	46	74	137	292	394	381	367	257	114	43	31
KUNMING												
Max/min (°C)	20/8	22/9	25/12	28/16	29/18	29/19	28/19	28/19	28/18	24/15	22/12	20/8
Max/min (°F)	68/46	72/48	77/54	82/61	84/64	84/66	82/66	82/66	82/64	75/59	72/54	68/46
rainfall (mm)	8	18	28	41	127	132	196	198	97	51	56	15
SHANGHAI												
Max/min (°C)	8/1	8/1	13/4	19/10	25/15	28/19	32/23	32/23	28/19	23/14	17/7	12/2
Max/min (°F)	46/34	46/34	55/39	66/50	77/59	82/66	90/73	90/73	82/66	73/57	63/45	54/36
rainfall (mm)	48	58	84	94	94	180	147	142	130	71	51	36

OPPOSITE FROM TOP DRAGON BACKBONE RICE TERRACES (P.609); TAIJI ON THE BUND SHANGHAI (P.352)

31

things not to miss

It's not possible to see everything that China has to offer in one trip – and we don't suggest you try. What follows, in no particular order, is a selective taste of the country's highlights: stunning scenery, distinctive cuisine, exuberant festivals and monumental architecture. All highlights have a page reference to take you straight into the Guide, where you can find out more. Coloured numbers refer to chapters in the Guide section.

1

1 TERRACOTTA ARMY, XI'AN
Page 212
These 2200-year-old, life-sized warriors protect the tomb of China's first emperor.

2 JIAYUGUAN FORT, GANSU
Page 806
Famously lonely desert outpost, guarding the remote western tail end of the Great Wall.

3 CENTRAL'S SKYLINE, HONG KONG
Page 549
Indulge in afternoon tea while admiring one of the world's most spectacular cityscapes.

16

17

21

22

25

26

27

23 LIJIANG, YUNNAN

Page 672

Attractive ancient town, now a lively tourist fairground of cobbled lanes and rustic wooden houses.

24 KASHGAR'S SUNDAY MARKET

Page 840

Watch Central Asian crowds trading in livestock, carpets and knives at Xinjiang's premier frontier bazaar.

25 FORBIDDEN CITY, BEIJING

Page 70

Once the sole preserves of emperors, the centre of the Chinese imperial universe is now open to all.

26 PEKING DUCK

Page 108

Tuck into this delicious northern Chinese speciality – all crispy skin and juicy meat, eaten in a pancake.

27 MEILI XUE SHAN

Page 689

A wilderness area in northwestern Yunnan, holy to Tibetans, which offers superlative hiking and staggering scenery.

30

31

Itineraries

China is vast, and you'll barely be able to scratch the surface on a single trip. The following itineraries will, however, give you an in-depth look at some of the country's most fascinating areas – the Grand Tour covers the essentials, while the other suggested routes cover the trip to the deserts of the west, and China's tropical southwestern corner.

GRAND TOUR

This tour ticks the major boxes – historical sights, gorgeous countryside and sizzling cities. Allow two weeks in a hurry, or three at a more leisurely pace.

❶ **Beijing** The Chinese capital is packed with essential sights, including the Forbidden City, the Summer Palace and the Great Wall. **See p.60**

❷ **Pingyao** Step back in time inside the walls of this charming, traffic-free Ming-dynasty town, spending the night at a traditional courtyard inn. **See p.252**

❸ **Xi'an** Dynastic capital for a millennium, Xi'an is filled with treasures, including the enigmatic Terracotta Army, built to guard the tomb of China's despotic first emperor. **See p.197**

❹ **Chengdu** The Sichuanese capital features traditional teahouses, fire-breathing opera, lively temples and locally bred pandas. **See p.715**

❺ **Three Gorges** Take a three-day cruise down this impressive stretch of the mighty Yangtze River, between Chongqing and the massive Three Gorges Dam. **See p.752**

❻ **Yangshuo** Cycle between jagged limestone peaks and brilliant green paddy fields surrounding Yangshuo village, looking like something straight off a Chinese scroll painting. **See p.603**

❼ **Hong Kong** Stunning cityscapes, modern conveniences, serious shopping, glorious beaches, wonderful mountain trails and superb cuisine – this bustling territory has it all. **See p.528**

WILD WEST

This three-week-long trip takes you from Beijing to China's Wild West, where you can ride horses across Mongolian grasslands, or soak up Uyghur culture in Xinjiang.

❶ **Beijing** Before setting out, get a taster of northwestern China in Beijing's Muslim quarter, where street hawkers sell delicious skewers of barbecued lamb. **See p.60**

❷ **Datong** Cycle around Datong's rebuilt city walls, then bus out to giant Buddhist sculptures at the Yungang caves, and the gravity-defying Hanging Temple. **See p.239**

❸ **Grasslands** Use pleasant Hohhot, the capital of Inner Mongolia, for exploring the never-ending grasslands to the north, galloping across the plains on a tiny steed. **See p.236**

❹ **Shapotou** See the mighty Yellow River flowing smoothly between desert dunes at this tiny, remote resort town in up-country rural Ningxia – a spellbinding sight. **See p.221**

❺ **Lanzhou** Slurp down outstanding beef noodles at this former garrison town along the fabled Silk Road, the gateway to China's Muslim northwest. **See p.781**

ABOVE PINGYAO, SHANXI; STEAMED BUNS FOR SALE

❻ Jiayuguan The fortress at the Great Wall's western extremity, over 2000km from Beijing, impressive for its mighty defences yet dwarfed by the stark desert scenery. **See p.806**

❼ Dunhuang Ride a camel across 300m-high dunes outside this small city, then explore the marvellous galleries of ancient Buddhist sculptures at the Mogao caves. **See p.808**

❽ Turpan Small, relaxed oasis town, with a main street shaded by grape trellises and a surrounding desert packed with historical relics from its former Silk Road heyday. **See p.828**

❾ Kashgar Frontier city where Chinese, Uyghur and Central Asian cultures mix: don't miss the astonishing Sunday Bazaar, crammed with metalwork, spices and livestock traders. **See p.837**

SIGHTS OF THE SOUTHWEST

The southwestern provinces offer spellbinding mountain vistas, karst-dotted rivers and rushing waterfalls, alongside fascinating minority villages and laidback cities.

❶ Emei Shan Join Buddhist pilgrims ascending this forested, temple-studded mountain up seemingly endless flights of stone steps. **See p.735**

❷ Dafo This gigantic Buddha statue was completed in 803 AD and remains one of the world's biggest religious sculptures. **See p.733**

❸ Jiuzhaigou Enchanting alpine valley of calcified waterfalls and stunningly blue lakes, all surrounded by magestically forested peaks – get in early to beat the crowds. **See p.758**

❹ Lijiang Exploring the rambling, cobbled lanes of this picturesque ancient town – once home to the Naxi minority, now crammed with sightseers – makes for an atmospheric few days. **See p.672**

❺ Dali Dali's laidback street life and outlying minority villages encourage unplanned long stays. **See p.663**

❻ Kunming The cheery, pleasantly warm Yunnanese capital retains considerable charm despite its modernity. Don't forget to try the famous "Crossing-the-Bridge" noodles. **See p.647**

❼ Kaili Jumping-off point for visiting villages of the Miao minority, famed for their festivals and spectacular embroideries. **See p.628**

❽ Li River Ride a boat down this magical river, lined with karst pinnacles, between Guilin and Yangshuo. **See p.601**

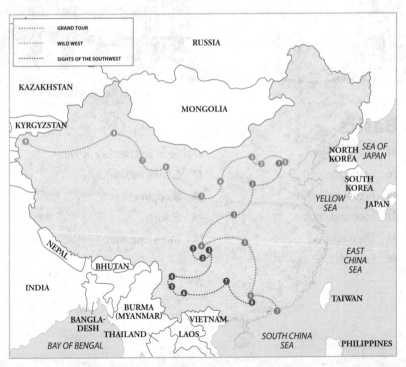

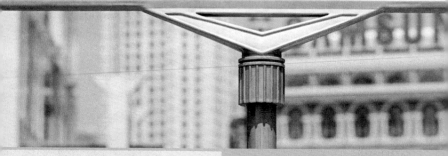

STREET SIGN IN ENGLISH AND CHINESE, SHANGHAI

Basics

Getting there

China's most important long-haul inter-national gateways are Beijing, Hong Kong, Guangzhou and Shanghai, though many other Chinese cities are served by international flights, operated mainly by airlines based in East Asia. There are also well-established overland routes into China – including road and rail links from its Southeast Asian neighbours, as well as the alluring Trans-Siberian Express from Moscow.

Fares to Hong Kong are at their highest during the fortnight before Christmas, the fortnight before Chinese New Year (see p.46) and from mid-June to early October. The cheapest time to fly there is in February (after Chinese New Year), May and November. For Beijing and Shanghai, peak season is generally in the summer. Flying on weekends is slightly more expensive; price ranges quoted below assume midweek travel.

Flights from the UK and Ireland

You can fly **direct** from London Heathrow to Beijing (10hr) with Air China or British Airways; to Hong Kong (12hr) with British Airways, Cathay Pacific or Virgin Atlantic; or to Shanghai with British Airways, China Eastern or Virgin Atlantic. Other airlines flying via a change of planes in a hub city include Aeroflot, Air France, KLM, Qatar, Singapore and Thai. Flying to China from other UK airports or from the Republic of Ireland involves either catching a connecting flight to London or flying via the airline's hub city.

From the UK, the lowest available **fares** to Beijing, Hong Kong or Shanghai start from around £450 in low season, rising to above £800 in high season. You may pay less with airlines such as Aeroflot and Qatar if you're prepared to transit.

Flights from the US and Canada

From North America, there are more flights to **Hong Kong** than to other Chinese destinations, though there's no shortage of flights to Beijing and Shanghai and there are some direct services to Guangzhou. Airlines flying **direct** include Air Canada, Air China, Cathay Pacific, United and China Eastern. You can also choose to fly to a Chinese provincial city – Chinese, Japanese, Korean and Hong Kong airlines offer services to cities throughout China via their respective hubs. It takes around 13hr to reach Beijing from the West Coast; add 7hr or more to this if you start from the East Coast (including a stopover on the West Coast en route). New routes over the North Pole shave off a couple of hours' flying time; these include Air Canada's routes from Toronto, Air China's from New York, United's from Chicago and Continental's flights from Newark to Beijing.

Round-trip fares to Hong Kong, Beijing and Shanghai are broadly comparable: in low season, expect to pay US$850–1200 from the West Coast (Los Angeles, San Francisco, Vancouver), or US$1100–1400 from the East Coast (New York, Montréal, Toronto). To get a good fare during high season it's important to buy your ticket as early as possible, in which case you probably won't pay more than US$250 above what you would have paid in low season.

Flights from Australia, New Zealand and South Africa

The closest entry point into China from Australia and New Zealand is Hong Kong, though from Australia it's also possible to fly direct to Guangzhou, Shanghai and Beijing. It's not a problem to fly elsewhere in China from either country if you catch a connecting flight along the way, though this can involve a long layover in the airline's hub city.

From eastern Australia, expect to pay from AU$800–1050 to Hong Kong with Cathay Pacific, China Airlines, EVA Airlines or Singapore Airlines; AU$1000–1200 to Shanghai with Royal Brunei, Singapore or Japan Airlines; and AU$1000–1200 to Beijing with Singapore, JAL, Malaysia or China Eastern. Cathay, Qantas, Air China and China Eastern

A BETTER KIND OF TRAVEL

At Rough Guides we are passionately committed to travel. We believe it helps us understand the world we live in and the people we share it with – and of course tourism is vital to many developing economies. But the scale of modern tourism has also damaged some places irreparably, and climate change is accelerated by most forms of transport, especially flying. All Rough Guides' flights are carbon-offset, and every year we donate money to a variety of environmental charities.

fly direct; other trips require a stopover in the airline's hub city. **From Perth**, fares to the above destinations are AU$100 or so more expensive. But the best deals by far are with Jetstar, who fly from Perth or Melbourne to Hong Kong and Hangzhou, via Singapore; one-way fares start at just over AU$300.

Flights **from New Zealand** are limited; the only direct flights are the Air New Zealand routes from Auckland to Shanghai and Hong Kong, which cost around NZ$1700–2000, and the Air Singapore, Air New Zealand and Malaysia Airlines flights to Hong Kong (around NZ$1800). Cheaper are the Jetstar flights from Auckland and Christchurch to Beijing, Hong Kong and Hangzhou, all via Singapore; one-way fares start at NZ$550.

From South Africa, South African Airlines have direct flights to Beijing (14hr) and more to Hong Kong (14hr), both costing ZAR10,000–18,000.

Round-the-World flights

If China is only one stop on a much longer journey, you might want to consider buying a **Round-the-World** (**RTW**) ticket (from around £1000/US$1800). Some travel agents can sell you an "off-the-shelf" RTW ticket that will have you touching down in about half a dozen cities (Beijing and Hong Kong are on many itineraries); others will have to assemble one for you, which can be tailored to your needs but is apt to be more expensive.

Airlines, agents and operators

When booking airfares, the cheapest online deals are often with stock operators such as STA, Trailfinders and Flight Centres, though it's always worth checking airline websites themselves for specials – and, often, a lot more flexibility with refunds and changing dates.

AIRLINES

Aeroflot W aeroflot.com/cms/en
Air Canada W aircanada.com
Air China W www.airchina.com.cn
Air France W airfrance.com
Air New Zealand W airnz.co.nz
Alitalia W alitalia.com
All Nippon Airways W www.anaskyweb.com
American Airlines W aa.com
Asiana Airlines W flyasiana.com
Austrian Airlines W aua.com
British Airways W ba.com
Cathay Pacific W cathaypacific.com
China Airlines W china-airlines.com

China Eastern Airlines W chinaeastern.co.uk
China Southern Airlines W cs-air.com
Continental Airlines W continental.com
Delta W delta.com
Emirates W emirates.com
EVA Air W evaair.com
Finnair W finnair.com
Japan Airlines W jal.com
Jetstar W jetstar.com
KLM W klm.com
Korean Air W koreanair.com
Lufthansa W lufthansa.com
Malaysia Airlines W malaysiaairlines.com
Nepal Airlines W nepalairlines.com.np
Qantas Airways W qantas.com
Qatar Airways W qatarairways.com
Royal Brunei W bruneiair.com
Royal Jordanian W rj.com
SAS W flysas.com
Singapore Airlines W singaporeair.com
Swiss W swiss.com
Thai Airways W www.thaiair.com
United Airlines W united.com
US Airways W usair.com
Vietnam Airlines W vietnamairlines.com
Virgin Atlantic W virgin-atlantic.com

AGENTS AND OPERATORS

Absolute Asia Can ☎ 1 212 627 1950, W absolutetravel.com. Numerous tours, all in first-class accommodation, from 6-day tasters to the 16-day "Silk Road" expedition.
Adventure Center US ☎ 1 866 338 8735, W adventurecenter .com. Dozens of tours in China and Tibet, from a week-long whizz around the highlights to a month of walking, hiking and biking expeditions.
Adventures Abroad US ☎ 1 800 665 3998, W adventures -abroad.com. Small-group specialists with two-week tours from Beijing and Shanghai to Hong Kong, plus interesting Silk Road trips from Uzbekistan to Beijing, and Yunnan/Tibet adventures.
Asian Pacific Adventures US ☎ 1 800 825 1680, W asianpacificadventures.com. Numerous tours of China, the most interesting focusing on southwestern ethnic groups and overlooked rural corners.
Backroads US ☎ 1 800 462 2848, W backroads.com. Cycling and hiking between Beijing and Hong Kong.
Bamboo Trails Taiwan ☎ 886 07 7354945, W bambootrails.com. A small travel company specializing in the Chinese world, offering some unique group itineraries (including Movie China and The Bamboo Trail), as well as high-end, tailor-made trips.
Bike Asia China ☎ 0773 8826521, W bikeasia.com. Guided bicycle tours ranging from day-long pedals around rural Guangxi to two-week epic rides across Southwestern China.
Birdfinders UK ☎ 01258 839066, W birdfinders.co.uk. Several trips per year to find rare and endemic species in Sichuan and northeast China.

China Holidays UK ☎ 020 7487 2999, ⓦ chinaholidays.co.uk. Aside from mainstream packages to the Three Gorges, Shanghai and Guilin, they also run themed tours, including cooking and birdwatching specials.

CTS Horizons UK ☎ 020 7868 5590, ⓦ ctshorizons.com. The China Travel Service's UK branch, offering an extensive range of tours including some cheap off-season hotel-and-flight packages to Beijing, and tailor-made private tours.

Exodus UK ☎ 020 3603 9372, ⓦ www.exodus.co.uk. Some interesting and unusual overland itineraries in the wilds of Tibet, Inner Mongolia and the Northwest.

Explore Worldwide UK ☎ 01252 760000, ⓦ explore.co.uk. Big range of small-group tours and treks, including Tibet and trips along the Yangzi. Their 21-day "shoestring" tour is particularly popular.

Geographic Expeditions US ☎ 1 888 570 7108, ⓦ geoex.com. Travel among the ethnic groups of Guizhou, Tibet, Yunnan and western Sichuan, as well as more straightforward trips around Shanghai and Beijing.

Intrepid Travel UK ☎ 0800 781 1660, Australia ☎ 03 9473 2673; ⓦ intrepidtravel.com. Small-group tours with the emphasis on cross-cultural contact and low-impact tourism; visits some fairly out-of-the-way corners of China.

Mir Corp US ☎ 206 624 7289, ⓦ mircorp.com. Specialists in Trans-Siberian rail travel, for small groups as well as individual travellers.

Mountain Travel Sobek US ☎ 1 888 831 7526, ⓦ mtsobek.com. Adventure tours to Tibet, northern Yunnan and along the Silk Road.

North South Travel UK ☎ 01245 608291, ⓦ northsouthtravel .co.uk. Friendly, competitive travel agency, offering discounted fares worldwide, including to Beijing. Profits are used to support projects in the developing world, especially the promotion of sustainable tourism.

On the Go Tours UK ☎ 020 7371 1113, Aus ☎ 07 3358 3385, ⓦ onthegotours.com. Runs group and tailor-made tours to China and other destinations, many tying in with the country's most interesting festivals.

Pacific Delight Tours US ☎ 1 800 221 7179, ⓦ pacificdelight tours.com. City breaks, cruises along the Li and Yangzi rivers, plus a range of tours to Tibet, the Silk Road and western Yunnan.

Regent Holidays UK ☎ 020 7666 1244, ⓦ regent-holidays.co.uk. Offers Trans-Siberian packages for individual travellers in either direction and with different possible stopover permutations, as well as interesting China tours.

REI Adventures US ☎ 1 800 622 2236, ⓦ rei.com/travel. Fascinating 11-day cycling and hiking tours through China.

The Russia Experience UK ☎ 0845 521 2910, Aus ☎ 1300 654 861, ⓦ trans-siberian.co.uk. Besides detailing their excellent Trans-Siberian packages, their website is a veritable mine of information about the railway.

STA Travel UK ☎ 033 321 0099, US ☎ 800 781 4040, Australia ☎ 134 782, New Zealand ☎ 0800 474 400, South Africa ☎ 0861 781 781; ⓦ statravel.co.uk. Worldwide specialists in independent travel; also student IDs, travel insurance, car rental, rail passes, and more. Good discounts for students and under-26s. China options include tours from 8 to 21 days in length, covering Beijing, Shanghai and the Yangzi and Li rivers, among others.

Sundowners Australia ☎ 03 9672 5300, ⓦ sundownersoverland .com. Tours of the Silk Road, plus Trans-Siberian rail bookings.

Trailfinders UK ☎ 020 7368 1200, Ireland ☎ 01 677 7888, Australia ☎ 1300 780 212; ⓦ trailfinders.com. One of the best-informed and most efficient agents for independent travellers. Numerous China options on offer.

Travel CUTS Canada ☎ 1 866 246 9762, US ☎ 1 800 592 2887; ⓦ travelcuts.com. Canadian youth and student travel firm.

Travel Indochina Australia ☎ 1300 138 755, ⓦ travelindochina .com.au. Covers the obvious China sights but goes a bit beyond them, too; also arranges cross-border visas for Thailand, Laos, Vietnam and Cambodia.

Wild China Beijing ☎ 010 6465 6602, ⓦ wildchina.com. Small group tours to out-of-the-way places, such as minority villages in Guizhou, as well as Tibet tours and tracking pandas in Sichuan.

World Expeditions UK ☎ 0800 074 4135, ⓦ worldexpeditions .co.uk; Australia ☎ 1300 720 000, ⓦ worldexpeditions.com.au; New Zealand ☎ 0800 350 354, ⓦ worldexpeditions.co.nz. Offers cycling and hiking tours in rural areas, including a Great Wall trek.

Overland routes

China has a number of **land borders** open to foreign travellers. Remember that Chinese visas must be used within three months of their date of issue, meaning that on a longer trip, you may have to apply for one en route. Visas are obtainable in the capitals of virtually all European and Asian countries, and are likely to take several days to be issued (see p.52 for embassy addresses). Note that most nationalities can easily pick up a Chinese visa in Hong Kong, though these are now attracting various restrictions.

Via Russia and Mongolia

One of the classic overland routes to China is through Russia by rail to Beijing. As a one-off trip, the rail journey is a memorable way to begin or end a stay in China; views of stately birch forests, misty lakes and arid plateaus help time pass much faster than you'd think, and there are frequent stops during which you can wander the station platform, purchasing food and knick-knacks – packages (see p.34) include more lengthy stopovers. The trains are comfortable and clean: second-class compartments contain four berths, while first-class have two and even boast a private shower.

There are actually two rail lines from Moscow to Beijing: the **Trans-Manchurian** (see p.34), which runs almost as far as the Sea of Japan before turning south through Dongbei (Manchuria) to Beijing; and the **Trans-Mongolian** (see p.34), which cuts through Mongolia from Siberia. The Manchurian train takes about six days, the Mongolian train about five. The latter is more popular with foreigners, a scenic route that rumbles past Lake Baikal and Siberia, the grasslands of Mongolia, and the desert of northwest China, skirting the Great Wall along the way. At the Mongolia/China border, you can watch as the undercarriage is switched to a different gauge.

Meals are included while the train is in China. In Mongolia, the dining car accepts payment in both Chinese and Mongolian currency; while in Russia, US dollars or Russian roubles can be used. It's worth having small denominations of US dollars as you can change these on the train throughout the journey, or use them to buy food from station vendors along the way – though experiencing the cuisine and people in the dining cars is part of the fun. Bring instant noodles and snacks as a backup, as well as that great long novel you've always wanted to read.

Tickets and packages

Booking tickets needs some advance planning, especially during the popular summer months. Sorting out travel arrangements from abroad is also complex – you'll need a visa for Russia, as well as for Mongolia if you intend to pass through there. It's therefore advisable to use an experienced **travel agent** who can organize all tickets, visas and stopovers (if required), in advance. Visa processing is an especially helpful time saver, given the queues and paperwork required for visas along the route.

You can cut complications and keep your costs down by using the online ticket booking system offered by **Real Russia** (W realrussia.co.uk); they mark up prices by about 20 percent but save you a lot of hassle. A second-class Moscow to Beijing ticket booked with them costs around £550 – they will then help you sort out your visas for a small fee (as will all other agencies). They also offer tours: a 9-day tour, including a couple of nights' accommodation in Moscow, costs £900 per person, a little less if you book as a group. Another agency offering a wide range of inexpensive tours is **Monkey Shrine** (W monkeyshrine.com); a Moscow to Beijing trip, including a couple of nights in a youth hostel, costs around £600 in standard class. Note that tours with Russian agencies offer good value for money; try **All Russia Travel Service** (W rusrailtravel.ru) or **Ost West** (W ostwest.com). Tailor-made tours from Western companies will be much more expensive, but offer the minimum hassle: the **Russia Experience** (W trans-siberian.co.uk) has a good reputation. For details of companies at home which can sort out Trans-Siberian travel, check the lists of specialist travel agents (see p.32).

Via the Central Asian republics

You can reach China through several Central Asian countries, though the obstacles reaching them can occasionally be insurmountable; contact the in-country agents listed on p.32, or Trans-Siberian

---

TRANS-SIBERIAN AND TRANS-MONGOLIAN TRAINS

Beijing's International Train Booking Office (Mon–Fri 8.30am–noon & 1.30–5pm; ☎ 010 6512 0507) is at the *International Hotel*, 9 Jianguomenwai Dajie (see map, p.85). Here you can buy **tickets to Moscow and Ulaan Baatar** with the minimum of fuss. BTG Travel have a desk for Trans-Siberian tickets that charges about the same. You can also buy tickets at the Foreigners' Ticket Booking Office in Beijing train station (see p.101) though they aren't much good on visa advice. Out of season, few people make the journey (you may get a cabin to yourself), but in summer there may well not be a seat for weeks.

Getting **visas** for Russia and/or Mongolia in China can be tricky, since regulations change all the time; it's always best (and, sometimes, essential) to organize them in your own country. If you want to apply in Beijing, check first whether it will be possible; you may need to show proof of inward and onward travel, and possibly hotel bookings and an official invitation too. See Beijing embassy websites and W seat61.com for the latest advice. It's a lot easier, but a lot more expensive, to book a **tour**; see p.32 for a few recommended organizations.

Chinese train #3, which follows the **Trans-Mongolian route**, leaves every Wednesday from Beijing station and takes five-and-a-half days. A bunk in a 2nd-class cabin with four beds – which is perfectly comfortable – costs around US$690. Trains leave Moscow for Beijing every Tuesday, though in this direction you'll likely have to buy tickets through an agency.

Russian train #19, which follows the **Trans-Siberian route**, leaves every Saturday from Beijing station and takes six days. A Mongolian train leaves for Ulaan Baatar every Tuesday and costs around US$200 for one bed in a four-bed berth.

See p.32 for details on companies offering Trans-Siberian tours and packages; of course they'll cost more than doing it yourself, but it'll save a world of hassle.

operators listed earlier in this section, for up-to-date practicalities. Once in the region, crossing into China from Kazakhstan is straightforward – there are comfortable weekly trains from Almaty (Mon) and Astana (Tues) to Ürümqi, which take two nights and cost about US$225 for a berth in a four-berth compartment. From Bishkek in Kyrgyzstan, Kashgar in the northwestern Chinese province of Xinjiang is an 11hr drive away, and the two cities are linked by buses in summer months. Foreigners, however, have had difficulties in trying to use these and have usually had to resort to expensive private transport, run by local tour operators, to help them across (see p.839). You may well be expected to bribe the border guards (a bottle of spirit will often suffice).

From Pakistan and Nepal

The routes across the Himalayas to China are among the toughest in Asia. The first is from Pakistan into Xinjiang province via the **Karakoram Highway**, along one of the branches of the ancient Silk Road. This requires no pre-planning, except for the fact that it is open only May–October, and closes periodically due to landslides; at the time of writing, however, most Western governments were advising against travel to Pakistan, thanks to fundamentalist militants and **attacks on Westerners**. See p.848 for practical information on the Karakoram Highway.

Another popular route is **from Nepal into Tibet**, but Nepal's political situation can be volatile, and you should check your government's travel advice on the latest situation – practical details are covered on p.865. It's advisable to arrive in Nepal with a Chinese visa already in your passport, as the Chinese Embassy in Nepal often does not issue visas at all and at the best of times will only issue group visas. The **Tibetan border** is closed to travellers during politically sensitive times, for example after the riots in 2010.

From **India** there are, for political reasons, no border crossings to China. For years, authorities have discussed opening a bus route from Sikkim to Tibet, north from Darjeeling, but despite both sides working on the road, the border remains closed.

From Vietnam

Vietnam has three border crossings with China – **Dong Dang**, 60km northeast of Hanoi; **Lao Cai**, 150km northwest; and the little-used **Mong Cai**, 200km south of Nanning. All three are open daily 8.30am–5pm. Officious Chinese customs officials at these crossings occasionally confiscate guidebooks, including this one; bury it at the bottom of your bag.

A **direct train** service from Hanoi is advertised as running all the way to **Beijing** (60hr), passing through **Nanning** and **Guilin**. In practice, though, you'll probably have to change trains in Nanning. Alternatively, there are daily trains from Hanoi to Lao Cai, 11hr away in Vietnam's mountainous and undeveloped northwest (near the pleasant minority hill-resort of Sa Pa), from where you can cross into Yunnan province at Hekou, and catch regular buses to Kunming. From Mong Cai, there are also regular buses to Nanning.

From Laos and Burma (Myanmar)

Crossing into China **from Laos** also lands you in Yunnan, this time at Bian Mao Zhan in the Xishuangbanna region. Formalities are very relaxed and unlikely to cause any problems, though it's prudent to take some hard cash along with you. It's 220km on local buses north from here to the regional capital, Jinghong. Alternatively, there are also direct daily buses between Luang Namtha in Laos and Jinghong (8hr), and Luang Prabang to Kunming (24hr).

Entering China **from Burma** (Myanmar) is a possibility, too, with the old Burma Road cutting northeast from Rangoon (Yangon) to Lashio and the crossing at Ruili in Yunnan. At present, this border is open only to groups travelling with a tour agency, which will sort out all the necessary paperwork in Yangon. Be aware that border regulations here are subject to change.

By ferry from Korea and Japan

There are a number of ferry routes linking China with Korea and Japan. Those **from Korea** take one night, and all depart from Incheon, a coastal city connected to Seoul by subway train; services to Tanggu, near Tianjin, land you closest to Beijing (see p.139), though there are other useful services to Dalian (p.170), Dandong (p.174), Qingdao (p.302) and Yantai (p.306). Trips take 16–24hr, services usually run two times a week, and fares and standards are similar across the board; the cheapest tickets (KRW110,000) will get you a berth in a common room (though often closed off with a curtain, and therefore surprisingly private), while paying a little more (from KRW150,000) will get you a bed in a private, en-suite room (at lower classes, you may have to share with other travellers).

From Japan, there are regular ferries from Fukuoka to Busan (2hr from Seoul by high-speed train), or you can take direct ferries from Osaka or Kobe to Shanghai (see p.372), and Fukuoka or

Shimonoseki to Qingdao (see p.302). All trips take two nights and leave once or twice per week, though standards are actually a little lower than those on Korean ferries; the cheapest tickets (¥1300) will buy you space on an often-crowded tatami floor, though for a little more (from ¥1600) you'll have a bed in a (sometimes shared) room.

Getting around

China's public transport is comprehensive and good value: you can fly to all regional capitals and many cities, the rail network extends to every region, and you can reach China's remotest corners on local buses. Tibet is the one area where there are widespread restrictions on independent travel (see p.865).

However, getting around such a large, crowded country requires planning, patience and stamina. This is especially true for long-distance journeys, where you'll find that travelling in as much comfort as you can afford saves a lot of undue stress. **Tours** are one way of taking the pressure off, and may be the only practical way of getting out to certain sights. China is also not the easiest country in which to travel independently: families and older travellers might prefer to book a tour with one of the agents on p.32.

Public holidays – especially the May, October and Spring Festival breaks (see p.46) – are rotten times to travel, as half of China is on the move between family and workplace: ticket prices rise (legally no more than 15 percent, though often by up to double), bus- and train-station crowds swell insanely, and even flights become scarce.

By rail

China's rail network is vast, efficient and reliable. The country invests billions of yuan annually on the network, considering a healthy transport infrastructure as essential to economic growth – and political cohesion. Recent years have seen some impressive developments: a rail line over the mountains between eastern China and **Tibet** completed in 2005; the country's first ultra-fast **bullet** trains, which began operation in eastern China in 2007; and an expanding web of **high-speed networks between major cities**.

Food, though expensive and ordinary, is always available on trains, either from trolleys serving snacks and polystyrene boxes of rice and stir-fries or in a dedicated restaurant car. You can also buy snacks from vendors at train stations during the longer station stops.

Timetables and tickets

It's easiest to check **train schedules** online; ⓦtravelchinaguide.com/china-trains is one good, and usually up-to-date, source of information.

Tickets – always **one-way** – show the date of travel and destination, along with the train number, carriage, and seat or berth number. They become available up to twenty days in advance, though it can be as little as four. **Station ticket offices** are all computerized, and while queues can tie you up for an hour or more of jostling, you'll generally get what you're after if you have some flexibility – note that you'll need to show your **passport** when booking tickets. At the counter, state your destination, the train number if possible, the day you'd like to travel, and the class you want, and have some alternatives handy. If you can't speak Chinese, get someone to write things down for you before setting out, as staff rarely speak English.

In all cities, you'll also find **downtown advance purchase offices**, where you pay a small commission (¥5/ticket); it makes sense to try these places first, as train stations – especially for high-speed services – are often located far from city centres. **Agents**, such as hotel travel services, can also book tickets for a commission of ¥30 or more each. The best way to **book tickets online**, and have them delivered to your hotel door in major Chinese cities, is through ⓦtravelchinaguide.com; you'll pay a surcharge of about 25 percent for this.

If you've bought a ticket but decide not to travel, you can get most of the fare **refunded** by returning the ticket to a ticket office. The process is called *tuipiao* (退票, **tuìpiào**), and there's usually a dedicated window for this at stations.

Types of train

The different **types of train** each have their own code on timetables. Swanky **high-speed** services (C-, D- and G-class), which travel up to 350km/h, now link many cities in the east of the country, and often travel from dedicated high-speed stations. The trains are kept in excellent condition, with surprisingly clean Western-style toilets, reclining seats, and a decent enough amount of legroom.

High-speed routes are supplemented by, and others are still reliant upon, regular Z-, T- and K-class trains, which can still reach 150–200km/h. These all have modern fittings with text tickers at the carriages' end scrolling through the temperature,

SAMPLE TRAIN FARES

The fares below are for one-way travel on express trains. As always in China, the faster services are more expensive.

	HARD SEAT	HARD SLEEPER	SOFT SLEEPER	HIGH SPEED
FROM BEIJING				
Guangzhou	¥250	¥460	¥780	¥860
Hong Kong	-	¥505	¥820	
Shanghai	¥309	-	-	¥555
Xi'an	¥150	¥270	¥415	¥515
FROM XI'AN				
Guangzhou	¥240	¥435	¥760	¥815
Turpan	¥265	¥475	¥735	-
Ürümqi	¥275	¥495	¥770	

arrival time at next station and speed. Toilets are usually Western-style in soft sleeper carriages, and squat elsewhere; the latter can be truly disgusting.

Ordinary trains (普通车, **pǔtōng chē**) have a number only and range from those with clean carriages and able to top 100km/h, to ancient plodders destined for the scrapheap with cigarette-burned linoleum floors and grimy windows. A few busy, short-haul express services, such as the Shenzhen–Guangzhou train, have **double-decker carriages**.

No-smoking rules are vigorously enforced on high-speed trains, though on slower services it's still common to see passengers puffing away between carriages.

Ticket classes

On **high-speed** services there are two seat classes, the only real difference between them being a two-two seat arrangement in first, compared to the three-two arrangement in second.

On regular trains, there are **four ticket classes**: soft sleeper, hard sleeper, soft seat and hard seat, not all necessarily available on each train. **Soft sleeper** (软卧, **ruǎnwò**) costs around the same as flying, and gets you a berth in a four-person compartment with a soft mattress, fan and optional radio. **Hard sleeper** (硬卧, **yìngwò**), about two-thirds the price of soft sleeper, is the best value. Carriages are divided into twenty sets of three-tiered **bunks**; the lowest bunk is the largest, but costs more and gets used as communal seating during the day; the upper bunk is cheapest but headroom is minimal. Each set of six bunks has its own vacuum flask of boiled water (topped up from the urn at the end of each carriage) – bring your own mugs and tea. There are fairly spacious **luggage racks**, though make sure you chain your bags securely while you sleep.

In either sleeper class, on boarding the carriage you will have your ticket exchanged for a metal tag by the attendant. The tag is swapped back for your ticket (so you'll be able to get through the barrier at the station) about half an hour before you arrive at your destination, whatever hour of the day or night this happens to be.

Soft seat (软座, **ruǎnzuò**) is widespread on services whose complete route takes less than a day. Seats cost around the same as express-bus fare, have plenty of legroom and are well padded. More common is **hard seat** (硬座, **yìngzuò**), which costs around half the soft-seat fare but is only recommended for relatively short journeys, as you'll be sitting on a padded three-person bench, with every available bit of floor space crammed with travellers who were unable to book a seat. You'll often be the focus of intense and unabashed speculation from peasants and labourers who can't afford to travel in better style.

Finally, if there's nothing else available, you can buy an **unreserved ticket** (无座, **wúzuò**; literally "no seat"), which lets you board the hard-seat section of the train – though you might have to stand for the entire journey if you can't upgrade on board.

Boarding the train

Turn up at the station with at least 30min to spare before your train leaves. You'll need to show your passport and ticket to be allowed into the station; all luggage is then **x-rayed** to check for dangerous goods such as firecrackers. You next need to work out which **platform** your train leaves from – most stations have electronic departure boards in

Chinese (high-speed stations have dual-language boards), or you can show your ticket to station staff who will point you in the right direction. Passengers are not allowed onto the platform until the train is almost in, which can result in some mighty stampedes out of the crowded waiting rooms when the gates open. Carriages are **numbered** on the outside, and your ticket is checked by a guard as you board. Once on the train, you can **upgrade** any ticket at the controller's booth, in the hard-seat carriage next to the restaurant car (usually #8), where you can sign up for beds or seats as they become available.

By bus and minibus

Buses go everywhere that trains go, and well beyond, usually more frequently but more slowly. Finding the departure point isn't always easy though; even small hamlets can have **multiple bus stations**, generally located on the side of town in which traffic is heading.

Bus station **timetables** – except electronic ones – can be ignored; ask station staff about schedules and frequencies, though they generally can't speak English. **Tickets** are easy to buy: ticket offices at main stations are computerized, queues are seldom bad, and – with the exception of backroad routes, which might only run every other day – you don't need to book in advance. In country towns, you sometimes buy tickets on board the bus. **Destinations** are always displayed in Chinese characters on the front of the vehicle. Take some **food** along, although buses usually pull up at inexpensive roadhouses at mealtimes. Only the most upmarket coaches have **toilets**; drivers stop every few hours or if asked to do so by passengers (roadhouse toilets are some of the worst in the country, however).

Downsides to bus travel include drivers who spend the journey chatting on their mobile phone or coast downhill in neutral, with the engine off; and the fact that vehicles are obliged to use the horn before overtaking anything – earplugs are recommended. **Roadworks** are a near-certainty too, as highways are continually being repaired, upgraded or replaced; in 2010, a 100km-long jam on the Tibet–Beijing highway, blamed on roadworks, took nine days to clear.

Types of buses

There are various **types of buses**, though there's not always a choice available for particular routes, and, if there is, station staff will assume that as a

foreigner you'll want the fastest, most comfortable and most expensive service.

Ordinary buses (普通车, pǔtōng chē) are cheap and basic, with lightly padded seats; they're never heated or air-conditioned, so dress accordingly. Seats can be cramped and luggage racks tiny; you'll have to put anything bulkier than a satchel on the roof or your lap, or beside the driver. They tend to stop off frequently, so don't count on an average speed of more than 30km/h.

Express buses (快车, kuài chē) are the most expensive and have good legroom, comfy seats that may well recline, air-conditioning and video. Bulky luggage gets locked away in the belly of the bus, a fairly safe option.

Sleeper buses (卧铺车, wòpù chē) have cramped, basic bunks instead of seats, minimal luggage space and a poor safety record, and are not recommended if there is any alternative.

The final option is **minibuses** (小车, xiǎochē; or 包车, bāochē) seating up to twenty people, common on routes of less than 100km or so. They cost a little more than the same journey by ordinary bus, can be extremely cramped, and often circuit the departure point for ages until they have filled up.

By plane

China's **airlines** link all major cities, and services are becoming more and more regular. The main operators are Air China (ⓦwww.airchina.com.cn), China Southern (ⓦcs-air.com), China Eastern (ⓦwww.ce-air.com) and Hainan Airlines (ⓦglobal .hnair.com); along with smaller regional companies they are overseen by the Civil Aviation Administration of China, or **CAAC**. Flying is a luxury worth considering for long distances, especially since prices can actually be lower than soft-sleeper train travel; planes are modern and well maintained and service is good.

Buying tickets from local airline offices or hotel desk tour agents is easy, and there are enough flights along popular routes to cope with demand. Agents often give substantial discounts on advertised fares, especially if you book a day or two in advance. Competitive fares are available if you **buy e-tickets online** at ⓦelong.net or ⓦenglish.ctrip .com. You'll need to provide a phone number to confirm the booking (your hotel's will do), and to book more than 24 hours in advance if using an overseas credit card.

Fares are based on one-way travel (so a return ticket is the price of two one-way tickets) and include all **taxes**. As an illustration, from Beijing, expect to pay at least ¥740 to Xi'an; ¥900 to Shanghai; ¥1120 to

Chengdu; ¥1230 to Shenzhen; ¥1000 to Kunming; ¥1440 to Ürümqi, and ¥2100 to Hong Kong.

There are usually **buses** running to and from the airport; check the individual city entries in this Guide. **Check-in time** for all flights is 90min before departure.

By ferry

Though there are few public ferries in China, you can make one of the world's great river journeys down the **Yangzi** between Chongqing and Yichang (see p.752), via the mighty **Three Gorges** – though the spectacle has been lessened by the construction of the giant Three Gorges Dam. Another favourite is the day-cruise down the **Li River** between Guilin and Yangshuo in southwestern Guangxi province, past a forest of pointy pinnacles looking just like a Chinese scroll painting (see p.601). By **sea**, there are **passenger ferries** between Hong Kong and Macau (see p.561), and between Guangxi and Hainan Island (p.617).

Conditions on board are greatly variable, but on overnight trips there's always a choice of **classes** – sometimes as many as six – which can range from a bamboo mat on the floor right through to private cabins. Don't expect anything too impressive, however; many mainland services are cramped and overcrowded, and cabins, even in first-class, are grimly functional.

By bicycle

China has the highest number of **bicycles** (自行车, zìxíngchē) of any country in the world, with about a quarter of the population owning one, despite a rising trend towards mopeds, motorbikes and cars. Few cities have any hills and some have **bike lanes**, though many of the bigger cities are in the process of banning bicycles from main roads in order to free them up for cars.

Rental shops or booths are common around train stations, where you can rent a set of wheels for ¥10–20 a day. You will need to leave a deposit (¥200–400) and/or some form of ID, and you're fully responsible for anything that happens to the bike while it's in your care, so check brakes, tyre pressure and gears before renting. Most rentals are bog-standard black rattletraps – the really deluxe models feature working bells and brakes. There are **repair shops** all over the place should you need a tyre patched or a chain fixed up (¥10–30). If the bike sustains any serious damage, it's up to the parties involved to sort out responsibility and payment on

the spot. Always use a **bicycle chain** or lock – they're available everywhere – and in cities, leave your vehicle in one of the ubiquitous designated **parking areas**, where it will be guarded by an attendant for a small fee.

An alternative to renting is to **buy a bike**, a sensible option if you're going to be based anywhere for a while. All department stores sell them: a heavy, unsophisticated machine will only set you back about ¥350, whereas a mountain bike will be upwards of ¥600. A **folding bike** (around ¥450) is a great idea, as you can cycle around all day and, when you're tired, put it in the boot of a taxi; plus, you can take it from one destination to another on the bus. You can also **bring your own bike** into China; international airlines usually insist that the front wheel is removed, deflated and strapped to the back, and that everything is thoroughly packaged. Inside China, airlines, trains and ferries all charge to carry bikes, and the ticketing and accompanying paperwork can be baffling. Another option is to see China on a **specialized bike tour** such as those offered by Bike China (W bikechina.com), Bike Asia (W bikeasia.com) or Cycle China (W cyclechina.com).

Tours

Local tour operators, who are listed throughout the Guide, offer excursions ranging from city coach tours to river cruises and multiday cross-country hikes or horse treks. While you always pay for the privilege, sometimes these tours are good value: travel, accommodation and food – usually plentiful and excellent – are generally included, as might be the services of an interpreter and guide. And in some cases, tours are virtually the only way to see something really worthwhile, saving endless bother organizing local transport and accommodation. In general, **foreign-owned operations** tend to give better service – or at least to understand better what Westerners want when they take a tour.

On the downside, there are disreputable operators who'll blatantly overcharge for mediocre services, foist unhelpful guides on you and spend three days on what could better be done in an afternoon. Bear in mind that many Chinese tour guides are badly paid, and supplement their income by taking tourists to souvenir shops where they'll receive commissions. It always pays to make exhaustive **enquiries** about the exact nature of the tour, such as exactly what the price includes and the departure/return times, before handing any money over.

City transport

All Chinese cities have some form of **public transit system**. An increasing number have (or are building) **light-rail systems** and underground **metros**; elsewhere, the **city bus** is the transport focus. These are cheap and run from 6am–10pm or later, but (Hong Kong's apart) they're usually slow and crowded. Pricier **private minibuses** often run the same routes in similar comfort but at greater speed; they're either numbered or have their destination written up at the front.

Taxis are always available in larger towns and cities; main roads, transit points and tourist hotels are good places to find them. They cost a fixed rate of ¥5–13 within certain limits, and then add from ¥1 per kilometre. You'll also find (motorized or cycle-) **rickshaws** in touristy areas, whose highly erratic rates are set by bargaining beforehand.

Accommodation

China's accommodation scene continues to improve at pace, with most cities boasting a range of good options from budget to top-end. Luxury hotels (mostly international brands) and backpacker hostels are as good as you'll find in the West, the latter supplemented by some excellent budget hotel chains. Mid-range hotels, however, are often lacking in character, many of them former state-run behemoths.

Price is not a good indicator of quality, with a good deal of overlap between the various places. The Chinese hospitality industry remains on a steep learning curve, so new places are often vastly better than old ones.

Security in accommodation is reasonably good, with budget dosshouses and youth hostels the only places where you'll really have to keep an eye on your stuff; the latter usually have places in which you'll be able to lock away valuables.

Finding a room

Increasingly, **booking ahead** by phone or online is a routine procedure. **Accommodation-booking websites,** such as elong (Ⓦelong.net) or China Trip (Ⓦenglish.ctrip.com), often have English-language content and offer massive discounts on selected mid-range to upmarket hotel rates. These two don't require pre-payment for rooms; you simply reserve

through the website and pay on arrival. Budget travellers should check out **hostel websites** such as Ⓦhostelworld.com and Ⓦhostelbookers.com.

For some hotels, however, the concept of booking ahead may be alien, and you won't make much headway without spoken Chinese – though it's a good idea to call (or to ask someone to call for you) to see if vacancies exist before lugging your bag across town. Be aware that **room rates** displayed at reception are almost always just the starting point in negotiations. Staff are generally amenable to **bargaining** and it's normal to get 30 percent off the advertised price, even more in low season or where there's plenty of competition. Always ask to **see the room first**. Rooms usually have either **twin beds** (双人房, shuāngrén fáng) or **single beds** (单人房, dānrén fáng), which often means "one double bed", rather than a small bed; some places also have triples or even quads.

New arrivals at city bus and train stations are often besieged by **touts** wanting to lead them to a hotel where they'll receive a commission for bringing guests in. Chinese-speakers might strike a bargain this way, but you do need to be very clear about how much you're willing to pay before being dragged all over town.

If you find yourself being turned away by cheaper hotels, it's not that they don't like you – they probably haven't obtained **police permission** to take foreigners, and would face substantial fines for doing so. The situation is dependent on the local authorities, and can vary not just from province to province, but also from town to town. Nothing is ever certain in China, however: being able to speak Chinese greatly improves your chances of negotiating a way into these cheaper places, as does being able to write your name in Chinese on the register (or having it printed out so the receptionist can do this for you) – in which case the authorities need never know that a foreigner stayed.

Checking in and out

Checking in involves filling in a **form** giving details of your name, age, date of birth, sex and address, places where you are coming from and going to, how many days you intend staying and your visa and passport numbers. Upmarket hotels have English versions, and might fill them in for you, but hotels unaccustomed to foreigners usually have them in Chinese only, and might never have seen a foreign passport before – which explains why hotel receptionists can panic when they see a foreigner walk in the door.

You always **pay in advance**, including a **deposit** which may amount to twice the price of the room. Assuming you haven't broken anything – make sure everything works properly when you check in – deposits are refunded; just don't lose the receipt.

In cheaper places, disconnect your **telephone** to avoid being woken by prostitutes calling up through the night.

At most mid-range and high-end hotels, **breakfast** will come as part of your room rate; you'll usually get a coupon for this when you check in. Breakfast is served a little earlier than most foreign travellers would like – some places stop service at 8am, though 7–9am is by far the most common timeframe.

Check-out time is noon, though you can ask to keep the room until later for a proportion of the daily rate. Make sure you arrange this **before** check-out time, however, as staff may otherwise refuse to refund room deposits, claiming that you have overstayed. Conversely, if you have to leave very early in the morning (to catch transport, for instance), you may be unable to find staff to refund your deposit, and might also encounter locked front doors or compound gates. This is most of a problem in rural areas, though often the receptionist sleeps behind the desk and can be woken up if you make enough noise.

Hotels

The different Chinese words for hotel are vague indicators of the status of the place. Sure signs of upmarket pretensions are **dajiudian** (大酒店, dà jiŭdiàn), which translates as "big wine shop", or, in the countryside, **shan zhuang** (山庄, shān zhuāng) or "mountain resort". **Binguan** (宾馆, bīnguǎn) and **fandian** (饭店, fàndiàn) are more general terms for hotel, covering everything from downmarket lodgings to smart new establishments; reliably basic are **guesthouse** (客栈, kèzhàn), **hostel** (招待所, zhāodàisuŏ) and **inn** (旅馆, lǚguǎn; or 旅舍, lǚshè). Sometimes you'll simply see a sign for "accommodation" (住宿, zhùsù).

Whatever type of hotel you are staying in, there are two things you can rely on: one is a pair of plastic or paper **slippers**, which you use for walking to the bathroom, and the other is a vacuum flask of drinkable **hot water** that can be refilled any time by the floor attendant – though upmarket places tend to provide electric kettles instead.

Upmarket

In the larger cities, you'll find **upmarket** four- or five-star hotels. Conditions in such hotels are comparable to those anywhere in the world, with all the usual **facilities** on offer – such as swimming pools, gyms and business centres – though the finer nuances of service are sometimes lacking. Prices for standard doubles in these places are upwards of ¥1200, with a 15 percent **service charge** on top; the use of credit cards is routine. In **Hong Kong** and **Macau**, the top end of the market is similar in character to the mainland, though prices are higher and service more efficient.

Even if you cannot afford to stay in the upmarket hotels, they can still be pleasant places to escape from the hubbub, and nobody in China blinks at the sight of a stray foreigner roaming around the foyer of a smart hotel. As well as air-conditioning and clean toilets, you'll find **cafés and bars** (sometimes showing satellite TV), telephone and internet facilities and seven-days-a-week money changing (though this is usually only for guests).

Mid-range

Many Chinese hotels built nowadays are **mid-range**, and every town in China has at least one hotel of this sort. The quality of mid-range places is the hardest to predict from the price: an old hotel with cigarette-burned carpets, leaking bathrooms and grey bedsheets might charge the same as a sparkling new establishment next door; newer places are generally better, as a rule. In remote places, you should get a twin in a mid-range place for ¥150, but expect to pay at least ¥300 in any sizeable city.

There's been a recent explosion in **urban budget hotels** aimed at money-conscious businessmen, which offer small (but not cramped) clean double rooms with showers, phones, TV and internet portals right in city centres. Some places like Kunming, Chengdu and Shanghai have local brands, but nationwide chains include *7 Days Inn* (Ⓦ7daysinn.cn), *Home Inn* (Ⓦhomeinns.com) and *Motel 168* (Ⓦwww.motel168.com). At around ¥200 a double, or even less, they're a very good deal, especially if you're able to take advantage of early-booking promotions (you'll need to speak Chinese for this, and possibly to have a local credit card too).

Cheap hotels

Cheap hotels, with doubles costing less than ¥150, vary in quality from the dilapidated to the perfectly comfortable. In many cities, they're commonly located near the train or bus stations, though they may need some persuading to take foreigners. Where they do, you'll notice that the Chinese routinely **rent beds** rather than rooms – doubling up with one or more strangers, and paying per bed

– as a means of saving money. Foreigners are seldom allowed to share rooms with Chinese people, but if there are three or four foreigners together it's often possible for them to share one big room; otherwise single travellers might have to negotiate a price for the whole room.

Hostels and guesthouses

China has a rapidly expanding network of **youth hostels** (青年旅舍, qīngnián lǚshè), many affiliated with the International Youth Hostel Association (IYHA). Contact details for individual hostels are given through the Guide, and **booking ahead** is always advisable – easiest on sites such as ⓦhostelworld.com and ⓦhostelbookers.com. At IYHA hostels, members get a small discount, usually ¥10, and you can join at any mainland hostel for ¥60.

Hong Kong, Macau and a few regions of China (mostly in southwestern provinces) also have a number of **privately run guesthouses** in everything from family mansions to Mongolian tents, whose variety comes as a relief after the dullness of mainland accommodation. Prices for double rooms in these guesthouses are generally lower than in hotels.

Camping

Camping is only feasible in Hong Kong – where there are free campsites scattered through the New Territories – and in wilderness areas of Tibet, Sichuan, Yunnan, Qinghai, Xinjiang, Gansu and Inner Mongolia, far away from the prying eyes of thousands of local villagers. Don't bother trying to get permission for it: this is the kind of activity that the Chinese authorities do not have any clear idea about, so if asked they will certainly answer "no".

Food and drink

The Chinese love to eat, and from market-stall buns and soup, right through to the intricate variations of regional cookery, China boasts one of the world's greatest cuisines. Meals are considered social events, and the process is accordingly geared to a group of diners sharing a variety of different dishes with their companions. Fresh ingredients are available from any market stall, though unless you're living long term in the country there are few opportunities to cook for yourself.

Ingredients

In the south, **rice** as grain, noodles, or dumpling wrappers is the staple, replaced in the cooler north by **wheat**, formed into buns or noodles. **Meat** is held to be invigorating and, ideally, forms the backbone of any meal. Pork is the most common meat used, except in areas with a strong Muslim tradition where it's replaced with mutton or beef. **Fowl** is considered especially good during old age or convalescence; most rural people in central and southern China seem to own a couple of chickens, and the countryside is littered with duck and geese farms. **Fish and seafood** are highly regarded and can be expensive, as are rarer **game** meats.

Eggs – duck, chicken or quail – are a popular nationwide snack, often flavoured by hard-boiling in a mixture of tea, soy sauce and star anise. There's also the so-called "thousand-year-old" variety, preserved for a few months in ash and straw – they look gruesome, with translucent brown albumen and green yolks, but actually have a delicate, brackish flavour. **Dairy products** serve limited purposes in China. Goat's cheese and yoghurt are eaten in parts of Yunnan and the Northwest, but milk is considered fit only for children and the elderly and is not used in cooking.

Vegetables accompany nearly every Chinese meal, used in most cases to balance tastes and textures of meat, but also appearing as dishes in their own right. Though the selection can be very thin in some parts of the country, there's usually a wide range on offer, from leafy greens to water chestnuts, mushrooms, bamboo shoots, seaweed and radish.

Soya beans are ubiquitous in Chinese cooking, being a good source of protein in a country where meat has often been a luxury. The small green beans are sometimes eaten straight in the south, but are more often salted and used to thicken sauces, fermented to produce **soy sauce**, or boiled and pressed to make white cakes of **tofu** (bean curd). Fresh tofu is flavourless and as soft as custard, though it can be pressed further to create a firmer texture, deep-fried until crisp, or cooked in stock and used as a meat substitute in vegetarian cooking. The skin that forms on top of the liquid while tofu is being made is itself skimmed off, dried, and used as a wrapping for spring rolls and the like.

Seasonal availability is smoothed over by a huge variety of **dried**, **salted** and **pickled vegetables**, meats and seafood, which often characterize local cooking styles. There's also an enormous assortment of regional **fruit**, great to clean the palate or fill a space between meals.

For a comprehensive menu reader and useful phrases for ordering food and drink, see p.965.

Breakfast, snacks and street food

Breakfast is not a big event by Chinese standards, more something to line the stomach for a few hours. Much of the country is content with a bowl of rice porridge flavoured with pickles and eaten with plain buns, or sweetened soya milk accompanied by a fried dough stick; dumplings, sometimes in soup, are another favourite. Guangdong and Hong Kong are the exceptions, where the traditional breakfast of **dim sum** (also known as **yum cha**) involves a selection of tiny buns, dumplings and dishes served with tea.

Other **snacks and street food** are served through the day from small, early-opening **stalls** located around markets, train and bus stations. These serve grilled chicken wings; kebabs; spiced noodles; baked yams and potatoes; boiled eggs; various steamed or stewed dishes dished up in earthenware **sandpots**; grilled corn and – in places such as Beijing and Sichuan – countless local treats. Also common are **steamed buns**, which are either stuffed with meat or vegetables (*baozi*) or plain (*mantou*, literally "bald heads"). The buns originated in the north and are especially warming on a winter's day; a sweeter Cantonese variety is stuffed with barbecued pork. Another northern snack now found everywhere is the ravioli-like **jiaozi**, again with a meat or vegetable filling and either fried or steamed; **shuijiao** are boiled *jiaozi* served in soup. Some small restaurants specialize in *jiaozi*, containing a bewildering range of fillings and always sold by weight.

Restaurants and eating out

The cheapest **hole-in-the-wall canteens** are necessarily basic, with simple food costing a few yuan a serve and often much better than you'd expect from the furnishings. Proper **restaurants** are usually bright, busy places whose preferred atmosphere is *renao*, or "hot and noisy", rather than the often quiet norm in the West. Prices at these places obviously vary a lot, but even expensive-looking establishments charge only ¥20–50 for a main dish, and servings tend to be generous.

While the cheaper places might have long hours, **restaurant opening times** are early and short: breakfast lasts from around 6–9am; lunch 11am–2pm; and dinner from around 5–9pm, after which the staff will be yawning and sweeping the debris off the tables around your ankles.

Ordering and dining

Pointing is all that's required at street stalls and small restaurants; they'll usually have the fare laid out, ready for cooking or already done. In **proper restaurants** you'll be given a **menu** – most likely Chinese-only, unless you're in a tourist area, though many now have pictures, and some are on tablets (more fiddly than useful). Alternatively, have a look at what other diners are eating – the Chinese are often delighted that a foreigner wants to eat Chinese food, and will indicate the best options on their table.

When **ordering**, unless eating a one-dish meal like Peking duck or a hotpot, try to select items with a **range of tastes and textures**; it's also usual to include a soup. In cheap places, servings of noodles or rice are huge, but as they are considered basic stomach fillers, quantities decline the more upmarket you go.

Dishes are all **served** at once, placed in the middle of the table for diners to share. With some poultry dishes you can crunch up the smaller bones, but anything else is spat out on to the table-cloth or floor, more or less discreetly depending on the establishment – watch what others are doing. **Soups** tend to be bland and are consumed last (except in the south where they may be served first or as part of the main meal) to wash the meal down, the liquid slurped from a spoon or the bowl once the noodles, vegetables or meat in it have been picked out and eaten. **Desserts** aren't a regular feature in China, though sweet soups and buns are eaten (the latter not confined to main meals) in the south, particularly at festive occasions.

Resting your chopsticks together across the top of your bowl means that you've **finished** eating. After a meal, the Chinese don't hang around to talk over drinks as in the West, but get up straight away and leave. In canteens, you'll **pay** up front, while at restaurants you ask for the bill and pay either the

---

CHINESE WEIGHTS

Note that dishes such as *jiaozi* and some seafood, as well as fresh produce, are **sold by weight**: a **liang** (两, liǎng) is 50g, a **banjin** (半斤, bànjīn) 250g, a **jin** (斤, jīn) 500g, and a **gongjin** (公斤, gōngjīn) 1kg.

waiter or at the front till. **Tipping** is not expected in mainland China, though in Hong Kong you generally leave around ten percent.

Western and international food

There's a fair amount of **Western and international food** available in China, though supply and quality vary. Hong Kong, Shanghai and Beijing have the best range, with some excellent restaurants covering everything from Russian to Brazilian cuisine, and there are international food restaurants in every Chinese city of any size, with Korean and Japanese the best represented. Elsewhere, upmarket hotels may have Western restaurants, serving expensive but huge **buffet breakfasts** of scrambled egg, bacon, toast, cereal and coffee; and there's a growing number of **cafés** in many cities, especially ones with large foreign expat populations. **Burger**, **fried chicken** and **pizza** places are ubiquitous, including domestic chains such as *Dicos* alongside *McDonald's*, *KFC* and *Pizza Hut*.

Self-catering

Self-catering for tourists is feasible to a point. **Instant noodles** are a favourite travel food with the Chinese, available anywhere – just add boiling water, leave for five minutes, then stir in the flavourings supplied. Fresh **fruit and veg** from markets needs to be washed and peeled before eating raw; you can supplement things with **dried fruit**, **nuts and seeds**, roast and cured meats, biscuits and all manner of snacks. In cities, these things are also sold in more hygienic situations in **supermarkets**; many provincial capitals also have branches of the international chain **Carrefour** (家乐福, jiālèfú), where you can generally find small caches of Western foods.

Drink

Water is easily available in China, but never drink what comes out of the tap. **Boiled water** is always on hand in hotels and trains, either provided in large vacuum flasks or an urn, and you can buy **bottled spring water** at station stalls and supermarkets.

Tea

Tea has been known in China since antiquity and was originally drunk for medicinal reasons. Over the centuries a whole **social culture** has sprung up around this beverage, spawning **teahouses** that once held the same place in Chinese society that the local pub or bar does in the West. Plantations of neat rows of low tea bushes adorn hillsides across southern China, while the brew is enthusiastically consumed from the highlands of Tibet – where it's mixed with barley meal and butter – to every restaurant and household between Hong Kong and Beijing. Unfortunately, in a land where a pot of tea used to be plonked in front of every restaurant-goer before they'd even sat down, you now usually have to pay for the privilege – and your tea can work out more expensive than the rest of your meal.

Chinese tea comes in red, green and flower-scented **varieties**, depending on how it's processed; only Hainan produces Indian-style **black** tea. Some regional kinds, such as *pu'er* from Yunnan, Fujian's *tie guanyin*, Zhejiang's *longjing* or Sichuan's *zhuye qing*, are highly sought after; indeed, after locals in Yunnan decided that banks weren't paying enough interest, they started investing in *pu'er* tea stocks, causing prices to soar.

The manner in which it's **served** also varies from place to place: sometimes it comes in huge mugs with a lid, elsewhere in dainty cups served from a miniature pot; there are also formalized **tea rituals** in parts of Fujian and Guangdong. When drinking in company, it's polite to top up others' cups before your own, whenever they become empty; if someone does this for you, lightly tap your first two fingers on the table to show your thanks. If you've had enough, leave your cup full, and in a restaurant take the lid off or turn it over if you want the pot refilled during the meal.

Chinese leaf tea is never drunk with milk or sugar, though recently **Taiwanese bubble tea** – Indian-style tea with milk, sugar and sago balls – has become popular in the south. It's also worth trying some **Muslim** *babao cha* or **Eight Treasures Tea**, which involves dried fruit, nuts, seeds and crystallized sugar heaped into a cup with the remaining space filled with hot water, poured with panache from an immensely long-spouted copper kettle.

Alcohol

The popularity of **beer** in China rivals that of tea, and, for men, is the preferred mealtime beverage (drinking alcohol in public is considered improper for Chinese women, though not for foreigners). The first brewery was set up in the northeastern port of Qingdao by the Germans in the nineteenth century (see p.301), and now, though the Tsingtao label is widely available, just about every province produces at least one brand of 4% Pilsner. Sold in 660ml bottles, it's always drinkable, often pretty good, and is actually cheaper than bottled water. Draught beer is becoming available across the country.

Watch out for the term "**wine**" on English menus, which usually denotes **spirits**, made from rice, sorghum or millet. Serving spirits to guests is a sign of hospitality, and they're always used for toasting at banquets. Again, local home-made varieties can be quite good, while mainstream brands – especially the expensive, nationally famous Moutai and Wuliangye – are pretty vile to the Western palate. China does have several commercial **wine labels**, the best of which is Changyu from Yantai in Shandong province, and there are ongoing efforts to launch wine as a stylish niche product, with limited success so far.

Western-style bars are found in all major cities. These establishments serve both local and imported beers and spirits, and are popular with China's middle class, as well as foreigners. Mostly, though, the Chinese drink alcohol only with their meals – all restaurants serve at least local brews and spirits. **Imported beers and spirits** are sold in large department stores and in city bars, but are always expensive.

Soft drinks

Canned drinks, usually sold unchilled, include various lemonades and colas. **Fruit juices** can be unusual and refreshing, however, flavoured with chunks of lychee, lotus and water chestnuts. **Milk** is sold in powder form as baby food, and increasingly in bottles for adult consumption as its benefits for invalids and the elderly become accepted wisdom.

Coffee

Coffee has long been grown and drunk in Yunnan and Hainan, and **coffee** culture is now taking off across China, with cafés in every major city across the land. The quality of what you'll get varies widely; it's pretty good in the trendy brunch-houses of Beijing and Shanghai, for example, though pretty wretched in the generic (and huge) local chains. If you simply need to staisfy your caffeine cravings, head to *McDonald's* or *KFC*, which serve passable coffee (with milk, if you'd like) for very low prices; or buy imported instant powder in any supermarket.

The media

Xinhua is the state-run news agency, and it supplies most of the national print and TV media. All content is Party-controlled and censored, though there is a limited openness about social issues and natural disasters as long as the government is portrayed as successfully combating the problem. Stories about corrupt local officials, armed confrontations between developers and peasants being forced off their land, or the appalling conditions of coal-mine workers, do occasionally get through the net, though both journalists and editors take a risk reporting such things: several doing so have been jailed for "revealing state secrets", or even beaten to death by the thugs they were trying to expose.

Newspapers and magazines

The national **Chinese-language newspaper** is the *People's Daily* (with an online English edition at Ⓦ english.peopledaily.com.cn), though all provincial capitals and many major cities produce their own dailies with a local slant. The only national **English-language newspaper** is the *China Daily* (Ⓦ chinadaily.com.cn), which is scarce outside big cities. **Hong Kong**'s English-language media includes the locally produced newspapers *South China Morning Post* and the *Standard*, published alongside regional editions of *Time*, *Newsweek*, the *Asian Wall Street Journal* and *USA Today*. These have so far remained openly critical of Beijing on occasion, despite the former colony's changeover to Chinese control.

Most big cities, including Beijing, Shanghai, Kunming, Chengdu and Chongqing, have free **English-language magazines** aimed at expats containing listings of local venues and events, plus classifieds and feature articles; they're monitored by the authorities, though this doesn't stop them sailing quite close to the wind at times.

Television and radio

Chinese **television** comprises a dozen or so channels run by the state television company, **CCTV**, plus a host of regional stations; not all channels are available across the country. Most of the content comprises news, flirty game shows, travel and wildlife documentaries, soaps and historical dramas, and bizarre song-and-dance extravaganzas featuring performers in fetishistic, tight-fitting military outfits entertaining party officials with rigor-mortis faces. Tune in to **CCTV 1** for news; **CCTV 5** is dedicated to sport; **CCTV 6** shows films (with at least one war feature a day, in which the Japanese will be mightily beaten); **CCTV News** broadcasts an **English-language** mix of news, documentaries and travel shows; and

CCTV 11 concentrates on Chinese opera. The **regional stations** are sometimes more adventurous, with a current trend for frank dating games, which draw much criticism from conservative-minded government factions for the rampant materialism displayed by the contestants.

On the **radio** you're likely to hear the latest soft ballads, or versions of Western pop songs sung in Chinese. For **news from home**, you'll need to bring a shortwave radio with you, or listen via the websites of the **BBC World Service** (🌐 bbc.co.uk /worldservice), **Radio Canada** (🌐 rcinet.ca), the **Voice of America** (🌐 voa.gov) and **Radio Australia** (🌐 abc.net.au/ra).

Festivals

China celebrates many secular and religious festivals, two of which – the Spring Festival (Chinese New Year) and National Day on October 1 – involve major nationwide holidays. Avoid travel during these times, as the country's transport network becomes severely overloaded.

Most festivals take place according to dates in the **Chinese lunar calendar**, in which the first day of the month is the time when the moon is at its thinnest, with the full moon marking the middle of the month. By the Gregorian calendar used in the West, such festivals fall on a different day every year – check online for the latest dates. Most festivals celebrate the turning of the seasons or auspicious dates, such as the eighth day of the eighth month

(eight is a lucky number in China), and are times for gift giving, family reunions, feasting and the setting off of firecrackers. It's always worth visiting temples on festival days, when the air is thick with incense, and people queue up to kowtow to altars and play games that bring good fortune, such as trying to hit the temple bell by throwing coins.

Aside from the following national festivals, China's **ethnic groups** punctuate the year with their own ritual observances, which are described in the relevant chapters of the Guide. In Hong Kong, all the national Chinese festivals are celebrated.

A HOLIDAYS AND FESTIVALS CALENDAR

January/February Two-week-long **Spring Festival** (see box below). Everything shuts down for a national holiday during the first week.

February Tiancang Festival On the twentieth day of the first lunar month, Chinese peasants celebrate Tiancang, or Granary Filling Day, in the hope of ensuring a good harvest later in the year.

March Guanyin's Birthday Guanyin, the Bodhisattva of Mercy, and probably China's most popular deity, is celebrated on the nineteenth day of the second lunar month.

April 4/5 Qingming Festival This festival, also referred to as Tomb Sweeping Day, is the time to visit the graves of ancestors and burn ghost money in honour of the departed.

April 13–15 Dai Water Splashing Festival Anyone on the streets of Xishuangbanna, in Yunnan province, is fair game for a soaking.

May 1 Labour Day A three-day national holiday when everyone goes on the move.

May 4 Youth Day Commemorating the student demonstrators in Tian'anmen Square in 1919, which gave rise to the Nationalist "May Fourth Movement". It's marked in most cities with flower displays.

June 1 Children's Day Most schools go on field trips, so if you're visiting a popular tourist site, be prepared for mobs of kids in yellow baseball caps.

SPRING FESTIVAL (CHINESE NEW YEAR)

The **Spring Festival** is two weeks of festivities marking the beginning of the lunar **New Year**, usually in late January or early February. In Chinese astrology, each year is associated with one of twelve animals, and the passing into a new phase is a momentous occasion. The festival sees China at its most colourful, with shops and houses decorated with good-luck messages. The first day of the festival is marked by a family feast at which *jiaozi* (dumplings) are eaten, sometimes with coins hidden inside. To bring luck, people dress in red clothes (red being a lucky colour) and eat fish, since the Chinese script for fish resembles the script for "surplus", something everyone wishes to enjoy during the year. Firecrackers are let off almost constantly to scare ghosts away and, on the fifth day, to honour **Cai Shen**, god of wealth. Another ghost-scaring tradition is the pasting up of images of door gods at the threshold. Outside the home, New Year is celebrated at **temple fairs**, which feature acrobats and clouds of smoke as the Chinese light incense sticks to placate the gods. The celebrations end with the **lantern festival**, when the streets are filled with multicoloured paper lanterns; many places also have flower festivals and street processions with paper dragons and other animals parading through the town. It's customary at this time to eat *tang yuan*, glutinous rice balls stuffed with sweet sesame paste.

June/July Dragon-boat Festival On the fifth day of the fifth lunar month, dragon-boat races are held in memory of the poet Qu Yuan, who drowned himself in 280 BC. The traditional food to accompany the celebrations is *zongzi* (lotus-wrapped rice packets). Another three-day public holiday.

August/September Ghost Festival The Chinese equivalent of Halloween, this is a time when ghosts from hell are supposed to walk the earth. It's not celebrated so much as observed; it's regarded as an inauspicious time to travel, move house or get married.

September/October Moon Festival On the fifteenth day of the eighth month of the lunar calendar, the Chinese celebrate what's also known as the Mid-Autumn Festival. Moon cakes, containing a rich filling of sugar, lotus-seed paste and walnut, are eaten, and plenty of spirits consumed. The public get a further three days off.

September/October Double Ninth Festival Nine is a number associated with *yang*, or male energy, and on the ninth day of the ninth lunar month such qualities as assertiveness and strength are celebrated. It's believed to be a good time for the distillation (and consumption) of spirits.

September 28 Confucius Festival The birthday of Confucius is marked by celebrations at all Confucian temples. It's a good time to visit Qufu, in Shandong province, when elaborate ceremonies are held at the temple there.

October 1 National Day Another week-long holiday when everyone has time off to celebrate the founding of the People's Republic. TV is even more dire than usual as it's full of programmes celebrating Party achievements.

December 25 Christmas This is marked as a religious event only by the faithful, but for everyone else it's an excuse for a feast and a party.

Sport and outdoor activities

Since 2008, when China hosted the Olympics, athletic passion has become almost a patriotic duty. But the most visible forms of exercise are fairly timeless; head to any public space in the morning and you'll see citizens going through all sorts of martial-arts routines, playing ping pong and street badminton, even ballroom dancing. Sadly though, facilities for organized sport are fairly limited.

The Chinese are good at "small ball" games such as squash and badminton, and, of course, table tennis, at which they are world champions, but admit room for improvement in the "big ball" games, such as **football**. Nevertheless, Chinese men follow foreign football avidly, with games from the European leagues shown on CCTV5. There's also a national obsession among students for **basketball**,

which predates the rise to international fame of NBA star **Yao Ming**, who plied his trade for the Houston Rockets.

If China has an indigenous "sport", however, it's the **martial arts** – not surprising, perhaps, in a country whose history is littered with long periods of civil conflict. Today, there are hundreds of Chinese martial-arts styles, often taught for exercise rather than for fighting.

As for **outdoor activities**, hiking for its own sake is slowly catching on, though tourists have plenty of opportunities for step-aerobic-type exercise up long, steep staircases ascending China's many **holy mountains**. Snow sports have become popular in Dongbei, which has several **ski resorts**, while the wilds of Yunnan and Sichuan, along with Qinghai and Tibet, are drawing increasing numbers of adventurous young city-born Chinese – always dressed in the latest outdoor gear – to **mountaineering** and four-wheel-drive expeditions.

Culture and etiquette

The Chinese are, on the whole, pragmatic, materialistic and garrulous. Many of the irritations experienced by foreigners – the sniggers and the unhelpful service – can almost invariably be put down to nervousness and the language barrier, rather than hostility. Visitors who speak Chinese will encounter an endless series of delighted and amazed interlocutors wherever they go, invariably asking about their country of origin, their job and the reason they are in China.

If you're **invited** to someone's home, take along a **gift** – a bottle of spirits, some tea or an ornamental trinket are good choices (anything too utilitarian could be considered patronizing) – though your hosts won't impolitely open this in front of you. **Restaurant bills** are not shared out between the guests; instead, people will go to great lengths to pay the whole amount themselves. Normally this honour will fall to the person perceived as the most senior, and as a foreigner dining with Chinese you should make some effort to stake your claim, though it is probable that someone else will grab the bill before you do. Attempting to pay a "share" of the bill will embarrass your hosts.

Privacy

Mainland Chinese have almost no concept of **privacy** – many public toilets are built with partitions so low that you can chat with your neighbour while squatting, and in some bus stations or hotel toilets, some have no partitions at all. All leisure activities including visits to natural beauty spots or holy relics are enjoyed in large noisy groups, and the desire of some Western tourists to be "left alone" can be interpreted by locals as eccentric or arrogant.

Exotic foreigners inevitably become targets for **blatant curiosity**. People stare and point, voices on the street shout out "helloooo" twenty times a day, or – in rural areas – people even run up and jostle for a better look, exclaiming loudly to each other, *laowai, laowai* ("foreigner"). This is not usually intended to be aggressive or insulting, though the cumulative effects of such treatment can prove to be annoying, perhaps even alienating.

Spitting and smoking

Various other forms of behaviour perceived as antisocial in the West are considered perfectly normal in China. The widespread habit of **spitting**, for example, though slowly on the wane, can be observed in buses, trains, restaurants and even inside people's homes. Outside the company of urban sophisticates, it would not occur to people that there was anything disrespectful in delivering a powerful spit while in conversation with a stranger. **Smoking**, likewise, is almost universal among men, and any attempt to stop others from lighting up is met with incomprehension. As in many countries, handing out cigarettes is a basic way of establishing goodwill, and non-smokers should be apologetic about turning down offered cigarettes.

Clothing

Chinese clothing styles lean towards the casual, though surprisingly for such an apparently conservative-minded country, summertime **skimpy clothing** is common in all urban areas, particularly among women (less so in the countryside). Even in potentially sensitive Muslim areas, many Han Chinese girls insist on wearing miniskirts and see-through blouses. Although Chinese men commonly wear shorts and expose their midriffs in hot weather, Western men who do the same should note that the bizarre sight of hairy flesh in public – chest or legs – will instantly become the focus of giggly gossip. The generally relaxed approach to clothing applies equally when visiting temples, though in **mosques** men and women alike should cover their bodies above the wrists and ankles. As for **beachwear**, bikinis and briefs are in, but nudity has yet to become fashionable.

Casual clothing is one thing, but **scruffy clothing** quite another. If you want to earn the respect of the Chinese – useful for things like getting served in a restaurant or checking into a hotel – you should make some effort with your appearance. While the average Chinese peasant might reasonably be expected to have wild hair and wear dirty clothes, a rich foreigner doing so will arouse a degree of contempt.

Meeting people

When **meeting people** it's useful to have a name or **business card** to flash around – Chinese with business aspirations hand them out at every opportunity, and are a little crestfallen if you can't produce one in return. It's polite to take the proffered card with both hands and to have a good look at it before putting it away – though not in your back pocket. If you don't speak Chinese but have your name in Chinese printed on them, they also become useful when checking in to hotels that are reluctant to take foreigners, as the staff can then copy your name into the register.

Shaking hands is not a Chinese tradition, though it is fairly common between men. Bodily contact in the form of embraces or back-slapping can be observed between same-sex friends, and these days, in cities, a boy and a girl can walk round arm in arm and even kiss without raising an eyebrow. **Voice levels** in China seem to be pitched several decibels louder than in most other countries, though this should not necessarily be interpreted as a sign of belligerence.

Sex and gender issues

Women travellers in China usually find **sexual harassment** less of a problem than in other Asian countries. Chinese men are, on the whole, deferential and respectful. A more likely complaint is being ignored, as the Chinese will generally assume that any man accompanying a woman will be doing all the talking, ordering and paying. Women on their own visiting remote temples or sights need to be on their guard – don't assume that all monks and caretakers have impeccable morals.

Prostitution, though illegal, is everywhere in China. Single foreign men are likely to be approached inside hotels; it's common practice for prostitutes to phone around hotel rooms at all hours of the night. Bear in mind that the consequence of a Westerner being caught with a prostitute may be unpleasant, and that AIDS is on the increase.

Homosexuality is increasingly tolerated by the authorities and people in general, though public displays may get you in trouble outside the more cosmopolitan cities. There are gay bars in most major cities, especially Beijing and Shanghai.

Dating a local won't raise many eyebrows in these relaxed times, though displays of mixed-race public affection certainly will.

Shopping

China is a good place to shop for tourist souvenirs, folk art, clothes, household goods and faked designer labels – but not for real designer brands or electronic goods (including mobile phones), which are all cheaper at home or online. Even small villages have markets, while larger cities will also have big department stores, shopping malls and even international supermarket chains.

Prices in stores are fixed, but **discounts** (折扣, zhékòu) are common: they're marked by a number between one and nine and the character "折", indicating the percentage of the original price you have to pay – "8折", for example, means that the item is on sale at eighty percent of its original price. At markets you're expected to **bargain** for goods unless prices are displayed. If you can speak Chinese, hang around for a while to get an idea what others are paying, or just ask at a few stalls selling the same things; Chinese shoppers usually state the price they're willing to pay, rather than beginning low and working up to it after haggling. Don't become obsessed about saving every last yuan; being charged more than locals and getting ripped off from time to time is inevitable.

Souvenirs popular with foreign tourists include "chops" (stone seals with your name engraved in characters on the base); all manner of reproduction antiques, from porcelain to furniture; mementos of Mao and the Cultural Revolution – Little Red Books and cigarette lighters that chime "*The East is Red*"; T-shirts and "old-style" Chinese clothes; scroll paintings; and ethnic jewellery and textiles. Chinese tourists also look for things like local teas, "purple sand" teapots and bright tack. Pretty much the same selection is sold at all tourist sites, irrespective of relevancy. For **real antiques**, you need specialist stores or markets – some are listed in the Guide –

where anything genuine is meant to be marked with a wax seal and requires an export licence to take out of the country. But be aware that, with world prices for Chinese art going through the roof, forgeries abound. The Chinese are also clued-up, avid collectors and value their culture highly, so don't expect to find any bargains.

Clothes are a very good deal in China, with brand stores such as Giordano, Baleno, Metersbonwe and Yishion selling high-quality smart-casual wear. Fashion-conscious places such as Shanghai and Hong Kong also have **factory outlet** stores, selling last year's designs at low prices, and all major cities have specialist stores stocking outdoor and hiking gear, though it often looks far better than it turns out to be for the price. Silk and other **fabrics** are also good value, if you're into making your own clothes, while **shoes** are inexpensive too. With the Chinese youth racing up in height, finding clothing in large **sizes** is becoming less of an issue.

All bookshops and many market stalls in China sell **music CDs** of everything from Beijing punk to Beethoven, plus **VCDs** and **DVDs** of domestic and international movies (often subtitled – check on the back). While extremely cheap, many of these are **pirated** (the discs may be confiscated at customs when you get home). Genuine DVD films may be region-coded for Asia, so check the label and whether your player at home will handle them; there are no such problems with CDs or VCDs.

Hong Kong is the only place with a comprehensive range of **Western goods**; on the mainland, your best bet is to head to provincial capitals, many of which have a branch of **Carrefour** (家乐福, jiālèfú) or **Wal-Mart** (沃尔玛, wòěrmǎ), where you may find small caches of foreign goodies.

Children

Children in China are, thanks to the one-child policy, usually indulged and pampered, and foreigners travelling with children can expect to receive lots of attention from curious locals – and the occasional admonition that the little one should be wrapped up warmer.

While **formula and nappies** might be available in modern, big city supermarkets, elsewhere you'll need to bring a supply (and any **medication** if required) with you – local kids don't use nappies, just pants with a slit at the back, and when baby wants to go, mummy points him at the gutter. Similarly, changing facilities and baby-minding services are virtually unknown on the mainland outside high-end international hotels.

Hong Kong is the only part of China where children are specifically catered to by attractions such as Ocean World and Disneyland; elsewhere, the way that most Chinese tourist sites are decked up like fairground rides makes them attractive for youngsters in any case. Things to watch for include China's poor levels of **hygiene** (keeping infants' and toddlers' hands clean can be a full-time occupation), spicy or just unusual food, plus the **stress levels** caused by the ambient crowds, pollution and noise found in much of the country – though this often seems to affect parents more than children.

Travel essentials

Costs

China is an **expensive** place to visit compared with the rest of Asia. Though food and transport are good value, accommodation can be pricey for what you get, and **entry fees** for temples, scenic areas and historic monuments are becoming high even on an international scale – so much so that the central government is trying to get local authorities to reduce them (with little effect so far). Actual prices vary considerably between **regions**: Hong Kong and Macau are as costly as Europe or the US; the developed eastern provinces are expensive by Chinese standards; and the further west you go, the more prices fall.

By doing everything cheaply and sticking mostly to the less expensive interior provinces, you can survive on £30/US$45/¥300 a day; travel a bit more widely and in better comfort and you're looking at £60/US$90/¥600 a day; while travelling in style and visiting only key places along the east coast, you could run up daily expenses of £150/US$225/¥1500 and above.

Discount rates for pensioners and students are available for many sights, though students may well be asked for a Chinese student card – the practice varies from place to place, even within the same city. Pensioners, on the other hand, can often just use their passports to prove they are over 60 (women) or 65 (men).

Crime and personal safety

While the worst that happens to most visitors to China is that they have their pocket picked on a bus or get **scammed** (see p.51), you do need to take care. Carry passports and money (and your phone,

if it fits) in a concealed money belt, and keep some foreign notes – perhaps around US$200 – separately from the rest of your cash, together with your insurance policy details and photocopies of your passport and visa. Be wary on **buses**, the favoured haunt of **pickpockets**, and **trains**, particularly in hard-seat class and on overnight journeys.

One of the most dangerous things you can do in China is **cross a road**: marked pedestrian crossings might as well not be there for all the attention shown them by motorists; and even when traffic lights flash green to show it's safe to cross, you'll find that vehicles are still permitted to turn in to or out of the road. **Hotel rooms** are on the whole secure, dormitories much less so, though often it's your fellow travellers who are the problem here. Most hotels should have a safe, but it's not unusual for things to go missing from these. Wandering around cities late at night is as bad an idea in China as anywhere else; similarly, walking alone across the countryside is ill-advised, particularly in remote regions. If anyone does try to rob you, run away or, if this isn't possible, stay calm and don't resist.

You may see stress-induced **street confrontations**, though these rarely result in violence, just a lot of shouting. Another irritation, particularly in the southern cities, is gangs of **child beggars**, organized by a nearby adult. They target foreigners and can be very hard to shake off; handing over money usually results in increased harassment.

The police

The **police**, known as the **Public Security Bureau** or **PSB**, are recognizable by their dark blue uniforms and caps, though there are a lot more around than you might at first think, as plenty are undercover. They have much wider powers than most Western police forces, including establishing the guilt of criminals – trials are used only for deciding the sentence of the accused (though this is changing and China now has the beginnings of an independent judiciary). If the culprit is deemed to show proper remorse, this will result in a more lenient sentence.

The PSB also have the job of looking after foreigners, and you'll most likely have to seek them

SCAMS

A good number of professional **con artists** target tourists – especially in places such as Shanghai, Beijing and Guilin – with variations on the following scam. A sweet-looking young couple, a pair of girls, or perhaps a kindly old man, will ask to practise their English or offer to show you round. Having befriended you – which may take hours – they will suggest some refreshment, and lead you to a teahouse, art gallery or restaurant. After eating or drinking, you will be presented with a bill for thousands of yuan, your new "friends" will vanish, and some large gentlemen will appear – who in some cases have forced people into handing over their card and PIN and raiding their bank account before letting them go. It's hard to believe just how convincing these scam artists can be: never eat or drink with a stranger unless you know how much you're expected to pay.

out for **visa extensions**, reporting theft or losses, and obtaining permits for otherwise closed areas of the country (mostly in Tibet). On occasion, they might seek you out; it's common for the police to call round to your hotel room if you're staying in a remote place – they usually just look at your passport and then move on.

While individual police often go out of their way to help foreigners, the PSB itself has all the problems of any police force in a country where corruption is widespread, and it's best to minimize contact with them.

Offences to avoid

With adjacent opium-growing areas in Burma and Laos, and a major Southeast Asian distribution point in Hong Kong, China has a massive **drug problem**. Heroin use has become fairly widespread in the south, particularly in depressed rural areas, and ecstasy is used in clubs and discos. In the past, the police have turned a blind eye to foreigners with drugs, as long as no Chinese are involved, but you don't want to test this out. In 2010, China **executed** a British national for drug trafficking, and annually holds mass executions of convicted drug offenders on the UN anti-drugs day in June.

Visitors are not likely to be accused of **political crimes**, but foreign residents, including teachers or students, may find themselves expelled from the country for talking about politics or religion. The Chinese they talk to will be treated less leniently. In Tibet, and at sensitive border areas, censorship is taken extremely seriously; **photographing** military installations (which can include major road bridges), instances of police brutality or gulags is not a good idea.

Electricity

The electricity supply runs on 220 volts, with the most common type of **plug** a dual flat prong, except in Hong Kong, where they favour the

UK-style square triple prong. Adaptors are widely available from neighbourhood hardware stores.

Entry requirements

Unless you're briefly transiting China via certain key cities (see box, p.52), all foreign nationals require a **visa** to enter mainland China, available worldwide from Chinese embassies and consulates and through specialist tour operators and visa agents, and online. In the past they've been easiest to obtain in **Hong Kong**, though at the time of writing there were restrictions being placed on visas issued here.

Visas must be used within three months of issue, and **cost** £30/$45 and up, depending on the visa type, the length of stay, the number of entries allowed, and your nationality. Your passport must be valid for at least another six months from your planned date of entry into China, and have at least one blank page for visas. You'll be asked your **occupation** – it's not wise to admit to being a journalist, photographer or writer since you might be called in for an interview, and in such instances it's best to say "consultant" or similar instead. At times of political sensitivity, you may be asked for proof of onward air travel and hotel bookings in your name. **Don't overstay your visa**: the fine is ¥500 a day, along with the possibility that you may be deported and banned from entering China for five years.

Tourist visas (L) are valid for between one and three months, and can be single- or multiple-entry – though multiple-entry visas usually require you to leave China every thirty days.

A **business visa** (F) is valid for between three months and two years and can be either multiple- or single-entry. To apply, you'll need an official invitation from a government-recognized Chinese organization. **Twelve-month work visas** (Z) again require an invitation, plus a **health certificate**.

VISA-FREE TRANSIT

Currently, visitors from the US, Canada, UK and many European countries arriving on international flights at Beijing, Shanghai, Guangzhou and Chengdu can spend up to 72 hours in transit **without a visa**. To be eligible, you must have proof of onward travel to a third country (so you can't, for instance, be on a round-trip from Hong Kong). You are also not allowed to leave the relevant city's boundaries during your stay.

Students intending to study in China for less than six months need an invitation or letter of acceptance from a college there and will be given an F visa. If you're intending study for longer than six months, there is an additional form, available from Chinese embassies and online, and you will also need a health certificate; then you'll be issued with an X visa, which allows you to stay and study for up to a year.

You're allowed to **import** into China up to 400 cigarettes and 1.5l of alcohol and up to ¥20,000 cash. Foreign currency in excess of US$5000 or the equivalent must be declared. It's illegal to import **printed or filmed matter** critical of the country, but this is currently only a problem with Chinese border guards at crossings from Vietnam, who have confiscated guidebooks to China that contain maps showing Taiwan as a separate country (such as this one); keep them buried in the bottom of your bags.

CHINESE EMBASSIES AND CONSULATES

Australia 15 Coronation Drive, Yarralumla, Canberra, ACT 2600 ☎ 02 6273 4780, ⓦ au.china-embassy.org/eng.

Canada 515 St Patrick St, Ottawa, Ontario K1N 5H3 ☎ 1 613 789 3434, ⓦ ca.chineseembassy.org/eng/.

Ireland 40 Ailesbury Rd, Dublin 4 ☎ 01 269 1707, ⓦ ie.china-embassy.org/eng.

New Zealand 2–6 Glenmore St, Wellington ☎ 04 474 9631, ⓦ www.chinaembassy.org.nz.

South Africa 972 Pretorius St, Arcadia, Pretoria ☎ 012 431 6500, ⓦ www.chinese-embassy.org.za.

UK 49–51 Portland Place, London W1B 1JL ☎ 020 7299 4049, ⓦ www.chinese-embassy.org.uk.

US 3505 International Place, Washington DC 20008 ☎ 1 202 495 2266, ⓦ www.china-embassy.org/eng/.

Visa extensions

Visa extensions are handled by the **Public Security Bureau** (**PSB**), so you can apply for one in any reasonably sized town – the department will be called something like "Aliens' Entry Exit Section". The cost, and the amount of hassle you'll have, varies greatly depending on where you are and your nationality. In particular, many places want to see a receipt from your accommodation, proving that you're staying in the town in which you're applying.

A **first extension**, valid for a month, is easy to obtain and costs ¥160 (though US citizens pay more). However, the particular PSB office may decide to levy extra charges on top, or even waive the fee completely. Processing the application takes seven working days, and you need to apply at least seven days in advance of your old visa expiring. The worst place to apply (bar Tibet, of course) is Beijing, then Shanghai.

A **second or third extension** is harder to get, and is impossible if your visa was originally issued in Hong Kong. In major cities, you will probably be turned away, though you'd be unlucky not to be given some kind of extension from PSB offices in small towns. You will be asked your reasons for wanting an extension – simply saying you want to spend more time in this wonderful country usually goes down well, or you could cite illness or transport delays. Don't admit to being low on funds. Fourth or even fifth extensions are possible, but you'll need to foster connections with a PSB office. Ask advice from a local independent travel agent – they often have the right sort of contacts. In Shanghai and Beijing, it is possible to get extra extensions from a visa agent – they advertise in expat magazines.

Health

No vaccinations are required to visit China, except for yellow fever if you're coming from an area where the disease is endemic. It's worth taking a **first-aid kit** with you, particularly if you will be travelling extensively outside the cities, where getting hold of the appropriate medicines might be difficult. Include bandages, plasters, painkillers, oral rehydration solution, medication to counter diarrhoea, vitamin pills and antiseptic cream. A sterile set of hypodermics may be advisable, as re-use of needles does occur in China. Note there is widespread ignorance of sexual health issues, and AIDS and STDs are widespread – always practise **safe sex**.

The most common health hazards in China are the **cold and flu infections** that strike down a large proportion of the population in the winter months. **Diarrhoea** is also common, usually in a mild form while your stomach gets used to unfamiliar food, but also sometimes with a sudden onset accompanied by stomach cramps and vomiting, which indicates **food poisoning**. In both instances, get plenty of rest, drink lots of water, and in serious cases replace lost salts with **oral rehydration solution** (**ORS**); this is especially important with young children. Take a few sachets with you, or make your own by adding half a teaspoon of salt and three of sugar to a litre of cool, previously boiled water. While down with diarrhoea, avoid milk, greasy or spicy foods, coffee and most fruit, in favour of bland foodstuffs such as rice, plain noodles and soup. If symptoms persist, or if you notice blood or mucus in your stools, consult a doctor as you may have **dysentery**.

To avoid stomach complaints, eat at places that look busy and clean and stick to fresh, thoroughly cooked food. Shellfish is a potential hepatitis A risk, and best avoided. Fresh fruit you've peeled yourself is safe; other uncooked foods may have been washed in unclean water. **Don't drink untreated tap water** – boiled or bottled water is widely available.

Hepatitis A is a viral infection spread by contaminated food and water, which causes an inflammation of the liver. The less common **hepatitis B** virus can be passed on through unprotected sexual contact, transfusions of unscreened blood, and dirty needles. Hepatitis symptoms include yellowing of the eyes and skin, preceded by lethargy, fever, and pains in the upper right abdomen.

Typhoid and cholera are spread by contaminated food or water, generally in localized epidemics; both are serious conditions and require immediate medical help. Symptoms of **typhoid** include headaches, high fever and constipation, followed by diarrhoea in the later stages. The disease is infectious. **Cholera** begins with sudden but painless onset of watery diarrhoea, later combined with vomiting, nausea and muscle cramps. Rapid dehydration rather than the infection itself is the main danger, and should be treated with constant oral rehydration solutions.

Summer outbreaks of **malaria** and **dengue fever** occur across southern China, usually in localized areas. Symptoms are similar – severe headaches, joint pains, fever and shaking – though a rash might also appear with dengue. There's no cure for dengue fever, whereas malaria can be prevented and controlled with medication; both require immediate medical attention to ensure that there are no complications. You can minimize your chances of being bitten by mosquitoes in the first place by wearing light-coloured, full-length clothing and insect repellent in the evenings when mosquitoes are active.

In tropical China, the **temperature and humidity** can take a couple of weeks to adjust to. High humidity can cause **heat rashes**, **prickly heat** and **fungal infections**. Prevention and cure are the same: wear loose clothes made of natural fibres, wash frequently and dry-off thoroughly afterwards. Talcum or anti-fungal powder and the use of mild antiseptic soap help, too.

Don't underestimate the strength of the sun in the tropics, desert regions such as Xinjiang or high up on the Tibetan Plateau. Sunscreen is not always easily available in China, and local stuff isn't always of sufficiently high quality anyway. Signs of **dehydration** and **heatstroke** include a high temperature, lack of sweating, a fast pulse and red skin. Reducing your body temperature with a lukewarm shower will provide initial relief.

Plenty of places in China – Tibet and the north in particular – also get very **cold**. Watch out here for **hypothermia**, where the core body temperature drops to a point that can be fatal. Symptoms are a weak pulse, disorientation, numbness, slurred speech and exhaustion. To prevent the condition, wear lots of layers and a hat, eat plenty of carbohydrates, and stay dry and out of the wind. To treat hypothermia, get the victim into shelter, away from wind and rain, give them hot drinks – but not alcohol – and easily digestible food, and keep them warm. Serious cases require immediate hospitalization.

High altitude, in regions such as Tibet and parts of Xinjiang, Sichuan and Yunnan, prevents the blood from absorbing oxygen efficiently, and can lead to **altitude sickness**, also known as **AMS** (acute mountain sickness). Most people feel some symptoms above 3500m, which include becoming easily exhausted, headaches, shortness of breath, sleeping disorders and nausea; they're intensified if you ascend to altitude rapidly, for instance by flying direct from coastal cities to Lhasa. Relaxing for the first few days, **drinking** plenty of water, and taking painkillers will ease symptoms. Having acclimatized at one altitude, you should still ascend slowly, or you can expect the symptoms to return.

If for any reason the body fails to acclimatize to altitude, serious conditions can develop including **pulmonary oedema** (characterized by severe breathing trouble, a cough and frothy white or pink sputum), and **cerebral oedema** (causing severe headaches, loss of balance, other neurological symptoms and eventually coma). The only treatment for these is **rapid descent**: in Tibet, this means flying out to Kathmandu or Chengdu without delay. You also need to see a doctor as soon as possible.

Hospitals, clinics and pharmacies

Medical facilities in China are best in major cities with large expat populations, where there are often high-standard clinics, and the hotels may even have resident doctors. Elsewhere, larger cities and towns have hospitals, and for minor complaints there are plenty of pharmacies that can suggest remedies, though don't expect English to be spoken.

Chinese hospitals use a mix of Western and traditional Chinese medicine approaches, and sometimes charge high prices for simple drugs and use procedures that aren't necessary – they'll put you on a drip just to administer antibiotics – so always ask for a second opinion from a Western-trained doctor if you're worried (your embassy should be able to recommend one if none is suggested in the Guide). In an **emergency**, you're better off taking a cab than waiting for an ambulance – it's quicker and will work out much cheaper. There's virtually **no free health care** in China even for its citizens; expect to pay around ¥500 as a consultation **fee**.

Pharmacies are marked by a green cross, and if you can describe your ailment or required medication, you'll find many drugs which would be restricted and expensive in the West are easily available over the counter for very little money. Be wary of **counterfeit drugs**, however; check for spelling mistakes in the packaging or instructions.

MEDICAL RESOURCES FOR TRAVELLERS

IN THE UK AND IRELAND
MASTA (Medical Advisory Service for Travellers Abroad) UK ⓦ masta-travel-health.com. Fifty clinics across the UK.
Tropical Medical Bureau Republic of Ireland ⓦ tmb.ie.

IN THE US AND CANADA
Canadian Society for International Health ⓦ csih.org. Extensive list of travel health centres in Canada.
CDC ⓦ cdc.gov. Official US government public health agency, with good travel-health information.
International Society for Travel Medicine ⓦ istm.org. A full list of clinics worldwide specializing in travel health.

IN AUSTRALIA, NEW ZEALAND AND SOUTH AFRICA
Netcare Travel Clinics ⓦ www.travelclinic.co.za/. Travel clinics in South Africa.
Travellers' Medical & Vaccination Centre ⓦ tmvc.com.au. Website lists travellers' medical and vaccination centres throughout Australia and New Zealand.

Insurance

China is a relatively safe place to travel, though traffic accidents, respiratory infections, petty theft and transport delays are all fairly common occurrences – meaning that it's sensible to ensure you've arranged some form of **travel insurance** before leaving home.

Internet

Internet bars (网吧, **wǎngbā**) with high-speed connections are everywhere in China, from big cities – where some seat hundreds of people – to rural villages. They're invariably full of network-gaming teenagers, and **charge** ¥2–5 per hour.

Having said this, since 2010 you've been required to show a Chinese ID card before being allowed to use a net bar – obviously impossible for most tourists. In some places this rule is strictly enforced; elsewhere nobody cares, or you'll be handed a fake ID at the front counter which will allow you to sign on. It's best not to rely on them: all large hotels have **business centres** where you can get online, but this is expensive, especially in the classier places (around ¥30/hr). Better value are the **backpacker hostels**, where getting online costs around ¥5/hr or is free. But the best deal is to tote a **laptop**, tablet or phone – major cities have cafés with free **wi-fi**, while almost all youth hostels and major hotels have it too (though the latter may charge you through the nose); hotels also often feature ADSL sockets in their rooms.

In an attempt to keep control of news and current affairs, China's internet censors have set up the dryly named "**Great Firewall**" or Net Nanny, which blocks access to any websites deemed undesirable by the state – currently including Twitter, YouTube and Facebook. To get around it, you need to use a **web proxy** or **VPN** (Virtual Private Network) such as WiTopia, Hotspot Shield or UltraSurf, all of which cost a few pounds a month and offer a free limited period trial. This is illegal, but the government pays no attention to foreigners who do this – just about every foreign business in China runs a VPN. For Chinese nationals, it's a different matter, and you will never find a public computer, such as in a hotel or business centre, running one.

Laundry

Big city hotels, and youth hostels all over, offer a **laundry service** for anything between ¥10 and ¥100; alternatively, some hostels have self-service facilities or you can use your room sink (every corner store in China sells **washing powder**). Otherwise, ask at accommodation either for the staff to wash your clothes or for the nearest **laundry**, where they usually charge by dry weight. Laundromats are virtually unknown in China.

Living in China

It is becoming increasingly easy for foreigners to live in China full time, whether as a student, a teacher or for work. Anyone planning to stay more than six months is required to pass a **medical** (from approved clinics) proving that they don't have any venereal disease – if you do have a VD, expect to be deported and your passport endorsed with your ailment.

Many mainland cities – including Beijing, Shanghai, Guangzhou, Kunming and Chengdu – have no restrictions on where foreigners can **reside**, though either you or your landlord must register with the local PSB. **Property rental** is relatively inexpensive if you avoid purpose-built foreign enclaves. The easiest way to find accommodation is to go through an **agent**, who will generally charge one month's rent as a fee. There are plenty who advertise in expat magazines and online.

Teaching

There are **schemes** in operation to place **foreign teachers** in Chinese educational institutions – contact your nearest Chinese embassy (see p.52 for addresses) for details. Some employers ask for a TEFL qualification, though a degree, or simply the ability to speak the language as a native, is usually enough.

The standard **teaching salary** for a foreigner – though this is heavily dependent on your location in China – is around ¥5500 per month for a bachelor's degree, ¥7500 for a master's degree and ¥10,000 for a doctorate. This isn't enough to put much away, but you should also get subsidized on-campus accommodation, plus a fare to your home country – one-way for a single semester and a return for a

year's work. The workload is usually fourteen hours a week, and if you work a year you get paid through the winter holiday. Most teachers find their students keen, hard-working, curious and obedient, and report that it is the contact with them that makes the experience worthwhile. That said, avoid talking about religion or politics in the classroom as this can get them into trouble. You'll earn more – say ¥12,000 a month – in a **private school**, though be aware of the risk of being ripped off by a commercial agency (you might be given more classes to teach than you'd signed up for, for example). Check out the institution thoroughly before committing yourself.

Studying

Many universities in China now host substantial populations of **Western students**, especially in Beijing, Shanghai and Xi'an. Indeed, the numbers of foreigners at these places are so large that in some ways you're shielded from much of a "China experience", and you may find smaller centres offer both a mellower pace of life and more contact with Chinese outside the campus.

Most foreign students come to China to study **Mandarin**, though there are many additional options available – from martial arts to traditional opera or classical literature – once you break the language barrier. Courses cost from the equivalent of US$2400 a year, or US$800 a semester. Hotel-style campus accommodation costs around US$10 a day; most people move out as soon as they speak enough Chinese to rent a flat.

Your first resource is the nearest Chinese embassy, which can provide a list of contact details for Chinese universities offering the courses you are interested in; most universities also have English-language **websites**. Be aware, however, that promotional material may have little bearing on what is actually provided. Though teaching standards themselves are high at Chinese universities, the administration departments are often confused or misleading places. Ideally, visit the campus first and be wary of paying course fees up front until you've spoken to a few students.

Working

There is plenty of **work** available for foreigners in mainland Chinese cities, where a whole section of expat society gets by as actors, cocktail barmen, Chinglish correctors, models, freelance writers and so on. To really make any money here, however, you need either to be employed by a foreign company or start your own business.

China's vast markets and WTO membership present a wealth of **commercial opportunities** for foreigners. However, anyone wanting to do business here should do thorough research beforehand. The difficulties are formidable – red tape and shady business practices abound. Remember that the Chinese do business on the basis of mutual trust and pay much less attention to contractual terms or legislation. Copyright and trademark laws are often ignored, and any successful business model will be immediately copied. You'll need to develop your *guanxi* – connections – assiduously, and cultivate the virtues of patience, propriety and bloody-mindedness.

Study and work programmes

AFS Intercultural Programs Ⓦ afs.org. Intercultural exchange organization whose China offerings include academic and cultural exchanges that are anywhere from one month to a year long.

Council on International Educational Exchange (CIEE) Ⓦ ciee.org. Leading NGO offering study programmes and volunteer projects around the world. China options include: an academic semester or year abroad; a gap year (US students only); summer study; and paid teaching for a semester or year.

Mail

The Chinese mail service is fast and efficient, with letters taking a day to reach destinations in the same city, two or more days to other destinations in China, and up to several weeks to destinations abroad. **Overseas postage rates** are fairly expensive and vary depending on weight, destination and where you are in the country. The International **Express Mail Service** (**EMS**), however, is unreliable, with items often lost in transit or arriving in pieces, despite registered delivery and online tracking. **DHL** (Ⓦ dhl .com), available in a few major cities, is a safer bet.

Main post offices are open daily, usually from 8am–8pm; smaller offices may keep shorter hours or close at weekends. As well as at post offices, you can post letters in green **postboxes**, though these are rare outside big cities.

To send **parcels**, turn up with the goods you want to send and the staff will sell you a box and pack them in for ¥15 or so. Once packed, but before the parcel is sealed, it must be checked at the customs window and you'll have to complete masses of paperwork, so don't be in a hurry. If you are sending valuable goods bought in China, put the receipt or a photocopy of it in with the parcel, as it may be opened for customs inspection farther down the line.

Maps

Street maps for almost every town and city in China are available from kiosks, hotel shops and bookshops. Most are in Chinese only, showing bus routes, hotels, restaurants and tourist attractions; local bus, train and flight timetables are often printed on the back as well. The same vendors also sell pocket-sized provincial **road atlases**, again in Chinese only.

Some of the major cities and tourist destinations also produce **English-language** maps, available at upmarket hotels, principal tourist sights or tour operators' offices. In Hong Kong and Macau, the local tourist offices provide free maps, which are adequate for most visitors' needs.

Countrywide maps, which you should buy before you leave home, include the excellent 1:4,000,000 map from GeoCenter, which shows relief and useful sections of all neighbouring countries, and the Collins 1:5,000,000 map. One of the best maps of Tibet is *Stanfords Map of South-Central Tibet; Kathmandu–Lhasa Route Map.*

Money

The mainland **Chinese currency** is formally called **yuan** (¥), more colloquially known as **renminbi** (RMB, literally "the people's money") or **kuai**. One yuan breaks down into ten **jiao**, also known as **mao**. **Paper money** was invented in China and is still the main form of exchange, available in ¥100, ¥50, ¥20, ¥10, ¥5 and ¥1 notes, with a similar selection of mao. One mao, five mao, and ¥1 **coins** are increasingly common, though less so in rural areas. China suffers regular outbreaks of **counterfeiting** – many people check their change for watermarks, metal threads and the feel of the paper.

The yuan floats within a narrow range set by a basket of currencies, keeping Chinese exports cheap (much to the annoyance of the US). At the time of writing, the **exchange rate** was approximately ¥6.1 to US$1, ¥9.5 to £1, ¥8.2 to €1, ¥5.9 to CAN$1, ¥5.5 to AU$1, ¥4.9 to NZ$1 and ¥0.6 to ZAR1. For exact rates, check Ⓦ www.xe.com.

Hong Kong's currency is the Hong Kong **dollar** (HK$), divided into one hundred cents, while in **Macau** they use **pataca** (usually written MOP$), in turn broken down into 100 avos. Both currencies are worth slightly less than the yuan, but while Hong Kong dollars are accepted in Macau and southern China's Special Economic Zones and can be exchanged internationally, neither yuan nor pataca is any use outside the mainland or Macau respectively. Tourist hotels in Beijing, Shanghai and Guangzhou also sometimes accept payment in Hong Kong or US dollars.

Banks and ATMs

Banks in major Chinese cities are sometimes open seven days a week, though **foreign exchange** is usually only available Monday to Friday, approximately 9am–noon and 2–5pm. All banks are closed for the first three days of the Chinese New Year, with reduced hours for the following eleven days, and at other holiday times. In Hong Kong, banks are generally open Monday to Friday from 9am to 4.30pm, until 12.30pm on Saturday, while in Macau they close thirty minutes earlier.

Cirrus, Visa and Plus **cards** can be used to make cash withdrawals from **ATMs** operated by the Bank of China, the Industrial and Commercial Bank of China, China Construction Bank and Agricultural Bank of China, as long as they display the relevant logo. In major east-coast cities, almost every one of these banks' ATMs will work with foreign cards, but elsewhere it's likely that only the main branch of the Bank of China will have a suitable machine. Note that most ATMs are inside banks or shopping centres, so close when they do, though some are accessible 24 hours a day. Your bank back home will charge a **fee** on each withdrawal, either a fixed rate or a percentage of the transaction. You can change your yuan into dollars or sterling at any branch of the Bank of China.

Travellers' cheques and foreign currency

Travellers' cheques can be replaced if lost or stolen (keep a list of the serial numbers separate from the cheques) and attract a slightly better rate of exchange than cash. The downsides include having to pay a fee when you buy them, and that they can be cashed only at branches of the Bank of China and at tourist hotels.

It's worth taking along a small quantity of **foreign currency** (US, Canadian or Australian dollars, British pounds or euros) as cash is more widely exchangeable than travellers' cheques. The notes will need to be in perfect condition, bright and crisp with no creases or tears. Don't try to change money on the **black market** – you'll almost certainly get ripped off.

Credit cards and wiring money

China is basically a cash economy, and **credit cards**, such as Visa, American Express and MasterCard, are only accepted at big tourist hotels and the fanciest restaurants, and by some tourist-oriented shops; there is usually a 4 percent handling charge. It's straightforward to obtain cash advances on a Visa card at many Chinese banks (however, the commission is a steep 3 percent). Visa card holders can also get cash advances using ATMs bearing the "Plus" logo, and book hotels and the like online.

It's possible to **wire money** to China through Western Union (Ⓦ www.westernunion.cn); funds can be collected from one of their agencies or branches of the Postal Savings Bank of China.

Opening hours

China officially has a **five-day week**, though this only really applies to government offices, which open Monday to Friday approximately 8am–noon and again from 1–5pm. Generalization is difficult, though: post offices open daily, as do many shops, often keeping long, late hours, especially in big cities. Although banks *usually* close on Sundays – or for the whole weekend – even this is not always the case.

Tourist sights open every day, usually 8am–5pm and without a lunch break. Most public **parks** open from about 6am. **Museums** tend to have more restricted hours, often closing on Mondays. If you arrive at an out-of-the-way place that seems to be closed, however, don't despair – knocking or poking around will often turn up a drowsy doorkeeper. Conversely, you may find other places locked and deserted when they are supposed to be open.

For dates of public holidays, see p.46.

Phones

Everywhere in China has an **area code**, which must be used when phoning from outside that locality; these are given for all telephone numbers throughout the Guide. **Local calls** are free from land lines, and **long-distance** China-wide calls are ¥0.3 a minute. International calls cost from ¥3.5 a minute (much cheaper if you use an IP internet phone card – see p.58).

Card phones, widely available in major cities, are the cheapest way to make domestic long-distance calls (¥0.2 for 3min), and can also be used for international calls (under ¥10 for 3min). They take **IC Cards** (IC卡, IC kǎ), which come in units of ¥20, ¥50 and ¥100. There's a 50 percent discount after 6pm and on weekends. You will be cut off when your card value drops below the amount needed for the next minute. A cheaper option is the **IP card**, which can be used with any phone, and comes in ¥100 units. You dial a local number, then a PIN, then the number you're calling. Rates are as low as ¥2.4 per minute to the US and Canada, ¥3.2 to Europe.

Both IC and IP cards are sold from corner stores, mobile-phone emporiums, and from street hawkers (usually outside the mobile-phone emporiums) all over the country. These cards can only be used in the places you buy them – move to another city and you'll have to buy a new card.

Mobile coverage in China is excellent and comprehensive; they use the GSM system. Assuming your phone is unlocked and compatible, buy a Chinese **SIM card** (SIM卡, SIM kǎ or 手机卡, shǒujīkǎ) from any China Mobile shop or street kiosk (you will have a new number). SIM cards **cost** upwards of ¥80 depending on how "lucky" the number is – favoured sixes and eights bump up the cost, unlucky fours make it cheaper. They come with ¥50 of time, which you extend with prepaid **top up cards** (充值卡, chōngzhí kǎ). Making and receiving domestic calls this way costs ¥0.6 per minute; an international call will cost around ¥8 a minute, though often you can only send texts overseas. The cheapest **mobile phones** to buy will cost around ¥200; make sure the staff change the operating language into English for you.

Photography

Photography is a popular pastime among the Chinese, and all big towns and cities have photo stores selling the latest cameras (especially Hong Kong – see p.574), where you can also download your digital images onto disc for around ¥30, though prints are expensive at ¥1 each. Camera batteries, film and memory cards are fairly easy to obtain in city department stores.

Chinese people are often only too pleased to have their picture taken, though many temples **prohibit photography** inside buildings, and you should avoid taking pictures of anything to do with the military, or that could be construed as having strategic value, including ordinary structures such as bridges in sensitive areas along borders, in Tibet, and so forth.

Time

Despite its huge east-west spread, the whole of China occupies a single time zone, 8hr ahead of GMT, 13hr ahead of US Eastern Standard Time, 16hr ahead of US Pacific Time and 2hr behind Australian Eastern Standard Time. There is no daylight saving.

Tourist information

The **internet** is your best source of information before you travel, as Chinese tourist offices overseas mostly sell packages and have little to offer individual travellers. Once you reach the mainland, you'll find the **CITS** (China International Travel Service; 中国国际旅行社, zhōngguó guójì lǚxíngshè) and alternatives such as the **CTS** (China Travel Service; 中国旅行社, zhōngguó lǚxíngshè) everywhere from large cities to obscure hamlets. While they book flight and train tickets, local tours and accommodation, their value to independent travellers is usually pretty low, even on the rare occasions that someone speaks English. Other sources of information on the ground include

---

DIALLING CODES

To **call mainland China** from abroad, dial your international access code (☎00 in the UK and the Republic of Ireland, ☎011 in the US and Canada, ☎0011 in Australia, ☎00 in New Zealand and ☎27 in South Africa), then ☎86 (China's country code), then area code (minus initial zero) followed by the number.

   To call **Hong Kong**, dial your international access code followed by ☎852, then the number; and for **Macau**, dial your international access code, then ☎853 and then the number.

PHONING ABROAD FROM CHINA

To **call abroad** from mainland China, Hong Kong or Macau, dial ☎00, then the country code (see below), then the area code minus initial zero (if any), followed by the number.

UK ☎44	Ireland ☎353	Australia ☎61
New Zealand ☎64	US & Canada ☎1	South Africa ☎27

accommodation staff or tour desks – especially at youth hostels – and backpacker cafés in destinations such as Dali and Yangshuo.

Cities with large expat populations (including Beijing, Shanghai, Chengdu and Guangzhou) have English-language **magazines** with bar, restaurant and other **listings**. These are usually distributed free in bars and upmarket hotels, and often have accompanying websites, listed throughout the Guide.

Hong Kong and Macau both have efficient and helpful tourist information offices, and several free listings magazines; see p.564 and p.587 for more on these.

CHINESE TOURIST OFFICES ABROAD

Australia and New Zealand Ⓦ cnto.org.au
Canada Ⓦ tourismchina.org
UK Ⓦ cnto.org.uk
US Ⓦ cnto.org

GOVERNMENT WEBSITES

Australian Department of Foreign Affairs Ⓦ dfat.gov.au, Ⓦ smartraveller.gov.au
British Foreign & Commonwealth Office Ⓦ fco.gov.uk
Canadian Department of Foreign Affairs Ⓦ dfait-maeci.gc.ca
Irish Department of Foreign Affairs Ⓦ foreignaffairs.gov.ie
New Zealand Ministry of Foreign Affairs Ⓦ mft.govt.nz
South African Department of Foreign Affairs Ⓦ www.dfa.gov.za/consular/travel_advice.htm
US State Department Ⓦ travel.state.gov

CHINA ONLINE

China Backpacker Ⓦ chinabackpacker.info. Heaps of trekking information for well-known and very off-the-beaten-path areas of China. Dated in parts but still a great resource.
China Bloglist Ⓦ chinabloglist.org. Directory with links to over 500 blogs about China, most of whose writers claim unique insights into the country, its people and culture. Check out the Angry Chinese Blogger.
China Daily Ⓦ chinadaily.com.cn. The official, state-approved version of the news. Read it and yawn.
China Expat Ⓦ chinaexpat.com. Aimed at foreign residents, but a generally useful English-language resource, with a wide range of China-related articles and plenty of links.
China From Inside Ⓦ www.chinafrominside.com. Glimpses into China's traditional martial arts, with dozens of English-language articles and interviews with famous masters.
China Hush Ⓦ chinahush.com. Translations of what Chinese net forums are saying about popular national press stories – but not the sort of stories that would ever surface in the China Daily.
chinaSMACK Ⓦ chinasmack.com. Similar to China Hush, but with a definite cruel and trashy tabloid slant. Gives a rare insight into the underbelly of contemporary Chinese life.

China Trekking Ⓦ chinatrekking.com. Inspiring trekking background; plenty of first-hand details you won't find elsewhere.
Danwei Ⓦ danwei.org. English-language analysis of highbrow and "serious" goings-on in the Chinese media. Thorough and worthy, but could do with an occasional injection of humour.
International Campaign for Tibet Ⓦ savetibet.org. An authoritative source of current news from Tibet.
Managing the Dragon Ⓦ managingthedragon.com. Blog commentary on economic subjects from investor-who-lost-millions Jack Perkowski (who has since bounced back).
Middle Kingdom Life Ⓦ middlekingdomlife.com. Online manual for foreigners planning to live and work in China, providing a sane sketch of the personal and professional difficulties they're likely to face.
Sexy Beijing Ⓦ sexybeijing.tv. Internet TV series whose Western host talks to young Chinese about mostly gender-related issues. Lighthearted and occasionally insightful.
Travel China Ⓦ travelchinaguide.com. Unusual in covering obscure places and small-group tours, as well as the normal run of popular sites and booking links.
Youku Ⓦ youku.com. One of the many YouTube-style clones in China, with a similar range of content (all in Chinese).
Zhongwen Ⓦ zhongwen.com. A handy online Chinese/English dictionary.

Travellers with disabilities

In **mainland China** the disabled are generally hidden away, so attitudes are not very sympathetic and little special provision is made. As it undergoes an economic boom, much of the country resembles a building site, with intense crowds and traffic, few ramps and no effort to make public transport accessible. Ribbed paving down every city street is intended to help blind people navigate, but frankly Chinese pavements are unevenly surfaced obstacle courses of trees and power poles, parked vehicles, market stalls and random holes – the last thing anyone designs them for is unobstructed passage. Only a few upmarket international hotel chains, such as *Holiday Inn*, have experience in assisting disabled visitors. The situation **in Hong Kong** is considerably better; check out the Hong Kong Tourist Association website (Ⓦ discoverhongkong.com) for their extensive Accessible Hong Kong listings.

Given the situation, it may be worth considering an organized tour. Take spares of any specialist clothing or equipment, extra supplies of drugs (carried with you if you fly), and a prescription including the generic name (in English and Chinese characters) in case of emergency. If there's an association representing people with your disability, contact them early on in the planning process.

Beijing and around

THE SUMMER PALACE

1

Beijing and around

By turns brash, gaudy, elegant, charming, filthy and historic, the Chinese capital of Beijing leaves an indelible impression on each and every traveller who passes through – this city is never, ever, ever dull. It has been this way for centuries: for a full millennium, the drama of China's imperial history was played out here, with the emperor enthroned at the centre of the Chinese universe in the Forbidden City, now one of Asia's most famous draws. Beijing was, according to some accounts, the first city in the world to hit a population of one million; as such, despite the setbacks which plagued the first decades of communist control, it should come as little surprise to see the remote control of urbanity stuck on permanent fast-forward here. Crisscrossed by freeways, spiked with high-rises and soaked in neon, this vivid metropolis is China at its most dynamic.

First impressions of Beijing are of an almost inhuman vastness, conveyed by the sprawl of apartment buildings, in which most of the city's population of 21 million are housed, and the eight-lane freeways that slice it up. It's a notion that's reinforced on closer acquaintance, from the magnificent **Forbidden City**, with its stunning wealth of treasures, the concrete desert of **Tian'anmen Square** and the gargantuan buildings of the modern executive around it, to the rank after rank of office complexes that line its mammoth roads. Outside the centre, the scale becomes more manageable, with parks, narrow alleyways and ancient sites such as the **Yonghe Gong**, the **Observatory** and, most magnificent of all, the **Temple of Heaven**, offering respite from the city's oppressive orderliness and rampant reconstruction. In the suburbs beyond, the two **summer palaces** and the **Western Hills** have been favoured retreats since imperial times. Unexpectedly, some of the country's most pleasant scenic spots also lie within the scope of a day-trip, and, just to the north of the city, another of the world's most famous sights, the long and lonely **Great Wall**, winds between mountaintops.

Beijing is an invaders' city, the capital of oppressive foreign dynasties – the Manchu and the Mongols – and of a dynasty with a foreign ideology – the Communists. As such, it has assimilated a lot of outside influence, and today has an international flavour reflecting its position as the capital of a major commercial power. As the front line of China's grapple with **modernity**, it is being ripped up and rebuilt at a furious pace – attested by the cranes that skewer the skyline and the character "demolish" (拆, chāi) painted on old buildings. Students in the latest fashions while away their time in

Highlights

❶ Forbidden City Imperial magnificence on a grand scale and the centre of the Chinese universe for six centuries. **See p.70**

❷ Nanluogu Xiang Artsy alley of laidback cafés, restaurants and bars, at the centre of a charming neighbourhood. **See p.83**

❸ Temple of Heaven This classic Ming-dynasty building, a picture in stone of ancient Chinese cosmogony, is a masterpiece of architecture and landscape design. **See p.88**

❹ Summer Palace Escape the city in this serene and elegant park, dotted with imperial architecture. **See p.95**

❺ 798 Art District This huge complex of galleries and studios provides the focus for a thriving contemporary arts scene. **See p.98**

❻ Peking duck A real Beijing classic, and worthy of its fame, as long as you can find the right place to eat it. **See p.108**

❼ Showtime Beijing's various shows are hugely popular with visitors, especially the breathtaking acrobatic displays. **See p.113**

❽ The Great Wall One of the world's most extraordinary engineering achievements, the old boundary between civilizations is China's must-see. **See p.120**

HIGHLIGHTS ARE MARKED ON THE MAP ON P.64 & PP.68–69

1

internet cafés, hip-hop has overtaken the clubs, businessmen are never without their laptops and schoolkids carry mobile phones in their lunchboxes. Rising incomes have led not just to a brash consumer-capitalist society that Westerners will feel very familiar with, but also to a revival of older **Chinese culture** – witness the re-emergence of the teahouse as a genteel meeting place and the interest in imperial cuisine. In the evening, you'll see large groups of the older generation performing the *yangkou* (loyalty dance), Chairman Mao's favourite dance once universally learned, and in the *hutongs*, the city's twisted grey stone alleyways, men sit with their pet birds and pipes as they always have done.

Brief history

It was in Tian'anmen, on October 1, 1949, that Chairman Mao Zedong hoisted the red flag to proclaim officially the **foundation of the People's Republic**. He told the crowds that the Chinese had at last stood up, and defined liberation as the final culmination of a 150-year fight against foreign exploitation. The claim, perhaps, was modest. Beijing's recorded **history** goes back a little over three millennia, to beginnings

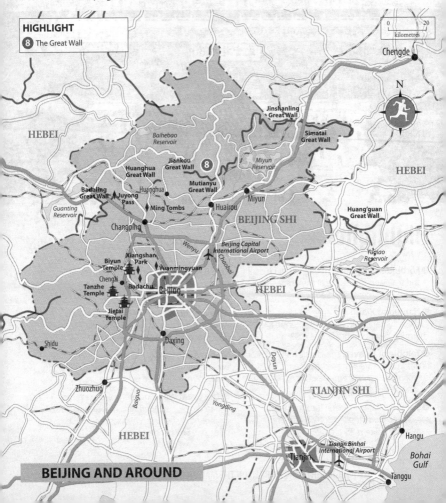

WHEN TO VISIT BEIJING

If the Party had any control over it, no doubt Beijing would have the best climate of any Chinese city; as it is, it has one of the worst. The **best time to visit** is in autumn, between September and October, when it's dry and clement. In winter, it gets very cold, down to -20°C, and the mean winds that whip off the Mongolian plains feel like they're freezing your ears off. Summer (June–Aug) is muggy and hot, up to 30°C, and the short spring (April & May) is dry but windy, with dust often blowing in from the northwestern deserts – you'll see it covering cars.

as a trading centre for Mongols, Koreans and local Chinese tribes. Its predominance, however, dates to the mid-thirteenth century, and the formation of **Mongol China** under Genghis and later Kublai Khan.

The Khans

It was Kublai who took control of the city in 1264, and who properly established it as a capital – then named **Khanbalik** – replacing the earlier power centres of Luoyang and Xi'an. Marco Polo visited him here, working for a while in the city, and was clearly impressed with the level of sophistication; he observed in *The Travels*:

So great a number of houses and of people, no man could tell the number. I believe there is no place in the world to which so many merchants come, and dearer things, and of greater value and more strange, come into this town from all sides than to any city in the world.

The **wealth** came from the city's position on the Silk Road, and Polo described "over a thousand carts loaded with silk" arriving "almost each day", ready for the journey west out of China. And it set a precedent in terms of style and grandeur for the Khans, later known as emperors, with Kublai building himself a palace of astonishing proportions, walled on all sides and approached by great marble stairways.

The Ming dynasty

With the accession of the **Ming dynasty**, who defeated the Mongols in 1368, the capital temporarily shifted to present-day Nanjing, but Yongle, the second Ming emperor, returned, building around him prototypes of the city's two greatest **monuments** – the Imperial Palace and Temple of Heaven. It was in Yongle's reign, too, that the basic **city plan** took shape, rigidly symmetrical, extending in squares and rectangles from the palace and inner-city grid to the suburbs, much as it is today.

The Qing dynasty

Subsequent, post-Ming history is dominated by the rise and eventual collapse of the Manchus, northerners who ruled China as the **Qing dynasty** from 1644 to the beginning of the twentieth century. Beijing, as the Manchu capital, was at its most prosperous in the first half of the eighteenth century, the period in which the Qing constructed the legendary **Summer Palace** – the world's most extraordinary royal garden, with two hundred pavilions, temples and palaces, and immense artificial lakes and hills – to the north of the city. With the central Imperial Palace, this was the focus of endowment and the symbol of Chinese wealth and power. However, in 1860, the Opium Wars brought British and French troops to the walls of the capital, and the Summer Palace was first looted and then razed to the ground by the British.

Foreign empires arrive

While the imperial court lived apart, within what was essentially a separate walled city, conditions for the civilian population, in the capital's suburbs, were starkly different. Kang Youwei, a Cantonese political reformer visiting in 1895, described this dual world:

1

No matter where you look, the place is covered with beggars. The homeless and the old, the crippled and the sick with no one to care for them, fall dead on the roads. This happens every day. And the coaches of the great officials rumble past them continuously.

The indifference, rooted according to Kang in officials throughout the city, spread from the top down. From 1884, using funds meant for the modernization of the nation's navy, the Empress Dowager Cixi had begun building a new Summer Palace of her own. The empress's project was really the last grand gesture of **imperial architecture** and patronage – and like its model was also badly burned by foreign troops in the aftermath of the Boxer Rebellion in 1900. By this time, with successive waves of occupation by foreign troops, the empire and the imperial capital were near collapse. The **Manchus abdicated** in 1911, leaving the Northern Capital to be ruled by warlords. In 1928, it came under the military dictatorship of Chiang Kai-shek's **Guomindang**, who moved the national capital south to Nanjing. Renamed Beiping, Beijing fell into temporary decline, even losing its status as provincial capital to Tianjin. It became capital once more after being seized by the Japanese in 1939, and at the end of **World War II**, the city was controlled by an alliance of Guomindang troops and American marines.

The communist era

The **Communists** took Beijing in January 1949, nine months before Chiang Kai-shek's flight to Taiwan assured final victory. The **rebuilding of the capital** was an early priority, since the city that Mao Zedong inherited for the Chinese people was in most ways primitive. Imperial laws had banned the building of houses higher than the official buildings and palaces, so virtually nothing was more than one storey high. The new plans aimed to reverse this but retain the city's sense of ordered planning, with Tian'anmen Square at its heart – unsurprisingly, the communists' initial inspiration was Soviet, with an emphasis on heavy industry and poor-quality high-rise housing programmes.

In the zest to be free from the past, much of **Old Beijing** was destroyed, or co-opted: the Temple of Cultivated Wisdom became a wire factory and the Temple of the God of Fire produced electric lightbulbs. In the 1940s, there were 8000 temples and monuments in the city; by the 1960s, there were only around 150. Even the city walls and gates, relics mostly of the Ming era, were pulled down and their place taken by ring roads and avenues.

More destruction was to follow during the **Cultural Revolution**. Under Mao's guidance, Beijing's students organized themselves into a political militia – the **Red Guards** – who were set loose to erase symbols of previous regimes, capitalism and the Soviet Union; few of the capital's remaining ancient buildings escaped desecration. Things improved with the death of Mao and the accession of pragmatic Deng Xiaoping and his fellow moderates, who embraced capitalism – though not, as shown by the massacre at Tian'anmen Square and the surrounding events of 1989, freedom (see p.925).

MODERN ARCHITECTURE IN BEIJING

Since dynastic times, Beijing has been an image-conscious city – anxious to portray a particular face to its citizenry, and to the world at large. In the early days of Communist rule, Soviet functionality predominated, though things have recently taken a turn towards the cool and stylish – indeed, Beijing has undergone the kind of urban transformation usually only seen after a war. Esteemed architects from across the globe have been roped in for a series of *carte blanche* projects and, though the overall results have been hit and miss, some of the buildings are truly astounding. The best include the fantastic **Olympic venues** from 2008 (the "Bird's Nest" and "Water Cube"); Paul Andreu's **National Theatre** (the "Egg"); and, perhaps most striking of all, the **CCTV headquarters** (the "Twisted Doughnut") by Dutch architect Rem Koolhaas, which appears to defy gravity with its intersecting Z-shaped towers.

1

Recent history

In 2008 Beijing succeeded in putting on a spectacular, if politicized, **Olympic Games**. This was the city's grand coming out party, and no expense was spared to show that the capital – and China – could hold its own on the world stage. The city's infrastructure was vastly upgraded, a process which continues today: in the past few years, six new subway lines have opened, along with a new airport terminal and a light-rail system. Some US$12bn has been spent on greening projects, including a 125km tree belt around the city to curb the winter sandstorms that rage in from the Gobi desert. Parks and verges have been prettified, fetid canals cleaned, and public facilities are better than anywhere else in China. Historic sites have also been renovated – or, it sometimes appears, invented.

The city gleams like never before, but what little antique character Beijing had is fast disappearing as old city blocks and *hutongs* are demolished. Now, the city's main problems are the pressures of **migration**, pollution and **traffic** – car ownership has rocketed, and the streets are nearing gridlock.

Beijing

北京, běijīng

BEIJING is a city that almost everyone enjoys. For new arrivals, it provides a gentle introduction to the country, and for travellers who've been roughing it round rural China, the creature comforts on offer are a delight. The place to start exploring is **Tian'anmen Square**, geographical and psychological centre of the city, where a cluster of important sights can be seen in a day, although the **Forbidden City**, at the north end of the square, deserves a day, or even several, all to itself. Heading north brings you to a city section with a more traditional and human feel, with some magnificent **parks**, **palaces and temples**, some of them in the *hutongs*. To the east, the **Sanlitun** area is a ghetto of expat services including some good upscale restaurants and plenty of bars; heading south will bring you to **Qianmen**, an important shopping area which ends in style with one of the city's highlights, the **Temple of Heaven** in Tiantan Park. An expedition to the outskirts is amply rewarded by the **Summer Palace**, the best place to get away from it all.

Beijing requires patience and planning to do it justice – wandering aimlessly around without a destination in mind will rarely be rewarding. This is also an essentially private city, whose surface is difficult to penetrate; sometimes, it seems to have the superficiality of a theme park. To get deeper into the city, wander what's left of the labyrinthine *hutongs*, and check out the little antique markets, the residential shopping districts, the smaller, quirkier sights, and the parks; the latter are some of the best in China, and you'll see Beijingers performing *tai ji* and hear birdsong – just – over the hum of traffic. Take advantage, too, of the city's burgeoning nightlife and see just how far the Chinese have gone down the road of what used to be called spiritual pollution.

BEIJING ORIENTATION

There's no doubt that Beijing's initial culture shock owes much to the artificiality of the city's **layout**. The main streets are huge, wide and dead straight, aligned east–west or north–south, and extend in a series of widening rectangles across the whole thirty square kilometres of the inner capital.

The pivot of the ancient city was a north–south road that led from the entrance of the Forbidden City to the city walls. This remains today as **Qianmen Dajie**, though the main axis has shifted to the east–west road that divides Tian'anmen Square and the Forbidden City and, like all major boulevards, changes its name every few kilometres along its length.

1

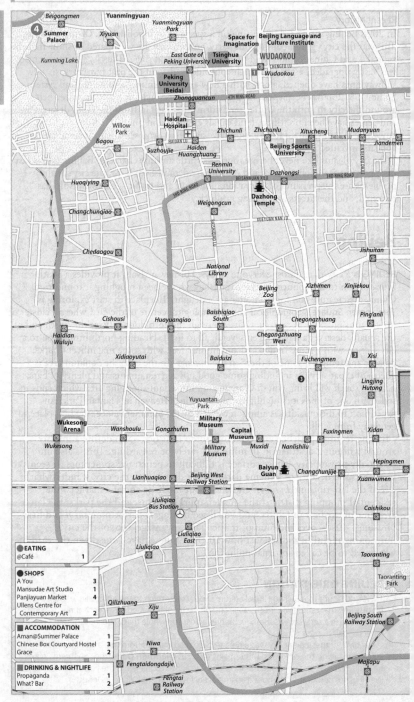

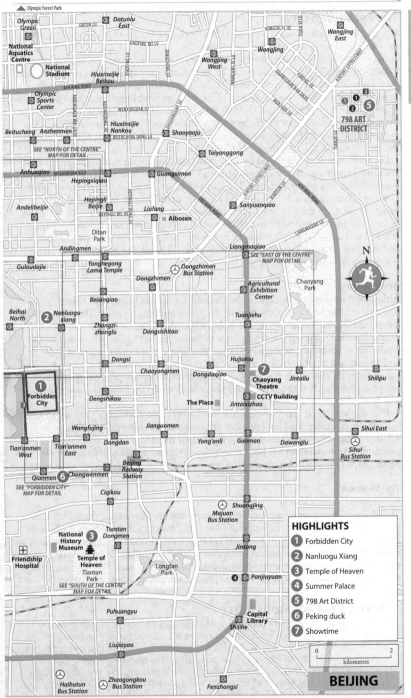

▲ Olympic Forest Park

Olympic Green
National Aquatics Centre
National Stadium
Olympic Sports Center
Datunlu
DATUN LU
Datunlu East
XIADYING BEI LU
HONGTAI XI JIE
Wangjing East
Wangjing
4TH RING ROAD
Hiuxinxijie Beikou
WENYUEGUAN LU
Wangjing West
GUANGSHUN NAN DAJIE
FURONG JIE
AIRPORT EXPRESSWAY
Beitucheng Anzhenmen
Hiuxinxijie Nankou
BEITUCHENG DONG LU
Shaoyaoju
HUIZHONG JIE
798 ART DISTRICT
Anhuaqiao
BEISANHUAN XILU
Hepingxiqiao
Guangximen
AIRPORT EXPRESSWAY
Sanyuanqiao
ANDINGLU
4TH RING ROAD
LIANGMAQIAO LU
Andelibeijie
Hepingli Beijie
HEPINGLI BEI JIE
Liufang
Aibosen
Taiyanggong
Ditan Park
Liangmaqiao
SEE "EAST OF THE CENTRE" MAP FOR DETAIL
Guloudajie
Andingmen
Yonghegong Lama Temple
Dongzhimen Bus Station
Chaoyang Park
SEE "NORTH OF THE CENTRE" MAP FOR DETAIL
Dongzhimen
Agricultural Exhibition Center
Beihai North
Nanluogu-xiang
Beixinqiao
Tuanjiehu
N
Zhangzi-zhonglu
Dongsishitao
Dongsi
Chaoyangmen
Dongdaqiao
Hujialou
Chaoyang Theatre
Jintailu
Shilipu
The Place
CCTV Building
Dengshikou
Jintaixizhao
Wangfujing
Jianguomen
Tian'anmen West
Tian'anmen East
Dongdan
Yong'anli
Guomao
Dawanglu
Sihui East
Forbidden City
Sihui Bus Station
Qianmen
Chongwenmen
Beijing Railway Station
Ciqikou
SEE "FORBIDDEN CITY" MAP FOR DETAIL
Shuangjing
Majuan Bus Station
National History Museum
Tiantan Dongmen
Jinsong
Friendship Hospital
Temple of Heaven
Tiantan Park
Longtan Park
Panjiayuan
SEE "SOUTH OF THE CENTRE" MAP FOR DETAIL
Puhuangyu
Capital Library
Shilihe
Liujiayao
Haihutun Bus Station
Zhaogongkou Bus Station
Fenzhongsi

HIGHLIGHTS

1 Forbidden City
2 Nanluogu Xiang
3 Temple of Heaven
4 Summer Palace
5 798 Art District
6 Peking duck
7 Showtime

0 ——————— 2
kilometres

BEIJING

1

The Forbidden City

故宫, gùgōng • Monday 8am–noon, Tues–Sun April–Oct 8.30am–5pm, Oct–March 8.30am–4.30pm • April–Oct ¥60, Nov–March ¥40 • audio-guide ¥40 • subway line #1 to Tian'anmen East or Tian'anmen West

Lying at the heart of the city, the **Forbidden City** – or, more accurately, the **Imperial Palace** – is Beijing's finest monument. To do it justice, you should plan to spend at least a whole day here; you could wander the complex for a week and keep discovering new aspects, especially now that many of the halls are doubling as museums of dynastic artefacts. The central halls, with their wealth of imperial pomp, may be the most magnificent buildings, but for many visitors it's the side rooms, with their displays of the more intimate accoutrements of court life, that bring home the realities of life for the inhabitants in this, the most gilded of cages.

The Forbidden City is encased by a moat and, within the turreted walls, employs a wonderful symmetry and geomantic structure to achieve a balance between *yin* and *yang*; positive and negative energy. The City's spine is composed of eleven south-facing Halls or Gates, all colossal, exquisite and ornate. Branching off from this central vertebrae are more than eight hundred buildings that share the exclusive combination of Imperial colours: red walls and yellow roof tiles. Elsewhere, jade green, gold and azure blue decorate the woodwork, archways and balconies. The doors to the central halls are heavy, red, thick and studded with gold. All in all, the intricacy of the city's design is quite astonishing.

Brief history

Although the earliest structures on the Forbidden City site began with Kublai Khan during the Mongol dynasty, the **plan** of the palace buildings is essentially Ming. Most date to the fifteenth century and the ambitions of the Emperor Yongle, the monarch responsible for switching the capital back to Beijing in 1403. The halls were laid out according to geomantic theories, and since they stood at the exact centre of Beijing, and Beijing was considered the centre of the universe, the harmony was supreme. The palace complex constantly reiterates such references, alongside personal symbols of imperial power such as the dragon and phoenix (emperor and empress) and the crane and turtle (longevity of reign).

After the Manchu dynasty was overthrown in 1911, the Forbidden City began to fall into disrepair, exacerbated by looting of artefacts and jewels by the Japanese in the 1930s and again by the Nationalists, prior to their flight to Taiwan, in 1949. A programme of **restoration** has been under way for decades, and today the complex is in better shape than it was for most of the last century.

The Wumen

午门, wǔmén

The **Wumen** (Meridian Gate) itself is the largest and grandest of the Forbidden City gates and was reserved for the emperor's sole use. From its vantage point, the Sons of Heaven would announce the new year's calendar to their court and inspect the army in times of war. It was customary for victorious generals returning from battle to present their prisoners here for the emperor to decide their fate. He would be flanked, on all such imperial occasions, by a guard of elephants, the gift of Burmese subjects.

VISITING THE FORBIDDEN CITY

The Forbidden City can only be entered from the south; you can exit here too, or from alternative gates to the north, east and west. If you're in a taxi, you can be dropped right outside the ticket office. Visitors have freedom to wander most of the site, though not all of the buildings. If you want detailed explanations of everything you see, take the **audio tour**, available at the main gate. If you take this option, it's worth retracing your steps afterwards for an untutored view, and heading off to the side halls that aren't included on the tour.

LIFE INSIDE THE FORBIDDEN CITY

The emperors rarely left the Foribidden City – perhaps with good reason. Their lives, right up to the fall of the Manchu in the twentieth century, were governed by an extraordinarily developed taste for **luxury and excess**. It is estimated that a single meal for a Qing emperor could have fed several thousand of his impoverished peasants, a scale obviously appreciated by the last influential occupant, the Empress Dowager Cixi (see p.96), who herself would commonly order preparation of 108 dishes at a single sitting. **Sex**, too, provided startling statistics, with the number of Ming-dynasty concubines approaching ten thousand. At night, the emperor chose a girl from his harem by picking out a tablet bearing her name from a pile on a silver tray. She would be delivered to the emperor's bedchamber naked but for a yellow cloth wrapped around her, and carried on the back of a servant, since she could barely walk with her bound feet.

The only other men allowed into the palace were **eunuchs**, to ensure the authenticity of the emperor's offspring. In daily contact with the royals, they often rose to considerable power, but this was bought at the expense of their dreadfully low standing outside the confines of the court. Confucianism held that disfiguration of the body impaired the soul, and eunuchs were buried apart from their ancestors in special graveyards outside the city. In the hope that they would still be buried "whole", they kept and carried around their testicles in bags hung on their belts. They were usually recruited from the poorest families – attracted by the rare chance of amassing wealth other than by birth. Eunuchry was finally banned in 1924 and the remaining 1500 eunuchs were expelled from the palace. An observer described them "carrying their belongings in sacks and crying piteously in high-pitched voices".

Jinshui He and Taihemen

North through the Wumen you find yourself in a vast paved court, cut east–west by the **Jinshui He** (金水河, jīnshuǐ hé), the Golden Water Stream, with its five marble bridges, decorated with carved torches, a symbol of masculinity. Beyond is a further ceremonial gate, the **Taihemen** (太和门, tàihémén), Gate of Supreme Harmony, its entrance guarded by a magisterial row of lions, and beyond this a still greater courtyard where the principal imperial audiences were held. Within this space the entire court, up to one hundred thousand people, could be accommodated. They would have made their way in through the lesser side gates – military men from the west, civilian officials from the east – and waited in total silence as the emperor ascended his throne. Then, with only the Imperial Guard remaining standing, they kowtowed nine times.

Taihedian

太和殿, tàihédiàn

Raised on a three-tiered marble terrace is the first and most spectacular of the three main **ceremonial halls**, the **Taihedian**, Hall of Supreme Harmony. This was used for the most important state occasions, such as the emperor's coronation or birthdays and the nomination of generals at the outset of a campaign, and last saw action in an armistice ceremony in 1918. A marble pavement ramp, intricately carved with dragons and flanked by bronze incense burners, marks the path along which the emperor's chair was carried. His golden dragon throne stands within.

Zhonghedian

中和殿, zhōnghédiàn

Beyond the Taihedian, you enter the **Zhonghedian**, Hall of Middle Harmony, another throne room, where the emperor performed ceremonies of greeting to foreigners and addressed the imperial offspring (the product of several wives and numerous concubines). The hall was used, too, as a dressing room for the major Taihedian events, and it was here that the emperor examined the seed for each year's crop.

1

Baohedian
保和殿, bǎohédiàn

The third of the great halls, the **Baohedian**, Hall of Preserving Harmony, was used for state banquets and imperial examinations, graduates from which were appointed to positions of power in China's bureaucratic civil service. Its galleries, originally treasure houses, display various finds from the site, though the most spectacular, a vast block carved with dragons and clouds, stands at the rear of the hall. This is a Ming creation, reworked in the eighteenth century, and it's among the finest carvings in the palace. It's certainly the largest – a 250-tonne chunk of marble transported here from well outside the city by flooding the roads in winter to form sheets of ice.

The imperial living quarters

To the north, paralleling the structure of the ceremonial halls, are the three principal palaces of the **imperial living quarters**. Again, the first chamber, the **Qianqinggong** (乾清宫, qiánqīnggōng), Palace of Heavenly Purity, is the most extravagant. It was originally the imperial bedroom – its terrace is surmounted by incense burners in the form of cranes and turtles (symbols of immortality) – though it later became a conventional state room. Beyond, echoing the Zhonghedian in the ceremonial complex, is the **Jiaotaidian** (交泰殿, jiāotàidiàn), Hall of Union, the empress's throne room.

The Kunninggong
坤宁宫, kūnínggōng

Last of the living quarters is the **Kunninggong**, Palace of Earthly Tranquillity, where the emperor and empress traditionally spent their wedding night. By law the emperor had to spend the first three nights of his marriage, and the first day of Chinese New Year, with his wife. The palace is a bizarre building, partitioned in two. On the left is a large sacrificial room with its vats ready to receive offerings (1300 pigs a year under the Ming). The wedding chamber is a small room, off to

---

FORBIDDEN CITY EXHIBITIONS

The Imperial Palace is increasingly being devoted to museum space – so much so that it arguably constitutes the best museum in China. The numerous buildings spreading out from the Forbidden City's central axis house a variety of fascinating permanent and temporary exhibitions of Chinese and international historical artefacts and treasures (check what's on at Ⓦ www.dpm.org.cn); you'll find a map showing their location on the back of your entrance ticket.

The Treasure Gallery In buildings surrounding the Hall of Supremacy (¥10). Gold, silver, pearl and jade items demonstrating the wealth, majesty and luxury of imperial life.

Hall of Clocks (¥10). This hall, always a favourite, displays the result of one Qing emperor's passion for liberally ornamented Baroque timepieces, most of which are English and French, though the rhino-sized water clock by the entrance is Chinese. There's even one with a mechanical scribe who can write eight characters. Some clocks are wound to demonstrate their workings at 11am and 2pm.

Ceramics Gallery Hall of Literary Brilliance (free). A wonderful, air-cooled selection of fine pots, statues and porcelain treasures; keep an eye out for the Ming and Qing vases.

Painting and Calligraphy Gallery Hall of Martial Valour (free). Pieces demonstrating the art, skill and beauty of artists and literary aesthetics.

Jade Gallery Palace of Accumulated Purity (free). A selection of intricate jade objects from the Imperial Court.

Gold and Silver Gallery Palace of Great Brilliance (free). Precious religious, decorative, dress and sacrificial items.

Opera Gallery Hall for Viewing Opera (free). Fascinating display of all the finery of the Chinese opera.

one side, painted entirely in red, and covered with decorative emblems symbolizing fertility and joy. It was last pressed into operation in 1922 for the child wedding of Pu Yi, the last emperor, who, finding it "like a melted red wax candle", decided that he preferred the Yangxindian.

Yangxindian
养心殿, yǎngxīndiàn

The **Yangxindian**, or Mind Nurture Palace, is one of a group of palaces west of the living quarters where emperors spent most of their time. Several of the palaces retain their furniture from the Manchu times, most of it eighteenth-century; in one, the **Changchungong** (Palace of Eternal Spring), is a series of paintings illustrating the Ming novel, *The Story of the Stone*.

The Imperial Garden

From the Inner Court, the Kunningmen (Gate of Terrestrial Tranquillity) opens north onto the **Imperial Garden**, by this stage something of a respite from the elegant buildings. There are a couple of **cafés** here amid a pleasing network of ponds, walkways and pavilions, designed to be reminiscent of southern Chinese landscapes. In the middle of the garden, the **Qin'andian**, or Hall of Imperial Tranquillity, was where the emperor came to worship a Taoist water deity, Xuan Wu, who was responsible for keeping the palace safe from fire. You can exit here into Jingshan Park, which provides an overview of the complex (see p.80).

Tian'anmen Square
天安门广场, tiānānmén guǎngchǎng • Daily sunrise–sunset • Free • subway line #1 to Tian'anmen East or Tian'anmen West, or subway line #2 to Qianmen

For many Chinese tourists, this gigantic square is a place of pilgrimage. Crowds flock to gaze at Chairman Mao's portrait on **Tian'anmen** gate, then head south to see the fellow himself (maybe) in his **mausoleum**, quietly bowing their heads by the **Monument to the People's Heroes** en route. The square itself is plain, and rather dull considering its colourful recent history (see p.925). It's sometimes better to look upwards, where you'll often see incredibly long chains of kites disappearing into Beijing's soup-like sky. It's worth popping by at **sunrise** or **sunset**, when the national flag at the northern end of the square is raised in a military ceremony. Crowds are usually large for both.

Tian'anmen
天安门, tiānānmén • Daily 8.30am–4.30pm • ¥15 • buy tickets from the Forbidden City ticket office, further north on the right

Tian'anmen, the "Gate of Heavenly Peace", was once the main entrance to the Forbidden City. The boxy gatehouse is familiar across the world, and occupies an exalted place in Chinese communist iconography, appearing on banknotes, coins, stamps and indeed virtually any piece of state paper you can imagine. As such, it's a prime object of pilgrimage, with many visitors milling around waiting to be photographed in front of the large **portrait of Mao** (one of the very few still on public display), which hangs over the central passageway.

The Reviewing Platform

From the reviewing platform above Tian'anmen, Mao delivered the liberation speech on October 1, 1949. For the entrance fee you can climb up to this platform yourself, where security is tight – all visitors have to leave their bags, are frisked and have to go through a metal detector before they can ascend. Inside, the fact that most people cluster around the souvenir stall selling official certificates of their trip reflects the fact that there's not much to look at.

1

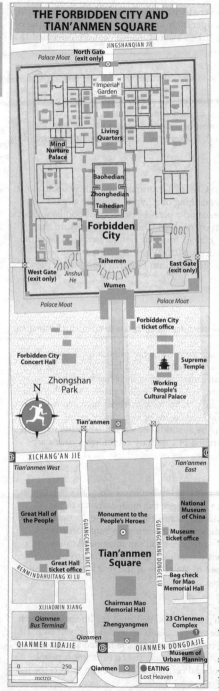

THE FORBIDDEN CITY AND TIAN'ANMEN SQUARE

JINGSHANQIAN JIE
Palace Moat
North Gate (exit only)
Imperial Garden
Living Quarters
Mind Nurture Palace
Baohedian
Zhonghedian
Taihedian
Forbidden City
Taihemen
West Gate (exit only)   Jinshui He   East Gate (exit only)
Wumen
Palace Moat   Palace Moat
Forbidden City ticket office
Forbidden City Concert Hall
Zhongshan Park
N
Supreme Temple
Working People's Cultural Palace
Tian'anmen
XICHANG'AN JIE
Tian'anmen West   Tian'anmen East
Great Hall of the People
Monument to the People's Heroes
National Museum of China
Museum ticket office
GUANGCHANG XICE LU
GUANGCHANG DONGCE LU
Tian'anmen Square
Great Hall ticket office
RENMINDAHUITANG XI LU
Bag check for Mao Memorial Hall
XIJIAOMIN XIANG
Chairman Mao Memorial Hall
23 Ch'ienmen Complex
Qianmen Bus Terminal
Zhengyangmen
QIANMEN XIDAJIE   QIANMEN DONGDAJIE
Qianmen
Museum of Urban Planning
0   250
metres
● EATING
Lost Heaven   1

The parks

Tian'anmen is flanked by two parks: **Zhongshan** to the west, and the grounds of the **Working People's Culture Palace** to the east. These are great places to escape the rigorous formality of Tian'anmen Square, not to mention the crowds of the Forbidden City; they also double as a highly pleasant alternative means of access to the latter.

Zhongshan Park

中山公园, zhōngshān gōngyuán • entrances on Xichang'an Jie and Nanchang Jie • Daily 6am–9pm • ¥3 • flower exhibition and Huifang Garden 9am–4.30pm, ¥5 • subway line #1 to Tian'anmen West

This delightful **park** boasts the ruins of the **Altar of Land and Grain**, a site of biennial sacrifice during the Qing and Ming dynasties. It was built during Yongle's reign in 1420, and hosts harvest-time events closely related to those of the Temple of Heaven (see p.88). You'll have to pay extra for the **flower exhibition** and the **Huifang Garden**; the former is a greenhouse full of so-so blooms, while the latter is a beautiful, bamboo-strewn section of the park.

Working People's Cultural Palace

劳动人民文化宫, láodòng rénmín wénhuàgōng • entrances on Dongchang'an Jie and Nanchizi Dajie • Daily 6.30am–7.30pm • ¥2, or ¥15 including Front Hall • subway line #1 to Tian'anmen East

This wonderful place is much more interesting than its pedestrian name suggests, the symbolic label highlighting the fact that ordinary Chinese were only allowed within this central sector of their capital following the communist takeover in 1949. Though far smaller than the Forbidden City, it's also far more manageable, infinitely less crowded, and equally beautiful in parts – proof of sorts is provided by its status as Beijing's number one venue for wedding photos. The park is centred on the **Supreme Temple** (太庙, tài miào), today a sort of Forbidden City annexe; this is a stupendously beautiful place, though you'll need an extra ticket to peek inside the first of its three halls (the other two are, sadly, closed off). Surrounding these are a number of exhibition halls, often worth checking out for their temporary art shows.

Monument to the People's Heroes
人民英雄纪念碑, rénmín yīngxióng jìniànbēi

Towards the northern end of Tian'anmen Square is this 38m-high **obelisk**, commemorating the victims of the revolutionary struggle. Its foundations were laid on the October 1, 1949, the day that the establishment of the People's Republic was announced. Bas-reliefs illustrate key scenes from China's revolutionary history; one of these, on the east side, shows the Chinese burning British opium (see p.918) in the nineteenth century. The calligraphy on the front is a copy of Mao Zedong's handwriting and reads "Eternal glory to the Heroes of the People". The platform on which the obelisk stands is guarded, and a prominent sign declares that commemorative gestures, such as the laying of wreaths, are banned.

The Chairman Mao Memorial Hall
毛主席纪念堂, máozhǔxí jìniàntáng • Tues–Sun 8.30am–noon • Free (bring ID) • bag & camera deposit ¥2–15

At the centre of the centre of China lies a corpse that nobody dare remove.
                                            Tiziano Terzani, *Behind the Forbidden Door*

Mao's **mausoleum**, constructed in 1977 by an estimated million volunteers, is an ugly building that looks like a drab municipal facility. It contravenes the principles of Chinese geomancy – presumably deliberately – by interrupting the line from the palace to Qianmen and by facing north. Mao himself wanted to be cremated, and the erection of the mausoleum was apparently no more than a power assertion by his would-be successor, Hua Guofeng. In 1980 Deng Xiaoping, then leader, said it should never have been built, although he wouldn't go so far as to pull it down.

Much of the interest of a visit here lies in witnessing the sense of awe of the Chinese confronted with their former leader and architect of modern China, who was accorded an almost god-like status during his life. The atmosphere is one of reverence, though once through the marble halls, you're herded past a splendidly wide-ranging array of tacky Mao souvenirs; the flashing Mao lighter that plays the national anthem is a perennial favourite, as is the waving-Mao wristwatch (shoddy batteries mean that Mao usually stops waving within the week).

Viewing the Chairman

After depositing your bag and camera at the bag check across the road to the east, join the orderly queue of Chinese – almost exclusively working-class out-of-towners – on the northern side. The queue advances surprisingly quickly, and takes just a couple of minutes to file through the chambers. Mao's pickled **corpse**, draped with a red flag within a crystal coffin, looks unreal, which it may well be; a wax copy was made in case the preservation went wrong. Mechanically raised from a freezer every morning, it is said to have been embalmed with the aid of Vietnamese technicians who had previously worked on the body of Ho Chi Minh. Apparently, 22 litres of formaldehyde went into preserving his body; rumour has it that not only did the corpse swell grotesquely, but that Mao's left ear fell off during the embalming process, and had to be stitched back on.

Zhengyangmen
正阳门, zhèngyángmén • Daily 8.30am–4pm • ¥20

For an overview of Tian'anmen Square, ascend its south gate, **Zhenyangmen**. Similar to Tian'anmen to the north, and 40m high, it gives a good idea of how much more impressive the square would look if Mao's mausoleum hadn't been stuck in the middle of it.

1

DISSENT IN TIAN'ANMEN SQUARE

Blood debts must be repaid in kind – the longer the delay, the greater the interest.

Lu Xun, writing after the massacre of 1926

Chinese history is about to turn a new page. Tian'anmen Square is ours, the people's, and we will not allow butchers to tread on it.

Wu'er Kaixi, student, May 1989

It may have been designed as a space for mass declarations of loyalty, but in the twentieth century **Tian'anmen Square** was as often a venue for expressions of popular dissent; against foreign oppression at the beginning of the century, and, more recently, against its domestic form. The first mass protests occurred here on May 4, 1919, when three thousand students gathered in the square to protest at the disastrous terms of the **Versailles Treaty**, in which the victorious allies granted several former German concessions in China to the Japanese. The Chinese, who had sent more than a hundred thousand labourers to work in the supply lines of the British and French forces in Europe, were outraged. The protests of **May 4**, and the movement they spawned, marked the beginning of the painful struggle of Chinese modernization. In the turbulent years of the 1920s, the inhabitants of Beijing again occupied the square, first in 1925, to protest over the **massacre in Shanghai** of Chinese demonstrators by British troops, then in 1926, when the public protested after the weak government's capitulation to the Japanese. Demonstrators marched on the government offices and were fired on by soldiers.

In 1976, after the death of popular premier Zhou Enlai, thousands of mourners assembled in Tian'anmen without government approval to voice their dissatisfaction with their leaders, and again in 1978 and 1979 groups assembled here to discuss new ideas of **democracy and artistic freedom**, triggered by writings posted along Democracy Wall on the edge of the Forbidden City. In 1986 and 1987, people gathered again to show solidarity for the **students** and others protesting at the Party's refusal to allow elections.

But it was in **1989** that Tian'anmen Square became the venue for a massive expression of **popular dissent**, when, from April to June, nearly a million protesters demonstrated against the slowness of reform, lack of freedom and widespread corruption. The government, infuriated at being humiliated by their own people, declared martial law on May 20, and on **June 4** the military moved in. The killing was indiscriminate; tanks ran over tents and machine guns strafed the avenues. No one knows how many died in the massacre – certainly thousands. Hundreds were arrested afterwards and many are still in jail. The event remains a taboo topic; look out for droves of undercover police on the massacre's anniversary.

Great Hall of the People

人民大会堂, rénmín dàhuìtáng • entrance off Tian'anmen Square • Daily 8.15am–4pm when not in session • ¥30 (bring ID) • subway line #1 to Tian'anmen West or line #2 to Qianmen

Taking up almost half the west side of Tian'anmen Square is the **Great Hall of the People**. This is the venue of the National People's Congress, and hundreds of black limos with tinted windows are parked outside when it's in session. When it isn't, it's open to the public: what you see on the mandatory route is a selection of the 29 reception rooms – all looking like the lobby of a Chinese three-star hotel, with badly fitted red carpet and armchairs lined up against the walls.

National Museum of China

中国历史博物馆, zhōngguó lìshǐ bówùguǎn • entrance off Tian'anmen Square • Daily 9am–5.30pm • Free (bring ID) • subway line #1 to Tian'anmen East

The monumental building to the east of Tian'anmen Square is now home to the **world's largest museum**. Large though it may be, it only opened in its present guise in 2011, and it feels as though the curators have yet to pack in any hard-hitting exhibits – a couple of hours here is plenty.

OPPOSITE THE TEMPLE OF HEAVEN >

1

The Ancient China exhibition

The museum's main attraction is the engrossing **Ancient China exhibition** in the basement, which traces China's history from Neolithic to pre-Communist times, heading through the various dynasties in a spellbinding succession of relics. Things to look out for here include bronze wine vessels from the Western Zhou, a jade shroud and mini terracotta army from the Liao, and a bronze acupuncture statue (and, inevitably, some great porcelain vases) from the Ming.

The other floors

Forget the ironically tiring **Road of Rejuvenation** exhibit on the second floor – a collection of bombastic national messages, paintings of Japanese imperial evil and innumerable photos of red-tied delegations, this one's aimed squarely at the locals. Instead, head upstairs to the third and fourth floors, where you'll find small exhibitions on bronze, jade, porcelain, fans, money and more.

Qianmen

前门, qiánmén • south of Tian'anmen Square • subway line #2 to Qianmen

Just south of Tian'anmen Square is one of Beijing's most famous **gates** – Qianmen, an imposing, double-arched edifice dating back to the fifteenth century. Before the city's walls were demolished, this controlled the entrance to the inner city from the outer, suburban sector, and in imperial days the shops and places of entertainment banned from the interior city were concentrated around here.

The Museum of Urban Planning

规划博物馆, guīhuà bówùguǎn • Qianmen Dong Dajie • Tues–Sun 9am–5pm • ¥30 • subway line #2 to Qianmen

This quirky museum is little visited; for some reason, displays on solid waste management and air quality have failed to galvanize the public. Given its focus on the future, it's also laughably old-fashioned – and, on occasion, unintentionally hilarious – but there are definite highlights in three excellent, and very different, mapping exhibits.

The maps

First, and visible on a wall from the escalator, is a fascinating **bronze model** showing the city as it used to look in imperial times, back when every significant building was part of an awesome, grand design. Then comes another TV screen, which slowly spools through a digitized version of an **ancient scroll**, heading through Old Beijing from south wall to north wall, via the Forbidden City. The star attraction, though, is an enormous and fantastically detailed underlit **model of the city** that takes up the entire top floor. At a scale of 1m:1km it covers more than three hundred square metres, and illustrates what the place will look like once it's finished being ripped up and redesigned by 2020.

Northern Beijing

The area north of the Forbidden City has a good collection of sights you could happily spend days exploring. Just outside the Forbidden City are **Jingshan and Beihai parks**, two of the finest in China; north of here, the peripheries of the **Shicha Lakes** – Qianhai and Houhai – are filled with bars, restaurants and cafés. These continue east to **Nanluogu Xiang**, an artsy, renovated *hutong* area that has proven wildly popular with young locals and foreign visitors alike. It's a great place for people-watching over a coffee, and boasts some great places to stay.

Around the lakes you'll also find a somewhat older *hutong* district, perhaps the last major one left in the city, and once the home of princes, dukes and monks. Its alleys are a labyrinth, with something of interest around every corner; some regard them as

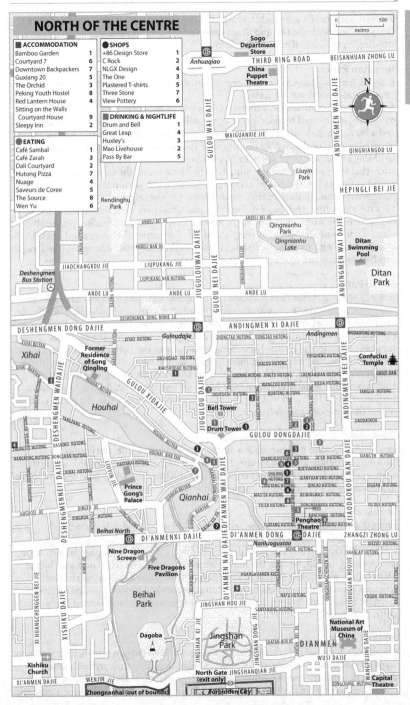

1

the final outpost of a genuinely Chinese Beijing. Buried deep within them is **Prince Gong's Palace**, with the **Bell and Drum towers**, once used to mark dawn and dusk, standing on the eastern edge of the district.

Jingshan Park

景山公园, jǐngshān gōngyuán • across from the north gate of the Forbidden City • Daily April–Oct 6.30am–9pm, Nov–March 6.30am–8pm • ¥2 • subway line #6 to Nanluoguxiang

Jingshan Park is a natural way to round off a trip to the Forbidden City. An artificial mound, it was created by the digging of the palace moat, and served as a windbreak and a barrier to malevolent spirits (believed to emanate from the north) for the imperial quarter of the city. Its history, most momentously, includes the suicide of the last Ming emperor, **Chong Zhen**, in 1644, who hanged himself here from a locust tree after rebel troops broke into the imperial city. The spot, on the eastern side of the park, is easy to find as it is signposted everywhere (underneath signs pointing to a children's playground), though the tree that stands here is not the original.

It's the **views** from the top of the hill that make this park such a compelling target: they take in the whole extent of the Forbidden City – giving a revealing perspective – and a fair swath of the city outside, a deal more attractive than at ground level. To the west is Beihai with its fat snaking lake; in the north, Gulou and Zhonglou (the Drum and Bell towers); and to the northeast, the Yonghe Gong.

Beihai Park

北海公园, běihǎi gōngyuán • just west of Jingshan Park • Daily April–Oct 6.30am–9pm, Nov–March 6.30am–8pm • sights close 5pm • ¥10, or ¥20 including all buildings • pedaloes/rowboats ¥40/¥50 per hour • subway line #6 to Beihai North for the north entrance

Over half of **Beihai Park** is water – the lake, stretching over 1km from south to north, is one of Beijing's favourite ice-skating spots in the winter months. The park was supposedly created by Kublai Khan, long before any of the Forbidden City structures were conceived, and its scale is suitably ambitious: the lake was man-made, an island being created in its midst with the excavated earth. Emperor Qianlong oversaw its landscaping into a classical garden, and Mao's widow, the ill-fated Jiang Qing, was a frequent visitor. Today, its willows and red-columned galleries make it a grand place to retreat from the city and recharge.

The Round

Just inside the main gate, which lies on the park's southern side, the **Round**, an enclosure of buildings behind a circular wall, has at its centre a courtyard, where there's a large jade bowl said to have belonged to Kublai Khan. The white-jade Buddha in the hall behind was a present from Burmese Buddhists.

The island

From the Round, a walkway provides access to the island, which is dotted with buildings – including the **Yuegu Lou**, a hall full of steles (stone slabs carved with Chinese characters); and the giant **dagoba** (a dumpy Tibetan-style pagoda) sitting on the crown of the hill, built in the mid-seventeenth century to celebrate a visit by the Dalai Lama. It's a suitable emblem for a park that contains a curious mixture of religious constructions, storehouses for cultural relics and imperial garden furniture. Nestling inside the dagoba is a shrine to the demon-headed, multi-armed Lamaist deity, Yamantaka.

North of the lake

On the north side of the lake stands the impressive **Nine Dragon Screen**, its purpose to ward off evil spirits. An ornate wall of glazed tiles, depicting nine stylized, sinuous dragons in relief, it's one of China's largest at 27m in length, and remains in good condition. Nearby are the **Five Dragon Pavilions**, supposedly in the shape of a dragon's spine. Even when the park is crowded at the weekend, the gardens and rockeries near here remain tranquil and soothing – it's easy to see why the area was so favoured by Qianlong. It's popular with courting couples today, some of whom like to dress up for photos in period costume (there's a stall outside the Nine Dragon Screen) or take boats out on the lake.

The Shicha Lakes: Qianhai and Houhai

24hr • Free • pedaloes/rowboats from docks around the lake from ¥40 per person per hour • subway line #6 to Beihai North or Nanluoguxiang, or line #2 to Jishuitan

Just north of Beihai Park is pretty **Qianhai** (前海, qiánhǎi) lake, an appealing, easygoing place away from the city traffic. Having been dredged and cleaned up, the area around it has become a drinking and dining hotspot, though be warned that the lakeside bars and restaurants are overpriced and rather tacky, and their staff rather pushy; it can be more relaxing to rent a pedal- or row-boat and have a drink on that instead.

Lakeside sights

As you head north along Qianhai, look out for the hardy folk who swim here every day; it may be tempting to join in, but foreigners who do so often end up getting sick. From the top of the cute humpback **Yinding Bridge** (银锭桥, yíndìng qiáo), spanning the lake's narrowest point and marking the divide between Qianhai and **Houhai** (后海, hòuhǎi), you can see the Western Hills on (very rare) clear days. Turn right, and you're on **Yandai Xie Jie** (烟袋斜街, yāndài xiéjiē), an alley of little jewellery and trinket shops that's one of the best places in Beijing to buy contemporary souvenirs.

Prince Gong's Palace

恭王府, gōngwáng fǔ • Qianhai Xijie • Daily March–Nov 7.30am–4.30pm, Dec–Feb 8am–4pm • ¥40 • subway line #6 to Beihai North, exit B, turn left up Sanzuoqiao Hutong, then left at the crossroads

The charming **Prince Gong's Palace** was once the residence of Prince Gong, the brother of Emperor Xianfeng and father of the last Qing emperor, Pu Yi. Its many courtyards, joined by covered walkways, have been restored to something like their former elegance. In the very centre is the **Yin'an Dian**, a hall where the most important ceremonies and rites were held; keep a lookout for the sumptuously painted ceiling of **Xi Jin Zhai**, used as a studio by Prince Gong. The northern boundary of the courtyard area is marked by a 151m-long wall; sneak around this and you'll be on the southern cusp of a gorgeous **garden** area, set around an attractive lake. One hall here was once used for **opera** performances, though these have sadly been discontinued; it's worth asking to see if these have resumed.

There are plenty of other **old palaces** in the area, as this was once something of an imperial pleasure ground and home to a number of high officials and distinguished eunuchs.

Song Qingling's Former Residence

宋庆龄故居, sòngqìnglíng gùjū • 46 Houhai Beiyan • Daily 9am–4pm • ¥20 • subway line #2 to Jishuitan, or lines #2 or #8 to Guloudajie

On the northern shore of Houhai, **Song Qingling's** former residence is a Qing mansion with an agreeable, spacious garden. The wife of Sun Yatsen, who was leader of the short-lived republic that followed the collapse of imperial China (see p.920), Song Qingling commands great respect in China, and the exhibition inside details her busy life. The collection of her personal effects, including letters and cutlery, is pretty dry, but check out the revolver Sun Yatsen (obviously not a great romantic) gave his wife as a wedding gift. More interesting is the building itself, whose interior gives a glimpse of a typical Chinese mansion from the beginning of the twentieth century – all the furnishings are pretty much as they were when she died.

1

Xu Beihong Museum

徐悲鸿纪念馆, xúbēihóng jìniànguǎn • 53 Xinjiekou Bei Dajie • Tues–Sun 9–11am & 1.30–4.30pm • ¥5 • subway line #2 to Jishuitan • bus #22 from Qianmen or #38 from the east end of Fuchingmennei Dajie

Just outside the quarter of *hutongs*, but easily combined with a visit to the Shicha lakes, is the **Xu Beihong Museum**; though closed for repair at the time of writing, it should have reopened by the time you read this. The son of a wandering portraitist, Xu (1895–1953) did for Chinese art what his contemporary Lu Xun did for literature – modernize an atrophied tradition. Following the death of his father, Xu had to look after his entire family from the age of 17 and spent much of his early life labouring in semi-destitution and obscurity before receiving the acclaim he deserved. His extraordinary talent is well in evidence here in seven halls, which display a huge collection of his works. These include many ink paintings of **horses**, for which he was most famous, and **Western-style oil paintings**, which he produced while studying in France (and that are now regarded as his weakest works); the large-scale **allegorical images** also on display allude to tumultuous events in modern Chinese history. However, the pictures it's easiest to respond to are his delightful sketches and studies, in ink and pencil, often of his infant son.

The Drum and Bell towers

Junction of Gulou Xidajie, Gulou Dongdajie and Di'anmenwai Dajie • Daily 9am–5pm • ¥20 per tower, or ¥30 combined ticket • subway lines #2 or #8 to Guloudajie

These two architecturally stunning towers stand directly to the north of the Forbidden City, providing yet more evidence that Beijing was once laid out according to a single, great scheme. Today's city planners have, belatedly, decided to go for something similar; the stretch from here to Jingshan is currently being gentrified, and the wonderful *hutong* area around the towers – which has been living on borrowed time – might well have disappeared within just a few years. It's easy to get to the towers from the lakes; they stand high above the surrounding buildings, so you can't really miss them.

The Drum Tower

鼓楼, gǔlóu • Drumming hourly 9.30–11.30am & 1.30–5pm

The formidable two-storey **Drum Tower**, a squat, wooden, fifteenth-century Ming creation set on a red-painted stone base, is the southern member of the pair. In every city in China, drums like these were banged to mark the hours of the day, and to call imperial officials to meetings. Nowadays, at regular intervals throughout the day, a troupe of drummers in traditional costume whack cheerfully away at the giant drums inside. They're not, to be blunt, terribly artful, but seeing them in action is still an impressive sight; as is the working replica of an ancient Chinese water clock, a *kelou*. Views from the top are fantastic, particularly after the steep slog up, but unfortunately only the southern end – the one facing the Bell Tower – is open.

The Bell Tower

钟楼, zhōnglóu

The **Bell Tower**, at the other end of the small plaza from the Drum Tower, is somewhat different in appearance, being made of stone and a bit smaller. The original structure was of Ming vintage, though the tower was destroyed by fire and rebuilt in the eighteenth century. It still, however, boasts its original iron bell, which, until 1924, was rung every evening at 7pm to give an indication of the time. A sign by the bell relates the legend of its creation: the bell-maker was under threat of execution for being unable to cast such a complex artefact, when at the last moment his daughter jumped into the molten mix – with added girl, the bell cast perfectly. The unobstructed panoramas from the top are even better than those from the Drum Tower – again, it's a short but tough pant up.

Nanluogu Xiang

南锣鼓巷, nánluógǔ xiàng • subway line #6 to Nanluoguxiang

There aren't, to be frank, too many streets in Beijing that could be called appealing, so the pedestrianized north–south *hutong* of **Nanluogu Xiang** is a little oasis. Dotted with cafés, boutiques and restaurants, it has become a playground for the city's bo-bos (bourgeois-bohemians). Though some expats sneer at this "Disney *hutong*", in the alleys shooting off to the east and west there are enough open-air mahjong games, rickety mom-and-pop stores, and old men sitting out with their caged birds to maintain that ramshackle, backstreet Beijing charm. If there seems to be a surfeit of bright and beautiful young things, that's because there's a drama school just around the corner. All in all, it's a great place to idle over a cappuccino, tuck into a meal or head for a drink in the evening – and there's some good accommodation in the area too (pp.104–105).

Eastern Beijing

Beijing's eastern districts are the most cosmopolitan and fashionable parts of the city. Just east of Tian'anmen, the madcap shopping district of **Wangfujing** buzzes by day and evening; the umpteen bars and restaurants of **Sanlitun**, to the northeast, crackle until a far later hour; south of here, **Guomao** bristles with high-rise buildings, and is also no slouch in the food or nightlife departments. Although the best places to see contemporary Beijing in action, none of these areas have much in the way of traditional sights: so step forward **Yonghe Gong** and the **Confucius Temple**, Beijing's two most spellbinding temple complexes.

Yonghe Gong

雍和宫, yōnghé gōng • Yonghegong Beidajie • Daily 9am–4pm • ¥25 • subway line #2 or #5 to Yonghegong Lama Temple

You won't see many bolder or brasher temples than this, built towards the end of the seventeenth century as the residence of Prince Yin Zhen. In 1723, when the prince became Emperor Yong Zheng and moved into the Forbidden City, the temple was re-tiled in imperial yellow and restricted thereafter to religious use. It became a **lamasery** in 1744, housing monks from Tibet and Inner Mongolia. The temple has supervised the election of the Mongolian Living Buddha (the spiritual head of Mongolian Lamaism), who was chosen by drawing lots out of a gold urn. After the civil war in 1949, Yonghe Gong was declared a national monument and closed for the following thirty years. Remarkably, it escaped the ravages of the Cultural Revolution, when most of the city's religious structures were destroyed or turned into factories and warehouses.

The lamasery nowadays functions as an active **Tibetan Buddhist centre**, though it's used basically for propaganda purposes, to show China guaranteeing and respecting the religious freedom of minorities. It's questionable how genuine the monks you see wandering around are – at best, they're state-approved.

The Yonghe Hall

雍和殿, yōnghédiàn

There are five main **prayer halls**, arranged in a line from south to north, and numerous side buildings housing Bodhisattva statues and paintings. The statues in the **Yonghe Hall**, the second one along, are gilded representations of the past, present and future Buddhas, respectively standing to the left, centre and right.

The Pavilion of Eternal Blessings

永佑殿, yǒngyòudiàn

Buddhas of longevity and medicine stand in the third hall, the **Pavilion of Eternal Happiness**, though they're far less interesting than the *nandikesvras*, representations of

1

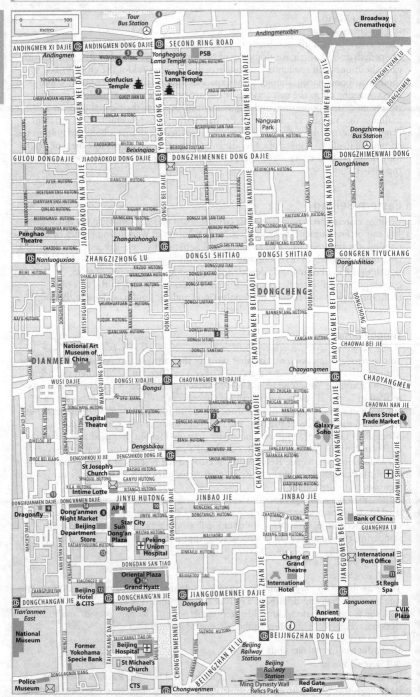

EAST OF THE CENTRE

● SHOPS

Aliens Street Market	7
Beijing Huashiweiye	3
Bookworm	6
Dong Liang Studio	5
Foreign Language Bookstore	8
Khawachen Tibetan Rugs	4
Page One	1
Shanghai Tang	9
Silk Market	10
Yashow Market	2

■ DRINKING & NIGHTLIFE

Apothecary	3
Atmosphere	11
Bling	5
Destination	8
Haze	10
Ichikura	9
Mesh	1
Migas	4
Tree	2
Vics	7
World of Suzie Wong	6
Xiu	12

■ ACCOMMODATION

Beijing	12
Cote Cour	8
Double Happiness Courtyard Hotel	5
Fly by Knight Courtyard Hostel	7
Hotel G	4
Ibis	6
Jianguo	13
Kapok	9
Opposite House	1
Park Hyatt	14
Peninsula Palace	10
St Regis	11
Sanlitun Youth Hostel	3
Yoyo	2

● EATING

Biteapitta	1
Bookworm	8
Confucius Café	7
Dong'anmen Night Market	14
The Elephant	11
Hatsune	3
Jin Ding Xuan	4
Justine's	17
Lime	12
Made in China	16
Najia Xiaoguan	18
Nali Patio	2
Qin Tang Fu	9
Renhe	13
Unban Bulgogi	10
The Veggie Table	6
Vineyard Café	5
Xiaochi Jie Night Market	15

Buddha having sex, in a side room. Once used to educate emperors' sons, the statues are now covered by drapes. The chamber behind, the **Hall of the Wheel of Law**, has a gilded bronze statue of Gelugpa, the founder of the Yellow Hats (the largest sect within Tibetan Buddhism) and paintings that depict his life, while the thrones at its side are for the Dalai Lama (each holder of the post used to come here to teach).

The Hall of Boundless Happiness

万福殿, wànfúdiàn

In the last, grandest hall, the **Wanfu Pavilion**, stands an 18m-high statue of the Maitreya Buddha, the world's largest carving made from a single piece of wood – in this case, the trunk of a Tibetan sandalwood tree. Gazing serenely out, the giant reddish-orange figure looms over you; details, such as his jewellery and the foliage fringing his shoulders, are beautifully carved. It took three years for the statue, a gift to Emperor Qianlong from the seventh Dalai Lama, to complete its passage to Beijing.

Confucius Temple

孔庙, kǒngmiào • Guozijian Jie • Daily May–Oct 8.30am–6pm, Nov–April 8.30am–5pm • ¥30 • performances hourly 9–11am & 2–5pm • subway line #2 or #5 to Yonghegong Lama Temple

Entered on a quiet *hutong* lined with shops selling incense, images and tapes of religious music, this **Confucius Temple** is one of Beijing's most pleasant sights, somewhere to sit on a bench in the peaceful courtyard among the ancient, twisted trees, and enjoy the silence – though there's plenty to look at inside, too. The complex is split into two main areas: the temple proper to the east, and the easy-to-miss, but equally large, old imperial college to the west; these are bisected by a hall containing the **Qianlong stone scriptures**, a Buddhist text consisting of 630,000 characters written between 1726 and 1738.

The temple complex

Constructed in 1306, the **temple** is a charming place filled with carved steles, red-lacquered wood and gnarled cypresses, some of which are over 700 years old; one, to the southwest of the complex, is now also a mulberry tree, the ambitious mulberry seed apparently dropped into the trunk by a bird. The buildings themselves are pretty ancient, too; parts of the colossal **Dacheng Hall** date back to 1411. The halls to its east and west were once sacrificial venues, but are now employed as **museums** of sorts, holding a diverse range of objects from every dynasty – though the Tang pottery, which includes images of pointy-faced foreigners, is most diverting. Small performances take place to the rear of the complex.

Guozi Jian

国子监, guózǐ jiàn

To the west of the temple complex is **Guozi Jian**, the old imperial college, the temple's junior by only two years and equally beautiful. After walking through the gigantic main gate, you'll be confronted by the **Memorial Arch**, clad with orange and green tiles and featuring the calligraphy of Emperor Qianlong. Behind this is the **Biyong Hall**, set in a circular lake filled with carp; Qianlong used to give speeches here, backed by an elaborate folding screen, and replicas of both are now in place.

Ditan Park

地坛公园, dìtán gōngyuán • Hepingli Xijie • Daily 6am–9.30pm • ¥2, extra ¥5 for altar and museum • subway line #2 or #5 to Yonghegong Lama Temple

Around 100m north from the Yonghe Gong, **Ditan Park** is more interesting as a place to wander among the trees and spot the odd *tai ji* performance than for its small **museum** holding the emperor's sedan chair and the enormous **altar** at which he performed sacrifices to the earth.

1

Dongyue Temple

东岳庙, dōngyuè miào · Chaoyangmenwai Dajie · Tues–Sun 8am–5pm · ¥40 · subway line #6 to Dongdaqiao

This intriguing **temple** stands in pointed contrast to all the shrines to materialism in nearby Santilun. Dating back to the Ming dynasty, it's been restored, and though rebranded as the "Beijing Folk Arts Museum" it's essentially still the same place, with a few vaguely diverting exhibitions. Pass under the **Zhandaimen archway** – originally constructed in 1322 – and you enter a courtyard holding around thirty annexes, each of which deals with a different aspect of Taoist life, the whole making up a sort of surreal spiritual bureaucracy. There's the "Department of Suppressing Schemes", "Department of Wandering Ghosts", even a "Department for Fifteen Kinds of Violent Death". In each, a statue of Taoist deity Lao Zi holds court over brightly painted figures, many with monstrous animal heads, too many limbs and the like.

Poly Plaza Museum

保利大厦博物馆, bǎolì dàshà bówùguǎn · Poly Plaza, Dongzhimen Nandajie · Mon–Sat 9.30am–4.30pm · ¥50 · subway line #2 to Dongsishitiao

Within the **Poly Plaza**, a boring-looking office block, lies a small **museum** that has one of the most select collections of **antiquities** in the capital. In the hall of ancient bronzes you'll find four of the twelve bronze animals that were **looted from the Old Summer Palace** (see p.96); the pig, tiger, ox and monkey were bought in the West by patriotic businessmen, and their return was much heralded. Another two were returned in 2013, and now take pride of place in the National Museum of China (p.76); the four here may follow in due course. The second hall displays ancient Buddha statues.

Sanlitun

三里屯, sānlǐtún · subway line #10 to Tuanjiehu or Agricultural Exhibition Centre

The most famous **nightlife district** in Beijing, if not all China, **Sanlitun** has come a long way since its first few watering holes opened up on "Bar Street". It's now full to the brim with fancy boutiques and shopping malls, a wonderfully cosmopolitan array of excellent cafés and restaurants, and some of Beijing's trendiest bars. The area is centred on **Tai Koo Li** (太古里, tài gǔ lǐ), a visually splendid mix of upper-class shops, bars and restaurants formally known as "The Village", and still often referred to as such. To the southwest is the **Workers' Stadium** (工人体育场, gōngrén tǐyùchǎng), colloquially known as "Gongti" to Beijingers, and itself surrounded by bars and clubs.

Ritan Park

日坛公园, rìtán gōngyuán · several entrances · 24hr · Free · subway line #1 to Yong'anli

Just south of the Sanlitun area, and part of Beijing's Central Business District (CBD), is **Ritan Park**, one of the imperial city's original four. Each park was the location for a yearly sacrificial ritual performed by the emperor, but today's Ritan Park is popular with embassy staff and courting couples, who make use of its numerous secluded nooks. It's a very attractive place, with paths winding between groves of cherry trees, rockeries and ponds.

The diplomatic district

The area surrounding Ritan Park has a casual, affluent, cosmopolitan atmosphere thanks to its large contingent of foreigners, many of them staff from the **Jianguomenwai diplomatic compound**, an odd place with neat buildings in ordered courtyards, and frozen sentries on plinths. Though their embassy lies elsewhere, you'll see plenty of Russians (and Cyrillic writing) here; many have set up shop in this area, most notably in the weird **Ritan International Trade Center** (most of whose shops have closed doors and no customers, and seem to be fronts). Perhaps more interesting is the **North Korean embassy**; though their grouchy staff are unlikely to give you a visa, you can eat North Korean food with them at the fantastic Unban Bulgogi restaurant nearby (see p.111).

1

The Ancient Observatory

古观象台, gǔguānxiàngtái • Off Jianguomennei Dajie • Tues–Sun 9am–5pm • ¥20 • subway line #1 or #2 to Jianguomen

Beside the concrete knot that is the intersection between Jianguomennei Dajie and the Second Ring Road, the **Ancient Observatory**, an unexpected survivor marooned amid the high-rises, comes as a delightful surprise. The first observatory on the site was founded in the thirteenth century on the orders of Kublai Khan; the astronomers were commissioned to reform the inaccurate calendar then in use. Subsequently the observatory was staffed by Muslim scientists, as medieval Islamic science enjoyed pre-eminence, but, strangely, in the early seventeenth century it was placed in the hands of Jesuit missionaries. Led by one **Matteo Ricci**, they proceeded to astonish the emperor and his subjects by making a series of precise astronomical forecasts. The Jesuits re-equipped the observatory and remained in charge until the 1830s.

The Observatory complex

The squat, unadorned observatory building was built in 1442; today it lies empty, and visitors aren't allowed inside – there'd be little point, really, since Beijing's present-day skies often make it impossible to see the *Marriott* down the road, let alone Mars. The best features of the complex are, however, accessible: its garden, a placid retreat; and the eight Ming-dynasty **astronomical instruments** sitting on the roof – stunningly sculptural armillary spheres, theodolites and the like, all beautifully ornamented with entwined dragons, lions and clouds, looking for all the world like gigantic Art Nouveau trinkets. The attached **museum**, displaying pottery decorated with star maps, and arrayed around a courtyard featuring navigational equipment dating from the Yuan dynasty onwards, is well worth a wander round.

Wangfujing

王府井, wángfǔjǐng • subway line #1 to Wangfujing

Wangfujing district is where the capital gets down to the business of **shopping** in earnest. The haunt of quality stores for over a century, it was called Morrison Street before the communist takeover. There are some giant malls here, including the biggest in Asia, the **Oriental Plaza**, which stretches east for nearly a kilometre.

Bar the shopping, and the opportunity to eat scorpions, testicles and the like at two fantastic **night markets**, there's little to see in Wangfujing bar the **National Art Museum of China**, a huge exhibition hall showcasing state-approved artworks.

Southern Beijing

Visitors usually head south of Tian'anmen Square for one main reason: the glorious **Temple of Heaven**, a visually arresting ancient building that counts as one of Beijing's must-see sights. However, there's plenty to distract you on your way: of most interest is the earthy, old-fashioned *hutong* area surrounding the famed **Dazhalan shopping street** (大栅栏路, dàzhàlán lù), which has been Beijing's prime backpacker base for decades, and remains the city's best area for aimless browsing, snacking and wandering. Forming a neat counterpoint is **Qianmen Dajie**, a shopping street stretching immediately south of Qianmen – a brand-new, though pleasing, pastiche of dynastic styles.

The Temple of Heaven

天坛, tiāntán • park 6am–9pm, temple 8am–6pm • park ¥15, park and temple ¥35 • subway line #5 to Tiantandongmen

Set in a large, tranquil park about 2km south of Tian'anmen, the **Temple of Heaven** is widely regarded as the pinnacle of Ming design. For five centuries it was at the very heart of imperial ceremony and symbolism, and for many modern visitors its architectural unity and beauty remain more appealing – and on a much more accessible scale – than the Forbidden City.

TIANTAN: BETWEEN HEAVEN AND EARTH

Construction of the Temple of Heaven was begun during the reign of Emperor Yongle, and completed in 1420. The temple complex was conceived as the prime meeting point of earth and heaven, and symbols of the two are integral to its design. **Heaven** was considered round, and the **earth** square; thus the round temples and altars stand on square bases, while the park has the shape of a semicircle beside a square. The intermediary between earth and heaven was, of course, the **Son of Heaven** – the emperor, in other words.

The temple was the site of the most important ceremony of the imperial court calendar, when the emperor prayed for the year's harvests at the **winter solstice**. Purified by three days of fasting, he made his way to the park on the day before the solstice, accompanied by his court in all its magnificence. On arrival at Tiantan, the emperor would meditate in the Imperial Vault, ritually conversing with the gods on the details of government, before spending the night in the Hall of Prayer for Good Harvests. The following day he sacrificed animals before the Altar of Heaven. It was forbidden for commoners to catch a glimpse of the great annual procession to the temple, and they were obliged to bolt their windows and remain, in silence, indoors. Indeed, the Tiantan complex remained sacrosanct until it was thrown open to the people on the first Chinese National Day of the Republic, in October 1912.

The last person to perform the rites was **General Yuan Shikai**, the second president of the Republic, on December 23, 1914. He planned to declare himself emperor but died a broken man, his plans thwarted by opponents, in 1916.

The temple is easiest to access via the park's east gate, which is the only one close to a subway station. Walking, cycling or coming by bus, you're more likely to enter Tiantan Park from the north or west. Exiting the park via its west gate, you can head a little north to the Museum of Natural History (p.90).

Altar of Heaven

This main pathway leads straight to the circular **Altar of Heaven**, consisting of three marble tiers representing (from the top down) heaven, earth and man. The tiers are comprised of blocks in various multiples of nine, cosmologically the most powerful number, symbolizing both heaven and emperor. The centre of the altar's bare, roofless top tier, where the Throne of Heaven was placed during ceremonies, was considered to be the middle of the Middle Kingdom – the very centre of the earth. Various acoustic properties are claimed for the altar; from this point, it is said, all sounds are channelled straight upwards to heaven. To the east of the nearby **fountain**, which was reconstructed after fire damage in 1740, are the ruins of a group of buildings used for the preparation of sacrifices.

Imperial Vault of Heaven

Directly north of the Altar of Heaven, the **Imperial Vault of Heaven** is an octagonal structure made entirely of wood, with a dramatic roof of dark blue, glazed tiles. It is preceded by the so-called **Echo Wall**, said to be a perfect whispering gallery, although the unceasing cacophony of tourists trying it out makes it impossible to tell.

Hall of Prayer for Good Harvests

At the north end of the park, the **Hall of Prayer for Good Harvest**, the principal temple building of the entire complex, amply justifies all this build-up. Made entirely of wood, without the aid of a single nail, the circular structure rises from another tiered marble terrace and has three blue-tiled roofs. Four compass-point pillars, representing the seasons, support the vault, enclosed in turn by twelve outer pillars (one for each month of the year and hour of the day). The dazzling colours of the interior, surrounding the central dragon motif on the coffered ceiling, give the hall an ultramodern look; it was in fact rebuilt, faithful to the Ming design, after the original was destroyed by lightning in 1889. The official explanation for this appalling omen was that it was divine

■ **ACCOMMODATION**
365 Inn	1
Leo Hostel	2

● **SHOPS**
Beijing Curio City	4
Neiliansheng Shoes	3
Panjiayuan Market	5
Ruifuxiang	2
Ten Fu	1

● **EATING**
Deyuan	5
Goubuli	4
Liqun	2
Quanjude	3
Starbucks	1

■ **DRINKING**
365 Inn	1

SOUTH OF THE CENTRE

punishment meted out on a sacrilegious caterpillar, which was on the point of crawling to the golden ball on the hall's apex when the lightning struck. Thirty-two court dignitaries were executed for allowing this to happen.

Museum of Natural History

自然博物馆, zìrán bówùguǎn • Tianqiao Nandajie • Tues–Sun 10am–5pm • ¥10 • subway line #5 to Tiantandongmen

Just north of Tiantan Park's east gate, this museum is highly popular with local and foreign kids alike – they never fail to be impressed by the **dinosaur skeletons**, set amid an array of local fossils. On upper levels of the building, China's prodigious wealth of animal life is portrayed in stuffed form, while sharks, manta rays and the like zip above your head in the basement **aquarium**.

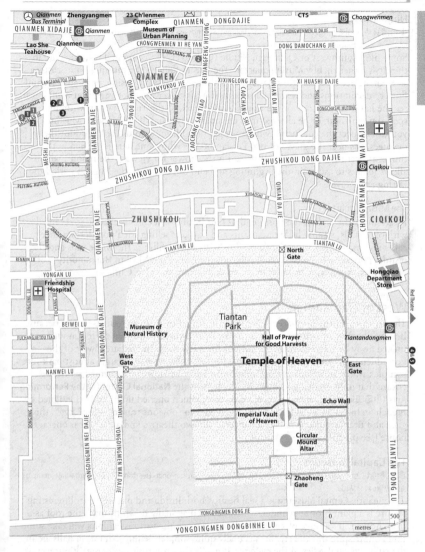

Museum of Architecture

古代建筑博物馆, gǔdài jiànzhù bówùguǎn • south of Nanwei Lu (look for the red arch) • Tues–Sun 9am–5pm • ¥15 • subway line #4 to Taoranting, or walking distance from the Temple of Heaven's west gate

One of Beijing's most underrated attractions, this museum is housed in the former **Xiannong Temple**, where the emperor ritually ploughed a furrow to ensure a good harvest. You can see the gold-plated plough he used in the Hall of Worship. The Hall of Jupiter has a fantastically ornate ceiling and cutaway models of famous buildings from all over the country. Anyone who has ever wondered how a *dougong* works – those ornate interlocking brackets seen on temples – can satisfy their curiosity here. There's also a great model of the city as it appeared in 1949, before the Communists ripped it up.

1

Niujie Mosque

牛街清真寺, niújiē qīngzhēnsì • Niu Jie • Daily from first to last prayers • ¥10, free for Muslims • subway line #4 to Caishikou subway, or bus #6 from the north gate of Tiantan Park

Some 3km southwest of Qianmen, **Niu Jie** (Ox Street) is a congested thoroughfare in the city's rather shabby **Muslim quarter**. The street's focus is the **mosque** on its eastern side, an attractive, colourful marriage of Chinese and Islamic design, with abstract and flowery decorations and text in Chinese and Arabic over the doorways. You won't get to see the handwritten copy of the Koran, dating back to the Yuan dynasty, without special permission, or be allowed into the main prayer hall if you're not a Muslim, but you can inspect the courtyard, where a copper cauldron, used to cook food for the devotees, sits near the graves of two Persian imams who came here to preach in the thirteenth century. Also in the courtyard is the "tower for viewing the moon", which allows imams to ascertain the beginning and end of Ramadan, the Muslim period of fasting and prayer.

The Muslim quarter

Head under the arch at the north end of Niu Jie and you enter a chaotic street lined with offal stalls, steamy little restaurants and hawkers selling fried dough rings, rice cakes and *shaobing*, Chinese-style muffins with a meat filling. The white caps and the beards sported by the men distinguish these people of the Muslim **Hui minority** – of which there are nearly 200,000 in the capital – from the Han Chinese.

West of Tian'anmen

The area west of the Forbidden City is rarely visited by western tourists, partly because Beijing's best restaurants and places to stay lie elsewhere. However, there's enough tucked away here to entertain the curious for a few days. Immediately west of the Forbidden City you'll find **Zhongnanhai** (中南海, zhōngnánhǎi), a large, almost park-like complex which functions as the Communist Party headquarters – armed sentries ensure that only invited guests get inside. It faces the **National Centre for the Performing Arts** (中国国家大剧院, zhōngguó guójiā dàjùyuàn), which opened up in 2007. Designed by French architect Paul Andreu and nicknamed – for obvious reasons – the "Egg", this glass and titanium dome houses a concert hall, two theatres and a 2500-seat opera house (see p.113).

The Capital Museum

首都博物馆, shǒudū bówùguǎn • Fuxingmenwai Dajie • Tues–Sun 9am–5pm • Free (bring ID) • ⓦ en.capitalmuseum.org.cn • subway line #1 to Muxidi

The gigantic **Capital Museum** is a real beauty, both inside and out. Its most interesting feature is a giant bronze cylinder, which shoots diagonally down through the roof as if from heaven. It's a huge place, and walking between the various exhibits will take some time, but despite this the layout is actually quite simple: Beijing exhibition halls are in the **cube**, cultural relics in the **cylinder**. If you're short on time or energy, skip the cube and head for the rarer pieces in the cylinder instead.

The cylinder: galleries

The ground-floor gallery in the **cylinder** holds Ming and Qing paintings, mostly landscapes. The calligraphy upstairs can be safely missed unless you have a special interest, but the bronzes on level three are pretty interesting: a sinister third-century BC owl-headed dagger, for example, or the strangely modern-looking three-legged cooking vessels decorated with geometrical patterns – which are more than three thousand years old. The display of jade on the fourth floor is definitely worth lingering over; some astonishing workmanship has gone into the buckles, boxes and knick-knacks here, and the white quail-shaped vessels are particularly lovely.

The cube: exhibition halls

The **cube** of exhibition halls on the building's west side can be travelled around rather faster than those in the cylinder. The bottom level hosts a confusing show on the history of Beijing – there aren't enough English captions to make any sense of the exhibition whatsoever – while the models of historical buildings on the next level up can be skipped in favour of the show-stealing Buddhist figurines on the top floor. As well as depictions of serene, long-eared gentlemen, there are some very esoteric Lamaist figures from Tibet; the Goddess Marici, for example, comes with her own pig-drawn chariot, and other fierce deities have lion heads or many arms.

Baiyun Guan

白云观, báiyún guàn • off Baiyun Lu • Daily 8.30am–4.30pm • ¥10 • subway line #1 to Muxidi

Once the most influential Taoist centre in the country, **Baiyun Guan**, the White Cloud Temple, has been extensively renovated after a long spell as a military barracks and is now the location for the **China Taoism Association**. There are thirty resident monks, and it's become a popular place for pilgrims, with a busy, thriving feel to it. Though laid out in a similar way to a Buddhist temple, Baiyun Guan has a few unusual features, such as the three gateways at the entrance, symbolizing the three worlds of Taoism – Desire, Substance and Emptiness. There are also three monkeys depicted in relief sculptures around the temple, and it is believed to be lucky to find all three: the first is on the gate, easy to spot as it's been rubbed black, and the other two are in the first courtyard. The place is at its most colourful during the New Year temple fair (see "Festivals", p.46).

The Military Museum

军事博物馆, jūnshì bówùguǎn • Fuxing Lu • Tues–Sun 8.30am–5pm • Free (bring ID) • subway line #1 or #9 to Military Museum

Now that all the communists have been to marketing school, it's almost refreshing to be confronted with the old-fashioned Soviet-style brutalism of this museum – the last public image of Marx in China hung here until 1999. The entrance hall is full of big, bad art, including photo-collages of Mao inspecting his army and soldiers performing an amphibious landing (as, perhaps, a not-so-subtle hint to Taiwan). The hall beyond has a wealth of Russian and Chinese weaponry on show, including tanks and rockets, with – in case martial feelings have been stirred – an air-rifle shooting gallery at the back. In the rear courtyard a group of miscellaneous old aircraft includes the shells of two American spy planes (with Nationalist Chinese markings) shot down in the 1950s. Upstairs, you'll find plaster casts of statues of military and political leaders.

Guangji Temple

广济寺, guǎngjì sì • Fuchengmennei Dajie • Daily 6am–4.30pm • Free • subway line #4 to Xisi

A quiet complement to the Baita temple further west, this working Buddhist temple is the headquarters of China's **Buddhist Association**. Though an unassuming place, it boasts an important collection of painting and sculpture, as well as a Ming-dynasty Tripitaka; these are, however, only on view to academics with a specialist interest in the art. Visitors can look around, though; keep an eye out for Trikala Buddhas made of yellow sandalwood.

Baita Temple

白塔寺, báitǎ sì • Fuchengmennei Dajie • subway line #2 to Fuchengmen, or line #4 to Xisi

The massive white **dagoba** of this famous temple is visible from afar, rising over the rooftops of the labyrinth of *hutongs* that surround it. Shaped like an upturned bowl with an inverted ice-cream cone on top (the work of a Nepali architect), the 35m-high dagoba was built in the Yuan dynasty; it's a popular spot with Buddhist pilgrims, who ritually circle it clockwise. The temple was closed for reconstruction at the time of writing, but when it reopens it'll be worth visiting simply for the collection of thousands of small statues of Buddha – mostly Tibetan – housed in one of its halls, very impressive en masse. Another hall holds bronze *luohans* (Buddha's original group of disciples), including one with a beak; small bronze Buddhas; and other, outlandish Lamaist figures.

Lu Xun Museum

鲁迅博物馆, lǔxùn bówùguǎn • Xisantiao Hutong, off Fuchengmennei Dajie • Tues–Sun 8am–5pm • Free (bring ID) • subway line #2 to Fuchengmen

A large and extensively renovated courtyard house, this museum was once home to **Lu Xun** (1881–1936), widely accepted as the greatest Chinese writer of the modern era. He gave up a promising career in medicine to write books, with the aim, so he declared, of curing social ills with his pithy, satirical stories. Lu Xun bought this house in 1924, but as someone who abhorred pomp, he might feel a little uneasy here nowadays. His possessions have been preserved like treasured relics, giving a good idea of what Chinese interiors looked like at the beginning of the twentieth century, and there's a photo exhibition lauding his achievements. Unfortunately there are no English captions, though a bookshop on the west side of the compound sells English translations of his work, including his lauded *The True Story of Ah Q*.

Beijing Zoo and Aquarium

动物园, dòngwùyuán • Xizhimenwai Dajie • Zoo daily April–Oct 7.30am–6pm, Nov–March 7.30am–5pm • Aquarium daily 10am–4.30pm • Zoo ¥40, combined ticket ¥130, children ¥70, children under 1.2m free • Aquarium dolphin show daily 10am & 2.30pm • subway line #4 to Beijing Zoo

Beijing's **zoo** is most worth visiting for its panda house. Here you can join the queues to have your photo taken sitting astride a plastic replica of the creature, then push your way through to glimpse the living variety – kept in relatively palatial quarters and familiar through the much-publicized export of the animals to overseas zoos for mating purposes. While the pandas lie on their backs in their luxury pad, waving their legs in the air, other animals – less cute or less endangered – slink, pace or flap around their miserable cells. The children's zoo, with plenty of farmyard animals and ponies to pet, is rather better, and the new **Beijing Aquarium**, in the northwest corner of the compound, is surprisingly good, with thousands of varieties of fish, including sharks.

Wuta Temple

五塔寺, wǔtǎ sì • Wutasi Lu, off Zhongguancun Nandajie • Daily 9am–4.30pm • ¥20, free to first 300 visitors on Wed • subway line #4 or #9 to National Library subway

Canal-side **Wuta Temple** boasts a central hall radically different from any other sacred building you'll see in the capital. Completed in 1424, it's a stone cube decorated on the outside with reliefs of animals, Sanskrit characters, and Buddha images – each has a different hand gesture – and topped with five layered, triangular spires. It's visibly Indian in influence, and is said to be based on a temple in Bodhgaya, where Buddha gained enlightenment. There are 87 steps to the top, where you can inspect the spire carvings at close quarters – including elephants and Buddhas, and, at the centre of the central spire, a pair of feet. The new halls behind the museum are home to statues of bulbous-eyed camels, docile-looking tigers, puppy-dog lions and the like, all collected from the spirit ways of tombs and long-destroyed temples.

Wanshou Temple

万寿寺, wànshòu sì • Guangyuanjia Lu • Daily 9am–4pm • ¥20, free to first 300 visitors on Wed • subway line #4 or #9 to National Library, or line #4 to Weigongcun

A Ming temple that was once a favourite of the Dowager Empress Cixi (see p.96), **Wanshou** is the last survivor of the several dozen places of worship which once lined the canalsides all the way up to the Summer Palace. It's now a small museum of ancient art, with five exhibition halls of Ming and Qing relics, mostly ceramics – not something to cross town for, but it's certainly worth popping by if you're in the area.

The far north

Beijing's far northern quarters are home to a number of attractions. In the city's northwest corner is the wonderful **Summer Palace**, an imperial retreat which has retained the charm of centuries gone by; Beijing's main **university district** lies nearby, and exudes a somewhat different atmosphere. Heading east will bring you to the **Olympic area**, somewhat neglected since the heady summer of 2008. East again, and on the way to the airport, is the superb **798 Art District** – tough to get to on public transport, but easily within taxi range.

The Summer Palace

颐和园, yíhé yuán • several entrances, but most commonly accessed from the north or northeast • Daily 8am–7pm, buildings close at 5pm • park ¥20, park and all buildings ¥50 • subway line #4 to Xiyuan or Beigongmen

One of Beijing's must-see attractions, the **Summer Palace** is a lavish imperial playground whose grounds are large enough to have an almost rural feel. Once the private haunt of the notorious **Empress Cixi** (see p.96), it functions today as a lovely public park, two-thirds of which is taken up by Kunming Lake. During the hottest months of the year, the imperial court would decamp to this perfect location, the site surrounded by hills, cooled by the lake and sheltered by judicious use of garden landscaping.

The palace buildings, many connected by a suitably majestic gallery, are built on and around **Wanshou Shan** (Longevity Hill), north of the lake and west of the main gate. Many of these edifices are intimately linked with Cixi – anecdotes about whom are the stock output of the numerous tour guides – but to enjoy the site, you need know very little of its history: like Beihai (see p.80), the park, its lake and pavilions form a startling visual array, akin to a traditional Chinese landscape painting brought to life.

Brief history

There have been imperial summer pavilions at the Summer Palace since the eleventh century, although the present park layout is essentially eighteenth-century, created by the Manchu Emperor Qianlong. However, the key character associated with the palace is the **Dowager Empress Cixi**, who ruled over the disintegrating Chinese empire from 1861 until her death in 1908. The Summer Palace was very much her pleasure ground; it was she who built the palaces here in 1888 after the original palace was destroyed by Western forces during the Opium Wars, and determinedly restored them after another bout of European aggression in 1900.

The palaces

The **palaces** are built to the north of the lake near the **East Gate**, on and around Wanshou Shan, and many remain intimately linked with Cixi. The main compound includes the **Renshou Dian**, a majestic hall where the empress gave audience. It contains much of the original nineteenth-century furniture, including an imposing throne. Beyond, to the right, is the **Dehe Yuan** (Palace of Virtue and Harmony), dominated by

---

BY BOAT TO THE SUMMER PALACE

The fastest route to the Summer Palace is to take the subway, but there's also a **boat service** from Zizhuyuan Park or behind the Beijing Exhibition Hall (hourly 10am–5pm, ¥70 including park ticket to palace) that takes the old imperial approach along the now dredged and prettified Long River. Your vessel is either one of the large, dragon-shaped cruisers or a smaller speedboat holding four people, passing the Wuta Temple, Zizhuyuan Park, and a number of attractive bridges and willow groves en route.

1

EMPRESS DOWAGER CIXI

The notorioius Cixi entered the imperial palace at 15 as Emperor Xianfeng's **concubine**, quickly becoming his favourite and bearing him a son. When the emperor died in 1861, she became regent, ruling in place of her boy for the next 25 years through a mastery of intrigue and court politics. When her son died of syphilis, she installed her nephew as puppet regent, imprisoned him, and retained her authority. Her fondness of extravagant gestures (every year she had ten thousand caged birds released on her birthday) drained the state's coffers, and her deeply conservative policies were inappropriate for a time when the nation was calling out for reform.

With foreign powers taking great chunks out of China's borders on and off during the nineteenth century, Cixi was moved to respond in a typically misguided fashion – impressed by the claims of the xenophobic **Boxer Movement**, she let them loose on all the foreigners in China in 1899 (see p.919). On her return, Cixi clung to power, attempting to delay the inevitable fall of her dynasty. One of her last acts, before she died in 1908, was to arrange for the murder of her puppet regent.

a three-storey **theatre**, complete with trap doors for the appearances and disappearances of the actors. Theatre was one of Cixi's main passions and she sometimes took part in performances, dressed as Guanyin, the goddess of mercy. The next major building along the path is the **Yulan Tang** (Jade Waves Palace), where the child emperor Guangxu was kept in captivity for ten years while Cixi exercised his powers. Just to the west is the dowager's own principal residence, the **Leshou Tang** (Hall of Joy and Longevity), which houses Cixi's hardwood throne, and the table where she took her infamous 108-course meals. The chandeliers were China's first electric lights, installed in 1903 and powered by the palace's own generator.

The Long Corridor and Kunming Lake

Boats for hire at any of the jetties ¥40 per hour • winter ice skate hire at the main entrance ¥10 per hour

From Leshou Tang, the **Long Corridor** runs to the northwest corner of **Kunming Lake**. Flanked by various temples and pavilions, the corridor is actually a 700m covered way, its inside walls painted with more than eight thousand restored images of birds, flowers, landscapes and scenes from history and mythology. Near the west end of the corridor is Cixi's ultimate flight of fancy, a magnificent lakeside pavilion in the form of a 36m-long **marble boat**, boasting two decks. Constructed using funds intended for the Chinese navy, it was regarded by Cixi's acolytes as a characteristically witty and defiant snub to her detractors, though her misappropriations caused China's heavy naval defeats during the 1895 war with Japan. Close to the marble boat is a **jetty** – the tourist focus of this part of the site – with rowing boats for hire. In winter, the Chinese **skate** on the lake here – a spectacular sight, as some of the participants are really proficient.

The south of the park

It's a pleasant fifteen-minute walk from the marble boat to the southern part of Kunming Lake, where the scenery is wilder and the crowds thinner. Should you need a destination, the main attraction to head for is the white **Seventeen-Arch Bridge**, 150m long and topped with 544 cute, vaguely canine lions, each with a slightly different posture. The bridge leads to **South Lake Island**, where Qianlong used to review his navy, and which holds a brace of fine halls, most striking of which is the **Yelu Chucai Memorial Temple**.

Yuanmingyuan (Old Summer Palace)

圆明园, yuánmíng yuán • Qinghua Xilu • Daily 7am–7pm, buildings close at 5pm • Grounds ¥10, all-inclusive ticket ¥25 • subway line #4 to Yuanmingyuan Park

Beijing's original summer palace, the **Yuanmingyuan** was built by the Qing Emperor Kangxi in the early eighteenth century. Once nicknamed China's Versailles for its elegant, European-influenced design, the palace boasted the largest royal gardens in the

1

world, containing some two hundred pavilions and temples set around a series of lakes and natural springs. Marina Warner re-creates the scene in *The Dragon Empress*:

Scarlet and golden halls, miradors, follies and gazebos clustered around artificial hills and lakes. Tranquil tracts of water were filled with fan-tailed goldfish with telescopic eyes, and covered with lotus and lily pads; a superabundance of flowering shrubs luxuriated in the gardens; antlered deer wandered through the grounds; ornamental ducks and rare birds nestled on the lakeside.

Today there is precious little left: in 1860, the entire complex was burnt and destroyed by British and French troops, who were ordered by the Earl of Elgin to make the imperial court "see reason" during the Opium Wars (see p.918). The troops had previously spent twelve days looting the imperial treasures, many of which found their way to the Louvre and British Museum. This unedifying history is described in inflammatory terms on signs all over the park and it's a favoured site for brooding nationalists. Still, don't let that put you off, as the overgrown ruins are rather appealing and unusual.

There are actually three parks here, the Yuanmingyuan (Park of Perfection and Brightness), Wanchunyuan (Park of Ten Thousand Springs) and Changchunyuan (Park of Everlasting Spring), all centred around the lake, Fuhai (Sea of Happiness). All together this forms an absolutely gigantic area, but the best-preserved structures are the fountain and the **Hall of Tranquillity** in the northeastern section. The stone and marble fragments hint at how fascinating the original must once have been, with its marriage of European Rococo decoration and Chinese motifs.

Dazhong Temple

大钟寺, dàzhōng sì • Beisanhuan Lu • Tues–Sun 8.30am–4.30pm • ¥15 • subway line #13 to Dazhongsi

The **Dazhong Temple** houses one of Beijing's most interesting little exhibitions, showcasing several hundred **bronze bells** from temples all over the country. These are considerable works of art, their surfaces enlivened with embossed texts in Chinese and Tibetan, abstract patterns and images of storks and dragons. The odd, scaly, dragon-like creature shown perching on top of each bell is a *pulao*, a legendary animal supposed to shriek when attacked by a whale (the wooden hammers used to strike the bells are carved to look like whales). The shape of Chinese bells dampens vibrations, so they only sound for a short time and can be effectively used as instruments: you can buy CDs of the bells in action.

The King of Bells

The Dazhong Temple derives its name from the enormous bell hanging in the back (*dazhong* means big bell); this Ming creation, known as the **King of Bells**, is as tall as a two-storey house. Hanging in the back hall, it is, at fifty tonnes, the biggest and oldest surviving bell in the world, and can reputedly be heard up to 40km away. You can climb up to a platform above it to get a closer look at some of the 250,000 Chinese characters on its surface, and join visitors in trying to throw a coin into the small hole in the top. The method of its construction and the history of Chinese bell-making in general is explained by displays, with English captions, in side halls.

Olympic Park

奥林匹克公园, àolínpǐkè gōngyuán • subway line #8 to Olympic Sports Center or Olympic Green

China used the 2008 Olympics to make an impact on the world stage, and facilities built for the occasion were accordingly lavish. The **Olympic Park** was placed on the city's north–south axis, laid down during the Yuan dynasty – so it's bang in line with the Forbidden City. In addition, subway line #8 – eight being a highly auspicious number in Chinese – was built for the occasion.

Several of the venues used for the Games are still standing, but most visitors come here to bear witness to two masterpieces of modern architecture: the astonishing **National Stadium**, and the **National Aquatics Centre**.

1

The National Stadium

奥林匹体育馆, àolínpīkè tǐyùguǎn • Daily 8am–5pm • ¥50

The 90,000-seater **National Stadium**, nicknamed the "Bird's Nest" on account of its exterior steel lattice, was built at a cost of over US$400m by Herzog and de Meuron, with input from Ai Weiwei. It made a grand stage for many memorable events, including the spectacular opening display, but since the Olympics it hasn't seen much use, hosting a couple of concerts and football games, and a winter theme park; it's eventually expected to become part of a larger shopping and event complex. A few hundred people visit every day, mostly out-of-towners; you can join them in wandering round the empty shell for the extortionate entry fee.

The National Aquatics Centre

国家游泳中心, guójiā yóuyǒng zhōngxīn • Daily 10am–9.30pm • ¥200

Next door to the National Stadium, the **National Aquatics Centre** quickly became known as the Water Cube, thanks to its bubble-like exterior membrane. Part of it is now occupied by the **Beijing Watercube Waterpark**, which though expensive is a lot of fun; it holds several pools, with wave machines, water slides, diving and an Olympic-sized competition pool.

798 Art District

798艺术区, qījiǔbā yìshùqū • Daily 24hr • Free • subway line #2 or #13 to Dongzhimen, then bus #915, #918 or #934 • taxi from Dongzhimen ¥35–50

Though it's way out on the way to the airport, the **798 Art District** is a hotspot for the arty crowd, and one of the most interesting of Beijing's attractions. Originally this huge complex of Bauhaus-style buildings was an electronics factory, built by East Germans; when that closed down in the 1990s, artists moved in and converted the airy, light and, above all, cheap spaces into studios. As the Chinese art market blossomed, **galleries** followed, then **boutiques** and **cafés** – a process of gentrification that would take fifty years in the West, but happened here in about five. The city government – terrified of unfettered expression – initially wanted to shut the area down, but now that 798's emphasis is ever more commercial, the future of the place looks secure.

THE 2008 OLYMPICS

It had to be China; it had to be Beijing. In a nation so obsessed with the number eight that SIM cards or apartments bearing that number cost more, it was unimaginable that they would not be selected to host the **Olympics** in 2008 – especially since a suitably auspicious quirk of the calendar meant that the eighth day of the eighth month fell on a Friday – the day on which the Opening Ceremony has to take place.

Beijing duly won the vote in 2001 (beating Toronto into second place, and Paris into third), and readied itself for the Games to end all Games – some put the final cost at over US$40bn, making it by far the most expensive sporting event in history. There were problems along the way, most notably protests by pro-Tibetan and human rights activists on the torch relay, but all venues were completed on time, and the Games duly began on August 8, 2008 in an utterly compelling Opening Ceremony.

Though over 10,000 athletes competed in the Games, two superstars stole the show. American swimmer **Michael Phelps** had won six golds at the previous Games in Athens; here he surpassed himself, and everyone in Olympic history, by winning an unprecedented eight gold medals. Then there was Jamaican sprinter **Usain Bolt**, who had broken the 100m world record a few months before the Games in only his fifth race at the distance; here he obliterated that mark, winning in a time of 9.69 seconds, a time even more amazing when replays showed that he started to celebrate (and decelerate) well before the finish line. China had plenty to cheer about too, winning 51 gold medals – far ahead of the USA in second place.

FROM TOP 798 ART DISTRICT (P.98); ACROBATS (P.114) >

1

Visiting 798

The 798 district has the feel of a campus, with a grid of pedestrianized, tree-lined streets dotted with wacky sculptures – a caged dinosaur, a forlorn gorilla – and the gnarliness of the industrial buildings (those in "Power Square" are particularly brutal) softened by artsy graffiti. It's surprisingly large, but there are maps throughout.

Exhibitions open every week, and every art form is well represented – though with such a lot of it about, it varies in quality. Many galleries close on Monday. Note that, unlike all other Beijing sites, it's actually better on the weekend, when there's a real buzz about the place; on weekdays it can feel a little dead.

See p.115 for a rundown of the most interesting galleries to visit; p.108 for restaurant and café recommendations; and p.116 for shops.

ARRIVAL AND DEPARTURE   BEIJING

Unless you arrive by train, it's a long way into the centre from either the bus stations or the airport, and even when you get into downtown you're still a good few kilometres from most hotels, which tend to cluster between the second and third ring roads. It's a good idea to hail a taxi from the centre to get you to your final destination rather than tussle with the buses, as the public transport system is confusing at first and the city layout rather alienating. Walking to your hotel isn't really an option, as distances are always long, exhausting at the best of times and unbearable with luggage. From Beijing, you can get just about anywhere in China via the extensive air and rail systems. You'd be advised to buy a ticket a few days in advance, though, especially in the summer or around Spring Festival. Few visitors travel long-distance by bus as it's less comfortable than the train and takes longer, though it has the advantage that you can usually just turn up and get on, as services to major cities are frequent.

BY PLANE

The first experience many visitors have of China is the smooth ride along Beijing's airport–city freeway, lined with hoardings and jammed with cars.

Beijing Capital Airport (北京首都机场, běijīng shǒudū jīchǎng; 24hr enquiries ☎010 64563604) was opened in 1999 on October 1, the 50th birthday of Communist rule. 29km northeast of the centre, it serves both international and domestic flights, and has three terminals (T1, T2 and T3) – if you're departing Beijing, be sure to figure out which one you'll be using before heading to the airport. There are banks and ATMs here, and commission rates are the same as everywhere else. Get some small change if you're planning to take any buses. The main outlet for tickets is the Aviation Office, at 15 Xichang'an Jie (open 24hr; information ☎010 66017755, domestic reservations ☎010 66013336, international reservations ☎010 66016667), and there are airline agents dotted around the city (ask at your accommodation for the nearest).

Destinations Baotou (1hr 30min); Beihai (4hr); Changchun (1hr 45min); Changsha (2hr); Chengdu (2hr 30min); Chongqing (2hr 40min); Dalian (1hr 20min); Dandong (1hr 20min); Fuzhou (2hr 50min); Guangzhou (3hr); Guilin (3hr); Guiyang (4hr 45min); Haikou (3hr 45min); Hangzhou (1hr 50min); Harbin (2hr); Hefei (2hr); Hohhot (1hr 10min); Hong Kong (3hr); Huangshan

---

AIRPORT TRANSPORTATION

By taxi A taxi between the airport and city centre will cost ¥70–150, including the ¥10 toll, and takes 35min–1hr, at least half an hour longer in rush hour. You'll be pestered in the arrivals hall by charlatan taxi drivers; ignore them and use the official ranks.

By subway The "Airport Express" light rail runs from T3 and stops at T2 (connected by walkway and free shuttle bus to T1); it then hits Sanyuanqiao (on line #10), before terminating at Dongzhimen (on lines #2 and #13). The ride from the airport to Dongzhimen takes about 30min from terminal 3, and 20min from terminal 2; tickets cost ¥25. The trains run every 15min, 6.30am–10.30pm. If you want to continue your journey from Dongzhimen by cab, note that cabbies at the Dongzhimen exit commonly gouge new arrivals, so walk a little way and hail a cab from the street.

By bus Airport buses (¥16) to the city depart from T3, stopping at T2 and T1 on the way; buy tickets from desks inside the terminals. They leave regularly on eleven routes; the most useful are line #1 for Guomao, and line #3 for Dongzhimen and the main train station. The same routes return to the airport from the city. Journeys take at least 1hr each way.

(2hr); Jilin (1hr 50min); Ji'nan (1hr); Jingjinag (2hr 30min); Kunming (3hr 30min); Lanzhou (2hr 20min); Lhasa (4hr); Luoyang (1hr 40min); Nanchang (2hr); Nanjing (1hr 45min); Nanning (3hr 30min); Qingdao (1hr 15min); Qiqihar (2hr); Sanya (5hr 20min); Shanghai (1hr 50min); Shenyang (1hr); Shenzhen (3hr 10min); Taiyuan (1hr 10min); Ürümqi (3hr 50min); Wenzhou (2hr 20min); Wuhan (2hr); Wuyishan (1hr 45min); Xiamen (2hr 50min); Xi'an (1hr 30min); Xining (2hr 30min); Yantai (1hr); Yibin (3hr 45min); Yinchuan (2hr); Zhangjiajie (3hr); Zhengzhou (1hr 20min); Zhuhai (3hr 30min).

BY TRAIN

Beijing has three train stations: main, West and South. The latter two host most high-speed services; these can save you hours in journey times – note that new high-speed lines are being added all the time – though of course tickets cost more. Tickets can be bought at the stations or, with a small surcharge, from hotels, the CITS and rail ticket outlets; as elsewhere in China, you'll need your passport to book and board. Tickets for busy routes should be booked at least a day in advance, and can be booked up to ten days ahead. All stations have left-luggage offices.

Beijing Station (北京站, běijīng zhàn) is the most central station, though it has few high-speed services. Most arrivals will catch a taxi to their destinations in the city (follow signs to the rank), or use the subway (it's on line #2). To buy train tickets here, the Foreigners' Ticket Booking Office (daily 5.30am–7.30am, 8am–6.30pm & 7–11pm) is in the soft-sleeper waiting room at the back of the station, on the left side as you enter, and is signposted in English. There's a timetable in English on the wall. As well as the following, there are weekly services to Moscow and Ulaan Baatar; see p.34 for details.

Destinations Baotou (3 daily; 9hr 30min–13hr); Beidaihe (many daily; 3–5hr); Changchun (many daily; 7–16hr); Changsha (5 daily; 14–19hr); Chengde (10 daily; 4hr 30min–6hr 15min); Dalian (9 daily; 7hr 45min–12hr); Dandong (2 daily; 14–22hr); Datong (6 daily; 6hr); Guangzhou (1 daily; 22hr); Hangzhou (3 daily; 13hr 30min–21hr); Harbin (many daily; 8–17hr); Hohhot (3 daily; 9–10hr); Ji'nan (7 daily; 6–10hr); Nanjing (5 daily; 11–15hr); Pingyao (5 daily; 10–16hr); Qufu (2 daily; 8hr 30min–10hr); Shanghai (2 daily; 14–20hr); Shanhaiguan (many daily; 2hr 30min–6hr); Shenyang (many daily; 5–12hr); Taishan (for Tai'an; 5 daily; 5–7hr); Tianjin (9 daily; 1hr 20min–2hr); Yantai (2 daily; 14–17hr); Zhengzhou (5 daily; 6–9hr).

Beijing West (北京西站, běijīng xī zhàn) is Asia's largest rail terminal, and serves destinations south and west of the capital, including the forthcoming high-speed line to Hong Kong. The Foreigner's Ticket Booking Office is on the second floor and is open 24 hours. Getting into the city is easy by taxi, since there's an official rank; the station is also on subway lines #7 & #9.

Destinations Baotou (5 daily; 12–18hr); Changsha (18 daily; 5hr 40min–21hr); Chengdu (4 daily; 28hr); Chongqing (5 daily; 24–31hr); Datong (4 daily; 6hr); Fuzhou (1 daily; 20hr); Guangzhou (6 daily; 8–29hr); Guilin (4 daily; 22–27hr); Guiyang (4 daily; 28–37hr); Hohhot (5 daily; 6–10hr); Hong Kong (1 daily; 24hr, or 11hr when high-speed services start in 2015); Kunming (2 daily; 37–44hr); Lanzhou (6 daily; 17–28hr); Lhasa (daily; 44hr; requires travel permit, see p.864); Luoyang (18 daily; 4–14hr); Nanchang (8 daily; 11hr 30min–18hr); Nanning (2 daily; 28–31hr); Taiyuan (many daily; 2hr 45min–5hr); Ürümqi (1 daily; 34hr); Xi'an (many daily; 4hr 40min–20hr); Zhengzhou (many daily; 2hr 30min–9hr).

Beijing South (北京南站, běijīng nán zhàn) is where most high-speed trains arrive. By far the most modern and attractive of Beijing's stations, it's easy to leave by taxi from the official rank, while it's also on subway line #4 (and, soon, #14).

Destinations Fuzhou (2 daily; 10hr 30min–15hr); Hangzhou (10 daily; 5hr–6hr 30min); Ji'nan (many daily; 1hr 30min–2hr 30min); Nanjing (many daily; 3hr 30min–4hr 30min); Qingdao (13 daily; 4hr 40min–5hr 45min); Qufu (18 daily; 2–3hr); Shanghai (many daily; 5–9hr); Tai'an (22 daily; 2hr); Tianjin (many daily; 33–38min).

Beijing North (北京北站, běijīng běi zhàn) is a minor terminal connected to Xixhimen subway station (lines #2, #4 & #13). You'll only really need it for services to the Great Wall (see p.120).

BY BUS

Beijing has many long-distance bus terminuses, each one serving only a few destinations. There is little point travelling far from Beijing by bus; journey times are far longer – and less comfortable – than by train. The most useful options are listed below; if you arrive at any other station, it's generally best to catch a taxi to the nearest subway.

Dongzhimen (东直门公共汽车站, dōngzhímén gōnggòng qìchēzhàn), northeast of the centre on subway lines #2 & #13, is the largest bus station, handling services from Dongbei.

Deshengmen (德胜门公共汽车站, déshèngmén gōnggòng qìchēzhàn), the north station serving Chengde (4hr) and Datong (8hr), is just north of the second ring road, near Jishuitan subway station (line #2).

Sihui (四惠公共汽车站, sìhuì gōnggòng qìchēzhàn), in the southeast on subway line #1, is good for buses to Chengde (3hr 30min–4hr).

1

GETTING AROUND

Beijing's scale militates against taking "bus number 11" – Chinese slang for walking – almost anywhere, and most of the main streets are so straight that going by foot soon gets tedious. The bus system is extensive, and the subway continues to improve, but many visitors quickly tire of the heaving crowds on public transport and take rather more taxis than they'd planned – they're still cheap. Cycling is a good alternative, with plenty of rental outlets in the city. A word of warning: be very wary of pickpockets on buses and the subway. Skilful thieves target Westerners, and especially backpackers, looking not just for money and phones but also coveted Western passports. If you'll be spending some time in Beijing, it'll save time investing in a transport card, available from all subway stations for a deposit of ¥20.

BY SUBWAY

Clean, efficient, user-friendly and very fast, the subway (see map, p.103) is by far the most convenient method of public transport. It's amazing how far the system has come in a short time: the third regular line only opened in 2007, but by 2013 there were almost a dozen lines, and the system had broken the world record for most passengers carried in a single day. It operates daily from 5.30am–11pm, and entrances are marked by a logo of a square inside a "G" shape; you're obliged to pass bags through an airport-style scanner on entry, though this is not necessary for handbags and manbags if you give staff a quick flash of what's inside. Tickets cost ¥2 per journey from station ticket offices, or when using a transport card. All stops are marked in English or *pinyin*, and announced in English after Chinese.

BY BUS

Services generally run 5.30am–11pm every day, though some operate 24hr. All routes are efficiently organized, though none is marked in English at the stops or on the buses – unless you speak Chinese, or can find an English-speaker, you may have to rely on luck, or instructions from your hotel or a tourist office.

City bus and trolleybus Even though the city's 200-plus bus and trolleybus services run extremely regularly, you'll find getting on or off at busy times hard work (rush hours are 7–9am & 4.30–8pm). The fare for ordinary buses is ¥1, or an incredibly cheap ¥0.40 when using a travel card. There are also some comfortable double-decker bus

services, costing ¥2 a trip. Buses numbered in the #200s only provide night services. Buses numbered in the #800s are modern, air-conditioned, and actually quite pleasant, but more expensive, with fares starting at ¥2.

Tourist bus These look like ordinary buses but have route numbers written in green and make regular trips (Apr–Oct) between the city centre and certain out-of-town attractions; useful routes are listed in the text.

BY TAXI

Taxis cost ¥2.3 per kilometre, with a minimum fare of ¥13. Using a taxi after 11pm will incur a surcharge of twenty percent. Drivers are generally honest (except the ones who hang around transport links), but if they don't put the meter on, you can insist by saying "*da biao*". If you're concerned about being taken on an expensive detour, have a map open on your lap, or your phone.

BY BIKE

As a positive alternative to relying on public transport, it's worth renting a bike. All hostels rent bikes; figure on a daily charge of ¥20–50 and a deposit of ¥200–500. You can buy used bikes for about ¥200 from shops all over town; a good bet is the strip of bike shops on the south side of Jiaodaokou, just west of the Ghost Street (see p.110) restaurants. Always test the brakes before riding off, and get the tyres pumped up. If you have any problems, there are plenty of bike-repair stalls on the pavement. See p.39 for general cycling advice.

INFORMATION

Tourist information Beijing Travel Service (BTS) is the official tourist information service, with offices strewn around town; they're mostly interested in selling tours and handing out leaflets, and are useless for actual travel

---

BIKING AROUND BEIJING

Chinese cycling pace is sedate, and with good reason. Chinese roads are unpredictable and at times fairly lawless, with aggressive trucks that won't get out of the way, impatient taxi drivers in the cycle lane, buses veering suddenly towards the pavement, and jaywalkers aplenty. Still, riding around Beijing is less daunting than riding around many Western cities, as there are bike lanes on all main roads; you'll be in the company of plenty of other cyclists. Ringing your bell is sometimes the only way of letting someone know you're there, even if they can actually see you. At junctions, cyclists cluster together and then cross en masse when strength of numbers forces other traffic to give way. If you feel nervous, just dismount and walk the bike across – plenty of Chinese do.

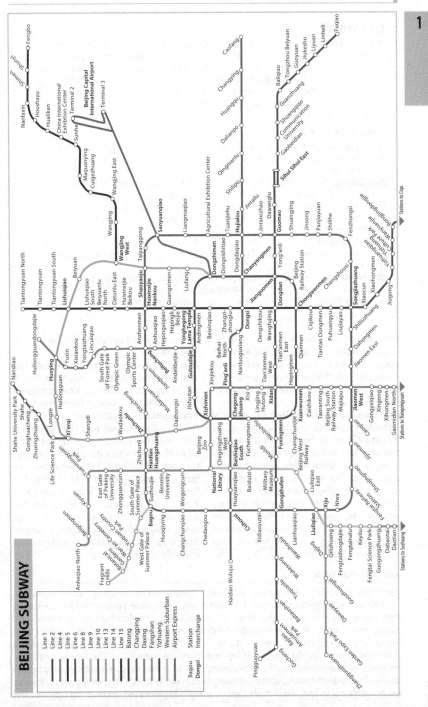

BEIJING SUBWAY

Line 1
Line 2
Line 4
Line 5
Line 6
Line 8
Line 9
Line 10
Line 13
Line 14
Line 15
Batong
Changping
Daxing
Fangshan
Yizhuang
Western Suburban
Airport Express

○ Station
◉ Interchange

Bagou Station
Dongsi Interchange

1

CITY TOURS

Organized tours of the city and its outskirts run by big hotels, CITS and other agents offer a painless way of seeing the main sights quickly. Though they're not cheap, the price will include lunch and a tour guide: a trip to the Summer Palace, Yonghe Gong and a pedicab jaunt around the *hutongs* is ¥360. The **one-day tours** offered by the cheaper hotels offer better value, and you don't have to be a resident of theirs to go along. All the youth hostels offer good-value evening trips to the acrobatics shows and the opera a few times a week (see p.114), and trips to the Great Wall (see p.120).

TOUR OPERATORS

Beijing Sideways (ⓦ beijingsideways.com). Dash around Beijing in a side-car, its adjoining motorbike driven by a local expat. Plenty of options available, including *hutong* tours, night tours, and trips to the Great Wall.

Bike Beijing (ⓦ bikebeijing.com). Offer some excellent bicycle tours of Beijing and its surrounding area, from half-day *hutong* trips to 15-day grassland journeys.

CITS A variety of one- and two-day tour packages on "Dragon Buses", which you can book from their offices (see below), from the BTS office (see p.102) or from the information desk in the Friendship Store.

City Bus Tour (ⓦ www.citybustour.com, ☎ 400 650 0760). The most convenient city tour operator; coaches are modern and you'll have an English-speaking guide. A day trip with them costs ¥380.

★ **The Hutong** (ⓦ thehutong.com). This excellent outfit runs some interesting tours, including informative culinary and tea-market trips.

UCCA (ⓦ ullens-center.org). Informative tours of their gallery in the 798 Art District (see p.98).

---

advice, even on the occasion that staff speak English. Hostels are generally a far better source of information, even putting many top hotels to shame in this regard. However, the city's official website (ⓦ ebeijing.gov.cn) is surprisingly informative, as is its new 24hr tourism hotline (☎ 010 65130828).

Magazines and guidebooks There are a number of English-language publications that will help you get the best out of the city. The *China Daily* (¥1), available from most bookshops and higher-end hotels, has a listings section detailing cultural events. Much more useful are the free magazines aimed at the large expat community, which contain up-to-date and fairly comprehensive entertainment and restaurant listings. Look for *The Beijinger* (ⓦ thebeijinger.com), *City Weekend* (ⓦ cityweekend.com.cn/beijing) and *Time Out* (ⓦ timeoutbeijing.com), all of which have listing and event sections, with addresses written in *pinyin* and

Chinese; you can pick up copies in most bars and other expat hang-outs.

Maps In these days of mobile phone apps and good subway connections, maps are less vital than before. There is, however, a wide variety available from hotels and bookshops, while street vendors also sell (mostly Chinese) maps too.

Travel agents CITS are at 103 Fuxingmennei Dajie (☎ 010 66011122); also in the *Beijing Hotel*, 33 Dongchang'an Jie (☎ 010 65120507) and the *New Century Hotel* (☎ 010 68491426), opposite the zoo. They offer expensive tours, a tour guide and interpreter service, and advance ticket booking for trains, planes and ferries (the latter from Tianjin), with a commission of around ¥30 added. Koryo Tours, at 27 Beisanlitun Nan (☎ 010 64167544, ⓦ koryogroup.com), are Beijing's most unusual tour agency, arranging visits (heavily controlled, of course) to the paranoid hermit kingdom of North Korea. Expect to pay at least US$1800 for the privilege.

ACCOMMODATION

Beijing hotels were once largely impersonal concerns, with standardized, rather nondescript, modern interiors. But newer accommodation options are placing more emphasis on design and character, the established places are sprucing themselves up, and now, whatever your budget, it's possible to stay somewhere that's not just functional but memorable; most notable are the huge number of traditional-as-it-gets courtyard options, set in Beijing's famed *hutongs* (see p.78). The city's cheapest beds are, of course, in its hostels, some of which are up there with Beijing's most atmospheric places to stay. Private rooms at Beijing's cheap chain hotels (see p.106) are safe, clean and comfortable, and sometimes cheaper than those at the hostels. Moving up a level to three-star places and above, rooms are more spacious; head up another notch, and there are usually facilities such as satellite TV, swimming pools and saunas. Luxury hotels are of an international standard and are generally foreign-run and -managed, and sometimes offer discounts of up to seventy percent off-season. See p.40 for general information and advice on Chinese accommodation. Most of the mid-range and high-class hotels are east of the centre, strung out along the international shopping streets of Wangfujing and Jianguomen or clustered around subway stations. Further north, the Sanlitun district has some good accommodation options for all budgets, with plenty of places to eat and drink nearby. The most charismatic places to stay are those hidden in the *hutongs* north of the centre around Houhai and Nanluogu Xiang, close to good eating and nightlife options; there's something here for all budgets.

HOSTELS

Beijing has a tremendous wealth of hostels, most of them clean and professionally run. You can expect them to feature a lounge with a TV and a few DVDs, self-service laundry (¥15 or so), bike rental (around ¥20 a day) and free wi-fi. They will also offer tours to sights outside the city such as the Great Wall, and will arrange train and plane tickets for a small commission (¥40 at most). Don't be put off if you don't fit the backpacker demographic; there are a few slightly pricier options in which you won't hear Bob Marley or see tables filled with empty Qingdao bottles. An added bonus of the places below is that they are actually more appealingly located than most of the larger mid-range hotels, in quiet neighbourhood *hutongs*.

NORTH OF THE CENTRE

Downtown Backpackers 东堂青年旅舍, dōngtáng qīngnián lǚshè. 85 Nanluogu Xiang ☎010 84002429, ⓦbackpackingchina.com; subway line #6 to Nanluoguxiang; see map, p.79. Long-time backpacker favourite, with an enviable location among the artsy boutiques of Beijing's trendiest *hutong*; you won't be short of eating and nightlife options. There are a couple of single rooms and doubles, which get rapidly booked up. Dorms **¥75**, rooms **¥170**

Peking Youth Hostel 北平国际青年旅舍, běipíng guójì qīngnián lǚshè. 113-2 Nanluogu Xiang ☎010 84039098; subway line #6 to Nanluoguxiang; see map, p.79. Superb new hostel, with immaculate rooms and a winning location; there's some great people-watching to be done from the rooftop café, the downstairs component of which is extremely popular with passers-by. They've a far quieter annexe a 15min walk away. Dorms **¥75**, rooms **¥230**

Red Lantern House 红灯笼宾馆, hóngdēnglóng bīnguǎn. 5 Zhengjue Hutong ☎010 83285771, ⓦredlanternhouse.com; subway line #4 to Xinjiekou; see map, p.79. A converted courtyard house in a quiet *hutong*, close to the Houhai bar area. The courtyard, with its jumble of lanterns and ornaments, is quite something. Offers bike rental, internet and laundry. They recently opened a highly appealing second venue; see website for details. Dorms **¥85**, rooms **¥220**

Sitting on the Walls Courtyard House 城墙客栈, chéngqiáng kèzhàn. 57 Nianzi Hutong ☎010 64027805; subway line #6 to Nanluoguxiang; see map, p.79. Another converted courtyard house that offers a bit of character, friendly staff, pets and dodgy plumbing. It's very central, just behind the Forbidden City, though a little tough to find first time; most taxi drivers won't know where it is. Wend your way through the alleyways, following the signs. Dorms **¥100**, rooms **¥480**

Sleepy Inn 丽舍什刹海国际青年旅店, lìshè shíshàhǎi guójì qīnnián lǚdiàn. 103 Deshengmennei Dajie ☎010 64069954; subway line #2 to Jishuitan; see map, p.79. This homely place has a great location, beside a canal just off Xihai Lake, and is probably the most laidback of Beijing's hostels. A good terrace and pleasant staff make up for slightly overpriced rooms; the dorms are good value, though. Dorms **¥100**, rooms **¥380**

EAST OF THE CENTRE

Fly By Knight Courtyard Hostel 夜奔北京四合院客栈, yèběn běijīng sìhéyuàn kèzhàn. 6 Dengcao Hutong ☎130 41095935; subway lines #5 or #6 to Dongsi; see map pp.84–85. Superb new courtyard hostel, tucked into an atmospheric *hutong* area east of the Forbidden City. It's a small, boutiquey place, and thus gets booked up early; those lucky enough to bag a room or bed will benefit from a relaxed atmosphere, punctuated with occasional martial arts lessons. Dorms **¥130**, rooms **¥500**

Sanlitun Youth Hostel 三里屯青年旅舍, sānlìtún qīngnián lǚshè. Off Chunxiu Lu ☎010 51909288; subway line #2 to Dongsishitiao; see map pp.84–85. Most notable for being the closest hostel to Sanlitun, this is a friendly place that boasts a good bar of its own. The only problem for most backpackers is its distance from the nearest subway station. Dorms **¥60**, rooms **¥220**

SOUTH OF THE CENTRE

365 Inn 365 安怡之家宾馆, 365 ānyí zhījiā bīnguǎn. 55 Dazhalan Xijie ☎010 63085956, ⓦchina365inn.com; subway line #2 to Qianmen; see map pp.90–91. Highly popular place on the bustling Dazhalan strip. Its warren of rooms are cheery and relatively spacious, though guests tend to spend more time in the street-facing restaurant, which morphs into a busy bar come evening. Dorms **¥50**, rooms **¥250**

Leo Hostel 广聚园青年旅舍, guǎngjùyuán qīngnián lǚshè. 52 Dazhalan Xijie ☎010 63031595, ⓦleohostel.com; subway line #2 to Qianmen; see map pp.90–91. Still the best hostel on Dazhalan, and particularly popular with younger backpackers on account of its cheap bar and fun vibe. Leafy and attractive communal spaces make up for rooms that are a bit tatty round the edges; some of the dorms can be a bit cramped. It's easy to find, and an easy walk from Tian'anmen Square and the Forbidden City. Dorms **¥50**, rooms **¥240**

WEST OF THE CENTRE

Chinese Box Courtyard Hostel 团圆四合院客栈, tuányuán sìhéyuàn kèzhàn. 52 Xisi Beiertiao ☎010 66186768, ⓦ chinesebox.hostel.com; subway line #4 to Xisi; see map pp.68–69. Charming little family-run courtyard hotel, hidden behind a sturdy red door in a *hutong*. It only has a couple of rooms, so you'll certainly need to book ahead; the dorms are pricey, but the incongruously luxurious double rooms are up there with the best in their price range. There are daily events such as musical performances, tea tastings and "dumpling parties". Small breakfast included. Dorms **¥120**, rooms **¥450**

HOTELS
NORTH OF THE CENTRE
See map, p.79.

Bamboo Garden 竹园宾馆, zhúyuán bīnguǎn. 24 Xiaoshiqiao Hutong ☎010 58520088, ⓦ bbgh.com.cn; subway line #2 or #8 to Guloudajie. A quiet, charming courtyard hotel in a *hutong* close to the Drum and Bell towers. It was converted from the residence of a Qing official, and today the courtyards and bamboo-filled gardens are by far its best features; recent renovations have added to its charm. **¥680**

Courtyard 7 秦唐府客栈七号院, qíntángfǔ kèzhàn qīhàoyuàn. 7 Qiangulouyuan Hutong ☎010 64060777; subway line #6 to Nanluoguxiang. Rooms in this courtyard hotel off Nanluogu Xiang might be on the small side, but it more than makes up for it with a peaceful ambience and good location. All the rooms face the courtyard, and are elegantly furnished throughout, with four-poster beds and colourful tiled bathrooms. Ask about discounts from the sky-high rack rate. **¥1500**

Guxiang 20 古巷20号商务会, gǔxiàng èrshí hào shāngwùhuì. 20 Nanluogu Xiang ☎010 64005566; subway line #6 to Nanluoguxiang. Well located in a trendy area, this swanky new place is done out in opium-den chic. The best doubles have four-poster beds, and there's a tennis court on the roof. It doesn't maintain much presence on the street, bar the *Starbucks* in the lobby. **¥580**

★ **The Orchid** 65 Baochao Hutong ☎010 84044818, ⓦ theorchidbeijing.com; subway line #6 to Nanluoguxiang. Located on newly popular Baochao *hutong*, this new boutique hotel is up there with the best-value places to stay in the whole city. Its rooms, arranged around a delightful courtyard, are an absolute delight, as is the food served for breakfast. Their rooftop area offers

superlative sunset views, and staff will encourage you to drink one of their delicious house cocktails up there. **¥700**

EAST OF THE CENTRE
See map, pp.84–85.

Beijing 北京饭店, běijīng fàndiàn. 33 Dongchag'an Jie ☎010 65137766; subway line #1 to Wangfujing. The most central hotel, just east of Tian'anmen Square, and one of the most recognizable buildings in Beijing. The view from the top floors of the west wing, over the Forbidden City, is superb. But it's pricey, renovations have expunged the historic feel and service is not up to scratch. **¥880**

Cote Cour 演乐宾馆, yǎnyuèbīnguǎn. 70 Yanyue Hutong ☎010 65237981, ⓦ hotelcotecourbj.com; subway line #5 or #6 to Dongsi, or line #5 to Dengshikou. Fourteen-room courtyard-style boutique hotel, in the middle of the city but in a quiet *hutong*. Skilfully decorated in oriental chic (though oddly it doesn't have the Chinese name you'd expect), it's a place to consider if you would rather pay for style and character than lavish facilities. Taxis sometimes won't go down the alley, so you'll have to walk for 5min after being dropped off – call the hotel before you arrive and they'll arrange a taxi to pick you up. **¥1068**

Double Happiness Courtyard Hotel 阅微庄四合院宾馆, yuèwēizhuāng sìhéyuàn bīnguǎn. 37 Dongsi Sitiao ☎010 64007762, ⓦ hotel37.com; subway line #5 or #6 to Dongsi. Located down a narrow, bustling alley, this courtyard hotel has larger rooms than most, with wooden floors and the usual traditional Chinese carved and lacquered decor. The courtyards are attractive, with red lanterns and plenty of foliage. **¥550**

Jianguo 建国饭店, jiànguó fàndiàn. 5 Jianguomenwai Dajie ☎010 65002233, ⓦ hoteljianguo.com; subway line #1 to Yong'anli. Well run and good-looking, with many of the rooms arranged around cloistered gardens, this place is deservedly very popular with regular visitors. The restaurant, *Justine's*, has some of the best French food in the city, and the Silk Market is close by. Many walk-in rates only include breakfast for one; book online for the best deals. **¥1235**

Kapok 木棉花酒店, mùmiánhuā jiǔdiàn. 16 Donghuamen Dajie ☎010 65259988, ⓦ kapokhotel beijing.com; subway line #1 to Tian'anmen East or Wangfujing. Swish boutique hotel a 10min walk from the Forbidden City, with clean lines, glass walls and a bamboo theme giving it a distinctive, modish look. There aren't too many luxury extras, but overall it's clean, chic, well located, and not too pricey. **¥700**

Park Hyatt 柏悦酒店, bóyuè jiǔdiàn. 2 Jianguomenwai Dajie ☎010 85671234, ⓦ beijing .park.hyatt.com; subway line #1 or #10 to Guomao. One of the most architecturally masterful hotels in the city, set atop a toy-like series of blocks illuminated rather beautifully at night. Rooms here offer all the pared-down luxury you'd expect of the chain, and there are stupendous views from all sides. There's a great bar and restaurant up top, and *Xiu* bar down below. **¥2300**

★ **Peninsula Palace** 王府饭店, wángfǔ fàndiàn. 8 Jingyu Hutong ☎010 85162888, ⓦpeninsula.com; subway line #5 to Dengshikou. A discreet, upmarket place with a very good reputation, and up to the standard of its sister in Hong Kong. It's well located, within walking distance of the Forbidden City, and rooms are decked out in pleasing earth tones. Nice touches include a non-smoking floor, and fresh fruit left in the room daily. **¥1800**

St Regis 国际俱乐部饭店, guójìjùlèbù fàndiàn. 21 Jianguomenwai Dajie ☎010 64606688, ⓦstarwoodhotels.com; subway line #1 or #2 to Jianguomen. One of the plushest hotels in the city, this is the first choice of visiting dignitaries, having housed both George Bush and Quentin Tarantino. It features real palm trees in the lobby, and there's a personal butler for guests. **¥2500**

SANLITUN AND AROUND

See map, pp.84–85.

Hotel G 极视酒店, jízhàn jiǔdiàn. A7 Gongti Xilu ☎010 65523600, ⓦhotel-g.com; metro to Dongsishiqiao. At night every window of this slick boutique hotel is lit up a different colour. The nightclubby impression is reinforced inside by sharp lines and subdued lighting; it's aimed squarely at the hip young crowd who like to party in nearby Sanlitun. Rooms are cosy and standards high, making this one of the best in its price range. **¥1100**

Ibis 宜必思酒店, yíbìsī jiǔdiàn. 30 Nansanlitun Lu ☎010 65088100, ⓦaccorhotels.com; subway line #6 to Dongdaqiao, or line #6 or #10 to Hujialou. One of the only reliably cheap options in this expensive part of town. Rooms are surprisingly large and attractive for the price, and the bars and restaurants of Sanlitun are only 10min up the road. **¥420**

Opposite House 瑜舍, yúshè. Sanlitun Lu ☎010 64176688, ⓦwww.theoppositehouse.com; subway line #10 to Tuanjiehu. This trendy modern hotel is filled with modern Chinese art, thanks to connections with UCCA in the 798 Art District (see p.98). Rooms offer minimalist chic with no stinting on comfort; bathrooms have oakwood tubs and waterfall showers. It's just around the corner from Sanlitun, so there's no shortage of restaurants and nightlife in the area. There's no sign on the outside – look for the green building next to the 3.3 Mall. **¥2560**

Yoyo 优优客酒店, yōuyōu kèjiǔdiàn. Due east of 3.3 Building ☎010 64173388, ⓦwww.yoyohotel.cn; subway line #10 to Tuanjiehu. A lovely little boutique-style hotel, located just a hop, skip and jump from Sanlitun on a (surprisingly) quiet alley. Rooms may be minuscule, but considering the location you won't do any better for price. **¥320**

THE FAR NORTH

See map, pp.68–69.

Aman@Summer Palace 安缦颐和, ānmàn yíhé. 1 Gongmenqian Jie ☎010 59879057, ⓦamanresorts .com; subway line #4 to Xiyuan. This is about as close as you'll be able to stay to the Summer Palace, both in terms of location – it's just outside the east gate – and feel. Parts of the complex are centuries old, and there's even a secret gate into the palace, which can be opened at night for a crowd-free stroll. As with most *Aman* resorts, this is a place to get away from it all, if you've got the cash; the restaurants, pool and spa facilities are top-notch, though staff have a little to learn about what's expected of luxury service. **¥3880**

Grace 格瑞斯酒店, géruìsī jiǔdiàn. 798 Art District ☎010 64361818, ⓦgracebeijing.com. A great little hotel sitting pretty in the 798 Art District. Sure, you're rather far away from central Beijing, but you're in one of the city's most characterful areas; cheaper rooms are a tiny bit small for the price, but they're all suitably artistic, and there's a nice Italian restaurant downstairs. **¥880**

EATING

Nowhere else on the Chinese mainland can compete with the culinary wealth of Beijing: splurging in classy restaurants is a great way to spend your evenings, as prices in even the most luxurious places are very competitive and a lot more affordable than their equivalent in the West. Every style of Chinese food is available, but among this abundance it's sometimes easy to forget that Beijing has its own culinary tradition – specialities well worth trying are Peking duck (see box, p.108) and Mongolian hotpot. Other Asian cuisines, including Japanese and Korean, are also widely available; Western food is easy to find too, with major chains prevalent, and a few good brunch places – also the city's best places for coffee – dotted around the city's trendier areas.

FAST FOOD AND STREET FOOD

While branches of *KFC*, *McDonald's* and *Subway* are ubiquitous, there are a number of local and Asian food chains worth trying; they're all over the city, but easiest to find in shopping malls or complexes, and outside the train stations. Every mall and shopping centre has a food court, usually in the basement but sometimes on the top floor, which offers inexpensive meals from a variety of outlets. Any backpacker worth their salt will be itching to have a crack at Beijing's wonderfully weird street food. The best place to indulge is at one of the designated night markets (see p.108), which are at their busiest and best in

1

PEKING DUCK

Succulent **roast duck** is Beijing's big culinary hitter. Every venerable restaurant has a different preparation technique, but once the duck has been brought to your table and carved, or vice versa, the routine is always the same; slather dark, tangy plum sauce onto pancakes, pop in a few scallions, add shreds of duck or duck fat (surprisingly delicious, if done correctly) with your chopsticks, roll it up and prepare for the local taste sensation. Nothing is wasted; the duck's entrails are usually made into a separate dish of their own, then served alongside the meat and fat.

Prices vary depending on where you go, what grade you'd like (there are usually two "classes" to choose from), and what you'd like served alongside the duck (some places charge for the sauce and scallions). These days it's tough to find a whole duck for under ¥100, while at the city's more famous duck restaurants you can expect to pay up to three times this price. Recommended places include: *Liqun* (p.111), *Deyuan* (p.111) and *Quanjude* (p.111).

the summer. The Noah's ark-worth of fare on offer includes chicken hearts, sparrows, crickets, silkworm pupae, scorpions, sheep testicles... the list goes on. At more regular street stands, which you'll find in every single part of the city, most popular are the skewers (串, chuàn, though pronounced "*chuar*" in Beijing's pirate-like accent) of heavily spiced, barbecued meat, often served up by Uyghurs from Xinjiang, China's far west; lamb skewers (羊肉串, yángròu chuàn) are the de facto choice, though there are usually various cuts of chicken to choose from too.

CHAIN RESTAURANTS

Bellagio 味千拉面, wèiqiānlāmiàn. Tai Koo Li complex, Sanlitun, and elsewhere. A Taiwanese chain, despite the Italian-sounding name, selling specialities such as *migao* (steamed glutinous rice flavoured with shrimp and mushroom) and *caipu dan* (a turnip omelette).

Hai Di Lao 海底捞, hǎidǐlāo. 24hr branch on the top floor of the Intime Lotte mall, Wangfujing. Reasonably priced Sichuan hotpot chain, with a good choice of broths and a make-your-own-dipping-sauce counter.

Yonghe King 永和大王, yǒnghé dàwáng. Fast-food chain known for its *youtiao* (fried dough sticks) and cheap noodle dishes.

Yoshinoya 吉野家, jíyějiā. ⓦyoshinoya.com. A Japanese chain offering bowls of rice topped with slices of meat – cheap, tasty and relatively healthy.

NIGHT MARKETS

Dong'anmen Night Market 东安门夜市, dōngānmén yèshì. Dong'anmen Dajie; subway line #1 to Wangfujing or line #5 to Dengshikou; map pp.84–85. Set up along the north side of this main road are red-canopied stalls offering all sorts of weird and wonderful goodies, generally of a higher quality and lower price than you'd get in Xiaochi Jie. Sadly, it shuts rather early for a "night" market. Daily 4–10pm.

Xiaochi Jie 小吃街, xiǎochī jiē. Xiagongfu Jie. Subway line #1 to Wangfujing; map pp.84–85. This pedestrianized alley is lined with stalls selling xiǎo chī – literally, "little eats" – from all over China. Though vendors are pushier than those at Dong'anmen, it's more atmospheric, and has the added bonus of tables at which you can actually sit down, perhaps with an ice-cold glass of beer. Daily 10am–midnight.

CAFÉS

Coffee culture has exploded in Beijing, though prices are as high as in any Western country, aimed at foreigners and well-to-do locals only. As well as places listed below, note that some bars are also great spots to linger over a cappuccino, notably *Pass By Bar* (see p.112). Conversely, some of the places below also do great food, most commonly of the western variety. All have free wi-fi.

@Café 798 Art District ⓣ010 64387264; map pp.68–69. The best café in the 798 District, with good coffee (surprisingly cheap for the area, at ¥20–30) and a nice range of meals. Try the pasta dishes (from ¥40), some of which use fresh, hand-made spaghetti. Daily 11am–6pm.

Bookworm 老书虫书吧, lǎo shūchóng shūbā. 4 Sanlitun Nanjie ⓣ010 65869507, ⓦbeijingbookworm .com; subway line #10 to Tuanjiehu; map pp.84–85. Despite awful coffee, and staff who often seem hell-bent on redefining the word "apathy", this remains hugely popular with Beijing's expat crowd, largely on account of its excellent book selection (see p.117), and regular literary events and lectures. Check the website for details. Daily 9am–2am.

Café Zarah 飒哈, sàhā. 42 Gulou Dongdajie ⓣ010 84039807, ⓦcafezarah.com; subway line #5 to Beixinqiao or line #6 to Nanluoguxiang; map p.79. Cosy, attractively converted courtyard house serving good continental breakfasts (from ¥45) and plenty of snacks, including tasty home-made ice cream and a few cakes plonked, rather unfairly, on the counter. Wed–Mon 10am–midnight.

Confucius Café 秀冠, xiùguān. 25 Guozijian Lu ⓣ010 64052047; subway line #5 to Yonghegong Lama Temple; map pp.84–85. Just down the road from

A REAL BEIJING BREAKFAST

Wherever you are at breakfast time in Beijing, you're within easy walking distance of a place selling *jianbing* (煎饼, **jiānbǐng**), a sort of **savoury pancake** usually sold from streetside windows. First the hot-plate will be greased up, then attacked with a scoop of batter. You'll be asked *la bu la*?: nod if you want chilli, shake your head if not. Chilli powder, if you want it, is flecked onto the rapidly frying mix, along with various bits of green veg; an egg is then cracked on top, to make a tasty, omelette-like layer. When it's nearly done, a rectangle of miscellaneous crispy substance is added, and in a flash the whole shebang will be folded and put in a plastic bag. The whole process takes well under a minute, even including the time it takes to hand over your ¥5 and say "*xie xie*".

You may also care to look out for the tell-tale baskets fronting places selling **dumplings**, which remain every old Beijinger's favourite form of morning sustenance. Also be sure to hunt down some Beijing **yoghurt** (老北京酸奶, **lǎo běijīng suānnǎi**) during your stay; sold in cute clay pots for ¥3–5 (including ¥1 deposit for the pot), it has a delicious, honey-like taste.

the Confucius Temple, this café has employed similar themes in its design – a bold move, but it works. Good coffee, too. Daily 9am–8pm.

Starbucks 星巴克, xīngbākè. 1 Qianmen Dajie; subway line #2 to Qianmen; map pp.90–91. Branches of *Starbucks* are all over the city, but their Qianmen branch stands out – as with the rest of the street, it's been decorated in a mock-dynastic style, and views from the upper levels are very pleasant indeed. Daily 9am–10pm.

★ **Vineyard Café** 葡萄院儿, pútáoyuàn'er. 31 Wudaoying Hutong ☏010 64027961, ⓦvineyardcafe .cn; subway line #2 or #5 to Yonghegong Lama Temple; map pp.84–85. Good Western wine and food, including pizza, makes this bright, cheery place popular with the local expats. Serves good brunches too, making it a good target before or after a trip to the Yonghe Gong. Tues–Sun 11.30am–midnight.

Wen Yu 文宇奶酪店, wényǔnǎilàodiàn. 49 Nanluogu Xiang; subway line #6 to Nanluoguxiang; map p.79. You'll spy people bearing blue-and-white plastic pots all along Nanluogu Xiang: they've all been to *Wen Yu*, a yoghurt café so popular that they've long thrown away the tables. ¥10–15 per pot; cold coffee ¥5. Daily noon–6pm.

RESTAURANTS

Visitors to Beijing will be amazed by how many restaurants the city has – not just on every corner, but everywhere between them too. Most ubiquitous are regular local restaurants, and the food served at them is generally fine (with the honourable exception of the Forbidden City area). The nature of restaurants changes as you shift throughout the city. Sanlitun and the Drum Tower areas have become trendy and cosmopolitan, and Wangfujing caters to the masses with its series of chain restaurants and night markets (see p.108); you'll find good duck south of Qianmen, Muslim food around Niujie Mosque and a mini Koreatown in Wudaokou. Expect to eat earlier than you

would in Western cities: lunch is around noon and dinner around 6pm or 7pm. Few places stay open after 11pm.

THE FORBIDDEN CITY & TIAN'ANMEN SQUARE

★ **Lost Heaven** 花马天堂, huāmǎ tiāntáng. 23 Qianmen Dongdajie ☏010 85162698, ⓦlostheaven .com.cn; subway line #2 to Qianmen; map p.74. The best of Beijing's many Yunnanese restaurants, set in the fashionable, newly renovated 23 Ch'ienmen complex. It's spellbindingly beautiful and surprisingly cheap (around ¥100 per head); the only mystery is that it's hardly ever full. Daily noon–2pm & 5pm–1am.

Renhe 仁和酒家, rénhé jiǔjiā. 19 Donghuamen Dajie; subway line #1 to Tian'anmen East subway; map pp.84–85. A short walk from the Forbidden City's east gate, this is a cut above the area's other (mostly horrendous) restaurants. Here you're far less likely to be ripped off or served yesterday's rice; in fact, the food is rather good, especially their tasty tofu dishes (from ¥22). Its outdoor seats are also a good place for evening beers. Daily 6am–1am.

NORTH OF THE CENTRE

Café Sambal 桑芭, sāng bā. 43 Doufuchi Hutong ☏010 64004875, ⓦcafesambal.com; subway line #2 or #8 to Guloudajie subway; map p.79. Authentic Malay food in a laidback courtyard restaurant, tucked away inside a *hutong* and actually quite easy to miss. Dishes start at ¥45, with the house chicken and tofu particularly recommended. Daily 10am–11pm.

Dali Courtyard 大理院子, dàlǐ yuànzi. 67 Xiaojingchang Hutong ☏010 84041430; subway line #5 to Beixinqiao subway; map p.79. A charming courtyard restaurant tucked down a *hutong*. It has no menu – you simply turn up, pay the fixed price (¥128, or ¥200 for a few extra dishes), then the chef gives you whatever Yunnanese food he feels like cooking; dishes are generally rice-based, and all sets will have a fish dish. Reservations recommended. Daily noon–2.30pm & 6–10.30pm.

GHOST STREET

Nicknamed "Ghost Street" (簋街, guǐ jiē), a 1km-long stretch of **Dongzhimennei Dajie** is lined with hundreds of restaurants, all festooned with red lanterns and neon – a colourful and boisterous scene, particularly on weekends. Note that staff in these restaurants will probably speak little or no English; few places will have an English menu, but plenty have a picture menu. It's an atmospheric place, for sure, though when the crowds arrive in the evening the whole street can resemble a car park.

Hutong Pizza 胡同批萨, hútóng pīsà. 9 Yindingqiao Hutong ☏010 83228916; subway line #6 to Beihai North; map p.79. A charming little courtyard restaurant serving up delicious pizzas, though at over ¥100 each they're a bit pricey. It's hidden away in an alley; follow the signs from the bridge over the lakes. Daily 11am–11pm.

Nuage 庆云楼, qìngyún lóu. 22 Qianhai Dongzhao ☏010 64019581; subway line #6 to Beihai North or Nanluoguxiang; map p.79. Decent Vietnamese food served in a smart upstairs bar-restaurant. Try the steamed garlic prawns and battered squid, and finish with super-strong Vietnamese coffee if you don't intend to sleep in the near future. You'll spend upwards of ¥100 per head. Daily 11am–2pm & 5.30–10.30pm.

Saveurs de Coree 韩香馆, hánxiāng guǎn. 128 Xiang'er Hutong ☏010 54715753, ⓦsaveursdecoree.com.cn; subway line #6 to Nanluoguxiang; map p.79. Trendy Korean bistro which prides itself on MSG-free dishes. Go for the ¥59 *bibimbap* (mixed rice, vegetables, egg and beef), or the barbecued *galbi* (marinated beef or pork). Ginseng-flavoured *baekseju* wine goes well with either. Daily 11am–10pm.

The Source 都江源, dūjiāng yuán. 14 Banchang Hutong ☏010 64003736; subway line #6 to Nanluoguxiang; map p.79. Artfully decorated courtyard restaurant serving set meals of the kind once favoured by Sichuanese aristocracy (they'll go easy on the spices if you ask). From ¥188 per person. Daily 10.30am–2pm & 5–10pm.

EAST OF THE CENTRE

Biteapitta 吧嗒饼, bā da bǐng. 2F Tongli Studio; subway line #10 to Tuanjiehu; map pp.84–85. Israeli-run restaurant whose falafel pitta wraps (¥25) are by far the best in the city – not that you'll notice, or care, after a few beers in the nearby bars. Daily 11am–11pm.

Hatsune 隐泉日本料理, yǐnquán rìběnliàolǐ. 3F Tai Koo Li South ☏010 64153939; subway line #10 to Tuanjiehu; map pp.84–85. Hip, young, American-styled Japanese restaurant with a reputation for good sashimi, which will cost you around ¥200 per head. Daily 11.30am–2pm & 5.30–10pm.

★ **Jin Ding Xuan** 金鼎轩, jīn dǐng xuān. 77 Hepingli Xijie ☏010 64978978; subway line #2 or #5 to Yonghegong Lama Temple; map pp.84–85. A stone's

throw from Ditan Park, this four-floor place is amazingly cheap considering the lavish-looking exterior. Choices include shrimp and pork dumplings (¥19), Sichuan noodles (¥12), wonton soup (¥16) and breakfast-style dough sticks (¥5). Leave room for the mango pudding (¥8). Daily 24hr.

Justine's. Inside Jianguo Hotel (建国饭店, jiànguó fàndiàn) 5 Jianguomenwai Dajie ☏010 65002233; subway line #1 to Yong'anli; map pp.84–85. Beijing's oldest French restaurant is suitably fancy – super-plush carpets, giant mirrors, golden chandeliers and stained glass. The menu switches around with pleasing regularity; try the lobster soup or grilled lamb. Service is attentive. Around ¥250 per person. Daily 6.30am–10.30am, noon–2pm & 6–10pm.

Lime 青柠, qīng níng. Building 15, Central Park ☏010 65970887; subway line #10 to Jintaixizhao; map pp.84–85. A friendly Thai venue serving fairly authentic food for ¥30–60 per dish. Their outdoor seats are the best place from which to gaze over Central Park, a cosmopolitan area that's one of Beijing's most impressive examples of urban rebuilding. Daily 11am–10pm.

★ **Made in China** Grand Hyatt (东方君悦大酒店, dōngfāng jūnyuè dàjiǔdiàn) 1 Dongchang'an Jie ☏010 65109608; subway line #1 to Wangfujing; map pp.84–85. One of the swankiest places in town, and the Chinese-with-a-twist food is reliably excellent; their signature menu goes for ¥398 per person (minimum two), but à la carte items go from around ¥100. Daily 11.30am–2.30pm & 5.30–10.30pm.

★ **Najia Xiaoguan** 那家小馆, nǎjiā xiǎoguǎn. 10 Yong'an Xili ☏010 65673663; subway line #1 to Yong'anli; map pp.84–85. Superb little eatery with friendly service, cheap prices and an attractive, tearoom-like interior. Their food is of the Manchu variety, with most dishes in the ¥50–70 range; go for one of the venison meals, or something more interesting like sweet potato and taro with cheese (¥36). Daily 11am–11pm.

Qin Tang Fu 秦唐府, qíntángfǔ. 69 Chaoyangmen Nanxiaojie ☏010 65598135; subway line #5 or #6 to Dongsi; map pp.84–85. The best place in town for a famous Xi'an dish known as *paomo* (泡馍, pāomó), a spicy, broth-like dish made with beef or lamb, and a disc of ripped-up bread. It's far, far more delicious than it may sound, and backpacker-friendly at just ¥28. Daily 11am–11pm.

The Elephant 大笨象, dàbènxiàng. Off Ritan Beilu

📍010 85614013; subway line #6 to Dongdaqiao; map pp.84–85. A popular, reasonably priced restaurant that keeps the area's sizeable Russian population happy with staples such as borshch (¥25), beetroot and walnut salad (¥25), and shashlik (¥50). Daily 9am–1am.

★ **Unban Bulgogi** 车轮烧烤, chēlún shāokǎo. 38 Chaowai Dajie; subway line #6 to Dongdaqiao; map pp.84–85. Decent Korean food, including barbecued meat from ¥32 per portion, and excellent *naengmyeon* (cold buckwheat noodles) for ¥24. All of the waitresses are North Korean, and here with the blessings of the government in Pyongyang, whose embassy is just around the corner. Most of the customers are, in fact, North Korean diplomats – look for anyone wearing a Kim Il-sung badge. Daily noon–3pm & 5–10pm.

Veggie Table 吃素的, chīsù de. 19 Wudaoying Hutong 📍010 64462073; subway line #2 or #5 to Yonghegong Lama Temple; map pp.84–85. Organic, vegan food makes this place absolute heaven for a certain chunk of Beijing travellers and expats. Couscous, curries and mezes (including superb hummus) are on the menu, though pride of place goes to their famed mushroom burger (¥62). Mon–Fri 11.30am–3.30pm & 5.30–10.30pm, Sat & Sun 11.30am–11.30pm.

SOUTH OF THE CENTRE

★ **Deyuan** 德缘, déyuán. 57 Dazhalan Xijie 📍010 63085371; subway line #2 to Qianmen; map pp.90–91.

Miraculously, this is a decent restaurant on tourist-heavy Dazhalan, serving a whole Peking duck for just ¥128, including all the trimmings (enough to feed two or three). The quality would put many more expensive places to shame. Daily 10am–2pm & 5–9pm.

Goubuli 狗不理, gǒubùlǐ. 31 Dazhalan Dajie 📍010 63032280; subway line #2 to Qianmen; map pp.90–91. Delicious steamed buns with various fillings (try the pork, shrimp and sea cucumber combo), for ¥48 and up per batch. You can eat them here or take away, while there's also good duck (¥88 for half) and other regular Chinese dishes on the menu. Daily 7.30am–9pm.

Liqun 利群烤鸭店, lìqún kǎoyādiàn. 11 Beixiangfeng Hutong 📍010 67025681; subway line #2 to Qianmen; map pp.90–91. A well-kept secret for years, though no longer: prices have shot up to ¥198 per duck, without the trimmings, and you'll likely have to queue even after you've made a reservation (essential, in any case). Quality remains high, however, and the earthy, courtyard-house atmosphere is just the same. Daily 11.30am–10pm.

Quanjude 全聚德, quánjùdé. 30 Qianmen Dajie 📍010 67011379; subway line #2 to Qianmen; map pp.90–91. Beijing's most famous duck restaurant by far; reservations are not essential, but advised if you don't want to spend ages in the queue. The duck remains up there with the city's best; with the trimmings, a whole one is ¥296. Daily 11am–1.30pm & 4.30–8pm.

BARS AND CLUBS

Plenty of bars are clustered around Sanlitun Lu, also called Jiu Ba Jie (literally, "Bar Street"), all within staggering distance of one another. An alternative bar scene exists around the prettified Shicha lakes (known locally as "Houhai") where lounge bars now proliferate the way pondweed once did. There are other small bar scenes nearby, around the Drum and Bell towers and around Nanluogu Xiang. Though Chinese beer can be cheaper than bottled water if bought in a shop, a 350ml

LUNCHTIME AT NALI PATIO

Just off Sanlitun's main road, and snuggled into the gap between Tai Koo Li's north and south malls at 81 Sanlitun Beilu, is **Nali Patio** (那里花园, nàli huāyuán; subway line #10 to Tianjiehu; map p.85), Beijing's current lunch venue of choice for expats and more affluent locals. This building's various levels are full of interesting choices, with most restaurants putting on good-value lunch sets noon–3pm; at the time of writing, tapas was the taste *du jour*, though this is the fastest-moving place in Beijing – by the time you visit, everything could have changed.

Agua 4F 📍010 52086188. Classy Spanish place with some outdoor seating. ¥88, plus ¥11 for dessert.

Jubang 2F 📍010 52086071. Korean food that's moderately priced through the day; no lunch specials.

Let's Seafood GF 📍010 52086038. No dedicated lunch sets, though their ¥98 mussels make a good meal at this time of day.

★ **Migas** 6F 📍010 52086061. Probably the best of the bunch (and also a great place to drink, with an

artfully decorated interior and tapas-like dishes from various Spanish regions. ¥85 for three courses.

Mosto 3F 📍010 52086030. Yet another Spanish place, and a very good one too. Keep your fingers crossed that their famed *ceviche* is on the menu. ¥95, plus ¥15 for dessert.

Mughal's 3F 📍010 52086082. Decent Indian and Pakistani restaurant offering a 35 percent lunchtime discount.

1

bottle of *Tsingtao* or the local *Yanjing* at a bar will usually cost ¥20–40. Many bars also sell British and Irish draught beers such as *Guinness* and *Boddingtons*, which cost at least ¥40. For up-to-the-minute bar reviews, check the expat magazines. Chinese clubs are quite slick these days, with hip-hop and house music proving to be crowd pleasers. If you just want to dance, and aren't too prissy about the latest music, see the bar reviews below for venues with their own dancefloor.

BARS

FORBIDDEN CITY & TIAN'ANMEN SQUARE

What? Bar 什么酒吧, shénme jiǔbā. 72 Beichang Jie, ☎133 4112 2757; subway line #1 to Tian'anmen West; map pp.68–69. Though primarily a live music bar, this tiny venue is a great place for a drink on any evening. They've got table football, and outdoor chairs on the super-quiet-at-night street running alongside the Forbidden City. Daily, usually 6pm–late.

NORTH OF THE CENTRE

Drum and Bell 鼓钟咖啡馆, gǔzhōng kāfēiguǎn. 41 Zhonglouwan Hutong ☎010 84033600; subway line #2 or #8 to Guloudajie; map p.79. With welcoming staff and a great location between the Drum and Bell towers, this little place is always crowded. The rooftop patio is an added bonus in summer, and they serve decent thin-crust pizza. Daily midday–2am.

★ **Great Leap** 悠航鲜啤, yōuháng xiānpí. 6 Doujiao Hutong, ☎slowboatbrewery.com; subway line #5 to Zhangzizhonglu; map p.79. Microbrewery that's hard to find the first time around, and perhaps even harder to leave if you end up having too many of their great ales, best imbibed in a bustling outdoor courtyard. Tues–Thurs 5–10.30pm; Fri 5–11pm; Sat 2–11pm; Sun 2–10pm.

Huxleys 德比酒吧, débǐ jiǔbā. 16 Yandai Xiejie; subway line #6 to Beihai North or Nanluoguxiang; map p.79. Cheap booze, no attitude and approachable staff – a total contrast to the places lining nearby Houhai. It's a real winner with young locals and expats alike. Daily 5pm–late.

Pass By Bar 过客酒吧, guòkè jiǔbā. 108 Nanluogu Xiang; subway line #6 to Nanluoguxiang; map p.79. A renovated courtyard house turned comfortable bar/restaurant, popular with backpackers and students. There are lots of books and pictures of China's far-flung places to peruse, and well-travelled staff to chat to. Daily 9am–4am.

EAST OF THE CENTRE

Apothecary 酒术, jiǔ shù. 3F Nali Patio ☎010 52086040; subway line #10 to Tuanjiehu; map pp.84–85. Superb cocktail bar; probably the best in town. If you're not a mixologist like the expert bartenders, check out the infomative menu, which will tell you all you need to know about what you're drinking. Cocktails from ¥80. Tues–Sun 7pm–late.

Atmosphere 云酷就把, yúnkù jiǔbā. 80F World Trade Center ☎010 85716459; subway line #1 or #10 to

Guomao; map pp.84–85. Eighty floors up, this is Beijing's loftiest bar – for now, at least – and sells costly cocktails. Book ahead to get a window seat; use the lifts facing the building's east entrance. Daily noon–2am.

Ichikura 一藏酒吧, yīcáng jiǔbā. Chaoyang Theatre, 36 Dongsanhuan Beilu ☎010 65071107; subway line #6 or #10 to Hujialou; map pp.84–85. This two-storey Japanese whisky bar is as tasteful and understated as the acrobatic shows next door are glitzy and vulgar. A great range of single malts – including superb Japanese varieties – and great attention to detail (check out the round ice cubes) make this dark, cosy venue a hidden gem. Daily 7pm–2am.

Mesh At the Opposite House (瑜舍, yúshè) 11 Sanlitun Lu ☎010 64105220; subway line #10 to Tuanjiehu; map pp.84–85. Cosy, classy lounge bar in the basement of a chic hotel, attracting a trendy, international crowd. Dress up, order a cocktail (from ¥80), and try to look sophisticated. Daily 5pm–2am.

Migas 6F Nali Patio (那里花园, nàli huāyuán) subway line #10 to Tuanjiehu; map pp.84–85. The bar sitting atop this excellent Spanish restaurant was Beijing's "it" place at the time of writing; views from here are simply superb, and there's barely room to wiggle your butt during the weekend DJ sets. Weekdays are a different story, with lounge music pulsing over a nattering crowd, all seated on funky furniture. Daily 7pm–late.

Tree 树酒吧, shù jiǔbā. Behind 3.3 Mall ☎010 64151954; subway line #10 to Tuanjiehu; map pp.84–85. Relaxed and unassuming little bar, with a selection of Belgian white beers and decent pizza; if you'd like to mix things up a bit, they've a great sister bar within stumbling distance. Daily midday–late.

Xiu 秀, xiù. 6F Park Hyatt, 2 Jianguomenwai Dajie; subway line #1 or #10 to Guomao; map pp.84–85. With some of the most wonderful views of any Beijing bar from its outdoor terrace, this bar has been up there with the most popular in the city for several years now. Drinks are good too, and there's a dancefloor inside. Daily 6pm–late.

SOUTH OF THE CENTRE

365 Inn 365 安怡之家宾馆, 365 ānyí zhījiā bīnguǎn. 55 Dazhalan Xijie ☎010 63085956; subway line #2 to Qianmen subway; map pp.90–91. The bar fronting this hostel is just about the best place to drink in the backpacker-heavy Dazhalan area; *Leo Hostel* across the road has a great bar too, but this one has the added benefit of being able to people-watch on one of Beijing's most intriguing streets. Daily 7am–late.

1

CLUBS

Bling Solana 5–1, 6 Chaoyang Park Lu ☎010 59056999, ⓦall-starclub.com; map pp.84–85. This hip-hop venue wows its beautiful, vapid clientele with features such as a DJ booth made out of a Rolls-Royce. ¥50 cover charge. Wed–Sat 9pm–3am.

Destination 目的地, mùdedì. Workers' Stadium West Gate; ⓦbjdestination.com; line #2 to Dongsishitiao; map pp.84–85. Beijing's biggest and most popular gay club by far, with two floors full of half-naked men (mainly local), as well as women who'd rather avoid non-gay fellas for the night. Entry ¥60. Daily 8pm–late.

Haze Inside Guanghualu Soho (光华路 SOHO, guānghuálù SOHO) Guanghua Lu ⓦhazebeijing .com; subway line #1 to Yong'anli; map pp.84–85. This was one of Beijing's most popular clubs at the time of writing – whatever that's worth, in this hectic city. House, nu-disco and techno pulse from two floors' worth of speakers, and the atmosphere is relaxed, rather than manic. Cover charge ¥50. Fri–Sat 8pm–late, occasionally open Thurs too.

Propaganda East Gate, Huaqing Jiayuan; subway line #13 to Wudaokou; map pp.68–69. "Oh god, *that* place..." is the stock reaction when mentioning this bar to someone who's been in Beijing for a while. This infamous Wudaokou student club is a shameless meat market, whose ¥50 all-you-can-drink nights (every Wed) are crazily popular. The spirits are dodgy for sure, though; stick to the beer. Daily 8pm–late.

Vics 威克斯, wēikèsī. Workers' Stadium north gate ☎010 52930333, ⓦvics.com.cn; subway line #2 to Dongsishitiao; map pp.84–85. Long-running hip-hop club, with a sweaty dancefloor filled with enthusiastic booty grinders. The low cover charge and cheapish drinks (bottled beer is ¥20) make it popular with students and embassy brats. ¥50 on weekends, free Mon–Thurs. Daily 9.30pm–2am.

World of Suzie Wong 苏西黄酒吧, sūxīhuáng jiǔbā. Outside west gate of Chaoyang Park; map pp.84–85. Not as fashionable as it was, but still a stalwart with its striking neo-Oriental decor – think lacquer and rose petals. Dancing downstairs and a cocktail bar above. ¥50 cover charge. Daily 7pm–late.

ENTERTAINMENT

Most visitors to Beijing make a trip to see Beijing opera and the superb Chinese acrobatics displays – both of which remain timeless arts. In contrast, the contemporary theatrical scene is changing fast as home-grown dramatists experiment with foreign forms. The live music scene continues to develop apace, while Western classical music can be heard at any of the concert halls. Check the expat magazines (see p.104) for event listings.

TRADITIONAL OPERA

A trip to see Beijing's famous opera (see box, p.114) is one of the most popular diversions for international travellers. If the regular shows seem too long, you could visit a teahouse to get your fix – such performances are short and aimed at foreigners.

★ **Chang'an Grand Theatre** 长安大戏院, cháng'ān dàxìyuàn. 7 Jianguomennei Dajie ☎010 65072421; subway line #1 or #2 to Jianguomen; map pp.84–85. A modern, central theatre putting on a wide range of performances throughout the day – it's probably the most popular place in town for Beijing opera. From ¥180.

Lao She Teahouse 老舍茶馆, lǎoshě cháguǎn. 3F Dawancha Building, 3 Qianmen Xidajie ☎010 63036830; subway line #2 to Qianmen; map pp.90–91. Teahouse theatre at which you can watch the 90min-long "Old Beijing Variety Show", which comprises song, dance and opera; popular with tour groups, the show gives a gaudy taste of traditional Chinese culture. ¥180–380. Daily 7.40pm.

Liyuan Theatre 梨园剧场, líyuán jùchǎng. 1F Jianguo Qianmen hotel, 175 Yong'an Lu ☎010 63016688, ⓦqianmenhotel.com; subway line #4 to Caishikou; map pp.90–91. Pricey, but perhaps the best place to see opera, with an emphasis on accessibility; as you go in you pass the actors putting on their make-up – a great photo op. The opera itself is a visitor-friendly bastardization, lasting an hour and jazzed up with some martial arts and slapstick. Tickets can be bought from the office in the front courtyard of the hotel (daily 9–11am, noon–4.45pm & 5.30–8pm; ¥70–180). Performances nightly 7.30pm.

National Centre for the Performing Arts 国家大剧院, guójiā dàjùyuàn. 2 Xichang'an Jie ☎010 66550000, ⓦchncpa.org; subway line #1 to Tian'anmen West; map pp.68–69. This is one venue you can't miss: it's that giant egg west of Tian'anmen Square. The opera hall seats over 2000, with fantastic acoustics and lighting; tickets start from ¥180 (box office opens daily from 9.30am, or ring to reserve). Nightly performances 7.30pm.

Zhengyici Theatre 正乙祠剧场, zhèngyǐcí jùchǎng. 220 Qianmen Xiheyanjie ☎010 63189454; subway line #2 to Hepingmen; map pp.90–91. The genuine article, performed in the only surviving wooden Beijing opera theatre and worth a visit just to check out the architecture. Tickets from ¥380. Performances nightly at 8pm.

DRAMA AND DANCE

Most evenings you can catch Chinese song and dance simply by turning on the TV, though there's plenty of opportunity to see it live. Some venues, such as the Beijing

1

BEIJING OPERA

Beijing opera (京戏; jīng xì) is the most celebrated of China's 350 or so regional operatic styles – a unique combination of song, dance, acrobatics and mime. Highly stylized, to the outsider the performances can often seem obscure and wearying, as they are punctuated by a succession of crashing gongs and piercing, discordant songs. But it's worth seeing once, especially if you can acquaint yourself with the story beforehand. Most of the plots are based on historical or mythological themes – two of the most famous sagas, which any Chinese will explain to you, are *The White Snake* and *The Water Margin* – and full of moral lessons. Offering an interesting, if controversial, variation on the traditions are those operas that deal with contemporary themes – such as the struggle of women to marry as they choose. The **colours** used on stage, from the costumes to the make up on the players' faces, are highly symbolic: red signifies loyalty; yellow, fierceness; blue, cruelty; and white, evil.

Exhibition Theatre, occasionally stage performances, in the original language, of imported musicals like *The Sound of Music*, which, with tickets at ¥50–100, are a lot cheaper to watch here than at home.

Beijing Exhibition Theatre 北京展览馆剧场, běijīng zhǎnlǎnguǎn jùchǎng. 135 Xizhimenwai Dajie ☎010 68354455, ⓦbjexpo.com; subway line #4 to Beijing Zoo; map pp.68–69. This giant hall, containing nearly 3000 seats, stages classical ballet, folk dance and large-scale song-and-dance revues. Check website for performance prices.

Capital Theatre 首都剧场, shǒudū jùchǎng. 22 Wangfujing Dajie ☎010 65121598, ⓦbjry.com; subway line #5 or #6 to Dongsi; map pp.84–85. Look out for the People's Art Theatre company here – their photo archive, documenting their history, is displayed in the lobby. Tickets generally start at ¥80. Most performances are in Chinese.

Penghao Theatre 蓬蒿剧场, pénghāo jùchǎng. 35 Dongmianhua Hutong ☎010 64006452, ⓦpenghaotheatre.com; subway line #6 to Nanluoguxiang; map pp.84–85. In a *hutong* just behind the Central Academy of Drama, this intimate, privately run theatre set in a beautifully converted courtyard house also has a rather nice rooftop bar. Check website for performance prices.

Puppet Theatre 中央木偶剧院, zhōngyāng mùǒu jùyuàn. Corner of Anhua Xili & Third Ring Road ☎010 64254798, ⓦpuppetchina.com; subway line #8 to Anhuaqiao; map p.79. Once as important for commoners as opera was for the elite, Chinese puppetry usually involves hand puppets and marionettes. Shows here, aimed at kids, involve Beijing opera, short stories and Western fairy tales; tickets cost from ¥100. Five shows daily 10am–3pm.

ACROBATICS AND MARTIAL ARTS

Beijing Workers' Club 北京工人俱乐部, běijīng gōngrén jùlèbù. 7 Hufang Lu ☎010 63528910; subway line #4 to Caishikou; map pp.90–91. Popular for

its "Legend of Jinsha" show, which adds a few interesting quirks to the old acrobatic routines – silk-rope dancing, water cannon, and some zany motorbike stunts. Tickets from ¥180. Daily 5.30pm & 7.30pm.

★ **Chaoyang Theatre** 朝阳剧场, cháoyáng jùchǎng. 36 Dongsanhuan Beilu ☎010 65072421, ⓦchaoyangtheatre.com; subway line #6 or #10 to Hujialou; map pp.84–85. If you want to see acrobatics, come to one of the shows here. At the end, the Chinese tourists rush off as if it's a fire drill, leaving the foreign tour groups to do the applauding. There are plenty of souvenir stalls in the lobby – make your purchases after the show rather than during the interval, as prices reduce at the end. Tickets from ¥180. Daily 7.15–8.30pm.

Red Theatre 红剧场, hóng jùchǎng. 44 Xingfu Dajie ☎010 67142473, ⓦredtheatre.cn; subway line #5 to Tiantandongmen; map pp.90–91. A lively kung fu routine, featuring smoke, fancy lighting and some incredible action. Tickets from ¥180. Daily 7.30–8.50pm.

LIVE MUSIC VENUES

Beijing has a glut of places in which to see music – everything from stadiums for superstars to small indie rock bars.

Beijing Concert Hall 北京音乐厅, běijīng yīnyuètīng. 1 Beixinhua Jie ☎010 66057006; subway line #1 to Tian'anmen West, or line #1 or #4 to Xidan; map pp.68–69. This hall seats 1000 people and hosts regular concerts of Western classical and Chinese traditional music by Beijing's resident orchestra and visiting orchestras from the rest of China and overseas. Tickets from ¥80.

Century Theatre 世纪剧院, shìjì jùyuàn. Sino-Japanese Youth Centre, 40 Liangmaqiao Lu, 2km east of the *Kempinski* hotel ☎010 64663311; map pp.84–85. An intimate venue for soloists and small ensembles. Mostly Chinese modern and traditional classical compositions. ¥120–150. Evening performances.

Forbidden City Concert Hall 北京中山公园音乐堂, běijīng zhōngshān gōngyuán yīnyuètáng.

THE MIDI FESTIVAL

The **Midi Rock Music festival** is held at the beginning of May in Haidian Park, just west of Beijing University campus (Ⓦ www.midifestival.com); it has always been controversial, banned in 2008 and with foreign acts occasionally refused permission to play. Still, plenty of local talent is on display, and the audience is enthusiastic. You can even camp, for the full-on "Chinese Glastonbury" experience. Tickets ¥280 for all three days, or ¥120 per day.

Zhongshan Park, Xichang'an Jie Ⓣ010 65598285, Ⓦ fcchbj.com; subway line #1 to Tian'anmen West; map p.74. A stylish hall, with regular performances of Western and Chinese classical music, and occasionally jazz too. Tickets from ¥80.

★ **National Centre for the Performing Arts** 国家大剧院, guójiā dàjùyuàn. 2 Xichang'an Jie Ⓣ010 66550000, Ⓦ chncpa.org; subway line #1 to Tian'anmen West; map pp.68–69. The giant egg-shaped structure just west of Tian'anmen Square hosts the best international performances in its huge concert hall. Note that you can't bring a camera.

Workers' Stadium 工人体育场, gōngrén tǐyùchǎng. Off Gongti Beilu Ⓣ010 65016655; subway line #2 to Dongsishitiao or line #6 to Dongdaqiao; map pp.84–85. This is where giant gigs are staged, mostly featuring Chinese pop stars, though the likes of Björk have also played here (though, given her views on Tibet, that'll never happen again).

INDIE ROCK BARS

★ **2 Kolegas** 两个好朋友, liǎnggè hǎopéngyǒu. 21 Liangmaqiao Ⓣ010 81964820, Ⓦ 2kolegas.com; map pp.68–69. This dive bar in the far northeast of the city is great for checking out the indie rockers and their fans, though it's a fair way out. In summer the crowd spills out onto the lawn.

Mao Livehouse 毛现场, mào xiànchǎng. 111 Gulou Dongdajie Ⓣ010 64025080, Ⓦ maolive.com; subway line #2 to Andingmen or line #6 to Nanluoguxiang; map p.79. Managed by Japanese music label Bad News, who know their stuff, this great, decent-sized venue hosts all the best local rock and punk bands. There may be no frills – not even a cloakroom – but it has the best sound system around, and drinks are refreshingly cheap (¥10).

★ **What?Bar** 什么酒吧, shénme jiǔbā. 72 Beichang Jie; subway line #1 to Tian'anmen West; map pp.68–69. Oddly, this rock and punk gig venue is within spitting distance of the Forbidden City. It's so small you'll probably get spattered with the guitarist's sweat. A good introduction to the local rock scene, and a great bar outside performance time too.

FILM

There are plenty of cinemas showing Chinese and dubbed Western films, usually action movies. Tickets cost around ¥80. Expect two showings daily of foreign movies, one dubbed into Chinese, the other subtitled; ring to check. These days most Beijingers have an impressive knowledge of world cinema, thanks to the prevalence of cheap, pirated DVDs.

★ **Broadway Cinematheque** F3 Building 4, MOMA North, 1 Xiangheyuan Lu Ⓣ010 84388258; subway line #2 or #13 to Dongzhimen; map pp.84–85. Cinema running regular themed events, often international in nature.

★ **Megabox** Tai Koo Li Ⓣ010 64176118, Ⓦ imegabox.com; subway line #10 to Tuanjiehu; map pp.84–85. Beijing's most reliable option for international, non-dubbed films.

Space for Imagination 5 Xiwangzhuang Xiaoqu, Haidian Ⓣ010 62791280; subway line #13 to Wudaokou; map pp.68–69. A charming cineastes' bar opposite the east gate of Qinghua University, showing avant-garde films every Saturday at 7pm.

Star City B1 Oriental Plaza Mall, 1 Dongchang'an Jie Ⓣ010 85186778; subway line #1 to Wangfujing; map pp.84–85. Another biggie, located in the highly presentable Oriental Plaza Mall.

Wanda Cineplex 3F Building 8, Wanda Plaza, 93 Jianguo Lu Ⓣ010 59603399, Ⓦ wandafilm.com; subway line #1 or #10 to Guomao; map pp.84–85. Big, comfortable cinema that usually has at least one international film showing.

CONTEMPORARY ART

Beijing is the centre for the vigorous Chinese arts scene and there are plenty of interesting new galleries opening up, particularly in the 798 Art District (see p.98 for a description of the area, and access details). Galleries in the city centre are rather more commercial than those in the suburban artsy areas; they tend to focus on selling paintings rather than making a splash with a themed show. The best place to find out about new shows is in the expat magazines.

798 ART DISTRICT

Galleria Continua 常青画廊, chángqīng huàláng. Ⓣ010 64361005, Ⓦ galleriacontinua.com. Shows international and home-grown art stars across three floors' worth of space – head up to the top for a nuts-and-bolts view (literally) of this former factory.

1

They tend to choose artists "with something to say", and rotate exhibitions 3–5 times per year. Tues–Sun 11am–6pm.

Mansudae Art Studio 万寿台创作社美术馆, wànshòutái chuàng zuòshè měishùguǎn. ☏ 010 59789317. Small studio displaying North Korean painting – every bit as fascinating as you might imagine, with a range from misty mountain scenes to brave Socialist Realism. There's also a small shop on site, where you can buy North Korean goodies. Tues–Sun 10am–6pm.

Tokyo Gallery+ 东京艺术工程, dōngjīng yìshùgōngchéng. ☏ 010 84573245, ⓦ tokyo-gallery .com. The first gallery to set up shop here, and still one of the best, with a large elegant space for challenging shows. Tues–Sun 10am–5.30pm.

Ullens Centre for Contemporary Art 尤伦斯当代 艺术中心, yóulúnsī dāngdài yìshùzhōngxīn. ☏ 010 64386675, ⓦ ucca.org.cn. This huge nonprofit space is more of a museum than a gallery; no artwork is for sale and it is the only space that charges an entrance fee. There are three exhibition halls and a programme of regular events (all detailed on the website), which mainly focus on Asian artists. Free on Thurs, otherwise ¥15. Tues–Sun 10am–7pm.

CITY-CENTRE GALLERIES

National Art Museum of China 中国美术馆, zhōngguó měishùguǎn. 1 Wusi Dajie ☏ 010 84033500, ⓦ namoc.org; subway line #5 or #6 to Dongsi; map p.79. This grand building usually holds a couple of shows at once. There's no permanent display; past exhibitions have included specialist women's and minority people's exhibitions, and even a show of Socialist-Realist propaganda. Free (bring ID); occasional charges for special exhibitions. Daily 9am–5pm.

Red Gate Gallery 红门画廊, hóngmén huàláng. Dongbianmen watchtower, Chongwenmen Dongdajie ☏ 010 65251005, ⓦ redgategallery.com; subway line #1 or #2 to Jianguomen; map pp.84–85. Commercial gallery, run by a Western curator, inside one of the last remnants of the old city wall. A little more adventurous than other Beijing galleries, it has a good reputation overseas. Daily 10am–5pm.

Today Art Museum 今日美术馆, jīnrì měishùguǎn. ☏ 010 58621100, ⓦ todayartmuseum.com; subway line #4 to Shuangjing; map pp.84–85. This promising gallery is one of China's first privately owned museums, with a focus on promoting contemporary Chinese art. Daily 10am–5pm.

SHOPPING

Appropriately for the capital of a major commercial power, Beijing has some great shopping – the best choice of souvenirs and consumables in the country is on sale here, and a collection of intriguing little markets offers an appealing and affordable alternative to the new giant malls. Clothes are particularly inexpensive; there's also a wide choice of antiques and handicrafts, but don't expect to find any bargains or particularly unusual items as the markets are well picked over.

ANTIQUES, CURIOS AND CARPETS

There's no shortage of antique stores and markets in the capital, offering opium pipes, jade statues, porcelain Mao figurines, mahjong sets, Red Guard alarm clocks, Fu Manchu glasses, and all manner of bric-a-brac – pretty much all of it fake. The jade is actually soapstone, the "antique" porcelain is reproduction, inset jewels are glass, and that venerable painting is a print stained with tea.

SHOPS

+86 Design Store 245 Gulou Dongdajie; subway line #2 to Andingmen; map p.79. Terrific little shop selling all sorts of arty paraphernalia. Cute backpacks, laptop cases, mugs, pens, pencils, T-shirts, small items of furniture... the list goes on. There's another branch in the 798 Art District (see map, p.69). Daily 10am–7pm.

Khawachen Tibetan Rugs 客瓦坚西藏手工地毯, kèwǎjiān xīzàng shǒugōng dìtǎn. 3–2FA, Solana Shopping Park, Chaoyang Park ☏ 010 59056311; subway line #10 to Liangmaqiao; map pp.84–85. Handmade Tibetan rugs from about ¥2000, plus custom designs produced to order. Daily 10am–10pm.

★ **Mansudae Art Studio** 万寿台创作社美术馆, wànshòutái chuàng zuòshè měishùguǎn. 798 Art District; map pp.68–69. This studio specializes in North Korean art, and also has a range of North Korean goodies on sale – buy a Kim Il-sung pin-badge, some English-language propaganda magazines, or (if you've got a big wad of cash) an authentic Pyongyangese painting. Tues–Sun 10am–6pm.

★ **The One** 69 Yandaixie Jie; subway line #6 to Nanluoguxiang; map p.79. The only real stand-out shop remaining on Yandaixie Jie (referred to as "tat alley" by some visitors); this is a quality place selling quirky, if slightly pricey, items – all sorts from pictures to cutlery, and cups to cuddly monk dolls. Daily 9am–8pm.

★ **Three Stone** 三石斋风筝坊, sāndànzhāi fēngzhēngfǎng. 25 Di'anmen Xidajie; subway line #6 to Nanluoguxiang; map p.79. A specialist kite shop with a rich history – the ancestors of the current owner once made kites for the Qing royals. Though there are plenty of fancy designs here, they also sell a fair few cheapies. Daily 9am–8pm.

View Pottery 视界, shì jiè. 1 Mao'er Hutong; subway

line #6 to Nanluoguxiang; map p.79. Despite its location on kitschy Nanluogu Xiang, this is a quality place, selling pretty teasets and other fired ware for decent prices. Daily 9.30am–6.30pm.

MARKETS

Beijing Curio City 北京古玩城, běijīng gǔwánchéng. Huawei Nanlu; subway line #10 to Panjiayuan; map pp.90–91. A giant arcade of more than 400 stalls, best visited on a Sunday, when other antique traders come and set up in the surrounding streets. Daily 9.30am–6.30pm.

★ **Panjiayuan Market** 潘家园市场 pānjiāyuán shìchǎng. Panjiayuan Lu; subway line #10 to Panjiayuan; map pp.90–91. Also called the "Dirt Market", this is Beijing's biggest antique market, with traders (some Tibetan) selling a huge range of souvenirs and secondhand goods. Mon–Fri 8am–6.30pm, with earlier opening at weekends.

BOOKS

Beijing can claim a better range of English-language literature than anywhere else in China. If you're starting a trip of any length, stock up here. Higher-end hotels sell copies of foreign newspapers and magazines, such as *Time* and *Newsweek*, for around ¥50.

★ **Bookworm** 老书虫书吧, lǎoshūchóng shūbā. 4 Sanlitun Nanjie ⓣ 010 65869507, ⓦ beijingbookworm.com; subway line #10 to Tuanjiehu; map pp.84–85. There are plenty of English-language books, both used and new, on sale in this popular café, which also hosts regular literary events and lectures. Check the website for details. Daily 9am–2am.

Foreign Language Bookstore 外文书店, wàiwén shūdiàn. 218 Wangfujing Dajie ⓦ bpiec.com.cn; subway line #1 to Wangfujing or line #5 to Dengshikou; map pp.84–85. The main store has the biggest selection of foreign-language books in mainland China. Books on offer downstairs include fiction, textbooks on Chinese medicine, translations of Chinese classics, and Japanese *manga*. Daily 8am–5pm.

★ **Page One** 叶壹堂, xiéyī táng. Tai Koo Li (south mall), Sanlitun Lu; subway line #10 to Tuanjiehu; map pp.84–85. Wonderful new bookshop, with a wide selection of English-language books, including travel guides, novels and artsy stuff. Daily 10am–10pm.

CLOTHES

SHOPS

A You 阿尤, āyóu. 108 Xinjiekou Beidajie ⓦ ayoufashion.com; subway line #4 to Xinjiekou subway; map pp.68–69. Trendy, ethnic-style designer clothes from an established local design brand. Prices start at around ¥200 for striking summer dresses. Mon–Sat 9am–5pm.

Dong Liang Studio 栋梁, dòngliáng. 26 Wudaoying Hutong ⓣ 010 84047648; subway line #2 or #5 to Yonghegong Lama Temple; map pp.84–85. Chic, elegant and affordable clothes by local designers; look out for beautiful dresses by JJ, Ye Qian and Shen Ye. Mon–Sat 9am–5pm.

Neiliansheng Shoes 内联升布鞋, nèiliánshēng bùxié. 34 Dazhalan ⓣ 010 63013041, ⓦ nls1853.com; subway line #2 to Qianmen; map pp.90–91. Look out for the giant shoe in the window. All manner of handmade flat, slip-on shoes and slippers in traditional designs, starting from ¥200 or so – they make great gifts. Daily 9am–8pm.

NLGX Design NLGX 设计, NLGX shèjì. 33 Nanluogu Xiang ⓣ 010 64048088, ⓦ nlgxdesign.com; subway line #6 to Nanluoguxiang; map p.79. Hipster streetwear from local designers, with much made from recycled materials. Designs are generally grouped around a theme, which changes regularly. There's another branch in Terminal 2 of the airport. Daily 10am–11pm.

★ **Plastered T-Shirts** 创可贴T恤, chuàngkětiē tīxù. 61 Nanluogu Xiang ⓦ plasteredtshirts.com; subway line #6 to Nanluoguxiang; map p.79. Hipster T-shirts and sweatshirts whose witty designs reference everyday Beijing life – subway tickets, thermoses and so on. It's a standard ¥180 per shirt. Daily 9am–7pm.

Ruifuxiang Store 瑞蚨祥丝绸店, ruìfúxiáng sīchóudiàn. 5 Dazhalan, off Qianmen Dajie ⓣ 010 63035313, ⓦ ruifuxiang.cn; subway line #2 to Qianmen; map pp.90–91. Silk and cotton fabrics and a good selection of shirts and dresses, with a tailor specializing in made-to-measure *qipaos*. You should aim to barter a little off the quoted price. Daily 9.30am–8.30pm.

Shanghai Tang 上海滩, shànghǎi tān. B1 Grand Hyatt Hotel, 1 Dongchang'an Jie ⓦ shanghaitang.com; subway line #1 to Wangfujing; map pp.84–85. This renowned Chinese designer label offers brightly coloured luxury chinoiserie. Nice bags and cufflinks, as well as cushions, purses, robes and neo-Mao jackets, though it's all a bit pricey. It's straight down the steps from the *Hyatt* lobby. Daily 10am–9.30pm.

★ **Ullens Centre for Contemporary Art** 798 Art District ⓦ ucca.org.cn; map pp.68–69. The shop down the road from, and owned by, this excellent gallery sells limited-edition fashions by local designers for around ¥1000, and handwoven bags for ¥300. Tues–Sun 10am–7pm.

MARKETS

Aliens Street Market 老番街, lǎofān jiē. Yabao Lu, north of Ditan Park; subway line #2 or #6 to Chaoyangmen; map pp.84–85. This bustling warren of stalls has a vast range of (cheap) goods, but it's particularly worth picking over for clothes and accessories; take a close

1

look at the stitching before you hand over your cash. Daily 9.30am–7pm.

Silk Market 秀水市场, xiùshuǐ shìchǎng. Off Jianguomenwai Dajie ⓦ xiushui.com.cn; subway line #1 to Yong'anli; map pp.84–85. This huge six-storey tourist mall has electronics, jewellery and souvenirs, but its main purpose is to profit through flouting international copyright laws, with hundreds of stalls selling fake designer labels. You'll need to haggle hard. Daily 9.30am–9pm.

Yashow Clothing Market 雅秀服装市场, yǎxiù fúzhuāng shìchǎng. 58 Gongren Tiyuchang Beilu; subway line #10 to Jinsong, then a taxi; map pp.84–85. A four-storey mall of stalls selling designer fakes, very like the Silk Market but a little less busy. The third floor is filled with tailors, and the fourth is for souvenirs. Daily 9.30am–8pm.

TEA

There are tea shops all over the city, with Zhang Yiyuan and Ten Fu the two biggest chains; you'll find branches all over the city, but perhaps the best are the two facing each other across Qianmen Dajie (see map, p.91); not only is the newly gentrified street beautifully finished, but English is spoken, and you'll be able to compare competing brews within seconds.

CDS AND DVDS

Beijing Huashiweiye West side of Yashow Market; subway line #10 to Tuanjiehu; map pp.84–85. Forget the name of this place, since even the proprietors aren't sure; it's marked from the outside as "CD DVD SHOP", and that's what they sell; thanks to a wide selection of films, they've a regular base of expat customers. Daily 8am–5pm.

C Rock 99 Gulou Dongdajie; subway line #2 to Andingmen; map p.79. One of the best places in the city to go hunting for CDs by local bands; the friendly owner will be pleased to make recommendations, and give you a listen to a few choice tracks. Hours vary; generally 11am–5pm.

SPORTS AND ACTIVITIES

During the 2008 Olympics, a passion for athletic activity became a patriotic duty. Now the dust has settled, the legacy of the Games includes a range of good sports facilities across the capital, from the outdoor workout machines placed in every neighbourhood to the showpiece stadiums themselves. However, the most visible kinds of exercise need no fancy equipment; head to any park in the morning and you'll see citizens going through all sorts of martial arts routines, walking backwards, chest slapping, and tree hugging.

SPECTATOR SPORTS

Beijing's football team, Guo'an, plays at the massive Workers' Stadium in the northeast of the city (see map, pp.84–85). There's a timetable outside the ticket office, which is just east of the north gate of the stadium. Tickets cost around ¥50, though you'll likely have to get them on the day from a tout. Basketball is almost as popular; the Beijing Ducks play at the superb Wukesong Arena (tickets ¥50), built for the Olympics.

SWIMMING

Avoid swimming pools at the weekends, when they're full of teenagers doing just about everything but swimming. As well as the pools listed below, bear in mind that some hotels open their lavish pools and gym facilities to non-guests; most impressive are the pools at the *Westin Chaoyang* (1 Xinyuan Nan Lu; ☎010 59228888; ¥250 for a weekend pass), the *Ritz-Carlton* (1 Jinchengfang Dong Jie; ☎010 66016666; ¥220) and the *Doubletree by Hilton* (168 Guang'anmen Wai Dajie; ☎010 63381888; ¥150).

Ditan Swimming Pool 8 Hepingli Zhong Jie ☎010 64264483; subway line #5 to Hepinglibeijie. If you just want a cheap swim, try this place, open year-round (entry ¥30). In the summer, there are outdoor pools open for the same price at nearby Qingnian Lake.

Olympic Water Cube Since the Games, this famous Olympic venue (see p.98) has reopened as a water theme park, featuring spas, slides and a wave pool. ¥200. Daily 10am–9.30pm.

MASSAGE & SPA

Beijing is full of dodgy massage joints, but plenty of reliable venues do exist. Prices are rising, but are still less than you'd pay in most Western countries.

Bodhi 17 Gongti Beilu, opposite Workers' Stadium ☎010 64130226, ⓦ bodhi.com.cn; subway line #2 to Dongsishitiao. Ayurvedic and Thai massages are among the many options available at this Southeast Asia-styled clinic. Ayurvedic massage ¥288 for 1hr. Daily 11am–12.30pm.

Chi Shangri-La Hotel, 29 Zizhuyuan Lu ☎010 68412211; subway line #10 to Chedaogou. Therapies at this luxurious New Age spa claim to use the five Chinese elements – metal, fire, wood, water and earth – to balance your *yin* and *yang*. It might look like a Tibetan temple, but there can't be many real Tibetans who could afford to darken its doors; a Chi Balance massage costs ¥1430, a Himalayan Healing Stone Massage ¥1700 (and there's a 15 percent service charge). Daily 10am–midnight.

Dragonfly 1F Eastern Inn, Sanlitun Nanlu ☎010 65936066, subway line #6 to Dongdaqiao; 60 Donghuamen Dajie, outside the east gate of the

Forbidden City; ☎010 65279368, subway line #1 to Tian'anmen East; ⓦdragonfly.net.cn. This well-reputed Shanghai chain has opened a couple of conveniently located centres in the capital. Their two-hour hangover release special (¥288) is always popular, as are the foot massages. Daily 10am–11pm.

Taipan 6 Ritan Lu ☎010 65025722, ⓦtaipan.com.cn. A popular chain, with branches all over the city – no frills, but clean and cheap. Around ¥198 for a 90min foot massage or a 60min body massage.

DIRECTORY

Banks and exchange There are banks all over Beijing, and ATMs at many accept foreign cards – machines at branches of the Bank of China are usually the most reliable, and they also have some in large malls or the lobbies of major hotels. Bank of China branches are also the best place to head if you need to exchange travellers' cheques or foreign currency; though many hotels are able to perform such functions, they usually do so at worse rates. To change money, you'll need to show your passport.

Courier service DHL has a 24hr office at 2 Jiuxianqiao Lu in the Chaoyang district (☎010 64662211). More convenient are the offices in the *New Otani Hotel* (daily 8am–8pm; ☎010 65211309) and at L115, China World Trade Centre (daily 8am–8pm).

Embassies Visa departments usually open for a few hours every weekday morning (phone for exact times and to see what you'll need to take; some places only accept US dollars). Remember that they'll take your passport from you for as long as a week sometimes, and it's very hard to change money, buy train tickets, or check in at a new hotel without it; stock up on cash before applying for any visas, and prepare to hunker down. You can get passport-size photos from machines all over town. Most embassies are either around Sanlitun in the northeast or in Jianguomenwai compound, north of and parallel to Jianguomenwai Dajie: Australia, 21 Dongzhimenwai Dajie ☎010 51404111; Canada, 19 Dongzhimenwai Dajie ☎010 51394000; India, 1 Ritan Donglu ☎010 65321908; Ireland, 3 Ritan Donglu ☎010 65322691; Japan, 7 Ritan Lu ☎010 65322361; Kazakhstan, 9 Sanlitun Dongliujie ☎010 65326182; Kyrgyzstan, 2-4-1 Tayuan Compound ☎010 65326458; Laos, 11 Sanlitun Dongsijie ☎010 65321224; Mongolia, 2 Xiushui Beijie ☎010 65321203; Myanmar (Burma), 6 Dongzhimenwai Dajie ☎010 65320359; New Zealand, 1 Ritan Dong'erjie ☎010 65322731; North Korea, Ritan Beilu ☎010 65321186; Pakistan, 1 Dongzhimenwai Dajie ☎010 65326660; Russian Federation, 4 Dongzhimen Beizhongjie ☎010 65321381; South Africa, 5 Dongzhimenwai Dajie ☎010 65320171; South Korea, 20 Dongfang Donglu ☎010 85310700; Thailand, 40 Guanghua Lu ☎010 65321749; visa and consular section 15F Building D, Twin Tower, Jianguomenwai Da Jie ☎010 85664469; UK, 11 Guanghua Lu ☎010 51924000; US, 55 Anjialou Lu ☎010 85313000; Vietnam, 32 Guanghua Lu ☎010 65321155.

Hospitals and clinics Most big hotels have a resident medic. The following two hospitals have foreigners' clinics where some English is spoken: Peking Union Medical College Hospital, 1 Shuaifuyuan, Wangfujing (Mon–Fri 8am–4.30pm; the foreigner unit is south of the inpatient building; ☎010 65295284, ⓦwww .pumch.ac.cn); and the Sino-Japanese Friendship Hospital, in the northeast of the city just beyond Beisanhuan Donglu (daily 8–11.30am & 1–4.30pm with a 24hr emergency unit; ☎010 64221122, ⓦzryhyy.com .cn). At each of the above you will have to pay a consultation fee of around ¥200. For services run by and for foreigners, try the Beijing International SOS Clinic, Suite 105, Kunsha Building, 16 Xinyuanli (daily 24hr; ☎010 64629112, ⓦinternationalsos.com); the International Medical and Dental Centre, S111 Lufthansa Centre, 50 Liangmaqiao Lu (☎010 64651384); the Hong Kong International Clinic, 3F, Swissôtel Hong Kong Macau Centre, Dongsishitiao Qiao (daily 9am–9pm; ☎010 65012288 ext 2346); or the United Family Hospital, 2 Jingtai Lu (appointment ☎010 59277000, emergency ☎010 59277120, ⓦwww.unitedfamilyhospitals.com). Expect to pay at least ¥500 for a consultation.

Internet Beijing's internet cafés are heavily regulated – you will be asked to show your passport before being allowed near a computer, and some places will refuse entry to those without a Chinese ID card. Internet cafés are all over town, and typically charge ¥5 per hour. All hotels have business centres with internet available, but it can be ridiculously expensive, especially in the classier places; you may prefer to head for a backpacker hotel or hostel, where access is generally free. Best of all, most cafés and bars now have wi-fi.

Kids There's an amusement park inside Chaoyang Park (daily 8.30am–6pm) with lots of rides, or they could try ice-skating on the basement level 2 of the China World Trade Centre (Mon, Wed, Fri & Sat 10am–10pm, Tues & Thurs 10am–5.50pm, Sun 10am–8pm; ¥30/hr) – though be aware that Chinese kids are very good. Sights that youngsters might enjoy are the zoo and aquarium (see p.94), pedal boating on Houhai and the Summer Palace, (see p.81 & p.95) the acrobat shows (see p.114), the Puppet Theatre (see p.114), and the Natural History Museum (see p.90). If you're tired of worrying about them in the traffic, try taking them to pedestrianized Liulichang, the Olympic Green, the 798 Art District, or the parks – Ritan Park has a good playground (see p.87) and Chaoyang Park has boating. Check ⓦbeijing-kids .com for more suggestions and advice. Note that most Beijing attractions are free for children under 1.2m high.

1

Language courses You can do short courses (from two weeks to two months) in Mandarin Chinese at Beijing Foreign Studies University, 2 Xi Erhuan Lu ☎010 68468167; at the Bridge School in Jianguomenwai Dajie ☎010 64940243, which offers evening classes; or at the Cultural Mission at 7 Beixiao Jie in Sanlitun ☎010 65323005, where most students are diplomats. For courses in Chinese lasting six months to a year, apply to Beijing International School at Anzhenxili, Chaoyang ☎010 64433151; Beijing University in Haidian ☎010 62751230; or Beijing Normal University, at 19 Xinjiekouwai ☎010 62207986. Expect to pay around US$1500 in tuition fees per semester.

Libraries The Beijing National Library (Mon–Fri 8am–5pm; ☎010 68415566), 39 Baishiqiao Lu, just north of Zizhuyuan Park, is one of the largest in the world, with more than ten million volumes, including manuscripts from the Dunhuang Caves and a Qing-dynasty encyclopedia. The oldest texts are Shang-dynasty inscriptions on bone. To take books out, you need to be resident in the city, but you can turn up and get a day pass that lets you browse around. The Library of the British Embassy, 4F Landmark Building, 8 Dongsanhuan Beilu, has a wide selection of books and magazines; anyone can wander in and browse.

Mail There are post offices all over town: just look for the green-and-gold logos. The International Post Office is on Chaoyangmen Dajie (Mon–Sat 8am–6pm), just north of the intersection with Jianguomen Dajie. This is where poste restante letters (addressed poste restante, GPO, Beijing) end up, dumped in a box; letters are only kept for one month, after which the officious staff are quick to send them back.

Pharmacies There are large pharmacies at 136 Wangfujing and 42 Dongdan Bei Dajie, or you could try the famous Tongrentang Medicine Store on Dazhalan, which also has a doctor for on-the-spot diagnosis. For imported non-prescription medicines, try Watsons at the *Holiday Inn Lido*, Shoudujichang Lu (daily 9am–9pm), in the northeast of the city, the basement of Raffles Mall, Dongzhimen, or at the Full Link Plaza on Chaoyangmenwai Dajie (daily 10am–9pm).

PSB The Foreigners' Police, at 2 Andingmen Dong Dajie (Mon–Fri 8am–noon & 1.30–4pm; ☎010 84015292), will give you a first visa extension for a fee of ¥160. It will take them up to a week to do it, so make sure you've got plenty of cash before you go, as you can't change money (or your hotel) without your passport.

Around Beijing

There are plenty of scenic spots and places of interest scattered in the plains and hills around the capital, and no visit would be complete without a trip to the **Great Wall**, accessible in three places within easy journey time of Beijing. The **Ming Tombs**, another remnant of imperial glory, are often combined with a trip to the nearby wall. In addition, the **Western Hills** shouldn't be overlooked, and if you're in the capital for any length of time, this large stretch of densely wooded parkland provides an invigorating breather from the pressures of the city. Further out, the **Jietai** and **Tanzhe temples** are pretty in themselves and, unlike the city's other temples, they're attractively situated.

The Great Wall

长城, chángchéng

This is a Great Wall and only a great people with a great past could have a great wall and such a great people with such a great wall will surely have a great future.

Richard M. Nixon

Stretching from Shanhaiguan, by the Yellow Sea (see p.144), to Jiayuguan Pass in the Gobi Desert, the **Great Wall** is an astonishing feat of engineering. The practice of building walls along China's northern frontier began in the fifth century BC and continued until the sixteenth century. Over time, this discontinuous array of fortifications and ramparts came to be known as **Wan Li Changcheng** (literally, "Long Wall of Ten Thousand Li", *li* being a Chinese measure of distance roughly equal to 500m), or "the Great Wall" to English-speakers.

Today, the wall is big business, and is touted by the government as a source of national pride. The restored sections are now besieged daily by rampaging hordes of

GREAT WALL, LONG HISTORY

The Chinese have walled their cities throughout recorded history, and during the Warring States period (around the fifth century BC) simply extended the practice to separate rival territories. The Great Wall's origins lie in these fractured lines of fortifications and in the vision of the first Emperor **Qin Shi Huang** who, having unified the empire in the third century BC, joined and extended the disparate sections to form one continuous defence against barbarians.

Under subsequent dynasties, whenever insularity rather than engagement drove foreign policy, the wall continued to be maintained; in response to shifting regional threats, it grew and changed course. It lost importance under the Tang, when borders were extended north, well beyond it. The Tang was, in any case, an outward-looking dynasty that kept the barbarians in check far more cheaply by fostering trade and internal divisions. With the emergence of the insular Ming, however, the wall's upkeep again became a priority; from the fourteenth to the sixteenth century, military technicians worked on its reconstruction. The Ming wall is the one that you see today.

The 7m-high, 7m-thick wall, with its 25,000 battlements, served to bolster Ming sovereignty for a couple of centuries. It restricted the movement of the nomadic peoples of the distant, non-Han minority regions, preventing plundering raids. Signals made by gunpowder blasts, flags and smoke swiftly sent news of enemy movements to the capital. In the late sixteenth century, a couple of huge Mongol invasions were repelled, at Jinshanling and Badaling. But a wall is only as strong as its guards, and by the seventeenth century the Ming royal house was corrupt and its armies weak; the wall was little hindrance to the invading Manchus. After they had established their own dynasty, the Qing, they let the wall fall into disrepair. Slowly it crumbled away, useful only as a source of building material – demolitions of old *hutongs* in Beijing have turned up bricks from the wall, marked with the imperial seal.

tourists, while its image adorns all manner of products, from wine to cigarettes, and is even used – surely rather inappropriately – on visa stickers.

Even the most over-visited section of the wall at **Badaling** is still easily one of China's most spectacular attractions. The section at **Mutianyu** is somewhat less crowded; distant **Simatai** much less so, and far more beautiful. To see the wall in its crumbly glory, head out to **Jinshanling**, **Jiankou** or **Huanghua**, as yet largely untouched by development. For other trips to unreconstructed sections, check out Ⓦwildwall.com or contact China Culture Centre (Ⓦccctravel.net).

Badaling

八达岭, bādálǐng • Daily 7am–6pm • ¥45

The best-known section of the wall is at **Badaling**, 70km northwest of Beijing. It was the first section to be restored (in 1957) and opened up to tourists. Here the wall is 6m wide, with regularly spaced watchtowers dating from the Ming dynasty. It follows the highest contours of a steep range of hills, forming a formidable defence, so much so that this section was never attacked directly but instead taken by sweeping around from the side after a breach was made in the weaker, low-lying sections.

Badaling may be the easiest part of the wall to get to from Beijing, but it's also the most packaged. At the entrance, a giant tourist circus – a plethora of restaurants and souvenir stalls – greets you. As you ascend to the wall, you pass a train museum (¥5), a cable car (¥30) and the **Great Wall Museum** (included in the main ticket). The wall museum, with plenty of aerial photos, models and construction tools, is worth a browse, though it's more interesting visited on the way down.

Once you're up on the wall, flanked by guardrails, it's hard to feel that there's anything genuine about the experience. Indeed, the wall itself is hardly original here, as the "restorers" basically rebuilt it wholesale on the ancient foundations. To get the best out of this part of the wall you need to walk – you'll quickly lose the crowds and, generally, things get better the further you go.

1

If you come with a tour you'll arrive in the early afternoon, when the place is at its busiest, spend an hour or two at the wall, then return, which really gives you little time for anything except the most cursory of jaunts and the purchase of an "I climbed the Great Wall" T-shirt. It's just as easy, and cheaper, to travel under your own steam.

By bus The easiest way to get here is on bus #919 from Deshengmen (near Jishuitan subway stop) – there's an ordinary service (2hr; ¥7) and a much quicker air-conditioned luxury bus (1hr; ¥12). Note that private minibuses also call themselves #919 and that you might get scalped on these; the real buses are larger and have "Deshengmen–Badaling" written in the window.

By train A nicer ride than the bus ia the train from Beijing North station to Badaling (12 daily; 1hr 15min); the wall entrance is a 2km walk from Badaling station. Five morning services leave Beijing, and the last one back is at 9.30pm.

By tourist bus Regular tourist buses leave from Qianmen, heading to Badaling (depart 7–11am; ¥120 return, including wall ticket); some also visit the Ming Tombs (p.126; ¥180 return, including tickets) on their way around. The last buses head back to Beijing at around 6pm – take care not to miss them.

Tours As well as CITS (see p.104), all the more expensive Beijing hotels (and a few of the cheaper ones) run tours to Badaling, usually with a trip to the Ming Tombs thrown in. Most such tours hover around the ¥240 mark, including the Ming Tombs and lunch, and will pick up from your hotel.

ACCOMMODATION

Commune by the Great Wall 长城脚下的公社 chángchéngjiǎo xiàde gōngshè. By the Shuiguan Great Wall, 4km east of Badaling ☏010 81181888, ⓦwww.communebythegreatwall.com. For the ultimate in luxury breaks, visit this "lifestyle retreat". Each of the eleven striking buildings was designed by a different architect (the complex won an architectural award at the 2002 Venice Biennale) and is run as a small boutique hotel. If you can't afford to stay here, you can take a tour of the complex for ¥120, or pop in for lunch (around ¥400). **¥1830**

Juyong Pass

居庸关, jūyōng guān • Daily 8am–6pm • ¥45

The closest section to Beijing, the wall at **Juyong Pass**, only fifteen minutes' bus ride south of the Badaling section, has been rather over-restored by enthusiastic builders. That said, it's not too popular, and thus not too crowded. Strategically, this was an important stretch, guarding the way to the capital, just 50km away. From the two-storey gate, the wall climbs steeply in both directions, passing through modern copies of the mostly Ming fortifications. The most interesting structure, and one of the few genuinely old ones, is the intricately carved stone base of a long-vanished stupa just beyond here. Access to unreconstructed sections is blocked, but you can walk for about an hour in either direction.

By bus You can catch the ordinary (not luxury) bus #919 (2hr; ¥7) from Deshengmen bus station (near Jishuitan subway stop) in Beijing.

By tourist bus Tourist buses from Qianmen (see above) stop here on their way to Badaling.

Mutianyu

慕田峪, mùtiányù • Daily 7am–6pm • ¥45 • cable car ¥80 return • chair-lift ¥40 each way

The **Mutianyu Great Wall**, 90km northeast of the city, is the second most popular point on the wall after Badaling, though since it receives relatively few tour buses it's a noticeably quieter place. It's geared towards families, with a cable car, chair-lifts and toboggsning facilities. The wall itself passes along a ridge through some lush, undulating hills; well endowed with guard towers, it was built in 1368 and renovated in 1983.

From the entrance, steep steps lead up to the wall; you can get a cable car up, though it's not far to walk. The stretch of wall you can walk here is about 3km long (barriers in both directions stop you continuing any further).

ARRIVAL AND DEPARTURE   MUTIANYU

However you reach Mutianyu, returning by other means shouldn't be a hassle, provided you do so before 6pm; plenty of minibuses wait in the car park to take people back to the city. If you can't find a minibus back to Beijing, get one to the town of Huairou (懷柔, huáiróu) from where you can get regular bus #916 back to the capital – the last bus leaves at 6.30pm.

By bus Take bus #916 from Dongzhimen to Huairou (1hr, ¥12); get off at Mingzhu Square, where you can catch a minibus to the wall (¥20 per person).

Tours Available from hotels and offices all over Beijing, these tend to cost around ¥280, including a visit to the Ming Tombs (p.126), lunch and all tickets.

ACCOMMODATION

Goose and Duck Ranch 鹅和鸭农庄 éhéyā nóngzhuāng. In Qiaozi, near Hauirou ☎010 64353778, ⓦgdclub.net.cn. This chirpy family holiday camp has plenty of outdoor pursuits on offer, including archery, go-karting and horseriding. Their all-inclusive weekend getaways (around ¥500 per person per day) are popular and convenient – turn up at the bar and they'll look after you from there. You'll have to book three days in advance. Cabins **¥300**, bungalows **¥880**

Mutianyu Great Wall Guesthouse 慕田峪长城宾馆 mùtiányù chángchéng bīnguǎn. Near eastern barrier, ☎010 69626867. Situated in a reconstructed watchtower 500m before the eastern barrier, this is a good place for a quiet overnight stay, though be aware it has no plumbing. Booking ahead advised. **¥180**

Shambhala@the Great Wall 新红资避暑山庄 xīnhóngzī bìshǔ shānzhuāng. Xiaguandi village, near Huairou, about 2hr north of Beijing ☎010 84018886, ⓦredcapitalclub.com.cn. This former hunting lodge is now an idyllic boutique hotel, set in attractive countryside. Each of the ten traditional courtyard buildings was constructed from local materials, with a mix of Chinese, Tibetan and Manchu themes; the rooms, all protected by a stone animal, feature Qing-style carved beds. There's also an on-site spa for some serious pampering, and the place is a short walk from the Great Wall. **¥1200**

Simatai

司马台, sīmǎtái • Daily 8am–4pm • ¥40 • cable car ¥20

Some 110km northeast of the city, **Simatai** was long famed as the most unspoilt section of the Great Wall around Beijing. With the wall snaking across purple hills that resemble crumpled velvet from afar, and blue mountains in the distance, it fulfils the expectations of most visitors more than the other sections. Most of Simatai dates back to the Ming dynasty, and sports a few late innovations such as spaces for cannon, with the inner walls at right angles to the outer wall to thwart invaders who breached the first defence.

At the time of writing, the whole area was closed for renovation; on reopening it will no doubt have been spruced up considerably, so take the information below as provisional. From the car park, a winding path takes you up to the wall, where most visitors turn right. Regularly spaced watchtowers allow you to measure your progress uphill along the ridge. If you're not scared of heights you can take the cable car to the eighth tower. The walk over the ruins isn't an easy one, and gets increasingly precipitous after about the tenth watchtower. The views are sublime, though. After about the fourteenth tower (2hr on), the wall peters out and the climb becomes quite dangerous, and there's no point going any further.

Turning left when you first reach the wall, you can do the popular hike to Jinshanling in three to four hours (see p.124). Most people, though, do the walk in the other direction, as it's more convenient to finish up in Simatai.

GREAT REFRESHMENTS

At all the less touristy places, each tourist or group of tourists will be followed along the wall by a villager selling drinks and postcards, for at least an hour; if you don't want to be pestered, make it very clear from the outset that you are not interested in anything they are selling – though after a few kilometres you might find that ¥5 can of Coke very welcome.

1

The journey out from the capital to Simatai takes about three hours by private transport. It's easiest to take a tour; you can travel here independently, but considering the logistical hassles and expense, this is only worth doing if you want to stay for a night or two.

By bus To get here under your own steam, take bus #980, #970 or #987 to Miyun (密云, mìyún; ¥15), and negotiate for a minibus (¥15) or taxi (over ¥100 return) to take you the rest of the way. To get from Simatai back to Beijing, you can either take a taxi from Simatai to Miyun (¥70 or so, after some negotiation), from where the last public bus back to Beijing is at 4pm, or wait at the Simatai car park for a tourist bus (see below).

By taxi A rented taxi will cost about ¥850 return, including a wait.

Tours Tours run from the backpacker hotels and hostels for around ¥180, and sometimes offer overnight stays. Most other hotels can arrange transport too (usually a minibus), though you should expect to pay a little more for these.

ACCOMMODATION AND EATING

For eating, head to one of the nameless places at the side of the car park, where the owners can whip up some very creditable dishes; if you're lucky, they'll have some locally caught wild game in stock.

Guesthouses Locals hang around the car park, renting out spare rooms in their houses, whose rates are set by negotiating. Facilities will be simple, with only cold water on tap; your host will bring a bucket of hot water to the bathroom for you on request. **¥50–100**

Jinshanling

金山岭长城, jīnshānlǐng chángchéng • Daily 8am–4pm • ¥60

Jinshanling, about 135km from Beijing and not far west of Simatai, is one of the least visited and best preserved parts of the wall, with jutting obstacle walls and oval watchtowers, some with octagonal or sloping roofs.

Turn left when you hit the wall and it's a three-hour walk to Simatai along an unreconstructed section. You won't meet many other tourists, and will experience something of the wall's magnitude; a long and lonely road that unfailingly picks the toughest line between peaks. Take the hike seriously, as you are scrambling up and down steep, crumbly inclines, and you need to be sure of foot. Watch, too, for loose rocks dislodged by your companions. When you reach Simatai a toll may be imposed at the suspension bridge. Note that this walk is still possible while Simatai is being renovated – you just can't go any further after the bridge.

Alternatively, if you head right when you get onto the wall at Jinshanling, you quickly reach an utterly abandoned and overgrown section. After about four hours' walk along here, you'll reach a road that cuts through the wall, and from here you can flag down a passing bus back to Beijing. This route is only recommended for the intrepid.

By bus This is one of those places that's far better reached on a tour. If you really fancy making the trip on public transport, take a bus to Chengde from Liuliqiao or Sihui in Beijing (see p.101); you're usually required to pay for the full ticket to Chengde (¥85). Get off at the Jinshanling intersection, from which minibuses run to the wall for ¥15.

Tours Plenty of hostels run tours out here from around ¥180; most drop you off in the morning, then pick you up post-hike at Simatai in the afternoon.

Huanghua

黄花长城, huánghuā chángchéng • Daily 8am–4.30pm • ¥25

The section of the wall at **Huanghua**, 60km north of Beijing, is completely unreconstructed. It's a good example of Ming defences, with wide ramparts, intact parapets and beacon towers. If arriving by minibus, you'll be dropped off on a road that cuts through the wall. The section to the left is too hard to climb, but the section on the right, past a little reservoir, shouldn't present too many difficulties for the agile; indeed, the climb gets easier as you go, with the wall levelling off along a ridge.

The wall here is attractively ruined – so watch your step – and its course makes for a pleasant walk through some lovely countryside. Keep walking the wall for about 2km, to the seventh tower, and you'll come to steps that lead south down the wall and onto a stony path. Follow this path down past an ancient barracks to a pumping station, and you'll come to a track that takes you south back to the main road, through a graveyard and orchards. When you hit the road you're about 500m south of where you started. Head north and after 150m you'll come to a bridge where taxis and buses to Huairou congregate.

ARRIVAL AND DEPARTURE   HUANGHUA

By bus Take bus #916 from Dongzhimen bus station to Huairou (懷柔, huáiróu; ¥12), and catch a minibus from there (¥10). The last bus from Huairou to Beijing is at 6.30pm.

Tours Backpacker hostels occasionally run tours this way, though you'll really have to ask around.

ACCOMMODATION AND EATING

There are a couple of restaurants in the village by the wall, though nothing to get too excited about.

Guesthouses Locals rent out spare rooms in their houses, with the usual spartan facilities: hard beds, bare furnishings and only cold water on tap which they might be able to heat up for you. Bargain hard over the rates. **¥50–100**

Jiankou

箭扣, jiànkòu • Daily 7am–5pm • ¥20

First it was Simatai, then Huanghua; now that these have become entrenched on the tourist trail, the new intrepid destination is **Jiankou**, about 30km north of Huairou. The wall here is white, as it's made of **dolomite**, and there is a **hikeable** and very picturesque section, about 20km long, that winds through thickly forested mountain. Don't make the trip without a local guide; much of the stonework is loose on the wall, which is a little tricky to find in the first place. You really need to watch your step, and some nerve-racking sections are so steep that they have to be climbed on all fours.

Hiking Jiankou

Only the most determined choose to make the full 20km hike from west to east at Jiankou; most people do the first 12km or so, or choose to walk the spectacular **middle section**, which is easier to get to and has no tricky parts. The far western end of the hike starts at **Nine Eye Tower**, one of the biggest watchtowers on the wall, and named after its nine peepholes. It's a tough 12km from here to the Beijing Knot, a watchtower where three walls come together. Around here the views are spectacular, and for the next kilometre or so the hiking is easier, at least until you reach a steep section called "Eagle Flies Vertically". Though theoretically you can scale this, then carry on for another 10km to Mutianyu, it is not recommended; the hike gets increasingly dangerous and includes some almost vertical climbs, such as the notorious "sky stairs".

ARRIVAL AND DEPARTURE   JIANKOU

It's possible to get to Jiankou and back in a day, if you leave very early, but you'd be better off planning to stay a night at Xizhazi village (西柵子, xīzhàzi). From here it takes an hour or so just to reach the wall – but without a local to guide you it's easy to get lost.

By bus Take bus #916 from Dongzhimen to Huairou (懷柔, huáiróu; 1hr, ¥12), then charter a minibus or taxi to Xizhazi village (minimum ¥100 one-way; 1hr 15min).

ACCOMMODATION

Jiankou Zhao's Hostel 箭扣赵家, jiànkòu zhào jiā. Near the car park in Xizhazi village ☎010 89696677. Plenty of local farmers rent out rooms, but it's recommended that you call in at this spartan but clean hostel. Mr Zhao is full of information on the hike, and will either guide you himself or sort out someone else to do it. The home-cooked food, incidentally, is excellent – ask if he has any trout. Dorms **¥15**, rooms **¥70**

1

The Ming Tombs

十三陵, shísān líng

After their deaths, all but three of the sixteen Ming-dynasty emperors were entombed in giant underground vaults, the **Shisan Ling** (literally, Thirteen Tombs), usually referred to in English as the **Ming Tombs**. Two of the tombs, Chang Ling and Ding Ling, were restored in the 1950s; the latter was also excavated. The tombs are located in and around a valley 40km northwest of Beijing. The location, chosen by the third Ming emperor, Yongle, for its landscape of gentle hills and woods, is undeniably one of the loveliest around the capital, the site marked above ground by grand halls and platforms.

That said, the fame of the tombs is overstated in relation to the actual interest of their site, and unless you've a strong archeological bent, a trip here isn't worth making for its own sake. The tombs are, however, very much on the tour circuit, being conveniently placed on the way to Badaling Great Wall (see p.121). The site also makes a nice place to picnic, especially if you just feel like taking a break from the city. To get the most out of the place, it's better not to stick to the tourist route between the car park and Ding Ling, but to spend a day here and hike around the smaller tombs further into the hills. You'll need a map to do this – you'll find one on the back of some Beijing city maps, or you can buy one at the site (¥2).

The Spirit Way

神道, shéndào • Daily 7am–7pm • ¥35

The approach to the Ming Tombs, the 7km-long **Spirit Way**, is Shisan Ling's most exciting feature, well worth backtracking along from the ticket office. The road commences with the **Dahongmen** (Great Red Gate), a triple-entranced triumphal arch, through the central opening of which only the emperor's dead body was allowed to be carried. Beyond, the road is lined with colossal stone statues of animals and men. Alarmingly larger than life, they all date from the fifteenth century and are among the best surviving examples of Ming sculpture. Their precise significance is unclear, although it is assumed they were intended to serve the emperors in their next life. The animals depicted include the mythological *qilin* (a reptilian beast with a deer's antlers and a cow's tail) and the horned, feline *xiechi*; the human figures are stern, military mandarins. Animal statuary reappears at the entrances to several of the tombs, though the structures themselves are something of an anticlimax.

Chang Ling

长陵, cháng líng • Daily 8.30am–5pm • ¥45

At the end of the Spirit Way stands the tomb of Yongle himself: **Chang Ling**, the earliest at the site. There are plans to excavate the underground chamber – an exciting prospect since the tomb is contemporary with some of the finest buildings of the Forbidden City in the capital. At present, the enduring impression above ground is mainly one of scale – vast courtyards and halls, approached by terraced white marble. Its main feature is the Hall of Eminent Flowers, supported by huge columns consisting of individual tree trunks which, it is said, were imported all the way from Yunnan province in China's southwest.

Ding Ling

定陵, dìng líng • Daily 8.30am–5pm • ¥35

The main focus of the Ming Tombs area is **Ding Ling**, the underground tomb-palace of the Emperor Wanli, who ascended the throne in 1573 at the age of 10. Reigning for almost half a century, he began building his tomb when he was 22, in line with common Ming practice, and hosted a grand party within on its completion. The mausoleum, a short distance east of Chang Ling, was opened up in 1956 and found to be substantially intact, revealing the emperor's coffin, flanked by those of two of his empresses, and floors covered with scores of trunks containing imperial robes, gold and silver, and even the imperial cookbooks. Some of the treasures are displayed in the tomb, a huge, musty stone vault, undecorated but impressive for its scale; others have been replaced by replicas.

ARRIVAL AND DEPARTURE   **THE MING TOMBS**

All transport drops you at a car park in front of Ding Ling.

By bus To get to the tombs on ordinary public transport, take bus #872 from Deshengmen (hourly; 1hr; ¥10). You can use this same bus to get from the spirit way to the tombs, though you may be waiting a while.
By tourist bus The easiest way to get to the Ming Tombs is to take one of the tourist buses that go to Badaling (see p.122), some of which visit the tombs on the way to and from Beijing. You can get off here, then rejoin another tourist bus later, either to continue to Badaling or to return to the city.
Tours There are few, if any, dedicated tours to the Ming Tombs alone; they're usually included with a visit to Badaling (see p.122).

The Western Hills

西山, xīshān

Like the Summer Palace (see p.95), Beijing's **Western Hills** are somewhere to escape urban life for a while, though they're more of a rugged experience. Thanks to their coolness at the height of summer, the hills have long been favoured as a restful retreat by religious men and intellectuals, as well as politicians in the modern times – Mao lived here briefly, and the Politburo assembles here in times of crisis.

The hills are divided into three parks, the nearest to the centre being the **Botanical Gardens**, 3.5km northwest of the Summer Palace. Two kilometres farther west, **Xiangshan** is the largest and most impressive of the parks, but just as pretty is **Badachu**, its eight temples strung out along a hillside 2.5km to the south of Xiangshan. You could explore two of the parks in one day, but each really deserves a day to itself. The hills take roughly an hour to reach from Beijing on public transport.

The Botanical Gardens

植物园, zhíwù yuán • Daily 6am–8pm • ¥10, or ¥45 including conservatory and temple

The **Botanical Gardens**, just over 5km west of the Summer Palace as the crow flies, feature over 2,000 varieties of trees and plants arranged in formal gardens (and usually labelled in English). They're at their prettiest in summer, though the terrain is flat and the landscaping is not as original as in the older parks. The impressive conservatory has desert and tropical environments and a lot of fleshy foliage from Yunnan. Behind the Wofo Temple is a bamboo garden, from which paths wind off into the hills; one heads northwest to a pretty cherry valley, just under 1km away, where Cao Xueqiao is supposed to have written *The Dream of Red Mansions* (see p.955).

Wofo Temple

卧佛寺, wòfó sì • Daily 8am–4.30pm • ¥5, or free with Botanical Gardens through ticket

The gardens' main path leads after 1km to the **Wofo Temple**, whose main hall houses a huge reclining Buddha, more than 5m in length and cast in copper. With two giant feet protruding from the end of his painted robe, and a pudgy baby-face, calm in repose, he looks rather cute, although he is not actually sleeping but dying – about to enter nirvana. Suitably huge shoes, presented as offerings, are on display around the hall.

ARRIVAL AND DEPARTURE   **THE BOTANICAL GARDENS**

By bus Bus #331 from outside the Yuanmingyuan (see p.96) travels via the north gate of the Summer Palace to the Western Hills. Bus #360 also heads this way from the zoo.
By taxi The quickest way here would be to get a cab (¥25) from Anheqiao North subway station, one stop along from the Summer Palace's Beigongmen station; you're less likely to be ripped off here, though drivers will still need persuading to use the meter.
By subway By the time you read this, the new Western Suburban line should have commenced operations, heading from Bagou subway station (on line #10) to the dedicated Botanical Gardens station.

1

Xiangshan Park

香山公园, xiāngshān gōngyuán • Daily 7am–6pm • ¥10 • cable car ¥30 one-way, ¥50 return

Around 2km west of the botanical gardens lies **Xiangshan Park**, a range of hills dominated by Incense Burner Peak in the western corner. It's at its best in the autumn (before the sharp November frosts), when the leaves turn red in a massive profusion of colour. Though busy at weekends, the park is too large to appear swamped, and is always a good place for a hike and a picnic. Take the path up to the peak (1hr) from where, on clear days, there are magnificent views down towards the Summer Palace and as far as distant Beijing. You can hire a horse to take you down again for ¥30, the same price as the cable car.

Zhao Miao

昭庙, zhāo miào • Daily 7am–4pm • Free with park entry

Right next to the north gate of the park is the **Zhao Miao** (Temple of Brilliance), one of the few temples in the area that escaped vandalism by Western troops in 1860 and 1900. It was built by Qianlong in 1780 in a Tibetan style, designed to make visiting Lamas feel at home.

Biyun Temple

碧云寺, bìyún sì • Daily 8am–5pm • ¥10

About 400m west of the park's north gate is the superb **Biyun Temple**. A striking building, it's dominated by a bulbous, north Indian-style dagoba and topped by extraordinary conical stupas. Inside, rather bizarrely, a tomb holds the hat and clothes of Sun Yatsen – his body was held here for a while before being relocated to Nanjing in 1924. The giant main hall is now a maze of corridors lined with *arhats*, five hundred in all, and it's a magical place. The benignly smiling golden figures are all different – some have two heads or sit on animals, one is even pulling his face off – and you may see monks moving among them and bowing to each.

ARRIVAL AND DEPARTURE   XIANGSHAN PARK

By bus Bus #331 heads from outside the Yuanmingyuan (see p.96) via the north gate of the Summer Palace, both of which are also on subway line #4. Bus #360 also heads this way from the zoo.

By taxi The quickest way here is to get a cab (¥30) from Anheqiao North subway (line 4), one stop along from the Summer Palace's Beigongmen station; you're less likely to

be ripped off here, though drivers will still need persuading to use the meter.

By subway By the time you read this, the new Western Suburban line should have commenced operations, heading from Bagou (on line #10) to the Fragrant Hills station at the end of the line.

ACCOMMODATION

Fragrant Hills Hotel 香山饭店, xiāngshān fàndiàn. Close to the main entrance of Xiangshan Park ☎010 62591166, ⓦxsfd.com. This hotel makes a good base for a weekend escape and some in-depth exploration of the Western Hills. A startlingly incongruous sight, the light,

airy hotel looks like something between a temple and an airport lounge. It was designed by I.M. Pei, also responsible for the pyramid at the Louvre in Paris, and the Bank of China building at Xidan. **¥688**

Badachu

八大处, bādàchù • Daily 8am–5pm • ¥10, cable car ¥50, sled ¥40 • bus #347 from the zoo, or ¥20 by taxi from Pingguoyuan station (on subway line #1)

A forested hill 10km south of Xiangshan Park, **Badachu** (Eight Great Sites) derives its name from the presence of eight temples here. Fairly small affairs, lying along the path that curls around the hill, the temples and their surroundings are nonetheless quite attractive, at least on weekdays; don't visit at weekends when the place is swamped.

At the base of the path is a pagoda holding what's said to be **one of Buddha's teeth**, which once sat in the fourth temple, about halfway up the hill. The third temple is a nunnery, and is the most pleasant, with a relaxing teahouse in the courtyard. There's a statue of the rarely depicted, boggle-eyed thunder deity inside the main hall. The other temples make good resting points as you climb up the hill.

Inevitably, there's a cable car that you can ride to the top of the hill; you'll see it as you enter the park's main (north) gate. To descend, there's also a metal sled that you can use to slide down the hill. You'll whizz to the bottom in a minute.

Tanzhe Temple and Jietai Temple

Due west of Beijing, two splendid temples sit in the wooded country outside the industrial zone that rings the city. Though the **Tanzhe** and **Jietai temples** are relatively little-visited by tourists, foreign residents rate them as among the best places to escape the city smoke. Getting there and back can be time-consuming, so take a picnic and enjoy the clean air, peace and solitude in the wooded hills.

Tanzhe Temple

潭柘寺, tánzhé sì • Daily 8am–5pm • ¥55, or ¥85 combined ticket with Jietai

Forty kilometres west of Beijing, **Tanzhe Temple** has the most beautiful and serene location of any temple near the city. It's also one of the oldest, having been constructed during the Jin dynasty (265–420), and one of the largest too. Although there are no longer any clergy living or working here, it once housed a thriving monastic community; these days, a terrace of stupas provides the final resting place for a number of eminent monks.

The temple complex

Wandering through the complex, past the stupas, you reach an enormous central courtyard, with an ancient, towering gingko tree at its heart that's over a thousand years old. Across the courtyard, a second, smaller gingko was once supposed to produce a fresh branch every time a new emperor was born. From here you can take in the other buildings, arrayed on different levels up the hillside, or look around the lush gardens, whose bamboo is supposed to cure all manner of ailments.

Jietai Temple

戒台寺, jiètái sì • Daily 8am–5pm • ¥45 or ¥85 combined ticket with Tanzhe

Sitting on a hillside 12km east of Tanzhe, **Jietai Temple**, looks more like a fortress than a temple, surrounded as it is by forbiddingly tall, red walls. First constructed during the Sui dynasty (581–600), it's an extremely atmospheric, quiet place, made slightly spooky by its venerable but eccentric-looking **pine trees**, all growing in odd directions. In the main hall is an enormous tenth-century platform of white marble at which novice monks were ordained. At 3m high, it's intricately carved with figures – monks, monsters (beaked and winged) and saints. Another, smaller side hall holds a beautiful wooden altar that swarms with dragon reliefs.

ARRIVAL AND DEPARTURE	**TANZHE AND JIETAI TEMPLES**

By public transport Ride the subway line #1 all the way to its western terminus at Pingguoyuan, then catch bus #931 (¥3; this bus has two routes, so make sure the driver knows where you're going) to Tanzhe Temple; it stops at Jietai too, but this is more easily visited on the return journey. If you don't fancy waiting for a bus, taxis between the two temples will cost around ¥35.

By taxi You can save yourself some hassle by hiring a taxi to visit both temples, which should cost around ¥400 return if you start from the city centre.

Hebei and Tianjin

CHENGDE, PUTUO ZONGCHENG ZHIMIAO

Hebei and Tianjin

A somewhat anonymous region, Hebei has two great cities at its heart – Beijing and Tianjin – both of which long ago outgrew the province and struck out on their own as separate municipalities. In the south, a landscape of flatlands is spotted with heavy industry and mining towns – China at its least glamorous – which are home to the majority of the province's seventy million inhabitants. The sparsely populated tableland to the north, rising from the Bohai Gulf, holds more promise. For most of its history this marked China's northern frontier, and was the setting for numerous battles with invading forces; both the Mongols and the Manchus swept through, leaving their mark in the form of the Great Wall, winding across lonely ridges. The first sections of the wall were built in the fourth century AD, along the Hebei–Shanxi border, in an effort to fortify its borders against aggressive neighbours.

Two centuries later, Qin Shi Huang's Wall of Ten Thousand Li – better known as **the Great Wall** – skirted the northern borders of the province. The parts of this barrier visible today, however, are the remains of the much younger and more extensive Ming-dynasty structure, begun in the fourteenth century as a deterrent against the Mongols. You can see the wall where it meets the sea at **Shanhaiguan**, a fortress town only a few hours by train from Beijing. If you're in the area, don't miss the intriguing seaside resort of **Beidaihe**, along the coast to the south, whose beaches host summer vacationers and dwindling numbers of Communist Party elite. Well north of the wall, the town of **Chengde** is the province's most visited attraction, an imperial base set amid the wild terrain of the Hachin Mongols and conceived on a grand scale by the eighteenth-century emperor Kangxi, with temples and monuments to match. All three towns are popular spots with domestic tourists, particularly Beijingers snatching a weekend away from the capital's bustle and stress. The Chinese like their holiday spots the way they like their restaurants – *renao* (literally "hot and noisy") – but it's easy to beat the crowds and find some great scenery.

Tianjin, an industrial giant and former concession town with a distinctly Western stamp, is worth a day-trip on the super-fast express train from Beijing to see its hodgepodge of colonial architecture and modern skyscrapers, or to hunt for "antiques" in its fascinating market area.

Tianjin

天津, tiānjīn

The third-largest city in China after the capital and Shanghai, dynamic **TIANJIN** is largely ignored by Western travellers – even those who enter or exit China via the nearby port of **Tanggu**. One reason is that Beijing, an infinitely more interesting city, is so close – just 130km to the northwest, a mere thirty minutes away by high-speed

Highlights

❶ **Tianjin** Glimpse dilapidated colonial architecture and browse the souvenir markets of this huge city. **See p.132**

❷ **Beidaihe beachfront** Once the pleasure preserve of colonists, then Communists, the summer sands are now chock-a-block with the bikini-clad masses. **See p.142**

❸ **Shanhaiguan** A dusty relic of a walled city on the Bohai Gulf, where you can follow the Great Wall until it disappears dramatically into the sea. **See p.144**

❹ **Chengde** The summer playground of emperors, whose many palaces and temples have been restored to the delight of Beijing day-trippers. **See p.148**

HIGHLIGHTS ARE MARKED ON THE MAP ON P.134

train. However, such proximity brings it within easy day-trip range of the capital; though the city has few actual sights, with a little time on your hands there certainly is merit to a Tianjin visit. Partly as a result of the wealth pouring in from the sea, it's actually richer than Beijing in terms of per capita GDP, and mushrooming flocks of brand-new skyscrapers bear testament to this fact. Thanks again to its maritime connections, Tianjin is also a place of substantial historical interest; its **streetscapes** – ageing nineteenth- and early twentieth-century foreign architecture, mostly European – are its most engrossing attractions.

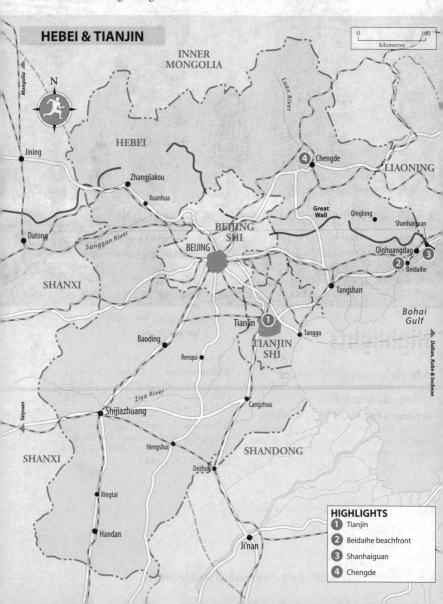

HEBEI & TIANJIN

HIGHLIGHTS
1 Tianjin
2 Beidaihe beachfront
3 Shanhaiguan
4 Chengde

TIANJIN ORIENTATION

The majority of Tianjin's colonial buildings are clustered in the grid of streets on the southern side of the Hai River (海河, hǎi hé), whose calm, newly gentrified banks are great for ambling. From the main train station, you can approach the Old Town via Jiefang Bridge, built by the French in 1903, which leads south along heavily restored and developed **Jiefang Bei Lu**, an area given an oddly continental feel by the pastel colours and wrought-iron scrollwork balconies of the French concession. This is at its most appealing around the glorified roundabout known as **Zhongxin Park** which marks the southeastern end of the main shopping district. Rising above all of this are the skyscrapers of new Tianjin, tallest of which at the time of writing was the 337m-high *Tianjin World Financial Center*; the *Goldin Finance 117* and the *Rose Rock IFC*, two near-600m-tall beasts, are scheduled to bring Tianjin into the world's select 100-storey-plus club in 2015.

2

Locals say, not altogether with pride, that the city has become a massive construction site, requiring a new map to be printed every three months. Though wide swaths of the city are being redeveloped, much of the colonial architecture has been placed under protection, though not from overzealous renovation – look for the distinctive plaques on the relevant buildings. **Feng Jicai**, one of China's best-known writers and a Tianjin resident, led a campaign to preserve the old city, noting that, "if you regard a city as having a spirit, you will respect it, safeguard it, and cherish it. If you regard it as only matter, you will use it excessively, transform it at will, and damage it without regret." Contemporary Tianjin is an illustration of the latter, an unwieldy fusion of Beijing's bustle and Shanghai's Bund, though delivered without the character of either.

Brief history

Though today the city is given over to industry and commerce, it was as a **port** that Tianjin first gained importance. When the Ming emperor Yongle moved the capital from Nanjing to Beijing, Tianjin became the dock for vast quantities of rice paid in tribute to the emperor and transported here from all over the south via the Grand Canal. In the nineteenth century, the city's strategically useful location caught the attention of the seafaring Western powers, not least during the Opium War (see p.918): with well-armed gunboats, the invaders were assured of victory, and the **Treaty of Tianjin**, signed in 1858, gave the Europeans the right to establish nine treaty ports on the mainland, from which they could conduct trade and sell opium.

Tianjin's own **concessions**, along the banks of the Hai River, were separate, self-contained, European fantasy worlds (see box, p.137). The Chinese were discouraged from intruding, except for servants, who were given pass cards. Tensions between the indigenous population and the foreigners exploded in the **Tianjin Massacre** of 1870, when a Chinese mob attacked a French-run orphanage, killing nuns, priests and the French consul in the belief that the Chinese orphans had been kidnapped and were merely awaiting the pot. The city had its genteel peace interrupted again by the **Boxer Rebellion** in 1900 (see p.919), after which the foreigners levelled the walls around the old Chinese city to enable them to see in and keep an eye on its residents.

Central Tianjin

The city centre is home to a fair few diverting sights, all within fairly easy walking distance of the train station. Here you'll find the bulk of Tianjin's **colonial architecture** (at its best on Jiefang Bei Lu), as well as the intriguingly designed **China House Museum**. It's also the city's main shopping area, centred on the pedestrianized Heping Lu and Binjiang Dao; the **antiques market** is, perhaps, of most interest to visitors. Arty types may care to check out the trendy new **6Haoyuan** complex, just north of the *Astor Hotel*, where there are several galleries and art shops.

2

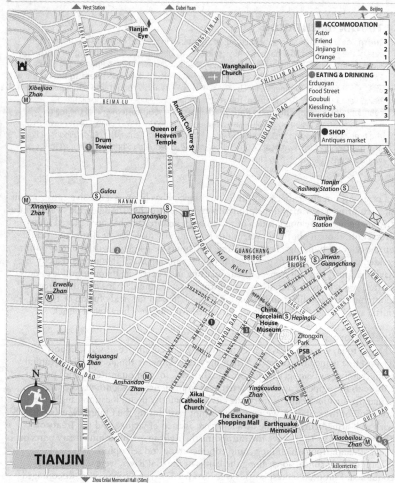

Yinyang International Center ▶
Airport ▶
Tanggu Port ▶

■ ACCOMMODATION

Astor	4
Friend	3
Jinjiang Inn	2
Orange	1

● EATING & DRINKING

Erduoyan	2
Food Street	1
Goubuli	4
Kiessling's	5
Riverside bars	3

● SHOP

Antiques market	1

TIANJIN

0 ————————— 1
kilometre

▼ Zhou Enlai Memorial Hall (50m)

China Porcelain House Museum

中国瓷房子博物馆, zhōngguó cífángzi bówùguǎn • Chifeng Dao • Daily 9am–6pm • ¥35 • metro line #3 to Hepinglu

While most people won't feel the need to go inside, the **China House Museum** is a must-see for its (frankly insane) premises – a colonial mansion clad entirely in broken pottery, replete with extensive additional curlicues. This is the work of Zhang Lianzhi, a Tianjin native who purchased the house in 2002; he has since gone on to fill it with thousands of porcelain pieces, mainly from the Qing dynasty, though some go back to the Tang (618–907). A couple of rooms at the front of the property function as small shops, though prices verge on the extortionate.

The antiques market

旧货市场, jiùhuò shìchǎng • Daily 8am–5pm • metro line #3 to Hepinglu

Tianjin's **antiques market**, centred on Shandong Lu, is a great attraction even if you have no intention of buying. The side-alleys here are lined with dark, poky shops, pavement vendors with their wares spread out in front of them on yellowed newspapers and stallholders waving jade and teapots in the faces of passers-by. The market expands and contracts according to the time of year (small in winter, big in summer), but it's always at its largest on Sundays, swelled by Beijingers here for the weekend.

The variety of goods on display is astonishing: among the standard jade jewellery, ceramic teapots, fans and perfume bottles are Russian army watches, opium pipes, snuffboxes, ornate playing cards, old photographs, pornographic paintings and rimless sunglasses, not to mention bizarre picture-postcards of revolutionary dramas depicting synchronized ballet dancers performing graceful, mid-air leaps with hand grenades. Prices are generally cheaper than in the capital (after mandatory bargaining), though be aware that few, if any, antiques are genuine.

2

Xikai Catholic Church

西开教堂, xīkāi jiàotáng • Daily 5.30am–4.30pm • English-language Mass Sun 11am • metro lines #1 or #3 to Yingkoudao

At the southern end of Binjiang Dao, this **Catholic Church** is a useful landmark and one of the most distinctive buildings in the city. Dedicated to St Joseph, it was built by the French in 1917, its odd facade of horizontal brown and orange brick stripes topped with three green domes; the interior is pleasing, if less interesting than the exterior.

Tangshan Earthquake memorial

抗震纪念碑, kàngzhèn jìniànbēi • metro lines #1 or #3 to Yingkoudao

The diffuse zone of unremarkable buildings east of the Catholic Church, around Nanjing Lu, is notable only for the **Earthquake Memorial** opposite the *Friendship Hotel*. More tasteful than most examples of Chinese public statuary, this hollow pyramid commemorates the 250,000 people who died in the 1976 earthquake in Tangshan, a city to the northeast – one of the world's worst ever natural disasters, and one which many Chinese believe foretold the subsequent death of Chairman Mao.

Northwest of the centre

There's another clutch of sights to the north and west of central Tianjin, an area bisected by the prettified Hai River; you can use its banks as a pleasant means of access from the train station. Off the east bank are two interesting places of worship, the Buddhist **Dabei Yuan** and the Christian **Wanghailou Church**. To the west of the river lies the mildly diverting **Ancient Culture Street**, and the **Drum Tower** area, both of which have been over-renovated in faux-dynastic style.

Dabei Yuan

大悲院, dàbēi yuàn • Tianwei Lu, off Wuma Lu • Daily 9am–4pm • ¥5 • metro line #3 to Jinshiqiao

The main sight in the northern part of the city, best reached by taxi, is the **Dabei Yuan**, located on a narrow lane off Zhongshan Lu. Tianjin's major Buddhist temple, it's easy to find as the alleys all around are crammed with stalls selling a colourful mix of religious knick-knacks: incense, tapes of devotional music, mirror-glass shrines and ceramic Buddhas with flashing lights in their eyes. Large bronze vessels full of water stand outside the buildings, a fire precaution that has been in use for centuries. Outside

> **OLD TIANJIN**
>
> The area northwest of the main train station, on the west side of the Hai River, was Tianjin's **old city**, strictly demarcated into national zones, and each section today retains a hint of its old flavour. Running from west to east along the north bank of the river were the Austrian, Italian, Russian and Belgian concessions, though most of the old buildings here have been destroyed. Unmistakeable are the chateaux of the French concession, which now make up the downtown district just south of the river, and the haughty mansions the British built east of here. Farther east, also south of the river, the architecture of an otherwise unremarkable district has a sprinkling of stern German constructions.

2

the first hall, which was built in the 1940s, the devout wrap their arms around a large bronze incense burner before lighting incense sticks and kowtowing. In the smaller, rear buildings – seventeenth-century structures extensively restored after the Tangshan earthquake – you'll see the temple's jovial resident monks, while small antique wood and bronze Buddhist figurines are displayed in a hall in the west of the complex.

Tianjin Eye

天津之眼, tiānjīn zhīyǎn • On Jingang Bridge • Daily 9.30am–9.30pm • ¥70 • metro line #3 to Jinshiqiao

The city's newest attraction, **Tianjin Eye** is perched just west of the Dabei Yuan on Jingang Bridge. Views of Tianjin's skyscrapers are good enough from the roads flanking the river, but you'll get even more of an eyeful from one of the Eye's pods.

Wanghailou Church

望海楼教堂, wànghǎilóu jiàotáng • Junction of Shizilin Dajie and Haihe Donglu • Open during services only (times vary) • metro line #3 to Jinshiqiao

The stern **Wanghailou Church** stands not far south of Dabei Yuan, over Shizilin Dajie on the north bank of the river. Built in 1904, it has an austere presence thanks to the use of dark stone and is the third church to stand on this site – the first was destroyed in the massacre of 1870 (see p.135), a year after it was built, and the second was burnt down in 1900 during the Boxer Rebellion. It's possible to visit during the week, but the Sunday morning Chinese-language services (7am) make a stop here much more interesting.

Ancient Culture Street

古文化街, gǔwénhuà jiē • metro line #2 to Dongnanjiao

Southwest of Wanghailou Church, the **Ancient Culture Street** runs off Beima Lu just west of the river, its entrance marked by colourful arches – and, at the southern end, a tank. This re-creation of a nineteenth-century Chinese street (minus the beggars and filth) is similar to others springing up in cities across China, but lacks conviction despite all the curling, tiled roofs, carved balconies and red-and-green wooden shop-fronts. Part of the problem, perhaps, is that it's relentlessly commercial, and one has to wonder how on earth *Doraemon* keyrings, ceramic snowmen and butt-wiggling dog dolls can be representative of ancient culture. More interesting are stalls selling *chatang*, soup made with millet and sugar; the stallholders attract customers by demonstrating their skill at pouring the boiling liquid from a long, dragon-shaped spout into four bowls, all held in one hand.

Queen of Heaven Temple

天后宫, tiānhòu gōng • Daily 9am–5pm • ¥10

The one actual piece of culture on Ancient Culture Street is the heavily restored **Queen of Heaven Temple**, originally built in 1326 and supposedly the oldest building in Tianjin; as with such places all along the Chinese coast, it's dedicated to the Sea Goddess, long deemed to be the protector of sailors and fishermen. There's an exhibition of local crafts in the side halls.

The mosque

清真寺, qīngzhēn sì • Dafeng Lu • metro line #1 to Xibeijiao

Tianjin's **mosque**, off Dafeng Lu, is an active place of worship, and though you're free to wander around the buildings, only Muslims may enter the prayer halls. It's a fine example of Chinese Islamic architecture, with some striking woodcarvings of floral designs in the eaves and around the windows.

ARRIVAL AND DEPARTURE   **TIANJIN**

By plane Binhai International airport (天津滨海国际 机场, tiānjīn bīnhǎi guójì jīchǎng) lies 15km east of Tianjin; it has connections to every major city in China, as well as services to Japan, Singapore, South Korea and Taiwan. Shuttle buses serve various parts of the city; most useful for travellers are those to the main train station (every 30min 6am–7.30pm; 20min; ¥15).

Destinations Changsha (4 weekly; 1hr 40min); Chengdu (1 daily; 2hr 20min); Dalian (daily; 50min); Fuzhou (3 weekly; 3hr 50min); Guangzhou (4 daily; 3hr); Guilin (2 weekly; 4hr 30min); Haikou (1 daily; 3hr 15min); Hangzhou (5 weekly; 1hr 30min); Harbin (1 daily; 3hr); Hong Kong (1 daily; 3hr 15min); Kunming (8 weekly; 3hr 20min); Nanjing (1 daily; 1hr 40min); Qingdao (1 daily; 1hr); Shanghai (1 daily; 1hr 45min); Shenyang (8 weekly; 1hr 20min); Shenzhen (1 daily; 2hr 45min); Taiyuan (1 daily; 1hr); Wuhan (7 weekly; 2hr 30min); Xiamen (5 weekly; 2hr 30min); Xi'an (1 daily; 2hr); Zhengzhou (1 daily; 1hr 10min).

By train The main train station (天津站, tiānjīn zhàn) sits at the nexus of metro lines #2, #3 and #9; the most stylish way to arrive is on one of the high-speed bullet trains (¥54.5) from Beijing South, which plough along at a top speed of 340km/h. Tianjin has several other train stations, including North, South and West, but you're unlikely to use these.

Destinations from main station: Beidaihe (many daily; 2hr 10min–7hr); Beijing (every 20min; 30–90min);

Guangzhou (3 daily; 25hr); Harbin (22 daily; 8–17hr); Shanhaiguan (many daily; 3–5hr); Shenyang (many daily; 5–12hr); Xi'an (4 daily; 17–19hr).

By bus There is no point in using buses to get to or from Tianjin: the city's train connections are faster and more numerous, while its confusing profusion of bus stations are all outside the centre.

By ferry Tanggu Port (天津港; tiānjīn gǎng), around 50km east of central Tianjin, has connections to Dalian, as well as international services to Incheon in South Korea and Kobe in Japan. Tickets can be purchased from travel agents all over Tianjin (ask your hotel for the closest one; many even sell tickets themselves), or at the port itself. There are frequent minibuses between Tanggu and Tianjin's main train station (¥10), and some shuttle services direct to Beijing (¥70); alternatively, it's ¥100–120 for a taxi from the port to central Tianjin, and you'll easily find others to share the cost if necessary.

Destinations Dalian (March–Oct daily; rest of year every other day; 13–15hr); Incheon (2 weekly; 26hr); Kobe (weekly; 51hr).

GETTING AROUND

Downtown and the old concession areas are just about small enough to explore on foot; the pretty banks of the Hai River provide a pleasant alternative to using the crowded bus and metro services.

By metro Tianjin's useful subway system (from ¥2 per journey) is still expanding in scope, and currently comprises lines #2, #3 and, bizarrely, #9. At the time of writing there was a small, two-station break in line #2, west of the train station; it should have been reconnected by the time you read this. In addition, lines #5 and #6 are scheduled to open in 2015.

By bus Buses run 5am–midnight, with fares a standard ¥1.5 throughout the city centre. The most useful route, by far, is the #600, which starts behind the main train station, then heads out on a circular route past (or close to) all the main city sights.

By taxi Cabs are plentiful – flag fall is ¥9, and ¥15 is sufficient for most journeys around town.

ACCOMMODATION

Thanks to the city's proximity to Beijing via the high-speed train, there is no need to stay overnight in Tianjin, but if a hotel is required there are some decent options.

Astor 利顺德饭店, lìshùndé fàndiàn. 33 Tai'er Zhuang Lu ☏ 022 23311688, ⓦ luxurycollection.com /astor. A truly charming hotel, and the only one in the city that exudes any colonial-era vibes whatsoever, this is located in a stylish British mansion dating back to 1863. It has kept itself up to date with careful restorations, and remains one of the most luxurious places to stay in Tianjin. ¥1100

Friend 富蓝特大酒店, fùlántè dàjiǔdiàn. 231 Xinhua Lu ☏ 022 83326399. Very welcoming, clean, and a bargain by Tianjin standards. Rooms are surprisingly well appointed for the price. ¥298

Jinjiang Inn 锦江宾馆, jǐnjiāng bīnguǎn. 17 Jinbu Dao ☏ 022 58215018. A cheap chain hotel close to the station (150m from south Exit #4), with clean, standard rooms. It's often full – book ahead if possible. ¥199

Orange 桔子酒店, júzi jiǔdiàn. 7 Xing'an Lu ☏ 022 27348333. Smart new cheapie by the riverside, with rooms that are a notch above those of the main budget chains. Try to nab a room with a river view; those from the upper levels are quite superb. Note that it's quite difficult to access the hotel, especially from the riverside itself. ¥328

EATING AND DRINKING

Tianjin has a few great restaurants to choose from, though for general snacking try Food Street (食品街, shípǐn jiē) east of Nanmenwai Dajie, on Qingyi Dajie; it's a highly atmospheric place to eat, and with so many restaurants crammed in, there's something to suit all budgets and tastes. For drinking, it's hard to beat the small curl of bars on the river bank opposite the train station; many sell draught beer from just ¥8, and their outdoor terraces are glorious places to sit on a sunny day.

2

Erduoyan 耳朵眼, ěrduoyǎn. Corner of Gulou Dongjie and Chengxiang Zhonglu. *Erduoyan* is a true Tianjin institution, a city-wide chain famed for their eponymous rice-powder cakes fried in sesame oil (the name literally means "ear hole"), and *mahua*, fried dough twists. Though little more than a hole in the wall, the Gulou branch is best, and forms part of the company headquarters, just east of the Drum Tower; it's just ¥3.5 for one of their greasy, but very tasty, snacks. Daily 10am–7.30pm.

Goubuli 狗不理包子铺, gǒubùlǐ bāozi pù. 99 Jianshe Lu. Another esteemed restaurant, and often packed to the gills despite occasionally awful service, this found fame on account of its succulent dumplings (from ¥10 each). It's also a great place in which to sample Tianjin cuisine – see the picture menu for details (dishes ¥30–60). Daily 10am–9pm.

Kiessling's 起士林西式餐厅, qǐshìlín xīshì cāntīng. 333 Zhejiang Lu, just off Nanjing Lu, hidden behind the be-domed and be-columned concert hall. Formerly Austrian-owned, this restaurant has been around for nearly 100 years, and still serves Western food: breaded fish fillets, mashed potatoes, pasta and so forth, all around ¥50–100 per dish. The beer hall and dining room on the top level is worth a stop, if only for its home-brewed dark beer (¥25). Restaurant daily 11am–2pm & 5–9pm.

DIRECTORY

Banks and exchange The main Bank of China (daily 8am–5pm) is at 80 Jiefang Bei Lu, on the corner of Datong Dao.
Mail The post office (daily 9am–6.30pm) is just east of Tianjin Station.
Travel agents CITS (☎022 28358866 ext 102) is at 22 Youyi Lu, opposite the Friendship Store. They don't impart much information, but they will book train and boat tickets for onward travel. Closer to the centre, CYTS (☎022 23035678), on the fourth floor at 166 Xinhua Lu, are helpful and speak some English.

The Bohai Gulf

On the **Bohai Gulf**, 300km east of Beijing, lies the rather bizarre seaside resort of **Beidaihe**. The coastline, reminiscent of the Mediterranean – rocky, sparsely vegetated, erratically punctuated by beaches – was originally patronized a hundred years ago by European diplomats, missionaries and businessmen, who can only have chosen it out of homesickness. They built villas and bungalows here, and reclined on verandas sipping cocktails after indulging in the new bathing fad. Most of Beidaihe's visitors nowadays are ordinary, fun-loving tourists, usually relatively well-heeled Beijingers; in high season (May–Aug), when the temperature hovers around the mid-20s Celsius and the water is warm, it's a fun place to spend the day.

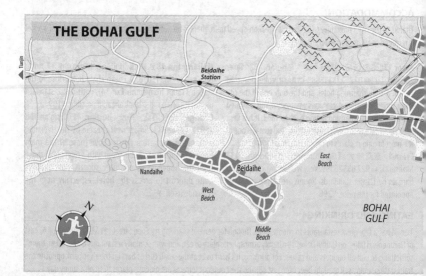

Only 25km or so to the northeast, historic attractions at **Shanhaiguan** have year-round appeal, and include some fine sturdy fortifications within the town and remnants of the **Great Wall** outside. With little nightlife and frustratingly little accommodation at present, however, Shanhaiguan is perhaps best visited on a day-trip.

Beidaihe

北戴河, běidàihé

China doesn't really do beach culture, especially up north, but they're learning fast in little **BEIDAIHE**. In fact, it wasn't so long ago that there were strict rules enforced here: West Beach was reserved for foreigners after they were granted access in 1979, with guards posted to chase off Chinese voyeurs interested in glimpsing their daringly bourgeois swimming costumes; for visiting Chinese, dark swimsuits were compulsory to avoid the illusion of nudity. These days things have changed and skimpy bikinis are now *de rigueur* on the town's three main beaches (and local girls are slowly learning that high heels and sand do not mix), while the streets by the shore are as gaudy and kitschy as any busy seaside resort. Away from the sea, up the hill, the tree-lined streets are much quieter, and the majority of the town seems to consist of nondescript compounds hosting guesthouses, **villas** and sanatoriums, some open to paying guests and others set aside for the Party, PLA or state-run companies who reward favoured members with trips to the seaside.

Note that much of Beidaihe shuts down during colder months; the streets along the seafront are at their liveliest from May to August.

Haining Lu

Beidaihe's central area is the southern stretch of **Haining Lu**, a busy stretch of hotels, seafood restaurants and tourist shops running down to the beach. This central area has been given a colonial German facelift, with older buildings restored and newer ones fitted out with timber-frame cladding; the overall flavour, however, is Sino-Russian, with signs in Cyrillic catering to the huge contingent of holiday-makers for whom Beidaihe represents a cheap break from Siberian climes. Most buildings are either

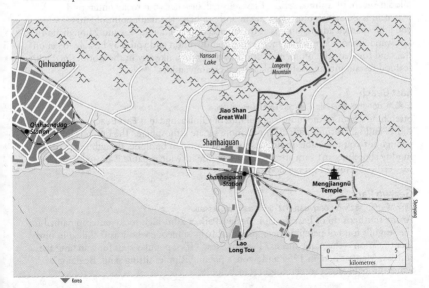

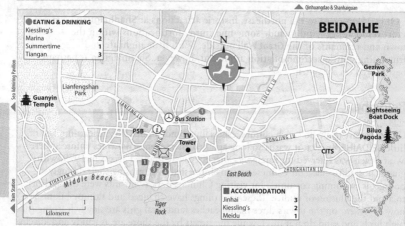

restaurants, with crabs and prawns bobbing about in outdoor tanks, or shops selling Day-Glo swimsuits, inflatables, snorkelling gear, souvenirs and a menagerie of animals tastefully sculpted from shells and raffia.

Lianfengshan Park

联峰山公园, liánfēngshān gōngyuán · Daily 7am–5pm · ¥20

On the far western side of town, 500m back from the beach, **Lianfengshan Park** is a hill of dense pines with picturesque pavilions and odd little caves, a good place to wander and get away from the crowds for a while, and also a popular spot with birdwatchers. Atop the hill is the **Sea Admiring Pavilion**, which has good views of the coast, and a quiet Guanyin Temple.

Middle Beach

中海滩, zhōnghǎi tān · ¥8

Middle Beach, in reality a series of several small beaches with rocky outcrops in between, is Beidaihe's most convenient and popular. The main point of entry – where you'll be charged admission – is at the intersection of Haining Lu and Zhonghaitan Lu, but wander about a hundred metres in either direction and you may be able to get on the sand for free. The promenade at the back is much like any in the world, lined with seafood restaurants and soft-drink and ice-cream vendors.

East Beach

东海滩, dōnghǎi tān · 24hr · Free · bus #1 or #34 from bus station

Stretching 15km to the industrial rail hub of Qinhuangdao is **East Beach**, popular with cadres and sanatorium patients for its more sedate atmosphere. The beach is long enough for you to be able to find a spot where you can be alone, though much of the muddy shoreline isn't very attractive. At low tide its wide expanse is dotted with seaweed collectors in rubber boots.

Geziwo Park

鸽子窝公园, gēzǐwō gōngyuán · ¥12 · bus #1 or #34 from bus station

At the southern tip of East Beach is **Geziwo Park**, a 20m-high rocky outcrop named for the seagulls fond of perching here, presumably by someone who wasn't skilled in bird identification – the name means "Pigeon's Nest". It's a popular spot for watching the sunrise. Mao sat here in 1954 and wrote a poem, "Ripples sifting sand: Beidaihe", which probably loses something in translation.

ARRIVAL AND DEPARTURE

By train Beidaihe train station (北戴河站, běidàihé zhàn) is on a branch line, and the train station is inconveniently located 15km west of town; some fast services from Beijing now arrive here, however. From a stop just outside the train station exit, bus #5 (¥1) heads to the central bus station; these finish at around 8pm. A taxi into the centre will cost around ¥40.

Destinations Beijing (many daily; 2–5hr); Shanhaiguan (many daily; 30min–1hr); Shenyang (17 daily; 2–7hr); Tianjin (many daily; 2hr 10min–7hr).

By bus Beidaihe bus station (北戴河汽车站, běidàihé qìchē zhàn) is off Haining Lu, a 15min walk from Middle Beach. Given the train station's inconvenient location, it's useful for getting to and from Shanhaiguan (1hr 30min), though you'll need to change buses halfway along in the gritty city of Qinhuangdao (秦皇岛, qínhuángdǎo): from Beidaihe, take the #34 (¥2) and let the bus attendant know you're going to Shanhaiguan, then they'll set you down in Qinhuangdao at the nexus with the #33 route (¥2), which you should take the remainder of the way – not a nice journey.

GETTING AROUND

By taxi Cabs around town cost ¥10, but once down by the beach Beidaihe is small enough to get around easily on foot.

By bicycle Stands at the beaches rent bicycles for up to three people on one machine (a thrandom?) at ¥20–40/hr,

depending on the number of saddles, plus ¥200 deposit.

By boat Just before Geziwo Park, the bus stops near the dock for Beidaihe's sightseeing boats, which in season leave regularly during the day to chug up and down the somewhat underwhelming coast (1hr; ¥32).

INFORMATION

Tourist information There's a small tourist information booth just outside the train station, and another near the bus station at the junction of Haining Lu and Lianfeng Lu;

these are only really good for the handing out of maps, which you can buy from street vendors in any case.

ACCOMMODATION

Beidaihe's accommodation is most in demand between May and August; out of season room prices are often slashed by half. Most of the budget hotels (some of which are pretty dodgy) are not licensed to accept foreigners, though hunt around a bit and you're sure to find one who'll take you, legally or otherwise.

Jinhai 金海宾馆, jīnhǎi bīnguǎn. Zhonghaitan Lu ☎ 0335 4030048. With an easy-to-find location next to the beach, and good sea views from many rooms, this is the best choice in its price range – as droves of visiting Russians will attest. **¥420**

Kiessling's 起士林西式餐厅, qǐshílín xīshì cāntīng. Off Dongjing Lu ☎ 0335 4033863. Small, upper-end hotel, its cream-coloured, red-roofed buildings arranged around a

fountain and badminton court; rooms are quiet, and appointed with a modicum of luxury. The hotel is connected to a bakery and restaurant of the same name. **¥700**

Meidu 美都饭店, měidōu fàndiàn. Xijing Lu ☎ 0335 4030053. The most reliable of Beidaihe's cheaper options – nowhere near as sleazy, institutional or noisy as others in its price range, and more than willing to accept foreigners. No breakfast. **¥200**

EATING AND DRINKING

Beidaihe is noted for its crab, cuttlefish and scallops. Try one of the innumerable small seafood places on Haining Lu, where you order by pointing to the tastiest-looking thing scuttling or slithering around the bucket. These are also the best places to drink; in summer, many stay open until after midnight.

Kiessling's 起士林西式餐厅, qǐshílín xīshì cāntīng. Off Dongjing Lu. Part of the hotel of the same name, this restaurant is connected to the far more illustrious Tianjin branch. It's split into two areas: the ho-hum bakery on Dongjing Lu (not a bad breakfast choice); and the far nicer restaurant within the hotel itself, which has been serving the foreign community for most of the last century. There's a pleasing range of Western-style food here, including tasty pasta dishes and German sausages; expect to pay up to ¥100 per head. Daily noon–2pm & 5–9pm.

Marina 玛丽娜西餐厅, mǎlìnà xīcāntīng. Haining

Lu. The best of the town's several Russian restaurants – they've tried hard to make Russian visitors at home with the lighting and seating. Simple Russian salads and stews available from ¥15–30 and borshch for ¥8, and there's also a range of okay-ish Chinese food on offer. Daily 9am–10pm.

★ **Summertime** 夏令咖啡, xiàlìng kāfēi. Haining Lu. What a lovely addition to Beidaihe this is – a relaxed café serving decent coffee (from ¥20), as well as pizza and waffles. There's free wi-fi too, making this a great place to check your emails over breakfast. Daily 9.30am–11pm.

Tiangan 天干海鲜大排档, tiāngān hǎixiān dàpái dàng. 9 Haining Lu. The most consistently popular of the seafood barbecue restaurants heading down Haining Lu. They'll grill you up shrimp, tofu, squid and other seafood for ¥5–15 a skewer, while bottles of beer are ¥5. You can also drop by in the morning for some cheap-as-chips Chinese breakfast: a variety of goods, mostly pickled, from ¥2 per saucer. Daily 8am–late.

Shanhaiguan

山海关, shānhǎiguān

A town at the northern tip of the Bohai Gulf, **SHANHAIGUAN** – "the Pass Between the Mountains and the Sea" – was originally built during the Ming dynasty as a fortress to defend the eastern end of the **Great Wall**. The wall crosses the Yanshan mountains to the north, forms the east wall of the town and meets the sea a few kilometres to the south. Far from being a solitary castle, Shanhaiguan originally formed the centre of a network of defences: smaller forts, now nothing but ruins, existed to the north, south and east, and beacon towers were dotted around the mountains. The town's obvious tourist potential is now being tapped, and extensive demolition and reconstruction continues within the city walls as the tide of tourist buses visiting the town grows ever larger. It's obvious that not much money has made its way into the town outside the battlements, and aside from the reconstructed streets (now given over to tourist shops and restaurants) the *hutongs* of the old town are squalid and crumbling. That said, Shanhaiguan is still arranged along its original plan of straight boulevards following the points of a compass, intersected with a web of alleys, and the odd courtyarded gem makes Shanhaiguan a good place to explore on foot, as well as an excellent base for visiting the Great Wall sites of **Lao Long Tou** and **Jiao Shan**.

First Pass Under Heaven

天下第一关, tiānxià dìyī gūan • Daily 7.30am–5.30pm • ¥50

Dominating the town is a fortified gatehouse in the east wall, the **First Pass Under Heaven**, which for centuries was the entrance to the Middle Kingdom from the barbarian lands beyond. An arch topped by a two-storey tower, the gate makes the surrounding buildings look puny: one can only imagine how formidable it must have looked when first built in 1381, with a wooden drawbridge over a moat 18m wide, and three outer walls for added defensive strength. The arch remained China's northernmost entrance until 1644, when it was breached by the Manchus. These days, the gate is overrun by hordes of marauding tourists, and is at its best in the early morning before most of them arrive; there are several **entrances**, with the main one west of the gate, another by the battlements to the south, and another way down the wall by the southeastern corner of the old town.

The gateway and wall

The gateway's name is emblazoned in red above the archway, calligraphy attributed to **Xiao Xian**, a Ming-dynasty scholar who lived in the town. A steep set of steps leads up from Dong Dajie to the impressively thick wall, nearly 30m wide. The tower on top, a two-storey, 10m-high building with regularly spaced arrow slits along its walls, is now a **museum** containing weapons, armour and costumes, as well as pictures of the nobility, who are so formally dressed they look like puppets. It's possible to stroll a little way **along the wall** in either direction; the walk is scattered with pay-per-view telescope and binocular stands, which afford a view of tourists on the Great Wall at Jiao Shan several kilometres to the north (see p.146), where the wall zigzags and dips along vertiginous peaks before disappearing over the horizon.

The Great Wall Museum

长城博物馆, chángchéng bówùguǎn • Daily 9am–4pm • Free

Follow the city wall south from the gate and you come to the **Great Wall Museum**. Its eight halls showcase the history of the region in chronological order from Neolithic times, and

the history of the wall from its beginnings. In addition to the tools used to build the wall, the vicious weaponry used to defend and attack it is also on display, including mock-ups of siege machines and broadswords that look too big to carry, let alone wield. The last three rooms contain dioramas, plans and photographs of local historic buildings. Inside the final room is a **model** of the area as it looked in Ming times, giving an idea of the extent of the defences, with many small outposts and fortifications in the district around.

ARRIVAL AND DEPARTURE   SHANHAIGUAN

By train The train station is a few hundred metres south of the city wall – easily walkable through a park-like area, though cabbies will try to persuade you otherwise (it's ¥5 if you're tempted). The station now receives some fast services from Beijing, and it's easy to buy tickets here. Destinations Beidaihe (many daily; 30min–1hr); Beijing (many daily; 2hr 30min–5hr 40min); Shenyang (many daily; 2hr 20min–6hr 30min); Tianjin (many daily; 2hr 45min–5hr 30min).

By bus The only useful bus links Shanhaiguan with Beidaihe – there are also fast trains between the two, but the remoteness of Beidaihe's station will eat up any time you save. You'll need to change buses halfway along in messy Qinhuangdao (秦皇岛, qínhuángdǎo); take the #33 (¥2) from points along Guancheng Nan Lu (there's a stop just outside the southern city gate), then change in Qinhuangdao for the #34 (¥2), which drops off at Beidaihe's bus station. All in all, it'll take at least 90min to get between the two cities.

ACCOMMODATION AND EATING

Frustratingly for budget travellers, accommodation options for foreigners are limited to the more expensive end of the market; at time of writing only one hotel inside the city walls accepted non-Chinese-ID holders, though some mum-and-pop operations may be willing to bend the rules. Shanhaiguan gets awfully boring in the evening, however, and is well within day-trip range from Beijing. Bar the restaurants at the *Shanhai Holiday* (expensive) and *Jingshan* (cheap and not too

2

bad), there's not a great deal going food-wise in Shanhaiguan either – another reason why visiting on a day-trip may not be such a bad idea.

Jingshan 京山宾馆, jīngshān bīnguǎn. Facing the First Pass Under Heaven ☎0335 5132188. Built to imitate a Qing mansion, with high ceilings, decorative friezes, curling roofs and red-brick walls and balconies, this hotel is slowly falling apart at the seams; it's overpriced too, unless you're able to chop a chunk from the rack rates. ¥580

Shanhai Holiday 山海假日酒店, shānhǎi jiàrì jiǔdiàn. Beima Lu ☎0335 5352888. This Qing-themed hotel lies within an entire Qing-styled part of town, west of

the drum tower – the most ambitious of Shanhaiguan's large-scale renovations. Some find it pleasing, others rather tacky, but the hotel itself is one of the town's few comfortable places to stay. ¥880

Super 8 速八酒店, sùbā jiǔdiàn. Xijing Lu ☎0335 5020888. Shanhaiguan's only recommendable place at budget level, this branch of the *Super 8* empire has carpeted rooms, comfortable beds and 24hr hot water, and is a mere 5min walk from the train station or old town. No breakfast. ¥298

The Great Wall beyond Shanhaiguan

Walk around Shanhaiguan's old town, and you'll be pestered continuously for rides to a series of nearby sights. It's well worth heading to a couple, especially the (reconstructed) sections of Great Wall to the north and south – the latter is where the wall finally runs into the sea, while the former marks its first steep rise into the mountains. Intrepid hikers could try and make it to **Yansai Lake** (燕塞湖, yànsài hú), up in the mountains directly north of Shanhaiguan, or to **Longevity Mountain** (长寿山, chángshòu shān), a hill of rugged stones east of the lake, where many of the rocks have been carved with the character *shou* (longevity). There's also a mountain pool here, a good place for a quiet swim.

Lao Long Tou

老龙头, lǎolóng tóu • Daily 7am–7.30pm • ¥50 • bus #25 from Laolongtou Lu • taxi ¥20

Follow the remains of the Great Wall south from Shanhaiguan and after 4km you'll reach **Lao Long Tou** (Old Dragon Head, after a large stone dragon's head that used to look out to sea here), the point at which the wall hits the coast – literally jutting out into the water. A miniature fortress with a two-storey temple in the centre stands right at the end of the wall. Unfortunately everything here has been so reconstructed it all looks brand new, and is surrounded by a rash of tourist development. The rather dirty beaches either side of the wall are popular bathing spots.

Walk for a few minutes past the restaurants west of Lao Long Tou and you'll come to the old British Army **barracks**, on the right; this was the beachhead for the Eight Allied Forces in 1900, when they came ashore to put down the Boxers. A plaque here reminds visitors to "never forget the national humiliation and invigorate the Chinese nation". Do your part by taking care not to trample the lawn.

Jiao Shan

角山, jiǎo shān • Daily 8am–4pm • ¥30 • cable car ¥30 one-way, ¥50 return • taxi from Shanhaiguan ¥20

A couple of kilometres to the north of Shanhaiguan lies **Jiao Shan**, a reconstructed section of the Great Wall. The ticket office is an easy walk from the town's north gate; from here, a steep path takes you through some dramatic scenery into the Yunshan mountains, or you can cheat and take the cable car.

The further along the wall you go the better it gets – the crowds peter out, the views become more dramatic, and once the reconstructed section ends, you're left standing beside – or on top of – the real, crumbly thing. Head a few kilometres further east and you'll discover a trio of passes in the wall, and a beacon tower that's still in good condition. You can keep going into the mountains for as long as you like, so it's worth getting here early and making a day of it.

Mengjiangnü Temple

孟姜女庙, mèngjiāngnǚ miào • Daily 7.30am–5pm • ¥30 • ¥20 by taxi

Some 6.5km northeast of town is **Mengjiangnü Temple**, dedicated to a legendary woman whose husband was press-ganged into one of the Great Wall construction squads. He died from exhaustion, and she set out to search for his body to give him a decent burial, weeping as she walked along the wall. So great was her grief, it is said, that the wall crumbled in sympathy, revealing the bones of her husband and many others who had died in its construction. The temple is small and elegant, with good views of the mountains and the sea. Statues of the lady herself and her attendants sit looking rather prim inside.

Chengde

承德, chéngdé

Relatively quiet and small for a Chinese city, unassuming **CHENGDE** boasts a highly colourful history; though the town itself is bland, on its fringes lie some of the most magnificent examples of imperial architecture in China, remnants from its glory days as the **summer retreat** of the Manchu emperors. In recent years Chengde has once more become a summer haven, justly popular with weekending Beijingers escaping the capital. Gorgeous temples punctuate the cabbage fields around town, and a palace-and-park hill complex, **Bishu Shanzhuang**, covers an area to the north nearly as large as Chengde itself. Farther north and to the east, on the other side of the river, stands a further series of imposing **temples**.

The majority of Chengde's one-million-strong population live in a semi-rural suburban sprawl to the south of the centre, leaving the city itself fairly small-scale – the new high-rises on its traffic-clogged main artery, **Nanyingzi Dajie**, are yet to obscure the view of distant mountains and fields.

Brief history

Originally called "Rehe", the town was discovered by the Qing-dynasty emperor **Kangxi** at the end of the seventeenth century. Attracted by the cool summer climate and rugged landscape, he built small lodges here from which he could indulge in a fantasy Manchu lifestyle, hunting and hiking like his northern ancestors. The building programme expanded when it became diplomatically useful for the Qing emperors to spend time north of Beijing, forging closer links with the troublesome Mongol tribes, whose princes he overawed with splendid audiences, hunting parties and impressive military manoeuvres.

Building Chengde

Construction began in 1703. By 1711, there were 36 palaces, temples, monasteries and pagodas set in a great walled park, its ornamental pools and islands dotted with beautiful pavilions and linked by bridges. Craftsmen from all parts of China were

---

THE BRITISH AT CHENGDE

The first **British Embassy** to China, under Lord Macartney, visited Qianlong's court in 1793. Having sailed up the river to Beijing in a ship whose sails were painted with characters reading "Tribute bearers from the vassal king of England", they were somewhat disgruntled to discover that the emperor had decamped to Chengde for the summer. However, they made the 150km journey there, in impractical European carriages, where they were well received by the emperor, though the visit was hardly a success. Macartney caused an initial stir by refusing to kowtow, while Qianlong was disappointed with the gifts the British had brought and, with Manchu power at its height, rebuffed all British trade demands, remarking: "We possess all things. I set no value on objects strange or ingenious, and have no use for your country's manufactures." His letter to the British monarch concluded, magnificently, "O king, Tremblingly Obey and Show No Negligence!"

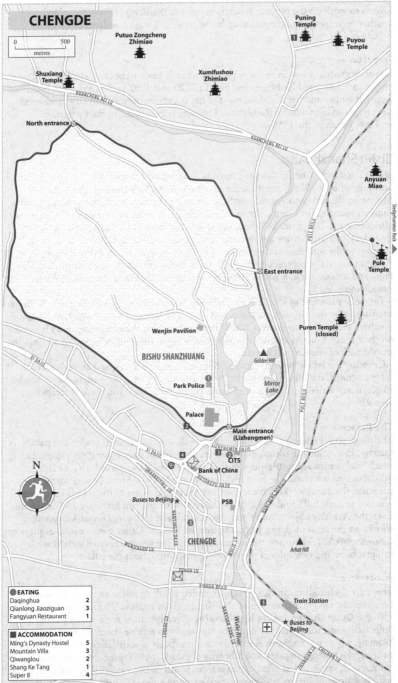

CHENGDE

0   500
metres

Puning
Temple

Puyou
Temple

Putuo Zongcheng
Zhimiao

Xumifushou
Zhimiao

Shuxiang
Temple

HUANCHENG BEI LU

North entrance

HUANCHENG BEI LU

Anyuan
Miao

Sledgehammer Rock

PULE BEILU

Pule
Temple

East entrance

Puren Temple
(closed)

Wenjin Pavilion

BISHU SHANZHUANG

Golden Hill

Mirror
Lake

PULE BEILU

Park Police

Palace

XI DAJIE

Main entrance
(Lizhengmen)

LIZHENGMEN DAJIE

CITS

@

Bank of China

DUTONGFU DAJIE

SHANXIYING JIE

Buses to Beijing ★

PSB

HUO CHENG DONGLU

WENJIAGOU LU

XINSHENGLU DAJIE

CHENGDE

Arhat Hill

YIHUA LU

XINHUA BEILU

Train Station

Wulie River

Buses to
Beijing ★

WULIE DONG LU

XINXIU LU

TIAN XIAN LU

CHEZHAN LU

East Bus Station

● EATING

Daqinghua	2
Qianlong Jiaoziguan	3
Fangyuan Restaurant	1

■ ACCOMMODATION

Ming's Dynasty Hostel	5
Mountain Villa	3
Qiwanglou	2
Shang Ke Tang	1
Super 8	4

2

invited to work on the project; Kangxi's grandson, **Qianlong** (1736–96), added another 36 imperial buildings during his reign, which was considered to be the heyday of Chengde.

Recent times

Chengde gradually lost imperial popularity when it came to be seen as unlucky after emperors Jiaqing and Xianfeng died here in 1820 and 1861 respectively. The buildings were left empty and neglected for most of the twentieth century, but largely escaped the ravages of the Cultural Revolution. Ongoing restorations, in the interests of tourism, began in the 1980s.

Bishu Shanzhuang

避暑山庄, bìshǔ shānzhuāng • Daily 8am–5.30pm • April 16–Oct 15 ¥120 • Oct 16–April 15 ¥90

Surrounded by a 10km-long wall, the enormous **Bishu Shanzhuang** (the Bishu Mountain Resort) occupies the northern third of the town's area. This is where, in the summer months, the Qing emperors lived, feasted, hunted and occasionally dealt with affairs of state. The palace buildings just inside the main entrance are unusual for imperial China as they are low, wooden and unpainted – simple but elegant, in contrast to the opulence and grandeur of Beijing's palaces. It's said that Emperor Kangxi wanted the complex to mimic a Manchurian village, to show his disdain for fame and wealth, though with 120 rooms and several thousand servants he wasn't exactly roughing it.

The same principle of idealized naturalness governed the design of the park. With its twisting paths and streams, rockeries and hills, it's a fantasy re-creation of the rough northern terrain and southern Chinese beauty spots that the emperors would have seen on their tours. Lord Macartney noted its similarity to the "soft beauties" of an English manor park of the Romantic style.

Covering the whole park and its buildings takes at least a day, and an early start is recommended; it's at its nicest in the early morning anyway. The park is simply too big to get overcrowded, and if you head north beyond the lakes, you're likely to find yourself alone.

The Palace

The **main gate**, Lizhengmen, is in the south wall, off Lizhengmen Dajie. The **palace quarter**, just inside the complex to the west of the main gate, is built on a slope, facing south, and consists of four groups of dark wooden buildings spread over an area of 100,000 square metres. The first, southernmost group, the Front Palace, where the emperors lived and worked, is the most interesting, as many of the rooms have been restored to their full Qing elegance, decked out with graceful furniture and ornaments. Even the everyday objects are impressive: brushes and ink stones on desks, ornate fly whisks on the arms of chairs, little jade trees on shelves. Other rooms house displays of ceramics, books and exotic martial-art weaponry. The Qing emperors were fine calligraphers, and examples of their work appear throughout the palace.

Front Palace

There are 26 buildings in this group, arranged south to north in nine successive compounds, which correspond to the nine levels of heaven. The main gate leads into the **Outer Wumen**, where high-ranking officials waited for a single peal of a large bell, indicating that the emperor was ready to receive them. Next is the **Inner Wumen**, where the emperor would watch his officers practise their archery. Directly behind, the **Hall of Frugality and Sincerity** is a dark, well-appointed room made of cedarwood, imported at great expense from south of the Yangzi River by Qianlong, who had none of his grandfather Kangxi's scruples about conspicuous consumption.

Topped with a curved roof, the hall has nine bays, and patterns on the walls include symbols of longevity and good luck. The **Four Knowledge Study Room**, behind, was where the emperor worked, changed his clothes and rested. A vertical scroll on the wall outlines the knowledge required of a gentleman: he must be aware of what is small, obvious, soft and strong.

Rear Palace

The main building in the **Rear Palace** is the **Hall of Refreshing Mists and Waves**, the living quarters of the imperial family, and beautifully turned out in period style. It was in the west room here that Emperor Xianfeng accepted the humiliating Beijing Treaty in 1860, giving away more of China's sovereignty and territory after their defeat in the Second Opium War. The **Western Apartments** are where Cixi, better known as the Empress Dowager (see p.96), lived when she was one of Xianfeng's concubines. A door connects the apartments to the hall, and it was through here that she eavesdropped on the dying emperor's last words of advice to his ministers, intelligence she used to force herself into power.

Outer complexes

The other two complexes are much smaller. The **Pine and Crane Residence**, a group of buildings parallel to the front gate, is a more subdued version of the Front Palace, home to the emperor's mother and his concubines. In the **Myriad Valleys of Rustling Pine Trees**, to the north of here, Emperor Kangxi read books and granted audiences, and Qianlong studied as a child. The group of structures southwest of the main palace is the **Ahgesuo**, where male descendants of the royal family studied during the Manchurian rule; lessons began at 5am and finished at noon. A boy was expected to speak Manchu at 6, Chinese at 12, be competent with a bow by the age of 14 and marry at 16.

The lake

Rowing boat rental ¥30–50/hr

The best way to get around the **lake area** of the park – a network of pavilions, bridges, lakes and waterways – is to rent a **rowing boat**. Much of the architecture here is a direct copy of southern Chinese buildings. In the east, the **Golden Hill**, a cluster of buildings grouped on a small island, is notable for a hall and tower modelled after the Golden Hill Monastery in Zhenjiang, Jiangsu province. The **Island of Midnight and Murmuring Streams**, roughly in the centre of the lake, holds a three-courtyard compound which was used by Kangxi and Qianlong as a retreat, while the compound of halls, towers and pavilions on **Ruyi Island**, the largest, was where Kangxi dealt with affairs of state before the palace was completed.

Wenjin Pavilion

Just beyond the lake area, on the western side of the park, is the grey-tiled **Wenjin Pavilion**, surrounded by rockeries and pools for fire protection. From the outside, the structure appears to have two storeys. In fact there are three – a central section is windowless to protect the books from the sun. Sadly, the building is closed to the public.

Grassland and hills

A vast expanse of **grassland** extends from the north of the lake area to the foothills of the mountains, comprising Wanshun Wan (Garden of Ten Thousand Trees) and Shima Da (Horse Testing Ground). The **hilly area** in the northwest of the park has a number of rocky valleys, gorges and gullies with a few tastefully placed lodges and pagodas. The deer, which graze on tourist handouts, were reintroduced after being wiped out by imperial hunting expeditions.

2

The temples

The **temples** in the foothills of the mountains around Chengde were built in the architectural styles of different ethnic nationalities, so that wandering among them is rather like being in a religious theme park. This isn't far from the original intention, as they were constructed less to express religious sentiment than as a way of showing off imperial magnificence, and also to make envoys from anywhere in the empire feel more at home. Though varying in design, all the temples share **Lamaist features** – Qianlong found it politically expedient to promote Tibetan and Mongolian Lamaism as a way of keeping these troublesome minorities in line.

The Puning Temple

普宁寺, pǔníng sì · Daily 8am–5.30pm · April–Oct ¥80, Nov–March ¥60 (joint ticket with Puyou Temple) · bus #6 from Lizhengmen Dajie

The **Puning Temple** was built in 1755 to commemorate the Qing victory over Mongolian rebels at Junggar in northwest China, and is based on the oldest Tibetan temple, the Samye. Like traditional Tibetan buildings, it lies on the slope of a mountain facing south. This is the only working temple in Chengde, with shaven-headed Mongolian monks manning the altars and trinket stalls, and though the atmosphere is not especially spiritual – it's usually clamorous with day-trippers – the temple and its grounds exude undeniable charm.

Hall of Heavenly Kings and East Hall

In the **Hall of Heavenly Kings**, the statue of a fat, grinning monk holding a bag depicts Qi Ci, a tenth-century character with a jovial disposition, believed to be a reincarnation of the Buddha. In the **East Hall**, the central statue, flanked by *arhats*, portrays Ji Gong, a Song-dynasty monk who was nicknamed Crazy Ji for eating meat and being almost always drunk, but who was much respected for his kindness to the poor.

Mahayana Hall

The rear section of the temple, separated from the front by a wall, comprises 27 Tibetan-style rooms laid out symmetrically, with the **Mahayana Hall** in the centre. Some of the buildings are actually solid (the doors are false), suggesting that the original architects were more concerned with appearances than function. The hall itself is dominated by the 23m-high **wooden statue of Guanyin**, the Goddess of Mercy. She has 42 arms with an eye in the centre of each palm, and three eyes on her face, which symbolize her ability to see into the past, present and future. The hall has two raised entrances, and it's worth looking at the statue from these upper viewpoints as they reveal new details, such as the eye sunk in her belly button, and the little Buddha sitting on top of her head.

Xumifushouzhi Zhimiao

须弥福寿之庙, xūmífúshòu zhīmiào · Daily 8am–5.30pm · April–Oct ¥80 Nov–March ¥60 (joint ticket with Putuo Zongcheng Zhimiao) · bus #118 from Lizhengmen Dajie

Recently restored, the **Xumifushouzhi Zhimiao**, just southwest of Puning Temple, was built in 1780 in Mongolian style for the ill-fated sixth Panchen Lama when he came to

---

SEEING THE TEMPLES

The temples are now in varying states of repair, having been left untended for decades. Originally there were twelve, but two have been destroyed and another three are dilapidated; the remaining seven stand in two groups: a string of five just beyond the northern border of Bishu Shanzhuang; and two more to the east of the park. If you're short on time the **Puning Temple** is a must, if only for the awe-inspiring statue of Guanyin, the largest wooden statue in the world.

A good itinerary is to see the northern cluster in the morning, return to town for lunch, and in the afternoon head for the Pule Temple and Sledgehammer Rock, a bizarre protuberance that dominates the eastern horizon of the town (see p.154).

CATCHING THE GHOST

On the thirteenth day of the first lunar month (Jan or Feb), monks at Puning Temple's Mahayana Hall observe the ritual of **catching the ghost**, during which a ghost made of dough is placed on an iron rack while monks dressed in white dance around it, then divide it into pieces and burn it. The ritual is thought to be in honour of a ninth-century Tibetan Buddhist, Lhalung Oaldor, who assassinated a king who had ordered the destruction of Tibetan Buddhist temples, books and priests. The wily monk entered the palace on a white horse painted black, dressed in a white coat with a black lining. After killing the king, he washed the horse and turned the coat inside out, thus evading capture from the guards who did not recognize him.

Beijing to pay his respects to the emperor (see p.154) – indeed, it's a near-copy of Tashilunpo Monastery in Shigatse, the Lama's home town in Tibet (see p.896). Though he was lavishly looked after – contemporary accounts describe how Qianlong invited the Lama to sit with him on the Dragon Throne – he went home in a coffin (see box, p.154).

The temple centrepiece is the **Hall of Loftiness and Solemnity**, its finest features the eight sinuous gold dragons sitting on the roof, each weighing over 1000kg.

Putuo Zongcheng Zhimiao

普陀宗乘之庙, pǔtuó zōngchéng zhīmiào • Daily 8am–5.30pm • April–Oct ¥80, Nov–March ¥60 (joint ticket with Xumifushouzhi Miao) • bus #118 from Lizhengmen Dajie

Next door to the Xumifushouzhi Zhimiao, the magnificent **Putuo Zongcheng Zhimiao** (Temple of Potaraka Doctrine) was built in 1771 and is based on the Potala Palace in Lhasa. Covering 220,000 square metres, it's the largest temple in Chengde, with sixty groups of halls, pagodas and terraces. The grand terrace forms a Tibetan-style facade screening a Chinese-style interior, although many of the windows on the terrace are fake, and some of the whitewashed buildings around the base are merely filled-in shapes. The roof of the temple has a good view over the surrounding countryside.

The West Hall

Inside Putuo Zongcheng, the **West Hall** is notable for holding a rather comical copper statue of the Propitious Heavenly Mother, a fearsome woman wearing a necklace of skulls and riding side-saddle on a mule. According to legend, she vowed to defeat the evil demon Raksaka, so she first lulled him into a false sense of security – by marrying him and bearing him two sons – then swallowed the moon and in the darkness crept up on him and turned him into a mule. The two dancing figures at her feet are her sons; their ugly features betray their paternity.

Other halls

The **Hall of All Laws Falling into One**, at the back, is worth a visit for the quality of the decorative religious furniture on display. Other halls hold displays of Chinese pottery and ceramics and Tibetan religious artefacts, an exhibition slanted to portray the gorier side of Tibetan religion and including a drum made from two children's skulls.

Pule Temple

普乐寺, pǔlè sì • Daily 8.30am–4.30pm • ¥50 (joint ticket with Anyuan Miao) • bus #10 from Lizhengmen Dajie

Due east of Bishu Shanzhuang, the **Pule Temple** (Temple of Universal Happiness) was built in 1766 by Qianlong as a place for Mongol envoys to worship, and its style is an odd mix of Han and Lamaist elements. The Lamaist back section, a triple-tiered terrace and hall, with a flamboyantly conical roof and lively, curved surfaces, steals the show from the more sober, squarer Han architecture at the front. The ceiling of the back hall is a wood-and-gold confection to rival the Temple of Heaven in Beijing. Glowing at its centre is a **mandala of Samvara**, a Tantric deity, in the form of a cross. The altar beneath holds a Buddha of Happiness, a life-size copper image of sexual congress; more cosmic

2

THE PANCHEN LAMA AT CHENGDE

In 1786, the **Panchen Lama** was summoned from Tibet by Qianlong for his birthday celebrations. This was an adroit political move to impress the followers of Lamaist Buddhism. The Buddhists included a number of minority groups who were prominent thorns in the emperor's side, such as Tibetans, Mongols, Torguts, Eleuths, Djungars and Kalmucks. Some accounts (notably not Chinese) tell how Qianlong invited the Panchen Lama to sit with him on the Dragon Throne, which was taken to Chengde for the summer season. He was certainly feted with honours and bestowed with costly gifts and titles, but the greatest impression on him and his followers must have been made by the replicas of the Potala and of his own palace, constructed at Chengde to make him feel at home – a munificent gesture, and one that would not have been lost on the Lamaists. However, the Panchen Lama's visit ended questionably in Beijing when he succumbed to smallpox, or possibly poison, and his coffin was returned to Tibet with a stupendous funeral cortege.

sex is depicted in two beautiful mandalas hanging outside. Outside the temple, the view from the car park is spectacular, and just north is the path that leads to Sledgehammer Rock and the cable car.

Anyuan Miao

安远庙, ānyuǎn miào • Daily 8.30am–4.30pm • ¥50 (joint ticket with Pule Temple) • bus #10 from Lizhengmen Dajie

Anyuan Miao (Temple of Appeasing the Borders) lies within walking distance to the north of the Pule Temple, and is decidedly less appealing though enjoying a delightful setting on the tree-lined east bank of the Wulie River. It was built in 1764 for a troop of Mongolian soldiers who were moved to Chengde by Qianlong,

Sledgehammer Rock

棒锤山, bàngzhōng shān • ¥50 • 2km walk from the Pule Temple, or cable car (¥50 return) • bus #10 from Lizhengmen Dajie

Of the scenic areas around Chengde, the one that inspires the most curiosity is **Sledgehammer Rock**. Thinner at the base than at the top, the towering column of rock is more than 20m high, and skirted by stalls selling little models and Sledgehammer Rock T-shirts. According to legend, the rock is a huge dragon's needle put there to plug a hole in the peak, which was letting the sea through. The rock's obviously phallic nature is tactfully not mentioned in tourist literature, but is acknowledged in local folklore – should the rock fall, it is said, it will have a disastrous effect on the virility of local men.

ARRIVAL AND DEPARTURE

CHENGDE

Unlike anywhere else in northeast China, it's usually faster to reach Chengde by bus.

By train Chengde sits on a spur-line between Beijing and Dongbei. The train station sits to the south of town; from Beijing you'll chug through rolling countryside, with a couple of Great Wall vistas on the way. Tickets are easy to buy at the station, though there's a helpfully located ticket office just east of the *Mountain Villa* hotel.
Destinations Beijing (8 daily; 5hr 30min–9hr); Dandong (1 daily; 16hr); Shenyang (2 daily; 12–13hr).
By bus Travelling to Chengde by bus, you'll pitch up in one of several locations. There's a station of sorts immediately in

front of the train station, though more and more services are using the East bus station, which lies 7km to the south of town (bus #118 to Bishu Shanzhuang, or ¥20 by taxi). From Beijing, the two best departure points are the Liuliqiao and Sihui bus stations. Heading back to Beijing you'll find buses in front of the train station; in addition, sleeper-style services (which are, oddly, a little cheaper than the regular buses; buy tickets from the driver) leave at 9.30pm from Nanyingzi Dajie, stopping at the train station (10pm) on the way.
Destinations Beijing (3–5hr); Tianjin (4hr).

GETTING AROUND

Getting around Chengde can be slow going – public transport is crowded and at peak hours during the summer the main streets are so congested that it's quicker to walk. The town itself is just about small enough to cover on foot, and it's easy to walk or cycle between the two westernmost temples, and even on to Puning Temple, though this last section is busy, tedious and best navigated by taxi.

By bus Local buses are infrequent and always crammed. Buses #5 and #11, which go from the train station to the mountain resort, Bishu Shanzhuang; bus #6 from the resort to the Puning Temple; and bus #118 to the northern temples are the most useful.

By taxi Taxis are easy to find, but the drivers are often unwilling to use their meters – flag fall is ¥5, and a ride around town shouldn't cost more than ¥10.

By minibus Hotels will be able to help with chartering a minibus for around ¥300 a day (bargain hard).

INFORMATION

Agents and tickets Onward tickets and tours can be booked from CITS on Lizhengmen Dajie (☎ 0314 2027483), but similar services are available at most hotels.

ACCOMMODATION

There are plenty of hotels in Chengde town itself, plus a couple of expensive places on the fringes of Bishu Shanzhuang. Unfortunately, as with elsewhere in Hebei, strict enforcement of local government rules means foreigners are barred from cheaper accommodation; if you're really slumming it, try the flophouses in the side-alleys opposite the *Super 8*. On the plus side, rates at approved hotels are highly negotiable and off-peak discounts of up to two-thirds are possible.

★ **Ming's Dynasty Hostel** 明朝国际城市青年酒店, míngcháo guójì chéngshì qīngnián jiǔdiàn. Chezhan Lu ☎ 0314 7610360, ⓦ mingsdynastyhostel .com. Just a few minutes on foot from the train station, this is a great addition to the town, especially for budget travellers. Rooms are simple but kept nice and clean, and staff here are more informative than those at Chengde's most expensive hotels. Dorms **¥100**, twins **¥330**

Mountain Villa 山庄宾馆, shānzhuāng bīnguǎn. 127 Xiaonanmen (entrance on Lizhengmen Dajie) ☎ 0314 2025588. This grand, well-located complex has huge rooms, high ceilings and a cavernous lobby, and is extremely popular with tour groups. The large rooms in the main building are nicer but a little more expensive than those in the ugly building round the back, and there are some very cheap rooms in the basement. Service can be patchy. **¥550**

Qiwanglou 倚望楼宾馆, yǐwànglóu bīnguǎn. Around the corner and uphill from the Bishu Shanzhuang main entrance ☎ 0314 2024385. A well-run (though hugely expensive) hotel in an imitation Qing-style building. Its flowery grounds make for an interesting walk even if you're not staying here. Service is excellent, and the staff among the few people in Chengde who speak some English. **¥1680**

★ **Shang Ke Tang** 上客堂宾馆, shàng kè táng bīnguǎn. Puning Temple ☎ 0314 2058888. This interesting hotel's staff wear period clothing and braided wigs befitting the adjoining Puning temple, and glide along the dim bowels of the complex to lead you to appealingly rustic rooms. You're a little away from the action here, though this is not necessarily a negative, and there are a few cheap restaurants in the area. **¥550**

Super 8 速八酒店, sùbā jiǔdiàn. 2 Lizhengmen Dajie ☎ 0314 2028887. One of the cheaper places foreigners are allowed to stay in, this is a cheery, well-located option with rooms overlooking the main roundabout. Staff speak no English, but are eager to please. **¥318**

EATING AND DRINKING

Chengde is, unfortunately, not a great place to eat. There are plenty of restaurants catering to tourists on Lizhengmen Dajie, around the main entrance to Bishu Shanzhuang; on summer evenings, rickety tables are put on the pavement outside, and plenty of diners stay on drinking well into the evening. The best place for a drink is busy Shaanxiying Jie, a stream-side street stretching west of Nanyingzi Dajie; there are a few quieter places across the road to the east.

Daqinghua 大清花, dàqīnghuā. 21 Lizhengmen Dajie ☎ 0314 2082222. Pine-walled dumpling restaurant that's the best option in the area around the Bishu Shanzhuang entrance. Their dumplings (¥12–20) are great and come with a variety of fillings, though there's a full menu of tasty Chinese staples to choose from. Daily 11.30am–8.50pm.

Fangyuan Restaurant 芳园居, fāngyuánjū. Inside Bishu Shanzhuang ☎ 0314 2161132. This snazzy restaurant serves imperial cuisine, including such exotica as "Pingquan Frozen Rabbit"; prices are pretty high, however, and you won't get much change from ¥150 per person, even without drinks. Daily 11am–5pm.

Qianlong Jiaoziguan 乾隆饺子馆, qiánlóng jiǎoziguǎn. Just off Centre Square, a park at the heart of the shopping district ☎ 0314 2076377. The best *jiaozi* in town are served here, and far more besides – the menu is full of Chinese staples, with a few more interesting items such as sauerkraut with lung, braised bullfrog in soy, and battered venison. The more interesting mains clock in at ¥60–100, though penny-pinchers will appreciate the spicy Sichuan noodles (¥8). Daily 11.30am–8.50pm.

Dongbei

CRANES AT ZHALONG NATURE RESERVE

Dongbei

Dongbei (东北, dōngběi) – or, more evocatively, Manchuria – may well be the closest thing to the "real" China that visitors vainly seek in the well-travelled central and southern parts of the country. Not many foreign tourists get up to China's northernmost arm, however, due to its reputation as an inhospitable wasteland: "Although it is uncertain where God created paradise", wrote a French priest when he was here in 1846, "we can be sure he chose some other place than this." Yet, with its immense swaths of fertile fields and huge mineral resources, Dongbei is metaphorically a treasure house. Comprising Liaoning, Jilin and Heilongjiang provinces, it is economically and politically among the most important regions of China, and, for much of its history, the areas has been fiercely contested by Manchus, Nationalists, Russians, Japanese and Communists. With 4000km of sensitive border territory alongside North Korea and Russia, Dongbei is one of China's most vulnerable regions strategically.

In addition, economic pressures have made it prone to internal unrest, with worker protests common and a widening gap between the haves and have-nots that is threatening to become a chasm. Redressing this imbalance is **tourism**, a good portion of it domestic, which has become the leading growth industry. The region is cashing in on its colourful history, seen most vividly in the preservation of long-ignored Russian and Japanese colonial architecture, some of which you can actually stay in.

Furthest south of the Dongbei provinces, **Liaoning** boasts the busy port of **Dalian**; the provincial capital **Shenyang**, home to China's "other" Forbidden City; and Dandong, which sits right on the North Korean border. Moving north is **Jilin** province, whose capital **Changchun** sports the Puppet Emperor's Palace, home to Puyi during his reign as "emperor" of the Japanese state Manchukuo. Lastly, and hogging most of China's border with Russia, is **Heilongjiang**: the province's capital and major city, **Harbin**, is a thoroughly likeable place, and world-renowned for its amazing Ice Festival.

Brief history

The history of Manchuria proper begins with **Nurhaci**, a tribal leader who in the sixteenth century united the warring tribes of the northeast against the corrupt central rule of Ming-dynasty Liaoning. He introduced an **alphabet** based on the Mongol script, administered Manchu law and, by 1625, had created a firm and relatively autonomous government that was in constant confrontation with the Chinese. Subsequently, **Dorgun** was able to go a stage further, marching on Beijing with the help of Wu Sangui, a Ming general who surrendered to the Manchus because the warlord Li Zicheng (whose assault on Beijing had driven the last Ming emperor to suicide) had captured his concubine.

Highlights

❶ The Imperial Palace, Shenyang
Pre-empting Beijing's Forbidden City, this was the historical seat of the Manchus before they seized the capital. **See p.164**

❷ Old Yalu Bridge, Dandong Walk halfway to North Korea on this structure, bombed by the US during the Korean War. **See p.173**

❸ Puppet Emperor's Palace, Changchun
The second act of the "last emperor" Puyi's life was played out here, where he was installed by the Japanese as leader of Manchuria. **See p.176**

❹ Changbai Shan The northeast's loveliest nature reserve – see the crater lake and root around for wild ginseng, though beware of North Korean border guards. **See p.179**

❺ Winter ice festivals Most Manchurian metropolises have one, but Harbin's is the biggest and best, with illuminated ice sculptures that tower higher by the year. **See p.184**

❻ Russian architecture, Harbin Harbin's a great summertime destination, too, with local beer guzzled by the truckload around the city's beautiful Russian buildings. **See p.184**

HIGHLIGHTS ARE MARKED ON THE MAP ON P.160

The Qing dynasty

In 1644, the **Qing dynasty** was proclaimed, and one of Nurhaci's grandsons, **Shunzhi**, became the first of a long line of Manchu emperors, with his uncle Dorgun as regent. Keen to establish the Qing over the whole of China, the first **Manchu emperors** – Shunzhi, Kangxi and Qianlong – did their best to assimilate Chinese customs and ideas. They were, however, even more determined to protect their homeland, and so the whole of the northeast was closed to the rest of China. This way they could guard their monopoly on the valuable **ginseng trade** and keep the agricultural Han Chinese

DONGBEI

0 — 300
kilometres

High Speed Rail line

HIGHLIGHTS

1. The Imperial Palace, Shenyang
2. Old Yalu Bridge, Dandong
3. Puppet Emperor's Palace, Changchun
4. Changbai Shan
5. Winter ice festivals
6. Russian architecture, Harbin

from ploughing up their land, a practice that often resulted in the desecration of the graves of the Manchus' ancestors. But isolationism was a policy that could not last forever, and the eighteenth century saw increasing migration into Manchuria. By 1878, these laws had been rescinded, and the Chinese were moving into the region by the million, escaping the flood-ravaged plains of the south for the fertile northeast.

Foreign occupation

All this time, Manchuria was much coveted by its neighbours. The **Sino-Japanese War** of 1894 left the Japanese occupying the Liaodong Peninsula in the south of Liaoning province; alarmed by Japan's victory and the quantity of Chinese territory it had taken, European nations forced the Japanese to hand Liaodong back to China. China then turned to **Russia**, also hungry for influence in the area. The deal was that the Russians be allowed to build a **rail line** linking Vladivostok to the main body of Russia, an arrangement that in fact led to a gradual and, eventually, complete occupation of Manchuria by the imperial Russian armies. This was a bloody affair, marked by atrocities and brutal reprisals, and was followed in 1904 by a Japanese declaration of war in an attempt to usurp the Russians' privileges for themselves.

Manchukuo

The **Russo-Japanese War** concluded in 1905 with a convincing Japanese victory, though Japan's designs on Manchuria didn't end there. Japan's population doubled between 1872 and 1925, creating the perceived need to expand its territories; this, coupled with a disastrous economic situation at home and an extreme militaristic regime, led to their invasion of the region in 1932, establishing the puppet state of **Manchukuo**. This regime was characterized by horrific and violent oppression – not least the secret germ-warfare research centre in **Pingfang**, where experiments were conducted on live human subjects.

DONGBEI'S MINORITY COMMUNITIES

After forcing **minority communities** to embrace official communist culture during the 1950s and 60s, the Chinese government now takes a more enlightened – if somewhat patronizing – approach to the nations of the north. The **Manchu** people, spread across Inner Mongolia and Dongbei, are the most numerous and assimilated. Having lived so long among the Han, they are now almost identical, though Manchus tend to be slightly taller, and Manchu men have more facial hair. Manchus are noted for an elaborate system of etiquette and will never eat dog, unlike their Korean neighbours, who love it. The "three strange things" that the southern Chinese say are found in the northeast are all Manchu idiosyncrasies: paper windows pasted outside their wooden frame, babies carried by their mothers in handbags and women smoking in public (the latter, of course, can be a habit of Han and every other ethnicity in large cities).

In the inhospitable northern margins of Dongbei live communities such as the **Hezhen**, one of the smallest minority nations in China with an estimated 1400 members. Inhabiting the region where the Songhua, Heilong and Wusuli (Ussuri) rivers converge, they're known to the Han Chinese as the "Fish Tribe", and their culture and livelihood centre around fishing. Indeed, they're the only people in the world to make clothes out of fish skin: the fish is gutted, descaled, then dried and tanned and the skins sewn together to make light, waterproof coats, shoes and gloves. More numerous are the **Daur**, 120,000 of whom live along the Nenjiang River. They are fairly seamlessly assimilated these days, but still retain distinctive marriage and funerary traditions, and have a reputation for being superb at hockey, a form of which they have played since the sixth century.

However, perhaps the most distinctive minority are the **Oroqen**, a tribe of nomadic hunters living in patrilineal clan communes called *wulileng* in the northern sub-Siberian wilderness. Although they have recently adopted a more settled existence, their main livelihood still comes from deer-hunting, while household items, tools and canoes are made from birch bark by Oroqen women. Clothes are fashioned from deer hide, and include a striking hat made of a roe deer head, complete with antlers and leather patches for eyes, which is used as a disguise in hunting.

Rice was reserved for the Japanese, and it was a crime for the locals to eat it. Japan's defeat at the end of World War II finally drew a line under all of this, although it was some time (and in spite of a vicious campaign backed by both Russia and the USA against the Communists) before Mao finally took full control of the northeast.

Recent history

Relations with Russia dominate recent history. In the brief romance between the two countries in the 1950s, Soviet experts helped the Chinese build efficient, well-designed factories and workshops in exchange for the region's agricultural products. These factories laid the foundation for China's automobile industry: the **First Automobile Works** (FAW) in Changchun, for example, began production then, and now has a joint venture with VW and Audi. In the 1960s, relations worsened, the Soviets withdrew their technical support and bitter **border disputes** erupted, notably around the Wusuli (Ussuri) River, where hundreds of Russian and Chinese troops died fighting over an insignificant island in the world's first military confrontation between communist states. An extensive network of nuclear shelters was constructed in northeastern cities. Following the collapse of the Soviet Union, military build-ups around the border areas and state paranoia have lessened, and the shelters have been turned into underground shopping malls. Russian faces can again be seen on the streets, often **traders** buying up consumer goods to take over the border.

INFORMATION

Transport Thanks to Dongbei's export-based economy, there's an efficient rail system between the cities – high-speed trains fire between Dalian and Harbin – as well as an extensive highway network.

Food The region's food is heavily influenced by neighbouring countries, and every town has a cluster of Korean, Japanese and, up north, Russian restaurants. The specialities are also quite diverse, ranging from fresh crabs in Dalian and *luzi yu* river fish in Dandong, to silkworms in the countryside (a mushy, pasty-tasting local delicacy).

Climate Dongbei's climate is one of extremes: in summer, it is hot, and in winter it is very, very cold, with temperatures as low as −30°C combining with howling gales. But there is skiing, sledding and skating all winter, plus January ice festivals in Jilin and Harbin.

Liaoning

辽宁, liáoníng

Of the Dongbei provinces, **LIAONING** has the most to see; there's also a pleasing amount of variety to proceedings. The thriving port of **Dalian** sports cleaned-up beaches, a cliffside drive, and restored Russian and Japanese neighbourhoods. Whoosh north by high-speed train and you'll soon arrive in Liaoning's capital, **Shenyang**, home to China's second Forbidden City – the restored **Manchu Imperial Palace** – and the tombs of the men who established the Qing dynasty. Head southeast and you'll eventually hit **Dandong**, the country's window on North Korea, which features a promenade on the Yalu River and a fascinating Korean War museum.

Shenyang

沈阳, shěnyáng

Capital of Liaoning province and unofficial capital of the northeast, **SHENYANG** is a railway junction and banking centre that has served as host to the Manchus, Russians, Japanese, Nationalists and then Communists. The city draws domestic tourists from all over the north-east of China, and their primary focus is all too obvious: as any cabbie here will delight in telling you, Shenyang has the only other **Imperial Palace** in China. Constructed by Manchus before their takeover of the Ming dynasty, many visitors find it far more user-friendly than its (much larger) counterpart in Beijing.

SHENYANG

Beiling Park

North Tomb

Xinyueyizhi (M)

CITS

N

BEILINGJIE

TAISHAN LU (M) Beilinggongyuan

HUANGHE JIE

(M) CHONGSHAN LU
Chongshan Lu

North Pagoda

WANGHUA JIE

September 18 History Museum

Qishan Lu

North Station Shenyangzhan
(M)

BEIZHAN LU

Long-distance Bus Station

3

Botanical Garden & East Tomb

Huigongguangchang
(M)

Liaoning Provincial Museum

Zhongjiedang
(M)

KOREA TOWN

TAIYUAN JIE SHOPPING STREET

SHIFU DA LU

Bank of China

JIAOXI LU

(M)

(M) Zhong Jie Imperial Palace

Mao Statue

PSB

Yunfeng Beijie
(M)

ZHONGSHAN LU

ZHONGSHAN SQUARE

(M) Shifuguangchang

Train Ticket Booking Office

Huaiyuanmen (M)

DAXI LU

CHAOYANG JIE

Nanyun River

South Station

Shenyang Station

ZHONGSHAN LU

Taiyuan Jie
(M)

(M) Manshichang

Qingnian Dajie
(M)

Airlines Office

Russian Consulate

Airport Bus

SHISIWEI LU

Japanese Consulate

SHISIWEI LU

US Consulate

Qingnian Park
(M)

QINGNIAN DAJIE

SHENGLIJIE

MINZU LU

HEPINGJIE

NANJING JIE

NANWU LU

Liaoning Industrial Exhibition Centre
(M)

0 _____ 1
kilometre

▼ Airport

■ **ACCOMMODATION**

7 Days Inn	2/3
Holiday Inn	5
Liaoning	4
Peace	1
Traders	6

● **SHOP**

Zhong Jie Shopping Street	1

● **EATING & DRINKING**

Korean Town	1
Laobian Jiaozi Guan	3
Pyongyang Mujigae	2
Shiyiwei Lu	5
Stroller's Bar	7
World and View Vegetarian	6
Yoshinoya	4

Though you're unlikely to need more than a couple of days in Shenyang, there are **other notable sights** dotted around this fast-moving city, including a stunning monument to Chairman Mao built during the frenzied height of the Cultural Revolution; the tombs of two former emperors; and architecture left over from Japan's occupation, including a real gem of a hotel. You'll have to time it right to enjoy another amusement: from December to February, the town hosts the **Shenyang International Ice and Snow Festival** – held at Qipanshan, 17km northeast of town, it's lower-key than Harbin's festivities (see p.184), but increasingly popular.

Brief history

Though well known in China as an important power base for the more radical hardline factions in Chinese politics (Mao's nephew, Yuanxin, was deputy Party secretary here until he was thrown in jail in 1976), Shenyang had its real heyday in the early seventeenth century. Nurhaci declared the city (then known as Mukden) the first capital of the expanding Manchu empire. He died in 1626, as work on his palace was just beginning, and was succeeded by his eighth son, **Abahai**, who consolidated and extended Manchu influence across northern China. When the Manchus, having defeated the resident Ming, moved to Beijing in 1644 and established the Qing dynasty, Shenyang declined steadily in importance. The city began to take on its modern, industrial role with the arrival of the Russians in the nineteenth century, who made it the centre of their rail-building programme. Years later, the puppets of the Japanese state also set up shop here, exploiting the resources of the surrounding region and building an industrial infrastructure whose profits and products were sent home to Japan.

Zhongshan Square

中山广场, zhōngshān guǎngchǎng

Shenyang has some great examples of uncompromising Soviet-style constructions, the most eye-catching of which is the giant **Mao statue** in **Zhongshan Square**. Erected in 1969 at the height of the Cultural Revolution, it comprises a pastiche of Communist iconography, its base lined with strident, blocky peasants, Daqing oilmen, PLA soldiers and students (though the Little Red Books the latter were waving have mostly been chipped off). Above them, the monolithic Mao stands wrapped in an overcoat, a bald superman whose raised hand makes him look as if he's directing traffic.

The Imperial Palace

沈阳故宫, shěnyáng gùgōng • Daily April–Oct 8.30am–5.30pm, Nov–March 8.30am–4.30pm • ¥50 • metro to Huaiyuanmen

Begun in 1626, this wonderful complex is essentially a vastly scaled-down replica of Beijing's Forbidden City. Entering from the south, you'll first come across the **Cong Zhen Dian**, a low, wooden-fronted hall where the Qing dynasty was proclaimed and which was used by ministers to discuss state affairs. Beyond here, in the second courtyard, stands the Phoenix Tower, most formal of the ceremonial halls, and the Qingning building, which housed bedrooms for the emperor and his concubines.

Da Zheng Dian

In the eastern section of the complex, the **Da Zheng Dian** is a squat, octagonal, wooden structure in vivid red and lacquered gold, with two pillars cut with writhing golden dragons in high relief. Here, the emperor Shunzhi was crowned before seizing Beijing – and the empire – in 1644. Colourful, dynastic-style performances take place just outside on the hour.

Shi Wang Ting

Just in front of the Da Zheng Dian stand the **Shi Wang Ting**, ten square pavilions once used as offices by the chieftains of the Eight Banners (military divisions) of the Empire, and now housing a collection of bizarrely shaped swords and pikes. Take time to wander away from the groups amid the side palaces, and note the Manchu dragons in bas-relief, unique to this palace.

Liaoning Provincial Museum

辽宁省博物馆, liáoníngshěng bówùguǎn • Tues–Sun 9am–5pm • Free (bring ID) • metro to Shifuguangchang

The **Liaoning Provincial Museum**, in the heart of the downtown, is one of the largest museums in the northeast. Though there's little information in English, it's certainly worth popping along for a look at the well-arranged exhibits, which include paintings, copperware, pottery and porcelain. Perhaps most interesting are the fragments of oracle bones used for divination, featuring some of the earliest examples of written Chinese.

North Tomb

北陵, běi líng • Daily 7am–5pm • park entry ¥6 • park plus tomb ¥50 • metro to Beilinggongyuan for south entrance, or Lingxi for west entrance

Located inside spacious **Beiling Park** (北陵公园, běilíng gōngyuán) – itself a fun place where families pedal boats around its various lakes in summer, and build snow sculptures or ice-skate in winter – the **North Tomb** is that of **Abahai** (1592–1643), founder of the Qing dynasty. The well-preserved complex, constructed in 1643, is entered through a gate to the south, either side of which are pavilions; the easternmost was for visiting emperors to wash and refresh themselves, the westernmost for sacrifices of pigs and sheep. A "spirit way" flanked with animal statues leads to the **Long En Hall**, which contains an altar for offerings and the spirit tablets of the emperor and his wife. Their tree-covered burial mounds are at the rear, where you'll also find a fine dragon screen.

September 18 History Museum

九一八历史博物馆, jiǔyībā lìshǐ bówùguǎn • 46 Wanghua Nanjie • Daily 9am–4.30pm • Free • bus #213 from the North Tomb

A short walk northeast of the North pagoda you'll find this huge concrete edifice, whose collection focuses on Japan's invasion of Shenyang in 1931; the story is told via a predictable array of black-and-white photos, maps and rusty weapons. It's a "patriotic education base", so the tone of the Chinese-only captions is easy to guess.

East Tomb

东陵, dōng líng • Daily 7am–6pm • park entry ¥6 • park plus tomb ¥50 • bus #168 or #218 from a stop one block north and one block east of the Imperial Palace

Built in 1629 as the last resting place of Nurhaci, the **East Tomb** is set among conifers next to **Dongling Park** (东陵公园, dōnglíng gōngyuán) in the east of the city. The tomb is less monumental in layout than Abahai's (see opposite) and shows more signs of age, but it's still an impressive structure, with fortified walls and a three-storey tower. One hundred and eight steps (the number of beads on a Buddhist rosary) lead into the main gate, while all around the tomb are walking trails into the woods covering Mount Tianzhu – a hill, really.

Shenyang Botanical Garden

沈阳世博园, shěnyáng shìbó yuán • Daily 9am–4pm • ¥50 • bus #168 from a stop one block north and one block east of the Imperial Palace

A half-hour bus ride outside town, **Shenyang Botanical Garden** is a vast area featuring formal gardens from all over China and the world. Some of the attempts at foreign gardens may be a little wide of the mark, but it makes for a great escape from the dust of the city.

ARRIVAL AND DEPARTURE
SHENYANG

By plane Shenyang Taoxian International Airport (沈阳桃仙国际机场, shěnyáng táoxiān guójì jīchǎng), 20km south of the city, is the busiest in the northeast; aside from a great number of domestic destinations, there are also flights to Thailand, Japan, Germany, Singapore, Canada, and both Koreas. Getting into town is as easy as boarding an airport bus (¥15); taxis will start the bidding at ¥150, though you can haggle this down. Heading to the airport, the bus stop is opposite the *Dunkin Donuts* off Zhonghua Lu; a taxi is cheaper in this direction as they'll agree to use the meter (¥90), while a seat in a shared cab costs ¥25 per person.

Destinations Beijing (7 daily; 1hr 15min); Chengdu (2 daily; 4hr 30min); Chongqing (3 daily; 3hr 15min); Dalian (1 daily; 50min); Fuzhou (1 daily; 2hr 50min); Guangzhou (3 daily; 3hr 45min); Guiyang (1 daily; 4hr 40min); Hangzhou (1 daily; 2hr 20min); Harbin (2 daily; 1hr); Hohhot (3 weekly; 1hr 30min); Hong Kong (1 daily; 4hr 35min); Ji'nan (4 daily; 1hr 20min); Kunming (2 daily; 5hr 10min); Lanzhou (1 daily; 3hr 10min); Nanjing (1 daily; 1hr 50min); Qingdao (2 daily; 1hr 10min); Shanghai (8 daily; 2hr); Shenzhen (4 daily; 4hr); Wuhan (1 daily; 3hr 25min); Xi'an (1 daily; 2hr 30min); Yanji (2 daily; 1hr 10min); Zhengzhou (1 daily; 2hr).

By train South train station (南站, nánzhàn) and North train station (北站, běizhàn) both handle similar services, including high-speed ones, but note when booking tickets that each train almost always stops at just the one station. Most Beijing services use the North station, though the area around the South station is a far nicer place to stay. You can buy tickets at either station, or from any number of ticket offices around town; ask at your accommodation for the one closest to you. Handily, both stations are on the new metro network.

Destinations Beijing (many daily; 4hr 40min–17hr); Changchun (many daily; 1hr 10min–4hr); Dalian (many daily; 2–6hr); Dandong (16 daily; 3hr 40min–6hr); Harbin (many daily; 2hr 20min–7hr); Jilin (21 daily; 2–9hr); Tonghua (8 daily; 6hr 30min–9hr).

By bus The gleaming, futuristic long-distance bus station (快速客运站, kuàisù kèyùnzhàn) is near the North station, though little used by foreigners since Shenyang is so well connected by train. To get to the centre from here, catch one of the many minibuses plying the route, or take a taxi (¥10).

Destinations Beijing (7–8hr); Changchun (3hr); Dalian (5hr); Harbin (6hr); Jilin (4hr).

3

GETTING AROUND

By taxi Cabs are widely available and start at ¥8 for 3km; a taxi to or between most of the sights is around ¥25, though getting to the East Tomb from the South station costs over ¥60.

By bus The extensive local bus system (tickets ¥1) is not too crowded; bus maps can be bought outside all stations for about ¥5.

Metro Shenyang's new metro system consists of two lines: one north–south, and one east–west. It's handy for getting across town from either of the train stations, and with stops just a short walk from the Imperial Palace, Beiling Park and some other sights. Tickets cost ¥2–4, depending upon the number of stations travelled, and run 5am–11pm.

ACCOMMODATION

7 Days Inn 7天连锁酒店, 7 tiān liánsuǒ jiǔdiàn. 3 Tongze Beijie ☎024 62661777, ⓦ7daysinn.cn. Forget what it looks like from the outside (awful), the rooms here are just fine for budget travellers; they all have showers with 24hr hot water, free wi-fi, small TVs and comfortable beds. It's a short walk from the South station. **¥167**

Holiday Inn 假日饭店, jiàrì fàndiàn. 204 Nanjing Beilu ☎024 23341888, ⓦholiday-inn.com. Modern high-rise in the heart of town, with health club and Irish bar; the entrance is just off Nanjing Lu. It's a popular place, and you're advised to book ahead in season; conversely, rates may be slashed in winter. **¥580**

★ **Liaoning** 辽宁宾馆, liáoníng bīnguǎn. 97 Zhongshan Lu ☎024 23839104. This historic lodging, constructed by the Japanese in 1927, overlooks the Chairman Mao statue on Zhongshan Square. Rooms are spacious and light. Stop over if only for a look at how things were eighty years ago – the fittings and furnishings are remarkably well preserved. **¥388**

Peace 和平宾馆, hépíng bīnguǎn. 104 Shengli Beijie ☎024 23498888. Conveniently near the South train station. Recently renovated rooms are smart, and staff friendly. Its travel service can organize train and plane tickets. You'll pay more if you want a private bathroom. **¥100**

Traders 商贸饭店, shāngmào fàndiàn. 68 Zhonghua Lu ☎024 23412288, ⓦshangri-la.com. The most luxurious place to stay in Shenyang, as befitting its *Shangri-La* connections, and priced to match. The opulence of the lobby is matched by that of the rooms, and the professionalism of the largely English-speaking staff. **¥750**

EATING AND DRINKING

★ **Laobian Jiaozi Guan** 老边饺子馆, lǎobiān jiǎoziguǎn. 6 Zhong Jie ☎024 24315666. Shenyang's most famous restaurant is a super-busy dumpling house on the city's main shopping drag – any local will be able to point you here. The food is utterly superb for the price: rounds of dumplings go from ¥18, with intriguing fillings including curry beef, "mandarin duck", and edible flowers. Then there's the non-dumpling selection; try spicy battered shrimp (¥55), goose stewed in beer (¥68), or even some donkey meat. Daily 10am–9.30pm.

Pyongyang Mujigae 平阳彩虹, píngyáng cǎihóng. South end of Xita Jie. The giant flag on the front gives the game away: this is a North Korean restaurant. Staff are no refugees; they're here with the blessing of the government in Pyongyang. Pop by at 7pm and you'll be treated to a surreal performance of North Korean music. The food's good too; try the cold *naengmyeon* noodles (¥25). Daily 10am–1pm.

Stroller's Bar 流浪者酒吧, liúlàngzhě jiǔbā. 36 Bei Wujing Jie, near the junction with Shiyi Weilu ☎024 22876677. The top pub in town, with a vast range of beers: eleven German and seventeen Belgian ones at the last count, as well as draught Guinness (¥60). The food's great too, with goulash, lasagne, moussaka and other dishes costing ¥60–80. Daily 10am–2am.

World and View Vegetarian 宽巷子素菜馆, kuānxiàngzi sùcàiguǎn. On the north side of Shiyi Weilu near the junction with Bei Yijing Jie ☎024 22848678. This curiously titled place is where to go if meat is off your menu; as with most such places, they try as hard as they can to show vegetarians what they're missing, with fake-meat dishes such as sausage and Peking duck. Dishes range around the ¥25 mark. Daily 10am–10pm.

Yoshinoya 吉野家, jíyějiā. Shengli Nanjie, opposite the South station. For a quick feed before or after your train ride, try this branch of Japan's favourite fast-food chain, which sells bowlfuls of beef on rice (牛肉饭, niúròu fàn) for under ¥20. Daily 8am–10pm.

DIRECTORY

Airline 117 Zhonghua Lu (daily 8am–6pm; ☎024 8939 2520). Plane tickets can also be bought from hotels or from CITS.

Banks and exchange Bank of China. 253 Shifu Da Lu (Mon–Fri 8.30am–5pm, Sat & Sun 9am–4pm).

Consulate Russia 31, Shisiwei Lu, in the south of the city (Mon–Fri 9am–noon; ☎024 23223927). Note that reports on the availability of Russian visas here aren't encouraging; it's better to apply in Beijing.

Mail and telephones Shenyang's main post office is at 32 Zhongshan Lu (Mon–Fri 8am–6pm).

PSB On Zhongshan Lu, by the Mao statue (Mon–Fri 8am–5pm; ☎ 024 86898711).

Travel agents The CITS has offices at 113 Nan Huanghe Dajie (☎ 024 86131251) and Shifu Dalu (☎ 024 85850808), at the junction with Xishuncheng Jie, next to the *Tesco* supermarket.

Dalian

大连, dàlián

Few Western tourists make it to **DALIAN**, a modern, sprawling city on the Yellow Sea. This is a pity, since it's an extremely agreeable place with swaths of colonial architecture, proximity to some good beaches, and some excellent seafood. It's also one of China's most cosmopolitan cities, partly because it has changed hands so often – in the years around the turn of the twentieth century, it found itself under Japanese, then Russian, then Japanese, then Soviet occupation.

The "foreign devils" are still here, though they're now invited: Dalian has been designated a Special Economic Zone, one of China's "open-door" cities, with regulations designed to attract overseas investment. Unlike most Chinese metropolises, the city boasts green spaces and an excellent traffic control system, both the handiwork of the high-flying former mayor turned national commerce minister and Politburo member Bo Xilai. Despite his leaving the city in 2003, locals still seem to admire him as much as they do the city's football team, the most successful in Chinese league history; they also contributed six players to the country's 2002 World Cup squad (the first, and so far only, time the national team qualified).

Brief history

As the only ice-free port in the region, Dalian was eagerly sought by the foreign powers that held sway over China in the nineteenth century. The Japanese took the city in 1895 yet soon ceded it back to China, who then allowed the Russians to build a rail line here – Moscow saw Dalian as an alternative to ice-bound Vladivostok. In 1905, after decisively

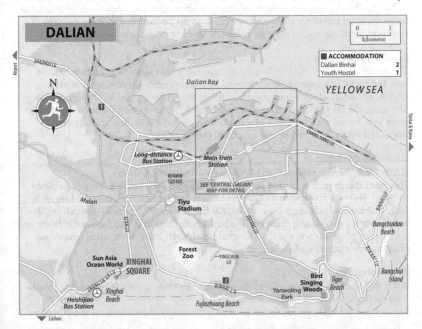

> ### DALIAN ORIENTATION
>
> Dalian sits at the southern tip of the Liaodong Peninsula, filling a piece of land that's shaped like a tiger's head – the result, local legend has it, of a mermaid flattening the animal into land as punishment for eating the fiancé of a beautiful girl. The city's hub is **Zhongshan Square** (中山广场, zhōngshān guǎngchǎng), really a circle, whose spokes are some of the most interesting streets in the city. Japanese and Russian buildings, *KFC* and *McDonald's*, girls in miniskirts and Western dance music blaring from the shops give the area an international flavour. To the west is **Renmin Square** (人民广场, rénmín guǎngchǎng), large, grassy and lit with footlights at night; the neighbourhoods to the south of the square retain their Russian colonial architecture, and their narrow, tree-lined streets make for excellent wandering.

defeating the Russian navy, the Japanese wrested it back and remained in control for long enough to complete the construction of the port facilities and city grid – still visible in the many traffic circles and axial roads. After World War II, the Soviet Union occupied the city for ten years, finally withdrawing when Sino–Soviet relations improved.

The Russian quarter
老俄罗斯风景区, lǎoéluósī fēngjǐngqū

Just over 1km northwest of Zhongshan Square is the old **Russian quarter**. This neighbourhood used to house Russian gentry, though today each peeling mansion is home to several families. The pedestrianized main street takes you past restored pistachio-coloured facades and street vendors selling Russian cigarettes, lighters, vodka and Soviet pins. Easy on the eye, and surprisingly calm, it's one of the most appealing parts of the city to base yourself in (see p.171).

The Japanese quarter

South of the train station is the former Japanese quarter, its hub (both then and now) the Japanese-designed **Laodong Park** (劳动公园, láodòng gōngyuán). A hilly zone with some great walking trails, it's a nice escape from urbanity. **Nanshan** (南山, nánshān), the neighbourhood across the street east of the park, was once home to the Japanese community; now, the cream-coloured, red-roofed villas are being renovated by nouveau riche Chinese.

South of the centre

The coastline south of the city is quite spectacular, with a series of good **beaches**, all free, and rocky outcrops; these are hugged by Dalian's most scenic road, **Binhai Lu** (滨海路, bīnhǎi lù), which winds past the villas of Party bigwigs and local sports stars. The turquoise sea stretches before you to the south, while the north side of the road is green year-round with trees and new grass. Attractions here include the city **zoo**, a wonderful **aviary**, and two hugely expensive **theme parks**.

Sun Asia Ocean World
圣亚海洋世界, shèngyà hǎiyán shìjiè • Daily 9am–5pm • ¥180 • taxi from the city ¥20–30

This giant theme park is located just off **Xinghai Beach** (星海公园浴场, xīnghǎi gōngyuán yùchǎng). Its main feature is a 118m-long underwater tunnel, reputedly the longest in Asia, which affords close-up views of 10,000 fish of over 200 species – though you'd have a tough job counting them all. The park's polar section is also fun, and is home to polar bears, penguins and the like. Xinghai Beach itself features the usual fairground rides, souvenir stands and restaurants.

Dalian Forest Zoo
森林动物园, sēnlín dōngwùyuán • Daily 8.30am–5pm, panda pavilion 8.30am–4pm • ¥120, children under 1.3m free • cable car ¥50 • taxi from the centre ¥20–30 • bus #801 from Zhongshan Square

The city zoo is hugely popular with local kids. Naturally, the stars of the show here are

CENTRAL DALIAN

■ ACCOMMODATION
Crystal Orange	4
Dalian Binguan	5
Dalian Binhai	8
Furama	3
Home Inn	2
Jinjiang Inn	1
Ramada	6
Tiantian Youth Hostel	7

● EATING & DRINKING
Niu Zhong Niu	2
Noah's Ark	4
Paris Baguette	3
Tiantian Yugang Jiulou	1
Tianyuan Vegetarian	5

the pandas, with both giant and smaller red varieties represented; there's also a caged "safari" area, a reptile pavilion, and an area for parrot performances. Opposite the entrance is a cable-car station, allowing an easy ascent of the small neighbouring peak; there are superlative views of city and sea from the top.

Fujiazhuang Beach

傅家庄公园浴场, fùjiāzhuāng gōngyuán yùchǎng • Daily dawn–dusk • bus • #5 from Jiefang Lu
Sheltered from the wind in a rocky bay, this is less developed than most beaches in the area, and a great place for seafood. There are a number of small islands offshore; a chartered speedboat from the seafront west to Xinghai Beach costs around ¥100, depending on your bargaining skills.

Yanwoling Park

燕窝岭公园, yànwōlǐng gōngyuán • Daily dawn–dusk • ¥10 • hourly tourist buses from Tiger Beach or the zoo
The entrance to this park is marked by a statue – made from shells – of a little boy with seagulls. From here, a profusion of maintained trails and stairs takes you down precipitous slopes to the sea. One particularly nice hike, signed in English, ends up at Sunken Boat Rock, a cove where starfish cling to rocks and the only sounds are those of the waves. Strong currents make swimming here dangerous, however.

Bird Singing Woods

鸟语林, niǎoyǔ lín • Daily 7.30am–5pm • ¥40 • hourly tourist buses from Tiger Beach or the zoo • bird show 1.30am, 1.30pm & 2.40pm • parrot performance 10am, 11.30am, 1pm, 2.10pm, 3.20pm & 4.30pm

Just south of Tiger Beach, this is one of the most enjoyable sights in Dalian, and far better value than the zoo. Few of the birds actually sing – the ostriches and crested cranes near the entrance merely race over to stare at you, while the fowl in the hilly area beyond cluck and squawk to get at your food, available in ¥5 packs. The same price will buy some fish for the highly comical spoonbills, though seagulls will try to snatch it away first. The shows are surprisingly entertaining; peacocks fly (or rather fall) in from the upper reaches of the park, pelicans save football penalties, and parrots perform their usual tricks.

Tiger Beach

老虎滩, lǎohǔ tān • Ocean Park daily 7.30am–5.30pm, ¥210 • boat 104 daily 8.30am–4pm, ¥20 • bus #2, #4, #30, #402 or #801

At Tiger Beach, the funfair of **Laohutan Ocean Park** seems to cover the entire bay area. A mind-boggling array of combination tickets covers attractions inside the park, such as the dolphin show and coral hall. Near the entrance, you'll find a quirky sight – **Boat 104**, a warship whose various nooks and crannies are a delight to explore. Amazingly, it used to function as a youth hostel – the familiar triangular hostelling logo is still in place.

ARRIVAL AND DEPARTURE | DALIAN

By plane Dalian Zhoushuizi airport (大连周水子国际机场, dàlián zhōushuǐzǐ guójì jīchǎng) is 12km northwest of the city; there are services to most major cities in China, as well as flights to Japan, Russia, Singapore and both Koreas. A taxi should cost ¥20–35; there's a regular airport bus (¥5) to and from Shengli Square; and city buses #701 and #710 (¥1) head to the train station and Zhongshan Square respectively.

Destinations Beijing (12 daily; 1hr 10min); Changchun (3 daily; 1hr); Chengdu (2 daily; 3hr 40min); Guangzhou (3 daily; 3hr 15min); Guilin (2 weekly; 4hr 25min); Hangzhou (2 daily; 2hr); Harbin (3 daily; 1hr 25min); Hong Kong (1 daily; 3hr 25min); Ji'nan (2 daily; 1hr); Kunming (1 daily; 5hr); Qingdao (5 daily; 40min); Shanghai (7 daily; 1hr 30min); Shenyang (1 daily; 50min); Xi'an (1 daily; 2hr 20min); Yantai (1 daily; 35min).

By train The main train station (大連站, dàlián zhàn) is an easy walk from Zhongshan Square, just 1km to the east. Tickets are easy enough to buy here (though there'll be a queue), or at a number of ticket offices around town. Dalian North station (大連北站, dàlián běizhàn),

located 20km to the north (on the subway line), is worth heading to if you need a high-speed service to Harbin; Harbin trains from the main station are super-slow only.

Destinations Beijing (5 daily; 7hr 30min–12hr); Dandong (1 daily; 10hr); Harbin (hourly; 4–13hr); Shenyang (many daily; 1hr 45min–6hr).

By bus It's hard to know which bus station you'll pitch up at in this vast, sprawling city, though many services arrive around the main train station. With high-speed trains to all major cities in Dongbei, and decent sleepers to Beijing, the only long-distance buses really worth bothering with are those to and from Dandong (7 daily; 4hr), which are much faster than the daily train; they leave from the plaza south of the train station.

By ferry Dalian's passenger-ferry terminal is 1km northeast of Zhongshan Square. Ferries to Yantai are a full day faster than the train, and cheaper (at least 2 daily; 6hr 30min; from ¥185). Tickets can be bought in advance from the passenger-ferry terminal, or from one of the many windows both at and around the train station. A twice-weekly service also runs to Incheon in South Korea (18hr; ¥920–1848).

GETTING AROUND

By bus Tourist buses (hourly; ¥10) from the train station circle the entire town, serving all sights and beaches to the south. You can hop on and off with your ticket, though hard-sell conductors will do their best to make you buy theme-park tickets too. Buses for specific sights are given in the main text.

By taxi As the city centre is compact, the minimum ¥8 fare will get you to most places. A taxi from the city centre to beaches is around ¥40.

By tram Line #202 (¥1) runs north–southwest roughly

along Zhongshan Lu, beginning in the shopping area around the north end of Xi'an Lu, a couple of kilometres west of the train station, before passing Xinghai Square and terminating at Heishijiao.

By metro An elevated line runs from the main station to northern parts of town (¥1–2), though it's of precious little use to tourists.

By bicycle Tandem and mountain bikes are available to rent at the beaches for ¥20/hr.

ACCOMMODATION

Dalian is choked with five-star hotels – *Holiday Inn*, *Ramada*, *Swissotel*, *Kempinski* and *Shangri-La* can all be found here – but budget options open to foreigners are scarce. The good news is that, as in many beach towns, off-season rates are usually half those of summers.

★ **Crystal Orange** 桔子水晶酒店, júzi shuǐjīng jiǔdiàn. 235 Huabei Lu ☎0411 84442458. Fantastic new boutique-style hotel, a short walk from the old Russian quarter. Rooms are phenomenal value, with a black-white-silver colour scheme, electronically powered Venetian blinds, iPhone speaker units, and Rubik cubes to play with. ¥368

Dalian Binguan 大连宾馆, dàlián bīnguǎn. 4 Zhongshan Square ☎0411 82633111, ⍟dl-hotel.com. A stylish old place, built by the Japanese in 1927. Bar occasionally indifferent service, it's a decent hotel, with an excellent sushi restaurant on the ground floor. ¥498

Dalian Binhai 大连滨海大厦酒店, dàlián bīnhǎi dàshà jiǔdiàn. 2 Binhai Lu ☎0411 82406666. The setting, overlooking Fujiazhuang Beach, is the main selling point for this two-star affair; it's overpriced, but the views just about balance things out. ¥450

Furama 富丽华大酒店, fùlìhuá dàjiǔdiàn. 60 Renmin Lu ☎0411 82630888, ⍟furama.com.cn. A very upscale Japanese venture whose gargantuan lobby is a luxury mall of sorts, the *Furuma* has every imaginable facility and palatial rooms. ¥780

Home Inn 如家酒店, rújiā jiǔdiàn. 92 Renmin Lu ☎0411 39858588, ⍟homeinns.com. Budget chain offering tidy, moderately priced rooms near the centre. It's also within easy walking distance of the ferry terminal – great if you've just stepped off the overnight ferry from Korea. ¥167

Jinjiang Inn 锦江之星, jǐnjiāng zhīxīng. 20 Laoleluosi Jie ☎0411 88105588. The pan-China budget chain has opened a branch in the old Russian quarter. This colonial-era structure is beautiful from the outside (local tourists stop just to take pictures of it), and the minimalist rooms aren't bad either. ¥219

Ramada 九洲华美达酒店, jiǔzhōu huáměidá jiǔdiàn. 18 Shengli Square ☎0411 82808888, ⍟ramada.com. Four-star luxury in the heart of town next to the train station, overlooking Shengli Square. ¥730

Tiantian Youth Hostel 天天国际青年旅馆, tiāntiān guójì qīngnián lǚguǎn. 235 Huabei Lu ☎0411 84442458. Great hostel in a gritty, slightly inconvenient area west of the train station. They've a pool table, cute pups to play with, and a decent little café-bar; rooms are comfy and pleasantly decorated. Dorms ¥60, rooms ¥220

EATING AND DRINKING

Dalian is full of restaurants, especially around Shengli Square, and just south and west of here on the pedestrian streets bordered by Qing Er Jie and Jiefang Lu. For simple, affordable fare, head south from Zhongshan Square toward the University of Foreign Languages: Yan'an Lu is lined with restaurants. There's a stretch of Korean barbecue joints along Gao Er Ji Lu, a block south of Renmin Square; simply follow the smoke and bustle, and the touts out front will wave you in. Dalian has lots of bars; the side-streets around Changjiang Lu are your best bet, though there are some good *izakaya* (Japanese-style bars, also serving food) tucked in behind *Niu Zhong Niu* restaurant.

★ **Niu Zhong Niu** 牛中牛, niúzhōngniú. Just off Renmin Lu ☎0411 82651006. This fancy-looking venue is a great place in which to try Korean food; barbecue some beef (from ¥30 per portion), go for a *bibimbap* (veggies on rice in a sizzling-hot bowl; ¥20), or try some cold *naengmyeon* noodles (¥16). They also serve good Japanese-style sashimi. Daily 11am–11pm.

Noah's Ark 诺亚方舟酒吧, nuòyà fāngzhōu jiǔbā. 32 Wusi Lu ☎0411 88993500. Across the street from Renmin Square (look for the wooden wagon out front), this is a long-standing favourite for live music, with a good local-expat mix and a mix of indoor and outdoor seating. Daily 1pm–2am.

Paris Baguette 比萨王, bǐsà wáng. Changjiang Lu. Korea has exported this bakery chain to China; a mix of baked treats (from ¥6) and drinkable coffee makes this a good bet for breakfast. Daily 8am–10pm.

★ **Tiantian Yugang Jiulou** 天天渔港酒楼, tiāntiānyúgǎng jiǔlóu. 10 Renmin Lu ☎0411 84549111. For seafood away from the beaches, don't miss one of Dalian's branches of *Tiantian*; come dinner time, they're usually packed with people enjoying draught beer and fresh steamed crab. They've eschewed the usual picture menu for foreigner-friendly wax versions of their dishes. Expect to pay around ¥100 per head. Daily 10am–10pm.

Tianyuan Vegetarian 天缘素食店, tiānyuán sùshídiàn. Tangshan Jie ☎0411 83673110. Vegetarians should head straight for this hard-to-find restaurant, near the small but colourful Songshan Temple. They have the usual mix of cheap, meat-like tofu dishes (from ¥20). Daily 9am–9pm.

DIRECTORY

Banks and exchange The Bank of China is at 9 Zhongshan Square (Mon–Fri 8.30am–noon & 1–5pm).

Football The Jinzhou Stadium, just southwest of Renmin Square on Wusi Lu, is the venue for Dalian Aerbin (formerly Dalian Shide) matches late March–Oct. Seats (¥50) are sold at the stadium.

Mail and telephones The post office (Mon–Sat 8am–6pm) is next to the main train station.

PSB Centrally located on the northeast side of Zhongshan Square (daily 8am–4.30pm; ☎0411 86766108). One of Dongbei's better bets for visa extensions.

Travel agents CITS (daily 8.30am–4.30pm; ☎0411 83691159, ⊛citsdl.com) is at 10F Wanda Plaza, Zhongshan Square, though they're not terribly useful. Most hotels also have their own ticketing and tour offices.

Dandong

丹东, dāndōng

Once an obscure port tucked away in the corner of Liaoning province at the confluence of the **Yalu River** and the Yellow Sea, **DANDONG** is now a popular weekend destination for Chinese and South Koreans, who come to gaze across the river at the listless North Korean city of Sinuiju. Foreigners from further afield are also drawn to the massive memorial and museum dedicated to the defence of China's communist neighbour against imperialists during the Korean War. All in all, Dandong makes a worthwhile weekend trip out of Beijing or a stopover while touring the sooty northeast, as well as a convenient departure point for Changbai Shan (see p.179).

Dandong remains small enough to feel human in scale, and the tree-lined main streets are uncrowded, clean and prosperous. A strong Korean influence can be felt: vendors along the riverfront promenade sell North Korean stamps bearing slogans such as "Become human gun bombs!", and North Korean TV is on view in Dandong hotels.

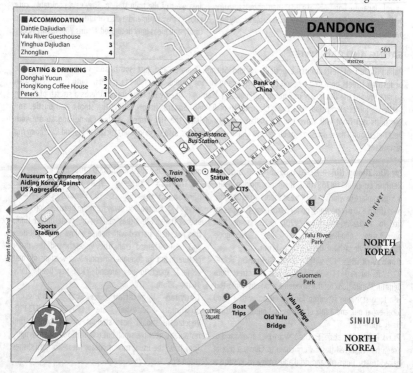

A NORTH KOREAN PLEASURE CRUISE

From 8am, **boats** set out from all along Dandong's promenade, by the bridge, on 30min trips across the river (costing ¥50 in a large boat that leaves when full, or ¥70 per person for a zippy six-seater). The boats take you into North Korean waters to within a few metres of shore, where you can do your part for international relations by waving at the soldiers shouldering automatic rifles. Photography is allowed, but don't try to snap anything vaguely military. If you've an interest in visiting, it's best to check the current situation with Dandong's CITS (☎0415 2132237), though foreigners will almost certainly be forbidden from joining their North Korean tour; try Koryo Tours (ⓦ koryogroup.com) instead.

Old Yalu Bridge

鸭绿江断桥, yālùjiāng duànqiáo · Daily 7am–6pm · ¥30

On foot, the nearest you can get to North Korean soil without a visa is halfway across the river, on the "broken" bridge in the south of town, next to the new bridge. The Koreans have dismantled their half but the Chinese have left theirs as a memorial, complete with thirty framed photos of its original construction by the Japanese in 1911, when the town was called Andong. The bridge ends at a tangled mass of metal that resulted from American bombing in 1950 during the Korean War. Several viewing platforms are on site, along with pay-telescopes trained on Sinuiju on the far bank. There isn't much to see on Sinuiju's desultory shore, save for some rusting ships and curious civilians.

Along the riverside

The **Dandong side** of the Yalu is a boomtown compared with what you can see of Sinuiju. The most scenic area is by the bridges, full of strolling tourists, particularly in the early evening. Nearby is **Yalu River Park** (鸭绿江公园, yālùjiān gōngyuán), where you can drive bumper cars and pay ¥1 to sit on a patch of downy green grass. At the western end of the riverside promenade, **Culture Square** (文化广场, wénhuà guǎngchǎng) is a well-lit local evening hangout.

The Museum to Commemorate Aiding Korea Against US Aggression

抗美援朝纪念馆, kàngměi yuáncháo jìniànguǎn · Daily 8am–4.30pm · Free with ID · buses #1, #3, #4 or #5 from the station stop at the sports stadium, from where it's a 5min walk north · taxis about ¥10

Built in 1993 this huge, macabre museum feels like a relic of the Cold War – though note the Coca-Colas for sale at the entrance, next to Jiang Zemin's plaque swearing eternal North Korean-Sino friendship. It has nine exhibition halls on the Korean War, full of maps, dioramas, machine guns, hand grenades, photographs (mostly captioned in English), and sculptures of lantern-jawed Chinese and Korean soldiers. A few large plaques in each hall spell out the basic theme of each room – tending to be along the lines of "the Americans were terrible aggressors, China heroically won the war after stepping in to help its Korean brothers and sisters." The trifling details that the North kicked off the war by invading the South, and that at best the conflict (which has never officially ended) was a draw, are conspicuous by their absence.

The outside exhibits

In a field behind the museum, a collection of Chinese and captured US aircraft and artillery is on display, while a paintball area, assault course and fighter plane simulator help crank up the fun factor. Climb up inside the huge memorial next to the museum – surrounded by statues of burly Chinese soldiers trampling US army helmets underfoot – for a view over Dandong and into North Korea.

ARRIVAL AND DEPARTURE   **DANDONG**

Arriving at Dandong train station, or at the long-distance bus station just to the north, puts you right in the centre of town – a gleaming, marble-paved square featuring a Mao statue, about 1km north of the Yalu River.

By plane Dandong's small airport (丹东浪头机场, dāndōng làng tóu jīchǎng) is 14km southwest of town; take a shuttle bus into town (¥10) or a taxi (about ¥50). CITS can book flights, though most hotels will either be able to reserve tickets for you or point you in the right direction.

Destinations Sanya (3 weekly; 6hr 25min); Shanghai (3 weekly; 2hr 20min); Shenzhen (3 weekly; 5hr 35min).

By train Dandong is well connected to the rest of northeast China, though journey times can be long. Tickets are easy enough to get from the train station, which sits right in the centre of town, and can also be booked through CITS.

Destinations Beijing (2 daily; 14–22hr); Changchun (3 daily; 8hr 20min–10hr); Dalian (1 daily; 12hr); Shenyang (11 daily; 3hr 30min–5hr 30min).

By bus The long-distance bus station is handily located in the thick of the action, very close to the train station. Rarely for this part of China, buses can be faster than the trains. If you're planning to head off to the Changbai Shan Nature Reserve, you'll need to get an early-morning bus to Tonghua (通化, tōnghuà), from where it's another 5hr by bus; buy a ticket the night before from the efficient bus station booking office.

Destinations Dalian (hourly; 3hr 30min); Shenyang (2 hourly; 3hr); Tonghua (2 daily; 7hr).

By taxi Shared cabs to Shenyang hunt for passengers on the west side of the train station concourse (¥90 per person; 2hr), which works out faster than taking the train.

By ferry Dandong's ferry terminal (丹东港, dāndōng gǎng), 38km to the southwest, handles vessels to South Korea. On days of departure, buses to the port (¥20) leave Dandong's train station at 1.30pm; arriving at Dandong port, buses to town leave when full, so board them as quickly as possible. Ferry tickets are most easily bought through a hotel travel agent. Note that the ferries themselves are probably the worst of those connecting China and Korea.

Destinations Incheon, South Korea (3 weekly; 20hr).

GETTING AROUND

By taxi Cabs charge a minimum of ¥5, which is sufficient for rides around town.

ACCOMMODATION

Dantie Dajiudian 丹铁大酒店, dāntiě dàjiǔdiàn. Train Station Square ☎ 0415 2307777. Situated within the station itself, this is convenient if arriving late or leaving early; rooms are not too shabby. **¥140**

Yalu River Guesthouse 鸭绿江大厦, yālùjiān dàshà. 87 Jiuwei Lu ☎ 0415 2125901. A Sino-Japanese effort – though the rooms have seen better days they are more than adequate, even coming equipped with satellite TV. Staff are helpful, and the ticket service is able to deal with onward travel requests. **¥280**

Yinghua Dajiudian 樱花大酒店, yīnghuā dàjiǔdiàn. 2 Liuwei Lu ☎ 041 5100999. Boasting views across the river and large rooms equipped with broadband internet access, this is a decent and reasonably priced bet if you're on a business trip. **¥180**

★ **Zhonglian** 中联大酒店, zhōnglián dàjiǔdiàn. 62 Binjiang Zhonglu ☎ 0415 2333333, ⊕ zlhotel .com.cn. The poshest accommodation in town, this waterfront hotel looks out across the bombed-out bridge toward North Korea. As well as smart rooms with great views, they offer an exceedingly helpful lobby travel service. **¥488**

EATING

Dandong's restaurants cater to masses of weekenders craving freshwater fish and Korean food, supplied by restaurants strung along San Jin Jie, north from its junction with Shiwei Lu, and also stretching the length of the promenade.

Donghai Yucun 东海渔村, dōnghǎi yúcūn. 42 Block E, west of the Yalu Bridge. Pick of the dishes here is the *luzi yu*, a local river fish; everything comes with glutinous rice, soup, bread and dumplings, and a feast for two is a bargain at around ¥80. Daily 9am–9pm.

Hong Kong Coffee House 香港咖啡厅, xiānggǎng kāfēitīng. 32 Block D. For an enlightening start to your morning, check out the latest North Korean TV news at this café, where Korean coffee is ¥20. Daily 7am–9pm.

★ **Peter's** 彼得咖啡, bǐdé kāfēi. 103 Building 3, Yanjiang Lu ☎ 0415 2168415. This welcoming, Canadian-run café-restaurant is the place to head if you're in the mood for some Western food – it feels like heaven if you've just been in North Korea for a week. They've plenty of good sandwiches and panini (¥14–32), great farmhouse breakfasts (¥32), burgers (¥32–48) and much more. Mon–Sat 8am–10pm, Sun midday–9pm.

DIRECTORY

Banks and exchange There is a Bank of China on the waterfront at Culture Square. US, Hong Kong and Japanese money can also be changed at the *Yalu River Guesthouse*.

Mail and telephones The central post office (daily 8am–5.30pm) is on Qi Jing Jie, the main road running east from the station and site of a bustling night market.

Jilin

吉林, jílín

JILIN must go down as one of China's least-visited provinces, and its two main cities have an air of neglect about them (as even locals will confess). The region bore the brunt of Japanese, Russian and Chinese communist planning more than anywhere in China: during the twentieth century, Jilin's vast deposits of coal and iron ore transformed the area into a network of sprawling industrial hubs.

Today, things are on the up: roads have been improved, the rail network is thorough and easy to use, most hotels are delighted to see foreigners, and winter brings low-cost skiing and sledding. The provincial capital, **Changchun**, boasts the Puppet Emperor's Palace memorializing Puyi's reign as "emperor" of the Japanese state Manchukuo; while **Jilin city** is famed for the ice-coated trees that line its riverfront in winter, and ski resorts on the outskirts of town. Popular with both domestic and South Korean tourists is the **Changbai Shan Nature Reserve**, a swath of mountain and forest scenery along the North Korean border in the far east of the province; for independent foreign travellers, however, the area is a little tricky (and costly) to get around.

Changchun

长春, chángchūn

CHANGCHUN has historical notoriety from its role as **Hsinking**, capital of Manchukuo, the Japanese-controlled state that, from 1932 to 1945, had the former Manchu princeling Xuantong (better known as Puyi) as its emperor. Now a huge, sprawling, industrial city, it's also renowned for its many colleges, its movie studio and the Number One Automobile Factory. The city retains its imperial architecture and design, with straight boulevards and squares throughout.

If you're short on time, or just don't feel like staying in Changchun (nobody would blame you), it's perfectly possible to rock up on a train in the morning or early afternoon, take a subway train to the **Puppet Emperor's Palace** – the city's most memorable sight – and then head off again in the evening.

The Puppet Emperor's Palace

伪皇宫, wěihuáng gōng • Daily 8.30am–4pm • ¥80 • museum free • subway to Weihuanggong

Changchun's only truly notable attraction is the **Puppet Emperor's Palace**, in the east of the city. Like its former occupant Puyi (see box opposite), the palace is really just a shadow of Chinese imperial splendour; in its defence, it does boast a swimming pool and horse-racing track. This luxurious retreat was only meant to be temporary, until his grand abode proper was completed south of Changchun's train station at Wenhua Square (the second-largest square in the world after Tian'anmen) – plans that led to nothing.

Inside the palace grounds, the **Museum of North East China's Occupation by Japan** documents Japan's brutal invasion and rule. On a lighter note, be sure to see the restored Japanese garden, one of Changchun's most tranquil spots.

BACKCHAT

Jilin province is famous for **er ren zhuan** – loosely translated as "Repartee for Two" – a form of theatre closer to vaudeville than Beijing opera, incorporating dancing, singing, baton-twirling, costume changes and soliloquies. A typical performance sees a man and woman regaling the audience with a humorous tale of their courtship and love. CDs of the genre are available at stores, and you may be able to get into a performance with translation via CITS, or you could just ask a cabbie or local to point you to a theatre.

THE LAST EMPEROR

In 1908, at the age of 2, Puyi ascended to the imperial throne in Beijing, at the behest of the dying Dowager Cixi. Although forced to abdicate four years later by the Republican government, he retained his royal privileges, continuing to reside as a living anachronism in the Forbidden City. Outside, the new republic was coming to terms with democracy and the twentieth century, and Puyi's life, circumscribed by court ritual, seems a fantasy in comparison. In 1924, he was expelled by Nationalists uneasy at what he represented, but the Japanese eventually found a use for him in Changchun as lending a symbolic legitimacy to their rule. After the war, he was re-educated by the Communists and lived the last years of his life as a gardener. His story was the subject of Bernardo Bertolucci's lavish film *The Last Emperor*.

ARRIVAL AND DEPARTURE

By plane Changchun Longjia airport (长春龙嘉国际机场, chángchūn lóngjiā guójì jīchǎng), 10km northwest of town, is connected to every major city in China, plus Seoul in South Korea. Airport buses (40min; ¥20) head to a few points in town, including Renmin Square and the *Civil Aviation Hotel* (☎0431 82988888) at 480 Jiefang Dalu, about 3km south of the train station.

Destinations Beijing (11 daily; 1hr 30min); Changbai Shan (1 daily; 50min); Dalian (4 daily; 1hr 10min); Guangzhou (1 daily; 5hr 40min); Hangzhou (1 daily; 2hr 50min); Hong Kong (1 daily; 4hr 30min); Ji'nan (1 daily; 1hr 55min); Qingdao (2 daily; 1hr 35min); Shanghai (3 daily; 2hr 30min); Xi'an (3 weekly; 4hr 10min); Yantai (1 daily; 2hr 25min).

By train The surprisingly attractive train station

CHANGCHUN

(长春火车站, chángchūn huǒchē zhàn) lies to the north of town on the subway line, and has frequent connections – including a fair few high-speed services – to the rest of the northeast. Tickets are easy to buy at the station (it's near-deserted at night).

Destinations Beijing (14 daily; 6hr 30min–13hr 30min); Dandong (2 daily; 8hr 40min); Harbin (many daily; 1–4hr); Jilin (many daily; 40min–2hr); Shenyang (many daily; 1hr 10min–4hr); Tonghua (2 daily; 7hr).

By bus The main station is just to the south of the train station. With Changchun's excellent rail connections, the only services worth bothering with are those to Dandong (1 daily; 6hr), which is a few hours shorter than the train ride; and Baihe, near the northern gate of Changbai Shan (2 daily; 6hr).

GETTING AROUND

By taxi Taxi fares begin at ¥5; most rides in town will be under ¥10. It can be tough to find a cab around the train station.

By subway Changchun's rather sloppy new subway

system currently has two lines (confusingly numbered #3 and #4); much of this is above ground. Tickets cost ¥2–4, depending upon distance travelled.

ACCOMMODATION

Chunyi Hotel 春谊宾馆, chūnyí bīnguǎn. South of the station plaza ☎0431 82096888. Built in 1909 by the Japanese, the province's oldest inn is hardly beautiful, but good value for cleanliness, location and price. It also has a good on-site restaurant. **¥380**

★ **Home Inn** 如家酒店, rújiā jiǔdiàn. On the station plaza ☎0431 89863000. The most appealing of the options in the train station area – the plaza actually looks quite nice from the upper floors. Rooms are small, it's true, but they're pretty, clean, quiet and safe, with free wi-fi. **¥180**

International Hotel 国际大厦酒店, guójì dàshà jiǔdiàn. 568 Xi'an Dalu ☎0431 88485116. Though its prices hint at budget-chain mediocrity, this is actually a comfortable and more than adequate business hotel, with rooms that are excellent value for the location. **¥288**

Shangri-La 香格里拉饭店, xiānggélǐlā fàndiàn. 569 Xi'an Dalu ☎0431 88981818, ⊛shangri-la.com. In the centre of the new commercial district, this is the city's five-star option – if a hugely expensive one. As you'd expect for the price, service is excellent, and the rooms extremely plush. **¥2000**

EATING AND DRINKING

The city's bar and restaurant area lies down Tongzhi Jie, running into side alleys between Qinghua Lu and Xikang Lu.

Chunyi Hotel 春谊宾馆, chūnyí bīnguǎn. South of the station plaza ☎0431 82096888. This old hotel (see above) has a good hotpot buffet restaurant on the second floor of its newer VIP wing – stuff your face for just ¥78 per person. Daily 5–8pm.

★ **Xiangyangtun** 向阳屯饭馆, xiàngyángtún fànguǎn. 433 Dong Chaoyang Lu, off Tongzhi Jie ☎0431 88982876. Changchun's best place to eat, by a long way. It's a traditional Dongbei restaurant – most things here are still cooked on wood-fired stoves.

They have a picture menu, though nothing is written in English; try the *zheng jidan jiang* (蒸鸡蛋酱, zhēng jīdànjiàng, ¥14), a spicy egg dish served in a metal bowl, or one of the many tofu, cured meat or mushroom dishes. And all this with Mao overlooking affairs – you won't miss him. Daily 11am–11pm.

DIRECTORY

Banks and exchange Bank of China is just north of the *Shangri-La* at 699 Xi'an Dalu (Mon–Fri 8.30am–4.30pm).

Mail and telephones The post office (daily 8.30am–4.30pm) is just to the left as you exit the train station.

Jilin

吉林, jílín

Known as Kirin during the Manchukuo time, **JILIN** is split in two by the Songhua River, with the downtown area spread along its northern shore. There's nothing as such to see here, but the waterside promenade makes for a pretty walk, especially in winter, when the trees are coated in frost – a phenomenon, known as *shugua* in Chinese, that results from condensation from the city's hydroelectric dam at Songhua Lake. It's Jilin's claim to fame, along with an **ice festival** in January and neighbouring parks for skiing and sledding. The city also makes a convenient jumping-off point for Changbai Shan.

City sights

There's not too much to see in the city itself, though if you're here overnight you could try visiting the pretty **Catholic church** (天主堂, tiānzhǔ táng) on Songjiang Lu (bordering the river promenade), or **Beishan Park** (北山公园, běishān gōngyuán) to the west of town; the latter is filled with pathways and temples, the most interesting of which is Yuhuangge (Jade Emperor's Temple), where rows of fortune-tellers gather out front.

Songhua Lake

松花湖, sōnghuā hú • taxi from town about ¥50

Twenty kilometers east of Jilin is deep **Songhua Lake**, very attractively surrounded by forested hills. Unlike most Chinese scenic attractions, the lake seems big enough to absorb all its visitors, and even on weekends it's possible to find some peaceful spots.

At the Songhua's southern end is the huge **Fengman Dam**, a source of great local pride. Although in recent years the Songhua River's level has dropped by half (a result of extensive tree felling in its catchment area), the river floods every year, and at least a couple of the dam's four sluice gates have to be opened. With ruthless Chinese pragmatism, cities in Dongbei have been graded in order of importance in the event that the annual floods ever become uncontrollable. Jilin is judged more important than Harbin, so if the river does ever flood disastrously, Jilin will be spared and Harbin submerged.

Zhuque Shan Park

朱雀山, zhūquè shān • bus #9 and #33 • taxi from the train station ¥40 • transport terminates 1km from the park

Fourteen kilometres southeast of Jilin, **Zhuque Shan park** is known for its hiking and temples, but is primarily the closest winter ski area to town. There are two small slopes, one for skiing and one for sledding. The sleds are actually two downhill skis nailed together with a piece of raised plywood, and they really fly if you get a running start and bellyflop. A good restaurant on-site seats guests on a *kang*, a heated raised platform that provides a nice vantage point over the hill. Foreigners are a rarity, and the staff and patrons a lot of fun.

ARRIVAL AND DEPARTURE   JILIN

If you've a long way to go from Jilin, consider first heading to Changchun, which offers many more destination options.

By plane Jilin's small airport is located 25km northwest of town; a taxi into the centre will cost ¥50.

Destinations Beijing (4 weekly; 1hr 40min); Dalian (3 weekly; 1hr 20min).

JILIN'S SKI RESORTS

Jilin has two first-class ski resort areas, which are considerably more expensive and better-equipped – not to mention vastly more professional – than those at Zhuque Shan.
Songhua Lake Huaxue Chang (松花湖滑雪场, sōnghuā hú huáxuěchǎng) ☎ 0432 4697666. 26km east of Jilin; take bus #9 or #33 to the small district of Fengman (丰满, fēngmǎn; 30min) and continue by taxi, or get a taxi all the way from Jilin city for about ¥75.
Beida Lake Huaxue Chang (北大湖滑雪场, běidàhú huáxuěchǎng) ☎ 0432 4202168. 56km southeast of Jilin; in winter months hourly buses make the trip (1hr 30min; ¥20), or charter a taxi (¥150).

By train The train station is right in the centre of town, around 2km north of the river. It receives a few high-speed services, too.

Destinations Beijing (3 daily; 7hr 20min–17hr); Changchun (many daily; 40min–2hr); Dalian (4 daily; 4hr 30min–14hr); Harbin (5 daily; 1hr 40min–6hr); Shenyang (many daily; 2–9hr).

By bus The bus station is in the centre of town, very close to the train station. As with much of Dongbei, good train connections render the buses near useless; the only exceptions are services to Baihe (2 daily; 5hr), near the northern gate of Changbai Shan.

GETTING AROUND

By taxi Taxi fares begin at ¥5; most rides in town will be under ¥10.

ACCOMMODATION AND EATING

Angel 天使宾馆, tiānshǐ bīnguǎn. 2 Nanjing Jie ☎ 0431 2481848. A smart choice in the centre of town, near the Catholic church. The rooms, all a/c, are a wee bit bare, but still manage to be attractive; in addition, the on-site restaurant makes good meals. **¥270**
Dongfang Jiaozi Wang 东方饺子王, dōngfāng jiǎozi wáng. South of the Jilin International, Chongqing Jie. This is a reliable option on a street filled with restaurants, where you'll be able to fill up on northern-style dumplings for under ¥20. Daily 8am–10pm.
Jilin International 吉林国际大酒店, jílín guójì dàjiǔdiàn. 20 Zhongxing Jie ☎ 0431 66571888. A comfortable, affordable place, right in front of the train station – you can't miss it, especially at night, when it pulses in soft neon. However, after passing through the cavernous lobby area, the rooms seem a bit small. **¥230**

DIRECTORY

Banks and exchange Just north of the bridge on Jilin Dajie; daily 8am–5pm.
Post office Just north of the bridge on Jilin Dajie; Mon–Sat 8am–5pm.

Travel agents CITS are on Jiangwan Lu (9am–5pm; ☎ 0432 2435819). Only really useful for their irregular Changbai Shan tours; figure on a minimum of ¥1000 per person, including transport and accommodation.

Changbai Shan

长白山, chángbái shān • ¥125

The **Changbai Shan** ranges run northeast to southwest for more than 1000km along the Chinese-North Korean border. With long, harsh winters and humid summers, this is the only mountain range in east Asia to possess alpine tundra, and its highest peak, Baitou Shan (2744m), is the tallest mountain on the eastern side of the continent. **Changbai Shan Nature Reserve**, with its jagged peaks emerging from swaths of lush pine forests, is one of the highlights of Dongbei, not least for its stunning lake, **Tian Chi**, which actually straddles the international border.

Despite Changbai Shan's remote location, both domestic and South Korean tourists come here in great numbers; a village has grown up on the mountain, and the scenery and atmosphere are somewhat marred by litter, souvenir stalls and hawkers. In fact the reserve averages around 10,000 visitors a day in summer – as you're herded from one spot to the next, it's easy to feel the outdoors experience has been diluted a bit, and getting away from the crowds is the key to a rewarding visit. You need to come well prepared with all-weather gear, whatever the time of year.

3

GINSENG

Ginseng has been collected as a medicinal plant for millennia, and the first Chinese pharmacopoeia, written in the first century, records its ability to nourish the five internal organs, sharpen intelligence, strengthen *yin* (female energy) and invigorate *yang* (male energy).

It is the ginseng root that is prized. Plants are rare and the hunt for them is shrouded in **superstition**. The roots are said to be guarded by snakes and tigers, and legend has it that if a hunter should dream of a laughing, white-bearded man or a group of dancing fairies, he must get up, remain silent, and walk off into the forest. His colleagues must follow without speaking to him, and he will lead them to a root.

Changbai ginseng is regarded as the finest in China. Ginseng hunters here work in summer, when the plant can be spotted by its red berries. One way to find it is to listen for the call of the Bangchui sparrow, which becomes hoarse after eating ginseng seeds. When a ginseng is found, a stick is planted in the ground and a red cloth tied to it: according to tradition, the cloth stops the ginseng child – the spirit of the root – from escaping.

Ginseng generally grows in the shade of the Korean pine, and it is said that a plant of real medicinal value takes fifty years to mature. The plants are low-growing, with their roots pointing upwards in the topsoil. Digging one out is a complex, nail-biting operation, because if any of the delicate roots are damaged, the value of the whole is severely diminished. Roots are valued not just by weight, but by how closely their structure resembles a human body, with a head and four limbs. If you find a wild root, you're rich, as Changbai ginseng sells for over ¥1000 a gram. Artificially reared ginseng is worth a fraction of this.

Northern route

Open 24hr • park buses 8.30am–about 3pm, ¥85

A huge, alpine-style hut marks Changbai Shan's northern entrance. From here, regular buses head through gorgeous, forested surrounds towards Tian Chi, though you'll need to hike or get a 4WD for the last section of the route. On your way up this flank of the mountain, you may care to stop by the **Underground Forest** (地下森林, dìxià sēnlín), an extremely attractive tree-filled canyon; **Small Tian Chi** (小天池, xiǎo tiānchí), a lake that's almost laughable when compared to its larger sibling; and a **hot spring** area in which the gushing, steaming water is used to boil eggs and corn (both ¥5). There are paths ascending from the spring area to Tian Chi, a journey of well over one thousand steps.

Western route

Open 24hr • park buses 8.30am–about 3pm, ¥85

Changbai Shan's western route is less interesting and less beautiful than its northern counterpart, though you'll have far fewer people to deal with. Buses stop by at a couple of **gardens** (only really worth visiting in warmer months), and a deep, rocky canyon. There is, as yet, no road for the last section up to Tian Chi, though it's possible to hike.

Tian Chi

天池, tiān chí • 4WD to lake from north or west "changing centres", where buses terminate, ¥80

It is surely only a matter of time before **Tian Chi**, a dramatic volcanic crater lake 5km across, encircled by angular crags, gushing waterfalls and snowcapped peaks, takes its place alongside China's must-see wonders. As long as the irascible weather cooperates, the effort of climbing the thousand or so concrete steps to reach the lake, not to mention all the trouble of getting to the reserve in the first place, is forgotten as you cross the boulder-strewn snow field to what must be one of the most spectacular views anywhere in the world.

Head off on your own and you can quickly be swallowed up in the wilderness, but be careful around Tian Chi, since the lake straddles the **Chinese-North Korean border** – if you stray across, you're subject to arrest and charges of espionage. At the height of the Cultural Revolution, Chairman Mao ordered that the line be demarcated, but it isn't clearly visible on the ground.

ARRIVAL AND DEPARTURE

CHANGBAI SHAN

Despite Changbai Shan's remote location, there are good train, bus and plane links. The vast majority of visitors are on a tour of some kind – it's tough to get around independently, though possible with a modicum of patience. You might not save any money though, as prices for tickets, transport and accommodation stack up quickly.

By plane The cute, new Changbai Shan airport (长白山 机场, chángbáishān jīchǎng) is close to the park's western entrance, and can save hours over catching a bus or train to the park. In theory, airport buses connect the airport with the west entrance (¥5) or Baihe town (¥28); unfortunately, bus timetables are out of kilter with flight schedules, and it's not unknown for services to rock up at the airport five minutes after the planes have left. To reach the airport from Baihe, buses depart from the *Jinhuishe International Hotel* (金水鹤国际酒店, jīnshuǐhè guójì jiǔdiàn), which sits in an inconvenient, isolated spot between Baihe train station and Erdao Baihe. There are also airport buses from the west gate. Taxis from the airport charge around ¥40 to the west gate, or ¥240 to Baihe.

Destinations Beijing (1 daily; 1hr 50min); Changchun (1 daily; 50min); Shenyang (1 daily; 50min).

By train Baihe train station (白河站, báihé zhàn) is the most useful jump-off point for independent visitors to Changbai Shan, though services hitting this station are few and far between; to get anywhere bar Changchun, Dandong, Jilin and Shenyang, you may have to change in Tonghua (通化, tōnghuà). Services on this extremely rural line are rarely full.

Destinations Changchun (1 daily; 15hr); Dandong (1 daily; 19hr); Jilin (1 daily; 17hr); Shenyang (4 daily; 13hr 30min); Tonghua (7 daily; 6–7hr).

By bus Baihe bus station is handily located just across the road from Baihe train station. Again, it's not terribly busy, though far faster than the train for Changchun (2 daily; 6hr) and Jilin (5 daily; 5hr).

Tours Changbai Shan is most easily reached on a three-day, two-night tour arranged through CITS in Jilin (see p.179). These cost over ¥1000 per person, including park entrance fees and accommodation, and cover all the must-see sights, including Tian Chi.

INFORMATION

ACCESS

Changbai Shan has two main entrances, both of which eventually converge on Tian Chi, the focal point of pretty much every visitor to the park. Shoddy Changbai Shan maps are available at both entrances.

Northern entrance The northern entrance is easiest to access for independent travellers via the scruffy mountain town of Baihe (白河, báihé) 20km away, the main base of operations with plenty of accommodation, as well as the area's main train and bus stations. The route to Tian Chi is also prettier and more rewarding from the northern entrance.

Western entrance Changbai Shan's western entrance is far less developed, though the new Changbai Shan airport nearby is becoming an increasingly popular option for tour operators and independent travellers alike.

WEATHER

Bear in mind that the weather in the region is not kind, and can change very suddenly. Summer brings torrential rain; winter snows can close roads; and year-round cloud and mist can make it impossible to see 10m ahead of you. The best chance for decent weather is between June and September. Conditions are posted at both park entrances, though your hotel should also be able to let you know how Tian Chi is looking at any given time.

GETTING AROUND

By bus From Baihe, there are a couple of morning buses (45min; ¥8.5) to the park's north entrance, and more through the day in summer. The last buses return to Baihe around 4pm. For buses between Baihe and the west gate, you'll need to board the irregular airport services (see above).

By taxi Given the awful state of public transport in Baihe, you're almost inevitably going to need a taxi at some point.

Rides start at ¥5, though it'll be more like ¥60 to the north gate. If you'll be descending late, it may be a good idea to grab your driver's business card for the return trip – if you miss the last bus, you'll otherwise be reliant upon the kindness of whichever tour groups are yet to head back down from the park. Those descending before 3pm should find it easy to share a cab (¥20 per person) down to Baihe.

ACCOMMODATION AND EATING

Most visitors stay at Baihe, a town 20km from the park's northern entrance. There are a few grubby accommodation options in the immediate vicinity of the train and bus stations, though most prefer to head into the main commercial area, Erdao Baihe (二道白河站, èrdào báihé zhàn), around 4km to the south; it's ¥5 by taxi, though you'll have to haggle it down from ¥10. More pleasant than this scruffy area is the unnamed zone surrounding the *Changbai Shan* hotel, which is around 4km southwest of the station (again ¥5 by taxi); this also has better (though not really good) restaurants than those in Erdao Baihe. An amazing number of places to eat specialize in dog meat – if in any doubt when ordering, ask if your dish features *gou rou* (狗肉, gǒuròu). Lastly, there are a few upmarket places to stay around both main park gates.

BAIHE

Changbai Shan Hostel 长白山国际青年旅舍, chángbáishān guójì qīngnián lǚshè. Just south of the train station ☎0433 5710800. Probably the best-organized place in the area, in terms of the service they offer indepdendent travellers – as well as running shuttle buses to both park entrances, they're able to organize overnight stays on the mountain. It's in an ugly part of town, though just a short walk from the train station – turn right when you hit the main road. Dorms ¥45, twins ¥200

Changbaishan 长白山大厦, chángbáishān dàshà. 50 Tongchang Lu ☎0433 5723333. Long-standing hotel in Baihe's nicest quarter, a large affair popular with tour groups, though more than happy to take independent travellers. Rooms are fine, if a little dated, and service courteous. A smaller, cheaper hotel was nearing completion at the time of writing one block west – it may be worth checking out. ¥300

Singie Art Hotel 星际酒店, xīngjì jiǔdiàn. Erdao Baihe ☎0433 5750222. At the northern end of Baihe's main commerical district, this recently renovated hotel is good value for money – even if said renovations focused exclusively on the trendy-looking lobby, rather than the somewhat mediocre rooms. ¥250

NORTH GATE

Lanjing Spa Resort 蓝景温泉度假酒店, lánjīng wēnquán dùjià jiǔdiàn. ☎0451 5052222. Changbai Shan's most luxurious accommodation lies just across from the park's north entrance. As its name implies, it boasts a hot spring centre; it also has excellent restaurants and admirable standards of service. ¥1600

WEST GATE

Days Hotel Landscape Resort 蓝景戴斯度假酒店, lánjīng dàisī dùjià jiǔdiàn. ☎0439 6337999. Attractive new lodge-style resort, located just down the road from the west gate. As well as wonderfully attractive rooms and forest surroundings, they've by far the best restaurants in the Changbai Shan area. ¥800

Heilongjiang

黑龙江, hēilóngjiāng

The province of **HEILONGJIANG** has always been considered a little remote to the Chinese – a perception that remains intact, even in these days of high-speed trains and cheap flights. "Black Dragon River" is a land of extremities: this is home to China's northernmost and easternmost points, as well as its coldest. Winter temperatures regularly plummet below -30°C, though this is actually high season in the provincial capital **Harbin**, which hosts a world-famous annual **ice festival**. Though the shuddering cold makes it hard to truly enjoy the city itself during this period, come summertime it's one of the most pleasant in the land.

Beyond Harbin, Dongbei's northeast is little visited by Western tourists, with the main draw being the **Zhalong Nature Reserve**, near Qiqihar. If you're journeying any further, it's likely you'll be on the **Trans-Manchurian train** and on your way to Russia, via Hailar and Manzhouli, both in **Inner Mongolia** (see p.227).

Harbin

哈尔滨, hāěrbīn

The capital of Heilongjiang province and laid out on the southern bank of the Songhua River, **HARBIN** is most famous for its wonderfully photogenic winter **Ice Festival**. While visiting at this time is highly recommended, it's certainly worth popping by in a warmer month too, for this is one of the few northern cities with a distinctive character. A few roads near Harbin's centre are lined with gorgeous colonial-era structures, most of them painted in soothing lemon tones. In fact, the city used to be nicknamed "Little Moscow", and though much of the old architecture has been replaced with sterile blocks and skyscrapers, corners of Harbin still look like the last threadbare outpost of imperial Russia – leafy boulevards are lined with European-style buildings painted in pastel shades, and bulbous onion domes dot the skyline. There are several **Russian restaurants**, and the locals have picked up on some of their neighbour's customs: as well as a taste for ice cream and pastries, the residents have a reputation as the hardest drinkers in China.

Brief history

Harbin was a small fishing village on the Songhua River until world history intervened. In 1896, the Russians obtained a contract to build a rail line from Vladivostok through Harbin to Dalian, and the town's population swelled to include 200,000 foreigners. More Russians arrived in 1917, this time White Russian refugees fleeing the Bolsheviks, and many stayed on. In 1932, the city was captured by Japanese forces invading Manchuria, then in 1945 it fell again to the Russian army, who held it for a year before Stalin and Chiang Kai-shek finally came to an agreement to return Harbin to China – though when the Russians withdrew, they took with them most of the city's industrial plants. Things haven't been totally peaceful since; Harbin was the scene of fierce factional fighting during the Cultural Revolution, and when relations with the Soviet Union deteriorated, the inhabitants looked anxiously north as fierce border skirmishes took place.

Zhongyang Dajie

中央大街, zhōngyāng dàjiē

Better than any of Harbin's actual sights is a walk down **Zhongyang Dajie**, the city's most charming road. Many shops along this pedestrianized stretch have been restored, with plaques out front detailing, in English, their past lives as colonial homes and stores. Make sure you go in the department store at no. 107, if only to see its spectacular skylight and rendition of a section from Michelangelo's Sistine Chapel

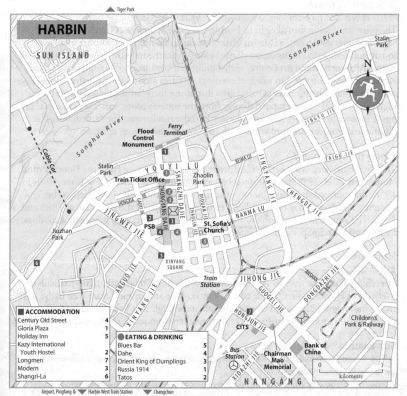

ACCOMMODATION
Century Old Street	4
Gloria Plaza	1
Holiday Inn	5
Kazy International Youth Hostel	2
Longmen	7
Modern	3
Shangri-La	6

EATING & DRINKING
Blues Bar	5
Dahe	4
Orient King of Dumplings	3
Russia 1914	1
Tatos	2

THE ICE FESTIVAL

In compensation for Harbin's cruel winter weather, the annual **Ice Festival** (冰灯节, bīngdēng jié), centred on Zhaolin Park, is held from January 5 to February 5 – though with the influx of tourists, the dates extend each year. Sculptors, some of them teenagers, work twelve-hour days in -20°C December weather to help transform the park into a fairy-tale landscape: the magnificent ice sculptures they create are sometimes entire buildings, complete with slides, stairways, arches and bridges. Carved with chainsaws and picks, the creations often have coloured lights inside to heighten the psychedelic effect. Highlights of past festivals have included detailed replicas of St Paul's Cathedral and life-size Chinese temples, though these days cartoon characters outnumber more traditional Chinese subject matter.

The festivities take place in various places around the city, though the two largest exhibitions are over the river on Sun Island. Here you'll find the Snow Sculpture Art Exhibition (8am–5.30pm; ¥240) and the Ice & Snow World (9am–midday ¥150; midday–9pm ¥300). Back in central Harbin, there's the smaller Ice Lantern Garden Party (2–9.30pm; ¥200) in Zhongshan Park. At all venues, festival's end is marked with fireworks and pickaxes; visitors are encouraged to destroy the icy artwork by hand.

3

mural, which hangs on the back wall. There are good restaurants and bars along the numbered streets running off the main road, which are paved with cobblestones and closed to cars and bicycles. At the north end, a modern shopping mall encroaches on the atmosphere, but can be useful for locating Western "essentials". In winter, ice sculptures line the street, while summer sees pavement cafés and bars set up.

St Sophia's Church
哈尔滨建筑艺术馆, hā'ěrbīn jiànzhú yìshùguǎn • Daily 8.30am–5pm • ¥20

The most interesting formal sight in Harbin has to be **St Sophia's Church** (哈尔滨建筑艺术馆, hā'ěrbīn jiànzhú yìshùguǎn), a Russian Orthodox cathedral built in 1907. Set in its own square and restored to all its onion-domed glory, the cathedral now houses the **Harbin Architecture and Art Centre**, with a photographic survey of Harbin's history as a Russian railway outpost. On summer evenings, the area around the cathedral comes alive with impromptu badminton games, ladies displaying their fan-dancing skills and – the highlight – a well-choreographed display from the square's fountains. They are roped off, but it is never long before someone charges into the maelstrom. The cathedral itself is illuminated from sunset until around 10pm – a truly enchanting sight.

Along the river bank

The river-bank area is a worthwhile district to explore, starting from the **Flood Control Monument** (防洪纪念碑, fánghóng jìniànbēi) at the bottom of Zhongyang Dajie. Built in 1958, the monument commemorates the many thousands who have died in the Songhua floods, and has been updated to mark floods from the summers of 1989 and 1998. The square here is a popular hangout for local people, who gather to walk dogs, fly kites and send paper lanterns into the night-time sky.

Stalin Park
斯大林公园, sīdàlín gōngyuán

Stretching along the river banks from the monument is **Stalin Park**, that's particularly lively on weekends, when people come to meet, chat and drink. Some even bathe in the river – not a good idea, as levels of pollution are so high that fish can no longer survive. Others cluster around palm-readers and storytellers who relate old Chinese folk legends.

Sun Island
太阳岛, tàiyáng dǎo • ferries from near Flood Control Monument ¥10 return • cable car ¥50 one-way • sightseeing bus ¥15 • tandem bikes ¥50 per hour, ¥200 deposit

Across from the city on the Songhua River's northern bank is the busy resort and

> ## HARBIN'S UNDERGROUND MALLS
>
> Due to frosty relations with the Soviet Union in the 1960s and 70s (subject of Ha Jin's excellent *Ocean of Words*, a book of short stories by a former PLA soldier who was based on the Siberian border), Harbin also boasts a network of underground bomb shelters turned shopping malls. You can enter at the train station and walk all the way to Dongdazhi Jie and beyond.

sanatorium village of **Sun Island**. In summer you can catch a ferry; in winter, the Songhua freezes solid and you can ride a horse carriage, rent a go-kart or walk across – the ice is so thick it will support a fully loaded bus or lorry, and it gets used as a road.

Sun Island Park

Daily 9am–5pm • ¥30 • Russia-Style Town daily 9am–5pm, ¥20 • Tiger Park daily 9am–4pm, ¥90

Sun Island Park is an enormous leisure complex with lakes for boating, swimming pools and fairground rides. Nearer the river is the small, and rather twee, **Russia-Style Town**, whose faux-colonial buildings are perhaps less impressive than the real ones south of the river. Then there's **Tiger Park**, supposedly a refuge and breeding centre for the critically endangered Siberian tiger; frankly, it smells more of commerce than conservation, especially since visitors are encouraged to feed the beasts with live chickens (for a price), and even cattle (for a much higher price). If none of these attractions floats your boat, it's pleasurable, not to mention free, simply to walk around the park.

Pingfang: unit 731

平方, píngfāng • Tues–Sun 9–11.30am & 1–3.30pm • ¥20 • buses #338 or #343 from train station

Harbin's most notorious location lies a forty-minute bus journey southwest of the centre at **PINGFANG**. This was the home of a secret Japanese research establishment during World War II, now open to the public as a **museum**. Here, prisoners of war were subjected to horrendous torture – being injected with deadly viruses, dissected alive, and frozen or heated slowly until they died – under the pretence of scientific experimentation. More than three thousand people from China, Russia and Mongolia were murdered by troops from unit 731 of the Japanese army. After the war, the Japanese tried to hide all evidence of the base, and its existence only came to light through the efforts of Japanese investigative journalists. It was also discovered that, as with scientists in defeated Nazi Germany, the Americans gave the Japanese scientists immunity from prosecution in return for their research findings.

The museum mostly comprises photographs labelled in Chinese. Looking at the displays, which include a painting of bound prisoners being used as bomb targets, you can begin to understand why Chinese antipathy towards Japan runs so deep.

ARRIVAL AND DEPARTURE   HARBIN

Train and plane tickets can be bought from ticket offices around town, and from many hotels – if your hotel doesn't sell tickets, they will at least be able to tell you where to go.

By plane Harbin airport (哈尔滨太平国际机场, hā'ěrbīn tàipíng guójì jīchǎng) is 50km southwest of the town and served by an airport bus (every 20min; 1hr or more; ¥20), which drops you near the *Holiday Inn*. A taxi will cost ¥120.
Destinations Beijing (13 daily; 1hr 50min); Chengdu (1 daily; 5hr 50min); Dalian (4 daily; 1hr 20min); Hangzhou (1 daily; 3hr 10min); Hong Kong (1 daily; 4hr 40min); Ji'nan (1 daily; 2hr 10min); Kunming (daily; 7hr); Qingdao (4 daily; 1hr 50min); Shanghai (7 daily; 2hr 40min); Shenyang (4

daily; 55min); Xi'an (1 daily; 3hr).

By train Harbin's main train station (哈尔滨站, hā'ěrbīn zhàn) lies a short walk from the centre of town, though you're just as likely to pitch up at Harbin West (哈尔滨西站, hā'ěrbīn xīzhàn), a huge, gleaming, high-speed-only station isolated some 10km from the centre. Taxis from the west station cost around ¥25, though the new metro line is nearing completion.
Destinations from main station Beijing (10 daily; 10–16hr); Changchun (many daily; 2hr 40min); Hailar (4

CROSSING INTO SIBERIA

From northern Heilongjiang, there are a number of crossing points into **Siberia**, of which Heihe, a large border town that sees a lot of traffic with the Russian town of Blagoveshchensk, is the best option. Trains go daily from Harbin station to Heihe (2 daily; 11hr 20min); upon arrival, Russia is a mere few strides and a mountain of paperwork away. A rail connection also exists between Harbin and Suifenhe (2 daily; 10hr), from where it's a 4hr bus ride to Vladivostok. In practice, however, these routes are fraught with difficulties; there is no tourist infrastructure, distances are long and conditions primitive. By far the simplest way to get into Russia from Dongbei is to hop on the Trans-Siberian train to Moscow (see p.34), which passes through Harbin every Sunday afternoon on its way west to the border at Manzhouli.

The biggest problem with crossing from Dongbei into Siberia is getting a **visa**, which is always easiest – and often essential – to sort out in your home country. It may also be possible in Beijing; if you're very lucky indeed, you may get one from the Russian consulate in Shenyang (see p.166).

daily; 10–23hr); Jilin (1 daily; 7hr 20min); Manzhouli (3 daily; 12hr 30min–14hr); Moscow (1 weekly; 6 days); Qiqihar (many daily; 2hr 45min–4hr); Shenyang (many daily; 4hr 30min–7hr); Yabuli (6 daily; 3hr).

Destinations from West station Beijing (6 daily; 7hr 45min–10hr); Changchun (many daily; 1hr); Jilin (4 daily; 1hr 50min); Shenyang (many daily; 2hr 15min–3hr).

By bus The long-distance bus station is on Songhuajiang Jie, across from the main train station. You can pretty much ignore it, though; distances from Harbin are long, and train connections almost always far faster.

GETTING AROUND

By bus The most useful bus is #103, which runs between Zhongshan Lu and Zhaolin Park (兆林公园, zhàolín gōngyuán) just east of Zhongyang Dajie.

By taxi Taxi fares around the city start at ¥8 for the first 3km; Harbin has lots of one-way streets, so don't panic if it seems your driver is lapping the block.

By subway The new Harbin metro system was still under construction at the time of writing; this should open in 2014, with another two following shortly afterwards. Given central Harbin's compact nature, it'll likely be most useful for trips to and from Harbin West train station, on line #3.

INFORMATION

Travel agents CITS at 68 Hongjun Jie (⏏0451 53633178) is friendly and dependable, though you'd be lucky to encounter an English-speaker. They can organize ski packages to Yabuli, but with transport to the resort so plentiful (see p.188), it can be just as easy to arrange independently.

Maps English maps of the city are sold in the gift shop at the *Holiday Inn*; Chinese-only versions are widely available (¥6).

ACCOMMODATION

The hotels around Zhongyang Dajie are the best option if you're staying for any length of time. There's a cluster of cheapies around the train station, but the area is noisy, dirty and crowded.

★ **Century Old Street** 百年老街酒店, bǎinián lǎojiē jiǔdiàn. 32 Zhongyang Dajie ⏏0451 8469969. This is probably the best-value accommodation in Dongbei, a baby blue-painted Russian beauty whose rooms almost live up to the expectations generated by the gorgeous exterior. Cheapest rooms lack windows, but their larger "luxury" options are still a steal. Standard doubles with window **¥198**, luxury **¥228**

Gloria Plaza 饥菜花园大酒店, jīcài huāyuán dàjiǔdiàn. 259 Zhongyang Dajie ⏏0451 8670000. Smart four-star affair perched at the top of Zhongyang Dajie, looking out across the river toward Sun Island. **¥488**

Holiday Inn 万达假日饭店, wàndájiàrì fàndiàn. 90 Jingwei Jie ⏏0451 84887205, ⏏holidayinn.com /harbinchn. One of the town's top choices, with a good location at the head of Zhongyang Dajie, and very helpful English-speaking staff. Rooms are pleasantly decorated, and extremely comfortable, but it's hard to get around the fact that they're well overpriced. **¥868**

Kazy International Youth Hostel 卡兹国际青年旅舍, kǎzī guójì qīngnián lǚshè. 27 Tongjiang Jie ⏏0451 87654211. What a pity that this hostel, formerly located in an old synagogue, moved down the road in 2013. Though its new location off a grubby courtyard is far less salubrious, staff here are perhaps even more informative than those at Harbin's five-stars. Dorms **¥198**

Longmen 龙门大厦, lóngmén dàshà. 85 Hongqi Jie

0451 86791999. A grand old place built in 1901 as the *Chinese Eastern Railway Hotel*, this restored gem is a snapshot of Harbin's bicultural past, with wood-panelled corridors and charmingly decorated rooms. It's worth visiting even if you don't stay – check out the lobby's ornate staircase and revolving door. **¥480**

Modern 马达尔宾馆, mǎdá'ěr bīnguǎn. 89 Zhongyang Dajie 0451 84884199, hotel .hrbmodern.com. The name is a misnomer, as this place was built in 1906 and survives as Harbin's oldest hotel. An elegant building on one of the city's busiest streets, it's bursting with character. From Zhongyang Dajie, you enter via a ground-floor restaurant. **¥680**

Shangri-La 香格里拉大饭店, xiānggélǐlā dàfàndiàn. 555 Youyi Lu 0451 84858888, shangri-la.com/harbin. A five-star hotel overlooking Stalin Park, Zhongyang Dajie and Zhaolin Park, making rooms here hard to come by during the Ice Festival – book early. Some rooms are simply gigantic, and all exude the luxury you'd expect from this upper-class chain. **¥1200**

EATING, DRINKING AND NIGHTLIFE

Aside from expensive regional delicacies such as bear paw and deer muzzle, available in upmarket hotels, food in Harbin is good value. Influenced by Russian cuisine, local cooking is characterized by the exceptionally heavy use of garlic – and a lot of potato. A favourite local dish is *xiaoji dunmogu* (chicken and stewed mushrooms). In summer and during the busy winter periods, tented areas resembling outdoor German beer halls spring up on the fringes of Zhongyang Dajie. They're great spots to enjoy piping-hot barbecued skewers and a stein or two of ice-cold *Harbin* beer (¥35 for a 2000ml jug).

Blues Bar 布蓝斯酒吧, bùlánsī jiǔbā. 100 Diduan Jie. Intriguing bar where Russian and Chinese students – plus a rogues' gallery of older folk – dance the night away on weekends. Occasional live music. Daily 5pm–late.

Dahe 大和美食日本菜, dàhé měishí rìběncài. 60 Xi 14 Dao Jie. Reasonably priced Japanese restaurant serving all the favourites, from steaming bowls of udon noodles to well-sculpted plates of sashimi. Look for the restaurant with the orange front. Daily 10am–10pm.

★ **Orient King of Dumplings** 东方饺子王, dōngfāng jiǎozi wáng. 81 Zhongyang Jie. A real Harbin institution – there are no fewer than eighteen branches of this dumpling chain in town. This one is by far the most attractive, a two-floor affair with photos of old Harbin on the walls. The dumplings themselves are simply superb, with intriguing fillings such as pumpkin, omelette, spicy sausage and honeydew pork; they're also amazing value at ¥10–20 per portion. Daily 9am–9pm.

★ **Russia 1914** 俄罗斯一九一四, éluósī yījiǔyīsì. 59 Xi Toudao Jie. Also known as *Russia Coffee & Food*, this is the perfect place for afternoon tea, with atmosphere to match – you can almost imagine yourself back in the early 1900s. Main meals are also served, but if you're just after a little pick-me-up, it's hard to beat a cup of Russian tea (¥12) with Russian bread and jam (¥10). Daily 10am–midnight.

★ **Tatos** 华梅饭店, huáméi fàndiàn. 127 Zhongyang Jie 0451 84688855. The best Russian restaurant in town, if only for the atmosphere – in this lavishly decorated basement venue, it's easy to forget that you're still in China. Unless you go for caviar, it won't break the bank as most mains are in the ¥30–50 range, with the shashlik particularly recommended. Daily 11am–11pm.

DIRECTORY

Banks and exchange The Bank of China is on Zhongshan Lu (Mon–Fri 8am–noon & 1–5pm). The foreign-exchange counter is upstairs. You can also change money at its branch at 37 Zhaolin Jie (same hours).

Mail and telephones The main post office is at 51 Jianshe Jie (Mon–Sat 8am–6pm).

PSB 6 Jingweitou Daojie (Mon–Fri 8–11am & 2–5pm; 0451 87661613). It's one of those PSBs that can be good, or very bad – some have had to wait over a week for their visa to be renewed.

Yabuli

亚布力, yàbùlì • Ski season Nov–Mar

Regarded as the premier ski destination in China, **YABULI** resort's 3800m piste spreads across the southern slopes of Guokui Shan (1300m), literally Pot-Head Mountain, 194km southeast of Harbin. Six lifts shuttle an average of 10,000 skiers per day during the winter months. Although popular, the pistes are nowhere near as good as those in Europe, North America or Japan, nor are they cheap to ski. If you're after a proper skiing holiday, this is not really the place, and the slopes cropping up outside most northern cities offer much better value for money and are easier to get to. Nevertheless, a trip can still be good fun if expectations are kept in check.

3

TO RUSSIA ON THE TRANS-MANCHURIAN

For those with time and a little bit of patience to spare, the evocatively named **Trans-Manchurian railway** is one of the best ways to enter or exit China. The line barrels northeast out of Beijing, eventually crossing the Russian border to connect with its far more illustrious sibling, the Trans-Siberian. Indeed, once a week **direct trains** run the route all the way between Beijing and Moscow, avoiding Mongolia and thus the necessity of acquiring an extra visa. The trip takes around six days, starting almost simultaneously in both Moscow and Beijing each Saturday evening; trains are comfortable, with private rooms and restaurant cars. **Visas** must be arranged in advance both ways, and the difficulty of acquiring a Russian one (not to mention buying the ticket itself) means that many choose to organize the trip through a travel agency; see p.32 for recommended operators. Prices vary enormously depending upon whether you go through an agency or do things by yourself.

With a little advance planning, it'll be possible to visit other Russian cities before hitting Moscow, with the Siberian city of Irkutsk a favourite thanks to its proximity to Lake Baikal, the world's largest body of fresh water. Easier to organize are stops at Chinese cities on the way: Shenyang (p.162), Changchun (p.176) and Harbin (p.182) all have their merits, and new high-speed services have cut travel times considerably. From Harbin, the train cuts through **Inner Mongolia** (see p.227 for more on this province's history and attractions) before hitting the Russian border, passing through the pleasant towns of Hailar and Manzhouli.

HAILAR

With rail connections as well as an airport, **Hailar** (海拉尔, hǎilā'ěr) is the main transport hub of the region, and a centre for grassland visits. The town itself is of minimal interest – the chief reason most visitors come to Hailar is to see the **Hulunbuir grasslands** (呼伦贝尔草原, hūlúnbèi'ěr cǎoyuán), an apparently limitless rolling land of plains and low grassy mountains. As elsewhere in Inner Mongolia, there are the CITS-approved villages of Mongol herders; though you could try to strike off independently, it's worth noting that the grassland **tours** here don't attract hordes of people. A day-trip from Hailar to eat a traditional mutton banquet on the grasslands, for a group of four people, costs around ¥420 each, or a little under double that to stay the night. For bookings and more information, contact Hailar's CITS (☎0470 8224017) at their office on the third floor of *Beiyuan Hotel* (北苑宾馆, běiyuàn bīnguǎn; ☎0470 8235888; **¥288**) on 20 Alihe Lu, one of the better accommodation options in town.

MANZHOULI

A few hours to the west of Hailar is **Manzhouli** (满洲里, mǎnzhōulǐ), a bustling centre for cross-border commerce whose wholesale demolition, renovation and development – much of which has involved the surreal addition of Versailles-inspired facades to communist tower blocks – has left it with little atmosphere. It's worth a visit for trips to the surrounding countryside, as well as air fresher than you may have experienced elsewhere in China. There are plenty of **hotels** in town, and **eating** is a treat if you love Russian food. Those staying the night may care to visit the great **Dalai Lake** (达赉湖, dálài hú; Hulun Nur in Mongolian), a shallow expanse of water set in marshy grazing country where flocks of swans, geese, cranes and other migratory birds come to nest. In June and July, the grasslands in this region are said to be the greenest in all Mongolia, and coming here may be the most rewarding – and least expensive – way to see the region's grasslands. A taxi from town will cost from ¥250 round-trip.

ARRIVAL AND INFORMATION   YABULI

Packages covering travel, accommodation and skiing can be booked at CITS and other travel agents in Harbin and throughout China, but it's fairly easy (and much cheaper) to organize your own trip independently.

By train Yabuli is served by a main station (亚布力站, yàbùlì zhàn), with trains daily to Harbin, Dalian and even distant Beijing. Shuttle buses (¥60) run from the station to the resort entrance. The brand-new Yabuli South station (亚布力南站, yàbùlì nánzhàn) is located far closer to the resort entrance, but as yet has only a single morning train from Harbin.

Destinations Beijing (2 daily; 19–22hr); Dalian (1 daily; 15hr); Harbin (7 daily; 3hr).

Information Few Chinese possess their own ski gear, so it should come as no surprise that you'll be able to rent everything you need at the resort entrance. Their pricing structure is in a constant state of flux; lift tickets will end up costing around ¥450/day, and equipment another ¥200 or so.

ACCOMMODATION

Sun Mountain Resort 阳光度假村, yángguāng dùjìacūn. ☎0451 53458888, ⓦyabuliski.com. Though overpriced (surprise, surprise), Yabuli's first hotel remains its best, and renovations have ensured that it's still a quality place. The ski lifts are a stone's throw away, rooms are large and well appointed, and the on-site restaurants are decent enough. **¥1200**

Yabuli Shanzhuang 亚布力山庄, yàbùlì shānzhuāng. ☎0451 53455030, ⓦyabuliski.com. The best "cheapie" on the slopes, though it's still very costly for what you get: a fair-sized room with a linoleum floor (not great in winter), though mercifully the hot water runs 24hr a day. **¥600**

Zhalong Nature Reserve

扎龙自然保护区, zhālóng zìrán beohùqū · ¥50

A four-hour bus ride west of Harbin, **QIQIHAR** (齐齐哈尔, qíqíhāěr) is one of the northeast's oldest cities, and still a thriving industrial centre. Alas, it's more fun to say the city's name aloud than to stay here for more than a day, and the sole reason to visit is the **Zhalong Nature Reserve**, 30km southeast of town. This marshy plain abounds in shallow reedy lakes and serves as the summer breeding ground of thousands of species of birds, including white storks, whooper swans, spoonbills, white ibis and – the star attractions – nine of the world's fifteen species of crane. Most spectacular of these is the endangered **red-crowned crane**, a lanky black-and-white bird over 1m tall, with a scarlet bald patch. It has long been treasured in the East as a paradigm of elegance and is a popular symbol of longevity, living up to sixty years. The birds mate for life, and the female only lays one or two eggs each season, over which the male stands guard.

Visiting Zhalong

The best time to visit the reserve is from April to June, when the migrants have just arrived, though the viewing season extends through September. Walking around the reserve, although not forbidden, is not encouraged by the keepers – or by the murderous swarms of mosquitoes. Come prepared, and bring binoculars if you can, too. Dedicated ornithologists might like to spend a few days here, but for most people an afternoon crouched in the reedbeds will be enough.

ARRIVAL AND DEPARTURE   ZHALONG

Qiqihar is accessible by plane and train; you'd be mad to go by bus, since journeys are long and tedious.

By plane Qiqihar's small airport (齐齐哈尔三家子机场, qíqíhāěr sānjiāzǐ jīchǎng) is 10km to the south of town. Buses (¥10) meet the few planes, or it's ¥25 to the centre by taxi.
Destinations Beijing (2 daily; 1hr 50min); Guangzhou (1 daily; 5hr 55min); Shanghai (1 daily; 2hr 50min).

By train Qiqihar's train station (齐齐哈尔站, qíqíhāěr zhàn) is 3km east of the city centre. Plenty of buses head into town, though it's far easier by taxi.
Destinations Beijing (4 daily; 14–22hr); Hailar (9 daily; 8–12hr); Harbin (many daily; 2hr 45min–5hr).

GETTING AROUND

By bus Buses to the reserve (1hr; ¥5) leave from Qiqihar's bus station, 1km south down Longhua Lu, on the left, and also from in front of the train station.
By taxi A taxi to the reserve will cost from ¥200 return,

though the exact price will obviously depend on how long you want the driver to wait around. If you want your driver to come back to pick you up, grab their business card so that you can phone them.

ACCOMMODATION

Visitors to Zhalong have to stay in Qiqihar, where a number of new business hotels have sprung up.

Ibis 宜必思酒店, yíbìsī jiǔdiàn. 2 Pukui Lu ☎0452 240000. A great addition to Qiqihar, close to the station (take a cab) and acceptable for travellers of all budgets. If

you've stayed at an *Ibis* before, you know what the rooms will be like: not too big, but clean and quiet. Discounts are not uncommon. **¥279**

The Yellow River

YUNGANG CAVES, DATONG

The Yellow River

From its lofty source on the Tibetan plateau, the famed Yellow River (黄河, huánghé) runs for almost 5500km before emptying into the Yellow Sea, making it China's second-longest waterway after the Yangzi, and the sixth longest in the world. The river's name stems from the vast quantities of loess it carries, a fertile yellow silt which has done much to benefit the region's agricultural potential over the millennia. However, the river's popular nickname, "China's Sorrow", hints at the regular floods and changes of course that have repeatedly caused devastation – the waterway is often likened to a dragon, a reference not just to its sinuous course, but also to its uncontrollable nature, by turns benign and malevolent. On the flipside, it provides much-needed irrigation to areas otherwise arid and inhospitable, and has created some of China's most distinctive landscapes, barrelling past colossal sand dunes before sliding along pancake-flat loess plains scarred with deep, winding crevasses.

4

Such is the length of the Yellow River that the first and last major cities it hits – Lanzhou and Ji'nan – are actually covered in other chapters (see p.708 & p.282). In between, the river flows through **Ningxia**, **Inner Mongolia**, **Shanxi**, **Shaanxi** and **Henan**, and has played a vital role in the history, geography and fortunes of each province – though sadly its capricious nature makes river travel impossible in the region.

The most famous sight in the Yellow River's catchment area is actually some distance from the river itself: the city of **Xi'an** is one of China's biggest tourist destinations, with as many temples, museums and tombs as the rest of the region put together, and with the **Terracotta Army** deservedly ranking as one of China's premier sights. Xi'an is also home to a substantial **Muslim** minority, whose cuisine is well worth sampling. East of the city, and also within **Shaanxi** province, is the spectacular **Hua Shan** range, whose temple-studded slopes offer superb – if occasionally terrifying – hiking opportunities.

Heading northwest into **Ningxia**, a tiny province with a substantial Hui minority, you can witness the river's mighty waters running between desert sand dunes at the resort of

Highlights

❶ **The Terracotta Army** No visit to China is complete without a peek at these warrior figurines, guarding the tomb of Qin Shi Huang near Xi'an. **See p.212**

❷ **Hiking Hua Shan** Within day-trip distance of Xi'an, this spectacular mountain range encourages a longer stay, and begs to be hiked around. **See p.217**

❸ **The grasslands** Explore the rolling green horizons of Inner Mongolia's "grass sea" – such as those near Hohhot – and sleep in a Mongol yurt. **See p.237**

❹ **The Hanging Temple** If you've a fear of heights, stay away from this incredibly photogenic temple, perched on stilts on a cliffside south of Datong. **See p.245**

❺ **Pingyao** An intact Ming-era walled city, home to winding back alleys and a number of atmospheric hotels and guesthouses. **See p.252**

❻ **Longmen Caves** Walk along a riverside promenade past caves peppering limestone cliff faces, containing more than 100,000 Buddhist carvings. **See p.261**

HIGHLIGHTS ARE MARKED ON THE MAP ON PP.194–195

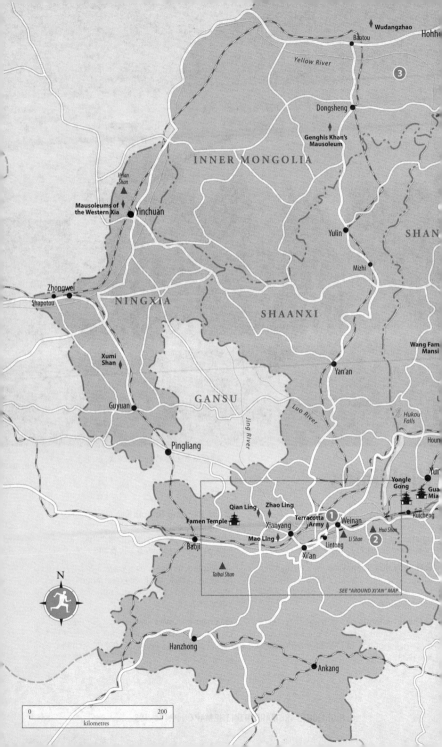

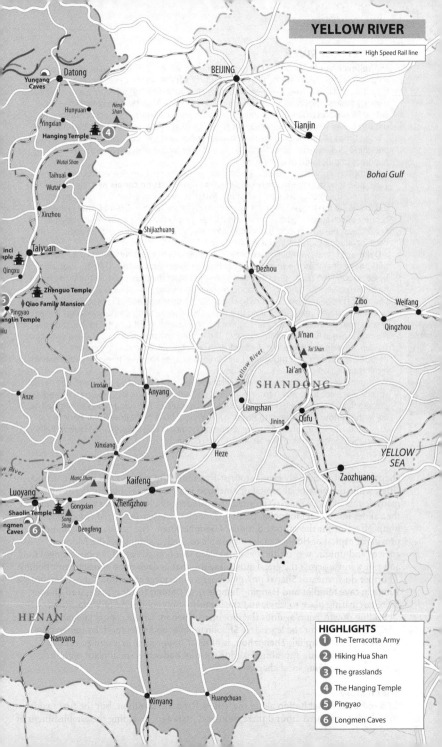

YELLOW RIVER

- - - - High Speed Rail line

Datong
Yungang Caves

Hunyuan   Heng Shan
Yingxian
Hanging Temple   4

Wutai Shan
Taihuai
Wutai

Xinzhou

inci ple   Taiyuan
Qingxu

Zhenguo Temple
Qiao Family Mansion
5   Pingyao
anglin Temple
iu

Anze
Linxian
Anyang

Luoyang   Mang Shan
Shaolin Temple   Gongxian
ngmen   Song Shan
Caves   6   Dengfeng

HENAN
Nanyang

Xinxiang

Kaifeng
Zhengzhou

Xinyang   Huangchuan

BEIJING

Tianjin

Bohai Gulf

Shijiazhuang

Dezhou

Zibo   Weifang
Qingzhou
Ji'nan
Tai Shan
Tai'an
SHANDONG
Liangshan
Jining   Qufu
Heze
YELLOW
SEA
Zaozhuang

Yellow River

N River

HIGHLIGHTS
1 The Terracotta Army
2 Hiking Hua Shan
3 The grasslands
4 The Hanging Temple
5 Pingyao
6 Longmen Caves

THE YELLOW RIVER

The **Yellow River** flows for 5500km through nine provinces, making it one of the world's mightiest waterways. However, the vast quantity of **silt** the river carries along its twisted length – 1.6 billion tonnes a year – has confused its course throughout history, and its unpredictable swings have always brought chaos. From 1194 to 1887, there were fifty major Yellow River **floods**, with three hundred thousand people killed in 1642 alone. Another disastrous event in 1933 was followed in 1937 by further tradgedy – this time man-made – when Chiang Kai-shek used the river as a weapon against the advancing Japanese, breaching its dykes to cut the rail line. A delay of a few weeks was gained at the cost of hundreds of thousands of Chinese lives.

Attempts to enhance the river's potential for creation rather than destruction began very early, at least by the eighth century BC, when the first **irrigation canals** were cut. In the fifth century BC, the Zheng Guo Canal irrigation system stretched an impressive 150km; it's still in use today. But the largest scheme was the building of the 1800km **Grand Canal** in the sixth century, which connected the Yellow and the Yangzi rivers and was used to carry grain to the north. It was built using locks to control water level, an innovation that did not appear in the West for another four hundred years.

Dykes, too, have been built since ancient times, and in some eastern sections the river bottom is higher than the surrounding fields, often by as much as 10m. Dyke builders are heroes around the Yellow River, and every Chinese knows the story of Da Yu, the legendary figure responsible for battling the capricious waters. It is said that he mobilized thousands of people to dredge the riverbed and dig diversionary canals after a terrible flood in 297 BC. The work took thirteen years, and during that period Yu never went home. At work's end, he sank a bronze ox in the waters, a talisman to tame the flow (a replica of the ox guards the shore of Kunming Lake in Beijing's Summer Palace). Today, **river control** continues on a massive scale. To stop flooding, the riverbed is dredged, diversion channels are cut and reservoirs constructed on the river's tributaries. Land around the river has been forested to help prevent erosion and so keep the river's silt level down.

Surrounded by colossal sand dunes, the Ningxia resort of **Shapotou** is probably the most spectacular place from which to view the Yellow River, but for most of its course it meanders across a flat flood plain with a horizon sharp as a knife blade. Two good places to witness this are at the **Yellow River Viewing Point** in Kaifeng and from the **Yellow River Park** outside Zhengzhou. To see the river in a more tempestuous mood, take a diversion to **Hukou Falls** (see p.257), farther north on the Shaanxi–Shanxi border.

Shapotou. Still a relatively exotic, tourist-free zone, Ningxia also offers quiet, attractive cities, while the provincial capital of **Yinchuan** is a base for fascinating sights such as the mausoleums of the Western Xia, ancient reminders of a long-extinct culture. The river then slides into **Inner Mongolia**, passing through the super-industrial city of **Baotou**, jump-off point for the supposed **tomb of Genghis Khan**. The grasslands surrounding the provincial capital of **Hohhot** make it possible to catch a glimpse of the Mongols' ancient and unique way of life – you can sleep in a nomad's yurt, sample Mongol food and ride a horse across the grasslands, all within half a day's train journey from Beijing.

Further downstream, **Shanxi** province boasts some great attractions, most notably the **Yungang cave temples** and **Hanging Temple** near **Datong** (itself turning into an ever more fascinating place to stay), and the beautiful holy mountain of **Wutai Shan**.

Heading downstream again is the province of **Henan**, whose capital **Luoyang** is a great jumping-off point for the legendary **Shaolin temple**, and the superb **Longmen cave temples**. Henan's capital, **Zhengzhou**, is of most importance as a transport nexus, though just east is the appealing lakeside town of **Kaifeng**, a small place with little grandeur but a strong local character.

Brief history

Sites of **Neolithic habitation** along the Yellow River are common, but the first major conurbation appeared around three thousand years ago, heralding the establishment of the Shang dynasty. For the next few millennia, every Chinese dynasty had its **capital** somewhere in the Yellow River area, and most of the major cities, from Datong in the north, capital of the Northern Wei, to Kaifeng in the east, capital of the Song, have spent some time as the centre of the Chinese universe. With the collapse of imperial China, the area sank into provincialism, and it was not until late in the twentieth century that it again came to prominence. The old capitals have today found new leases of life as industrial and commercial centres, and thus present two sides to the visitor: a rapidly changing, and sometimes harsh, modernity; and a static history, preserved in the interests of tourism. This latter feature contrasts strongly with, for instance, southwestern China, where temples might double as tourist attractions but are also clearly functional places of worship; here, most feel much more like museums – even if they seldom lack grandeur.

Shaanxi

陕西, shǎnxī

SHAANXI province is dusty, harsh and unwelcoming, with a climate of extremes: in winter, strong winds bring yellow dust storms, while summer is hot and wet. However, it's remarkable for the depth and breadth of its history, best exemplifed in the provincial capital, **Xi'an**: famed for the renowned **Terracotta Army** to the east, it was used as a dynastic capital over the course of 2000 years. Mysterious terracotta figures aside, there's other evidence of the city's former glories, in the shape of the tomb of the great emperor Qin Shi Huang, and a host of nearby temples and museums; it's a far bigger, busier place than many visitors expect, and perhaps the country's most cosmopolitan city outside the eastern seaboard.

Shaanxi, however, is more than just Xi'an. If you've had enough of the relics of ancient cultures, head east of Xi'an to **Hua Shan**, a spectacular mountain range which offers superb, easy-to-access hikes.

4

Xi'an

西安, xī'ān

XI'AN is a name tingling with intrigue. One of China's most famous cities, it's synonymous with the mysterious **Terracotta Army**, standing in inscrutable silence just to the east. These are the most famous remnant from Xi'an's extraordinarily long history – between 1000 BC and 1000 AD, it served as the **imperial capital** for no fewer than eleven dynasties, and as such it comes as no surprise that the place is filled with,

---

XI'AN ORIENTATION

Central Xi'an is bounded by city walls, with a bell tower marking the crossroads of the four main streets. Getting around this area is a doddle, since the street layout closely follows the ordered **grid plan** of the ancient city; the only exception is the **Muslim Quarter**, northwest of the Bell Tower, around whose unmarked winding alleys it's easy (and not necessarily unpleasurable) to get lost.

Downtown Xi'an, inside the walls, is just about compact enough to get around on foot, with enough sights to fill a busy day. To the southeast you'll find the **Beilin Museum**, which holds a massive collection of steles, next to the **city walls**, imposing remnants of Imperial China.

The area south of the Ming-dynasty city walls is scattered with architecture from the Han and Tang dynasties. The excellent **Shaanxi History Museum** and the small **Daxingshan Temple** sit between the two **Goose pagodas** and their temples, which are some of Xi'an's oldest buildings, and certainly the most distinctive.

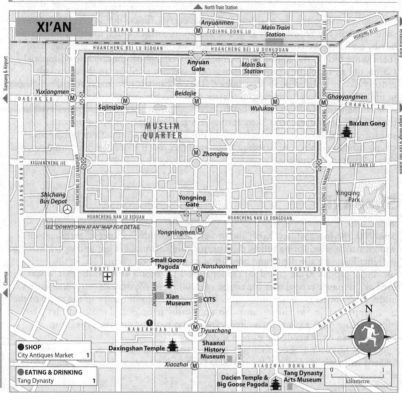

XI'AN

SHOP
City Antiques Market 1

EATING & DRINKING
Tang Dynasty 1

and surrounded by, a wealth of important sites and relics. The list of newly discovered treasures grows with each passing decade; in addition to the Terracotta Army, highlights include **Neolithic Banpo**, and the Han and Tang **imperial tombs**. In the city itself, you'll find two Tang-dynasty **pagodas**, the **Bell and Drum towers** and the **Ming city walls**, as well as two excellent **museums** holding a treasury of relics from the most fabled chapters of Chinese history.

However, visitors are also advised to prepare for a modicum of disappointment. Historically significant though it may be, today's Xi'an is a manufacturing metropolis of five million inhabitants, filled with traffic and prone to heavy **pollution** – issues that can make trips to the outlying sights a bit of a chore. Yet most travellers are able to see past these failings, perhaps best evidenced by a large foreign community, many of whom come to study, since the colleges are regarded as some of the best places to learn Chinese outside of Beijing.

Brief history

Some 3000 years ago, the western Zhou dynasty, known for their skilled bronzework, built their capital at **Fenghao**, a few kilometres west of Xi'an. When Fenghao was sacked by northwestern tribes, the Zhou moved downriver to **Luoyang** and, as their empire continued to disintegrate into warring chiefdoms, the nearby Qin kingdom expanded. In 221 BC, the larger-than-life **Qin Shi Huang** united the Chinese in a single empire, the Qin, with its capital at **Xianyang**, just north of Xi'an. The underground **Terracotta Army**, intended to guard his tomb, are this tyrant's inadvertent gift to today's tourist prosperity.

The Han

The Qin dynasty's successors, the **Han**, ruled from 206 BC to 220 AD, building themselves a new, splendid and cosmopolitan capital a few kilometres northwest of Xi'an, which they called **Chang'an** – Eternal Peace. Its size reflected the power of their empire, and records say that its walls were 17km round with twelve great gates. Chang'an was the start of the **Silk Road**, along which, among many other things, Chinese silk was carried to dress Roman senators and their wives at the court of Augustus. There was also a brisk trade with south and west Asia; Han China was an outward-looking empire.

When the dynasty fell, Chang'an was destroyed, though the imperial **tombs** remain, including Emperor Wu's mound at **Mao Ling**. It was not until 589 that the **Sui** dynasty reunited the warring kingdoms into a new empire, but their dynasty hardly lasted longer than the time it took to build a new capital near Xi'an, called **Da Xingcheng** – Great Prosperity.

The Tang

The **Tang**, who replaced the Sui in 618, took over the capital, overlaying it with their own buildings in a rational grid plan that became the model not only for many other Chinese cities, but also the contemporary Japanese capital Hei'an (now Kyoto). During this time, the city became one of the biggest in the world, with over a million inhabitants. The Tang period was a **golden age** for China's arts, and ceramics, calligraphy, painting and poetry all reached new heights. Its sophistication was reflected in its religious tolerance – not only was this a great period for **Buddhism**, with monks busy translating the sutras that the adventurous monk **Xuan Zong** had brought back from India, but the city's **Great Mosque** dates from the Tang, and one of the steles in the Provincial Museum bears witness to the founding of a chapel by Nestorian Christians.

Decline

After the fall of the Tang, Xi'an went into a long **decline**. It was never again the imperial capital, though the Ming emperor Hong Wu rebuilt the city as a gift for his son; today's great walls and gates date from this time. Occasionally, though, the city did continue to provide a footnote to history. When the Empress Dowager Cixi had to flee Beijing after the Boxer Rebellion, she set up her court here for two years. In 1911, during the uprising against the Manchu Qing dynasty, the Manchu quarter in Xi'an was destroyed and the Manchus massacred. And in 1936, Chiang Kai-shek was arrested at Huaqing Hot Springs nearby in what became known as the Xi'an Incident (see p.212).

The Bell Tower

钟楼, zhōng lóu • Daily 8am–10pm • ¥35, or ¥50 including Drum Tower

In the heart of town, the **Bell Tower** stands at the centre of the crossroads where the four main streets meet. The original tower was raised two blocks west of here in 1384, at the centre of the Tang-dynasty city; the present triple-eaved wooden structure standing on a brick platform was built in 1582 and restored in 1739. You can enter only via the subway on Bei Dajie, where you buy your ticket and where you must leave any large bags. Inside is an exhibition of chimes and a bronze bell (not the original). A balcony all the way around the outside provides a view of the city's traffic; if you'd rather see the tower from the outside instead, there are a couple of upper-level cafés to the northwest.

The Drum Tower

鼓楼, gǔlóu • Daily 8am–10pm • ¥35, or ¥50 including the Bell Tower

Just west of the Bell Tower is the **Drum Tower**. It's a triple-eaved wooden building atop a 50m-long arch straddling the road. You enter up steps on the eastern side, to find a row of drums that used to be banged at dusk, a complement to the bell in the Bell Tower, which heralded the dawn.

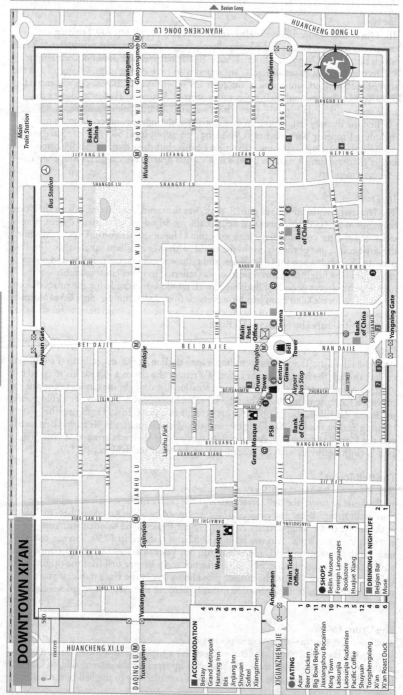

DOWNTOWN XI'AN

Baxian Gong

HUANCHENG DONG LU

Chaoyangmen

Changlemen

Main Train Station

Bank of China

Bus Station

Lianhu Park

Great Mosque

Drum Tower

Bell Tower

Century Ginwa

Main Post Office

Cinema

Bank of China

Bank of China

Bank of China

Yongning Gate

West Mosque

Zhonglou Tower

PSB

Airport Bus Stop

Andingmen

Train Ticket Office

ACCOMMODATION

Bestay	4
Grand Metropark	5
Hantang Inn	2
Ibis	6
Jinjiang Inn	3
Shuyuan	8
Sofitel	1
Xiangzimen	7

EATING

Azur	1
Beer Chicken	9
Big Bowl Beijing	11
Jiaxiangshou Bocaimian	10
King Town	7
Laosunjia	3
Laosunjia Kudaimian	5
Pacific Coffee	12
Shuyuan	4
Tongshengxiang	8
Xi'an	2
Xi'an Roast Duck	6

SHOPS

Beilin Museum	3
Foreign Languages Bookstore	2
Huajue Xiang	1

DRINKING & NIGHTLIFE

Belgian Bar	1
Muse	1

The Muslim Quarter

North of the Drum Tower, the scale of Xi'an's streets constricts, and the narrow alleys lined with cramped half-timbered, two-storey buildings feel more like a village than a sprawling provincial capital. This is the **Muslim Quarter**, for centuries the centre for Xi'an's Hui population; numbering thirty thousand today, they're said to be descended from eighth-century Arab soldiers. **Beiyuanmen**, the street that runs north from the Drum Tower gate, is flagstoned and lined with Muslim restaurants, all packed out and lively in the evening.

The Great Mosque

清真大寺, qīngzhēn dàsì • Daily 8am–5.30pm • April–Oct ¥25, Nov–March ¥15

Just north of the Drum Tower, the narrow, covered alley of **Huajue Xiang** – essentially one long line of tourist tat – heads to the **Great Mosque**; a more interesting approach can be made on the small roads running up the western and northern sides of the complex. The largest mosque in China, it was originally established in 742, then rebuilt in the Qing dynasty and heavily restored. An east–west-facing complex that integrates Arabic features into a familiar Chinese design, it's a calm place, untouched by the hectic atmosphere of the streets outside.

Around the south gate

Heading south from the Bell Tower along Nan Dajie, a street of department stores and offices, you come to Yongning, the huge **south gate**. A turn east takes you along **Shuyuanmen**, a pleasant, cobbled street of souvenir shops, art stores and antique shops traversing the heart of Beilin, a touristy artists' quarter.

Beilin Museum

碑林博物馆 • bēilín bówùguǎn • Daily 8.30am–6.30pm • March–Sept ¥45, Oct–Feb ¥30

About 500m east of the south gate, near an access point for the city walls, is the **Beilin Museum**, a converted Confucian temple. Aside from an annexe on the west side, which holds an exhibition of chronologically arranged **Buddhist images** where you can follow the evolution of styles over the centuries, the museum's main focus is six halls containing more than a thousand **steles**.

The first and second halls

The **first hall** contains the twelve Confucian classics – texts outlining the Confucian philosophy – carved onto 114 stone tablets, a massive project ordered by the Tang emperor Wenzong in 837 as a way of ensuring the texts were never lost or corrupted by copyists' errors. The **second hall** includes the **Daqing Nestorian tablet**, on the left as you go in, recognizable by a cross on the top, which records the arrival of a Nestorian priest in Chang'an in 781 and gives a rudimentary description of Christian doctrine.

The third and fourth halls

In the **third hall**, one stele is inscribed with a **map of Chang'an** at the height of its splendour, when the walls were extensive enough to include the Big Goose Pagoda within their perimeter. Rubbings are often being made in the **fourth hall**, where the most carved drawings are housed; thin paper is pasted over a stele and a powdered ink applied with a flat stone wrapped in cloth. Among the steles is an image called the "God of Literature Pointing the Dipper", with the eight characters that outline the Confucian virtues – regulate the heart, cultivate the self, overcome selfishness and return propriety – cleverly made into the image of a jaunty figure. "To point the dipper" meant to come first in the exams on Confucian texts, which controlled entry to the civil service.

The city walls

Daily Dec–Feb 8am–6pm, March–Nov 8am–10pm • entry after 6pm through South Gate only • ¥40 • electric shuttle ¥50 for circuit, or ¥5 per station • bike rental ¥20 for 100min, plus ¥200 deposit

Imposing enough to act as a physical barrier between the city centre and the suburbs, Xi'an's **city walls** were originally built in the Tang dynasty, though they took their modern form in 1568, when they were faced with brick. Recently restored, the walls are the most distinctive feature of the modern city, forming a 12m-high rectangle whose perimeter is nearly 14km in length. Some 18m wide at the base, they're capped with crenellations, a watchtower at each corner and a fortress-like gate in the centre of each side. Originally, the city would have been further defended with a moat and drawbridges, but today the area around the walls is a thin strip of parkland. You can **ascend** the wall from the **four main gates**, from where you can explore the top of the wall on foot, by pushbike (the 100min rental period gives just enough time to get around, though don't dawdle too much) or on an **electric shuttle**. If prepared with food and drinks, you can spend the better part of a day up here.

The Small Goose Pagoda

小雁塔, xiǎoyàn tǎ • Youyi Xi Lu, southwest of the Yongning gate • Daily 8am–6pm • March–Sept ¥25, Oct–Feb ¥18 • metro to Nanshaomen

The delicate, 45m-high **Small Goose Pagoda** was founded during the Tang dynasty in 707 to store sutras brought back from India, and sits in what remains of the Jianfu Temple. Two of the pagoda's original fifteen storeys were damaged in an earthquake, leaving a rather abrupt jagged top to the roof, to which you can ascend for a view of the city. A shop at the back of the complex sells Shaanxi folk arts.

Xi'an Museum

西安博物馆, xī'ān bówùguǎn • Wed–Mon 9am–5pm • Free (bring ID) • visitor numbers limited to 3000 per day

Sited in the grounds of the Small Goose Pagoda, the **Xi'an Museum** compares favourably with the more illustrious, and far more crowded, Shaanxi Museum (see below). Its design echoes the ancient Chinese concept of a round heaven surrounding a square earth, and over 130,000 relics are on display across its three floors. Best of all is the **underground hall** which, rather appropriately, shows objects unearthed from in and around Xi'an – take time to linger around the superb Han-dynasty pottery. Up on the **first floor** you'll find Buddhist regalia and an interesting "virtual" display, while the **second floor** has dedicated halls for jades, seals, paintings and the like.

Daxingshan Temple

大兴善寺 • dàxīngshàn sì • Xingshan Xijie • Daily 8am–5pm • Free • metro to Xiaozhai

The **Daxingshan Temple** is usually overlooked by visitors, but the absence of teeming crowds makes a visit even more worthwhile – this is one of the calmest, most pleasant places in noisy Xi'an. It's also the only working Buddhist temple in the city; destroyed during the late Tang's persecution of the religion, today's buildings are mainly Qing. If your time is short, make a beeline for the main hall, which features a giant sandalwood statue of Guanyin; look for monks in baggy orange trousers around the periphery of the hall, who'll write your name on a prayer sheet for a donation.

Shaanxi History Museum

陕西历史博物馆 • shǎnxīlìshǐ bówùguǎn • Tues–Sun 8am–5pm • Free (bring ID) • visitor numbers limited to 4000 per day • metro to Xiaozhai

One of the city's major highlights, the **Shaanxi History Museum** is an impressive modern building within walking distance of the Daxingshan Temple and the Big Goose Pagoda. The exhibition halls are spacious, well laid out, and have English captions, displaying to full advantage a magnificent collection of more than 3000 relics.

The **lower floor**, which contains a general survey of the development of civilization until the Zhou dynasty, holds mostly weapons, ceramics and simple ornaments – most impressive is a superb set of Western Zhou and Shang bronze vessels covered in geometric designs suggestive of animal shapes, used for storing and cooking ritual food. The **western hall** holds bronzes and ceramics, in which the best-looking artefacts are Tang. Large numbers of ceramic funerary objects include superbly expressive and rather vicious-looking camels, guardians and dancers. The **eastern hall** features a display of Tang gold and silver, mainly finely wrought images of dragons and tiny, delicate flowers and birds, and an exhibition of Tang costume and ornament. Highlights of the two **upstairs galleries** include the Han ceramic funerary objects, particularly the model houses.

The Dacien Temple

大慈恩寺 • dàcíēn sì • Daily 8am–6.30pm • ¥25 • metro to Xiaozhai then a 2km walk

The **Dacien Temple**, 4km south of the city walls at the end of Yanta Lu, is the largest temple in Xi'an. The original, destroyed during the fall of the Tang dynasty in 907, was even bigger: founded in 647, it had nearly 2,000 rooms, and a resident population of more than three hundred monks. The surrounding area is a bit of a circus nowadays, with the armies of souvenir sellers dwarfed by a crowd-pulling **musical fountain**, arranged in steps, which fills the northern approach to the temple. The main entrance, however, is to the south, and inside the walls the atmosphere is much calmer, though still oriented towards tourism rather than worship, even though there are resident monks here.

The Big Goose Pagoda

大雁塔 • dàyàn tǎ • Daily March–Nov 8am–6.30pm, Dec–Feb 8.30am–6pm • ¥50, plus ¥30 to climb

The most famous person associated with Dacien Temple is **Xuanzang**, the Tang monk who made a pilgrimage to India and returned with a trove of sacred Buddhist texts (see p.830). At his request, the **Big Goose Pagoda** was built of brick at the centre of the temple grounds as a fireproof store for his precious sutras. More impressive than its little brother, the Big Goose Pagoda is sturdy and angular, square in plan, and more than 60m tall. As you go in, look for a famous **tablet** on the right showing Xuanzang dwarfed by his massive bamboo backpack. The pagoda has **seven storeys**, each with large windows (out of which visitors throw money for luck). The area surrounding the complex has been heavily redeveloped in recent years, to the delight of some locals, and the chagrin of others.

The Baxian Gong

八仙宫 • bāxiān gōng • ¥3 • bus #203 or #502

The **Baxian Gong**, Xi'an's largest Taoist temple, lies in a shabby area east of the city walls. It's said to be sited over the wine shop where **Lü Dongbin**, later one of the Eight Immortals, was enlightened by Taoist master Han Zhongli. Containing an important collection of steles, including pictures of local scenic areas and copies of complex ancient medical diagrams of the human body, the temple is the setting for a popular **religious festival** on the first and fifteenth day of every lunar month. However, it is probably of most interest to visitors for the **antiques market** that takes place outside every Wednesday and Sunday (see p.204).

ARRIVAL AND DEPARTURE
XI'AN

BY PLANE

Xi'an airport (西安咸阳国际机场, xī'ān xiányáng guójì jīchǎng), 40km northwest of the city, is connected to town by regular airport buses (6am–8pm; ¥25; 1hr), which terminate at five locations around town; the most useful are the *Rainbow Hotel* and main train station. A taxi costs ¥100–120 for the vehicle (or ¥25–30 per person if you share), and it's best to fix the fare in advance rather than risk being taken a long way round on the meter; cabs hover around the airport bus departure points looking for passengers. Air tickets can

SHOPPING IN XI'AN

Xi'an is an excellent place to pick up souvenirs and antiques, which are generally cheaper and more varied than in Beijing, though prices have to be bartered down and the standard of goods, especially from tourist shops, is sometimes shoddy. Shopping is also an enjoyable evening activity, since the markets and department stores are open until 10pm – the Muslim Quarter and Beilin make for an entertaining stroll under the stars, where the nocturnal hawkers sell everything from dinner to souvenir silk paintings.

ARTWORK

Xi'an has a strong artistic pedigree, and the **paintings** available here are much more varied in style than those you see elsewhere in China. As well as the widespread line-and-wash paintings of legendary figures, flowers and animals, look for bright, simple **folk paintings**, usually of country scenes. A traditional Shaanxi art form, appealing for their decorative, flat design and lush colours, these images were popular in China in the 1970s for their idealistic, upbeat portrayal of peasant life. A good selection is sold in a shop just behind the Small Goose Pagoda and in the temple compound, as well as outside the Banpo Museum (see p.208). For **rubbings** from steles, much cheaper than paintings and quite striking, try the Big Goose Pagoda and Shuyuanmen, especially around the Beilin Museum, which is also a great area to find **calligraphy and paintings**. The underground pedestrian route at the South Gate includes an interesting diversion down an old bomb shelter tunnel to Nan Shang Jie, where **papercuts** are for sale.

Strong competition means you can pick up a painting quite cheaply if you're prepared to **bargain**. Beware the bright young things who introduce themselves as art students whose class happens to be having an exhibition. They're essentially touts who will lead you to a room full of mediocre work at inflated prices.

SOUVENIRS

Beiyuanmen and Huajue Xiang, the alley that runs off to the Great Mosque, are the places to go for **small souvenirs**, engraved chopsticks, teapots, chiming balls and the like. Clusters of stalls and vendors swarm around all the tourist sights, and are often a nuisance, though the stalls around the Great Mosque are worth checking out – you'll see curved Islamic **shabaria** knives among the Mao watches and other tourist knick-knacks.

For a personalized souvenir, try the **seal engravers** along Shuyuanmen, where you'll also find a variety of calligraphy sets and other **artists' materials**.

ANTIQUES

Antiques abound in Xi'an, but be aware that many – however dusty and worn – are reproductions. The best place to go is the **City Antiques Market**, about a block south of the Small Goose Pagoda, on Zhuque Dajie; this has some genuine antiques and oddities (such as old military gear) at reasonable prices, and Mao-era artwork with price tags that show the dealers here know how much these things sell for overseas. Another good place is the market outside **Baxian Gong**, which is biggest on Wednesdays and Sundays; many vendors are villagers from the outlying regions who look as if they are clearing out their attics. You can find some unusual items here, such as books and magazines dating from the Cultural Revolution containing rabid anti-Western propaganda, Qing vases, opium pipes and even rusty guns.

be arranged through all accommodation; if hostels attempt to charge a booking fee, go elsewhere.

Destinations Beijing (10 daily; 2hr); Chengdu (8 daily; 50min); Chongqing (8–9 daily; 1hr 15min); Dalian (3–4 daily; 2hr); Dunhuang (2–3 daily; 2hr 50min); Guangzhou (11–13 daily; 2hr 25min); Guilin (6 daily; 1hr 40min); Hong Kong (3 daily; 2hr 30min); Ji'nan (3–4 daily; 1hr 30min); Kunming (2–3 daily; 2hr); Lanzhou (6–8 daily; 1hr 10min); Nanjing (7 daily; 1hr 50min); Qingdao (5–6 daily; 1hr 50min); Shanghai (hourly; 1hr 50min); Taiyuan (2–4 daily; 1hr).

BY TRAIN

Train tickets are a nightmare to get at the station; either use your accommodation (hostels charge around ¥40 a ticket) or one of several advance-ticket offices scattered around (¥5). Ask at your accommodation for the closest one to you. **Main station** (西安站, xīān zhàn) The busy main train station, just outside the north wall, is a major stop on routes from Zhengzhou, Beijing, Chengdu and Lanzhou. It will, by 2016, be on metro line #4; for now, buses #206, #205, #201 and #610 (aka tourist bus #8) will get you to the

Bell and Drum tower area from the south exit, while taxis congregate on the western side of the station concourse.

Destinations Baoji (many daily; 1hr 40min–3hr); Beijing (11 daily; 11hr–16hr); Datong (1 daily; 16hr 30min); Guangzhou (7 daily; 21 30min–30hr); Hua Shan (many daily; 1hr 30min); Lanzhou (many daily; 6hr 30min–8hr 30min); Lhasa (2 daily; 33hr); Luoyang (many daily; 4hr 30min–6hr 30min); Shanghai (10 daily; 14hr 30min–20hr 30min); Taiyuan (10 daily; 9hr 50min–11hr 30min); Ürümqi (10 daily; 28–34hrs); Xining (8 daily; 9hr 15min–12hr); Zhengzhou (many daily; 6hr–8hr 30min).

Xi'an North (西安北站, xī'ān běizhàn) This is a high-speed only station lying a full 15km north of the city walls; from here, the city centre is easily accessible on metro line #2. At the time of writing no high-speed services headed further west from Xi'an.

Destinations Beijing (11 daily; 4hr 40min–6hr); Guangzhou (7 daily; 7hr 40min–9hr); Hua Shan (15 daily; 30–50min); Luoyang (22 daily; 1hr 30min–2hr); Shanghai (1 daily; 10hr 50min); Zhengzhou (many daily; 2hr–2hr 50min).

BY BUS

Xi'an is so well connected by train that fewer and fewer people are arriving by bus.

The main station (省汽车站, shěng qìchēzhàn) faces the train station at the top of Jiefang Lu; it's most notable for the services to Luoyang (5 daily; 5hr), Pingyao (5 daily; 7hr) and Zhengzhou (hourly; 6hr).

The east bus station (客运东站, kèyùn dōngzhàn), 2km outside the walls on Changle Lu, is best for services to Hua Shan (hourly; 2hr).

GETTING AROUND

By bus The largest concentration of city buses is found outside the train station at the northern end of Jiefang Lu. There are other clusters just outside the South Gate (a gigantic mess at the time of writing), and at the southern end of Yanta Lu, just north of the Big Goose Pagoda. Normal buses cost ¥1, fancier ones with air conditioning ¥2.

By metro Xi'an's new metro system provides a welcome relief from the city's crowded, congested buses. Line #1 crosses the city east–west; line #2 runs north–south; and lines #3 and #4 should follow by 2016. Fares cost ¥2–4, depending upon the distance travelled.

By taxi Cabs are plentiful, though drivers here are even more berserk than those in other Chinese cities, and such is demand that taxis are next to impossible to pick up after around 6pm. Rides start at ¥6, and ¥12 should be enough to get you almost anywhere within the city walls.

By bicycle As Xi'an's streets are wide and flat, and the main roads have cycle lanes, controlled at major intersections by officials with flags. There are, however, few bike parks, and most people risk a (rarely enforced) ¥10 fine by leaving their bikes padlocked to railings. Hostels rent bikes for around ¥20 per day, with a deposit of up to ¥200.

INFORMATION

Maps City maps (¥5), some in English, are available everywhere and are worth picking up immediately, as bus routes are continually amended.

Travel agents All hostels can book you on local tours, and some act as agents for Yangzi ferries, too; you don't have to be staying with them either. Hotels and motels also have tour desks, though you're likely to be bundled in with Chinese-speaking groups if you use them. The main CITS office is at 48 Chang'an Lu (daily 8am–6pm; ☎029 85399999); they can arrange tours and hire minibuses seating 5–6 for ¥650 per day.

ACCOMMODATION

Xi'an is firmly on the tourist itinerary, and accommodation abounds for all budgets. As plenty of options are located within the city walls, close to the most interesting bits of Xi'an and with easy access to the tourist sights, there seems little point in staying outside, in the drabber, more modern parts of town. Hostels all offer internet, laundry, food and beer, and usually free pick-up from the train station. The following all appear on the map on p.200.

HOSTELS

★ **Hantang Inn** 汉唐旅舍, hàntáng lǚshè. 7 Nanchang Xiang ☎029 87231126, ⊕itisxian.com. The most pleasant hostel in the city, with a fun bar downstairs, decent rooms, and a ping-pong table, sunbeds (!) and a small sauna up on the roof. Rooms are comfortable too. Their sister operation just up the road, *Hantang House*, offers much the same but is marginally cheaper, flashier

---

BUS #610

Bus #610 (labelled as tourist bus #8 in Chinese) is particularly useful, as it links most of the sights: it runs from the train station via Bei Xin Jie, Bei Dajie, the Bell and Drum towers, then south off Xi Dajie down Guangji Jie to Small Goose Pagoda, Daxingshan Temple, the History Museum and on to the Big Goose Pagoda.

and noisier. Daily events are shared across the two hostels. Dorms **¥50**, twins **¥220**

Shuyuan 书院旅舍, shūyuàn lǚshè. West of the South Gate ☎029 87287721, ⓦhostelxian.com. Owned by the *Hantang* team, who may or may not have plans to commandeer the whole city, this is an appealingly ramshackle hostel facing the city walls. The building is based on a traditional courtyard plan, and rooms are generally fine, if occasionally a little musty; their restaurant is also popular. Dorms **¥45**, rooms **¥220**

Xiangzimen 湘子门国际青年旅舍, xiāngzǐmén guójì qīngnián lǚshè. 16 Xiangzimiao Jie ☎029 62867888, ⓦyhaxian.com. Beautiful old courtyard mansion hostel with wooden fittings – there's nothing else like this closer than Pingyao. The downstairs doubles are decent but windowless and claustrophobic; better to try rooms in the new wing. Dorms **¥35**, rooms **¥140**

HOTELS

Bestay 百时快捷酒店, bǎishí kuàijié jiǔdiàn. 110 Jiefeng Lu ☎029 87436868, ⓦwww.bestay.com.cn. Cheapie on a quiet, atmospheric (and occasionally stinky) road featuring umpteen restaurants. They've gone for artsy decoration in the common areas, though rooms themselves are, mercifully, kept simple. All in all, a good budget choice for those who'd rather not join the backpackers at a hostel; note, however, that there's no lift. **¥189**

Grand Metropark 维景国际大酒店, wéijǐng guójì dàjiǔdiàn. 158 Dong Dajie, just east of Heping Lu ☎029 87691234, ⓦmetroparkhotels.com. Little changed since its previous incarnation as the *Hyatt*, including the signature pyramidal atrium. Rooms are well appointed, and suitably popular with tour groups and business folk. **¥700**

Ibis 宜必思酒店, yíbìsī jiǔdiàn. 59 Heping Lu ☎029 87275555, ⓦaccorhotels.com. Blocky and unadventurous it may appear from the outside, but rooms here are a real bargain, even if the beds are a little firm for some tastes. Staff speak English and score good service marks. **¥428**

Jinjiang Inn 锦江之星旅馆, jǐnjiāng zhīxīng lǚguǎn. 110 Jiefang Lu ☎029 87452288, ⓦjinjianginns.com. Exactly what you'd expect of a *Jinjiang Inn*: low rates, smartly furnished modern rooms, efficient service and free wi-fi. There's another, slightly more expensive, branch a stone's throw from the Drum Tower, on 1 Shehui Lu. **¥289**

★ **Sofitel** 索菲特国际饭店, suǒfēitè guójì fàndiàn. 319 Dongxin Jie ☎029 87928888, ⓦsofitel .com. Part of a large complex of high-class hotels, the twin *Sofitel* buildings boast scented lobbies, intricately designed interiors, and plush rooms, presided over by a young and energetic staff, all of whom are bilingual. Their restaurants are excellent; try *Azur* (see below), or *Churrasco* for Brazilian barbecue. **¥1200**

EATING

Xi'an is a great place to eat, though the best of the **local food** is fairly rough and ready, most enjoyably consumed in the Muslim Quarter's hectic, open-fronted restaurants – an excellent primer for those pushing on west to Xinjiang. Here you'll find *liang fen* (cold, translucent noodles shaved off a block of beanstarch jelly and served with a spicy sauce), *hele* (buckwheat noodles) and *mianpi* (flat noodles made of refined wheat dough); *kudai mian* (super-thick, "belt" noodles, served in a spicy sauce); huge rounds of flat bread, which make an excellent accompaniment to a handful of grilled mutton skewers; **sweets** such as steamed "eight treasure pudding" (glutinous rice cooked in a tiny wooden pot and dusted with sugar and sesame); and preserved fruits heaped on plates. The most widely touted Xi'an dish, however, is *paomo* (see below). The following all appear on the map on p.200.

Azur. 319 Dongxin Jie, in the east wing of the Sofitel. Entered through a panoply of hanging cuboid lanterns, this is perhaps the most stylish venue in town, blending the cuisines of North Africa, southern Europe and the eastern Mediterranean. The lunch (¥168) and dinner buffets (¥278) are immaculate, if pricey, though there's a cheaper *à la carte* selection (pastas from ¥85). It's also a good place to drop in for an evening tipple. Daily 11.30am–10.30pm.

Beer Chicken 啤酒鸡, píjiǔ jī. 3 Duanlumen. If you're

PAOMO

It would be a shame to leave Xi'an without sampling **paomo**, its signature dish. This is basically a meat soup – there are both lamb (羊肉泡馍, yángròu pāomó) and beef (牛肉泡馍, niúròu pāomó) versions – poured over a bowlful of tiny bread cubes. At many restaurants, diners are given discs of bread and encouraged to do the cubing themselves. Most foreigners seem to prefer the taste and texture of larger chunks – this will likely be met with a scornful look from your waitress, since locals take their time with this process, producing something almost akin to breadcrumbs. The bowl is then taken to the kitchen and piled with shredded meat and noodles, and it's all served with cloves of pickled garlic and chilli paste for you to tip in as required.

in the mood for something a little different, head to this simple place, which specializes in beer-cooked chicken. A ¥50 portion is enough to feed at least two people, though do note that there's no English-language or picture menu. Daily 9am–9pm.

Big Bowl Beijing 老碗, lǎo wǎn. 55 Xiangzimiao Jie ☏ 029 68893666. Cheap yet highly attractive choice in Xi'an's most important backbacker base, this is a long, skinny restaurant so popular that people have to queue at mealtimes. Staples from ¥16, with some Shaanxi specials; see the English menu for details. Daily 9am–9pm.

Jiaxiangshou Bocaimian 家乡手菠菜面, jiāxiāngshǒu bōcàimiàn. Nanchang Xiang, opposite the Hantang Inn. This simple place serves scrumptious bocai mian (green spinach noodles) for the backpacker-friendly price of ¥10. They'll even serve you in the restaurant of the hostel across the road – the staff don't mind at all. Daily 10.30am–9pm.

King Town 秦唐一号中国餐馆, qíntáng yīhào zhōngguó cānguǎn. 176 Dongmu Tuoshi ☏ 029 87235888. Smart, excellent Sichuanese restaurant, with a casual snack area at street level and a more formal restaurant upstairs where you can pay over ¥50 a head. Daily 9am–2pm & 4.30–10pm.

Laosunjia 老孙家, lǎosūnjiā. Corner of Nanxin Jie and Dong Dajie, 5F of Go Go Happy Building ☏ 029 87421858. No list of Xi'an restaurants is complete without this yangrou paomo venue, whose fame is such that every second restaurant in the Muslim quarter has appropriated the name. This one is the real deal; they've been in business since 1898, though recently relocated to a disappointingly modern venue. Paomo goes from ¥28 a bowl; for a bit more, you can have it with decidedly non-traditional ingredients such as ostrich and deer. Daily 9am–9pm.

Laosunjia Kudaimian 老孙家裤带面, lǎosūnjiā kùdài miàn. Behind Drum Tower. Reliable, earthy

choice for kudai mian, Xi'an's famous "belt" noodles (so named on account of their thickness), served luke-warm in a spicy, oily sauce. ¥15, or ¥25 including more meat and vegetables. Daily 7am–10pm.

Pacific Coffee 太平洋咖啡, tàipíngyáng kāfēi Off northwest corner of Bell Tower. Western-style café serving adequate coffee (¥30 or so), though most notable for its stunning views of the Bell Tower. Daily 7.30am–11.30pm.

Shuyuan 书院旅舍, shūyuàn lǚshè. West of the South Gate ☏ 029 87287721. This hostel's restaurant is hugely popular with travellers and expats alike for its pizza (¥30 and up), made in a proper oven. The large ones are enough to feed a whole hutong. Daily 8am–10pm.

Tongshengxiang 同盛祥, tóngshèngxiáng. Xi Dajie, in an eleborately styled building between the Drum and Bell Towers. This multistoreyed Muslim place is famous for its paomo and tangbao (soup buns); it's far more pleasant than the more illustrious Laosunjia, and the paomo (from ¥26) is just as good. Daily 7.30am–10pm.

Xi'an 西安宾馆, xīān bīnguǎn. 298 Dong Dajie. A restaurant famed as the place where the plotters of the Xi'an Incident (see p.212) formulated their plan to kidnap Chiang Kai-shek – a history that has, so far, afforded it protection from the wrecking balls swung liberally around the area. The downstairs canteen is all right, with set breakfasts and lunch buffets for ¥15–30, but the upstairs restaurant is excellent, with banquet dishes such as gourd-shaped chicken. Expect to pay over ¥60 a head. Daily 10am–2pm & 5–10pm.

Xi'an Roast Duck 西安烤鸭店, xīān kǎoyādiàn. 368 Dong Dajie. This otherwise unassuming restaurant near the bell tower is usually packed to the gills at lunch. A whole duck (enough for 2–3 people) costs around ¥148. Daily 10am–2pm & 5.30–10pm.

DRINKING AND ENTERTAINMENT

Xi'an has a large student population and general prosperity that make it more exciting at night than many other Chinese cities. The easiest place to start is the bar street area on Defu Xiang, just north of the Xiangzimen hostel, which is lined with Western-style pubs – none are particularly remarkable, but since all can be peeked inside from the street it's easy to find the best venue. Alternatively, all of the hostels listed on opposite have great bars, in which it's easy to round up fellow travellers for an extended night out elsewhere.

Belgian Bar East of the South Gate ☏ 029 87264019. A far more appealing venue than those you'll find on Bar Street, just to the west. Authentic Belgian beer from ¥40 per pint of draught; cheaper Chinese beer is also available. Happy hour from 3–8pm. Daily 3pm–midnight.

Muse Corner of Xi Dajie and Nanguangji Lu. The most popular club in town, at the time of writing. The music, generally of the hip-hop variety, is typically overloud, though the wiggling bodies inside don't seem to care

– perhaps because there's almost never a cover charge to get in. Daily 8pm–5am.

Tang Dynasty 唐乐宫, tánglè gōng. 75 Chang'an Beidajie ☏ 029 87822222, ⓦ xiantangdynasty.com. Theatre-restaurant with performances of traditional song and dance – too gaudy for most tastes, though some seem to enjoy the show. Nightly 90min performances ¥220, or ¥500 with banquet dinner; some hotels and hostels sell tickets at a discounted rate, and provide transport.

DIRECTORY

Banks and exchange Banks with ATMs are strewn all over town; a few convenient branches of the Bank of China are marked on the map, p.200.

Bookshop The Foreign Languages Bookstore on Duanlumen has a wide selection of books about China – and Xi'an in particular – together with the standard English-language novels.

Cinema Few cinemas in Xi'an show foreign films, and even those that do usually dub rather than subtitle. One honourable exception is the Oscar Cinema in the Century Ginwa Shopping Mall, southwest of the walled city at the corner of Gaoxin Lu and Keji Lu. It's ¥50 or so per ticket.

Hospital The Provincial Hospital is on Youyi Xi Lu, just west of the intersection with Lingyuan Lu.

Mail and telephones The central post office (8am–8pm) faces the Bell Tower at the intersection of Bei Dajie and Dong Dajie. The "Telecom district", with phone emporiums and card sellers, is around the intersection of Bei Dajie and Xixin Jie.

PSB 138 Xi Dajie (Mon–Sat 8am–noon & 3–5pm). Xi'an being such a popular place, many travellers try to extend their visa here, but service is not that great – go elsewhere if possible.

Around Xi'an

You could spend days on excursions **around Xi'an**. People swarm to see the **Terracotta Army** and **Banpo Museum**, and if your stay in Xi'an is short then the army is still the must-see sight. However, with a little more time, recommended attractions off the tour-group itinerary include the **Famen Temple**, with a superb museum attached, which is a little too remote for most visitors; and the **Tomb of Jingdi**, which has become extremely popular with backpackers.

Banpo Museum

半坡博物馆, bànpō bówùguǎn • Daily 8am–5pm • ¥45 • bus #105, #240 or #715 from train station area (1hr)

The **Banpo Museum**, 8km east of the centre, is the first stop on most eastern tours. It sits over the excavated site of a **Neolithic village**, discovered in 1953, which was occupied between around 4500 BC and 3750 BC. Banpo is the biggest and best-preserved site so far found of **Yangshao culture**, and is named after the village near the eastern bend of the Yellow River where the first relics of this type were found.

That said, the covered excavation area is a lunar landscape of pits, craters and humps, navigated on raised walkways, and it can be hard to relate these to the buildings and objects described on the signs in whimsical English. Outside the museum, the **Culture Village** is a crude attempt to bring the prehistoric settlement to life – it's basically a Neolithic theme park entered through the nether regions of an enormous fibreglass woman.

> ## TOURS AROUND XI'AN
>
> The easiest way to see the sights around Xi'an is to get up early and take one of the many **tours** on offer. There are two routes: the popular **eastern route** covers the Huaqing Pool and the Lintong Museum, the Terracotta Army, the Tomb of Qin Shi Huang and the Banpo Museum; the **western route**, going to the Imperial Tombs and the Famen Temple, is less popular as more travel time is involved, and it's more expensive (it's also harder to find anyone running it off season). The best tours leave by 8am.
>
> Most hotels, and all hostels, can arrange such tours, sometimes even with no advance notice; the hostels are usually both the cheapest and most reliable, though you should still ask about exactly what you're getting, and expect to be taken to some shops on the way. Prices for the eastern route are around ¥260 for the Terracotta Army plus the Tomb of Qin Shi Huang, or ¥350 including the Banpo Museum; a day-trip to Hua Shan will be around ¥450 including the cable car. A tour of the western route will cost from ¥340 – some operators tempt customers by knocking the price down, then also knock Famen Temple off the itinerary, so clarify its inclusion beforehand.
>
> One unusual option offered by the hostels is a full day-trip southwest to a **panda reserve** at Foping in the Qingling mountains (¥200–300), where you can see captive animals and tour the research centre.

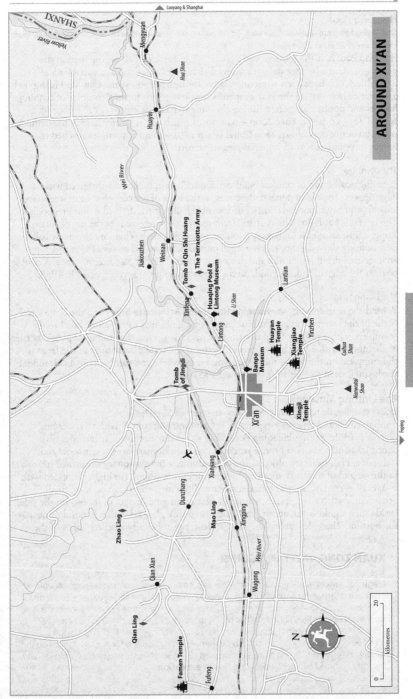

AROUND XI'AN

Luoyang & Shanghai

SHANXI

Yellow River

Mengyuan

Hua Shan

Huayin

Wei River

Jiakouzhen

Weinan

Tomb of Qin Shi Huang

The Terracotta Army

Xinfeng

Huaqing Pool & Lintong Museum

Lintong

Li Shan

Lantian

Yinzhen

Huayan Temple

Xiangjiao Temple

Cuihua Shan

Tomb of Jingdi

Banpo Museum

Nanwutai Shan

Xi'an

Xingji Temple

Xianyang

Dianzhang

Mao Ling

Xingping

Zhao Ling

Wei River

Qian Xian

Wugong

Qian Ling

Fufeng

Famen Temple

Foping

N

0   20

kilometres

4

Huaqing Pool

华清池, huáqīng chí • Daily 8am–5pm • March–Oct ¥70, Nov–Feb ¥40 • private bathhouse ¥70, public pool ¥20 • bus #306 (tourist bus #5) from east side of train station square

Huaqing Pool is at the foothills of Li Shan, 30km east of Xi'an on the road to the Terracotta Army. Its **springs**, with mineral-rich water emerging at a constant and agreeable 43°C, have been attracting people for nearly 2500 years. Qin Shi Huang had a residence here, as did the Han emperors, but its present form, a complex of **bathing houses and pools**, was created during the Tang dynasty. It was under the reign of the second Tang emperor, **Xuan Zong** – who spent much of the winter here in the company of his favourite concubine, **Yang Guifei** (see p.210) – that the complex reached its height of popularity as an imperial pleasure resort.

The complex

Huaqing's collection of classical buildings is usually unromantically thronged with day-trippers. The old **imperial bathhouses**, at the back of the complex, must once have looked impressive, but today they just resemble half-ruined, drained swimming pools. The largest is **Lotus Pool**, more than 100m square, once reserved for the use of Xuan Zong; a little smaller is **Crabapple Pool**, for concubine Yang. There are also a few halls, now housing souvenir shops, and a small **museum**, where fragments of Qin and Tang architectural detail – roof tiles and decorated bricks – hint at past magnificence. A marble boat, at the edge of Jiulong Pond, on the left as you enter, was constructed in 1956.

The bathhouses

Behind the marble boat, the **Huaqing Hot Spring Bathhouse** offers you the chance to bathe in the waters; you are shut in a room that looks like a mid-range hotel room (complete with a photo of a glossy tropical paradise on the wall and little plastic bottles of shampoo) with a bath and a shower. Better is the **public bathhouse** at the front of the complex, on the left of the gate as you go in, where you can bathe in a communal pool; you'll need to take your own towel and soap.

The Lintong Museum

临潼博物馆, líntóng bówùguǎn • Daily 8am–6pm • ¥25 • 150m from Huaqing Pool

Though small and relatively expensive, the **Lintong Museum** provides a rewarding diversion while visiting Huaqing Pool, with a varied collection that includes silver chopsticks and scissors, a bronze jar decorated with human faces, a crossbow and numerous Han funerary objects. The best exhibit, a **Tang reliquary** unearthed nearby, is in the second of the three rooms. Inside a stone stupa about 1m high, decorated with images of everyday life, was found a silver coffin with a steep sloping roof, fussily ornamented with silver spirals, strings of pearls and gold images of monks on the side. Inside this, a gold coffin about 7cm long held a tiny glass jar with a handful of dust at the bottom. These delicate relics, and the dust, optimistically labelled "ashes of the

---

XUAN ZONG AND YANG GUIFEI

The tale of Emperor Xuan Zong and his concubine Yang Guifei is one of the great Chinese **tragic romances**, the equivalent to the Western Antony and Cleopatra, and is often depicted in art and drama, most famously in an ode by the great Tang poet Bai Juyi. Xuan Zong took a fancy to Yang Guifei – originally the concubine of his son – when he was over 60, and she was no spring chicken. They fell in love, but his infatuation with her, which led to his neglect of affairs of state, was seen as harmful to the empire by his officials, and in part led to the rebellion of the disgruntled general, **An Lushan**. As An Lushan and his troops approached the capital, the emperor and his retinue were forced to flee southwest into Sichuan; along the way, his army mutinied and demanded Yang Guifei's **execution**.

CENTRAL STREET AND TOWER, PINGYAO (P.252) >

THE XI'AN INCIDENT

Huaqing Pool's modern claim to fame is as the setting for the **Xi'an Incident** in 1936. As Japanese troops continued to advance into China, Chiang Kai-shek virtually ignored them, concentrating instead on pursuing his policy of national unification – meaning the destruction of the Communists before all else. In December 1936, he flew to Xi'an, which was then under the control of **Marshal Zhang Xueliang** and his Manchurian troops. Although GMD supporters, they, like many others, had grown weary of Chiang's policies, fuelled by the fact that their Manchurian homeland was now occupied by the Japanese. In secret meetings with Communist leaders, Zhang had been convinced of their genuine anti-Japanese sentiments, and so, on the morning of December 12, Nationalist troops stormed Chiang's headquarters at the foot of Li Shan, capturing most of the headquarters staff. The great leader himself was eventually caught halfway up the slope in a house at the back of the complex, behind the pools – a neo-Grecian pavilion on the lower slopes of the mountain marks the spot. Still in his pyjamas and without his false teeth, he had bolted from his bed at the sound of gunfire. Chiang was forced to pay a heavy ransom but was otherwise unharmed, his captors allowing him to remain in control of China – provided that he allied with the Communists against the Japanese. Today, tourists line up here to don GMD uniforms and have their pictures taken.

Buddha", though crudely exhibited in what look like Perspex lunchboxes, are more interesting than anything at Huaqing Pool.

The Terracotta Army

兵马俑 • bīngmǎ yǒng • army and tomb ticket ¥150 during high season, otherwise ¥120 • photography permitted, but not tripods or flash • bus #306 (¥7) or minibuses (¥26) from the east side of the Xi'an train station

No historical records exist of the **Terracotta Army**, which was set to guard **Qin Shi Huang's tomb** over two thousand years ago, and was only discovered accidentally by peasants sinking a well 28km east of Xi'an in 1974. Three rectangular vaults were found, constructed of earth with brick floors and timber supports. Today, hangars have been built over the excavated site so that the ranks of soldiers – designed never to be seen, but now one of the most popular tourist attractions in China – can be viewed *in situ*.

The army is probably the highlight of any trip to Xi'an, so don't be discouraged by what greets arrivals: a vast car park and a tourist complex of industrial proportions whose main purpose seems to be to channel visitors through a kilometre-long gauntlet of overpriced, mediocre restaurants and souvenir stalls.

Vault 1

Vault 1 is the largest, and has so far yielded more than a **thousand figures** (out of an estimated eight thousand) ranked in battle formation and assembled in a grid of 6m-deep corridors. Facing you as you enter the hangar, this is one of the most memorable sights in China; you can inspect the static soldiers at closer range via raised walkways running around their perimeter. Averaging 1.8m in height, the figures are hollow from the thighs up; head and hands were modelled separately and attached to the mass-produced bodies. Each soldier has **different features** and expressions and wears marks of rank; some believe that each is a portrait of a real member of the ancient Imperial Guard. Their hair is tied in buns and they are wearing knee-length battle tunics; some figures wore leather armour, now decayed, and traces of **pigment** show that their monochrome grey dress was once bright yellow, purple and green.

A central group of **terracotta horses** is all that remains of a set of chariots. These wore harnesses with brass fittings and have been identified as depicting a breed from Gansu and Xinjiang. Each has six teeth, an indication that they are in their prime.

QIN SHI HUANG

As a silkworm devours a mulberry leaf, so Qin swallowed up the kingdoms of the Empire.

The first-century BC historian Sima Qian

Though only 13 when he ascended the throne of the western state of Qin in 246 BC, within 25 years **Qin Shi Huang** had managed to subjugate all the quarrelsome eastern states, thus becoming the first emperor of a unified China. During his eleven years as the sole monarch of the Chinese world, Qin Shi Huang set out to transform it, hoping to create an empire that his descendants would continue to rule for "ten thousand years". His reign was marked by centralized rule, and often **ruthless tyranny**. As well as standardizing weights and measures (even the width of cartwheels) and ordering a unified script to be used, the First Emperor decreed that all books, except those on the history of the Qin and on such practical matters as agriculture, be destroyed, along with the scholars who produced them. It was only thanks to a few Confucian scholars, who hid their books away, that any literature from before this period has survived.

As well as overseeing the construction of roads linking all parts of the empire, mainly to aid military operations, Qin Shi Huang began the construction of the **Great Wall**, a project that perhaps – more than any of his harsh laws and high taxes – turned the populace, drummed into constructing it, against him. Ambitious to the end, Qin Shi Huang died on a journey to the east coast seeking the legendary island of the immortals and the secret drug of longevity they held. His entourage concealed his death – easy to do as he lived in total seclusion from his subjects – and on their return installed an easily manipulated prince on the throne. The empire soon disintegrated into civil war, and within a few years Qin Shi Huang's capital at Xianyang had been destroyed, his palace burnt and his tomb ransacked.

It is possible that Qin Shi Huang, seen as an archetypal tyrant, has been harshly judged by history, as the story of his reign was written in the Han dynasty, when an eastern people whom he subjugated became ascendant. They are unlikely to have been enamoured of him, and the fact that the Terracotta Army faces east, the direction from where Qin Shi Huang thought threats to his empire would come, indicates the animosity that existed. The outstanding artistry of the terracotta figures has revised the accepted view of the Qin dynasty as a time of unremitting philistinism, and his reign has been reassessed since their discovery. Mao Zedong, it is said, was an admirer of his predecessor in revolution.

Vault 2

Vault 2 is a smaller, L-shaped area, still under excavation; it's thought to hold more warriors than vault 1. The four groups here – crossbowmen, charioteers, cavalry and infantry – display more variety of posture and uniform than the figures in the main vault, though a large number of smashed and broken figures make the scene look more like the aftermath of a battle than the preparation for one. **Four exceptional figures** found here are exhibited at the side: a kneeling archer, a cavalryman leading a horse, an officer with a stylish goatee and the magnificent figure of a general, 2m tall, wearing engraved armour and a cap with two tails. Also on show are some of the weapons discovered at the site (including a huge bronze battle-axe); made of sophisticated alloys, some were still sharp after 2000 years underground. At times, you'll find a half-blind peasant signing postcards in the shop at vault 2; this is **Yang Zhifa**, the man who discovered it all in 1974.

Vault 3

The much smaller **vault 3**, where over 70 figures and a chariot have been found, seems to have been battle headquarters. Armed with ceremonial *shu*, a short bronze mace with a triangular head, the figures are not in battle formation but form a guard of honour. Animal bones found here provide evidence of ritual sacrifices, which a real army would have performed before going into battle. A photo exhibition of plaster replicas gives some idea of how the figures would have been painted.

The museums

At the side of vault 2 is a small **museum** where two magnificent **bronze chariots**, found in 1982 near Qin Shi Huang's tomb, are displayed in glass cases. They're about half actual size. The front one, depicting the Imperial Fleet leader's chariot, has four horses and a driver, and is decorated with dragon, phoenix and cloud designs, with a curved canopy and a gold-and-silver harness. Behind the driver is a large compartment featuring a silver door-latch and windows that open and close. The chariot at the back was the emperor's and has seats and beds in the rear. Both chariots were made with astonishing attention to detail; even the driver's knuckles, nails and fingerprints are shown. Another museum holds small artefacts found around the area, including a skull with an arrowhead still embedded in it, and a few kneeling pottery attendants, the only **female figures** depicted.

The Tomb of Qin Shi Huang

秦始皇陵, qínshǐhuáng líng • same ticket as Terracotta Army

The **Tomb of Qin Shi Huang** is now no more than an artificial hill, nearly 2km west of the Terracotta Army; there's no transport so you'll have to walk. The burial mound was originally at the southern end of an inner sanctuary with walls 2.5km long, itself the centre of an outer city, none of which remains. The tomb has yet to be excavated and there's not much to see here; hassled at every step by souvenir sellers, you can walk up stone steps to the top of the hill, where you have a view of fields scraped bare for agriculture. According to accounts by **Sima Qian** in his *Historical Records*, written a century after the entombment, 700,000 labourers took 36 years to create a subterranean imperial city, full of wonders: the heavens were depicted on the ceiling of the central chamber with pearls, and the geographical divisions of the earth were delineated on a floor of bronze, with the seas and rivers represented by pools of mercury and made to flow with machinery. Automatic crossbows were set to protect the many gold and silver relics. Abnormally high quantities of **mercury** have been found in the surrounding soil, suggesting that at least parts of the account can be trusted.

The Tomb of Jingdi

汉阳陵, hànyánglíng • Daily 8.30am–6pm • ¥90 • hostel tours from ¥160

Most of Xi'an's sights have been consistent draws since the dawn of international tourism to China, but every now and then a new one sees its popularity start to bubble. The tomb of **Jingdi** (188–141 BC) has recently become one of most popular out-of-town excursions with Xi'an hostel-goers, and deservedly so – especially since it's still largely off the tour-bus circuit. This is the tomb of the sixth emperor of the great Han dynasty; Jingdi is recognized as one of its main drivers, having centralised control and put down the rebellions threatening to tear the nascent dynasty apart.

The **tomb** here is, as with so many sights in Xi'an, still being excavated; you'll be able to see some of this for yourself at close range, with the aid of glass floor panels and well-placed lighting - an atmospheric experience. Some of the relics unearthed here, including a wide range of terracotta figures, are on display in a superb on-site **museum**.

Xianyang

咸阳, xiányáng • buses (1hr 30min) from Xi'an's main bus station; ask to be dropped off at museum

XIANYANG, now a nondescript city 60km northwest of Xi'an, was the centre of the country a couple of millennia ago, and capital of **China's first dynasty**, the Qin. Little evidence remains of the era, however, except a flat plain in the east of the city that was once the site of Qin Shi Huang's palace, and relics on display at the city museum.

The city museum

咸阳博物馆, xiányáng bówùguǎn • Tues–Sun 8am–5.30pm • ¥20

Xianyang's **city museum**, in a converted Confucian temple, displays a range of Qin-era artefacts of most interest to archeologists – roof tiles, water pipes, bricks and so on. Star of the collection is a **miniature terracotta army** unearthed from a tomb 20km away, probably belonging to a high official, and a lot less sinister than Qi Shi Huang's as each of the nearly three thousand figures stands just 50cm high. Some still have traces of their original bright paint scheme, which show that the designs on their shields varied widely. The warriors are fairly crude, but the horses are well done.

Mao Ling

茂陵, màolíng • Daily 8am–5pm • ¥28

The resting place of the fifth Han emperor, Wu Di (157–87 BC), **Mao Ling**, 40km west of Xi'an, is the largest of the twenty Han tombs in the area. It's a great green mound against the hills, which took more than fifty years to construct and contains, among many treasures, a full **jade burial suit** – jade was believed to protect the corpse (and the soul) from decay. A dozen **smaller tombs** nearby belong to the emperor's court and include those of his favourite concubine and his generals, including the brilliant strategist Huo Qubing who fought several campaigns against the northern tribes and died at the age of 24. A small **museum** displays some impressive relics, including many massive stone sculptures of animals that once lined the tombs' spirit ways, simplified figures that look appealingly quirky; look for the frogs and a cow, and the horse trampling a demonic-looking barbarian with its hooves, a macabre subject made to look almost comical.

Qian Ling

乾陵, qiánlíng • Daily 8am–5pm • March–Oct ¥45, Nov–Feb ¥25 • bus #2 from east side of train station departs 8am (2hr 30min; ¥28)

Qian Ling is 80km northwest of Xi'an, and usually the second tomb tour after Mao Ling. This hill tomb, on the slopes of Liang Shan, is where **Emperor Gao Zong** and his empress **Wu Zetian** were buried in the seventh century.

The **Imperial Way** leading to the tombs is formed from two facing rows of carved stone figures of men and flying horses, and with two groups of (now headless) mourners – guest princes and envoys from tribute states, some with their names on their backs. The tall stele on the left praises Gao Zong; opposite is the uninscribed **Wordless Stele**, erected by the empress to mark the supreme power that no words could express.

Tomb of Prince Zhang Huai

章怀幕, zhānghuái mù • entry with Qian Ling ticket

Seventeen **lesser tombs** are contained in the southeast section of Qian Ling. Among the five excavated since 1960 here is the **tomb of Prince Zhang Huai**, second son of Gao Zong, forced to commit suicide by his mother Wu Zetian during one of her periodic purges of those opposing her rise to power. At this tomb you walk down into a vault frescoed with army and processional scenes, a lovely tiger with a perm in the dip on

---

EMPRESS WU ZETIAN

The rise to power of **Empress Wu Zetian** is extraordinary. Originally the **concubine** of Emperor Gao Zong's father, she emerged from her mourning to win the affections of his son, bear him sons in turn, and eventually marry him. As her husband ailed, her power over the administration grew until she was strong enough, at his death, to usurp the throne. Seven years later she was declared empress in her own right, and ruled until being forced to abdicate in favour of her son shortly before her death in 705 AD. Her reign was notorious for intrigue and bloodshed, but even her critics admit that she chose the right ministers for the job, often solely through merit. The heavy negative historical criticism against her may be solely because she was a woman, as the idea of a female in a position of authority is entirely contrary to Confucian ethics (her title was "Emperor", there being no female equivalent for so exalted a position). For more about Wu Zetian, see also p.730.

either side. One fresco shows the court's welcome to visiting foreigners, with a hook-nosed Westerner depicted. There are also vivid frescoes of polo playing and, in the **museum** outside, some Tang pottery horses.

Tomb of Princess Yong Tai

永泰幕, yŏngtài mù • ¥20

Princess Yong Tai's tomb is the finest at Qian Ling – no surprise, considering the fact that she was the emperor's granddaughter. Niches in the wall hold funeral offerings, and the vaulted roof still has traces of painted patterns. The passage walls leading down the ramp into the tomb are covered with murals of animals and guards of honour. The court ladies are still clear, elegant and charming after 1300 years, displaying Tang hairstyles and dress. At the bottom is the great tomb in black stone, lightly carved with human and animal shapes. Some 1300 gold, silver and pottery objects were found here and are now in Xi'an's Shaanxi Museum. At the mouth of the tomb is the traditional **stone tablet** into which the life story of the princess is carved – according to this, she died in childbirth at the age of 17, but some records claim that she was murdered by her grandmother, the empress Wu Zetian.

Zhao Ling

昭陵, zhāolíng • Daily 8am–6pm • ¥15 • see p.208 for details of tours

At **Zhao Ling**, east of Qian Ling and 70km northwest of Xi'an, lie nineteen **Tang tombs**. It was emperor Tai Zong who introduced the practice of building tombs into the hillside, instead of as a tumulus on an open plain, and his own mausoleum, begun in 636 AD, took thirteen years to complete. From the main tomb, a great cemetery fans out southeast and southwest, which includes 167 lesser tombs of the imperial family, generals and officials. A small **museum** displays stone carvings, murals and pottery figures from the smaller tombs.

Famen Temple

法门寺, fǎmén sì • Daily 8am–6pm • March–Oct ¥120, Nov–Feb ¥90 • bus from Big Goose Pagoda departs 8am (3hr; ¥30)

The extraordinary **Famen Temple**, 120km west of Xi'an, home of the finger bone of the Buddha, and the nearby **museum** containing an unsurpassed collection of Tang-dynasty relics, are worth the long trip it takes to get out here.

Brief history

In 147 AD, King Ashoka of India, to atone for his warlike life, had precious **Buddhist relics** (*sarira*) distributed throughout Asia. One of the earliest places of Buddhist worship in China, the Famen Temple was built to house his gift of a **finger**, in the form of three separate bones. During the Tang dynasty, these were ceremonially removed every thirty years; the bones would be taken to the court at Chang'an at the head of a procession, and when the emperor had paid his respects, they'd be closed back up in the **crypt** underneath the temple stupa, together with a lavish collection of offerings. After the fall of the Tang, the vault was forgotten about until the stupa above collapsed in 1981, revealing the most astonishing array of precious objects, and at the back, concealed inside box after box, the legendary finger of the Buddha.

The stupa and crypt

Today, the temple is a popular place of pilgrimage. The stupa and crypt have been rebuilt, with a **shrine** holding the finger at the crypt's centre. A praying monk is always in attendance, sitting in front of the finger, next to the safe in which it is kept at night (if it's not being exhibited elsewhere, as happens periodically). Indeed, the temple's monks are taking no chances, and the only entrance is protected by a huge metal door of the kind usually seen in a bank. You can look into the original crypt – at 21m long, the largest of its kind ever discovered in China – though there's not much to see now.

The museum

Don't miss the **museum** west of the temple, which houses the well-preserved Tang relics found in the crypt. Exhibits are divided into sections according to their material, with copious explanations in English. On the lower floor, the **gold and silver** are breathtaking for the quality of their workmanship: especially notable are a silver incense burner with an internal gyroscope to keep it upright; a silver tea basket, the earliest physical evidence of tea-drinking in China; and a gold figure of an elephant-headed man. Some unusual items on display are twenty **glass plates and bottles**, some Persian with Arabic designs, some from the fifth-century Roman Empire. Glassware, imported along the Silk Road, was more highly valued than gold at the time, as none was made in China.

At the centre of the main room is a gilded **silver coffin**, which held one of the finger bones, itself inside a copper model of a stupa, inside a marble pagoda. Prominent upstairs is a gold-and-silver **monk's staff**, which, ironically, would have been used for begging alms, but the main display here is of the **caskets** that the other two finger bones were found in – finely made boxes of diminishing size, of silver, sandalwood, gold and crystal, which sat inside each other, while the finger bones themselves were in tiny jade coffins.

Hua Shan

华山, huáshān • ¥180 • bus to cable car ¥40 • cable car ¥80 one-way March–Nov, ¥45 one-way Dec–Feb • "Danger Trail" ¥30

The five peaks of **Hua Shan** provide some of the best mountain scenery in China – crowded though their trails may be, they make for thoroughly enjoyable hiking nonetheless. They rise in a series of rugged, occasionally tree-dappled granite crags from the plains 120km east of Xi'an; here you can choose your desired level of energy expenditure, from low (cable car) to medium (a hike up the North Peak), to hard (a terrifying hike along the "Danger Trail"). Though the summits aren't that high, the gaunt rocky cliffs, twisted pines and rugged slopes certainly look like genuine mountains as they swim in and out of the misty trails.

Hua Shan was originally known as Xiyue (Western Mountain), because this is the westernmost of the five sacred **Taoist** mountains. It's always been a popular place for pilgrimage, though these days people puffing up the steep, narrow paths or enjoying the dramatic views from the peaks are more likely to be tourists – or the astonishingly hardy porters who shuttle up and down the mountain, often several times a day, to deliver supplies.

Ascending Hua Shan

There's a Chinese saying, "There is one path and one path only to the summit of Hua Shan", meaning that sometimes the hard way is the only way. These days the saying is redundant, since the **North Peak** is accessible by cable car; however, anyone in decent health will be able to make it up this far on foot. The original, arduous **old route** begins at the west gate and **Yuquan Temple** (玉泉院, yùquán yuàn), dedicated to the tenth-century monk Xiyi, who lived here as a recluse. From here, every few hundred metres you'll come across a wayside refreshment place offering stone seats, a burner, tea, soft drinks, maps and souvenirs – the higher you go, the more attractive the knobbly walking sticks on sale seem. In summer, you'll be swept along in a stream of Chinese, mostly young couples, dressed in their fashionable, but often highly impractical, holiday finest, including high-heeled shoes.

To the North Peak

Known as the **Eighteen Bends**, the deceptively easy-looking climb up the gullies in fact winds for about two hours before reaching the series of stone steps that ascend to the first summit, **North Peak** (1615m). At one point there's a (poorly signed) fork in the path; go left and the steps continue, go right and the path gets so steep that you'll have to drag your way up (or, if you're even more unfortunate, down) part of the way along a series of chains. On the way you'll pass plenty of small **temples**, some of which can be peeked inside – a chance, at least, to get your breath back. All in all, it'll take from two-and-a-half to four hours to get up to the peak, depending upon your level of fitness, and the weather.

Beyond the North Peak

Many people turn back at the North Peak, although you can continue to **Middle Peak** next, then East, South and West peaks (each at around 2000m), which make up an **eight-hour circuit trail**. If you're going to do this in a single day, you'll likely need to get the cable car up to the North Peak first. Some people arrive in the evening and climb by moonlight in order to see the **sunrise** over the Sea of Clouds from Middle or East Peak; if you plan to climb at night, be sure to take some warm clothes and a flashlight with spare batteries.

The Danger Trail

Of most interest to daredevil travellers is the "Danger Trail" near the South Peak. The going is rough in places and you'll need a head for heights (and, preferably, a bit of rock-climbing experience), with chain handrails, wooden galleries and rickety ladders attached at difficult points. The most nerve-racking stretch traverses a cliff-hugging wooden boardwalk perched above a sheer 1000m drop, after which you'll need to use a harness with chain-links to complete the walk.

ARRIVAL AND DEPARTURE   HUA SHAN

As Hua Shan lies between Xi'an and Luoyang, you can take in the mountain en route between the two cities, or as an excursion from Xi'an.

By train Hua Shan station (华山站, huáshān zhàn) is located near the park's east gate, and around ¥10 by taxi from the west gate and surrounding accommodation. The new Hua Shan North high-speed station (华山北站, huáshān běizhàn) is 10km away; take any bus departing here (¥2) and they'll tell you where to transfer to another bus for the west gate; it'll be around ¥25 by taxi.
Destinations from main station Beijing (2 daily; 14hr 30min); Luoyang (20 daily; 3hr 30min); Xi'an (many daily; 1hr 30min).
Destinations from North station Beijing (3 daily; 5hr);

Luoyang (10 daily; 1hr–1hr 40min); Xi'an (15 daily; 30min).
By tour bus and minibus Tour bus #1 (2hr) goes from Xi'an's train station concourse to Hua Shan's east gate. The last buses back to Xi'an leave at around 5.30pm, but walk to the main road and you'll find private minibuses leaving as late as 8pm.
By day-tour Day-tours organized by hostels in Xi'an, including transport, cable car, entry and occasionally a light breakfast, cost around ¥450 per person. Do check, before you sign up, exactly what is included, as you don't want to be stung unexpectedly once you're there.

ACCOMMODATION AND EATING

Most visitors stay in the motley selection of hotels downhill from the west gate; if you're doing so, the most enjoyable place to eat in the area is the line of restaurants on the other side of the main road (Yuquan Jie), which have pleasant outdoor seating in warmer months (note that it can get very windy). There are also a few places to stay on and around the peaks themselves, though the nicest thing to be said about the food on the mountain – available from tiny path-side restaurants – is that it's palatable. It's also more expensive the higher you go; if you're on a tight budget, stock up beforehand.

WEST GATE AREA

★ **Huashan** 华山客栈, huáshān kèzhàn. 2 Yuquan Dongjie ☎0913 4658111. The classiest place to stay near the west gate, with attentive staff and moderately plush rooms. Try to bag one that faces south – away from the main road and, more importantly, towards the mountains. The small garden area behind the

main building is a pleasant place to nab a beer. **¥380**
Jinse Nianhua 金色年华酒店, jīnsè niánhuá jiǔdiàn. Yuquan Xi Jie ☎0913 8373666. Modern place on the main road near the bottom of the west gate entrance road; look for the clock tower-style entrance. Staff are generally rather flustered, but rooms are okay – check the bathrooms, though, as they can be a tiny bit dodgy.

You'll often be able to slice up to ¥100 from the rack rate – good value. **¥268**

Mingzhu Jituan 明珠集团, míngzhū jítuán. Corner of Yuquan Xi Jie and west gate access road ☎0913 4369099. Don't expect too much here: musty rooms, though generously sized, and next to no frills whatsoever besides patchy wi-fi signals. They'll come down to ¥100 most days. **¥180**

ON THE MOUNTAIN

Dongfeng 东峰宾馆, dōngfēng bīnguǎn. East

Peak, no phone. This is the best place from which to see the sunrise; rooms are spartan but they've a great restaurant that isn't too much of a rip-off, considering the location. Dorms from **¥145**, doubles **¥440**

Yuntai 云台饭店, yúntái fàndiàn. North Peak ☎1571 9136466. A hop, skip and jump from the North Peak, this is a popular base from which to embark upon a morning bash around the peak circuit. Rooms are nothing special, but the little café-restaurant comes in handy. Dorms from **¥95**, doubles **¥380**

Ningxia

宁夏, níngxià

Squeezed between Inner Mongolia, Gansu and Shanxi, **Ningxia** is the smallest of China's provinces, and an autonomous region for the **Hui** minority (see below). Geographically, the area is dominated by coalfields and the **Yellow River**, without which the hilly south of the province, green and extremely beautiful, would be barren and uninhabitable desert. In the west of the province, however, the river does actually run past desert dunes at **Shapotou**, near the city of **Zhongwei** – one of the most visually arresting sights in China. Other sights include the capital **Yinchuan**, which makes a pleasant stopover, and one relic from an obscure northern branch of the Silk Road, the delightful **Xumi Shan Grottoes**, located well away from the Yellow River in the southern hills.

Despite a certain degree of industrialization in modern times, Ningxia remains an underdeveloped area. For visitors, the rural scenes provide the charm of the place, but this province is one of the poorest in the country.

Brief history

Historically, the area within what is now Ningxia has never been a secure one for the Chinese: almost every dynasty built its section of **Great Wall** through here and, in the nineteenth century, the Hui people played an active part in various Muslim rebellions,

---

THE HUI

Hui (回, húi) is a vague term, applied to followers of the **Muslim faith** all over China who have no other obvious affiliation bar Islamic dress and the absence of pork in their diets. Most Hui are descended from Middle Eastern traders who arrived in China over a thousand years ago; men can usually be distinguished by their skullcaps, women often wear headscarves or veils, while the sprouting of minarets is the most obvious sign that you're in a Hui-populated area. While remaining Muslim, the Hui have otherwise long since integrated with Han culture; barring a few Persian or Islamic words, they speak Chinese as their mother tongue.

Ningxia is the officially designated homeland of the Hui, who today make up about 30 percent of the province's tiny population of four million. However, most Hui do not live in Ningxia at all, but are scattered around neighbouring regions – particularly Gansu and Shaanxi – to the point where they often seem strangely absent within what is supposed to be "their" land. In Ningxia, as with all the autonomous regions of the Northwest, the central government has steadily encouraged **Han immigration** – or colonization – as a way of tying the area to the Chinese nation, but the situation of the Hui people is not comparable with that of the disaffected Uyghurs or Tibetans, since there is no talk whatsoever of secession.

The Hui population of Ningxia's major cities is rather low, but to immerse yourself more fully in the culture take a trip to Guyuan (see p.220), the Muslim districts in Xi'an (see p.201), or the Lanzhou–Linxia route in Gansu province (see p.787).

which were subsequently put down with great ferocity by the Qing authorities. Until recent times, Ningxia's very existence as a separate zone remained an open question; having first appeared on the map in 1928, the region was temporarily subsumed by Gansu in the 1950s before reappearing again in 1958. It appears that the authorities of the People's Republic could not make up their minds whether the Hui population was substantial enough to deserve its own autonomous region, in the same way as the Uyghurs and the Mongols.

Unsurprisingly, the science of **irrigation** is at its most advanced here: 2000 years ago the great founding emperor of China, Qin Shi Huang, sent a hundred thousand men here to dig irrigation channels. To those ancient systems of irrigation, which are still used to farm cereal crops, have now been added ambitious reforestation and desert reclamation projects.

Guyuan

固原, gùyuán

Located in the remote, impoverished southern part of Ningxia province, the town of **GUYUAN** is itself of no special interest. Aside from a ruinous stretch of the **Great Wall** 5km north, built in the Qin dynasty, Guyuan's main tourist function is as a base for visiting the Buddhist grottoes at **Xumi Shan**, a major relic of the Silk Road, curiously marooned far to the north of the favoured route from Lanzhou to Xi'an. In addition, the great Taoist complex of **Kongtong Shan** at Pingliang in Gansu (see p.780) is also only two hours from Guyuan, another possible day-trip.

The Xumi Shan grottoes

须弥山, xūmí shān • Daily 8am–6pm • ¥50

The dramatic **Xumi Shan grottoes** lie about 55km northwest of Guyuan. No less than 138 caves have been carved out from the rusty red sandstone cliff face on five adjoining hillsides, and a large number of statues – primarily from Northern Wei, Sui and Tang dynasties – survive, in a somewhat diminished state. With a beautifully secluded natural backdrop, the grottoes occupy a huge site, the red cliffs and shining tree-covered slopes commanding panoramic views. The last stage of the journey there takes you through one of the remotest corners of rural China where, at the height of summer, you can occasionally see the golden wheat being cut by hand, then spread out over the road to be threshed by passing vehicles.

The caves

The site takes at least two hours to walk around. After entering the cliffs area, bear left first for Cave 5 and the **Dafo Lou**, a statue of a giant 20m-high Maitreya Buddha facing due east. Originally this Buddha was protected by a wall that has long since fallen away. Head back to the entrance and you'll see the five hillocks lined up along an approximate east–west axis, each with one key sight and a cluster of caves.

After the Dafo Lou, the second major sight you come to is the **Yuanguang Temple**, a temple housing caves 45, 46 and 48, where statues were built during the North Zhou and Tang dynasties. You'll need to ask the nun to open the caves. Looking at their smoky-coloured surface today, it is hard to imagine that all Buddha statues were once coated in gold. From here you have to cross a bridge and bear left to reach **Xiangguo Temple**, centred around the magnificent Cave 51 with its 5m-high Buddha seated around a central pillar. Returning to the bridge, walk underneath it and up the dry river bed towards the cliff, to reach **Taohua Dong** (Peach Blossom Cave).

ARRIVAL AND DEPARTURE

By train Guyuan's train station (固原站, gùyuán zhàn), on the Zhongwei–Baoji line, is on the northeastern edge of town. Note that it can be hard to buy tickets for the single overnight sleeper to Xi'an at short notice; if you're

planning on doing this, it's a good idea to arrange your departure from Guyuan before you arrive.
Destinations Lanzhou (1 daily; 9hr 30min); Xi'an (4 daily; 7–8hr); Yinchuan (5 daily; 6–9hr); Zhongwei (7 daily; 3hr 30min).
By bus The long-distance bus station is in the west of town

but, with the exception of Yinchuan, trains are far more convenient.
Destinations Lanzhou (2 daily; 8hr); Sanying (hourly; 1hr); Xi'an (5 daily; 7hr); Yinchuan (every 30min; 5hr); Zhongwei (3 daily; 4hr).

GETTING AROUND

By bus Bus #1 (¥1) links the train station and the bus station in town. There's one daily direct bus to Xumi Shan, but at the wretchedly inconvenient time of 2pm – you'd have to stay the night. To make a day-trip of it, head from Guyuan to the small town of Sanying (三营, sānyíng),

and tell the driver that you want to see the grottoes. From the drop-off point in Sanying, hire a minivan for the thirty-minute drive to the caves; a return trip (including 2hr wait while you look around) should cost about ¥100.
By taxi A taxi to anywhere in Guyuan costs ¥5.

ACCOMMODATION AND EATING

There's plenty of accommodation, mostly rather insalubrious, outside Guyuan's bus and train stations; and don't expect anything wonderful, food-wise. At Xumi Shan, there's a drinks and snacks kiosk at the grottoes' car park, plus a basic hotel if you need to stay the night.

Hongbao 红宝宾馆, hóngbǎo bīnguǎn. 231 Zhongshan Nanlu ☏ 0954 2066866. Though nothing to write home about, moderately plush rooms make this one of the more reliable choices in Guyuan, and walkable from the train station if your luggage is light. Mercifully, the noise from the on-site KTV doesn't carry up to the rooms. **¥230**

Zhongwei

中卫, zhōngwèi

ZHONGWEI – a mini-city based around a simple crossroads, with a traditional **drum tower** (鼓楼, gǔlóu) at the centre – lies right alongside one of the most curious stretches of the **Yellow River**. Just west of town at **Shapotou**, the waterway can be seen roaring past an expanse of **sand dunes**, providing a rare opportunity to see a river of such size in desert terrain; it's a splendid sight and is definitely worth a visit if you are in the area.

Gao Miao

高庙, gāomiào • a short walk north of the Drum Tower • Daily 8am–7pm • ¥30

Zhongwei itself has one intriguing sight, the **Gao Miao**, a quite extraordinary temple catering for a number of different religions, including Buddhism, Confucianism and Taoism. Originally constructed in the early fifteenth century, and rebuilt many times, the temple is now a magnificent jumble of buildings and styles. From the front entrance you can see dragon heads, columns, stairways and rooftops spiralling up in all directions; the left wing contains vivid sculptures of five hundred *arhats*, while the right wing is a mock hell. Altogether, there are more than 250 temple rooms, towers and pavilions.

The Desert Research Institute

The Yellow River has essentially moulded the Zhongwei of today: historically, the old walled city was said to have had no north gate, simply because there was nothing more to the north of here. It remains in a potentially awkward location, between the fickle river to the south and the sandy **Tenger Desert** to the north, but today Zhongwei is surrounded by a rich belt of irrigated fields, in part thanks to the **Shapotou Desert Research Institute**, which has been based here for forty years, working on ways to conquer the sands. Travelling either by bus or train between Zhongwei and Shapotou, you'll see some of the fruits of their labour in the chequerboard grid of straw thatch implanted to hold the sands in place and provide irrigation.

Shapotou

沙坡头 • shāpōtóu • ¥90, Nov–March ¥65 (optional activities extra) • minibus from central Zhongwei every 30min (¥5) • taxi ¥30

By the banks of the Yellow River 16km west of Zhongwei, **SHAPOTOU** is a tourist resort whose main pleasure is the contrast between the leafy, shady banks of the river, and the harsh desert that lies just beyond. The resort is a Disneyfied place, with cafés, outdoor restaurants and various activities on hand – ferry rides, ziplines over the river, sand-sledding and camel rides. There's very little shade, so bring a hat and sunscreen. There are two main entrances, one to the south, and another high up to the north; the latter is preferable, since from here you can slide down a huge sand dune to get to the main resort area. Most people come on a day-trip, but you can easily spend an enjoyable night here at the nearby *Shapo Shanzhuang* (see below).

ARRIVAL AND DEPARTURE

ZHONGWEI

By train Zhongwei's train station (中卫站, zhōngwèi zhàn) is just off the north arm of the city's crossroads, off Renmin Square; from here, you can walk to everything of note in Zhongwei. All trains on the main Lanzhou–Beijing (via Inner Mongolia) rail line call here, but services are not that regular. Branch lines also serve Wuwei in Gansu province and Baoji in Shaanxi.

Destinations Guyuan (7 daily; 3hr 30min); Hohhot (3 daily; 12–15hr); Lanzhou (7 daily; 5–6hr); Yinchuan (9 daily; 2hr 45min); Wuwei (4 daily; 3hr 30min–6hr 30min).

By bus The long-distance bus station (中卫汽车站, zhōngwèi qìchē zhàn) is 3km east of the centre; walkable, though you can take bus #1 (¥1) or a taxi (¥5). Yinchuan services run frequently, either regular buses or more expensive express coaches that utilize the new highway.

Destinations Guyuan (3 daily; 4hr); Wuwei (3 daily; 4hr); Yinchuan (every 30min; 2hr 30min).

GETTING AROUND

By taxi Zhongwei's centre is small enough to walk everywhere, although an absurd number of taxis – perhaps more numerous than any other vehicle – are available to ferry you around. Flag fall is ¥5, and it'll cost at least ¥30 to get to Shapotou.

By minibus Minibuses to Shapotou (¥5) depart when fullish from a point on Changcheng Xijie, just southwest of the train station.

INFORMATION

Travel Agents Shapotou Travel Service (☎0955 7014880), just outside the *Zhongwei Binguan*, a few minutes' walk west of the Drum Tower, offers tours of the Tenger Desert, as well as Yellow River excursions and camping trips.

ACCOMMODATION

If you're arriving in Zhongwei by train, you'll find scores of accommodation options right outside the station, though the cheapest usually turn foreigners away. Such is the popularity of Shapotou that all establishments can be fully booked on weekends.

ZHONGWEI

Aijia Easy Hotel 爱家酒店, àijiā jiǔdiàn. Changcheng Donglu ☎0955 7037777. This well-run little hotel is superb value for money, its clean rooms a welcome change from the grotty neighbouring options available for similar prices – no wonder it's often fully booked. Cross the square in front of the train station, then turn left on the main road; it's right there. **¥180**

★ **Zhongwei Dajiudian** 中卫大酒店, zhōngwèi dàjiǔdiàn. Bei Dajie ☎0955 7025555. Plush place offering generous discounts out of season, with fair-sized rooms and decent beds. It's more or less opposite the entrance to the Gao Miao. **¥388**

SHAPOTOU

★ **Shapo Shanzhuang** 沙坡山庄, shāpō shānzhuāng. Shapotou ☎0955 7689073. Delightful hotel in a very cool and pleasant location near the Shapotou tourist complex, with gardens full of trees and vine trellises. It has well-designed doubles with bath and, despite the tourist draw just down the road, is rarely busy; given the remote location, its tiny, simple restaurant is a pleasant relief. Only open April–Oct. **¥288**

EATING

The train station square is alive most evenings with stands peddling barbecued meat; sitting on a plastic chair overlooking a small stream, this is Zhongwei's most pleasant and atmospheric place to eat. Elsewhere, you'll find a clutch of places selling beef noodles (牛肉面, niúròumiàn) in an alley just south of the Gao Miao – great value at just ¥4 per bowl.

DIRECTORY

Bank The main Bank of China is immediately to the southeast of the Drum Tower. The ATM here accepts foreign cards, though given the remoteness of the town it's advisable to arrive with at least enough cash to cover your stay.

Mail and telephones There's a post office on Zhongshan Jie, a small lane several minutes' walk along Xi Dajie from the centre; you can also make long-distance phone calls from here.

Yinchuan

银川, yínchuān

The capital of Ningxia, **YINCHUAN** is a bland modern city possessing little of essential interest bar the Islamic designs incorporated into many of its buildings, some of which pulse with green neon at night. From 1038, however, Yinchuan was capital of the **Western Xia kingdom**, an independent state which survived for less than 200 years (see p.226). It was virtually forgotten about until the early twentieth century, when archeological remains started being recognized for what they were; you should definitely make a visit to their weathered **mausoleums**, some 20km outside the city.

Yinchuan is frustratingly spread out, and divided into three parts from east to west, though almost everything of interest – bar the excellent regional museum – is in **Xingqing district**, the de facto city centre.

Xingqing district

兴庆区, xīngqìng qū

The best place to start exploring **Xingqing** is around the eastern part of Jiefang Jie, which is dominated by a couple of well-restored, traditionally tiered Chinese towers guarding the main intersections. The first of these is the **Drum Tower** (鼓楼, gǔlóu) at Gulou Jie, while the second, one block farther east, is the 400-year-old **Yuhuang Pavilion** (玉皇阁, yùhuáng gé; ¥5) at Yuhuangge Jie, which also contains a tiny exhibition room.

Nanguan Grand Mosque

南关清真寺, nánguān qīngzhēn sì • Off Yuhuangge Nanlu • Daily 8am–7pm • ¥10, free to Muslims

Nanguan Grand Mosque, the biggest mosque in Yinchuan, is one of the few places in town you'll find Hui in any appreciable numbers. Founded in 1915, it was rebuilt in 1981 after years of damage and neglect during the Cultural Revolution, but now looks something like a leisure centre with minarets. It's located a short walk south of the Yuhuang Pavilion.

Chengtiansi Pagoda

承天寺塔, chéngtiānsì tǎ • Daily 9am–5pm • ¥3, plus ¥15 to climb pagoda

The **Chengtiansi pagoda**, also known as the West Pagoda, stands in a pleasant, leafy courtyard in the west of Xingqing. A place of worship for Buddhists, this classic Chinese twelve-storey tower was first built around 1050 during the time of the Western Xia; the top six storeys were rebuilt during the Qing dynasty. You can climb the octagonal tower right to the top for excellent views.

Ningxia Museum

宁夏博物馆, níngxià bówùguǎn • East side of Renmin Guangchang • Daily 9am–5pm • Free (bring ID) • Bus #102 from Xingqing or train station

Plonked next to Renmin Square, halfway between Xingqing district and the train station, Ningxia's brand-new **Provincial Museum** is a great place to get a handle on Hui culture. A typically huge affair, it has been designed with Islamic motifs aplenty – in fact, when you first sight it over the large concourse, it may well appear to be some kind of large, Brutalist mosque. It contains some interesting English-labelled exhibitions, including relics from the Xixia mausoleum (see p.225), a superb display of rock art, and pottery dating back to Silk Road times.

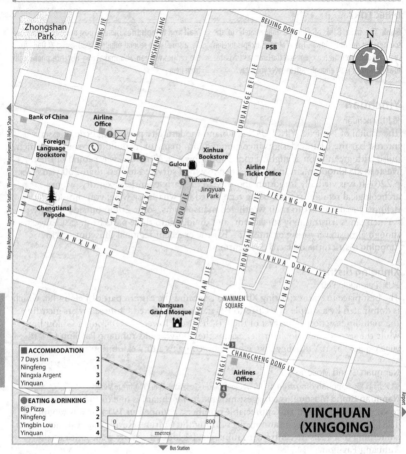

ACCOMMODATION

7 Days Inn	2
Ningfeng	1
Ningxia Argent	3
Yinquan	4

EATING & DRINKING

Big Pizza	3
Ningfeng	2
Yingbin Lou	1
Yinquan	4

0 — 800
metres

YINCHUAN (XINGQING)

▼ Bus Station

ARRIVAL AND DEPARTURE
YINCHUAN

By air Yinchuan's little airport (银川河东国际机场, yínchuān hédōng guójì jīchǎng) lies 15km southeast of Xingqing. Airport buses (¥15) depart from outside the *Ningxia Argent Hotel* on the hour; a taxi into Xingqing will cost more like ¥50. Rather conveniently, it's possible to buy flight tickets from an office right next to the bus departure point. The main airlines office is at the intersection of Changcheng Dong Lu and Shengli Jie (daily 8am–10.30pm; ☏ 0951 6913456).

Destinations Beijing (9 daily; 2hr); Chengdu (2 daily; 2hr); Guangzhou (4 weekly; 4hr); Lanzhou (1 daily; 50min); Nanjing (2 daily; 3hr 30min); Shanghai (1 daily; 3hr 30min); Ürümqi (3 daily; 3hr); Xi'an (12 daily; 50min).

By train The beautiful, Islamically styled train station (银川站, yínchuān zhàn) is inconveniently sited at the west end of Jinfeng district; a taxi for the 12km run to

Xingqing will cost ¥20, or take bus #102. Buy tickets in Xingqing at the booking office on Xinhua Xi Jie (daily 9am–6pm), or the office by the airport bus departure point.

Destinations Baotou (5 daily; 6–10hr); Beijing (3 daily; 13–20hr); Guyuan (5 daily; 7–10hr); Hohhot (5 daily; 8–12hr); Lanzhou (4 daily; 8–9hr); Xi'an (4 daily; 13hr 30min–15hr); Zhongwei (9 daily; 2hr 45min).

By bus The main long-distance station (银川长途汽车站, yínchuān chángtú qìchēzhàn) is frustratingly located 7km to the south of central Xingqing, from where a taxi into town will cost about ¥20. It's only really worth heading out this way for express services to Guyuan (every 30min; 5hr) and Zhongwei (every 30min; 2hr 30min); the bus journey to Xi'an (4 daily; 10hr) is faster than the train, but it's a long haul.

ACCOMMODATION

Accommodation in Yinchuan can be amazingly tight in midsummer: Chinese tourists flock here, and you may end up doing a lot of traipsing around to find a room. There's a clutch of scruffy guesthouses directly to the left outside the train station, but since there's absolutely nothing to see in the area, it's best to stay in Xingqing district – all places listed below are located in this part of the city.

7 Days Inn 7天连锁酒店, 7 tiān liánsuǒ jiǔdiàn. 74 Gulou Nanjie ☎0951 5612888. Great cheapie with a central, though secluded, location near the drum tower. It's highly popular, and you may have to book ahead. **¥177**

Ningfeng 宁丰宾馆, níngfēng bīnguǎn. 6 Jiefang Dongjie ☎0951 6090222. Smart-looking place in a highly central location. It's a solid choice with comfy rooms, a neat little bar, and a good Brazilian restaurant. **¥488**

Ningxia Argent 宁夏银座酒店, níngxià yínzuò jiǔdiàn. 553 Changcheng Donglu ☎0951 6020777. Swanky place near the mosque, with super-comfy rooms and attentive staff. Very convenient for the airport, too, since the shuttle bus stops right outside. **¥468**

Yinquan 银泉大酒店, yínquán dàjiǔdiàn. 157 Shengli Jie ☎0951 3999888. A good-value place near the mosque. Rooms are quiet, and there's a superb hotpot restaurant on the ground floor. **¥288**

EATING

Yinchuan's culinary scene is pretty poor. Your best bet is probably finding a hotpot restaurant, though there's plenty of fast food – Chinese and Western – in the drum tower area.

Big Pizza 比格比萨, bǐgé bǐsà. Gulou Nanjie ☎0951 5111117. There's no shame indulging in some Western food if you've made it as far as Ningxia. This restaurant is better value than the *Pizza Hut* down the road; it's ¥55 per person for a pizza-and-salad-bar buffet, and around the same to have a large pizza made fresh. Daily 10am–10pm.

Ningfeng 宁丰宾馆, níngfēng bīnguǎn. 6 Jiefang Dongjie ☎0951 6090222. It's worth popping by this hotel for the Brazilian restaurant, tucked away upstairs. The Chinese love Brazilian buffet barbecues at the moment, and you can get your fill of succulent meat (plus a selection from the salad bar) for ¥108 per head. Daily 6–10pm.

Yingbin Lou 迎宾楼, yíngbīn lóu. Jiefang Xijie. Muslim restaurant serving lamb hotpots, kebabs, noodles and eight-treasure tea. The food's good, and around ¥20–50 per main dish, but service can be absolutely atrocious. Daily 10am–2pm & 5–10pm.

★**Yinquan** 银泉大酒店, yínquán dàjiǔdiàn. 157 Shengli Jie ☎0951 3999888. A cut above most hotpot restaurants in town – more attractive, and with far more helpful staff (though they can't speak any English), yet meals will cost more or less the same. ¥100 will buy more than enough to fill two hungry bellies. Daily noon–10pm.

DIRECTORY

Banks The main Bank of China is in the western part of Xingqing, on Jiefang Xi Jie; the branch on Yuhuangge Beijie has an ATM.

Bookshop The Foreign Language Bookstore (daily 9am–6.30pm), at the corner of Jiefang Xijie and Jining Jie, is well stocked with English novels as well as local maps.

PSB At the corner of Beijing Donglu and Yuhuangge Beijie (☎0951 6915080; Mon–Thurs 8am–noon & 2.30–6.30pm, Fri 2.30–6.30pm). Ningxia being an autonomous province, it's best to extend your visa elsewhere.

Western Xia Mausoleums

西夏王陵, xīxià wánglíng • Daily 8am–6pm • ¥60

The **Western Xia Mausoleums**, about 10km west of Yinchuan's sprawl and thus around 40km west of Xingqing district, stand as monuments to the nine kings of Western Xia (see box, p.226). The site is spectacular and atmospheric, with towering, haystack-shaped piles of brown mud bricks, slowly disintegrating and punctuating the view around the Helan Mountain range. The entrance fee includes transport within the complex to the museum, figure gallery and the biggest mausoleum of the nine. Interesting items in the museum include the original pieces of the Lishi pillar support and some terracotta bird ornaments with human faces.

ARRIVAL AND DEPARTURE

WESTERN XIA MAUSOLEUMS

By minibus and taxi Getting here from Yinchuan's Xingqing district is either expensive or difficult. If you favour the expensive option, just grab a cab – drivers will start the bidding at ¥150 (or more) one-way, though you

THE WESTERN XIA KINGDOM

The ancient **Western Xia kingdom** (1038–1227 AD) encompassed a vast expanse of land, overlapping regions of what is now Ningxia, Gansu and Shaanxi provinces. Established by the nomadic Dangxiang clan of Qiang ancestry, the kingdom had twelve kings and developed its own **written language**, which combines influences from Mongolian, Tibetan and Chinese. The Western Xia territory survived prior to independence by playing off the Song or Liao dynasties against each other. In 1038, **Li Yuanhao**, leader of Western Xia, was militarily powerful enough to oppose Song jurisdiction and thus this third kingdom was created. A prosperous period ensued as the kingdom benefited from controlling the trade routes into central Asia. The new era saw a time of great **cultural development**, a state academy was erected, and future officials took Confucian examinations. Less emphasis, however, was placed on military matters, and in 1227 the Western Xia were obliterated by the Mongol empire of **Genghis Khan**.

should be able to get them down to ¥200 return, including waiting time. Alternatively, green and red buses (no number, though with Xixia written on the front) run from a stop just east of Nanmen Square; these cost just ¥2, though they take up to 2hr to reach the tombs. Finally, you could split the difference and take a bus to Xixia district (1hr; ¥1), from which it's a far cheaper taxi-ride to the ruins (¥25 each way).

Helan Shan
贺兰山, hèlán shān

The rugged **Helan Shan** ranges rises up behind the Western Xia mausoleums, and race away to the north, where there are a number of sights on and around the eastern (ie, Yinchuan-facing) slopes. Of most interest here is a series of wonderful **rock carvings**, while there's also ample opportunity for **hiking** in a couple of park areas. Sights listed here run north to south, from the mountain range's main access point; Yinchuan starts about 20km to the southeast, and the Xingqing district another 20km further along.

The rock carvings
贺兰山岩画, hèlánshān yánhuà • Daily 9am–6pm • ¥70, including ride from entrance

The **rock carvings** here date back to the early Neolithic period – some have been dated to just under 10,000 years of age. There are over 1500 here, set in a pretty valley, though only a few are on view to tourists; the images of hunting, animals and Neolithic faces are quite wonderful, and the mind boggles at how many generations have passed since their creation.

Suyukou National Park
苏峪口国家公园, sūyùkǒu guójiā gōngyuán • ¥60 • Cable car ¥30 each way

About 7km south of the rock art galleries is **Suyukou National Park**, an expanse of pine trees that's home to the Helan range's best hiking trails – swaths of pine forest, with wonderful vistas of the flat Yinchuan area to the east. You can hike way up to the peak of Helan Shan, though these days most prefer to take the cable car.

Baisikou Shuang Ta
拜寺口双塔, bàisìkǒu shuāng tǎ • Daily 8am–6pm • ¥10

Another 7km south of Suyukou are the **Baisikou Shuang Ta**, a pair of 12m-high pagodas guarding a pass. You won't stay here for too long, but the towers – set a short distance away from each other – are highly photogenic, jutting from the ground like giant pencils with the Helan Shan range rippling away behind.

West Film Studio
镇北堡西部影视城, zhènběibǎo xībù yǐngshìchéng • Daily 8am–6pm • ¥60 • bus #16 from Nanmen Square, or #17 from train station

East of the Helan mountain range, and easily visited on the way back, is the **China West Film Studio** where the film *Red Sorghum*, directed by Zhang Yimou, was shot. The stunning film depicts village life in northwest China during the period leading up to World War II – in part a rural idyll, in part a brute struggle to survive. The scenes of dry, dusty hillsides alternating with the lush fields of sorghum are a fair record of how parts of Ningxia still look today. The studio itself is immensely popular with Chinese tourists, who flock to take pictures of each other in and around faux-dynastic buildings.

ARRIVAL AND DEPARTURE HELAN SHAN

By bus and taxi Bus #16 from Nanmen Square, or #17 from train station, only go as far as the film studios. You could board one of these, then try to cab it from there to the other sights – it'll save you a bit of money. From Xingqing it'll cost at least ¥300 to hire a driver for a half-day.

Inner Mongolia

内蒙古, nèi měnggǔ

Mongolia is an almost total mystery to the outside world, its very name synonymous with remoteness. Landlocked between the two Asian giants of Russia and China, it seemed to have been doomed to obscurity, trapped in a hopeless environment of fleeting summers and interminable, bitter winters. And yet, 700 years ago the people of this benighted land suddenly burst out of their frontiers, and for a century subjugated and terrorized almost all of the Eurasian landmass.

Visitors to the **Inner Mongolia Autonomous Region** will not necessarily find many signs of this today. The modern-day heirs of the Mongol hordes are not only placid – quietly going about their business of shepherding, herding horses and entertaining tourists – but, even here, are vastly outnumbered by the Han Chinese (by almost nineteen million to fewer than four million). In addition, this is, and always has been, a sensitive border area, and there are still restrictions on the movements of tourists in some places.

Nevertheless, traces of the "real" Mongolia remain, in terms of both landscape and people – and not just the **Mongol script**, used alongside Chinese throughout the province. Dotting the region are enormous areas of **grassland**, gently undulating plains stretching to the horizon and still used by nomadic peoples as pastureland for their horses. Tourists are able to visit the grasslands and even stay with the Mongols in their yurts, though the only simple way to do this is on an **organized tour** out of the regional capital **Hohhot** – an experience rather short on authenticity. If you don't find what you are looking for in the Hohhot area, however, a whole vast swath of Mongol territory lies across the border in Dongbei province, much of it untouched by Western tourists – see p.188.

Brief history

One man's name is synonymous with unleashing Mongol armies on an unsuspecting world: the great **Genghis Khan** (1162–1227), under whose rule much of China and pretty much the whole of Central Asia were conquered (see p.916). After his immediate successors had wrested control of Eastern Europe, Mongol forces were poised in 1241 to make the relatively short final push across Europe, when a message came from deep inside Asia that the invasion was to be cancelled. The decision to spare Western Europe cleared the way for the **final conquest of China** instead.

The Yuan dynasty

By 1271 the Mongols had established their own dynasty in China – the **Yuan**. It was the first time the country had come under foreign rule, and the Yuan is still an era about which Chinese historians can find little good to say, though the empire was expanded considerably by incorporating Yunnan and Tibet for the first time. The magnificent zenith of the dynasty was achieved under **Kublai Khan**, as documented in Marco Polo's *Travels* (see p.953). Ironically, however, the Mongols were able to sustain their power only by becoming Sinicised, and abandoning the traditional nomadic

Mongol way of life. Kublai Khan and his court soon forgot the warrior skills of their forefathers, and in 1368, after less than a century on the imperial throne, the Yuan were **driven out of China** by the rising Ming dynasty. The Mongols returned to Mongolia, and reverted to their former ways, hunting, fighting among themselves and occasionally skirmishing with the Chinese down by the Wall.

Post-Khan decline

Thereafter, Mongolian history moves gradually downhill, though right into the eighteenth century they maintained at least nominal control over many of the lands won by Genghis Khan. These included **Tibet**, from where **Lamaist Buddhism** was imported to become the dominant religion in Mongolia. Over the years, as well, came **settlers** from other parts of Asia: there is now a sizeable Muslim minority in the region, and under the Qing many Chinese settlers moved in too, escaping overpopulation and famine at home, a trend that has continued under the Communists. The incoming settlers tried ploughing up the grassland with disastrous ecological results – wind and water swept the soil away – and the Mongols withdrew to the hills. Only recently has a serious programme of land stabilization and reclamation been established.

Recent history

Sandwiched between two imperial powers, Mongolia found its independence constantly threatened. The Russians set up a protectorate over the north, while the rest

---

4

KUBLAI KHAN

In Xanadu did Kubla Khan
A stately pleasure-dome decree…

Samuel Taylor Coleridge

Immortalized not only in the poetry of Coleridge but also in the memoirs of Marco Polo, **Kublai Khan** (1215–94) – known to the Chinese as Yuan Shizu – is the only emperor popularly known by name to the outside world. And little wonder: as well as mastering the subtle statecraft required to govern China as a foreigner, this grandson of Genghis Khan commanded an **empire** that encompassed the whole of China, Central Asia, southern Russia and Persia – a larger area of land than perhaps anyone in history has ruled over, before or since. And yet this king of kings had been born into a nomadic tribe which had never shown the slightest interest in political life, and which, until shortly before his birth, was almost entirely illiterate.

From the beginning, Kublai Khan had shown an unusual talent for politics and government. He managed to get himself elected **Khan of the Mongols** in 1260, despite considerable opposition from the so-called "steppe aristocracy" who feared his disdain for traditional Mongolian skills. He never learned to read or write Chinese, yet after audaciously establishing himself as **Emperor of China**, proclaiming the Yuan dynasty in 1271, he soon saw the value of surrounding himself with advisers steeped in Confucianism. This was what enabled him to set up one hundred thousand Mongols in power over perhaps two hundred million Chinese. As well as **reunifying China** after centuries of division under the Song, Kublai Khan's contributions include establishing **paper money** as the standard medium of exchange, and fostering the **development of religion**, Lamaist Buddhism in particular. Above all, under his rule China experienced a brief period of **cosmopolitanism** which saw not only foreigners such as Marco Polo promoted to high positions of responsibility, but also a final flowering of the old Silk Road trade, as well as large numbers of Arab and Persian traders settling in seaports around Quanzhou in southeastern China.

Ironically, however, it was his admiration for the culture, arts, religion and sophisticated bureaucracy of China – as documented so enthusiastically by Marco Polo – that aroused bitter hostility from his own people, the Mongols, who despised what they saw as a betrayal of the ways of Genghis Khan. Kublai Khan was troubled by skirmishing nomads along the Great Wall just as much as his more authentically Chinese predecessors, forcing the abandonment of **Xanadu** – in Inner Mongolia, near the modern city of Duolun – his legendary summer residence immortalized in Coleridge's poem *Kubla Khan*. Today virtually nothing of the site remains.

effectively came under the control of China. In the 1930s, Japan occupied much of eastern Inner Mongolia as part of Manchukno, and the Chinese Communists also maintained a strong presence. In 1945 Stalin persuaded Chiang Kai-shek to recognize the independence of **Outer Mongolia** under Soviet protection as part of the Sino-Soviet anti-Japanese treaty, effectively sealing the fate of what then became the Mongolian People's Republic. In 1947, **Inner Mongolia** was designated the first autonomous region of the People's Republic of China.

Baotou

包头, bāotóu

Inner Mongolia's biggest and bleakest city, **BAOTOU**'s primary significance is as the chief iron- and steel-producing centre in China: if you're arriving at night from the direction of Yinchuan, your first glimpse of the city is likely to be of satanic fires burning in the great blast furnaces, and the sky over the western half of Baotou glows a more or less permanent yellow, orange and purple. For visitors, there can be something magnificent about Soviet ugliness on such a scale, but otherwise, apart from providing a springboard to a few distant sights – including **Wudangzhao**, an attractive Tibetan-style monastery, and what is possibly **Genghis Khan's Mausoleum** – Baotou has nothing to offer.

Inner Mongolia Museum

内蒙古博物馆, nèi měnggǔ bówùguǎn • A'erding Dajie • Tues–Sun 9am–5pm • Free • bus #1 from train station

Compared with other provincial museums, most of which are giant, gleaming structures, the **Inner Mongolia Museum** is decidedly shabby – nevertheless, and despite a total absence of English captioning, it still constitutes the most worthwhile sight in Baotou. The first floor features Yuan-dynasty relics from the nearby site of Yanjialing, and local treasures from other nearby areas; a few pieces feature designs which, if not conclusively Mongolian, are at least not distinctively Chinese. The second floor, and part of the first, feature temporary exhibition halls; frustratingly for travellers to the region (and perhaps a fair few locals), they're usually used to showcase the delights of other, non-Mongolian, Chinese minority groups.

The Yellow River

黄河, huáng hé • bus #18 (¥2) from Baotou East station • taxi from Baotou station ¥20

The main sight in the immediate vicinity of Baotou (about 8km away) is the **Yellow River**, worth having a look at, if only to ruminate on its historical significance; as seen from the park-like viewing point, the river here is around 1km wide, shallow, sluggish and chocolate brown. When the Chinese built the Great Wall far to the south, the area between the Inner Mongolian loop of the Yellow River and the Wall became known as the **Ordos** and remained the dominion of the nomad. To the Chinese, however, the Yellow River seemed like the logical northern limit of China. The Qing eventually decided matters once and for all not only by seizing control of the Ordos, but also by moving north of the river into the heart of Mongolia. Today, the whole Yellow River region, from Yinchuan in Ningxia province up to Baotou and across to Hohhot, is thoroughly irrigated and productive land – without the river, it would be pure desert.

BAOTOU ORIENTATION

A colossal city stretching for kilometres in all directions, Baotou comprises three main areas: **Donghe** (东河, dōnghé), the ramshackle, oldest part of town, to the east; west lies the pleasant shopping and residential area of **Qingshan** (青山, qīngshān); and, further west again, the iron- and steelworks at **Kundulun** (昆都仑, kūndū lún). Qingshan is bisected by A'erding Jie, a wide road which zooms straight as an arrow to A'erding Square – empty, with nothing of note on its periphery and vast to the point of ridicule, it's beautiful in a very strange way.

ARRIVAL AND DEPARTURE

BAOTOU

By air Baotou's airport (包头机场, bāotóu jīchǎng) is just 2km south of Baotou East train station. There's no airport bus, as yet; taxis will take you into town for ¥20–40, but it can be hard to persuade drivers to use the meter. The airlines office (☎0472 2118966) is on the south side of Gangtie Dajie, east of the post office, though the better hotels can also book tickets for you.

Destinations Beijing (5 daily; 55min); Shanghai (3 daily; 2hr 25min); Xi'an (2 daily; 1hr 15min).

By train There are two major train stations: Baotou station (包头站, bāotóu zhàn) to the west, and Baotou East (包头东站, bāotóu dōngzhàn) over 20km down the line. Almost all through trains stop at both stations; times

given here are from the main station. Train tickets can be bought at a booking office on the east of A'Erding Square; there are others about town too.

Destinations Beijing (11 daily; 10–16hr); Dongsheng (4 daily; 1hr 45min–3hr); Hohhot (many daily; 2hr); Lanzhou (4 daily; 16hr); Yinchuan (6 daily; 6–8hr).

By bus The city's main bus station (包头长途汽车站, bāotóu chángtú qìchēzhàn) is right opposite the East train station, and connected by bus #17 to Qingshan. Baotou is a long way from almost anywhere; you'll only really need this station to get to Dongsheng (every 30min; 2hr 30min) for Genghis Khan's Mausoleum, or Shiguai (hourly; 1hr) for Wudangzhao.

GETTING AROUND

By bus The three parts of the city are well connected by frequent buses (¥2), which take 30–40min to travel between Donghe and Kundulun.

By taxi Fares begin at ¥6 for the first 3km, charging ¥1.5 per additional kilometre. Traversing Baotou, this can add up quickly.

INFORMATION

Travel agents There's a CITS office (☎0472 2118966) just northwest of the *Baotou Hotel* on Wulan Dao; they can organize trips to the surrounding sights at cheaper prices than the hotel travel desks. To Wudangzhao it's ¥240 per

person (minimum of two) for a trip, including a short desert tour, and it's ¥360 to Genghis Khan's mausoleum. Hotels will typically charge ¥350 and ¥440 per person, respectively, when there's a tour going.

ACCOMMODATION AND EATING

Of the two ends of town, Donghe is the more convenient place to stay for trips to Genghis Khan's mausoleum, though sadly there isn't much choice here. Qingshan has far more choice, and makes a more appealing place to stay. Baotou isn't famous for its cuisine, and restaurants here are average to say the least. However, there are some good cheapies off Gangtie Dajie, in the area behind the *KFC*.

DONGHE

West Lake 西湖宾馆, xīhú bīnguǎn. 10 Nanmenwai Dajie, ☎0472 4187101. The best of the very limited

options in this part of town. From the train station, walk straight up Nanmenwai Dajie; the hotel is on the right, before the intersection with Bayan Tala Dajie. **¥248**

STAYING IN A YURT

In regions that still harbour semi-nomadic herders, such as Inner Mongolia's grasslands (see p.237) and around Tian Chi (see p.821) in Xinjiang, it's often possible to ask a local family to put you up in their **yurt** (蒙古包, ménggǔ bāo). The genuine article is a circular felt tent with floor rugs as the only furniture, horsehair blankets, a stove for warmth, and outside toilets. Though it's a well-established custom to offer lodging to travellers, remember that few people in these regions have had much contact with foreigners, and misunderstandings can easily arise. You'll need to haggle over the price with your hosts; around ¥80 should cover bed and simple meals of noodles and vegetables. In addition, it's a good idea to bring a **present** – a bottle of *baijiu*, a clear and powerful vodka-like spirit, rarely goes amiss. Liquor stores, ubiquitous in Chinese cities and towns, are the obvious place to buy the stuff, but you'll also find it on sale at train and bus stations, restaurants, hotels, shops and airports. You might also want to bring a torch and bug spray for your own comfort.

Local tour companies may be able to arrange yurt accommodation, though where Chinese tour groups are commonplace, you may be treated to a very artificial experience – often basically just a concrete cell "dolled" up in yurt fashion, with karaoke laid on in the evenings. If you want something better than this, it's worth at least asking to see photos of the interior when making a booking.

KUNDULUN

Bao Yuan Binguan 包院宾馆, bāoyuàn bīnguǎn. 43 Gangtie Dajie ☎0472 6942628. For low prices and a good location, look no further than this hotel, opposite the entrance to Bayi Park – just don't expect much in the way of a cheery welcome or decor. **¥95**

Baotou Hotel 包头宾馆, bāotóu bīnguǎn. 33 Gangtie Dajie ☎0472 6911222. A good bet, just a few hundred metres west of A'Erding Square. Following a makeover, the old building is now very comfortable, so push for a room here rather than in the "new" block. **¥288**

Haide 海德酒店, hǎidé jiǔdiàn. 56 Gangtie Dajie ☎0472 5365555, 🌐hd-hotel.com.cn. The most upmarket hotel in town (and sometimes known as the *Header*) is a five-star establishment, with all the service and facilities you would expect. It's pricey but often gives 25 percent discounts. **¥756**

Shenhua International 神华国际大酒店, shénhuá guójì dàjiǔdiàn. 17 Shaoxian Lu ☎0472 5368888. A tall edifice a block to the southeast of A'Erding Square, a professionally run outfit with its own pool, sauna and gym. Rooms are quite lovely, with soft duvets and good carpets – after a couple of hours here it can be quite a surprise to see the ugly city lurking out of the window. **¥450**

Wudangzhao

五当召, wǔdāng zhào • Daily 8am–6pm • ¥60 • bus #7 (¥10) from East train station to Shiguai (石拐, shíguǎi), then taxi (¥90 return) for the final 25km • round-trip taxi hire from Baotou about ¥400 • tours from Baotou ¥240–350 per person

Set in a pretty, narrow valley about 70km northeast of Baotou, **Wudangzhao** is the best-preserved Lamaist monastery still functioning in Inner Mongolia, one of the results of the Mongolian conquest of Tibet in the thirteenth century. For centuries afterwards, the roads between Tibet and Mongolia were worn by countless pilgrims and wandering monks bringing Lamaist Buddhism to Mongolia. This particular monastery, of the Yellow Sect, was established in 1749 and at its height housed twelve hundred lamas; seven generations of Living Buddhas were based here, the ashes of whom are kept in one of the halls. Today, however, the few remaining monks are greatly outnumbered by tourists from Baotou, and sadly their main duties now seem to involve hanging around at the hall entrances to check tourists' tickets.

Beyond the monastery you can hike off into the surrounding hills and, if you're keen, you should be able to **stay** in the pilgrims' hostel in the monastery as well.

Genghis Khan's Mausoleum

成吉思汗陵园, chéngjísīhàn língyuán • Daily 7am–7pm • ¥120

The first thing to be said about **Genghis Khan's Mausoleum** – located around 150km south of Baotou – is that it's not all it's cracked up to be: it probably isn't the tomb of Genghis Khan, and it isn't a particularly attractive place anyway, but nonetheless it provides a fascinating insight into the modern cult of the famous warrior. There are no English captions for the exhibits.

Special **sacrificial ceremonies** take place here four times a year on certain days of the lunar calendar – the fifteenth day of the third lunar month, the fifteenth day of the fifth lunar month, the twelfth day of the ninth month and the third day of the tenth month. On these occasions, Mongolian monks lead solemn rituals that involve piling up cooked sheep before the statue of the khan. The ceremonies are attended not only by local people, but also by pilgrims from the Republic of Mongolia itself.

The site

Genghis Khan is known to have died in northern China, but while his funeral cortege may have passed through this region on its way back to Mongolia, the story that the wheels of his funeral cart got stuck in the mud here, resulting in his burial on the spot, is almost certainly apocryphal. At best, scholars believe, the site contains a few of the warrior's relics. The real tomb is thought to be on the slopes of Burkhan Khaldun, in the Hentei Mountains, not far to the east of Ulaan Baatar in Outer Mongolia. The reason it came to be so strongly believed that the Khan was buried here in China

---

GENGHIS KHAN

Genghis Khan (1162–1227) was born, ominously enough, with a clot of blood in his hand. Under his leadership, the Mongols erupted from their homeland to ravage the whole of Asia, butchering millions, razing cities and laying waste to all the land from China to eastern Europe. It was his proud boast that his destruction of cities was so complete that he could ride across their ruins by night without the least fear of his horse stumbling.

Even before Genghis exploded onto the scene, the nomadic Mongols had long been a thorn in the side of the city-dwelling Chinese. Construction of the **Great Wall** had been undertaken to keep these two fundamentally opposed societies apart. But it was always fortunate for the Chinese that the early nomadic tribes of Mongolia fought as much among themselves as they did against outsiders. Genghis Khan's achievement was to weld together the warring nomads into a fighting force the equal of which the world had never seen: the secret of his success was skilful **cavalry tactics**, acquired from long practice in the saddle on the wide-open Mongolian plains. Frequently his armies would rout forces ten or twenty times their size.

Led by Genghis, the Mongols unleashed a massive onslaught on China in 1211. The Great Wall proved no obstacle, and with two hundred thousand men in tow Genghis cut a swath across northwest China towards Beijing. It was not all easy progress, however – so great was the destruction wrought in northern China that **famine and plague** broke out, afflicting the invader as much as the invaded. Genghis Khan himself died (of injuries sustained in falling from his horse) before the **capture of China** had been completed. His body was carried back to Mongolia by a funeral cortege of ten thousand, who murdered every man and beast within 16km of the road so that news of the Great Khan's death could not be reported before his sons and viceroys had been gathered from the farthest corners of his dominions. The whereabouts of his **tomb** is uncertain, though according to one of the best-known stories his ashes are in the mausoleum outside Dongsheng (see below).

---

appears to be that the tribe who were charged with guarding the real sepulchre eventually drifted down across the Yellow River to the Ordos – but continued to claim the honour of being the official guardians of the tomb.

The mausoleum

The main part of the cement mausoleum is formed by three connecting halls, shaped like Mongolian yurts. The corridors connecting the halls are adorned with bizarre murals supposedly depicting the life of Genghis Khan – though note the women in Western dress (1890s-style). In the middle of the main hall stands a 5m-high marble **statue** of Genghis before a map of his empire. Whatever the truth about the location of his burial place, the popular view among Mongolians, both in China and in the Republic of Mongolia, is that this is a holy site: the side halls, all very pretty, have ceremonial yurts, altars, burning incense, hanging paintings and Mongolian calligraphy, and offerings as though to a god. Some bring offerings – not the usual apples and bread, but bottles of rotgut *baijiu* on sale in the souvenir shop – and bow in penitence. Others, including several of the female staff, get drunk early and keep sipping until they're either surly or extremely affectionate; be prepared for anything as the site attracts its fair share of dodgy characters, including about fifteen "hairdressers" just outside.

The museum and relics

There's a small, free **museum** by the mausoleum ticket office with a few alleged **relics**, which have a murky political history. Several times they have been removed, and later returned, the most recent occasion being during World War II, when the Japanese seized them. Apparently the Japanese had plans to set up a puppet Mongol state, centred around a Genghis Khan shrine. They even drew up plans for an elaborate mausoleum to house them – plans that were then commandeered by the Chinese Communists who, having safely returned the relics from a hiding place in Qinghai, built the mausoleum for themselves in 1955 as a means of currying favour with the Mongolian people.

<table>
<tr><td>**ARRIVAL AND DEPARTURE**</td><td>**GENGHIS KHAN'S MAUSOLEUM**</td></tr>
</table>

It would be possible, if you left Baotou early in the morning, to reach the mausoleum and make it back the same evening.

By bus and minibus From Baotou, catch a bus to the up-and-coming mid-point town of Dongsheng (东胜, dōngshèng; 1hr), then change services to the mausoleum (1hr). To return to Dongsheng, flag down a passing minibus, but note that services tend to dry up after 1pm or so.

ACCOMMODATION AND EATING

There are some (very) fake yurts on the mausoleum grounds (no showers; beds ¥40–50); but Dongsheng makes a more pleasant place to stay the night, with plenty of cheap hotels and some good noodle restaurants.

Hohhot

呼和浩特, hūhé hàotè

Although it's now a large city, with a majority Han population, **HOHHOT** manages to present an interesting blend of the old and the new: as well as the shiny modern banks and department stores downtown, most of the historic buildings are crowded into the interesting – though fast-disappearing – old southwestern part of the city, where you can enjoyably spend half a day simply ambling around. Fittingly, Hohhot is a relatively green and leafy place in summer – the town's Mongolian name means "green city".

Brief history

There has been a settlement at Hohhot since the time of the Ming dynasty some 400 years ago, though it did not become the capital of Inner Mongolia until 1952. Until relatively modern times, it was a small town centred on a number of **Buddhist temples**. The temples are still here, and it's also worthwhile tracking down the vanishing **Mongol** districts, not

NAADAM IN HOHHOT

Summer is a good time to be in Hohhot, coinciding as it does with Mongolia's famed **Naadam festival**. Shows of horsemanship, wrestling and other games take place at the gigantic **Inner Mongolia horse racecourse**, 2km north of the train station; built in the shape of two circular Mongolian yurts, adjacent and connected to each other to form the elongated shape of a stadium, it's the biggest racecourse in China by far. The dates vary, but Naadam usually falls between late July and early August. Outside the holiday, displays of Mongolian riding and dancing sometimes take place here too.

---

least to try some of their distinctive food. The other reason for visiting Hohhot is its proximity to some of the famous Mongolian **grasslands** within a 100km radius of the city; in summer, travellers arriving by train, in particular, are often subjected to furious and persistent harassment by travel agents' touts trying to sell them grassland tours.

Jiangjun Yashu

将军衙署, jiāngjūn yáshǔ • Xincheng Xijie • Daily April–Oct 8am–6.30pm; Nov & March, 9am–5pm; Dec–Feb 9am–3pm • ¥25 • bus #3 (¥1) from the train station

There is just one historic building marooned in the new part of town: this is the **Jiangjun Yashu**, a former military headquarters, even though it looks like a temple. Now it's a tiny museum with some bizarre modern Buddhist art mingling with Qing office furniture at the back. The best reason to come here is to see the scale model of ancient Hohhot, back before the city walls and temples were replaced with boulevards and banks.

Inner Mongolia Museum

内蒙古博物馆, nèiménggǔ bówùguǎn • Off Xinhua Donglu • Tues–Sun 9am–5pm • Free (bring ID) • bus #3 • taxi from train station ¥20

Some 6km east of the Jiangjun Yashu, the brand-new **Inner Mongolia Museum** is infinitely better than its counterpart in Baotou (see p.229). Even before you get in, you'll be struck by the space-age architecture's swooping roofs, with a small tract of grassland (the Mongol connection) racing up to meet them. The museum's curators are still experimenting with the layout, though the pick of the exhibits includes a tremendous display of **ethnic Mongolian items**, such as costumes, saddles, long leather coats and cummerbunds, as well as hunting and sporting implements, including hockey sticks and balls. There's also a good **paleontology** display, with complete fossils of a woolly rhinoceros and a sizeable dinosaur. Then there are the halls dedicated to the **Khans**, with interesting maps and objects outlining the exploits of Genghis Khan and the huge Mongol empire of the thirteenth century.

Great Mosque

清真大寺, qīngzhēn dàsì • Zhongshan Lu • Open from first to last prayers • Free • Only Muslims allowed inside • Bus #6, #7 or #8 from the train station • taxi ¥20

Hohhot's attractive black-brick **Great Mosque** is easily spotted on account of its minaret, topped with a pagoda roof in a fine fusion of Chinese and Arabic styles. The Hui people who worship here are extremely friendly, and will probably be delighted if you ask to look round the mosque complex (though not the prayer halls). The surrounding streets comprise the Muslim area of town, and besides a lot of old men with wispy beards and skullcaps, you'll find a good, if dwindling, array of noodle and kebab shops in the immediate area.

Dazhao

大召, dàzhāo • Da Nanjie • Daily 8am–6.30pm • ¥35 • Bus #6, #7 or #8 from the train station • taxi ¥25

Constructed in 1579, and recently the subject of a typically gaudy renovation, the **Dazhao** temple was dedicated in the late seventeenth century to the famous Qing emperor Kangxi – a gold tablet with the words "Long Live the Emperor" was set before the silver statue of Sakyamuni, and in the main hall murals depicting the visit of Kangxi can still be seen.

Xilituzhao

席力图召, xílìtú zhào • Da Nanjie • Daily 8am–6.30pm • ¥30 • Bus #6, #7 or #8 from the train station • taxi ¥25

Xilituzhao is a temple of similar scale and layout to the Dazhao, and dates from the same era, though it too has been restored. The dagoba is interesting for featuring Sanskrit writing above Chinese dragons above Tibetan-style murals. Since 1735 this has been the official residence of the reincarnation of Hohhot's Living Buddha, who is in charge of Buddhist affairs in the city.

Wuta Temple

五塔寺, wǔtǎ sì • Wutasi Qianjie • Daily 8.30am–5.30pm • ¥35 • best accessed by taxi (¥20)

Around 1km east of the Dazhao temple, the **Wuta Temple** was built in 1727, in an Indian style, and remains Hohhot's most attractive piece of architecture. This composite of five pagodas originally belonged to the Ci Deng Temple, which no longer exists. It's relatively small, but its walls are engraved with no fewer than 1563 Buddhas, all in slightly different postures. Currently stored inside the pagoda building is a rare, antique Mongolian cosmological map that marks the position of hundreds of stars.

ARRIVAL AND DEPARTURE
HOHHOT

By air Hohhot's Baita airport (呼和浩特白塔国际机场, hūhéhàotè báitǎ guójì jīchǎng) lies 35km east of the city, and the airport bus (30min; ¥10) drops arriving passengers at the airlines ticket office on Xilin Guole Lu, just south of Xinhua Square (Mon–Sat 8am–9pm; ☎0471 6963160). A taxi costs around ¥40.
Destinations Beijing (9 daily; 1hr 10min); Guangzhou (1–3 daily; 3hr); Shanghai (5 daily; 2hr 30min); Shenyang (1–3 daily; 1hr 30min); Shenzhen (2–3 daily; 3hr); Tianjin (2–4 daily; 1hr); Xi'an (2 daily; 1hr 30min).
By rail Hohhot's station (呼和浩特站, hūhéhàotè zhàn), to the north of the city centre, has good connections east and west, as well as trains across the border to Ulaan Baatar in Outer Mongolia (see p.238). As the station ticket office is often hideously crowded, travel agents can procure train tickets for a ¥5 commission; ask at your hotel for the

nearest. There's also an East station (呼和浩特东站, hūhéhàotè dōngzhàn) 12km up the track, which though quite handy for reaching the museum is otherwise of little use.
Destinations from main station Baotou (many daily; 2hr); Beijing (11 daily; 6–11hr); Datong (10 daily; 3hr 30min–6hr); Taiyuan (1 daily; 10hr); Ulaan Baatar (2 weekly; 25hr); Xi'an (2 daily; 13hr–15hr 30min); Yinchuan (4 daily; 8hr 30min–10hr).
By bus The main long-distance station (呼和浩特长途汽车站, hūhéhàotè chángtú qìchēzhàn), right outside the train station exit on the west, is useful for services to Datong (every 30min; 2hr 30min), which are faster than the train, and Xilamuren (hourly; 2hr) for the grasslands. Coming into town, you may also rock up at one of two depots off the main road to the west.

GETTING AROUND

By bus The local bus network is a bit of a nightmare, but the #1, #6, #7 or #8, which head from the train station area to sights in the west part of town, can be useful.

By taxi The minimum fare is ¥6, though traffic and distance mean that the meter regularly ticks over the ¥20 level.

INFORMATION AND TOURS

Travel agents There are numerous travel agents in town, many of whom will find you before you find them. They nearly all have English-speaking employees, and deal in grassland tours as well as booking train tickets. These are the

best form of access to the grasslands: your accommodation will also be able to organize trips, but for a much higher price. Honourable exceptions are the *Anda* hostel and *Zhaojun* hotel, both of which are pretty fair with their tours.

ACCOMMODATION

Hohhot's accommodation scene is changing rapidly, and as older places by the train station fall prey to the wrecking ball, demand is being met by more modern and central establishments.

Anda Guesthouse 安达宾馆, āndá bīnguǎn. Qiaokou Xijie ⊙0471 6918039, ⓦandaguesthouse.com. Friendly little youth hostel, with cheap dorm beds, and pleasant private rooms. The owner is a fountain of local knowledge, and will be able to rustle up a tailor-made grasslands trip in no time. The hostel is almost impossible to find independently – call ahead for a train station pick-up. Dorms ¥60, rooms ¥180

★ **Jia Yuan** 家源酒店, jiāyuán jiǔdiàn. Off Xilinguole Beilu ⊙0471 6263338. This is a lovely place, located just off the main road in a quiet, residential area. The phoney Miró at the entrance hints at what they're about: cheap, but trying hard. Rooms are cheerfully decorated too. ¥129

★ **Shangri-La** 香格里拉酒店, xiānggélǐlā jiǔdiàn. Xilinguole Nanlu ⊙0471 3366888, ⓦshangri-la .com. You'll have to travel for hundreds of kilometres to find better rooms – this is Hohhot's plushest hotel, with superb standards of service and great views from the higher floors. ¥1288

Zhaojun 昭君大酒店, zhāojūn dàjiǔdiàn. 69 Xinhua Dajie ⊙0471 6668888, ⓦzhaojunhotel.com.cn. A well-organized and comfortable place in the centre of town, diagonally across from Xinhua Square. The travel service in the lobby has information in English on their grassland and Genghis Khan Mausoleum tours. ¥320

EATING AND DRINKING

The highlight of eating in Hohhot is dining on Mongolian food, best experienced in the Mongolian quarter at the southeast of town (bus #4, get off at Daxue Xijie). For an excellent breakfast or lunch, order a large bowl of sugary milk tea, along with *chaomi* (buckwheat), *huangyou* (butter), *nailao* (hard white cheese) and *naipi* (a sweetish, biscuit-like substance formed from the skin of boiled milk). Toss everything into the tea, and eat it with chopsticks – it's surprisingly delicious. Mongolian hotpot is best shared with friends and beer.

Alekaoba 阿乐烤吧, ālè kǎobā. Xincheng Xijie ⊙0471 6967510. Family restaurant serving a mix of Chinese and Korean food. There's meat to barbecue from ¥30 per portion, *bibimbap* (veggies on rice) for ¥15, and *kimbap* (California rolls) for ¥20. Daily 24hr.

Ashes of Time Cafe 时光简影咖啡馆, shíguāng jiǎnyǐng kāfēi guǎn. Daxue Xilu. A thoroughly pleasant café that wouldn't look out of place in Beijing, though in Hohhot it comes as a wonderful little surprise. They've a range of coffees (including, rarely for China, some iced ones too) and teas for ¥30 and up; the menu's Chinese-only, but it should be easy to communicate with the friendly Mongolian staff. Daily 10am–10pm.

★ **Hotpot 518** 快东518火锅, kuàidōng 518 huǒguō. Da Dongjie ⊙0471 6301933. A brilliant hotpot for dummies: gone is the regular menu full of indecipherable ingredients, replaced here with a supermarket-style aisle from which you select your food (¥5 for things in a white dish, ¥10 for red, ¥18 for green and ¥28 for black). Also gone is the copper boiler; instead, you eat from an electric hob. Throw in friendly staff, free fruit and dips, and you're onto a winner. Daily 10am–11pm.

★ **Malaqin** 马拉沁饭店, mǎlāqin fàndiàn. Xincheng Xijie ⊙0471 6926685. The most famous restaurant in town, with a menu bursting with Chinese goodies, many of a notably Mongolian bent. Try your mutton in a potato stew (¥78), or heavily seasoned then served on a sizzling platter (¥68); alternatively, go for the Genghis Khan steak (¥98). All can be followed up with mashed yam with blueberry sauce (¥22). Daily 11am–2.30pm & 5.30–9pm.

DIRECTORY

Banks and exchange There are banks with ATMs all around town; as usual, Bank of China branches are your best bet. The main post office handles Western Union money transfer services should you find yourself in dire straits.

Consulate The Republic of Mongolia consulate (Mon, Tues & Thurs 8.30am–noon; ⊙0471 4303254) is in the east of the city, at 5 Dongying Nanlu. Visas are fairly easy to obtain, and cost ¥290 for a month; you can get one the next day for ¥500. Note that Mongolian entry requirements have a habit of changing – ask your own embassy for the latest advice.

Mail and telephones The main post office (daily 8am–6pm) is on the northeastern corner of the train station square. There's another on the south side of Zhongshan Lu, just east of Xilin Guole Lu (Mon–Sat 8am–7pm). The Telecom Centre is adjacent (daily 8am–6pm), with a small 24hr office.

PSB In the government building to the south of the junction between Zhongshan Lu and Xilin Guole Lu. It's surprisingly useful for a PSB in an autonomous province, and there are usually no problems with visa extensions.

Around Hohhot

Hohhot has become a pleasant place to hunker down in for a few days, and there are a few sights nearby to keep you occupied – these include the Tang-dynasty **Tomb of Wang Zhaojun**, beautiful **Wusutu Zhao** temple, and the **Bai Ta** pagoda. Bar the pagoda, all are easily accessible on public transport, though taxis are pretty cheap for small groups.

TOURING THE GRASSLANDS

Mongolia isn't all one giant steppe, but three areas in the vicinity of Hohhot are certainly large enough to give the illusion of endlessness. These are **Xilamuren** (希拉穆仁草原, xīlāmùrén cǎoyuán), which begins 80km north of Hohhot; **Gegentala** (格根塔拉草原, gégēntǎlā cǎoyuán), 70km further north; and **Huitengxile** (辉腾锡勒草原, huīténgxīlè cǎoyuán), 120km northeast of Hohhot. It's hard to differentiate between them, except that Xilamuren – the only one of the three that can feasibly be reached independently – is probably the most visited and Gegentala the least. Bear in mind that your grassland experience in the immediate area of the regional capital is likely to be a rather packaged affair, and a visit to a grassland in another, remoter part of the region (such as Hailar – see p.188) may well give you a more authentic flavour of Mongolia.

Most people visit by taking one of the **grassland tours**, which Westerners rarely enjoy but East Asian tourists seem to love – or at least put up with in good humour. The tours all follow the same pattern, with visitors based at a site comprising a number of **yurts**, plus a dining hall, kitchen and very primitive toilets. The larger sites, at Xilamuren, are the size of small villages. Transport, meals and accommodation are all included in the price, as are various unconvincing "Mongolian entertainments" – wrestling and horseriding in particular – and visits to typical Mongol families in traditional dress. Only the food is consistently good, though watch out for the local firewater, *baijiu*, which you're more or less forced to drink when your Mongolian hosts bring silver bowls of the stuff round to every table during the evening banquet. The banquet is followed by a fairly degenerate evening of drinking, dancing and singing.

If you accept the idea that you are going on a tour of the grasslands to participate in a bizarre social experience, then you'll get much more out of it. Besides, it is perfectly possible to escape from your group by hiring your own horse, or heading off for a hike. If your stay happens to coincide with a bright moon, you could be in for the most hauntingly beautiful experience of your life.

PRACTICALITIES

A **two-day tour** (with one night in a yurt) is definitely enough – in a group of four or five people, this should come to around ¥450 each. Some travel services can tack smaller parties onto existing groups. Bear in mind that you may find yourself sleeping crushed into a small yurt with six others who don't speak your language, and that the tour may not be in English, even if you've requested that it should be.

Travelling independently to the Xilamuren grassland can work out a good deal cheaper than taking a tour. Store your luggage at your hotel in Hohhot, and catch a bus from the long-distance bus station (90min; ¥20); these set down adjacent to the grassland. When you get off you will be accosted by people offering to take you to their yurts – try to negotiate an all-inclusive daily rate of about ¥80 per person, for food and accommodation, before you accept any offer. You aren't exactly in the wilderness here, but you can wander off into the grass and soon find it. Return buses to Hohhot run regularly throughout the day, though if they're already full they won't even pass through town. If this occurs (which it often does), enterprising taxi drivers will take carfuls of people to the scruffy mid-point town of Wuchuan (武川, wǔchuān), then buy your onward ticket and pop you on the bus for Hohhot – meaning that you don't usually spend any more than you would have done for the direct bus.

Tomb of Wang Zhaojun

昭君墓, zhāojūn mù · Daily 8am–6pm · ¥35 · minibus #44 (¥1.5) from Hohhot train station

The **Tomb of Wang Zhaojun**, about 8km to the south of Hohhot, is the burial site of a Tang-dynasty princess, sent from present-day Hubei to cement Han–Mongol relations by marrying the king of Mongolia. It isn't spectacular – a huge mound raised from the plain and planted with gardens, in the centre of which is a modern pavilion – but the romantic story it recalls has important implications for modern Chinese politics, signifying the harmonious marrying of the Han with the minority peoples. In the rose garden, among pergolas festooned with gourds, is a little museum devoted to Zhaojun, containing some of her clothes, including a tiny pair of shoes, plus jewels, books and a number of steles.

Wusutu Zhao

乌素图召, wūsùtú zhào • Daily 8am–6pm • ¥25 • bus #23 from Hohhot train station

Well worth the effort to reach, the **Wusutu Zhao** complex is the only temple in Mongolia to have been designed and built solely by Mongolians. Boasting Mongolian, Tibetan and Han architectural styles, it lies 12km northwest of Hohhot, south of the Daqing Shan ranges and in attractive countryside separated from the city by the new expressway. Admission is collected by an elderly monk who will probably be surprised to see you. There are still no souvenir stands or gaudy refurbishments, so take the time to scour the Ming-era murals within and the ornate woodcuts attached to sticks at the base of the Buddhas. The surrounding grasslands and trails into the mountains make for a relaxing day out.

Bai Ta

白塔, bái tǎ • Daily dawn–dusk • ¥35 • taxi from town around ¥35

The **Bai Ta**, or White Pagoda, lies about 17km east of the city along Xincheng Xi Jie – it's a possible stop on the way to the airport, which was named after it. An attractive, 55m-high wood-and-brick construction erected in the tenth century, it's covered in ornate carvings of coiling dragons, birds and flowers on the lower parts of the tower.

Shanxi

山西, shānxī

With an average height of 1000m above sea level, **Shanxi province** is effectively one huge highland plateau. Its name, not to be confused with Shaanxi (home to Xi'an; see p.197), means "west of the mountains", though rocky peaks indeed stream happily throughout the provinces, ending abruptly at all borders bar its northeast and southwestern corners. Tourism staff in the province call it a "museum above the ground", a reference to the many unrestored but still intact **ancient buildings** that dot the region, some from dynasties almost unrepresented elsewhere in China.

Just outside the coal-mining city of **Datong** lie the **Yungang cave temples** – one of China's major Buddhist art sites – and the gravity-defying **Hanging Temple**. To the south lies Shanxi's major mountain drawcard: the beautiful, if seasonally inaccessible, **Wutai Shan** range. South again, past the uninteresting provincial capital, **Taiyuan**, is a host of little places worth a detour, the highest profile of which is **Pingyao**, an old walled town preserved entirely from its Qing-dynasty heyday as a banking centre. Southwest of here and surprisingly time-consuming to reach, the Yellow River presents its fiercest aspect at **Hukou Falls**, as its chocolate-coloured waters explode out of a short, tight gorge.

ON TO OUTER MONGOLIA

Should you require them, visas for the Republic of Mongolia, otherwise known as **Outer Mongolia**, are available in Hohhot (see p.236) and Beijing (p.119). At the time of writing, there were no direct flights from Hohhot to the Outer Mongolian capital, Ulaan Baatar, though both Mongolian Airlines and Tianjin Airlines have flown the route in the past.

In the absence of planes, the fastest way from Hohhot to Ulaan Baatar is by train. There are two weekly departures, with trains leaving Hohhot just before 10pm Mon & Fri (tickets from ¥950). Alternatively, you can do the journey in stages: the first leg is to get to the border at Erlianhot (二连浩特; èrlián hàotè), shortened to Erlian on timetables (2 daily; 9hr; tickets from ¥30).

Crossing the border at the curious, bustling border town of Erlianhot will take a fair bit of time if you are not on a through train. Assuming you arrive in the evening, you'll certainly have to spend one night here; there's plenty of cheap accommodation. After crossing the border (figure on at least ¥50 by taxi), you should have plenty of time to kill before the evening train on to Ulaan Baatar (18hr).

CAVE HOUSES

A common sight among the folds and fissures of the dry loess plain of northern Shanxi (and neighbouring Shaanxi) are **cave dwellings**, a traditional form of housing that's been in use for nearly two thousand years. Hollowed into the sides of hills terraced for agriculture, they house more than eighty million people, and are eminently practical – cheap, easy to make, naturally insulated and long-lasting. In fact, a number of intact caves in Hejin, on the banks of the Yellow River in the west of the province, are said to date back to the Tang dynasty. Furthermore, in a region where flat land has to be laboriously hacked out of the hillside, caves don't take up land that could be cultivated.

The **facade** of the cave is usually a wooden frame on a brick base. Most of the upper part consists of a wooden lattice – designs of which are sometimes very intricate – faced with white paper, which lets in plenty of light, but preserves the occupants' privacy. Tiled eaves above protect the facade from rain damage. Inside, the **single-arched chamber** is usually split into a bedroom at the back and a living area in front, furnished with a *kang*, whose flue leads under the bed and then outside to the terraced field that is the roof – sometimes, the first visible indication of a distant village is a set of smoke columns rising from the crops.

Such is the popularity of cave homes that prosperous cave dwellers often prefer to build themselves a new courtyard and another cave rather than move into a house. Indeed, in the suburbs of towns and cities of northern Shaanxi, new concrete apartment buildings are built in imitation of caves, with three windowless sides and an arched central door. It is not uncommon even to see soil spread over the roofs of these apartments with vegetables grown on top.

Brief history

Strategically important, bounded to the north by the Great Wall and to the south by the Yellow River, Shanxi was for centuries a buffer territory against the northern tribes. Today, the significance is economic: this is China's most **coal-rich** province, with 500 million tonnes mined here annually, a quarter of the national supply. Physically, Shanxi is dominated by the proximity of the Gobi Desert, and wind and water have shifted sand, dust and silt right across the province. The land is farmed, as it has been for millennia, by slicing the hills into steps, creating a plain of ribbed hillocks that look like the realization of a cubist painting. Erosion and increasing desertification are serious problems, presently being combated by extensive tree-planting and dune stabilization projects.

Datong

大同, dàtóng

Famed for being gritty, polluted and ugly, **DATONG** has recently been the subject of one of China's biggest urban makeovers – though there's some way to go until the city could be described as attractive. The knobbly remains of the earthen **ramparts** that once bounded the old city have been lovingly rebuilt, and by the time you read this it should be possible to cycle their full perimeter. Inside the walls, and spreading east and west of a centrally located Ming-dynasty **Drum Tower** (鼓楼, gǔlóu), you'll also find a new, rather successfully contrived Qing-style district. The unrestored parts of town exude a rugged atmosphere that those who don't have to live here might just find appealing, and a good number of small temples and old monuments are hidden away in the backstreets. Despite these definite improvements, though, many visitors merely use the city as a springboard to outlying sights, especially the **Yungang Caves** (see p.243) and **Hanging Temple** (p.245).

Brief history

The Turkic **Toba** – a non-Han people from Central Asia – took advantage of the internal strife afflicting central and southern China to establish their own dynasty, the **Northern Wei** (386–534 AD), taking Datong as their capital in 398 AD. Though the period was one of discord and warfare, the Northern Wei became fervent Buddhists and commissioned a magnificent series of **cave temples** at Yungang, just west of the

city. Over the course of almost a century, more than a thousand grottoes were completed, containing over fifty thousand statues, before the capital was moved south to Luoyang, where construction began on the similar Longmen Caves (see p.261).

A second period of greatness came with the arrival of the Mongol **Liao dynasty**, also Buddhists, who made Datong their capital in 907. Their rule lasted two hundred years, leaving behind a small legacy of statuary and some fine temple architecture, notably in the **Huayan** and **Shanhua temples** in town, and a **wooden pagoda**, the oldest in China, in the nearby town of Yingxian. Datong remained important to later Chinese dynasties for its strategic position just inside the Great Wall, south of Inner Mongolia, and the tall **city walls** date from the early Ming dynasty.

Nine Dragon Screen

九龙壁, jiǔlóng bì · south side of Da Dongjie · Daily 7.30am–7.30pm · ¥10

The **Nine Dragon Screen** is the largest of several similar Ming-dynasty screens around the city: a lively 45m-long relief of nine sinuous dragons depicted in 426 multi-coloured glazed tiles, rising from the waves and cavorting among suns. The only other dragon screens of this age are in Beijing, the main difference being that Datong's are four-clawed, indicating the dwelling of a prince, not an emperor (whose dragons had five claws). Originally, the screen stood directly in front of a palace, destroyed in the fifteenth century, as an unpassable obstacle to evil spirits, which, it was believed, could only travel in straight lines. A long, narrow pool in front of the screen is meant to reflect the dragons and give the illusion of movement when you look into its rippling surface.

Huayan Temple

华严寺, huáyán sì · Accessible from Huayuan Jie · Daily 8am–6.30pm · ¥80, covers both complexes

A short walk west of the drum tower are the remaining buildings of the large **Huayan Temple**, originally dating to 1062 AD during the Liao dynasty and now forming two complexes. The **Upper Temple**, the first one you come to, is a little shabby, but its twelfth-century **Main Hall** is one of the largest in China, and is unusual for facing east – it was originally built by a sect that worshipped the sun. The roof is superb, a Tang-style design with two vertical "horns" fashioned to look like lions doing handstands. The cavernous interior has some wonderful Ming statuary including twenty life-size guardians, gently inclined as if listening attentively, but the main draw is the Qing-dynasty **frescoes** completely covering the walls, depicting Buddha's attainment of nirvana.

The Lower Temple

Turn right out of the entrance to this complex and you come to the **Lower Temple**, notable for its rugged-looking hall, a rare Liao-dynasty construction from 1038, complete with contemporary statues. Halls surrounding the front courtyard form a **museum** of regional discoveries spanning the Liao, Jin, Khitan and Yuan eras.

Shanhua Temple

善化寺, shànhuà sì · Da Nanjie · Daily 8am–6.30pm · ¥50

South of the Drum Tower lies the **Shanhua Temple**, a pretty place of solace in which birdsong replaces traffic noise. Founded during the Tang dynasty, what you see is a Ming restoration of a Jin structure. The buildings have a solid presence very different from the delicate look of later Chinese temples, and are impressive for their obvious age alone – one dates from 1154. The Jin-era statues in the main hall, five Buddhas in the centre with 24 *lokapalas* (divine generals) lined up on either side, are exceptionally finely detailed. One of the outlying courtyards sports a **five-dragon screen**, relocated from a monastery that once stood to the south of the city.

The city walls

Daily 8am–6pm · ¥30 · Bike rental ¥10/hr · golf buggies ¥10 per ride · only accessible via south and east gates at time of writing, though more points to open

Anyone who visited Datong prior to 2011 will be astonished by what has happened to its old city wall. Within the space of a few years, more or less the whole 10km circumference was rebuilt from scratch – no mean feat, even for a city long associated with hard work. Work was still being conducted on the western side at the time of writing, though it'll eventually be possible to cycle clean around the perimeter, making for an extremely enjoyable way to get a view of the city.

ARRIVAL AND DEPARTURE   DATONG

By air Datong's tiny airport (大同云冈机场, dàtóng yúngāng jīchǎng) is 15km east of the city centre. A shuttle bus (¥10) heads to and from a departure point on Yingbin Lu, opposite the *Datong Hotel* (大同宾馆, dàtóng bīnguǎn); you can buy tickets here too, though the main airlines office is one block north at 1 Nanguan Nanjie (daily 8.30am–5pm; ☏0352 2052777). Alternatively, a taxi costs ¥50.

Destinations Beijing (1 daily; 1hr); Shanghai (2 weekly; 2hr 10min).

By train The train station (大同站, dàtóng zhàn) – served largely by clunkers – is on the city's northern edge, on several bus routes, or a ¥15–20 taxi ride from town. Tickets are straightforward enough to buy at the station, or

at the advance-ticket office (daily 8am–12.30pm & 2.30–6pm) at the corner of Nanguan Nanjie and Nanguan Xijie.

Destinations Beijing (11 daily; 6hr); Hohhot (10 daily; 3hr 30min–6hr); Lanzhou (1 daily; 23hr); Linfen (4 daily; 10hr); Taiyuan (12 daily; 5hr 30min–6hr); Xi'an (1 daily; 16hr).

By bus Xinnan bus station (新南站, xīnnán zhàn), 5km south of the centre on the #30 bus route (which also links with the train station), is Datong's main long-distance depot. There's a more central Regional bus station (长途汽车站, chángtú qìchēzhàn), off Xinjian Beilu just west of the walled city; both serve similar destinations, so ask at your accommodation for the best one to head to.

Destinations Hohhot (hourly; 3hr 30min); Taiyuan (hourly; 3hr 30min); Wutai Shan (2 daily; 5hr).

GETTING AROUND

By bus Datong has numerous bus services (¥1), though ongoing reconstruction means that you should check routes on arrival. Currently, #4 heads from the train station

into town.

By taxi Flag fall is ¥6, and a ride within town should be under ¥20.

INFORMATION

Travel agents On arrival at the train station you may be grabbed by a representative of the helpful CITS office, based at the *Taijia* hotel (6.30am–6.30pm; ☏130 08088454), just north of the station exit. They offer day-trips from ¥100/person (transportation only; more if fewer than 5 people) to

Yungang Caves and the Hanging Temple; you can add the Wooden Pagoda for ¥100/group. They're nice enough, but not beyond giving false public transport information in order to get you onto a tour. The team at the *Datong Youth Hostel* are able to book taxi tours at similar prices.

ACCOMMODATION

The city's budget accommodation options are clustered around the train station, with some good-value mid-range options in the city centre. Very little stands out at the cheapest end of the scale, so budget travellers – or anyone, really – may care to arrive in the morning, see the sights and then grab transport out.

★ **Datong Youth Hostel** 大同国际青年旅舍, dàtóng guójì qīngnián lǚshè. Huayuan Jie ☎0352 2427766. A very welcome addition to the city, with neat rooms centred around a friendly common area. There's little English spoken by the staff, though they'll try their best to arrange tours for you if necessary – they're not too pushy selling their own, though these are usually good value. Dorms ¥50, doubles ¥150

Garden 花园大饭店, huāyuán dàfàndiàn. 59 Da Nanjie ☎0352 5865825. The city centre's top-end option, with good service, crisp linen on the beds and an excellent location. There's also a Brazilian buffet (see p.225). ¥378

★ **Holiday Inn** 假日酒店, jiàrì jiǔdiàn. Off Yingbin Lu ☎0352 2118888. Now the top place to stay in town, this immaculately designed hotel lies just to the south of the city wall, beyond a pleasingly grubby area that's great for street eats. Rooms are spick and span, and there are excellent restaurants on site, as well as a lovely swimming pool. ¥588

Taijia 泰佳宾馆, taìjiā bīnguǎn. Jianbei Jie ☎0352 5101816. This shabby hotel is pretty much the cheapest acceptable lodging near the station, and the base of the city's CITS office, who will probably try to push you here. Have a good look at the room before agreeing to stay, though; you'll pay double if you want a private bathroom. ¥88

EATING AND DRINKING

Datong is far enough north for mutton hotpot to figure heavily in the local cuisine, along with potatoes, which you can buy, processed into a starchy jelly and seasoned with sauces, from street stalls. Other typically northern dishes available are *zongzi* (glutinous rice dumplings) and *yuanxiao* (sweet dumplings). There are plenty of inexpensive places in the very centre of town, in the area to the east of the hostel.

★ **Fenglinge Shaomai** 风临阁烧麦, fēnglíngé shāomài. Gulou Xijie ☎0352 2059699. Datong's most attractive restaurant by far, with temple-style woodwork, silky cushions and smartly dressed staff. It's set in a (totally rebuilt) venue said to be over 500 years old – they claim to have provided food to Dowager Cixi (see p.96) on her flight from the Allied Forces in 1900. Try the *shaomai* dumplings (¥18–98 per portion), of which the "flower" varieties are the best. There are some very cheap dishes on the menu, and it's possible to eat for under ¥30 per person – considering the beauty of the place, it's surprising that staff don't get sniffy. Daily 11.30am–2pm & 5.30–8.30pm.

Latina 59 Da Nanjie, at the Garden Hotel (see above). This restaurant serves Brazilian barbecue – incongruous in dusty Datong, but quite a pleasant surprise – for a princely ¥218 per person. There's suitably samba-style music performed most evenings. Daily 11.30am–2pm & 6–9pm.

Old Tibet 西藏往事, xīzàng wǎngshì. 2 Huayuan Jie. Tucked down inside a shop within staggering distance of the hostel, this great little basement bar's pleasing, Tibetan-style interior encourages casual conversation rather than raucous drinking. It doubles as a café during the day, with coffee from ¥30 and beers from ¥10. Daily noon–2am.

DIRECTORY

Banks and exchange The main Bank of China (Mon–Fri 8am–6pm) on Yingbin Xilu can cash travellers' cheques, and there's a small branch with an ATM at the southern end of Da Nanjie.

Hospital People's Hospital No. 3 is in the south of the city on Yingbin Xi Lu, just west of the crossroads with Xinjian Nanlu.

Left luggage There's an office outside the train station on the western side of the concourse (¥5).

Mail and telephones The large, Russian-looking building fronting Hongqi Square, south of Da Xijie, houses both the post office (daily 8am–6pm) and a 24hr telecom office.

PSB The police station (Mon–Sat 8.30am–noon & 2.30–6pm) is on Xinjian Beilu, 200m north of the post office; take along a Mandarin-speaker, since they're not particularly heedful of travellers' needs.

Around Datong

Datong is the main jumping-off point for two of northern China's most spectacular sights: the phenomenal **Yungang Caves** and the gravity-defying **Hanging Temple**, which can both be seen in a single day. The latter can also be combined with a visit to **Heng Shan**, one of the five holy mountains of Taoism, or as a stop on the way to **Wutai Shan** (see p.245). Roads are sometimes bumpy and often blocked in winter, when transport times can double, but at least journeys are enlivened by great views: the lunar emptiness of the fissured landscape is broken only occasionally by villages whose mud walls seem to grow out of the raw brown earth. Some of the villages in the area still have their **beacon towers**, left over from when this really was a wild frontier.

Yungang Caves

云冈石窟, yúngāng shíkū • Daily 8am–6.30pm • ¥150 • bus #3 from Xinjian Nanlu in Datong (¥1, up to 1hr) • taxi ¥40–50 each way

Just 16km west of Datong, the monumental **Yungang Caves**, a set of Buddhist grottoes carved into the side of a sandstone cliff, are a must. Built around 400 AD at a time of religious revival, the caves were the first and grandest of the three major Buddhist grottoes, the other two being the Longmen Caves in Luoyang (p.261) and the Mogao Caves in Gansu (p.811). These are the best preserved, but prepare to be disappointed by their surroundings – the atmosphere has for years been blighted by nearby coal mines, and the benefits afforded by the recent addition of parkland have been eroded by a huge and even more recently built shopping mall. However, it's still well worth the trip.

Caves 1–5

The easternmost caves are slightly set apart from, and less spectacular than, the others. **Caves 1 and 2** are constructed around a single square central pillar, elaborately carved in imitation of a wooden stupa but now heavily eroded, around which devotees perambulated. **Cave 3**, 25m deep, is the largest in Yungang – an almost undecorated cavern, it may once have been used as a lecture hall – while **cave 4** has a central pillar carved with images of Buddha.

Being suddenly confronted and dwarfed by a huge, 17m-high Buddha as you walk into **cave 5**, his gold face shining softly in the half-light, is an awesome, humbling experience. Other Buddhas of all sizes, a heavenly gallery, are massed in niches that honeycomb the grotto's gently curving walls, and two Bodhisattvas stand attentive at his side.

Cave 6

At the spectacular **cave 6**, a wooden facade built in 1652 leads into a high, square chamber dominated by a thick central pillar carved with Buddhas and Bodhisattvas in deep relief, surrounded by flying Buddhist angels and musicians. The vertical grotto walls are alive with reliefs depicting incidents from the **life of the Buddha** at just above head height, which form a narrative when read walking clockwise around the chamber. Easy-to-identify scenes at the beginning include the birth of the Buddha from his mother's armpit, and Buddha's father carrying the young infant on an elephant. Buddha's first trip out of the palace, which is depicted as a schematic, square Chinese building, is shown on the east wall of the cave, as is his meeting with the grim realities of life, in this case a cripple with two crutches.

Caves 7–15

Caves 7 and 8 are a pair, both square, with two chambers, and connected by an arch lined with angels and topped with what looks like a sunflower. The figures here, such as the six celestial worshippers above the central arch, are more Chinese in style than their predecessors.

TOURING AROUND DATONG

There's public transport to the separate sights around Datong (see individual accounts for details), though many visitors choose to go with a tour (see p.241). If you want to rent your own vehicle, a **taxi** for a day-trip to the Yungang caves and the Hanging Temple will cost around ¥300, though you may be able to haggle this down slightly; while ¥250 will cover a round-trip to the Hanging Temple and Wood Pagoda. Add an extra ¥100 to either for adding on Heng Shan too; and another ¥50 if you'd like to continue to Wutai Shan rather than head back to Datong afterwards.

Note that there are also regular public buses through the day between Hunyuan (for the Hanging Temple and Heng Shan) and Yingxian (for the Wood Pagoda), and plenty of cheap hotels and restaurants in either should you feel like staying the night – though Yingxian is more appealing by far.

BUILDING THE YUNGANG CAVES

Construction of the Yungang Caves began in 453 AD, when Datong was the capital of the Northern Wei dynasty, and petered out around 525, after the centre of power moved to Luoyang. The caves were made by first hollowing out a section at the top of the cliff, then digging into the rock, down to the ground and out, leaving two holes, one above the other. As many as forty thousand craftsmen worked on the project, coming from as far as India and Central Asia, and there is much **foreign influence** in the carvings: Greek motifs (tridents and acanthus leaves), Persian symbols (lions and weapons), and bearded figures, even images of the Hindu deities Shiva and Vishnu, are incorporated among the more common dragons and phoenixes of Chinese origin. The soft, rounded modelling of the **sandstone figures** – China's first stone statues – lining the cave interiors has more in common with the terracotta sculptures of the Mogao Caves near Dunhuang in Gansu, begun a few years earlier, than with the more linear features of Luoyang's later limestone work. In addition, a number of the seated Buddhas have sharp, almost Caucasian, noses.

The caves' present condition is misleading, as originally the cave entrances would have been covered with wooden facades, and the sculptures would have been faced with plaster and brightly painted; the larger ones are pitted with regular holes, which would once have held wooden supports on which the plaster face was built. Over the centuries, some of the caves have inevitably suffered from weathering, though there seems to have been little vandalism, certainly less than at Luoyang.

Today a 1km-long fragment of the original array survives, arranged in **three clusters** (east, central and west) and numbered east to west from 1 to 51. The earliest group is caves 16–20, followed by 7, 8, 9 and 10, then 5, 6 and 11 – the last to be completed before the court moved to Luoyang. Then followed 4, 13, 14 and 15, with the caves at the eastern end – 1, 2 and 3 – and cave 21 in the west, carved last.

The columns and lintels at the entrances of **caves 9, 10 and 12** are awash with sculptural detail in faded pastel colours: Buddhas, dancers, musicians, animals, flowers, angels and abstract, decorative flourishes (which bear a resemblance to Persian art). Parts of cave 9 are carved with imitation brackets to make the interior resemble a wooden building.

The outstretched right arm of the 15m-high Buddha inside **cave 13** had to be propped up for stability, so his sculptors ingeniously carved the supporting pillar on his knee into a four-armed mini-Buddha. The badly eroded sculptures of **caves 14 and 15** are stylistically some way between the massive figures of the early western caves and the smaller reliefs of the central caves.

The western caves

Compared to the previous caves, the figures in these **earliest caves** are simpler and bolder, though they are at least as striking. Constructed between 453 and 462 AD, under the supervision of the monk Tan Hao, all are in the same pattern of an enlarged niche containing a massive Buddha flanked by Bodhisattvas. The **giant Buddhas**, with round faces, sharp noses, deep eyes and thin lips, are said to be the representations of five emperors.

The Buddha in **cave 16**, whose bottom half has disintegrated, has a knotted belt high on his chest, Korean-style. The Buddhas were carved from the top down, and when the sculptors of the Buddha in **cave 17** reached ground level they needed to dig down to fit his feet in. The same problem was solved in **cave 18** by giving the Buddha shortened legs. The 14m-high Buddha in **cave 20**, sitting open to the elements in a niche that once would have been protected by a wooden canopy, is probably the most famous, and certainly the most photographed.

The small and unspectacular caves 21–51 are not much visited, but the ceiling of **cave 50** is worth a look for its flying elephants, and in **caves 50 and 51** there are sculptures of acrobats.

The Hanging Temple

悬空寺, xuánkōng sì • Daily 7am–6pm • ¥130 • Summertime minibuses from outside Datong train station • bus from Datong to Hunyuan (浑圆, húnyuán) and then a taxi (¥15–20) • see p.241 for tours

Clinging to the side of a sheer cliff face in a gorge some 80km southwest of Datong, the **Hanging Temple** is one of the most visually arresting sights in all China. It's not, however, an attraction for those nervous of heights – literally translating as "Temple Suspended in the Void", its buildings are anchored by wooden beams set into the rock.

There's been a temple on this site since the Northern Wei, though the buildings were periodically destroyed by the flooding of the Heng River (now no longer there, thanks to a dam upstream), occasioning the temple to be rebuilt higher and higher each time. Your first glimpse of it will be spectacular enough, but things get a great deal more atmospheric once you're inside the rickety, claustrophobic structure. Tall, narrow stairs and plank walkways connect the six halls – natural caves and ledges with wooden facades – in which shrines exist to Confucianism, Buddhism and Taoism, all of whose major figures are represented in nearly eighty statues in the complex, made from bronze, iron and stone.

Heng Shan

恒山, héngshān • Daily 8am–6pm • ¥60 • return cable car to Hengzong Temple ¥60 • bus from Datong to Hunyuan (浑圆, húnyuán) and then take a taxi (¥30) • see p.241 for tours

The Hanging Temple sits on the valley road that runs up to **Heng Shan**, a range of peaks that constitutes one of China's five main Taoist mountains – its history as a religious centre stretches back more than two thousand years, and plenty of emperors have put in an appearance here to climb the highest peak, Xuanwu (2000m), a trend begun by the very first emperor, Qin Shi Huang. From the base of the mountain, an easy climb takes you to Heng Shan's main place of worship, **Hengzong Temple**, via switchbacking paths through other smaller temples, about a thirty-minute walk up and twenty minutes down. Heng Shan's peak lies another 40min uphill from Hengzong Temple, and might be the quietest place left on the mountain.

The Wood Pagoda

应县木塔, yìngxiàn mùtǎ • Daily April–Oct 7.30am–7pm, Nov–March 8am–5.30pm • ¥60 • bus to Yingxian then taxi (¥5) • see p.241 for tours

At the centre of the small town of **YINGXIAN** (应县, yìngxiàn), 75km south of Datong, the stately **Wood Pagoda**, built in 1056 in the Liao dynasty, is one of the oldest wooden buildings in China, a masterful piece of structural engineering that looks solid enough to stand here for another millennium – however, it's not possible to ascend. During a recent renovation, a cache of **treasures** was found buried underneath the pagoda, including Buddhist sutras printed using woodblocks dating back to the Liao.

The pagoda

The tower reaches nearly 70m high and is octagonal in plan with nine internal storeys, though there are only six layers of eaves on the outside. The first storey is taller than the rest with extended eaves held up by columns forming a cloister around a mud-and-straw wall. The original pagoda was constructed without nails, though there are plenty in the floors nowadays. Originally, each storey had a statue inside, but now only one remains, an 11m-tall Buddha with facial hair and stretched-out earlobes – characteristic of northern ethnic groups, such as the Khitan, who came to power in Shanxi during the Liao dynasty (916–1125 AD).

Wutai Shan

五台山, wǔtái shān • ¥218, including park buses • extra fees apply for temples

One of China's four Buddhist mountains, the five flat peaks of **Wutai Shan** – the name means "Five-terrace Mountain" – rise around 3000m in the northeastern corner of

> ## DOUGONGS
>
> The ceilings and walls of the Wood Pagoda's spacious internal halls are networks of beams held together with huge, intricate **wooden brackets**, called *dougongs*, of which there are nearly sixty different kinds. Interlocking, with their ends carved into curves and layered one on top of another, these give the pagoda a burly, muscular appearance, and as structural supports they perform their function brilliantly – the building has survived seven earthquakes.

Shanxi province, near the border with Hebei. Its main base, the village of **Taihuai**, lies on a backroads route linking Datong and Taiyuan, and it's possible to access the mountains from either of those cities. The long bus ride here is rewarded with fresh air, superb scenery, some fascinating temple architecture and a spiritual (if not always peaceful) tone. Though increasingly accessible, many of Wutai Shan's forty temples have survived the centuries intact and remain functioning, full of resident clergy.

Despite a surprising number of ordinary Chinese people here as **pilgrims** – thumbing rosaries and prostrating themselves on their knees as they clamber up the temples' steep staircases – it has to be said that intense summertime tourism at Wutai Shan can put paid to feelings of remoteness, and might make you regret the effort taken to reach here. Crowds fade away between October and April, though during this period you will have to come prepared for some low temperatures and possible blizzards. Note that all temples are **open** daily from sunrise to sunset.

Brief history

Wutai Shan was an early bastion of Buddhism in China, a religious centre at least since the reign of Emperor Ming Di (58–75 AD). At that time, a visiting Indian monk had a vision in which he met **Wenshu** (Manjusri), the Buddhist incarnation of Wisdom, who is usually depicted riding a blue lion and carrying a manuscript (to represent a sutra) and a sword to cleave ignorance. By the time of the Northern Wei, Wutai Shan was a prosperous Buddhist centre, important enough to be depicted on a mural at the Dunhuang Caves in Gansu. The mountain reached its height of popularity in the Tang dynasty, when there were more than two hundred temples scattered around its peaks. In the fifteenth century, the founder of the **Yellow Hat order**, now the dominant Buddhist sect in Tibet, came to the area to preach; Manjusri is particularly important in Tibetan and Mongolian Buddhism, and Wutai Shan remains an important pilgrimage place for Lamaists.

Taihuai

台怀, táihuái

The monastic village of **TAIHUAI**, a strip of tourist facilities and temples spread along about 1km of road, sits in a depression at the centre of the Wutai area, surrounded by the five holy peaks. Orientation is easy: uphill along the road is north, with the main batch of temples jammed alongside one another immediately to the west, and a smaller group of pavilions studding the steep hillside to the east across a river. Many visitors stay for only one night, but the relaxed atmosphere – together with the physical exertion of climbing the hills – may encourage a longer stay.

Tayuan Temple

塔院寺, tǎyuàn sì • ¥10 • Mao hall ¥2 extra

Easily visible west of the main road, and first on most itineraries, is the 50m-tall, Tibetan-style **White Stupa** of the **Tayuan Temple**. The stupa is a staggering sight against the temple's dark grey roofs, a bulbous, whitewashed peak hung with 250 bells whose chiming can be heard across the valley on a windy day. The largest of many such bottle-shaped pagodas on Wutai Shan, it testifies to the importance of the mountain to Lamaism, which is also represented by the tall **wooden poles** with bronze caps standing inside many of the temple's entrances.

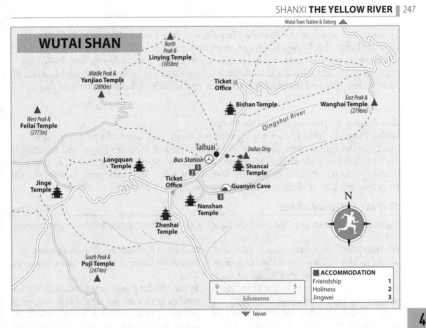

Wutai Train Station & Datong

WUTAI SHAN

North Peak & Linying Temple (3058m)

Middle Peak & **Yanjiao Temple** (2890m)

Ticket Office

Bishan Temple

East Peak & **Wanghai Temple** (2796m)

West Peak & **Feilai Temple** (2773m)

Qingshui River

Taihuai

Dailuo Ding

Longquan Temple

Bus Station

Shancai Temple

Jinge Temple

Ticket Office

Guanyin Cave

Nanshan Temple

Zhenhai Temple

South Peak & **Puji Temple** (2474m)

N

0   5 kilometres

■ ACCOMMODATION
Friendship	1
Holiness	2
Jingwei	3

Taiyuan

4

Inside a hall behind the pagoda, a Ming-dynasty, two-storey library was built to house a bizarre and beautiful revolving **wooden bookcase**, much older than the rest of the complex. Its 33 layers of shelves, split into cubbyholes and painted with decorative designs, hold volumes of sutras in Tibetan, Mongolian and Chinese. Not far from **Shanhai Lou**, the chunky main gate of the temple – which you can climb for views – is the **Chairman Mao Memorial Hall**, whose placement at the heart of one of Buddhism's most sacred sights is in decidedly poor taste.

Luohou Temple
罗睺寺, luóhóu sì • Free

Just north of Tayuan Temple's entrance, under-visited **Luohou Temple** is a Ming-dynasty reconstruction of a Tang temple. Those who do pop by gather to gawk at the spinning round wooden altar in the main hall with a wave design at its base supporting a large wooden lotus with moveable petals. A mechanism underneath opens the petals to reveal four Buddhas sitting inside the flower.

Xiantong Temple
显通寺, xiǎntōng sì • ¥10

The **Xiantong Temple**, just uphill from the Tayuan Temple, reputedly dates back to 68 AD, and if so is one of the oldest Buddhist sites in China. The main sights here are the whitewashed **Beamless Hall**, built in brick to resemble a wooden structure; and the dazzling 5m-high **Bronze Palace**, constructed entirely of the metal and recently gilded. Its walls and doors are covered with animal and flower designs on the outside and rank upon rank of tiny Buddhas on the inside, along with an elegant bronze Manjusri Buddha sitting on a human-faced lion. The grounds also house an interesting sundial, which uses zodiac animals to depict the hours.

Yuanzhao Temple
圆照寺, yuánzhào sì • ¥10

Sitting on the hill behind Luohou Temple, via a splendid statue of Manjusri surrounded by *arhats* and clouds at the **Yuanzhao Temple**, and atop a stone staircase of 108 steps, is the **Pusa Ding**. This Ming and Qing complex once accommodated emperors Kangxi and Qianlong, hence the yellow roof tiles and dragon tablet on the stairway, both indicating imperial patronage. This is a great destination for a first day in town, as it affords an aerial view of the valley and is a good way to warm up for longer hikes to higher temples.

Dailuo Ding

黛螺顶, dàiluó dǐng • ¥8 • cable car ¥50 one-way, ¥85 return

Dailuo Ding, the hillside overlooking the town to the east, offers the most accessible hiking in the Taihuai area, and provides superb vistas of the town below and mountains beyond. You can walk up the steep stone staircase in about twenty minutes, or take a (highly popular) cable car most of the way. At the top is **Shancai Temple** (山财寺, shāncái sì), a tiny but beautiful temple with unpretentious halls dedicated to Wenshu.

ARRIVAL AND DEPARTURE   TAIHUAI

Note that Taihuai is also known as "Wutai Shan" (but not just "Wutai", which is another township) on transport timetables.

By train Wutai Shan train station (五台山站, wǔtáishān zhàn) is 20km north at Shahe town, on the Beijing–Taiyuan line. It's connected through the day to Taihuai by taxis and shuttle buses (1hr 30min). There's nowhere to buy tickets in Taihuai itself.
Destinations Beijing (3 daily; 6–7hr); Pingyao (2 daily; 5hr 40min–7hr 20min); Taiyuan (7 daily; 3hr 30min–6hr).
By bus Taihuai's bus station is a few kilometres south of the main temple clutch. Note that the Datong road crosses a high pass, which can see it closed at short notice by snow.

Buy tickets at the station, and on all park bus routes.
Destinations Datong (2 daily; 5hr); Taiyuan (hourly; 3hr 30min).
By taxi Note that if you're coming to Wutai Shan by taxi from Datong, you'll also have to pay the park entry fee for your driver. It's usually cheaper to leave your driver at the gate, and head into town with a local cab; they typically ask for ¥50. The ticket inspectors may also take pity on you, and try to pop you into a tour bus.

GETTING AROUND

By bus Free park buses out to the sights shunt up and down the park's main road at regular intervals. You'll receive bus tickets when buying your park entry ticket, and though few drivers will ask for them, it's worth keeping them to hand. There are a couple of routes, both passing

Taihuai's bus station, though #1 is the one you want for the temples.
By taxi Locals gather on corners throughout Taihuai, offering their cars as taxis. ¥10 is the minimum they'll ask, even for a short trip.

ACCOMMODATION AND EATING

The number of hotels in Taihuai has increased steadily in recent years, and even in peak season it shouldn't be hard to find a place to stay. Few stand out in any way; you're best off looking at the area west of the main road to the south of Taihuai, near the Nanshan Temple turn-off. Taihuai's restaurants are plentiful, bar the area around the main temples, which only has a couple; however, as you'd expect with a trapped market, the food is mediocre and expensive. Fortunately, there are a few supermarkets around, including a great one just around the corner from the hostel.

Friendship 友谊宾馆, yǒuyì bīnguǎn. West of the main road, south of the bus station ☎ 0350 6542678. Clean, safe and quiet, this hotel is a reliably comfortable choice in an area with few reliably comfortable choices, and not too expensive at all. There's a good restaurant and small café on site. **¥288**
Holiness Youth Hostel 善斋青年旅馆, shànzhāi qīngnián lǚguǎn. West of the main road, south of the bus station ☎ 180 13141900. One of the cheapest places in town, this simple guesthouse has made an effort to tart itself up in hostel style. The owners speak very little English,

but try their best to help out with travel queries. **¥130**
Jingwei 经委大酒店, jīngwěi dàjiǔdiàn. Across the river between Nanshan Temple and the Guanyin Temple ☎ 0350 6542129. For something different, try this hotel, tucked on a nameless road on the other side of Dailuo Ding from Taihuai. Unless there's a group staying, there's a real (though pleasant) *Shining* feel to the large, empty corridors. Positives are that the rooms and on-site restaurant are just fine, and that you'll be well away from the crowds. The main Taihuai road is less than a 15min walk away, as are the wonderful Nanshan and Guanyin temples. **¥388**

FROM TOP VIEW OVER TAIHUAI VILLAGE, WUTAI SHAN (P.246); TERRACOTTA WARRIORS, XI'AN (P.212) >

DIRECTORY

Bank The Bank of China in Taihuai village has an ATM which works with foreign cards and can usually change money, but it's wise to arrive with enough yuan to last the duration of the visit.

South of Taihuai

Few tourists get very far out of Taihuai; it's certainly worth the effort, however, as not just the temples, but also the views and the scenery, are gorgeous. All of the following temples can be accessed in a single day, using the park buses to cut distances. Taxi drivers will be glad to drive you around; you'll pay ¥80–100 for a simple tour of the following sights.

Nanshan Temple

南山寺, nánshān sì • Free

The **Nanshan Temple** sits in a leafy spot halfway up Yangbai Shan, a hilltop 5km south of Taihuai. It's approached by a steep flight of stairs, with the entrance marked by a huge screen wall of cream-coloured brick. Decorated brickwork, including fake brackets and images of deities in flowing robes, is the temple's most distinctive feature. Ming images of *luohans* in the main hall are lifelike and expressive; one gaunt figure is sleeping with head propped up on one knee, his skin sagging over his fleshless bones. Come here in the late afternoon, if possible – the sunset views are out of this world, the vista centring on two bucolic valleys, which barrel into the mountains beyond.

Guanyin Temple

观音洞, guānyīn dòng • ¥5

The small temple around this **Guanyin Cave**, a twenty-minute walk east up the road from Nanshan Temple, is an unexpected delight. It's free from tourists generally, and many of those who do pop by are Tibetan pilgrims. Steep staircases make their way between various buildings to the cave itself; there are great mountain views all the way down. If you fancy a countryside walk, take the road heading to the left of the temple as you exit.

Zhenhai Temple

镇海寺, zhènhǎi sì • ¥5

About 2km southwest of Nanshan Temple, the **Zhenhai Temple**, sitting at an altitude of 1600m just off the road, seems an odd place to build a temple celebrating the prevention of floods, although legend has it that Wenshu tamed the water of the spring that now trickles past the place. During the Qing dynasty, a monk called **Zhang Jia**, reputed to be the living Buddha, stayed here; he is commemorated with a small pagoda south of the temple.

Longquan Temple

龙泉寺, lóngquán sì • Free

The **Longquan Temple** is on the west side of the Qingshui River, 5km southwest of Taihuai, just off the main road. Its highlight is the decorated **marble entranceway** at the top of 108 steps, whose surface is densely packed with images of dragons, phoenixes and foliage. The rest of the temple seems sedate in comparison, though the Puji Pagoda inside is a similar confection – a fat stupa carved with guardians, surmounted by a fake wooden top and guarded by an elaborate railing. Both structures are fairly late, dating from the beginning of the twentieth century.

OFF THE TRAIL IN WUTAI SHAN

There's some decent **hiking** in the area south of Taihuai; whatever the time of year, don't head off into the hills without some warm, weatherproof gear, food and water, and a torch, even though in good weather the trails here present no special difficulties. Allow plenty of time for hikes, as the paths are hard to find in the dark and even in summer the temperature drops sharply at sundown.

Taiyuan

太原, tàiyuán

Industrial powerhouse and the capital of Shanxi province, sprawling **TAIYUAN** is a victim of its own excellent transport connections – with Pingyao so close, and Beijing just a few hours away, there's no real need to stay the night here. If you've time, however, it's definitely worth setting aside half a day to visit the **Jinci Temple**, southwest of the city, a large complex with some unexpectedly venerable architecture.

Shuangta Temple

双塔寺, shuāngtǎ sì • Shuangta Beilu • Daily 8am–6pm • ¥30 • bus #820 from train station

No tour of the city's ancient buildings would be complete without a look at the two 50m-tall pagodas of the **Shuangta Temple**, south of the train station. These were built by a monk called Fu Deng in the Ming dynasty, under the orders of the emperor, and today have become a symbol of the city. You can climb the thirteen storeys for a panoramic view of Taiyuan.

Jinci Temple

晋祠寺, jìncí sì • Daily 7.30am–6.30pm • ¥40 • bus #804 from train station

About 25km southwest of Taiyuan, **Jinci Temple** contains perhaps the finest Song-dynasty buildings in the country, though the complex is oriented towards tourism rather than worship. A temple has stood on the site since the Northern Wei, and today's buildings are a diverse collection from various dynasties. The **Hall of the Holy Mother** is the highlight, its facade a mix of decorative flourishes and the sturdily functional, with wooden dragons curling around the eight pillars that support the ridge of its upward-curving roof.

ARRIVAL AND DEPARTURE

TAIYUAN

By plane Taiyuan's airport (太原武宿国际机场, tàiyuán wǔsù guójì jīchǎng) is 15km southeast of the city, a ¥60 taxi ride away; bus #201 (¥2) links the airport to the train station. There are numerous places to buy tickets around town, including a China Eastern airlines office on Yingze Dajie (daily 9am–6pm).

Destinations Beijing (7 daily; 1hr); Chengdu (2–3 daily; 2hr); Chongqing (3 daily; 1hr 50min); Guangzhou (6–7 daily; 2hr 40min); Nanjing (6–7 daily; 1hr 35min);

Shanghai (10 daily; 1hr 55min); Tianjin (3 daily; 1hr); Xi'an (2–4 daily; 1hr).

By train The train station (太原站, tàiyuán zhàn) is at the eastern end of Yingze Dajie. It hosts express services to Beijing and Zhengzhou, and slow-moving clunkers southwest to Pingyao and Xi'an, though in time many of the high-speed services will shift to a new station, being constructed to the south of the city.

Destinations Beijing (many daily; 2hr 30min–7hr);

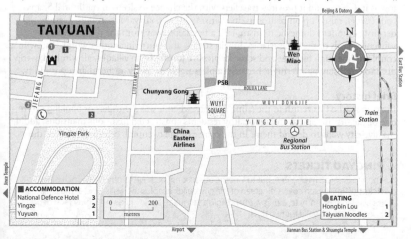

TAIYUAN

Beijing & Datong

N

East Bus Station

Wen Miao

PSB

HOUJIA LANE

Jinci Temple

TIEFANG LU

LUJIANG LU

Chunyang Gong

WUYI SQUARE

WUYI DONGJIE

Yingze Park

China Eastern Airlines

YINGZE DAJIE

Train Station

Regional Bus Station

■ ACCOMMODATION
National Defence Hotel   3
Yingze   2
Yuyuan   1

0   200
metres

● EATING
Hongbin Lou   1
Taiyuan Noodles   2

Airport

Jiannan Bus Station & Shuangta Temple

Datong (12 daily; 5hr 30min); Luoyang (2 daily; 12hr); Pingyao (16 daily; 1hr 30min); Xi'an (8 daily; 8hr 30min–12hr); Zhengzhou (6 daily; 3hr 30min–11hr).

By bus The Jiannan bus station (建南站, jiànnán zhàn), 3km south of the centre on Dicun Jie, handles traffic to Pingyao (hourly; 2hr–2hr 30min); it's on many bus routes heading south of the train station. Note, however, that regular traffic problems mean that it's far better to go to Pingyao by train instead. The East bus station (东客站, dōng kèzhàn), 1.5km east of the train station on Wulongkou Jie, handles Wutai Shan services (hourly; 4hr); take a taxi to the train station for ¥8, or walk.

ACCOMMODATION

National Defence Hotel 国防宾馆, guófáng bīnguǎn. 12 Yingze Dajie ☏ 0351 8822209. Far better than its official-sounding name may suggest, even if rooms don't live up to the promise of the presentable lobby. Good value nonetheless. ¥198

Yingze 迎泽宾馆, yíngzé bīnguǎn. 189 Yingze Dajie ☏ 0351 8828888, ⊕ sxyzhotel.com. This stylish four-star hotel has its own café, bookshop and tour company, and is thick with visiting dignitaries and upmarket domestic tourists. Not to be confused with another, much less presentable, the *Yingze* just to the east. ¥800

Yuyuan 豫园宾馆, yùyuán bīnguǎn. Kaihuasi Jie, just east off Jiefang Lu ☏ 0351 8823333. A good, if slightly expensive, mid-range option, set in a quiet street in an interesting part of town. ¥398

EATING

Taiyuan isn't exactly a gourmand's paradise. Perhaps most notable are the inexpensive Muslim noodle houses surrounding the old Mosque on Jiefang Lu; if you're in transit, you'll find the regular Chinese and Western fast-food chains huddled en masse around the train station.

Hongbin Lou 鸿宾楼, hóngbīn lóu. 22 Jiefang Lu ☏ 351 2027118. There's good roast duck (¥98) on offer at this highly presentable Muslim restaurant, together with a mammoth assortment of standard Chinese dishes. It's a pity that they've written pinyin, instead of actual translations, on the picture menu. Daily 10am–2pm & 5.30–10pm.

Taiyuan Noodles 太原面馆, tàiyuán miànguǎn. Jiefang Lu. Try Taiyuan's famed vinegary noodles (from ¥8) at this upper-floor venue; no English menu, but the noodles, and a host of other dishes (¥20–40), can be selected from pictures on the wall. Daily 11am–3pm & 5–9pm.

Pingyao

平遥, píngyáo

The tiny town of **PINGYAO** has become a firm travel favourite in recent times, and for good reason: not only does it form a logical stopover point between Beijing and Xi'an, but its wall-bound core – almost entirely filled with traditional eighteenth- and nineteenth-century buildings – provides a step back in time. This is one of the most authentic, old towns in China, and it provides travellers with the chance to sleep on traditional Shanxi beds (*kang*), raised up on platforms, in charismatic old courtyard mansions. Despite the density of modern domestic tourism, take a few steps away from the restaurants and souvenir stands of the pedestrianized main streets, and you're in another world. Throw in a couple of fine rural **temples** and some impressive **fortified clan villages**, all within day-trip distance, and staying overnight becomes a pleasurable necessity, rather than a possibility.

Brief history

Pingyao reached its zenith in the Ming dynasty, when it was a prosperous **banking centre**, one of the first in China, and its wealthy residents constructed luxurious **mansions**, adding massive **city walls** to defend them. In the course of the twentieth century, however, the

---

PINGYAO TICKETS

Entry to Pingyao itself is free, but to visit the attractions you have to buy an **all-inclusive ticket** (¥150), which covers nineteen of the city buildings, plus the walls. Sold at most places it's used to gain entry to, along with an English-language audio-guide (¥40, plus ¥100 deposit; bring ID too), it's valid for two days.

town slid rapidly into provincial obscurity, which kept it largely unmodernized. Inside the walls, Pingyao's narrow streets, lined with elegant Qing architecture – no neon, no white tile, no cars – are a revelation, harking back to the town's nineteenth-century heyday. This is especially true at night, when the glow from nearby houses shows the way – though small kids stay off the street after dark, haunted by their parents' tales of returning Ming-era **ghosts** who, it's said, navigate the unchanged alleys with ease. Few buildings are higher than two storeys; most are small shops much more interesting for their appearance than their wares, with ornate wood-and-painted-glass lanterns hanging outside, and intricate wooden latticework holding paper rather than glass across the windows.

The town walls

Daily 8am–6.30pm

From various access points around their 6km length, steps lead up to Pingyao's Ming **town walls**, 12m high and crenellated, and punctuated with a watchtower every 50m or so. You can walk all the way around them in two hours, and get a good view into some of the many courtyards inside the old town. A belt of sculpted **parkland** has been created to the south and east, and it's the corresponding walls that provide the best views. The structures where the wall widens out are *mamian* (literally, horse faces), where soldiers could stand and fight. At the southeast corner of the wall, the **Kuixing Tower** (奎星楼, kuíxīnglóu), a tall, fortified pagoda with a tiled, upturned roof, is a rather flippant-looking building in comparison to the martial solidity of the battlements.

City Tower

市楼, shìlóu • Ming Qing Jie • Daily 8am–7pm • ¥5, city ticket not valid

It's possible to climb the **City Tower** on Pingyao's central crossroads – for some reason, it's the only sight in Pingyao not covered by the city's ticketing scheme. This charming little building provides a fantastic rooftop view of the old city; its eave decoration includes colourful reliefs of fish and portly merchants, and guardian statues of Guanyin and Guandi face north and south respectively. Just watch out on your way around – it's easy to bump your head.

Rishengchang

日升昌, rìshēngchāng • western end of Dong Dajie • Daily 9am–5pm

Rishengchang, established in 1824, was China's first bank and one of the first places in the world where cheques were used. During the Qing, more than four hundred financial houses operated in Pingyao, handling over eighty million ounces of silver annually. After the Boxer Rebellion, Dowager Empress Cixi came here to ask for loans to pay the high indemnities demanded by the Eight Allied Forces. Soon after, the court defaulted, then abdicated, and the banks dried up. Hong Kong and Shanghai took over Pingyao's mantle, rendering the city an isolated backwater.

Town museums

Daily, approximately 8am–6pm

There are many, many **museums** in town, but after visiting a few you'll find the exhibits are repetitive and nowhere near as interesting as the buildings themselves, which are probably much like your accommodation in any case. Still, they give a good excuse to wander, and some – like the two **armed escort museums** and former **Hui Wu Lin martial arts training hall** (汇武林博物馆, huìwǔlín bówùguǎn) – are, given the need to protect the city's financial reserves from banditry, also relevant to Pingyao's history. Worthwhile options include the **Former County Yamen** (平遥县衙门, píngyáoxiàn yámén), a massive complex on Yamen Jie, which housed the town's administrative bureaucracy (the prisons here were in use until the 1960s); the **Former Residence of Lei Lütai** (雷履汰故居, léilǚtài gùjū), Rishengchang's founder; the ramshackle **City God Temple** (城隍庙, chénghuáng miào) on Chenghuang Miao Jie; and the large **Confucian Temple** (文庙, wénmiào), also on Chenghuang Miao Jie.

ARRIVAL AND DEPARTURE | PINGYAO

Pingyao is most easily accessed by train, though there are also plentiful bus connections with Taiyuan. It's a 15–30min walk to accommodation from arrival points, but if your bags are heavy a swarm of bicycle rickshaws and electric buggies will offer to carry you – ¥10 is a decent fare.

By train Pingyao should soon be receiving high-speed trains on the new Taiyuan–Xi'an line; until then, you'll have to head to the tiny station just northwest of the walls. Seats are easy enough to buy yourself at the station, where some staff speak a little English. Sleepers are harder to get, though hotels in Pingyao have sorted out a system where they book your ticket through Beijing or Xi'an and then get a photocopy of it, which you use in place of the real thing – it sounds like a scam, but reports say that it works. Expect a ¥40 fee per ticket for this.

Destinations Beijing (4 daily; 9hr 20min–14hr); Linfen (2hr 30min); Taiyuan (16 daily; 1hr 30min); Xi'an (5 daily; 8hr 30min–10hr 30min).

By bus There's a small bus depot 1km to the northeast of the train station, though most buses will set you down outside the latter. Other than the services to Taiyuan (hourly; 2hr–2hr 30min), for which the train is better in any case, the only ones you're likely to want are the services to Xi'an (5 daily; 7hr); you can book these through some accommodation, or at the *Zhongdu Binguan* just across from the train station.

GETTING AROUND

Cars are banned from Pingyao's central streets, though at the height of summer these are usually congested with bicycles and pedestrians instead.

By bicycle Cycling around Pingyao's interior perimeter road is almost as much fun as walking around the wall itself, providing views of Pingyao at its most attractive.

Bikes are available from some of the guesthouses, and from agencies with English signs along Xi Dajie (¥10 per day, plus ¥100 deposit).

INFORMATION

Tour agents Most hotels will be able to offer tours of surrounding sights; *Harmony* is best for individuals and

Tianyuankui for small groups. *Harmony* offer daily Zhangbi Castle tours (¥85 per person), and Qiao Family Mansion (¥120

per person) if there's sufficient demand. *Tianyuankui* bundle groups into a car: it's ¥350 for the Qiao Family Mansion; ¥400 for the Wang Family Mansion and Shuanglin Temple; or ¥450 for the Wang Family Mansion and Zhangbi Castle.

ACCOMMODATION

Staying overnight in Pingyao is a must: all of the following places are housed in atmospheric mansions with stone courtyards, wooden window screens, traditional furniture and *kang* to sleep on. Although offering much the same in the way of decor, prices vary quite a lot – you'll pay most along Xi Dajie, since that's where Chinese groups tend to head. Lodgings can fill up quickly – especially at weekends or during holidays – so it's best to book in advance.

★ **Harmony** 和议昌客栈, héyìchāng kèzhàn. 165 Nan Dajie ☎0354 5684952. Presided over by a cheery, English-speaking local couple, this is a tremendous place whose rooms, arrayed around the courtyards of an old mansion, are the equal of some far more expensive alternatives, decorated with silk drapes and carved bedheads. In addition, the excellent facilities include bike rental, free internet, free train station pick-up and a good bar, while they also run tours to Zhangbi castle (see p.257). Dorms from **¥30**, doubles **¥180**

★ **Jing's Family Residence** 锦宅, jǐn zhái. 16 Dong Dajie ☎0354 5841000, ⊛jingsresidence.com. A 200-year-old courtyard mansion, lovingly renovated as a smart boutique hotel – think decorative lacquered bed screens, charming courtyards dotted with lanterns, and expensive beauty products in the bathrooms. You'll also be able to indulge in a spa session, or be served afternoon tea. The breakfasts are delicious, too. **¥1500**

★ **Tianyuankui** 天元奎客栈, tiānyuánkuí kèzhàn. 73 Nan Dajie ☎0354 5680069, ⊛pytyk.com. This is the liveliest of the central guesthouses, and for good reason. Accessible through labyrinthine, lantern-strewn courtyards, their immaculate rooms will make you want to whip out your camera before putting your bag down. The on-site restaurant is great too, and staff are fonts of local knowledge. **¥280**

Yide 一得客栈, yídé kèzhàn. 16 Sha Xiang, just south off Xi Dajie ☎0354 5685988, ⊛yide-hotel.com. Eighteenth-century building hidden at the end of a quiet lane, and surrounded by several other courtyard homes. Rooms are cosy, and the restaurant is a good place to dine even if you're not staying. **¥400**

EATING AND DRINKING

Eating in Pingyao is fun, with a score of tasty, well-presented **local dishes**. Umpteen restaurants serve these, though prices are tourist-inflated, and portions not always that large – you're best off heading to one of the hotels. Things to look for include salted, five-spiced beef; wild greens; yams; flat "mountain noodles" (served on their edges in a steamer); and "cat's ear noodles" (triangular flecks of dough flicked into boiling water). For cheap Chinese staples, head to the western end of Xi Dajie, or to the streets between the West Gate and the train station.

Harmony 165 Nan Dajie. Run by (and just along from) the guesthouse of the same name, this is usually Pingyao's most kicking bar, with backpacker-friendly music, a pool table, a calm upstairs chill-out zone, and good cocktails (¥35 and up). They also make a fine espresso (¥15). Daily 4pm–midnight.

Sakura 6 Dong Dajie. A backpacker institution, this is the city's best option for Western food, if that's what you're after – homemade bread, pizzas (¥60), Yunnanese coffee (¥30–40) and the like. However, it really comes into its own come sundown, when it morphs into a hugely popular bar; there's another location, often rowdier, on Nan Dajie. Daily 10am–11pm.

★ **Tianyuankui** 73 Nan Dajie. The lobby restaurant at this hotel is one of the best in the city, and prices are backpacker-friendly. Staff have been drilled well, and know what foreigners like and dislike. Local specialities (see above) have been marked with stars on the menu, though try their special "fried and juicy" aubergine dish (¥38), which arrives on your table looking more like a dressed fish. Daily 7.30am–11pm.

★ **Yide** 16 Sha Xiang. Yet another excellent hotel restaurant, and one of the best places in which to sample Pingyao specialities. Amazingly, despite the luxurious appearance, their dishes (at ¥15–50 each) are hardly any more expensive than those at the motley shack-restaurants lining the main roads – and in some cases, they're cheaper. There's also Western breakfast fare and good coffee, extremely inexpensive rice and noodle dishes, and yummy caramel-dipped yam for dessert (¥30). Daily 7am–10pm.

DIRECTORY

Banks and exchange There are a few banks, with ATMs, outside the west gate on the way to the station.

Mail The post office is at 1 Xi Dajie (daily 8am–6pm).

Shopping Anywhere along Ming Qing Jie and the first section of Xi Dajie that isn't a restaurant or hotel will be selling souvenirs – lacquerware, papercuts, embroideries and the usual run of "new antiques", along with martial-arts weaponry. Prices are good after haggling.

Around Pingyao

You could easily spend a couple of days in the countryside around Pingyao, though you'd only need a few hours to visit either of two nearby **temples** – one full of superb statues, the other interesting for its age. Further afield, a couple of Ming-dynasty **fortified mansions** standing starkly among the surrounding hills would be even more impressive if you hadn't seen Pingyao first, but are anyway worth the effort it takes to reach them.

Shuanglin Temple

双林寺, shuānglín sì • Daily 8am–6pm • ¥40 • within cycle range of Pingyao • bus to Jiexiu (介休, jièxiū; ¥6) and get off en route • round-trip by taxi ¥35 or so after haggling

The fortress-like **Shuanglin Temple** stands 5km southwest of Pingyao, just off the main road to Jiexiu. Originally built in the Northern Wei, the present buildings, ten halls arranged around three courtyards, are Ming and Qing. Once you're inside, the fine architecture pales beside the contents of the halls, a treasury of 1600 coloured terracotta and wood **sculptures** dating from the Song to the Qing dynasties. They're arranged in tableaux, with backgrounds of swirling water or clouds, turning the dusty wooden halls into rich grottoes. Some of the figures are in bad shape but most still have a good deal of their original paint, although it has lost its gaudy edge. It's worth hiring a **guide** (ask at your accommodation), as each hall and each row of statues have intriguing histories attached.

The halls

The horsemen dotted in vertical relief around the **Wushung Hall**, the first on the right, illustrate scenes from the life of Guandi, the god of war, but the figures in most of the halls are depictions of Buddha or saints and guardians. The **eighteen arhats** in the **second hall**, though unpainted, are eerily lifelike, and somewhat sinister in the gloom with their bulging foreheads, long tapering fingernails and eyes of black glass that follow you round the room. In the **third hall**, the walls are lined with elegant 20cm-high Bodhisattvas inclined towards a set of larger Buddha figures at the centre like so many roosting birds. The statue of **Guanyin** – sitting in a loose, even provocative, pose – is probably a reflection of the confidence and pride Pingyao enjoyed during its economic heyday.

Zhenguo Temple

镇国寺, zhènguó sì • Daily 8am–6pm • ¥25 • bus #9 from train station

Out in the fields 12km northeast of Pingyao, **Zhenguo Temple** is a quiet, forgotten place, fronted by gnarled old trees. It's surprising then to find one of China's **oldest wooden buildings** here: the Wanfo Hall was built in 963 AD and looks like it hasn't been touched since, with an amazingly complex system of brackets holding the roof up and full of contemporary, Indian-influenced statuary. At the rear, the upper hall has some Qing frescoes of the life of Buddha, all set in a Chinese context, while the Ming-dynasty **Dizang Hall** is a riot of paintings of the King of Hell and his demons handing out punishments to sinners.

The Wang Family Mansion

王家大院, wángjiā dàyuàn • Daily 8am–5pm • ¥66 • bus from Pingyao's bus depot to Jiexiu (介休, jièxiū; 50min; ¥9), then minibus #11 to the mansion (30min, ¥4) • see p.254 for tours

Some 45km southwest of Pingyao, the **Wang Family Mansion** is more like a huge, fortified castle than a private residence. Set among stark brown hills, the location, enormous scale and – especially – the details of the mansion buildings are all astounding, with high brick walls surrounding an intricate and vast collection of interconnected Qing-dynasty courtyards, halls (around a thousand), gardens, galleries, triumphal archways and screens, all built in carved grey stone along a rigidly symmetrical plan. The Wangs settled here at the end of the Mongol dynasty and built this complex in the early nineteenth century, after the family struck it rich not only in commerce but also political appointments; the infamous **Empress Dowager Cixi** stayed

---

HUKOU FALLS

Isolated way out in Shanxi's western backblocks, **Hukou Falls** (壶口瀑布, húkŏu pùbù; March–Nov ¥90, Dec–Feb ¥45) are the Yellow River at its most impressively turbulent. Flowing north, the mighty river's span approaches 400m at this point, yet it suddenly finds itself forced through a gap only 20m wide – the resultant torrent is predictably fierce, and predictably loud. The falls are regarded by the Chinese as one of their premier beauty spots, though you may question whether reaching them is worth the effort: they're accessed via **Linfen** (临纷, línfēn), itself 140km south of Pingyao and still a further 150km-long, 4hr-plus bus-ride from the falls. Linfen's CITS (☎0357 3330281) often runs tours from the south side of the city's train station plaza, or can recommend where to pick up a **tourist minibus**.

---

a night here in 1900 while fleeing to Xi'an after the Boxer Rebellion. The complex is in two sections, joined by a stone bridge over a gully, and you could easily spend half a day here getting lost among the architecture.

The Qiao Family Mansion

乔家大院, qiáojiā dàyuàn • Daily 8am–5pm • ¥72 • see p.254 for tours

The comfortably scaled **Qiao Family Mansion** lies 25km northeast of Pingyao near the hamlet of **Leguan Zhen**. An enchanting maze of attractive details including carved screens and tiled roofing, the mansion was used as a setting by Zhang Yimou for his film *Raise the Red Lantern*, in which the labyrinthine layout of the place symbolizes just how restricted life was for women in classical China.

Zhangbi Castle

张壁古堡, zhāngbì gŭbăo • ¥60 including guide • see p.254 for tours

About 40km southwest of Pingyao, **Zhangbi Castle** was built at the beginning of the seventh century, yet was only recently added to Shanxi's litany of tourist sights. Though pleasant enough on the surface, the castle is more famed for its network of **underground tunnels**, most of which were added by the Sui dynasty for protection against Tang invasion. The Tang themselves later added a few tunnels of their own, and explorations of the resultant warren – a multilayered maze which dives over 20m beneath the surface – are thoroughly enjoyable. The labyrinthine nature of the tunnels makes hiring a guide all but essential, even more so since doing so will also get you a tour of **Zhangbi Village**, a pleasing, ramshackle hotchpotch of Yuan, Ming and Qing buildings.

Henan

河南, hénán

China's third most populous province, **HENAN**'s modern-day industrial trappings conceal a rich history watered by the great **Yellow River**. The wonderful **Longmen Caves** lie due south of **Luoyang**, an ancient dynastic capital thought by the Chinese of antiquity to be the centre of the universe – it may, at one time, have been the largest city on earth. Luoyang also makes a good jumping-off point for one sight whose name, at least, is familiar to many Westerners: **Shaolin Temple**, home to the famed fighting monks. Henan's modern capital, **Zhengzhou**, is unremarkable, but further to the east is the old city of **Kaifeng**, which wears its history rather better than others in the province – particularly in the form of the ancient wall still enclosing its centre.

Luoyang

洛阳, luòyáng

Sprawling, increasingly industrial **LUOYANG** lies in the middle reaches of the Yellow

Museum of Ancient Tombs & Airport

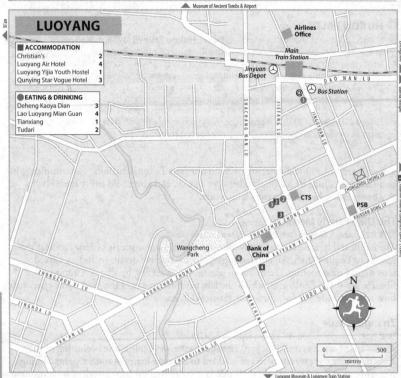

LUOYANG

■ ACCOMMODATION
Christian's	2
Luoyang Air Hotel	4
Luoyang Yijia Youth Hostel	1
Qunying Star Vogue Hotel	3

● EATING & DRINKING
Deheng Kaoya Dian	3
Lao Luoyang Mian Guan	4
Tianxiang	1
Tudari	2

Luoyang Museum & Longmen Train Station

River valley. While the drab modern city itself retains little hint of past glories, bar its astonishingly good **museum**, there's plenty to see in the surrounding area and Luoyang makes a convenient hub for visiting the famed **Longmen Caves**, one of China's three major rock art galleries, which lie just to the south. In addition, the city is within striking distance of several important religious complexes, including **Shaolin Temple** (see p.265). These ancient sights hint at a rich history – Luoyang has, indeed, been occupied since Neolithic times, and served as China's capital at various points from the Zhou dynasty through to 937 AD. Confucius once studied here, and this is where Buddhism first took root in China in 68 AD.

Luoyang Museum

洛阳博物馆, luòyáng bówùguǎn • Nietai Lu • Tues–Sun 9am–5pm • Free (bring ID) • bus #77 from train station • taxi from the city centre ¥20–25

The dynamic new **city museum**, slightly inconveniently located south of the Luo River, is an absolutely gigantic place, though well laid out for viewing the profusion of extraordinary treasures from Luoyang's days as the capital of eight dynasties. As the museum is still shifting exhibitions around, take the following rundown as a guide only; they'll also hopefully improve some poor room signage (though the explanations on exhibits themselves are excellent).

The main halls

On the first floor you'll find a huge exhibit of **ancient stone carving**, an amazing collection of statues, steles and the like from various points in Luoyang's history. The rest of the floor is given over to temporary exhibition space – usually well worth a look.

LUOYANG'S PEONIES

It's said that in 800 AD the Tang Empress Wu Zetian, enraged that the **peonies**, alone among flowers, disobeyed her command to bloom in the snow, banished them from her capital at Chang'an. Many were transplanted to Luoyang (the secondary capital) where they flourished, and have since become one of the city's most celebrated attractions, the subject of countless poems and cultivation notes. Luoyang now boasts over 150 varieties of peony, which have found their way onto every available patch or scrap of ground – including central Wangcheng Park (王成公园, **wángchéng gōngyuán**; ¥55 during the April Peony Festival) – a splendid sight when they flower in spring. The peony motif is also everywhere in the city, from trellises to rubbish bins.

Head up to the second floor, where you'll find halls for **Han and Tang pottery** and **Qing-dynasty relics**. Given Luoyang's history, the former is by far the more interesting; look out for a glazed incense burner of Eastern Han vintage (25–220), found in Wangcheng Park in 2004. A side-hall features a dedicated display on **funerary pottery** from throughout the dynasties – pay attention to the stylistic shifts, essentially moving from simple to decorative, from the Han to the Tang. The latter are more eye-catching; look out for multicoloured, expressive camels and several hook-nosed, pointy-chinned foreigners.

Luoyang Ancient Treasures Hall

In the **Luoyang ancient treasure** hall you'll find all sorts of goodies. The area around Luoyang entered the Bronze Age before the rest of China, so the **Shang bronzes** are especially extensive; look, too, for an endearing **jade tiger** from the Zhou, as well as some Indian-influenced **Wei statuary**, and a model farm from a Han tomb, with a sow and her row of piglets. Lastly, ornate **gold and silver** from the Tang shows the influence of Persian and Roman styles.

ARRIVAL AND DEPARTURE
LUOYANG

By air Luoyang's airport (洛阳北郊机场, luòyáng běijiāo jīchǎng) lies 20km north of town; from here, bus #83 will bring you to the train station, or it's around ¥35 by taxi. Destinations Beijing (2 daily; 1hr 30min); Chengdu (3 weekly; 1hr 50min); Guangzhou (4 weekly; 2hr); Hangzhou (3 weekly; 1hr 40min); Shanghai (daily; 1hr 30min); Shenzhen (2 weekly; 2hr).

By train Luoyang has two train stations. The main station (洛阳站, luòyáng zhàn) is just north of the city centre, while the gleaming new Longmen station (洛阳龙门站, luòyáng lóngmén zhàn), which handles high-speed services only, is 10km south. Both stations are on innumerable bus routes; it costs around ¥30 to get to or from Longmen station by taxi. Advance-purchase offices all over town charge a ¥5 fee per ticket – particularly handy

for booking services from far-flung Longmen station. Destinations from main station Beijing (7 daily; 7hr 30min–11hr); Hua Shan (18 daily; 3hr 30min); Ji'nan (10 daily; 5–10hr); Kaifeng (17 daily; 2hr 30min–3hr); Shanghai (6 daily; 12–17hr); Xi'an (many daily; 5hr); Zhengzhou (many daily; 1hr 30min–2hr).

Destinations from Longmen station Beijing (7 daily; 3hr 50min); Hua Shan (10 daily; 1hr–1hr 30min); Shanghai (1 daily; 9hr); Xi'an (many daily; 1hr 30min–2hr); Zhengzhou (many daily; 40min).

By bus There are bus stations either side of the main train station, both serving similar destinations. Destinations Kaifeng (1 hourly; 3hr); Shaolin Temple (every 30min; 1hr 30min); Xi'an (several daily; 4hr); Zhengzhou (every 30min; 1hr 30min).

GETTING AROUND

By bus The train station area is also the place to pick up city buses, including those to Baima Temple and the Longmen Caves (see accounts for details), while touts for buses to Shaolin Temple (p.265) hang around outside the

main bus station, and are not shy of grabbing customers. **By taxi** Taxis are plentiful, and have a ¥5 flag fare; Luoyang is big, meaning that you may end up paying more than ¥20 for a ride.

INFORMATION

Travel agents If your accommodation can't help out, the CTS (☎0379 6537 2020) are in the *Yinyan* hotel on Tanggong Xi Lu. A standard day-tour of the sights in the

vicinity of town, including Baima Temple and Shaolin Temple (excluding entry tickets), costs around ¥100 per person.

ACCOMMODATION

Basing yourself in one of the budget options near Luoyang's train station isn't such a bad idea, as there are good connections to the sights and transport out once you've finished. Yet the centre of town is cleaner, and the accommodation more upmarket. There's even an option out near the Longmen Caves (see opposite).

★ **Christian's** 克丽司汀酒店, kèlìsītīng jiǔdiàn. 56 Jiefang Lu ☎0379 63266666, ⓦwww.5xjd.com. Chic new hotel with friendly, young staff, and a shark swimming in the lobby. Rooms have been designed with rare attention, with internet-ready computers in each, and plush carpets; each floor has been given a theme, meaning that you can stay in European, Chinese or even Balinese style. Note that the bathrooms are rather visible from a few of the bedrooms – check first. **¥1390**

Luoyang Air Hotel 洛阳航空大厦, luòyáng hángkōng dàshà. Junction of Fanglin Lu and Kaixuan Xi Lu ☎0379 3944668. Staff at this nine-storey place wear the most stylish uniforms of any Luoyang hotel, and the guests – plenty of pilots and flight attendants – are pretty chic, too. The lobby, appropriately, looks like an airport lounge. **¥580**

Luoyang Yijia Youth Hostel 洛阳一家国际青年旅舍, luòyáng yìjiā guójì qīngnián lǚshè. 329 Zhongzhou Donglu ☎0379 63512311. Located in a nice, older area to the east of the centre (¥10 by taxi, ¥1 on bus #5), this is the best of Luoyang's several youth hostels (there's a fusty one near the main train station, if you're desperate). Staff are helpful, dorms cosy (ie, a bit cramped) and the private rooms well appointed. Dorms from **¥40**, rooms **¥250**

Qunying Star Vogue Hotel 群英之皇的尚酒店, qúnyīng zhīhuángdeshàng jiǔdiàn. 266 Zhongzhou Zhong Lu ☎0379 62683198. Cute boutique motel with colourful, frivolous decor usually alien to Chinese accommodation. Relatively pricey, though you can haggle them down a fair bit. **¥300**

EATING

As far as restaurants go, the Sichuanese have landed and taken over Luoyang, though there are a couple of places where dishes don't arrive smothered in chillies. It's a shame that Luoyang's famous water-feast meals (水席, shuǐxí) are so hard to find; so named because they're largely soup-based, they can be extremely expensive too. For cheap noodles and dumplings, try the snack stalls near the station. There's also a knot of cafés at the south end of Shachang Nan Lu, near the junction with Kaixuan Xi Lu.

Deheng Kaoya Dian 德恒烤鸭店, déhéng kǎoyā diàn. Tanggong Xi Lu. Famous roast-duck restaurant with smart antique-style furnishings, but not especially expensive – a whole duck is around ¥100. Daily 9am–9pm.

★ **Lao Luoyang Mian Guan** 老洛阳面馆, lǎo luòyáng miànguǎn. 17 Wangcheng Lu, just south of Wangcheng Park. This is the place to go for *shuixi* meals; though instead of an expensive banquet, which is the usual way to go, you'll be able to select individual dishes from a picture menu. Dishes cost around ¥26 per bowl, though don't order too many as servings are absolutely gigantic. Regular Chinese staples also available at single-figure

prices. Daily 11am–2.30pm & 5.30–10.30pm.

Tianxiang 天香饭店, tiānxiāng fàndiàn. 56 Jingyuyuan Lu. Crowded, smoky and inexpensive Sichuanese restaurant, very popular and with decent food; dishes clock in at ¥30–50. They have an English menu of sorts, too. Part of a hotel of the same name. Daily 9.30am–11pm.

Tudari 土大力, tǔdàlì. Off Jiefang Lu. This Korean restaurant, sitting on the northern cusp of a fancy new shopping area just east of *Christian's* hotel, serves up tasty portions of *naengmyeon* (cold noodles, ¥19), *bibimbap* (veggies on rice), and various Japanese *yakitori* sticks. Daily 11am–11.30pm.

DIRECTORY

Airlines The airlines office is at 196 Dao Bei Lu (☎0379 3935301), 200m north of the station. There's also a China Southern office on Zhongzhou Zhong Lu, just east of Jiefang Lu.

Banks and exchange The Bank of China (daily 8am–5pm) is on the corner of Zhongzhou Zhong Lu and

Shangchang Nan Lu.

Mail The post office (Mon–Sat 8am–6pm) is on the north side of Zhongzhou Zhong Lu, near the junction with Jinguyuan Lu.

PSB The PSB is at 1 Kaixuan Xi Lu (Mon–Sat 8am–noon & 2–6pm).

Around Luoyang

The main destination around Luoyang lies south at the **Longmen Caves**. However little you know about Buddhism or about sculpture, you'll be impressed by the scale and complexity of the work here and by the extraordinary contrast between the power of the giant figures and the intricate delicacy of the miniatures. On the way to the caves you can also visit **Guanlin Miao**, a memorial temple to Three Kingdom hero Guan Di. The other major sight is the Buddhist **Baima Temple**, which lies east of the city; and there's also an interesting, if not very well-presented, **Museum of Ancient Tombs** northwest of Luoyang, where you can see the interiors of the mounds that dot the local fields. All these can be visited on various **buses** from Luoyang, and you could pack the lot into one very busy day. Alternatively, all but the museum are served by private **tourist minibuses**, which run from outside the station.

The Longmen Caves

龙门石窟, lóngmén shíkū • Daily 7.30am–5.30pm • ¥120 • Bus #81 from Luoyang train station (¥1.5) • taxi ¥50–70

A UNESCO World Heritage Site, the **Longmen Caves** are a spectacular parade of Buddhist figurines and reliefs only 12km south of Luoyang. Caves pockmark the cliffs lining a meandering river, hosting figures ranging in size from the miniature to the monumental. It's an extremely popular place in the summer, though even the teeming crowds can't lessen the spectacle; try to visit early on in the day, however, as the exposed site can be rather hot.

Longmen's roadhead is almost 2km short of the caves; if you don't fancy a walk through the souvenir stalls, head down to the river and follow it to the entrance. Starting from the northern end and moving south down the group, the following are the most important carvings, which stand out due to their size.

The Bingyang Caves

The three **Bingyang caves** are among the earliest at the site; the central one, commissioned by Emperor Xuan Wu to honour his parents, supposedly took 800,000 men working from 500 to 523 AD to complete. The eleven statues of Buddha inside show northern characteristics – long features, thin faces, splayed fishtail robes – and traces of Greek influence. The side caves, completed under the Tang, are more natural and voluptuous, carved in high relief.

The Cave of Ten Thousand Buddhas

Just south of the Bingyang Caves you'll find **Wanfo**, the Cave of Ten Thousand Buddhas. Built in 680 by Gao Zong and his empress Wu Zetian, it contains not ten but fifteen thousand Buddhas carved in tiny niches, each one different and the smallest just 2cm high.

CREATING THE LONGMEN CAVES

Over the years, 1350 caves, 750 niches and 40 pagodas containing 110,000 statues were carved out of the limestone cliffs bordering the Yi River to create the Longmen Caves. Stretching more than 1km in length, the carvings were **commissioned** by emperors, the imperial family, other wealthy families wanting to buy good fortune, generals hoping for victory, and religious groups. The Toba Wei began the work in 492 AD, when they moved their capital to Luoyang from Datong, where they had begun the Yungang Caves (see p.243). At Longmen, they adapted their art to the different requirements of a harder, limestone surface. Three sets of caves, Guyang, Bingyang and Lianhua, date from this early period. Work continued for five hundred years and reached a second peak under the Tang, particularly under Empress Wu Zetian, a devoted adherent of Buddhism.

There's a clearly visible progression from the early style brought from Datong, of simple, rounded, formally modelled holy figures, to the complex and elaborate, but more linear, Tang carvings, which include women and court characters. In general, the Buddhas are simple, but the sculptors were able to show off with the attendant figures and the decorative flourishes around the edges of the caves.

Other caves

Lianhua (Lotus Flower Cave) is another early one, dating from 527, and named after the beautifully carved lotus in its roof; while at **Moya Sanfo** you can see an incomplete trinity, abandoned when the Tang dynasty began to wobble. But by far the most splendid is **Fengxian** (Ancestor Worshipping Cave), where an overwhelming seated figure of Vairocana Buddha, 17m high with 2m-long ears, sits placidly overlooking the river, guarded by four enormous warrior attendants (though the westerly two are almost completely gone) who are grinding malevolent spirits underfoot.

Medical Prescription Cave, built in 575, details several hundred cures for everything from madness to the common cold. **Guyang** is the earliest collection of all, begun in 495, where you can still see traces of the vivid paintwork that originally gave life to these carvings. There's a central Buddha and nineteen of the "Twenty Pieces", important examples of ancient calligraphy.

ACCOMMODATION
LONGMEN CAVES

Dongshan Hotel 东山宾馆, dōngshān bīnguǎn. Longmen Caves ☏ 0379 64686000, ⌨ www .lydongshanhotel.cn. On a hilltop overlooking the Longmen Caves, this resort-style hotel boasts almost 100 elegant rooms, a free gym and a few interesting quirks, such as piped spring water and a superb night-time view of the caves from a fourth-floor bar. The downside of its remote location is that you're almost obliged to dine on site. **¥880**

Guanlin Miao

关林庙, guānlín miào • Daily 8am–5pm • ¥40 • Bus #81

Some 7km south of Luoyang and easily combined with a trip to the Longmen Caves, the red-walled **Guanlin Miao** is a temple complex dedicated to **Guan Di** – also known as Guang Gong and Guan Yu – the famously loyal Three Kingdoms general (see p.393). Guan Di was captured and executed by the King of Wu, who then sent the head to Cao Cao, the King of Wei; Cao Cao neatly sidestepped this grisly game of pass-the-parcel by burying the head with honour in a tomb behind the temple, now a wooded, walled mound. Since his death, Guan Di has become the patron saint of martial virtue, worshipped by the military, police and the criminal underworld.

The temple and grounds

Despite its military theme, the temple is beautiful and rather peaceful, the elegant Ming buildings highly carved and richly decorated. Especially fine are the carved stone lionesses lining the path to the Main Hall. Each has a different expression and a different cub, some riding on her mother's back, some hiding coyly behind her paws. In the first hall, look carefully at the eaves for rather comical images of Guan Di fighting – he's the one on the red horse, a faithful animal called **Red Hare** – and leading an army engaged in sacking a city engulfed by carved wooden flames. Inside stands a 7m-tall statue of the general, resplendent in technicolour ceremonial robes with a curtain of beads hanging from his hat.

The Baima Temple

白马寺, báimǎ sì • Daily 7.30am–5.30pm • ¥50 • bus #56 from main train station (¥1.50) • taxi around ¥45 • also visited on some Shaolin Temple tours

Historic, leafy **Baima Temple** (White Horse Temple), 12km east of Luoyang, was founded in 68 AD, and has some claim to being the first Buddhist temple in China. Home to a thriving monastic community, the Baima Temple is primarily a place of worship, and over-inquisitive visitors are tactfully but firmly pointed away from closed buildings. Inside the temple, you'll find this a placid place, its silence only pricked by the sound of gongs or the tapping of stonemasons carving out a stele.

Brief history

Legend says that the Emperor Mingdi of the Eastern Han dreamed of a golden figure with the sun and moon behind its head, and so sent two monks westwards to find out what his dream meant. They reached India and returned, riding white horses with two Indian monks in tow, laden down with Buddhist sutras. Baima Temple was built to honour them, and its layout is in keeping with the legend: there are two stone horses, one on either side of the entrance, and the tombs of the two monks, earthen mounds ringed by round stone walls, lie in the first courtyard.

The Main Hall

Beyond the Hall of Celestial Guardians, the **Main Hall** holds a statue of Sakyamuni flanked by the figures of Manjusri and Samantabhadra. Near the Great Altar is an ancient bell weighing more than a tonne; as in the days when there were over ten thousand Tang monks here, it is still struck in time with the chanting. The inscription reads: "The sound of the Bell resounds in Buddha's temple causing the ghosts in Hell to tremble with fear".

The Cool Terrace

Behind the Main Hall is the **Cool Terrace** where, it is said, the sutras brought back from India were translated. Offerings of fruit on the altars, multicoloured cloths hanging from the ceilings and lighted candles in bowls floating in basins of water, as well as the heady gusts of incense issuing from the burners in the courtyards, indicate that, unlike other temples in the area, this is the genuine article.

The Museum of Ancient Tombs

洛阳古墓博物馆, luòyáng gǔmù bówùguǎn • Daily 8am–5pm • ¥20 • bus #83 from main train station

In a patch of open land around 6km northwest of Luoyang, the **Museum of Ancient Tombs** contains the relocated brick interiors of two dozen tomb mounds from the area, dating from the Western Han to Northern Song periods. Most had been robbed in antiquity, and the museum is neglected, but, compared with Longmen's overwhelming scale, it does give a more human view of the times.

The tombs

The tombs are arranged underground around a central atrium, into which you descend from beside souvenir stalls (there are no signs, but the helpful stallholders will point the way). Each is entered through a short tunnel, and is very small – you can barely stand in a couple – but decorated brickwork and frescoes liven the whole thing up. Best, however, is **Jing Ling**, the tomb of Xuan Wu of the Northern Wei, which stands just outside the museum grounds – again, there's no sign but you can't miss the huge earth hillock. This hasn't been relocated, and you descend a 50m-long ramp into Xuan Wu's tomb chamber – guarded by two sneering demons – where his sarcophagus remains.

Dengfeng

登封, dēngfēng

Halfway between Luoyang and Zhengzhou, **Dengfeng** sits among the seventy peaks of the 1500m-high **Song Shan** range. When Luoyang became the Zhou capital in 771 BC, these hills were considered to be at the axis of the **five sacred Taoist mountains**, with Hua Shan to the west, Tai Shan to the east, Heng Shan to the south and another Heng Shan to the north. Given the importance to Taoism, it's ironic that the busiest sight around Dengfeng today is the **Shaolin Temple**, a Buddhist complex famed not just as one of the earliest dedicated to the Chan (Zen) sect, but also where **Chinese kung fu** is said to have originated. A major Taoist temple survives, however, in the **Zhongyue Miao**, and there are some other interesting sights nearby, though to be honest Dengfeng itself is a messy place which doesn't really encourage an overnight stay, and you can see most of the regional attractions on day-trips from Luoyang or Zhengzhou.

Zhongyue Miao

中岳庙, zhōngyuè miào · Daily 7am–6pm · ¥30 · bus #2 from Dengfeng

The **Zhongyue Miao**, on the eastern edge of Dengfeng, is a huge Taoist temple founded as long ago as 220 BC, though the buildings here today date from the Ming. Inside, the spacious, wooded courtyards and brilliantly coloured buildings stand out against the muted green of the mountain behind. If you've just come from crowded Shaolin, the calm atmosphere of this working Taoist monastery is particularly striking.

The temple grounds

A series of gateways, courtyards and pavilions leads to the **Main Hall** where the emperor made sacrifices to the mountain. The Junji Gate, just before the hall, has two great sentries, nearly 4m high, brightly painted and flourishing their weapons. The courtyard houses gnarled old cypresses, some of them approaching the age of the temple itself, and also features four Song-dynasty **iron statues** of guardian warriors in martial poses. The **Bedroom Palace** behind the Main Hall is unusual for having a shrine that shows a deity lying in bed. Contemporary worshippers tend to gravitate to the back of the complex, where you may see people burning what look like little origami hats in the iron burners here, or practising *qi gong*, exercises centring around control of the breath.

Songyang Academy

嵩阳书院, sōngyáng shūyuàn · Daily 7am–6pm · ¥30 · buses #2 or #6 from Dengfeng

3km north of Dengfeng at the top end of Songshan Lu, the **Songyang Academy** consists of a couple of lecture halls, a **library** and a memorial hall, founded in 484 AD, which was one of the great centres of learning under the Song. Many famous scholars from history lectured here, including Sima Guang and Cheng Hao. In the courtyard are two enormous cypresses said to be over 4000 years old, as well as a stele from the Tang dynasty.

Songyue Temple Pagoda

嵩岳寺塔, sōngyuèsì tǎ · Daily 7am–6pm · ¥30 · buses #2 and #6 from Dengfeng

The path beyond the Songyang Academy climbs to Junji Peak and branches off to the **Songyue Temple Pagoda**, 5km north of Dengfeng. Built at the beginning of the sixth century by the Northern Wei, this 45m-tall structure is both the oldest pagoda and the oldest complete brick building in China, rare for having twelve sides.

ARRIVAL AND DEPARTURE

DENGFENG

If you're only interested in the Shaolin Temple, it's not worth making a point of stopping in Dengfeng – catch a direct bus or tour from either Luoyang or Zhengzhou.

By bus Dengfeng's small bus station (登封汽车站, dēngfēng qìchēzhàn) is located to the southeast of town, of most use for connections to Luoyang or Zhengzhou.

The last buses from Dengfeng depart around 6pm.
Destinations Luoyang (many daily; 1hr 30min); Zhengzhou (many daily; 1hr 30min).

GETTING AROUND

By bus All sights in this area, including Shaolin Temple, can be accessed by bus from Dengfeng's bus station, though it can be tricky to track them down – even locals get confused, though you'll soon find people willing to help out. Most buses operate from the main road in front of Dengfeng's bus station; white minibuses to Shaolin Temple (¥5) use the station itself.

By taxi Taxis are useful for accessing sights or accommodation around Dengfeng; the basic fare is ¥7.
By tour Hotels in both Luoyang and Zhengzhou are able to organize taxi tours of the Song Shan area; figure on ¥600–900 for the day. Those with a decent command of Chinese can cut this down considerably by negotiating directly with taxi drivers.

ACCOMMODATION AND EATING

Dengfeng's accommodation is OK, though the town itself is grubby and functional and you might be tempted to stay out at Shaolin Temple instead (see p.267). For eating, there are numerous dumpling places scattered around, or head to the frenetic night market in the lane directly facing the *Shaolin* hotel for street food.

Shaolin International 少林宾馆, shàolín bīnguǎn.
66 Zhongyue Dajie ☎ 0379 62856188. A pricey place,
though amenable to bargaining, this motel-like four-star is
the best option in town; the same can be said of the on-site
restaurant. Rooms are a little musty for the rate. **¥680**

Very Pear 梨花酒店, líhuā jiǔdiàn. 1 Shaolin Dadao,
within a 10min walk of the bus station ☎ 0379
62900000. Not bad, considering the weird name: it's a
modern place with decent rooms, though nothing in the
way of facilities. **¥280**

Shaolin Temple

少林寺, shàolín sì • Daily 8am–6pm • ¥100 • Kung fu shows daily 10am–4pm, included in ticket price

Sitting 13km west of Dengfeng on the road to Luoyang, **Shaolin Temple** is a place of
legends. This is the temple where the sixth-century founder of Buddhism's Chan (Zen)
sect, **Bodhidarma**, consolidated his teachings in China, and also where – surprisingly,
given Buddhism's peaceful doctrines – **Chinese kung fu** is said to have originated.
Today, it's a tourist black spot, packed with noisy groups and commercial enterprises,
and a complete non-starter if you're seeking any form of spiritual enlightenment
– though as an entertaining look into modern China's kung fu cult, it's a lot of fun. In
autumn, the place is particularly busy, filling up with martial-arts enthusiasts from all
over the world who come to attend the international **Wushu Festival** in nearby
Zhengzhou.

Brief history

The original Shaolin Temple was built in 495 AD. Shortly afterwards, the Indian monk
Bodhidarma (known as **Da Mo** in China) came to live here after visiting the emperor in
Nanjing, then crossing the Yangzi on a reed (depicted in a tablet at the temple). As the
temple has been burned down on several occasions – most recently in 1928, by the
warlord Shi Yousan – the buildings you see here today are mostly reconstructions in the
Ming style, built over the last twenty years. Despite this, and the incredible density of
tourists, the temple and surroundings are beautiful, and the chance to see some
impressive martial-art displays here makes it well worth the trip.

The kung fu show hall

Once through the gates, the road passes two huge open areas packed in the morning
and afternoons with hundreds of **martial-arts students** in tracksuits, arranged in small
groups and practising jumps, throws, kicks and weapons routines. Just on from here
and to the right is the **kung fu show hall**, with performance times posted outside. The
half-hour performance is a cut-down version of the stage show that regularly tours the
world, with demonstrations of Shaolin's famous stick fighting and animal-style kung
fu, all pretty electrifying if you haven't seen it before. You may care to sit on the upper
level – foreigners on the lower level sometimes get pushed into showing off their
(usually awful) kung fu skills for a delighted audience.

The temple

The **temple entrance** is about 200m further up the path from the show hall, and
inside you should look for trees whose bark has been drilled with holes by kung fu
practitioners' fingers. At the end of the entranceway is a boxy pavilion housing two
fearsome demon statues that tower overhead, fists raised. On the right in the
courtyard beyond are two large glassed-in tablets from 728 AD, raised by the
emperor **Taizong** after thirteen of Shaolin's monks had aided him against the rebel
Wang Shichang; in gratitude, he passed an edict allowing monks at the temple to eat
meat and drink wine. The temple's halls are quite small and simple, but two at the
rear of the complex are worth attention: **Qianfo Hall**, whose brick floor is dented
from where the monks used to stamp during their kung fu training; and the **White
Robe Hall**, where Ming-dynasty **murals** covering two walls depict Taizong being saved
by the monks.

SHAOLIN KUNG FU

Kung fu was first developed at the Shaolin Temple as a form of gymnastics to counterbalance the immobility of meditation. The monks studied the movement of animals and copied them – the way snakes crawled, tigers leapt and mantises danced – and coordinated these movements with meditational breathing routines. As the temple was isolated it was often prey to bandits, and gradually the monks turned their exercises into a form of self-defence.

The monks owed their strength to rigorous **discipline**. From childhood, monks trained from dawn to dusk, every day. To strengthen their hands, they thrust them into sacks of beans, over and over; when they were older, into bags of sand. To strengthen their fists, they punched a thousand sheets of paper glued to a wall; over the years, the paper wore out and the young monks punched brick. To strengthen their legs, they ran around the courtyard with bags of sand tied to their knees, and to strengthen their heads, they hit them with bricks.

Only after twenty years of such exercises could someone consider themselves proficient in kung fu, by which time they were able to perform incredible **feats**, examples of which you can see illustrated in the murals at the temple and in photographs of contemporary martial-arts masters in the picture books on sale in the souvenir shops. Apart from breaking concrete slabs with their fists and iron bars with their heads, the monks can balance on one finger, take a sledgehammer blow to the chest, and hang from a tree by their neck. Their **boxing routines** are equally extraordinary, their animal qualities clearly visible in the vicious clawing, poking, leaping and tearing that they employ. One comic-looking variation that requires a huge amount of flexibility is **drunken boxing**, where the performer twists, staggers and weaves as if inebriated – useful training given that Shaolin monks are allowed alcohol.

Yet the monks were not just fighters; as many hours were spent **meditating and praying** as in martial training. They obeyed a moral code, which included the stricture that only fighting in self-defence was acceptable, and killing your opponent was to be avoided if possible. These rules became a little more flexible over the centuries as emperors and peasants alike sought their help in battles, and the Shaolin monks became legendary figures for their interventions on the side of righteousness.

The monks were at the height of their power in the Tang dynasty, though they were still a force to be reckoned with in the Ming, when **weapons** were added to their discipline. However, the temple was sacked during the 1920s and again in the 1960s during the Cultural Revolution, when Shaolin's monks persecuted and dispersed. Things picked up again in the 1980s when, as a result of Jet Li's enormously popular first film *Shaolin Temple*, there was a **resurgence** of interest in the art. The old masters were allowed to teach again, and the government realized that the temple was better exploited as a tourist resource than left to rot.

Evidence of the popularity of kung fu in China today can be seen not just at the tourist circus of the Shaolin Temple, but in any cinema, where **kung fu films**, often concerning the exploits of Shaolin monks, make up a large proportion of the entertainment on offer. Many young Chinese today want to study kung fu, and to meet demand numerous **schools** have opened around the temple. Few of them want to be monks, though – the dream of many is to be a movie star.

Inevitably, such attention and exploitation has taken its toll on Shaolin Temple's original purpose as a Buddhist monastery. The temple's primary drive today seems less towards the spiritual and more about the travelling shows and protecting commercial interests – they are currently pursuing efforts to trademark the name "Shaolin", in order to capitalize on its use by everything from martial-arts outfits to beer companies. For a good account of what it's like to live and train here, and the challenges that the modern temple faces, read *American Shaolin* by Matthew Polly (see p.253).

Ta Lin

塔林, tǎlín

The **Ta Lin**, 200m up the hill past the temple entrance, is where hundreds of stone pagodas, memorials to past monks, are tightly grouped together in a "forest". Up to 10m tall, and with stepped, recessed tops, these golden stone structures are visible from a wooden walkway that circles the area; they look particularly impressive against the purple mountain when snow is on the ground. The earliest dates to 791 AD and commemorates a monk named Fawan, while the forest is still being added to as monks die.

The mountains
Songyang cable car ¥50 • Shaolin cable car ¥60

The mountains beyond Ta Lin can be ascended by cable car or stone steps. There are two main routes to choose from, with the **Songyang** route the more popular; this heads up Shaoshi Shan, the highest peak in the area at 1512m, past a cave where Bodhidarma supposedly passed a nine-year vigil, sitting motionless facing a wall in a state of enlightenment. There are some spectacular views of rugged hills from these lofty paths, though on busy days crowds can dampen the effect somewhat. The Songyang cable car is most popular, but far fewer people take the new **Shaolin** cable car, which starts a little further along the path from Ta Lin and heads up a neighbouring mountain; views here are just as good.

ARRIVAL AND DEPARTURE   SHAOLIN TEMPLE

By bus and minibus There's no bus station at Shaolin; services just pull up at a vehicle park between the main road and temple. Leaving, search out direct buses to Luoyang or Zhengzhou here, or catch one of the white minibuses to Dengfeng and change there.
Destinations Dengfeng (many daily; 30min); Luoyang (10 daily; 1hr 15min); Zhengzhou (several daily; 1hr 45min).
By tour For tours from Luoyang or Zhengzhou, see p.270.

ACCOMMODATION AND EATING

There is a whole bunch of cheap places to stay around the temple – you'll be offered rooms as soon as you step off the bus – and a decent hotel within the grounds. If you plump for a cheapie, bring some snack food, since there are few restaurants in this area; within the Shaolin Temple, a large building near the kung fu hall offers Western fast food and cheap Chinese staples.

Zen International 禅居国际饭店, chánjū guójì fàndiàn. Behind the kung fu hall ☎ 0371 62745666. Located within the grounds of the temple itself, this is an upmarket hotel – if a somewhat ageing one. There's a decent on-site restaurant, offering huge (and mostly vegetarian) lunch buffets at ¥38 a head. Ignore the rack rates, as you can usually halve these. **¥680**

Zhengzhou
郑州, zhèngzhōu

Close to the south bank of the Yellow River, **ZHENGZHOU** lies almost midway between Luoyang to the west and Kaifeng to the east. The walled town that existed here 3500 years ago was probably an early capital of the Shang dynasty, and excavations have revealed bronze foundries, bone-carving workshops and sacrificial altars. Today's Zhengzhou, however, is an entirely modern city, rebuilt virtually from scratch after heavy bombing in the war against Japan. Despite the resultant dearth of historical sights, and the industrial trappings inevitably springing from a position atop China's two main rail routes, Zhengzhou is not all that unpleasant, its broad, leafy avenues lined with shopping malls and boutiques.

Erqi Pagoda
二七塔, èrqī tǎ

The hub of downtown Zhengzhou is the **Erqi Pagoda**, made up of two conjoined nine-storey towers. It was built to commemorate those killed in a 1923 Communist-led rail strike that was put down with great savagery by the warlord Wu Pei Fu, though it's sadly no longer open for viewing.

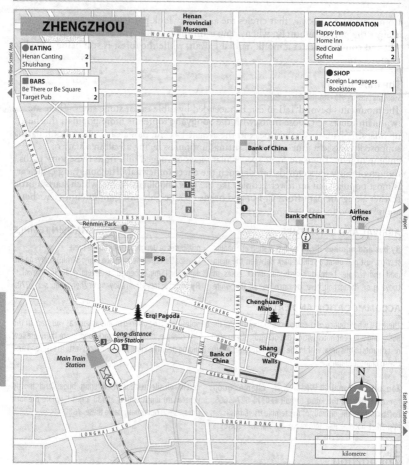

The city walls

East of the Erqi Pagoda, there's a remnant of old Zhengzhou in its ancient **city walls**, rough earthen ramparts 10m high, originally built more than two thousand years ago. There's a path along the top, and you can walk for about 3km along the south and east sections (the west section has been destroyed by development), descending to cross the main roads along the way. Planted with trees, the walls are now used by the locals as a short cut and a park, full of courting couples, kids who slide down the steep sides on metal trays, and old men who hang their cagebirds from the trees and sit around fires cooking sweet potatoes – it doesn't seem to occur to anyone to treat it as a historical monument.

Chenghuang Miao

城隍庙, chénghuáng miào • Daily 9am–5pm • Free

Chenghuang Miao, on the north side of Shangcheng Lu, is the most interesting of Zhengzhou's temples, with well-observed images of birds decorating the eaves of the first hall, underneath roof sculptures of dragons and phoenixes. Murals in the modern Main Hall owe much to 1950s socialist realism, and surround a sculpture of a stern-looking Chenghuang, magisterial defender of city folk, who sits flanked by two attendants.

Henan Provincial Museum

河南省博物院, hénánshěng bówùyuàn • northern end of Jingqi Lu • Daily 8.30am–6.15pm • Free (bring ID) • English audio guide • ¥30 • bus #32 or #118 from the main train station

A giant stone pyramid, the modern **Henan Provincial Museum** boasts an outstanding collection of relics unearthed in the region, dating back to when Henan was the cradle of Chinese civilization. As you move clockwise, each hall covers a particular stage of regional history, beginning with the Stone Age: look for **oracle bones** inscribed with the ancestors of modern Chinese script unearthed from **Anyang**, 200km north of Zhengzhou, site of China's Shang-dynasty capital; and some superb **bronzes**, from the Shang to Tang periods, including large tripods and tiny animal figures used as weights. By far the most interesting pieces, however, are the **Han pottery**, with scale models of houses showing defensive walls and towers, models of domestic animals, and huge numbers of human figurines – dancers, musicians, soldiers, court ladies – all leaving the impression that the Han were an articulate, fun-loving people who liked to show off.

The Yellow River Scenic Area

黄河公园, huánghé gōngyuán • Daily 8am–6pm • ¥60 • bus #16 (¥5) from Minggong Lu, just outside Zhengzhou's train station

The Yellow River slides by just 28km to the north of town at the **Yellow River Scenic Area**, really a stretch of typical Chinese countryside incorporating villages and allotments. Despite the dusty environs, parts of this large, semi-wild park are surprisingly verdant, incorporating forested hills, crumbly temple buildings, lakeside pavilions and large statues of dynastic emperors (including one Mount Rushmore-like design). You can spend an afternoon here walking, **horse-trekking** – an escorted, hour-long trot should cost about ¥20 – or taking a speedboat ride along the river. From the hilltops you have a good view over the river and the plain of mud either side of it. It's hard to imagine that in 1937, when Chiang Kai-shek breached the dykes 8km from the city to prevent the Japanese capturing the rail line, the Yellow River flooded this great plain, leaving more than a million dead and countless more homeless.

ARRIVAL AND DEPARTURE — ZHENGZHOU

Book plane and train tickets through Henan Tourism (☎0371 65959892), north of the Sofitel on Jinshui Lu.

BY PLANE

Zhengzhou airport (郑州新郑国际机场, zhèngzhōu xīnzhèng guójì jīchǎng) lies well to the east of the city; a taxi into the centre should cost ¥100, while airport buses (every 30min; ¥15) terminate at, and depart back to the airport from, the Aviation Building at 3 Jinshui Lu (open 24hr; ☎0371 599 1111).

Destinations Beijing (7 daily; 1hr 10min); Chengdu (3–4 daily; 1hr 40min); Guangzhou (9 daily; 2hr); Hong Kong (1 daily; 2hr 35min); Kunming (6 daily; 2hr 20min); Lanzhou (3 daily; 1hr 40min); Qingdao (3 daily; 1hr 10min); Shanghai (11 daily; 1hr 40min).

BY TRAIN

Tickets can be hard to buy at the main station due to the overwhelming crowds, and the East station is a bit far away – there are advance-booking booths dotted around town, all charging a ¥5 fee per ticket.

Zhengzhou's main station (郑州站, zhèngzhōu zhàn) is well located, just to the southwest of the city centre; it receives a few high-speed services per day.

Destinations Beijing (many daily; 3hr 20min–9hr); Guangzhou (19 daily; 5hr 30min–21hr); Kaifeng (many daily; 45min); Luoyang (many daily; 40min–2hr); Qufu (2 daily; 4–6hr); Shanghai (19 daily; 7–15hr); Taiyuan (3 daily; 8–11hr); Xi'an (many daily; 2hr 30min–7hr).

Zhengzhou East station (郑州东站, zhèngzhōu dōngzhàn), around 6km east of the main station, hosts the vast majority of high-speed services, and is ¥30 from the centre by taxi; it'll also be on the new subway system, when that starts up.

Destinations Beijing (many daily; 2hr 30min–3hr 15min); Guangzhou (13 daily; 5hr 30min–6hr 30min); Luoyang (12 daily; 40min); Taiyuan (3 daily; 3hr 30min); Xi'an (15 daily; 2hr 15min–3hr).

BY BUS

The long-distance bus station (郑州长途站, zhèngzhōu chángtú zhàn) is opposite the train station, though there is also the usual run of other depots scattered around the city's edges. Bus tickets to all major regional destinations are easy to get at the horde of windows surrounding the main bus station.

Destinations Dengfeng (1hr 30min); Kaifeng (1hr 30min); Luoyang (2hr 30min).

GETTING AROUND

By bus The main city bus terminuses lie either side of the train station plaza. Routes can be hard to ascertain for non-Chinese-speakers; maps in Chinese with details of bus routes are available outside the train station. Fares cost ¥1–2.

By subway At the time of writing, the city was putting the

BY MINIBUS

Shaolin minibuses Day-trips to Shaolin leave from in front of the train station around 8–11am, when you'll find minibuses lined up.

finishing touches to its new subway system; lines #1 and #2 are scheduled to open in 2015.

By taxi Cabs have an ¥8 minimum charge, though Zhengzhou is a big city – you could be looking at fares of up to ¥30.

ACCOMMODATION

If you've only come to Zhengzhou in transit, it makes sense to stay around the train station area, where there's plenty of inexpensive, decent accommodation, though it can get noisy. There are also a couple of motel and upmarket hotel options further out, in less crowded settings.

★ **Happy Inn** 喜鹊家旅馆, xǐquèjiā lǚguǎn. 9 Jingliu Lu ☎ 0371 87559666. This boutique hotel is a lovely surprise, full of neat little touches: cartoon shows are projected behind reception, which features a small magazine library and DVDs laid out for rent. The rooms are quiet and clean, and the place is located on Zhengzhou's most appealing nightlife street. **¥309**

Home Inn 如家酒店, rújiā jiǔdiàn. Off Fushou Lu ☎ 0371 66970055, ⓦ homeinns.com. You can't miss this bright yellow, friendly motel, whose smart modern doubles have free wi-fi access and passably comfy beds. An easy walk from the main train station. **¥199**

Red Coral 红珊瑚酒店, hóngshānhú jiǔdiàn. 20 Erma Lu ☎ 0371 66652226. The best of the motley crew of mid-rangers outside the train station, with large, comfortable rooms, a filling breakfast buffet, helpful staff – and Kenny G, the original epic sax man, playing 24hr in the lift. **¥280**

Sofitel 索菲特国际饭店, suǒfēitè guójì fàndiàn. 289 Chengdong Lu ☎ 0371 65950088, ⓦ sofitel.com. Don't let the ugly exterior throw you – this is the most comfortable of Zhengzhou's five-stars, and the most popular with business travellers, thanks to appealing rooms and a clutch of excellent bars and restaurants. **¥1198**

EATING, DRINKING AND ENTERTAINMENT

Zhengzhou has abundant eating options, though you'll likely want to escape the train station area, which is as crowded with Western fast-food eateries as it is with people. A number of shops here also sell travellers' nibbles – walnuts, oranges and dates – which testify to the great number of people passing through here every day. For drink, it's best to head to Jingliu Lu, where there's a pleasing range of bars.

Be There or Be Square 不见不散, bùjiàn bùsàn. 108 Jingliu Lu. A great little bar – attractive and friendly, it's a good place to meet people. Also hosts occasional live music. Daily 6pm–2am.

Henan Canting 河南餐厅, hénán cāntīng. Off Dongtaikang Lu ☎ 0371 66222108. A surprisingly smart place in which to sample some excellent Henan cooking. Pick from a picture menu; one interesting choice is the *liyu beimian* (鲤鱼焙面), a real Henan favourite consisting of a whole carp covered with sauce and noodles. Daily 10am–10pm.

★ **Shuishang** 水上餐厅, shuǐshàng cāntīng.

100 Beierqi Lu ☎ 0371 66249599. Straddling a small river, this is a delightful, old-fashioned venue serving Hong Kong-style dim sum. There's a menu, but you may not need it – waitresses will soon bus their trolleys over to your table with rounds of succulent goodies, most of which cost around ¥9 per plate. Daily 10am–2pm & 5pm–10pm.

Target Pub 目标酒吧, mùbiāo jiǔbā. 10 Jingliu Lu. Get your fill of Guinness and darts at this deliberately ramshackle-looking pub, which is popular with expats a nd some of Zhengzhou's more colourful locals. Daily 5–2am.

DIRECTORY

Banks and exchange The main Bank of China is on Jinshui Lu; the closest branch to southern accommodation is on Dong Dajie – both have ATMs.

Mail and telephones The principal post office (Mon–Fri

8am–8pm) is next to the train station on the south side, with a 24hr telecom office next door.

PSB The visa section is at 70 Erqi Lu (Mon–Fri 8.30am–noon & 3–6pm; ☎ 0371 69620359).

Kaifeng

开封, kāifēng

Located on the alluvial plains in the middle reaches of the Yellow River 70km east of Zhengzhou, **KAIFENG** is an ancient capital with a history stretching back over three thousand years. However, unlike other ancient capitals in the region, the city hasn't grown into an industrial monster, with most of its sights in a pleasingly compact area within the **town walls**, which enclose a 5km-long rectangle. These tamped-earth ramparts have been heavily damaged and there's no path along them, but they do present a useful landmark. The town is also crisscrossed by **canals**, part of a network that connected it to Hangzhou and Yangzhou in ancient times. While not especially

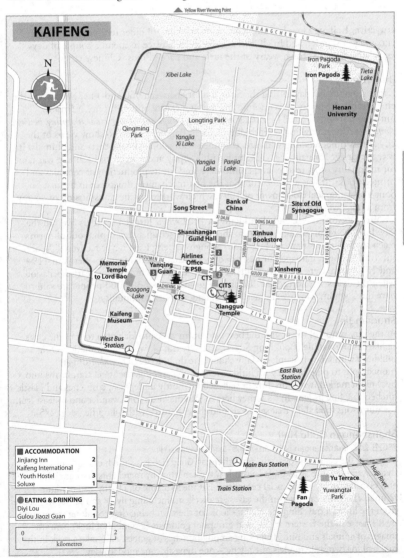

KAIFENG

Yellow River Viewing Point

BEIHUANGCHENG LU

N

Xibei Lake

Iron Pagoda Park
Iron Pagoda

Tieta Lake

BEIMEN DAJIE

Henan University

Longting Park

Qingming Park

Yangjia Xi Lake

Yangjia Lake   Panjia Lake

XIHUANCHENG LU

DONGHUANCHENG LU

Song Street

Bank of China

Site of Old Synagogue

XIMEN DAJIE

XI DAJIE

DONG DAJIE

BEIDAMEN JIE

Shanshangan Guild Hall

Xinhua Bookstore

NEIHUAN DONG LU

Memorial Temple to Lord Bao

XIHOUMEN JIE

Yanqing Guan

Airlines Office & PSB

CTS

ZHONGSHAN LU

SIHOU JIE

GULOU JIE

MADAO JIE

MUJIAQIAO JIE

BEITUI JIE

SHUDIAN JIE

Xinsheng

Baogong Lake

DAZHIFANG JIE

CTS

CITS

Xiangguo Temple

ZIYOU LU

Kaifeng Museum

YINGBIN LU

WOLONG JIE

ZIYOU LU

GONGYUAN LU

West Bus Station

East Bus Station

BINHE LU

MUYI LU

ZHONGSHAN LU

XINMENGUAN JIE

TIELUBEI YUAN

Huji River

WUFU XI LU

■ ACCOMMODATION
Jinjiang Inn	2
Kaifeng International Youth Hostel	3
Soluxe	1

● EATING & DRINKING
Diyi Lou	2
Gulou Jiaozi Guan	1

Main Bus Station

MUYI LU

POTA LU

Train Station

Fan Pagoda

Yu Terrace

Yuwangtai Park

0   2
kilometres

KAIFENG'S JEWS

A number of families in Kaifeng trace their lineage back to the **Jews**, though their origins remain a mystery. It's likely that their ancestors arrived from central Asia around 1000 AD, when trade links between the two areas were strong. The community was never large, but it seems to have flourished until the nineteenth century, when – perhaps as a result of disastrous floods, including one in 1850 that destroyed the synagogue – the Kaifeng Jews almost completely died out. However, following the atmosphere of greater religious tolerance in contemporary China, many Jews have begun practising their faith again. You can see a few relics from the synagogue in the museum, including three steles that once stood outside it, but most, such as a *Torah* in Chinese now in the British Museum, are in collections abroad.

attractive, Kaifeng's low-key ambience and sprinkling of older temples and pagodas encourage a wander, and in all, this is a worthwhile place to spend a couple of days, especially if you've grown weary of the scale and pace of most Chinese cities.

Brief history

Kaifeng had its heyday during the Song dynasty between 960 and 1127 AD, when the city became the political, economic and cultural centre of the empire. A famous 5m-long horizontal **scroll** by Zhang Azheduan, *Qingming Shang He* (*Qingming Festival Along the River*), now in the Forbidden City in Beijing, unrolls to show views of the city at this time, teeming with life, crammed with people, boats, carts and animals. It was a great age for painting, calligraphy, philosophy and poetry, and Kaifeng was famed for the quality of its textiles and embroidery, and for its production of ceramics and printed books. It was also the home of the first mechanical timepiece in history, Su Song's **astronomical clock tower** of 1092, which worked by the transmission of energy from a huge water wheel.

Kaifeng's Golden Age ended suddenly in 1127 when Jurchen invaders overran the city. Just one royal prince escaped to the south, to set up a new capital out of harm's reach beyond the Yangzi at Hangzhou, though Kaifeng itself never recovered. What survived has been damaged or destroyed by repeated **flooding** since – between 1194 and 1887 there were more than fifty severe incidents, including one fearful occasion when the dykes were breached during a siege and at least 300,000 people are said to have died, whom which were many of Kaifeng's **Jewish community**.

Shudian Jie

At the very centre of town, and the best place from which to kick off a tour of the city's sights, lies **Shudian Jie** (Bookshop Street), a scruffy run of two-storey imitation Qing buildings with fancy balconies. Many shops here do indeed sell books, from art monographs to pulp fiction with lurid covers. In the evening, the street transforms into a busy **night market**, when brightly lit stalls selling mostly underwear, cosmetics and plastic kitchenware line its length; it's somewhere to join the locals for a wander and to feast from the numerous **food stalls** that set up around the crossroads with Sihou Jie (see p.275).

Shanshangan Guild Hall

陕山甘会馆, shǎnshāngān huìguǎn • Xufu Jie • Daily 8am–6.30pm • ¥30

Very near the centre of town, the **Shanshangan Guild Hall** is a superb example of Qing-dynasty architecture at its most lavish. It was established by merchants of Shanxi, Shaanxi and Gansu provinces as a social centre and has the structure of a flashy, ostentatious temple. The woodcarvings on the eaves are excellent, including lively and rather wry scenes from the life of a travelling merchant – look for the man being dragged along the ground by his horse in the Eastern Hall – and groups of gold bats (a symbol of luck) beneath images of animals and birds frolicking among bunches of grapes. Also take a peek in the first hall for two scale models of Kaifeng – one dynastic, one modern-day.

Xiangguo Temple

相国寺, xiàngguó sì • Ziyou Lu • Daily 8am–6pm • ¥45

A short walk south of the guild hall, across an appealingly ramshackle part of the Old Town, is the **Xiangguo Temple**, founded in 555 AD. The simple buildings here today are Qing style, with a colourful, modern frieze of *arhats* at the back of the Main Hall, and an early Song-dynasty bronze Buddha in the Daxiong Baodian (Great Treasure House). In an unusual octagonal hall at the back you'll see a magnificent four-sided Guanyin carved in ginkgo wood and covered in gold leaf, about 3m high.

Yanqing Guan

延庆观, yánqìng guān • Ziyou Lu • Daily 8.30am–6.30pm • ¥30

One kilometre west of Xiangguo Temple, on the way to Baogong Lake, is the **Yanqing Guan**, whose rather odd, knobbly central building, the **Pavilion of the Jade Emperor**, is all that remains of a larger temple complex built at the end of the thirteenth century. The outside of this octagonal structure of turquoise tiles and carved brick is overlaid with ornate decorative touches; inside, a bronze image of the Jade Emperor sits in a room that is by contrast strikingly austere. The rest of the complex looks just as old, though the images of kangaroos among the animals decorating the eaves suggest otherwise.

Memorial Temple to Lord Bao

包公祠, bāogōng cí • Daily 8am–6pm • ¥40

On a promontory jutting out into the western side of Baogong Lake (包公湖, bāogōng hú), the **Memorial Temple to Lord Bao** is a modern imitation of a Song building holding an exhibition of the life of this legendary figure who was Governor of Kaifeng during the Northern Song. Judging from the articles exhibited, including modern copies of ancient guillotines and the scenes from his life depicted in paintings and waxworks, Lord Bao was a harsh but fair judge, who must have had some difficulty getting through doors if he really wore a hat and shoes like the ones on display.

Kaifeng Museum

开封博物馆, kāifēng bówùguǎn • Tues–Sun 9am–5pm • main exhibition free (bring ID) • steles ¥50

A substantial mansion on the south side of Baogong Lake houses the **Kaifeng Museum**. The lower levels host a predictable, though interesting, chronologically arranged collection of Kaifeng relics, and a good exhibition of local folk art. Of more note are the upper floors, where you'll find a series of **steles** recording the history of Kaifeng's Jewish community that used to stand outside the synagogue – you'll need an extra ticket for these.

Song Street

宋都御街, sòngdū yùjiē

At the north end of Zhongshan Lu and under a stone archway, **Song Street** is the most interesting access point for the **lakes** dotting the northern half of Kaifeng's old town. The street itself is lined with antique-style tourist shops built over the site of the Song-dynasty Imperial Palace. The shops sell handmade paper, paintings, reproduction classical scrolls and, around Chinese New Year, brightly coloured woodblock prints of animals and legendary figures, which people paste on their doors for good luck.

Yangjia Lake

杨家湖, yángjiā hú • Daily 24hr • Free

At the northern end of Song Street is a large **plaza**, often full of people strolling and flying kites, beyond which is **Yangjia Lake**, originally part of the imperial gardens but now at the centre of a large warren of carnival-like tourist traps arranged around the lakeshore.

The canal leading south from Yangjia Lake and Qingming Park to Baogong Lake has been newly gentrified, and is Kaifeng's best place for an evening stroll (unless you hate bats or mosquitoes, of which there are plenty).

Qingming Park

清明上河园, qīngmíng shànghéyuán • Daily 9am–10pm • tickets from ¥80

At **Qingming Park**, a kitschy theme park west of Yangjia Lake, you can walk through a realized version of *Qingming Shang He*, wandering to your heart's content past costumed courtesans and ingratiating shopkeepers. It's a good place for families, and perhaps those who want an interesting (though expensive) window into China's current means of packaging history for local consumption.

Iron Pagoda Park

铁塔公园, tiětǎ gōngyuán • accessible only off Beimen Dajie • Daily 8am–6pm • ¥50, plus ¥30 to climb the tower • buses #1 and #3 from the centre of town

Kaifeng's far northeast corner is occupied by **Iron Pagoda Park**. At its centre you'll find the 13-storey, 56m-high pagoda that gives it its name, a striking Northern Song (1049 AD) tower so named because its surface of glazed tiles gives the building the russet tones of rusted iron. Its base, like all early buildings in Kaifeng, is buried beneath a couple of metres of silt deposited during floods. Most of the tiles hold relief images, usually of the Buddha, but also of Buddhist angels, animals and abstract patterns.

The Fan Pagoda

繁塔, fán tǎ • 7am–7pm • ¥10 • taxi from train station ¥10

The dumpy, hexagonal **Fan Pagoda** pokes out of a labyrinthine maze of alleyways, about 3km southeast of the city centre. Built in 997 AD, and the oldest standing building in Kaifeng, it was once 80m tall and had nine storeys; three remain today. It's not in a park, as city maps suggest; instead, it sits between a car repair yard and a set of courtyards. The fact that the local inhabitants tie their washing lines to the wall around the base and peel sweetcorn in the courtyard adds to the charm of the site.

Yuwangtai Park

禹王台公园, yǔwángtái gōngyuán • Daily 7am–7pm • ¥30 • taxi from train station ¥10

Yuwangtai Park surrounds the **Yu Terrace**, an earthen mound now thought to have been a music stage that was once the haunt of Tang poets. The park, dotted with pavilions and commemorative steles, is pleasant in summer when the many flower gardens are in bloom – it's well overpriced, though.

Yellow River Viewing Point

黄河公园, huánghé gōngyuán • bus #6 from the west side of Beimen Dajie, opposite the entrance to Iron Pagoda Park

It's worth catching a bus to the **Yellow River Viewing Point**, 11km north of town, especially if you haven't seen the river before. From the pavilion here you can look out onto a plain of silt that stretches to the horizon, across whose dramatic emptiness the syrupy river meanders. Beside the pavilion is an **iron ox**, which once stood in a now submerged temple. It's a cuddly-looking beast with a horn on its head that makes it look like a rhino sitting on its hind legs. An inscription on the back reveals its original function – as a charm to ward off floods, a tradition begun by the legendary flood-tamer Da Yu.

ARRIVAL AND DEPARTURE   KAIFENG

By plane The nearest airport to Kaifeng is at Zhengzhou (see p.269); buy tickets at the airlines office (8am–7pm; ☎0378 595 5555) at the southwest corner of Zhongshan Lu and Sihou Jie.

By train Kaifeng's small train station (开封站, kāifēng zhàn) sits 2km south of the old town, and receives services from all over the area. You can buy tickets here, though there are several booking offices in the centre, including a convenient one diagonally across from the hostel; they'll also be able to sell tickets for high-speed services from Zhengzhou.

Destinations Beijing (2 daily; 13hr); Luoyang (22 daily; 2hr 30min); Qufu (1 daily; 3hr 40min); Shanghai (11 daily; 6hr 30min); Xi'an (19 daily; 7–9hr); Zhengzhou (many daily; 45min).

By bus The main long-distance station (开封汽车站,

kāifēng qìchē zhàn) is in front of the train station to the east, though you might also wind up at the smaller west or east bus stations, near the southern walls. The only notable

destinations are Zhengzhou (hourly; 1hr 30min) and Luoyang (hourly; 2hr 30min); for anywhere else, it's far better to go by train.

GETTING AROUND

By bus City buses cost ¥1 and are useful for arrival points – numbers #1 and #9 head into town from the station – though taxis are more convenient elsewhere.

By taxi Taxis are cheap: flag fall is ¥5, and ¥15 will get you almost anywhere you need to go. Note that drivers waiting at the station will likely refuse to use their

meters; head to the main road and pick up a cruising cab.

By rickshaw Rickshaw drivers pester new arrivals at the station, but be wary of using them – they often rip tourists off.

By bicycle Surprisingly few places rent out bikes; try the hostel, which will give you one for ¥20 per day (¥200 deposit).

ACCOMMODATION

Despite Kaifeng's small size, it has several good-value budget hotels; pickings are somewhat slimmer at the upper end of the scale.

★ **Jinjiang Inn** 锦江之星旅馆, jǐnjiāng zhīxīng lǚguǎn. 88 Zhongshan Lu ☎ 0378 3996666. The best, and most usefully located, of Kaifeng's chain-hotel cheapies. Rooms are actually rather plush for the price – monochrome, minimalist affairs which put most of the city's four-stars to shame. **¥179**

Kaifeng International Youth Hostel 开封天福国际青年旅舍, kāifēng tiānfú guójì qīngnián lǚshè. 30 Yingbin Lu ☎ 0378 3153789, ☺ kfyha.com. Kaifeng's sole hostel option is a bit grubby around the edges: rooms could

do with a clean, and beds are a bit creaky. Nevertheless, most enjoy their stay, largely because the staff are friendly and informative, there's a good bar with cheap happy hour deals, Western breakfasts are served, and there's a pool table to bash balls about on. Dorms **¥50**, rooms **¥140**

Soluxe 阳光酒店, yángguāng jiǔdiàn. 41 Gulou Jie ☎ 0378 5958888. This is the classiest place in town – or, at least, the only upper-end place that doesn't feel horribly institutional. It's very well located in the very centre of things, and there's a good duck restaurant on the ground level. **¥560**

EATING

Kaifeng's best place to eat is the new night market in the area between Shudian Jie and Sihou Jie, where the food, as well as the ambience, is fun. You'll find *jiaozi*, made in front of you; skewers of mutton cooked by Uyghur peddlers; shock-the-folks-back-home favourites like sparrow, snails and silkworm; and a local delicacy consisting of hot liquid jelly, into which nuts, berries, flowers and fruit are poured. You can spot jelly stalls by their huge bronze kettles, with a spout in the form of a dragon's head. Those visiting during the Mid-Autumn Festival should look out for Kaifeng's unique mooncakes – the usual thickness, but nearly half a metre wide. Lastly, those needing coffee should head to Shudian Jie, where a couple of trendy(ish) cafés have opened up near the north end of the road.

★ **Diyi Lou** 第一楼, diyīlóu. 43 Sihou Jie ☎ 0378 5998688. This smart spot is famous for Kaifeng's own take on the humble *baozi*; flat and circular, they look a little like wagon wheels. The ones served here (¥25 per round) are utterly delectable, though often take up to 30min to prepare; there are six different varieties available, of which the seafood (海米, hǎimǐ) are the tastiest. Dumplings aside, there's a full menu of Chinese staples to choose from;

figure on around ¥40 per head, without drinks. Daily 11.30am–2pm & 5.30–8pm.

Gulou Jiaozi Guan 鼓楼饺子馆, gǔlóu jiǎoziguǎn. Corner of Shudian Jie and Sihou Jie. Housed in a mock Qing structure at the corner of Gulou Jie and Shudian Jie, this three-storey venue whips up round after round of succulent dumplings, and boasts tremendous views of the night market from its upper levels. Daily 10am–2pm & 5–8pm.

DIRECTORY

Banks and exchange The main Bank of China is on the corner of Xi Dajie and Song Jie, and there are several major banks with ATMs on Zhongshan Lu.

Mail and telephones There's a large post office (Mon–Fri 8am–noon & 2.30–6pm) on Ziyou Lu, with a 24hr telecom office next door.

PSB 86 Zhongshan Lu (daily 9am–noon & 3–5pm, ☎ 0378 5322242). Windows #3 and #4 deal with visas; it's a

relatively easy place in which to get a visa extension (¥160), which can take as little as 10min.

Shopping Kaifeng is a good place to find paintings and calligraphy, among the best buys in China. The obvious thing to pick up is a full-size reproduction of the *Qingming Shang He* scroll, which shouldn't set you back more than ¥80, or renowned New Year woodblock prints produced at the nearby town of Zhuxian. Try the shops on Song Jie and Shudian Jie.

The eastern seaboard

HUMBLE ADMINISTRATOR'S GARDEN, SUZHOU

5

The eastern seaboard

Encompassing the provinces of Shandong, Jiangsu and Zhejiang, China's eastern seaboard stretches for almost 2000km between the mouths of the Yellow and Yangzi rivers. These waterways have played a vital part in the cultural and economic development of China for the last two thousand years, and the area today remains one of the country's economic powerhouses. Including Shanghai, a city flanked by Jiangsu and Zhejiang, the eastern seaboard is home to nearly 250 million people – meaning that, if somehow cleaved from China, it would be the world's fourth most populous country. This makes for great transport infrastructure: comfortable, modern buses run along the many inter-city expressways, while the area has the country's highest concentration of high-speed rail routes. Yet, however modernized the eastern seaboard might be, with cities which rank among the most sophisticated in the land, there's plenty of visible history to get your teeth into as you journey around the region.

Shandong province is home to some small and intriguing places: **Ji'nan**, a large city in which you can go swimming in a hutong spring; **Qufu**, the birthplace of Confucius, with its giant temple and mansion; **Tai Shan**, one of the major pivots of the Taoist religion; and the coastal city of **Qingdao**, which offers a couple of beaches, swath of colonial architecture, lots of beer and seafood, and a ferry service to South Korea. Over in Jiangsu province there's **Nanjing**, China's large but likeable "southern capital", and wonderful **Suzhou**, whose centre is crisscrossed by gorgeous canals, and dotted with classically designed gardens. Heading further south to Zhejiang province one will undoubtedly stumble across **Hangzhou**, which Marco Polo termed "the most beautiful and magnificent city in the world"; its Xi Hu (West Lake), still recognizable from classic scroll paintings, is deservedly rated as one of the most scenic spots in China. The same can be said of the enchanting island of **Putuo Shan**, which juts out of the sea just east of the mainland.

The region's prosperity means that its **accommodation** is on the expensive side, though there are excellent youth hostels in almost all tourist centres. The **climate** varies a fair bit from north to south: Shandong's is similar to that of Beijing; while the Yangzi River region, despite being low-lying and far from the northern plains, is unpleasantly cold and damp in winter, yet also unbearably hot and sticky during the summer

GRAND CANAL, XITANG

Highlights

❶ Wangfu Chizi, Ji'nan Swim with China's fittest pensioners at this open-air pool, fed by spring water. **See p.284**

❷ Qufu Delve into the world of Confucius in the sage's charming home town. **See p.293**

❸ The Grand Canal The original source of the region's wealth, and a construction feat to rival the Great Wall. **See p.307**

❹ Suzhou A striking medley of tree-lined canals, ramshackle homes, old stone bridges and traditional Chinese gardens. **See p.318**

❺ Xi Hu, Hangzhou You will get great vistas from this beautiful lake, best appreciated by cycling the area. **See p.328**

❻ Moganshan An old colonial hill resort that has become fashionable as a summer retreat – it's a great spot for a brisk hike. **See p.335**

❼ Shaoxing Charismatic backwater once home to writer Lu Xun, whose elegant mansion – now a museum – offers a glimpse into a vanished world. **See p.336**

HIGHLIGHTS ARE MARKED ON THE MAP ON P.280

HIGHLIGHTS

1. Wangfu Chizi, Ji'nan
2. Qufu
3. The Grand Canal
4. Suzhou
5. Xi Hu, Hangzhou
6. Moganshan
7. Shaoxing

THE EASTERN SEABOARD

EAST CHINA SEA

— — — High Speed Rail line

0   100
kilometres

– Nanjing's reputation as one of the "three furnaces" of China is well justified. If possible, try to visit in spring (mid-April to late May), during which a combination of rain showers, sunshine and low humidity gives the terrain a splash of green as well as putting smiles on the faces of residents emerging from the harsh winter.

Brief history

The murky Yellow River oozes slowly across Shandong province and into the sea, and its dusty basin provided China with its original heartland – human settlements have existed in Shandong for more than six thousand years, with Neolithic remains indicating a sophisticated agricultural society. In the Warring States Period (720–221 BC), Shandong included the states of Qi and Lu, and the province is well endowed with ancient tombs and temples, not least thanks to the efforts of its most illustrious son, Confucius (see box, p.293).

The Yangzi basin

It was the lower Yangzi basin, however, which provided the power base for China's first empire. As early as the sixth century BC, the basin's flat terrain, large crop yield and superb communications offered by coastal ports and navigable waterways enabled the principal towns of the area to develop quickly into important trading centres. These presented an irresistible target for the expanding Qin dynasty, and in 223 BC the region was annexed, immediately developing into one of the empire's economic hubs. After the end of the Han dynasty in the third century AD, several regimes established short-lived capitals in southern cities; however, the real boost for southern China came when the Sui (589–618 AD) extended the Grand Canal to link the Yangzi with the Yellow River and, ultimately, to allow trade to flow freely between here and the northern capitals. With this, China's centre of gravity took a decisive shift south. Under later dynasties, Hangzhou and then Nanjing became the greatest cities in China, each serving as capital of the country at some point, and acting as counterweights to the bureaucratic tendencies of Beijing since its own accession to power.

Recent history

The area's recent history, though, has been dominated by foreign influence and its ramifications. The Treaty of Nanking, which ceded Hong Kong to Britain, was signed in Nanjing in 1842, after which the city itself became a treaty port. In 1897, the Germans arrived in Shandong, occupying first the port of Qingdao and then the capital, Ji'nan, their influence spreading further as they built a rail system across the province. Resentment at this interference, exacerbated by floods and an influx of refugees from the south, combined at the turn of the twentieth century to make Shandong the setting for the Boxer Rebellion (see p.919). Moving on a few decades, Nanjing was to suffer one of the world's worst ever massacres, with an estimated 300,000 civilians killed by Japanese soldiers in what is now known as the Rape of Nanking (see p.308).

Shandong

山东, shāndōng

Shandong province, encompassing a fertile plain through which the Yellow River completes its journey, was once one of the poorest regions of China, overpopulated and at the mercy of the river, whose course has continually shifted, bringing chaos with every move. Times have changed, and it is now one of the most **prosperous** provinces in the land. Visitors may also remark upon the friendliness of the people, who are proud of their reputation for hospitality, a tradition that goes right back to **Confucius**, a Shandong native who declared in *The Analects*, "Is it not a great pleasure to have guests coming from afar?"

5

Despite Shandong's new-found wealth, some of its most appealing attractions are as old as the hills. One actually *is* a hill, albeit a rather large one – **Tai Shan**, China's holiest Taoist mountain, and a favourite with hikers and temple-hunters alike. Also popular is little **Qufu**, formerly home to Confucius, and where a magnificent temple complex stands in his honour. The coast is lined with colossal cities, of which **Qingdao** proves the most attractive to visitors, as much for its beer as its ferry connections to Korea.

As far as tourists are concerned, there's little reason to stray from these areas, though other port cities offer **ferries** to South Korea and elsewhere in China, while highways are good and bus services frequent. The province is also home to new **high-speed rail** lines, which effortlessly zip from Beijing to Ji'nan, and thence south to Tai Shan and Qufu, or east to Qingdao.

Ji'nan

济南, jǐnán

Looking at the gleaming high-rises, wide boulevards and a modern maze of flyovers that characterize Shandong's capital, **JI'NAN**, it's hard to believe that this is the site of one of China's **oldest settlements**, inhabited for the last four thousand years. Though regularly ranked among China's most liveable cities, Ji'nan would barely register on the travel radar were it not for its **natural springs**, a series of clear blue upwellings set

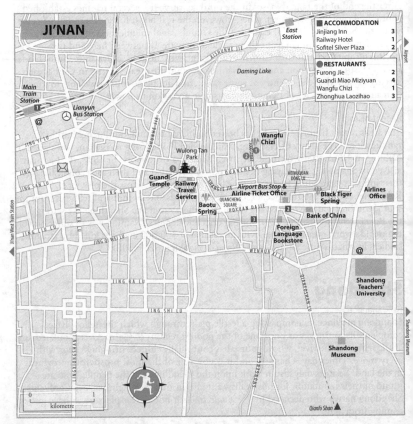

JI'NAN

East Station

■ **ACCOMMODATION**
Jinjiang Inn 3
Railway Hotel 1
Sofitel Silver Plaza 2

● **RESTAURANTS**
Furong Jie ....
Guandi Miao Miziyuan 4
Wangfu Chizi 1
Zhonghua Laozihao 3

Daming Lake

Main Train Station

Lianyun Bus Station

DAMINGHU LU

Wangfu Chizi

Wulong Tan Park

QUANCHENG LU

Guandi Temple

Railway Travel Service

HEIHUQUAN DONG LU

Airport Bus Stop & Airline Ticket Office

Black Tiger Spring

Airlines Office

Baotu Spring

QUANCHENG SQUARE

POYUAN DAJIE

Bank of China

Foreign Language Bookstore

WENHUA

Shandong Teachers' University

JING BA LU

JING SHI LU

N

Shandong Museum

0   1
kilometre

Qianfo Shan

5

> ### JI'NAN BY BOAT
>
> You can now explore parts of Ji'nan by boat, with regular departures heading clockwise around the city's waterways (¥10 per person per stop; ¥100 for the whole trip); they stop at ten stations on this 7km route, including Wulong Tan Park, Baotu Spring, Black Tiger Spring and Daming Lake.

among several urban parks – some of the cleanest water available in any Chinese city. These springs are close enough to each other to be connected on foot, but these days it's also possible to explore them by **boat** (see box above). Ji'nan has non-watery attractions too, particularly the **provincial museum** and the steep hillside at **Qianfo Shan**, respectively to the east and south of the city centre.

Wulong Tan Park

五龙潭公园, wǔlóngtán gōngyuán • Gongqingtuan Lu • Daily 7am–6pm • ¥5

The **Wulong Tan springs** have some serious pedigree – they were mentioned in the *Spring and Autumn Annals*, government texts of 694 BC. Nowadays the park enclosing them is a family favourite, with goldfish-filled ponds, flower-scented paths, and local kids spraying each other with pipe-like water-shooters; in the summer, it is tempting to take off your shoes and wade with them through the shallower ponds. In the east of the park is a modern hall to one of China's most famous female poets, **Li Qingzhao**, who was born in 1084 in Ji'nan – it contains extracts from her work and paintings by well-known contemporary artists.

Guandi Temple

关帝庙, guāndì miào • Daily 7am–7pm • Free

Just outside Wulong Tan's south gate is a tiny **Guandi Temple**, noted as the site where eunuch An Dehai, manipulative confidant of the Qing Empress Dowager Cixi, was executed by governor Ding Baozhen in 1869 after making an outrageously pompous, imperial-style tour of the nearby countryside. If you're peckish, try the wonderful *Guandi Miao Miziyuan* restaurant next door (see p.285).

Baotu Spring

趵突泉, bàotū quán • Luoyuan Lu • Daily 7am–6pm • ¥40

Ji'nan's famous **Baotu springs** are set in a captivating park full of shaded walkways, intricate flower gardens, delicate bridges and charming pagodas; elderly gents hone their calligraphy skills on the floor with spring water, while those visiting at the right time may well get to witness a musical performance of some kind. However, despite the park's undoubted splendour, it's worth noting that the Wulong Tan Springs (see above) are almost as good, and far cheaper to visit.

Black Tiger Spring

黑虎泉, hēihǔ quán • 24hr • Free

Behind a wall on Heihuquan Dong Lu, the famous **Black Tiger Spring** rises from a subterranean cave and emerges through tiger-headed spouts into a canal that once formed the old city's moat. People come here to fill up jerrycans from the spring and play in the water.

Daming Lake

大明湖, dàmíng hú • Daily 6am–6pm • ¥30

Large and handsome, and just north of the city centre, **Daming Lake** is surrounded by some quaint gardens, pavilions and bridges, edged with willow trees and sprinkled with water lilies. It makes a nice counterpoint to the city's springs, especially when accessed by boat (see above).

5

JI'NAN'S SECRET SPRING

Ji'nan is justly famed for its springs, but very few outsiders are aware of the quirkiest one in town – possibly the best-kept travel secret in the whole of Shandong. You won't find **Wangfu Chizi** (王府池子, *wángfǔ chízi*) on any tourist maps, and the pool's location at the centre of a labyrinthine tangle of alleyways makes it doubly difficult to track down, but your efforts will not go unrewarded. Edged with grey *hutong* buildings, this is essentially an **open-air swimming pool**, and the fact that it remains such an integral part of local life makes for quite a spectacle – lines of elderly men bob up and down on their daily laps, housewives engage in casual conversation while local youths whoop and shout as they scrub themselves clean on the western bank. The water quality isn't superb – spit, cigarette butts and ice-cream wrappers are inevitable – but it's hard to resist the temptation to join in the fun, even more so when being persuaded by a gaggle of bronzed and finely chiselled pensioners.

There's also a bit of **history** in the air – as may be inferred from its name, which roughly translates as "King's Abode Pool". Wangfu Chizi was once the property of a local prince, and the family still living on the north bank are descendants of former royal bodyguards. The pool maintains a temperature of around 16°C (ie, pretty cold) throughout the year, making for an ethereal effect in the winter, when mist rises from the waters and makes silhouettes of the swimmers. It's also worth dropping by in the late evening, when locals drain draught beer on the south bank while listening to the gentle lapping of waves.

Qianfo Shan

千佛山, qiānfó shān • Daily 8am–6pm • ¥30 • city bus routes include the #K51 and #K54 • taxi from the centre ¥15

A scenic spot worth a trip is **Qianfo Shan**, about 5km south of the city. Most of the original Buddha and Bodhisattva statues that once dotted the slopes of this "Thousand Buddha Mountain" were destroyed by Red Guards, but new ones are being added, largely paid for by donations from overseas Chinese. The mountainside is leafy and tracked with winding paths, the main one lined with painted opera masks; it's quite a climb to the summit (2hr), but the sculptures, and the view, get better the higher you go. Behind the **Xingguo Temple** near the top, you'll find some superb sixth-century Buddhist carvings.

Shandong Museum

山东博物馆, shāndōng bówùguǎn • Jingshiyi Lu • Tues–Sun 9am–5pm • Free (bring ID) • bus routes include the #18, #62 & #63 • taxi from the centre ¥20 • W sdmuseum.com

This beautifully designed new museum portrays the long history of Ji'nan city, and Shandong province as a whole. Exhibits are arranged over three large floors; the upper levels are of greatest interest, particularly the exhibits from excavations at Longshan and Dawenkou, two nearby Neolithic sites noted for the delicate black pottery unearthed there; the remains date back to 5000–2000 BC. Elsewhere there are a number of fine Buddhist carvings, Han **pictorial tomb reliefs**, Tang-dynasty tombstones, and a 22m-long Ming-dynasty **wooden boat**; the latter was excavated from the marshes southwest near Liangshan, the setting for China's Robin Hood epic, *Outlaws of the Marsh*.

ARRIVAL AND DEPARTURE	JI'NAN

BY PLANE

Yaoqiang International Airport (济南遥墙国际机场; *jǐnán yáoqiáng guójì jīchǎng*), which boasts international connections to Japan, South Korea and Hong Kong, is 40km northeast of the city. A taxi ride will set you back at least ¥100, while airport shuttles (6am–7pm; ¥20; hourly; 1hr) pick up and drop off at the airline ticket office opposite the *Sofitel Silver Plaza* hotel. This is also an easy place to buy flight tickets, though the main airlines office is at 95 Jiefang Lu (8am–5.30pm; 0531 86988777).

Destinations Beijing (3 daily; 1hr); Chengdu (5–6 daily; 2hr 25min); Chongqing (6 daily; 2hr); Guangzhou (6 daily; 2hr 30min); Kunming (5–6 daily; 3hr); Nanjing (2 daily; 1hr); Shanghai (hourly; 1hr 20min); Xi'an (3–4 daily; 1hr 30min); Yantai (4 daily; 50min).

BY TRAIN

Train tickets are not hard to get at the stations, though if there's a queue head to the desk in the *Railway Hotel*, on the station plaza; alternatively, there are ticket offices strewn across the city, including one opposite Wulong Tan Park (daily 8.30am–5pm; ☎0531 81817171).

Ji'nan station (济南站, jǐnán zhàn). Ji'nan's main train station is just to the northwest of the city centre. It receives some high-speed services, though for the rest you'll have to head to the West station.

Destinations Beijing (15 daily; 2–6hr); Qingdao (many daily; 2hr 30min–5hr 30min); Qufu (7 daily; 40min–2hr 30min); Shanghai (many daily; 4–14hr); Taishan (many daily; 17min–1hr); Yantai (10 daily; 6hr–7hr 30min).

Ji'nan West station (济南西站, jǐnán xīzhàn), handles many high-speed connections to Beijing, Shanghai and Qingdao. From here, a number of bus routes (¥1) head into the centre, or it's ¥10–15 by taxi from a surprisingly orderly rank.

Destinations Beijing (many daily; 1hr 30min–2hr); Qingdao (17 daily; 3hr); Qufu (19 daily; 30–50min); Shanghai (many daily; 3hr 20min–4hr); Tai'an (for Taishan; 17 daily; 18min).

BY BUS

Lianyun bus station (联运车站, liányùn chēzhàn) is the most convenient of several in the city, located on the train station square. Ji'nan is so well connected by train that the only buses you may need are those to Tai'an (1hr 30min) or Qufu (2hr 30min).

GETTING AROUND

By bus Many of the city's bus routes (¥1) begin from the train station, though given the layout of the city it's generally far easier to get a cab to your accommodation.

By taxi Taxis start at ¥8, and nowhere in the centre is more than ¥20 away.

ACCOMMODATION

Ji'nan's hotel situation is a little limited, as foreigners are excluded from the cheapest places.

Jinjiang Inn 锦江之星, jǐnjiāng zhīxīng. 5 Luowen Lu ☎0531 61316666, ⓦjinjianginns.com. The most central of Ji'nan's many branches of this budget option, with a winning location just off Quancheng Square; from here, pretty much all of the city's sights are within walking distance. Rooms are a little poky but will suffice for the price. **¥218**

Railway Hotel 铁道大酒店, tiědào dàjiǔdiàn. On the train station square ☎0531 86328888. Comfy three-star attached to the main train station; as such it's convenient for transport, though the surrounding area is not exactly appealing. Ask about discounts – rack rates can often be halved. **¥458**

Sofitel Silver Plaza 索菲特银座大酒店, suǒfēitè yínzuò dàjiǔdiàn. 66 Luoyuan Dajie ☎0531 86068888, ⓦsofitel.com. The pinnacle of luxury in Ji'nan, right in the heart of the city with views of Quancheng Square. The fittings here are quite superb, and rates are often discounted by half or more. **¥776**

EATING

The train station area is surrounded by the usual local and international chains, though there are far more appealing options in the city centre. The trendiest area at the time of writing – at least in a studenty, snack-style sense – was Furong Jie, an alley north of Quancheng Lu, and immediately west of the Wangfu Chizi spring (see p.284).

★ **Guandi Miao Miziyuan** 关帝庙 蜜脂园, guāndì miào mǐzhīyuán. Gongqingtuan Lu, near Wulong Tan Park ☎0531 86011251. Connected to the Guandi Temple (see p.283), though the door is sometimes closed, this is the city's best place in which to sample local Lu cuisine, all served up in a ramshackle courtyard filled with bamboo, carp and caged birds. Top picks from the helpful picture menu include tofu made with local spring water (¥48), and delicious local dumplings (¥58). Daily 11.30am–1.30pm & 5.30–8.30pm.

★ **Wangfu Chizi** 王府池子, wángfǔ chízi. The no-name snack shack at the Wangfu Chizi is the most atmospheric place to eat in town, with old men in bathing suits dropping by for snails, peanuts, barbecued shrimp and the like between swims, and occasionally somersaulting into the pool from above your head. Also a grand place for beer in the evenings – the local draught uses water from the Baotu Springs. Daily 9am–11pm.

Zhonghua Laozihao 中华老字号, zhōnghuá lǎozìhào. Puli Jie, just west of Wulong Tan Park's southern entrance. This decades-old dumpling restaurant is something of a local institution, and handily located. They've a few different varieties, each costing around ¥15 per portion; the pork and shrimp ones are usually best. Daily 8.30am–8.30pm.

DIRECTORY

Banks and exchange The Bank of China (Mon–Fri 8.30am–5pm) is on Poyuan Dajie, just east of the *Sofitel*.
Bookshop The Foreign Language Bookstore is on Chaoshan Jie, southwest of the *Sofitel*.

Mail and telephones Ji'nan's main post office (8am–4.30pm) is a red-brick building on Jing Er Lu, just west of Wei Er Lu. There's a 24hr telecom office inside.

5

Tai'an

泰安, tài'ān

Though one million visitors pass through scruffy **TAI'AN** each year, almost none of them is interested in the town itself – they're all here to see **Tai Shan**, the hulking mountain just to the north. Tai'an has, for centuries, served as a base for pilgrims, and on certain holy days ten thousand people at one time might be making their way up the crowded path to the peak.

Before heading off to join them, however, you should definitely visit **Dai Miao**, an important and ancient temple at Tai'an's centre. Just to the north of this temple are some busy **market streets** selling medicinal herbs that grow on the mountain, such as ginseng, the tuber of the multiflower knotweed and Asian puccoon, along with strange vegetables, bonsai trees and potted plants.

Dai Miao

岱庙, dài miào • Dongyue Lu • Daily 8am–5.30pm • ¥30

Dai Miao, the temple where emperors once made sacrifices to Tai Shan, is the traditional starting point for the procession up the mountain. It's a magnificent complex, with yellow-tiled roofs, red walls and towering old trees; there's a blend of buildings from different belief systems here, with veneration of the mountain as the only constant factor – the peak is, suitably, visible from many parts of the temple. Be sure to head up the steps by the north or south entrances; whether you're looking inside the halls or out to the mountains, the view from the perimeter path is quite spectacular.

Tiankuang Dian

Tiankuang Dian (Hall of the Celestial Gift), is matched in size only by halls in the Forbidden City and at Qufu. Construction started as early as the Qin dynasty (221–206 BC), though expansion and renovation have gone on ever since, particularly during the Tang and Song dynasties. Inside is a huge **mural** covering three of the walls, a Song-dynasty masterpiece depicting the Emperor Zhen Zong as the God of Tai Shan

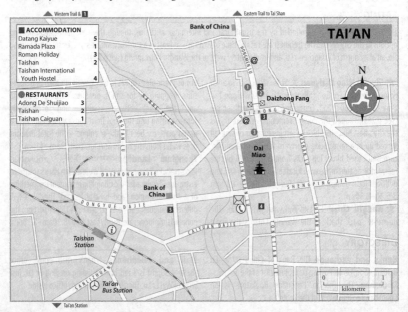

on an inspection tour and hunting expedition. The mural is fairly worn overall, but you can still see thousands of figures, each rendered in painstaking detail. There is also a **statue** of the God of Tai Shan, enthroned in a niche and dressed in flowing robes, holding the oblong tablet that is the insignia of his authority. The five sacrificial vessels laid before him bear the symbols of the five peaks.

The courtyards

The surrounding courtyards, halls and gardens are used as a museum for **steles**; the oldest, inside the **Dongyuzuo Hall**, celebrates the visit of Emperor Qin and his son in the third century BC. Many of the great calligraphers are represented here and even the untrained Western eye can find something to appreciate. Charcoal rubbings of the steles can be bought from the mercifully discreet souvenir shops inside the temple complex. The courtyards are also well wooded with cypresses – including five supposedly planted by the Han emperor Wu Di – ginkgos and acacias.

Temple of Yanxi

In a side courtyard at the back of the complex is the **Temple of Yanxi**. A Taoist resident on the mountain, Yanxi was linked with the mountain cult of the Tang dynasty. A separate hall at the rear is devoted to the Wife of the Mountain, a deity who seems somewhat of an afterthought, appearing much later than her spouse.

ARRIVAL AND DEPARTURE   TAI'AN

By train Tai'an has two stations, and it's important to note which one you'll be using. Tai'an station (泰安站, tài'ān zhàn) is a high-speed-only affair over 10km to the west of the centre; the central station, confusingly called Taishan (泰山站, tàishān zhàn), receives slower services. Bus #18 (¥2; 25min) connects the two stations at regular intervals, or it's ¥25 by taxi. For Ji'nan, you might as well take a slower train, since the time saved on a faster one will be cancelled out by the trip to the high-speed station; Qufu is best reached by bus, since Qufu's train stations are far from the centre.

Destinations from Taishan station Beijing (4 daily; 7–10hr); Ji'nan (many daily; 50min); Qingdao (10 daily; 6–7hr); Qufu (3 daily; 1hr 30min).
Destinations from Tai'an station Beijing (19 daily; 2hr); Ji'nan (many daily; 20min); Qingdao (1 daily; 3hr); Qufu (6 daily; 20min).
By bus The most useful by far of the city's many depots is Tai'an bus station (泰安汽车站, tài'ān qìchē zhàn) on Sanlizhuang Lu, south of the train station, which handles traffic from Ji'nan and Qufu.
Destinations Ji'nan (1hr 30min); Qufu (1hr).

GETTING AROUND

By bus Most of Tai'an's city buses run east–west through town along Dongyue Dajie: bus #3 connects to the mountain's western and eastern trailheads; #14 also goes to the eastern trailhead via Daizhong Dajie.
By taxi The minimum fare of ¥6 is sufficient for rides around town, with no more than ¥12 required to reach the mountain.

INFORMATION

Tourist office There is a small tourist office (24hr) in front of the train-station exit; they're well versed in the handing out of Tai Shan maps (¥5), and may be able to rustle up some train times, though don't expect anything as regards accommodation advice.

ACCOMMODATION

There's a mess of places to stay around Tai'an's arrival points, with a slightly more upmarket group of hotels clustered up between Dai Miao and the mountain's eastern trail on Hongmen Lu. While there's also accommodation on Tai Shan itself, it's expensive for what you get – see p.292.

Datang Kaiyue 大堂凯悦酒店, dàtáng kǎiyuè jiǔdiàn. 53 Dongyue Dajie ☎0538 8169999. Surprisingly plush for the price, the corridors of this hotel are lined with carpets of brown and gold, which lead to well-appointed rooms with flatscreen televisions. **¥388**

Ramada Plaza 东尊华美达大酒店, dōngzūnhuá měidá dàjiǔdiàn. 16 Yingsheng Dong Lu ☎0538 8368666, ⓦramadaplazataian.com. This superlative five-star resort basks in a stupendous location amid Tai Shan's rocky foothills. Decorated with the chain's signature

5

gold and dark reds, its rooms are little havens of comfort, and most provide stunning mountain views. It's a little outside town, but the on-site restaurants are the only upscale places to eat in Tai'an in any case. Ask about discounts – rack rates are regularly halved. **¥1160**

Roman Holiday 罗马假日商务酒店, luómǎ jiàrì shāngwù jiǔdiàn. 18 Hongmen Lu ☎ 0538 6279999. Motel-like venue that's excellent value for the price, and usefully located just north of Dai Miao, on the way to the eastern trailhead. Frosted glass walls mean that some bathrooms are a little visible from the beds, but some strategic curtain placement may come to the aid of those who want a little privacy. Do ensure first that your room has a window – some don't. **¥258**

Taishan 泰山宾馆, tàishān bīnguǎn. 26 Hongmen Lu ☎ 0538 8224678, ✆ www.taishan-hotel.com. Five-storey venue with smart, unfussy rooms; those on the northern side of the complex boast terrific Tai Shan views. They've also a decent on-site restaurant, located in an annexe across the car park. **¥498**

★ **Taishan International Youth Hostel** 泰山国际 青年旅舍, tàishān guójì qīngnián lǚshè. 8 Fuqian Lu ☎ 0538 6285196. Handily located a short walk from Dai Miao, this is a bit of a treat, with friendly staff, pine-clad dormitories and a reception desk that doubles as a café and bar of sorts. It's tucked away in a small alley behind a covered shopping arcade. Dorm beds **¥45**, doubles **¥150**

EATING AND DRINKING

Tai'an cuisine can be exquisite, particularly red-scaled carp, fresh from pools on the mountain and fried while it's still alive. In reality, few places now serve such delicacies, and the town is one of those places where you're best off hunting down a street shack for kebabs and beer – try the alleys south of the youth hostel, or the river bank just off Dongyue Dajie.

Adong De Shuijiao 阿东的水饺, ādōng de shuǐjiǎo. Hongmen Lu. Straightforward place serving simple, reliable Chinese staples – a decent option if you've just been hiking Tai Shan and are walking back into town. Daily 9am–8pm.

Taishan 泰山宾馆, tàishān bīnguǎn. 26 Hongmen Lu ☎ 0538 8224678. In theory, this hotel restaurant is one of the best places to eat in town, and one of the few places serving

carp prepared in the local style (¥170). In practice, it's in use more often as a conference or wedding venue. Hours vary.

Taishan Caiguan 泰山菜馆, tàishān càiguǎn. Hongmen Lu, directly opposite the Taishan hotel. A far more reliable and cheaper option than the hotel's own restaurant, specializing in tofu dishes: for ¥18 a serve, try the tofu dumplings (豆腐水饺 dòufu shuǐjiǎo) or fried tofu balls (豆腐丸子 dòufu wánzi). Daily 10am–8pm.

DIRECTORY

Banks and exchange The main Bank of China is located at 48 Dongyue Dajie, though a small branch with an ATM is uphill from the *Taishan* hotel.

Left luggage Both the train station and Tai'an bus station

have left-luggage facilities.

Mail The post office (Mon–Fri 8am–6pm) is on Dongyue Dajie, near the junction with Qingnian Lu.

Tai Shan

泰山, tàishān • Feb–Nov ¥127, Dec–Jan ¥102

Tai Shan is not just a mountain, it's a god. It's the easternmost and holiest of China's five major Taoist peaks (the other four being Hua Shan, the two Heng Shans and Song Shan), and has been worshipped by the Chinese throughout recorded history: the ascent is engrossing and beautiful – and very hard work.

Once host to emperors and the devout, Tai Shan is now Shandong's biggest tourist attraction, a religious theme park whose paths are thronged with a constant procession

---

TAOISM AT TAI SHAN

Taoism, after a long period of communist proscription, is again alive and flourishing at Tai Shan, and you're more than likely to see a bearded Taoist monk on the way up. Women come specifically to pray to **Bixia Yuan Jun**, the Princess of the Rosy Clouds, a Taoist deity believed to be able to help childless women conceive. Tai Shan also plays an important role in the **folk beliefs** of the Shandong peasantry (tradition has it that anyone who has climbed Tai Shan will live to be 100).

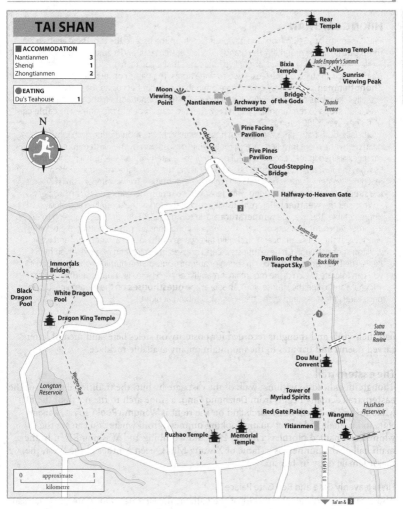

TAI SHAN

■ ACCOMMODATION

Nantianmen	**3**
Shenqi	**1**
Zhongtianmen	**2**

● EATING

Du's Teahouse	**1**

of tourists – alongside a significant number of genuine **pilgrims**. There are photo booths, souvenir stalls, soft-drinks vendors and teahouses; halfway up, there's a **bus station** and **cable car**. Yet Tai Shan retains an atmosphere of grandeur; the temples here – and the mountain itself – are magnificent enough to survive their trivialization.

Brief history

More so than any other holy mountain, Tai Shan was the haunt of **emperors**, and owes its obvious glories – the temples and pavilions along its route – to the patronage of the imperial court. From its summit, a succession of emperors surveyed their empires, made sacrifices and paid tribute. Sometimes, their retinues stretched right from the top to the bottom of the mountain, 8km of pomp and ostentatious wealth. In 219 BC, Emperor Qin Shi Huang had **roads** built all over the mountain so that he could ride here in his carriage under escort of the royal guards when he was performing the grand ceremonies of *feng* (sacrifices to heaven) and *chan* (offerings to earth). Emperors also

5

HIKING TAI SHAN

Tai Shan looms at 1545m high, and it's about 8km from the base to the top. There are **two main paths** up the mountain: the grand historical eastern trail, and a quieter, more scenic western trail. The ascent takes four or five hours, half that if you rush it, and the descent – almost as punishing on the legs – two to three hours. The paths converge at **Zhongtianmen**, the midway point (more often than not, climbers using the western route actually take a **bus** to Zhongtianmen, costing ¥30). After Zhongtianmen, the path climbs for over 6000 **steps** to the summit, though the sedentary can complete the journey by **cable car** (¥100 one-way, ¥200 return).

Officially, both path gates are open 24 hours; evening hikers should bring flashlights and head up by the more travelled eastern route while descending by the western route (the circuit explained in the account that follows). For the eastern route, walk uphill on Hongmen Lu from the *Taishan* hotel, or catch bus #3 or #9 along the way or from the train station. To reach the western route, take bus #3 (¥1) to its other terminus, Tianwaicun, or a taxi (¥7). Cross the street, ascend the stairs dotted with decorated columns, then descend to the bus park.

Whatever the **weather** in Tai'an, it's usually cold at the top of the mountain and always unpredictable. The average **temperature** at the summit is 18℃ in summer, dropping to -9℃ in winter, when the sun sets by 5pm. The summit conditions are posted outside the ticket windows at the park entrances. You should take warm clothing and a waterproof and wear walking shoes, though Chinese tourists ascend dressed in T-shirts and plimsolls, even high heels. The **best time to climb** is in spring or autumn, outside the humid months, though if you can tolerate the cold, the mountain is magnificent (and virtually untouristed) in winter.

If you want to see the sunrise, you can stay at the **guesthouses** on the mountain – though prices are almost as steep as the trail – or risk climbing at night.

---

had their visits and thoughts recorded for posterity on steles here, and men of letters carved poems and tributes to the mountain on any available rockface.

The eastern trail

Though most head to within a walk of the east gate by bus, the traditional ascent of the **eastern trail** actually begins from **Daizhong Fang**, a stone arch to the north of the Dai Miao in Tai'an. North of the arch and on the right is **Wangmu Pool** (王母池, wángmǔ chí), and a small and rather quaint-looking nunnery, from where you can see the whimsically named Hornless Dragon Pool and Combing and Washing River. In the main hall of the nunnery is a statue of Xiwang Mu, Queen Mother of the West, the major female deity in Taoism.

First Heavenly Gate and Red Gate Palace

About 500m up is the official start of the path, at the **First Heavenly Gate** (一天门, yītiān mén). This is followed by a Ming arch, said to mark the spot where Confucius began his climb, and the **Red Gate Palace** (红门宫, hóngmén gōng), where emperors used to change into sensible clothes for the ascent, and where you buy your ticket. Built in 1626, Hongmen Gong is the first of a series of temples dedicated to the Princess of the Rosy Clouds. It got its name from the two red rocks to the northwest, which together resemble an arch.

There are plenty of buildings to distract you around here. Just to the north is the Tower of Myriad Spirits, and just below that the Tomb of the White Mule is said to be where the mule that carried the Tang emperor Xuan up and down the mountain finally dropped dead, exhausted. Xuan made the mule a posthumous general, and gave it a decent burial.

Dou Mu Convent
斗母宫, dǒumǔ gōng
It's over 2km to the first sight of note on the hard slog uphill from the Red Gate Palace: the former **Dou Mu Convent**, a hall for Taoist nuns. Its date of founding is uncertain,

but it was reconstructed in 1542. Today, there are three halls, a drum tower, a bell tower and an ancient, **gnarled tree** outside, which is supposed to look like a reclining dragon. Like all the temple buildings on the mountain, the walls are painted with a blood-red wash, here interspersed with small grey bricks.

Sutra Stone Ravine

经石谷, jīngshí gǔ

North of Dou Mu Convent, a path veers east off the main route for about 1km to the **Sutra Stone Ravine**, where the text of the Buddhist Diamond Sutra has been carved on the rockface. This is one of the most prized of Tai Shan's many calligraphic works, and makes a worthwhile diversion as it's set in a charming, quiet spot.

Du's Teahouse

杜家茶馆, dùjiā cháguǎn · Daily 7am–sunset

One quirky sight, just off the main path, is **Du's Teahouse**, built on the spot where, more than a thousand years ago, General Cheng Yao Jin planted four pines, three of which are still alive. The teahouse, as well as everything in it, is quaintly built out of polished tree roots; the "maiden tea" is excellent, and a speciality of this mountain area.

Around Zhongtianmen

Reached through a tunnel of cypress trees, the **Teapot Sky Pavilion** (壶天阁, hútiān gé) is so called because the peaks all around supposedly give the illusion of standing in a teapot, and here you will see a sheer cliff rising in front of you, called **Horse Turn Back Ridge** (回马岭, huímǎlǐng); this is where Emperor Zhen Zong had to dismount because his horse refused to go any farther.

Not far above the ridge is **Halfway-to-Heaven Gate** (中天门, zhōngtiān mén), the midpoint of the climb. There are some good views here, though the **cable car** will be the most welcome sight if you're flagging. Confusingly, you have to descend two staircases and then follow the road round to continue the climb.

Cloud Stepping Bridge and Five Pines Pavilion

The first landmark north of Zhongtianmen is **Cloud Stepping Bridge** (云步桥, yúnbù qiáo). A stroll east you'll find **Five Pines Pavilion**, where the first Qin emperor took shelter from a storm under a group of pines. The grateful emperor then promoted the lucky pine trees to ministers of the fifth grade. From here you can see the lesser peaks of Tai Shan: the Mountain of Symmetrical Pines, the Flying Dragon Crag and Hovering Phoenix Ridge.

Archway to Immortality

升仙房, shēngxiān fáng

It's a tough climb from Cloud Stepping Bridge to the **Archway to Immortality**; no matter, since according to mountain myth, those who have made it this far are assured their longevity. It was the view from this point which inspired Tang poet Li Bai to write: "In a long breath by the heavenly gate, the fresh wind comes from a thousand miles away"; though by this point most climbers are long past being able to appreciate poetry.

To the summit

The **final section** of the climb is the hardest, as the stone stairs are steep and narrow, and ascend almost vertically between two walls of rocks, often through thick white mist – by this point, almost everyone is unashamedly grasping the handrails as they haul themselves upwards. And then suddenly you're at the top on **Tian Jie** (Heaven Street), a tourist strip where you can buy "I climbed Tai Shan" T-shirts, slurp a pot noodle and get your picture taken dressed as an emperor. There are a couple of **restaurants** here, **hotels** and a few **shops**. This thriving little tourist village represents a triumph of the profit motive over the elements; it's often so misty you can hardly see from one souvenir stall to the next.

Bixia Temple

碧霞寺, bìxiá sì

On the southern slopes of the summit, **Bixia Temple** is the final destination for most genuine pilgrims, where offerings are made to a bronze statue of the princess in the main hall. It's a splendid building, the whole place tiled with iron to resist wind damage, and all the decorations are metal, too. The bells hanging from the eaves, the mythological animals on the roof, and even the two steles outside are bronze. From 1759 until the fall of the Qing, the emperor would send an official here on the eighteenth day of the fourth lunar month each year to make an offering. Just below is a small **shrine to Confucius**, at the place where he was supposed to have commented, "the world is small".

Jade Emperor Temple

玉皇寺, yùhuáng sì

At the **Jade Emperor Temple**, you have truly arrived at the **highest point** of the mountain, and a rock with the characters for "supreme summit" and "1545m" carved on it stands within the courtyard. In Chinese popular religion, which mixes Taoism with much earlier beliefs, the Jade Emperor is the supreme ruler of heaven, depicted in an imperial hat with bead curtains hanging down his face. Outside the temple is the **Wordless Monument**, thought to have been erected by Emperor Wu more than two thousand years ago. The story goes that Wu wanted to have an inscription engraved that would do justice to his merits. None of the drafts he commissioned came up to scratch, however, so he left the stele blank, leaving everything to the imagination.

Sunrise Peak

Southeast of the Jade Emperor Temple is the peak for **watching the sunrise** (4.45am in June, 7am in December). It was here that the Song emperor performed the *feng* ceremony, building an altar and making sacrifices to heaven. On a clear day, you can see 200km to the coast, and at night you can see the lights of Ji'nan. There are numerous **trails** from here to fancifully named scenic spots; if the weather is good, and you've some energy left, it's a great place for aimless wandering.

The western trail

The best way down – and the one less likely to make jelly of your legs – is along the **western trail**, which is longer, quieter and has some impressive views. It diverges from the east trail at Zhongtianmen, loops round and joins the main trail back at the base of the mountain. Midway is the **Black Dragon Pool**, a dark, brooding pond, home of the Tai Shan speciality dish, red-scaled carp, once so precious that the fish was used as tribute to the court. Near the bottom, the **Puzhao Temple** (普照寺, pǔzhào sì) is a pretty, mostly Qing, temple complex. It's actually located between the eastern and western trails, and access is via the road that runs around the base of the mountain.

ACCOMMODATION AND EATING   **TAI SHAN**

There are plenty of places to eat along the eastern route to Zhongtianmen, but it's a good idea to take your own snacks as well; the food on offer past the midway point is unappealing and gets more expensive the higher you go. In all hotels, hot water is generally only available in the evening; some may be closed in the winter, when it's imperative to phone ahead.

Nantianmen 南天门宾馆, nántiānmén bīnguǎn. Near Nantianmen gate ☎ 0538 8330988. This basic hotel is wildly overpriced for what you get – many doubles have share bathrooms and you'll pay a fair bit more for en-suite. They have dormitory-style accommodation too, but you're usually required to book the whole room. Also has a restaurant serving simple Chinese staples. **¥480**

Shenqi 神憩宾馆, shénqì bīnguǎn. ☎ 0538 8223866.

Within sprinting distance of Sunrise Peak, this is the fanciest place to stay on the mountain, with passably comfy rooms. However, don't expect anything more than a place to bed down for the night – the televisions, for example, rarely work. **¥1600**

Zhongtianmen 中天门宾馆, zhōngtiānmén bīnguǎn. Near Tai Shan's midway point ⊕0538 8226740. Simple hotel though comfortable enough for a night. There's an on-site restaurant, but you'll save money by eating in one of the alternatives nearby. **¥480**

Qufu

曲阜, qǔfù

Though it may, at first glance, appear to be little more than a small town in the south of Shandong, **QUFU** is of immense importance. **Confucius** (孔子, kǒngzǐ) was born here around 551 BC, and, having spent his life teaching his moral code – largely unappreciated by his contemporaries – was buried just outside the town, in what became a sacred burial ground for his clan, the Kong. His teachings caught on after his death, however, and despite periodic purges, they have become firmly embedded in the Chinese psyche. All around Qufu is architectural evidence of the esteem in which he was held by successive dynasties – most monumentally by the Ming, who were responsible for the two dominant sights, the **Confucius Temple** and the **Confucius Mansion**, whose scale seems more suited to Beijing. For more on Confucius and Confucianism, see p.929.

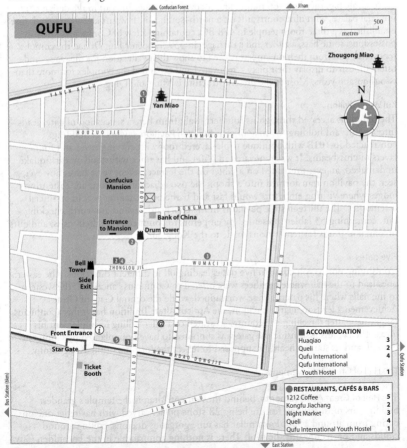

QUFU

ACCOMMODATION
Huaqiao	3
Queli	2
Qufu International	4
Qufu International Youth Hostel	1

RESTAURANTS, CAFÉS & BARS
1212 Coffee	5
Kongfu Jiachang	2
Night Market	3
Queli	4
Qufu International Youth Hostel	1

5

QUFU COMBINATION TICKETS

If you're interested in seeing the Confucius Temple, Mansion and Forest in a single day (quite possible, even if you start around midday), you'll save a little money by buying a **combination ticket** (¥150), sold at many hotels (usually for no extra charge), and outside the entrances to each site.

Qufu is an interesting place to spend a few days, with plenty to see concentrated in a small, walkable area, mostly within the confines of Qufu's flag-studded old town walls. As a major tourist destination, expect the usual crowds and hustles – especially around the end of September, **on Confucius's birthdate** in the lunar calendar, when a **festival** is held here and reconstructions of many of the original rituals are performed. If it all gets too much, there are places to escape amid old buildings, trees and singing birds, such as the **Confucian Forest** to the north.

Confucius Temple

孔庙, kǒng miào • Daily 8am–5pm • ¥90 • Ticket office is unmarked in English, just to the southeast of the Star Gate • audio-guides ¥20, plus ¥200 deposit

The **Confucius Temple** ranks among the greatest classical architectural complexes in China. It's certainly big: there are 466 rooms, and it's over 1km long, laid out in the design of an imperial palace, with nine courtyards on a north–south axis. It wasn't always so grand, first established as a three-room temple in 478 BC, containing a few of Confucius's lowly possessions: some hats, a zither and a carriage. In 539, Emperor Jing Di had the complex renovated, and from then on emperors keen to show their veneration for the sage – and ostentatiously to display their piety – renovated and expanded the complex for more than two thousand years. Most of the present structure is Ming and Qing.

Kui Wen Pavilion

The temple is accessed through its southern wall; from here a succession of gates leads into a courtyard holding the magnificent **Kui Wen Pavilion**, a wooden building constructed in 1018 with a unique triple-layered roof with curving eaves and four layers of crossbeams. It was renovated in 1504 and has since withstood an earthquake undamaged, an event recorded on a tablet on the terrace; recent years have, however, seen the pavilion transformed into a shop. The two adjacent pavilions are abstention lodges where visiting emperors would fast and bathe before taking part in sacrificial ceremonies. The **thirteen stele pavilions** in the courtyard beyond are worth checking out, containing 53 tablets presented by emperors to commemorate their visits, and gifts of land and funds for renovations made to the Kong family.

Five gates

Continuing north, you come to **five gates** leading off in different directions. The eastern ones lead to the hall where sacrifices were offered to Confucius's ancestors, the western to the halls where his parents were worshipped, while the central Gate of Great Achievements leads to a large pavilion, the **Apricot Altar**. Tradition has it that Confucius taught here after travelling the country in search of a ruler willing to implement his ideas. The cypress just inside the gate was supposed to have been planted by Confucius himself, and its state of health is supposed to reflect the fortunes of the Kong family.

The Hall of Great Achievements

大成殿, dàchéng diàn

The **Hall of Great Achievements**, behind the Apricot Altar, is the temple's grandest building, its most striking feature being 28 **stone pillars** carved with bas-relief dragons, dating from around 1500. Each pillar has nine gorgeous dragons, coiling around clouds and pearls towards the roof. There is nothing comparable in the Forbidden City

CONFUCIANISM IN MODERN CHINA

When the Communists came to power they saw Confucianism as an archaic, feudal system and an **anti-Confucius campaign** was instigated, which came to a climax during the Cultural Revolution. Now, however, conservatives frightened by the growing generation gap and the new materialism of China are calling for a **return to Confucian values** of respect and selflessness, just as their nervous counterparts in the West preach a return to family values. Confucian social morality – obeying authority, regarding family as the seat of morality and emphasizing the mutual benefits of friendship – is sometimes hailed as one of the main reasons for the success of East Asian economies, just as Protestantism provided the ideological complement to the growth of the industrialized West. As one Chinese visitor commented, "Confucius is the one Chinese leader who never let the people down".

in Beijing, and when emperors came to visit, the columns were covered with yellow silk to prevent imperial jealousy. Originally, the temple was solely dedicated to the worship of Confucius, but in 72 AD, Emperor Liu Zhuang offered sacrifices to his 72 disciples, too. Emperors of later dynasties (not wishing to be outdone) added more, and there are presently 172 "eminent worthies".

Hall to Qi Guan

Behind the Hall of Great Achievements is an inner hall for the worship of **Confucius's wife**, Qi Guan, who also, it seems, merited deification through association (though Confucian values placed women way down the social hierarchy, with wives less important than their sons, and daughters-in-law less important than anybody). The phoenixes painted on its columns and ceiling are symbols of female power, in the same way as the dragon symbolizes masculinity.

The Hall of Poetry and Rites

诗社堂, shīshè táng

Next to the Hall of Great Achievements, the eastern axis of the temple is entered through the **Gate of the Succession of the Sage**. Here is the **Hall of Poetry and Rites** where Confucius was supposed to have taught his son, Kong Li, to learn poetry from the *Book of Odes* in order to express himself, and ritual from the *Book of Rites* in order to strengthen his character.

The Lu Wall

A solitary wall in the courtyard is the famous **Lu Wall**, where Kong Fu, a ninth-generation descendant of Confucius, hid the sage's **books** when Qin Shi Huang, the first emperor (see p.213), persecuted the followers of Confucius and burned all his books. Several decades later, Liu Yu, prince of Lu and son of the Emperor Jing Di, ordered Confucius's dwelling to be demolished in order to build an extension to his palace, whereupon the books were found, which led to a schism between those who followed the reconstructed version of his last books, and those who followed the teachings in the rediscovered originals.

Site of Confucius's home

In the east wall of the temple, near the Lu Wall, an unobtrusive gate leads to the legendary **site of Confucius's home**, sandwiched between the spectacular temple and the magnificent mansion, a tiny square of land just big enough to have held a couple of poky little rooms.

The western section

The temple's **western section** is entered through the Gate of He Who Heralds the Sage, by the Hall of Great Achievements. A paved path leads to a high brick terrace on which stands the five-bay, green-tiled **Hall of Silks and Metals** and the **Hall of He Who Heralds the Sage**, built to venerate Confucius's father, **Shu Lianghe**. He was originally a minor military

5

official who attained posthumous nobility through his son. Behind is, predictably, the Hall of the Wife of He Who Heralds the Sage, dedicated to Confucius's mother.

Confucius Mansion

孔府, kǒng fǔ • Daily 8am–5pm • ¥60 • entrance just northwest of the Drum Tower

The First Family Under Heaven – the descendants of Confucius – lived continuously at the **Confucius Mansion** for more than 2500 years, spanning 74 generations. The opulence and size of the mansion testifies to the power and wealth of the **Kong clan** and their head, the **Yansheng Duke**. Built on a north–south axis, the mansion is loosely divided into living quarters, an administrative area and a garden. In the east is a temple and ancestral hall, while the western wing includes the reception rooms for important guests and the rooms where the rites were learned. Intricate and convoluted, this complex of twisting alleyways and over 450 rooms (most of them sixteenth-century) has something decidedly eccentric about it. Unfortunately, one reason is that so many of these rooms have been converted into shops – you only have to head a few kilometres north of town to see whether Confucius really is rolling in his grave.

The Great Hall and Hall of Withdrawal

In past the **old administrative departments** and through the **Gate of Double Glory**, the **Great Hall** was where the Yansheng Duke sat on a wooden chair covered with a tiger skin and proclaimed edicts. The flags and arrow tokens hanging on the walls are symbols of authority. Signs next to them reading "Make way!" were used to clear the roads of ordinary people when the duke left the mansion.

The residential apartments

The **residential apartments** of the mansion are to the north, accessible through gates that would once have been heavily guarded; no one could enter of their own accord under pain of death. Tiger-tail cudgels, goose-winged pitchforks and golden-headed jade clubs used to hang here to drive the message home. Even the water-carrier was not permitted, and emptied the water into a stone trough outside that runs through the apartment walls. A fire here during the twentieth century raged for three days as only twelve of the five hundred hereditary servants were allowed to go into the area to put it out.

THE YANSHENG DUKE AND THE KONG FAMILY

The status of the **Yansheng Duke** – the title given to Confucius's direct male descendant – rose throughout imperial history as emperors granted him increasing **privileges and hereditary titles**; under the Qing dynasty, he was uniquely permitted to ride a horse inside the Forbidden City and walk along the Imperial Way inside the palace. Emperors presented the duke with large areas of sacrificial fields (so called because the income from the fields was used to pay for sacrificial ceremonies), as well as exempting him from taxes.

The Kongs remained a close-knit family, practising a severe interpretation of **Confucian ethics** – any young family member who offended an elder was fined two taels (about 70g) of silver and battered twenty times with a bamboo club. A female family member was expected to obey her father, her husband and her son. One elderly Kong general, after defeat on the battlefield, cut his throat for the sake of his dignity. When the news reached the mansion, his son hanged himself as an expression of filial piety; after discovering the body, his wife hanged herself out of female virtue. On hearing this, the emperor bestowed the family with a board, inscribed "A family of faithfulness and filiality".

The Kong family enjoyed the good life right up until the beginning of the twentieth century. **Decline** set in rapidly with the downfall of imperial rule, and in 1940, the last of the line, **Kong Decheng**, fled to Taiwan during the Japanese invasion, breaking the tradition of millennia. His sister, **Kong Demao**, penned *In the House of Confucius*, a fascinating account of life lived inside this strange family chained to the past. Half of Qufu now claims descent from the Kongs, and it's by far the most common family name in the city.

The first halls

The first hall is the seven-bay **Reception Hall**, where relatives were received, banquets held and marriage and funeral ceremonies conducted. Today, the only remnants of its once-salubrious past are several golden throne chairs and ornate staffs. Directly opposite the Reception Hall, the **central eastern room** contains a set of furniture made from tree roots, presented to the mansion by Emperor Qianlong – an original imperial decree lies on the table.

Front Main Building

Past the outbuildings and through a small gate, you reach the **Front Main Building**, an impressive two-storey structure in which are displayed paintings and clothes. The eastern central room was the home of **Madame Tao**, wife of Kong Lingyi, the 76th duke. Their daughter, Kong Demao, lived in the far eastern room, while Kong Lingyi's concubine, Wang, originally one of Tao's handmaids, lived in the inner western room. It doesn't sound like an arrangement designed for domestic bliss; indeed, whenever the duke was away, Madame Tao used to beat Wang with a whip she kept for the purpose. When Wang produced a male heir, Tao poisoned her. A second concubine, Feng, was kept prisoner in her rooms by Tao until she died.

The rear building

The duke himself lived in the **rear building**, which has been left as it was when the last duke fled to Taiwan. Behind that is the garden where, every evening, flocks of **crows** come to roost noisily. Crows are usually thought to be inauspicious in China, but here they are welcome, and said to be the soldiers of Confucius, who protected him from danger on his travels. To the southeast of the inner east wing is a four-storey building called the **Tower of Refuge**, a planned retreat in the event of an uprising or invasion. The first floor was equipped with a moveable hanging ladder, and a trap could be set in the floor. Once inside, the refugees could live for weeks on dried food stores.

The temple

In the east of the complex you'll find the family temple, the Ancestral Hall and residential quarters for less important family members. The **temple** is dedicated to the memory of Yu, wife of the 72nd duke, and daughter of Emperor Qianlong. The princess had a mole on her face, which, it was predicted, would bring disaster unless she married into a more illustrious family. The Kongs were the only clan to fulfil the criteria, but the daughter of the Manchu emperor was not allowed to marry a Han Chinese. This inconvenience was got around by first having the daughter adopted by the family of the Grand Secretary Yu, and then marrying her to the duke as Yu's daughter. Her dowry included twenty villages and several thousand trunks of clothing.

Yan Miao

颜庙, yán miào • Daily 8am–5pm • ¥10

A little way northeast of the Confucius Mansion is the **Yan Miao**, a smaller temple dedicated to Yan Hui, who was regarded as Confucius's greatest disciple and sometimes called "The Sage Returned". A temple has been situated here since the Han dynasty, though the present structure is Ming. It's attractive, quieter than the Confucius Temple, and contains some impressive architectural details, such as the dragon pillars on the main hall, and a dragon head embedded in the roof. The eastern building now contains a display of locally excavated Neolithic and Zhou pottery.

Zhougong Miao

周公庙, zhōugōng miào • Daily 7.30am–4.30pm • ¥5

This temple, in the northeast of town, is dedicated to a Zhou-dynasty duke, a statue of whom stands in the main hall, together with his son Bo Qin and Bo Qin's servant.

5

Legend has it that Bo Qin was a rasher man than his father, and the duke, worried that his son would not act sensibly in state matters, inscribed a pithy maxim from his own political experience on a slate and directed the servant to carry it on his back. Whenever Bo Qin was about to do something foolish, the ever-present servant would turn his back so Bo Qin would think again. The open terrace before the hall, where sacrifices were made to the duke, contains a striking stone incense burner carved with coiling dragons.

The Confucian Forest

孔林, kǒng lín • Daily 8am–5pm • ¥40 • bus #1 via Gulou Nanjie and Gulou Beijie • taxi ¥10

The **burial ground** of the Kongs, this large, forested tract of land is situated 3km north of the town centre. The forest, like the temple, expanded over the centuries from something simple and austere to a grand complex, in this case centring around a single grave – **the tomb of Confucius**. Confucian disciples collected exotic trees to plant here, and there are now thousands of different varieties. It's an atmospheric place, sculptures half concealed in thick undergrowth, tombstones standing aslant in groves of ancient trees and wandering paths dappled with sunlight. A great place to spend an afternoon, it's one of the few famous scenic spots in China that it's possible to appreciate unaccompanied by crowds.

The Confucian cemetery

The imperial carriageway runs north, then west, from the forest's chunky main gate. Before long, you'll see a gateway and an arched stone bridge to your right; beyond this is the spot where Confucius and his son are buried. The **Hall of Deliberation**, just north of the bridge, was where visitors put on ritual dress before performing sacrifices. An avenue leads to the **Hall of Sacrifices**, and behind that to a small grassy mound – the **grave**. Just to the west of the tomb, a hut, looking like a potting shed, was where Confucius's disciples each spent three years watching over the grave. Confucius's son is buried just north of here. His unflattering epitaph reads: "He died before his father without making any noteworthy achievements".

According to legend, before his death Confucius told his disciples to bury him at this spot because the *feng shui* was good. His disciples objected, as there was no river nearby. Confucius told them that a river would be dug in the future. After the first Qin emperor, Qin Shi Huang, unified China, he launched an anti-Confucian campaign, burning books and scholars, and tried to sabotage the grave by ordering a river to be dug through the cemetery – thus inadvertently perfecting it.

ARRIVAL AND DEPARTURE   QUFU

The #K01 bus (¥3) links town to the bus terminal and both train stations; a taxi from the centre costs around ¥15 to the bus or main train stations, and ¥30–35 to the high-speed station.

By train Qufu station (曲阜站, qǔfù zhàn), served by very slow trains only, is inconveniently located 5km east of central Qufu. High-speed trains use new Qufu East station (曲阜东站, qǔfù dōngzhàn), a full 20km to the east. Tickets are easy to buy at either station, and there are several ticket offices in the town centre. Note that if you're going to Tai'an, it's easier to take the bus.
Destinations from main station Beijing (2 daily; 9–11hr); Ji'nan (4 daily; 2hr 40min); Kaifeng (1 daily; 8hr); Qingdao

(2 daily; 3hr 20min); Taishan (4 daily; 1hr 30min–2hr).
Destinations from East station Beijing (19 daily; 2hr 10min); Ji'nan (many daily; 30min); Kaifeng (1 daily; 4hr); Tai'an (8 daily; 20min).
By bus The bus station is 6km to the west of town on Jingxua Lu; you'll only really need it to get to Tai'an, and possibly Ji'nan. Buses on these routes dry up by 6pm.
Destinations Ji'nan (2hr 30min); Tai'an (1hr).

GETTING AROUND

By bus Once in town, the only city bus you'll need is the #1, which runs via Gulou Nanjie and Gulou Beijie to the Confucian Forest.

By taxi Taxis to anywhere in the town centre costs about ¥5.
By bicycle Qufu is a great place to get around by bike; the youth hostel rents them out (¥4 for 4 hours). Unfortunately,

the town's most bike-friendly sight – the Confucian Forest – did not allow bikes inside at the time of writing. It's worth asking at the hostel to see whether this has changed. **Local transport** A cycle-rickshaw ride, where the passenger is slung low in the front, giving an uninterrupted dog's-eye view of the street, costs from ¥5. Horse-drawn carts aimed strictly at tourists are not cheap; start the bidding at ¥30 for a ride to the Forest.

ACCOMMODATION

Accommodation in Qufu is surprisingly patchy, given the city's popularity with domestic tourists, and higher-end places are few and far between.

Huaqiao 华侨宾馆, huáqiáo bīnguǎn. Nanmadao Xijie ☎139 53711550. A comfy but basic hotel, conveniently located just east of the Star Gate – a busy area through the day, but near silent at night. **¥180**

Queli 阙里宾舍, quèlǐ bīnshè. 1 Queli Jie ☎0537 4866523, ⓦquelihotel.com. Located right next to the Confucius Temple and Mansion, this is the only real higher-end accommodation in town. Because of their trapped market, rooms are relatively poor value for money, but have satellite TV, 24hr hot water and English-speaking staff. Their on-site restaurant is the best place to eat in town. **¥568**

Qufu International 曲阜国际饭店, qǔfù guójì fàndiàn. 2 Hongdao Lu ☎0537 4418888. A typical Chinese tourist hotel, located just outside the city walls and hence underpatronized – which means it's easier to bargain rates down. Their rooms are absolutely fine, though the a/c doesn't always cool them down enough in summer. **¥380**

★ **Qufu International Youth Hostel** 曲阜国际青年旅舍, qǔfù guójì qīngnián lǚshè. Gulou Beijie ☎0537 4418989, ⓦwww.yhachina.com. What a lovely place this is: a pleasant, well-run hostel with decent bedrooms and amiable staff. Their bar/restaurant is a good place to make new travel buddies, and worth a visit even if you're not staying here. Dorm **¥45**, twins **¥128**

EATING AND DRINKING

Qufu's local specialities are great in number, and include such delicacies as fragrant rice and boiled scorpions soaked in oil. The Kong family also developed its own cuisine, featuring dishes such as "Going to the Court with the Son" (pigeon served with duck) and "Gold and Silver Fish" (a white and a yellow fish together); unfortunately, fewer and fewer places are serving these dishes. At night, Wumaci Dajie fills up with open-air food stalls, offering tasty-looking hotpots and stews. The food's not bad and the atmosphere is lively, though make sure you know the price before you order anything.

1212 Coffee 1212 咖啡, 1212 kā fēi. 9 Nanmadao Xijie. This three-level café is a neat recent addition to Qufu, a quiet, cutesey place with a lengthy coffee list (¥20–35). Quite out of keeping with the Chinese norm, they even have a few iced varieties, which can really help out on a hot day. Daily 10am–11pm.

Kongfu Jiachang 孔府家常, kǒngfǔ jiācháng. West of the Drum Tower. Overpriced but good-quality Qufu cuisine, with nice evening views of the Drum Tower, which stands a stone's throw away. There's no English or picture menu; their *yipin doufu* (一品豆腐, yīpǐn dòufu; ¥48), a slab of tofu stuffed with snail and all sorts of other goodies, is probably best. Daily 9am–10.30pm.

★ **Queli** 阙里宾舍, quèlǐ bīnshè. 1 Queli Jie. Good-value hotel restaurant, which whips up tasty local delicacies. Try the Qufu pancake, essentially a thin omelette smeared with shrimp paste and chicken mince (¥48), the yipin tofu (¥58), or spicy tofu soup (¥28). You could really push the boat out with the Gold and Silver Fish (¥208), while on the budget side there are plenty of Chinese staples in the ¥20–40 range. Daily 11am–2pm & 5–8pm.

★ **Qufu International Youth Hostel** 曲阜国际青年旅舍, qǔfù guójì qīngnián lǚshè. Gulou Beijie. This is as good as Western soul food gets in town, with a range of pizza, spaghetti and sandwiches, all backpacker friendly at ¥20–60. They also make superb shakes and good coffee, while at night it's a great place for a beer over a game of pool. Restaurant daily 8am–11pm, bar sometimes open a little later.

DIRECTORY

Banks and exchange There's a Bank of China near the corner of Dongmen Dajie and Gulou Nanjie.

Mail The post office is near the corner of Dongmen Dajie and Gulou Beijie.

Shopping There are plenty of stalls and shops selling tourist gimmicks all through town, exploiting the Confucian connection to the hilt. Most appropriate perhaps are books of translated Confucian sayings; these are available at the *Queli* hotel, but beware price tags covering their actual printed price. On Queli Jie, it's worth checking out the chops (which can be carved with your name in a few minutes), rubbings taken from steles in the temple, and locally crafted pistachio carvings. Get your scorpion essence – a local product, advertised as a general tonic – in the department stores on Wumaci Jie.

5

Qingdao

青岛, qīngdǎo

There's a lot to like about **QINGDAO** – and not just on account of its status as the home of **Tsingtao**, China's most famous beer. This fresh, modern city enjoys a charming, windswept location right next to the famed **Yellow Sea**, where you can chomp down superb seafood, hunt down a nearby beach, or prise sea creatures from their shells at low tide. It's also surprisingly cosmopolitan for a provincial Chinese city, the result of its former status as a German military base; take time to wander amid the red-roofed **Bavarian architecture** of the hilly old city centre. Modern Qingdao remains an important **port**, the fourth largest in the land; the city is connected by ferry to both Japan and South Korea, and is highly recommended as an introduction, or full stop, to a trip around China.

For all Qingdao's colourful history, its progress is relentlessly modern. The **2008 Olympics**, whose sailing events were held here, accelerated the rate of change, most evident in the skyscraper-filled new city sprouting to the east. For tourists, most places of interest are within the walkable, compact **old German town**; exceptions include a series of **beaches** dotted along the shoreline, and day-trips east to the famous peak of **Lao Shan**.

Brief history

Qingdao sprang to prominence in 1897, after two German missionaries were murdered here in a prelude to the **Boxer Rebellion** (see p.919). Following a hysterical speech by Germany's **Kaiser Wilhelm** (which coined the phrase "Yellow Peril"), the feeble Manchu court ceded the territory for 99 years, along with the right to build the Shandong rail lines. Qingdao made an ideal deep-water base for the German navy, and while they were here they established a **brewery** producing the now world-famous Tsingtao beer

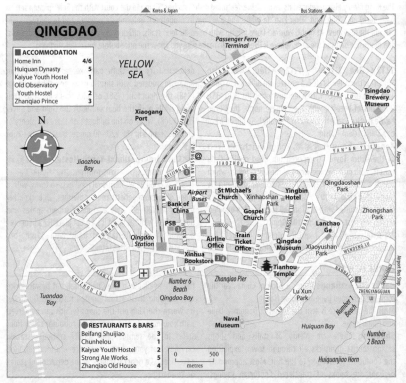

QINGDAO

■ ACCOMMODATION
Home Inn	4/6
Huiquan Dynasty	5
Kaiyue Youth Hostel	1
Old Observatory Youth Hostel	2
Zhanqiao Prince	3

● RESTAURANTS & BARS
Beifang Shuijiao	3
Chunhelou	1
Kaiyue Youth Hostel	2
Strong Ale Works	5
Zhanqiao Old House	4

YELLOW SEA

Korea & Japan

Bus Stations

Passenger Ferry Terminal

Xiaogang Port

Jiaozhou Bay

Tsingtao Brewery Museum

St Michael's Church

Airport Buses

Bank of China

PSB

Qingdao Station

Airline Office

Xinhua Bookstore

Yingbin Hotel

Xinhaoshan Park

Gospel Church

Train Ticket Office

Qingdao Museum

Tianhou Temple

Qingdaoshan Park

Lanchao Ge

Xiaoyushan Park

Zhongshan Park

Number 6 Beach

Qingdao Bay

Tuandao Bay

Zhanqiao Pier

Lu Xun Park

Naval Museum

Huiquan Bay

Number 1 Beach

Number 2 Beach

Huiquanjiao Horn

Airport

Airport Bus Stop

0   500
metres

5

("Tsingtao" being the old transliteration of Qingdao). However, the city was forcibly taken from Germany in 1914 by the **Japanese** and later gifted to Japan at the Treaty of Versailles, an event that led to nationwide demonstrations which eventually saw Qingdao returned to China in 1922.

The churches

Gospel Church daily 8am–5pm • ¥7

Anchoring the old German town is the fine **St Michael's Church** (天主教堂, tiānzhǔ jiàotáng), whose distinctive double spires can be seen from all over the western parts of the city; it's a favourite with those taking wedding photos. Poke down the streets east of here – some are cobbled affairs lined with pink buildings, whose black iron balconies overlook the street. Farther east on Jiangsu Lu, there's the 1908 **Gospel church** (基督教堂, jīdū jiàotáng), built of solid stone and with a dark blue tin clocktower; you can climb up for a closer look at the various cogs and pulleys.

Qingdao Museum

青岛市博物馆, qīngdǎoshì bówùguǎn • Daxue Lu • Tues–Sun 9am–4.30pm • Free

The **Qingdao Museum** is housed in a beautiful, temple-like building, which in the 1930s was the headquarters of the sinister-sounding Red Swastika Association, a welfare institute. There's a collection of paintings here from the Yuan through to Qing dynasties, and four large **Buddhas** dating back to 500–527 AD – slim striking figures with bulbous, smiling heads, one hand pointing upward to heaven, the other down to the earth. Some halls double as space for contemporary art exhibits.

Tsingtao Brewery Museum

青岛啤酒博物馆, qīngdǎo píjiǔ bówùguǎn • 56 Dengzhou Lu • Daily 8.30am–4.30pm • ¥50 • ☏ 0532 83833437

For a great many visitors to Qingdao – Chinese as well as foreign – one essential city sight is the **Tsingtao brewery**, a pretty red-brick affair built in 1903. There's a small, rather tame, museum located here, though happily the ticket includes a few glasses of beer from the brewery lines themselves. You'll be able to buy more from the on-site bar, or "Beer Street", opposite the gates.

The seafront

Qingdao's **beaches**, with fine white sand, are busy places in the summer, when holidaymakers come to promenade or just slump and look out to sea against a backdrop of pine trees. **Kite flying** is popular, too – some of the country's best kites are made at the nearby city of Weifang. Closest to the old town, **Number 6 beach** is at the

---

TSINGTAO BEER

Many a Western traveller arrives in Qingdao with a nagging sense of familiarity regarding the city's name: this is the home of **Tsingtao**, China's undisputed number-one beer. The confusion stems from its non-pinyin romanization, which can be directly attributed to the brewery's age; it was started way back in 1903 (when Chinese used the Wade-Giles transliteratory system) as a German-British joint venture, before coming under **Japanese** control during their occupation of Qingdao. The Japanese ramped up production and essentially transformed Tsingtao from a pumped-up microbrewery to a national success story. During the first decades of **Communist control**, Tsingtao beer was pretty much the only product exported from China.

As in the rest of China, bottles of Tsingtao can be bought all over the city. However, it would be a shame to leave Qingdao without buying the unpasteurized **draught** version, sold in plastic bags on the streetsides – getting the nectar into the bag without spillage is something of an art form. Tsingtao also takes pride of place during the August **International Beer Festival** (see ⓦ thatsqingdao.com for information), which is held at the International Beer City, way out to the east of town.

5

bottom of Zhongshan Lu; it's small but has the liveliest social scene, with crowds promenading along **Zhanqiao Pier** and numerous little stalls lining Taiping Lu selling gaudy swimsuits and cheap souvenirs.

Naval Museum

海军博物馆, hǎijūn bówùguǎn • off Laiyang Lu • Daily 8am–5pm • ¥50

This quirky museum is easily visible from the southern boundary of the old town – its halls comprise one **submarine** and one **destroyer** which, though decommissioned long ago, still bob up and down in the water. The submarine is the more interesting of the two, its narrow, dark rooms arrayed with masses of chunky old valves, dials, levers and knobs, many of them bearing Russian markings. Note that you may be asked to leave your camera at the ticket booth – a little oversensitive, since both exhibits are virtually antiques.

Number 1 beach

The old town ends abruptly with a flurry of high-rises and paved plazas at **Number 1 beach**, which is the best in town – and the longest too, at over 580m. In season, it's packed with ice-cream vendors, trinket stalls and a rash of photographers. There are beachball-shaped changing huts, showers, multicoloured beach umbrellas, and designated swimming areas marked out with buoys and protected by shark nets. The water, however, is like Chinese soup – murky and warm, with unidentifiable things floating in it – so swimming is not recommended.

ARRIVAL AND DEPARTURE   QINGDAO

By air Liuting International Airport (青岛流亭国际机场, qīngdǎo liútíng guójì jīchǎng) links Qingdao with Germany, Japan, Singapore, South Korea and Taiwan, as well as many domestic destinations. It lies 30km to the northeast of the centre, the intervening distance spanned by taxis (¥100) or airport buses (¥20; 1hr). There are three bus lines to choose from: take the one heading to Zhongshan Lu, which drops off outside an airlines office (📞 0532 2895577). To head to the airport, you can find this stop just up the road from the *KFC* (and opposite *McDonald's*); the buses leave at 40 minutes past the hour.
Destinations Beijing (hourly; 1hr 15min); Chengdu (5 daily; 2hr 30min); Chongqing (4 daily; 1hr 30min); Guangzhou (8 daily; 3hr); Hangzhou (10 daily; 1hr 30min); Hong Kong (1–2 daily; 3hr); Kunming (2 daily; 3hr); Nanjing (3–5 daily; 1hr); Shanghai (hourly; 1hr 15min); Xi'an (5–6 daily; 1hr 50min); Zhengzhou (3 daily; 1hr 10min).
By rail Qingdao station (青岛站, qīngdǎo zhàn), built along German architectural lines, is conveniently located in the area of greatest tourist interest; trains run north to Yantai, and west to Ji'nan and beyond. High-speed trains stop here, though in due course most services will shift to a new station being constructed to the north. There are ticket

offices dotted all over the city (usually open 8am–6pm); ask at your accommodation for the one closest to you.
Destinations Beijing (12 daily; 4hr 30min–5hr 20min); Ji'nan (many daily; 2hr 30min–4hr 30min); Qufu (2 daily; 3hr 20min); Shanghai (4 daily; 6hr 40min); Tai'an (11 daily; 3–7hr); Xi'an (3 daily; 21hr); Yantai (1 daily; 4hr 45min).
By bus Qingdao's main bus terminal (青岛汽车站, qīngdǎo qìchē zhàn) is over 6km north of town; bus #5 runs from here down to the seafront at Taiping Lu. The most useful services are to Yantai (2 hourly; 3hr), though departures to a multitude of destinations are available.
By ferry The passenger-ferry terminal (大港客运站, dàgǎng kèyùnzhàn) hosts ferries from Japan and South Korea. It's located just north of the old town – bus #303 heads to the train station area and #8 to Zhongshan Lu, though it'll only cost around ¥12 by taxi. The cheapest tickets buy comfy capsule-like berths with dividing curtains; paying a bit more gets you a berth in a private room, in which instance you'll likely be bundled in with another foreigner. In addition to the ticket, expect to pay around ¥60 in fuel and port surcharges.
Destinations Incheon, Korea (Mon, Wed & Fri; 16hr; ¥750–1090); Shimonoseki, Japan (Mon & Thurs; 36hr; ¥1100–1800).

GETTING AROUND

By bus Qingdao has a decent bus system, but you may not need to use it – the city centre is compact, and actually quite interesting to walk around (if, on occasion, a little hilly).
By taxi Flagfall is ¥9, and you should be able to get anywhere in the centre for under ¥20; note that some

"luxury" taxis start at ¥12 instead, and rise in price far more quickly.
By subway The first line of the new Qingdao Metro system – confusingly named Line #3 – is scheduled to commence operations in late 2014, heading to the new town from the Taiping Lu seafront area.

INFORMATION

Magazines There's plenty of expat-oriented information in *Red Star* (ⓦ myredstar.com), an excellent monthly magazine. The team also puts out a quirky pack of cards highlighting 52 top Qingdao venues.

ACCOMMODATION

Qingdao's old town has abundant accommodation and, though the city's newest, flashest places are much further east, there's a good range here.

Home Inn 如家酒店, rújiā jiǔdiàn. 52 Danxian Lu, just off Guizhou Lu ⓣ0532 82669000, ⓦhomeinns .com. Usual good value offered by this motel chain – book ahead if possible. There's another branch nearby at 62 Fuzhou Lu, if they're full here. **¥188**

Huiquan Dynasty 汇泉王朝大酒店, huìquán wángcháo dàjiǔdiàn. 9 Nanhai Lu ⓣ0532 82999888, ⓦwww.hqdynasty.com. A well-located five-star hotel – the beach is directly opposite, and there's a nice indoor pool if you fancy cleaner water to swim in. Many rooms have fantastic views, as does the nifty revolving restaurant way up on top, which serves a mix of local and international food. **¥850**

★ **Kaiyue Youth Hostel** 凯越国际青年旅馆, kǎiyuè guójì qīngnián lǚguǎn. 31 Jining Lu ⓣ0532 82845450, ⓦyhaqd.com. Situated near some of the town's older colonial quarters, and inside what was once a church, this is a lovely place to stay, and the staff can

organize all watersports plus kite-flying activities. The basement bar is also hugely popular. Dorms from **¥40**, doubles **¥149**

Old Observatory Youth Hostel 奥博维特国际青年旅馆, àobówéitè guójì qīngnián lǚguǎn. 21 Guanxiang Er Lu ⓣ0532 82822626, ⓦyhachina.com. Housed in a former observatory, this offers (predictably) good views, best taken in over coffee or beer from its rooftop café. Pick-up is available from the train station or ferry terminal. Dorms from **¥70**, doubles **¥380**

Zhanqiao Prince 栈桥宾馆, zhànqiáo bīnguǎn. 31 Taiping Lu ⓣ0532 82888666, ⓦzhanqiaoprince hotel.com. Elderly hotel with heaps of character from the wood-panelled lobby upwards, and featuring the excellent *Zhanqiao Old House* restaurant on the lobby floor. Sun Yatsen stayed here once, too, though he probably didn't have to pay ¥130 extra for a sea view. **¥628**

EATING AND DRINKING

Qingdao has ample restaurants to choose from. The speciality is seafood; mussels and crabs here are particularly good, and there are plenty of small, noisy and busy seafood places in the streets leading down to the coast, where competition means standards are high, and, with some exceptions, costs are reasonably low. Nightlife isn't as exciting in the Old Town as you'll find out east in the city centre – see ⓦ myredstar.com for up-to-date listings information. In the centre, you'll see umpteen bars selling draught Tsingtao from large outdoor barrels; the stout version is available in stubby bottles from restaurants around the city.

Beifang Shuijiao 北方水饺, běifāng shuǐjiǎo. 26 Hubei Lu. At the corner of Henan and Hubei streets, this friendly place specializes in seafood; try their black-ink rice, served with pine nuts and slices of meat pancake (¥50). They also serve jiaozi and simple rice-and-noodle staples. Daily 6am–9pm.

Chunhelou 春和楼饭店, chūnhélóu fàndiàn. 146 Zhongshan Lu ⓣ0532 82824346. Dating back to 1891, this is one of Qingdao's most famous eateries, and is suitably heaving in the evenings – head up to the top floor for generous portions of spiced chicken (around ¥30 per head). Daily 11am–3pm & 5–10pm.

Kaiyue Youth Hostel 凯越国际青年旅馆, kǎiyuè guójì qīngnián lǚguǎn. 31 Jining Lu ⓣ0532 82845450. The basement restaurant-bar in this excellent hostel is extremely popular – not just with travellers, but young locals, and the elements of the Qingdao expat crowd. Pizzas (from ¥50) are the pick of the food choices; beer runs from ¥18 a bottle, and is best enjoyed with new

friends, over the pool or table football. Daily 8am–midnight.

★ **Strong Ale Works** 10 Daxue Lu, opposite the museum. Sometimes referred to as the *SAW House* or the *Taphouse*, this American-run microbrewery pumps out rounds of delectable bitter, coffee stout, pale ale, and whatever else they've been brewing; they go for ¥25 a glass, and for ¥10 more you can have them served with a German sausage. Daily from noon until custom dies down.

★ **Zhanqiao Old House** 栈桥宾馆, zhànqiáo bīnguǎn. 31 Taiping Lu ⓣ0532 82888666. Surprisingly reasonable prices at this restaurant, which sits pretty in the bowels of the *Zhanqiao Prince* hotel, and offers shimmery ocean views. Fish is the speciality, including sea bass and Japanese-style sashimi, but simple mains (¥20 or so) are on offer for those who want a promenade view without breaking the bank. The seafood soup (¥48) is highly recommended. Daily 10am–10pm.

5

DIRECTORY

Banks and exchange The Bank of China (Mon–Fri 8.30am–5pm, Sat & Sun 9.30am–4pm), which has an ATM, is at 62 Zhongshan Lu.

Bookshop The Xinhua Bookstore is at 10 Henan Lu, just south of Hubei Lu.

Mail and telephones The main post office and telecom building (Mon–Sat 8am–6pm) is about halfway along Zhongshan Lu.

PSB The PSB (Mon–Sat 8am–noon & 2–7pm) is at 29 Hubei Lu, not far from the train station.

Lao Shan

崂山, láo shān

The **Lao Shan** area, 400 square kilometres of rugged, mountainous coast 40km northeast of Qingdao, makes an easy day-trip from the city. It's a good place to **hike** around, dotted with caves, springs and waterfalls amid striking scenery, among which it's possible to lose the crowds and trinket stalls. Writers have been inspired by the landscape for centuries – *Strange Stories from a Chinese Studio* by the Qing-dynasty author **Pu Songling** (see p.956) was written here – and have left noble graffiti in the form of poems and sage reflections cut into rocks all round the area. Jiushui Valley here is also the source of **Lao Shan mineral water**, which gives Tsingtao beer its taste; it's one of the few Chinese mineral waters that doesn't taste of swimming pools.

Ju Feng

巨峰, jù fēng • April–Oct ¥80, Nov–March ¥50 • cable car ¥40 each way

Rising 1133m above sea level, **Ju Feng** is Lao Shan's apex. From the bus drop-off point a pathway of stone steps, constructed a century ago by the enterprising German Lao Shan Company to cater for their compatriots' weakness for alpine clambering, runs all the way to the summit and then back down a different route on the other side. The **path** climbs past gullies and woods, streams and pools, and the ascent should take around three hours; you're able to shorten this with a cable-car ride from the base. There's a temple halfway up, where you can fortify yourself with fruit and tea for the final haul. At the **summit**, a ruined temple now houses a meteorological station. The view is great, and gets even better as you descend by the alternative route back to the village.

Taiqing Gong

太清宫, tàiqīng gōng • park entry (including temple ticket) April–Oct ¥90, Nov–March ¥60 • temple ¥20 • cable car ¥35 one-way, ¥60 return

Taiqing Gong, a temple to the south of Lao Shan, is the oldest and grandest of local temples, consisting of three halls set amid old trees – some dating back to the Han and Tang dynasties – and gardens. Outside the first hall are two camellias about which Pu Songling wrote a story. There are nine other temples nearby, which, are peaceful places.

ARRIVAL AND DEPARTURE   LAO SHAN

By bus Public bus #304 (¥8; 1–2hr) leaves frequently from the east side of the train station, dropping you at Yakou (哑口, yākǒu), the easternmost part of the Lao Shan area. Plenty of other buses come here from other parts of Qingdao.

By minibus Early-morning minibuses depart Qingdao from Taiping Lu, west of the pier, and do rounds of Lao Shan

sights. The drivers are extremely unlikely to speak any English, but should be able to point out where they're going on a map. They can cost anything from ¥30–130 per person, depending upon whether Lao Shan tickets are included, and how many shopping stops they make on the way there and back.

GETTING AROUND

Buses There are shuttle buses between the various sights in each area of the park, and these will be included within the price of your ticket.

DIRECTORY

Maps It's definitely worth getting a map of Lao Shan – detailed spreads are printed on the back of most Qingdao city maps.

Yantai

烟台, yāntái

On the Yellow Sea in northern Shandong, **YANTAI** is a bustling place with a burgeoning port. Tourist sights are thin on the ground, however, and things are rather pricey – the main reason to visit the area is to pick up **ferries** to Dalian, or even Korea (see p.306). Away from the transit points along scruffy Beima Lu, Yantai is quite a modern place, with a busy shopping district on **Nan Dajie** south of the port.

Yantai Folk Museum

烟台民俗博物馆, yāntái mínsú bówùguǎn • 2 Yulan Jie • Tues–Sun 8am–4.30pm • Free (bring ID)

Yantai's **folk museum** is housed in a beautiful old guild hall, set up around the turn of the nineteenth century by Fujianese merchants and shipowners. It remains most notable for its architecture; the main building here is the **Tian Hou Miao**, a temple to the southern Chinese sea goddess, whom sailors trust to guide ships to safety. The temple itself was brought from Fujian by ship in 1864 and is a good example of southern architecture, with its richly carved wooden roof beams, eaves and panels illustrating historical scenes, and sweeping, pronged roofline fancifully ornamented with mythical figures in wood, stone and glazed ceramics. The whole temple complex is set in a little garden with pools and a stage (the goddess is said to have been fond of plays).

Wine Museum

张继酒文博物馆, zhāngjì jiǔwén bówùguǎn • Beima Lu • Daily 9am–5.30pm • ¥50, including wine tasting

Yantai's **Wine Museum** is worth a look, not so much for the humdrum historical exhibits but because – rarely for China – they produce a grape wine that is actually drinkable. Make sure you descend in to the vast **cellar** where, sitting proud and beribboned among lesser casks, are the three-century-old "Barrel Kings", each holding fifteen tonnes. You can have a go at bottling in cellar 4, or make your way straight to the **bar** in cellar 5 for your samples – the twelve-year-old red is excellent, as is their brandy, both of which are on sale in the museum shop.

The seafront

Yantaishan Park • Daily 7am–6pm • ¥30

After seeing the museums you've pretty well exhausted Yantai's attractions, though the **seafront** is pleasant on a good day. **Yantaishan Park** (烟台山公园, yāntáishān gōngyuán), marking the eastern edge of the port area, features a steep hill where the locals used to keep an eye out for pirates, all latticed with twisting paths, pavilions, a couple of former consulates and an old Japanese military camp. The city's two **beaches** are both east of

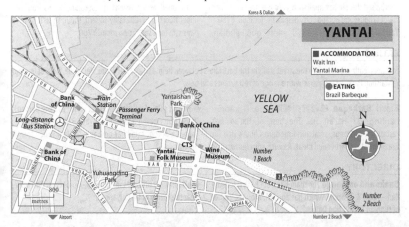

5

FERRIES TO KOREA

In addition to services from Qingdao (see below), two other Shandong ports – Yantai and Weihai – offer ferry connections to **Incheon** in South Korea, only one hour from Seoul by subway train. **Tickets** can be bought in advance from travel agencies, or at the terminals themselves. There are several classes on each vessel, with gradations in price as you move down the scale. You will also have to pay a **departure tax** and **fuel surcharge**, totalling around ¥60.

Ferries leave **Yantai** on Monday, Wednesday and Friday; the journey takes 12 hours and tickets start at ¥960. Tickets can be bought at the terminal, or from CTS (☎0535 6231539, 6216533 or 6611582), on Beima Lu. From **Weihai** (威海, wēihǎi), 80km east of Yantai, ferries leave on Sunday, Tuesday and Thursday; the journey takes 14 hours and tickets start at ¥750.

---

here, but they're not great – littered, windy and hemmed in by unattractive buildings. Number 2 beach, the farther of the two, is the better, though the water is very polluted.

ARRIVAL AND DEPARTURE   YANTAI

By air Yantai's airport (烟台莱山国际机场, yāntái láishān guójìjīchǎng) is 15km south of the city; shuttle buses (¥10) run from here to the bus station, or a taxi will cost around ¥60. There are plenty of airline offices in town, including one (☎0535 6669777) on Da Haiyang Lu, near the train station.

Destinations Beijing (7–8 daily; 1hr 15min); Hong Kong (2 weekly; 3hr 30min); Ji'nan (1–2 daily; 50min); Nanjing (1–2 daily; 1hr 20min); Shanghai (9 daily; 1hr 30min).

By train The station (烟台站, yāntái zhàn) is handily located just to the west of the centre, though out of keeping with most of eastern China, it's yet to receive high-speed services.

Destinations Beijing (2 daily; 15–17hr); Ji'nan (10 daily; 7–8hr); Qingdao (1 daily; 4hr 30min).

By bus Yantai's main bus station (汽车总站; qìchē zǒngzhàn) is about 1km west of the train station on Qingnian Lu, though sometimes you get dropped in the train station forecourt. The only connections you're likely to need are those to Qingdao (2 hourly; 3hr), since there's still only one daily train connecting the two cities.

By ferry The port (烟台港, yāntái gǎng), just east of the train station, handles international services to Korea, as well as domestic ferries to Dalian (4–6 daily; 6–7hr; ¥170–800); some of the latter run overnight, in which case you're advised to book a sleeper berth. There are ticket offices in the terminal – you'll have to run between the various companies' booths to find the service you need – and several more around the train station.

ACCOMMODATION

The rail and port areas are flooded with hotels charging just ¥100 for a double, though not all will take foreigners.

Wait Inn 维特酒店, wéitè jiǔdiàn. 78 Beima Lu ☎0535 2120909. Visible from the train station exit, this newly refurbished cheapie has small rooms but is otherwise a good budget choice, and not too noisy despite the location. **¥180**

Yantai Marina 烟台国际酒店, yāntái guójì jiǔdiàn.

128 Binhai Beilu ☎0535 2129999, ⓦytmarina.com. A gleaming white edifice rising up 25 storeys over the bay, and topped with a revolving restaurant. Views from the upper floors are predictably superb, though you'll have to pay extra for a sea-facing room. **¥780**

EATING

For cheap eating, you can try the street stalls in the back lanes between Beima Lu and Nan Dajie; Hai'an Jie, a street up near Yantaishan Park, is far classier, with a range of restaurants and bars.

Brazil Barbeque 巴西烤肉餐厅, bāxī kǎoròu cāntīng. 23 Hai'an Jie. The best of Hai'an Jie's restaurant offerings, scratching modern China's itch for Brazilian-style barbecued meat. As with any *churrascaria*

worth its salt, it's all served buffet style (¥58 per person); if you fancy being an omnivore rather than a carnivore, there's a decent salad bar on hand. Daily 11am–2pm & 5–9pm.

DIRECTORY

Banks and exchange The main Bank of China (Mon–Fri 8am–noon & 2–5pm), which has an ATM, is on the corner of Qingnian Lu and Nan Dajie.

Mail The post office (Mon–Fri 8am–6pm) is on Nan Dajie, near the corner of Da Haiyang Lu.

Jiangsu

5

江苏, jiāngsū

Jiangsu is a long, narrow province hugging the coast south of Shandong. Low-lying, flat and wet, it is one of China's most fertile and long-inhabited areas. Today, much of it is industrial sprawl, but there are a few gems among all the new factory towns; provincial capital **Nanjing** is one of the country's great historical cities, while ancient **Suzhou** is famous throughout China for its gardens and silk production.

Visiting the region, you find yourself in a world of **water**. The whole area is intensively drained, canalized, irrigated and farmed, and the rivers, canals and lakes which web the plain give it much of its character. The traditional way to travel here was by **boat**, with the **Grand Canal** (see below) once navigable all the way from Hangzhou in Zhejiang province to Beijing. The province's other great water highway – the **Yangzi River** – connects Nanjing with Shanghai, ensuring that trade from both east and west continues to bring wealth to the region.

Nanjing

南京, nánjīng

Formerly known in the West as Nanking, **NANJING** – the "Southern Capital" – stands as a direct foil to the "Northern Capital" of Beijing, and the city is still considered China's rightful hub by many Overseas Chinese, particularly those from Taiwan. Its current prosperity derives both from its proximity to Shanghai and from its gateway position on the **Yangzi River**, which stretches away west deep into China's interior. With leafy, shaded avenues and a laidback air, it's one of those cities that's perhaps better to live in than visit, though a wealth of historic sites means that it's well worth a few days of anyone's time.

THE GRAND CANAL

The **Grand Canal** (大运河, dàyùnhé) is, at 1800km, the longest canal on earth. The first sections were dug about 400 BC, probably for military purposes, but the historic task of linking the Yellow and the Yangzi rivers was not achieved until the early seventh century AD under the Sui emperor Yang Di, when as many as six million men may have been pressed into service for its construction.

The original function of the canal was specifically to join the fertile rice-producing areas of the Yangzi with the more heavily populated but barren lands of the north, and to alleviate the effects of regular crop failures and famine. Following its completion, however, the canal became a vital element in the expansion of **trade** under the Tang and Song, benefiting the south as much as the north. Slowly the centre of political power drifted south – by 800 AD the Yangzi basin was taking over from the Yellow River as the chief source of the empire's finances, a transformation cemented when the Song dynasty established its capital at **Hangzhou** and the Ming emperors subsequently based themselves in **Nanjing**. For centuries afterwards, the canal was constantly maintained and the banks regularly built up. A Western traveller, Robert Morrison, journeying in 1816 from Tianjin all the way down to the Yangzi, described the sophisticated and frequent locks and noted that in places the banks were so high and the country around so low that from the boat it was possible to look down on roofs and treetops.

Not until early in the twentieth century did the canal seriously start falling into **disuse**. Contributing factors included the frequent flooding of the Yellow River, the growth of coastal shipping and the coming of the rail lines. Unused, much of the canal rapidly silted up. But since the 1950s its value has once more been recognized, and renovation undertaken. The stretch **south of the Yangzi**, running from Zhenjiang through Changzhou, Wuxi and Suzhou, is now navigable year-round, at least by flat-bottomed barges, since passenger services have been killed off by new highways and high-speed trains. **North of the Yangzi**, the canal is seasonally navigable virtually up to Jiangsu's northern border with Shandong, and major works are going on to allow bulk carriers access to the coal-producing city of Xuzhou. Beyond here, towards the Yellow River, sadly the canal remains impassable.

5

Brief history

Occupying a strategic site on the south bank of the Yangzi River, Nanjing has had an important role from the earliest times, though not until 600 BC were there the beginnings of a walled city. By the time the Han empire broke up in 220 AD, Nanjing had been the capital of half a dozen local dynasties, and when the Sui reunited China in 589, the building of the Grand Canal began to considerably increase the city's economic importance. During the Tang and Song periods, the city rivalled nearby Hangzhou as the wealthiest in the country, and in 1368 the first emperor of the Ming dynasty decided to establish Nanjing as the **capital** of all China.

Turmoil and revolution

Although Nanjing's claims to be the capital would be usurped by the heavily northern-based Qing dynasty, subsequent anti-authoritarian movements associated themselves with efforts to restore the old capital. In the wake of the first Opium War – when the humiliating **Treaty of Nanking** was signed here – the **Taiping rebels** (see p.312) set up the capital of their Kingdom of Heavenly Peace at Nanjing. The siege and final recapture of the city by the foreign-backed Qing armies in 1864 was one of the saddest and most dramatic events in China's history. Following the overthrow of the Qing dynasty in 1911, however, the city flowered again, chosen as the national capital by both Sun Yatsen's Republican government, and the Nationalist administration under Chiang Kai-shek.

Modern times

In 1937, the name Nanjing became synonymous with one of the worst atrocities of World War II, after the **Rape of Nanking**, in which invading Japanese soldiers butchered an estimated 300,000 civilians. Subsequently, Chiang Kai-shek's government escaped the Japanese advance by moving west to Chongqing, though after Japan's surrender and Chiang's return, Nanjing briefly resumed its status. Just four years later, however, in 1949, the victorious Communists decided to abandon Nanjing as capital altogether, choosing instead the ancient – and highly conservative – city of Beijing in which to base the country's first "modern" government.

Xuanwu Lake Park

玄武湖公园, xuánwǔhú gōngyuán • Daily 24hr • Free • ☎ 025 83612204, Ⓦ xuanwuhu.net • metro to Xuanwumen

North of the centre, to the east of Zhongyang Lu and south of the train station, the enormous **Xuanwu Lake Park** comprises mostly water, with hills on three sides and the city wall skirting the western shore. Formerly a resort for the imperial family and once the site of a naval inspection by Song emperor Xiaowu, it's a pleasant place to mingle with the locals who come here en masse at weekends. The lake contains five small **islets** linked by causeways and bridges, with restaurants, teahouses, pavilions, rowing boats, paddle boats, places to swim, an open-air theatre and a zoo. The southern end of the park contains one of the better-preserved reaches of the city wall.

NANJING ORIENTATION

Nanjing's broken Ming **walls** are still a useful means of orientation, and the main streets run across town between gates in the city wall. Xinjiekou and Fuzi Miao are the most interesting areas for simply wandering, with historic buildings, pedestrianized shopping streets, canals and some good restaurants.

Many of the main sights can be taken in on the convenient **metro line 1 route** from the train station in the north to Yuhuatai Park in the south. This will get you to **Xuanwu Lake Park** and its glorious lake, the opulent **Presidential Palace** and **Temple of Confucius**. To the west there are a number of sights around the **Yangzi River**, while rising to the east are the slopes of **Zijin Shan**, a mountain spotted with historical sights.

5

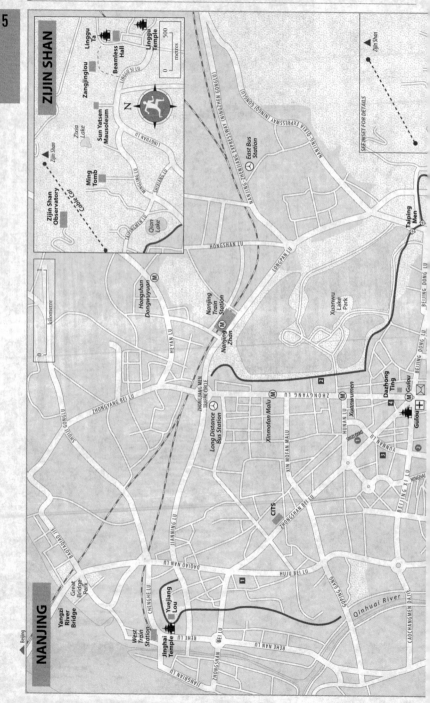

ZIJIN SHAN

Linggu Ta

Linggulou
Beamless
Hall

Zangjinglou

Linggu
Temple

500
metres
0

N

Zixia
Lake

Sun Yatsen
Mausoleum

Ming
Tomb

Zijin Shan
Observatory

Cable Car

Zijin Shan

Qian
Lake

SEE INSET FOR DETAILS

Zijin Shan

HONGSHAN LU

East Bus
Station

Taiping
Men

NANJING

Beijing

Yangzi
River
Bridge

Great
Bridge
Park

West
Train
Station

Jinghai
Temple

Yuejiang
Lou

kilometre
0

Hongshan
Dongwuyuan

Nanjing
Train
Station

Nanjing
Zhan

Xuanwu
Lake
Park

ZHONGYANG BEI LU

ZHONGYANG MEN
TRAFFIC CIRCLE

Long Distance
Bus Station

Xinmofan Malu

XIN MOFAN MALU

ZHONGYANG LU

Xuanwumen

HUNAN LU

YUNNAN LU

Dazhong
Ting

Gulou

BEIJING DONG LU

BEIJING XI LU

NINGHAI

CITS

ZHONGSHAN BEI LU

JIANNING LU

DAQIAO NAN LU

CHENGHE LU

REHE LU

ZHONGSHAN

JIANGBIAN LU

HUJU BEI LU

REHE NAN LU

GUPING GANG

Qinhuai River

CAOCHANGMEN DAJIE

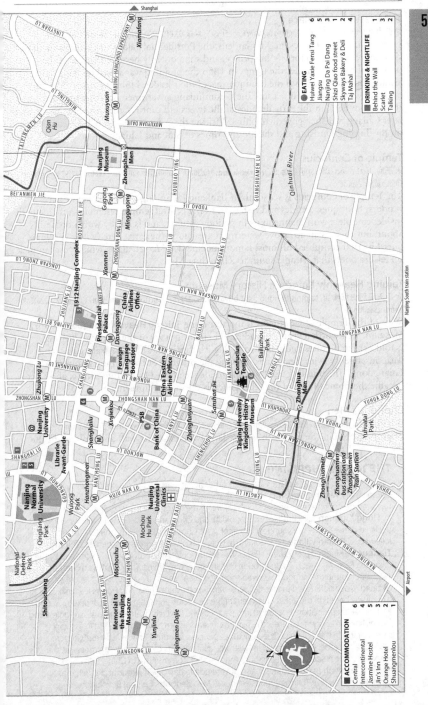

EATING
Huiwei Yaxie Fensi Tang	6
Jiangsu	5
Nanjing Da Pai Dang	3
Shizi Qiao food street	1
Skyways Bakery & Deli	2
Taj Mahal	4

DRINKING & NIGHTLIFE
Behind the Wall	1
Scarlet	3
Talking	2

ACCOMMODATION
Central	6
Intercontinental	4
Jasmine Hostel	5
Jin's Inn	3
Orange Hotel	2
Shuangmenlou	1

5

The Presidential Palace

总统府, zŏngtŏng fŭ • 292 Changjiang Lu • Daily 8am–5pm • ¥40 • ☎ 025 84578700, ⓦ njztf.cn • Metro to Daxinggong

Located in the Suzhou-esque Xu Gardens, the **Presidential Palace** was built more than six hundred years ago for a Ming prince, and subsequently became the seat of the provincial governor under the Qing. In 1853 the building was seized by the Taiping armies and converted into the headquarters of their leader, Hong Xiuquan. After the overthrow of the Qing, it became the Guomindang government's Presidential Palace. It was from here, in the early decades of the twentieth century, that first Sun Yatsen and later Chiang Kai-shek governed China. Visiting the palace today, you'll see exhibitions on the Taiping Uprising and the life and times of Sun and Chiang.

Temple of Confucius

夫子庙, fūzĭ miào • Daily 8am–9.30pm • Free • electric boats ¥40/30min • paddle boats ¥20/30min • ☎ 025 52209788 ⓦ njfzm.net • metro to Sanshan Jie

The **Temple of Confucius** is set south of Jiankang Lu among a noisy welter of street vendors, boutiques, arcades and restaurants. The central **temple** resembles a theme park inside, complete with mannequins in period costume, and is hardly worth bothering about, but there is an attractive waterfront area along the canal here (where the Tang poet Liu Yuxi composed his most famous poem, *Wuyi Lane*), along which you can pick up **leisure boats** that trundle south to Zhonghua Men.

Taiping Heavenly Kingdom History Museum

太平天国历史博物馆, tàipíng tiānguó lìshĭ bówùguăn • 128 ZhanYuan Lu • Daily 8am–5pm • ¥30 • ☎ 025 52201849 • metro to Sanshan Jie

West of the Temple of Confucius is the absorbing **Taiping Heavenly Kingdom History Museum**, well worth a visit. The sad but fascinating story of the Taiping Uprising is told here in pictures and relics, with English captions. There are seals, coins, and weapons aplenty, with clear maps showing the progress of the Taiping army from Guangdong. The building itself was the residence of Xu Da, a Ming prince, and became the home of one of the rebel generals during the uprising.

Zhonghua Men

中华门, zhōnghuá mén • Daily 8.30am–9pm • ¥35 • ☎ 025 86625435, ⓦ zhmgls.com • metro to Zhonghuamen

Zhonghua Men in the far south is now largely bereft of its wall and isolated in the

---

THE TAIPING UPRISING

One of the consequences of the weakness of the Qing dynasty in the nineteenth century was the extraordinary **Taiping Uprising**, an event that would lead to the slaughter of millions, and which has been described as the most colossal civil war in the history of the world. The Taipings were led by **Hong Xiuquan**, failed civil-service candidate and Christian evangelist, who, following a fever, declared himself to be the younger brother of Jesus Christ. In 1851, he assembled 20,000 armed followers at **Jintian village**, near Guiping in Guangxi province, and established the **Taiping Tianguo**, or Kingdom of Heavenly Peace. This militia routed the local Manchu forces, and by the following year was sweeping up through Hunan into central China. They **captured Nanjing** in 1853, but though the kingdom survived another eleven years, this was its last achievement. Poorly planned expeditions failed to take Beijing or win over western China, and Hong's leadership – originally based on the enfranchisement of the peasantry and the outlawing of opium, alcohol and sexual discrimination – devolved into paranoia and fanaticism. After a gigantic struggle, **Qing forces** finally managed to unseat the Taipings when Western governments sent in assistance, most notably in the person of Queen Victoria's personal favourite, Charles "Chinese" Gordon.

Despite the rebellion's ultimately disastrous failure and its overtly Christian message, the whole episode is seen as a precursor to the arrival of Communism in China. Indeed, in its fanatical rejection of Confucianism and the incredible damage it wrought on buildings and sites of historic value, it finds curious echoes in Mao Zedong's Cultural Revolution.

NANJING'S CITY WALLS

Though Nanjing was walled as many as 2500 years ago, the present **city wall** is basically the work of the first Ming emperor, who extended and strengthened the earlier walls in 1369–73. Built of brick and more than 32km long, construction followed the contours of the country, skirting Xuanwu Lake in the north, fringing Xijin Shan in the east, and tracing the Qinhuai River (which doubled as a moat) to the west and south. The wall was mainly paid for by rich families resettled here by the emperor: one third of it was "donated" by a single native of Wuxiang in Zhejiang province. Its construction employed 200,000 conscripts, who ensured that the bricks were all the same size and specification, each one bearing the names of the workman and overseer. They were held together, to an average height of 12m and a thickness of 7m, by a mortar of lime and glutinous rice paste.

The original structure, of red rock in places, is still plainly visible along a 300m section of the wall at the so-called **Shitoucheng**, in the west of the city between Caochangmen Dajie and Fenghuang Jie. You can see it from bus #18, which runs outside the walls between Xinjiekou and the west train station.

middle of a traffic island, just inside the river moat near a metro station of the same name. This colossal gate actually comprises four gates, one inside another, and its seven enclosures were designed to hold three thousand men in case of enemy attack, making it one of the biggest of its kind in China. Today you can walk through the central archway and climb up two levels, and, up above, there's a tremendous view of the city spread out beyond and you can stroll for a short distance in both directions.

Jinghai Temple

静海寺, jìnghǎi sì • 228 Jianning Lu, off Rehe Lu • Daily 8am–8pm • ¥6 • ☎ 025 58802973 • metro to Gulou then bus #32

Jinghai Temple lies in the far northwest of town near the Yangzi River and the west train station. It was here that the British and Chinese negotiated the first of the many unequal treaties in the wake of the Opium War in 1842 (the treaty was later signed on a British naval ship in Nanjing harbour), and the temple buildings now house the **Nanjing Treaty Museum**. Unfortunately, the museum's detailed exposition of fractious Sino-British relations throughout the nineteenth and twentieth centuries is in Chinese only, but the temple is pleasant to stroll around nonetheless. It was originally built in the Ming dynasty by Emperor Chengzu to honour the Chinese Muslim naval hero **Zheng He**, who led the Chinese fleet on exploratory voyages to East Africa and the Persian Gulf; you'll see his name commemorated throughout the city.

Shizi Shan

狮子山, shīzishān • Daily 7am–6pm • ¥40 • elevator ¥3 • ☎ 025 58815369

Rising up behind the Jinghai Temple is **Shizi Shan**, a small mountain topped with an ornate, multi-storey building, the **Yuejiang Lou** (阅江楼, yuèjiāng lóu). While the structure is of little historical importance, its 52m height alone makes it worth a look, and from the top level there's a tremendous view of the city on one side and the Yangzi on the other.

Memorial to the Nanjing Massacre

南京大屠杀纪念馆, nánjīng dàtúshā jìniànguǎn • 195 Chating Dong Jie • Tues–Sun 8.30am–4.30pm • Free • metro to Yunjinlu

Some way west of the river is the must-see **Memorial to the Nanjing Massacre**. This grim, gravelly garden includes a gruesome display of victims' skulls and bones, half-buried in the dirt, as well as a clearly labelled (in English) photographic account of the sufferings endured by the Chinese at the hands of the Japanese army during World War II.

5

The Nanjing Museum

南京博物馆, nánjīng bówùguǎn • 321 Zhongshan Dong Lu • Daily 9am–4pm • ¥20 • ☎ 025 84807923, ⓦ njmuseum.com • metro to Minggugong

East of the centre, the huge **Nanjing Museum** is one of the best provincial museums in China, especially in terms of clarity of explanations – nearly everything is labelled in English. Highlights include some superb silk-embroidered sedan chairs and several heavy cast bronzes, dating from as early as the Western Zhou (1100–771 BC). The jade and lacquer work sections, as well as the model Fujian trading ships, are also well worth seeing. Currently under renovation and due to reopen sometime in 2014.

Zijin Shan

紫金山, zǐjīn shān • Free • cable car (one-way ¥35, return ¥60) • ☎ 025 84446111, ⓦ zschina.org.cn • bus #9 or #Y2 from Xinjiekou

Just east of the city, **Zijin Shan** (Purple Gold Mountain) is a cool and shady spot to escape the furnace heat of Nanjing's summer, with fragrant woods and stretches of long grass, but also here are the three most visited sites in Nanjing. Of these, the centrepiece, right in the middle of the hill, is **Zhongshan Ling**, the magnificent mausoleum of China's first president, Sun Yatsen. To the east of Zhongshan Ling is the **Linggu Temple** complex, and to the west are the **tombs** of the Ming emperors who ruled China from Nanjing. Visiting all three sites can easily take a full day, though each can be reached independently using public transport. Note that in some tourist literature and on maps it may be called Zhongshan Mountain Scenic Area.

Linggu Temple

灵谷寺, línggǔ sì • Daily 6.30am–6pm • ¥35 • buses #9 or #Y2 from Xinjiekou

On the eastern side of Zijin Shan, the highlight of **Linggu Temple** complex is the so-called **Beamless Hall**. Completed in 1381, and much restored since, it's unusual for its large size and particularly for its self-supporting brick arch construction, with five columns instead of a central beam. The hall was used to store Buddhist sutras before the Taiping rebels made it a fortress; now it's an exhibition hall. A couple of minutes' walk southeast from the Beamless Hall is Linggu Temple itself, a surprisingly small place attended by yellow-robed monks.

Linggu Ta

灵谷塔, línggǔ tǎ

Leading northwest from the Linggu buildings and part of the same complex, a delightful footpath through beautiful cypresses and pines leads to **Linggu Ta**, an octagonal, nine-storey, 60m-high pagoda, built during the 1930s as a monument to the more than 30,000 Guomindang members killed in the fighting against insurgent Communists. It's well worth climbing up for the views over the surrounding countryside.

Sun Yatsen Mausoleum

中山陵, zhōngshān líng • Tues–Sun 8.30am–5pm • Free • ☎ 025 84446111 • bus #9 from Xinjiekou

Dr Sun Yatsen, the first president of post-imperial China, is the only hero revered by Chinese jointly on both sides of the Taiwan Straits. The former leader's **mausoleum** is an imposing structure of white granite and blue tiles (the Nationalist colours) set off by the green pine trees. The mausoleum was completed in 1929, four years after Sun Yatsen's death. From the large bronze statue at the bottom, 392 marble steps lead up to the Memorial Hall, dominated by a 5m-tall seated white marble figure of the great man himself. Beyond the figure is the burial chamber, with another marble effigy lying on the stone coffin; according to unsubstantiated rumours, the bones were removed from the coffin to Taiwan by fleeing Guomindang leaders in 1949. The Guomindang ideals – Nationalism, Democracy and People's Livelihood – are carved above the entrance to the burial chamber in gold on black marble.

The Ming Tomb

明孝陵, míng xiàolíng • Daily 8.30am–5.30pm • ¥70 • ☎ 025 84446111 • metro to Muxuyuan, or buses #3 or #20 from Gulou

About 2km west of the Sun Yatsen Mausoleum, the **Ming Tomb** marks the burial place of Zhu Yuanzhang, founder of the Ming dynasty and the only one of its fourteen emperors to be buried at Nanjing (his thirteen successors are all buried in Beijing; see p.126). So colossal was the task of moving earth and erecting the stone walls that it took two years and a hundred thousand soldiers and conscripts to complete the tomb in 1383. The site was originally far larger, but its halls and pavilions, and 22km-long enclosing vermilion wall, were mostly destroyed by the Taipings. Today what remains is a walled collection of trees, stone bridges and dilapidated gates leading to the lonely mound at the back containing the (as yet unexcavated) burial site of the emperor and his wife, as well as the fifty courtiers and maids of honour who were buried alive to keep them company.

The Sacred Way

石像路, shíxiàng lù • Daily 8.30am–6.30pm • ¥10

The site comprises two parts, the tomb itself and the approach to the tomb, known as Shandao (Sacred Way) or, more commonly, **Shixiang Lu** – which leads to the tomb at an oblique angle as a means of deterring evil spirits, who can only travel in straight lines. It's a strange and magical place to walk through, the road lined with twelve charming pairs of stone animals – including lions, elephants and camels – and four pairs of officials. Most people visit the tomb first and the approach afterwards, simply because the road from Zhongshan Ling arrives immediately outside the tomb entrance. To reach the Sacred Way from the tomb entrance, follow the road right (with the tomb behind you) and then round to the left for about fifteen minutes.

ARRIVAL AND DEPARTURE
NANJING

BY AIR

The China Eastern Airlines' office (daily 8.30am–5.30pm; ☎ 025 8456 7158) is at 334 Hongwu Nan Lu.

Nanjing Lukou International Airport (南京禄口国际机场, nánjīng lùkǒu guójì jīchǎng) lies 42km southeast of the city. Express buses (every 15min; ¥20) run two routes into town, both terminating at the main railway station – buy tickets at a booth just inside the arrivals building. A taxi costs ¥100–150, depending on your destination in the city.

Destinations Beijing (10 daily; 1hr 30min); Chengdu (9 daily; 2hr 25min); Chongqing (7 daily; 2hr 10min); Dalian (7 daily; 1hr 30min); Guangzhou (17 daily; 2hr 10min); Guilin (15 daily; 2hr); Haikou (4 daily; 2hr 40min); Hong Kong (7 daily; 2hr 20min); Kunming (8 daily; 3hr); Qingdao (4 daily; 1hr); Shenzhen (13 daily; 2hr 10min); Xiamen (8 daily; 1hr 30min); Xi'an (4 daily; 2hr).

BY TRAIN

Although Nanjing has seventeen train stations, you're likely to arrive at either of the following.

Nanjing train station (南京站, nánjīng zhàn) is a large and fairly chaotic station northeast of the city wall, connected by metro to the city centre. Departures go from the second and third floors; arrivals, the left luggage (6am–11pm; ¥1–5) and the metro entrance are on the first.

Nanjing South train station (南京南火车站, nánjīng nán huǒchē zhàn). Enormous and brand-new station (claimed to be the largest in Asia) for high-speed trains to Beijing, Shanghai and other major destinations. Linked to the centre by blue metro line #1 in under 20min.

Destinations Beijing (57 daily; 3hr 39min–9hr); Chengdu (7 daily; 18–35hr); Guangzhou (2 daily; 24–26hr); Hangzhou (70 daily; 1hr 14min–8hr 40min); Shanghai (frequent; 1hr 7min–5hr); Suzhou (frequent; 49min–3hr 37min); Xi'an (12 daily; 8hr 13min–16hr).

BY BUS

Nanjing long-distance bus station (南京长途巴士总站, nánjīng chángtú bāshì zǒngzhàn) is on Jianning Lu at Zhongyang Men, a 10min walk northwest of Nanjing train station. Nanjing's main bus station used in general by buses coming from and departing to points north and east of Nanjing (Shanghai and Yangzhou among them). You can only buy tickets for same- or next-day departure.

Nanjing South (Zhonghuamen) station (中华门汽车站, zhōnghuámén qìchē zhàn) is next to Zhonghuamen metro station, and serves many destinations in Anhui province.

Destinations Hangzhou (4hr); Hefei (6–7hr); Huang Shan (4hr); Qingdao (11hr); Shanghai (4–5hr); Suzhou (2hr 30min–3hr).

5

GETTING AROUND

By taxi Cabs are plentiful, though can be difficult to stop (a red sign means it's available), and you're advised to take the metro during rush hour as the traffic is terrible. Flag fall is ¥9 (plus ¥1 fuel surcharge).

By metro Nanjing has seventeen lines planned, of which two were running at the time of writing, though the immediate future should see a new extension to the airport. Trains run 5am–11pm and fares cost ¥2–4.

By bus Buses have a flat fare of ¥2 and give no change. There is no English information, and announcements are only in Chinese, so having an electronic map with GPS is handy.

INFORMATION

Travel agents CITS is at 202 Zhongshan Bei Lu (Mon–Fri 8.30am–noon & 2–5pm, Sat & Sun 9am–4pm; ☎025 83538590) and can book train, bus and airplane tickets. The number above is for "Mark", who speaks excellent English and can help sort out any requests or information. Buses #16, #34 & #100 stop nearby.

Nearly all hotels have their own travel agencies, able to arrange half-day bus tours of the city's sights and a host of private operators cover Zijin Shan's various attractions from the train station square.

Websites For English-language listings, reviews and the latest on expat nightlife, check ⊛ hellonanjing.net.

ACCOMMODATION

Outside the summer months, you should be able to bargain a healthy discount on hotel rooms. There are plenty of hostels around, but unfortunately none is particularly good – cheap motels are an option.

Central 中心大酒店, zhōngxīn dàjiǔdiàn. 75 Zhongshan Lu ☎025 83155888, ⊛www.njcentralhotel .com. Adventurously designed from top to toe, this is one of the most luxurious places in town – in some cases, the en-suite facilities are almost as large as the rest of the room. Service can be a little scratchy, though. **¥788**

★ **Intercontinental** 绿地洲酒店, lǜdìzhōu jiǔdiàn. 1 Zhongyang Lu ☎025 83538888, ⊛ichotelsgroup.com/ intercontinental. There are few more stunning hotels in all China than this behemoth, filling many floors of the Greenland Financial Center. At the time of writing, it was the seventh-tallest building in the world, and very similar in appearance to the first – Dubai's Burj Khalifa – since it was designed by the same team. Every single room is superbly stylish, and the same can be said of the many on-site bars and restaurants, which simply purr with quality. **¥1250**

Jasmine Hostel 茉莉国际青年旅舍, mòlì guójì qīngnián lǚshè. 7 Hequn Xincun, Shanghai Lu ☎025 83300517, ⊛jasminehostel@gmail.com. Decent hostel with a good location amid the culinary and alcoholic opportunities of Shanghai Lu. Staff can occasionally be unhelpful, but speak competent English and rooms are generally kept clean. Dorms beds **¥45**, Female-only dorm beds **¥60**, doubles **¥345**

Jin's Inn 金一村大方巷店, jīnyīcūn dàfāngxiàng diàn. 26 Yunnan Lu ☎025 83755666 ⊛jinsinn.com. There are several of these good-value budget hotels around town but this is in a prime location, being central and handy for the best bars. Rooms might be small but they're neat and comfortable, and have free internet and wi-fi. **¥188**

★ **Orange Hotel** 桔子水晶酒店, júzi shuǐjīng jiǔdiàn. 224 Zhongyang Lu ☎0400 8190099, ⊛orangehotel.com.cn. Terrific lakeside cheapie whose rooms are stylish, comfortable and remarkable value for the price – doubles can go for as little as ¥250 at quiet times, and deluxe rooms are only a little more. **¥348**

Shuangmenlou 双门楼宾馆, shuāngménlóu bīnguǎn. 185 Huju Bei Lu, near the intersection with Zhongshan Bei Lu ☎025 58800888. Surrounded by large gardens and carrying a vague colonial air, this is a perfectly decent place popular with tour groups, though a little far from the interesting parts of town. Rooms are comfortable and the service is helpful and friendly (though not much English spoken). **¥420**

EATING

Nanjing has a wide selection of local, regional Chinese and foreign foods; it's an especially great place to sample Jiangsu cuisine, the best areas for which are north of Gulou along Zhongyang Lu and northwest along Zhongshan Bei Lu. The presence of a heavy contingent of foreign students in the city, as well as a growing population of expat and home-grown business people, ensures a scattering of highly Westernized restaurants and bars, which are not necessarily expensive. Xinjiekou and the Confucius Temple area are generally good districts to browse, but for just about every kind of Chinese cuisine – plus Indian, Japanese and Thai – head for pedestrianized Shizi Qiao, off Hunan Lu to the west of Xuanwu Lake Park.

Huiwei Yaxie Fensi Tang 回味鸭血粉丝汤, huíwèi yāxiě fěnsī tāng. 42 Zhanyuan Lu ☎025 52211360.

The name means "Duck's Blood Soup" and that's what you're here for. Fast-food chain serving one of Nanjing's signature dishes at a very affordable price – around ¥20 a head. Not the most romantic of surroundings, but the food's good and it's close to the Confucius Temple. Daily 8am–10pm.

Jiangsu 江苏, jiāngsū. 26 Jiankang Lu, just east of Zhonghua Lu. Fairly upmarket place to try Jiangsu food, though not as expensive as you might think – the brine duck is their speciality and only ¥30 a dish. Ordering is no problem as there's no menu; you pick your food from plastic reproductions in the brightly lit lobby. Daily 11am–11pm.

★ **Skyways Bakery & Deli** 160 Shanghai Lu ☎025 83317103. Fantastic deli sandwiches on offer at this expat magnet: they bake their own baguettes, ciabatta and cookies, and have a case of handmade confections and cakes, as well as *Illy* coffee. A big, well-filled sandwich and a drink costs ¥25. Daily 9am–9pm.

Nanjing Da Pai Dang 南京大牌档, nánjīng dàpái dàng. Deji Plaza, 18 Zhongshan Lu ☎025 8472 2777, ⓦnjdapaidang.com. Fabulous place to try the local grub in a great atmosphere, with classical Chinese decor and uniforms, and local Ping Tan singing performances while you eat. There's a picture menu, and it's always busy, so arrive early or expect to wait. Prices are around ¥40 upwards per person – the salted duck and the pork in glutinous rice are highly recommended. Daily 8am–11pm.

Taj Mahal 泰姬玛哈印度料理, tàijīmǎhā yìndù liàolǐ. 117 Nanjing Lu ☎025 84214123, ⓦtajmahalrestaurant.com.cn. The kind of curry-house you'd love to have near your house, this place has chefs from the subcontinent, and serves authentic, reasonably priced North Indian fare in plain but clean surroundings. Mains go for ¥40–50 and the samosas are excellent. They will deliver free (min ¥100 order) within 3km, or you can pay the taxi-fare beyond that. Daily 10.30am–3pm & 5–10.30pm.

DRINKING AND ENTERTAINMENT

Most foreign students and expats after Nanjing nightlife head for the boozy delights of Shanghai Lu, but for a more civilized time, the 1912 Nanjing complex, on Taiping Bei Lu, is the local answer to Shanghai's Xintiandi; a pedestrianized zone of restored buildings now housing upscale bars and restaurants. There's not a huge amount of cultural entertainment in town; check the expat-oriented listings magazine *Map* (ⓦmaiqiu.cn) for the latest.

Behind the Wall 答案吧, dá'àn ba. 150 Shanghai Lu ☎025 83915630. Head a few metres uphill along Nan Xiu Cun alley, and go up the nondescript staircase on the left, which leads to the patio entrance. Although the Mexican food is best avoided, the bar really comes alive in the evenings, with a good range of imported bottled beers (¥25), excellent cocktails (¥35), and even better sangria (¥20). Also has a nightly live flamenco guitarist (8.30–11.30pm) as well as occasional impromtu jam sessions. Daily 4.30pm–midnight.

Scarlet 盛世佳人, shèngshì jiārén. 8-1 at the northern end of the 1912 Nanjing complex ☎025 86270999. Two-storey bar that's the late-night venue of choice with most expat residents, with the occasional Western DJ playing mostly Latin music though dance sounds and rock come later. Not too dark and serves mid-price Western food, as well as some good cocktails for around ¥50. Also has outdoor seating. Daily 8.30pm–4am.

Talking talking 西餐厅, talking xī cāntīng. 9-101 Ninghai Lu, with 4 other locations around the city ☎025 83200844. Cheap beer (from ¥25/pint) and a lively atmosphere mean that the five *Talking* bars are hugely popular with local expats, as well as locals that fancy practising their English. Also serves mid-price Western staples, with pizzas starting at ¥38. Daily 10am–2am.

DIRECTORY

Banks and exchange The main Bank of China (daily 8.30am–5pm), with a 24hr ATM, is due south of Xinjiekou on Zhongshan Nan Lu.

Hospital The most central English-speaking medical care is the Global Doctor-run Nanjing Universal Clinics, at the eastern end of Shuiximen Jie (☎025 86519991, ⓦwww.globaldoctor.com.au).

Mail Nanjing's main post office (daily 8am–6.30pm) faces the Gulou traffic circle. There's also a post office at 19 Zhongshan Lu, just north of Xinjiekou.

5

Suzhou

苏州, sūzhōu

With its centre riddled with **classic gardens** and picturesque **canals**, **SUZHOU** is justly one of eastern China's biggest tourist draws. Whereas most Chinese cities are busy building themselves up from the inside out, parts of central Suzhou remain remarkably quaint and calm – no mean feat in a city of around six million. As if greenery and waterways were not enough, Suzhou has also long been famed for its **silk** production, making it one of China's best places in which to shop for said commodity.

Just forty minutes from Shanghai by high-speed train, many choose to visit Suzhou on a day-trip, though those who stay the night will see the soft light of innumerable **paper lanterns** dappling the canal sides, whose paved lanes make Suzhou one of those rare places that looks fantastic in the rain. Additionally, beyond the industrial areas which surround the city are several smaller **canal towns**, and the majestic lake of **Tai Hu**.

Brief history

He Lu, semi-mythical ruler of the Kingdom of Wu, is said to have founded Suzhou in 600 BC as his capital, but it was the arrival of the **Grand Canal** more than a thousand years later that marked the beginning of the city's prosperity. The **silk trade** too was established early here, reaching its zenith when the whole imperial court moved south under the Song. With the imperial capital close by at Hangzhou, Suzhou attracted an overspill of scholars, officials and merchants, bringing wealth and patronage with them. In the late thirteenth century, Marco Polo reported "six thousand bridges, clever merchants, cunning men of all crafts, very wise men called Sages and great natural physicians". These were the people responsible for carving out the intricate gardens that now represent Suzhou's primary attractions.

North Temple Pagoda

北寺塔, běisì tǎ • Renmin Lu • Daily 7.45am–5pm • ¥25 • bus #4 from the train station

A short way south from the train station, the **North Temple Pagoda** looms up unmistakeably. On the site of the residence of the mother of Wu Kingdom king Sun Quan, the structure was first built in the third century AD, and rebuilt in 1582. The pagoda is, at 76m, the tallest Chinese pagoda south of the Yangzi, though it retains only nine of its original eleven storeys. Climbing it gives an excellent view over some of Suzhou's more conspicuous features, and there's also a very pleasant teahouse on site.

The Silk Museum

丝绸博物馆, sīchóu bówùguǎn • 2001 Renmin Lu • Daily 9am–5pm • ¥15 • ☎ 0512 82112636, ⓦ szsilkmuseum.com • buses #1 or #102

Suzhou's well-presented **Silk Museum** illustrates the development of silk production from ancient times to the present day. There are looms, weaving machines and faded reproductions of early silk patterns, and although none of them is particularly exciting, the main reason to come here is to see the fascinating room full of silkworms munching mulberry leaves and spinning cocoons. There's also a shop which, although slightly overpriced, is more likely to sell genuine items than other places in town.

SUZHOU ORIENTATION

Lying within a rectangular moat formed by canals, the historic town's clear grid of streets and waterways makes Suzhou a relatively easy place in which to get your bearings. The traditional commercial centre of the city lies around **Guanqian Jie**, halfway down Renmin Lu, an area of cramped, animated streets thronged with small shops, teahouses and restaurants, though savvy travellers are now heading to **Pingjiang Lu**, a canal-side street which is fast becoming a local version of Beijing's Nanluogu Xiang (see p.83), blending a traditional vibe with modern cafés and galleries.

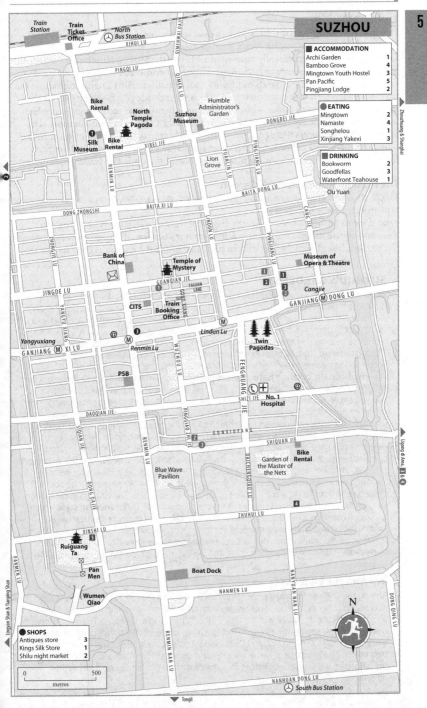

SUZHOU

■ ACCOMMODATION

Archi Garden	1
Bamboo Grove	4
Mingtown Youth Hostel	3
Pan Pacific	5
Pingjiang Lodge	2

● EATING

Mingtown	2
Namaste	4
Songhelou	1
Xinjiang Yakexi	3

■ DRINKING

Bookworm	2
Goodfellas	3
Waterfront Teahouse	1

● SHOPS

Antiques store	3
Kings Silk Store	1
Shilu night market	2

Train Station
Train Ticket Office
North Bus Station
XIHUI LU
PINGQI LU
QIMEN LU
QIWANGU DAJIE
Bike Rental
North Temple Pagoda
Suzhou Museum
Humble Administrator's Garden
Silk Museum
Bike Rental
XIBEI JIE
DONGBEI JIE
Lion Grove
YUANLIN LU
PINGJIANG LU
REMMIN LU
BAITA DONG LU
BAITA XI LU
LINDUN LU
CANG JIE
Ou Yuan
DONG ZHONGSHI
ZHONGJIE LU
YANGYU XIANG
Bank of China
Temple of Mystery
GUANQIAN JIE
TAIJIAN LANE
Museum of Opera & Theatre
Cangjie
GANJIANG M DONG LU
JINGDE LU
CITS
Train Booking Office
Lindun Lu
M
Yangyuxiang
GANJIANG M XI LU
Renmin Lu
WUZHOU LU
Lindun Lu
M
Twin Pagodas
PSB
FENGHUANG JIE
SHIZI JIE
No.1 Hospital
DAQQIAN JIE
SQUAN JIE
RENMIN LU
PINGHAO ZHI JIE
GUNXIUFANG
SHIQUAN JIE
DONG DAJIE
DAICHENGQIAO LU
Garden of the Master of the Nets
Bike Rental
Blue Wave Pavilion
ZHUHUI LU
XINSHI LU
Ruiguang Ta
Pan Men
Boat Dock
NANYUAN NAN LU
Wumen Qiao
NANMEN LU
PANMEN LU
RENMIN NAN LU
DONG QING LU
NANHUAN DONG LU
South Bus Station

N

0	500
	metres

Zhouzhuang & Shanghai
Luzhi di area 3 & 4
Lingyan Shan & Tianping Shan
Tongli

5

Suzhou Museum

苏州博物馆, sūzhōu bówùguǎn • 204 Dongbei Jie • Tues–Sun 9am–4pm • Free • ☎ 0512 67575666, ⓦ szmuseum.com • limited numbers of visitors allowed at any time, meaning queues in peak season

Designed by the internationally renowned I.M. Pei, the **Suzhou Museum** is a successful attempt to update the city's characteristic white-wall-and-black-beam architectural style. The collection itself stands out for its quality (and detailed English captions): the first two galleries feature exquisitely delicate china and jade pieces – look out for the ugly toad carved out of jasper – but the museum's highlight is the craft gallery, which holds some fantastically elaborate carvings of Buddhist scenes in bamboo roots. The adjacent **Prince Zhong's Residence** (included in the same ticket) is a monument to the Taiping Rebellion, a collection of period maps, battle plans, paintings and artefacts housed in the nineteenth-century mansion of one of the uprising's leaders.

The Humble Administrator's Garden

拙政园, zhuózhèng yuán • Dongbei Jie • Daily 7.30am–5.30pm • ¥70 • ☎ 0512 67537002, ⓦ szzzy.cn • free Mandarin-language tours every ten minutes include a short boat trip

Next door to Suzhou Museum lies the largest of the Suzhou gardens, covering forty thousand square metres, the **Humble Administrator's Garden**. It's based on water and set out in three linked sections: the eastern part (just inside the entrance) consists of a small

---

SUZHOU'S GARDENS

Gardens, above all, are what Suzhou is all about. Some were founded during the Song dynasty, a thousand years ago, and in their Ming and Qing heyday it is said that the city had two hundred of them. Some half-dozen major gardens have now been restored, as well as a number of smaller ones, mostly in enclosed areas behind high compound walls.

Chinese gardens do not set out to improve upon a slice of nature or to look natural: they are a serious art form, the designer working with rock, water, buildings, trees and vegetation in subtly different combinations. As with painting and poetry, the aim is to produce for contemplation the **balance**, **harmony**, **proportion** and **variety** which the Chinese seek in life. The wealthy scholars and merchants who built Suzhou's gardens intended them to be enjoyed either in solitude or in the company of friends over a glass of wine and a poetry recital or literary discussion. Their designers used little pavilions and terraces to suggest a larger scale, undulating covered walkways and galleries to give a downward view, and intricate interlocking groups of rock and bamboo to hint at, and half conceal, what lies beyond. Glimpses through delicate lattices, tile-patterned openings or moon gates, and reflections in water created cunning perspectives which either suggested a whole landscape or borrowed outside features (such as external walls of neighbouring buildings), in order to create an illusion of distance.

Among the essential features of the Suzhou gardens are the white pine trees, the odd-shaped rocks from Tai Hu and the stone tablets over the entrances. The whole was completed by animals – there are still fish and turtles in some ponds today. **Differences in style** among the various gardens arise basically from the mix and balance of the ingredients; some are dominated by water, others are mazes of contorted rock, yet others are mainly inward-looking, featuring pavilions full of strange furniture. Almost everything you see has some symbolic significance – the pine tree and the crane for long life, mandarin ducks for married bliss, for example.

VISITING THE GARDENS

Among the Chinese, Suzhou is one of the most highly favoured tourist destinations in the country, and the city is packed with visitors from far and wide – meaning that you are rarely able to appreciate the gardens in the peace for which they were designed. The most famous ones attract a stream of visitors year-round, but many of the equally beautiful yet lesser-known gardens, notably Canglang Ting and Ou Yuan, are comparatively serene and crowd-free; the best strategy is to visit one or two of the popular gardens before 10am and spend the rest of the day in the smaller gardens. **Prices** for many of these sights are slightly lower in the off-season.

lotus pond and pavilions; the centre is largely water, with two small islands connected by zigzag bridges, while the western part has unusually open green spaces. Built during the Ming by Wang Xianchen, a retired imperial censor, the garden was named by its creator as an ironic lament on the fact that he could now administer nothing but gardening.

Lion Grove

狮子林, shīzi lín • 23 Yuanlin Lu • Daily 7.30am–5.30pm • ¥30 • buses #2, #4 or #5

South of the Suzhou Museum is another must-see garden, the **Lion Grove**. Tian Ru, the monk who laid this out in 1342, named it in honour of his teacher, Zhi Zheng, who lived on Lion Rock Mountain, and the rocks of which it largely consists are supposed to resemble the big cats. Once chosen, these strange water-worn rocks were submerged for decades in Tai Hu (p.325) to be further eroded. Part of the rockery takes the form of a convoluted labyrinth, from the top of which you emerge occasionally to gaze down at the water reflecting the green trees and grey stone. The Qing emperors Qianlong and Kangxi were said to be so enamoured of these rockeries that they had the garden at the Yuanmingyuan Palace in Beijing (p.96) modelled on them.

The Temple of Mystery

玄妙观, xuánmiào guān • Gong Chedao, just off Guanqian Jie • Mon–Fri 7.30am–4.30pm, Sat & Sun 7.30am–4.45pm • ¥20 • bus #1, #2, #20 or #101 to Guanqian Jie

Right at the heart of the downtown area, the intriguingly named **Temple of Mystery** is rather incongruously located at the heart of the modern city's consumer zone. Founded during the third-century Jin dynasty, the temple has been destroyed, rebuilt, burned down and put back together many times, and for centuries was the heart of a great bazaar where travelling showmen entertained the crowds. Nowadays the complex, still an attractive, lively place, basically consists of a vast entrance court full of resting locals with, at its far end, a hall of Taoist deities and symbols; it's all encircled by a newly constructed park.

The Museum of Opera

戏曲博物馆, xìqǔ bówùguǎn • 14 Zhangjia Chedao • Daily 8.30am–4.30pm • Free • opera performances Sun at 2pm (90min; ¥30; buy tickets 15min in advance on-site) • buses #202 or #204

East from Guanqian Jie, the rooms of the unusual and memorable **Museum of Opera and Theatre** are filled with costumes, masks, musical instruments, and even a full-sized model orchestra, complete with cups of tea, though the building itself is the star, a Ming-dynasty theatre made of latticed wood. The Suzhou area is the historical home of the 500-year-old **Kunqu Opera** style, China's oldest operatic form – Beijing Opera has existed for a mere 300 years. Along with the other local opera styles **Suqu** and **Pingtang**, Kunqu is distinguished by storytelling and ballad singing, performed in the Suzhou dialect.

Ou Yuan

耦园, ǒu yuán • 5–9 Xiaoxinqiao Chedao • Daily 8am–5pm • ¥20 • buses #701, #301 or #305

Northeast of the opera museum, abutting the outer moat and along a canal, is the **Ou Yuan**, whose greatest asset is its comparative freedom from the loudhailer-toting tour groups that crowd the other gardens. Built by a husband and wife during the 1920s, it's also called The Couple's Garden Retreat. Here a series of hallways and corridors opens onto an intimate courtyard, with a pond in the middle surrounded by abstract rock formations and several relaxing teahouses. The surrounding area houses some of Suzhou's loveliest architecture, bridges and canals.

Twin Pagodas

双塔, shuāng tǎ • 22 Dinghuisi Chedao • ¥3 • Daily 7am–4.30pm • ¥4 • buses #5, #2, #27, #46, #47, #51 or #68

Several blocks east of Renmin Lu and immediately south of Ganjiang Lu, the twin towers known as **Shuang Ta** are matching slender brick pagodas built during the Song dynasty by a group of students wishing to honour their teacher. Too flimsy to climb,

5

the pagodas sprout from a delightful patch of garden. At the other end is a teahouse crowded in summer with old men fanning themselves against the heat.

Blue Wave Pavilion

沧浪亭, cānglàng tíng • 3 Canglangting Jie • Daily 7.30am–5.30pm • ¥20 • ☎ 0512 65293190 • buses #1, #14, #28, #30, #51, #101, #102, #103 or #701

Just beyond Shiquan Jie and Renmin Lu towards the river, the under-visited but intriguing **Blue Wave Pavilion** is the oldest of the major surviving gardens, near the corner of Renmin Lu and Zhuhui Lu. Originally built in 1044 AD by the Song-dynasty scholar Su Zimei, it's approached through a grand stone bridge and ceremonial marble archway. The central mound inside is designed to look like a forested hill, making it very cool on hot days.

Garden of the Master of the Nets

网师园, wǎngshī yuán • 11 Touxiang Chedao • Daily 7.30am–5.30pm & March–Nov 7–10pm • ¥30 daytime, ¥80 at night including performance • ☎ 051 265293190 • buses #2, #4, #14 or #31

The **Garden of the Master of the Nets** is a tiny, intimate place considered the finest of Suzhou's gardens by many a connoisseur. Started in 1140, it received its curious name because the owner, a retired official, decided he wanted to become a fisherman. Nowadays, it boasts an attractive central lake, minuscule connecting halls, pavilions with pocket-handkerchief courtyards, delicate latticework and carved wooden doors – and rather more visitors than it can cope with. The garden is said to be best seen on moonlit nights, when the moon can be seen three times over from the Moon-watching Pavilion – in the sky, in the water and in a mirror. Between March and November, the garden also plays host to nightly performances of traditional performing arts (see p.325).

Pan Men

盘门, pánmén • 1 Dong Dajie • Daily 8am–4.45pm • ¥25 • buses #5, #7, #30 or #701

In the far southwestern corner of the moated area is one of the city's most pleasant districts, centred around **Pan Men** and a 300m stretch of the original city wall, built in 514 BC by King Helu of the Wu Kingdom; the gate is the only surviving one of eight that once surrounded Suzhou. There are two entrances, with the main and busiest on Dong Lu, but the best approach to this area is from the south, via **Wumen Qiao** (吴门桥, wúmén qiáo), a delightful high-arched bridge (the tallest in Suzhou) with steps built into it; it's a great vantage point for watching the canal traffic. Just inside Pan Men sits the dramatic **Ruiguang Ta** (瑞光塔, ruìguāng tǎ), a thousand-year-old pagoda now rebuilt from ruins, once housing a rare Buddhist pearl stupa (since moved to the Suzhou Museum).

ARRIVAL AND DEPARTURE	SUZHOU

By air There's no airport at Suzhou, though regular buses to both of Shanghai's airports depart from Suzhou's China Eastern Airlines ticket office at 115 Ganjiang Xi Lu (hourly; 6.20am–2.50pm; ¥80). Air tickets can also be booked here or at the CITS.

By train Suzhou's newly refurbished station (苏州火车站, sūzhōu huǒchē zhàn) lies immediately north of town over a canal, servicing the main Shanghai–Nanjing rail line. A number of tourist bus routes head into the centre (#Y2 and #Y5 are most convenient), or it's a short taxi ride. There's a train ticket booking office (daily 8am–8pm) 50m south of Xuanmiao Guan on the west side of Gong Xiang; most hotels will also book tickets for a commission.

Destinations Hangzhou (frequent; 1hr 29min–5hr 47min); Nanjing (frequent; 49min–4hr 22min); Shanghai (frequent; 22min–2hr).

By bus Suzhou's North bus station (苏州北汽车站, sūzhōu běi zhàn), at 29 Xihui Lu, serves destinations to the north; buses #6, #26, #29 and #178 head the short distance into town, or a taxi costs ¥10–15. The South bus station (苏州南汽车站, sūzhōu nán zhàn), at the junction of Yingchun Lu and Nanhuan Dong Lu, sees arrivals from points south including Shanghai, Hangzhou and Nanjing. Buses #29, #30, #31 and #101 all run into town, or it's under ¥11 by taxi. Destinations Hangzhou (4hr); Nanjing (3hr); Shanghai (1–2hr); Tongli (1hr).

5

GETTING AROUND

By bicycle Suzhou is made for cycling around, and many gift shops along Shiquan Jie rent bikes, as does accommodation, along with a couple of shops just north of the Silk Museum. Expect ¥25–30/day with a deposit of a few hundred yuan (or a passport).

By taxi Cabs are your best bet for getting around Suzhou's small centre. Fares start at ¥11 for the first 3km.

By metro The city's first metro line opened in 2012, with three more under construction, though of no particular use to the casual visitor. Fares start at ¥2.

By boat Canal boat tours of the city cost from ¥120 and can be arranged at the Boat Dock to the south of town, and booths just south of the Humble Administrator's Garden. The trips last 55min, and as well as commentary (in English if you're lucky), they also include a performance of Suzhou singing. Enterprising freelance boatmen may also offer you a ride – it's around ¥100 per boat for a 40min trip.

INFORMATION

Travel Agents CITS (Mon–Sat 8.30am–5.30pm; ☎ 0512 65155207) is next to the *Lexiang Hotel* on Dajing Xiang, and can book tours, flights and train tickets. Nearly all hotels also have their own travel agencies.

Websites For general tourist information in English, try ⓦ en.visitsz.com or ⓦ eng.2500sz.com.

ACCOMMODATION

Suzhou has some excellent accommodation options for all budgets, although be warned that many of the cheapies near the station are terrible. The main hotel area is in the south of the city, around Shiquan Jie, though travellers are increasingly falling for the more rustic appeal of Pingjiang Lu, to the east. Prices tend to fall heavily out of season.

★ **Archi Garden** 筑园, zhúyuán. 31 Pingjiang Lu ☎ 0512 65810618, ⓦ www.archi-garden.com. A place for Suzhou's artier visitors, featuring just four spartan but immaculate rooms – sliding doors, white linen and an atmosphere so quiet you could hear a pin drop. The lobby also functions as a café, gallery and style-book library. **¥450**

Bamboo Grove 竹辉饭店, zhúhuī fàndiàn. 168 Zhuhui Lu ☎ 0512 65205601, ⓦ www.bg-hotel.com. A tour-group favourite, this efficient Japanese-run four-star hotel imitates local style with black-and-white walls and abundant bamboo in the garden. Fabulous rooms, with a couple of good restaurants too. **¥988**

★ **Mingtown Youth Hostel** 明堂青年旅舍, míngtáng qīngnián lǚshè. 28 Pingjiang Lu ☎ 0512 65816869. Filled with character, this friendly canal-side venue is hugely popular with budget travellers – singles and doubles are remarkably stylish for the price, with wooden furniture and excellent en-suite facilities. Dormitories can get a little stuffy, though. Dorm beds **¥60**, doubles **¥205**

Pan Pacific 吴宫泛太平洋酒店, wúgōngfàn tàipíngyáng jiǔdiàn. 259 Xinshi Lu ☎ 0512 65103388, ⓦ panpacific.com. This top-end hotel was modelled on the old city gate, a design which strangely enough works well. Rooms are superb, the staff are sprightly and informative, and the outside gardens could function as a tourist draw in themselves. **¥650**

Pingjiang Lodge 平江客栈, píngjiāng kèzhàn. 33 Pingjiang Lu ☎ 0512 65233888, ⓦ the-silk-road.com. Part of a small yet nationwide chain of "culture hotels", this appealingly rustic venue seeks to re-create the charm of old Suzhou. Its rooms have been traditionally styled, and prove particularly popular with Chinese families. **¥450**

EATING

Suzhou cooking, with its emphasis on fish from the nearby lakes and rivers, is justly renowned; specialities include *yinyu* ("silver fish") and *kaobing* (grilled pancakes with sweet filling). The town is well stocked with restaurants for all budgets – in addition to those reviewed below, flanking *Songhelou* on Taijian Lane are four other big, busy restaurants of repute: the *Dasanyuan*, *Deyuelou*, *Wangsi* and *Laozhengxing*, all of which are good for a splurge on local dishes, with foreigner-friendly staff and menus.

Namaste 娜玛斯提印度餐厅, nàmǎsītí yìndù canting. A7, 1912 Bar Street ☎ 0512 62720369. Quite a treat if you've been racing around the provincial backwaters, this high-end curry-house serves up authentic North Indian food in a classy environment, where you can see the Indian chefs at work in the kitchen through a window. There's outdoor seating too, and very friendly service. Mains are ¥40–80. Daily 11am–2pm & 5–11pm.

Mingtown 明堂, míngtáng. 28 Pingjiang Lu ☎ 0512 65816869. Just down the road from the hostel, and popular with backpackers on account of tasty food, decent coffee and an only-slightly-wonky pool table. Good for a Western breakfast (¥20–28), and turns into a bar of sorts in the evening. Daily 8am–11pm.

Songhelou 松鹤楼菜馆, sōnghèlóu càiguǎn. Taijian Xiang, just south of the Temple of Mystery ☎ 0512 67700688. The most famous restaurant in town – it claims to be old enough to have served Emperor

Qianlong. The menu is elaborate and long on fish and seafood (crab, eel, squirrel fish and the like), though not cheap at around ¥150 a head. There are four good places nearby on Taijian Lane; see opposite. Daily 11am–2pm & 5–8.30pm.

Xinjiang Yakexi 新疆亚克西酒楼, xīnjiāng yǎkèxī

jiǔlóu. 768 Shiquan Jie ☎0512 65291798. Xinjiang comfort food – pulled noodles with vegetables (*latiaozi*) and naan bread, among others – in a bright dining room bustling with local Uyghurs and tourists. Also sells lamb kebabs cooked on a grill outside for just ¥4, though most mains ¥20–30. Daily 9am–midnight.

DRINKING

Suzhou's nightlife is fairly well developed, with the oldest bars (as well as the oldest profession) along Shiquan Jie. However, the Ligong Di area (especially the 1912 Bar Street) on the southeastern corner of Jinji Lake is fast overtaking it as the nightlife centre of the city, especially with the expat community.

Bookworm 老书虫, lǎo shūchóng. 77 Gunxiu Fang, corner and round the back of Shiquan Jie ☎152 50074471, ⓦsuzhoubookworm.com. Like sister operations in Beijing and Chengdu, this place is ground zero for local expats, and popular with locals too. Visitors will also be able to take part in the many events such as art/ literary festivals, open-mics, and pub quizzes that they organize, or just pop by for coffee or an evening drink. Western food here is also good at around ¥45 for mains. Daily 9am–midnight.

Goodfellas 菲拉主题吧, fēilā zhǔtí ba. A9, 1912 Bar Street ☎0512 62962789, ⓦsoutherncrosssz.com. The best of the foreigner-friendly bars in this area, this place

has live music (Tues–Sat 9pm–1am) on its ample stage, as well as pool, darts and dancing later in the night. There's also a good range of foreign beer, some fine cocktails and a mix of both Chinese and foreigner clientele. Daily 6.30pm–2am.

Waterfront Teahouse 运河茶馆, yùnhé cháguǎn. 36 Pingjiang Lu. Traditional canal-side venue with tiny seats on the outside veranda, and slightly fancier places to park your posterior inside. The former are recommended for the splendid views of local canal life, over a latte or herbal tea. Walk past at night if you can – the sight of soft light pouring through its latticed windows is rather magical. Daily 8am–8pm.

ENTERTAINMENT

Garden of the Master of the Nets 11 Touxiang Chedao ☎051 265293190. Between March and November, this classical Chinese garden hosts nightly

performances of Chinese opera, folk dancing and storytelling. ¥80 includes admission to garden. Daily March–Nov 7.30–10pm.

SHOPPING

There are numerous opportunities to shop for silk in Suzhou, although beware of outrageous prices – often ten times the going rate – especially in the boutiques along Shiquan Jie and Guanyin Jie, and the night market on Shi Lu pedestrian street (石路步行街, shí lù bùxíng jiē), over on the west side of the old town. The King Silk Store next to the Silk Museum has a good selection, including great duvets starting at just over ¥300. The Antique Store on Renmin Lu is the place for old furniture, while paintings and embroidery are on hand in a pavilion near the corner of Renmin Lu and Baita Xi Lu, and in the shops along Shiquan Jie.

DIRECTORY

Banks and exchange The Bank of China head office (daily 8.15am–5.15pm) is at 1450 Renmin Lu, in the centre of town, just north of Guanqian Jie, and has money exchange and international ATMs.

Hospital The best hospital in the city for foreigners is the Suzhou Kowloon Hospital (苏州九龙医院, sūzhōu jiǔlóng yīyuàn) at 118 Wangsheng Jie, in the Suzhou Industrial Park Zone; it's about a ¥60 taxi-ride from the centre.

Internet The best place to find internet cafés is on Moye Road just east of Shiquan Street, and costs ¥2.5/hr. Most cafés, bars and hotels will have wi-fi and often computers you can use.

Mail Suzhou's main post office (daily 9am–6pm) is at the corner of Renmin Lu and Jingde Lu.

PSB At 201 Renmin Lu, at the junction with the small lane Dashitou Xiang.

Tai Hu

太湖, tàihú • buses #62, #500, #502 or #621 from Suzhou train station to Dongshan 1hr, ¥15

Thirty-five kilometres west of Suzhou lies the enormous **Tai Hu**, one of the largest freshwater lakes in China. It's a popular focus for a day out, though there's not much to

5

do but wander the wooded hills around the shore. Be warned that, in summer, algae blooms will make the lakeside slightly smelly.

Dongshan and the lake
Xishan island ferries ¥10

Tai Hu's access point is rural **DONGSHAN** (东山, dōngshān), which sits at the end of a long promontory. Here, you can pop into the lovely **Zijin An Nunnery** (紫金庵, zǐjīn' ān; daily 7.30am–5pm; ¥20), notable for its ancient statuary and location in a secluded wood surrounded by sweet-smelling orange groves. Then it's an easy hike up to Longtou Shan, or Dragon's Head Mountain. If the peak's not shrouded, there are stunning views of the surrounding tea plantations and the lake. Head back to Dongshan and walk northwest and you'll come to the pier for ferries (¥10) to the nearby island of **Xishan** (西山, xīshān). There are plenty of woods to wander through before returning to Dongshan for a bus back to Suzhou.

Zhejiang
浙江, zhèjiāng

ZHEJIANG, one of China's smallest provinces but also one of the wealthiest, is made up of two quite different areas. The northern part shares its climate, geography, history and the Grand Canal with Jiangsu – the land here is highly cultivated, fertile and netted with waterways, hot in summer and cold in winter. The south, however, has much more in common with Fujian province, being mountainous and sparsely populated in the interior, thriving and semitropical on the coast.

Cities throughout the province tend to have an attractive, prosperous air. **Hangzhou**, the terminus of the Grand Canal, is one of the greenest and most visually appealing cities in China, with its famous lake a former resort of emperors; it's still a centre for silk, tea and paper-making. Nearby **Shaoxing**, a charming small town threaded by canals, offers the chance to tour its beautiful surroundings by boat. Off the coast, and accessible from Shanghai, **Putuo Shan** is a Buddhist island with more temples than cars; as fresh, green and tranquil as eastern China gets.

Hangzhou
杭州, hángzhōu

Few cities are as associated with a tourist draw as the Zhejiang capital of **HANGZHOU**, which has found fame for one simple reason – **Xi Hu**, a large lake right in the centre of the action. Encircled by gardens and a wreath of willow trees, crisscrossed with ancient walkways and bridges and punctuated by the odd temple or pagoda, the lake exudes an old-style air increasingly hard to find in modern China, and is a must-see if you're in this part of the land.

Hangzhou is particularly busy at weekends, when it's packed with trippers escaping from the concrete jungle of Shanghai, and in summer, when the whole country seems to be jostling for space around the lakeshore. This popularity has pushed up hotel prices, but it also brings advantages: there are plenty of restaurants, the natural environment is being protected and the bulk of the temples and gardens on the lakeside are in superb condition. Most of the places to see can be visited on foot or by bicycle, though those following the latter course of action should avoid evening rush hour – this is a city of almost nine million people, and the lake makes for something of a traffic obstacle.

Brief history

Hangzhou has little in the way of a legendary past or ancient history, for the simple reason that the present site was originally under water. Xi Hu itself started life as a wide

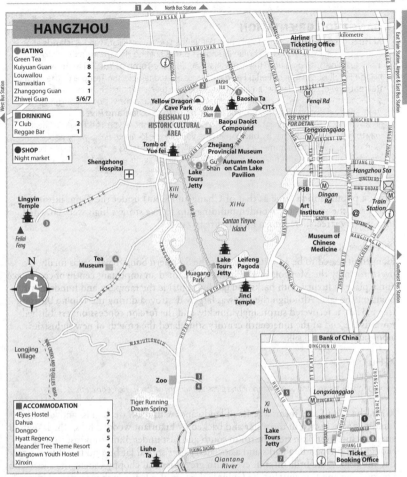

HANGZHOU

EATING
Green Tea	4
Kuiyuan Guan	8
Louwailou	2
Tianwaitian	3
Zhanggong Guan	1
Zhiwei Guan	5/6/7

DRINKING
7 Club	2
Reggae Bar	1

SHOP
Night market	1

ACCOMMODATION
4Eyes Hostel	3
Dahua	7
Dongpo	6
Hyatt Regency	5
Meander Tree Theme Resort	4
Mingtown Youth Hostel	2
Xinxin	1

inlet off the bay, and it is said that Emperor Qin Shihuang sailed in from the sea and moored his boats on what is now the northwestern shore of the lake. Only around the fourth century AD did river currents and tides begin to throw up a barrier of silt, which eventually resulted in the formation of the lake.

Development of the city

Hangzhou rapidly made up for its slow start. The first great impetus came from the building of the **Grand Canal** at the end of the sixth century (see p.307), and Hangzhou developed with spectacular speed as the centre for trade between north and south, the Yellow and Yangzi river basins. But the city really flourished from 1138, when the Song imperial family, chased south from Kaifeng by Mongol invasions, chose Hangzhou as the Chinese **capital**. There was an explosion in the silk and brocade industry, and indeed in all the trades that waited upon the court and their wealthy friends. Marco Polo, writing of Hangzhou towards the end of the thirteenth century, spoke of "the City of Heaven, the most beautiful and magnificent in the world". So glorious was the reputation of the city that it rapidly grew overcrowded: over a million people were crammed onto Hangzhou's sand

5

HANGZHOU ORIENTATION

Xi Hu is, of course, Hangzhou's focal point. Within the lake area itself are various **islands** and causeways, while the shores are home to endless **parks** holding Hangzhou's most famous individual sights, ranging from the extravagant and historic **Tomb of Yue Fei** to the ancient hillside Buddhist carvings of **Feilai Feng** and its associated temple, the **Temple of the Soul's Retreat**, one of China's largest and most renowned. Farther afield the terrain becomes semi-countryside, where beautiful tea plantations nestle around the village of **Longjing**, while there are excellent walking opportunities south down to the **Qiantang River**.

With most of Hangzhou's sights located on or near the lakeshore, you'll find that the ideal way to get between them is by **bike**; otherwise you can use local buses or simply walk. Outside the sweltering summer, it's possible to walk round the lake's entire circumference in one day, but you wouldn't have time to do justice to all the sights en route.

bank, a population as large as that of Chang'an (Xi'an) under the Tang, but in a quarter of the space – tall wooden buildings up to five storeys high were crowded into narrow streets, creating a ghastly fire hazard.

Post-imperial times

Hangzhou ceased to be a capital city after the Southern Song dynasty was finally overthrown by the Mongols in 1279, but it remained an important centre of commerce and a place of luxury, with **parks and gardens** outside the ramparts and hundreds of boats on the lake. Although the city was largely destroyed during the **Taiping Uprising** (see p.312), it recovered surprisingly quickly, and the **foreign concessions** established towards the end of the nineteenth century stimulated the growth of new industries alongside traditional silk.

Xi Hu

西湖, xīhú

A voyage on this lake offers more refreshment and pleasure than any other experience on earth…

Marco Polo

Xi Hu, the West Lake, forms a series of landscapes with rock, trees, grass and lakeside buildings all reflected in the water and backed by luxuriant wooded hills. The lake itself stretches just over 3km from north to south and just under 3km from east to west, though the surrounding parks and associated sights spread far beyond this. On a sunny day the colours are brilliant, but even with grey skies and choppy waters, the lake views are soothing and tranquil; for the Chinese they are also laden with literary and historic associations. Although the crowds and hawkers are sometimes distracting, the area is so large that you can find places to escape the hubbub.

As early as the Tang dynasty, work was taking place to control the waters of the lake with dykes and locks, and the two **causeways** that now cross sections of the lake, Bai Di across the north and Su Di across the west, originated in these ancient embankments. Mainly used by pedestrians and cyclists, the causeways offer instant escape from the noise and smog of the built-up area to the east. Strolling the causeways at any time, surrounded by clean, fresh water and flowering lilies, is a pleasure and a favourite pursuit of Chinese couples. The western end of Bai Di supposedly offers the best vantage point over the lake.

Bai Di

白堤, báidī

Bai Di is the shorter and more popular of the two causeways, about 1500m in length. Starting in the northwest of the lake near the *Shangri-La* hotel, it runs along the outer edge of Gu Shan before crossing back to the northeastern shore, enclosing a small strip known as Beili Hu (North Inner Lake).

Gu Shan (Solitary Hill)

孤山, gūshān · bus #850

In the middle of Bai Di, the little island of **Gu Shan** is one of Hangzhou's highlights, a great place to relax under a shady tree. Bursting with chrysanthemum blossoms in the spring and sprinkled with pavilions and pagodas, this tiny area was originally landscaped under the Tang, but the present style dates from when the Qing Emperor Qianlong built himself a palace here, surrounded by the immaculate **Zhongshan Park** (中山公园, zhōngshān gōngyuán). On the southeastern side of the hill by the water is another of Qianlong's buildings, the **Autumn Moon on a Calm Lake Pavilion**, which is the perfect place to watch the full moon. It's a teahouse now, very popular after sunset and full of honeymooners. The popular view-point of the low stone **Broken Bridge**, at the far eastern end of the causeway, gets its name because winter snow melts first on the hump of the bridge, creating the illusion of a gap.

Zhejiang Provincial Museum

浙江博物馆, zhèjiāng bówùguǎn · Tues–Sun 8.30am–4.30pm · Free · 25 Gushan Lu · ☎ 0571 87980281, ⓦ zhejiangmuseum.com · bus #850

Part of the Gu Shan palace itself, facing south to the centre of the lake, is now the **Zhejiang Provincial Museum**, a huge place with clear English captions throughout and a number of different wings. The main building in front of the entrance houses historical relics, including some superb bronzes from the eleventh to the eighth centuries BC. Another hall centres on coin collections and has specimens of the world's first banknotes, dating to the Northern Song. Modern galleries outside hold displays of painting and Tibetan Buddha statues.

Xiling Seal Engravers' Society

西泠印社, xīlíng yìnshè · Daily 9am–5pm · ¥5

The curious **Xiling Seal Engravers' Society**, founded in 1904, occupies the western side of Gu Shan, next to the *Louwailou* restaurant. Its tiny park encloses a pavilion with a pleasant blend of steps, carved stone tablets, shrubbery and, nearby, a small early Buddhist stupa; drop by here in summer and you can often see the engravers at work.

Su Di

苏堤, sūdī

The longer of the lake's two causeways, **Su Di** is named after the Song-dynasty poet-official Su Dong Po, who was governor of Hangzhou; it extends from the southwest corner of the lake and runs its full length to the northern shore close to Yue Fei's Tomb. Consisting of embankments planted with banana trees, weeping willows and plum trees, linked by six stone-arch bridges, the causeway encloses **Xili Hu**, a narrow stretch of water.

Santan Yinyue

三潭印月, sāntán yìnyuè · ¥20

East of the Su Di causeway and in the southern part of the lake is the largest of the islands here, **Xiaoying**, built up in 1607. It's better known as **Santan Yinyue**, meaning

---

BOAT TRIPS ON XI HU

One of the loveliest things to do in Hangzhou is take a boat trip on the lake. Tourist boats (¥45, including entrance fees for Santan Yinyue) launch from the two lake tour jetties and head directly for the **islands**. Then there are the freelance boatmen in small canopied boats with four comfortable seats, who fish for tourists along major lakeside gathering points, especially the causeways, and charge around ¥100 per person for 40 minutes. You can also take out a boat of your own – either electric putt-putters for four people (¥80/40min; ¥200 deposit), or paddle boats (¥40/30min).

5

"Three Flags Reflecting the Moon", after the three "flags" – actually stone pagodas – said to control the evil spirits lurking in the deepest spots of the lake. Bridges link across from north to south and east to west so that the whole thing seems like a wheel with four spokes, plus a central hub just large enough for a pavilion, doubling as a shop and a restaurant. The admission fee to get onto the island is usually included if you take one of the tourist boat rides here.

Beishan Lu Historic Cultural Area

北山街历史文化节街区, běishān jiē lìshǐ wénhuàjié jiē qū

This large area, accessed from Beishan Lu, begins northeast of the lake with the seven-storey **Baoshu Ta** (报数塔, bǎoshū tǎ), a 1933 reconstruction of a Song-dynasty pagoda. You can follow hillside tracks from here right up to **Lingering Rosy Cloud Mountain** (栖霞山, qīxiá shān) above the lake. About halfway along this path you'll see a yellow-walled monastery with black roofs lurking below to your left, the **Baopu Taoist Compound** (包朴道远, bāopǔ dàoyuàn; daily 7am–5pm; ¥5). It's well worth a stop, especially in the late afternoon, if only because you might be able to discreetly watch one of the frequent ancestral worship ceremonies that are held here, with widows clutching long black necklaces to pay tribute to their husbands.

Above the monastery is **Sunrise Terrace**, traditionally the spot for watching the spring sun rise over the lake and Gu Shan. Further west, some steep stone stairs descend back down to the road, close to the Tomb of Yue Fei at the northwest end of the lake, next to the *Shangri-La* hotel.

Tomb of Yue Fei

岳飞墓, yuèfēi mù • Daily 7.30am–5.30pm • ¥25 • 80 Beishan Lu, at the western end • ☎ 0571 87986653 • buses #K7, #Y1, #Y2 or #Y3

The **Tomb of Yue Fei** is one of Hangzhou's big draws, the twelfth-century Song general being considered a hero in modern China thanks to his unquestioning patriotism. Having emerged victorious from a war against barbarian invaders from the north, Yue Fei was falsely charged with treachery by a jealous prime minister, and executed at the age of 39. Twenty years later, the subsequent emperor annulled all charges against him and had him reburied here with full honours. Walk through the temple to reach the tomb itself – a tiny bridge over water, a small double row of stone men and animals, steles, a mound with old pine trees and four cast-iron statues of the villains, kneeling in shame with their hands behind their backs. The calligraphy on the front wall of the tomb reads, "Be loyal to your country".

Yellow Dragon Cave Park

黄龙洞公园, huánglóngdòng gōngyuán • Daily 8am–6pm • ¥15 • bus #Y3

Immediately west of Yue Fei's tomb is a lane leading away from the lake and north into the hills behind. Thirty minutes' walk along here leads to the **Yellow Dragon Cave Park**, to the north of Qixia Shan, passing several small caves and temples on the way. For those of a less ambulatory nature, the park can also be approached from the north via an entrance at 69 Shuguang Lu. The main area of the park is charmingly secretive, sunk down between sharply rising hills with a pond, teahouses, a shrine to Yue Lao (the Chinese god of matchmaking), cherry blossoms in the early spring, and a pavilion where musicians perform traditional music. A nice touch is that all the staff wear Song-dynasty costumes.

Huqingyu Tang Museum of Chinese Medicine

胡清余堂中药博物馆, húqìngyútáng zhōngyào bówùguǎn • Daily 8am–5pm • ¥10 • on Hefang Jie, look for the white wall with seven large characters and turn down the first alley along its west side; the museum is on the right after about 30m

A kilometre east of the lake is the Huqingyu Tang Museum of Chinese Medicine, which traces the complicated history of Chinese medicine from its roots several thousand years ago. There's not really much to see other than endless exhibits of the various plants and animals (of a stuffed variety) used in Chinese Medicine, but the museum is housed in a traditional apothecary, an architectural gem of aged dark wooden beams, gold inlay and intricately carved panels, and also bustles with shop assistants mixing up traditional concoctions.

Feilai Feng

飞来峰, fēilái fēng • Daily 5.30am–5.30pm • ¥45 • bus #7 from the Yue Fei Tomb to its terminus

Three kilometres west of the lake, Hangzhou's other famous sights are scattered around **Feilai Feng**, "The Hill that Flew Here". The hill's bizarre name derives from the tale of an Indian Buddhist devotee named Hui Li who, upon arrival in Hangzhou, thought he recognized the hill from one back home in India, and asked when it had flown here. Near the entrance is the **Ligong Pagoda**, constructed for him.

The main feature of Feilai Feng is the hundreds of **Buddhist sculptures** carved into its limestone rocks. These date from between the tenth and fourteenth centuries and are the most important examples of their type to be found south of the Yangzi. Today the little Buddhas and other figurines are dotted about everywhere, moss-covered and laughing among the foliage. It's possible to follow trails right up to the top of the hill to escape the tourist hubbub.

Lingyin Temple

灵隐寺, língyǐn sì • Daily 7am–5.30pm • ¥30 • ☎0571 87968665 • buses #Y1, #Y2, #Y4, #7 & #807

Deep inside the Feilai Feng tourist area you'll eventually arrive at the **Temple of the Soul's Retreat**, one of the biggest temple complexes in China, and the oldest in Hangzhou. Founded in 326 AD by Hui Li, who is buried nearby, it once had three thousand monks, nine towers, eighteen pavilions and 75 halls and rooms. Today it is an attractive working temple with daily services, usually in the early morning or after 3pm.

In the 1940s the temple was so badly riddled with woodworm that the main crossbeams collapsed onto the statues; the 18m-high Tang statue of Sakyamuni is a replica, carved in 1956 from 24 pieces of camphorwood. Elsewhere in the temple, the old frequently brushes against the new – the **Hall of the Heavenly King** contains four large and highly painted Guardians of the Four Directions made in the 1930s, while the Guardian of the Buddhist Law and Order, who shields the Maitreya, was carved from a single piece of wood eight hundred years ago.

Tea Museum

茶博物馆, chá bówùguǎn • Tues–Sun 8.30am–4.30pm • Free • 88 Longjing Lu • ☎0571 87964221 • bus #27 or #Y3 from Pinghai Lu in the town centre to the former Zhejiang Hotel, then follow a small lane, running parallel to the main road, southwest to the museum

Down in the southwestern quarter of the lake, in the direction of the village of Longjing, the dominant theme is **tea production**: gleaming green tea bushes sweep up and down the land, and old ladies pester tourists into buying fresh tea leaves. Fittingly, this is where you'll find the **Tea Museum**, a smart place with lots of captions in English, covering themes such as the history of tea and the etiquette of tea drinking.

Longjing

龙井, lóngjǐng • bus #K27 from the northwestern lakeshore, near the Tomb of Yue Fei • can hike from "Nine Creeks and Eighteen Gullies" area

A couple of kilometres southwest of the Tea Museum, the village of **LONGJING**, with tea terraces rising on all sides behind the houses, is famous as the origin of **Longjing tea**, perhaps the finest variety produced in China. Depending on the season, a stroll around here affords glimpses of leaves in different stages of processing – being cut, sorted or dried. You'll be pestered to sit at an overpriced teahouse or to buy leaves when you get off the bus – have a good look around first, as there is a complex grading system and a huge range in quality and price. "Longjing" means **Dragon Well**, and the spring itself is at the end of the village, surrounded by a group of buildings done up in a rather touristy fashion.

5

Tiger Running Dream Spring

虎跑梦泉, hǔpǎomèng quán • Daily 8am–5pm • ¥15 • bus #504 or tourist bus #5 from the city centre, down the eastern shore of the lake • tourist bus #3 from Longjing passes close by

The area to the south and southwest of Xi Hu, down to the Qiantang River, was long a popular site for hermits to settle and is now a large forested area dotted with teahouses, shrines, waterfalls and pagodas. Of all the parks in this area, perhaps the nicest is the **Tiger Running Dream Spring**. The spring (originally found by a ninth-century Zen Buddhist monk with the help of two tigers, according to legend) is said to produce the purest water around, the only water that serious connoisseurs use for brewing the best Longjing teas – you can try a cuppa yourself for ¥20.

Liuhe Ta

六和塔, liùhé tǎ • Daily 7am–5.30pm • ¥20, plus ¥10 to ascend • ☎0571 86591364 • buses #318, #354, #808, #K280 or #K291

South of the lake on Zhijiang Lu is the 1000-year-old **Liuhe Ta**, a pagoda occupying a spectacular site overlooking the Qiantang River, a short way west of the rail bridge. The story goes that a Dragon King used to control the tides of the river, wreaking havoc on farmers' harvests. Once a massive tide swept away the mother of a boy named Liuhe to the Dragon King's lair. Liuhe threw pebbles into the river, shaking the Dragon Palace violently, which forced the Dragon King to return his mother to him and to promise never again to manipulate the tides. In appreciation villagers built the pagoda, a huge structure of wood and brick, hung with 104 large iron bells on its upturned eaves. Today, ironically, the pagoda is a popular vantage point from which to view the dramatic **tidal bores** during the autumn equinox.

Nine Creeks and Eighteen Gullies

九小溪和十八沟, jiǔ xiǎoxī hé shíbā gōu • bus #K27 or #Y3 from north-west of lake

Twenty minutes' walk upriver west from the Liuhe pagoda, a lane known as **Nine Creeks and Eighteen Gullies** runs off at right angles to the river and up to Longjing. This is a delightful narrow way, great for a bike ride or a half-day stroll, following the banks of a stream and meandering through paddy fields and tea terraces with hills rising in swelling ranks on either side. Halfway along the road, a restaurant serving excellent tea and food straddles the stream where it widens into a serene lagoon.

ARRIVAL AND DEPARTURE
HANGZHOU

BY PLANE
Hangzhou's airport (杭州萧山国际机场, hángzhōu xiāoshān guójì jīchǎng) is 27km east of town. The airport bus (daily 5.45am–8pm; around 1hr depending on traffic; ¥20) runs via Hangzhou train station to the airport ticketing office at 390 Tiyuchang Lu (daily 7.30am–8pm; reservations ☎0571 85154259), in the north of the centre next to a *KFC*.

Destinations Beijing (frequent; 2hr); Chengdu (10 daily; 2hr 45min); Guangzhou (frequent; 2hr); Guilin (5 daily; 2hr); Hong Kong (11 daily; 2hr); Kunming (8 daily; 3hr); Qingdao (8 daily; 1hr 30min); Shenzhen (19 daily; 2hr); Xiamen (11 daily; 1hr 20min); Xi'an (8 daily; 2hr 15min).

BY TRAIN
Tickets for both stations can be bought at a booking office at 147 Huanshan Lu (daily 8am–8pm) just north of the junction with Jiefang Lu, with others scattered across the city.
Hangzhou train station (杭州火车站, hángzhōu huǒchē zhàn) is 2km east of the city centre. Reaching

the lake from here on foot takes about 40min; otherwise, take the metro to Ding'an Lu (for southeastern lake) or Longxiangqiao (for northeastern lake). Alternatively, you can get bus #K7 direct to the lake or #K290 as far as Yan'an Lu. The ticket office and left-luggage office (8am–midnight; ¥15) are upstairs on the second floor and ticket window #19 is bilingual in English.
Hangzhou East train station (杭州东站, hángzhōu dōng zhàn) Hangzhou's high-speed rail hub has services to Ningbo and Nanjing, with others to Shanghai starting soon. The easiest way to get to the northeastern lakefront is on the metro or bus #K28.

Destinations Beijing (13 daily; 5–20hr); Guangzhou (4 daily; 16hr 30min–20hr 30min); Nanjing (frequent; 1hr 29min–5hr 47min); Shanghai (frequent; 45min–3hr); Shaoxing (frequent; 21min–1hr 16min); Suzhou (frequent; 1hr 38min–4hr 20min).

BY BUS
The long-distance bus stations are fairly logical, with the

HANGZHOU'S FREEDOM BIKE RENTAL NETWORK

Hangzhou's authorities have provided an astonishing 50,000 bicycles for the city's **Freedom Bike Rental Network** which, costing just ¥10 a day, is one of the best ways to get around Hangzhou's sights. You pay ¥300 for an electronic card which covers a ¥200 deposit, and they subtract the rental fee from the remaining ¥100. In fact the first hour is free, and young Chinese travellers have cottoned onto the fact that they don't have to pay at all if they simply change bikes every 55 minutes or so. You can change bikes at marked booths all over the city, but only a few of these issue cards and return deposits – there's one at the Hangzhou train station.

North, East, South and West bus stations serving the corresponding points of the compass.

East (Jiubao) bus station (九堡汽车站, jiǔbǎo qìchē zhàn) at Desheng Dong Lu, for traffic to Shaoxing and Fuzhou. Buses #69, #100, #101 and #B-4 run to the centre of town.

North bus station (汽车北站, qìchē běi zhàn), 9km out on Moganshan Lu, serves Shanghai and Jiangsu. Buses #K15, #K67 and #K290 run to the centre, with frequent private buses to the train station square.

West bus station (汽车西站, qìchē xī zhàn), 8km west on Tianmushan Lu, services Huang Shan (see p.404). Buses #K49, #K310 and #K502 travel to the centre.

South bus station (汽车南站. qìchē nán zhàn). South of the main train station on the corner of Dongbao Lu and Qiutao Lu. Useful for Wenzhou and Fujian province; it's a 2min walk north to Wujiang Lu metro station and red line #1 to the northeastern lakefront.

Destinations Huang Shan (3hr); Nanjing (4hr); Shanghai (2–3hr); Shaoxing (1hr 30min); Suzhou (2–3hr); Wenzhou (4hr–4hr 30min).

GETTING AROUND

By taxi Taxis are a convenient way to get around town, with the meter starting at ¥11 for the first 3km.

By bus The useful tourist buses are marked with a "Y" plus their route number, and cost ¥3–5. Otherwise normal buses cost ¥1–1.5, and a/c buses ¥2.

By metro The new metro system (daily 5.30am–11pm; ¥2–8) currently only has one line, but usefully connects all the train stations with the lake area.

By boat It would be a shame to leave Hangzhou without taking a boat ride on Xi Hu (see p.329)

INFORMATION

Tourist information Hangzhou Tourist Centre (daily 8am–8pm; ☎0571 96123) is in front of the train station, between the public bus stops; they run one-day tours of Hangzhou and surrounding canal towns and cities, as well as shuttles to Shanghai's Pudong airport. They can also supply you with a free, annually updated guide in English to the city which contains many maps and useful information. There are also offices at the airport and on Yan'an Lu with

several visitor information booths dotted around town. CITS (daily 8.30am–5pm; ☎0571 85059033) is on the north shore of the lake, on a hillock above the junction of Beishan Lu and Baoshu Lu. Nearly all Hangzhou hotels have their own travel agencies, usually more helpful than CITS.

Websites For the expat view of town – including eating and nightlife listings – check out ⓦ hihangzhou.com. The official tourist website is ⓦ www.gotohz.gov.cn.

ACCOMMODATION

Hangzhou has some excellent hotels and a handful of hostels on and around the lakefront – there's not much point in staying anywhere else in this huge city unless you're pinching pennies. There is a nice spot south of Xi Hu at Siyanjing Village, which although a little far from the action, is quieter and less expensive than anywhere else around the lake.

4Eyes Hostel 四眼睛青年旅舍, sìyǎnjīng qīngnián lǚ shè. 66 Siyanjing Village ☎0571 86435731, ⓦhostelhangzhou.com. Very tranquil location, with clean dorms and rooms as well as a nice outdoor seating area where you can sup draught beer or coffee and enjoy the reasonably-priced cook-ups they do. Funky-ethnic decor on the inside where you'll also find the bar. Dorm beds **¥40**, double rooms **¥166**

Dahua 大华饭店, dàhuá fàndiàn. 171 Nanshan Lu, on the lakeside, several blocks south of Jiefang Lu ☎0571 87181888, ⓦdh-hotel.com. Spacious grounds

with comfortable rooms and attentive service justify the prices – this hotel is actually better value than many of its competitors. Mao Zedong and Zhou Enlai stayed here whenever they were in town. Also has a good and reasonably priced restaurant overlooking the lake. **¥1380**

Dongpo 东坡宾馆, dōngpō bīnguǎn. 52 Renhe Lu ☎0571 28973333. Smart rooms, a beautiful six-storey central atrium and friendly staff make this hotel just about the best deal in Hangzhou as rooms are often half the listed price. Those at the front can get noisy, though. **¥888**

★ **Hyatt Regency** 凯悦酒店, kǎiyuè jiǔdiàn.

5

28 Hubin Lu ☎0571 87121234, ⓦhangzhou.regency .hyatt.com. Bill Clinton's abode of choice in Hangzhou, this hotel offers views of Xi Hu from its deluxe rooms (even from the bathtubs, if you're in a suite), which have been decorated with splashes of red and gold. There are excellent restaurants on site, as well as a swimming pool which makes you feel like you're paddling in the lake. ¥1000 extra for lake views. **¥2300**

Meander Tree Theme Resort 漫居主题度假酒店, mànjū zhǔtí dùjià jiǔdiàn. 58 Siyanjing Village ☎0571 87979158, ⓦmanju58.com. Candidate for the most psychedelic hotel in China, the outside and grounds of this resort are decorated with dozens of colourful mosaic walls and sculptures. The themed rooms are individually decorated, some with bright primary colours, others in eclectic or ethnic styles; all have very comfy beds, though some rooms have been more recently renovated than others. **¥350**

Mingtown Youth Hostel 明堂国际青年旅舍, míngtáng guójì qīngnián lǚshè. 101 Nanshan Lu ☎0571 87918948, ⓔmingtown@foxmail.com. A pleasant range of rooms, including a few with lake views and private bathroom. Has all the hostel facilities you'd expect, plus a decent restaurant-bar and a pleasant rooftop overlooking the lake. Take bus #Y2 from the train station, or it's about 1km southwest of Dingban Lu metro stop. Dorm beds **¥70**, rooms **¥375**

Xinxin 新新饭店, xīnxīn fàndiàn. 58 Beishan Lu ☎0571 87999090, ⓦthenewhotel.com. Recently refurbished to an old-style look, with antique furniture and wood panelling in the rooms. This grand old building occupies one of the nicest locations in town, overlooking the northern shore of the lake; the ground-floor restaurant overlooks the waters and serves high-class local dishes. Also called *The New Hotel* in English. ¥200 extra for lake views. **¥1180**

EATING AND DRINKING

As a busy tourist resort, Hangzhou has plenty of good places to eat. The wedge-shaped neighbourhood between Hubin Lu and Yan'an Lu is home to a number of Chinese restaurants and fast-food joints, while Hefang Jie is also a good spot for Chinese restaurants and snacks. Lastly, the area between Shuguang Lu and the park has its own little cultural microclimate – downmarket and sometimes downright seedy, but fascinating nonetheless. Many Chinese tourists make it a point to visit one of the famous historical restaurants in town: both *Louwailou* (Tower Beyond Tower) and *Tianwaitian* (Sky Beyond Sky) serve local specialities at reasonable prices, though a third, *Shanwaishan* (Mountain Beyond Mountain), has garnered a bad reputation over the years. All three were named after a line in Southern Song poet Lin Hejin's most famous poem: "Sky beyond sky, Mountain beyond mountain and tower beyond tower/Could song and dance by West Lake be ended anyhow?"

Green Tea 绿茶餐厅, lǜchá cāntīng. 83 Longjing Lu ☎0571 87888022. Sitting amid tea plantations, and opposite the Tea Museum itself, this out-of-the-way yet very popular restaurant is quite a treat, a rickety pine structure sitting lakeside above the lily pads. Its collection of dishes is extensive but the barbecued beef deserves a special mention – mains start at around ¥40. Packed most evenings, so book ahead. Daily 11am–10pm.

Kuiyuan Guan 奎元馆面店, kuíyuán guan miàndiàn. 154 Jiefang Lu ☎0571 87029012. This busy place is just west of Zhongshan Zhong Lu – go through the entrance with Chinese lanterns hanging outside, and it's on the left, upstairs. Specializes in more than forty noodle dishes for all tastes, from the mundane (beef noodle soup) to the acquired (pig intestines and kidneys). Also offers a range of local seafood delicacies. Daily 8am–9pm.

Louwailou 楼外楼, lóuwài lóu. Gu Shan Island ☎0571 87969023. The best-known and seemingly most popular restaurant in Hangzhou, whose specialities include *dongpo* pork, fish-shred soup, and beggar's chicken (a whole chicken cooked inside a ball of mud, which is broken and removed at your table). Lu Xun and Zhou Enlai, among others, have dined here. Standard dishes cost surprisingly little, only around ¥45. Daily 11am–11pm.

Tianwaitian 天外天, tiānwài tiān. 2 Lingzhu Lu, at the gate to Feiliai Feng and Lingyin Temple ☎0571

87960599. Chinese tourists flock here to sample the fresh seafood, supposedly caught from Xi Hu. Not as good as *Louwailou*, but a great location under some immense trees by the lake. Dishes are local cuisine and around ¥50 for mains – the West Lake Vinegar Carp is great if you can afford it. Daily 7am–9pm.

Zhanggong Guan 张功馆, zhānggōng guǎn. 3 Baoshi 1 Lu ☎0571 86586609. Very rustic despite the stylish interior, with a room-full of live fish and chickens replacing the conventional menu. Choose your beast (or use a picture menu on the wall for other dishes) and they'll dispatch and cook it for you. The live fish is obviously quite pricey, but the regular dishes start at ¥25 and include a very fine slow-stewed *dongpo* pork. There are two adjacent branches; the other one serves only inexpensive noodle dishes. Daily 10am–11pm.

Zhiwei Guan 知味观, zhīwèi guǎn. 71 Gaoyin Jie downtown, and 10 Yanggongdu in the southwest of the lake ☎0571 87010200, ⓦzhiweiguan.com.cn. In a very urbane atmosphere, with piped Western classical music, you can enjoy assorted *dianxin* by the plate, including *xiao long bao* (small, fine stuffed dumplings) and *mao erduo* (fried, crunchy stuffed dumplings). The *huntun tang* (wuntun soup) and *jiu miao* (fried chives) are also good. At least ¥100 per person. Daily 11am–10pm.

NIGHTLIFE

For nightlife, Nanshan Lu and Shuguang Lu are the best bar strips in the Xi Hu area, but they tend to be a bit touristy; the local hangouts are slightly outside the centre, especially in the area north of Shugang Lu. For good information about bars and restaurants, check ⓦ morehangzhou.com.

7 Club 7club 杭州, 7club hángzhōu. 43 Shuguang Lu (behind the florists) ☎ 0571 86431517. Intimate and friendly basement bar with mostly local, but some expat, customers. An outstanding selection of Belgian and British bottled beers, as well as cocktails and single-malt scotch, though prices for all of them start at ¥50. Very laid back, and the eclectic mix of music is kept at a reasonable volume. Some English spoken. Daily 6pm–2am.

Reggae Bar 黑根酒吧, hēigēn jiǔbā. 131 Xue Yuan Lu ☎ 0571 86575749. About 3 km north of Shuguang Lu, this happy, three-floor bar, and old favourite of local and foreign students, sees plenty of action at the weekend. Decor is very squat-party, though drinks include imported beers at reasonable prices (bottles ¥20–45). Has live music, usually student bands (Tues–Sun 8.30–10pm), as well as some crazy Chinese DJs to get the dancefloor going. Daily 6pm–5am.

DIRECTORY

Banks and exchange The Bank of China head office is at 140 Yan'an Bei Lu (daily 8am–5pm), immediately north of Qingchun Lu.

Hospital The Sir Run Run Shaw Hospital at 3 Qingchun Dong Lu (☎ 0571 86006613, ⓦ english.srrsh.com) is the best-equipped hospital in town, and has English-speaking staff. It's named after a Hong Kong movie tycoon.

Mail The most central post office is at 139 Qing Chun Lu, just east of Zhonghe Bei Lu.

PSB For visa extensions, enquire at the PSB in the centre of town, just south of Dingan Road metro stop at 35 Huaguang Lu (Mon–Fri 8.30am–noon & 2.30–5pm; ☎ 0571 87280561).

Shopping The most touristy concentration of souvenir outlets – selling silk, tea and crafts – is along Hefang Jie. An L-shaped night market bends around the western end of Renhe Lu, with street sellers peddling a proletarian jumble of wares, ranging from watches to DVDs to Little Red Books. The ritziest brand names are all on Hubin Lu, right on the waterfront.

Moganshan

莫干山, mògān shān • ¥80 per day, ticket office daily 8am–6.30pm

The hill station of **MOGANSHAN**, 60km north of Hangzhou, was popular before World War II with the fast foreign set, and is currently reprising its former role as a resort to escape the stifling summer heat. The old European-style villas and po-faced communist-style sanatoriums here are being restored and turned into guesthouses, bars and cafés; there's little to do here but wander the incongruously European-looking village, hike in the bamboo forest with its many pagodas to rest in, and enjoy the views. The centre of the village is already starting to get pretty spoiled and overly-busy at weekends and in the summer, but a thirty-minute walk in any direction will take you into peace and quiet.

ARRIVAL AND DEPARTURE

MOGANSHAN

Moganshan transport terminates at the foot of the mountain at a hamlet known as both Deqing (德清, déqīng) and Wukang (武康, wǔkāng). From here, a taxi or minivan the rest of the way up the mountain costs around ¥80–100; avoid using the three-wheeler rickshaws for the same journey – they're slow and often cheat tourists.

By train Regular trains depart Hangzhou train station for the 40min–1hr ride to Deqing/Wukang.

By bus Buses leave hourly from Hangzhou's north bus station for the 1hr run to Wukang/Deqing.

ACCOMMODATION AND EATING

Moganshan has a surfeit of faded, Chinese-style two-star accommodation from ¥200, though better rooms in old lodges are preferable. For food, main street Yinshan Jie (it's only 50m long) is lined with restaurants offering local specialities such as wild game.

Moganshan Lodge 莫干山旅馆, mògànshān lǚguǎn. In a wing of the *Songliang Shanzhuang* (松梁山庄, sōngliáng shānzhuāng) at the southern end of the main street ☎ 0572 8033011, ⓦ moganshanlodge.com. Foreign-owned bar-cum-café-cum-restaurant in an old lodge with fantastic coffee and

5

even better views from the patio. Also serves pukka British breakfasts, light lunches, and set-dinners (¥125–145). The helpful owners can also help arrange good accommodation at various forest venues from ¥380.

DIRECTORY

Banks There are no ATMs in town, so arrive with enough money to last your stay.

Shaoxing

绍兴, shàoxīng

Located south of Hangzhou Bay in the midst of a flat plain crisscrossed by waterways and surrounded by low hills, **SHAOXING** is one of the oldest cities in Zhejiang, having established itself as a regional centre in the fifth century BC. During the intervening centuries – especially while the Song court was based in neighbouring Hangzhou – Shaoxing remained a flourishing city, though the lack of direct access to the sea has always kept it out of the front line of events. Even so, some of the nation's more colourful characters came from here, including the mythical tamer of floods Yu the Great, the wife-murdering Ming painter Xu Wei, the female revolutionary hero Qiu Jin and the great twentieth-century writer Lu Xun, all of whom have left their mark on the city.

For the visitor, Shaoxing is a quieter and more intimate version of Suzhou, combining attractive little sights with great opportunities for boating around classic Chinese countryside. Although the immediate centre comprises a standard shopping street, elsewhere there are running streams, black-tiled whitewashed houses, narrow lanes divided by water, alleys paved with stone slabs and back porches housing tiny kitchens that hang precariously over canals.

Cang Qiao Heritage Street

仓桥直街, cāngqiáo zhíjiē · opera performances every evening at 7.30pm, ¥50–160

East of Fushan Park along Fushanheng Lu, **Cang Qiao Heritage Street** is a charming alleyway of poky restaurants, wine shops and the like, where the smell of street vendors' *chou dofu* – "stinky tofu" – is all-pervasive. Just north at City Square there's a collection of architectural oddities, the grandest of which is the **Shaoxing Grand Theatre** (绍兴大剧院, shàoxīng dàjùyuàn; ⓦ sxdjy.com), built to resemble the Sydney Opera House and almost the same size. It's disliked by locals, and is something of a white elephant, though it does make a great place to experience the local **Yue opera** style, which is considerably softer and more melodious than Beijing opera – check the website for details.

Qingteng Library

青藤书屋, qīngténg shūwū · Houguan Xiang, an alley west off Jiefang Lu · Daily 8am–5pm · ¥10

The Jiefang Lu area houses the former residences of a number of famous people. The tranquillity of the **Qingteng Library**, a perfect little sixteenth-century black-roofed building, belies the fact that it was once the home of eccentric Ming painter Xu Wei (1521–93), whose expressive, free-handed brush style proved incredibly influential to later generations of artists, but who is also notorious for attempting to commit suicide on multiple occasions, and for having murdered his wife.

SHAOXING WINE

Near Shaoxing is **Jian Hu**, a lake whose unusual clarity has made the city known throughout China for its alcohol. Most famous are the city's sweet **yellow rice wine**, made from locally grown glutinous rice and available in Chinese supermarkets around the globe; and ruby-coloured **nu'er hong wine**, traditionally the tipple brides sipped to toast their new husbands – it was bought when the bride was born, and buried in the back yard to age.

Yingtian Pagoda

应天塔, yìngtiān tǎ • 558 Jiefang Nan Lu • Daily 8am–5pm • ¥5

Further down Jiefang Lu, the 38m **Yingtian Pagoda** crowns a low hill, Tu Shan. Part of a temple founded by the Song, burnt down by the Taiping rebels and subsequently rebuilt, the pagoda repays the stiff climb with splendid views over the town's canals and black-tiled roofs.

Qiu Jin's former residence

秋瑾故居, qiūjǐn gùjū • 100m off Jiefang Lu at 35 Hechangtang • Daily 8am–5pm • ¥15

A block to the south of the Yingtian Pagoda, situated on a small lane, is the former residence of the radical woman activist **Qiu Jin**. Born here in 1875, Qiu Jin studied in Japan before returning to China and joining Sun Yatsen's clandestine revolutionary party. After editing several revolutionary papers in Shanghai and taking part in a series of abortive coups, she was captured and executed in Hangzhou in 1907 by Qing forces.

Lu Xun's former residence

鲁迅故居, lǔxùn gùjū • Luxun Lu • Daily 8.30am to 5.30pm • Free with passport • ☎ 0575 85129163

Several sights associated with the writer **Lu Xun** (see p.955), whose childhood and early youth were spent in Shaoxing, are clustered together on Luxun Lu. The most interesting is **Lu Xun's former residence**, now converted into a **Folk Museum**. If you've seen the high, secretive outer walls so many compounds have, you'll find it a refreshing change to get to look at the spacious interior and numerous rooms inside a traditional house; drop in here for a wander through the writer's old rooms and for a stroll in his garden.

Sanwei Shuwu

三味书屋, sānwèi shūwū • Luxun Lu • Free with passport

Immediately across the road from Lu Xun's former residence is the **Sanwei Shuwu**, the

5

small school where he was taught as a young boy. In the one room to see, there's a small desk on which you'll find a smooth stone and a bowl of water, in former times the only available tools for calligraphy students too poor to buy ink and paper. Visitors are supposed to write their names in water on the stone for luck.

Bazi Qiao

八子桥, bāzī qiáo • Baziqiao Zhi Jie, a small alley off Zhongxing Zhong Lu • Free

In the east of the town and in the heart of one of Shaoxing's most picturesque and traditional neighbourhoods is the most famous of all the town's old bridges, **Bazi Qiao**. This thirteenth-century piece of engineering, which acquired its name because it looks like the Chinese character for the number eight, is still very much in use.

Dong Hu

东湖, dōnghú • Daily 7am–5.30pm • ¥40 • 20min boat rental for up to 3 people ¥85 • ☎ 0575 8601841 • bus #1 or #28 from town

Easily accessible from Shaoxing, the photogenic **Dong Hu** is 6km and a twenty-minute bus ride away. Despite appearances, the lake is not a natural one. In the seventh century the Sui rulers quarried the hard green rock east of Shaoxing for building, and when the hill streams were dammed, the quarry became a lake to which, for picturesque effect, a causeway was added during the Qing dynasty. The cliff face and lake are now surrounded by a maze of streams, winding paths, pagodas and stepping-stone bridges. Once inside the site, you can rent a little boat to take you around the various caves, nooks and crannies in the cliff face. On the opposite shore, a flight of steps leads up to a path running to the cliff top, offering superb views over the surrounding paddy fields.

Yu Ling

禹陵, yǔlíng • Daily 8am–4pm • ¥50 • bus #2 from the city square

Yu Ling – Yu's Mausoleum – is a heaped-up chaos of temple buildings in a beautiful setting of trees, mossy rocks and mountains some 6km southeast of Shaoxing. Yu, who founded the Xia dynasty around 2000 BC, earned his title "Tamer of Floods" by tossing great rocks around and dealing with the underwater dragons who caused so many disasters. It took him eight years to control a great flood in the Lower Yangzi. The original temple here was probably built around the sixth century AD, while Yu's tomb may be Han dynasty. Restored in the 1930s, the temple complex contains a large painted figure of Yu and scores of inscribed tablets. Outside, Yu's tall, roughly shaped **tombstone** is sheltered by an elegant open pavilion. The vigorous worshipping you'll see inside the temple shows what a revered figure Yu still is in flood-stricken eastern China.

ARRIVAL AND DEPARTURE	**SHAOXING**

By plane Shaoxing has no airport, but regular buses (hourly 6am–7.30pm; ¥25) run direct to Hangzhou's from next to the *Margaret Centre Hotel* at 25 Chezhan Lu, opposite the train station.

By train Shaoxing's train station (绍兴火车站, shàoxīng huǒchēzhàn) is in the far north of town, on a spur line between Hangzhou and the port of Ningbo. Bus #2 runs from here along Jiefang Lu to the southern end of the city. Tickets can be bought in town at the railway

booking office at 108 Xi Er Huan Lu (daily 8am–8pm), at the junction with Shanyin Lu.

Destinations Hangzhou (frequent; 21min–1hr 16min).

By bus Shaoxing's transit centre (绍兴市公路客运中心, shàoxīng shì gōnglù kèyùn zhōngxīn), in the far northeast of town, is where you'll most likely arrive. Buses #8, #88 and #312 run to the city centre; taxis should only cost ¥15, but queues are quite bad (touts will charge ¥30).

Destinations Hangzhou (1hr 30min).

INFORMATION

Tourist office There is a fairly useful tourist office at Lu Xun's Former Residence (daily 8.30am–5pm; ☎ 0575 85129163). They speak some English, and can book city tours (including canal boats) as well as dole out a map.

CITS at 288 Zhongxing Zhong Lu (☎ 0575 5200079) can arrange English-speaking guides for the surrounding area (¥400/day) as well as book flights. They're quite informative and helpful, and speak good English.

ACCOMMODATION

Shaoxing Fandian 绍兴饭店, shàoxīng fàndiàn. 9 Huanshan Lu ☎0575 5155888, ⓦwww.hotel-shaoxing .com. The most upmarket hotel in town is this charming Ming-style complex in grounds so large that you can travel around them by boat. Rooms are modern and comfortable and it has all the facilities expected of a 4-star, including a very good restaurant. Online rates offer heavy discounts. **¥900**

Shaoxing Laotai Men 绍兴老台门旅店, shàoxīng lǎotáimén lǔdiàn. 558 Xinjian Nan Lu ☎0575 85080288. Housed in an old courtyard building, it's all rather rickety, but with its period fittings has something of the feel of a country inn. A little hard to find; cross the bridge south off Luxun Zhong Lu by the *Xianheng Hotel*, then follow Baiya Long to the east. **¥180**

EATING

While walking around town you might be struck by the huge number of stalls selling that malodorous staple of Chinese street life, *chou doufu* (smelly tofu). The recipe was allegedly created by a Shaoxing woman who, tired of her limited cooking prowess, decided to experiment by throwing a variety of spices into a wok with some tofu. Dried freshwater fish is a great speciality in Shaoxing, as is the yellow rice wine that's these days more commonly used for cooking than drinking – *shaoxing ji* (Shaoxing chicken) is a classic dish prepared with it. You'll find a few restaurants around the northern half of Jiefang Bei Lu.

Da Bao Kou Fu Tea Restaurant 大宝口福茶餐厅, dàbǎokǒufú chácāntīng. 186 Jiafeng Bei Lu ☎0575 58583866. Not local food, but this Cantonese joint serves excellent dishes in very pleasant surroundings, with dim sum and congee (¥12–20), as well as their great-value signature hotpot rice dishes (¥38–50). Daily 6.45am–2pm & 5pm–2am.

Shaoxing Fandian 绍兴饭店, shàoxīng fàndiàn. 9 Huanshan Lu ☎0575 5155888, ⓦwww.hotel-shaoxing .com. To sample local cuisine in upscale surroundings, visit the swanky Chinese restaurant here, which serves several dishes in the local *mei* (charcoal-grilled) style; the Shaoxing Zao chicken is also excellent. Expect to pay around ¥100 per person for a feast. Daily 11am–10pm.

DIRECTORY

Banks The main Bank of China (daily 7.30am–5.30pm) is on Renmin Xi Lu.

Putuo Shan

普陀山, pǔtuó shān • ¥160

The Buddhist island of **Putuo Shan** is undoubtedly one of the most charming places in eastern China. A combination of religious reverence and relative inaccessibility means that it has no honking cars or department stores, only endless vistas of blue sea, sandy beaches and lush green hills dotted with ancient monasteries. As such, it's an ideal place to escape the noise, traffic and dirt of the big cities, but only midweek – Putuo Shan is just twelve square kilometres in area, and can get swamped with tourists on weekends. Indeed, the best times to come are April, May, September and October, when the weather is warm and the island not especially busy. Bring walking shoes, too; you'll get much more out of the place if you walk between the attractions rather than taking the bus. If it's crowded, remember that there are over eighty temples here, and the vast majority of tourists will only be at the big ones – grab a map and just walk off, and you'll soon be on your own. Be warned, thanks to the "Buddhist Buck" and the fact everything has to be shipped in, prices are relatively high here for both food and accommodation.

Brief history

Over the years more than a hundred monasteries and shrines were built at Putuo Shan, with magnificent halls and gardens to match. At one time there were four thousand monks squeezed onto the island, and even as late as 1949 the religous community numbered around two thousand. Indeed, until that date secular structures were not permitted on the island, and nobody lived here who was not a monk. Although there was a great deal of destruction on Putuo Shan during the Cultural Revolution, many treasures survived, some of which are in the Zhejiang Provincial Museum in Hangzhou (see p.329). Restoration continues steadily, and the number of monks has grown from

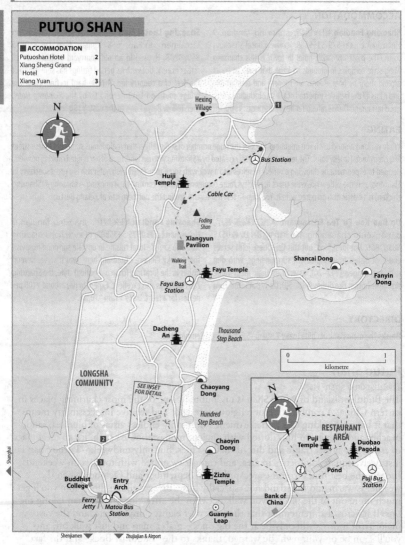

PUTUO SHAN

ACCOMMODATION

Putuoshan Hotel	**2**
Xiang Sheng Grand Hotel	**1**
Xiang Yuan	**3**

only 29 in the late 1960s to several hundred. Three principal monasteries survive – **Puji**, the oldest and most central; **Fayu**, on the southern slopes; and **Huiji**, at the summit.

Puji Temple

普济寺, pǔjì sì • Daily 6am–9pm • ¥5 • bus #1

The three main monasteries on the island are in extremely good condition, recently renovated, with yellow-ochre walls offsetting the deep green of the mature trees in their forecourts. This is particularly true of **Puji Temple**, right in the centre of the island, built in 1080 and enlarged by successive dynasties. Standing among magnificent camphor trees, it boasts a bridge lined with statues and an elegantly tall pagoda with an enormous iron bell.

THE CULT OF GUANYIN

Putuo Shan has been attracting Buddhist pilgrims from all over northeast Asia for at least a thousand years, and there are many tales accounting for the island's status as the centre of the **cult of Guanyin** (观音; guānyīn), the Boddhisatva of Compassion. According to one, the goddess attained enlightenment here; another tells how a Japanese monk named Hui'e, travelling home with an image of the goddess, took shelter here from a storm and was so enchanted by the island's beauty that he stayed, building a shrine on the spot. With the old beliefs on the rise again, many people come specifically to ask Guanyin for favours, often to do with producing children or grandchildren. The crowds of Chinese tourists carry identical yellow cotton bags which are stamped with symbols of the goddess at each temple, sometimes in exchange for donations.

South of the temple and just to the east of the square ponds is the five-storey **Duobao Pagoda** (多宝塔, duōbǎo tǎ). Built in 1334 using stones brought over from Tai Hu in Jiangsu province, it has Buddhist inscriptions on all four sides.

Zizhu Temple

紫竹寺, zǐzhú sì · Daily 6am–6pm · ¥5 including admission to Chaoyin Dong · bus #2

Down on the southeastern corner of the island, **Zizhu Temple** is slightly less touristed than most and, for that reason alone, is a good spot to observe the monks' daily rituals. Just down from the temple is a cave, **Chaoyin Dong** (潮音洞, cháoyīn dòng); the din of crashing waves here is remarkable, and thought to resemble the call of Buddha (and hence this was a popular spot for monks to commit suicide in earlier days).

Guanyin Leap

观音跳, guānyīn tiào · Daily 6am–6pm · ¥6 · bus #2

On the island's southern tip is Putuo's most prominent sight, the **Guanyin Leap**, a headland from which rises a spectacular 33m-high bronze-plated statue of the Boddhisatva, visible from much of the island. In her left hand, Guanyin holds a steering wheel, symbolically protecting fishermen from violent sea storms. The pavilion at the base of the statue holds a small exhibit of wooden murals recounting how Guanyin aided Putuo villagers and fishermen over the years, while in a small room directly underneath the statue sit four hundred statues representing the various spiritual incarnations of Guanyin. The view from the statue's base over the surrounding islands and fishing boats is sublime, especially on a clear day.

The northern temples

The two temples in the **northern half of the island**, Huiji and Fayu, make for a pleasant day-trip from town and tend to be less busy than those in the south. A paved marked path, called the Xiangyun Road, connects them, the whole walk taking under an hour. About halfway along is the **Xiangyun Pavilion**, where you can rest and drink tea with the friendly monks, who have sofas outside.

Huiji Temple

慧济寺, huìjì sì · Daily 6am–9pm · ¥5 · cable car daily 7am–5pm, ¥50/return, ¥30 one-way · bus #2

Huiji Temple stands near the top of **Foding Shan** (佛顶山, fódǐng shān), whose summit provides spectacular views of the sea and the surrounding islands. You can hike up or use the **cable car** from the minibus stand. The temple itself, built mainly between 1793 and 1851, occupies a beautiful site just to the northwest of the summit, surrounded by green tea plantations. The halls stand in a flattened area between hoary trees and bamboo groves, the greens, reds, blues and gold of their enamelled tiles gleaming magnificently in the sunshine. There's also a vegetarian restaurant here.

5

Fayu Temple

法雨寺, fǎyǔ sì • Daily 6am–9pm • ¥5 • bus #2

Approaching **Fayu Temple**, listen out for cheesy Buddhist muzak wafting in from the forest – see if you can spot the speakers disguised as rocks. The temple itself forms a superb collection of more than two hundred halls amid huge green trees, built up in levels against the slope. With the mountain behind and the sea just in front, it's a delightful place to sit in peaceful contemplation. The Daxiong Hall has been brilliantly restored, and the Dayuan Hall has a unique beamless arched roof and a dome, around the inside of which squirm nine carved wooden dragons. This hall is said to have been moved here from Nanjing by Emperor Kangxi in 1689. Its statue of **Guanyin**, flanked by monks and nuns, is the focal point of the goddess's birthday celebrations in early April, when thousands of pilgrims and sightseers crowd onto the island for chanting and ceremonies that last all evening.

Fanyin Dong

梵音洞, fányīn dòng • Daily 8am–4.30pm • ¥5 • bus #3

Occasional minibuses head out along the promontory immediately east of Fayu Temple to **Fanyin Dong**, a cave whose name derives from the resemblance of the sound of crashing waves to Buddhist chants. The cave is set in the rocky cliff, with a small shrine actually straddling a ravine. Walking around on the promontory is a pleasure given the absence of crowds and the difficulty of getting lost.

ARRIVAL AND DEPARTURE   PUTUO SHAN

Upon arrival, you can reach Putuo Shan's main "town" near Puji Temple by following either the road heading west or the one east from the jetty, or by picking up a bus from the car park just east of the arrival gate. The westerly route is slightly shorter and takes you past most of the modern buildings and facilities on the island including the banks.

BY AIR

Zhoushan Putuoshan Airport (舟山普陀山机场, zhōushān pǔtuóshān jīchǎng) is, confusingly, actually on the neighbouring island of Zhujiajian (朱家尖, zhūjiājiān). On arrival, catch a bus (every 30min, 5.45am–8pm; ¥15) to Zhujiajian's Wugongshi Wharf (吴宫市码头, wúgōngshì mǎtóu), from where ferries (15min; ¥28) zip over to Putuo Shan. Airline tickets can be bought from the Zhoushan Haixing Tourist Distribution Center, by the Wugongshi Wharf.

BY FERRY

The ferry jetty, where all visitors arrive, is in the island's far south. There's a hotel booking counter here, which can also

provide transport to accommodation – though it's cheaper to get there yourself. When you need to move on from Putuo Shan, you can buy tickets for outbound boats from any of the island's hotels or at the jetty office (daily 6am–6pm).

Shanghai ferries There are two classes of ferries to Shanghai's Luchao Wharf (芦潮港码头, lúcháo gǎng mǎtóu): the fast ferry (1 daily; 4hr; ¥250–349 depending on level of comfort); and the overnight slow boat (Tues, Thurs & Sun; 13hr; ¥200). The slow boat back to Shanghai chugs into the city just after sunrise, providing a memorable view of the awakening metropolis.

Shenjiamen ferries Putuo Shan also has ferries to the transport hub of Shenjiamen (沈家门, shěnjiāmén) on

PUTUO'S BEACHES

You'll appreciate Putuo's beauty much more by making the trip to Huiji Temple and Fayu Temple **on foot** via the two excellent **beaches** that line the eastern shore: the windswept and empty Qianbu Sha (Thousand Step Beach) and more civilized Baibu Sha (Hundred Step Beach). Swimming is only permitted on Hundred Step Beach where there are overly-keen lifeguards with whistles, and also showers (¥10). Be careful where you swim and when, though, as the waters can be extremely dangerous. In summer, it's possible to bring a sleeping bag and camp out on either beach; both are in easy reach of the restaurants along the road. The beaches are separated by a small headland hiding the cave of **Chaoyang Dong**. One kilometre south of Fayu Temple, the **Dacheng Nunnery** (大乘庵, dà chéng' ān; daily 6am–6pm; ¥5) is notable for the reclining Buddha downstairs in the main hall, and the thousands of tiny seated Buddhas upstairs.

neighbouring Zhoushan Island (舟山, zhōushān), from where you can catch direct buses to Shanghai and Hangzhou. Ferries run from Putuo Shan to Shenjiamen's Banshendong Wharf (阪神洞码头, bǎnshéndòng mǎtóu; every 15min, 6.30am–5.30pm): slow ferries (¥14) take 25min, while the fast boats (¥28) take just 10min. From the wharf, catch local bus #6 to Shenjiamen's Chenbei bus station (埕北汽车站, chéng běi qìchē zhàn).

GETTING AROUND

By minibus Putuo Shan's three minibus routes connect the ferry port with Puji Temple and other sights farther north; they run 6am–6pm in summer and autumn, and 6.30am–5.30pm in the winter and spring (¥4–10). Each major attraction has its own minibus station, with the destinations (and price) written in English at the stops – which is just as well, as vehicles aren't numbered.

INFORMATION

Tourist information Staff at the ferry terminal tourism desk speak a little English, can book hotels, and also sell maps of the island in Chinese (¥10). However, Puji Temple's Tourism Information Centre (daily 9am–7pm) is better, whose staff not only speak excellent English and know what they're talking about, but also hand out free English-language guides and maps.

ACCOMMODATION

Much of the island's accommodation is spread between the ferry terminal and Putuo Shan's main "town", a tiny collection of buildings 1km north near Puji Temple, with a recognizable central square around three ponds. Options include a number of converted monasteries, but be warned that during the weekend stampede out of Shanghai, rooms are scarce and expensive; prices given here represent weekend rates, outside of which (even in summer) they fall sharply. Another option is to stay in a private house; though technically illegal for foreigners, it's not hard to find people with rooms to let – they congregate at the jetty pier, and you should be able to bargain them down to around ¥150 per room. A third option, pursued especially by younger foreign travellers, is to crash on one of the island's two beaches for the night (see box opposite).

★**Putuoshan Hotel** 普陀山大酒店, pǔtuóshān dàjiǔdiàn. On the main west road from the jetty to the town ☎0580 6092828. Very easy to spot, thanks to its spacious grounds and opulent design, this is the best hotel in the south of the island, with cheaper prices than some less salubrious competitors. Traditional Chinese furniture in the classier rooms, and an on-site vegetarian restaurant. **¥1568**

Xiang Sheng Grand Hotel 祥生大酒店, xiángshēng dàjiǔdiàn. ☎0580 6696666, ⓦwww.xsdjhotel.com. Perched up on a headland overlooking the sea by Fuding Shan in the north, this new 5-star has big, comfortable rooms and most have balconies with fantastic views. Staff are friendly, the service is good and there are three restaurants serving seafood, Cantonese and Southeast Asian cuisine. Has all the facilities you'd expect, and runs a private minibus fleet for getting around the island. **¥1880**

Xiang Yuan 翔园宾馆, xiángyuán bīnguǎn. ☎0580 6095298, ⓦwww.ptsxybg.com. In the little square on the western road from the jetty before the Bank of China, this is one of the cheapest hotels on the island, and its rooms are fairly comfortable and clean, if slightly old and decrepit. There are three other slightly more expensive places nearby, whose rooms are the same but new. **¥580**

EATING

Most food must be brought in from the mainland and is, therefore, expensive. The lane running northeast away from Puji Temple, and the road between the jetty departure and arrival points, both have some dingy-looking places specializing in seafood (fish, molluscs, eel) though they also do standard dishes and noodles starting at around ¥40. All the main temples have simple vegetarian restaurants which serve breakfast (5.30–6.30am), lunch (10.30–11.30am), and supper (4.30–5.30pm) for just ¥2.5–10 a person. There's also an upscale vegetarian place attached to the *Putuoshan Hotel*, which serves food at more convenient times.

DIRECTORY

Banks and exchange The Bank of China (daily 8–11am & 1–4.30pm; ATM 24hr) is on the westerly route into town from the ferry jetty.

Mail The post office (8am–4.30pm) is just past the Bank of China, up a small lane to the right.

Shanghai

THE BUND

Shanghai

上海, shànghǎi

6

After years of stagnation, the great metropolis of Shanghai is undergoing one of the fastest economic expansions the world has ever seen. As Shanghai begins to recapture its position as East Asia's leading business city, a status it last held before World War II, the skyline is filling with high-rises – there are well over a thousand now. Gleaming shopping malls, luxurious hotels and prestigious arts centres are rising alongside, while underneath everything snakes the world's longest subway system. Shanghai's 23 million residents enjoy the highest incomes on the mainland, and there's plenty for them to splash out on; witness the rash of celebrity restaurants and designer flagship stores. In short, it's a city with a swagger, bursting with nouveau-riche exuberance and élan. And yet, for all the modernization, Shanghai is still known in the West for its infamous role as the base of European imperialism in mainland China during the 1930s.

Whichever side you were on, life in Shanghai then was rarely one of moderation. China's most prosperous city, in large part European- and American-financed, Shanghai introduced Asia to electric light, boasted more cars than the rest of the country put together, and created for its rich citizens a world of European-style mansions, tree-lined boulevards, chic café society, horse-racing and exclusive gentlemen's clubs. Alongside, and as much part of the legend, lay a city of singsong girls, warring gangsters and millions living in absolute poverty.

Then came the Japanese invasion, civil war and the communist victory. With their egalitarian, anti-Western stance, China's new rulers despised everything that pre-war Shanghai had stood for and deliberately ran the city down, siphoning off its surplus to other parts of the country. Shanghai came to resemble a living museum, housing the largest array of **Art Deco architecture** in the world. Yet the Shanghainese never lost their ability to make waves for themselves. The present boom dates back to 1990, with the opening of the "New Bund" – the Special Economic Zone across the river in Pudong. Ever since, the city has enjoyed double digit growth, and if present plans for a new economic free trade zone come to pass, it will likely one day rival Hong Kong as Asia's financial centre.

Yet old Shanghai has not disappeared. Most of the urban area was partitioned between foreign powers until 1949, and their former embassies, banks and official residences still give large sections of Shanghai an early twentieth-century European flavour. It's still possible to make out the boundaries of what used to be the foreign concessions, with the bewildering tangle of alleyways of the old Chinese city at its heart. Only along the Huangpu waterfront, amid the stolid grandeur of the **Bund**, is there some sense of space – and here you feel the past more strongly than ever. It's ironic that the relics of hated foreign imperialism are now protected as city monuments.

HUXIN TING TEAHOUSE, YU YUAN

Highlights

❶ The Bund Fusty colonial architecture and brash modernity stare each other down over the Huangpu River. **See p.352**

❷ Huangpu boat trips Get out on the river for a sense of the maritime industry that's at the heart of the city's success. **See p.353**

❸ Shanghai Museum A candidate for the best museum in the country, with a wide range of exhibits housed in a building that's shaped like an ancient Chinese pottery vessel. **See p.358**

❹ Yu Yuan An elegant Chinese garden with opportunities to snack and sip tea in the vicinity. See p.360

❺ Tianzifang Intriguing, fun shopping district of traditional housing turned into boutiques. See p.363

❻ Shanghai World Financial Centre observation platform The view from the top floor of Shanghai's finest building is simply awesome. See p.366

❼ Cocktail bars Dress up, and enjoy a drink with the smart set: Shanghai has the most sophisticated nightlife on the mainland. See p.380

HIGHLIGHTS ARE MARKED ON THE MAP ON PP.350–351

Shanghai does not brim with obvious attractions, however. Besides the Shanghai Museum, the Suzhou-reminiscent gardens of Yu Yuan, and the Huangpu River cruise, there are few tourist sights with broad appeal. But the place absolutely excels in all materialistic pleasures, so make sure you sample the fantastic restaurant and nightlife scenes, and budget some time for serious shopping. Perhaps the greatest fascination is in simply absorbing the splendour of a city so extravagantly on the up. Shanghai is also one of the few Chinese cities that rewards aimless wandering, and

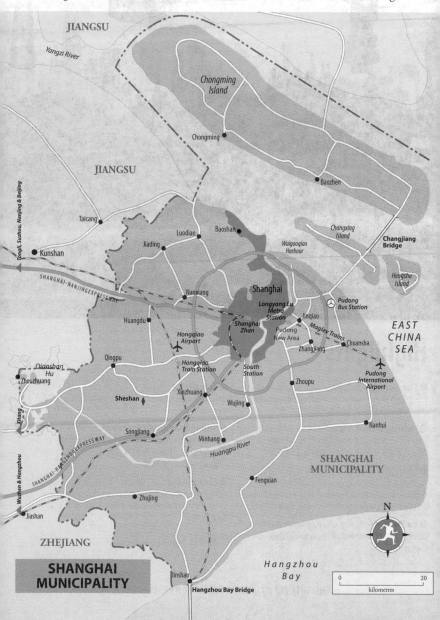

it's fascinating to stroll the Bund, explore the pockets of colonial architecture in the former French Concession, or get lost in the old city's alleys.

Brief history

Located at the confluence of the Yangzi River, the Grand Canal and the Pacific Ocean, Shanghai served as a major commercial port from the Song dynasty, channelling the region's extensive cotton crop to Beijing, the hinterland and Japan. By the Qing dynasty, vast **mercantile guilds** had established economic and, to some extent, political control of the city. In the words of East India Company representative Hugh Lindsay, "the city had become the principal emporium of Eastern Asia" by the 1840s.

The Concession Era

Following the **Opium Wars**, the British moved in under the Treaty of Nanking in 1842, to be rapidly followed by the French in 1847. These two powers set up the first **foreign concessions** in the city – the British along the Bund and the area to the north of the Chinese city, the French in an area to the southwest, on the site of a cathedral a French missionary had founded two centuries earlier. Later the Americans (in 1863) and the Japanese (in 1895) came to tack their own areas onto the British Concession, which expanded into the so-called International Settlement. Traders were allowed to live under their own national laws, policed by their own armed forces, in a series of privileged enclaves that were leased indefinitely. By 1900, the city's favourable position, close to the main trade route to the major silk- and tea-producing regions, had allowed it to develop into a sizeable port and manufacturing centre. At this time, it was largely controlled by the "Green Gang", the infamous Chinese crime syndicate founded in the 1700s by unemployed boatmen, which by the 1920s ran the city's vast underworld. Businessmen and criminals who flouted the Green Gang's strict code of behaviour were subject to "knee-capping" punishment – having every visible tendon severed with a fruit knife before being left to die on a busy pavement.

Shanghai's cheap workforce was swollen during the Taiping Uprising (see p.312) by those who took shelter from the slaughter in the foreign settlements, and by peasants attracted to the city's apparent prosperity. Here China's first urban proletariat emerged, and the squalid living conditions, outbreaks of unemployment and glaring abuses of Chinese labour by foreign investors made Shanghai a natural breeding ground for **revolutionary politics**. The Chinese Communist Party was founded in the city in 1921, only to be driven underground by the notorious massacre of hundreds of strikers in 1927.

The Communist era

Inevitably, after the Communist takeover in 1949, the bright lights dimmed. The foreign community may have expected "business as usual", but the new regime was determined that Shanghai should play its role in the radical reconstruction of China. The worst slums were knocked down to be replaced by apartments, the gangsters and prostitutes were taken away for "re-education", and foreign capital was ruthlessly taxed if not confiscated outright (although Chiang Kai-shek did manage to spirit away the gold reserves of the Bank of China to Taiwan, leaving the city broke). For 35 years, Western influences were forcibly suppressed.

Even after 1949, the city remained a centre of radicalism – Mao, stifled by Beijing bureaucracy, launched his Cultural Revolution here in 1966. Certain Red Guards even proclaimed a Shanghai Commune, before the whole affair descended into wanton destruction and petty vindictiveness. After Mao's death, Shanghai was the last stronghold of the Gang of Four in their struggle for the succession, though their planned coup never materialized.

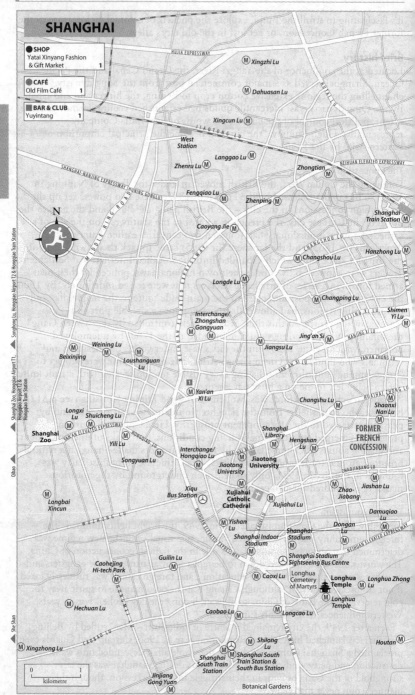

SHANGHAI

● SHOP	
Yatai Xinyang Fashion & Gift Market	1

● CAFÉ	
Old Film Café	1

■ BAR & CLUB	
Yuyintang	1

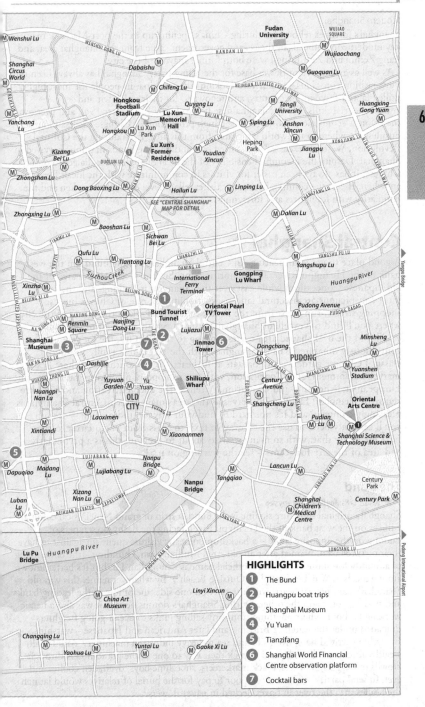

HIGHLIGHTS

1. The Bund
2. Huangpu boat trips
3. Shanghai Museum
4. Yu Yuan
5. Tianzifang
6. Shanghai World Financial Centre observation platform
7. Cocktail bars

6

Modern Shanghai

Shanghai's fortunes rebounded during China's opening up in the post-Mao era: many key modernizing officials in the central government came from the Shanghai area, and Jiang Zemin and Zhu Rongji were both former mayors of the city.

As well as an important power base for the ruling party, Shanghai has always been the most fashion-conscious and **outward-looking** city in China, its people the most highly skilled labour force in the country, and renowned for their quick wit and entrepreneurial skills. Many Shanghainese fled to Hong Kong after 1949 and oversaw the colony's economic explosion, while a high proportion of Chinese successful in business elsewhere in the world emigrated from this area. Even during the Cultural Revolution, Western "excesses" like curled hair and holding hands in public survived in Shanghai. Despite the incomprehensibility of the local Shanghainese dialect to other Chinese, it has always been easier for visitors to communicate with the locals here than anywhere else in the country, because of the excellent level of English spoken and the familiarity with foreigners and foreignness.

Central Shanghai

A good place to get your bearings in Central Shanghai is at the **Bund**, on the west bank of the Huangpu River. To the north, across Suzhou Creek, is the area of the old Japanese Concession; while east over the Huangpu is Pudong, and the city's most conspicuous architectural landmarks. **Nanjing Lu**, one of China's busiest shopping streets, runs west from the Bund, to **Renmin Park** in the centre of the city, where you'll find the excellent Shanghai Museum. South and west of the Bund, you'll find the oval-shaped area corresponding to the **Old City**, the longest continuously inhabited part of Shanghai, with the Yu Yuan – a fully restored classical Chinese garden – and bazaars at its heart. To the southwest of here lies the marvellous **former French Concession**, with its cosmopolitan cooking traditions, chic European-style housing and revolutionary relics. The energetic eating and nightlife centre of Shanghai, Huaihai Lu, serves as the area's main artery. Central Shanghai is pleasingly compact, and it's not hard to find your way around on foot – though you'll certainly need to use the subway or taxis to cross from one quarter to the next. Be aware that, with so many tourists about to prey on, this is a particularly bad area of the city for **scams** – see the warning on p.51.

The Bund

外滩, wàitān • Nanjing Dong Lu subway stop

Shanghai's original signature skyline is the **Bund**, a strip of grand Neoclassical colonial edifices on the west bank of the Huangpu River, facing the flashy skyscrapers of Pudong on the opposite shore – a backdrop domestic visitors queue up against to have their picture taken. Named after an old Anglo-Indian term, "bunding" (the embanking of a muddy foreshore), the Bund's official name is Zhongshan Lu, but it's better known among locals as Wai Tan (literally "Outside Beach"). By whatever name, this was old Shanghai's commercial heart, with the river on one side, the offices of the leading banks and trading houses on the other. During Shanghai's riotous heyday it was also a hectic working harbour, where anything from tiny sailing junks to ocean-going freighters unloaded under the watch of British – and later American and Japanese – warships. Everything arrived here, from silk and tea to heavy industrial machinery. Amid it all, wealthy foreigners disembarked to pick their way to one of the grand hotels through crowds of beggars, hawkers, black marketeers, shoeshine boys, overladen coolies and even funeral parties – Chinese too poor to pay for the burial of relatives would launch the bodies into the river in boxes decked in paper flowers.

Shanghai Post Museum

上海邮政博物馆, shànghǎi yóuzhèng bówùguǎn • 276 Suzhou Bei Lu • Wed, Thurs, Sat & Sun 9am–4pm • Free • ☎ 021 63936666, ⓦ www.shpost.com.cn • Tiantong Lu subway stop

Before tackling the Bund, have a look at the Main Post Office, just north of it, built in 1931, and easily recognizable by its clocktower. It's the only Bund building that has never been used for anything but its original function. It houses the **Shanghai Post Museum** on the third floor, which is more interesting than it sounds. The collection of letters and stamps is only mildly diverting, but the new atrium is very impressive, and the view of the Bund from the grassed-over roof is superb.

6

Waibaidu Bridge

外白渡桥, wàibáidù qiáo • Nanjing Dong Lu subway stop

Waibaidu Bridge, whose arched metal frame spans Suzhou Creek, marks the Bund's northern edge. It was built by the British in 1908, and was China's first steel truss bridge. At the outbreak of the Sino-Japanese War in 1937, the bridge formed a no-man's-land between the Japanese-occupied areas north of Suzhou Creek and the **International Settlement** – it was guarded at one end by Japanese sentries, the other by British. Today it's a popular spot for wedding photographs, and you'll see brides-to-be braving the traffic in order to be briefly framed by its striking girders.

The first building south of the bridge was one of the cornerstones of British interests in old Shanghai, the former **British Consulate**, once ostentatiously guarded by magnificently dressed Sikh soldiers. The blue building just to the northeast of here across the Suzhou Creek still retains its original function as the **Russian Consulate**.

Huangpu Park

黄浦公园, huángpǔ gōngyuán • Zhongshan Dong Yi Lu • Free • Nanjing Dong Lu subway stop

Right on the corner of the Huangpu and Suzhou Creek, **Huangpu Park** was a British creation, the British Public Gardens, established on a patch of land formed when mud and silt gathered around a wrecked ship. Though it's firmly established in the Chinese popular imagination as a symbol of Western racism, there's no evidence that there ever was a sign here reading "No Dogs or Chinese Allowed". However, Sikh troops enforced a ban on Chinese from entering, unless they were servants accompanying their

---

HUANGPU RIVER TOURS

One highlight of a visit to Shanghai, and the easiest way to view the edifices of the Bund, is to take one of the **Huangpu River tours** (黄浦江旅游, huángpǔ jiāng lǚyóu). On the tour, you're introduced to the vast amount of shipping that uses the port, and you'll also be able to inspect all the paraphernalia of the shipping industry, from sampans and rusty old Panamanian-registered freighters to sparkling Chinese navy vessels. You'll also get an idea of the colossal construction that is taking place on the eastern shore. Evening cruises offer spectacular views, as Shanghai is lit up like a pinball machine at night.

Cruises leave from Shiliupu Wharf at the south end of the Bund, opposite Jinling Dong Lu at 171 Zhongshan Nan Lu. You can buy tickets at the wharf or at the Bund Tourist Information Centre, beside the entrance to the Bund Tourist Tunnel. You can also book direct with one of the many cruise operators, such as the Huangpu River Company (☎021 63740091; ⓦpjrivercruise.com). You can book tickets a few days in advance over the phone and they will deliver to your hotel.

Departure times vary depending on season and weather. Ninety-minute long cruises (¥128) depart at least twice an hour daily between 11am and 9.30pm. Hour-long cruises (¥100) are rarer, usually hourly, and there is one daily three-hour cruise (¥150) at 2pm, which goes all the way to the mouth of the Yangzi and back. Cruises that include a buffet dinner run between 7pm and 9pm (¥200).

It is also possible to take half-hour cruises from Pudong. These leave from the Pearl Dock, every half hour between 10am and 1.30pm (¥100).

6

employer. After protests, the regulations were relaxed to admit "well-dressed" Chinese, who had to apply for a special entry permit. These days, the park contains a stone monument to the "Heroes of the People", and is also a popular spot for citizens practicing *tai ji* early in the morning, but it's best simply for the promenade that commands the junction of the two rivers.

Rockbund Art Museum

外滩美术馆, wàitān měishùguǎn · 20 Huqiu Lu · Tues–Sun 10am–6pm · ¥15 · ☎ 021 33109985, ⓦ www.rockbundartmuseum.org · Nanjing Dong Lu subway stop

The narrow streets leading back from the Bund hold some fine Art Deco buildings, and the **Rockbund Art Museum**, a strikingly tall and angular hulk tucked behind the *Peninsula Hotel*, is one of the best. It dates back to the 1930s, when it was the headquarters of the Royal Asiatic Society. Now it's been skilfully restored and converted into a four-storey gallery of contemporary art, hosting shows that usually mix China's biggest hitters with international artists. There's no permanent exhibition so check the website for what's on, and for the programme of events and lectures.

The Fairmont Peace Hotel

和平饭店, hépíng fàndiàn · 20 Nanjing Dong Lu · ☎ 021 63216888, ⓦ fairmont.com/peace-hotel-shanghai · Nanjing Dong Lu subway stop

Straddling the eastern end of Nanjing Lu is one of the most famous hotels in China, the **Fairmont Peace Hotel**, formerly the *Cathay*. The place to be seen in prewar Shanghai, it offered guests a private plumbing system fed by a spring on the outskirts of town, marble baths with silver taps, and vitreous china lavatories imported from Britain. The sensitively restored *Peace* is well worth a visit today, just to walk around the lobby and corridors to take in the Art Deco elegance. On the first floor, a little **museum** of the hotel's history (daily 10am–7pm) displays relics such as room keys and lampshades from the thirties, and plenty of old photographs, including one of Mao meeting Monty.

The Bank of China

中国银行, zhōngguó yínháng · 19 Zhongshan Dong Yi Lu · Nanjing Dong Lu subway stop

Next door to the *Peace Hotel*, at no. 19 on the Bund, the **Bank of China** was designed in the 1920s by Shanghai architectural firm Palmer & Turner, who brought in a Chinese architect to make the building "more Chinese" after construction was complete. The architect placed a pagoda-like roof onto the Art Deco edifice, creating a delightful juxtaposition of styles, an idea that is being endlessly and much less successfully copied across the nation today.

Number 18 The Bund

外滩18号, wàitān shíbā hào · Contemporary Art Gallery Tues–Sun, 11am–9pm ☎ 021 63238099, ⓦ www.bund18.com/art-culture/18gallery · Nanjing Dong Lu subway stop

Number 18 The Bund was originally the Chartered Bank of India and Australia, but today is home to the city's ritziest shops, given gravitas by the building's Italian marble columns. As well as top-end retail outlets such as Cartier, the building houses swanky *Bar Rouge* (see p.380) above, which has a fantastic roof terrace with views of Pudong. There's also a **contemporary art gallery** on the third floor.

The Customs House

海关楼, hǎiguān lóu · 13 Zhongshan Dong Yi Lu · Nanjing Dong Lu subway stop

The **Customs House** is one of the few Bund buildings to have retained its original function, though its distinctive clocktower was adapted to chime *The East is Red* at six o'clock every morning and evening during the Cultural Revolution (the original clockwork has since been restored). The clocktower was modelled on the one in London housing Big Ben, and after its completion in 1927, local legend had it that the

> **GREAT BRITISH DRUG DEALERS**
>
> **Jardine Matheson**, founded by William Jardine – the man who did more than any other individual to precipitate the Opium Wars and open Shanghai up to foreign trade – was the first foreign concern to buy land in Shanghai. Their former base (they lost all of their holdings in China after 1949), just north of the *Peace Hotel*, is now occupied by the China Textiles Export Corporation.
>
> The wealth of the **Sassoon** family, too, was built on opium, but by the early years of the last century, the family fortune had mostly been sunk into Shanghai real estate, including the *Cathay* (originally known as *Sassoon House*). The flamboyant Victor Sassoon lived long enough to see his hotel virtually destroyed by the Japanese, including his rooftop private apartment, with 360-degree views and dark oak panelling (it has recently been restored), but also long enough to get most of his money away to the Bahamas.

6

chimes that struck each fifteen minutes confused the God of Fire: believing the chimes were a firebell, the god decided Shanghai was suffering from too many conflagrations, and decided not to send any more. You can step into the downstairs lobby for a peek at some mosaics of maritime motifs on the ceiling.

Hong Kong and Shanghai Bank

汇丰中国, huì fēng zhōngguó · 12 Zhongshan Dong Yi Lu · Nanjing Dong Lu subway stop

Right next to the Customs House, and also with an easily recognizable domed roofline, the former headquarters of the **Hong Kong and Shanghai Bank** (built in 1921) has one of the most imposing of the Bund facades. Each wall of the marble octagonal entrance originally boasted a mural depicting the Bank's eight primary locations: Bangkok, Calcutta, Hong Kong, London, New York, Paris, Shanghai and Tokyo. It's considered lucky to rub the noses of the bronze lions that stand guard outside.

Five and Three on the Bund

Nanjing Dong Lu subway stop

The section of the Bund south of Fuzhou Lu boasts some very posh addresses. Number five, officially known as **Five on the Bund** (外滩5号, wài tān wǔ hào), is entered on Guangdong Lu. Here you'll find the ritzy *Glamour Bar* (see p.380) and the upscale restaurant, *M on the Bund* (see p.377) which kicked off the area's renaissance when it opened in 1999.

Three on the Bund

外滩3号, wài tān sān hào; Gallery of Art daily 11am–9pm; ☎ 021 63215757, ⓦ shanghaigalleryofart.com

A little further down, **Three on the Bund** is perhaps the most luxurious of the new developments: there's an Armani flagship store, Evian spa, five swish restaurants, and continuingly changing contemporary exhibitions at the Shanghai Gallery of Art.

Waldorf Astoria Hotel

华尔道夫酒店, huá'ěr dàofū jiǔdiàn · 2 Zhongshan Dong Yi Lu · ☎ 021 63229988, ⓦ www.waldorfastoriashanghai.com · Nanjing Dong Lu subway stop

When this building opened in 1910, it was a private members' club for well-heeled Brits. It closed its doors with the arrival of the communists, then languished, semi-derelict, for decades. Happily, it has recently been restored to its full glory as the **Waldorf Astoria Hotel**. As with the other heritage hotels in the area, it is forbiddingly expensive to stay in, but worth a visit to check out the stylish interior – in this case, Neoclassical opulence. Don't miss the **Long Bar**, a fine evocation of 1930s Shanghai, reconstructed from photos after the original was torn out at some point in the 1980s. The eastern end of the original 12m-long bar commanded a view of the Huangpu, and only the club's elite members were allowed to sit there.

6

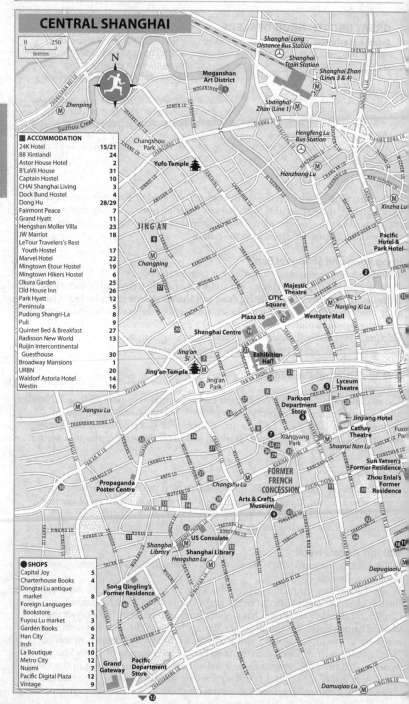

CENTRAL SHANGHAI

0   250
metres

ACCOMMODATION

24K Hotel	15/21
88 Xintiandi	24
Astor House Hotel	2
B'LaVii House	31
Captain Hostel	10
CHAI Shanghai Living	3
Dock Bund Hostel	4
Dong Hu	28/29
Fairmont Peace	7
Grand Hyatt	11
Hengshan Moller Villa	23
JW Marriot	18
LeTour Travelers's Rest Youth Hostel	17
Marvel Hotel	22
Mingtown Etour Hostel	19
Mingtown Hikers Hostel	6
Okura Garden	25
Old House Inn	26
Park Hyatt	12
Peninsula	5
Pudong Shangri-La	8
Puli	9
Quintet Bed & Breakfast	27
Radisson New World	13
Ruijin Intercontinental Guesthouse	30
Broadway Mansions	1
URBN	20
Waldorf Astoria Hotel	14
Westin	16

SHOPS

Capital Joy	5
Charterhouse Books	4
Dongtai Lu antique market	8
Foreign Languages Bookstore	1
Fuyou Lu market	3
Garden Books	6
Han City	2
Insh	11
La Boutique	10
Metro City	12
Nuomi	7
Pacific Digital Plaza	12
Vintage	9

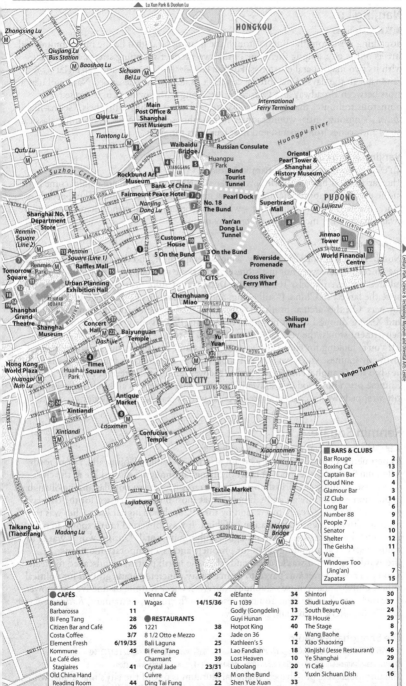

■ BARS & CLUBS

Bar Rouge	2
Boxing Cat	13
Captain Bar	5
Cloud Nine	4
Glamour Bar	3
JZ Club	14
Long Bar	6
Number 88	9
People 7	8
Senator	10
Shelter	12
The Geisha	11
Vue	1
Windows Too (Jing'an)	7
Zapatas	15

● CAFÉS

Bandu	1
Barbarossa	11
Bi Feng Tang	28
Citizen Bar and Café	26
Costa Coffee	3/7
Element Fresh	6/19/35
Kommune	45
Le Café des Stagiaires	41
Old China Hand Reading Room	44
Vienna Café	42
Wagas	14/15/36

● RESTAURANTS

1221	38
8 1/2 Otto e Mezzo	2
Bali Laguna	25
Bi Feng Tang	21
Charmant	39
Crystal Jade	23/31
Cuivre	43
Ding Tai Fung	22
elEfante	34
Fu 1039	32
Godly (Gongdelin)	13
Guyi Hunan	27
Hotpot King	40
Jade on 36	4
Kathleen's 5	12
Lao Fandian	18
Lost Heaven	39
Lubolang	20
M on the Bund	5
Shen Yue Xuan	33
Shintori	30
Shudi Laziyu Guan	37
South Beauty	24
T8 House	29
The Stage	8
Wang Baohe	9
Xiao Shaoxing	17
Xinjishi (Jesse Restaurant)	46
Ye Shanghai	29
Yi Café	4
Yuxin Sichuan Dish	16

6

Nanjing Lu

南京路, nánjīng lù

Stretching west from the Bund through the heart of Shanghai lie the main commercial streets of the city, among them one of the two premier shopping streets, **Nanjing Lu**, with its two major parallel arteries, **Fuzhou Lu** (福州路, fúzhōu lù) and **Yan'an Lu** (延安路, yán'ān lù). In the days of the foreign concessions, expatriates described Nanjing Lu as a cross between Broadway and Oxford Street; along with Fuzhou Lu, it housed numerous teahouses that functioned as the city's most exclusive brothels. Geisha-like *shuyu* ("singsong" girls) would saunter from teahouse to teahouse, performing classical plays and scenes from operas, and host banquets for guests.

Nanjing Dong Lu

南京东路, nángjīng dōng lù · Nanjing Dong Lu subway stop

The garish neon lights and window displays of **Nanjing Dong Lu** are iconic; come here in the evening to appreciate the lightshow in its full tacky splendour. The spectacle is more diverting than the shopping – which is generally cheap rather than chic – and be aware that foreign men will be pestered by pimps.

Some stores

Number 635 was once the glorious **Wing On** emporium, and diagonally opposite was the **Sincere**. These were not just stores: inside, there were restaurants, rooftop gardens, cabarets and even hotels. The **Shanghai Department Store** near Guizhou Lu at no. 800, once the largest in China, is still going, and is still a place of pilgrimage for out-of-towners. Off the circular overhead walkway at the junction between Nanjing Dong Lu and Xizang Zhong Lu, just northeast of Renmin Park, is the grandest of the district's department stores, the venerable **Shanghai No. 1 Store**.

If you're looking for cheap clothes, you'll be spoilt for choice, but for something distinctly Chinese you'll have to look a bit harder. Your best bet for curiosities is to head to the **Shanghai First Food Store** at the west end of the street, at no. 720. The Chinese often buy food as a souvenir, and this busy store sells all kinds of locally made gift-wrapped sweets, cakes and preserves, as well as tea and tasty pastries.

Renmin Square

人民广场, rénmín guǎngchǎng · Renmin Square subway stop

Its perimeters defined by the city's main arteries – Xizang, Nanjing and Yan'an roads – **Renmin Square** is the modern heart of Shanghai, though it started life as the city's racecourse, built by the British in 1862. The races became so popular among Shanghai's population – both foreign and Chinese – that most businesses closed for the ten-day periods of the twice-yearly meets, and by the 1920s the Shanghai Race Club was the third-wealthiest foreign corporation in China. It was converted into a sports arena in 1941 by Chiang Kai-shek, who thought gambling immoral. During World War II the stadium served as a holding camp for prisoners and as a temporary mortuary; afterwards, most of it was levelled, and while the north part was landscaped to create Renmin Park, the rest was paved to form a dusty concrete parade ground for political rallies. Only the racecourse's **clubhouse** survives; check out the distinctive clocktower, once nicknamed Little Ben. You can head up to the rooftop restaurant, *Kathleen's 5* (see p.377), for afternoon tea and good views.

The Shanghai Museum

上海博物馆, shànghǎi bówùguǎn · 201 Renmin Avenue · Daily 9am–5pm · Free · ☎ 021 63723500, ⓦ www.shanghaimuseum.net/en · audio-guide ¥40 plus ¥400 deposit · Renmin Square subway stop

The unmistakeable pot-shaped **Shanghai Museum** is one of the city's highlights, with a fantastic, well-presented collection. On the ground floor, the gallery of ancient **bronzes** holds cooking vessels, containers and weapons, many covered with intricate geometrical designs that reference animal shapes – check out the cowrie container from the Western Han dynasty, with handles shaped like stalking tigers. Most of the exhibits in the sculpture gallery next door are of religious figures – boggle-eyed temple guardians, serene Buddhas and the like, including a row of huge, fearsome Tang-dynasty heads. Tang-dynasty figurines again steal the show in the first-floor ceramics gallery, in the form of multicoloured ferocious-looking beasties placed to guard tombs.

The upper floors

On the second floor, skip the calligraphy and carved seals unless you have a special interest and investigate the **painting** gallery, which shows some amazingly naturalistic Ming-dynasty images of animals. The colourful top-floor exhibition dedicated to Chinese **minority peoples** is the museum highlight. One wall is lined with spooky lacquered masks from Tibet and Guizhou, while nearby are colourfully decorated boats from the Taiwanese minority, the Gaoshan. The silver ceremonial headdresses of southwest China's Miao people are breathtaking for their intricacy, if rather impractical to wear. Elaborate abstract designs turn the Dai lacquered tableware into art. In the section on traditional costumes, look out for the fish-skin suit made by the Hezhen people of Dongbei, in the far north.

Shanghai Urban Planning Exhibition Hall

城市规划展示馆, chéngshì guīhuà zhǎnshìguǎn • 100 Renmin Avenue • Tues–Sun 9am–5pm, last entry 4pm • ¥30 • Ⓦ supec.org/english/english_page.htm • People's Square subway stop

It's revealing of the Shanghai mindset that one of the city's grandest museums is dedicated not to the past but the future: the **Shanghai Urban Planning Exhibition Hall** is interesting for its insight into the vision of the city planners, though if you're not keen on slick propaganda presentations it can be safely skipped. Most worthy of note is the tennis-court-sized model of the city on the second floor, showing what it will (hopefully) look like when the current round of mordernizations is finished in 2020. There's no room in this brave new world for shabby little alleyways; it's a parade ground of skyscrapers and apartment blocks in which, according to this model, the whole of the Old City (see p.360) is doomed.

Renmin Park

人民公园, rénmín gōngyuán • Free • People's Square subway stop

Renmin Park is surprisingly quiet, with rocky paths winding between shady groves and alongside ponds – the only sign that you are in the heart of a modern city is the view of skyscrapers looming above the treetops. At weekends the north section of the park serves as an informal marriage market, and is rammed with busybody parents setting up dates for their unmarried adult children.

Museum of Contemporary Art (MoCA)

上海当代艺术馆 shànghǎi dāngdài yìshùguǎn • Daily 10am–6pm • ¥20, students free • ☎ 021 63279000, Ⓦ mocashanghai.org

This attractive little two-storey art gallery nestles in a bamboo grove, beside a lotus pond. There is no permanent collection but its themed shows are imaginatively curated, and there are regular talks and tours; check the website for details.

Nanjing Xi Lu

南京西路, nánjīng xīlù • Nanjing Xi Lu subway stop

The western end of Nanjing Xi Lu was known to "**Shanghailanders**" (the Europeans who made their homes here) as Bubbling Well Road, after a spring that used to gush at the far end of the street. Then, as today, it was one of the smartest addresses in the city, leading into tree-lined streets where Westerners' mock-Tudor mansions sheltered behind high walls. Now it's also the location of a number of malls and luxury hotels, including the **Shanghai Centre** (上海商城, shànghǎi shāngchéng), a complex of shops, restaurants and residential flats centred around the five-star *Portman Hotel*.

The Pacific and Park hotels

The historic **Pacific and Park hotels** also stand on Nanjing Xi Lu opposite Renmin Park. The *Park* (国际饭店, guójì fàndiàn), for many years the tallest building in Shanghai, once had a reputation for superb food as well as for its dances, when the roof would be rolled back to allow guests to cavort under the stars. Latterly, Mao Zedong always stayed here when he was in Shanghai. Today, however, the interior has been stripped of most of its old-world charm. The *Pacific* (金门大酒店, jīnmén dàjiǔdiàn), by contrast, a few metres to the east of the *Park*, is still worth having a look at, both for its ostentatious facade and for the fabulous plaster reliefs in the lobby.

Jing'an Temple

静安寺, jìng'ān sì • 1686 Nanjing Xi Lu • Daily 7.30am–5pm • ¥10 • Jiang'an Si subway stop • bus #20 from Renmin Square

Jing'an Temple is a small, active temple nestling beside the tiny **Jing'an Park** and under looming high-rises. Building work first began on the temple during the Three Kingdoms period, and its apparent obscurity belies its past as the richest Buddhist foundation in the city, headed by legendary abbot Khi Vehdu, who combined his abbotly duties with a gangster lifestyle. The abbot and his seven concubines were shadowed by White Russian bodyguards, each carrying a leather briefcase lined with bulletproof steel, to be used as a shield in case of attack.

Today, the temple is the primary place of ancestral worship in the city, although an equal number of people come to pray for more material reasons – worshippers eagerly throw coins into incense burners in the hope that the gods will bestow financial success. The three main halls have recently been lavishly renovated with Burmese teak.

The Old City

老城, lǎochéng

Shanghai's **Old City** is that strange oval on the map, circumscribed by two roads, Renmin Lu and Zhonghua Lu, which follow the old path of the city walls. The Old City never formed part of the International Settlement and was somewhat contemptuously known by resident foreigners as the **Chinese City**. Based on the original **walled city** of Shanghai, which dated back to the eleventh century, the area was reserved in the nineteenth and early twentieth centuries as a ghetto for vast numbers of Chinese who lived in conditions of appalling squalor, while the foreigners carved out their living space around them.

Ring roads had already replaced the original walls and moats as early as 1912, and sanitation has obviously improved vastly since the last century, but to cross the boundaries into the Old City is still to glimpse a different world. The twisting alleyways are a haven of free enterprise, bursting with makeshift markets selling fish, vegetables, cheap trinkets, clothing and food. Ironically, for a tourist entering the area, the feeling is like entering a Chinatown in a Western city. The centre of activity today is an area known locally as **Chenghuang Miao** (after a local temple), where one of the city's main draws, the peaceful **Yuyuan Garden**, sits at the centre of a busy tourist bazaar.

Yu Yuan

豫园, yù yuán • Daily 8.30am–5.30pm • ¥40 • Yu Yuan subway stop

A classical Chinese garden featuring pools, walkways, bridges and rockeries, the **Yu Yuan** was created in the sixteenth century by a high official in the imperial court in honour of his father. The Yu Yuan is less impressive than the gardens of nearby Suzhou, but given that it predates the relics of the International Settlement by some three hundred years, the Shanghainese are understandably proud of it. Despite fluctuating fortunes, the garden has surprisingly survived the passage of the centuries. It was spared from its greatest crisis – the Cultural Revolution – apparently because the anti-imperialist "Little Sword Society" had used it as their headquarters in 1853 during the Taiping Uprising.

Inside the garden
Undulating **dragon walls** – literally shaped like dragons, with scales, heads and all – divide the five-acre site into six areas, each of which is designed as a pocket landscape, to be viewed from a well-placed hall or pavilion. Particularly impressive is the rockery outside the **Sansui Hall**, a miniature mountain range of peaks, grottoes and caves. At the centre of the garden, next to the Yuhua Hall, stands the craggy "Exquisite Jade Rock" – a five-tonne boulder riddled with holes, which was much admired as a wonder of nature in its day. Tour guides burn a joss stick under it, and the smoke emerges through a dozen holes at once.

Yu Yuan is perhaps at its brightest during the Lantern Festival on the fifteenth day of the traditional New Year, when ten thousand lanterns (and an even larger number of spectators) decorate the garden.

Huxin Ting
湖心亭茶馆, húxīntíng cháguǎn · 257 Yuyuan Lu · Daily 8am–9pm · Yu Yuan subway stop

After visiting the garden, check out the charming **Huxin Ting**, a two-storey teahouse on an island at the centre of an ornamental lake, reached by a zigzagging bridge. The Queen of England and Bill Clinton, among other illustrious guests, have dropped in for tea. It's cute but decidedly pricey – at least ¥60 for a cup, though it will be refilled as often as you like. Rely on the waiter's recommendation and you'll be given the most expensive option, so insist on seeing the menu.

Fuyou Lu antique market
福佑路, fúyòu lù · 457 Fangbang Zhong Lu · Sun, busiest 8–11am though trade continues into mid-afternoon · Yu Yuan subway stop

If you're in the Chenghuang Miao area on Sunday morning, you can visit a great indoor **market** on Fuyou Lu, the small street running east–west along the northern edge of Yu Yuan. The market has a raw, entrepreneurial feel about it; all sorts of curios and antiques – mostly fakes – ranging from jade trinkets to Little Red Books can be found here, though you'll have to bargain fiercely if you want to buy.

Dongtai Lu antique market
东台路, dōngtāi lù · Daily 10am–4pm · Laoximen subway stop

Just outside the Old City, in a small alley called Dongtai Lu leading west off Xizang Nan Lu, is the largest permanent **antique market** in Shanghai. Even if you're not interested in buying, this is a fascinating area to walk around. The range is vast, from old Buddhas, coins, vases and teapots to mahjong sets, renovated furniture and Cultural Revolution badges. As with all antique markets in China, the vast majority of goods are fake.

The former French Concession
法租界, fǎzūjiè

Established in the mid-nineteenth century, the **former French Concession** lay to the south and west of the International Settlement, abutting the Chinese City. Despite its name, it was never particularly French: before 1949, in fact, it was a low-rent district mainly inhabited by Chinese and White Russians. Other Westerners looked

6

down on the latter as they were obliged to take jobs that, it was felt, should have been left to the Chinese.

Huaihai Lu is the main street running through the heart of the area. Not as crowded as Nanjing Lu, it is considerably more upmarket, particularly in the area around **Maoming Lu** and **Shanxi Lu**, where you'll find plenty of fashion boutiques and department stores. West of Changshu Lu station you get a good idea of what the French Concession is all about, with attractive streets lined with plane trees and villas. The largest villas have been converted to embassy properties (some guarded by soldiers), upmarket restaurants and cafés, a fair few beauty salons and, oddly, not that many shops. It's more a place to soak up the atmosphere on a sunny day than to take in specific sights, and a bicycle is the best way to explore.

Brief history

The French Concession was notorious for its lawlessness and the ease with which police and French officials could be bribed, in contrast to the well-governed areas dominated by the British. This made it ideal territory for gangsters, including the king of all Shanghai mobsters, **Du Yuesheng**, the right-hand man of Huang Jinrong. For similar reasons, political activists also operated in this sector – the first meeting of the Chinese Communist Party took place here in 1921, and both Zhou Enlai and Sun Yatsen, the first provisional President of the Republic of China after the overthrow of the Qing dynasty, lived here. The preserved former homes of these two in particular (see opposite) are worth visiting simply because, better than anywhere else in modern Shanghai, they give a sense of how the Westerners, and the Westernized, used to live.

Xintiandi

新天地, xīntiāndì • ⓦ www.xintiandi.com • Xintiandi or Huangpi Nan Lu subway stops

Although it might seem like an obvious idea, the **Xintiandi** development, which comprises two blocks of renovated and rebuilt *shikumen* converted into a genteel open-air mall, was the first of its kind in China. It has met with such success that now town planners all over the country are studying its winning formula. Paved and pedestrianized, with narrow lanes (*longtang*) opening out onto a central plaza, Xintiandi is a great place to wind down or linger over a coffee, with upscale restaurants and shops, and plenty of outside seating for people-watching.

Shikumen Open House Museum

石库门民居陈列馆, shíkùmén mínjū chénlièguǎn • 25 Xintiandi north block • Daily 10am–10pm • ¥20 • ⓣ 021 33070337

The **Shikumen Open House Museum**, at the south end of Xintiandi north block, does an excellent job of evoking early twentieth-century Chinese gentility. This reconstruction of a typical *shikumen* is filled with everyday objects – typewriters, toys, a four-poster bed and the like – so it doesn't look as bare as the "former residences" elsewhere in the city. A top-floor display details how Xintiandi came about, admitting that most of it was built from scratch. A quote on the wall is perhaps more revealing than was intended: "Foreigners find it Chinese and Chinese find it foreign".

The First National Congress of the Chinese Communist Party

中国一大会址纪念馆, zhōngguó yīdàhuìzhǐ jìniànguǎn • 76 Xingye Lu, at junction with Huangpi Nan Lu • Daily 9am–5pm, last admission 4pm • Free (bring ID)

On the east side of the complex you'll find, rather incongruously, one of the shrines of Maoist China, the **First National Congress of the Chinese Communist Party**. The official story is that on July 23, 1921, thirteen representatives of the Communist cells that had developed all over China – including its most famous junior participant, Mao Zedong – met here to discuss the formation of a national party. The meeting was discovered (it was illegal to hold political meetings in the French Concession) and, on July 30, the delegates fled north to nearby Zhejiang province, where they resumed their talks in a boat. Quite how much of this really happened is unclear, but it seems probable that there were in fact more delegates than recorded – the missing names would have been expunged according to subsequent political circumstances.

There's a little exhibition hall downstairs, where relics from the period such as maps, money and a British policeman's uniform and truncheon are more interesting than the comically outdated propaganda rants. The last room has a waxwork diorama of Mao and his fellow delegates.

6

Fuxing Park

复兴公园, fùxīng gōngyuán • 105 Fuxing Zhong Lu • Daily 6am–6pm • Free • Xintiandi subway stop

Attractive **Fuxing Park** was laid out by the French in 1909, and remains rather European in feel, which makes the statue of Marx and Engels in the northwest corner look incongruous. Come in the morning or at dusk and you'll see groups of middle-aged locals performing *tai ji*, ballroom dancing and opera singing. Later in the evening, the area is the haunt of a much younger crowd, attracted by the restaurants and clubs on the park's edges.

Former Residence of Sun Yatsen

孙中山故居, sūnzhōngshān gùjū • 7 Xiangshan Lu • Daily 9am–4.30pm • ¥20 • ☎ 021 64372954 • Xintiandi subway stop

From Xintiandi it's a short walk to the **Former Residence of Sun Yatsen**, the first president of the Chinese Republic, and his wife, Song Qingling. The first building contains a dry exhibition of the man's books and artefacts, and can be safely skipped, but the elegantly furnished period house beside it is worth a look.

Former Residence of Zhou Enlai

周恩来故居, zhōuēnlái gùjū • 73 Sinan Lu • Daily 9am–4pm • Free • ☎ 021 64730420 • Xintiandi subway stop

The southern end of Sinan Lu constitutes a smart neighbourhood of old houses, among them, the **Former Residence of Zhou Enlai**. Zhou was Mao's right-hand man, but he has always been looked upon with rather more affection than the Chairman. When he lived here he was head of the Shanghai Communist Party, and as such was kept under surveillance from a secret outpost over the road. There's not, in truth, a great deal to see, beyond a lot of hard beds on a nice wooden floor. The house has a terrace at the back with rattan chairs and polished wooden floors, and its garden, with hedges and ivy-covered walls, could easily be a part of 1930s suburban London.

Tianzifang

田子坊, tiánzifāng • main entrance 210 Taikang Lu • ☎ 021 54657531 • Dapuqiao Lu subway stop

Heading south from the former residences down Sinan Lu, the area begins to feel earthier; but turning right from the end of the road onto **Taikang Lu** (泰康路, tàikāng lù) will bring you to the latest fashionably artsy shopping and lunching quarter, **Tianzifang**. The unassuming entrance, an arch over alley 210 on the north side of the road, leads onto Taikang Art Street, a narrow north–south alleyway off which you'll find an expanding web of alleys filling up with trendy boutiques, coffee shops, handmade jewellery stores, art galleries and restaurants, all housed in converted *shikumen* houses. At its northern end, Tianzifang exits onto Sinan Lu, but don't even try to come in from there – the entrance is really tough to find.

Inevitably, Tianzifang gets compared with Xintiandi; but whereas the architecture there is modern pastiche, this is a set of real, warts-and-all *longtangs*, with the result that it's quainter, shabbier, more charming. If you're looking for an artsy knick-knack or accessory, quirky souvenir, tasteful homeware or a designer original, this is the place to come (see p.383), though try to visit on a weekday as the narrow lanes get very crowded at weekends. For a coffee stop, central *Kommune* (see p.377) is a local institution.

6

Ruijin Guesthouse

瑞金宾馆, ruìjīn bīnguǎn • 18 Ruijin Er Lu, just south of Fuxing Zhong Lu • ☎ 021 64725222, ⓦ ruijinhotelsh.com • Shaanxi Nan Lu subway stop

The south section of **Ruijin Er Lu** (瑞金二路, ruìjīn èr lù) is busy and cramped, but there's a wonderful escape in the form of the stately **Ruijin Guesthouse**. This Tudor-style country manor was home in the early twentieth century to the Morris family, owners of the *North China Daily News*; Mr Morris raised greyhounds for the Shanghai Race Club and the former Canidrome dog track across the street. The house, having miraculously escaped severe damage during the Cultural Revolution because certain high-ranking officials used it as their private residence, has now been turned into a pleasant hotel. Even if you're not a guest, you're free to walk around the spacious, quiet grounds, where it's hard to believe you're in the middle of one of the world's most hectic cities.

Arts and Crafts Museum

工艺美术博物馆, gōngyì měishù bówùguǎn • 79 Fenyang Lu • Daily 9am–4pm • ¥8 • ☎ 021 64314074 • Changshu Lu subway stop

This grand French mansion from 1905 has been rather haphazardly converted into Shanghai's **Arts and Crafts Museum**. Visitors are first confronted with a gamut of overpriced craft shops; ignore these and head upstairs, and you will find an intriguing collection of jade, ivory, wood and embroidery pieces, as well as craftspeople practising their trades. A lot of the works are very well made but seem fussy. The most striking exhibits are the ivories, carved in the 1960s, that depict communist subjects such as political meetings; they're brilliantly done but look very kitsch now.

Propaganda Poster Centre

宣传画年画艺术中心, xuānchuánhuà niánhuà yìshù zhōngxīn • Building 4, 868 Huashan Lu • the security guard at the entrance will give you a name card with a map on the back showing you the centre's location within the complex • Daily 9.30am–4.30pm • ¥25 • ☎ 021 62111845 • Changshu Lu subway stop

The **Propaganda Poster Centre** provides a fascinating glimpse into communist China – you will not come across a more vivid evocation of the bad old days of Marx and Mao. The walls are covered with Chinese Socialist Realist posters, over three thousand examples arranged chronologically from the 1950s to the 1970s. There are, fortunately, English captions: with slogans like "the Soviet Union is the stronghold of world peace" and "hail the over-fulfillment of steel production by ten million tons" and images of sturdy, lantern-jawed peasants and soldiers defeating big-nosed, green-skinned imperialists or riding tractors into a glorious future, the black-and-white world view of communism is dramatically realized.

Calendar poster exhibition

The style of this dry communist art owes much to images with a very different message – pre-war calendar posters – and the exhibition concludes with a room of these. These images, once disseminated all over China, show fetching Chinese girls in fashionable dress and make-up and once served to introduce the Chinese to the delights of consumer culture, such as cigarettes and hair curlers.

Former Residence of Song Qingling

宋庆龄故居, sòngqìnglíng gù jū • 1843 Huaihai Xi Lu • Daily 9–11am & 1–4.30pm • ¥20 • ☎ 021 64747183 • Hengshan Lu subway stop

As the wife of Sun Yatsen, **Song Qingling** was part of a bizarre family coterie – her sister Song Meiling was married to Chiang Kai-shek and her brother, known as T.V. Soong, was finance minister to Chiang. Song Qingling lived in Shanghai between 1948 and 1981, and her house serves as a charming step back into a residential Shanghai of the recent past. The trappings on display – including lovely wood panelling and lacquerwork, and her enormous limousines – are largely post-1949.

Pudong

浦东, pǔdōng

Historically, **Pudong** – the district opposite the Bund on the east bank of the river
– was known as the "wrong side of the Huangpu"; before 1949, the area was
characterized by unemployed migrants, prostitution, murders and the most appalling
living conditions in the city. It was here that bankrupt gamblers would "*tiao huangpu*",
commit suicide by drowning themselves in the river. Shanghai's top gangster, **Du
Yuesheng**, more commonly known as "Big-eared Du", learned his trade growing up in
this rough section of town. In 1990, however, fifteen years after China's economic
reforms started, it was finally decided to grant the status of Special Economic Zone
(SEZ) to this large tract of mainly agricultural land, a decision which, more than any
other, is now fuelling Shanghai's rocket-like economic advance. The skyline has since
been completely transformed from a stream of rice paddies into a sea of cranes, and
ultimately a maze of skyscrapers that seemingly stretches east as far as the eye can see.

6

ARRIVAL AND DEPARTURE PUDONG

By subway Subway line #2 runs from Renmin Square to
Lujiazui in less than 5min, and carries on to Century Park;
lines #4, #6 and #9 also have stops in Pudong.

By ferry A double-decker ferry (¥2) from the south end of
the Bund, opposite Jinling Dong Lu, crosses to Dongchang
Lu in Pudong (daily 7am–10pm, every 15min).

By tourist tunnel The Tourist Tunnel (外滩观光隧道,
wàitān guānguāng suìdào; ¥50 one-way, ¥70 return;
entrance in the subway opposite Beijing Dong Lu), in which
you're driven in a train past a silly light show, crosses under
the river to emerge near the Oriental Pearl Tower.

Lujiazui

陆家嘴, lùjiāzuǐ • Lijiazui subway stop

Lujiazui is, above all, an area of commerce, with few activities of interest to the visitor
besides giving your neck a good workout as you gaze upwards at the skyline. Here
you'll find the bulbous **Oriental Pearl TV Tower**, the sturdy **World Financial Centre** and
the elegant **Jinmao Tower**, all of which offer sublime views across the city. The latest
edition, the Shanghai Tower, is set to open in the immediate future, and will dwarf
them all; at 632m it will be the world's second-tallest building.

Several attractions have been plonked here, to take advantage of the huge crowds of
Chinese tourists who flock to the Pearl TV Tower. They can be safely ignored, with the
exception of the fascinating **History Museum**.

Oriental Pearl TV Tower

东方明珠广播电视塔, dōngfāng míngzhū guǎngbō diànshìtǎ • Fenghe Lu • Daily 8am–9.30pm • ¥70 to go to the
top bauble • W orientalpearltower.com/en • Liujiazui subway stop

The 457m-high **Oriental Pearl TV Tower** is an iconic symbol of the city and a visit has
become a mandatory pilgrimage for most Chinese visitors to Shanghai, despite the
high entrance fee, long queues and rather tatty interior. The building is showing its age,
and if you want views you are better off visiting one of its taller and classier neighbours.
There are three viewing platforms.

Shanghai History Museum

上海城市历史发展馆, shànghǎi chéngshìlìshǐ fāzhǎnguǎn • Fenghe Lu • Daily 8am–9.30pm • ¥35 •
T 021 58798888 • Liujiazui subway stop

The **Shanghai History Museum**, in the basement of the TV tower, is surprisingly decent;
the majority of exhibits, which focus on the nineteenth century onwards, do a good job
of evoking the old glory days, with convincing waxwork figures in dioramas of
pharmacies, teahouses and the like. One of the old bronze lions from outside the
HSBC building (see p.355) is on display, as well as a boundary stone from the

International Settlement, and there's a detailed model of the Bund as it would have looked in the 1930s.

Jinmao Tower

金茂大厦, jīnmào dàshà · 88 Century Avenue, enter from the building's north side · Daily 7am–9.30pm · observation deck ¥120 · ☎ 021 50475101, ⓦ www.jinmao88.com · Liujiazui subway stop

This beautiful building, an elegantly tapering postmodern take on Art Deco, has an observation deck on the 88th floor. An ear-popping lift whisks you up 340m to the top in a matter of seconds. The spectacle of the city spread out before you is of course sublime, but turn round for a giddying view down the building's glorious galleried atrium. If you baulk at the price, you can find decent views for free by going in the front door (on the east side) and up to the *Hyatt*'s hotel lobby on the 54th floor, where you can take advantage of the comfy, window-side chairs. For grand night-time views, visit the hotel bar *Cloud Nine*, on the 87th floor (see p.374).

World Financial Centre

环球金融中心, huánqiú jīnróng zhōngxīn · 100 Century Avenue · Daily 8am–11pm, last admission 10pm · little deck (423m) ¥120, larger deck (439m) ¥150, top deck (474m) ¥300 · ☎ 021 58780101, ⓦ www.swfc-observatory.com · Liujiazui subway stop

The best views of the city are from the observation deck at the top of the 492m Shanghai **World Financial Centre**, China's tallest building (at least until the neighbouring Shanghai Tower is complete). In contrast to nearby Jinmao Tower, its lines are simple: it's just a tapering slab whose most distinctive feature is the hole in the top, and locals call it "the bottle opener". That hole was originally meant to be circular, but was redesigned as an oblong when the mayor complained that it would look like a Japanese flag hovering over the city.

The entrance and ticket office is in the southwest side. The top level – the top bar of the bottle opener – features hardened glass tiles in the floor that allow you to look right down between your feet. Landmarks are pointed out in the booklet that comes with your ticket, and you can get a photo printed for ¥50. The view is at least as impressive at night.

Century Avenue

世纪大道, shìjì dàdào

Century Avenue runs arrow-straight for 4km southeast from the river to Century Park. The simplest way to travel along its length is by subway; the Shanghai Science and Technology Museum station plays host, incongruously, to a huge **fake market** (see p.383). It's a ten-minute walk from there to the Park, and you'll see plenty of skateboarders and kite flyers on the way; this is where Shanghai residents go for a sense of space.

The Science and Technology Museum

上海科技馆, shànghǎi kējìguǎn · Daily 9am–5pm · ¥60, students ¥45 · ⓦ www.sstm.org.cn · Science and Technology Museum subway stop

The **Science and Technology Museum** is huge; rather too big perhaps, as the cavernous halls make some of the twelve exhibitions look threadbare – there isn't much English explanation or quite enough interactivity. The section on space exploration is good – a hot topic in China right now, with the nation fully intending to get to the moon as soon as possible – with real spacesuits and plenty of models of spacecraft, and in the section on robots you can take on a robotic arm at archery and play a computer at Go. The most interesting sections, however, are the cinemas: the space theatre (every 40min; ¥40) shows films on astronomy; the two IMAX domes in the basement (hourly 10.30am–4.30pm; ¥40) show cartoons; while the IWERKS dome on the first floor (every 40min; ¥30) is an attempt to take the concept of immersive realism even further – as well as surround sound and images there are moving seats, and water and wind effects.

Century Park

世纪公园, shìjì gōngyuán • Daily 7am–6pm • ¥10 • Century Park subway stop

The park is spacious and clean, and it's possible to feel that you have escaped the city. You can hire a tandem bike (¥50/hr) – sadly you're not allowed to ride your own bicycle – and pedalos are available to rent on the central lake (¥60/hr).

6 North of Suzhou Creek

North across the Waibaidu Bridge from the Bund, you enter an area that, before the war, was the Japanese quarter of the International Settlement. The area immediately north of the bridge is tipped for a big renovation – you'll see some flashy new buildings, such as the bulbous International Cruise Terminal, and many more are planned. For the moment, the obvious interest lies further north, in the Lu Xun Park area (also known as Hongkou Park) and its monuments to the political novelist Lu Xun, although the whole district is lively and architecturally interesting.

Duolun Lu

多伦文化名人街, duōlún wénhuà míngrénjiē • Baoxing Dong Lu subway stop

Duolun Lu is a heritage street of antique and bric-a-brac shops housed in elegant imitation Qing buildings, and plenty of public statuary. Here you'll find the *Old Film Café* (see p.377), charmingly decorated with film posters, and, at the north end of the street, the four-storey **Duolun Museum of Modern Art** (多伦现代美术馆, duōlún xiàndài měishùguǎn; ⓦduolunmoma.org), which shows modern Chinese and international artists, though it has no permanent exhibition.

Lu Xun Park

鲁迅公园, lǔxùn gōngyuán • Daily 6am–7pm • Free • Hongkou Stadium subway stop

Lu Xun Park is one of the best places for observing Shanghainese at their most leisured. Between 6am and 8am, the masses undergo their daily *tai ji* workout; later in the day, couples frolic on paddle boats in the park lagoon and old men teach their grandkids how to fly kites. The park is also home to the pompous **Tomb of Lu Xun**, complete with a seated statue and an inscription in Mao's calligraphy, which was erected here in 1956 to commemorate the fact that Lu Xun had spent the last ten years of his life in this part of Shanghai. The tomb went against Lu Xun's own wishes to be buried simply in a small grave in a western Shanghai cemetery.

Lu Xun Memorial Hall

鲁迅纪念馆, lǔxùn jìniànguǎn • Daily 9–11am & 1.30–4pm • Free

The novelist is further commemorated in the **Lu Xun Memorial Hall**, also in the park, to the right of the main entrance. Exhibits include period photographs of the city, portraits of Lu Xun and original correspondence, among them letters and photographs from George Bernard Shaw.

Former Residence of Lu Xun

鲁迅故居, lǔxùn gùjū • Shanyin Lu, Lane 132, House 9 • Daily 9am–4pm • ¥8 • ☏ 021 56662608 • Hongkou Stadium subway stop

A block southeast of Lu Xun park, the **Former Residence of Lu Xun** is worth going out of your way to see, especially if you have already visited the former residences of Zhou Enlai and Sun Yatsen in the French Concession (see p.363). The sparsely furnished house where Lu Xun and his wife and son lived from 1933 until his death in 1936 offers a fascinating glimpse into typical Japanese housing of the period – a good deal smaller than their European counterparts, but still surprisingly comfortable.

Western Shanghai

Due west from the city centre there is less to see, with a sprinkling of widely scattered sights, much too far apart to walk between. Moganshan Art District is worth a visit to experience the commercial side of China's modern art movements; while the Longhua and Yufo temples are two of Shanghai's most important surviving religious sites.

6

Yufo Temple

玉佛寺, yùfó sì • 170 Anyuan Lu • Daily 8am–5pm • ¥15 • Changshou Lu subway stop

Two and a half kilometres northwest of Renmin Square is the **Yufo Temple**, a much more interesting and attractive complex than the Jing'an Temple. The pretty temple buildings have flying eaves, complicated brackets and intricate roof and ceiling decorations. It's a lively place of worship, with gusts of incense billowing from the central burner, and worshippers kowtowing before effigies and tying red ribbons to the branches of trees, decorative bells and the stone lions on the railings.

The two Buddhas

The temple was built to house **two jade Buddhas**, brought here from Burma in 1882 and now the star attractions. The larger, at nearly 2m tall, sits in its own separate building in the north of the temple, and costs an extra ¥10 to see. It was carved from a single block of milky-white jade and is encrusted with agate and emerald. The second statue, in the Western Hall, is a little smaller, around 1m long, but easier to engage with. It shows a recumbent Buddha, at the point of dying (or rather entering nirvana), with a languid expression on his face, like a man dropping off after a good meal.

Great Treasure Hall

Yufo's central **Great Treasure Hall** holds three huge figures of the past, present and future Buddhas, as well as the temple drum and bell. The gods of the twenty heavens, decorated with gold leaf, line the hall like guests at a celestial cocktail party, and a curvaceous copper Guanyin stands at the back. It's all something of a retreat from the material obsessions outside, but it's still Shanghai; religious trinkets, such as fake money for burning and Buddhas festooned with flashing lights, are for sale everywhere and the monks are doing a roaring trade flogging blessings.

Moganshan Art District

莫干山路50号, mògānshānlù wǔshíhào • 50 Moganshan Lu • Shanghai Zhan subway stop, then a ¥14 cab ride

Moganshan Arts District (or **M50**) is a complex of studios and galleries located in an old textile mill beside Suzhou Creek, just west of Shanghai train station. Attracted by cheap rents, artists took over the abandoned buildings in the 1990s and used them as studios; then the art galleries moved in, and now the design studios, cafés and arty shops are arriving. It's an intriguing mix of shabby and sophisticated, jumbling together paint-spattered artists, pretentious fashionistas and baffled locals. Recently a glut of lame commercial galleries have opened, but there are enough good ones left, including those listed below. Many of the galleries are closed on Mondays, and there's a map on the wall to the right of the entrance. When you're arted out, have a coffee at the nearby *Bandu* café (see p.376).

6

MOGANSHAN'S GALLERIES

New galleries tend to show insipid copies of the works of famous artists. Below are some established and worthwhile venues.

ShanghART Buildings 16 and 18 (daily 10am–6pm; ☎021 63593923, ⊛shanghartgallery.com). One of the first galleries in China to show work by modern Chinese artists, now with a stable of more than forty and a reputation for exciting work.

Island 6 Art Centre Building 6, first floor (daily 10am–7pm; ☎021 62277856, ⊛island6.org). This collective prides itself on its technological nous, and puts together lively multi-media shows.

M97 Second floor, 97 Moganshan Lu (Tues–Sun 10am–6pm; ☎021 62661597, ⊛m97gallery .com). The best photography gallery in the area – it's over the road from the main M50 complex, but worth seeking out.

OV Gallery Room 207, building 4 (Tues–Sun 11am–6pm; ☎021 54667768, ⊛ovgallery.com). Themed shows from up-and-coming artists, mostly Chinese.

Xujiahui Catholic Cathedral

圣依纳爵主教座堂, shèngyīnàjué zhǔjiào zuòtáng · 156 Puxi Lu · Xujiahui subway stop

The **Xujiahui Catholic Cathedral** (also called St Ignatius Church) was built in 1910, on the grave of Paul Xu Guangqi, the first Jesuit convert, and was lauded as the finest church in the Far East. It was vandalized during the Cultural Revolution, then used as a granary, but has now been well restored to its former glory, with some pretty new stained-glass windows. The cathedral's library, with 200,000 volumes, as well as the meteorological centre (built at the same time as the cathedral and now housing the Shanghai Municipal Meteorology Department), survive on the grounds.

Longhua Cemetery of Martyrs

龙华烈士陵园, lónghuá lièshì língyuán · 180 Longhua Xi Lu · Daily 6.30am–4pm · cemetery ¥1, exhibition hall ¥5 · Caoxi Lu subway · bus #41 from Huaihai Zhong Lu, near Shanxi Nan Lu, to its terminus, then a short walk south

Southeast of the Xujiahui Cathedral, **Longhua Cemetery of Martyrs** is a park commemorating those who died fighting for the cause of Chinese communism in the decades leading up to the final victory of 1949. In particular, it remembers those workers, activists and students massacred in Shanghai by Chiang Kai-shek in the 1920s – the site of the cemetery is said to have been the main execution ground. In the centre is a glass-windowed, pyramid-shaped **exhibition hall** with a bombastic memorial to 250 communist martyrs who fought Chiang's forces. With fountains and well-tended lawns, it's a pleasant place for a stroll.

Longhua Temple

龙华寺, lónghuá sì · 2853 Longhua Lu · Daily 5.30am–4pm · ¥10 · Longcao Lu subway stop

Just south of the Cemetery of Martyrs is one of Shanghai's main religious sites, the **Longhua Temple**. Though there has been a temple on the site since the Han dynasty, the halls are only around a century old. It's the most active Buddhist site in the city, and a centre for training monks. On the right as you enter is a bell tower: on Chinese New Year, a monk bangs the bell 108 times, supposedly to ease the 108 "mundane worries" of Buddhist thought. You can whack it yourself, any time, for ¥10; three hits is considered auspicious.

The pagoda

The temple's associated tenth-century **pagoda** is an octagonal structure about 40m high (until the feverish construction of bank buildings along the Bund in the 1910s, the pagoda was the tallest edifice in Shanghai), its seven brick storeys embellished with wooden balconies and red-lacquer pillars. After a long period of neglect (Red Guards saw it as a convenient structure to plaster with banners), an ambitious re-zoning project has spruced up the pagoda and created the tea gardens, greenery and shop stalls that now huddle around it.

The Botanical Gardens

上海植物园, shànghǎi zhíwùyuán • 1111 Longwu Lu • Daily 7am–4pm • ¥15 • bus #56 south down Longwu Lu, from just to the west of the Longhua Temple

More than nine thousand plants are on view in these large and rather sprawling **Botanical Gardens**, including two pomegranate trees that are said to date from the reign of Emperor Qianlong in the eighteenth century; despite their antiquity, they still bear fruit. Look out, too, for the orchid chamber, where more than a hundred different varieties are on show, and the bonsai garden.

Qibao

七宝, qībǎo • Daily 8.30am-4.30pm • ¥45 for an all-inclusive ticket • Qibao subway stop

This "water town" is a historical theme park in Shanghai's western suburbs. It's basically alleys of rather twee souvenir shops and snack stalls alongside a couple of canals, but it is worth a look if you aren't visiting one of the larger water towns (see p.385), or want to get all your souvenir shopping done at once. The ticket allows access to several historical buildings – the most rewarding is the cute little bell tower – and some small exhibitions. There are plenty of places to snack, many serving local specialities such as smoked toad and red braised pork. As the easiest way to escape the city (it's right on the subway, an hour from the centre), it gets very busy at weekends.

ARRIVAL AND DEPARTURE   SHANGHAI

Shanghai's transport links were upgraded considerably for the 2010 World Expo, and now it enjoys the best infrastructure on the mainland. All main arrival points are integrated with the subway system.

BY PLANE

PUDONG INTERNATIONAL AIRPORT

Pudong International Airport (浦东国际机场, pǔdōng guójì jīchǎng), 40km east of the city near the mouth of the Yangzi River, handles most international flights. There are two terminals at present, with a third due to open in 2015. New arrivals note that ATMs are on the departures floor, upstairs from Arrivals.

By Maglev train (磁悬浮列车, cíxuánfú lièchē; daily 7am–9pm; every 20min). The train is suspended above the track and propelled by the forces of magnetism. It whizzes from Pudong to Longyang Lu subway station in the eastern suburbs in 8min, at 300km/hr. Unfortunately Longyang Lu subway is still a long way from the centre of town. Tickets cost ¥50, or ¥80 for a return trip.

By subway Pudong airport is on subway Line #2, which will take you to the centre in just over an hour (¥7). You will have to change train at Guanglan, where there will be a wait of up to 20min, so this option isn't as convenient as it might be.

By airport bus There are stops opposite the gates, and eight routes to choose from, with departures every 15min until the last plane lands; tickets cost around ¥20. The journey into town takes around 90min. Bus #2 is generally the most useful as it goes to the Jing'an subway stop in the city centre. Bus #1 goes to Hongqiao Airport; bus #3 goes to the *Galaxy Hotel*, in the Hongqiao business district in the west of the city, and then to Xujiahui; bus #4 goes to Hongkou Stadium, in the north; bus #5 goes to Shanghai Zhan train station; bus #6 goes to Zhongshan Park, bus #7 to the south railway station, in the southern suburbs. The only one with a drop-off in Pudong is bus #5 (Dongfang Hospital).

By taxi A taxi to Pudong or the Bund should cost around ¥150, to Nanjing Xi Lu around ¥130. Avoid touts and take a cab from the rank.

By long-distance coach On the second floor of the airport opposite exit 18, there are long-distance coaches, leaving hourly, which will take you to Suzhou, Nanjing and Hangzhou; tickets cost around ¥50–80.

HONGQIAO AIRPORT

Hongqiao Airport (虹桥机场, hóngqiáo jīchǎng), 15km west of the city, services domestic flights. It has recently had a huge upgrade, and is well integrated with Hongqiao train station (for Beijing and Suzhou) and the subway.

By bus Buses leave from the parking lot: bus #1 goes to Pudong International Airport; the airport shuttle goes to

6

Jing'an Temple subway stop in the city centre; bus #925 goes to Renmin Square; and bus #941 goes to the Shanghai train station. Journeys can take up to an hour depending on traffic.

By subway line #2 will get you into the centre of town in under an hour.

By taxi A taxi to Nanjing Xi Lu only costs about ¥45, and to the Bund about ¥60. On busy times such as Friday nights, you can wait more than an hour for a cab at the rank – walk to departures and pick up one that's just dropped someone off, or get on any bus for a couple of stops and hail one there.

Destinations Baotou (3 daily; 2hr 50min); Beijing (16 daily; 12hr 20min); Changsha (12 daily; 1hr 45min); Changchun (11 daily; 2hr 25min); Chengdu (23 daily; 3hr 10min); Chongqing (19 daily; 2hr 40min); Dalian (14 daily; 1hr 50min); Fuzhou (10 daily; 1hr 30 min); Guangzhou (26 daily; 2hr 20min); Guilin (8 daily; 2hr 20min); Haikou (2 daily; 2hr 45min); Harbin (8 daily; 2hr 50min); Hefei (1 daily; 1hr 15min); Hohhot (4 daily; 4hr 45min); Huangshan (1 daily; 1hr); Kunming (17 daily; 3hr 10min); Lanzhou (6 daily; 3hr); Lhasa (4 weekly; 6hr 40min); Lijiang (1 daily; 3hr 50min); Nanning (8 daily; 2hr 45min); Qingdao (7 daily; 1hr 20min); Shenzhen (6 daily; 2hr 30min); Taiyuan (1 daily; 2hr 30min); Tianjin (3 daily; 2hr 15min); Ürümqi (2 daily; 5hr 20min); Wenzhou (7 daily; 1hr 10min); Wuhan (7 daily; 1hr 45min); Xiamen (19 daily; 1hr 30min); Xi'an (23 daily; 2hr 25min); Xining (3 daily; 3hr 30min); Yichang (2 daily; 2hr).

BY TRAIN

Buy tickets up to a week in advance from a hotel (sometimes for a small commission), the CITS in the Shanghai Centre (daily 8.30–11.30am & 1–4.45pm), or from a train-ticket booking office, where you'll rarely have to queue. There are handy ones (all open daily 8am–5pm) at 77 Wanhangdu Lu (near Jing'an Temple); 2 Jinling Dong Lu; 627 Nanjing Xi Lu; 124 Guizhou Lu; 296 Taixing Lu, close to Beijing Xi Lu; and, in Pudong, 10721 Zhangyang Lu.

Shanghai train station (上海火车站, shànghǎi huǒchēzhàn) is to the north of Suzhou Creek. The station is not particularly well served by buses but is handy for the metro; it's on lines #1, #3 and #4. Tickets are sold in a separate building on the western side of the central plaza. It has services to most cities in the country, a few high-speed trains to Nanjing and Xi'an, and services to Hong Kong.

Destinations Beijing (2 daily; 11hr); Changzhou (frequent; 2–3hr); Chengdu (3 daily; 21–42hr); Guangzhou (1 daily; 16hr); Harbin (1 daily; 33hr); Hefei (13 daily; 3–7hr); Hong Kong (2 daily; 19hr); Huangshan (2 daily; 12hr); Lanzhou (4 daily; 22–30hr); Nanjing (frequent; 2–4hr); Shenyang (5 daily; 25–31hr); Suzhou (frequent; 30min–1hr); Ürümqi (1 daily; 45hr); Wuxi (frequent; 40min–1hr 30min); Xi'an (10 daily; 10–21hr); Zhengzhou (13 daily; 10–15hr); Zhenjiang (frequent; 1hr30 min–3hr).

Shanghai South station (上海南站, shànghǎi nánzhàn) is new and high-tech; you might end up here if you have come from cities south of Shanghai, such as Hangzhou; it's on the subway lines #1 and #3.

Destinations Changsha (3 daily; 14hr); Chongqing (2 daily; 30–44hr); Fuzhou (2 daily; 17hr); Guilin (4 daily; 22hr); Hangzhou (frequent; 2–3hr); Kunming (3 daily; 36hr); Nanchang (7 daily; 10hr); Nanning (2 daily; 28hr); Ningbo (frequent; 3hr); Xiamen (1 daily; 26hr).

Hongqiao station (上海虹桥站, shànghǎi hóngqiáo zhàn). Shanghai's new high-speed terminus; all bullet trains use this station. It's on metro lines #2 and #10, and right beside the domestic airport.

Destinations Beijing (frequent; 5hr); Suzhou (frequent; 30min); Hangzhou (frequent; 1hr); Nanjing (frequent; 1hr).

BY BUS

For a few destinations, for example Suzhou and Hangzhou, buses might offer a convenient way to leave the city: they're slightly cheaper than trains, and it's easy to get a seat. The two biggest bus stations are listed below.

Shanghai South bus station (上海南站, shànghǎi nán zhàn, 666 Shiliong Lu, ☎021 54362835) is new and, despite the huge crowds, comparatively easy to reach and get around. It's underneath Shanghai South train station, on subway lines #1 and #3.

Destinations Hangzhou (¥78; 2hr); Nanjing (¥112; 4hr); Suzhou (¥38; 1hr 30min); Wuzhen (¥58; 2hr); Xitang (¥32; 1hr 30min); Zhouzhuang (¥25; 1hr).

Shanghai Long Distance Bus Station (上海长途客运总站, shànghǎi chángtú kèyùn zǒngzhàn, 1662 Zhongxing Lu, ☎021 56720594). This huge old station is behind Shanghai train station, a circuitous walk from the subway stop there.

Destinations Hangzhou (¥78; 2hr); Nanjing (¥112; 4hr); Suzhou (¥38; 1hr 30min).

BY BOAT

International Ferry Terminal (国际客运码头, guójì kèyùn mǎtóu, 500 Dong Daming Lu) is about 10min walk east of the Waibaidu Bridge, handling ferries to Kōbe and Ōsaka in Japan. The ferries are perfectly comfortable, but take some food as the restaurant is expensive. When you arrive in Japan you'll find yourself dumped in an industrial port with no banks or foreign exchanges nearby, so take some Japanese yen with you. The ferry to Ōsaka (⊕shanghai-ferry.co.jp) leaves on Tuesdays at 11am and takes two nights, arriving on Thursday morning; fares start at ¥1300 for a roll-up bed on the floor of a common room, though a bunk in a four-bed cabin is not much more expensive. Return tickets cost an extra fifty percent or so. Book a ticket at CITS (see p.374) or by emailing ✉ zhangyz@suzhaohao.com; you'll be given a reference number and can pick up and pay for your ticket at the ferry port on the day.

The ship to Kōbe (⊕ chinajapanferry.com) leaves every Saturday at 1pm and arrives on Monday at 10.30am; fares for this trip start at ¥1300 – book tickets online.

GETTING AROUND

By subway The Shanghai Subway (上海地铁; shànghǎi dìtiě; daily 5.30am–11pm) comprises twelve lines, but not all are particularly useful for visitors. Line #1 runs north–south, with useful stops at the railway station, Renmin Square, Changshu Lu (for the Old French Concession), Xujiahui and Shanghai Stadium. Line #2 runs east–west with stops at Jing'an Temple, Henan Lu and, in Pudong, Lujiazui and the Science and Technology Museum. The lines intersect at the enormous People's Square station (take careful note of the wall maps here for which exit to use). Line #8 is north–south, with handy stops at Hongkou Stadium, Qufu Lu, and Laoximen (for the Old City); and east–west line #10 has useful stops at Yu Yuan and Xintiandi.

Tickets cost from ¥3 to ¥10, according to the distance travelled. They can be bought either from touch-screen machines (there's an option for English) or from vendors. Alternatively, you can purchase a stored-value card for a refundable ¥20, which you can top up with as much as you like.

By bus City buses run everywhere from around 4am to 10.30pm, but they are crowded and slow, stops are far apart, and few lines travel from one side of the city to the other. Fares are ¥2; buy your ticket from the conductor on board or drop your cash into the tray by the driver. Services with numbers in the 300s are night buses; those in the 400s cross the Huangpu River. Most large fold-out city maps show bus routes, usually as a red or blue line with a dot indicating a stop. Sightseeing buses for tourist sights in the outskirts leave from the Shanghai Stadium (see p.386).

By taxi Cabs are very easy to get hold of and, if you're not on a very tight budget, they are often the most comfortable way to get around – there's a flag fall of ¥14 (¥18 at night), and fares usually come to ¥20–40 for rides within the city. Few drivers speak English, so it helps to have your destination written in Chinese.

INFORMATION

Maps Various glossy English-language maps are available, including the *Shanghai Official Tourist Map*, which is paid for by advertising and is issued free in hotels and from the tourist kiosk in the Renmin Square subway station. Additionally, bus routes can be found on the *Shanghai Communications Map*, which is widely available from street vendors, though this has street names in Chinese only.

Tourist information You can pick up free leaflets, containing basic tourist information, at the upmarket

hotels and at the airport. Much more useful, though, are the free magazines aimed at the foreign community, such as *City Weekend* (⊕ cityweekend.com.cn/shanghai) and *Time Out Shanghai* (⊕ timeoutshanghai.com), which you can pick up at most expat hangouts. All have listings sections including restaurants, club nights and art events, with addresses written in *pinyin* and Chinese, but no maps. Smart Shanghai (⊕ smartshanghai.com) is a good listings website that includes maps and user-submitted reviews.

USEFUL SHANGHAI BUS ROUTES

NORTH–SOUTH

#18 (trolleybus) From Lu Xun Park, across Suzhou Creek and along Xizang Lu.

#41 Passes Tianmu Xi Lu, in front of Shanghai train station, and goes down through the former French Concession to Longhua Cemetery.

#64 From Shanghai train station, along Beijing Lu, then close to Shiliupu wharf on the south of the Bund.

#65 From the top to the bottom of Zhongshan Lu (the Bund), terminating in the south at the Nanpu Bridge.

EAST–WEST

#19 (trolleybus) From near Gongping Lu wharf in the east, passing near the *Astor House Hotel* and roughly following the course of Suzhou Creek to Yufo Temple.

#20 From Jiujiang Lu (just off the Bund) along Nanjing Dong Lu, past Jing'an Temple, then on to Zhongshan Gongyuan in the west of the city.

#42 From Guangxi Lu (just off the Bund), then along Huaihai Lu in the former French Concession.

#135 From Yangpu Bridge in the east of the city to the eastern end of Huaihai Lu, via the Bund.

6

Travel agents CITS has an office at 66 Nanjing Dong Lu (☎021 63233384), providing travel and entertainment tickets, with a small commission added on. There's another CITS office at 1277 Beijing Xi Lu (☎021 62898899; daily 8.30am–5pm), as well as a transport ticket office just off the Bund at 2 Jinling Dong Lu (☎021 63238770); all branches are open daily 8.30am–5pm. Most hotels have travel agencies offering the same services.

ACCOMMODATION

Accommodation in Shanghai is plentiful, and in places extremely stylish, but prices are higher than elsewhere in China. The grand old-world hotels that form so integral a part of Shanghai's history cost at least US$150 per night, and for comfort and elegance have been overtaken by new arrivals, such as the clutch of boutique hotels. If you want to be near the centre of the action, go for somewhere around Renmin Park or the Bund; there are options here for all budgets. For style and panache, head to the genteel former French Concession, where attractive mid-range hotels are close to upmarket dining and nightlife. For the latest in corporate chic, Pudong has the fanciest options, but the area is rather dull. If you're simply looking for somewhere that's good value and convenient, stay in the outskirts near a subway station.

THE BUND AND AROUND

Astor House Hotel 浦江饭店, pǔjiāng fàndiàn. 15 Huangpu Lu ☎021 63246388, ⓦastorhousehotel.com. Located across the Waibaidu Bridge, opposite the blue Russian Consulate building. Dating back to 1846, this is a pleasingly old-fashioned place with creaky wooden floors and high ceilings, and the antiquated look of a Victorian school. It's a bit cheaper, and a bit rougher round the edges, than other historic Bund hotels, but represents good value for money. **¥640**

Captain Hostel 老船长青年酒店, lǎochuánzhǎng qīngnián jiǔdiàn. 37 Fuzhou Lu ☎021 63235053, ⓦwww.yhachina.com. Doubles at this place just off the Bund can be pokey, but it's of most interest for its clean, cheap dorms, all made to look like cabins. Staff are dressed in sailor suits – though it hasn't made them any jollier. The *Captain Bar* on the sixth floor has great views of Pudong (see p.380). Internet access is a steep ¥20/hr, bike rental ¥2/hr (guests only), and there's free use of the washing machine. All bathrooms are communal. Beds in an eight-bed dorm **¥80**, rooms **¥358**

★ **CHAI Shanghai Living** 上海灿客栈, shànghǎi cànkèzhàn. 400 Suzhou Bei Lu ☎021 63561812, ⓦchailiving.com. Luxury serviced apartments in a genteel Art Deco apartment block. There's no lobby to speak of – you'll be met on arrival by the service manager, Mr. Li – and your neighbours will be locals who hang their washing and practise *tai ji* in the corridors. Each well-designed apartment has underfloor heating and fully equipped kitchens; go for one with a view of Pudong. **¥1210**

Dock Bund Hostel 外滩源青年旅舍, wàitānyuán qīngnián lǚshě. 55 Xianggang Lu, ☎021 53500077. This well-located cheapie, just off the Bund, has virtually no lobby, and corridors are shabby, but staff are helpful and rooms clean and spacious. Patchy wi-fi. Dorms **¥55**, rooms **¥180**

★ **Fairmont Peace** 和平饭店, hépíng fàndiàn. Junction of the Bund and Nanjing Dong Lu ☎021 63216888, ⓦ shanghaipeacehotel.com. Occupying both sides of the road, this was formerly the *Cathay*, the most famous hotel in Shanghai, home to the *Jazz Bar* and still well worth a visit to admire the Art Deco interior (see p.354). The long list of illustrious former guests includes Charlie Chaplin and Noël Coward. In the modern era its star faded thanks to bad management, but its fortunes have been turned around by new owners, the *Fairmont* group, and it's now the iconic Shanghai hotel. **¥2200**

Mingtown Hikers Hostel 明堂上海旅行者国际青年旅馆, míngtáng shànghǎi lǚxíngzhě guójì qīngnián lǚguǎn. 450 Jiangxi Zhong Lu ☎021 63297889. Very well located just northwest of the Bund, this cheap-and-cheerful hostel is friendly and has wi-fi and a lively bar with a pool table. Four- and six-bed dorms **¥55**; rooms with shared bathrooms **¥220**

Peninsula 上海半岛酒店, shànghǎi bàndǎo jiǔdiàn. 32 Zhongshan Dong Lu ☎021 23272888, ⓦpeninsula.com/shanghai. The latest incarnation of the exclusive Hong Kong luxury brand. In keeping with the area, it's gone for a traditional, Art Deco look; black marble corridors lead to the white columned lobby, where a quartet plays and the local elite drink afternoon tea. **¥2300**

Shanghai Mansions (**Broadway Mansions**) 上海大厦, shànghǎi dàshà. 20 Suzhou Bei Lu ☎021 63246260. This is the huge, ugly lump of a building on the north bank of Suzhou Creek, visible from the north end of the Bund. Rooms get pricier the higher up you go, and depending on the view. **¥880**

PUDONG

Grand Hyatt 浦东金茂凯悦大酒店, pǔdōng jīnmàokǎiyuè dàjiǔdiàn. Jinmao Tower, 88 Shijia Dadao ☎021 50491234, ⓦshanghai.hyatt.com. Taking up the top floors of the magnificent Jinmao Tower, there's no doubt the place is fantastic – awesome views, great design, lots of lucky numbers (555 rooms, 88 storeys). *Cloud Nine Bar* (see p.380) is on the top floor. **¥2500**

Park Hyatt 柏悦酒店, bǎiyuè jiǔdiàn. 100 Century Ave ☎021 68881234, ⓦshanghai.park.hyatt.com. This stylish, ultra-modern business hotel, located on floor 79 in the World Financial Centre, has stolen the "highest hotel in the world" crown from its sister in the Jinmao Tower. Surprisingly large rooms have great views, and on-site attractions include an infinity pool and a spa. **¥2700**

Pudong Shangri-La 浦东香格里拉大酒店, pǔdōng xiānggélǐlā dàjiǔdiàn. 33 Fucheng Lu ☎021 68828888, ⓦshangri-la.com. The other monster hotel in Pudong, with almost a thousand rooms. Popular with upscale business travellers for comfort, convenience and, of course, the views through the huge windows. **¥2450**

THE FORMER FRENCH CONCESSION

88 Xintiandi 88 新天地, bāshíbā xīntiāndì. 380 Huangpi Bei Lu ☎021 53838833, ⓦ88xintiandi.com. Fifty-room boutique hotel at the edge of the yuppie theme park that is the Xintiandi complex. There's a pool, and guests can use the adjacent spa and fitness centre. The best rooms have a view of the lake, and the no-smoking floors are a nice touch. Convenient for Huangpi Nan Lu subway stop. **¥1800**

B'LaVii House 宝丽会馆, bǎolì huìguǎn. 285 Hunan Lu ☎021 64677171. This elegant, well-appointed French concession mansion has rooms arranged around a courtyard, all individually decorated, though a common theme is dark wood furniture and red lacquer. The area is quiet and civilized, and there are plenty of dining options nearby. Booking essential. **¥1080**

Dong Hu 东湖宾馆, dōnghú bīnguǎn. 70 Donghu Lu, one block north of Huaihai Zhong Lu ☎021 64158158, ⓦdonghuhotel.com. Of the seven buildings that make up the *Dong Hu*, the villas on the south side are the most interesting, with a chequered past; they served as an opium warehouse and the centre of gangland operations in the 1920s and 1930s. Make sure you get a room in here (Building One), and not the dull new annexe over the road, where the cheap rooms are. The good location and the pleasant gardens make this a solid mid-range choice. New annexe **¥480**, Building One **¥1340**

Hengshan Moller Villa 衡山马勒别墅饭店, héngshān mǎlèshù fàndiàn. 30 Shaanxi Nan Lu ☎021 62478881, ⓦmollervilla.com. Describing itself as a boutique heritage hotel, the main building here is a gorgeous Scandinavian gothic fantasy built in the 1930s. You can stay in the villa's well-appointed rooms, with their balconies and fireplaces, but they're expensive; most rooms are in a three-storey block just behind. Service is a little creaky. **¥1500**

Okura Garden 花园饭店, huāyuán fàndiàn. 58 Maoming Nan Lu ☎021 64151111, ⓦwww.garden hotelshanghai.com. Japanese-managed mansion; the grounds are lovely, and the lobby, which used to be the Cercle Sportif French Club, has some great Art Deco detailing; but the rooms, in a giant monolith looming at the back, are a little nondescript. **¥2200**

Old House Inn 老时光餐厅酒吧, lǎoshíguāng

cāntīng jiǔbā. 16 Lane 351, Huashan Lu, by Changshu Lu ☎021 62486118. A small guesthouse in a sympathetically restored *shikumen* house. The dozen rooms are comfortable, though the corridors are authentically poky. Free wi-fi. You'll need to book in advance. **¥1180**

★**Quintet Bed & Breakfast** 五重奏旅店, wǔchóngzòu lǚdiàn. 808 Changle Lu, near Changshu Lu ☎021 62499088, ⓦquintet-shanghai.com. This courtyard house has been smartly converted into an exclusive guesthouse, with each room designed around a theme. Staff are knowledgable, and the whole place is non-smoking. Not many business facilities, but this would be ideal for tourists looking for something a little different. Reservations essential. **¥1080**

Ruijin Intercontinental Guesthouse 瑞金宾馆, ruìjīn bīnguǎn. 118 Ruijin Er Lu (main entrance on Fuxing Lu) ☎021 64725222, ⓦruijinhotelsh.com. Cosy and exclusive Tudor-style villas in manicured gardens. Occasionally lacklustre service, but things are certain to improve with the *Intercontinental* group now at the helm. Ask for Building One, where Mao used to stay. **¥1320**

JING'AN

LeTour Travelers's Rest Youth Hostel 乐途国际青年旅舍, lètú guójì qīngnián lǚshè. Lane 36, 319 Jiaozhou Lu ☎021 62671912, ⓦletourshanghai.com. This huge hostel was once a factory, and though it's been livened up, concrete floors give it an industrial feel. Rooms are small, but this place boasts the most facilities of any hostel; as well as kitchen, rooftop bar, bike rental and free wi-fi, there's a DVD room, a mini gym and a ping pong table. It's a 10min walk north from Jing'an Lu subway stop, and can be hard to find first time, as it's located down a narrow alley just off busy Bai Lan Lu. Look out for the big green building and if you reach Wuding Lu you've gone too far. Dorms **¥70**, rooms **¥280**

Puli 璞丽酒店, púlì jiǔdiàn. 1 Changde Lu ☎021 32039999, ⓦthepuli.com. This attractive new hotel is coolly minimal, with a handsome library and spa attached. Rooms have wooden floors, grey slate walls and stylish if rather impractical sinks. Ask for a view of Jing'an Park. **¥2200**

URBN Hotel 雅悦酒店, yǎyuè jiǔdiàn. 183 Jiaozhou Lu ☎021 51534600, ⓦurbnhotels.com. Though it doesn't quite live up to its considerable hype, this hip little hotel is still pretty good value for this price range. The typical Shanghai idea of stylishness – low lighting and rough grey brick – is leavened with quirky touches, such as porthole-like doors and a wall made of leather suitcases behind reception. Breakfast is not included, and is rather pricey, so pop to the *Aura* café next door. **¥1500**

AROUND RENMIN SQUARE

24K Hotel 24K国际连锁酒店, 24K guójì liánsuǒ jiǔdiàn. 155 Weihai Lu ☎021 51181222 and 555

6

Fuzhou Lu ☎021 51503588. This no-frills business hotel chain scores for chirpy design and good value. Not much English is spoken. Both branches are on busy roads not far from Renmin Square, and walkable from the subway. Free wi-fi, and there's even a machine that dispenses medicines in the lobby. **¥168**

JW Marriot 明天广场JW万怡酒店, míngtiān guǎngchǎng JW wànyí jiǔdiàn. Tomorrow Square, 399 Nanjing Xi Lu ☎021 53594969, ⍅marriott.com. Housed in the top floors of one of Shanghai's most uncompromising landmarks (something like an upraised claw), this swanky venue is both well located and has magnificent views, making it one of the finest top-end destinations. **¥2180**

Marvel Hotel 商悦青年会大酒店, shāngyuè qīngniánhuì dàjiǔdiàn. 123 Xizang Nan Lu ☎021 33059999. Clean, good-value business hotel. Rooms can be on the small size and the Chinese breakfast is so-so, but the location – right on Renmin Square – puts you at the centre of the action. **¥780**

★ **Mingtown Etour Hostel** 上海明堂新易途国际青年旅馆, shànghǎi míngtáng xīnyìtú guójì qīngnián lǚguǎn. 57 Jiangxi Zhong Lu ☎021 63277766. This is the best of the cheapies, being very well located – tucked in the alleyway behind Tomorrow Square, right beside Renmin Park – yet quiet and surprisingly affordable. Everything centres on a relaxing courtyard bar that features fish pond and pool table. Rooms vary, so ask to see a few – one or two have balconies. Bathrooms are shared between two or three rooms. Internet is free, but there are only two computers. Dorms **¥80**, rooms **¥180**

Radisson New World 新世界丽笙大酒店,xīn shìjiè lìshēng dàjiǔdiàn. 88 Nanjing Dong Lu ☎021 63599999, ⍅radisson.com. A new and swish venue that has quickly become popular, offering a convenient location right at the corner of bustling Nanjing Lu, and, in general, a slick upscale experience. **¥2024**

Westin 威斯汀大酒店, wēisītīng dàfàndiàn. 88 Henan Zhong Lu ☎021 63351888, ⍅westin.com/shanghai. Chinese luxury hotels usually try to impress with either a water feature or palm trees in the lobby; the over-the-top *Westin* goes for both, and then, as if that weren't enough to declare its intentions, the building has a crown on top. Rooms aren't so flashy, which is a good thing; ask for one with a view. Good on-site restaurants and spa. **¥2660**

EATING

Food in Shanghai is fantastic; though there is fairly little in the way of cheap street food, most forms of international and Chinese cuisine are widely available and there are plenty of stylish and classy restaurants. It's hard to believe that up until the early 1990s, simply getting a table in Shanghai was a cut-throat business. Compared to, for example, Sichuan or Cantonese, Shanghai cuisine is not particularly well known or popular among foreigners. Most of the cooking is done with added ginger, sugar and Shaoxing wine, but without heavy spicing. There are some interesting dishes, especially if you enjoy exotic seafood. Fish and shrimp are considered basic to any respectable meal, and eels and crab may appear as well. In season (Oct–Dec), you may get the chance to try *dazha* crab, the most expensive and, supposedly, the most delicious. Inexpensive snack food is easily available in almost any part of the city at any time of night or day – try *xiao long bao*, a local dumpling speciality.

BREAKFAST, CAFÉS AND FAST FOOD

Global fast-food chains are everywhere; but rather better (and certainly healthier) are Asian chains such as *Yoshinoya*, *KungFu* and *Ajisen* (for noodles and rice dishes). Every mall and shopping centre has a cluster of fast-food restaurants, either in the basement or on the top floor. A good one is in the basement of Raffles Mall on Fuzhou Lu; *Megabite* on the sixth floor is a huge food court. Shanghai does cafés very well. As any tourist itinerary here involves lots of fairly unstructured wandering around, visitors might find themselves spending more time than they thought people-watching over a cappuccino. All the cafés listed below have free wi-fi. Visitors craving a good Western breakfast should head to a *Wagas* or *Element Fresh*.

Bandu 半度音乐, bàndù yīnyuè. 50 Moganshan Lu, near Changhua Lu ☎021 62768267, ⍅bandumusic.com. The best of the Moganshan Art District (see p.369) cafés, this intimate hideaway hosts performances of Chinese folk music every Sat at 8pm. Mon–Fri 10am–7pm, Sat & Sun 10am–11pm.

Barbarossa 芭芭露莎, bābālùshā. 231 Nanjing Xi Lu, inside Renmin Park ☎021 63180220. This mellow, onion-domed Arabian fantasy is beautifully situated by the lotus pond in Renmin Park. It's also a bar and a restaurant, but don't eat here as the food is overpriced. Makes a great pit stop for anyone doing the sights in nearby Renmin Square. Daily 10am–2am.

★ **Citizen Bar and Café** 天台餐厅, tiāntái cāntīng. 222 Jinxian Lu ☎021 62581620, ⍅citizenshanghai.com. A great continental-style café tucked away in a gentrified neighbourhood. A good brunch place, with a wide choice of bar snacks, and a very civilized venue for a pre-dinner cocktail or a slice of apple pie. Daily 11am–1am.

Costa Coffee 科斯塔咖啡, kēsīda kāfēi. 388 Nanjing Xi Lu and elsewhere ☎021 63346035. The latest coffee colonizers are from the UK, and they're spreading fast, with eighty branches in Shanghai. Hard to get excited about, but at least it's better than *Starbucks*. This branch is handy, as there aren't too many cafés in the area. Daily 9am–10pm.

Element Fresh 新元素, xīnyuán sù. Shanghai Centre (east side), 1376 Nanjing Xi Lu and elsewhere ☎021 62798682, ⓦwww.elementfresh.com. This airy, informal bistro is the best place in town for a Western breakfast (they're open early), with plenty of options both hearty and healthy. Breakfasts ¥80 including limitless coffee. Free delivery. Daily 7am–11pm.

★ **Kommune** 公社酒吧, gōngshè jiǔbā. 210 Taikang Lu, Building 7, near Sinan Lu ☎021 64662416. Hip, if pricey, café at the heart of Tianzifang (see p.363) – head north up Lane 210, take the first left and you're there. Very popular with the designer set, especially for weekend brunch, when the courtyard outside fills up. There's an Australian-style barbecue (¥100) every Wednesday night. Deli sandwiches from ¥38. Daily 8am–10pm.

Le Café des Stagiaires 54–56 Yongkang Lu, near Xiangyang Lu ☎021 34250210, ⓦcafedesstagiaires .com. This artsy bar and café in a buzzing, newly gentrified neighbourhood has plenty of panache. As well as strong coffee, there's a decent wine list and simple French food and pizza on offer. Daily 9am–11pm.

Old China Hand Reading Room 汉源书屋, hànyuán shūwū. 27 Shaoxing Lu, by Shaanxi Nan Lu ☎021 64732526, ⓦhan-yuan.com. Bookish but not fusty, this is the place to come for leisured reflection. There's a huge collection of tomes to peruse or buy, many printed by the café press, which specializes in coffee-table books about French Concession architecture. Afternoon coffee with a scoop of ice cream and biscuits is ¥45. No meals. Daily 10am–midnight.

Old Film Café 老电影咖啡吧, lǎodiànyǐng kāfēibā. 123 Duolun Lu, by Sichuan Bei Lu ☎021 56964763. If you're in the area, this charming old house full of period detail and wallpapered with old film ads is great for refreshments. Film buffs will be excited by the possibility of the owners screening their fine collection of old Chinese and Russian films – just ask. Daily 10am–1am.

Vienna Café 维也纳咖啡馆, wéiyěnà kāfēiguǎn. 25 Shaoxing Lu, near Ruijin Lu ☎021 64452131, ⓦviennashanghai.com. Popular and charming Austrian-style French Concession café, almost managing that fin-de-siécle vibe. You can't fault their strudel or *Kaiserchmarn* – pancake served with apple sauce. Daily 8am–8pm.

Wagas 沃ան斯, wògěsī. CITIC Square basement, 1168 Nanjing Xi Lu, near Jiangning Lu and elsewhere ☎021 52925228, ⓦwww.wagas.com.cn. Good-looking and wholesome food, decor and staff at this New York-style

deli. Order their Western breakfast before 10am and it's half price (only ¥32) – and add coffee for ¥10. Smoothies and frappés start at ¥38; wraps and sandwiches are a little more. Daily 7.30am–11pm.

RESTAURANTS

Restaurants are more expensive in Shanghai than elsewhere in China, although prices remain reasonable by international standards, and even the most upmarket Western restaurants have affordable lunch specials. Note that the Chinese are early diners, so many Chinese restaurants stop serving at 9pm; expat-oriented ones will open much later.

THE BUND, NANJING DONG LU, RENMIN PARK AND AROUND

8 1/2 Otto e Mezzo 6–7/F, Rockbund, 169 Yuanmingyuan Lu, near Beijing Dong Lu ☎60872890, ⓦottoemezzobombana.com/shanghai. The best of the new fine dining venues in the area. Chef Umberto Bombana has created a menu of northern Italian cuisine; home-made pastas, raviolis and ragout, all wonderfully done. There are great views of the Pearl Tower too. ¥500 per person. Daily 4pm–late.

Godly 功德林素食馆, gōngdélín sùshíguǎn. 445 Nanjing Xi Lu ☎021 63270218. A vegetarian restaurant with temple decor, specializing in fake meat dishes. It's all rather hit-and-miss; try the meatballs, roast duck, crab and ham, but avoid anything meant to taste like fish or pork, and be wary of ordering just vegetables, as they'll turn up too oily. Staff could be livelier. Around ¥80/head. Daily 6am–2pm, 5–9pm.

Kathleen's 5 赛马餐饮, sàimǎ cānyǐn. 5F, 325 Nanjing Xi Lu ☎021 63272221, ⓦkathleens5.com. Great location – an elegant glass box on top of the old racecourse building (that's the one with the clocktower), with views over Renmin Square. Well-presented Western food; the three-course lunch sets (¥188 for three courses) are decent value, and the afternoon tea set (¥138) is a treat. Dinner will be considerably pricier. Try the beef carpaccio as a starter and follow with the bass or lamb. Good for a date. Daily 10.30am–midnight.

★ **Lost Heaven** 花马天堂, huāmǎ tiāntáng. 17 Yan'an Dong Lu, near Sichuan Nan Lu ☎021 63300967, ⓦwww.lostheaven.com.cn. This expat favourite specializes in the cuisine of Yunnan province. The decor is as seductive and exotic as the food, though the lighting is on the dark side. The chicken with coriander and the lamb ribs are excellent. About ¥200 per person; reservation advised. Daily noon–2pm, 5.30–10.30pm.

M on the Bund 米氏西餐厅, mǐshì xīcāntīng. 7F, 5 Wai Tan, entrance at Guang Dong Lu ☎021 63509988, ⓦwww.m-restaurantgroup.com/mbund. This is the oldest of the luxury Bund restaurants, and is worth eating

6

at just for the extraordinary view. Chef Hamish Pollit's menu mixes European and north African dishes, and sticks to the classics. Lunch won't break the bank at ¥128 for a main course. Serves a civilized afternoon tea at weekends (3–5pm, ¥138). Daily 11.30am–2.30pm and 6–10.30pm.

The Stage Level 1, The Westin Bund Center, 88 Henan Zhong Lu, near Guangdong Lu ☎021 3350577. The "it" place for a buffet brunch – ¥538 for as much as you can eat and drink, including champagne and caviar. On Sunday there are acrobats to entertain you too. Come hungry and not too hungover, and pig out. Reservations necessary. Daily 6am–midnight; brunch 11.30am–2.30pm.

Wang Baohe 王宝和酒家, wáng bǎohé jiǔjiā. 603 Fuzhou Lu ☎021 63223673. Wang Baohe bills itself as the "king of crabs and ancestor of wine". It's been around for more than 200 years, so it must be doing something right. It gets very busy in hairy crab season (Nov and Dec). Crab set meals start at ¥228/person. 11am–2pm, 5pm–9pm.

Yuxin Sichuan Dish 渝信川菜, yúxìn chuāncài. 3F, 333 Chengdu Bei Lu ☎021 52980438. This huge no-nonsense dining hall serves probably the best Sichuan food in Shanghai. Very popular with families and the white-collar crowd, so a reservation is recommended. Go for the *koushui ji* (mouth-watering chicken) and *shaguo yu* (fish hotpot) and work on developing a face as red as the peppers. Little English is spoken, but there's a picture menu. 11am–2.30pm, 5–9.30pm.

YU YUAN AREA

The Yu Yuan area has traditionally been an excellent place for snacks eaten in unpretentious surroundings. Although quality is generally good and prices low, there is a drawback in the long queues that form at peak hours. Try to come outside the main eating times of 11.30am to 1.30pm, or after 5.30pm. For quick bites, check out the satay, noodle and corn-on-the-cob stands lining the street bordering the western side of Yu Yuan bazaar.

Ding Tai Fung 鼎泰豐, dǐngtàifēng. 168 Fangbang Zhong Lu ☎021 63341008. This popular Taiwanese chain has done very well out of making upmarket versions of Chinese snack food – dumplings, steamed buns and noodles – which you will rarely eat in more elegant surroundings. It's probably the best *xiaolong bao* in Shanghai, and perhaps the priciest at ¥45. Daily 11am–2pm, 5pm–9pm.

Lao Fandian 老饭店, lǎofàndiàn. 242 Fuyou Lu, just north of Yu Yuan ☎021 63111777, ⓦlaofandian.com. This venerable venue is one of the most famous restaurants in town for local Shanghai food, though prices are slightly inflated. Try the stuffed duck or the mandarin fish. Daily 11am–2pm, 5–8.30pm.

Lubolang 绿波廊, lǜbōláng. 131 Yuyuan Lu ☎021 63280602. Cantonese-style *dim sum* and Shanghai dishes. A good place for dumplings and noodles, though don't neglect classic local staples such as crab meat and cabbage. 11am–2pm, 5–8.30pm.

THE FORMER FRENCH CONCESSION AND WESTERN SHANGHAI

The French Concession area is where most expats eat and correspondingly where prices begin to approach international levels. The compensation, for travellers tired of Chinese food, is that the area brims with international cuisine: menus are bilingual, English is often spoken, and a lot of thought will have gone into the establishment's ambience.

1221 一二二一酒家, yī èr èr yī jiǔjiā. 1221 Yan'an Xi Lu ☎021 6213 6585. A little out of the way, a 10min walk east of Yan'an Lu subway stop (though bus #71 stops right outside), this is foreigner-friendly Shanghai cuisine; a good place to sample local staples such as drunken chicken, fragrant crispy duck and lion's head meatballs. The teaboy's long spouted teapots, and the deftness with which they are wielded, will give you something to talk about. Daily 11.30am–11pm.

Bali Laguna 巴厘岛, bālí dǎo. 189 Huashan Lu, inside Jing'an Park, near Yan'an Lu ☎021 62486970. A popular Indonesian restaurant whose food, such as seafood curry served inside a pineapple, is actually nothing special – but the park location makes for a lovely ambience on a fine day. Note that it is closed in the evenings. ¥160/person. Daily 11am–2.30pm.

Bi Feng Tang 避风塘, bìfēngtáng. 175 Changle Lu ☎021 64670628. This cheap and tasty Cantonese fast-food chain diner makes a great last spot on a night out (though beware the merciless lighting). There's a picture menu, and you can't go far wrong with their many *dim sum* and dumpling options. Finish off with custard tarts. Open 24hr.

Charmant 小城故事, xiǎochéng gùshì. 1414 Huaihai Zhong Lu ☎021 64318027. Great Taiwanese place – convenient, cheap, functioning as much as a café as a restaurant – that's open till the early hours, handy after a night of drinking in the former French Concession. Go for Taiwanese-style pork and tofu dishes, and finish with a peanut butter smoothie. Daily 11.30am–4am.

Crystal Jade 翡翠酒家, fěicuì jiǔjiā. Unit 12A-B, 2F, Building 7, South Block, Xintiandi ☎021 63858752. Great Hong Kong food, sophisticated looks and down-to-earth prices make this the place to eat in Xintiandi, and one of the best places in town for *dim sum*. Try the barbecued pork – and leave room for mango pudding. Cheaper than it looks, at around ¥120/head. Daily 11am–11.30pm.

Cuivre 1502 Huaihai Zhong Lu ☎021 64374219,

6

ⓦcuivre.cn. This glamorous, upscale French restaurant would be a great place for a date. It's hip – menus are on ipads – but not pretentious; the food is reliably good and there's an extensive wine list. The lobster risotto is recommended. Reservations essential. Mon & Wed–Fri 6–10.30pm, Sat–Sun noon–2pm & 6–10.30pm.

★ **elEfante** 20 Donghu Lu ⓣ021 54048085, ⓦel-efante.com. Chef Willy Trullas cooks up Mediterranean fare in this stylish and upmarket venue. The long menu includes good tapas and seafood dishes. When it's sunny out, ask for a table on the patio. ¥400 per person. Tues–Sun 11am–3pm & 6–10.30pm.

★ **Fu 1039** 福 1039, fú yīlíngsānjiǔ. 1039 Yuyuan Lu, near Jiangsu Lu ⓣ021 52371878. The best place in the city for Chinese-style fine dining: great Shanghai food in an elegant colonial villa. Indulge in local classics such as smoked Mandarin fish and red glazed pork and enjoy the view of the garden. Staff don't speak much English but there's a picture menu. Expect to pay around ¥400 per person. Note that finding the entrance is tricky; it's actually down a narrow, unmarked alley off the main road. Daily 11am–2pm, 5–11pm.

Guyi Hunan 古意湘味浓, gǔyì xiāngwèinóng. 89 Fumin Lu, near Julu Lu ⓣ021 62495628. This lively, popular place is the best in the city to sample Hunan cuisine – known for being hot and spicy and for its liberal use of garlic, shallots and smoked meat. Go for the chilli-spinkled spare ribs, fish with beans and scallions, or tangerine-peel beef, which tastes better than you might expect, or try the chef's speciality, open face fish. About ¥140/head. Daily 11.30am–10.30pm.

Hotpot King 来福楼, láifúlóu. 2F, 146 Huaihai Zhong Lu, by Fuxing Xi Lu ⓣ021 64736380. English menus, understanding staff and tasteful decor make this an accessible way to sample a local favourite. Order lamb, glass noodles, mushrooms and tofu (at the least) and chuck them into the pot in the middle of the table. Perfect for winter evenings. ¥80/person. Daily 11am–4am.

Shen Yue Xuan 申粤轩饭店, shēnyuèxuān fàndiàn. 849 Huashan Lu ⓣ021 62511166. The best Cantonese place in Shanghai, with scrumptious *dim sum* at lunchtime and pleasant, if cavernous, decor. In warmer weather, you can dine alfresco in the garden, a rarity for a Cantonese restaurant. Dinner for two comes to around ¥120/head, drinks included. Daily 11am–11pm.

Shintori 新都里餐厅, xīndūlǐ cāntīng. 803 Lulu Lu, three blocks south of Hengshan Lu ⓣ021 64672459. Take someone you want to impress to this nouvelle Japanese trendsetter: the buffet will set you back around ¥350. Entertaining presentation (such as plates made of ice) will give you something to talk about, though you'd better order a lot or you'll be bitching about the small portions. Finish with green tea tiramisu (¥60). Mon–Fri 5.30–10.30pm, Sat–Sun 11.30am–10.30pm.

Shudi Laziyu Guan 蜀地辣子鱼馆, shǔdì làzīyú guǎn. 187 Anfu Lu, on the corner with Wulumuqi Zhong Lu ⓣ021 54037684. Never mind the tacky decor; concentrate on the excellent, inexpensive Sichuan and Hunanese cuisine. A big pot of Sichuan spicy fish is a must, but also recommended is *zhu xiang ji* (bamboo fragrant chicken) and old favourite, *mala doufu* (spicy tofu). 11.30am–10pm.

South Beauty 俏江南, qiàojiāngnán. 881 Yan'an Lu, opposite the Exhibition Hall ⓣ021 62475878. Upmarket Sichuan food in what looks like an English country house. The house speciality is beef in boiling oil – cooked at your table. ¥220/person. Daily 11am–11pm.

T8 House 8 North Block, Xintiandi, Taicang Rd ⓣ021 63558999. ⓦT8shanghai.com. Fine continental-style dining, courtesy of a Swedish chef, in an elegant reconstruction of a courtyard house. Reserve, and ask for one of the booths at the back. Start with a lobster congee and follow with a goat cheese roulade, or splash out on the seven-course tasting menu (¥888). Fabulous desserts include a chocolate addiction platter. ¥500/head. Daily 11.30am–11.30pm.

Xiao Shaoxing 小绍兴饭店, xiǎoshàoxīng fàndiàn. 118 Yunnan Nan Lu (east side), immediately north of Jinling Dong Lu ⓣ021 63260845. This big, bright restaurant wouldn't win any prizes for its looks, but it's famous in Shanghai for its *bai qie ji* (chicken simmered in wine). Adventurous diners might also wish to sample the blood soup or chicken feet. It's three storey: prices and comfort rise the higher you go. No English menu. Daily 11am–10pm.

Xinjishi (**Jesse Restaurant**) 新吉士餐厅, xīnjíshì cāntīng. 41 Tianping Lu and elsewhere ⓣ021 62829260, ⓦwww.xinjishi.com. The decor is a bit tatty at the tiny, original branch on Tianping Lu, but there's nothing wrong with the tasty homestyle cooking, with dishes from all over the country. Go for the red cooked pork, braised fish head and other local faves. The second branch at Xintiandi, with its traditional styling, looks better, but the food is not as good. You'll certainly have to reserve. Daily 11am–11.30pm.

★ **Ye Shanghai** 夜上海, yè shànghǎi. House 6, North Block, Xintiandi, 338 Huangpi Nan Lu ⓣ021 63112323. Shanghai cuisine in a quiet and classy venue with a European ambience. A good introduction to local tastes – particularly recommended are the drunken chicken, prawns with chilli sauce and the many crab dishes. Around ¥200/person. The lunch menu, at ¥88, is perhaps the best value in Xintiandi. Daily 10.30am–10.30pm.

PUDONG

Jade on 36 36F, Tower 2, Pudong Shangri-La, 33 Fucheng Lu ⓣ021 68823636, ⓦshangri-la.com. Celebrity chef Franck-Elie Laloum's classic French food in a grand venue, which has an amazing view of the Bund. Foie gras, prawn and beef rib are recommended, but it's pricey; at least ¥600/head. Mon–Sat 6–10.30pm, Sun brunch 11.30am–3pm, closed Sun evening.

Yi Café Level 2, Tower 2, Pudong Shangri-La, 33 Fucheng Lu ☏021 58775372, ⓦshangri-la.com. This slickly designed place with ten show kitchens is the best of the hotel buffets. It's all you can eat – weekday lunch is ¥238; and the very popular weekend brunch (11am–3pm) is ¥298; dinner is always ¥308 (plus fifteen percent service charge). Daily 6am–1am.

DRINKING AND NIGHTLIFE

BARS

Bars are found mostly in the French Concession area, nearly all of which serve food, and some of which have room for dancing. You'll find the full range of drinks available, though beer is usually bottled rather than draught and prices are on the high side; reckon on at least ¥30 per drink in most places.

Bar Rouge 7F, Bund 18, 18 Zhongshan Dong Yi Lu, near Dianchi Lu ☏021 63391199, ⓦbar-rouge-shanghai .com. This is one of the oldest Bund bars, and the most well known. Staff are snobbish, clientele are pretentious, but the terrace has unrivalled views over the Bund. ¥100 cover on weekends and you won't get much change from a red bill for a drink either. Daily 6pm–3am, later on weekends.

Boxing Cat 拳击猫, quánjī māo. 82 Fuxing Lu ☏021 64312091, ⓦboxingcatbrewery.com. American pub grub and excellent beers from the on-site microbrewery. Barbecues on the outside patio in the summer. Mon–Fri 5pm–2am, Sat–Sun 11am–3am.

Captain Bar 船长酒吧, chuánzhǎng jiǔbā. 6F, Captain Hostel, 37 Fuzhou Lu, by Sichuan Zhong Lu ☏021 63235053. This relaxed venue scores for its terrace with a great view of Pudong. It sits atop a backpacker hotel (see p.374) and is accessible via the grotty lift. Most hotel guests are put off by the prices – draught beer ¥40 – though that's still cheaper than anywhere else in the area. Happy hour until 8pm. Daily 5pm–late.

Cloud Nine 87th floor, Grand Hyatt, Jinmao Tower, 88 Shiji Dadao, Pudong ☏021 50491234. Inside, it's all rather dark and metallic, but the view is great. Pick a cloudless day, and arrive soon after opening time to bag one of the coveted windowside tables facing Puxi. ¥120 minimum spend/person, which will only get you one cocktail. Mon–Fri 5pm–1am, Sat & Sun 2pm–2am.

★ **Glamour Bar** 魅力酒吧, mèilì jiǔbā. 6F, M on the Bund, 20 Guangdong Lu, by Zhonghsan Dong Yi Lu ☏021 63293751, ⓦm-glamour.com. Pink, frivolous and fabulous, this local institution is one of Shanghai's best bars (and one of the world's best, according to Condé Nast). Good view of the Bund, and there's a schedule of cultural events. Cocktails from ¥85 (great mojitos). Daily 5pm–late.

Long Bar Waldorf Astoria Hotel, 2 Zhongshan Dong Yi Lu, near Guangdong Lu ☏021 63229988. A sophisticated and upmarket lounge with an Art Deco look and a very, very long bar – modelled on the original that once graced this address (see p.355). The drinks menu is also huge, with some great whiskies, and there are frequent live jazz performances. Mon–Sat 4pm–1am, Sun 2pm–1am.

People 7 805 Julu Lu, close to Fumin Lu ☏021 54040707. This hip bar trades on its exclusivity; not only is there no sign, there's even a special code to get in: put your hands into some of the nine lighted holes outside (they'll give you the code if you call). A door slides back revealing a two-storey lounge bar with walls of exposed concrete, spotlights, comfy white sofas and a long, eerily lit bar. The quirky elements – glasses with curved bottoms so they keep rolling round, baffling toilet doors with fake handles – will either delight or annoy. Daily 11.30am–2pm & 6pm–midnight.

★ **Senator** 98 Wuyuan Lu, near Wulumuqi Zhong Lu ☏021 54231330. This stylish speakeasy is intimate and cosy and the staff really know their cocktails; tell them your mood and tastes and they'll suggest a drink to fit. Daily 5pm–1am.

Vue 32–33F, Hyatt on the Bund hotel, 199 Huangpu Lu, north of Suzhou Creek ☏021 63931234. Another *Hyatt*-run Shanghai "must do", this sleek designer bar has fantastic views of the Bund, and there's a jacuzzi on the outdoor terrace so take your swimwear (or rent it from the bar). Cocktails for around ¥80. Tues is ladies' night, cover ¥100 at weekends. Sun–Thurs 6pm–1am, Fri–Sat 6pm–2am.

Windows Too (Jing'an) 2/F, City Plaza, 1618 Nanjing Xi Lu ☏021 62889007, ⓦwindowsbars.com. A popular staple thanks to a simple formula – cheap drinks and no pretensions. A predominantly student crowd keeps the dancefloor bouncing to commercial hip-hop. No points for style but it's fun. Daily 10am–late.

Zapatas 长廊酒吧, chángláng jiǔbā. 5 Hengshan Lu, near Dongping Lu ☏021 64334104, ⓦzapatas -shanghai.com. No self-respecting Mexican anarchist would be seen dead in the company of this lascivious frat-house crowd. Never mind, it's a heaving party on their Mon and Wed "free margaritas for the ladies before midnight" special. You enter through the garden of *Sasha's*, the nearby restaurant. Happy hour Mon–Fri 5–8pm. Daily 5pm till late.

CLUBS

Shanghai has perhaps the best club scene in China, which will feel eerily familiar to anyone who's been clubbing in any Western capital – you won't hear much in the way of local sounds – but at least door prices are cheaper, never more than ¥100. One Chinese innovation is the addition of karaoke booths at the back; another, much less welcome, is the annoying practice of having to pay to sit at a table. Most places have international DJs, and plenty of famous faces have popped in for a spin of the decks. Wed is (usually) ladies' night, Thur is hip-hop night, and, of course, the weekends are massive.

JZ Club 特别演出预告 tèbié yǎnchū yùgào. 46 Fuxing Xi Lu, near Yongfu Lu ☎021 64310269, ⓦjzclub .cn. This old Shanghai staple is dark but not smoky, with live jazz every night from 10pm. Pricey drinks (starting at ¥45) but there's usually no cover. Daily 7pm–2am.

Number 88 88酒吧, bāshíbā jiǔbā. A Mansion, 2/F, 291 Fumin Lu, near Donghu Lu ☎021 61360288. This Chinese disco is fun to check out, if you're in the right frame of mind – it's fiercely tacky but exuberant. Young, moneyed Chinese bop to club classics or play dice at the back, in what looks like a Tomb Raider wonderland. Daily 8.30pm–6am.

★ **The Geisha** 芸, yún. 390 Shanxi Nan Lu, near Fuxing Lu ☎021 64030244, ⓦthegeisha-shanghai .com. This small but well-formed club has a Japanese theme to the decor and the cocktails, and plays club standards to a nicely mixed crowd. It gets rammed on the weekend; there's an open-air lounge bar upstairs, specializing in saki, for when the dancefloor gets too busy. Wed night is ladies' night – free martinis till midnight. Happy hour Mon–Fri 5–8pm. Daily 5pm–late.

Shelter 5 Yongfu Lu, near Fuxing Xi Lu ☎021 64370400. This disused bomb shelter is now the centre of Shanghai's underground music scene, hosting hip-hop, dubstep, and electro DJs. It's dark and sweaty, so don't dress up, but do be ready to dance. It doesn't really get going till after midnight. ¥30 cover, ¥50 on weekends, and beers are a reasonable ¥30. Wed–Sat 10pm–late.

Yuyintang 育音堂, yùyīntáng. 851 Kaixuan Lu, by Yan'an Xi Lu subway stop ☎021 52378662; ⓦwww .yytlive.com. This is ground zero for the Converse-and-black-nail-varnish set. Rock/punk and electro gigs every weekend with a varying cover of around ¥40. With concrete floors and graffitied walls, it's all pretty rough and ready, but the sound system is surprisingly good, and bottles of beer are only ¥15. Daily 9.30pm–late.

ENTERTAINMENT

Most visitors take in an acrobatics show, but equally worthy of note are the flourishing contemporary art and music scenes. The Shanghai Arts Festival (ⓦwww.artsbird.com) is held from mid-October to mid-November – though you'd be forgiven for not noticing it – when the city receives a lot of visiting shows. For listings of big cultural spectaculars such as visiting ballet troupes, check the *China Daily*, but for the lowdown on punk gigs, underground art shows and the like, get an up-to-date expat magazine such as *cityweekend*, or check ⓦsmartshanghai.com. The simplest way to buy tickets is at the box office before the show starts, or a few days earlier if there's any danger that it will sell out. You can also buy tickets from the booking centre behind the Westgate Mall on Nanjing Xi Lu. The contemporary art scene can be conveniently checked out at the Moganshan Art District (see p.369). The Shanghai Biennale, held in venues all over town, is held on even-numbered years (ⓦshanghaibiennale.com).

ACROBATICS

Shanghai Circus World 上海马戏城, shànghǎi mǎxìchéng. 2266 Gonghe Xin Lu, in the far north of the city ☎021 66527750, ⓦera-shanghai.com. Their nightly show "ERA: the Intersection of Time" is a good old-fashioned spectacular, in a specially built dome.

Performances daily at 7.30pm; tickets ¥120–600.

Shanghai Centre's Theatre 上海商城剧院, shànghǎi shāngchéng jùyuàn. 1376 Nanjing Xi Lu, by Xikang Lu ☎021 62798948, ⓦshanghaicentre.com. Lighter on the glitz but slick and full of breathtaking feats. Performances daily at 7.30pm; tickets ¥100–280.

CELLULOID SHANGHAI

China's first movie studios were in Shanghai, in the 1930s (see p.946), and you can see old classics such as *Sister Flower* and *The Goddess* – both surprisingly hard-hitting naturalistic tragedies – at the *Old Film Café* (see p.377). The old studios that produced these movies might have gone-but, increasingly, you can find Shanghai depicted on film, most successfully in Lou Ye's tragic love story *Suzhou Creek* (2002). The best of many concession-era "lipstick and qipao" films is *Shanghai Triad* (1995). The brutal end to those days is shown in Steven Spielberg's decent adaptation of J.G. Ballard's classic novel, *Empire of the Sun* (1987). Shanghai is successfully made to look like a city of the future in the neat and twisty sci-fi thriller, *Looper* (2012).

6

CINEMA

Despite a glut of fantastically talented film makers, the Chinese film scene is stifled by government interference, and most cinemas are restricted into showing popcorn or propaganda pics. In mid-June the city hosts the Shanghai International Film Festival (ⓦsiff.com) when heartier fare is on offer. For art-house flicks, there's a popular screening club at the *Vienna Café* (see p.377) every Thursday at 7.30pm. The following cinemas show foreign blockbusters in their original languages and the latest Chinese releases in Mandarin Chinese only. Tickets start at ¥50.

Broadband International Cineplex 万裕国际影城, wànyù guójì yīngchéng. Sixth Floor, Times Square, 99 Huaihai Lu, near Huangpi Nan Lu subway station ☎021 63910363, ⓦwww.wyfilm.com.

Paradise Warner International City 永华电影城, yǒnghuá diànyǐng chéng. Sixth Floor, Grand Gateway, 1 Hongqiao Lu, Xujiahui ☎021 64076622.

UME International Cineplex 新天地国际影城, xīntiāndì guójì yīngchéng. Fifth Floor, South Block, Xintiandi ☎021 63733333, ⓦume.com.cn. An English schedule follows the Chinese when you call.

MUSIC

A number of new world-class venues are sating local demand for classical music and imported musicals. The Shanghai Cultural Information and Booking Centre has a comprehensive website with the schedules of all the most popular venues (ⓦwww.culture.sh.cn/English, reservations on ☎021 62172426). Tickets (upwards of

¥120) can be booked over the phone then delivered to your hotel or home at no extra charge, provided you book more than three days before the performance. Jazz is perennially popular; check out JZ Club (see p.381). The indie music scene is not as good as Beijing's, but it's there, and it is well worth dipping a toe into.

Majestic Theatre 美琪大剧院, měiqí dà jùyuàn. 66 Jiangning Lu, near Nanjing Xi Lu ☎021 62174409. When built in 1941 this was one of Asia's best theatres. It usually shows musicals and drama.

Oriental Arts Centre 上海东方艺术中心, shànghǎi dōngfāng yìshù zhōngxīn. 425 Dingxiang Lu, near Century Ave ☎021 68541234, ⓦwww.shoac.com.cn. This is a fantastic, forty-thousand-square-metre behemoth, shaped like an opening flower. Hosts a little bit of everything, but comes into its own as a concert venue, as the acoustics are superb.

Shanghai Concert Hall 上海音乐厅, shànghǎi yīnyuètīng. 523 Yan'an Dong Lu, near Xizang Zhong Lu ☎021 63862836, ⓦwww.shanghaiconcerthall.org. This beautiful old building was moved 60m east in 2003, at tremendous cost, to get it away from the din of Yan'an Lu. Today, it's the premier venue for classical music. Tickets from ¥50.

Shanghai Grand Theatre 上海大剧院, shànghǎi dàjùyuàn. 300 Renmin Dadao ☎021 63273094, ⓦshgtheatre.com. Lovely building that puts on popular contemporary dramas, operas and classical ballets, and plays host to most of the visiting musicals. Regular performances by the in-house Shanghai Symphony Orchestra.

SHOPPING

The shopping is great in Shanghai, and it's a rare visitor who doesn't end up having to buy another bag to keep all their new goodies in. The Shanghainese love luxury goods, and it's not uncommon to find young women spending several months' salary on a handbag, but all those glitzy brand names that give the streets such a lot of their shine are not good value; high-end goods and international brands are generally twenty percent more expensive than they would be in the West. Ignore them, and instead plunge into the fascinating world of the backstreet boutiques and markets.

BOOKS

Charterhouse Basement of Times Square, 93 Hauihai Zhong Lu ☎021 63918237. Good selections of imported English-language books cost a little more than they would at home. Daily 10am–7pm.

Foreign Languages Bookstore 外文图书公司, wàiwén túshū gōngsī. 390 Fuzhou Lu ☎021 23204994. A useful resource, with plenty of English-language guides, coffee-table tomes and the like; the out of copyright English-language novels, published by Chinese publishers, are cheap. Daily 9.30am–7pm.

Garden Books 韬奋西文书局, tāofèn xī wénshújú. Changle Lu, near Shanxi Nan Lu ☎021 54048728, ⓦgardenbooks.cn. The best selection of

foreign-language books in the city and a charming café, known for its tasty ice cream, to sample them in. Daily 10am–10pm.

CLOTHES

Sartorial elegance is something of a local obsession, so you're spoilt for choice if you're looking for clothes. If you want to see international designer clothes in showpiece stores head to Nanjing Xi Lu or the Bund. The choicest shopping is to be had in the former French Concession; central Huaihai Zhong Lu itself is full of familiar brands, but the streets off it – such as Nanchang, Shanxi Nan Lu and Maoming Lu – are full of fascinating little boutiques, which make this the place to forage for fashionable gear. For

MADE TO MEASURE

Getting tailored clothes is a recommended Shanghai experience, as it will cost so much less than at home and the artisans are skilled (provided you're clear about exactly what you're after) and quick. At the textile market in the Old City, near Liushui Lu at 399 Lujiabang Lu (南外滩轻纺面料市场, nánwàitān qīngfǎng miànliào shìchǎng; daily 10am–7pm), on-site tailors will make you a suit for around ¥500, including material (you'll have to barter a bit), which will take a couple of days; a shirt should be around ¥150. It's all a bit hit and miss, but Jennifer at Unit 237, Andy at 295 and Xia at 326 are all considered a good bet.

If you're looking for a more sedate experience, or a tailored *qipao*, your best bet is to head to one of the dozen or so specialist tailors on Maoming Nan Lu, just south of Huaihai Lu. Three shirts in one of these stores should come to around ¥800, a suit will be around twice that.

designer clothes at bargain basement prices, head to a factory overstock shop. These will be unpromising from the outside, possibly won't have a name, and will usually carry their own lines in the window, with the good stuff hung rather negligently on a rail at the back. The place to start looking is Ruijin Er Lu, at the intersection with Huaihai Zhong Lu. Head south down the street then turn onto Nanchang Lu – look in any clothes shop that's busy on the way. A second concentration of these stores is on Fuxing Zhong Lu, east of Baoqing Lu. The place to start looking for interesting local designers is Tianzifang (see p.363).

Capital Joy 158 Jinxian Lu, near Maoming Nan Lu, ☎021 62560134. Elegant and affordable smart clothes for men, from Hong Kong designers. Off the peg suits start at ¥900, shirts at ¥400. Daily 11am–10pm.

Insh 200 Taikang Lu, Tianzifang ☎021 64665249, ⊚insh.com.cn. Check out local designer Helen Lee's fun and sexy takes on vintage Chinese designs. Daily 10am–9pm.

La Boutique 250–254 Taikang Lu ☎021 64317999. Stylish boutique serving as a showcase for the most hyped local designers. Daily 10.30am–10.30pm.

Nuomi 196 Xinle Lu, near Donghu Lu ☎021 54034199, and Lane 12, Tianzifang ☎021 64663952. This design collective makes stylish childrenswear and elegant women's clothes from natural fabrics. Daily 10am–9.30pm.

Vintage 84 Fenyang Lu, near Fuxing Zhong Lu. Browse this cluttered space for affordable retro dresses, starting at around ¥400, and quirky jewellery and womenswear from local designers. Daily 10am–6pm.

ELECTRONICS

The best places to shop for electronic goods are the giant tech-souks listed below. Obscure brand laptops, MP3 players, memory sticks, RAM, and low-end accessories such as headphones can be very cheap. Shop around, as many of the stalls sell the same things, and barter (though this isn't the fake market; you'll get at most twenty percent off the asking price). Test everything thoroughly, and remember that for the majority of this stuff the warranty is not valid internationally.

Metro City 美罗城, měiluó chéng. 111 Zhaojiabang Lu, by Caoxi Bei Lu. This mall, shaped like a giant bubble (Xujiahui subway), is full of electronics stores. Daily 10am–7pm.

Pacific Digital Plaza 太平洋数码广场, tàipíngyáng shùmǎ guǎngchǎng. 117 Zhaojiabang Lu, Xujiahui subway. Great for low-end tech products and computer components. Daily 10am–8pm.

FAKE MARKETS

There are several fake markets catering largely to foreigners. As well as clothes, stalls have trainers, sunglasses, bags and watches on sale, and plenty of souvenirs.

Han City 580 Nanjing Xi Lu. The most convenient fake market, on three floors of a mall. Barter hard, as the persistent sales people consistently start at ten times the real price. Daily 9am–9pm.

Yatai Xinyang Fashion & Gift Market 亚太新阳服饰礼品市场, yàtài xīnyáng fúshì lǐpǐn shìchǎng. Inside the Science and Technology Museum subway station, its entrance close to the ticketing machines. This is the biggest of the fake markets; as well as the usual fake shoes, bags and clothes there are plenty of tailors, and there's a whole zone for jewellery. Daily 8.30am–7.30pm.

DIRECTORY

American Express Room 206, Shanghai Centre, 1376 Nanjing Xi Lu (Mon–Fri 9am–noon, 1–5.30pm; ☎021 62798082).

Banks and exchange The head office of the Bank of China is at 23 Zhongshan Lu (The Bund), next to the *Peace*

Hotel (Mon–Fri 9am–noon & 1.30–4.30pm, Sat 9am–noon). Next door is a Citibank ATM machine with 24hr access.

Consulates Australia, 22F, CITIC Square 1168 Nanjing Xi Lu ☎021 22155200, ⊚shanghai.china.embassy.gov.au;

Canada, Room 604, West Tower, Shanghai Centre, 1376 Nanjing Xi Lu ☎021 32792800, ⓦchina.gc.ca; New Zealand, Room 1605, The Centre, 989 Changle Lu, ☎021 54075858; Republic of Ireland, 700A Shanghai Centre, 1376 Nanjing Xi Lu ☎021 62798729, ⓦembassyofireland .cn; South Africa, Room 2706, The Bund Centre, 220 Yanan Dong Lu ☎021 53594977; UK, Room 301, West Tower, Shanghai Centre, 1376 Nanjing Xi Lu ☎021 32792000; US, 1469 Huaihai Zhong Lu ☎021 62797662, ⓦshanghai .usembassy-china.org.cn.

Football Shanghai's team, Shenhua (ⓦshenhuafc.com .cn), play every other Sun at 3.30pm at the impressive 35,000-seat Hongkou Football Stadium, 444 Dongjianwan Lu, in the north of town. Tickets start at ¥80 and can be bought at the ground on the day, from the ticket office or from scalpers, or in advance from ⓦwww.mypiao.com.

Hospitals A number of the city's hospitals have special clinics for foreigners, including the Huadong Hospital at 221 Yan'an Xi Lu (☎021 62483180) and the Hua Shan Hospital at 12 Wulumuqi Lu (go to the eighth floor; ☎021 62483986). You'll find decent medical care at Parkway Medical and Dental Centres, Suite 203 of the Shanghai Centre West Tower at 1376 Nanjing Xi Lu

(☎021 62797688, ⓦwww.parkwayhealth.cn); and JJife, 1N01, Jinmao Tower, 88 Century Avenue, Pudong, and Fourth floor, Tomorrow Square, 389 Nanjing Xi Lu (☎021 64455999, daily 9am–5pm). Expect to pay ¥800/ consultation.

Internet Netbars are dotted around the backstreets (¥3/ hr; 24hr); you'll need to show your passport before you're let near a computer. There's a handy internet office in the basement of the Shanghai Library at 1555 Huaihai Zhong Lu (daily 8.30am–8pm; ¥4/hr).

Mail The main post office is at 276 Suzhou Bei Lu, just north of and overlooking Suzhou Creek (☎021 63936666; daily 7am–10pm). It offers a very efficient parcel service; the express option can get packages to Britain or the US within two days. Branch post offices dot the city, with convenient locations along Nanjing Dong Lu, Huaihai Zhong Lu, in the Portman Centre, and near the Huangpu River ferry jetties at the corner of Jinling Dong Lu and Sichuan Bei Lu.

PSB 210 Hankou Lu, near the corner of Henan Zhong Lu. Their visa extension office is on Floor 3, 1500 Minsheng Lu, Pudong, near Yinchun Lu (Science and Technology Museum subway stop; Mon–Fri 9am–11.30pm & 1.30–4.30pm).

Around Shanghai

Shanghai Municipality covers approximately two thousand square kilometres, comprising ten counties and extending far beyond the limits of the city itself. Very little of this huge area is ever visited by foreigners, though there are a couple of interesting sights – notably the attractive **water towns**, very popular with domestic tourists – which make enjoyable excursions from downtown Shanghai.

She Shan

余山, shéshān • Daily 8am–4pm • metro line #9 to She Shan station, then a free tourist bus to West Hill

Such is the flatness of the surrounding land some 30km southwest of Shanghai that **She Shan**, a low range which only rises about 100m, is visible for many kilometres around. The park is divided in two; the East Hill has a forest park, while the more attractive West Hill has the historical attractions.

West Hill

西山, xīshān • Free

It's a pleasant walk up west hill at any time of year, or a cable-car ride if you prefer (¥10), past bamboo groves and the occasional ancient pagoda. The peak here is crowned by an impressive **basilica**, a legacy of nineteenth-century European missionary work – She Shan has been under the ownership of a Catholic community since the 1850s – though the present church was not built until 1925. Also on the hill are a **meteorological station** and an old **observatory** (daily 8am–5pm, ¥12), the latter containing an astronomical exhibition, including an ingenious earthquake-measuring device: dragon heads, with balls in their mouths, ring a pendulum; when the pendulum swings due to an earthquake, it knocks a ball out, thus pointing out the earthquake's direction.

East Hill

东山, dōngshān • ¥80

East Hill has been redeveloped as a woodland park, including the artificial Moon Lake. A ten-minute walk west from the entrance brings you first to a sculpture park; the road curves south to get around the hill itself. There's nothing particularly distinguished about the thirty or so works of art, but they serve as handy way-stations on a pleasant walk. With a long artificial beach around a lake, manicured lawns and plenty of playgrounds, this makes a good retreat to take the kids and is busy with families at the weekend. Rowing boats can be rented for ¥60 an hour. If you want to escape the crowds, just head uphill into the woods.

6

The water towns

The extensive canal system surrounding Shanghai was once part of a network which transported goods all around imperial China, and the attractive **water towns** that grew up around them present some of eastern China's most distinctive urban environments. Whitewashed Ming and Qing timber buildings back onto the narrow waterways, which are crossed by charming humpback stone bridges; travel is by foot or punt as the alleys are too narrow for cars.

Today, these sleepy towns are a popular escape from the city, and each has become a nostalgia theme park for the urban sophisticate. They're fine as day-trips but don't expect much authenticity – there are far more souvenir shops than dwellings – and don't come on weekends, when they're overrun. All charge an **entrance fee**, which also gets you into the historical buildings, mostly the grand old houses of wealthy merchants.

It is possible to **stay over** in all the canal towns, which are attractively lit up, and much quieter, at night; if you are contemplating staying over, Wuzhen is the best choice (see p.386).

Zhouzhuang

周庄, zhōuzhuāng • 60km west of Shanghai, just across the border into Jiangsu province • ¥100 • boat ride round the canals ¥100

ZHOUZHUANG is the most accessible of the canal towns. Lying astride the large Jinghang Canal connecting Suzhou and Shanghai, Zhouzhuang grew prosperous from the area's brisk grain, silk and pottery trade during the Ming dynasty. Many rich government officials, scholars and artisans moved here and constructed beautiful villas, while investing money into developing the stately stone bridges and tree-lined canals that now provide the city's main attractions. Zhouzhuang's most highly rated views are of the pretty sixteenth-century twin **stone bridges** in the northeast of town. Also firmly on the itinerary is **lunch** – there is no shortage of restaurants, all offering the local specialities of pig's thigh, meatballs and clams as a set meal (around ¥60/head).

Shen House

South side of Fuan Bridge • Daily 8.30am–4.30pm • Free

The biggest mansion in Zhouzhuang is the **Shen House** in the east of town, built in 1742. Over a hundred rooms (not all of them open) are connected by covered colonnades, with grand public halls at the front and the more intimate family chambers at the back. Period furnishings help evoke a lost age of opulence, though it is all rather dark; the neat gardens offer a pleasant contrast.

Xitang

西塘, xītáng • Free on Sun afternoon and Fri morning, otherwise ¥50, or ¥100 including all entrance fees

Eighty kilometres south west of Shanghai, **XITANG** is short on specific sights, although the lanes, canals and bridges are undeniably picturesque. And if it rains, at least you'll be dry: the locals, tired of the wet climate, built roofs over the main

6

alleyways, the biggest of which is over 1km long. It runs alongside the central canal, and is lined with restaurants and stalls housed in half-timbered buildings. There are plenty of riverside restaurants serving up local specialities such as pork with sweet potatoes.

Tongli

同里, tónglǐ · ¥80

Of all the canal towns, **TONGLI**, around 80km southwest from Shanghai, has the best sights, and with more than forty humpback bridges (some more than a thousand years old) and fifteen canals it offers plenty of photo ops.

Tuisi Garden

退思园, tuìsī yuán · Daily 8am–6pm · ¥40

The town's highlight is the UNESCO World Heritage Site **Tuisi Garden**, built by disillusioned retired official Ren Lansheng in 1886 as a place to retreat and meditate – though you'll have to come in the early morning, before the tour groups arrive, to appreciate the peacefulness of the place. With its harmonious arrangements of rockeries, pavilions and bridges, zigzagging over carp-filled ponds, it is comparable to anything in Suzhou.

Sex Museum

中华性文化博物馆, zhōnghuá xìngwénhuà bówùguǎn · Daily 8am–5.30pm · ¥20

Housed in a former girls' school, this has plenty of striking exhibits – figurines of Tang-dynasty prostitutes, special coins for use in brothels and a wide range of occasionally eye-watering dildos.

Wuzhen

乌镇, wūzhèn · ¥120 · pick up a map at the nearby visitor's centre

As it's a little further out than other canal towns (120km southwest and two hours by bus), sedate **WUZHEN** is less busy; if you're headed out on the weekend, this is the one to go to as the others will be choked, and if you stay at a hotel within the confines of the old town, the entrance fee is waived and you'll get to see the place lit up by hundreds of red lanterns.

Around the town

Wuzhen's prime draw is the cute little **Xiuzhen Taoist Temple** and its collection of folk art, including intricate wood carving and leather shadow puppets; you can watch the latter in action at the nearby playhouse, which has shows every hour until 5pm. Several of Wuzhen's houses are used to demonstrate local crafts such as silk painting or printing using dyes made from tea leaves, or as museums; check out the intricately carved pieces of the **Hundred Bed Museum**. The **Fanglu Pavilion**, near the centre of town, is today a teahouse with picturesque views over the canal, and makes a good place for a rest, though as ever in these places, you won't find it cheap (¥60 a pot).

ARRIVAL AND DEPARTURE
THE WATER TOWNS

By bus There are plentiful buses to all the water towns from the Shanghai South bus station.

By tour bus Day-trips to the canal towns depart from the Shanghai Stadium Sightseeing Bus Centre (上海体育馆旅游集散中心, shànghǎi tǐyùguǎn lǚyóu jísàn zhōngxīn; information ☏021 64265555) at 666 Tianyaoqiao Lu, on the south side of the Shanghai Stadium in the southwest of the city, a 10min walk from the Shanghai Stadium subway stop. Tour buses leave between 7.30am and 9.30am, returning in the afternoon. Tickets, priced around ¥120 (which includes the entrance fee), are available up to a week in advance from the main booking office, where staff speak English, or you can order tickets up to three days in advance from a freephone number (☏021 4008872626) and they'll deliver them to your hotel for a fee of between ¥10 and ¥30. A guide is provided (non-English-speaking), though you are free to wander off on your own.

ACCOMMODATION

WUZHEN

Wuzhen Guesthouse 乌镇民宿, wūzhèn mínsù. 137 Xizha Jie ☎ 0573 88731230, ⓦ wuzhen.com.cn. Not a single guesthouse, this is a cooperative of properties all over town, run in B&B style by local families, who will cook your meals for you. It's worth paying a little extra for a riverside view. **¥450**

XITANG

Jinshui Lou Ge 近水楼阁客栈, jìnshuǐ loúgé kèzhàn. 10 Chaonan Dai ☎ 133 75731700. Simple place with whitewashed walls and exposed wooden-beam decor. The small rooms are attractively decorated with reproduction Ming-dynasty furniture, including four-poster beds. **¥180**

Xitang Youth Hostel 西塘忆水阑庭国际青年旅舍, xītáng yìshuǐ lántíng guójì qīngnián lǚshè. 6 Tangjia Lane, off Xi Xia Jie on the west side of town ☎ 0512 65218885, ⓦ www.yhachina.com. Traditional white walls and black tiles on the outside; inside there's a pleasant courtyard with bamboos overlooked by balconies, a small café and simple, clean rooms, some with wooden floors. Dorms **¥45**, doubles **¥120**

ZHOUZHUANG

International Youth Hostel 周庄国际青年旅馆, zhōuzhuāng guójì qīngnián lǚguǎn. 86 Beishi Jie ☎ 0512 57204566, ⓦ www.yhachina.com. Cosy repeat of their Xitang establishment, though rooms – even the dorms – tend to be more spacious; the staff here are especially helpful and there's the inevitable café on site. Rates rise by fifty percent or more at weekends. Dorm beds **¥45**, doubles **¥130**

6

The Yangzi basin

GOLDEN MONKEYS, SHENNONGJIA

The Yangzi basin

Having raced out of Sichuan through the narrow Three Gorges, the Yangzi (here known as the Chang Jiang) widens, slows down and loops through its flat, low-lying middle reaches, swelled by lesser streams and rivers that drain off the highlands surrounding the four provinces of the Yangzi basin: Anhui, Hubei, Hunan and Jiangxi. As well as watering one of China's key rice- and tea-growing areas, this stretch of the Yangzi has long supported trade and transport; back in the thirteenth century, Marco Polo was awed by the "innumerable cities and towns along its banks, and the amount of shipping it carries, and the bulk of merchandise that merchants transport by it". Rural fringes away from the river – including much of Anhui and Jiangxi provinces – remain some of the least developed regions in central China, a situation the mighty Three Gorges Dam on the border between Hubei and Chongqing, whose hydroelectric output powers a local industrial economy to rival that of the east coast, is going some way to address.

The river basin itself is best characterized by China's two largest freshwater lakes: **Dongting**, which separates Hunan and Hubei, and **Poyang**, in northern Jiangxi, famed for porcelain produced at nearby **Jingdezhen**. While all four provincial capitals are located near water, only **Wuhan**, in Hubei, is actually on the Yangzi, a position that has turned the city into central China's liveliest urban conglomeration. Long settlement of the capitals has, however, left a good deal of history in its wake, from well-preserved Han-dynasty tombs to whole villages of Ming-dynasty houses, and a smattering of sites from the Three Kingdoms (see box, p.393). Many cities also remain studded with hefty European buildings, a hangover from their being forcibly opened up to foreign traders as **Treaty Ports** in the 1860s, following the Second Opium War. Perhaps partly due to these unwanted intrusions, the Yangzi basin can further claim to be the **cradle of modern China**: Mao Zedong was born in Hunan; Changsha, Wuhan and Nanchang are all closely associated with Communist Party history; and the mountainous border between Hunan and Jiangxi was both a Red refuge during right-wing purges in the late 1920s and the starting point for the subsequent Long March to Shaanxi.

Away from the river, wild mountain landscapes make for excellent hiking, the prime spots being Anhui's **Huang Shan**, followed by **Zhangjiajie National Forest Reserve** in Hunan's far west. Pilgrims also have a selection of Buddhist and Taoist holy mountains to scale – Hubei's **Wudang Shan** is outstanding – and less dedicated souls can find pleasant views at the mountain resort town of **Lushan** in Jiangxi.

HUIZHOU BUILDINGS, YIXIAN

Highlights

❶ Yixian An amazing collection of antique Ming villages, used atmospherically in Zhang Yimou's film *Raise the Red Lantern*. **See p.403**

❷ Huang Shan Arguably China's most scenic mountain, wreathed in narrow stone staircases, contorted trees and cloud-swept peaks. **See p.404**

❸ Hubei Provincial Museum, Wuhan On show here are 2000-year-old relics from the tombs of aristocrats, including a lacquered coffin and an orchestra of 64 giant bronze bells. **See p.412**

❹ Shennongjia Forest Reserve Wild and remote mountain refuge of the endangered golden monkey and (allegedly) the enigmatic *ye ren*, China's Bigfoot. **See p.420**

❺ Wudang Shan Temple-covered mountains at the heart of Taoist martial-art mythology; it's said this is where *tai ji* originated. **See p.422**

HIGHLIGHTS ARE MARKED ON THE MAP ON P.392

In theory, **getting around** isn't a problem, as high-speed rail lines and highways link all but the remotest of corners. Autumn is probably the most pleasant time of year, though even winters are generally mild, but near-constant rains and consequential lowland flooding plague the summer months.

Anhui

安徽, ānhuī

Despite a government vision of **Anhui** as a wealthy corridor between coast and interior, the region continues to live up to its reputation as eastern China's poorest province. It has a long history, however, and million-year-old remains of the proto-human *Homo erectus* have been found here, while Shang-era copper mines in southern Anhui fuelled China's Bronze Age. The province later became known for its artistic refinements, from decorative Han tombs through to Ming architecture.

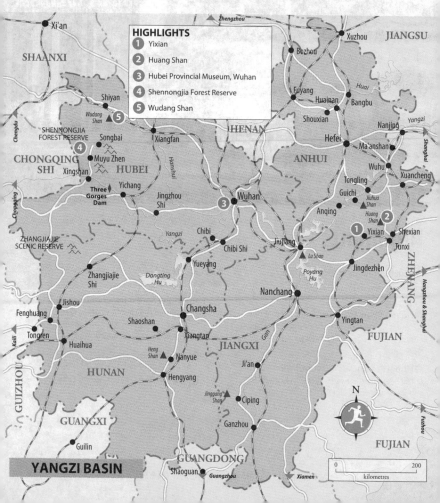

HIGHLIGHTS

1. Yixian
2. Huang Shan
3. Hubei Provincial Museum, Wuhan
4. Shennongjia Forest Reserve
5. Wudang Shan

YANGZI BASIN

SANGUO: THE THREE KINGDOMS

The empire, long divided, must unite; long united, must divide. Thus it has ever been.

So, rather cynically, begins China's great fourteenth-century historical novel, **Romance of the Three Kingdoms**. Covering 120 chapters and a cast of thousands, the tale touches heavily on the Yangzi basin, which, as a buffer zone between the Three Kingdoms, formed the backdrop for many major battles. Some surviving sites are covered in this chapter and elsewhere in the Guide.

Opening in 168 AD, the *Romance* recounts the decline of the Han empire and how China was subsequently split into three states by competing warlords. The two original protagonists were the villainous **Cao Cao** and the virtuous **Liu Bei**, whose watery character was compensated for by the strength of his spirited sworn brothers **Zhang Fei** and **Guan Yu** – the latter eventually becoming enshrined in the Chinese pantheon as the red-faced god of war and healing. A political dispute between Cao and Liu eventually broke down into forthright conflict, their armies fighting numerous campaigns through the Yangzi basin – both sides all the time claiming to represent the emperor's wishes. Cao was eventually defeated in Hubei at the **Battle of the Red Cliffs** (208 AD), after Liu engaged the aid of the wily adviser **Zhuge Liang**, who boosted Liu's heavily outnumbered forces by enlisting the help of a third warlord, **Sun Quan** – a campaign recently brought to life in John Woo's blockbuster Red Cliff movies.

Consolidating their positions, each of the three formed a private kingdom: Cao Cao retreated north to the Yellow River basin where he established the state of **Wei** around the ailing imperial court; Sun Quan set up **Wu** farther south along the lower Yangzi; while Liu Bei built a power base in the riverlands of Sichuan, the state of **Shu**. The alliance between Shu and Wu fell apart when Sun Quan asked Guan Yu to betray Liu. Guan refused and was assassinated by Sun in 220 AD. At this point Cao Cao died, and his ambitious son, **Cao Pi**, forced the emperor to abdicate and announced himself head of a new dynasty. Fearing retaliation from the state of Shu after Guan Yu's murder, Sun Quan decided to support Cao Pi's claims, while over in Shu, Liu Bei also declared his right to rule.

Against Zhuge Liang's advice, Liu marched against Wu to avenge Guan Yu's death, but his troops mutinied, killing Zhang Fei. Humiliated, Liu withdrew to Baidicheng in the Yangzi Gorges and died. With him out of the way, Cao Pi attacked Sun Quan, who was forced to renew his uncomfortable alliance with Shu – now governed by Zhuge Liang – to keep the invaders out of his kingdom. By 229 AD, however, things were stable enough for Sun Quan to declare himself as a rival emperor, leaving Zhuge to die five years later fighting the armies of Wei. Wei was unable to pursue the advantage, as a coup against Cao Pi started a period of civil war in the north, ending around 249 AD when the **Sima clan** emerged victorious. Sun Quan died soon afterwards, while Shu abandoned all claim to the empire. Wei's Sima clan founded a new dynasty, the **Jin**, in 265 AD, finally overpowering Wu and uniting China in 280 AD.

7

Any success, however, has been in the face of Anhui's unfriendly geography. Arid and eroded, the north China plains extend into its upper third as far as the **Huai River**, and while the south is warmer and wetter, the fertile wooded hills soon climb to rugged mountains, where little can grow. Historically, though, the flood-prone **Yangzi** itself has ensured Anhui's poverty by regularly inundating the province's low-lying centre, which would otherwise produce a significant amount of crops. Despite the expansion of highways and railways – not to mention several huge bridges across the Yangzi – Anhui's economy still trails its booming neighbours, though there are compensations for this underdevelopment. Superlative mountain landscapes at **Huang Shan** and the collection of Buddhist temples at **Jiuhua Shan** have been pulling in sightseers for centuries, and there's a strong cultural tradition stamped on the area, with a substantial amount of antique rural architecture surviving intact around **Tunxi**.

Hefei

合肥, héféi

Nestled in the heart of the province but generally overlooked in the rush to reach Huang Shan, Anhui's capital, **HEFEI**, gets few chance visitors. Once ringed by parkland and canals – the remains of Ming-dynasty moats – the outskirts of Hefei are now dominated by hundreds of identikit apartment blocks, and the city's sole points of interest are a couple of **historical sites** and an excellent new **museum**. Nevertheless it's a comfortable enough place to stay, can be a handy transport hub and the locals will be happy, if perhaps surprised, to see you.

Mingjiao Temple

明教寺, míngjiào sì • Huaihe Lu • Daily 6am–6pm • ¥10

The busy, pedestrian eastern half of Huaihe Lu seems an unlikely location for **Mingjiao Temple**, a restored sixteenth-century complex whose fortress-like walls front unpretentious halls and a plum garden. The temple occupies a Three Kingdoms site where the northern leader **Cao Cao** drilled his crossbowers during the winter of 216 AD. A glassed-in well in the temple's main courtyard reputedly dates from this time; it definitely looks ancient, a worn stone ring set close to the ground, deeply scored over the centuries by ropes being dragged over the rim.

Li Hongzhang's Former Home

李鸿章居, lǐhóngzhāng jū • Huaihe Lu • Daily 8.30am–6.30pm • ¥20

Just west of the Mingjiao Temple, the former home of controversial Qing dynasty politician **Li Hongzhang** is a similarly anachronistic mansion, whose surrounding grey brick wall hides a series of tastefully decorated courtyards and halls embellished with opulently carved wooden furniture. Li was heralded a hero for his role in quelling the

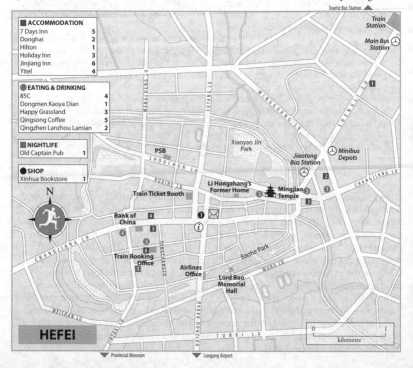

ACCOMMODATION
7 Days Inn	5
Donghai	2
Hilton	1
Holiday Inn	3
Jinjiang Inn	6
Yitel	4

EATING & DRINKING
85C	4
Dongmen Kaoya Dian	1
Happy Grassland	3
Qingsong Coffee	5
Qingzhen Lanzhou Lamian	2

NIGHTLIFE
| Old Captain Pub | 1 |

SHOP
| Xinhua Bookstore | 1 |

HEFEI

Taiping Rebellion, but later fell from favour after signing a number of unequal treaties with foreign powers. Knighted by Queen Victoria, by the end of his life Li was as reviled in China as he was respected in the West, although having spent much of his career attempting to reform dynastic China.

Lord Bao Memorial Hall

包公祠, bāogōng cí • Daily 8am–6pm • ¥50

Down at the southeastern side of town, **Baohe Park** (包河公园, bāohé gōngyuán) is a nice strip of lakeside willows and arched bridges off Wuhu Lu, where the **Lord Bao Memorial Hall** identifies Hefei as the birthplace of Bao, the famous Song-dynasty administrator (see p.273). Lord Bao's ability to uncover the truth in complex court cases, and his proverbially unbiased rulings, are the subject of endless tales – he also often appears as a judge in paintings of Chinese hell. Along with gilded statues, some waxworks bring a couple of well-known stories to life: look for Lord Bao's dark face, improbably "winged" hat and the three guillotines – shaped as a dragon, tiger and dog, according to the status of the condemned – he had made for summary executions.

The Provincial Museum

省博物馆, shěng bówùguǎn • Huaining Lu • Tues–Sun 9am–5pm • Free • ☎ 0551 63736677 • bus #162 or #166 from Shifu Guangchang

Hefei's new **Provincial Museum** opened its doors in 2011 and provides sound evidence of Anhui's contributions to Chinese culture, all displayed in state-of-the-art fashion 10km southwest of the centre. The museum traces the passage of time in the region, starting with the dinosaurs and moving through the arrival of man – the *Homo erectus* cranium from Taodian in the south of the province is one of the museum's most treasured exhibits. Comparatively recent history emerges in a few Stone Age items and an exceptional Shang bronze urn decorated with tiger and dragon motifs. Elsewhere, there's an exhibit of the "Four Scholastic Treasures" for which the province is famed: high-quality ink sticks, heavy carved inkstones, weasel-hair writing brushes and multicoloured papers.

ARRIVAL AND DEPARTURE	HEFEI

BY PLANE

Luogang airport (合肥骆岗机场, héféi luògǎng jīchǎng) is about 11km south of the city, and reachable by taxi (¥40), or hourly airport bus (¥25) from the airlines office (daily 6am–7pm; ☎ 0551 2886626) on Fuyang Lu. You can also buy plane and train tickets here.

Destinations Beijing (6 daily; 1hr 45min); Changsha (3 daily; 1hr 10min); Guangzhou (7 daily; 1hr 55min); Nanchang (1 daily; 1hr 15min); Shenzhen (6 daily; 2hr); Tunxi (1 daily; 50min); Xiamen (7 daily; 1hr 20min); Xi'an (5 daily; 1hr 35min).

BY TRAIN

The train station (合肥火车站, héféi huǒchē zhàn) is 3km northeast of the centre at the end of Shengli Lu – bus #119 runs down Shengli Lu and into town along Changjiang Lu. The station is the hub for both regular and high-speed lines and destinations. Tickets can be bought at the station, at the airlines office on Fuyang Lu (see above), or at the train booking office on Lujiang Lu.

Destinations Beijing (10 daily; 4–14hr); Jingdezhen (2

daily; 8hr 30min–10hr 30min); Jiujiang (11 daily; 4hr 30min–6hr); Nanchang (11 daily; 6–8hr); Nanjing (many daily; 1–4hr); Shanghai (many daily; 3–6hr); Tunxi (3 daily; 6–7hr); Xian (5 daily; 14hr 30min–17hr).

BY BUS AND MINIBUS

Hefei's confusing array of bus and minibus stations often offer overlapping services, so try the closest one first.

Jiaotong bus station (交通返点车站, jiāotōng fǎndiǎn chēzhàn) Shengli Lu. Serves major cities including Changsha, Shanghai and Wuhan.

Main bus station (客运总站, kèyùn zǒngzhàn) opposite the train station. Best for destinations within Anhui, including Tunxi.

Tourist bus station (旅游汽车站, lǚyóu qìchē zhàn) Zhan Qian Lu, 600m northwest of the train station. The best bet for Jiuhua Shan, although there are also services from the motley collection of minibus stands on Shengli Lu.

Destinations Jiuhua Shan (4hr); Jiujiang (5hr); Nanchang (6hr); Nanjing (3hr); Tunxi (4hr); Wuhan (6hr).

7

GETTING AROUND

Hefei's countless underpasses and traffic lights make large parts of the city troublesome to negotiate on foot. Fortunately taxis are both readily available and inexpensive.

By bus Buses cost ¥1–2 and operate 6am–8pm (or later).

By taxi Flag fall is ¥8 for the first 2.5km, then ¥1.4 per km.

ACCOMMODATION

7 Days Inn 7天连锁酒店, qītiān liánsuǒ jiǔdiàn. 299 Changjiang Zhong Lu ☏0551 62248177. Right in the centre of town, this characterless but scrupulously clean chain hotel is undeniably great value. **¥187**

Donghai 东海饭店, dōnghǎi fàndiàn. 139 Mingguang Lu ☏0551 64693004. Ignore the dated lobby and corridors and focus on the clean, modern rooms, which offer some of the best-value budget accommodation in town. **¥175**

Hilton 希尔顿酒店, xīěrdùn jiǔdiàn. 198 Shengli Lu ☏0551 62808888, ⓦhilton.com. A huge, opulent lobby, quality rooms and all the other services you would expect at a *Hilton*. Access is currently limited due to the construction work on Shengli Lu, but this should be finished in 2014. **¥630**

Holiday Inn 古井假日酒店, gǔjǐng jiàrì jiǔdiàn. 1104 Changjiang Lu ☏0551 62206666, ⓦholiday-inn.com.cn. Recently renovated and great value, *Holiday Inn* offers the usual range of facilities, along with a surprisingly good and inexpensive 24hr noodle bar. There's also a coffeeshop alongside the fifth-floor reception. **¥468**

★**Jinjiang Inn** 锦江之星, jǐnjiāng zhīxīng. 123 Lujiang Lu ☏0551 62641559, ⓦjinjianginns.com. Hefei's downtown Jinjiang offers a great location on a leafy street just a few minutes back from Changjiang Lu. Inside you'll find the usual generic but clean and comfortable rooms with internet access. **¥189**

Yitel 和颐酒店, héyí jiǔdiàn. Changjiang Lu ☏0551 62620088, ⓦwww.yitel.com. Owned and operated by the same group as *Motel 168*, this upmarket business chain hotel offers a very central location and stylish rooms with all mod cons. A touch of local flavour is added by the pictures of old Anhui which adorn the walls. **¥399**

EATING AND DRINKING

Off the Huaihe Lu pedestrian street, a warren of alleys holds stalls and canteens where you can fill up on stir-fries, noodle soups and river food, and a night market sets up here in the evenings.

85C 85度C, bāshíwǔ dù C. Jinzhai Lu ☏0551 62836785. This Taiwanese coffee chain is gradually taking hold in the mainland, and offers good coffee and cakes at significantly lower prices than the city's *Starbucks*. Daily 24hr.

★**Dongmen Kaoya Dian** 东门烤鸭店, dōngmén kǎoyā diàn. Changjiang Lu ☏0551 64299869. A fantastic, hugely popular example of a dying breed of basic Chinese canteen – no frills, but the open kitchen turns out delicious roast duck for ¥16 per 500g, along with a host of tasty accompanying dishes for just a few yuan each. Daily 6am–9.30pm.

Happy Grassland 欢乐牧场火锅, huānlè mùchǎng huǒguō. Basement location next door to Mingjiao Temple on pedestrianized Huaihe Lu ☏0551 62679177. A basic *yuanyang* hotpot (a divided pot with one spicy broth half and one clear broth half) costs ¥22, and friendly staff in this cavernous basement restaurant will help you pick out the best ingredients from the vast placemat menu. Daily 9am–2am.

Old Captain Pub Hongding Xintiandi, south of Changjiang Lu. Housed in Hongding Xintiandi, a low-grade version of Shanghai's gentrified shopping, dining and drinking zone, this pub offers a fair approximation of a Western bar. Daily 6pm–late.

Qingsong Coffee 青松咖啡店, qīngsōng kāfēidiàn.

THE DEMISE OF THE YANGZI RIVER DOLPHIN

The baiji, or **Yangzi river dolphin** (白鳍豚, báijì tún), was once a common sight along the middle Yangzi, and one of only four freshwater dolphin species worldwide. The animals – 2.5m long, with a long thin snout and a stubby dorsal fin – were seen as a good omen by fishermen, lending their name to Anhui's Baiji beer, which had their Latin name, *Lipotes vexillifer*, stamped on the bottle cap. But as China's population expanded, new forms of fishing, industrial pollution, river traffic and dam projects quickly decimated the numbers of sonar-guided baiji. A six-week, 3200km survey in 2006 failed to find a single dolphin and they have since become the first aquatic mammal to be declared functionally extinct for the past 50 years.

Lujiang Lu ⊕0551 62639118. Warm, cosy, and a little bit smoky, this coffeeshop does a good line in steak meals (¥39–129), albeit with some unusual side dishes including fruit salad with mayonnaise. Daily 9am–2am.

Qingzhen Lanzhou Lamian 清真兰州拉面

qīngzhēn lánzhōu lāmiàn. North of Changjiang Lu. This tiny little canteen bustles with diners who come for just one thing – a hearty bowl of Lanzhou stretched noodles with beef and coriander for just ¥7. Daily 8am–10pm.

DIRECTORY

Banks and exchange The Bank of China (Mon–Fri 8.30am–5.30pm) is on Changjiang Lu.

Bookshops The Xinhua Bookstore on Changjiang Lu has some books in English – including translated Chinese novels – on the second floor.

Hospital There's one with English-speaking doctors at the

junction of Tongchang Lu and Changjiang Lu.

Internet Upstairs at the post office.

Mail The post office (daily 8am–6pm) is on the corner of Suzhou Lu and Changjiang Lu.

PSB Open Mon–Fri 9am–5pm and centrally located at 6 Huoqiu Lu, at the junction with Lu'an Lu (⊕0551 2624550).

Jiuhua Shan

九华山, jiǔhuá shān • March–Nov ¥190, Dec–Feb ¥140 • temple hours daily approximately 6.30am–9pm

Some 60km south of the Yangzi, **Jiuhua Shan** has been one of China's sacred Buddhist mountains ever since the Korean monk **Jin Qiaojue** (believed to be the reincarnation of the Bodhisattva Dizang, whose doctrines he preached) died here in a secluded cave in 794 AD. Today, there are more than seventy temples – some

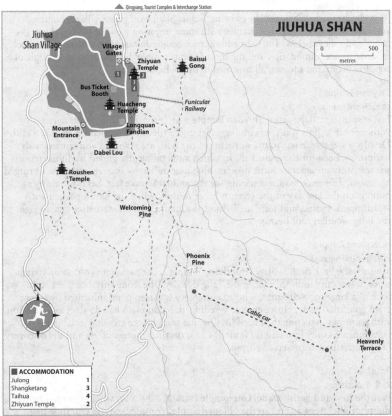

JIUHUA SHAN PRACTICALITIES

The mountain's official "entrance" is marked by a huge ornamental gateway and temple at the back of Jiuhua Shan village, though well-concealed, smaller flagstoned paths ascend from behind Zhiyuan Temple and at the corners of the main road in the village itself. Using these access points, you can do a good, easy circuit walk on the lower ridges in about an hour, or extend this to a full day's hike up around Jiuhua's higher peaks – though again, you can save time by using park buses and the cable car. Market stalls along the village road sell postcards, trinkets, and waterproof maps and umbrellas for the frequently sodden weather. It's fine to take photographs in the temples, but ask permission before photographing any monks.

founded back in the ninth century – containing a broad collection of sculptures, religious texts and early calligraphy, though intense tourism and some outsized building projects threaten to overwhelm Jiuhua Shan's otherwise human scale. Fortunately most of these developments – including a 99m-tall golden Buddha – are focused around the enormous new **tourist complex** at the base of the mountain; higher up the slopes, you'll find an atmosphere of genuine devotion in the austere halls of **Jiuhua Shan village**'s temples.

Jiuhua Shan Village

九华山, jiǔhuá shān

As it climbs the lower slopes the twisting Jiuhua Shan road passes villages scattered amid the moist green bamboo stands, with some inspiring views of bald, spiky peaks above and valleys below. The road ends at picturesque **Jiuhua Shan village**, where the mountain's accommodation and the most famous temples huddle around a couple of cobbled streets and squares, all hemmed in by encircling hills.

Zhiyuan Temple

执园寺, zhíyuán sì

Just inside the village gates, **Zhiyuan Temple** is an imposing Qing monastery built with smooth yellow walls, upcurving eaves and a tiled roof nestled up against a cliff. Despite a sizeable exterior, the numerous little halls are cramped and stuffed with sculptures; head for the main hall, in which a magnificently gilded Buddhist trinity sits solemnly on separate lotus flowers, blue hair dulled by incense smoke, and ringed by *arhats*. This makes quite a setting for the annual **temple fair**, held in Dizang's honour on the last day of the seventh lunar month, when the hall is packed with worshippers, monks and tourists. Behind the altar, Guanyin statuettes ascend right to the lofty wooden roof beams.

Huacheng Temple

化城寺, huàchéng sì

Towards the back of the village, **Huacheng Temple** is the mountain's oldest surviving place of worship, founded during the Tang dynasty. The stone entrance is set at the back of a large cobbled square whose centrepiece is a deep pond inhabited by some giant goldfish. Inside, Huacheng's low-ceilinged, broad main hall doubles as a museum, with paintings depicting the life of Jin Qiaojue from his sea crossing to China (accompanied only by a faithful hound) to his death at the age of 90, and the discovery of his miraculously preserved corpse.

Roushen Temple

肉身寺ròushēn sì

Past the new and garish **Dabei Lou temple** (大悲楼, dàbēi lóu), where the road bends sharply right, steps ascend to the "Flesh Temple" complex, whose entrance-hall atrium contains some gruesomely entertaining, life-size sculptures of Buddhist hell. These are so graphic that it's hard not to feel that the artists enjoyed their task of depicting sinners being skewered, pummelled, strangled, boiled and bisected by demons, the virtuous looking down, doubtless exceedingly thankful for their salvation.

Baisui Gong

百岁宫, bǎisuì gōng • funicular railway (缆车站, lǎnchē zhàn) from the main street ¥55 one-way, ¥100 return

The path up the mountain diverges at **Welcoming Guest Pine** (迎客松, yíngkè sōng). Bear left and it's a couple of kilometres past several pavilions and minor temples to **Baisui Gong**, a plain, atmospheric monastery whose interior is far from weatherproof, with clouds drifting in and out of the main hall. A rear room contains the mummy of the Ming priest Wu Xia, best known for compiling the Huayan *sutras* in gold dust mixed with his own blood; his tiny body is displayed seated in prayer, grotesquely covered in a thick, smooth skin of gold leaf. Steps descend to Zhiyuan Temple, or you can take the funicular railway down to the main street.

The upper peaks

Cable car (索道站, suōdào zhàn) between Phoenix Pine and Heavenly Terrace • March–Nov ¥75 one-way • Dec–Feb ¥55

To reach the upper peaks, turn right at Yingke Song, and it's a two-hour climb to the uppermost ridges via **Phoenix Pine** (凤凰松, fènghuáng sōng), more temples, wind-scoured rocks, and superb scenery surrounding the **Heavenly Terrace** (天台正顶, tiāntái zhèngdǐng) summit area. The indolent can also get here from the village by a combination of minibus and cable car.

ARRIVAL AND DEPARTURE   JIUHUA SHAN

By bus The enormous new Jiuhua Shan Tourist Interchange Station is part of the tourist complex at the base of the mountain. There's also a left luggage office here if you don't want to lug your pack around the mountain.

Destinations Hefei (4hr); Nanjing (4hr); Shanghai (8hr); Tangkou (4hr); Tunxi (2hr).

GETTING AROUND

By bus On arrival at the Interchange Station you'll need to buy a 3-day bus pass (¥50), which covers transport to and from Jiuhua Shan village, plus limited journeys within the scenic area.

ACCOMMODATION AND EATING

Aside from the following places in Jiuhua Shan village, there are also places to stay down at the tourist complex, but these are only worth considering if you arrive too late to ascend the mountain. There's no shortage of places to eat, serving everything from buns to expensive game dishes, and it's worth trying some of Jiuhua Shan's excellent vegetarian fare.

Julong 聚笼大酒店, jùlóng dàjiǔdiàn. To the right of the village gates behind an illuminated fountain ☎ 0566 2831368, ⊛ jiuhuashan.cc. Some of the best rooms on the mountain, with flat-screen TVs and good bathrooms, but very overpriced. The restaurant serves equally expensive vegetarian fare, and there's also a wine bar. **¥680**

★ **Shangketang** 上客堂宾馆 shàng kètáng bīnguǎn. Just beyond Zhiyuan Temple ☎ 0566 2833888, ⊛ vistahotel.cn. This temple-owned hotel reminds you where you are, whether by the views from the rooms, the Buddhist ornaments in the corridors, or the vegetarian breakfast. Rooms sport Qing-style furnishings, and the restaurant serves an excellent selection of vegetarian dishes including fried fava beans (¥25), mashed yam and blueberry (¥28), and pickled vegetables prepared by the monks. **¥580**

Taihua 太华山庄, tàihuá shānzhuāng. Next to the funicular railway ☎ 0566 2831340. Clean, comfortable rooms with a/c, flat-screen TV, hot water and internet connection make this friendly guesthouse the best value on the mountain. **¥200**

Zhiyuan Temple 执园寺, zhíyuán sì. By far the cheapest option on the mountain, the pilgrims' dormitory offers hard beds in a barebones room, but the sound of monks chanting in the background might add character to an otherwise austere night. **¥20**

Tunxi, Shexian and Yixian

The most obvious reason to stop in **Tunxi**, down near Anhui's southernmost borders, is for its transport connections to Huang Shan, 50km off to the northwest (see p.404): Tunxi has the closest airport and train station to the mountain, and many long-distance buses pass through as well. However, if you've even the slightest interest in **Chinese architecture**, then Tunxi and its environs are worth checking out in their own right, with a liberal sprinkling of seventeenth-century monuments and homes nearby at **Shexian** and **Yixian**.

Tunxi

屯溪, túnxī

An old trading centre, **TUNXI** (aka Huang Shan Shi) is set around the junction of two rivers, with the original part of town along the north bank of the Xin'an Jiang at the intersection of Huang Shan Lu and Xin'an Lu, and a newer quarter focused around the train station 1km or so to the northeast.

Lao Jie

老街, lǎojiē

Tunxi's historic, flagstoned **Lao Jie** (Old Street) forms a long stretch of elderly, restored **shops** selling local teas, medicinal herbs and all manner of artistic materials and "antiques" – inkstones, brushes, Mao badges, decadent advertising posters from the 1930s and carved wooden panels prised off old buildings. Some, particularly around Zhong Ma Lu, have re-branded themselves as coffee shops, bars and restaurants, and make great perches to watch the world wander by beneath the characteristic **horse-head gables** which rise up above the roof lines in steps. These originated as fire baffles between adjoining houses, stopping the spread of flames from building to building, but also served to discourage thieves, and became increasingly decorative over time.

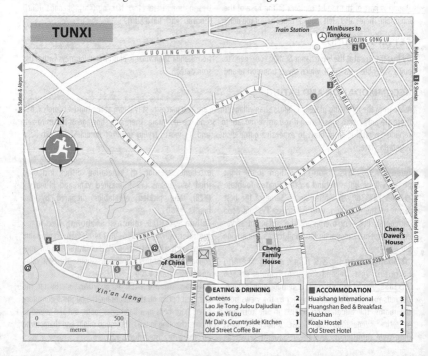

TUNXI

Train Station
Minibuses to Tangkou
GUOJING GONG LU
Huaishan Gucun & Shexian
Bus Station & Airport
GUOJING GONG LU
WEISHAN LU
XIN'AN BEI LU
QIANYUAN BEI LU
QIANYUAN NAN LU
Tiandu International Hotel & CITS
HUANGSHAN XI LU
XINYUAN LU
YANAN LU
LAODONGLI GANG
DONGLI GANG
Cheng Dawei's House
N
Cheng Family House
CHANGGAN DONG LU
LAO JIE
Bank of China
BINJIANG XI LU
Xin'an Jiang
XIN'AN NAN LU

0 ———— 500
metres

● EATING & DRINKING	
Canteens	2
Lao Jie Tong Julou Dajiudian	4
Lao Jie Yi Lou	3
Mr Dai's Countryside Kitchen	1
Old Street Coffee Bar	5

■ ACCOMMODATION	
Huaishang International	3
Huangshan Bed & Breakfast	1
Huashan	4
Koala Hostel	2
Old Street Hotel	5

HUIZHOU HOUSES

One of the highlights of a visit to southern Anhui is the chance to see **Huizhou houses**, whose plan of two floors of galleried rooms based around a courtyard became the template for urban domestic architecture in eastern China. Tunxi's best two examples are hidden in the eastern backstreets, both threatenend by ever-encroaching modern buildings. The more easterly house is that of the mathematician **Cheng Dawei** (程大位居, chéngdàwèi jū; ¥30; 8am–5pm); the other, closer to the old town, is known as the **Cheng Family House** (程氏三宅, chéngshì sānzhái; ¥30; 8am–5pm). Further examples can be found at the new riverside park development of **Hubian Gucun** (湖边古村, húbiān gǔcūn), where some 40 original Huizhou houses and two *paifang* memorial arches have been relocated, and you'll find plenty more at Shexian or Yixian.

ARRIVAL AND DEPARTURE

TUNXI

By plane Busy Huang Shan airport (黄山机场, huángshān jīchǎng) is 10km west of town. The only way into town is by taxi, which should cost ¥20–30 on the meter. Plane tickets can be bought at the airport, or from the airlines office near the *Huangshan International Hotel* on Huashan Lu.
Destinations Beijing (2 daily; 2–4hr); Guangzhou (1 daily; 1hr 45min); Hefei (daily; 50min); Shanghai (daily; 1hr).

By train The train station (黄山火车站, huángshān huǒchē zhàn) is at the end of Qianyuan Bei Lu on the northern city limits; aside from services to major destinations, there are also fast trains to Jingdezhen. Tickets can be hard to come by, especially sleeper berths, so it's worth buying your outbound ticket as soon as you arrive. From the train station, #6 takes a back road into town, while #12 follows Huang Shan Xi Lu southwest from the bus station – either route is a 20min walk.

Destinations Beijing (1 daily; 20hr); Hefei (3 daily; 6hr 30min–8hr); Jingdezhen (11 daily; 2hr 30min–5hr); Nanchang (daily; 8hr); Nanjing (10 daily; 5hr 30min–8hr 30min); Shanghai (2 daily; 12–14hr).

By bus Tunxi's bus station (黄山汽车站, huángshān qìchē zhàn), serving long-distance and local destinations, is inconveniently located in the middle of nowhere, several kilometres west of town; catch bus #1 from the train station, or a taxi (¥9).
Destinations Beijing (17hr); Hefei (4hr); Jiuhua Shan (4hr); Nanjing (6hr); Qingyang (2hr); Shanghai (7hr); Shexian (1hr); Tangkou (1hr); Yixian (2hr).

By minibus Minibuses to Tangkou (¥15–20), the gateway for Huang Shan, prowl the train station forecourt, leaving only when full. Some vehicles take the old route, which is slightly slower and cheaper than taking the expressway.

INFORMATION

Tourist information Local B&B owner Steven Huang (see *Huangshan B&B* below) is a great source of information and can also assist with ticket and taxi booking. Alternatively, try the CITS in the *Tiandu International Hotel* at 5 Tiandu Lu (☎0559 2512771).

GETTING AROUND

Tunxi's centre is small enough to walk around, though you might need transport for arrival points.

By bus City buses cost ¥1–2. There is also an electric bus service which runs from the riverside park (Hubian Gu Cun) to Lao Jie for ¥2.
By taxi Flag fall is ¥5 for the first 3km, plus a ¥2 fuel surcharge, though drivers don't like using the meter. Hiring a cab for trips to Shexian, Yixian or Huangshan should cost around ¥250–300 per full day.
By cycle rickshaw These anachronistic vehicles will also try to draw your business – just make sure that you agree the *total* price before starting the journey.

ACCOMMODATION

As the gateway to Huang Shan, Tunxi has a decent range of accommodation choices, mainly concentrated around the train station and on the other side of town near Lao Jie and the river.

Huaishang International 徽商国际大酒店, huīshāng guójì dàjiǔdiàn. 19 Qianyuan Lu ☎0559 520888. This big, bold modern edifice is the best hotel in this part of town. Rooms are spacious, comfortable and well kept, and fitted with Qing-style furnishings and LCD TVs. Bathrooms have a separate shower and tub. Major discounts usually available. **¥390**
Huangshan Bed & Breakfast 黄山市屯溪湖边农家乐客栈, huángshānshì túnxī húbiān nóngjiālè kèzhàn. East of the train station, north

of Guojing Gong Lu, Hubian Cun ☏0559 2585268, ⓦwww.huangshanbedbreakfast.com. Isolated and with some train noise, but this hospitable, family-run B&B is great value. Rooms are fitted to high specifications given the price, and downstairs there's free wi-fi, an enormous flat-screen TV and great food prepared by Steven's wife. Steven used to be a local guide and is also a great source of information on the region. It's difficult to find by yourself, so call in advance to arrange free pick-up. ¥100

Huashan 华山宾馆, huáshān bīnguǎn. 3 Yan'an Lu ☏0559 2328888. In a prime position overlooking the river at the end of Lao Jie, this enormous hotel has decent rooms, although the bathrooms are on the small side given the price. ¥530

Koala Hostel 考拉旅舍, kǎolā lǚshè. 58-4 Beihai Lu ☏0559 2328000, ⓔyhahuangshan@126.com. A decent location near the train station, comfortable and well-priced rooms and dorms, and the opportunity to meet other travellers, makes Koala popular with international backpackers. There's free wi-fi and the ground-floor café has a pool table and a choice of Western and Chinese meals. Dorms ¥40; doubles ¥100

★ **Old Street Hotel** 老街客栈, lǎojiē kèzhàn. 1 Lao Jie ☏0559 2534466, ⓦoldstreet-hotel.com.cn. An excellent location at the heart of the town's attractions, reasonable rates, friendly staff and traditionally furnished and comfortable rooms make this the best mid-range choice in Tunxi. ¥280

EATING AND DRINKING

Tunxi has plenty of good restaurants in which to sample the local *huicai* fare. As well as the listings below there are numerous small restaurants around the Xin'an Nan Lu-Lao Jie intersection. Near the train station, cheap eats can be found at the string of canteens off Qianyuan Lu on Hehuachi Zaochi Yitiao Jie (荷花池早吃一条街, héhuāchí zǎochī yìtiáojiē).

Lao Jie Tong Julou Dajiudian 老街同聚楼大酒店, lǎojiē tóngjùlóu dàjiǔdiàn. Lao Jie ☏0559 2572777. The basic English menu at this lively restaurant offers dishes including spicy Mandarin fish (¥58) and local speciality Yixian pork (¥28). In the summer you can dine outdoors. Daily 9.30am–2am.

Lao Jie Yi Lou 老街一楼食业 lǎojiē yīlóu shíyè. Lao Jie ☏0559 2359999. Lao Jie's most famous restaurant is spread over several dining areas, all replete with ornate stone carving, Qing-style furnishings and traditionally dressed staff. Always busy, the restaurant's cuisine lives up to the decor, and choosing is made easier by the second-floor *huicai* buffet spread of every dish on the menu. Expect ¥65 per head. Daily 11am–1.30pm & 5–9pm.

Mr Dai's Countryside Kitchen 戴记土菜馆 dàijì tǔcàiguǎn. 62-2 Beihai Lu ☏0559 2120988. Handy for a meal before a train journey (or if you're staying at Koala Hostel, next door), Mr Dai and family turn out delicious local specialities including Huangshan fried chicken with sweet nuts (¥48) in their simple restaurant. Daily 8am–10pm.

Old Street Coffee Bar 老街咖啡吧, lǎojiē kāfēiba. 26 Zhong Ma Lu, off Lao Jie ☏0559 25311298. One of the first trendy cafés to open its doors on atmospheric Zhong Ma Lu, this cosy place does good coffee and a mix of Chinese and Western dishes (from ¥35). On summer evenings the outdoor seats offer perfect people-watching prospects, to the backdrop of the picture-pretty Huizhou houses. Daily 1–11pm.

DIRECTORY

Bank The Bank of China (Mon–Fri 8am–5.30pm) is at the Huang Shan Lu/Xin'an Lu intersection.

Internet There are numerous internet cafés around town, including one in the train station square, several on Lao Jie,

and another just across the Yan'an Lu bridge by the turn for Huaxi Fandian.

Post office The main post office (Mon–Fri 8am–8pm) is on the same intersection as the Bank of China.

Shexian
歙县, shèxiàn

Anhui owes a good deal to **SHEXIAN**, an easy forty-minute minibus ride 25km northeast of Tunxi up the Xin'an River and once the regional capital – the name "Anhui" is a telescoping of Anqing (a Yangzi town in the southwest) and Huizhou, Shexian's former name. The region blossomed in the seventeenth century after local salt merchants started raising elaborate townhouses and intricately carved stone archways, some of which survive today, in a showy display of their wealth. The province's opera styles were formalized here, and the town became famous for *hui* inkstones and fine-grained *she* ink sticks, the latter still considered China's best. One

> **PAIFANG**
>
> Any exploration of Shexian will reveal traditional Ming and Qing architectural features, most notably the *paifang* or ornamental archways – there are over eighty of these in She County alone. Wood or stone, *paifang* can be over 10m in height, and are finely carved, painted or tiled, the central beam often bearing a moral inscription.
>
> They were constructed for a variety of reasons, foremost among which, cynics would argue, was the ostentatious display of wealth. This aside, the gateways were built to celebrate or reward virtuous behaviour, family success, important historical events or figures, and to reflect prevailing values such as filial piety; as such, they provide a valuable insight into the mores of the time.

of Shexian's charms is that most buildings remain in everyday use, and there's a genuinely old-world ambience to soak up.

The old town

From the bus station, take the bridge over the river and carry straight on past 100m of uninspiring, concrete-and-tile buildings; at the end of the road turn right, then take the first left, and you're walking up **Jiefang Jie**, off which run the narrow lanes that comprise the older part of town. To the sides you'll see the restored **Nan Lou** (南楼, nánlóu) and **Yanghe Men** (阳和门, yánghé mén) gate towers; straight ahead, Jiefang Jie runs under the smaller but highly decorative **Xuguo archway** (许国石坊, xǔguó shífāng), one of the finest in the region. You could just walk at random, snacking on traditional "pressed buns", but for a detailed look, seek out **Doushan Jie** (斗山街, dǒushān jiē), a street full of well-preserved Huizhou-style homes – choose one or more that looks appealing and pay (¥20) at the door for a poke around.

The Tangyue arches

堂越牌坊, tángyuè páifāng · ¥130 · taxi from Shexian ¥30, from Tunxi ¥60

The **Tangyue arches** form a strange spectacle of seven ornamental gates standing isolated in a row in a field about 5km west of Shexian. Given that there are plenty of other *paifang* to be seen in the region, the steep entry fee deters many would-be visitors, but these really are the best-preserved examples of Ming and Qing dynasty memorial arches anywhere in China. A sentimental story lies behind the construction of each archway – a father and son's fight to save the other's life in the face of execution was rewarded by the sparing of both of their lives and ultimately the "Filial Piety Archway".

ARRIVAL AND DEPARTURE SHEXIAN

By bus Shexian's bus station is out on the highway, across from the old town, and has regular services to Tunxi (45min).

Yixian

黟县, yīxiàn

YIXIAN, a county town 60km due west of Tunxi, is not of interest in itself and should only be seen as a stepping stone to the surrounding picturesque villages, two of which have been recognized as UNESCO World Heritage sites.

Xidi

西递, xīdì · ¥104 · bus from Yixian (15min)

XIDI is the pick of the local villages and hence the most visited; a particularly attractive place comprising some 120 eighteenth-century houses set along a river bank. There are endless examples of carved and gilded wooden screens and panels inside the houses, as well as thin line paintings on front walls showing pairs of animals or "double happiness" characters. Mirrors placed above the three-tiered door lintels reflect bad luck or reveal a person's true character – a useful tool for judging the nature of strangers.

Hongcun and Nanping Villages

Hongcun ¥104, Nanping ¥40 • bus from Yixian (15–20min)

HONGCUN (宏村, hóngcūn) is another attractive collection of antique buildings, whose street plan resembles (with some imagination) the body of a buffalo, complete with horns, body and legs. Nearby **NANPING village** (南屏村, nánpíng cūn), of similar vintage, was used as a set in Zhang Yimou's disturbing film *Judou*.

Mukeng

木坑竹海, mùkēng zhúhǎi • ¥30 • taxi or motorbike from Hongcun ¥20–30 return

The magical bamboo forests at **Mukeng**, 5km from Hongcun, is where the gravity-defying fight scene between Chow Yun Fat and Zhang Ziyi's characters was filmed in the epic *Crouching Tiger, Hidden Dragon*. Despite its popularity, you can lose the crowds along a two-hour trail, which gradually climbs above an enchanting pond and then loops around the hillside giving spellbinding views before descending back to the entrance. If you want to try and relive some of the movie's astounding wirework there's a flying fox (¥40) which speeds you from the highest point of the path nearly down to the bottom in an astoundingly fast thirty seconds.

ARRIVAL AND DEPARTURE
YIXIAN

By bus Tourist buses from Tunxi bus station run direct to Xidi and Hongcun, while more regular buses serve Yixian county town itself, from where there are minibus shuttles to the villages.

By taxi A cab from Yixian should cost around ¥200 for the day, or ¥300 from Tunxi, but either way you'll need to haggle.

ACCOMMODATION

Given the ticket price it's worth staying overnight at Xidi, which offers the chance to experience the village in the soft light of evening without the crowds.

Xidi Travel Lodge 西递行馆, xīdì xíng guǎn. Xidi village ☎ 0559 2317070. Beautifully atmospheric guesthouse built in the traditional style, with grey-tiled roof, whitewashed walls and simple modern rooms with a/c, featuring attractive wooden window screens. **¥120**

Huang Shan

黄山, húangshān • March–Nov ¥230, Dec–Feb ¥120

Rearing over southern Anhui, **Huang Shan** – the Yellow Mountains – are staggeringly scenic, with pinnacles emerging from thick bamboo forests, above which rock faces dotted with ancient, contorted pine trees disappear into the swirling mists. This magical landscape has left an indelible impression on Chinese art, with painters a common sight on mountain paths, huddled in padded jackets and sheltering their

---

ASCENDING HUANG SHAN

Huang Shan barely rises above 1870m, but as you **hike** up either of the staircases on the trails it can begin to feel very high indeed. You'll need between two and eight hours to walk up, depending on whether you follow the easier eastern route or the lengthy and demanding western route. Alternatively, **cable cars** take upwards of twenty minutes to ascend, though queues can be horrendous (there's usually less of a wait to go down), and services are suspended during windy weather. Once at the top, there's a half-day of relatively easy hiking around the peaks.

Ideally, plan to spend two or three days on the mountain to allow for a steady ascent and circuit, though it's quite feasible to see a substantial part of Huang Shan in a full day. Accommodation in Tangkou and Wenquan will store surplus gear: just bring a daypack, suitable footwear and something warm and weatherproof for the top – not forgetting the likelihood of year-round rain, and winter snow.

work from the drizzle beneath umbrellas. Indeed, so great is Huang Shan's influence on the national psyche – it's said that once you've ascended these peaks you will never need to climb another mountain – that it's the ambition of every Chinese to conquer it at least once in their lifetime. Consequently, don't expect to climb alone: noisy multitudes swarm along the neatly paved paths, or crowd out the three cable-car connections to the top. All this can make the experience depressingly like visiting an amusement park, but then you'll turn a corner and come face to face with a huge, smooth monolith topped by a single tree, or be confronted with views of a remote square of forest growing isolated on a rocky platform. Nature is never far away from reasserting itself here.

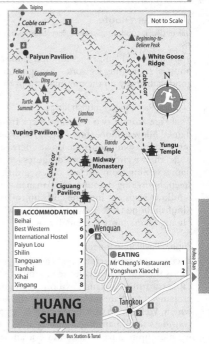

Tangkou

汤口, tāngkǒu

Some 50km northwest of Tunxi on Huang Shan's southern foothills, **TANGKOU** is a large blob of hotels and restaurants, anchored around where roads from Tunxi and Jiuhua Shan meet. Buses drop you at the tourist service centre at the entrance to the **new town** where there's a *KFC* and a *7 Days Inn*, but no sights or particular charm. If you've arrived early enough to move on, do so, at least as far as the **old town**, right at the base of the mountain, where a hint of character still exists between the cranes, and there are lovely but daunting views up to the peak.

Wenquan

温泉, wēnquán • bus from Tangkou service centre ¥11

A further 3km uphill from Tangkou, where the mountain's two main ascent routes diverge, **WENQUAN** ("Hot Springs") is an altogether more pleasant prospect than Tangkou, surrounded by pine and bamboo forest and perched above the clear blue Taoyuan Stream and a noisy waterfall. The first thing you'll see here is the arched bridge over the gully, where the road heads on 8km to the eastern route's trailhead; follow the footpath upstream and it's about half an hour to **Ciguang Pavilion** (慈光阁, cíguāng gé), at the start of the western route. The town is named for its 42.3ºC thermal pools, but for the moment these can only be enjoyed at the luxurious *Wenquan Hot Spring Resort*, where it costs ¥238 per person to soak in the 23 different spas which all look out towards the mighty mountain.

The Eastern Route

Cable car (索道, suǒdào) daily 8am–4.30pm, March–Nov ¥85, Dec–Feb ¥65 • bus from Tangkou service centre to Yungu Temple ¥19

The **eastern route** is by far the easier of the two trails: the road from Wenquan ends at **Yungu Temple** (云谷寺, yúngǔ sì), where a cable car can whisk you to the summit area at **White Goose Ridge** (白鹅峰, bái'é fēng) in twenty minutes – once you've queued two hours or so for your turn. Alternatively, you can climb the steps to Bai'e Feng in under three hours, though the forest canopy tends to block views and the path is thick with **porters** ferrying laundry, rubbish and building materials up and down the slopes.

The Western Route

Cable car (索道, suǒdào) daily 8am–4.30pm, March–Nov ¥85, Dec–Feb ¥65 • bus from Tangkou service centre to Ciguang Pavilion ¥19

The exceptional landscapes on the 15km **western route** are accompanied by up to eight hours of exhausting legwork – though you can shorten things by catching another gondola halfway up the mountain from the trailhead at Ciguang Pavilion.

Ciguang Pavilion to Kingfish Ridge

There are around two thousand steps from the **Ciguang Pavilion** to the misleadingly named **Midway Monastery** (半山寺, bànshān sì), after which things start to get interesting as you continue up an increasingly steep and narrow gorge. The rocks are huge, their weirdly contorted figures lending some credence to the usual gamut of names hailing from ancient times, and the broken hillside is riddled with caves. A steep, hour-long detour from Banshan – not a climb for those nervous of heights – follows steps cut into the cliffs up to **Tiandu Peak** (天都峰, tiāndū fēng), where **Kingfish Ridge** (鲫鱼背, jìyú bèi), a narrow path extending over a precipice, provides Huang Shan's most spectacular views.

Yuping Pavilion to the top

Back on the main track, the beautifully positioned **Yuping Pavilion** (玉屏楼, yùpíng lóu) is the true halfway house at around three hours into the journey, where the cable car from Ciguang Pavilion terminates. The vegetation thins out here, exchanged for bare rocks with only the occasional wind-contorted tree, one of which, **Welcoming Guest Pine** (迎客松, yíngkèsōng), has been immortalized in countless scroll paintings, photographs, cigarette packets and beer labels. The steps wind on up to a pass where more strange rocks jut out of the mist; bear right for the climb to Huang Shan's 1864m-high apex at **Lianhua Peak** (莲花峰, liánhuā fēng) or press on to accommodation at the *Tianhai Binguan*. From here, it's just a short climb to where you finally reach the peak circuit at **Guangming Ding** (光明顶, guāngmíng dǐng), with a TV tower and weather station off to the right, and **Feilai Shi** (飞来石, fēilái shí) ahead.

The Peak Circuit

It takes around three hours to make the beautiful but often busy **circuit around the peaks**. If you're staying on the mountain, early morning or late afternoon typically gives the least crowds and best light.

White Goose Ridge and Beginning to Believe Peak

North (anticlockwise) from the eastern steps and **White Goose Ridge** (白鹅峰, bái é fēng) cable-car terminus, the first stop is where a track leads out to **Beginning to Believe Peak** (始信峰, shǐxìn fēng). This cluster of rocky spires makes a wonderful perch to gaze down to lowland woods and rivers, with white-rumped swifts and pine and rock silhouettes moving in and out of shifting silver clouds. Tour groups concentrate on the higher levels, so the lower stairs are more peaceful.

Beihai and Xihai

From Beginning to Believe Peak, the path continues round to the first of a few accommodation options at Beihai (北海, běihǎi). Crowds congregate each morning on the terrace nearby to watch the sunrise over the "northern sea" of clouds, one of the most stirring sights on the mountain. The views are good even without the dawn, and the area tends to be busy all day. Another twenty minutes on the main path brings you to the well-placed *Xihai Fandian*, the perfect spot to sip drinks on the terrace and watch the sunset over the "western cloud sea".

Three Ways down the mountain

A short way from Xihai the track splits: ahead is the Taiping **cable-car station** down to Songgu town on the mountain's northern foothills. Stay on the main track for **Paiyun Pavilion** (排云亭, páiyún tíng); on a clear day you'll see a steep gorge squeezed between jagged crags below, all covered in pine trees and magnolias. Farther round, the lonely tower of **Feilai Shi**, the "Far-flying Rock" (飞来石, fēilái shí), looks across at cascades that are especially evident after rain. Beyond here, the path undulates along the cliff edge to where the western steps descend on the right (below the TV tower and weather station), and then winds back to the White Goose Ridge cable car.

ARRIVAL AND DEPARTURE   HUANG SHAN

Transport pours into the Huang Shan region from all over eastern China. There are direct buses from Shanghai, Hangzhou and Nanjing, as well as Jiuhua Shan, Hefei and other places within Anhui. Much of this, and all rail and air traffic, passes through Tunxi (aka Huang Shan Shi; see p.400), with regular shuttle buses connecting the train and bus stations here with Huang Shan's main gateway at Tangkou. Some long-distance buses go directly to Tangkou, and also might refer to it as "Huang Shan" on their timetables.

By bus Tangkou's long-distance bus station is in the tourist service centre on the edge of the new town, connected to the old town by tourist buses, local minibuses, or a 30min walk. Buying outbound tickets at the station is straightforward.

Destinations Hefei (4hr); Jiuhua Shan (3–4hr); Shanghai (6hr 30min); Tunxi (1hr).

GETTING AROUND

By bus An efficient local bus service connects Tangkou service centre with the old town and the trailheads, although given the short distances prices are high.

By private vehicle Private minibuses and cars also tout for business and can be bargained to lower than bus prices if there are enough people.

ACCOMMODATION

There are no accommodation bargains anywhere at Huang Shan, but spending extra to stay overnight on the mountain top will allow you to see it without the crowds at dawn and dusk, and is highly recommended. Local agencies might get you discounted rates, but during the week you can usually haggle a similar deal yourself at even the most expensive places. Note that in winter, hotels either drop their prices or close shop until spring.

TANGKOU

International Hostel 黄山温泉国际青年旅舍, huángshān wēnquán guójì qīngnián lǚshè. Just off the main road by the bridge ☎0559 5562478, ⓦyhhuangshan.com. Not much in the way of character or comfort, but cheap, friendly and in a decent location on the road down to the river. The downstairs café serves Chinese meals and has free wi-fi. Dorms ¥40, doubles ¥80

Tangquan 汤泉大酒店, tāngquán dàjiǔdiàn. On the road out of town towards the mountain ☎0559 5583333. When (or if) the construction boom finally ends in Tangkou, the *Tangquan's* quiet location on the edge of town will come into its own. Set in an imposing block behind a government building, the hotel's rooms are spacious and tastefully styled and feature all mod cons. ¥390

Xingang Dajiudian 黄山新港大酒店, huángshān xīngǎng dàjiǔdiàn. ☎0559 5562648. On the main road up the hill from the bridge, this ageing property has rooms overlooking a pleasant central courtyard. Carpets and furniture are a little shabby but more expensive rooms have updated fittings including flat-screen TVs and computers. ¥160

WENQUAN

Plans to convert Wenquan into a five-star villa and hotel complex have left most of the small hotels in this pretty valley closed for the time being.

★ **Best Western** 温泉大酒店, wēnquán dàjiǔdiàn. ☎0559 5585788, ⓦbestwestern.com It might not be on the mountain top, but this hotel's simply styled, clean and comfortable rooms in an incredible setting make it one of the best choices in the area. ¥460

PEAKS

Beihai 北海宾馆, běihǎi bīnguǎn. ☎0559 5582555. Despite its mountain-top location, the four-star *Beihai Binguan* boasts a Bank of China ATM, although its rooms are lacklustre for the money, despite a standard 30 percent discount on off-peak weekdays. Dorm beds ¥200, doubles ¥1680

Paiyun Lou 排云楼宾馆, páiyúnlóu bīnguǎn. ☎0559 5581558. *Paiyun Lou* offers a quiet location and has been attractively remodelled from its formerly distraught state, but there are no views from the rooms

7

– though you haven't far to go to find one. Dorms ¥120, doubles ¥1200

Shilin 石林大酒店, shílín dàjiǔdiàn. ☎0559 5584040, ⓦshilin.com. A good range of comfortable and functional rooms, with views from the better ones. Dorms are comfortable but, as ever on the mountain, wildly over-priced. Dorms ¥200, doubles ¥1680

★ **Xihai** 西海饭店, xīhǎi fàndiàn. ☎0559 5588888, ⓦhsxihaihotel.cn. Great location, well-kept rooms with a range of price options, and the forethought to provide bright-blue down jackets for snowy sunrise mornings makes this the best choice at the top of the mountain. Dorms ¥200, doubles ¥1280

EATING

As Tangkou expands there are increasingly more dining choices in town, but up on the peak it's mostly plain Chinese fare at inflated prices, occasionally justified by delicious mountain produce. The main road through Tangkou, and the path along the river, are lined with small canteens and restaurants; some have bilingual menus offering arresting delights such as squirrel hotpot and scrambled mountain frog. If there's no price on the menu, agree the cost in advance to avoid being ripped off.

Mr Cheng's Restaurant 程先生餐馆, chéngxiānshēng cānguǎn. Opposite the post office, Old Tangkou ☎130 85592603. Small café run by friendly and helpful Simon Cheng. The kitchen rustles up a host of reasonably priced Chinese classics (¥25–40), plus traveller favourites including pancakes and Western breakfasts. Simon can also assist with travel arrangements and mountain-top hotel bookings, plus he offers luggage storage. Daily 7am–10pm.

Yongshun Xiaochi 永顺小吃, yǒngshùn xiǎochī. Down by the river, Old Tangkou. A hole-in-the-wall canteen, typical of many in this part of town, turning out fresh and tasty noodles with veg and pork for ¥10 per bowl. Daily 6am–9pm.

DIRECTORY

Banks and ATMs There are branches of the Bank of China in Tangkou and on the mountain top at the *Beihai* hotel.
Internet Tangkou has a couple of internet cafés down by the river.

Mountain essentials You can pick up umbrellas, walking sticks, warm clothes and mountain maps from hawkers and stalls around Tangkou.

Hubei

湖北, húběi

Hubei is Han China's well-watered agricultural and geographic centre. Until 280 BC this was the independent state of **Chu**, whose sophisticated bronzeworking skills continue to astound archeologists, but for the last half-millennium the province's eastern bulk, spliced by waterways draining into the Yangzi and Han rivers, has become an intensely cultivated maze of rice fields so rich that, according to tradition, they alone are enough to supply the national need. More recently, Hubei's central location and mass of transport links into neighbouring regions saw the province become the first in the interior to be heavily industrialized. The colossal **Three Gorges hydroelectric dam** upstream from Yichang (see p.417), car manufacturing – up and running with the help of foreign investment – and long-established iron and steel plants provide a huge source of income for central China.

As the "Gateway to Nine Provinces", skirted by mountains and midway along the Yangzi between Shanghai and Chongqing, Hubei has always been of great strategic importance. The central river regions feature prominently in the *Romance of the Three Kingdoms*, while the capital, **Wuhan**, thrives on industry and played a key role in China's early twentieth-century revolutions. In the west, the ranges that border Sichuan contain the holy peak of **Wudang Shan**, alive with Taoist temples and martial-arts lore, and the remote **Shennongjia Forest Reserve**, said to be inhabited by China's yeti.

Wuhan

武汉, wǔhàn

One way or another, almost anyone travelling through central China has to pass through **WUHAN**, Hubei's vast capital. The name is a portmanteau label for three original settlements, separated by the Han and Yangzi rivers but connected by bridges, tunnels and ferries. On the west bank of the Yangzi, **Hankou** is the city's trade and business centre and boasts the best services and accommodation. South across the Han River is lightly industrial **Hanyang**, while **Wuchang** recedes southeast of the Yangzi into semi-rural parkland.

Wuhan's sheer size lends atmosphere and significance, even if the metropolis not a traditional tourist centre. Hankou's former role as a foreign concession has left plenty of colonial European heritage in its wake, while Wuchang's **Provincial Museum** in is one of China's best. There are also a couple of temples and historical monuments to explore, some connected to the **1911 revolution** that ended two thousand years of imperial rule. On the downside, Wuhan's continued growth and development and the ongoing metro construction mean that the city currently feels like an enormous building site, and can make it a challenge even to cross the road. Furthermore, the city has a well-deserved reputation – along with Chongqing and Nanjing – as one of China's three summer "furnaces": between May and September you'll find the streets melting and the gasping population surviving on a diet of watermelon and iced treats.

Brief history

Wuhan first boomed during the nineteenth century Taiping Rebellion, when trade was deflected away from the rebel capital, downstream at Nanjing. During the 1880s, the provincial viceroy **Zhang Zhidong** founded the country's first modern steelworks here, and the city became known as "the Chicago of China". But the twentieth century was not kind to Wuhan: on October 10, 1911, a **bomb** exploded prematurely at the Hankou headquarters of a revolutionary group dedicated to replacing imperial rule with a democratic government. Imperial troops executed the ringleaders, sparking a citywide uprising against the Manchus, which levelled Hankou and soon spread across China, forcing the last emperor, Pu Yi, to abdicate. Hankou's foreign concession area was rebuilt, but anti-Western riots broke out in 1925 and again in 1927, prompting their return to Chinese administration. A few months later, the Guomindang stormed through on their Northern Expedition, returning briefly in 1937 to establish a national government in town before being forced farther west by the Japanese. Thirty years later, Wuhan saw more fighting, this time between the PLA and various Red Guard factions, who had been slugging it out over differing interpretations of Mao's Cultural Revolution.

Hankou

汉口, hànkǒu

The largest of Wuhan's districts, **Hankou** was a simple fishing harbour until it opened as a treaty port in 1861 – a move greatly resented by the Chinese, who took to stoning any foreigners bold enough to walk the streets. Consequently, the Chinese were barred from the riverside concession area, which over the following decades was developed as a smaller version of Shanghai, complete with a racetrack and a **Bund** (flood-preventing embankments built by the British in the 1860s) lined with Neoclassical European architecture. Many of their facades survive today, as does Hankou's commercial emphasis: bursting with traffic and crowds, this is a place to walk, shop, eat, spend money and watch others doing the same along busy **Zhongshan Dadao**, a packed, 3km-long stretch of restaurants, stores and shopping plazas.

The colonial quarter

Metro line #1 runs underground above Jinghan Dadao with stops every kilometre or so, or line #2 to Jianghan Lu

Hankou's **colonial quarter** – located mostly between the eastern half of Zhongshan

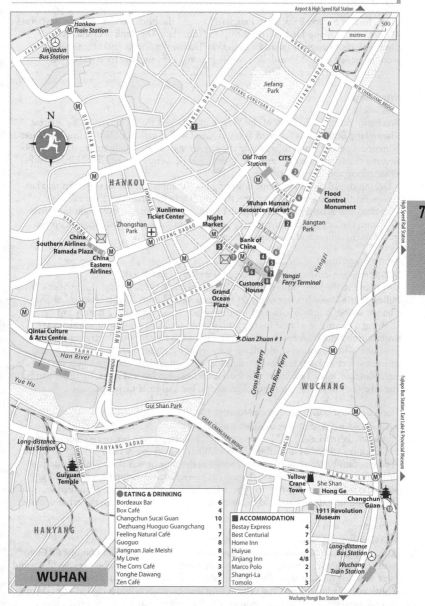

EATING & DRINKING

Bordeaux Bar	6
Box Café	4
Changchun Sucai Guan	10
Dezhuang Huoguo Guangchang	1
Feeling Natural Café	7
Guoguo	8
Jiangnan Jiale Meishi	8
My Love	2
The Corrs Café	3
Yonghe Dawang	9
Zen Café	5

ACCOMMODATION

Bestay Express	4
Best Centurial	7
Home Inn	5
Huiyue	6
Jinjiang Inn	4/8
Marco Polo	2
Shangri-La	1
Tomolo	3

WUHAN

Dadao and the river – survives largely intact, restored during a big clean-up project in 2001. The best sections are along the former Bund, renamed Yanjiang Dadao, and the pedestrianized Jianghan Lu; the Bund itself has been turned into parkland, a popular place to stroll of a stifling summer evening.

Some older buildings to look for include the mighty **Customs House** (武汉海关, wǔhàn hǎiguān) on Yanjiang Dadao, a solid Renaissance edifice with imposing grey-stone portico and Corinthian capitals; the unusual seven-storey Art Deco/Modernist exterior of the former **Siming Bank** at 45 Jianghan Lu; and the brick "**Wuhan Human Resources Market**" on Yanjiang Dadao – once the US Consulate. **The Bank of China**, at the intersection of Jianghan Lu and Zhongshan Dadao, retains its period interior of wooden panelling and chandeliers, while Hankou's defunct **old train station** on Chezhan Lu still sports its French Gothic shell.

Wuchang

武昌, wǔchāng

Wuchang, on the right bank of the Yangzi and reached from Hanyang via the **Great Changjiang Bridge**, was founded as Sun Quan's walled capital of Wu during the Three Kingdoms period. Tang rulers made the city a major port, which, under the Mongols, became the administrative centre of a vast region covering present-day Hunan, Hubei, Guangdong and Guangxi provinces.

During the 1910 insurrection, Wuchang hosted appalling scenes when ethnic Han troops mutinied under a banner proclaiming "Long live the Han, Exterminate the Manchu" and accordingly slaughtered a Manchu regiment and over eight hundred civilians. The city and its bureaucracy survived, and nowadays Wuchang comprises government offices and the huge Wuhan University campus.

Yellow Crane Tower

黄鹤楼, huánghè lóu • Daily 7am–6pm • ¥80 • metro to Pangxiejia, or bus #10, #401 or #402

Overlooking the river from the low ridge of She Shan (蛇山, shé shān), the 50m-high **Yellow Crane Tower** is a riot of bright tiles and red columns. Legend has it that She Shan was once home to a Taoist Immortal who settled his tab at a nearby inn by drawing a picture of a crane on the wall, which would fly down at intervals and entertain the guests. A few years later the Immortal flew off on his creation, and the landlord, who doubtless could afford it by then, built the tower in his honour. The current structure is no less magnificent for being an entirely modern Qing-style reproduction, sited 1km from where an earlier version burned down in 1884; climb (or take the lift) to the top to see Wuhan and the Yangzi at their best.

Hong Ge and the 1911 Revolution Museum

Tues–Sun 9am–5pm • Free with ID • metro to Pangxiejia, or bus #401 or #402

At the southern foot of She Shan, **Hong Ge** (红阁, hónggé) is an imposing colonial-style red-brick mansion that housed the Hubei Military Government during the 1910 uprising. A bronze Sun Yatsen stands in front, though at the time he was abroad raising funds. A little further south the striking V-shaped **1911 Revolution Museum** (武汉辛亥革命博物馆, wǔhàn xīnhài gémìng bówùguǎn) was opened in 2011 to commemorate a hundred years since the revolution, although its bold red exterior is more memorable than the exhibits inside.

Changchun Guan

长春观, chángchūn guān • Wuluo Lu • ¥10 • bus #15, #18 or #25

Around 1km east of Hong Ge, the russet-walled Taoist complex of **Changchun Guan** made its name through the Yuan-dynasty luminary Qiu Chuzi, who preached here and later founded his own sect. The halls are simply furnished with statues of the Three Purities, the Jade Emperor and other Taoist deities, while a side wing has been co-opted as a pharmacy, where Chinese-speakers can have their vital signs interpreted by a traditional doctor and buy medicines. Next door, Changchun's **vegetarian restaurant** is well worth a visit (see p.416).

Hubei Provincial Museum

湖北省博物馆, húběi shěng bówùguǎn • Donghu Lu • Tues–Sun 9am–5pm, last admission 3.30pm • Free • bus #14, #401 or #402

The **Hubei Provincial Museum** features a display of items unearthed from the Warring States Period's tomb of the Marquis Yi, and deserves a good hour of your

---

BELLS OF BRONZE

The Hubei Provincial Museum's impressive orchestra of 64 **bronze bells**, ranging in weight from a couple of kilos to a quarter of a tonne, were found in the marquis' waterlogged tomb along with the wooden frame from which they once hung in rows. Played with hand-held rods, each bell can produce two notes depending on where it is struck; the knowledge of metals and casting required to achieve this initially boggled modern researchers, who took five years to make duplicates. Brief performances (¥15) can be enjoyed in the museum's auditorium at 10.30am, 11.30am, 2.30pm and 3.30pm.

---

time. The marquis died in 433 BC and was buried in a huge, multilayered, wooden lacquered coffin at nearby Suizhou, then a major city of the state of Zeng. His corpse was accompanied by fifteen thousand bronze and wooden artefacts, 21 women and a dog. The museum's comprehensive English explanations of contemporary history and photos of the 1978 excavation put everything in perspective. More than a hundred musical instruments are on display, including **bronze bells**, stone chimes, drums, flutes and zithers, along with spearheads and a very weird brazen crane totem sprouting antlers – an inscription suggests that this was the marquis's steed in the afterlife.

7

East Lake

东湖, dōnghú • Botanical Gardens daily 8am–5.30pm, ¥60 • bus #114, #401 or #402

The shores of Hankou's vast **East Lake** not only host the high-speed rail station, the provincial museum and the university, but also have designated **scenic areas** in their own right. It is a lovely spot, and locals will proudly tell you that their East Lake is five times the size of Hangzhou's considerably more famous West Lake. **Moshan** (磨山风景区, móshān fēngjǐng qū), the pick of the scenic locations, is known for its springtime plum and cherry blossoms, on view at Wuhan's **Botanical Gardens** (磨山植物园, móshān zhíwùyuán).

ARRIVAL AND DEPARTURE WUHAN

More than 10km across, Wuhan has an extensive choice of transit points – there are four train stations and at least three main long-distance bus stations. Train and bus timetables usually spell out the district where services arrive, though the new high-speed rail terminal is simply written on tickets as "Wuhan Station".

BY PLANE

Tianhe airport (天河飞机场, tiānhé fēijīchǎng) sits 30km to the north of Wuhan, with bus links (every 30min, ¥16–41) running to the long-distance bus stations and the China Southern airline office on Hangkong Lu in Hankou. There's also a direct hourly bus to the high-speed rail station. Alternatively, a taxi into town will cost at least ¥80. Tickets can be purchased through most hotels or at the Xunlimen Ticket Centre (daily 8am–6pm; ☏ 027 8580055) next to the *Xunlimen Hotel* (循礼门饭店, xúnlǐmén fàndiàn).

Destinations Beijing (15 daily; 1hr 40min); Guangzhou (8 daily; 1hr 35min); Hong Kong (2–3 daily; 1hr 50min); Shanghai (16 daily; 1hr 25min).

BY TRAIN

Hankou train station (汉口火车站, hànkǒu huǒchēzhàn) is an enormous new "European style" construction on Fazhan Dadao. It mostly handles services from the north, along with express trains from Yichang. The station is well equipped with left luggage (¥10/24hr), internet cafés (¥5/hr), a China Post and plenty of fast-food outlets and shops. Bus #38 or #595 will get you down to Hankou's waterfront – as will the metro – while #507 continues over the river to Wuchang train station.

Wuchang train station (武昌火车站, wǔchāng huǒchēzhàn), southeast of the Yellow Crane Tower on Zhongshan Lu. Trains from southern China tend to favour this station; bus #507 will take you over the river to Hankou train station via the Customs House on Yanjiang Dadao; or exit the station, turn right up the road and Pangjiaxia metro station is 1km away.

High-speed rail station (武汉高铁站, wǔhàn gāotiě zhàn). High-speed G-Trains from across the country arrive at this station in northeast Wuchang. The station will eventually be connected to the city via metro line #4, but buses #610 (¥2) and #725 (¥1) also run into Hankou. A taxi to the town centre will cost around ¥50.

Destinations Beijing (many daily; 4hr 30min–18hr); Changsha (many daily; 1hr 30min–6hr); Guangzhou (many daily; 3hr 30min–15hr); Nanchang (many daily; 2hr 45min–9hr 30min); Shanghai (many daily; 5–15hr); Shiyan (many daily; 4hr–9hr 30min); Wudang Shan (14 daily; 5–8hr); Xi'an (many daily; 5–15hr); Yueyang (many daily; 1–4hr); Yichang (many daily; 1hr 45min–5hr).

BY BUS

Wuhan has several major long-distance bus stations, each handling services from all over the country – although note there are more services to Zhangjiajie from Wuchang's station.

Fujiapo (付家坡车站, fùjiāpō chēzhàn) 358 Wuluo Lu, Wuchang. Wuchang's main station has services all over the country, including Shanghai, Yichang and Zhangjiajie. Bus #15, #18 or #25 run into town.

Jinjiadun (金家墩汽车站, jīnjiādūn qìchē zhàn) 170 Fazhan Dadao, Hankou. Opposite the train station, this major depot is connected to the city by metro line #2, or bus #38 to Yanjiang Dadao.

Wuchang Hongji (宏基汽车站, hóngjī qìchē zhàn) 519 Zhongshan Lu, Wuchang. Not far from Fujiapo, Hongji has yet more services for the same destinations. Bus #402 or #503 from Hankou.

Destinations Changsha (4hr); Hefei (6hr); Jingzhou (3hr 30min); Jiujiang (4hr); Nanchang (6hr); Shanghai (12hr); Yichang (4hr); Yueyang (4hr); Zhangjiajie (12hr).

INFORMATION

Tours CITS, 909 Zhongshan Dadao, Hankou (☏027 82822120), are a well-informed, English-, German- and French-speaking agency which can organize Three Gorges cruises and trips to Shennongjia and Wudang Shan. The tourist information centre at the high-speed rail terminal (daily 8.30am–midnight) has little to offer foreign visitors, least of all any spoken English. The best information sources are the five-star hotels, most of which have a good selection of free maps and government-issued tourist brochures and leaflets about things to do in the city.

Maps Maps (¥8) of Wuhan showing transport routes can be picked up at kiosks and hotels around town, though English is currently lacking.

GETTING AROUND

By bus The main city-bus terminals are at Hankou and Wuchang train stations, and near the Customs House on Yanjiang Dadao. Services are regular and cheap – it only costs ¥2 between Wuchang and Hankou stations – and crawl out to almost every corner of the city between around 6am and 10pm.

By metro Hankou's line #1 is an elevated rail roughly following the curve of the river along Jinghan Dadao, while line #2 starts at Hankou Train Station and heads south across the river. Tickets are a very reasonable ¥1.5 for the first 5 stops, then ¥2 for 6 or more. Seven more lines are due to open by 2017.

By taxi Cabs are ubiquitous and, at ¥6–8 for the first 2km, not too expensive.

By ferry During daylight hours, there are passenger ferries across the Yangzi between the southern end of Hankou's Yanjiang Dadao and Wuchang's city-bus terminus, below and just north of the Changjiang Bridge; trips cost ¥1.5 and take about 15min.

By bicycle It might not seem the most appealing prospect, but Wuhan's free bike rental service is worth using if you're in town for a while. To rent a bike you'll need to get a rental card, which is available for ¥300 deposit outside most metro stations.

ACCOMMODATION

Wuhan's hotels are fairly upmarket, but there are some cheaper options, and mid-range places can be good value. All of the following are located in Hankou.

Bestay Express 百时快捷酒店, bǎishí kuàijié jiǔdiàn. 5 Nanjing Lu ☏027 59353280, ⓦbestay.com.cn. Part of the *Jinjiang* chain, *Bestay* offers cheaper, even more no-frills accommodation, but it's clean, has in-room internet connection, beds are comfortable and the location is good. **¥89**

Best Centurial 好百年饭店, hǎobǎinián fàndiàn. 131 Yanjiang Dadao ☏027 82777798. This is one of the few options to stay in a bona-fide colonial-era building, though the facade is more impressive than the interior. The modern styling of the rooms is fading fast, and the cheaper rooms come in all shapes and sizes, some of which only have interior windows, so ask to see a few. River views are more expensive, but also noisier. Still, it's comfortable enough, has cabled internet and is in a great location. **¥278**

Home Inn 如家酒店, rújiā jiǔdiàn. 141 Yanjiang Dadao ☏027 59207111, ⓦhomeinns.com. Another identikit budget business hotel, Wuhan's *Home Inn* enjoys a fantastic location in a courtyard next to the historic National Bank of New York City building. A little threadbare, but with all the facilities you could want for the price. **¥179**

Huiyue 汇悦宾馆, huìyuè bīnguǎn. 109 Jianghan Lu ☏027 82779069. This hard-to-spot guesthouse, marked only by a doorway beside a department store, is

WUHAN TOURIST BUS ROUTES

A convenient bus for **sightseeing** is the "Electric Special #1" (电一专路, diànyī zhuānlù), not to be confused with any other #1 bus or trolleybus – the Chinese characters are displayed either side of the number. It runs from Yanhe Dadao in Hankou, via Hanyang and the Great Changjiang Bridge (长江大桥, chángjiāng dàqiáo), and then links the Yellow Crane Tower with Changchun Guan and the Provincial Museum. Similarly, bus **#401** covers the main sights including Changchun Guan, Guiyuan Temple, Yellow Crane Tower and the Provincial Museum.

A more expensive option is the **sightseeing bus**, which covers all of the city's principal attractions in 120-minute loops every 30 minutes. Tickets cost ¥30 (with choice of English, French or Japanese audio) and can be purchased from any of the 18 station stops (including Yellow Crane Tower, the Provincial Museum, Guishan Park and the Ancient Lute Platform).

nothing glamorous, but it is central and cheap. Often full despite basic rooms. **¥149**

Jinjiang Inn 锦江之星, jǐnjiāng zhīxīng. 5 Nanjing Lu ⊕ 027 59353666 & 2 Jianghan Lu ⊕ 027 82776600, ⊛ jinjianginns.com. Two of Wuhan's *Jinjiang Inns* offer great locations for travellers. Of the two, the Nanjing Lu branch is slightly nicer, but both have the same clean and comfortable rooms with internet access. **¥189**

Marco Polo 马哥孛罗酒店, mǎgē bóluó jiǔdiàn. 159 Yanjiang Dadao ⊕ 027 82778888, ⊛ marcopolohotels.com. The lap of luxury on the waterfront, but good discounts during quiet times mean this international hotel can be a comparative bargain. Rooms are super sleek in blond wood-and stand-alone tubs overlook the river in the better rooms. **¥863**

Shangri-La 香格里拉大酒店, xiānggélǐlā dàjiǔdiàn. 700 Jianshe Dadao ⊕ 027 85806868, ⊛ shangri-la.com. Wuhan's first international five-star may have been superseded in some ways by the *Marco Polo*, but the prize for the city's comfiest bed is still safe with the *Shangri-La*, and visiting celebs choose to stay here (David Beckham recently graced the Presidential Suite). Several restaurants and all the usual five-star amenities make for a smooth stay. **¥658**

Tomolo 天美乐饭店, tiānměilè fàndiàn. 56 Jianghan 3 Lu ⊕ 027 82757288, ⊛ yzjhotel.com. Boutique hotel in a great location just off pedestrianized Jianghan Lu. Rooms have a simple, modern style and attractive mosaic-tiled bathrooms, although some smell a little smoky. **¥348**

EATING AND DRINKING

Wuhan's food reflects its position midway between Shanghai and Chongqing, and restaurants offer a good balance of eastern-style steamed and braised dishes – particularly fish and shellfish – along with some seriously spicy flavours. There's also a strong snacking tradition in town, with many places specializing in dumplings: various types of *shaomai*; *tangbao*, soup buns stuffed with jellied stock which burst messily as you bite them, much to the amusement of other diners; and *doupi*, sticky rice packets stuffed with meat and rolled up in a beanpaste skin.

HANKOU

Bordeaux Bar 波尔图酒吧, bōěrtú jiǔbā. Yanjiang Dadao ⊕ 027 82778779. One of many such café-bars in the area, replete with pavement tables and dimmed lighting. The Western-style pasta and steak dishes, along with Chinese fare, are expensive; expect at least ¥100/ head. Daily 10.30am–1.30am.

Box Café 盒子咖啡, hézǐ kāfēi. Yanjiang Dadao end of Chezhan Lu. Cosy and friendly little coffee shop opposite the former US embassy. Coffees from ¥20, beers from ¥12. Daily 11am–11pm.

The Corrs Café 可儿咖啡, kě é kāfēi. Zhongshan Dadao ⊕ 027 82830131. Housed in a beautiful colonial-era building and decked out in cosy but classical style, this is a great place to take a break from the steamy streets of Hankou. Coffees and beers both cost ¥20–¥40. Daily 11am–midnight.

Dezhuang Huoguo Guangchang 德庄火锅广场, dézhuāng huǒguō guǎngchǎng. Corner of Yanjiang Dadao and Eryao Lu ⊕ 027 82781789. If you're craving northern-style hotpot, this is the place to come – big, bright, noisy and inexpensive, with the more raucous customers playing drinking games. Daily 10.30am–10.30pm.

Feeling Natural Café 西餐酒吧, xīcān jiǔba. Jianghan 1 Lu ⊕ 027 82825919. Big, open, airy and friendly café-bar just off Jianghan Lu. A good range of Western meals including breakfasts (¥25–30), burgers (¥20–25), pastas and salads. Special deals every night make this place a popular drinking spot, and you can also partake in a shisha (¥50) if that's your thing. Daily 10am–3am.

★ **Guoguo** 锅锅, guōguō. Jiaotong Lu. Ridiculously popular canteen serving excellent, inexpensive breaded dumplings dripping in chilli oil. Order at the counter, then wait in line. Daily 11am–8pm.

Jiangnan Jiale Meishi 江南家乐美食, jiāngnán jiālèmeǐshí. Jiaotong Lu. Two doors up from *Guoguo*, this busy canteen serves up the whole range of local delicacies at just a fraction of the cost of the more proper restaurants. Daily 11am–8pm.

My Love 麦乐屋, màilèwū. Shengli Jie ☎ 153 7752 0521. Not worth a visit in its own right, but great for a snack if you're taking a wander through Hankou's colonial backstreets, *My Love* offers a tasty range of filled pancakes – the bacon and egg version (¥9) is as close as you'll get to a breakfast butty in Wuhan. Daily 8am–8pm.

Yonghe Dawang 永和大王, yǒnghé dàwáng. Jianghan Lu, and elsewhere. Open around the clock, this restaurant chain's logo looks suspiciously like *KFC*'s but the food is very different: big bowls of beef noodle soup or *doujiang*, steamed buns and fried rice. Daily 24hr.

Zen Café 禅石餐饮, chánshí cānyǐng. 163 Yanjiang Dadao ☎ 027 82849126. The cool, dark, industrial interior of this trendy coffee and pub chain is in stark contrast to the classical colonial exterior. Decent coffee (from ¥20), beers (from ¥12) and a range of meals (from ¥30) are served. There are plenty of quiet little nooks to relax in, plus there's free wi-fi, and even a mini casino if you're feeling lucky. Daily 11.30am–12.30pm.

WUCHANG

Changchun Sucai Guan 长春素菜馆, chángchūn sùcàiguǎn. Wulou Lu, just east of the Changchun temple. Vegetarian restaurant with Ming decor and a resolutely Chinese menu. The "beef" and "chicken" are made from bean-curd sheets, "prawns" from bean starch, and so on. Portions are good, liberally laced with chillies and aniseed, and very tasty. Mains from ¥30 or so. Daily 8.30am–8.30pm.

DIRECTORY

Banks and exchange The Bank of China (Mon–Sat 8.30am–5pm) is on Zhongshan Dadao, in Hankou.

Bookshop The Xinhua Bookstore, just west of the Jianghan Lu/Zhongshan Dadao intersection in Hankou, has plenty of maps and some English titles, including abridged texts of Chinese classics.

Cinema There are several theatres in Hankou, although English screenings are few and far between. If this doesn't deter, then try the Smile Wuhan Insun Cine City on Yanjiang Dadao.

Hospitals The Tongji, east of the Jiefang Dadao/Qingnian Lu crossroads in Hankou, is considered Wuhan's best. Another good place to go for acupuncture and massage is the hospital attached to the Hubei Traditional Medicine College, just north of She Shan, Wuchang.

Internet There are internet cafés at all of the major transport stations.

Left luggage There are booths charging ¥5–10 a bag at the bus (daily 8am–8pm) and train stations (24hr).

Mail and telephones The main post offices, with IDD phones, are on Zhongshan Dadao and at the junction of Hangkong Lu and Qingnian Lu, Hankou (daily 8am–6pm).

Pharmacies In addition to smaller places elsewhere, Hankou's Hangkong Lu has a string of pharmacies stocking traditional and modern medicines, the biggest of which is the Grand Pharmacy, or, according to the English sign, the "Ark of Health". The most modern pharmaceutical chain in town is Professional Phuan Pharm, and they have branches at the northern end of Jianghan Lu and on Jiefang Dadao near the junction with Qingnian Lu.

PSB The Foreign Affairs Department of the PSB (Mon–Fri 8am–noon & 2.30–5.30pm; ☎ 027 85395370) is contained within the eco-friendly but somehow daunting Wuhan Citizens Home, set just off Jinqiao Dadao, a 30min bus ride northeast of Hankou (bus #229 and #248). In spite of the sheer size of the building and the number of staff, expect long queues and strict requirements – better to head elsewhere.

Shopping For "antique" souvenirs, try the shops at the Hubei Provincial Museum, Wuchang. Like most Chinese cities, Hankou is a very good place to buy clothes – hit the new Grand Ocean Plaza or the Walmart Super Centre, both on Zhongshan Dadao, or numerous smaller shops nearby, many with unfortunate names such as the "Ebola" clothes shop on Zhongshan Dadao.

Jingzhou

荆州市, jīngzhōu shì

Around 240km west of Wuhan, **JINGZHOU** lies on the north bank of the Yangzi, where the Wuhan–Yichang expressway joins the highway up to Xiangfan in northern Hubei. The city divides into two districts: easterly **Shashi** is an indifferent modern port, while **Jingzhou** itself, 10km west, is ringed by around 8km of moats and well-maintained, 7m-high battlements built by the Three Kingdoms hero Guan Yu.

Jingzhou Museum

荆州博物馆, jīngzhōu bówùguǎn • Jingzhong Lu • Daily 8.30am–5.30pm • Free • city bus #1 from Shashi's long-distance bus station

Jingzhou Museum includes a fantastic collection of Western Han (221 BC–24 AD) funerary remains that were excavated from more than 180 tombs located to the north.

The exhibition here focuses on the tomb of a court official named Sui; in many regards the items on display are similar to those in Wuhan's provincial museum (see p.412) – the house-like sarcophagi and copious lacquerwork, for example – but the bonus here is Sui's astoundingly well-preserved **corpse**, along with some comfortingly practical household items and wooden miniatures of his servants.

Xiongjia Tombs

熊家冢, xióngjiā zhǒng • Daily 9.30am–4.30pm • ¥30 • buses from Jingzhou (¥8, 1hr) or charter a round-trip taxi for ¥100–150

The site where Jingzhou Museum's artefacts were found is 40km north of the city in the small village of Zhangchang. Sometimes compared to the Terracotta Warriors, the **Xiongjia Tombs** (presumed to belong to one of the Chu emperors and his family) offers an eerie glimpse into a 2000-year-old burial chamber, replete with legions of horse skeletons and painted wooden chariots ready to do battle in a giant burial pit. Many of the 100 chambers have yet to be excavated, but archeologists have already discovered China's largest cache of jade.

ARRIVAL AND DEPARTURE   JINGZHOU

Since the advent of high-speed trains to Jingzhou most people arrive this way, but there are also long-distance buses to Shashi.

By train Jingzhou's train station is northeast of the centre on the bus #1 route. Tickets for high-speed trains can easily be secured at the station on the day of travel.
Destinations Wuhan (many daily; 1hr 30min–3hr); Yichang (many daily; 30min–1hr).

By bus Buses arrive at Shashi's long-distance bus station on Taqiao Lu. Bus #101 connects the station with Jingzhou, or taxis are readily available.
Destinations Wuhan (4hr); Yichang (2hr).

Yichang

宜昌, yíchāng

You may well end up spending a night at **YICHANG**, a transport terminus on the Yangzi 120km upstream from Jingzhou and virtually in the shadow of the **Three Gorges Dam**. Ringed by car showrooms (western Hubei has long been a car manufacturing centre), the town is where visitors land after riding ferries and hydrofoils down through the Three Gorges – or it can be used as a staging post for visiting the dam itself. To the north, wild **Shennongjia Forest Reserve** is just a bus ride away.

The town

The town itself is of little interest, though remnants of Yichang's treaty port days provide a dash of character, such as the **St Francis Cathedral** (圣方济各堂, shèngfāngjǐ gè táng) on Zili Lu. In the face of the rapidly encroaching Japanese, Yichang also played a critical role in the 1938 evacuation of 30,000 people and nearly 100,000 tonnes of equipment west to Chongqing – a monument on Yanjiang Dadao commemorates this mammoth undertaking. Early evening is a good time to head down to the river and watch crowds flying kites, gorging themselves on shellfish at nearby street restaurants or cooling off with an ice cream.

ARRIVAL AND DEPARTURE   YICHANG

All plane, ferry, hydrofoil and train tickets are most easily booked through accommodation tour desks – you don't have to be staying to use these – though train tickets come with a fee, so you might want to buy them yourself at the station, or at one of the numerous train ticket offices to be found around the city (¥5 service charge). The ticket centre next to the *Yiling Hotel* on Yunji Lu also sells airline tickets.

BY PLANE
By plane Sanxia airport (三峡机场, sānxiá jīchǎng) is 10km east of town, covered by an hourly shuttle bus from

the Air China office on Dongshan Dadao, or a ¥60 taxi fare. Be warned that fares are expensive.
Destinations Beijing (2 daily; 2–2hr 30min); Chongqing (2

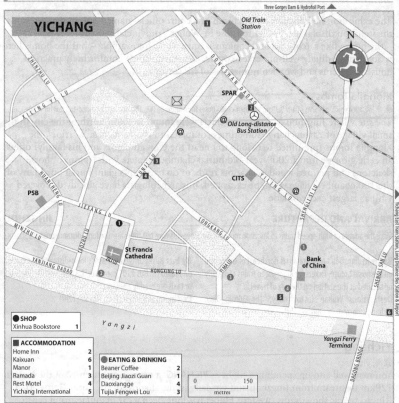

daily; 1hr); Guangzhou (daily; 1hr 50min); Shanghai (1 daily; 1hr 35min).

BY TRAIN

Yichang Train Station (宜昌 火车站, yíchāng huǒchē zhàn). The old train station is at the north side of town atop a broad flight of steps; this station is on the line north to Zhengzhou in Henan, or south to Zhangjiajie in Hunan.

Yichang East Station (宜昌 火车东站, yíchāng dōng chángqìchē zhàn). High-speed trains for Wuhan and beyond leave from the enormous new East Station which can be reached by bus #1 (¥1) or a ¥20 taxi ride. There's left luggage and an internet café here.

Destinations Beijing (4 daily; 8–21hr); Jingzhou (many daily; 30min–1hr); Xi'an (1 daily; 15hr 30min); Wuhan (many daily; 1hr 45min–6hr); Zhangjiajie (2 daily; 4hr 30min–5hr).

BY BUS

There are information desks and left-luggage offices at both terminals.

Yichang East long-distance bus station (宜昌东长汽车运站, yíchāng dōng chángqìchē zhàn; ☏0717 6445314) is next to Yichang East train station, and has services all over the province and the rest of the country.

Old long-distance bus station (长汽车客运站, chángqìchē kèyùnzhàn), 500m to the east of the train station on Dongshan Dadao. A few long-distance buses originate and terminate here, although as they all travel via the new East station, it's far better to buy tickets and start your journey there.

Destinations Changsha (6hr); Jingzhou (2hr); Jiujiang (8–10hr); Muyu Zhen (5hr); Wuhan (4hr); Xiangfan (5hr); Xing Shan (4hr); Wudang Shan (6hr).

BY BOAT

By hydrofoil For those without the time or money for a full Three Gorges cruise, taking the hydrofoil will give glimpses of the grandeur, albeit accompanied by a noisy engine. Hydrofoils run from Taiping Xi hydrofoil port (太平溪码头, tàipíngxī mǎtóu) above the Three Gorges Dam to Badong (for Shennong Stream), Wushan (for Lesser

Three Gorges) and Fengjie; at the time of writing they continued to Wanzhou, though Fengjie will be the terminus once regional highways are completed. The hydrofoil company lays on free transport between the port and their offices in town. There are five departures daily to Wanzhou (5hr; ¥300); when you buy your ticket, get the agent to write down the address of their office to show a cab driver, as this is where the bus to the port leaves from. Staff on board the hydrofoil sell bus tickets from the terminus to Chongqing.

By ferry Public ferry tickets for the 2-day journey upstream to Chongqing can be bought through accommodation – see p.753 for more about classes and conditions. Fares to Chongqing range from ¥152 for a berth in an open dorm to ¥1042 (per person) for a private cabin. Some boats also stop at Wushan, Fengjie, Wanxian, Shibaozhai and Fengdu.

INFORMATION

Travel agents Yichang's CITS office at 100 Yiling Lu (☎ 0717 6911998 or 6908582) is staffed by helpful English-speakers and can also arrange all Three Gorges cruise tickets, plus tours to Zhangjiajie (p.435) and Shennongjia (p.420). They can also organize tickets for daily bus-and-boat tours, taking in the Gezhou Dam and the Three Gorges Dam, after which passengers board the ominously named "Good Luck" for the trip through the Xiling Gorge. Tickets cost ¥280 including all entry fees and lunch, and will have you back in Yichang by 6pm.

7

GETTING AROUND

By taxi A cab costs a fixed ¥6 within the city centre.

ACCOMMODATION

Home Inn 如家酒店, rújiā jiǔdiàn. 126 Dongshan Dadao ☎ 0717 6915818 Ⓦ homeinns.com. The usual clean, comfortable rooms and a good location next to the long-distance bus station make Yichang's *Home Inn* fine value for an overnight stay. **¥159**

Kaixuan 凯旋宾馆, kǎixuán bīnguǎn. 133 Yanjiang Dadao ☎ 0717 6908000. A new hotel with plushly carpeted rooms and a pleasant location overlooking the Yangzi, plus helpful staff and attractive discounts. **¥220**

Manor 山庄商务酒店宜昌凯旋宾馆, shānzhuāng shāngwù jiǔdiàn. 105 Dongshan Dadao ☎ 0717 6084500. A pleasant situation set above Dongshan Dadao and decent-sized (if slightly damp) rooms at reasonable prices makes this place enduringly popular. **¥150**

Ramada 华美达酒店 huáměidá jiǔdiàn. 27 Yunji Lu ☎ 0717 6528888, Ⓦ ramadayichang.com.cn. Rooms and bathrooms are a little small for the money, but this is still far and away Yichang's most comfortable hotel, with a great location and all of the amenities you'd expect from this international chain. **¥618**

Rest Motel 锐思特汽锁酒店, dùisītè qìsǔo jiǔdiàn. 31 Yunji Lu ☎ 0717 6236888, Ⓦ restmotel.com.cn. A very central location, low prices and more character than the average budget business chain motel make the *Rest Motel* a good option, although some rooms suffer from road noise. **¥130**

Yichang International 国际大酒店, guójìdà jiǔdiàn. 121 Yanjiang Dadao ☎ 0717 6222888. Once Yichang's best, these days the *International* still offers a good location, views and decent discounts, although some of the cheaper rooms come in unusual shapes and sizes – ask to see another room if you're not happy. **¥260**

EATING, DRINKING AND NIGHTLIFE

You certainly won't go hungry in Yichang. Canteens and street stalls seem to line every back alley, and there's a good collection of local places on Yi Ma Lu (including *Tujia Fengwei Lou*, below). Western fast food can be found near the old long distance bus station in the centre of town and there are also a growing number of coffee shops. Nightlife centres on the pubs at the southern end of Yunji Lu, many of which have live music every night – try *N Zone*, or *Star Pub*.

Beaner Coffee 宾乐美式咖啡, bīnlè měishì kāfēi. Yunji Lu. Generic Western-style café serving expensive coffee and a reasonable imitation of Western food including sandwiches (¥21–25), pasta and steaks. The location just off Yanjiang Dadao makes it a good place to take a break after a riverside wander. Daily 11am–11pm.

Beijing Jiaozi Guan 北京饺子馆, běijīng jiǎoziguǎn. Shengli Si Lu. A simple restaurant which serves up a variety of cheap and tasty northern-style dumplings; plain pork and cabbage are by far the best. Daily 11am–9pm.

Daoxiangge 稻香阁, dàoxiāng gé. 31 Shengli Si Lu ☎ 0717 6222107. Enduringly popular place specializing in fish, but whose menu also stretches to dumplings (¥20) and game meats. Expect to pay ¥50–¥100 per person. Daily 9am–2pm & 4.30–9pm.

Tujia Fengwei Lou 土家风味楼, tǔjiā fēngwèi lóu. 33 Yi Ma Lu ☎ 0717 6230577. Small, friendly and very popular place serving homestyle dishes – the Tujia are a local ethnic group, scattered through the Yangzi gorges – including very spicy hotpots and tasty sweet-and-sour ribs (¥38). Daily 9.30am–9.30pm.

The Three Gorges Dam

长江三峡大坝, chángjiāng sānxiá dàbà · ¥105, includes ninety-minute tour of site in a perspex-roofed minibus

The vast **Three Gorges Dam**, 35km west of Yichang at Sandouping, is the most obvious target for a day-trip. Completed in 2006, the dam wall has raised water levels upstream by up to 175m and holds back a 660km-long lake. Now that the dam is fully operational it is the world's largest producer of hydroelectric power, capable of generating 22,500 megawatts, or the equivalent of over fifteen nuclear power plants.

Part of the dam's stipulated purpose is also to control the disastrous summer **flooding** which has long afflicted the lower Yangzi. The dam received its first serious test in 2010, when torrential "once-in-a-century" monsoonal rains upstream were just contained. **Critics** of the dam, meanwhile, label it a vanity project that has submerged countless archeological sites in the Three Gorges, required the relocation of millions of people, and which will become redundant through siltation within seventy years. But with its electricity consumption increasing every year, China desperately needs the power that the dam provides.

7

ARRIVAL AND DEPARTURE

THE THREE GORGES DAM

Note that if you're travelling on a Yangzi cruise boat, the dam may be an option on your itinerary, so you shouldn't need to set aside an extra day for the trip from Yichang.

By bus Take a northbound bus #4 from Yunji Lu in front of the train station to the Yemingzhu stop, then bus #8 (¥10) to Liuzhashou Reception Centre (六闸首游客接待中心, liùzháshŏu yóukè jiēdài zhōngxīn) – ask the drivers where to get off and expect the whole journey to take an hour and a half.

By bus tour Daily bus tours depart from the old ferry terminal on Yanjiang Dadao. Tours leave at 8am and return at 1pm, and cost ¥150 including entry ticket.

Shennongjia Forest Reserve

神农架林区, shénnóngjià línqū · ¥140

Hidden away 200km northwest of Yichang in Hubei's far west, **Shennongjia Forest Reserve** encloses a rugged chain of mountains, culminating in the 3053m-high Da Shennongjia, the tallest peak in central China. The area has been famed for its plant life ever since the legendary Xia king Shennong – credited with introducing mankind to farming, medicine and tea – scoured these heights for herbs. More recently, the plant hunter Ernest Wilson found several new species here in the early twentieth century. And more fancifully, Shennongjia has been the setting for numerous sightings of the Chinese **wild man** – even if he eludes you, there's a chance of seeing endangered **golden monkeys** here.

Muyu

木鱼镇, mùyú zhèn

From Yichang the road climbs through well-farmed, increasingly mountainous country overloaded with hydroelectric stations, passing tea fields and immense tower karst formations before following the narrow Shennong gorge to emerge at the rapidly expanding settlement of **MUYU ZHEN**, 17km south of the reserve. Foreigners are only allowed to visit one of the park's four zones, accessed from Muyu, and for the meanwhile the town manages to feel quite remote, with locals still using woven basket backpacks to haul produce up and down the mountain, and wild honey collectors selling their hard-earned wares on the main street. However, a new motorway and airport are under construction, and "luxury" apartments are being built on the edge of town – like everywhere else in China, Muyu is changing, and fast.

ARRIVAL AND DEPARTURE

MUYU

By bus The bus station is located at the northern end of town, a short walk to accommodation options and restaurants. Tickets are easily available, although it's worth buying them the day before if you plan on leaving early.

Destinations Yichang (4hr).

By tour Yichang's CITS run Chinese-language tours at ¥400 per person, including transport, overnight accommodation and a whip around the highlights. For more comfort, longer on site and an English-speaking guide, you're looking at double this price.

INFORMATION

Tourist office The Shennong Tourism Office (☏0719 3456018) on the main street doesn't seem to open very often, but theoretically can provide information.

GETTING AROUND

By minibus To reach the reserve gates at Yazikou from Muyu, flag down one of the plentiful early-morning Songbai-bound minivans on the main road (¥10). Hiring the whole minibus for the day costs ¥300–400.

By taxi Taxis to the reserve gates at Yazikou can be bargained to ¥20.

ACCOMMODATION

There's abundant accommodation at Muyu Zhen, though things can get busy at weekends and holidays. Most of the cheaper places are to be found on the main road through town, so it's quite easy to haggle over a few places before deciding. Aside from the upscale hotels it's always worth checking the hot water situation before you check in.

Holiday Hotel 假日酒店, jiàrì jiǔdiàn. Set off the main road at the bottom of town ☏0719 3452600. An enormous property recently redeveloped by Shennong Tourism with clean and comfortable, if spartan, rooms, but no views. The larger and better furnished deluxe rooms are worth the extra money. Double **¥260**, deluxe **¥320**

Laojin Shanzhuang 老金山庄, lǎojīn shānzhuāng. Above and behind *Holiday Hotel* ☏0719 3313555. This small and simple hotel has cheap, clean and spacious rooms with the odd glimpse of mountain. The rooms have 24-hour hot water and flat-screen TVs and the owners are friendly but don't speak any English. **¥80**

Shennong Shanzhuang 神农山庄, shénnóng shānzhuāng. Above the *Holiday Hotel* ☏0719 3452513. Shennongjia's smartest property enjoys commanding views across the hills, although the facade of the grand villa itself is starting to show signs of age. Rooms at the front are bright and attractive, while those at the back are gloomy, but they all have modern amenities and good bathrooms. **¥420**

Teafield Farmstay 茶园农庄, cháyuán nóngzhuāng. Above *Shennong Shanzhuang* ☏158 97876848. Halfway up the hill, this farmstay has clean, simple rooms and delicious fresh food served by the friendly owners in the small dining room. The rooftop terrace is a great place to enjoy a cuppa surrounded by tea fields. Get a Chinese-speaker to call ahead to arrange pick-up from town. **¥140**

EATING

The hills are alive with wonderful medicinal herbs and exotic game and Muyu's cuisine reflects this, but most places also serve a selection of favourites from around the country.

Luanchao Luanchi 乱炒乱吃, luànchǎo luànchī. Top end of the main street ☏138 86843410. Local specialities plus a good selection of Sichuan dishes including *yuxiang qiezi* (¥18) are best enjoyed in the upstairs open-sided dining room. Daily 8.30am–10pm.

Xiaolou Yushui Renjia 小楼渔水人家, xiǎolóu yúshuǐ rénjiā. Across the bridge south of the Shennong Tourism Office ☏0717 6222107. Delicious mountain dishes served in a lovely location right on the river. Bamboo rice, mountain mushrooms, "wild" vegetables and spicy pork (¥48) all feature on the menu. Ask if you can eat outside if the weather is nice. Daily 9am–2pm & 4–9pm.

The reserve

Once at the reserve entrance, known as **Yazikou** (鸭子口, yāzikǒu), you hand over the entry fee and add your name and passport number to the list of the few foreigners who make it here each year.

Xialong Tan
小龙潭, xiǎolóng tán

From the gates, 6km of gravel track runs southwest up a valley to the couple of Forestry Department buildings that comprise **Xiaolong Tan**, where close-up views of **golden monkeys** (金丝猴, jīnsīhóu) are available at the "animal hospital".

There's also a **Wild Man museum**, where paintings, newspaper clippings, maps and casts of footprints document all known encounters with the gigantic, shaggy, red-haired **ye ren**, first seen in 1924. The creature was most recently spotted in June 2003 by a party of six, including a local reporter, who described the beast as being 1.65m tall, of greyish hue, with shoulder-length hair and a footprint measuring some 30cm.

Jinhou Ling
金猴岭, jīnhóu lǐng

There are some good walks around Xiaolong Tan. One route (much of it along a vehicle track) climbs south, for around 2.5km, to a forest of China firs on the slopes of **Jinhou Ling**, a prime spot to catch family groups of golden monkeys foraging first thing in the morning. Favouring green leaves, stems, flowers and fruit, the monkeys live through the winter on lichen and moss, which cover the trees here. The males especially are a tremendous sight, with reddish-gold fur, light blue faces and huge lips. A far rougher trail continues to the top of the mountain in four hours, although you'll need a guide for this route.

Dalong Tan
大龙潭, dàlóng tán

A relaxed, 3km stroll north of Xiaolong Tan is **Dalong Tan**, a cluster of run-down huts by a stream, from where there's an undemanding 8km walk up the valley to **Guanyin Cave** (观音洞, guānyīn dòng). Most of this is through open country, which gets plenty of wildflowers in the spring; birders can spot **golden pheasants** (红胸山鸡, hóngxiōng shānjī) and grouse-like **tragopans** (红胸角稚, hóngxiōng jiǎozhì).

The Banbi Yan road

The gravel road from Xiaolong Tan curves westwards up the valley, climbing almost continually along the ridges and, in clear weather, affording spectacular views. On the way, you'll cross **Da Shennongjia** (大神农架, dà shénnóngjià), though the rounded peak is barely noticeable above the already high road. Better are the cliffscapes about 10km along at **Fengjing Ya** (风景垭, fēngjǐng yà) and the "forest" of limestone spires where the road finally gives up the ghost 17km due west of Xiaolong Tan at **Banbi Yan** (板壁岩, bǎnbì yán).

Wudang Shan
武当山, wǔdāng shān · ¥140 · unlimited use of mountain buses ¥70

Way up in northwestern Hubei, the 72 peaks of **Wudang Shan**, the Military Mountain, are steeped in legends surrounding its Taoist temples and fighting style. Wudang is associated with **Zhen Wu**, a martial deity whose portly statue graces many local temples, and whose birthday is celebrated on the third day of the third lunar month – a good

---

WUDANG'S MARTIAL ARTS

Wudang is most famous for its **martial arts**, which command as much respect as those of Henan's Shaolin Monastery (see p.265). It's said that the Song-dynasty monk **Zhang Sanfeng** developed Wudang boxing – from which *tai ji* is derived – after watching a fight between a snake and a magpie, which revealed to him the essence of *neijia*, an internal force used (in typical Taoist manner) to control "action" with "non-action".

For those interested in learning some Wudang *wushu*, there are several academies: try the Jing Wu Martial Arts School (☏0719 5666666) or Chuanzhen Martial Arts Institute (☏139 2471458, ⓦgongfuchina.com.cn), where you should be able to negotiate a course from around ¥2000 per week.

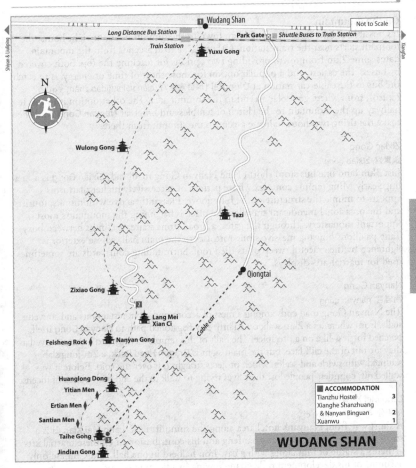

time to visit the mountain. Wudang's martial arts would have come in handy considering the vast number of outlaws who've inhabited these mountains over the centuries, not least the rebel peasant Li Zicheng, who amassed his forces and eventually deposed the last Ming emperor from here.

Many temple buildings here date to an imperial building frenzy during the fifteenth century – the work took three hundred thousand labourers ten years to complete – and the mountain is currently enjoying a bloom of tourist-funded religious fervour. A relatively easy ascent, coupled with the mountain's splendid scenery and the availability of transport connections, makes this an appealing trip.

Wudang Shan town

武当山市镇, wǔdāngshān shìzhèn

The market town of **Wudang Shan**, base for ascents of the mountain, sits with the famed ranges rising immediately to its south. It's not a big place, stretching thinly for a few kilometres along the main road, **Taihe Lu** (太和路, tàihélù), with a few side streets branching off. South down Huangbang Lu is the new **Wudang Shan Museum** (武当山博物馆, wǔdāngshān bówùguǎn; free), which traces the history of martial arts here and includes plenty of English.

On the mountain

It's possible to **hike** from Wudang Shan town to the summit in about eight hours; the footpath starts near the train station. Otherwise, a road ascends from the **mountain gates** some 2km from town, providing two options for reaching the top, both covered by buses. The easiest, and a popular option for those short of time or energy, is to catch the bus to the cable-car station at **Qiongtai** (琼台索道站, qióngtái suǒdào zhàn; ¥80 return), from where gondolas ascend to the summit area. The other option is to bus it halfway up the mountain to the clutch of temples and hotels at **Nanyan Gong**, and then make the tiring two-hour staircase ascent to the summit from there.

Zixiao Gong

紫霄宫, zǐxiāo gōng

Just 3km (and one bus stop) short of the Nanyan Gong roadhead, **Zixiao Gong** is a huge early Ming temple complex whose pattern of successively higher platforms appears to mimic the structure of the hills above. Pleasantly active with monks, tourists and the occasional mendicant traveller, the place is becoming the mountain's most important monastery. Through the gates, a broad stone staircase climbs between boxy Tang pavilions housing massive stone tortoises to the main hall, whose exterior is lightened by the graceful sweep of its tiled roof. Surrounding courtyards are sometimes used for martial-arts displays.

Nanyan Gong

南岩宫, nányán gōng

The Nanyan Gong road ends among a mess of accommodation, restaurants and souvenir stalls, from where it's a 2km walk on a fairly easy flagstoned path to **Nanyan Gong** itself, perched fortress-like on a precipice. The halls of this temple are tiny and austere, carved as they are out of the cliff face, but the main sight is **Dragon Head Rock**, a 2m-long slab sculpted with swirls and scales, which projects straight out over the void. Before it was walled off, countless people lost their lives trying to walk to the end with a stick of incense.

Lang Mei Xian Ci

郎梅仙祠, lángméi xiān cí

A short way from Nanyan's hotel area along the summit track, **Lang Mei Xian Ci** is a small shrine dedicated to Zhang Sanfeng and his contribution to Chinese martial arts – there's a statue of him along with a cast-iron halberd in one hall, and Chinese-only accounts of his development of Wudang boxing in adjoining rooms.

The summit staircase

The path from Nanyan Gong to the summit is only 4km long, but, with much of it being up and down stone steps, it takes two to three hours to complete. One way to keep your mind off the endless steps is to watch out for the colourful variety of **birds** in the forest, including boisterous red-billed magpies with graceful blue tails, and magnificent golden pheasants.

Halfway up to Tianzhu the path divides at **Huanglong Dong** (黄龙洞, huánglóng dòng; Yellow Dragon Cave) to form an eventual circuit via the peak. Turn left for the longer but less steep "hundred-step-ladder" (a lie, it's considerably more), with superb views through the canopy of cloud-swept, apparently unscalable cliffs. Alternatively, bearing right puts you on the even steeper, dangerously uneven staircase to the summit area via **Santian Men** (三天门, sāntiān mén), the Three Sky Gates – a route perhaps best saved for the descent.

Tianzhu Peak

天主蜂, tiānzhǔ fēng

Whichever route you take, paths converge outside an encircling wall that has turned 1600m-high **Tianzhu Peak** and its temples into a well-defended citadel. Inside, the

Ming-dynasty **Taihe Gong** (太和宫, tàihé gōng) is impressive for the atmosphere of grand decay enclosed by the thick green tiles and red walls of **Huangjing Hall** (皇经堂, huángjīng táng), where monks stand around the cramped stone courtyards or pray in the richly decorated, peeling rooms squeezed inside.

Jindian Gong
金殿宫, jīndiàn gōng • ¥20

Above Taihe Gong, and accessed via yet another steep staircase, the mountain is literally crowned by **Jindian Gong** (Golden Palace Temple), a tiny shrine with a gilded bronze roof embellished with cranes and deer, whose interior is filled by a statue of armour-clad Zhen Wu sitting behind a desk in judgement. It's a magical place: views from the front terrace (clearest in the morning) look down from the top of the world, with sharp crags dropping away through wispy clouds into the forest below.

ARRIVAL AND DEPARTURE
WUDANG SHAN

By train Wudang's train station on Chezhan Lu is served by trains from around the country, but sleeper tickets can be scarce, so it's worth booking your ticket out as soon as you arrive.
Destinations Beijing (3 daily; 19–22hr); Hefei (1 daily; 15hr); Shanghai (3 daily; 22–25hr); Wuhan (9 daily; 5hr 30min–7hr 30min).

By bus Wudang Shan's long-distance bus station is at the junction of Taihe Lu and Chezhan Lu.
Destinations Wuhan (8–10hr); Yichang (6hr).

ACCOMMODATION

Accommodation in Wudang Shan town is plentiful along Taihe Lu and tends toward the cheap, no-frills end of the market, though en-suite rooms are the norm. Prices can climb unreasonably at peak times, however.

WUDANG SHAN TOWN
Xuanwu Jiudian 玄武酒店, xuánwǔ jiǔdiàn. 8 Taihe Lu ⊙ 0719 5666013. A large, ageing property, but the renovated rooms are clean, comfortable and have a/c and hot water, although those facing the front are a little noisy. **¥150**

NANYAN
Places to stay line the road at Nanyan for the few hundred metres between the bus drop-off and the start of the hiking trails up the mountain. Advertised rates are outrageous, but only apply when demand outstrips supply – come on a Sunday or at the beginning of the week when it's quieter and you can pretty much name your price. Quality of rooms is similar across the board – modern, prematurely aged and basically clean – but check when hot water is available.

Xianghe Shanzhuang 祥和山庄, xiánghé shānzhuāng. The first hotel after the bus stop ⊙ 0719 5689018. Plain rooms at eminently bargainable prices, this place is absolutely typical of Nanyan's offerings. Rooms with cabled internet cost ¥20 more. **¥100**
Nanyan Binguan 南岩宾馆, nányán bīnguǎn. ⊙ 0719 5689182. Slightly better-than-average choice of large doubles and twins with decent amenities, or smaller budget rooms with basic bathrooms. There's also a reasonable on-site restaurant. **¥120**

THE SUMMIT
Tianzhu hostel Next to the upper cable-car terminus, just outside the Tianzhu Feng temple complex. A good place to stay overnight, with a chance to catch the sunrise and experience the mountain without attendant tourist hordes. **¥150**

DIRECTORY

Banks There's a Bank of China with ATM on Taihe Lu in Wudang Shan town.
Left luggage There's a left luggage office at the park gates where you can drop off any luggage you don't want to haul up the mountain (¥10/item/day).

Hunan
湖南, húnán

In many ways, **Hunan** is a pastiche of the tourist image of rural China – a view of endless muddy tracts or paddy fields rolling past the train window, coloured green or gold depending on the season. But the bland countryside, or rather the peasants farming it, has greatly affected the country's recent history. Hunan's most famous peasant son, **Mao Zedong**, saw the crushing poverty inflicted on local farmers by landlords and a corrupt government, and the brutality with which any protests were suppressed. Though Mao is no longer accorded his former god-like status, monuments to him litter the landscape around the provincial capital **Changsha**, which is a convenient base for exploring the areas where he spent his youth.

Both Hunan and Hubei – literally "south of the lake" and "north of the lake" respectively – take their names from **Dongting Hu**, China's second-largest lake, which also provided the origins of dragon-boat racing. South of Changsha, **Heng Shan** houses a pleasant assortment of mountain temples, while **Zhangjiajie Scenic Reserve** in the far west boasts inspiringly rugged landscapes. A few hours south of here lies the picturesque town of **Fenghuang**, where you'll find remnants of the Southern Great Wall.

Changsha

长沙, chángshā

CHANGSHA, Hunan's high-rise-filled capital, had been an important river town for millennia before its demarcation as a treaty port in 1903. Europeans had hoped to exploit the city's trading position, upstream from Dongtine Lake astride the Xiang river, but found that the Hunanese had a very short fuse (something other Chinese already knew): after the British raised the market price of rice during a famine in 1910, the foreign quarter was totally destroyed by rioting. Guomindang forces torched much of the rest of the city in 1938 as they fled the Japanese advance, and recent modernizations have finished the job of demolishing the past. Today, away from the bustling shopping district and vibrant nightlife, sights linked to Chairman Mao account for the majority of Changsha's formal attractions, though there are also some parks to wander around and a fascinating **Provincial Museum**.

Qingshui Tan

清水潭, qīngshuǐ tán • Bayi Lu • Daily 8am–4.30pm • Free • bus #113 stops outside

Qingshui Tan is Mao's former Changsha home and the site of the first local Communist Party offices. Outside, on Qingshuitan Lu, are a number of antiques stores, and at weekends an informal and jolly antiques market lines the pavement. A white marble statue of Mao greets you at the gate, and the garden walls are covered with stone tablets carved with his epigrams. Near the **pool** is a scruffy vegetable patch and the reconstructed room in which Mao and his second wife, Yang Kaihui (daughter of Mao's influential teacher, Yang Changji), lived after moving here from Beijing in 1921. Also within the grounds, a brightly tiled **museum** contains a low-key but interesting collection of historical artefacts, including a clay tomb figurine of a bearded horseman and a cannon that was used to defend the city against Taiping incursions in 1852.

Hunan Provincial Museum

湖南省博物馆, húnán shěng bówùguǎn • Daily 8.45am–4pm • Free • bus #113 or #126 from the train station stops outside

Inside **Martyrs' Park** (烈士公园, lièshì gōngyuán), the **Hunan Provincial Museum** is one of Changsha's highlights, dominated by relics from the Han-era tomb of **Xin Zui**, the Marquess of Dai. Xin Zui died around 160 BC, and her subterranean tomb was one of three discovered in 1972 during construction work at Mawangdui, about 4km northeast (the others contained her husband and son). Thanks to damp-proof walls of clay and charcoal, a triple wooden sarcophagus, and wrappings of linen and silk, the marquess' body was so well preserved that modern pathologists were able to determine that she suffered from tuberculosis, gallstones, arteriosclerosis and bilharzia when she died at age 50.

FROM TOP MAKING PORCELAIN BOWLS, JINGDEZHEN (P.447); WUDANG KUNG FU, WUDANG SHAN (P.422) >

CHANGSHA

■ **ACCOMMODATION**
Changsha International Youth Hostel	1
Civil Aviation Hotel	6
Days Hotel & Suites	3
Dolton	8
Green Tree Inn	7
Home Inn	5
Wanyi	2

● **EATING & DRINKING**
Fifth Tone Cafe	1
Fire Palace	3/7/8
Nutshell Coffee	5
Songhuajiang Jiaozi Guan	2
Xiangdangnian Canting	4
Ying Xiong Tie	6

● **SHOP**
Antique stores	1

CHANGSHA AND THE CHAIRMAN

Primarily, Changsha is known for its links with **Mao Zedong**, who arrived here in 1911 at the age of eighteen as nationwide power struggles erupted following the collapse of the Manchu dynasty. By 1918 there was a real movement for Hunan to become an independent state and, for a time, this found favour with local warlord **Zhao Hendi**, though he soon turned violently on his own supporters. Mao, back in his hometown of Shaoshan heading a Communist Party branch, was singled out for persecution and in 1925 fled to Guangzhou, taking up a teaching post at the Peasant Movement Training Institute. Within three years he returned to Hunan, organizing the abortive **Autumn Harvest Uprising** and establishing guerrilla bases in rural Jiangxi.

Mao was by no means the only young Hunanese caught up in these events, and a number of his contemporaries surfaced in the Communist government, including **Liu Shaoqi**, Mao's deputy until he became a victim of the Cultural Revolution; and **Hua Guofeng**, Mao's lookalike and briefly empowered successor.

7

The tomb relics

The sarcophagi are in a side hall, while access to the mummy is through a basement display of embroideries, lacquered bowls and coffins, musical instruments, wooden tomb figures and other funerary offerings. Taoist texts written on silk were also found in the tomb, and one piece illustrating *qi gong* postures is on display. Xin Zui herself lies in a fluid-filled tank below several centimetres of perspex, a gruesome white doll, with her internal organs displayed in jars.

Tangerine Island

桔子岛, júzi dǎo

Changsha's name – literally "Long Sand" – derives from a narrow midstream bar now called **Tangerine Island**. The lengthy Xiangjiang Bridge spans the river above, affording a good opportunity to gaze down on the island, which was settled by Europeans following the riots of 1910. Several of their former homes are still standing, though they've suffered overenthusiastic renovation, while the northern two-thirds of the island holds a new pavilion and hotel complex. The southern tip is a neatly laid-out park, centring on an enormous bust of a young and wild-haired Mao Zedong, gazing out over the river which he famously swam across on his 65th birthday.

ARRIVAL AND DEPARTURE **CHANGSHA**

Changsha is well connected to the rest of the country by planes, high-speed and regular trains and buses, and moving on is generally straightforward. The majority of destinations are most easily reached by train, although Fenghuang is best served by bus.

BY PLANE

Huanghua airport (黄花飞机场, húanghūa fēijīchǎng), 15km east of town, is connected to the city by taxi (¥100) or shuttle bus (¥16) to the airline office (daily 6.30am–8pm; ☎0731 84112222), which is in the same buiding as the *Civil Aviation* hotel on Wuyi Dadao.

Destinations Beijing (15 daily; 2hr–2hr 30min); Chongqing (11 daily; 1hr–1hr 15min); Guangzhou (4 daily; 1hr 15min); Hefei (3 daily; 1hr–1hr 30min); Hong Kong (1 daily; 1hr 40min); Shanghai (15 daily; 1hr 30min–2hr); Shenzhen (3 daily; 1hr 15min); Tianjin (5 weekly; 2hr); Zhangjiajie (1 daily; 50min).

BY TRAIN

Changsha is served by an impressive choice of trains, but ticket offices at both stations are always crowded so it's better to use one of the in-town kiosks, which also sell bus tickets. There's a ticket office (☎0731 854614180) just around the corner from *Nutshell Coffee* on Jiefang Lu.

Changsha Train Station (长沙火车站, chángshā huǒchēzhàn). Regular trains depart from this conveniently central station at the eastern end of Wuyi Dadao. Trains head north from Changsha to Zhangjiajie, Yueyang and Hubei province; west to Guizhou, Jishou and Zhangjiajie; east to Nanchang in Jiangxi; and south via Hengyang to Guangdong and Guangxi. There's also a special tourist train daily to Shaoshan.

Changsha South High Speed Rail Station (长沙南高铁站, chángshānán gāotiě zhàn). Changsha sits on the new high-speed rail line running between Wuhan and Guangzhou, and the higher ticket prices can prove money well spent by slashing journey times. The huge, airport-like station is several kilometres south of the city centre – around ¥30 in a taxi.

Destinations Beijing (23 daily; 5–20hr); Guangzhou (many daily; 2hr 40min–9hr); Guilin (10 daily; 7–11hr); Guiyang (6 daily; 12–13hr); Hengyang (many daily; 30min–2hr); Jishou (6 daily; 7–9hr); Nanchang (4 daily; 3hr 30min–5hr 30min); Shaoshan (daily; 2hr 30min); Shenzhen (32 daily; 2hr 50min–12hr); Wuhan (many daily; 1hr 30min–5hr); Yueyang (many daily; 30min–2hr); Zhangjiajie (8 daily; 5–11hr).

BY BUS

Changsha's three main long-distance bus stations are all way out of town in the suburbs.

East bus station (汽车东站, qìchē dōngzhàn) lies 4km from the centre on Shiyuan Dayi Lu, reached by city bus #126. Hefei, Nanchang and easterly destinations.

West bus station (汽车西站, qìchē xīzhàn), 8km out on Xiaoxiang Bei Lu; catch city bus #302. Mostly provincial destinations within Hunan.

South bus station (汽车南站, qìchē nánzhàn), Shizhongyi Lu, 10km from the centre on the city bus #7 route. Southern Hunan, and down into Guangxi.

Destinations Fenghuang (6hr); Heng Shan (3hr); Jiujiang (12hr); Nanchang (6hr); Nanyue (3hr); Wuhan (4hr); Yichang (6hr); Yueyang (3hr); Zhangjiajie (6hr).

INFORMATION

Travel agents CITS are at 160 Wuyi Dadao (☎0731 84468904), and can organize Chinese-guided day-trips to

Shaoshan (from ¥120) and Hengshan (¥390).

GETTING AROUND

By bus Changsha's city buses run about 6am–9pm and almost all travel via the train-station square. Regular buses cost ¥1 and a/c services are ¥2.
By metro A metro system is currently under construction,

due to open in 2015.
By taxi Flag fall is ¥6 for the first 2km, and each additional kilometre costs ¥1.8.

ACCOMMODATION

Changsha has a good selection of hotels, most of which are to be found on near central Wuyi Dadao.

Changsha International Youth Hostel 长沙国际青年旅舍, chángshā guójì qīngnián lǚshè. 61 Gongshang Lane, off Dongfeng Lu, north of the Provincial Museum ☎0731 82990202, ⊚www .yhachina.com. A friendly hostel with English-speaking staff set in an attractive old building close to the Provincial Museum. A little out of the way, but the only place in town you're likely to bump into backpackers – give reception a call and they will guide you in. Dorm beds ¥40, doubles ¥108

Civil Aviation Hotel 民航大酒店, mínháng dàjiǔdiàn. 47 Wuyi Dadao ☎0731 829125888. A well-run, tidy and slightly worn airlines-owned operation inside an ugly block of a building, featuring the standard mid-range amenities. It can get busy with tour groups. ¥288

Days Hotel & Suites 小天鹅戴斯酒店, xiǎotiāné dàisī jiǔdiàn. 648 Wuyi Dadao ☎0731 89899999, ⊚daysinn.com. Changsha's newest five-star enjoys a great location and offers plush modern styling and attentive service, although the rooms are on the small side for the price. ¥658

Dolton 通程国际大酒店, tōngchéng guójì dàjiǔdiàn. 159 Shaoshan Lu ☎0731 84168888, ⊚www.dolton-hotel.com. Once the best hotel in Changsha, the Dolton is an opulent sprawl of marble and chandeliers, with five-star service, although rooms are

starting to look dated. There's also a swimming pool and an ATM in the lobby. ¥689

Green Tree Inn 格林豪泰酒店, gélín háotài jiǔdiàn. 98 Shaoshan Lu ☎0731 88186998, ⊚998 .com. Chain hotel offering decent, good-value rooms with a/c, showers and moderately soft beds, though some are better kept than others – don't be shy about asking to see several options. ¥169

Home Inn 如家酒店, rújiājiǔdiàn. 34 Wuyi Dadao ☎0731 82918666. Very close to the train station, with the usual stripped-down but comfortable en-suite rooms with internet access. Rooms facing the main road are noisy though. ¥209

★ **Milkyway** 银河大酒店, yínhé dàjiǔdiàn. 59 Wuyi Dadao ☎0731 84111818. Don't be fooled by the tacky glass-and-chrome exterior, as most of the interior has had an overhaul, and attentive staff make for a pleasant stay. Standard rooms are comfortable enough, but higher up the building the bright and airy deluxe rooms are worth the extra money. Standard ¥198, deluxe ¥358

Wanyi 万怡商里务酒店, wànyí shānglǐwù jiǔdiàn. Train Station Square ☎0731 82279988. The smarter of two hotels in the station square – as usual you're paying for location rather than comfort, but it's a fair-ish deal for the standard rooms with internet connection. ¥168

EATING, DRINKING AND ENTERTAINMENT

Strong flavours and copious chillies are the signatures of Hunanese food – Mao himself claimed that it was the fiery food that made locals so (politically) red. Pungent regional specialities include air-cured and chilli-smoked meat; *dong'an ji*, chicken seasoned with a vinegar-soy dressing; *gualiang fen*, a gelatinous mass of cold rice noodles covered in spicy sauce; and *chou doufu* (literally "stinky tofu"), deep-fried fermented bean curd. Western-style cafés and bars are concentrated around Taiping Jie – a sympathetically reconstructed old street – and the western end of Jiefang Lu. For something a little more club-like head around the corner to Jiefang Xi Lu, Changsha's nightlife hub where DJs and live shows at a few mega-clubs, including *Soho*, contend for your twilight hours.

Fifth Tone Café 第五调咖啡店, dìwǔdiào kāfēidiàn. Just off Xinmin Lu, west over the river and close to Hunan University ☎0731 8805303. Relaxed and über-friendly American-run coffee shop with decent espresso, a selection of freshly baked cakes and free wi-fi. Call if you need directions. Mon–Sat 2–10pm.

★ **Fire Palace** 火宫殿, huǒgōng diàn. 507 Shaoshan Bei Lu, also at Wuyi Dadao and the western end of Jiefang Lu ☎0731 84114808. The original of this riotously good restaurant is on Shaoshan Lu – a busier, noisier and more enjoyable place to wolf down Hunanese food would be hard to imagine. Get an order card from the waitress, request some Baiwei beer, and stop trolleys loaded with small plates of goodies as they pass. Expect to pay ¥50–¥100 per person. Daily 11am–2pm & 5pm–2am.

Nutshell Coffee 果壳森林咖啡店, guǒké sēnlín kāfēi diàn. 2F 18, Jiefang Lu ☎0731 84592100. This cute mall coffee shop serves decent coffee, sandwiches and Western-style snacks (¥20–40), though the "spaghetti" looks suspiciously like *lamian*. Daily 10am–9pm.

Songhuajiang Jiaozi Guan 松花江饺子馆, sōnghuājiāng jiǎozǐ guǎn. Eastern end of Wuyi Dadao ☎0731 8805303. Big open dumpling house with delicious *jiaozi* (¥5–7 for 6, depending on the filling), plus plenty of other dishes to choose from. Daily 10am–2am.

★ **Xiangdangnian Canting** 湘当年餐厅, xiāngdāngnián cāntīng. Off Taiping Jie ☎0731 84863798. A filmreel banner of old Changsha photographs leads the way from Taiping Jie to this atmospheric Hunan restaurant. Specialities include Hunan taro (¥49) and Mao Zedong braised pork (¥31). Daily 9am–2pm & 4.30–9.30pm.

★ **Ying Xiong Tie** 英雄帖, yīngxióng tiē. Hidden away in a courtyard just off Jiefang Lu. Lively and traditional, this Hunanese restaurant dispenses with the hassle of a menu. Instead just tell the staff what you want – chicken, beef, pork, fish, tofu, vegetables, etc – and a few minutes later they'll bring you a steaming plate of spicy deliciousness. 10am–9pm.

DIRECTORY

Banks and exchange The principal Bank of China (Mon–Sat 8am–noon & 2.30–5pm) is near the train station on Wuyi Dadao. Upmarket hotels such as the *Dolton* also change travellers' cheques, and might not mind whether you're staying.

Hospital Global Doctor Clinic, 4F Hunan brain hospital, 427 Furong Zhong Lu, Section 3 (☎0731 85230250).

Internet There are internet cafés throughout the city, generally charging ¥3/hr; a convenient option is on the right side of the train station, while there are others near the airlines office on Wuyi Dadao and near the entrance to Qingshui Tang on Bayi Lu.

Left luggage Both the train and bus stations have left-luggage offices.

Mail and telephones The most convenient post office – with parcel post and international phones – is in the train-station square.

PSB The Foreign Affairs Department of the PSB (Mon–Fri 8am–noon & 2.30–5.30pm; ☎0731 84590788) is in the Hexi Jiaojing Building, west of the river on the north side of Wuyi Dadao.

Shopping Changsha has long had a reputation for silk embroidery, which you can buy at various stores along Wuyi Dadao. Taiping Jie has a smattering of shops selling pottery and other souvenirs, and there are antique stores along Qingshuitang Lu. For everyday needs there's a *Carrefour* on Wuyi Dadao, and a *Watsons* on Cai'e Lu.

Shaoshan

韶山, sháoshān

Mao Zedong's birthplace, the hamlet of **SHAOSHAN**, lies 90km to the southwest of Changsha, a fine day-trip from the provincial capital through the Hunanese countryside. Established as a pilgrimage site for idolatrous Red Guards during the Cultural Revolution, Shaoshan seethes with Chinese tourists, who – following a low point in Mao's reputation through the 1980s – have started to flock back to visit the Great Helmsman's hometown.

Shaoshan contains two settlements: a knot of hotels and services that have sprung up around the railhead and long-distance bus depot, and **Shaoshan Dong**, the village itself, some 6km distant. Patriotic jingles and a large portrait of Mao greet arrivals at the train station, as do minibuses heading up to the village.

Mao's Family Home

毛泽东故居, máozédōng gùjū • Daily 8am–5pm • Free

The first place to visit lies just before the village proper at **Mao's Family Home**, a compound of bare adobe buildings next to a lotus-filled pond, where Mao was born on December 26, 1893. The home is neatly preserved, with a few pieces of period furniture, the odd photograph, and wonderfully turgid English explanations completing the spartan furnishings. Here he led a thoroughly normal childhood, one of four children in a relatively wealthy peasant household that comfortably survived the terrible famines in Hunan during the first decade of the twentieth century. Though a rebellious youth, he did not become politicized until he moved to Changsha in his late teens.

Mao Zedong Exhibition Hall

毛泽东纪念馆, máozédōng jìniànguǎn • Daily 8am–5pm • ¥15

Just off the huge village square, next to a bronze statue of an elderly Mao and a swarm of souvenir stalls, stands the **Mao Zedong Exhibition Hall**. Photos and knick-knacks chart Mao's career, though today there's a great distinction between Mao the heroic revolutionary and the character who inflicted the **Great Leap Forward** – the disastrous movement which was meant to bring Chinese industrial output up to Western levels – and Cultural Revolution on his country. The exhibition reflects this: noticeable omissions include the Little Red Book and just about any mention of the years between 1957 and his funeral in 1976.

Dripping Water Cave

滴水洞, dīshuǐ dòng • ¥30

After his Great Leap Forward had begun to falter, Mao returned to Shaoshan in 1959 to interview peasants on the movement's shortcomings. He can't have liked what he heard; on his final visit in 1966 at the start of the Cultural Revolution, he kept himself aloof near the reservoir in a secret retreat, poetically named **Dripping Water Cave**, to which you can catch a minibus. Alternatively, the elegant pavilion atop Shaoshan peak

---

QU YUAN AND THE DRAGON BOAT FESTIVAL

The former state of **Chu**, which encompassed northern Hunan, was under siege in 278 BC from the first stirrings of the ambitious Qin armies, who later brought all of China under their control. At the time, the lakeside town of Yueyang was the haunt of the exiled poet-governor **Qu Yuan**, a victim of palace politics but nonetheless a great patriot of Chu. Hearing of the imminent invasion, Qu picked up a heavy stone and drowned himself in the nearby Miluo River rather than see his beloved state conquered. Distraught locals raced to save him in their boats, but were too late. They returned later to scatter *zongzi* (packets of meat and sticky rice wrapped up in reeds and lotus leaves) into the river as an offering to Qu Yuan's spirit.

The **Dragon Boat Festival**, held throughout China on the fifth day of the fifth lunar month (June or July), commemorates the rowers' hopeless rush – though many historians trace the tradition of food offerings and annual boat races to long before Qu's time. At any rate, it's a festive rather than mournful occasion, with the consumption of huge quantities of steamed *zongzi* and keen competition between local dragon-boat teams, who can be seen practising in their narrow, powerful crafts months before the event to the steady boom of a pacing drum. It's a lively spectator sport, with crowds cheering the rowers along, but you need to be up early to get the most from the ceremonies (for example, the dedication of the dragon-headed prows) as the race itself lasts only a few minutes.

overlooks the local landscape – not really typical, given the amount of tourist revenue, but a nice scene of healthy fields and bamboo thickets.

ARRIVAL AND DEPARTURE	SHAOSHAN

By train The best way to get here is on the special train from Changsha, which departs daily at 6.30am for the two-and-a-half-hour journey (¥101 return; returns from Shaoshan at 4.30pm).

By tour bus Tour buses leave from the square outside Changsha train station ticket office at 7am (guided day-tour in Chinese from ¥120).

Heng Shan
衡山, héngshān

Some 120km south of Changsha, the **Heng Shan** region is one of China's holiest sites. Spread over 80km or so, the ranges form scores of low peaks dressed in woodland with a smattering of **Buddhist and Taoist temples**, some of which were established more than 1300 years ago. It's somewhere to relax and admire the scenery (frosted in winter, golden in autumn and misty year-round), either tackling the easy walks between shrines on foot, or resorting to local transport and cable cars to ascend the heights.

Nanyue
南岳, nányuè

Banners strung across the highway welcome visitors to the village of **NANYUE**, home to the two largest and most architecturally impressive temple complexes in the area, **Nanyue** and **Zhusheng**. The Changsha–Hengyang highway runs along the eastern side of the village; midway along, an ornamental stone archway forms the "entrance" to the village proper and leads through to the main street, Dongshan Lu.

Nanyue Temple
南岳大庙, nányuè dàmiào · ¥50

Off Dongshan Lu, streets lead through the old village centre to **Nanyue Damiao**. The site has served as a place of worship since at least 725 AD, but the older buildings succumbed to fire long ago and were replaced in the nineteenth century by a smaller version of Beijing's Forbidden City. It's a lively place, echoing with bells and thick with smoke from incense and detonating firecrackers – there are furnaces in the courtyards to accommodate the huge quantities offered up by the crowds. Seventy-two pillars, representing Heng Shan's peaks, support the massive wooden crossbeams of the main hall's double-staged roof, and gilt phoenixes loom above the scores of kneeling worshippers paying homage to Taoist and Buddhist deities. Other halls in the surrounding gardens are far more humble but boast detailed carvings along their eaves and exterior alcoves.

Zhusheng Temple
祝圣寺, zhùshèng sì · ¥10

Far quieter than Nanyue Damiao, with fewer tourists and more monks in evidence, is **Zhusheng Temple**. A purely Buddhist site, the entire monastery – whose name translates as "Imperial Blessings" – was reconstructed for the anticipated visit of **Emperor Kangxi** in 1705, but he never showed up. The smaller scale and lack of pretence here contrast with Nanyue's extravagances, though there's a series of five hundred engravings of Buddhist *arhats* set into the wall of the rear hall, and a fine multifaced and many-handed likeness of Guanyin to seek out among the charming courtyards.

In the hills
¥100 · includes entry to all temples and a bilingual map of the mountain

There's a good day's walking to be had between Nanyue and **Zhurong Gong**, a hall perched on Heng Shan's 1290m apex, 15km from town. The main road through Nanyue leads to the park gates behind Nanyue Damiao; from here there's the choice of hiking, catching a minibus or taking the cable car (¥80) to the halfway point. Even major temples along the way are small and unassuming, requiring little time to explore, and tracks are easy, so around eight hours should be sufficient for a return hike along the most direct route.

Nanyue to Banshan Ting

On foot the first two hours are spent passing occasional groups of descending tourists and black-clad Taoists, as the road weaves past rivers and patches of farmland before reaching the temple-like Martyrs' Memorial Hall, built to commemorate those killed during the 1911 revolution. Entering pine forests shortly thereafter, you'll arrive at the cable car terminus at **Banshan Ting**, (literally "halfway pavilion"; 半山亭, bànshān tíng), where accommodation is available at the Duxiu Binguan.

Xuandu Temple

玄都寺, xuándū sì

Not far from Banshan Ting, **Xuandu Temple** is Hunan's Taoist centre, founded around 700 AD. Even so, an occasional Buddhist saint graces side shrines, but the best feature is the unusually domed ceiling in the second hall, watched over by a statue of Lao Zi holding a pill of immortality.

To the summit

From the cable-car station the rest of the ascent passes a handful of functioning, day-to-day temples with monks and nuns wandering around the gardens – **Danxia Temple** (丹霞寺, dānxiá sì) and **Zushi Gong** (祖师宫, zǔshī gōng) are larger than most – before arriving outside **Shangfeng Temple**'s red timber halls, which mark the minibus terminus. Overpriced **hotels** here cater to those hoping to catch the dawn from the sunrise-watching terrace, a short walk away below a radio tower. On a cloudy day, it's better to push on for a further twenty minutes to the summit, where **Zhurong Gong** (祝融宫, zhùróng gōng), a tiny temple built almost entirely of heavy stone blocks and blackened inside from incense smoke, looks very atmospheric as it emerges from the mist.

ARRIVAL AND DEPARTURE HENG SHAN

Nanyue village, the trailhead for getting up into the hills, has its own bus station but the regional train stations are all some distance away.

BY TRAIN

There are three train stations on two separate train lines serving Nanyue village, all connected by direct buses.

Hengshan station (衡山火车站, héngshān huǒchēzhàn). 20km east of Nanyue at Xintang town, with minibuses making the run in 30min.

Hengshan West (衡山西, héngshān xi). The closest station to the mountain is just 5km west of Nanyue, a 15min minibus transfer.

Hengyang East (衡阳东, héngyáng dōng). Located 25km south of Nanyue at Hengyang town, this station is on the Changsha South-Guangzhou high-speed line. Buses to Nanyue can take over an hour.

Destinations Changsha (10 daily; 1hr 30min–2hr); Changsha South (many daily; 40min); Guangzhou (2hr–6hr 30min); Shenzhen (10 daily; 2hr 30min–10hr).

BY BUS

Nanyue bus station At the southern end of the village, just off the highway; map sellers, rickshaw drivers and hotel touts descend on new arrivals. If you can't find direct buses to your destination here, head first for Hengyang (衡阳, héngyáng), whose bus and train stations offer a wider range of options.

Destinations Changsha (3hr); Guilin (6hr); Hengyang (1hr–1hr 30min).

BY TOUR

Tour agents Changsha CITS runs daily Chinese-only tours to Nanyue from ¥120 (see p. 000 for details).

GETTING AROUND

Minibuses (¥10) run between Nanyue town and Shangfeng Temple, below the summit, in under an hour.

ACCOMMODATION AND EATING

There's accommodation both in Nanyue village and up on the mountain itself, although Heng Shan is also fairly easily visited as a day-trip from Changsha. In Nanyue you'll find a mass of restaurants on Dongshan Lu; up on the mountain, food stalls lurk at strategic points, so there's no need to carry much.

Duxiu Binguan 独秀宾馆, dúxiù bīnguǎn. Banshan Ting, halfway up the mountain ☎0734 5661541. Attractive doubles, twins and triples, some with mountain views, surrounded by greenery and very handy for the cable car. There's also a reasonably priced restaurant. **¥168**

Guofeng Hotel 国峰宾馆, guófēng bīnguǎn. Opposite the bus station in Nanyue ☎0734 5678526. Clean, modern rooms, if a little plain, with LCD TVs and internet connection. More expensive rooms have computers. **¥128**

Zhangjiajie

张家界, zhāngjiājiè • also known as Wulingyuan Scenic Reserve 武陵源风景区, wǔlíngyuán fēngjǐngqū • ticket ¥248 valid for three days, or ¥301 for a week • tickets scanned with your fingerprint to prevent re-selling

Hidden away in the northwestern extremities of Hunan, **Zhangjiajie** protects a mystical landscape of sandstone shelves and fragmented limestone towers splintering away from a high plateau, often misted in low clouds and scored by countless streams, with practically every horizontal surface hidden under a primeval, subtropical green mantle. Among the 550-odd tree species (twice Europe's total) within its 370 square kilometres are rare **dove trees**, **ginkgos** and dawn **redwoods** – the last identified by their stringy bark and feathery leaves; now popular as an ornamental tree, until 1948 they were believed extinct. The region is also home to several million ethnic **Tujia**, said by some to be the last descendants of western China's mysterious prehistoric Ba kingdom.

On the downside, Zhangjiajie is beginning to suffer from its popularity, with more accessible parts of the reserve often almost invisible under hordes of litter-hurling tour groups. Fortunately the reserve is big enough that even on the main circuit it's easy to lose the crowds, and the majesty of the scenery comfortably overrides manmade intrusions. The reserve is best explored over two or three days, and you'll need comfortable walking shoes and the right seasonal dress – it's humid in summer, cold from late autumn, and the area is often covered in light snow early in the year.

Zhangjiajie village

森林公园, sēnlín gōngyuán

Having exited the train or long-distance bus stations at **Zhangjiajie city**, 33km from the reserve entrance, most visitors catch transport directly to the southern boundaries of the reserve at **ZHANGJIAJIE VILLAGE**. Despite comprising little more than a couple of streets in the valley, the village makes a good base and there's certainly enough nearby to keep you occupied for a few days. The road through the village leads downhill to the park entrance, past accommodation, restaurants and a throng of Tujia selling medicinal flora and cheap plastic ponchos.

Suoxi Village

索溪峪镇, suǒxīyù zhèn

With many of the same facilities as Zhangjiajie Village, **SUOXI** makes a good base for exploring the east and north of the reserve. Set in the **Suoxi Valley**, it's 10km as the crow flies from Zhangjiajie but the better part of a day away on foot (you can also get between the two by local bus). Attractions here include groups of rhesus monkeys and relatively open river gorges where it's possible to **cruise** – or even go white-water rafting – between the peaks.

The Suoxi Valley

Around the 2km-long **Baofeng Hu** (宝峰湖, bǎofēng hú), a lake accessed by a ladder-like staircase from the valley floor, there's a chance of encountering golden pheasants, the

7

ZHANGJIAJIE DAY-TRIPS

It's worth spending several days in the region, but if your time is limited you can still get to grips with Zhangjiajie's astounding natural beauty in as little as half a day: walk (or take the very short bus ride) to the cable car station (索道站, suǒdào zhàn; ¥118 return or ¥65 one-way) then ride up to **Huangshi village** (黄石寨, huángshí zhài), where the cable car terminates. From here hike the 2-hour circuit anticlockwise (most tour groups go the other way) around this minor, island-like plateau, surrounded by breathtaking views of the sea of pinnacles. Towards the end of the circuit, bearing left at the police station before Star Picking Tower will put you on the 45-minute trail back down to the park entrance.

For more of a hike, the left path from the park entrance follows a valley up to Huangshi, a trail which takes around two or three hours. Once at the top you can pick up the plateau circuit and walk or take the cable car back down. Alternatively, bearing right at the park entrance offers several more hiking loops, the shortest of which (around 4hr) runs along **Golden Whip Stream**, branching off to the right and returning to base through a particularly dense stand of crags below two facing outcrops known as the **Yearning Couple** (engraved tablets along the path identify many other formations). Alternatively, bearing left after a couple of kilometres – consult a map – takes you up past **Bewitching Terrace** (迷魂台, míhún tái) into the **Shadao Valley**. From here, basic trails continue through magnificent scenery around the western edge of the plateau to **Black Dragon village** (黑龙寨, hēilóng zhài), then circuit back to the park gates. This is a lengthy day's walk, and you won't see many other tourists along the way.

grouse-like tragopans and, if you're very lucky, **giant salamanders** – secretive, red-blotched monsters which reach 2m in length; once considered a great delicacy, these endangered creatures are now protected, and wild populations are being supplemented by captive bred animals. There's also **Huanglong Dong** (黄龙洞, huánglóng dòng; Yellow Dragon Cave), a few kilometres east of Suoxi, a mass of garishly lit limestone caverns linked by a subterranean river, and **Hundred Battle Valley**, where the Song-dynasty Tujia king, Xiang, fought imperial forces.

Tianmen Shan
天门山, tiānmén shān

The **Tianmen Shan** region basically covers the north of the park, and is named after an isolated 1250m-high peak which is now readily accessible from Zhangjiajie City by a 7km-long mountain cableway (天门山索道, tiānménshān suǒdào; ¥258 return including park entrance). The 11km road which covers the route incorporates 99 hairpin bends and is an equally impressive feat of engineering. At the top, steps lead to a giant natural rock arch, which has attracted high-wire walkers, jet-fly-throughs and even French free climber "Spiderman" Alain Robert. You can also access the area from Suoxi village, where there's a possible circuit of 30km setting off along the **Ten-li Corridor** (十里画廊, shílǐ huàláng). High points include the mass of lookouts surrounding **Shentangwan** (神堂湾, shéntáng wān), a valley thick with needle-like rocks; **Immortals' Bridge** (仙人桥, xiānrén qiáo), a narrow strip of rock bridging a deep valley; and the astounding, 330m-high **Bailong Elevator** (袁家界百龙电梯, yuánjiājiè bǎilóng diàntī; ¥56 each way) at Yuanjiajie.

ARRIVAL AND DEPARTURE | ZHANGJIAJIE

Zhangjiajie city (张家界市, zhāngjiājiè shì) is the regional hub, 33km south of the reserve gates, and accessible by planes, trains and buses from all over China.

By plane Zhangjiajie airport is 10km west of Zhangjiajie city. An airport bus connects with the city for ¥5, or taxis cost ¥15. Destinations Beijing (2 daily; 2hr–2hr 30min); Changsha (1 daily; 50min); Chengdu (1 daily; 1hr 30min); Guangzhou (1 daily; 1hr 45min); Nanjing (1 daily; 1hr 45min); Shanghai (2 daily; 1hr 45min).

By train The train station is in the south of Zhangjiajie city. Outside the station there are minibuses to the reserve, taxis and local buses. Train tickets are in short supply, especially at weekends, so book your outbound ticket on arrival. Direct services head east to Changsha, north to Yichang in Hubei, and south to Jishou and Liuzhou in Guangxi. For

Guizhou and points west you'll have to change trains at the junction town of Huaihua, four hours to the southwest – sleeper tickets out of Huaihua are hard to come by at the station, but you may be able to upgrade on board.
Destinations Changsha (8 daily; 5–11hr); Huaihua (for connections to Guiyang or Changsha; 13 daily; 3hr 20min–7hr 15min); Jishou (for Fenghuang; 12 daily; 2–4hr);

Yichang (2 daily; 5hr).
By bus The bus station is just across from the train station and shares the same park transport links. Leaving, there are regular buses covering the journey to Changsha and down to Fenghuang (or Jishou if you don't want to wait for a direct bus). Destinations Changsha (6hr); Fenghuang (4hr); Jishou (for Fenghuang; 2hr); Wuhan (12hr).

GETTING AROUND

By minibus Minibuses prowl the train station square for the hour-long journey to the reserve at either Zhangjiajie village (¥12) or Suoxi (¥19). Minibuses also run from Zhangjiajie village to Suoxi (¥10).
By taxi Taxis from transit points charge around ¥70 for the journey to Zhangjiajie village, or ¥100 for Suoxi.

By tour If you're on a Chinese package tour to Zhangjiajie, they may try to sting you for ¥50–100 based on a supposedly higher foreigners' entrance fee to the reserve; this is rubbish, and if the tour staff won't back down, tell them you'll pay the surcharge yourself at the gates.

INFORMATION

Guides and tour agents English-speaking freelance guides congregate inside the entrance at Zhangjiajie Village and charge ¥100 per day; and the travel service at

the *Xiangdian International Hotel* offers general hiking advice and arranges white-water rafting day-tours in the Suoxi Valley (¥250 per person).

ACCOMMODATION AND EATING

There's food and accommodation available at Zhangjiajie's villages, but take water and snacks on long journeys. Note that accommodation prices double at weekends and holidays, when crowds are at their worst. If you have a few days you should ask around about basic hotels within the reserve, which are recommended for getting away from it all – local guides can also take you.

ZHANGJIAJIE CITY
It's only worth staying here if you arrive too late to get the last bus to the park (around 7pm).

Home Inn 如家酒店, rújiājiǔdiàn. Jiefang Lu ☎0744 8209222. Zhangjiajie's *Home Inn* is set just off central Renmin Square and offers the usual comfortable, sterile rooms with internet connection. **¥209**

ZHANGJIAJIE VILLAGE
Farm Features Business Restaurant 农家特色商务酒楼, nóngjiā tèsè shāngwù jiǔlóu. Towards the top of the main road on the left ☎0744 5713999. A big, bright restaurant with an English menu featuring classic dishes (¥25–50) from around the country. Upstairs there are clean and cosy rooms with mountain views, although they can be noisy. Restaurant daily 8am–10pm. **¥150**
Hollyear Inn 和一宾馆, héyī bīnguǎn. Halfway

down the main street on the right ☎0744 5718989. Shabby rooms set around nice quiet gardens, although the silence is broken by an incredible frog chorus on summer evenings. **¥168**
Minsu Shanzhuang 民俗山庄, mínsú shānzhuāng. Halfway along the village on the left ☎0744 5719188. Ths Tujia-run wooden building is definitely past its best, with fairly basic facilities, but it's cheap and the owners are friendly. **¥120**
★ Xiangdian International Hotel 香殿山庄, xiāngdiàn shānzhuāng. Top of the village towards the park gate ☎0744 5712999, ⓦ xiangdianhotel.com .cn. Easily the best accommodation in the village, with comfortable, if small, traditionally styled rooms with all mod cons, set around a series of attractive courtyard gardens, complete with koi carp ponds, and the mighty peaks looming high on the skyline. There's also billiards, a bowling alley, and a helpful travel service. **¥468**

Fenghuang
凤凰, fènghuáng • ¥148 all-inclusive ticket, including boat ride on river

Tucked away close to the border with Guizhou, 160km south of Zhangjiajie, **Jishou** is the traditional jumping-off point for the charming town of **FENGHUANG**, with its stilted houses, flagstoned streets and communities of Miao and Tujia peoples. Fenghuang is a great place to unwind for a couple of days, although its popularity with domestic tourists means it is no longer a peaceful retreat. Almost every house has been

7

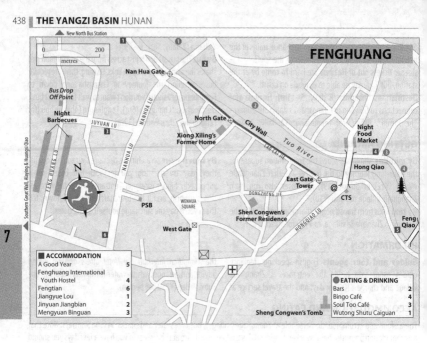

FENGHUANG

New North Bus Station

Bus Drop Off Point

Night Barbecues

Nan Hua Gate

North Gate

Xiong Xiling's Former Home

City Wall

Tuo River

Night Food Market

Hong Qiao

East Gate Tower

@

CTS

PSB

WENHUA SQUARE

Shen Congwen's Former Residence

Feng Qiao

West Gate

0 200
metres

ACCOMMODATION
A Good Year 5
Fenghuang International
Youth Hostel 4
Fengtian 6
Jiangyue Lou 1
Jinyuan Jiangbian 2
Mengyuan Binguan 3

EATING & DRINKING
Bars 2
Bingo Café 4
Soul Too Café 3
Wutong Shutu Caiguan 1

Sheng Congwen's Tomb

converted into some sort of commercial enterprise, and in the evenings bars and clubs blare out music over the water until the early hours. On the plus side Fenghuang's development gives great accommodation and dining choices, while the myriad narrow backstreets still offer plenty of genuine local life and a sense of the town's twelve-hundred-year history. Fenghuang is also a good base to explore smaller outlying settlements and the renovated **Southern Great Wall**.

Xiong Xiling's former home

熊希龄故居, xióngxīlíng gùjū · Daily 8am–5.30pm

Fenghuang is the hometown of several important Chinese, including **Xiong Xiling**, an ethnic Miao who became premier of China's first republican government. Near the North Gate, you can visit his **former home**, a simple affair preserved as it was and holding a few photos, including those of his three wives, with some English captions.

Shen Congwen's former residence

沈从文故居, shěncóngwén gùjū · just off Dongzheng Jie · Daily 8am–5.30pm

Shen Congwen (1902–88), one of China's greatest writers and also Miao, was from Fenghuang, and many of his stories centre on the Miao people and the local landscapes (*Recollections of West Hunan* is available in English). In 1949, Shen's writing was banned in both mainland China and Taiwan after he failed to align with either, effectively ending his career, but his works have enjoyed a recent revival. His **former residence**, a pleasantly proportioned traditional grey-brick courtyard building, evokes a soulful ambience, though there's little to see beyond some period wooden furniture.

Shen Congwen's tomb

沈从文墓地, shěncóngwén mùdì

Shen Congwen's **tomb** is 1km east of his former home, in a wooded spot along the river's south bank at Tingtao Shan. The epitaph on the jagged gravestone translates as "Thinking in my way you can understand me. And thinking in my way you can understand others".

The Southern Great Wall

南方长城, nánfāng chángchéng • ¥45 • bus from a roundabout at the western end of Jianshe Lu (30min)

The pretty countryside near Fenghuang has some worthwhile and easily accessible sights, the nearest being the **Southern Great Wall**, which, astonishingly, wasn't recognized for what it was until 2000. Originally constructed in 1554 as a defence against the Miao, the wall ran from Xiqueying in western Hunan to Zhenyuan Guizhou. There are several hundred metres of intact, newly renovated wall at a site 13km west from Fenghuang which, while not as rugged as its northern counterpart, is nevertheless impressive and significantly less visited; if you come in winter you'll probably have the place to yourself.

Alaying

阿拉营, ālāyíng • buses from the western end of Jianshe Lu in Fenghuang (¥7; 1hr)

Alaying, a Miao village 7km west of the Southern Great Wall, makes a useful transit point for visiting Huangsi Qiao (see below), though it's also worth a visit in itself on **market days** (on dates ending with a 2 or 7, as is the local practice), when you can buy Miao handicrafts and mingle with villagers from the outlying hills.

Huangsi Qiao

黄丝桥, huángsīqiáo • bus from Alaying (¥2; 15min)

Just a few kilometres from Alaying, **Huangsi Qiao** (Huang's Silk Bridge) is another ancient settlement, which prospered after Huang, a silk merchant, decided to build a bridge to attract people to the town. A smaller version of Fenghuang, with attractive stilted houses, the town is only half a kilometre across and has gate towers to the north, east and west.

ARRIVAL AND DEPARTURE   FENGHUANG

By plane The nearest airport to Fenghuang is at Tongren (铜仁市, tóngrénshì) in Guizhou province, 40km away. To catch a bus to Fenghuang, walk 1.5km from the airport to the main road and flag down one of the regular Tongren–Fenghuang services (1hr); heading to the airport from Fenghuang, ask the driver to set you down at the intersection. Alternatively, a taxi between the two costs ¥120–150 (40min). In Fenghuang plane tickets can be purchased through the CTS by the southern entrance to Hong Qiao.
Destinations Beijing (1 daily; 3hr); Guangzhou (1 daily; 1hr 30min).

By train Fenghuang's nearest train station is 45km away at Jishou (吉首, jíshǒu), on the line to Guiyang, Zhangjiajie and Changsha. From Jishou train station a bus or a taxi (¥5) over the bridge takes you to the bus station on Wuling Lu. From here, hop one of the regular shuttle buses to Fenghuang (¥12; 1hr 10min). If you arrive too late to travel on to Fenghuang, try the *7 Days Inn* opposite Jishou's station. In Fenghuang, onwards bus tickets can be purchased from the CTS by the southern entrance to Hong Qiao.
Destinations Changsha (6 daily; 7–9hr); Guiyang (3 daily; 8–12hr); Zhangjiajie (12 daily; 2–4hr).

By bus Fenghuang's North Station (北站, běizhàn) is a kilometre or so out of town up Fenghuang Lu, though on arrival buses will either drop you at Nanhua Lu bridge or halfway down Fenghuang Lu.
Destinations Changsha (5hr); Jishou (1hr); Tongren (1hr); Zhangjiajie (4hr).

7

GETTING AROUND

By taxi Old Fenghuang is small enough to walk around, but outside of the maze of narrow lanes it's easy to find taxis which should cost ¥5 for anywhere in town. A taxi to the outlying sights can be negotiated for ¥250–300 per day.

By tour Chinese-language day-trips covering Alaying, Huangsi Qiao and Daxiagu (a nearby gorge and waterfall) can be arranged through CTS for ¥100 per person, including lunch.

INFORMATION

Travel agent There's a friendly and helpful English-speaking CTS (7am–11pm; ☏ 0743 3221360) on the south side of the Hong Qiao bridge. They can arrange local tours; bus, train and plane tickets; plus car and driver hire for ¥250–300 per day.

ACCOMMODATION

Fenghuang is overloaded with hotels and hostels, and outside summer weekends or Chinese national holidays it's easy to find a room. Unless you really need your home comforts there's little point in staying in the new town; the character, charm and history of the old town is best enjoyed from the riverside balcony of your room. Fenghuang has developed a raucous nightlife scene centred on the north bank of the river near Nanhua Bridge; avoid the area if you like peace and quiet.

A Good Year 一年好时光, yìnián hǎoshíguāng. Lao Cai Jie ☏ 0743 3222026. Cosy little rooms with balconies overlooking the prettiest stretch of river, or cheaper rooms at the back. Rooms have bathroom and a/c but are chilly in winter. Doubles **¥80**, with riverside views **¥120**

Fenghuang International Youth Hostel 凤凰中天青年旅馆, fènghuáng zhōngtiān qīngnián lǚguǎn. 11 Shawan, near Hong Qiao ☏ 0743 3260546, ⍟ www.yhachina.com. Usually staffed by students, whose lack of experience is tempered by their eagerness to help; beautiful old facade, low prices, wi-fi and an excellent location aid the cause. Dorm beds **¥35**, doubles **¥108**

Fengtian Hotel 凤天宾馆, fèngtiān bīnguǎn. 8 Nanhua Lu ☏ 0743 3501000. Recently built four-star affair, tastefully furnished, with 24hr hot water and heating to boot. A nice way to treat yourself if you have been enduring unheated guesthouses, although it feels very removed from the old city. **¥400**

Jiangyue Lou 江月楼, jiāngyuè lóu. North side of the river, north of Nanhua Bridge ☏ 0743 3228588. Riverside hotel with pleasant, simple rooms and great balconies, near enough to see the twinkling lights of the bar zone, but not so close as to be affected by their noise. Bathrooms have good showers but squat loos. **¥160**

Jinyuan Jiangbian Binguan 金源江边宾馆, jīnyuán jiāngbiān bīnguǎn. 94 Lao Gong Shao ☏ 139 74346711. Ideally situated by the river, just below the Nanhua bridge, this traditional-style, family-run hotel boasts good views, but the rooms can be icy outside of summer. **¥120**

Mengyuan Binguan 梦源宾馆, mèngyuán bīnguǎn. Ju Yuan Lu, just off Nanhua Lu ☏ 0743 2150721. A good budget choice outside the old town and close to bus drop-off points. Spotless rooms, hot water and a good on-site restaurant make it a viable option. **¥120**

EATING, DRINKING AND NIGHTLIFE

One of the major pleasures in Fenghuang – taken between alley wanderings – is eating, especially if you're on the adventurous side. At restaurants by the East Gate Tower and along Hong Qiao Lu, cages and tubs of live chickens, ducks, pheasants, rabbits, bamboo rats (looking like a cross between a giant sewer rat and a guinea pig), frogs, snakes, crayfish, crabs, newts and catfish line the doorways – not to mention dead stuff resembling roadkill; they all await their turn in the pot. In the evenings the streets come alive with barbecues, particularly around Hong Qiao and along Nanhua Lu, where you can stuff your face for a few yuan. Fenghuang also has a decent selection of Western cafés and pubs, most of which have English menus.

Bingo Café 边各咖啡, biāngè kāfēi. Hui Long Ge, on the north bank of the river near the pagoda ☏ 0743 3260411. Light, airy and quiet café serving sandwiches (¥30), pasta (¥28–35) and pizzas (¥48–58). Also a good spot for a quiet evening drink, and there's an interesting variety of imported beers including Indian Kingfisher and Laotian Beerlao. Daily 8am–11pm.

★ **Soul Too Café** 素咖啡馆, sù kāfēiguǎn. Hui Long Ge, on the north bank of the river by the water wheel ☏ 0743 8882433. Good coffee, home-made yoghurt, Italian-style ice cream, cheesecake, and tasty pizza (¥49–65), pasta (¥35–38) and sandwiches. There are several other branches around the old town, all of which also serve cocktails and hookahs. Daily 8am–midnight.

Wutong Shutu Caiguan 梧桐树土菜馆, wútóng shù tǔcàiguǎn. North bank of the river near Nanhua Bridge ☏ 133 27255756. Large, noisy open-plan local restaurant where you can enjoy giant river clams (¥38) and Hunan hotpots (¥48–88) looking out to the river. Daily 9am–11pm.

DIRECTORY

Bank There's a Bank of China (Mon–Fri 9am–5pm) on Nanhua Lu.

Hospital On Hong Qiao Lu, near the junction with Fenghuang Lu.

Internet Two cafés are on the south side of the Hong Qiao bridge (¥3/hr).

Mail The post office is in the new town on Hong Qiao Lu, between the West and South gates to the old town.

Jiangxi

江西, jiāngxī

Caught between the Yangzi in the north and a mountainous border with Guangdong in the south, **Jiangxi** is generally considered a bit of a backwater, but to dismiss it out of hand is to ignore some significant attractions – namely, some major revolutionary history and a town that has been producing the highest-quality ceramics for almost six and a half centuries.

A network of rivers covering the province drains into Poyang Hu, China's largest freshwater lake. When the construction of the Grand Canal created a route through Yangzhou and the lower Yangzi in the seventh century, Jiangxi's capital, **Nanchang**, became a key point on the great north–south link of inland waterways. The region enjoyed a long period of quiet prosperity until coastal shipping and the opening up of treaty ports took business away in the 1840s. The twentieth century saw the province's fortunes nosedive: the population halved as millions fled competing warlords and, during the 1920s and 30s, fighting between the Guomindang and Communist forces raged in the southern **Jinggang Shan** ranges. This conflict eventually led to an evicted Red Army starting on their Long March across China.

Things picked up after the Communist takeover, and a badly battered Nanchang licked its wounds and reinvented itself as a centre of heavy industry. Transport links provided by the Poyang and Yangzi tributaries have also benefited the east of the province, where **Jingdezhen** retains its title as China's porcelain capital. North of the lake the mountain area of **Lushan** is easily visited from Nanchang and offers a pleasant reminder of Jiangxi's past, when it served as a summer retreat for Chinese literati and colonial servants.

Nanchang

南昌, nánchāng

Hemmed in by hills, **NANCHANG** sits on Jiangxi's major river, the Gan Jiang, some 70km south of where it flows into Poyang Hu. Built on trade, Nanchang has served as a **transport hub** for central-southern China and established itself as a handy base for car and plane manufacturers – Ford now has a plant here assembling vans. More recently, the city has traded in its reliance on heavy industry – which gave the city a sullen, Soviet atmosphere – for consumerism, tossing up office blocks and shopping malls with abandon.

The city centre

Nanchang sprawls eastward from the Gan Jiang, but the centre is a compact couple of square kilometres between the river and Bayi Dadao.

The Cold-War-era **Exhibition Hall** and revolutionary **Bayi Monument** (八一纪念塔, bāyī jìniàntǎ) are overshadowed by their modern neighbours, skyscrapers and shopping malls, which surround **Renmin Square** (人民广场, rénmín guǎngchǎng). Popular with locals, the square is a great place for an early-evening wander, when you'll see fan dancing, tai ji and kite-flying. Running west of the square, Zhongshan Lu takes you to the heart of Nanchang's bustling shopping district, past the water and greenery of **Bayi Park** (八一公园, bāyī gōngyuán) to the north.

NANCHANG

August 1 Uprising Museum

八一纪念馆, bāyī jìniànguǎn • Daily 9am–5pm, last entry 3.30pm • Free (bring your passport)

The Nationalist army occupied Nanchang in December 1926, but when Chiang Kai-shek broke with the Communists the following year, Zhou Enlai and Zhu De, two Communist officers, mutinied and took control of the city with thirty thousand troops. They were soon forced to flee into Jiangxi's mountainous south, but the anniversary of the uprising – August 1, 1927 – is still celebrated as the birth of the People's Liberation Army and the PLA flag remains emblazoned with the Chinese characters "8" and "1" (八一, bāyī) for the month and day.

Formerly a hotel, the imposing grey edifice of the **August 1 Uprising Museum** was occupied by the embryonic PLA as their 1927 headquarters and is mostly of interest as an example of Nanchang's colonial architecture. Inside, the meeting room has been preserved as it was, and there is the usual collection of military memorabilia including guns, medals and uniforms, with some English descriptions.

Tengwang Pavilion

滕王阁, téngwáng gé • Yanjiang Lu • Daily, summer 7.30am–6.30pm, winter 8am–5pm • ¥50

The mighty **Tengwang Pavilion** overlooks the river, 1km or so west of Youmin Temple. There have been 26 consecutive towers built here since the first was raised more than a thousand years ago in memory of a Tang prince. The present "Song-style" building was completed in 1989 but has an impressive pseudo-old exterior nonetheless. Climbing (or taking the lift) to the top affords views to the skyscrapers of the new city emerging west across the river.

Provincial Museum

省博物馆, shěng bówùguǎn • Xinzhou Lu • Tues–Sun 9am–4.30pm • Free

Half a kilometre south of the Tengwang Pavilion, the surreal **Provincial Museum** is a huge, futuristic complex of marble and green glass towers. There's an impressive ceramics collection, with pieces from as early as the Shang dynasty, all the way through to the blue and white porcelain of the Ming and Qing dynasties, for which the province is famous. English explanations detail the development of pottery production in the region, and identify the trade routes used to transport Jingdezhen's ceramics around the globe. Many Hakka settled in Jiangxi and neighbouring Fujian, and there's a small section on their traditions and fortified houses.

Shengjin Pagoda

绳金塔, shéngjīn tǎ • Daily 7am–6pm • ¥15 • bus #5 from Xiangshan Lu

West of the Fushan roundabout off Zhan Qian Lu, you'll find the **Shengjin Pagoda**. Legend has it that the city will fall if the seven-storey tower is ever destroyed, a warning still taken fairly seriously despite the fact that Shengjin has already been demolished several times, most recently in the early eighteenth century.

Bada Shanren Museum

八大山人纪念馆, bādàshānrén jìniànguǎn • Tues–Sun 9am–4.30pm • ¥20 • bus #20 from Yanjiang Lu

For a reprieve from the city, head 5km south to the **Bada Shanren Museum**. This whitewashed Ming-era compound set in parkland was the studio of the painter Zhu Da, also known as Bada Shanren, a wandering Buddhist monk of imperial descent who came to live in this former temple in 1661 and was later buried here. He is said to have painted in a drunken frenzy – his pictures certainly show great spontaneity. There are a number of originals displayed inside and some good reproductions on sale.

ARRIVAL AND DEPARTURE   **NANCHANG**

BY PLANE

Changbei International Airport (昌北国际机场, chāngběi guójì jīchǎng) is 23km north of the centre; the airport bus (¥15) terminates at the *Civil Aviation Hotel* (民航大酒店, mínháng dàjiǔdiàn) on Hongcheng Lu. Alternatively, taxis can whisk you into town for ¥70. Zhan Qian Lu is teeming with airline agents, and most hotels can book flights. China Eastern (📞 0791 8514195) is on Beijing Lu.

Destinations Beijing (9 daily; 2hr); Chengdu (2 daily; 2hr); Guangzhou (5 daily; 1hr 30min); Hefei (1 daily; 1hr 15min); Kunming (5 daily; 2hr 15min); Shanghai (1 daily; 1hr 15min).

BY TRAIN

Nanchang train station (南昌火车站, nánchāng huǒchē zhàn) is 700m east of the Fushan roundabout at the end of Zhan Qian Lu. Nanchang lies on the Kowloon–Beijing train line and just off the Shanghai–Kunming line, with connections through easterly Yingtan down into Fujian province. The city is also now connected to Hangzhou and Shanghai by high-speed D-trains. Sleeper tickets are easy to obtain, but prepare for mighty queues at the station or book through a downtown travel agency or train ticket booking office:

there's one at the Long-distance Bus Station on Bayi Dadao and another on Jianshe Lu, around the corner from the Xufang Bus Station.

Destinations Beijing (10 daily; 11hr 30min–18hr); Changsha (4 daily; 3hr 30min–6hr); Fuzhou (8 daily; 10hr–12hr 30min); Guangzhou (8 daily; 10hr 45min–14hr); Hefei (8 daily; 6–8hr); Jingdezhen (3 daily; 4hr 45min); Jinggang Shan (3 daily; 3–4hr); Jiujiang (50 daily; 1–2hr); Shanghai (10 daily; 6hr 15min–13hr); Shenzhen (14 daily; 10hr–14hr 30min); Tunxi (1 daily; 8hr); Wuhan (76 daily; 2hr 30min–9hr); Xiamen (4 daily; 14–17hr); Yingtan (31 daily; 1hr–2hr 30min).

BY BUS

Nanchang has four principal bus stations, of which the following three are most useful to travellers.

Long-distance Bus Station (长途汽车站, chángtú qìchēzhàn). Nanchang's biggest station is conveniently located just south of the centre on Bayi Dadao and can be reached by bus #1. The station is huge and often crowded, but ticket offices are user-friendly and there's usually no problem getting seats. Good for services to all over the country, except for Jingdezhen and Lushan.

Qingshan Passenger Station (青山客运站, qīngshān kèyùnzhàn) well north of the centre on

7

Qingshan Nan Lu and reached by bus #123. This is the only station with direct buses to Lushan (9.30am & 3.40pm; ¥62); alternatively, catch one of the regular services to Jiujiang and change there.

Xufang Passenger Station (徐坊客运站 xúfāng kèyùnzhàn) on Jinggang Shan Dadao in the south of town; reached on bus #1. Services to Jingdezhen,

Changsha, Hefei, Jiujiang (for Lushan), Shanghai and Wuhan. Chaotic and crowded, but tickets are readily available outside of peak holidays.

Destinations Changsha (5hr); Ciping (8hr); Hefei (6hr); Jingdezhen (3hr); Jinggang Shan (6hr); Jiujiang (2hr); Lushan (4hr); Shanghai (12hr); Wuhan (5hr); Yingtan (2hr 30min).

GETTING AROUND

By bus City bus #2 runs from the train station along Bayi Dadao and then makes a circuit of the central area, passing or coming close to all the hotels.

By taxi Cabs cruise downtown arrival points, with a ¥6 standing charge.

ACCOMMODATION

There's plenty of accommodation in town, although good budget choices are a little thin on the ground.

7 Days Inn 7天连锁酒店, qītiān liánsuǒ jiǔdiàn. 142 Bayi Dadao ☎0791 88857688. Excellent location across from the main long-distance bus station, with clean, modern rooms and attentive staff. **¥218**

Ganjiang 赣江宾馆, gànjiāng bīnguǎn. 138 Bayi Dadao ☎0791 8856888, ⓦgjhotel.com. Upscale hotel set in pleasant grounds. Rooms are spread out over several buildings and range in price, but even the cheapest are comfortable, spacious and have all modcons. **¥358**

Gloria Grand 凯莱大酒店, kǎilái dàjiǔdiàn. 88 Yanjiang Bei Lu ☎0791 86738855, ⓦgloriahotels.com. Modern, international-style joint-venture hotel, the most foreigner-friendly in Nanchang and worth visiting for its Western food. **¥608**

Hua Guang 华光宾馆, huáguāng bīnguǎn. 58 Xiangshan Bei Lu ☎0791 86777222. Shabby hotel with plain, faded (if clean) rooms, hard beds and brusque staff, but about the cheapest deal you'll find in the heart of town. **¥148**

Jinjiang Inn 锦江之星, jǐnjiāng zhīxīng. 255 Minde Xi Lu ☎0791 86788111, ⓦjinjianginns.com. Hard to fault for the central location with smart, bright rooms and modern amenities – though don't expect much extra space. There's a fair-value restaurant here too. **¥170**

Ruidu 瑞都大酒店, ruìdū dàjiǔdiàn. 399 Guangchang Lu ☎0791 86201888. An upmarket place, nicely located on the southeast corner of Renmin Square. Rooms are attractive and well kept, but don't have fridges or bathtubs, which you might expect at this price. **¥340**

EATING AND DRINKING

Nanchang's gastronomy covers everything from dumpling houses and spicy Hunanese restaurants to the regional Gan cooking – lightly sauced fresh fish, crayfish, snails and frogs. Soups are a Jiangxi favourite – egg and pork soup is a typical breakfast – often served in huge pots as communal affairs. Restaurants are spread all over the city, though the streets around Bayi Park have the highest concentration and Yongshu Lu is lined with eateries, from holes in the wall to fancy banquet dining halls.

Fengwei Xiaochi Cheng 凤味小吃城, fēngwèi xiǎochīchéng. 54 Zhongshan Lu. The name translates as Regional Flavour Snack City, and there's certainly plenty on offer at this no-frills crowded canteen where you can fill up for less than ¥20. Ordering is easy (the food's on display), and regular dishes include eggs with tomato, sweet-and-sour pork and delicious pickled cucumbers. Daily 10am–9pm.

Hunan Wang Caiguan 湖南王菜馆, húnánwáng càiguǎn. Supu Lu ☎0791 86243433. Popular, mid-range Hunanese restaurant where you can sweat over your red-braised pork (¥58), while enjoying the views overlooking Bayi Park. Daily 11am–2pm & 5–9pm.

Ming Dynasty 明朝铜鼎煨汤府, míngcháo tóngdǐng wēitāngfǔ. 144 Bayi Dadao ☎0791

6293683. The big bronze cauldron outside marks this as a Jiangxi-style soup restaurant, traditionally a breakfast favourite with locals, but filling enough to make a good lunch or dinner. A variety of flavours, including black chicken and young pigeon is on offer and individual pots start at ¥18, while three- to four-person pots cost from ¥30. Daily 7am–2pm & 5–9pm.

My Café 湖南王贩卖灵魂深处的品味, húnánwáng fànmài línghúnshēnchùde pǐnwèi. Minde Lu near Supu Lu ☎015377520521. High ceilings, comfy sofas and laid-back staff make this a cosy and relaxing place to spend a couple of hours reading and sipping Earl Grey tea (¥30). Daily 9am–midnight.

New Oriental Restaurant 新东方大酒店, xīndōngfāng dàjiǔdiàn. 18 Yanjiang Zhong Lu

📞 0791 86700777. This vast, opulent and gaudy Gan-style restaurant looks straight onto the river and the Tengwang Pavilion, and also serves Cantonese dishes. Expect to pay ¥50–¥100 per person. Daily 11am–2pm & 4.30–10pm.

DIRECTORY

Bank and exchange The main Bank of China is on Zhan Qian Xi Lu just off the Fushan roundabout, and there's another large branch in the southeastern corner of Renmin Square (both Mon–Fri 9am–5pm).

Hospital First City Hospital, Xiangshan Lu 📞 0791 88862261.

Internet There are internet bars scattered across the city, including one on Xiangshan Lu near the intersection with Dieshan Lu, and another just west of Bayi Park on Minde Lu.

Left luggage Offices at train and bus stations open roughly daily 6am–7pm.

Mail and telephones The main post office and the telecommunications building (both daily 8am–6pm) are near each other at the corner of Bayi Dadao and Ruzi Lu.

PSB On Shengli Lu, just north of Minde Lu (daily 8am–noon & 2.30–5.30pm; 📞 0791 88892000).

Shopping Nanchang Department Store, the city's largest and best-stocked department store, hides behind a 1950s frontage west of Renmin Square along Zhongshan Lu. Zhongshan Lu itself and the pedestrianized southern stretch of Shengli Lu are rife with clothing stores and boutiques. A good supermarket is *Walmart*, on the second floor of the shopping centre at the northern end of Renmin Square. For a big range of porcelain, name chops and paintings, try the Jiangxi Antique Store on Minde Lu.

Lushan

庐山, lúshān • ¥180 • park buses ¥80

Lushan's range of forested peaks rises abruptly from the level shores of Poyang Hu to a dizzying 1474m, its cool heights bringing welcome relief from the summer cauldron of the Yangzi basin. Developed in the late nineteenth century by Methodist minister-turned-property-speculator **Edward Little** as a hill-station-style resort for European expats, it saw the Chinese elite move in soon after foreigners lost their grip on the region. Chiang Kai-shek built a summer residence and training school for officials here in the 1930s, and, twenty years later, Lushan hosted one of the key meetings of the Maoist era. Today, proletarian holidaymakers pack out its restaurants and tramp its paths, and the mansions have been converted into hotels to accommodate them. Crowds reach plague proportions between spring and autumn, so winter – though very cold – can be the best season to visit, and a weekend's walking is enough for a good sample of the scenery.

Guling

牯岭, gǔlǐng

Some 30km uphill from the lowlands on a sharply twisting road, **GULING** township comprises a handful of quaintly cobbled streets, European stone villas and bungalows in Lushan's northeastern corner. There are some sights here, though these are generally only of interest to those making revolutionary pilgrimages: a bigger attraction for most foreign visitors is the combination of stunning scenery and cool mountain air.

Some revolutionary sights

All daily 8am–6pm

The **Meilu Villa** (美庐别墅, měilú biéshù; ¥25 with Zhou Enlai's Residence) is a former home of both Chiang Kai-shek (it's named after his wife, Song Meiling) and Mao Zedong. Not far away are **Zhou Enlai's Residence** (周恩来故居, zhōuēnlái gùjū) and the **People's Hall** (人民剧院, rénmín jùyuàn; ¥50), venue of many a historic meeting – including one in 1959 when Marshal Peng Dehui openly criticized the Great Leap Forward, and was subsequently denounced as a "Rightist" by Mao, triggering the Cultural Revolution.

Into the hills

Covering some 500 square kilometres, Lushan's highlands form an elliptical platform tilted over to the southwest, comprising a central region of lakes surrounded by pine-clad hills, with superb rocks, waterfalls and views along the vertical edges of the plateau. **Hiking** is undoubtedly one of the area's greatest pleasures, and there are a number of trails laid out within the park – maps of varying detail are widely available. Although it can be tempting to try to walk everywhere, some of the paths lie quite a distance from Guling and it's well worth taking advantage of park transport to save your energy for the trails proper.

The Floral Path

For an easy walk out from town (3hr round-trip), follow the road downhill to the southwest from Guling Lu and the Jiexin Garden to the far end of **Ruqin Lake** (如琴湖, rúqín hú), where you pick up the Floral Path. This affords impressive views of the Jinxui Valley as it winds along Lushan's western cliff edge past **The Immortal's Cave** (仙人洞, xiānrén dòng), once inhabited by an ephemeral Taoist monk and still an active shrine, complete with a slowly dripping spring.

Southern Lushan

The most spectacular scenery can be found on Lushan's **southern fringes**. Proper exploration requires a full day's hike, and this is one even hardened walkers should hop on a bus for. **Lulin Hu** (芦林湖, lúlín hú) is a nice lakeside area with the attractive Dragon Pools and elderly Three Treasure trees over to the west. Due east of here – about 5km by road but less along walking tracks – is one of China's few subalpine **botanical gardens** (植物园, zhíwù yuán), the finest spot in Lushan to watch the sunrise, though the peaks are famously often obscured by mist and clear days are a rarity; even the local brew is suitably known as "Cloud Fog Tea".

ARRIVAL AND DEPARTURE   LUSHAN

Lushan is most easily reached direct from Nanchang or via Jiujiang (九江, jiǔjiāng) a Yangzi port near the foot of the mountain, where the closest airport, train and long-distance bus stations are located.

BY PLANE

Jiujiang airport lies 40km south of the city. A taxi from the airport to Lushan costs ¥100–150; or you can take one of the regular buses to Jiujiang bus station, and then transfer to a Lushan service.

Destinations Beijing (1 daily; 2hr 15min); Guangzhou (1 daily; 1hr 30min).

BY TRAIN

Jiujiang train station is 3km southeast of the city centre – catch bus #1 to the bus station for services to Lushan.

Destinations Ganzhou (22 daily; 6–9hr); Hefei (7 daily; 4hr 30min–7hr); Nanchang (50 daily; 1–2hr); Shanghai (3 daily; 12–15hr).

BY BUS

Lushan is served by few direct long-distance services, so go first to Jiujiang for Wuhan and points east, and Nanchang for southern or westerly destinations.

Lushan bus station Buses from Nanchang stop on He Dong Lu, while minibuses from Jiujiang (¥15) might drop passengers anywhere.

Jiujiang bus station Jiujiang's long-distance bus station is on Xunyang Lu, from where there are regular buses to Lushan until 5pm, earlier in winter.

Destinations from Lushan Jiujiang (1hr); Nanchang (2hr). Destinations from Jiujiang Changsha (8hr); Hefei (5hr); Wuhan (4hr); Yichang (8–10hr).

GETTING AROUND

It's easy to make short excursions around Lushan on foot, but to reach further-flung destinations it's worth taking the odd cable car or bus.

By bus A bus network extends throughout the scenic area and week-long bus passes are available for ¥80.
By cable car Numerous cable cars and ropeways offer

easy access to some of Lushan's most scenic spots including: Three Cascades (¥80 return); Hanpo Pass (¥50 return); and Xiufeng Peak (¥80 return).

ACCOMMODATION AND EATING

Summers are very busy – arrive early on in the day to ensure a room – and expensive, with hotel-owners raising their rates and refusing to bargain. Rates tumble (from the summer prices listed below) during the winter months, when it gets cold enough to snow, so check the availability of heating and hot water. There are plenty of restaurants in Guling, mostly good value, and some post their menus and prices outside. For local flavours – mountain fungus and fish – try the stalls and open restaurants around the market.

Guling Dajiudian 牯岭大酒店, gǔlǐng dàjiǔdiàn. 7 He Xi Lu ☎0792 8282435. Handy for the buses, this remodelled three-star has comfortable rooms, a swimming pool and a gym, plus friendly staff. ¥360

Lushan Binguan 庐山宾馆, lúshān bīnguǎn. 70 He Xi Lu ☎0792 8282060. This is a heavy stone mansion set among parkland on the edge of the woods, with pleasant, comfortable rooms, good-value suites and a fine restaurant. ¥400

Lushan Dasha 庐山大厦, lúshān dàshà. 506 He Xi Lu ☎0792 8282178. A regimental exterior betrays this hotel as the former Guomindang Officers' Training Centre; rooms are fittingly well furnished and comfortable. ¥320

Lushan International Youth Hostel 庐山国际青年旅舍, lúshān guójì qīngnián lǚshè. 1 Hubei Lu ☎0792 8288989, ⊛hihostels.com. Set below Five Old Man Peak, Lushan's affiliated YH offers cheap comfortable accommodation nestled into the pine forest. The hostel has doubles, twins and dorm beds and offers free wi-fi, and friendly travel advice. Dorms ¥35, doubles ¥120

DIRECTORY

Bank and exchange The Bank of China on Hemian Jie has an ATM.

Internet There are a couple of internet cafés on Guling Jie.

Mail The post office (9am–5pm) is on Guling Jie.

Shopping Stores selling maps, raincoats and provisions can be found on Guling Jie.

Jingdezhen

景德镇, jīngdézhèn

Across Poyang Hu from Nanchang and not far from the border with Anhui province, **JINGDEZHEN** has been producing **ceramics** for at least two thousand years. Lying in a river valley not only rich in clay but also the vital feldspar needed to make porcelain, the city's defining moment came in the fourteenth century: China's capital was at Nanjing, and Jingdezhen was considered conveniently close to produce porcelain for the Ming court. An imperial kiln was built in 1369 and its wares became so highly regarded – "as white as jade, as thin as paper, as bright as a mirror, as tuneful as a bell" – that Jingdezhen retained official favour even after the Ming court moved to Beijing fifty years later.

Today, in spite of attempts to smarten up the place with ceramic lampposts and public bins, Jingdezhen remains a scruffy, heavily polluted city, mostly as a result of the scores of smoky kilns that still employ some fifty thousand people. Nonetheless, Jingdezhen is worth a day-trip to visit the expansive Museum of Ceramic History, and maybe even pick up some pottery.

KAOLIN AND SHIPWRECKS

The popularity of Jingdezhen pottery brought revenues and expertise which provided a platform for innovation. Workshops experimented with new glazes and a classic range of decorative styles emerged: *qinghua*, blue and white; *jihong*, rainbow; *doucai*, a blue-and-white overglaze; and *fencai*, multicoloured famille rose. The first examples reached Europe in the seventeenth century and became so popular that the English word for China clay – *kaolin* – derives from its source nearby at Gaoling. Factories began to specialize in **export ware** designed for Europe and Chinese colonies throughout Southeast Asia, which reached the outside world via the booming Canton markets: the famous **Nanking Cargo**, comprising 150,000 pieces salvaged from the 1752 wreck of the Dutch vessel *Geldermalsen* and auctioned for US$15 million in 1986, was one such shipment. Foreign sales petered out after European production technologies improved at the end of the eighteenth century, but Jingdezhen survived by sacrificing innovation for cheaper manufacturing processes, and more recently has reinvented itself as a centre of ceramic study and research.

The markets

There are plenty of shops aimed at tourists, but it's more fun to head to the **markets**. On Jiefang Lu, south of the central square, the pavements are clogged with stacks of everything that has ever been made in porcelain: metre-high vases, life-sized dogs, Western- and Chinese-style crockery, antique reproductions including yellow- and green-glazed Tang camels, ugly statuettes and simple porcelain pandas. Haggling can be fun, but it's just as entertaining to watch other people and wonder how they are going to get their new acquisitions home – and where on earth they'll put them once they do.

Museum of Ceramic History

陶瓷历史博物馆, táocí lìshǐ bówùguǎn • out of town on the west side of the river • Daily 8am–5pm • ¥95 • English-speaking guides ¥100 • bus #1, #16 or #17 to Cidu Dadao, then cross the road and head under the ornamental arch

To experience the manufacturing side of things, either join a CITS factory tour or visit the **Museum of Ceramic History**. From the main road, a fifteen-minute forested walk leads to a surprising collection of antique buildings divided into two sections. A Ming mansion houses the museum itself, and its ornate crossbeams, walled gardens and gilt eave screens are a great backdrop to the ceramics display which covers everything from 1000-year-old kiln fragments through to the Ming's classic simplicity and overwrought, multicoloured extravagances of the late nineteenth century. The museum also puts on hourly musical performances in its Waterside Pavilion, with all of the performers playing ceramic instruments.

Ancient Porcelain Workshop

Next door to the museum building, another walled garden conceals the **Ancient Porcelain Workshop**, complete with a Confucian temple and working pottery, where the entire process of throwing, moulding and glazing takes place. Out back is a rickety two-storey kiln, packed with all sizes of unglazed yellow **saggar**, pottery sleeves commonly seen outside local field kilns – these shield each piece of porcelain from damage in case one explodes during the firing process.

ARRIVAL AND DEPARTURE   JINGDEZHEN

By train Jingdezhen's train station is 1.5km southeast of the town centre on Tongzhan Lu and the #28 bus route. Buying tickets is simple enough at the station, or there's a booking office (8am–6pm; ☎0798 8522756) next to the *Jinjiang Inn* on Zhushan Lu.
Destinations Hefei (2 daily; 11hr); Nanchang (3 daily; 5hr); Shanghai (1 daily; 17hr); Tunxi (10 daily; 2hr 30min–4hr 30min).

By bus The long-distance bus station is 3km west across the river – take bus #28 into town.
Destinations Changsha (8hr); Ganzhou (9hr); Hangzhou (6hr); Jiujiang (2hr); Nanchang (3hr); Shanghai (9hr); Tunxi (3hr 30min); Wuhan (5hr); Yingtan (3hr).

GETTING AROUND

By bus Jingdezhen has a basic bus network with regular and a/c services costing ¥1–2.

By taxi Many taxi drivers refuse to use their meters, and are eager to show you the long way round, but you should be able to negotiate a fare of ¥10 for anywhere in town.

By motorbike taxi At ¥5 for anywhere in town, motorbike taxis are the quickest and cheapest – if not the safest – way to get around for solo travellers.

INFORMATION

Travel agents For factory tours or ticket booking there's a CITS at 1 Zhushan Xi Lu (Mon–Sat 9am–5.30pm; ☎0798 8515111).

ACCOMMODATION AND EATING

It's just as well that many visitors treat Jingdezhen as a day-trip, as accommodation prospects are mediocre. Food stalls offering hotpots and stir-fries can be found east of Guangchang along Tongzhan Lu, while Western fast-food choices can be found near the bridge on Zhushan Lu. If you're looking to pass the time before a train journey there are also a few Western-style coffee shops on Zhejiang Lu.

Bandao International Hotel 半岛国际酒店, bàndǎo guójì jiǔdiàn. 121 Tongzhan Lu ☎0798 8533333. By far the smartest option near the train station is clean and modern, although rooms are bare and a little small for the price. Generous Chinese breakfast included. ¥238

Jinsheng Dajiudian 金盛大酒店, jīnshèng dàjiǔdiàn. North side of Zhushan Zhong Lu, west of the square ☎0798 8207818. Welcoming, good-value hotel in the heart of town with surprisingly chirpy en-suite rooms and free wi-fi. Try to get one of the quieter rooms at the back. ¥138

DIRECTORY

Bank The main Bank of China is opposite the entrance to the Museum of Ceramic History on Cidu Dadao, but there's also a branch of Zhushan Lu.

Internet There's a small internet bar (¥3/hr) on Ma'anshan Lu near the junction with Tongzhan Lu

Mail The main post office is west of the river on Zhushan Lu.

Jinggang Shan

井岗山, jīnggāng shān • ¥260, tickets valid three days and include admission to all sights • park buses ¥70

When Zhou Enlai and Zhu De were driven out of Nanchang after their abortive uprising, they fled to the **Jinggang Shan** ranges, 300km southwest along the mountainous border with Hunan. Here they met up with Mao, whose Autumn Harvest Uprising in Hunan had also failed, and the remnants of the two armies joined to form the first real PLA divisions. Their initial base was near the country town of **Ciping**, and, though they declared a Chinese Soviet Republic in 1931 at the Fujian border town of Ruijin, Ciping was where the Communists stayed until forced out by the Guomindang in 1934.

Today, Jinggang Shan is reasonably accessible thanks to new roads, though it doesn't attract huge numbers of tourists, making the picture-perfect forest scenery and meandering hiking trails an attractive proposition.

Ciping

茨坪, cípíng

Once site of the Communist guerrillas' headquarters, **CIPING** is little more than a village, the main streets forming a 2km elliptical circuit, the lower half of which is taken up with a lake surrounded by well-tended gardens. Completely destroyed by artillery bombardments during the 1930s, it was rebuilt after the Communist takeover and has recently been remodelled to take better advantage of tourism – though the austere historical monuments here can be breezed through fairly quickly, as it's the surrounding hills that best re-create a feeling of how Communist guerrillas might have lived.

Revolutionary Museum

井岗山博物馆, jīnggāngshān bówùguǎn • Daily 8am–4pm

Opposite watery Yicuihu Park on Hongjun Lu lies the almost comically overbearing **Revolutionary Museum**, built in the monumental style so beloved of totalitarian regimes. Steps lead up behind to a vast statue commemorating the Communist struggle, from where there would be a great view across the valley – if the museum were not blotting it out. Exhibitions mainly consist of maps and dioramas showing battlefields and troop movements up until 1930, after which the Communists suffered some heavy defeats. There are also busts of prominent revolutionaries, paintings of a smiling Mao preaching to his peasant armies and cases of the spears, flintlocks and mortars that initially comprised the Communist arsenal.

Former Revolutionary Headquarters

革命旧居群, gémìng jiùjūqún • Daily 8am–4pm

On the east side of Yicuihu Park, a group of mud-brick rooms forms a reconstruction

7

THE LONG MARCH

In 1927, **Chiang Kai-shek**, leader of the Nationalist Guomindang (GMD) government, began an obsessive war against the Chinese Communist Party. Driven underground, the Communists set up remote rural bases, or soviets, across central China. The main **Jiangxi soviet** in the Jinggang Mountains was led by **Mao Zedong** and **Zhu De**, the Communist Commander-in-Chief. Ignoring Japanese incursions into Manchuria, Chiang blockaded the mountains with a steadily tightening ring of bunkers and barbed wire, systematically clearing areas of guerrillas with artillery bombardments. Hemmed in and facing eventual defeat, the First Front army, comprising some eighty thousand Red soldiers, broke through the blockade in October 1934 and retreated west to team up with the Hunan soviet – marking the beginning of the **Long March**.

Covering a punishing 30km a day, the Communists moved after dark whenever possible, but still faced daily skirmishes. After incurring severe losses during a battle at the Xiang River near Guilin in Guangxi, the marchers found their progress north impeded by massive GMD forces, and were obliged to continue west to Guizhou, where they took the town of Zunyi in January 1935, and an emergency meeting of the Communist Party hierarchy was called – the **Zunyi Conference**. Mao emerged as the undisputed leader of the Party, with a mandate to "go north to fight the Japanese" by linking up with **Zhang Guotao** in Sichuan. In one of the most celebrated and heroic episodes of the march, they took the Luding Bridge across the Dadu River (see p.763), only to negotiate the Great Snowy Mountains, where hundreds died from exposure before the survivors met up on the far side with the Fourth Front army.

The meeting between these two branches of the Red Army was tense. Mao wanted to start resistance against the Japanese, but Zhang Guotao favoured founding a Communist state in Sichuan's far west. Zhang eventually capitulated, and he and Mao took control of separate columns to cross the last natural barrier they faced, the Aba grasslands in northern Sichuan. Here, while Mao was bogged down by swamps, hostile nomads and dwindling food reserves, Zhang's column suddenly retreated to Ganzi, where Zhang set up an independent government. Mao struggled through southern Gansu, finally arriving in Communist-held Yan'an, Shaanxi province, in October 1935. While the mountains here were to become a Communist stronghold, only a quarter of those who started from Jiangxi twelve months before had completed the 9500km journey.

Immediately after the Long March, Mao admitted that in terms of losses and the Red Army's failure to hold their original positions, the Nationalists had won. Yet in a more lasting sense, the march was an incredible success, uniting the Party under Mao and defining the Communists' aims, while cementing their popular image as a determined and patriotic movement. After Zunyi, Mao turned the march into a deliberate propaganda mission to spread the Communist faith among the peasantry and minority groups. As Mao said, "Without the Long March, how could the broad masses have learned so quickly about the existence of the great truth which the Red Army embodies?"

of the **Former Revolutionary Headquarters**. As the site marking where Mao and Zhu De coordinated their guerrilla activities and the start of the Long March, it is the town's biggest attraction as far as visiting cadres are concerned.

In the hills

Having waded through the terribly serious displays in town, it's nice to escape into Jinggang Shan's surprisingly wild countryside. Some of the peaks provide glorious views of the **sunrise** – or frequent mists – and there are colourful plants, natural groves of pine and bamboo, deep green temperate cloudforests, and hosts of butterflies and birds.

Wulong Tan

五龙潭, wǔlóng tán

One of the nicest areas to explore is **Wulong Tan** (Five Dragon Pools), about 8km north along the road from the Martyrs' Tomb. A footpath from the roadhead leads past some poetically pretty waterfalls dropping into the pools (of which there are actually eight) between a score of pine-covered peaks.

Wuzhi Peak

五指峰, wǔzhǐ fēng

Less than 10km south of town is Jinggang Shan itself, also known as **Wuzhi Feng**, apex of the mountains at 1586m. The more well-trodden trails are obvious and well signposted in English, though they can become slippery in the wet. As the trees and waterfalls below slide in and out of the clouds, the peace and beauty make it hard to imagine it as the cradle of guerrilla warfare for the Communists back in the 1920s and 30s.

ARRIVAL AND DEPARTURE   JINGGANG SHAN

There's a bus station at Ciping, but the nearest airport and train station are at newly built Jinggang Shan town (井岗山市, jīnggǎng shān shì), which lies a good forty minutes by bus (¥10) or taxi (¥60–70) from Ciping.

By plane Jinggang Shan airport (井岗山机场, jīnggǎng shān jīchǎng) is served by an expensive daily flight from Beijing and another from Guangzhou. There is no direct transport to Ciping so you'll need to transfer to Jinggang Shan city bus station and then change to a Ciping service.

Destinations Beijing (1 daily; 2hr 30min); Guangzhou (1 daily; 1hr).

By train Jinggang Shan's train station is on the Nanchang–Shenzhen line. In Ciping there's a booking office on Hongjun Lu, just north of the *Green Lake Hotel*.

Destinations Ganzhou (1 daily; 4hr); Nanchang (3 daily; 4hr); Shenzhen (1 daily; 11hr).

By bus Ciping's bus station is on the northeastern side of the village's circuit, served by buses from Nanchang and elsewhere across the region. Heading south you'll need to change at Ganzhou (赣州, gànzhōu), down towards the Guangdong border.

Destinations Ganzhou (5hr); Hengyang (8hr); Nanchang (8hr).

ACCOMMODATION

As well as the following there is a host of budget and mid-range places to stay near the bus station.

Cuihu Hotel 翠湖宾馆, cuìhú bīnguǎn. 2 Hongjun Nan Lu ☎ 0796 6557666. One of Ciping's more affordable hotels, though with a rather institutional atmosphere, the *Cuihu* has standard-issue Chinese rooms complete with hard beds and dated furnishings. **¥200**

Jinggang Shan Binguan 井岗山宾馆, jīnggǎngshān bīnguǎn. 16 Hongjun Bei Lu ☎ 0796 6552272. Housed in a clearly Soviet-inspired building, this was a former favourite with party cadres. Despite a recent makeover, the rooms are plain and the prices a little too high. **¥328**

Nanhu Binguan 南湖宾馆, nánhú bīnguǎn. 19 Hongjun Nan Lu ☎ 0796 6556666. Palatial, marble-clad lobby and surprisingly spacious rooms in this conference-sized effort. There's a wood-decked terrace too, with splendid mountain views, and – of all things – a pool table. **¥400**

DIRECTORY

Bank There's a Bank of China (Mon–Fri 9am–5pm) with ATM just downhill from the Former Revolutionary Headquarters.

Fujian, Guangdong and Hainan Island

HAKKA ROUNDHOUSE, YONGDING

Fujian, Guangdong and Hainan Island

There's something very self-contained about the provinces of Fujian, Guangdong and Hainan Island, which occupy 1200km or so of China's convoluted southern seaboard. Though occasionally taking centre stage in the country's history, the provinces share a sense of being generally isolated from mainstream events by the mountain ranges surrounding Fujian and Guangdong, physically cutting them off from the rest of the empire. Forced to look seawards, the coastal regions have a long history of contact with the outside world: this is where Islam entered China, and porcelain and tea left it along the Maritime Silk Road; where the mid-nineteenth-century theatricals of the Opium Wars, colonialism, the Taiping Uprising and the mass overseas exodus of southern Chinese were played out; and where today you'll find some of China's most Westernized cities. Conversely, the interior mountains enclose some of the country's wildest, most remote corners, parts of which were virtually in the Stone Age a century ago.

8

Possibly because its attractions are thinly spread, the region receives scant attention from foreign visitors, except those transiting between the mainland and Hong Kong or Macau. And it must be admitted that a superficial skim through the region – especially the enormous industrial sprawl surrounding the Guangdong capital, **Guangzhou** – can leave a gloomy impression of uncontrolled development and its attendant ills. Yet below the surface, even Guangzhou has some antique architecture and a strangely compelling, lively atmosphere, while smaller cities – including the Fujian port of **Xiamen**, and **Chaozhou** in eastern Guangdong – seem partially frozen in time, staunchly preserving their traditions in the face of the modern world. Scenically, the **Wuyi Shan** range in northeastern Fujian contains the region's lushest, most picturesque mountain forests; while way down south on **Hainan Island** lie the country's best and busiest **beaches** where you can also **surf** and **scuba dive**.

As one of the longest-developed areas of the mainland, getting around the region is seldom problematic, though **accommodation** can be expensive and suffers huge seasonal fluctuations in price. The **weather** is nicest in spring and autumn, as summer storms from June to August bring sweltering heat and humidity, thunder,

CANTONESE STIR-FRY

Highlights

❶ Wuyi Shan Dramatic gorges and great hiking trails among some of the finest scenery in southern China. **See p.460**

❷ Gulangyu Island Uniquely relaxing island sporting vehicle-free streets, European-style colonial mansions and sea views. **See p.470**

❸ Hakka mansions These circular mud-brick homes, sometimes housing upwards of four hundred people, are China's most distinctive traditional architecture. **See p.474**

❹ Cantonese food Sample China's finest cuisine, from dim sum to roast goose, in one of Guangzhou's restaurants. **See p.493**

❺ Chaozhou Old town with Ming-dynasty walls, some great street life, the famous Kaiyuan Temple – and more good food. **See p.507**

❻ Hainan Island Soak up the sun while swimming, diving or surfing at the country's best beaches. **See p.513**

HIGHLIGHTS ARE MARKED ON THE MAP ON P.456

downpours and floods. In contrast, the higher reaches of the Guangdong-Fujian border can get very cold in winter.

Fujian

福建, fújiàn

Fujian, on China's southeastern coast, is well off the beaten track for most Western travellers, which is a pity because the province possesses not only a wild mountainous interior, but also a string of old ports, including **Xiamen**, probably China's most relaxed coastal city.

Contacts between the coastal area and the outside world have been flourishing for centuries. In the Tang dynasty, the port of **Quanzhou** was considered on a par with Alexandria, and teemed with Middle Eastern traders, some of whose descendants still live in the area today. Fujian's interior, however, remains largely unvisited, with the

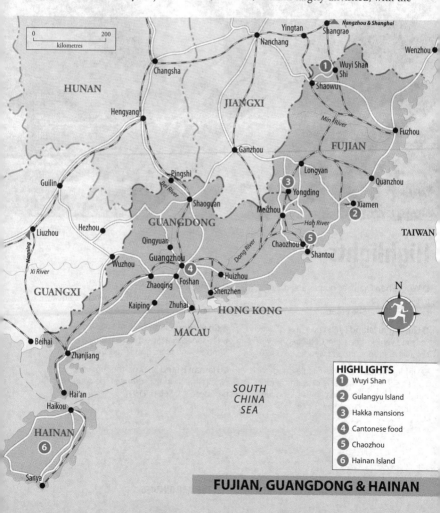

HIGHLIGHTS

1 Wuyi Shan

2 Gulangyu Island

3 Hakka mansions

4 Cantonese food

5 Chaozhou

6 Hainan Island

FUJIAN, GUANGDONG & HAINAN

exception of the scenic **Wuyi Shan** area in the northwest of the province, and the **Hakka regions** around southwesterly **Yongding**.

Fuzhou

福州, fúzhōu

Capital of Fujian province, **FUZHOU** is a modern city, with shiny skyscrapers looming over the main roads. Long an important trading centre, during the fifteenth century, Fuzhou's shipbuilders earned themselves the distinction of building the world's largest ocean-going vessel, the *Baochuan*, sailed by the famous Chinese navigator **Zheng He**, who used it to travel all around Asia and Africa. Marco Polo visited too, noting the high-profile presence of Mongol armies to suppress any potential uprisings; the city is no less well defended today, forming the heart of Fujian's military opposition to Taiwan. There's precious little to detain casual visitors, however, and Fuzhou is probably best used as a springboard for reaching the wilds of Wuyi Shan.

Wuyi Square

五一广场, wǔyī guǎngchǎng

Fuzhou is centred around **Wuyi Square**, an open expanse dominated by a gleaming-white **statue of Mao Zedong** (毛塑像, máo sùxiàng) looking south while making what appears to be an almost fascist salute and flanked by two horses so rampant that they would have made Mussolini proud. This statue commemorates the Ninth Congress of the Chinese Communist Party in 1969, an event that ratified Maoism as the "state religion" of China, and named the (subsequently disgraced) Lin Biao as official heir to Mao's throne.

Lin Zexu Memorial Hall

林则徐纪念馆, línzéxú jìniànguǎn • corner of Daoshan Lu and Nanhou Jie • Daily 8.30am–5pm • Free • buses #8 & #101 stop nearby outside the mosque on Bayiqi Bei Lu

A kilometre west from Wuyi Square is the **Lin Zexu Memorial Hall**, which comprises a quiet, attractive couple of halls and courtyards with funereal statues of animals. Lin Zexu (1785–1850) is fondly remembered as the patriotic Qing-dynasty official who fought against the importation of opium by foreigners – even writing a letter to Queen Victoria on the subject. His destruction of thousands of chests of the drug in 1840 sparked the first Opium War and, rather unfairly, he was exiled to Xinjiang.

Fuzhou Provincial Museum

福建省博物馆, fújiànshěng bówùguǎn • inside Xihu Park • Tues–Sun 9am–5pm • Free • ☏ 0591 83757627

Among the modern but unfrequented **Fuzhou Provincial Museum**'s thousands of pieces of porcelain and examples of primitive iron tools is a 3500-year-old coffin-boat removed from a Wuyi Shan cave, but the real highlight for children young and old has to be the dinosaur collection in the Natural History building. Regular art exhibitions are also hosted in the museum's ground-floor gallery.

Gu Shan

鼓山, gǔshān • Daily 8am–4pm • ¥40 • Gu Shan special line bus from Wuyi Square, ¥10 • cable car ¥80

Fuzhou's most-touted tourist attraction is **Gu Shan**, about 9km east of the city, offering woodland walks as well as scattered sights. The best of these is the heavily restored **Yongquan Temple** (永泉寺, yǒngquán sì), which boasts two 7m-high pottery pagodas covered with over a thousand images of the Buddha, and a collection of classics written by monks in their own blood. It also has a great vegetarian restaurant, though the whole complex gets phenomenally crowded at weekends. One way to escape the crowds is to climb the 2500 stone steps behind the temple to Gu Shan's wooded **summit** – allow at least an hour including rest-stops at the seven pavilions along the way. Alternatively, you could take the cable car up in ten minutes, or a taxi along the 8km-long, winding road.

8

ARRIVAL AND DEPARTURE

BY PLANE

Buy tickets at the airlines office, 183 Wuyi Lu (daily 8am–8pm; ☎0591 968899 or 83345988, ⓦwww.fzcaac .com).

Fuzhou Changle International Airport (福州长乐 国际机场, *fúzhōu chánglè guójì jīchǎng*) is 50km southeast of the city, from where airport buses run to either the *Apollo Hotel*, north of the South Bus Station on Wuyi

Zhong Lu (daily 5.30am–8.30pm; every 25min; ¥20), or the *Minjiang Hotel* (daily 5.50am–4.50pm; hourly; ¥20); both take around an hour. A taxi to the centre takes slightly less time, costs around ¥100 with hard bargaining, or ¥25 per person sharing – touts will find you.

Destinations Beijing (6 daily; 2hr 25min); Guangzhou (1 daily; 1hr 30min); Haikou (6 weekly; 2hr); Hong Kong (3 daily; 1hr 30min); Macau (1 daily; 1hr 35min); Shanghai

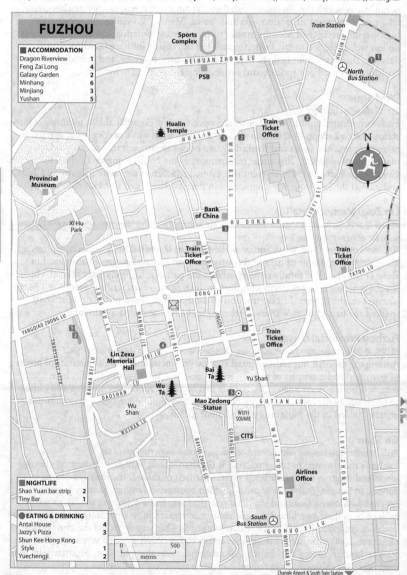

FUZHOU

◼ ACCOMMODATION	
Dragon Riverview	1
Feng Zai Long	4
Galaxy Garden	2
Minhang	6
Minjiang	3
Yushan	5

◼ NIGHTLIFE	
Shao Yuan bar strip	2
Tiny Bar	1

● EATING & DRINKING	
Antai House	4
Jazzy's Pizza	3
Shun Kee Hong Kong Style	1
Yuechengji	2

Sports Complex

BEIHUAN ZHONG LU

PSB

Train Station

HUALIN LU

North Bus Station

Hualin Temple

HUALIN LU

Train Ticket Office

Provincial Museum

Xi Hu Park

WUYI BEI LU

LIUYI BEI LU

Bank of China

HU DONG LU

Train Ticket Office

Train Ticket Office

TATOU LU

LINGDA LU

DONG JIE

YANGQIAO ZHONG LU

TONG HU LU

NANHOU JIE

BAYIQI BEI LU

JINGDA LU

WUYI BEI LU

Train Ticket Office

SHUIBU XI LU

BAIMA BEI LU

JIBI LU

Lin Zexu Memorial Hall

LU

Bai Ta

Yu Shan

DAOSHAN

Wu Ta

Wu Shan

Mao Zedong Statue

WUYI SQUARE

GUTIAN LU

WUSHAN LU

BAYIQI ZHONG LU

GUANGDA LU

CITS

WUYI ZHONG LU

LIUYI ZHONG LU

Go Shan

Airlines Office

WUYI ZHONG LU

South Bus Station

GUOHUO XI LU

WUYI NAN LU

0   500

metres

Changle Airport & South Train Station ▽

N

8

(7 daily; 1hr 10min); Shenzhen (2 daily; 1hr 50min); Wuyi Shan (5 weekly; 30min).

BY TRAIN

Fuzhou is Fujian's rail hub, and the terminus for lines northwest to Wuyi Shan and the rest of China; be aware that most trains to Guangdong province also travel this way and so take much longer than you'd expect, unless you get a high-speed one. Buy tickets at the stations, or in-town ticket offices (daily 8am–9pm) at 203-1 Hualin Lu, 77 Wuyi Bei Lu; 62 Tatou Lu (just off Liuyi Bei Lu), and Jingda Lu (just off Hu Dong Lu). Reserve sleeper berths at least a day in advance.

Fuzhou train station (福州火车站, fúzhōu huǒchē zhàn) is in the far northeast of town, from where bus #51 runs straight down Wusi and Wuyi roads to the South Bus Station and the Min River, while buses #K2 and #2 cover the same places but along a circuitous route. Allow plenty of time to get to the station as gates close 10min before departure.

Fuzhou South train station (福州南火车站, fúzhōu nán huǒchē zhàn) is inconveniently located about 12km south from the centre, with the #K2 bus connecting it with Fuzhou train station; a taxi costs about

¥50. Of most use for the high-speed service to Shanghai.
Destinations Beijing (3 daily; 15hr 30min–36hr); Chongqing (2 daily; 36hr), Longyan (11 daily; 3–10hr); Nanchang (9 daily; 10hr 15min–12hr 32min); Shanghai (18 daily; 6hr 27min–16hr 28min); Shenzhen (1 daily; 18hr 35min); Wuyi Shan (14 daily; 4hr 29min–6hr 43min); Yongding (1 daily; 11hr).

BY BUS

Both north and south bus stations handle traffic to just about everywhere outside of the city including overnight sleeper-buses to Hong Kong, Shenzhen and Guangzhou.

North station (北站, běizhàn), a few minutes' walk south of the train station; bus #51 runs straight down Wusi and Wuyi roads to the South Bus Station and the Min River, while buses #K2 and #2 do the same run but round the houses. Note that Longyan and Nanchang buses leave only from here.

South station (南站, nánzhàn) at the junction of Guohuo Lu and Wuyi Lu; overnight sleeper buses to Hong Kong run from here.

Destinations Guangzhou (12hr); Hong Kong (14hr); Longyan (7hr); Nanchang (9hr); Quanzhou (2hr 30min); Shenzhen (12hr); Wuyi Shan (7hr); Xiamen (4hr).

INFORMATION

Travel agencies CITS, 73 Guangda Lu just south of Wuyi Square (Mon–Sat 8.30am–5.30pm; ☎0591 88371588),

are useful for buying plane tickets and booking Wuyi Shan tours.

ACCOMMODATION

Most of Fuzhou's accommodation is upmarket, though touts for budget options approach arrivals at the train and North bus stations – despite many of these places not being able to take foreigners.

Dragon Riverview 龙城豪景, lóngchéng háojǐng. Apt 1118, Kowloon City Plaza, Wusi Lu ☎0591 87598335. Great budget choice and much nicer than all the other cheapies around the train station, this place rents clean, airy and largish mini-apartments with balconies. A little tricky to find, it's in an apartment building down the end of a small street of restaurants, immediately north of the North bus station – the entrance is left and left again, just past the underground garage. No English spoken. **¥118**

Feng Zai Long 丰灾隆酒店, fēngzāilóng jiǔdiàn. 96 Wuyi Lu ☎0591 87760123. One of the less expensive of the hotels near the centre, this place has pretty good rooms with clean bathrooms, soft beds and computers, though cheapest rooms can be a little dark. The red neon sign reading "Ba Emperor Li Island Home That Will Let Beauty" is pretty unmistakable. **¥199**

Galaxy Garden 银河花园大饭店, yínhéhuāyuán dàfàndiàn. 243 Wusi Lu, cnr with Hualin Lu ☎0591 87831888, ✉galaxy88@126.com. Close to the train and North bus stations, this business-oriented hotel has large

rooms, crisp bedding, smart furnishings and attentive, helpful staff, although their English is limited. Usually charges under half the advertised rate. **¥800**

Minhang 民航大厦, mínháng dàshà. Next to airlines office, 185 Wuyi Zhong Lu ☎0591 83343988. Also known as the *Civil Aviation Hotel*, this has spacious, comfortable and clean rooms which come with very thick curtains to guarantee a good night's sleep. Fair value for money. **¥380**

Minjiang 闽江饭店, mǐnjiāng fàndiàn. 130 Wusi Lu ☎0591 87557895, ☻mjht.com.cn. High-rise hotel with smart, luxurious rooms, decorated in soft colours, which can be a bargain as they usually discount to a third of the stated price. Served by the airport bus. **¥1184**

Yushan 于山宾馆, yúshān bīnguǎn. 10 Yushan Lu, off Gutian Lu ☎0591 83351668. A fine location just below Yu Shan and next to an old pagoda, with large, wooden-floored rooms in a very nice traditional-style buiding. Rooms are comfortable enough, if a little spartan, though the staff are helpful. **¥548**

8

EATING AND DRINKING

The highest concentration of places to eat is along downtown Dong Jie, although the junction of Gutian Lu and Baiqi Lu hosts several swanky Chinese and foreign restaurants – you're looking at over ¥100 a head, however. For snacks, hole-in-the-wall operations surround transit points, while street vendors peddle small, bagel-like "cut buns" (刮包, guābāo), stuffed with vegetables or a slice of spiced, steamed pork.

Antai House 安泰楼酒家, āntàilóu jiǔjiā. 39 Jibi Lu ☎0591 87550890. A Fuzhou institution, this three-floor place serves up relatively inexpensive local Min cuisine, much of it flavoured with taro. The soups are very good, and their seafood dishes are recommended. Under ¥50 per person. Daily 11.30am–10pm.

Jazzy's Pizza 圣杰士比萨餐厅, shèngjiéshì bǐsà cāntīng. 258 Wusi Lu, by the junction with Haulin Lu ☎0591 87855877. Chinese reboot of *Pizza Hut*, with crispy American-style pizzas, as well as passable pastas, salads and steak. Pizzas start at ¥49, and one person can probably fill up on under ¥100 whatever they order. Mon–Fri 11am–10pm, Sat & Sun 10.30am–10.30pm.

Shun Kee Hong Kong Style 顺记港式烧腊套餐, shùnjì gǎngshì shāolà tàocān. Wusi Lu ☎0591 87842737. Last and cleanest in a line of cheap canteens on the small street immediately north of the North Bus Station, serving filling plates of surprisingly good Cantonese food for under ¥20. Daily 9.50am–8.20pm.

Yuechengji 岳成纪, yuèchéngjì. 2F, 259 Hualin Lu ☎0591 63331111, ⓦyuechengji.com. For a city that is sweltering for most of the year, spicy Sichuan-style hotpot is inordinately popular – this busy branch of a chain is not far from the North bus station, where a pot for 2–3 people will set you back under ¥100. Daily 9am–midnight.

NIGHTLIFE

Currently, the most popular after-dark area with foreigners is the new Shao Yuan bar strip (芍园一号, sháoyuán yīhào), located on the river between Baima Bei Lu and Shaoyuanyi 47th. By law, all nightlife in Fuzhou must cease at 2am – the kind of place that opens later is usually less-than-reputable.

Tiny Bar 小酒吧, xiǎo jiǔbā. Shao Yuan bar strip, on right-hand side of entrance (no phone). This intimate bar is partly (and convivially) Irish-owned and very popular with expats and Chinese alike. Serves imported beers and very nice cocktails, though the quality of the drinks comes with a cost. Also shows foreign sports on TV. Daily 3pm–2am.

DIRECTORY

Banks and exchange There is a huge Bank of China on Wusi Lu with exchange facilities and ATMs.
Post office Fuzhou's main post office is at the southeastern intersection of Dong Jie and Bayiqi Bei Lu.

Taxis Fares start at ¥8, plus a fuel surcharge of ¥2. CCTV cameras discourage drivers from picking up in many areas, so if you can't flag one down, try to find one of the blue taxi-signs to stand next to.

Wuyi Shan

武夷山风景区, wǔyíshān fēngjǐng qū • tickets for individual sights ¥60–180 • two-day pass for all sights, including minibus transfers, ¥235; buy at the office next to the bridge in Dujia Qu, or the trailhead for the Thirty-Six Peaks

Away in Fujian's northeast, 370km from Fuzhou and close to the Jiangxi border, the

RAFTING THE JIUQU

The traditional way to appreciate Wuyi Shan is to take a two-hour **bamboo-raft trip** along the Jiuqu River (¥100). At busy times the river becomes a noisy bamboo conveyor belt, but there's stupendous gorge scenery all the way from the first crook in the meandering river right up to the ninth, and it's well worth the ticket. Watch out for the odd, boat-shaped **coffins** in caves above the fourth crook, which are said to be four thousand years old.

During the busy summer months or at weekends or holidays, it's essential to book tickets in advance at the tourist ticket office in Wuyi Shan. Rafts leave year-round (daily 6.40am–4.30pm) from the small village of **Xingcun**, accessible on public bus #6 from Wuyishan Shi and Wuyigong (daily 8am–9pm; every 15min; ¥2.5). The wharves themselves are in the hamlet of Jiuquxi (九曲溪, jiǔqū xī), down a side lane just off the main road 1km before town, so tell the bus driver when you get on and it'll save you the trek from the station.

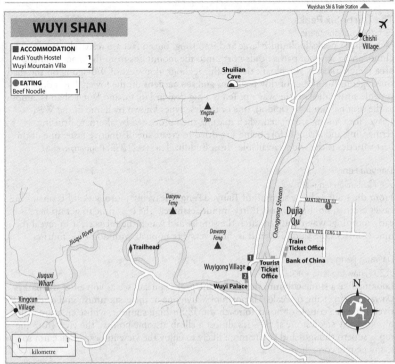

sixty-square-kilometre **Wuyi Shan Scenic Area** contains some of the most impressive scenery in southern China. It's about the only part of inland Fujian regularly visted by tourists, and consists of two principal parts: the **Jiuqu River**, which meanders at the feet of the mountains; and the **Thirty-Six Peaks**, which rise up from the river, mostly to its north. The river runs its crooked course for some 8km eastwards between **Xingcun village** (腥村, xīng cūn), and the main village in the area, **Wuyigong**. The scenery is classic Chinese scroll-painting material and the park, dotted with small, attractive villages, can be a tremendous place to relax for a few days, offering clean mountain air and leisurely walks through a landscape of lush green vegetation, deep red sandstone mountains, soaring cliff faces, rock pools, waterfalls and caves. Despite the remoteness, Wuyi is surprisingly full of tourists – especially Taiwanese – in high summer, so a visit off-season might be preferable, when you'll also see the mountaintops cloaked with snow.

Dujia Qu and Wuyigong

Around 10km south of the main long-distance arrival point, Wuyishan Shi, **DUJIA QU** (度假区, dùjià qū) sits on the east bank of the Chongyang Stream, providing a functional blob of amenities and services. It's nicer to push on over the river for 1km to **WUYIGONG** (武夷宫, wǔyí gōng), set in the cleft between the confluence of the Jiuqu and Chongyang, where there are further facilities and the **Wuyi Palace**, a Song-dynasty complex (currently under renovation) after which the village is named. Just under the bridge south of here is an area popular in the late afternoon with swimmers: the water is usually pretty sedate and Chinese "no swimming" signs are just as effective, it seems, as their "no smoking" signs.

The Thirty-Six Peaks

三十六峰, sānshíliùfēng

Wuyi Shan's **peaks** look quite large and imposing, but in fact are relatively easy to climb, and a series of paths heads north into the mountains from the **main trailhead area** (where there is also a park ticket office), about 4km west of Wuyigong on the road to Xingcun. A number of tiny pavilions and **tea gardens** on the lower slopes can provide sustenance on the way up. **Tea** is a big deal in Fujian, and Wuyi Shan is famous as the original home of **Oolong**, one of the few types known by name in the West. Leaves for Oolong are picked when mature, then processed by alternate bruising, fermenting and airing before being fire-dried to create the distinctive taste; one of the best varieties is the widely available "Iron Buddha Tea" (铁观音茶, tiěguānyīn chá).

Tianyou Feng

天游峰, tiānyóu fēng • ¥60

From the trailhead, the summit of **Tianyou Feng** (Heavenly Journey Peak) is one of the easier ascents, no more than a thirty-minute clamber. The best time to get up here is early morning, when you can catch the sunrise and watch the mists clear to reveal the nine crooks in the Jiuqu River. It is, however, very popular with domestic tourists.

Dawang Feng

大王峰, dàwáng fēng • ¥60

Looking like a stone column, the first of the peaks you can see as you enter the park, **Dawang Feng** (King of Peaks), is north of Wuyigong at the easternmost end of the river. It takes a couple of hours to reach the 580m-high summit, whose cliffs are scaled by extremely steep stone steps – it's almost a climb at some points. The view from the top is superb though, and you're more likely to enjoy the view in peace, since not so many people come here.

Shuilian Cave

水帘洞, shuǐlián dòng • minibus from the Tianyou Feng area or Wuyigong • ¥80

Ensure you set aside time for **Shuilian Cave**, about 6km north of the river; you can walk along easy trails, cycle or take a minibus. The cave – more of an overhang, really – is at the bottom of a red sandstone cliff inscribed with Chinese characters, down which a large waterfall cascades in the summer months (at other times it's more of a trickle). Behind the water curtain is the wooden **Hall of the Three Sages** (三圣大厅, sānshèng dàtīng), an antique-style complex; one enterprising local has also domesticated the pigeons that live in the cliffs, and for ¥3 he'll supply you with corn and command his birds to peck it from your hands. He sells cold drinks too.

ARRIVAL AND DEPARTURE   WUYI SHAN

Most long-distance transport arrives 15km north of the park at Wuyishan Shi (武夷山市, wǔyíshān shì), the regional town.

By plane Wuyi airport (武夷山机场, wǔyíshān jīchǎng) is at the village of Chishi (赤石, chìshí), a few kilometres to the northeast of the scenic area and to the south of Wuyishan Shi. Frequent minibuses connect it with Dujia Qu and Wuyishan Shi. There's a Xiamen Airlines office (daily 9am–5.30pm; ☏ 0599 5252777) next to the Bank of China on Dawangfeng Lu.
Destinations Beijing (6 weekly; 2hr 15min); Guangzhou (1 daily; 1hr 20min); Shanghai (1 daily; 1hr); Xiamen (6 daily; 46min); X'ian (1 daily; 2hr).
By train Wuyishan train station (武夷山火车站, wǔyíshān huǒchē zhàn) is on the eastern side of Wuyishan Shi, and connected by frequent minibuses with Dujia Qu, the main hotel area, from where a 5min rickshaw journey will see you across the river to the better accommodation at Wuyigong. A taxi from the train station to Wuyigong will cost around ¥50. There are plenty of trains to Fuzhou, but departing northwards, aim first for the rail junction town of Shangrao (上饶, shàngráo), on the Shanghai and Hangzhou line. There's a railway booking office (8.30am–5.30pm) next to the Bank of China on Dawangfeng Lu.

Destinations Beijing (1 daily; 15hr); Fuzhou (13 daily; 4hr 28min–7hr); Shanghai (3 daily; 10hr); Shangrao (3 daily; 3hr); Xiamen (1 daily; 12hr 30min).

By bus The main bus station (武夷山汽车站, wǔyíshān qìchē zhàn) is in the north of Wuyishan Shi

on Wujiu Lu, connected to the scenic area by minibuses (40min).

Destinations Fuzhou (7hr); Xiamen (8hr); Shangrao (3hr).

By tour bus Fuzhou's CTS (see p.459) runs tour buses direct to Wuyigong.

GETTING AROUND

By bus Regular bus #6 runs until early evening between the scenic area, Wuyishan Shi and Xingcun (¥2–4). Stand by the road to flag them down anywhere.

By tourist bus These buses travel around all the sights until 6pm, though you can only use them with the 2-day entrance ticket. The main terminal is at Wuyigong Palace.

By bicycle A pleasant way to get around, though you'll need to be fit for the hills. Rent bikes from *Andi Youth Hostel* (¥25 per day, plus ¥300 deposit). Beware tourist buses on the road: they are badly driven, and drivers seem tipsy by the end of the day.

ACCOMMODATION

Dujia Qu holds a plethora of identikit hotels, although, apart from the ease of access to amenities and restaurants, either Wuyigong or even Xingcun (which is far less touristy) are more mellow spots to stay. Prices at the more expensive places are generally flexible outside of summer and weekends, and hard bargaining should secure a hotel room for as little as ¥150.

Andi Youth Hostel 安邸青年旅舍, āndǐ qīngnián lǚshě. 16 Lantang Village, Wuyigong ✆0599 5231369, ✉ad513@sina.cn. Very Chinese-feeling youth hostel, with dorms and doubles in a converted house decorated with classic Chinese calligraphy and pictures. Serves good tea, basic food at mealtimes, and has a small bar. Also has wi-fi and rents bikes too, but no

English spoken. Rooms ¥138, dorm beds ¥40

Wuyi Mountain Villa 武夷山庄, wǔyíshān zhuāng. Wuyigong ✆0599 5251888. Nicest of Wuyigong's options, this is an upmarket place with comfortable rooms in a marvellous setting, resting hard under Dawang Feng and built around a Suzhou-style ornamental garden. ¥588

EATING

Foodwise, it's the local Shilin bullfrogs that make Wuyi cuisine special; along with other popular items such as bamboo shoots and fungus, they're served almost everywhere, along with pheasant, rabbit and other game such as venison and what is claimed to be bear. Most places have ingredients on show outside to make ordering as easy as pointing, but be warned that tourists are regarded as fair game for serious overcharging – always check the price of everything when ordering.

Beef Noodle 牛肉面馆, niúròu miànguǎn. Mantuoyuan Lu ✆0591 83301668. It's the red restaurant along this small road of inexpensive canteens, and there are no prizes for guessing the

house speciality. A hearty bowl of outstanding noodles in soup will set you back ¥15–20, which is ¥5 more than the local competition, but worth it. Daily 8am–8.30pm.

DIRECTORY

Banks and exchange The main Bank of China (Mon–Fri 8.30am–5.30pm) with an ATM is on Dawangfeng Lu, in

Dujia Qu, just off the main crossroads.

Quanzhou

泉州, quánzhōu

QUANZHOU, a small, prosperous and sympathetically preserved town 150km southwest of Fuzhou on the coastal highway to Xiamen, was for centuries a great port. Sitting astride trade routes that reached southeast to Indonesian Maluku, and west to Africa and Europe, the city became uniquely cosmopolitan, with tens of thousands of Arabs and Persians settling here, some of them to make colossal fortunes – the Arabs of Quanzhou are also believed responsible for introducing to the West the Chinese inventions of the compass, gunpowder and printing.

The Song dynasty saw the peak of Quanzhou's fortunes, when the old Silk Road through northwestern China into Central Asia was falling prey to banditry and war,

deflecting trade seawards along the **Maritime Silk Road**. Marco Polo visited Quanzhou around this time; the Italian **Andrew Perugia**, Quanzhou's third Catholic bishop, died here in 1332, having supervised the building of a cathedral; and fourteen years later the great Moroccan traveller **Ibn Battuta** saw the port bustling with large junks. But by the Qing era, the city was suffering from overcrowding and a decaying harbour, and an enormous exodus began, with people seeking new homes across Southeast Asia.

Guandi Miao

关帝庙, guāndì miào • junction of Tumen Jie and Mingquan Lu • Daily 6am–6pm • Free

Guandi Miao, a splendid and busy temple, is dedicated to the Three Kingdoms' hero turned god of war and healing, Guan Yu (see p.393). The temple's roofline is typically florid and curly, and the atmospheric interior – guarded by life-sized statues of soldiers on horseback – features low-ceilinged halls, smoke-grimed statues and wall engravings showing scenes from Guan Yu's life.

Qingjing Mosque

清净寺, qīngjìng sì • Tumen Lu • Daily 8am–5.30pm • ¥3 • ☏ 0595 22982505

The granite **Qingjing Mosque** provides proof of just how established the Arabs became in medieval Quanzhou. Founded by Arab settlers in 1009, Qingjing ranks as one of the oldest mosques in China and is highly unusual in being Middle Eastern in design, though only parts of the original buildings survive. The gate tower is said to be an exact copy of a Damascus original, its leaf-shaped archway embellished with Arabic calligraphy and designs, while parts of the walls and supporting pillars of the original prayer hall stand alongside. A side room has a detailed account of the Arab presence in

Quanzhou; the small, tiled building next door is the modern prayer hall. Behind the mosque, the "**Houcheng Tourism and Culture Street**" (后成街, hòuchéng jīe) is not as hokey as it sounds, containing some original buildings, most of which now hold souvenir shops and teahouses.

Fuwen Miao

府文庙, fǔwén miào • Daily 9am–5.30pm • Free • ☎ 0595 22281076

Between the Qingjing Mosque and Zhongshan Lu, an ornamental gateway leads north past a motorbike park to a broad paved square, at the back of which is **Fuwen Miao**, the largest Confucian complex in southern China. Though unexceptional in itself, there's an exhibition of Confucian texts as well as quite scary waxworks of local notables, and the square outside is dotted with freshly restored examples of Quanzhou's **traditional domestic architecture**, houses built of granite blocks and characteristic red bricks marked with dark chevrons, the roof ridges pulled up into projecting forks.

Yuan Miao Guan

元妙观, yuánmiào guān • Zhuangyuan Jie • Daily 5am–6pm • Free

The renovated **Yuan Miao Guan**, a colourful Taoist temple shoehorned between modern buildings, is small but perfectly formed – the quality of the workmanship, especially the carved pillars, is probably the best in the city. Little visited by tourists, it's highly recommended if you want to experience an authentic, working temple.

Kaiyuan Temple

开元寺, kāiyuán sì • Xi Jie • Daily 7.30am–5.30pm • ¥10 • ☎ 0595 22394182 • bus #2 from the old long-distance bus station

Quanzhou's most impressive historical remains are at the huge **Kaiyuan Temple**, a restful complex dotted with magnificent trees. Founded in 686, Kaiyuan was built, legend has it, after the owner of a mulberry grove dreamed a Buddhist monk asked him to erect a place of worship on his land. "Only if my mulberry trees bear lotus flowers", replied the owner dismissively – whereupon the lotus flowers duly appeared. The temple is highly regarded architecturally, not least for its details, which include one hundred stone columns supporting the roof of the main hall, most of which are carved with delicate musicians holding instruments or sacrificial objects.

The pagodas and exhibition hall

Having survived everything from earthquakes to the Red Guards, the temple's two unimaginably solid **stone pagodas** were added in the thirteenth century and are carved on each of their eight sides with two images of the Buddha; inside, one of them has forty Buddhist stories inscribed on its walls. The temple grounds also hold a special **exhibition hall** housing the hull of a twelfth- or thirteenth-century wooden sailing vessel found in 1974 (a series of photos details the stages of the excavation), still with the herbs and spices it had been carrying preserved in its hold.

The Maritime Museum

海外交通史博物馆, hǎiwàijiāotōngshǐ bówùguǎn • Dong Hu Lu, just past its junction with Tian'an Bei Lu • Tues–Sun 8.30am–5.30pm • Free • ☎ 0595 22100561 • bus #19 or #23 from near the bus station on Quanxiu Jie

Over on the northeast side of town, the **Maritime Museum** illustrates how advanced medieval Chinese shipbuilders were, compared to their European contemporaries. A corner devoted to the "Recovery of Taiwan from the Greedy Grasp of the Dutch Invaders and the Development of Foreign Trade" reinterprets Koxinga's exploits in a modern light (see p.471), but the museum's heart is its collection of hundreds of lovingly made **wooden models**. These illustrate everything from small, coastal junks to Zheng He's mighty *Baochuan* – possibly the largest wooden vessel ever made – and ornate pleasure boats used by the wealthy for touring China's famous lakes and rivers. Don't miss the first-floor collection of tombstones dating back to Quanzhou's heyday.

Most of these are Muslim, but you'll also find those of Italians and Spaniards, Nestorian Christians from Syria, and the fourteenth-century Bishop, Andrew Perugia.

Qingyuan Shan

清源山, qīngyuán shān • Daily 5.30am–4pm • ¥40 • bus #3 from Tumen Jie via Zhongshan Zhong Lu

The **Qingyuan Shan** scenic area is 3km to the north of Quanzhou, with good views over the town from small crags and pavilions, though most people come out here for the huge, Song-dynasty **sculpture of Laozi** (老君岩, lǎojūnyán) which is said to aid longevity if you climb onto its back and rub noses. There's also a lovely teahouse near the top of the park where you can get a set tea for around ¥55.

ARRIVAL AND DEPARTURE   QUANZHOU

Quanzhou's CTS office (daily 8am–9.30pm ☎ 0595 22332168), near the *Overseas Chinese Hotel* on Daxi Jie, can make train bookings and also runs night-buses to Guangzhou and Shenzhen.

BY PLANE

Quanzhou Jinjiang Airport (泉州晋江机场; quánzhōu jìnjiāng jīchǎng) is about 12km south of the city centre; a taxi costs ¥50, or the slower #16 bus costs ¥1.
Destinations Beijing (5 daily; 1hr 15min); Changsha (1 daily; 1hr 20min); Chengdu (2 daily; 2hr 10min); Chongqing (2 daily; 1hr 50min); Guangzhou (5 daily; 1hr 15min); Hangzhou (3 daily; 1hr 10min); Hong Kong (4 daily; 1hr 20min); Ji'nan (1 daily; 3hr 35min); Kunming (1 daily; 4hr); Macau (2 daily; 1hr 15min); Nanchang (1 daily; 1hr); Nanjing (2 daily; 1hr 30min); Nanning (1 daily; 2hr); Shanghai (5 daily; 1hr 35min); Shenzhen (2 daily; 1hr 15min); Wuhan (3 daily; 1hr 35min); Zhengzhou (1 daily; 3hr 35min).

BY TRAIN

Tickets can be bought in town at the Train Ticket Office (泉秀路火车售票处, quánxiù lù huǒchē shòupiào chù) on Quanxiu Lu, next to the Agricultural Bank of China and opposite the old bus station.
Quanzhou train station (泉州火车站, quánzhōu huǒchē zhàn) is a new station located about 12km north of the centre, and handles high-speed traffic to Xiamen, Hangzhou, Shenzhen and Shanghai. Bus #3 connects it to the centre; taxis cost about ¥50.
Quanzhou East train station (泉州火车东站, quánzhōu huǒchē dōngzhàn) is about 5km northeast

of the centre up Chenghua Nan Lu, and has slow connections to the interior of Fujian, including Wuyi Shan. Bus #23 connects it to the old bus station; a taxi is about ¥30.
Destinations Fuzhou (many daily; 56min–1hr 25min); Hangzhou (9 daily; 6hr 28min–7hr 24min); Longyan (8 daily; 1hr 40min); Shanghai (6 daily; 8hr–8hr 44min); Wuyi Shan (1 daily; 14hr); Xiamen (many daily; 30min–1hr).

BY BUS

There are frequent daytime buses from both new and old long-distance bus stations to Xiamen and Fuzhou, and to practically anywhere between Ningbo and Shenzhen. There's no reason to depart from the new bus station, but you may get dropped there.
Old long-distance bus station (泉州汽车站, quánzhōu qìchē zhàn). Just on the edge of the centre, it's within walking distance, or ¥10 by taxi, to all accommodation and sights.
New long-distance bus station (客运中心站, kèyùn zhōngxīnzhàn). Located 3km southeast of town down Quanxiu Jie, bus #15 from outside will take you northwest up to Wenling Lu and the old bus station (get off when you see the giant stone column on a roundabout). A taxi, motorcycle or rickshaw will cost under ¥10.
Destinations Fuzhou (2hr 30min); Guangzhou (10hr); Hangzhou (11hr); Shenzen (10hr); Xiamen (1hr 30min).

DAY-TRIPS FROM QUANZHOU

About 60km east of Quanzhou, **Chongwu** (崇武古城, chóngwǔ gǔchéng) is an old walled city built entirely of stone, now nicely restored as a huge museum piece. The adjacent new town has one of southern China's largest fishing fleets, with just about every man employed in this industry – the women work in local stone quarries, carting huge rocks around on carrypoles and wearing characteristic blue jackets and wide-brimmed straw hats.

Slightly closer to the southeast is the town of **Shishi** (石狮, shíshī), from where you can pick up a ride for the 5km to the beautiful **Sisters-in-law Tower** (姑嫂塔, gūsǎo tǎ), another Song-dynasty monument, overlooking the coast. Finally, 30km south, just off the expressway to Xiamen and outside the town of Anhai, the spectacular 2km-long, 800-year-old **Anping Bridge** (安平桥, ānpíng qiáo) actually crosses a section of sea

ACCOMMODATION

Hengxin 泉州恒信, quánzhōu héngxìn. Opposite the old bus station on Quanxiu Lu ☏0595 22597777. Spacious and comfortable rooms, and by far the best value of any of the nearby hotels. Beds are soft, bathrooms clean, and the service is friendly. Has quite a good attached Chinese restaurant too. ¥150

Jinzhou 金州大酒店, jīnzhōu dàjiǔdiàn. 615 Quanxiu Lu ☏0595 22586788. Next to the old long-distance bus station, this reasonably smart place has very nice, comfortable rooms that are actually better than the Quanzhou, but without the Disneyland exterior or facilities. There are plenty of eating options nearby. ¥458

Overseas Chinese Business Hotel 华侨之家宾馆, huáqiáo zhījiā bīnguǎn. 159 Wenling Lu ☏0595 22175395. The least expensive of local options which will go above board and register you with the police. Rooms are large, and clean enough, if slightly tatty, though it looks set for renovation in the near future. ¥130

Quanzhou 泉州酒店, quánzhōu jiǔdiàn. 22 Zhuangfu Xiang ☏0595 22289958, ⓦquanzhouhotel.com. A fantastically Baroque white-and-gold monstrosity, right in the centre of town. Rooms are of an international standard but, disappointingly, do not quite live up to the kitschy grandeur of the hotel's exterior, though they are comfortable enough. ¥592

Quanzhou Overseas Chinese Hotel 泉州华侨大厦, quánzhōu huáqiáo dàshà. Baiyuan Lu ☏0595 22282192, ⓦoverseaschinesehotel.com. Smart four-star business hotel right in the centre of town which has just had a major refit inside and out, and rooms come with all mod cons. A little bland, but well run. ¥625

EATING AND DRINKING

Northern Zhongshan Lu, the area around the Kaiyuan Temple and the backstreets off Tumen Jie are all thick with cheap noodle stalls and canteens. Between the long-distance bus stations, look for inexpensive food outlets serving imitation Western fare; better Chinese and foreign food is available at the new Liveshow Wonderland Entertainment Complex (领秀天地, lǐngxiù tiāndì), just south of Quanxiu Jie – also the best place to find nightlife.

Qingqi Shen teahouse 请其神茶店, qǐngqíshén chádiàn. 22 Houcheng Lu ☏0595 28275777. Housed in an old brick home in the lane over the bridge at the back of the Houcheng Tourism and Culture Street, this serves traditional teas, juices and dry snacks in a most atmospheric and serene environment. Tea for two will set you back upwards of ¥48. Daily 9am–midnight.

The Brickyard Unit 101, Building 6, Liveshow Wonderland ☏0595 22779179, ⓔthebrickyardqz @live.com. Friendly, partly Canadian-owned bar in the new nightlife complex, this place is the most foreigner-friendly in town, with imported booze and a comfortable brick interior with guitars on the walls. Also serves pretty good Western food. A little expensive, but then everywhere in Wonderland is. Daily 2pm–2am.

Three Virtues Vegetarian Restaurant 三德素食馆, sāndé sùshíguǎn. Upstairs at 124 Nanjun Lu ☏0595 22276705. Good veggie food is available in a tranquil ambience with an ample picture menu and mains in the ¥15–52 range. Particularly good are the pineapple stuffed with fragrantly spiced fried rice, and the fake meat kebabs. Daily 9am–10pm.

DIRECTORY

Banks and exchange The main Bank of China (Mon–Fri 8am–5.30pm) is on Nanjun Lu, with many other branches with ATMs around town.

Internet There are several internet cafés in the lane north of the Qingjing Mosque and more near the *Quanzhou* hotel.

Left luggage Note that the left-luggage office at the new bus station closes at 8pm sharp – anything still inside at the end of the day will stay locked there until morning.

Post office The enormous post office (Mon–Sat 8am–8pm) is at 155 Wenling Lu on the corner of Jiuyi Jie.

8

Xiamen

厦门, xiàmén

Joined to the mainland by a 5km-long causeway, **XIAMEN**, an island city formerly known to the West as **Amoy**, is more focused, clean and prosperous than the provincial capital, Fuzhou. It also offers more to see: the old streets and buildings, shopping arcades and a bustling seafront all contrast with the city centre's twenty-first-century skyscrapers. A ten-minute ferry ride to the southwest of town, little **Gulangyu island** was once the preserve of colonial Europeans and Japanese, whose mansions still line the island's traffic-free streets – staying here is highly recommended, though weekends and holidays sees the whole city overcrowded.

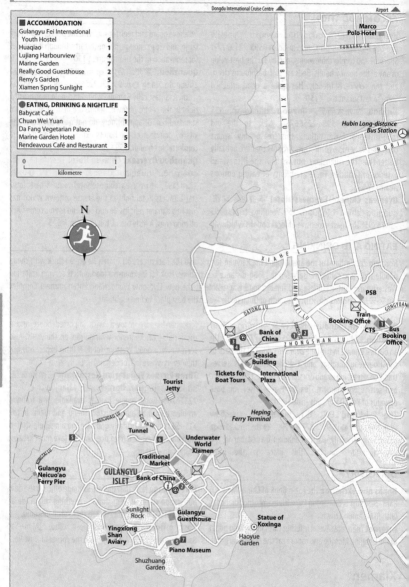

Dongdu International Cruise Centre

Airport

ACCOMMODATION

Gulangyu Fei International Youth Hostel	6
Huaqiao	1
Lujiang Harbourview	4
Marine Garden	7
Really Good Guesthouse	2
Remy's Garden	5
Xiamen Spring Sunlight	3

EATING, DRINKING & NIGHTLIFE

Babycat Café	2
Chuan Wei Yuan	1
Da Fang Vegetarian Palace	4
Marine Garden Hotel	5
Rendeavous Café and Restaurant	3

Marco Polo Hotel

YUNXANG LU

HUBIN XI LU

Hubin Long-distance Bus Station

HUBIN

XIAHE LU

SIMING BEI LU

PSB

DATONG LU

Train Booking Office

GONGYUAN

Bank of China

CTS

Bus Booking Office

ZHONGSHAN LU

Seaside Building

Tickets for Boat Tours

International Plaza

SIMING NAN LU

Tourist Jetty

Heping Ferry Terminal

NEICUOAO LU

FUJIAN LU

Tunnel

Underwater World Xiamen

Traditional Market

GULANGYU ISLET

Bank of China

LONGTOU LU

Gulangyu Neicuo'ao Ferry Pier

TONGAN LU

Sunlight Rock

Gulangyu Guesthouse

Statue of Koxinga

Yingxiong Shan Aviary

Haoyue Garden

Piano Museum

Shuzhuang Garden

0 — 1
kilometre

N

Brief history

Xiamen's strategic value as a port, midway between Guangzhou and Shanghai – and just a short hop across the straits to Taiwan – was noticed by the **British**, who took root on Gulangyu island after the city was opened up to foreign trade in 1842. By the start of the twentieth century, Xiamen's prosperity was supported by a steady turnover in trade and the trickling back of wealth from the city's emigrants, who had used its status as an international port to find work overseas.

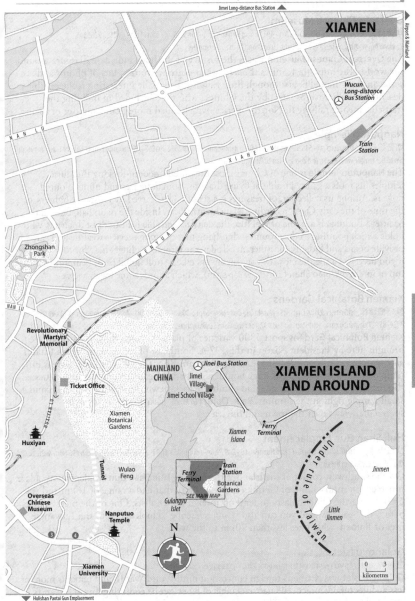

Jimei Long-distance Bus Station ▲

XIAMEN

Wucun
Long-distance
Bus Station

Train
Station

NAN LU

XIAHE LU

WENYUAN LU

Zhongshan
Park

NAN LU

Revolutionary
Martyrs'
Memorial

Ticket Office

Xiamen
Botanical
Gardens

Huxiyan

Tunnel

Wulao
Feng

Overseas
Chinese
Museum

Nanputuo
Temple

Xiamen
University

▼ Hulishan Paotai Gun Emplacement

**MAINLAND
CHINA**

Jimei Bus Station

Jimei
Village

Jimei School Village

**XIAMEN ISLAND
AND AROUND**

Xiamen
Island

Ferry
Terminal

Ferry
Terminal

Train
Station

Botanical
Gardens

SEE MAIN MAP

Gulangyu
Islet

Under rule of Taiwan

Jinmen

Little
Jinmen

N

| 0 | 3 |
kilometres

8

The **arrival of the Communists** in 1949 saw total chaos around Xiamen, with
thousands of Nationalists streaming across the straits to Taiwan to escape Red forces.
Today, although the small islands of **Jinmen** and **Mazu** – visible offshore – are still
Taiwanese territory, the threat of conflict has receded as the mutual economic gains
brought by closer cooperation have increased. Today, Xiamen's pleasant climate, healthy
economy and relatively sympathetic urban development mean it is recognized as having
among the best standards of living of any city in China.

Overseas Chinese Museum

华侨博物馆, huáqiáo bówùguǎn • 493 Siming Nan Lu • Tues–Sun 9.30am–4pm • Free • ☎0592 2085345, Ⓦ www.hqbwy.org.cn • bus #96 from Xiahe Lu or Zhong Shan Lu/Siming Bei Lu

The **Overseas Chinese Museum** traces the history of the huge Fujianese diaspora around the world. The museum features three floors of pottery, bronzes, lots of photos and some amazing model boats, though little English. Especially interesting is the exhibit describing the hardships faced by the Chinese who were included in building the transcontinental railway in North America, which killed more than a quarter of them.

Nanputuo Temple

南普陀寺, nánpǔtuó sì • 515 Siming Nan Lu • Daily 4am–6pm • ¥3 • ☎0592 2088554, Ⓦ nanputuo.com • buses #1, #87 & #96 all run to the temple via Xiahe Lu and Zhong Shan Lu/Siming Bei Lu

The **Nanputuo Temple** is one of China's most organized, modern-looking Buddhist temples, its roofs a gaudy jumble of flying dragons, human figures and multicoloured flowers. Among its collection of treasures is a set of tablets carved by resistance fighters at the time of the early Qing, recording Manchu atrocities. Inside the main hall, behind the Maitreya Buddha, is a statue of **Wei Tuo**, the deity responsible for Buddhist doctrine, who holds a stick pointing to the ground – signifying that the monastery is wealthy and can provide board and lodging for itinerants. Today the temple is a huge draw for tour groups; if you need to escape the crowds, you can always take a stroll uphill from Nanputuo to the top of forested **Wulao Shan** (五老山, wǔlǎo shān), which affords some lovely views.

Xiamen Botanical Gardens

厦门植物馆, xiàmén zhíwùguǎn • Wanshi Lu • Daily May–Sept 5.30am–6.30pm, Oct–April 6.30am–6pm • ¥40 • ☎0592 2024785, Ⓦ xiamenbg.com • four stops on bus #87 from the Xiahe Lu-Bailuzhou Lu junction

Xiamen Botanical Gardens sport 5300 varieties of plant life, including a redwood tree brought here by President Nixon in the 1970s. Southeast of the gardens' north (main) gate, you can climb up the hillside to Tiger Stream Rock (虎溪岩, hǔxī yán), a great little temple nestling amid a pile of huge boulders and crammed with gilded stone staues; slip through the cave to one side and climb the rock-hewn steps to the top. A second small temple right at the summit, **Bailu Dong** (白鹿洞, báilù dòng), commands spectacular views over the town and the sea.

Huli Shan Gun Emplacement

胡里山炮台, húlǐ shān pàotái • Nan Huandao Lu • Daily 9am–6pm • ¥25 • ☎0592 2084184 • buses #86 & #96 from Xiahe Lu or ZhongShan Lu/Siming Bei Lu

On the southwest corner of the island is the hulking **Huli Shan Gun Emplacement**, a late nineteenth-century hunk of German heavy artillery that had a range of 16km and was used during the Qing dynasty to fend off foreign imperialists. One of the nicest things here is the sea view, and you can also rent a telescope to look across to the Taiwanese islet of **Jinmen**, which lies less than 20km to the west.

Gulangyu Islet

鼓浪屿, gǔlàng yǔ • joint ticket for attractions ¥100 • golf buggies ¥50 per day

Gulangyu Islet was Xiamen's foreign concession until World War II, and remains more or less architecturally intact. The narrow tangle of lanes can be confusing, but the island's size (it's less than two square kilometres) means you can't go very far wrong. A stroll

---

SPYING ON TAIWAN

Several kiosks along the Xiamen waterfront and on Gulangyu itself sell tickets for boat trips offering circuits of Gulangyu (30min; ¥15) or, more adventurously, out towards neighbouring Jinmen island (1hr 40min; ¥136) – you don't get too close, so bring binoculars for good views of Taiwan's front line.

> **GULANGYU FERRIES**
>
> The **main ferry** (every 10–15min, 5.45am–midnight; ¥8 return) runs from the pier across from the *Lujiang* to the main Gulangyu ferry dock. Keep your ticket for the return; travelling on the upper deck costs ¥1 extra, which is collected by an inspector.
>
> This ferry is horrendously packed at weekends and during holidays, when it's better to get the far less busy ferry from the same place to **Gulangyu Neicuo'ao ferry pier** (鼓浪屿内厝, gŭlàngyŭ nèicuò) on the west of the island, which runs every 30min from 8.35am–6pm (¥8 return).

through the streets will uncover plenty of attractions, especially along **Fuzhou Lu** (福州路, fúzhōu lù) and **Guxin Lu** (鼓新路, gŭxīn lù), overhung with flowers and blossom throughout the year. Crowds tend to gravitate to the main sights in the south of the island; on busy days you'll find the northwest far quieter, with a surprising amount of lovely colonial buildings, along with three wooded hills and a small, near-deserted beach. Note that the only vehicles allowed on Gulangyu are battery-powered golf buggies.

Underwater World

海底世界, hăidĭ shìjiè • Daily 9.30am–6.30pm • ¥90, children and students ¥50

From the disembarkation point, a splendid bronze sculpture of a giant octopus diagonally to your right marks the entrance to **Underwater World Xiamen**, with walk-through aquariums, seal displays, penguins, turtles and a massive whale skeleton.

The tunnel

Just east of the disused tourist jetty on the northeast of the island off Sanming Lu, you'll find the mouth of a **tunnel**, built in the 1950s when the threat of military confrontation with Taiwan seemed imminent, which burrows right underneath the hill. Entering the tunnel, the temperature drops and you can join locals and tourists using it as an air-conditioned short cut to Neicuo'ao Lu.

Haoyue Garden

皓月园, hàoyuè yuán • Daily 7.30am–7.30pm • ¥15

On the southeast corner of the island, you can find a number of grand old buildings, including the former British and German consulates. The road continues on to the island's rocky eastern headland, now enclosed by **Haoyue Garden**, containing a gigantic granite **statue of Koxinga** (郑成功塑像, zhèngchénggōng sùxiàng). A seveteenth-century freebooter who rose to become naval commander at the close of the Ming dynasty, Koxinga – also known as **Zheng Chenggong** – fought the Manchu conquest of China before fleeing to Taiwan, where he threw out the Dutch overlords and dreamed of reconquering the mainland. The statue here shows him dressed in grand military attire and staring meaningfully out towards Taiwan.

Piano Museum

鼓浪屿钢琴博物馆, gŭlàngyŭ gāngqín bówùguăn • 7 Ganghou Lu • Daily 8.15am–5.45pm • ¥30 • ☎ 0592 2060238

The **Piano Museum** (the only one in China) is a reflection of the island's history with the instrument; foreigners began teaching locals here at the start of the twentieth century and the island has produced some of China's finest pianists. There are over eighty instruments on display, and if you join the half-hourly guided tours (in Chinese), you can also hear a piano or pianola performance at the end.

Sunlight Rock

日光岩, rìguāng yán • Daily 6am–8pm • ¥60 includes cable-car ride

The clean, sandy **beach** running west from the piano museum is tempting for swimming when it's not too packed, and is overlooked to the north by **Sunlight Rock**,

8

the highest point on Gulangyu (93m) and a magnet for tourists who ride up to the viewing platform to survey the entire island. At the foot of the rock (and covered by the same entrance ticket) is the **Koxinga Memorial Hall** (郑成功纪念馆, zhèngchénggōng jìniànguǎn), which contains various relics, including Koxinga's jade belt and bits of his "imperial" robe.

ARRIVAL AND DEPARTURE

BY PLANE

Xiamen airport (厦门高崎国际机场, xiàmén huǒchēzhàn) is 12km north of town, connected to the waterfront area by bus #27 (¥6) or taxi (¥40). As well as domestic services, the city has less frequent international flights to South Korea, Japan, Malaysia, the Philippines, Singapore, Thailand and recently even Amsterdam.

Destinations Beijing (16 daily; 2hr 40min); Guangzhou (13 daily; 1hr 5min); Hefei (5 daily; 1hr 20min); Hong Kong (7 daily; 1hr 15min); Macau (2 daily; 1hr 20min); Shanghai (23 daily; 1hr 30min); Shenzhen (8 daily; 1hr); Wuyi Shan (6 daily; 46min).

BY TRAIN

Buying tickets is not too problematic, though there is an in-town booking office at the Heping Ferry Terminal and another next door to the *Huaqiao* hotel.

Xiamen train station (厦门火车站, xiàmén huǒchē zhàn) is on Xiahe Lu, about 4km east from the seafront and connected by city bus #1. Rail lines run north to Wuyi Shan and Jiangxi province, and west into Guangdong province via Longyan. Services to Fuzhou are very circuitous; it's much faster to take the bus.

Destinations Guangzhou (3 daily; 14hr 30min); Nanchang (5 daily; 15–17hr); Nanjing (1 daily; 30hr); Shanghai (2 daily; 8hr); Shenzhen (20 daily; 14hr–16hr 45min); Wuyi Shan (1 daily; 13hr 30min); Xi'an (1 daily; 37hr).

BY BUS

Xiamen's multiple stations have frequent departures to Fuzhou and Quanzhou; several daily to Longyan and Yongding; at least one daily to Guangzhou; and fourteen daily to Shenzhen. Most long-distance services leave before 10am, so organizing beforehand is a good idea. It's best to book through your hotel or at a travel agent, as finding the best bus station is horrendously complex; otherwise, the three options below have the most departures to the destinations listed. There's a bus booking

office opposite the *Huaqiao* hotel.

Hubin (湖宾汽车站, húbīn qìchēzhàn), 2km northeast of the centre on Hubin Nan Lu; exit the station, turn right and it's 100m to the stop for city bus #23 to the seafront. Probably your best bet for most destinations regional and national.

Jimei Bus Station (集美汽车站, jíměi qìchēzhàn) 159 Yinjiang Lu, on the mainland just north of Xiamen. From 400m east of the station on Jiyuan Lu, catch bus #903 or #981 to Jimei Dadao, then change to get the #1 to seafront Xiahe Lu.

Wucun (捂村汽车站, wǔcūn qìchēzhàn), about 200m north of the train station, is useful only for its frequent connections to Quanzhou (every 15min; 6.20am–9.30pm). Transport into town is as for the train station.

Destinations Chaozhou (4hr); Fuzhou (4hr); Guangzhou (9hr); Longyan (5hr); Quanzhou (1hr 30min); Shenzhen (9hr); Yongding (3–4hr).

BY PRIVATE BUS

CTS operates private buses to Guangzhou, Shenzhen and Quanzhou, departing from their office on Xinhua Lu next to the *Huaqiao* hotel.

BY FERRY

Daily ferries (hourly 8.30am–5.30pm; ¥170/NT$700) operate between Xiamen's two international ports and Jinmen/Kinmen, in the Republic of China (Taiwan). You'll need a valid Taiwanese visa to buy a ticket.

Dongdu International Cruise Centre (东渡厦门国际邮轮中心, dōngdù xiàmén guójì yóulún zhōngxīn) at the northern end of Hubin Xi Lu, from where the ferry takes about an hour to Jinmen.

Wutong Ferry Terminal (五通客运码头, wǔtōng kèyùn mǎtóu), is in the northeast of the city close to the airport; it's less convenient to get to than Dongdu, but less hectic and the ferry is thirty minutes faster.

GETTING AROUND

By taxi Cabs are plentiful, but in high demand and cost upwards of ¥8 to hire, plus a ¥3 fuel surcharge and a twenty-percent night surcharge (11pm–5am).

There are also private cars which may approach you in the street, which are slightly more expensive (and technically illegal).

INFORMATION

Tourist office The only useful place is the Gulangyu Visitor's Center at 100 Longtou Lu (daily 9am–5.15pm;

📞0599 2060777, 🌐glyylq.com), where the staff speak English and are very helpful – it's also well air-conditioned and has seating if you fancy a sit down. For general information, try the city-wide website ⓦvisitxm.com.

Maps Vendors sell city maps with bus routes marked (¥6) near the Gulangyu ferry terminal and outside the stations.

Travel agents CS, at the *Huaqiao* hotel, Xinhua Lu (☎0592 2660888; daily 9am–5.30pm). They can book domestic and international flights, private long-distance buses, and Chinese-language one-day tours to the Hakka homelands (see p.474; ¥150–210 including lunch).

ACCOMMODATION

Finding low-end accommodation can be hard, especially during the summer, and the majority is near the train station. Some of Xiamen's best places to stay are on Gulangyu – note that you'll have to carry your own luggage as there are no buses or taxis on the island. Note that at weekends, and especially in the summer months, booking ahead is absolutely essential.

DOWNTOWN XIAMEN

Huaqiao 华侨宾馆, huáqiáo bīnguǎn. 70–74 Xinhua Lu ☎0592 2660888, ⓦxmhqhotel.com.cn. Very smart, modern and well-serviced hotel, with train, bus and airline agents conveniently located outside. Rooms are comfortable and there are also good Chinese and Western dining facilities, as well as a gym and swimming pool. **¥913**

Lujiang Harbourview 鹭江宾馆, lùjiāng bīnguǎn. 54 Lujiang Lu ☎0592 2022922, ⓦlujiang-hotel.com. Occupying a prime site on the seafront in a well-maintained colonial building, this is an excellent hotel with comfortable rooms and the ideal place to stay for views over Gulangyu Islet, especially from the rooftop terrace. **¥1380**

The Really Good Guesthouse 好实在家庭旅馆, hǎoshízài jiātíng lǚguǎn. 18 Jukou Jie ☎0592 2121097. No English sign, but this tiny guesthouse down an alley probably has the some of the cheapest rooms in the centre. Although the rooms are on the small side and have hard beds, they're quite clean and good enough for a couple of days. **¥118**

Xiamen Spring Sunlight 厦门春光酒店, xiàmén chūnguāng jiǔdiàn. 36 Haihou Lu ☎0592 2665558. Useful location opposite the Gulangyu ferry terminal. Behind its colonial-style facade the rooms are modern and spotless, if a little bland, though the price is much less than other places on the seafront. Worth paying the ¥50 extra for a seaview. **¥399**

GULANGYU ISLET

★**Gulangyu Fei International Youth Hostel** 国际青年旅舍, guójì qīngnián lǚshè. 20 Guxin Lu ☎0592 2082678, ⓦyhalf.cn. Located in a charming three-storey Mediterranean-style villa on a hill about 400m from the main ferry terminal towards the middle of the island, this hostel is by far the best of Gulangyu's three hostels, being prettier and in a much quieter spot – follow the signs for the Organ Museum and it's about 50m away. Clean, light and airy dorms and rooms, plus all the amenities you'd expect, and a peaceful patio, with an inexpensive Chinese restaurant next door. Dorms **¥75**, rooms **¥260**

Marine Garden 海上花园酒店, hǎishàng huāyuán jiǔdiàn. 27 Tianwei Lu ☎0592 2062688, ⓦmarinegardenhotel.com.cn. Just above Shuzhuang Garden, this plush, mildly garish faux-colonial place has quality rooms, a pool, tennis court and good views over the beach. Probably the best accommodation on the island, and a thoroughly pleasant oasis of calm, with an excellent Chinese restaurant. **¥1680**

Remy's Garden 雷米的酒店, léimǐde jiǔdiàn. 65 Kang Tai Lu ☎0592 2196957, ⓦremygardenhotel.com. A very romantic option, this small, German-owned hotel housed in an old colonial building has just eight rooms, all of which are uniquely and beautifully decorated. Also serves a range of reasonably priced European wines, and excellent coffees, which you can consume in the courtyard garden. Shared bathroom **¥468**, private bathroom **¥568**

EATING, DRINKING AND NIGHTLIFE

Xiamen has plenty of places to eat fresh fish and seafood, particularly oysters, crabs and prawns. Head for the restaurants around Gulangyu's market area, or the backstreets behind the *Lujiang Harbourview*, and establish a price in advance: seafood is generally sold by weight (see p.43). Otherwise, the vibrant and cramped market street down Renhe Lu (just off Lujiang Lu past the *Xiamen Spring Sunlight Hotel*) contains a cornucopia of inexpensive snack-stalls, tiny restaurants and barbecue seafood places – you can get half a lobster here for ¥30–50. For nightlife, the area around the *Marco Polo Hotel*, just north of Yundang Lu, is awash with new bars, clubs and restaurants. Check out ⓦwhatsonxiamen.com, for English-language reviews and listings.

Babycat Café 小猫茶馆, xiāomāo cháguǎn. 43 Longtou Lu ☎0592 2063651. Laidback coffee shop and café that does brisk trade in its famous traditional Amoy pies – has simple Western food, internet access and a

resident celebrity feline. A good, calm place to get your bearings, with old plaster and cute artworks on the walls, though it's not cheap. Daily 9am–9.30pm.

Chuan Wei Yuan 川味园香牌坊, chuānwèiyuán

xiāngpáifāng. 2F, 19 Jukou Jie ☎0592 2036288. Slightly earthy but clean restaurant specializing in local and Sichuan food, and claypots, for a mostly local crowd. The majority of dishes are fairly spicy, though the fantastic deep-fried tofu isn't as hot as some of the other dishes (like the dry-pot fragrance shrimp, or spicy duck tongues). Has an English menu and mains are ¥16–70. Daily 11am–4am.

Da Fang Vegetarian Palace 大方素食馆, dàfāng sùshíguǎn. 3 Siming Nan Lu ☎0592 2093236. Two minutes up the road from Nanputuo Temple and far better value than their restaurant, this great vegetarian option serves fine food in a sophisticated ambience. The fake meat and fish dishes are fantastic, especially the black pepper steak. Also recommended are the rice noodles (¥20), with other mains ¥20–30. Daily 9.30am–10pm.

Marine Garden Hotel 海上花园酒店, hǎishàng huāyuán jiǔdiàn. 27 Tianwei Lu ☎0592 2062688, ⓦmarinegardenhotel.com.cn. The nicest hotel on Gulangyu also has a great Chinese restaurant which will allow you to enjoy an after-meal stroll in their uncrowded gardens. They specialize in Fujianese and Cantonese cuisine and prices are reasonable, with mains in the ¥36–186 range. Particularly good are whelk and leek wrapped in lettuce leaf, and the Hainan coconut porridge. Daily 11am–2pm & 5.30–9.30pm.

Rendeavous Café and Restaurant 朗地咖啡, lǎngdì kāfēi. 35 Minzu Lu ☎0592 2196199. Best of a clutch of arty cafés along this road, this bohemian place is in a slightly shabby but beautiful colonial house, its nooks and crannies furnished with the original tile floors, sofas and bookcases. Also has a nice outdoor terrace, and serves great coffee and decent Western food (mains ¥38–68), though service is slow. Daily 1am–11.30pm.

DIRECTORY

Banks and exchange There are branches of the Bank of China (Mon–Fri 8.30am–noon & 2.30–5pm, Sat 8am–12.30pm) on Gulangyu Islet and on Zhongshan Lu, back from the seafront, and ATMs accepting foreign cards everywhere.

Consulates Philippines, near the geographic centre of Xiamen at 2 Lianhua Bei Lu ☎0592 5130355.

Mail Xiamen's main post office (8am–6.30pm) is on the seafront, just north of the *Xiamen Spring Sunlight*, and there's another large branch on Xinhua Lu, south of the junction with Siming Dong Lu.

PSB Across from the post office on Gongyuan Nan Lu ☎0592 2262203.

The Hakka homelands

Fujian's hilly southwestern border with Guangdong is an area central to the **Hakka**, a Han subgroup known to locals as *kejia* (客家, kèjiā; guest families) and to nineteenth-century Europeans as "China's gypsies". Originating in the Yangzi basin during the third century and dislodged ever southward by war and revolution, the Hakka today form large communities in Guangdong, Fujian and Southeast Asia. They managed to retain their original languages and customs by remaining aloof from their neighbours in the lands in which they settled, a habit that caused resentment and led to their homes being well defended. Traditional villages and hamlets sport fortress-like **mansions** (*tulou*, literally "mud building"), of which there are more than thirty thousand spread across the countryside. The largest are four or five storeys high, circular, and house entire clans.

Entry to the area is at **YONGDING** (永定, yǒngdìng), a heavily built-up city around 120km west and inland from Xiamen, from where local transport heads out to the sights.

Hongkeng

洪坑村, hóngkēngcūn • Daily 8am–7pm • ¥90

An hour's bus ride east of Yongding, **Hongkeng village** – where you can stay overnight (see p.476) – features a collection of traditional Hakka buldings, many still lived in, laid out along a small stream. Those worth investigating include a 1920s schoolhouse; **Fuyu Lou**, the old courthouse building; **Rushen Lou**, one of the smallest multistorey roundhouses; and **Kuijiu Lou**, a splendid, 165-year-old square-sided Hakka mansion, its interior like a temple squeezed into a box.

Zhencheng Lou

振城楼, zhènchéng lóu

Hongkeng's well-maintained centrepiece is the century-old **Zhencheng Lou**, considered to be the most perfect Hakka roundhouse. Plain and forbidding on the outside, the huge outer wall encloses three storeys of galleried rooms looking inwards to a central courtyard where guests were entertained, and which contained the clan shrine. The galleries are vertically divided into eight segments by thick fire walls, a plan that intentionally turns the building into a giant *bagua*, Taoism's octagonal symbol. This powerful design occurs everywhere in the region, along with demon-repelling mirrors and other Taoist motifs.

Other villages

From Hongkeng it's easy to organize trips to surrounding *tulou*, including **Chengqi Lou** (承启楼, chéngqǐ lóu), the largest roundhouse of them all, built in 1709, with more than 300 rooms housing more than 400 people; **Tianluo Keng** (田螺坑, tíanluó kēng), a remote grouping of five large houses – including three roundhouses, one square walled house and one oval – that date back three centuries and still house around six hundred people; and **Yuchang Lou** (裕唱楼, yùchàng lóu), the oldest and tallest of the roundhouses – Yuchang's five storeys have stood since 1309, despite a drunken, 15-degree lean to its 21m-tall uprights.

ARRIVAL AND DEPARTURE

THE HAKKA HOMELANDS

All long-distance transport terminates at Yongding.

By train Yongding Station (永定火车站, yǒngdìng huǒchē zhàn) is 3km north of the town with relatively infrequent connections to the rest of Fujian and eastern Guangdong. A taxi to most places in town costs under ¥10. Destinations Guangzhou (2 daily; 7hr 30min); Fuzou (2 daily; 10hr 45min); Shanghai (1 daily; 23hr); Shenzhen (5 daily; 7hr 20min); Xiamen (8 daily; 4hr 50min).

By bus Yongding's main bus station (永定汽车站, yǒngdìng qìchēzhàn) is on the large roundabout just east of the river, about 2km south of the train station. Seven daily direct buses head between Yongding and Xiamen's Hubin bus station, and two connect with Quanzhou's new bus station.

Destinations Longyan (1hr); Quanzhou (5hr); Xiamen (4hr 30min); Zhiling (1hr).

GETTING AROUND

By bus Direct services (1hr; ¥16) depart Yongding's bus station and drop you at Hongkeng outside a row of guesthouses, close to Zhencheng Lou itself.

By minibus Minibuses in the region are plentiful but seem to run fairly randomly, so be prepared to stand by the road and flag down whatever comes along. Services dry up by mid-afternoon.

By taxi and motorbike taxi In Yongding or Hongkeng it's easy to organize taxis and your accomodation can usually help – reckon on around ¥200 for a full day, which would mean around four or five sites, but be prepared to haggle. If you're on your own, a motorcyle taxi will cost about ¥120 for the day.

ACCOMMODATION AND EATING

Places to eat surround Yongding's bus station and main streets; you'll find all sorts of rice noodles, snacks and *kourou* (口肉, kǒuròu), a Hakka dish made from slices of soya-braised pork belly on a bed of bitter kale.

YONGDING

Dongfu 东府酒店, dōngfǔ jiǔdiàn. 1–2 Wenquan Lu ☏ 0597 5830668. Large, white, fancy-looking and good-value business hotel which has clean, pleasant rooms and helpful staff. Located on the large roundabout, close to the bus station and a couple of kilometres south of the train station, it's also handy for the restaurants on Dong Jie, though the rooms at the front are nosiy. **¥148**

HONGKENG

★ **Fuyulou Changdi Inn** 福裕楼常棣客栈, fúyùlóu chángdì kèzhàn. Hongkeng village ☏ 0597 55322800, ⓦ fuyulou.net. Friendly, twenty-room hostel inside a large *tulou* built in 1880 and located by the river, next to Kuijulou near Zhencheng Lou. It has clean but basic rooms (some with bathrooms), wi-fi, and also serves well-priced local food. English is spoken. Dorm beds **¥50**, rooms **¥100**

DIRECTORY

Bank Yongding's Bank of China is on Jiuyi Xi Jie at the junction with Nanmen Jie, west across the river from the main roundabout.

Guangdong

广东, guǎngdōng

Halfway along **Guangdong**'s 800km coastline, rivers from all over the province and beyond disgorge themselves into the South China Sea through the tropically fertile **Pearl River Delta**, one of China's most densely cultivated and developed areas. Perched right at the delta's northern apex and adjacent to Hong Kong and Macau, the frenetic provincial capital, **Guangzhou**, is not everyone's favourite city, but its famous **food** merits a stop, as does an assortment of museums, parks, monuments and pretty colonial quarters. Outlying delta towns have some history to pick up in passing, but in truth the area is emphatically focused on industry and commerce – as demonstrated by the border city of **Shenzhen** (深圳, shēnzhèn) where China's "economic miracle" took its first baby steps.

Farther afield, the rest of the province is more picturesque. Over in the east near Fujian, the ancient town of **Chaozhou** (潮州, cháozhōu) has well-preserved Ming architecture peppered among a warren of narrow streets, though the regional highlight lies to the east in the form of the fantastical towers around the town of **Kaiping** (开平, kāipíng).

8

Guangzhou

广州, guǎngzhōu

GUANGZHOU, once known to the Western world as **Canton**, was for centuries where China met the rest of the world – commercially, militarily and otherwise. Increased competition from elsewhere in China may have diminished Guangzhou's role as a centre of international commerce, but with the money continuing to roll in from the industrial and manufacturing complexes which cover the surrounding Pearl River Delta, there is little suggestion that the city is a fading power.

For visitors, however, Guangzhou's attractions are limited and mainly business-oriented, as the biannual **Canton Trade Fair** attests. The city is vast, untidy and unbelievably crowded, and actual tourist sights are relatively trivial, though a peek at the European colonial enclave of Shamian Island and the fascinating 2000-year-old tomb prove the city's lengthy and varied cultural heritage. Often the pervading impression is of endless anonymous blocks of chrome and concrete blurring together as you zip over the multiple elevated expressways in a taxi. Yet there's something about this chaotic caricature of Hong Kong that somehow manages to be enjoyable. The Cantonese are compulsively garrulous, turning Guangzhou's two famous obsessions – eating and business – into social occasions, and filling streets, restaurants and buildings with the sounds of *yueyu*, the Cantonese language.

Brief history

Legend tells how Guangzhou was founded by **Five Immortals** riding five rams, each of whom planted a sheaf of rice symbolizing endless prosperity – hence Guangzhou's nickname, Goat City. Myths aside, a settlement had sprung up here by the third century BC, when a rogue Qin commander founded the **Nanyue Kingdom** and made it his capital. Remains of a contemporary shipyard uncovered in central Guangzhou during the 1970s suggest that the city had contact with foreign lands even then: there were merchants who considered themselves Roman subjects here in 165 AD, and from Tang times, vessels travelled to Middle Eastern ports, introducing **Islam** into China and

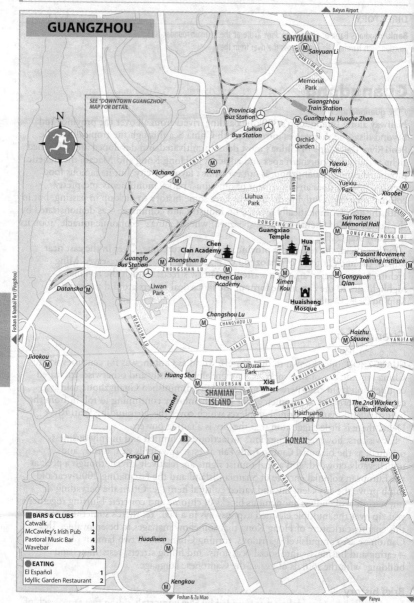

BARS & CLUBS
Catwalk	1
McCawley's Irish Pub	2
Pastoral Music Bar	4
Wavebar	3

EATING
El Español	1
Idyllic Garden Restaurant	2

exporting porcelain to Arab colonies in distant east Africa. By 1405, Guangzhou's foreign population was so large that the Ming emperor Yongle founded a special quarter for them.

From the Opium Wars to communism

Yet this contact with other nations, especially the **British**, proved to be Guangzhou's undoing, ending as it did with the Opium Wars and China's humiliation during the

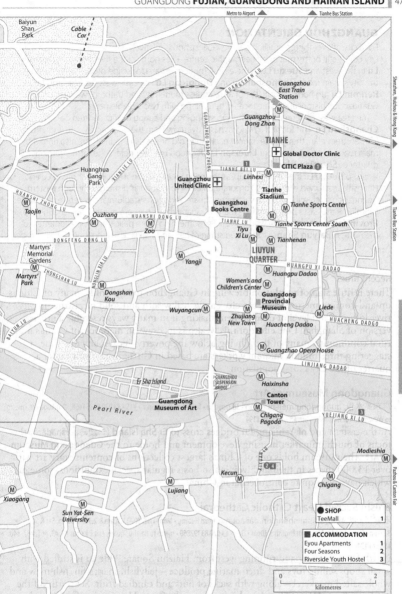

mid-nineteenth century (see p.918). The following decades saw Guangzhou develop into a revolutionary cauldron. It was here that Hong Xiuquan formulated his **Taiping Uprising** in the 1840s (see p.312), and sixty years later the city hosted a premature attempt by **Sun Yatsen** to kick out China's royal Qing rulers. When northern China was split by warlords in the 1920s, Sun Yatsen chose Guangzhou as his **Nationalist capital**, while a youthful Mao Zedong and Zhou Enlai flitted in and out between mobilizing rural peasant groups.

GUANGZHOU ORIENTATION

For a city of over thirteen million people, Guangzhou is relatively easy to navigate. The original city core – still pretty much the geographic centre – lies north of the river between **Renmin Lu** in the west and **Yuexiu Lu** in the east. A modern urban landscape predominates, cut by the city's main roads: **Zhongshan Lu** and **Dongfeng Lu** run east–west, and **Jiefang Lu** and **Renmin Lu** run north–south. It's not all relentless modernity and traffic, however: most of Guangzhou's historical sites are located here, along with two sizeable parks.

The area west of Renmin Lu is a thriving shopping and eating district centred on **Changshou Lu**. This formed a Ming-dynasty overflow from the original city, and it retains its former street plan, though the narrow back lanes, old houses and markets are also ringed by main roads, such as waterfront **Liuersan Lu**. Right on the river here is the former foreigners' quarter of **Shamian Island**.

East of Yuexiu Lu the city opens up, as the main roads – Zhongshan Lu, Dongfeng Lu and Huanshi Lu, all lined with glassy corporate offices – run broad and straight through eastern Guangzhou to culminate in the vast, open square and sports stadium at the centre of **Tianhe**. Nightlife is the east's biggest draw – many of Guangzhou's bars are out this way, though the **Provincial Museum** is well worth a visit. For something more peaceful, a few kilometres to the north is **Baiyun Shan**, a formalized string of hills and parkland just beyond the city proper.

Recent times

There is little sign of revolution brewing in Guangzhou today. Unlike many of China's up-and-coming metropolises, the city enjoys real wealth and solid infrastructure, its river location and level of development making it in many ways resemble a grittier version of Shanghai. One effect of this wealth is its draw on members of China's mobile rural community, many of them living below the poverty line. At any one time, a staggering three million **migrant workers** are based in Guangzhou – just under a quarter of the city's total population.

Guangdong Museum of Art

广东美术馆, guǎngdōng měishùguǎn • 38 Yanyu Lu • Tues–Sun 9am–5pm • ¥15 • ☎ 020 87351468, ⓦ gdmoa.org • metro to Wuyangcun or Haixinsha • bus #89, #131 or #194

At the eastern end of Yanjiang Lu bridges cross to **Er Sha Island** (二沙岛, èrshādǎo), the focus of much upmarket housing development and home to the **Guangdong Museum of Art**. The museum holds one of China's largest collections of contemporary art with over 13,000 pieces in their archives; it also hosts regular special exhibitions, some of which have been quite controversial in China.

Shishi Sacred Heart Catholic Cathedral

石室圣心大教堂, shíshì shèngxīn dàjiàotáng • Yuzi Hutong • Mon–Fri 8.30–11.30am & 2.30–5.30pm, Sat & Sun 8.30am–5pm • Sunday Masses in English 3.30pm • Free • ☎ 020 83392860 • metro to Haizhu Square, exit B1 • bus #8, #9, #61, #82, #40, #58 or #194

North from the river and running west from Haizhu Square, **Yide Lu** is stuffed with small shops selling toys and dried marine produce – jellyfish, shark's fin, fish maw and whole salted mackerel – along with sacks of nuts and candied fruit. Set north off the road, the **Sacred Heart Church** – also known as the Stone House – is a Gothic-style cathedral completed in 1888, impressive for its size and unexpected presence as well as being a working church.

Five Immortals' Temple

五仙观, wǔxiān guān • junction of Huifu Xi Lu and Liurong Lu • Daily 9am–noon & 1.30–5pm • ¥10 • ☎ 020 83336853 • metro to Haizu Square • buses #3, #5, #6, #8, #33, #39, #66, #72, #82, #106, #110, #124 & #206

Despite dating to 1377, the **Five Immortals' Temple** building itself isn't of much interest, though there are some obviously ancient statues around the place: weathered guardian lions flank the way in, and some stylized Ming sculptures at the back look like giant chess pieces. The Five Immortals – three men and two women – are depicted too, riding their goatly steeds as they descend through the clouds to found Guangzhou. More impressive is a fourteenth-century **bell tower** behind the temple, in which hangs a 3m-high, five-tonne bronze bell, silent since being blamed for a plague which broke out shortly after its installation in 1378 – it has been called the "Forbidden Bell" ever since.

Huaisheng Mosque

怀圣清真寺, huáishèng qīngzhēnsì sì • 56 Guangta Lu • Daily 8.30am–5pm • Free • metro to Ximen Kou, exit B • bus #56

Huaisheng Mosque and its grey, conical tower, **Guangta**, loom over a surrounding wall that bars entry to non-Muslims. Looking like a lighthouse, Guangta is possibly the world's oldest minaret outside Mecca and something of a stylistic fossil, said by some to have been built by the seventh-century Islamic missionary Abu Waqas. During the fifteenth century, Huaisheng's environs were known as Fanfang, the foreigners' quarter; today there's a smattering of halal canteens and restaurants in the vicinity, including the famous **Huimin Fandian** (see p.492).

Liurong Temple

六榕寺, liùróng sì • 87 Liurong Lu • Daily 9am–5pm • ¥5, plus ¥10 extra to climb the pagoda • Gongyuan Qian metro exit B, then a 500m walk

Liurong Temple lies north of the Huaisheng Mosque and is associated with the poet-governor **Su Dongpo**, who named the temple on a visit in 1100 and drew the characters for "Liu Rong" (Six Banyan Trees) on the two stone steles just inside the gates. Very little of the temple itself survives, and the site is better known for the 57m-high, seventeen-storey **Hua Ta** (花塔, huātǎ), a contemporary pagoda enshrining relics brought from India by Emperor Wu's uncle. Carvings of lions, insects and birds adorn the pagoda's wooden eaves. At the top is a gigantic bronze pillar covered with over a thousand reliefs of meditating figures rising up through the roof, solid enough to support the five-tonne begging bowl and pearl that you can see from ground level.

Guangxiao Temple

光孝寺, guāngxiào sì • 109 Jinghui Lu • Daily 5am–5.30pm • ¥5 • ☎ 020 81077170, ⊛ gzgxs.org • Ximen Kou metro exit B and turn right up Guangxiao Lu

The spacious and peaceful **Guangxiao Temple** is the oldest of Guangzhou's Buddhist complexes. In 113 BC this was the residence of **Zhao Jiande**, last of the Nanyue kings

---

PEARL RIVER CRUISES

Second only to the Yangzi in importance as an industrial channel, the oily grey **Pearl River** (珠江, zhūjiāng) originates in eastern Yunnan province and forms one of China's busiest waterways, continually active with ferries and barges loaded down with coal and stone. Its name derives from a legend about a monk who lost a glowing pearl in its waters, and although it shone on the riverbed night after night, nobody was ever able to recover it.

Evening cruises depart daily between 7.20pm and 9.20pm from **Xidi Wharf** (西堤码头, xīdī mǎtóu), roughly opposite the Customs House on Yanjiang Lu, or 1km east at the more popular **Tianzi Wharf** (天字码头, tiānzì mǎtóu), which has more luxurious and expensive boats – ticket offices line the waterfront. These cruises last 75–90min and prices start at ¥48, or ¥98 including dinner. You can sit back and watch the lights of the city slip slowly past your table, with fine views of Guangzhou's busy waterfront, flanked by ever-higher buildings and dominated by coloured lights from the Canton Tower, China's tallest structure (see p.488). The route also takes you past the *White Swan* on Shamian Island, back under Renmin Bridge, past Haizhu Bridge and then down to the grand Guangzhou suspension bridge at the far end of Er Sha Island.

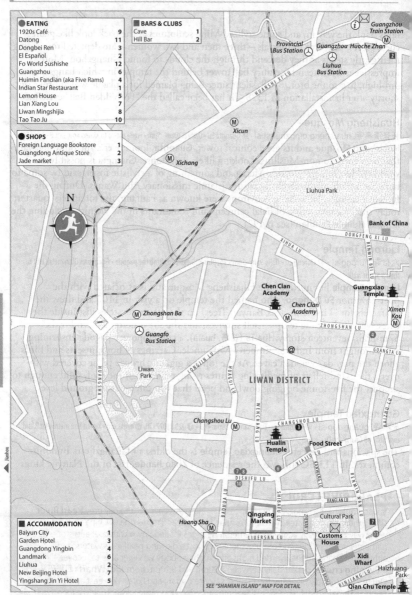

● EATING	
1920s Café	9
Datong	11
Dongbei Ren	3
El Español	2
Fo World Sushishe	12
Guangzhou	6
Huimin Fandian (aka Five Rams)	4
Indian Star Restaurant	1
Lemon House	5
Lian Xiang Lou	7
Liwan Mingshijia	8
Tao Tao Ju	10

■ BARS & CLUBS	
Cave	1
Hill Bar	2

● SHOPS	
Foreign Language Bookstore	1
Guangdong Antique Store	2
Jade market	3

■ ACCOMMODATION	
Baiyun City	1
Garden Hotel	3
Guangdong Yingbin	4
Landmark	6
Liuhua	2
New Beijing Hotel	7
Yingshang Jin Yi Hotel	5

(see p.485), becoming a place of worship only after the 85-year-old Kashmiri monk Tanmo Yeshe built the first hall in 401 AD. The temple was later visited by Buddhist luminaries such as the sixth-century monk Zhiyao Sanzang, who planted the fig trees still here today; the Indian founder of Chan (Zen) Buddhism, **Bodhidharma** (see p.265); and Chan's Sixth Patriarch, Huineng. Though none of the original buildings survives, the grounds are well ordered and enclose pavilions concealing wells and engraved tablets from various periods, while three halls at the back contain some

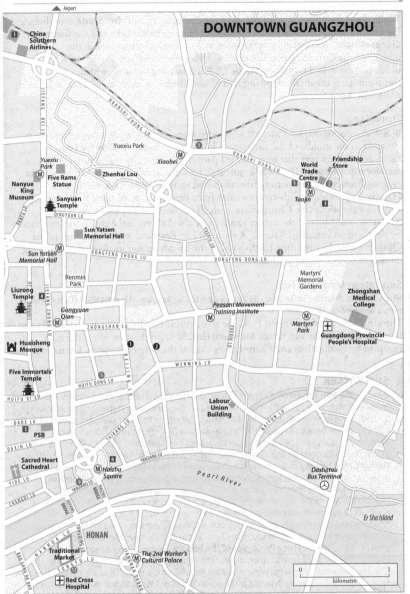

DOWNTOWN GUANGZHOU

imposing Buddha images; the westerly one is unusually reclining, while a more ordinary trinity fills the central hall.

Yuexiu Park

越秀公园, yuèxiù gōngyuán • 988 Jiefang Bei Lu • Daily 6am–10pm • Free • ☎ 020 86662357 • metro to Yuexi Park, exit B1

Yuexiu Park is China's biggest urban park, encompassing almost a square kilometre of sports courts, historic monuments, teahouses, three artificial lakes and shady groves.

While there are entrances at all points of the compass, Yuexiu's **front gate** is on Jiefang Bei Lu; to the north of the porcelain dragons here are **Beixiu Lake** and the **Garden of Chinese Idiom**, where many strange stone and bronze sculptures lurk in the undergrowth, illustrating popular sayings. Head south, and you'll wind up at the much-photographed **Five Rams Statue** (五羊石像, wǔyáng shíxiàng), which commemorates the myth of Guangzhou's foundation – at least one of these is definitely not a ram, however.

Zhenhai Lou

镇海楼, zhènhǎi lóu · Daily 9am–5.30pm · ¥10, free middle Wed of each month · ☎ 020 83545253, Ⓦ guangzhoumuseum.cn

Roughly in the middle of the park atop a hill, paths converge at **Zhenhai Lou**, a three-storey gate tower that once formed part of the Ming city walls. Today it houses the **Municipal Museum** (广州博物馆, guǎnzhōu bówùguǎn), full of locally found exhibits ranging from Stone Age pottery fragments and ivory from Africa found in a Han-dynasty tomb, to fifth-century coins from Persia, a copy of *Good Words for Exhorting the World* (the Christian tract which inspired the Taiping leader, Hong Xiuquan), and nineteenth-century cannons tumbled about in the courtyard (two made by the German company, Krupp). A statue of Lin Zexu and letters from him to the Qing emperor documenting his disposal of the British opium stocks always draws big crowds of tongue-clicking Chinese.

Sun Yatsen Memorial Hall

中山纪念堂, zhōngshān jìniàn táng · 259 Dongfeng Zhong Lu · Daily 8am–6pm · ¥10 · ☎ 020 83561631, Ⓦ zs-hall.com · metro to Sun Yatsen Memorial Hall, exit C

Directly to the south of Yuexiu Park, the most visible building is the large rotunda and blue-tiled roof of the **Sun Yatsen Memorial Hall**, built on the spot where the man regarded by Nationalists and Communists alike as the father of modern China took the

---

SUN YATSEN

Born in 1866, **Sun Yatsen** grew up during a period when China laboured under the humiliation of colonial occupation, a situation widely blamed on the increasingly feeble Qing court. Having spent three years in Hawaii during the 1880s, Sun studied medicine in Guangzhou and Hong Kong, where he became inspired by that other famous Guangdong revolutionary, Hong Xiuquan (see p.312), and began to involve himself in covert anti-Qing activities. Back in Hawaii in 1894, he abandoned his previous notions of reforming the imperial system and founded the **Revive China Society** to "Expel the Manchus, restore China to the people and create a federal government". The following year he incited an uprising in Guangzhou under **Lu Haodong**, notable for being the first time that the green Nationalist flag, painted with a white, twelve-pointed sun (which still appears on the Taiwanese flag), was flown. But the uprising was quashed, Lu Haodong was captured and executed, and Sun fled overseas.

Orbiting between Hong Kong, Japan, Europe and the US, Sun spent the next fifteen years raising money to fund revolts in southern China, and in 1907 his new Alliance Society announced its famous **Three Principles of the People** – Nationalism, Democracy and Livelihood. He was in Colorado when the Manchus finally fell in October 1911; on returning to China he was made provisional president of the Republic of China on January 1, 1912, but was forced to resign in February in favour of the powerful warlord **Yuan Shikai**. Yuan established a Republican Party, while Sun's supporters rallied to the Nationalist People's Party – **Guomindang** – led by **Song Jiaoren**. Song was assassinated by Yuan's henchmen following Guomindang successes in the 1913 parliamentary elections, and Sun again fled to Japan. Annulling parliament, Yuan tried to set himself up as emperor, but couldn't even control military factions within his own party, which plunged the north into civil war on his death in 1916. Sun, meanwhile, returned to his native Guangdong and established an independent Guomindang government. By the time of his death in 1925 he was greatly respected by both the Guomindang and the four-year-old Communist Party for his lifelong efforts to unite the country.

presidential oath in 1912. Inside it's a plain auditorium with seating for two thousand people, and is occasionally used as a concert hall.

Sanyuan Temple

三元宫, sānyuán gōng • 11 Yinguan Lu • Daily 8am–5pm • ¥1 • ☎ 020 83551548 • metro to Sun Yatsen Memorial Hall, exit C

Just north of the Sun Yatsen Memorial Hall, **Sanyuan Temple** can be found by simply heading for the gaggle of hawkers touting brightly wrapped packs of ghost money and incense. This is actually the largest Taoist temple in Guangzhou, and the oldest, too – it was first consecrated in 319 – though the current arrangement of spartan halls occupied by statues of Taoist deities is Qing. Despite being a busy place of worship, the temple is also a bit of a hidden gem, splashed in red- and gold-painted bats, cranes and other Taoist motifs, its dark wooden benches presenting an opportunity to sit in a serene spot.

Mausoleum of the Nanyue King Museum

西汉南越王墓, xīhàn nányuèwángmù • 867 Jiefang Bei Lu • ☎ 020 36182920 • Daily 9am–5.30pm, last admission 4.45pm • ¥12 • Yuexiu Gongyuan metro stop

Five hundred metres north of Yuexiu Park looms the red sandstone facade of **The Museum of the Mausoleum of the Nanyue King**. Discovered in 1983 during foundation-digging for a residential estate, it houses the 2000-year-old site of the tomb of **Zhao Mo**, grandson of the Nanyue Kingdom's founder Zhao Tuo, and really deserves an hour of your time – an English-language video provides background to the mass of exhibits. The museum's building itself has won several awards for combining modern and traditional Chinese style, although the actual tomb is quite drab.

8

The exhibition

Zhao Mo made a better job of his tomb than running his kingdom, which disintegrated shortly after his death: excavators found the mausoleum stacked with gold and priceless trinkets. They're on view in the museum, including a **burial suit** made from more than a thousand tiny jade tiles (jade was considered to prevent decay), and the ash-like remains of slaves and concubines immured with him. Several artefacts show Central Asian influence in their designs, illustrating how even at this early stage in Guangzhou's history there was contact with non-Chinese peoples.

Chen Clan Academy

陈家祠, chénjiā cí • Daily 8.30am–5.30pm, last admission 5pm • ¥10 • ☎ 020 81814559 • Chen Clan Academy metro exit D

Just north off Zhongshan Lu's western arm, a pedestrian walkway leads to the **Chen Clan Academy**. The complex was founded after subscriptions were invited from anyone named **Chen** (one of the most common Chinese surnames) and the result – part ancestor temple, part school – is a maze of rooms and courtyards, all decorated with the most garish tiles and gorgeously carved screens and stonework that money could buy in the 1890s. Have a look at the extraordinary brick reliefs under the eaves, both inside and out. One of the first, on the right as you enter, features an opera being performed for what looks like a drunken horse, which lies squirming on the floor with mirth. Other cameos feature stories from China's "noble bandit" saga, *Outlaws of the Marsh*, and some of the sights around Guangzhou.

Liwan

荔湾区, lìwān qū

Below the western end of Zhongshan Lu lies **Liwan** district, where the ring of part of the old city walls can be traced along **Longjin Lu** in the north, and **Dishifu Lu** and others to the south. Though a couple of wide, modern main roads barge through, most of this district, with east–west **Changshou Lu** at its core, retains its Ming-dynasty street plan and a splash of early twentieth-century architecture, making for excellent random walks. In addition to some of Guangzhou's biggest shopping plazas and a crowd of markets spreading into each other south from Changshou Lu right down to the river, several famous **restaurants** are located here, and the area is particularly busy at night.

Hualin Temple

华林寺, huálín sì • Wenchang Nan Lu • Daily 8am–5.30pm • ¥8 • Changshou Lu metro exit A

Shops and markets selling jade run all the way from the pedestrian square on Xiajiu Lu right up to Changshou Lu, culminating in two multistorey jade shopping malls built on either side of the Buddhist **Hualin Temple**, which was founded as a modest nunnery by the Brahman prince Bodhidharma in 527. After his Chan teachings caught on in the seventeenth century, the main hall was enlarged to house five hundred *arhat* sculptures ranged along the cross-shaped aisles, and Hualin remains the most lively temple in the city – during festivals you'll be crushed, deafened and blinded by the crowds, firecrackers and incense smoke.

Dishifu Lu and Xiajiu Lu

The area south of Hualin Temple is a great place to throw away your map and roam through the maze of alleys and Qing-era homes (some of which are protected historic relics), and just enjoy the atmosphere of a bustling and living city. In the middle of this are two streets, lined with restored 1920s facades and pedestrianized at the weekends: **Dishifu Lu** to the west, and **Xiajiu Lu** to the east. Places to shop and eat in the area are legion, the pavements always crammed to capacity.

Qingping Market

清平市场, qīngpíng shìchǎng • Huangsha metro exit D, then follow Liu'ersan Lu east

Between Xiajiu Lu and the river, **Qingping Market** was once one of China's most challenging – not to say gory – markets, full of large-scale streetside butchering in the interests of local culinary demands. Scaled back considerably in recent years, it remains a lively and busy affair, amply illustrating the Cantonese interest in fresh and unusual food, with each intersecting east–west lane forming dividing lines for the sale of different goods: dried medicines, spices and herbs, fresh vegetables, livestock, birds and fish – a great place to experience real Cantonese life.

Shamian Island

沙面岛, shāmiàn dǎo • Huangsha metro exit D, then cross the bridge

South of Liuersan Lu across a muddy canal, **Shamian Island** is a tear-shaped sandbank about 1km long and 500m wide which was leased to European powers as an Opium War trophy, the French getting the eastern end and the British the rest. Here the colonials re-created their own backyards, planting the now massive **trees** and throwing up solid, Victorian-style **villas**, banks, embassies, churches and tennis courts – practically all of which are still standing. Shamian todays serves as a quiet bolt hole for many long-term travellers in the city, and as a picturesque backdrop for wedding photographers. There's restricted traffic flow, and the well-tended architecture, greenery and relative peace make it a refreshing place to visit, if only to sample the restaurants and bars.

Around the island

The main thoroughfare is east–west **Shamian Dajie**, with five numbered streets running south across the island. Though sharing such a tiny area, the British and French seemingly kept themselves to themselves, building separate bridges, churches and customs houses. Wandering around, you'll find facades have largely been restored to their original appearance – most were built between the 1860s and early twentieth century – with plaques sketching their history. Next to the atypically, and looming, modern *White Swan* hotel on the **Shamian Nan Jie** esplanade, a focus of sorts is provided by **Shamian Park** (沙面公园, shāmiàn gōngyuán), where two **cannons**, cast in

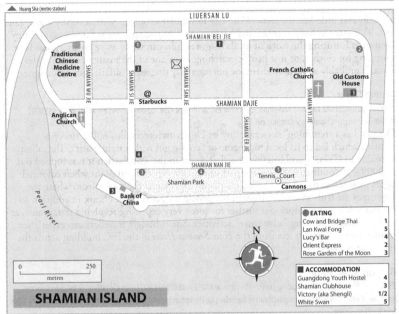

● EATING	
Cow and Bridge Thai	1
Lan Kwai Fong	5
Lucy's Bar	4
Orient Express	2
Rose Garden of the Moon	3

■ ACCOMMODATION	
Guangdong Youth Hostel	4
Shamian Clubhouse	3
Victory (aka Shengli)	1/2
White Swan	5

SHAMIAN ISLAND

nearby Foshan during the Opium Wars, face out across the river. You might catch Cantonese opera rehearsals here on Saturday afternoons.

Tianhe

天河, tiānhé • Metro to Linhexi

Guangzhou's new business district, **Tianhe** coalesced around a sports stadium built in 1986 as a showcase for the National Games, and is where to get a taste of the city's modern side. The district is worth at least a day, sporting some of China's tallest buildings and the marvellous **Guandong Provincial Museum** in the **Zhujiang New Town** area, whose many bars, clubs and restaurants all cater to Western expatriate tastes. Tianhe also has a few nooks and crannies hiding Guangzhou's artistic side (though the **Guangzhou Opera House** here is possibly the ugliest building dedicated to the arts in the world), alongside small designer boutiques dotted through **Liuyun** Quarter's leafy streets.

Guangdong Provincial Museum

省博物馆, shěng bówùguǎn • 2 Zhujiang Dong Lu • Daily 9am–5pm • Free but must show passport • ☎ 020 38046886, ⓦ gdmuseum.com • APM subway line to Opera House station exit B, or Zhujiang New Town metro exit B1

In Zhujiang New Town, the multimillion-dollar **Guangdong Provincial Museum** is, according to its promotional material, shaped "like a moonlight treasure box". It boasts some of the best natural history exhibitions in the country, including dinosaurs and whales, as well as its top-notch exhibits of Duanzhou inkstones, and Chaozhou woodcarving and porcelain. Don't miss the History of Guangdong section on the fourth-floor, despite its slightly nationalistic tone, which includes a real dragonboat. As well as being free, it's also one of the best air-conditioned museums in the city, making it a must in the summer.

Liuyun Quarter

六运季度, liùyùn jìdù • Tiyu Xilu metro exit H

Just across the road from the enormous TeeMall, the **Liuyun Quarter** is one of the most pleasant and little-known areas of the city to wander about in. With a faintly European feel, it's a maze of leafy avenues and backstreets, low-rise apartment buildings, and tiny boutiques featuring the work of local designers. You can while away an afternoon here shopping for clothes, or just people-watching from one of the many pavement cafés – you'll probably spot more than one outrageously dressed wannabe fashion designer.

Canton Tower

广州塔 guǎngzhōu tǎ · Daily 9am–11pm · 30th Floor ¥50, 107th Floor ¥150, Top Observation Deck ¥488 · ☎ 020 89338222, Ⓦ cantontower.com · Chigang Pagoda metro, exit A

Designed as a "feminine" skyscraper by its Dutch architects, this 600m tower is twisted, which led to its local nickname of "young girl with a tight waist". The tallest structure in China – and briefly the tallest tower in the world when it was topped out in 2009 – it dominates the eastern part of the city, especially at night when coloured lights play across its sinewy curves. It's possible to ascend the tower, from where the cityscapes are truly awesome, though the privilege doesn't come cheap; in addition to the entry fee, you can fork out further for some very expensive revolving restaurants, as well as vertigo-inducing "adventure" activities. Smart budget travellers can experience similar views for much less from the *Four Seasons Hotel* in the IFC building across the river (see p.492).

Baiyun Shan Park

白云山公园, báiyún shān gōngyuán · ¥5 · cable car ¥20–25 · ☎ 020 37222222 · bus #24 (30min) to the gates from the south side of Renmin Park, immediately northeast of the Jiefang Lu/Zhongshan Lu crossroads · Metro line #3 to Meihuayuan, about 1.2km from the Plum Garden

Just 7km north of downtown, **Baiyun Shan**, the White Cloud Mountains, are close enough to central Guangzhou to reach by city bus, but open enough to leave all the city's noise and bustle behind. Once covered with monasteries, Baiyun's heavily wooded slopes, dotted with refreshment stalls and restaurants, now offer lush panoramas out over Guangzhou and the delta region.

Routes to the top

The park encloses almost thirty square kilometres, and it's a good three-hour walk from the entrance off Luhu Lu to **Moxing Ling** (Star-touching Summit), past strategically placed teahouses and pavilions offering views and refreshments. There's also a **cable car** from the entrance as far as the **Cheng Precipice**, a ledge roughly halfway to the top, which earned its name when the Qin-dynasty minister **Cheng Ki** was ordered here by his emperor to find a herb of immortality. Having found the plant, Cheng nibbled a leaf only to see the remainder vanish; full of remorse, he flung himself off the mountain but – being now immortal – was caught by a stork and taken to heaven. Sunset views from the precipice are spectacular.

ARRIVAL AND DEPARTURE
GUANGZHOU

Guangzhou has multiple transit points spread all over the city, making it a daunting place to arrive at or depart from. Leaving, you'll generally need a few days to arrange tickets or at least check out the options, especially for the train.

BY PLANE

The regional airline, China Southern (daily 9am–6pm; ☎ 020 86120330), has its headquarters just east of Guangzhou train station at 181 Huanshi Xi Lu, with its well-organized ticket office upstairs.

Baiyun International Airport (白云国际飞机场, báiyún guójì fēijīchǎng) lies 20km north of the city centre. The second-busiest in China, it deliberately rivals Hong Kong's, but has considerably cheaper fares, and is well connected to cities across China, Southeast Asia and worldwide, and has free wi-fi throughout (☎ 020 36066999, Ⓦ www.gbiac.net/en/web/guest/byhome).

The easiest way to get into town is on metro line #1 from the Airport South station, which takes just 30min (daily 6.10am–11pm; ¥12–13). Taxis into town should cost ¥100–150 on the meter. Airport bus line #1 (5am–11pm; every 10–15min; ¥13–16) connects with the China Southern office at Guangzhou train station, although other routes run to various places in the city including CITIC Plaza in Tianhe.

Destinations Beijing (30 daily; 2hr 40min–3hr 40min); Changsha (4 daily; 1hr 15min); Chengdu (23 daily; 2hr 15min); Chongqing (18 daily; 1hr 40min); Dalian (9 daily; 4hr); Fuzhou (9 daily; 1hr 30min); Guilin (4 daily; 1hr 10min); Guiyang (12 daily; 1hr 40min); Haikou (16 daily; 1hr 10min); Hangzhou (23 daily; 2hr); Harbin (8 daily; 4hr); Hefei (7 daily; 1hr 55min); Hohhot (1 daily; 3hr 20min); Hong Kong (5 daily; 1hr 10min); Kunming (18 daily; 2hr 30min); Lanzhou (4 daily; 3hr–4hr 40min); Nanchang (10 daily; 1hr 25min); Nanjing (16 daily; 2hr); Nanning (7 daily; 1hr 20min); Qingdao (10 daily; 3–4hr); Sanya (10 daily; 1hr 25min); Shanghai (37 daily; 2hr 15min); Tianjin (7 daily; 3hr); Ürümqi (5 daily; 3hr 30min); Wuhan (9 daily; 1hr 45min); Xiamen (13 daily; 1hr 10min); Xi'an (15 daily; 2hr 30min); Yichang (1 daily; 1hr 55min); Zhengzhou (10 daily; 2hr 15min).

BY TRAIN

Demand for train tickets out of Guangzhou is very high. Tickets become available seven days before departure, but all classes sell out swiftly. There are several advance-ticket offices around town, where there's no commission and the queues are usually shorter than at the stations: the most convenient are in the Liwan Plaza (Changshou Lu metro, exit A); and at 305 Huanshi Zhong Lu (Haizu Square metro, exit B1). Trains to the same destination can leave from any one of the following, so make sure you double-check the departure point on your ticket.

Guangzhou Station (广州火车站, guǎngzhōu huǒchēzhàn), just north of the city centre, is pretty confrontational, the vast square outside perpetually seething with passengers, hawkers and hustlers. Mainline services from most central, northern and western destinations terminate here. The ticket hall is at the eastern end of the station; crowds are horrendous at peak times, when entry is through guarded gateways that are closed off when the interior becomes too chaotic. New arrivals exit on the west side of the square, convenient for the metro, which is just to the right of the bus station, but not easily visible or signposted.

Guangzhou East (东方火车站, dōngfāng guǎngzhōu chēzhàn) is 5km east of the centre at Tianhe and is handily located on metro line #1. The Kowloon Express trains from Hong Kong all terminate here

as well as many services from Shenzhen – although it's busy, it's by far the the most convenient and comfortable station to use in the city.

Guangzhou South Station (广州南站, guǎngzhōu nánzhàn) is in the city's Panyu district, around 17km south of the centre and a 30min ride on metro line #1. Most useful for trains heading to the Macau border at Zhuhai. The ticket office is just outside the main station as you come out of the metro, and to the right, though there is also a small ticket office upstairs on level 3.

Destinations Beijing (8 daily; 10–29hr); Changsha (50 daily; 2hr 25min–8hr 44min); Chaozhou (3 daily; 6hr 25min); Chengdu (4 daily; 30hr 36min–40hr 35min); Foshan (21 daily; 24–51min); Guilin (2 daily; 11hr 43min–12hr 51min); Guiyang (5 daily; 19hr 30min–22hr); Haikou (4 daily; 10hr 30min–13hr); Kowloon, Hong Kong (13 daily; 2hr); Kunming (3 daily; 23–27hr); Nanchang (9 daily; 10hr 30min–14hr); Nanning (6 daily; 12hr 30min–13hr 45min); Shanghai (4 daily; 16–22hr); Shenzhen (many daily; 36min–2hr 19min); Wuhan (many daily; 3hr 37min–20hr); Xiamen (2 daily; 13hr); Xi'an (13 daily; 7hr 40min–27hr 30min); Zhaoqing (22 daily; 1hr 40min–2hr 40min); Zhuhai (30 daily 1hr–1hr 19min).

BY BUS

Guangzhou has over seventeen bus stations. Although most of them are busy, especially at rush hour, buying tickets is often far easier than for any train services. Below are the main central bus stations with almost all major destinations served by multiple departure points – check which is best at ⑩ chinabusguide.com.

The provincial bus station (省汽车客运站, shěng qìchē kèyùnzhàn), west of Guangzhou train station at 145 Huanshi Xi Lu, handles arrivals from almost the entire country. It's always full to bursting, but tickets are easy to get – the ticket office is on the first floor – and there are at least daily departures to everywhere in Guangdong.

Liuhua station (流花车客运站, liúhuāchē kèyùnzhàn) is at 158 Huanshi Xi Lu, across the road from the provincial bus station. This is a clutch of depots handling destinations within 100km or so of Guangzhou – including all delta towns and Qingyuan.

Tianhe bus station (天河客运站, tiānhé kèyùnzhàn), at 633 Yanling Lu, is 7km out towards the eastern suburbs, and handles traffic from eastern Guangdong and central China. It's easily accessable by

8

THE YANGCHENG TRAVEL PASS

If you don't like queuing for tickets, invest in a **Yangcheng Pass** (羊城通, yángchéng tōng) stored-value card, which can be used on the metro, buses, some taxis, and even at convenience stores. These can be bought at metro station ticket offices but can only be charged at branches of *7-11* and other convenience stores inside stations (look for a free-standing sign and queue outside the shop). The standard card costs ¥70 with a ¥20 deposit.

metro and is the terminus for a branch of the orange line #1. You can buy tickets for departures from here at the provincial bus station – they'll stamp your ticket on the back for a free shuttle bus to the Tianhe station, which takes around 30min

Dashatou bus terminus (大沙头巴士总站, dàshātóu bāshì zǒngzhàn) 466 Yanjiang Dong Lu, by the Dashatou ferry pier. Dedicated station for direct, non-stop buses to Tsim Sha Tsui in Hong Kong (8 daily; 2–3hr; ¥85) and Macau (6 daily; 2–3hr; ¥75). About 1.5km south of Dongshankou metro station; buses #7 and #89 can get you to either Tianhe or Guangzhou railway station.

Express buses to Hong Kong are also run by CTS (☎020 83374810, ⓦctsbus.hkcts.com), take 3–4hr and depart from various hotels between 5.15am and 7.35pm; buy tickets at the departure points. Remember, during rush hours it may be a good idea to get the MTR from the border at Shenzen Bay Port (around 3hr; ¥65) which will save you time and money.

Destinations Beihai (13hr); Changsha (20hr); Chaozhou (6hr); Foshan (30min); Fuzhou (13hr); Guilin (6hr); Haikou (10hr); Hangzhou (10hr); Kowloon (2hr); Nanjing (22hr); Nanning (10hr); Panyu (1hr); Qingyuan (1hr); Sanya (14hr 30min); Shenzhen (1hr 30min); Xiamen (10hr); Zhaoqing (1hr 30min); Zhuhai (1hr 30min).

GETTING AROUND

Though Guangzhou is too big to walk everywhere, and bicycles are not recommended because of heavy traffic, the ever-expanding metro system makes getting around fairly straightforward, with almost everywhere within easy reach of a station.

By metro Guangzhou's extensive metro system has eight lines in service, with three more scheduled by 2020. Metro stations can be hard to locate at street level, but are signposted from nearby roads; keep an eye out for the red posts with yellow bands, and the metro logo at the top – something like a split "Y". Fares are ¥2–19, according to the number of stops from your starting point, and trains run every 2–3min approximately 6am–11pm. Carriages have bilingual route maps, and each stop is announced in Mandarin and English. Avoid rush hour, as carriages and stations are crammed to bursting, and metal crowd-control barriers go up – which is why the carrying of balloons is strictly forbidden on the system (in case you were wondering).

By bus Guangzhou's cheap and slow bus network covers most of the city from ¥2 a ride (no change given). Finding which bus to get on, however, is tricky if you don't read

Chinese, but many buses now announce stops in both Mandarin and English.

By taxi Taxis are plentiful except at rush-hour (when they often take longer than the metro anyway). Fares start at ¥10 for the first 2.5km, and ¥2.6 for each succeeding kilometer; larger vehicles charge more. All cabs are metered and drivers rarely try any scams, though the city's complex traffic flows can sometimes make it seem that you're heading in the wrong direction.

By motorbike taxi Outside many stations you may be accosted by a variety of motorcycle taxis, from beat-up regular motorcycles to three-wheelers that carry two people. These should cost about two-thirds the price of regular taxis for short journys, though be warned that drivers generally disregard not only the rules of the road, but seemingly the laws of physics too.

INFORMATION

Magazine For Guangzhou's eating, drinking and bar scene, as well as other expat-related and tourist information, try ⓦcityweekend.com.cn/guangzhou.

Tourist information offices (daily 9am–5.30pm) are located around the city, including at the airport, but they speak

no English and are of little use apart from getting a free map – and most hotels can supply you with one of these anyway.

Travel information Guangzhou has an English-speaking travellers' information and emergency line (☎020 86666666), which can be of use if you get into a jam.

ACCOMMODATION

Guangzhou's business emphasis means that budget accommodation is limited; resign yourself to this and plan accordingly. Prices rise during the fortnight-long trade fairs (see box below), when beds will be in short supply, but can be discounted

---

THE CANTON FAIR

The **China Import and Export Fair** (to give it its official name) is a bi-annual event held in Guangzhou since 1957. It is the largest of its kind in China, with 15,800 stands available at its gargantuan purpose-built halls in Pazhou, southeast of the city. The Spring session runs from April 14 to May 5 while the Autumn session runs from October 15 to November 4, both in three phases for different categories of products. During these times, accommodation prices in the city double or triple, and metro lines and buses to Pazhou become unbelievably busy. For more details see ⓦcantonfair.org.cn/en or phone ☎020 28888999.

by as much as fifty percent at other times. Shamian Island is the best place for travellers to stay, a pleasant spot with well-tended parks, a bit of peace and plenty of places to eat. Otherwise, there are several relatively inexpensive hotels in central Guangzhou, mostly near the riverfront, and upmarket accommodation in the city's north and eastern quarters, where you will also find a few budget options near Guangzhou train station.

SHAMIAN ISLAND

The places reviewed below are marked on the map on p.487, unless otherwise noted.

Guangdong Youth Hostel 广东青年招待所, guǎngdōng qīngnián zhāodàisuǒ. 2 Shamian Si Jie ☎020 81218298. Across from the lavish *White Swan*, this is one of Shamian's cheaper options. The ten-person dorm rooms are airy and comfortable and free internet is available, though despite the name, it's not an actual IYHF hostel. Dorm beds ¥60, rooms ¥270

★ **Riverside Youth Hostel** 广州江畔国际青年旅舍, guǎngzhōu jiāngpàn guójì qīngnián lǚshě) 15 Changdi Jie, Luju Lu ☎020 2239 2500, ☎rsjiangpan @yahoo.com.cn; see map, pp.478–479. Just across the water in a vibrant part of Liwan, this is Guangzhou's only genuine IYHF hostel. Very clean and efficient, but a little hard to reach; catch the metro line #1 to Fancun, take exit B2, then follow Luju Lu to Changdi Jie, turn right and walk 200m. Dorm beds ¥65, doubles ¥185

★ **Shamian Clubhouse** 沙面会馆, shāmiàn huìguǎn. 6 Shamian Dajie ☎020 81102388, ☎gzchotel.com. By far the most atmospheric hotel on the island, and housed in an old red-brick French customs house, this place has opulent, high-ceilinged rooms with period furniture and fittings, and even a wrought-iron lift. Utterly charming, though few of the staff speak any English. If you like character and luxury, this is the place to stay. ¥2680

Victory (aka Shengli) 胜利宾馆, shènglì bīnguǎn. Shamian Lu and Shamian Si Jie ☎020 81216688, ☎vhotel.com. Formerly the *Victoria* in colonial days, this upmarket choice covers two separate buildings; the newly renovated annexe (on Si Jie) is both more luxurious and more expensive. ¥518

White Swan 白天鹅宾馆, báitiān'é bīnguǎn. Shamian Nan Jie ☎020 81886968, ☎www .whiteswanhotel.com. A monolithic eyesore looming over Shamian, and a Chinese-Disneyland of new-money opulence inside, this was once Guangzhou's most upmarket place to stay. It's probably still the city's most famous, and a favourite with US citizens in town to adopt Chinese orphans. Currently under renovation.

CENTRAL GUANGZHOU

The places reviewed below are marked on the map on pp.482–483.

Guangdong Yingbin 广东迎宾馆, guǎngdōng yíng bīnguǎn. 603 Jiefang Bei Lu ☎020 83332950, ☎yingbinhotel.cn. Centrally located and just a 3min walk from the Gongyuanqian metro station, this four-star is a huge complex of square concrete wings, cunningly disguised as traditional Chinese with green tiling and flared eaves. Quite comfortable, and recently renovated. ¥980

Landmark 华厦大酒店, huáxià dàjiǔdiàn. 8 Qiaoguang Lu ☎020 83355988, ☎hotel-landmark .com.cn. Towering four-star business hotel with a great location between Haizu Square and the river, this place has all the facilities you might need, and is also the starting point for most of the CTS buses to Hong Kong. ¥630

New Beijing Hotel 北京新盛大酒店, běijīng xīnshèng dàjiǔdiàn. 10 Xihao 2 Lu ☎020 81232388. A typical inner-city Chinese hotel, but centrally located and fair value. The road it's on isn't the cleanest, but is full of some authentic, and very earthy, street restaurants where you can dine cheaply. ¥180

★ **Yingshang Jin Yi Hotel** 迎商金艺宾馆, yíngshāng jīnyì bīnguǎn. 318 Dade Lu ☎020 83391188. Comfortable and conveniently located hotel just 600m from Haizu Square and the river. Even though it doesn't look so great from the lobby, the rooms are large and clean, with good bathrooms, and it's altogether excellent value. The beds are supremely comfortable. ¥162

NORTHERN GUANGZHOU

The places reviewed below are marked on the map on pp.482–483.

Baiyun City 白云城市酒店, báiyún chéngshì jiǔdiàn. 179 Huanshi Xi Lu ☎020 86666889, ☎baiyuncityhotel.com. Right next to the China Southern office and the east side of the Guangzhou train station plaza, it's reasonably priced and very handy for early departures or late arrrivals from/to the station. Rooms are comfy, if a little on the small side. ¥330

Garden Hotel 花园酒店, huāyuán jiǔdiàn. 368 Huanshi Dong Lu ☎020 83338989, ☎thegardenhotel .com.cn. The city's most opulent accommodation, this offers a stunning marble-floored lobby decorated with gold-inlay wood panelling and piano bar. It also features a restaurant in its formal gardens that boasts its own waterfall. ¥1193

Liuhua 流花宾馆, liúhuā bīnguǎn. 194 Huanshi Xi Lu ☎020 86668800, ☎www.lh.com.cn. Probably the most comfortable hotel near Guangzhou station, it's located just over the road from Liuhua bus station, and has a broad range of rooms with good facilities, including a gym and sauna. ¥528

8

EASTERN GUANGZHOU

The places reviewed below, both at Zhuijiang New Town, are marked on the map on pp.478–479 and are close to the Canton Fair.

★ **Eyou Apartments** 亦友雅家短租公寓, yìyǒu yǎjiā duǎnzū gōngyù. 1318, Block A, International Apartment, 16 Huacheng Dadao ⓣ 020 38017199. One of the best options in Tianhe, it's literally just round the corner from *McCawley's Irish Pub* and rents out mini-apartments which have small kitchens, and even washing machines. A little hard to find: catch the metro to Wuyangcun, take exit B, cross the road, then turn right at the ABC bank, and it's on the left after a bakery. ¥178

Four Seasons 广州四季酒店, guǎngzhōu sìjì jiǔdiàn. IFC Building, 5 Zhujiang Xifang Lu ⓣ 020 88833888, ⓦ fourseasons.com/guangzhou. Undoubtably the highest accommodation in Guangzhou, occupying as it does the top part of the 103-storey IFC building. Phenomenal views, luxurious rooms, attentive staff and all mod cons; also a coffee shop on the 70th floor, a bar on the 99th, and various restaurants, all of which are open to non-guests and sport stunning cityscapes. ¥1780

EATING

Eating out is the main recreation in Guangzhou, something the city is famous for and caters to admirably, and it would be a real shame to leave town without having eaten in one of the more elaborate or famous restaurants. Once it was hard to find anything but Cantonese food, though now you can also track down a good variety of Asian, European and even Indian – not to mention regional Chinese. Restaurants aside, the city's numerous food stalls are never far away (streets off Beijing Lu have the best selection). Here you can pick up a few slices of roast duck or pork on rice, meat and chicken dumplings, or noodle soups, usually for less than ¥10 a plate. Be sure to try a selection of cakes and the fresh tropical fruits too; local lychees are so good that the emperors once had them shipped direct to Beijing.

CENTRAL GUANGZHOU

8

The following are all on the map on pp.482–483.

1920s Café 一九二零餐厅, yījiǔèrlíng cāntīng. 183 Yanjiang Lu, ⓣ 020 83336156, ⓦ 1920cn.com; Haizu Square metro, exit D. This refined German restaurant, with mains (¥50–130) including bratwürst, schnitzel, German noodles and sauerkraut, also has a pleasant, almost-riverside outdoor patio – perfect if you fancy knocking back a beer or two. Daily 11am–1am.

Datong 大同大酒家, dàtóng dàjiǔjiā. 63 Yanjiang Xi Lu ⓣ 020 81888988. If you're after an authentically noisy, crowded *dim sum* session with river views, head upstairs to floors 5 or 6 between 7am and noon. They pride themselves on their roast suckling pig. Window seats are in high demand, so arrive early. Daily 7am–11pm.

Huimin Fandian (aka Five Rams) 回民饭店, huímín fàndiàn. 325 Zhongshan Liu Lu ⓣ 020 81303991. At the crossroads with Renmin Lu, the city's biggest and most popular Muslim restaurant serves lamb hotpots, roast duck, lemon chicken, spicy beef and a few vegetarian options at reasonable prices. Just head up the stairs past the live seafood. Daily 7am–10pm.

★ **Lemon House** 越茗苑, yuèmíng yuàn. 507 Huifu Dong Lu ⓣ 020 83189715. Serving up succulent, spicy Southeast Asian fare, *Lemon House* is locked in competition with the much busier and harder-to-get-into *Tiger Prawn* across the street for the mantle of best Vietnamese in town. Few people realize, however, that it's more or less the same food, and owned by the same people. Mains ¥30–50. Daily 10am–11pm.

NORTHERN AND EASTERN GUANGZHOU

The following are all on the map on pp.482–483.

Dongbei Ren 东北人, dōngběi rén. 668 Renmin Bei Lu ⓣ 020 81361466 and at 1 Taojin Bei Lu ⓣ 020 83576277. Hugely popular nationwide chain serving Manchurian food. The sautéed corn kernels with pine nuts, steamed chicken with mushrooms, or eggs and black fungus are all good, and there are plenty of vegetarian options. No English spoken, but they have a photo menu. Around ¥20–50 per person, more if you go for seafood. Daily 10am–11pm.

El Español 爱思达西班牙餐厅, àisīdá xībānyá cāntīng) 2F, World Trade Center, Huanshi Dong Lu, & 9 Xingsheng Lu, Zhujiang New Town ⓣ 020 87302610. If you want to meet Spanish people then come to either branch, where they congregate to enjoy the fine tapas and especially rice dishes (*arrozes*) served in cheerful surroundings. It's not cheap with mains at ¥100–250, but stick to pasta, rice or pizza and you can eat here for under ¥100. Daily noon–midnight.

★ **Idyllic Garden Restaurant** 田园牧歌园林餐厅, tiányuán mùgē yuánlín cāntīng. Off Yiyuan Lu, Kecun metro, exit A ⓣ 136 02854747. Deep inside the northern end of the *T.I.T. Creative Zone*, this rooftop place offers mid-price barbecued meats to an artistic clientele. Recommended dishes include the lamb chops, and barbecued aubergine (烧烤茄子, shāokǎo qiézi), although the latter doesn't appear on the menu. You should be able to eat for under ¥50. Daily 11am–2pm & 5pm–2am.

Indian Star Restaurant 印度星餐厅, yìndù xīng cāntīng. 3F, Honghui International Trading Mall, Heng'an Lu T020 22812527, ⓦ indiastarrestaurant.com; Xiaobei metro exit D. Easy to find and clean Indian canteen serving mainly North Indian dishes for around

CANTONESE COOKING

Cantonese cooking is one of China's four major regional styles and is unmatched in the clarity of its flavours and its appealing presentation. Spoiled by good soil and a year-round growing season, the Cantonese demand absolutely fresh ingredients, kept alive and kicking in cages, tanks or buckets at the front of the restaurant for diners to select themselves. Westerners can be repulsed by this collection of wildlife, and even other Chinese comment that the Cantonese will eat anything with legs that isn't a piece of furniture, and anything with wings that isn't an aeroplane. The cooking itself is designed to keep textures distinct and flavours as close to the original as possible, using a minimum amount of mild and complementary seasoning to prevent dishes from being bland.

No full meal is really complete without a simple plate of rich green and bitter **choi sam** (*cai xin* in Mandarin), Chinese broccoli, blanched and dressed with oyster sauce. Also famous is **fish and seafood**, often simply steamed with ginger and spring onions; and nobody cooks **fowl** better than the Cantonese, always juicy and flavoursome, whether served crisp-skinned and roasted or fragrantly casseroled. Guangzhou's citizens are also compulsive snackers, and outside canteens you'll see **roast meats**, such as whole goose or strips of barbecued pork, waiting to be cut up and served with rice for a light lunch, or burners stacked with **sandpots**, a one-person dish of steamed rice served in the cooking vessel with vegetables and slices of sweet *lap cheung* sausage. **Cake shops** selling heavy Chinese pastries and filled buns are found everywhere across the region – make sure you try roast-pork buns and flaky-skinned **mooncakes** stuffed with sweet lotus seed paste.

DIM SUM

Perhaps it's this delight in little delicacies that led the tradition of **dim sum** (*dian xin* in Mandarin) to blossom in Guangdong, where it's become an elaborate form of breakfast most popular on Sundays, when entire households pack out restaurants. Also known in Cantonese as **yum cha** – literally, "drink tea" – *dim sum* involves little dishes of fried, boiled and steamed snacks being stuffed inside bamboo steamers or displayed on plates, then wheeled around the restaurant on trolleys, which you stop for inspection as they pass your table. On being seated, you're given a pot of tea, which is constantly topped up, and a card, which is marked for each dish you select and which is later surrendered to the cashier. Try *juk* (rice porridge), spring rolls, buns, cakes and plates of thinly sliced roast meats, and small servings of restaurant dishes like spare ribs, stuffed capsicum, or squid with black beans. Save most room, however, for the myriad types of little fried and steamed **dumplings** which are the hallmark of a *dim sum* meal, such as *har gau*, juicy minced prawns wrapped in transparent rice-flour skins, and *siu mai*, a generic name for a host of delicately flavoured, open-topped packets.

¥35–80 while Hindi movies play in the background. Has much cheaper (and lower-quality) Western food too. Daily 10.30am–11.30pm.

WESTERN GUANGZHOU

The following are all on the map on pp.482–483

Guangzhou 广州酒家, guǎngzhōu jiǔjiā. 2 Wen Chang Nan Lu, on the corner with Xiajiu Lu ☎020 8138 0388, ⊛gzr.com.cn. The oldest, busiest and most famous restaurant in the city, with entrance calligraphy by the Qing emperor Kangxi and a rooftop neon sign flashing "Eating in Guangzhou". The menu is massive, and you won't find better crisp-skinned chicken or pork anywhere – bank on at least ¥80 a person for a decent feed. Daily 7.30am–3pm & 5.30–10pm.

Lian Xiang Lou 莲香楼, liánxiāng lóu. 67 Dishifu Lu ☎020 81811638. Established in 1889 and famous for its mooncakes (baked dough confections stuffed with sweet

lotus paste), which you can buy from the downstairs shop. The upstairs restaurant does commendable roast suckling pig, brown-sauced pigeon, and "Lotus 8" fried duck with lotus flowers (¥138), with other mains about ¥35–80 a portion. Daily 7am–10pm.

Liwan Mingshijia 荔湾名食家, lìwān míngshíjiā. 99 Dishifu Lu ☎020 81391405. Ming-style canteen and teahouse decked in heavy marble furniture, crammed with diners wolfing down *dim-sum*-style snacks. Some of the finest *sheung fan* (stuffed rice rolls), *zongzi* (steamed packets of rice and meat) and *tangyuan* (glutinous riceballs filled with chopped nuts in a sweet soup) you'll find. The English menu-card is without prices, though most dishes are only around ¥10. Daily 7am–11.30pm.

★ **Tao Tao Ju** 陶陶居, táotáo jū. 20 Dishifu Rd ☎020 81396111. Looks upmarket, with huge chandeliers, wooden shutters and coloured leadlight windows, but prices are very good value. Roast goose is the house speciality, and they also do cracking seafood – plain boiled prawns or fried bean-noodle crab are both excellent – along with crisp-skinned chicken, lily-bud and beef sandpots, and a host of Cantonese favourites. Comprehensive English menu, with mains ¥18–120. Daily 7am–4pm & 5.30–11pm.

SHAMIAN ISLAND

The following are all on the map on p.487.

★ **Cow and Bridge Thai** 泰国牛桥, tàiguó niúqiáo. 54 Shamian Bei Lu ☎020 81219988. Great place to dine on what is unquestionably the finest Thai food in Guangzhou. The food is beautifully presented and the service impeccable. Main dishes are pricey, with curries starting at ¥50, but there are much cheaper weekday lunch sets starting at ¥35 (noon–2pm). Daily 11am–11pm.

Lan Kwai Fong 兰桂坊, lánguìfāng. Shamian Nan Lu ☎020 81216523. Taking its name from Hong Kong's central bar and restaurant district, this mid-price Guangdong restaurant's two outlets – one overlooking the tennis courts and one at the eastern end of the park – are extremely popular with locals, especially at the weekend. Mains from ¥35. Daily 11am–3pm & 5–9.30pm.

Lucy's Bar 露丝吧, lùsī bā. 3, Shamian Nan Lu ☎020 81366203, ⓦlucyscafe.cn. Pleasant "American" restaurant to sit outside in the evening and eat reasonable Mexican, Thai and Indian-style dishes, along with burgers, pizza and grills. Mains ¥35–170; beer ¥33 a pint. Daily 11am–1am.

Orient Express 车站西餐酒廊, chēzhàn xīcān jiǔláng. 1 Shamian Bei Lu ☎020 81218882. Fancy French gastronomy is available at this Gallic-owned restaurant which will serve you dinner either in the garden, or aboard one of two luxury train carriages. The à la carte is quite pricey (about ¥200 upwards per head), but the two-course ¥78 set menu is a bargain. Daily 11am–11pm.

Rose Garden of the Moon 玫瑰园西餐厅, méiguìyuán xīcāntīng. 3 Shamian Nan Lu ☎020 81218008, ⓦgzshamian.com.cn. Romantic, open-air restaurant set in the park and popular with couples. Reasonable Western-style menu from around ¥80 a head, but best for the riverside views, when tables and a barbecue are set up next to the water after 6pm. Daily 11am–2am.

SOUTH OF THE RIVER

See the map on pp.482–483.

Fo World Sushishe 佛世界素食社, fóshìjiè sùshìshè. 2–8 Niu Nai Chang Jie, south of Tongfu Lu ☎020 84243590; 2nd Workers' Cultural Palace metro stop. Down a small alley, this is hard to find: look for the sign reading "Fut Sai Kai". Huge portions of vegetarian food; crispy chicken drumsticks in sweet-and-sour sauce, salt-fried prawns, chicken-ball casserole and the rest are all made from bean curd, with heaps of straightforward vegetable dishes too. Full English menu and most mains are under ¥30. Daily 7am–9pm.

DRINKING, NIGHTLIFE AND ENTERTAINMENT

Guangzhou's clubs range from warehouse-sized discos to obscure, almost garage-like affairs. There are a few in the centre on Changdi Dama Lu (长堤大马路, chángdī dàmǎlù), just behind the waterfront, which is an up-and-coming clubbing area, and out in the east of the city is the new and very trendy Party Pier (琶醍珠江啤酒文化创意, páxǐng zhūjiāng píjiǔ wénhuà chuàngyì), attractively located on Yuejiang Xi Lu, between the river and the Zhujiang beer factory. Some places have a cover charge though most make their money from pricey drinks. Expats favour the bars located in Guangzhou's eastern reaches, where the booze is cheaper (¥20–35 a pint), pub-style meals can be had for ¥40, and the music is directed to Western tastes. Club hours are from 8pm to 2am; bars are open anytime from lunch to 2am, but don't expect much to be happening before 9pm. For the latest in an ever-changing scene, check ⓦgzstuff.com, ⓦcityweekend.com.cn/guangzhou or ⓦguangzhounightlife.com.

BARS

Hill Bar 小山吧, xiǎoshān bā. 367 Huanshi Dong Lu, Tao Jin metro exit B ☎020 83590206; map pp.482–483. Probably the nicest (though slightly more expensive) in a trio of adjacent expat bars, with a bigger mix of international and local clientele. Serves imported beers, cocktails and wine, has a comfortable outdoor terrace with wicker chairs, and a roadhouse feel inside. It also has a wide range of bar meals from ¥40, and occasional live music. The nearby *Mango* has a couch surfing night on Fridays, when backpackers can meet up. Both show big sporting events. Daily 10.30am–3.30am.

McCawley's Irish Pub and Restaurant 麦考利酒吧西餐厅, màikǎolì jiǔbā xīcāntīng. 16 Huacheng Dadao, Zhujiang New Town, metro exit B1 ☎020 38017000, ⓦmccawleys.com; map pp.478–479. Immensely popular two-floor faux Irish pub, with oakpanelling and flock wallpaper, especially busy when they're showing international sports on one of their three big screens. Unlike the drinks, the average pub grub is overpriced unless you order the week-night food specials, though the Tex-Mex is good. One of many foreign-style bars, coffeeshops and restaurants in the area. Daily 10am–2am.

Pastoral Music Bar 田园音乐酒吧, tiányuán yīnyuè jiǔbā. Off Yiyuan Lu, Kecun metro, exit A ☎020 87992345; see p.479. Deep inside the northern end of the *T.I.T. Creative Zone*, this is a Chinese bar is the place to come if you are musical or artistic, as the clientele are mostly creative folk who work in the zone; there's live music nightly (of varying quality) from 10pm to midnight. After that it's an alcohol-fuelled jamming free-for-all till the sun's up and, although few people speak English, everyone is very friendly and welcoming. You'll probably be the only foreigner. Daily 7pm–2am or later.

CLUBS

Catwalk 163 Tianhe Bei Lu ☎020 62869999; see the map on p.479. Guangzhou's biggest "super-club", where you can expect to find international DJs and a wealthy clientele dressed to kill inside its glamorous, state-of-the-art interior. Get in early or you'll either not get in at all, or not get a spot at the bar – which means paying a minimum table charge of ¥1200 on Fri & Sat (for 4–5 people). Security is, unfortunately, fairly annoying, and don't expect to be let in if you've dressed down. Daily 9pm–3am.

Cave 墨西哥餐厅酒吧, mòxīgē cāntīng jiǔbā. 360 Huanshi Dong Lu ☎020 83863660; map pp.482–483. Located in a basement and perhaps best visited in a group, this place offers leather-sofa booths around a stage where nightly dance shows start at 10pm: Chinese-, Latin-, belly- and "sexy"-dance all precede DJ sets at the small UV-lit dancefloor. A very Chinese clubbing experience. Daily 9pm–4am.

Wavebar A16, Party Pier, Yue Jiang Xi Lu ☎020 34489898; see the map on p.479. Foreigners often complain about this bar (bad service and bad drinks), yet it remains one of the most popular with expats and visitors alike, mainly due to its funky interior and funkier music – a mix of house, hip-hop and techno. It has enough room to dance and is still one of the better offerings inside the Party Pier complex, which includes quieter bars where you can sit overlooking the river. Daily 7.30pm–3am.

SHOPPING

Antiques and curios Wende Lu, running south from Zhongshan Lu, and various small shops in the streets between Dishifu Lu and Liuersan Lu, have varying selections of authenticated antiques, jade, lacquerwork, scrolls, chops and cloisonné artefacts.

Clothes For general outlets, try Dishifu Lu; the TeeMall in Tianhe is one of the biggest in Asia, good for designer labels. Many local designers have small boutiques in the Liyuan Quarter (see p.487), also in Tianhe.

Souvenirs The streets running east off the southern end of Renmin Lu are good for very Chinese things: Yide Lu has

several huge wholesale warehouses stocking dried foods and toys – action figures from Chinese legends, rockets and all things that rattle and buzz; other shops in the area deal in home decorations, such as colourful tiling or jigsawed decorative wooden dragons and phoenixes, and at New Year you can buy those red-and-gold good-luck posters put up outside businesses and homes. For out-and-out tourist souvenirs, such as batiks and clothing, carved wooden screens and jade monstrosities, try the streets of Shamian Island. The enormous jade market near Hualin Temple (see p.486) is also worth a snoop.

DIRECTORY

Acupuncture The tourist-oriented Shamian Traditional Chinese Medicine Centre on Shamian Island (85–87 Shamian Bei Jie ☎020 81218383, ⓦgzshamian.com.cn /yao/index.asp) offers foot massages (60min; ¥128), herbal baths (¥118), acupuncture (¥50 upwards) and hot cupping (¥60). Daily 9am–6pm.

Banks and exchange Most Bank of China branches can exchange money, including the enormous office at 197 Dongfeng Zhong Lu and outside the *White Swan*, Shamian Island (both open for currency exchange Mon–Fri 9am– noon & 2–5pm). Counters at almost all upmarket hotels can change currency for non-guests. Many banks have at least one ATM that accepts foreign cards.

Bookshop The city's biggest bookshop, Guangzhou Books Centre, is at the southwest corner of Tianhe Square, Tianhe Lu, but there's little in English.

Consulates Further information on consulates can be found on the Guangzhou local government's website (ⓦenglish.gz.gov.cn). Visa sections are usually only open around 9–11.30am, and getting served isn't always easy. Australia, 12th Floor, Development Centre, No. 3 Linjiang Lu, Zhujiang New City ☎020 38140111, visa office ☎020 38140250, ⓦguangzhou.china.embassy.gov.au; Canada, Suite 801, China Hotel Office Tower, Liu Hua Lu ☎020 86660569; France, Room 801-3, *Guangdong International*, 339 Huanshi Dong Lu ☎020 28292000; Germany, Floor 14, TeeMall, 208 Tianhe Lu ☎020 83130000, ⓦkanton.diplo .de; Italy, Room 1403, Heijing International Financial Plaza, 8 Huaxia Lu, Zhujiang New Town, Tianhe ☎020 38396225; Japan, *Garden* hotel, 368 Huanshi Dong Lu ☎020 83343009; Malaysia, Floor 19, CITIC Plaza, 233 Tianhe Bei Lu ☎020 38770765; Netherlands, Floor 34, TeeMall, 208 Tianhe Lu ☎020 38132200; Philippines, Room 709, *Guangdong International*, 339 Huanshi Dong Lu ☎020 83311461; Thailand, Floor 2, *Garden* hotel, 368 Huanshi Dong Lu ☎020 83804277; UK, Floor 2, *Guangdong International*, 339 Huanshi Dong Lu ☎020 83143000; US, 43 Hua Jiu Lu, Zhujiang New Town ☎020 38145775, ⓦguangzhou.usembassy-china.org.cn; Vietnam, Floor 2, Building B, *Hotel Landmark Canton*, 8 Qiaoguang Lu, Haizhu Square ☎020 83305911.

Hospitals The Guangzhou United Family Clinic, PICC Building, 301 Guangzhou Dadao Zhong, Tianhe (daily 8.30am–5.30pm; ☎020 87106000, 24hr emergency

8

hotline 📞 020 87106060; 🌐 www.unitedfamilyhospitals .com), has overseas-qualified doctors. Other options include the Global Doctor Clinic, Tianyu Garden, 136 Linhe Zhong Lu, Tianhe (daily 24hr; 📞 020 38906699, 24hr emergency hotline 📞 139 24001705, 🌐 globaldoctor.com.au), which has a pickup service for patients within 20km. There are English-speaking dentists at AllSmile Dental Clinic, Room 603–604, 6/F, Metro Plaza, 183 Tianhe Bei Lu (Mon–Sat 9am–6pm; 📞 020 87553380).

Internet Most hotels, coffeeshops and bars offer fee wi-fi and many hotels have their own terminals.

Left luggage There are offices at the train stations (daily 7am–11pm; ¥10/day), bus stations (daily 8am–6pm; ¥10/day) and most hotels.

Mail There are major post offices with parcel post on the western side of the square outside Guangzhou train station (daily 8am–8pm), and across from the Cultural Park entrance on Liuersan Lu (daily 8am–6pm). Shamian Island's post counter is open Mon–Sat 9am–5pm for stamps, envelopes and deliveries.

PSB Visa and residence applications are handled on the 6th Floor, 155, Jiefang Nan Lu 📞 020 83111895 (Haizu Square metro, exit B2; Mon–Fri 9am–noon & 1–5pm).

The Pearl River Delta

At a glance, the **Pearl River Delta** seems entirely a product of the modern age, dominated by industrial complexes and the glossy, high-profile cities of **Shenzhen**, east on the crossing to Hong Kong, and westerly **Zhuhai**, on the Macau border. Back in the 1980s these were marvels of Deng Xiaoping's reforms, rigidly contained **Special Economic Zones** of officially sanctioned free-market activities, previously anathema to Communist ideologies. Today, below the Delta's modern mantle of intense industrialization, there are a few places worth a day-trip from Guangzhou: don't miss **Foshan**'s splendid **Ancestral Temple**, or **Kaiping**'s bizarre antique architecture; historians might also wish to visit **Humen**, where the destruction of British opium in 1839 ignited the first Opium War.

Foshan

佛山, fóshān

Twenty-five kilometres southwest of Guangzhou, the satellite suburb of **FOSHAN** was once very much a town in its own right, with a history dating back to the seventh century. Along with neighbouring **Shiwan**, Foshan became famous for its ceramics and the splendour of its guildhall-temples, two of which survive on **Zumiao Lu**, a kilometre-long street shaded by office buildings and set in the heart of what was once the old town centre.

Zumiao Temple Complex

祖庙, zǔmiào • 21 Zumiao Lu • Daily 8.30am–6pm • ¥20 • metro to Zumiao

Zu Miao is a masterpiece of southern architecture, founded in 1080 as a metallurgists' guild temple. Ahead and to the left of the entrance is an elevated garden fronted by some locally made Opium War **cannons** – sadly for the Chinese, poor casting techniques and a lack of rifling made these inaccurate and liable to explode. Nearby, magnificent glazed **roof tiles** of frolicking lions and characters from local tales were made in nearby Shiwan for temple restorations in the 1830s. The temple's **main hall** is on the left past here, its interior crowded with minutely carved wooden screens,

---

MARTIAL ARTS AT FOSHAN

Foshan is renowned as a **martial-arts centre**, and at the rear of the Zumiao Temple (and included on the same ticket) is a museum dedicated to local master **Yip Man** (Bruce Lee's instructor and subject of the hit 2008 biopic *Ip Man*). The adjacent and more substantial **Huang Feihong Memorial Hall** is dedicated to the Hung Gar stylist Wong Feihung, who died in 1924 and has since been virtually canonized by the martial arts community, the hero of countless kung fu movies. An excellent reason to visit the hall is the **free martial-arts shows**, held at 10.30am and 3pm daily.

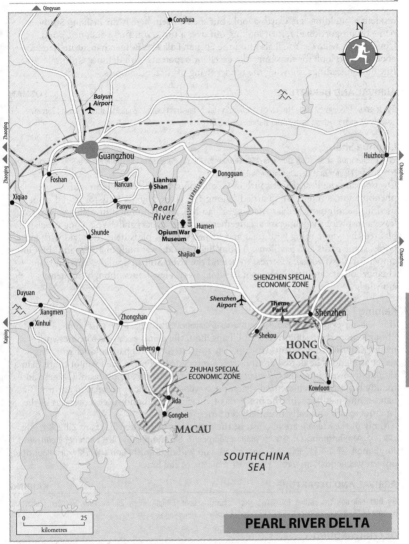

PEARL RIVER DELTA

oversized guardian gods leaning threateningly out from the walls, and a three-tonne
statue of Beidi, God of the North, who in local lore controlled low-lying Guangdong's
flood-prone waters – hence this shrine to snare his goodwill. Outside, the highly
decorative Wanfu stage dates to 1685; Foshan is considered the birthplace of Cantonese
opera, and halls nearby house the **Guangdong Museum of Cantonese Opera**.

Liang Yuan and the Folk Art Institute

梁园, liángyuán • entrance off Songfeng Lu, just past the police station • Daily 9am–5pm • ¥10

About 1km due north of Zumiao, **Liang Yuan** is one of the delta's historic **gardens**,
built between 1796 and 1850 by a family of famous poets and artists of the period.
There are artfully arranged ponds, trees and rocks, and the tastefully furnished

residential buildings are worth a look, but the real gem here is the **Risheng Study**, a perfectly proportioned retreat looking out over a tiny, exquisitely designed pond, fringed with willows. You'll also find the **Foshan Folk Arts Research Institute** here, a good place to look for souvenirs like excellent **papercuts** with definite Cultural Revolution leanings, showing the modernizing of rural economies.

ARRIVAL AND DEPARTURE — FOSHAN

By metro The easiest way to reach Foshan is on Guanzhou's metro system: from Xilang station, catch a GF line train south to Zumiao station in around 25min.

Lianhua Shan

莲花山, liánhuā shān • Daily 8am–4pm • ¥50 • ☎ 020 84861298, ⓦ pylianhuashan.com • metro line #4 to Shiqi station, then taxi (¥15) or bus #92 from outside the station for the final 3km

Overlooking the Pearl River south of Guangzhou, **Lianhua Shan** is an odd phenomenon, a mountain quarried as long ago as the Han dynasty for its red stone, used in the tomb of the Nanyue king, Zhao Mo. After mining it in such a way as to leave a suspiciously deliberate arrangement of crags, pillars and caves, Ming officials planted the whole thing with trees and turned it into a pleasure garden laid with lotus pools, stone paths and pavilions. A 50m-high pagoda was built in 1612, and the Qing emperor Kangxi added a fortress to defend the river. Still a popular excursion from Guangzhou, it's an interesting spot to while away a few hours, though frequently crowded.

Kaiping

开平, kāipíng • each village ¥50 • multiple-entry tickets ¥180 • additional ¥20 to climb Ruishi Lou • ⓦ kptour.com

Though more than 100km west of Guangzhou, the delta's excellent road network makes **KAIPING** an excellent day-trip. The town itself has no particular charm – its secret attractions lie dotted around the countryside beyond in the form of more than a thousand towers known as *diaolou* (碉楼, diāolóu). A fusion of European, Chinese and frankly fantastical architectural styles, the towers were built as protection against bandits and paid for with the proceeds of villagers who found success overseas in the late nineteenth and early twentieth centuries.

Many of the *diaolou* are in clusters, the main sites being the villages of **Zili** (自力村, zìlìcūn), **Majianglong** (马降龙村, mǎjiànglóng cūn), **Sanmenli** (三门里村, sānménlǐ cūn) and **Jingjiangli** (锦江里村, jǐnjiānglǐ cūn), where you will find **Ruishi Lou** (瑞石楼, rùishílóu; open only at weekends), arguably the most majestic of the lot.

ARRIVAL AND DEPARTURE — KAIPING

By bus Kaiping's Yici Station (义祠站, yìcí zhàn) handles traffic to Guangzhou's Fengcun bus station (daily 6am–7.10pm; every 20min; ¥57), Shenzen, Zuhai and Hong Kong.

GETTING AROUND

By bus Buses crisscross between Kaiping's Yici bus station and the sites, and it is perfectly possible – if slow – to make it round by hopping on and off these.

By taxi or minibus You can hire one of the many waiting taxis or minibuses for a day-tour of Kaiping's sights for around ¥400–500, but be prepared to negotiate. To organize this beforehand, there are four official tour taxi companies, the biggest of which is *Volkswagen* (☎ 0750 2228222), but it'll cost a bit more.

Humen

虎门, hŭmén

The routine industrial face of **HUMEN** (pronounced "Fumen" locally) ensures most visitors pass without a second look, but it also belies a colourful history. In 1839, after enduring a six-week siege of their warehouses in Guangzhou, the British were finally forced to hand over 1200 tonnes of **opium** to the Chinese authorities. The cargo was

THE ZHUHAI–MACAU BORDER

The mainland **border with Macau** is at the coastal city of Zhuhai (珠海, zhūhǎi), around 150km southwest of Guangzhou. The crossing point itself is in the Gongbei district (拱北口岸, gǒngběi kǒuàn), located a couple of hundred metres east of Zhuhai's bus and train stations. The **border crossing** itself (open 7am–midnight) is pretty straightforward in either direction, and takes about 30 minutes to an hour depending on how busy it is. Be very careful of your possessions either end, as pickpocketing is apparently rife.

Zhuhai is well connected to Guangzhou via the Guangzhu Intercity Railway to Guangzhou South station (daily 7am–10.35pm; every 30min; 43min; ¥70). **Buses** between Gongbei bus station and Guangzhou take between two to four hours (daily 6.10am–9.15pm; every 20min; ¥70–80); when buying tickets in Zhuhai, be careful to identify which of Guangzhou's many bus stations you want to go to. There are also 6 daily **non-stop bus** departures running direct between Macau itself and the Dashatou bus terminus, right in the centre of Guangzhou (3hr; ¥75).

brought to Humen, mixed with quicklime, and dumped in two 45m pits on the beach at **Shajiao** (沙角, shājiǎo), later to be flushed out to sea. Incensed, the British massacred the Chinese garrisons at Humen, and attacked Guangzhou. The Guangdong governor, Lin Zexu, got the blame and was replaced by an ineffectual nephew of the emperor, Qishan, who infuriated his uncle by unilaterally agreeing to hand over Hong Kong to Britain as compensation for the lost opium.

Opium War sites

Humen's bloody associations are recounted at the **Lin Zexu Park Opium War Museum** (林则徐公园 鸦片战争博物馆, lín zéxú gōngyuán yāpiàn zhànzhēng bówùguǎn; ☏0769 85512065; daily 8.30am–5pm; free) on Jiefang Lu, a twenty-minute walk between the skyscrapers northwest of Humen's bus station. If you can take another battering of justifiable moral outrage after this, follow this up with a visit to the diorama-rich **Sea Battle Museum** (海战博物馆, hǎizhàn bówùguǎn; daily 8.30am–5pm; free) on Weiyuan Island – reached at the end of the #9 bus route. Nearby, **Weiyuan Fort** (威远炮台, wēiyuán pàotái; daily 8.30am–6pm, ¥8), almost underneath Humen Bridge, provides a pleasant break from the city and a chance to see an actual historical site in the flesh – though most is covered by trees, the thick outer walls still look impregnable.

Shenzhen

深圳, shēnzhèn

Some Westerners may be familiar with **SHENZHEN** as the global centre of iPod production, but the city's role in determining China's technology boom ensures that it's well known to all its countrymen: it was in this one-time fishing village that China's modern "economic miracle" was born. Today, the city's gleaming skyscrapers – and ongoing construction – are testament to a continued success, as is the daily flow of thousands of commuters across the border, not just from Shenzhen to Hong Kong, but increasingly in the opposite direction. This doesn't necessarily mean there's much of interest to the casual visitor: the much-vaunted shopping is in decline, though a decent eating scene remains alongside a downright border-town seediness in areas – an atmosphere compounded by pushy touts, beggars and pickpockets.

Some history

Thanks to its proximity to then-British-colony Hong Kong, Shenzhen – then a tiny hamlet called Bao'an – was chosen in 1979 as the country's first "Special Economic Zone", a free-market experiment that provided both the model for the subsequent move away from a controlled economy and the spark for meteoric growth. By 1990 the city had four harbours, its manufacturing industries were turning over $2 billion a year

and a new nuclear power station was needed to cope with the energy demand. Delegations from all over China poured in to learn how to remodel their own businesses, cities and provinces.

Shenzhen may not have been the cause of capitalism in the People's Republic, but it has provided invaluable propaganda to those who promoted its virtues. It is no coincidence that in 1992, Deng Xiaoping chose Shenzhen as the place to make his memorable statement, "Poverty is not Socialism: to get rich is glorious", voicing the Party's shift away from Communist dogma – and opening the gate for China's financial explosion.

The city centre

For an up-close glimpse of the city and its myriad shopping and eating options, a stroll along Renmin Lu, running northeast from the train station and **Luo Hu border crossing** (罗湖, luóhú; in Hong Kong you'll see the Cantonese rendering, Lo Wu), is a good introduction. Over Jiefang Lu and you're in the tangle of narrow lanes that formed the **old town** of Bao'an; now a pedestrianized warren of shops selling cheap phones, clothes, shoes, bags and the ubiquitous DVDs. Here, on Qingyuan Lu, was the historic site of China's first ever *McDonald's* restaurant, since replaced with larger premises and joined by *KFC*, *Starbucks* and *Pizza Hut*, among others.

Lizhi Park

荔枝公园, lìzhī gōngyuán • Shennan Zhong Lu • Free • Da Ju Yuan metro

Lizhi Park is a surprisingly refreshing open space with a fun boating lake. South of the park, on Shennan Zhong Lu, the **Shenzhen Museum** (深圳博物馆, shēnzhèn bówùguǎn; Tues–Sun 10am–6pm; free) holds thousands of relics dug up during the construction of the city, paintings and works of calligraphy, as well as many historical items on loan from museums around China.

Diwang Commercial Center

地王大厦, dìwáng dàshà • junction of Shennan Lu and Bao'an Nan Lu • Daily 8.30am–11.30pm • ¥80 • ☎ 0775 82462230 • Grand Theatre metro • buses #1, #2, #3 & #10

A bird's-eye view of Shenzhen can be taken from the observation platform 384m up on the 69th floor of the **Diwang Center**. At the viewing platform there are big windows with telescopes as well as some rather desperate exhibits, including a waxwork reconstruction of the handover talks between Deng Xiaoping and Margaret Thatcher. From here downtown Shenzhen is revealed as a 5km-wide semicircle of high-rises immediately north of the Hong Kong border, bisected by the rail line descending straight down Jianshe Lu to the Luo Hu border crossing.

Lianhua Shan Park

莲花山公园, liánhuāshān gōngyuán • Hongli Xi Lu • Daily 6am–7pm • Free • ☎ 0775 83067950 • Lianhuacun, Children's Palace or Lianhua West metro stops

For a shot of greenery, **Lianhua Shan Park** – about 3km north of the border and train station – has some beautiful gardens and is one of the main public spaces where local people hang out. After enjoying the day-glo marvels flying at Kite Square (if you're there in the autumn), head up the hill for a great view of the city where a giant bronze Deng Xiaoping gazes happily across the skyline – a sight for which he is largely responsible – toward Hong Kong. Otherwise just enjoy the genial atmosphere of people relaxing and enjoying their precious free time; it's also a magnet for eccentrics.

Theme Parks

Daily 9am–10pm • ¥120–140 each • Window on the World metro station, Hua Qiao Cheng metro station (for Splendid China) and Shi Jie Zhi Chuang metro station (for the Folk Culture Village)

For Shenzhen's biggest guilty pleasure, head thirty minutes west to the city's three biggest **theme parks**, situated next to each other on the Guangshen Expressway – look for a miniaturized Golden Gate Bridge spanning the road.

8

By far the best of these, **Window on the World** (世界之窗, shìjiè zhīchuāng), is a collection of scale models of famous monuments such as the Eiffel Tower and Mount Rushmore, while **Splendid China** (锦绣中华, jǐnxiù zhōnghuá) offers the same for China's sights. The latter's ticket also includes admission to the **Folk Culture Village** (民俗文化村, mínsú wénhuàcūn), an enjoyably touristy introduction to the nation's ethnic groups – there are yurts, pavilions, huts, archways, rock paintings and mechanical goats, with colourful troupes performing different national dances every thirty minutes.

Happy Valley

欢乐谷, huānlègǔ • Mon–Fri 9.30am–9pm, Sat & Sun 9am–10pm • adults ¥180, children 1.2–1.5m ¥90, smaller children free • ☎ 0755 26949184, ⓦ sz.happyvalley.cn • Window on the World metro station, exit A

Just north of the theme parks is **Happy Valley**, Shenzhen's bigger answer to Hong Kong's Disneyland – and, many would say, considerably better. It's best avoided at weekends and national holidays when waits can be interminable, but there are some genuinely exciting rides here.

ARRIVAL AND DEPARTURE SHENZHEN

BY PLANE

Shenzhen Bao'an International Airport (深圳宝安国际机场, shēnzhèn bǎo'ān guójì jīchǎng; ⓦ eng .szairport.com) is 32km northwest of town. It's one of China's busiest airports, being far cheaper to fly out of than Hong Kong and so swamped by travellers from south of the border. The airport is at the end of the green Luobao metro line to Shenzhen (¥9); there are also buses to Kowloon (¥100) and Hong Kong Airport (¥180) for which you buy tickets from a booth in the arrival terminal. A taxi to Shenzhen costs ¥100–150.

Destinations Beijing (28 daily; 3hr); Changsha (3 daily; 1hr); Chengdu (17 daily; 2hr 15min); Chongqing (13 daily; 2hr); Fuzhou (2 daily; 1hr); Guilin (2 daily; 1hr); Guiyang (9 daily; 1hr 45min); Haikou (9 daily; 1hr 10min); Hangzhou (14 daily; 2hr); Harbin (2 daily; 4hr); Hefei (6 daily; 1hr 50min); Kunming (8 daily; 2hr 10min); Nanchang (7 daily; 1hr 30min); Nanjing (13 daily; 2hr); Nanning (5 daily; 1hr); Sanya (2 daily; 1hr 15min); Shanghai (37 daily; 2hr 10min); Wuhan (7 daily; 1hr 45min); Xiamen (3 daily; 1hr); Xi'an (3 daily; 2hr 40min).

BY TRAIN

Shenzhen train station (深圳站, shēnzhèn zhàn) is ideally located at Luo Hu, just north of the Hong Kong border. Buy tickets for the bullet train to Guangzhou East and Guanzhou main stations on the ground floor; ticket counters for other destinations are on the second floor, though with fairly few long-distance departures from here you're probably better off heading to Guanzhou first. There's a metro stop, local bus terminus and long-distance bus station next door.

Shenzen North (深圳北站, shēnzhèn běi zhàn). Located just north of the centre in Bao'an, this shiny new station is the terminus for the ultra high-speed rail services to Guangzhou South and onwards to Changsha (25 daily; 2hr 52min–3hr 44min) and Wuhan (11 daily;

4hr 15min–5hr). It's easy to reach, being on metro lines #4, #5 and #6.

Destinations Changsha (26 daily; 9hr–10hr 50min); Fuzhou (1 daily; 18hr); Guangzhou (many daily; 29min–2hr 20min); Wuhan (5 daily; 18hr 20min–19hr 20min).

Futian train station (福田火车站, fútián huǒchē zhàn), over in Shenzhen's western reaches. Shenzhen's new train station is due to open in the immediate future, and will probably take over some of the city's high-speed services.

BY BUS

Because of the Pearl River Delta's popularity with migrant workers, almost every village across the country has a bus service to Shenzhen, and there are rumoured to be over forty long-distance stations here. Below is listed the most convenient, and the biggest.

Luohu (罗湖汽车站, luóhú qìchē zhàn) is conveniently located next to the train station and serves the delta, Guangzhou, the rest of Guangdong and many places in central China. Note that there is no ticket office here; after finding where your bus leaves from, buy a ticket from the conductor. Has many services to Guangzhou, but make sure you know which of Guangzhou's bus stations you're headed for before buying a ticket.

Shenzhen Futian Transport Hub (福田综合交通枢纽, fútián zōnghé jiāotōng shūniǔ shūniǔ) is at 8001 Shennan Dadao, 8km west of downtown Shenzhen at Futian District. Has its own metro station which is on the blue Longgang line and orange Shekou line. Best bet for more or less anywhere in China. Note that there is an under-used border crossing to Hong Kong at Futian, about a 10min taxi ride from the Transport Hub (see opposite).

Destinations Chaozhou (5–6hr); Fuzhou (13hr); Guangzhou (3hr); Guilin (9–15hr); Haikou (14hr); Hong Kong (1–2hr); Nanning (8–10hr); Yangshuo (8–10hr).

BY FERRY

Shekou ferry port (蛇口码头, shékǒu mǎtóu) lies 15km west of the centre, with direct connections to Macau, Hong Kong and Hong Kong Airport (☏0755 26691213, ⊛www.cksp.com.hk). Access is easiest on orange metro line #2 which takes around 30–40min to the centre; buses between the port and Lo Wu include the #204 to Jianshe Lu, or a taxi will set you back around ¥80.

Destinations Hong Kong (daily 7.30am–9pm; every 30min; 1hr; ¥110); Hong Kong Airport (hourly; 7.45am–9pm; 30min; ¥260); Macau (6 daily; 7.45am–7.30pm; 1hr; ¥180).

BY FOOT

The two pedestrian border crossings to Hong Kong are open daily 6.30am–midnight. Border formalities are streamlined, and shouldn't take more than an hour at either option.

Luo Hu (罗湖口岸, luóhú kǒu'àn). Crossing from Shenzhen, there's a lack of directional signs; you need to get on to the overpass from upstairs at the train station and then head south past souvenir stalls, roasted-meat vendors and pet shops. The Hong Kong side, known here as Lo Wu, is on the MTR East Rail Line into town.

Futian (福田口岸, fútián kǒu'àn) An option if you've just arrived at the huge Futian Transport Hub nearby, though otherwise 8km distant from downtown Shenzhen. It can be more hassle than Luo Hu, as it's favoured by screaming hordes of Chinese tour groups. Called Lok Ma Chau on the Hong Kong side, and on the MTR East Rail Line into Kowloon.

GETTING AROUND

If you're spending any length of time in the city, consider buying a Shenzhen Pass (深圳通, shēnzhèn tōng), a stored-value card for use on Shenzhen buses and the metro, which can be bought and recharged at metro stations.

By metro Shenzhen's efficient metro system isn't as comprehensive as you might expect, but is growing rapidly and connects to the airport, all the train stations, most of the bus stations, and the ferry terminals (¥2–9; daily, every 3min or so, 6.30am–11pm; ⊛www.szmc.net).

By bus The city has almost 500 bus lines which operate from 7am–11pm, with "N" night buses running on busier routes. Most buses are air-conditioned and announce stops in Mandarin and English. Tickets are ¥1–10, with night buses starting at ¥2.

By taxi Taxis are plentiful; flag fall starts at ¥10, with burgundy and silver non-electric taxis adding a ¥3 fuel surcharge – the less plentiful sky-blue electric taxis are bigger, have "E-taxi" on the side, and don't have a surcharge. Few drivers speak English so it's best have your destination written down in Chinese.

INFORMATION

Websites Shenzhen's expat websites include ⊛www.shenzhenparty.com and ⊛www.shenzhenstuff.com, which can be handy for the latest entertainment and practical info. There's also a government website (⊛english.sz.gov.cn), although it doesn't seem to be regularly updated.

ACCOMMODATION

Shenzhen has a glut of business-oriented hotels – including the international standbys *Shangri-La, Novotel, Sheraton, Holiday Inn* and *Best Western* – though a host of cheap (¥100–180), uninspiring and slightly sleazy options are to be found running north from the train station along Heping Lu. Chinese budget chains such as *7 Days Inn* and *Home Inn* are dotted around the city.

Anshine Shenzhen 深圳安轩, shēnzhèn ānxuān. 3035 Bao'an Nan Lu ☏0755 25582333. About a ¥15 taxi-ride and away from the sleaze of the cheaper hotels near the train station, this slightly tatty hotel actually has pretty large rooms, with firm beds, and is somewhere you could bring your kids. Also handy for the more economical and interesting restaurants on Boa'an Nan Lu, but no wi-fi. **¥140**

Crowne Plaza Landmark 深圳富苑酒店, shēnzhèn fùyuàn jiǔdiàn. 3018 Nanhu Lu, corner of Shennan Zhong Lu ☏0755 82172288, ⊛crowneplaza.com. One of Shenzhen's most upmarket venues, boasting a beautifully furnished neo-colonial interior with chandeliers in the lobby, a very classy spa, swimming pool, and three restaurants. It even has a wine and cigar lounge. **¥1251**

★ **Loft Youth Hostel** 侨城旅友国际青年旅舍, qiáochéng lǚyǒu guójì qīngnián lǚshè. 3 Enping Lu ☏0755 86095773, ✉loftyha@yahoo.com. IYHF hostel backing onto the achingly cool "Loft Creative Area", a former factory now housing art galleries, cafés, bars and trendy offices. Clean and modern with dorms, doubles, twins and triples, some en suite. Take green metro Luobao line to Qiaochengdong and leave by exit A. Turn right and right again at the petrol station and you'll find the hostel behind the Konka building, just beyond the Loft complex. A bit out of the centre, but far cleaner, newer and more comfortable than options around the train station. Dorm beds **¥60**, doubles **¥180**

Petrel 海燕大酒店, hǎiyàn dàjiǔdiàn. Jiabing Lu ☏0755 82232828, ⊛www.petrel-hotel.com. Smart, friendly three-star option, centrally located with views of Shenzhen's skyline, which can also be enjoyed from the Cantonese restaurant on the top 29th floor. Discounts of up to 50 percent often available. **¥987**

EATING

The cheapest places to eat are in the streets just north of Jiefang Lu and along Bao'an Nan Lu, where Chinese canteens can fill you up with tasty dumplings, soups and stir-fries for a nice price.

Burning Goose Restaurant 燃烧鹅餐厅, ránshāo é cāntīng. 1038 Jianshe Lu ☎0775 82327315. Right next to the *Café de Coral*, this is a good, basic Cantonese joint where you can pick up delicious steamed *dim sum* at the door for ¥10 a plate, or order from the menu from under ¥20. The "burning goose" is of course delicious. Just a couple of hundred metres north from the train station. Daily 7am–11.30pm.

★ **Dengpin Vegetarian** 登品素食府, dēngpǐn sùshífǔ. All but hidden on the third floor of the Jun Ting Ming Yuan, north of Bao'an Nan Lu's junction with Hongbao Lu ☎0755 25908588. Serves an absolutely marvellous all-you-can-eat vegan buffet for ¥57 including *dim sum* and fake meat dishes – or order from the menu for a little more. Daily 11am–2pm (buffet served 11.30am–2pm & 6–9pm).

Laurel 丹桂轩酒楼, dānguìxuān jiǔlóu. Fifth floor of Louhu Commercial City in Railway Station Square ☎0755 82323668. Some of the best Cantonese food in town, though not all of the specialities (snake, for instance) make it on to the English menu. Serves excellent *dim sum*, and the roast pork is sublime. Very popular, so expect to wait at busy times; well worth the ¥100 per person expense. Daily 7am–11.30pm.

Little Sheep Hotpot 小肥羊火锅, xiǎoféiyáng huǒguō. 3041 Renmin Lu, at the junction with Shennan Zhong Lu ☎0755 82227179. Seat yourself at a bubbling cauldron of the nationwide chain's signature spicy broth and order meat and vegetables to stew in it – best enjoyed by groups of three or more although they also do one-person versions. Under ¥60 a head. Daily 10am–1am.

DRINKING AND NIGHTLIFE

The two main areas of foreigner-friendly nightlife are the Shekou Port Area, 15km west of the downtown (Sea World metro station on the orange Shekou line), and slightly closer to the centre at Coco Park in Futian (Shopping Park metro station on the blue Longgang and green Luobao lines). For something more laidback and less commercial, try the Loft Creative Area near Qiaochengdong metro (see "accommodation"). For up-to-date info on Shenzhen's (predominantly expat and overseas Chinese) nightlife, check out ⓦ www.shenzhenparty.com.

McCawley's Irish Pub and Restaurant 麦考利酒吧 西餐厅, màikǎolì jiǔbā xīcāntīng. 118 SeaWorld Shekou, and 115–152 Gou Wu Gong Yuan, Coco Park ☎0755 26684496, ⓦmccawleys.com. Faux Irish pub chain with two branches in Shenzhen, either of which makes a reasonable place to start the night. Plenty of wood panelling and folksy knick-knacks with English menus and imported beers and wines. Western food is better than average, if slightly expensive, but they're a magnet for expats, especially when they're showing international sports. Daily 10am–2am.

DIRECTORY

Banks There are banks at the border crossing, the airport, ferry terminal and some hotels, and an oversized Bank of China at 2022 Jianshe Lu (Mon–Fri 9am–5pm).
Left Luggage There's an office at the northeastern corner of the train station square (daily 7am–10pm; ¥5–40 per day, depending on size).

PSB For visa extensions go to the office at 4016 Jiefang Lu in Luo Hu (☎0755 84465490, ⓦwww.sz3e.com; Mon–Fri 9.30–noon & 2–4pm).
Post office The main downtown branch is at 3040 Jianshe Lu (Mon–Sat 8am–8pm), with a smaller office (same hours) just inside Luo Hu bus station.

Qingyuan

清远, qīngyuǎn

Sitting on the banks of the **Bei River**, about 80km northwest of Guangzhou, **QINGYUAN** is an industrial jumble solely of interest as a jumping-off point for river trips 20km upstream to the poetically isolated, elderly temple complexes at Feilai and Feixia – and the fact that the resort at the **Sankeng Hot Spring** (三坑温矿泉, sānkēng wēnkuàngquán),

FROM TOP ASCENDING WUYI SHAN (P.460); BEACH HUTS AND BEACH, HAINAN (P.521) >

FEILAI AND FEIXIA FERRIES

Qingyuan's **Wuyi Dock** (五一马头, wǔyī mǎtóu) lies about 1km north of the train station, or 14km east of the town centre (about ¥30 in a taxi). Charter boats seating up to ten people for a return trip to Feilai and Feixia cost ¥400–500, depending on your bargaining skills. On your own, try heading here at the weekend, when you may find other small groups with whom to split the cost of a single boat-hire, or it's sometimes possible to join a package group if you're lucky.

---

just north of the town, is favoured by some of China's best professional football teams. The city centre lies to the north of the river, and if you find yourself at a loose end, a walk down on the promenade along Yanjiang Lu is a pleasant way to spend an evening.

Feilai Temple

飞来古寺, fēilái gǔsì • Daily 8am–5.30pm • ¥15

Taking the boat from Qingyuan's Wuyi dock, it's a placid, hour-long journey upstream past a few brick pagodas, bamboo-screened villages and wallowing water buffalo being herded by children. Hills rise up on the right, then the river bends sharply east into a gorge and past the steps outside the ancient gates of **Feilai Temple**, a romantically sited Buddhist monastery whose ancestry can be traced back 1400 years. You'll need about forty minutes to have a look at the ornate ridge tiles and climb up through the thin pine forest to where a modern pavilion offers pretty views of the gorge scenery. If you have time to spare before your boat heads on, the temple gates are a good place to sit and watch the tame cormorants sunbathing on the prows of their owners' tiny sampans in the early morning and evening.

Feixia Temple

飞霞古寺, fēixiá gǔsì • Daily 8am–5.30pm • ¥35 • ☎ 0763 3780168

Some 3km farther upstream from Feilai Temple at the far end of the gorge, **Feixia Temple** is both far more recent and much more extensive. The complex comprises two entirely self-sufficient Taoist monasteries, founded in 1863 and expanded fifty years later, which were built up in the hills in the Feixia and Cangxia grottoes, with hermitages, pavilions and academies adorning the 8km of interlinking, flagstoned paths in between. A couple of hours is plenty of time to have a look around.

The temple buildings

A broad and not very demanding set of steps runs up from Feixia's riverfront through a pleasant woodland where, after twenty minutes or so, you pass the minute Jinxia and Ligong temples, cross an ornamental bridge, and encounter Feixia itself. Hefty surrounding walls and passages connecting halls and courtyards, all built of stone, lend Feixia the atmosphere of a medieval European castle. There's nothing monumental to see – one of the rooms has been turned into a **museum** of holy relics, and you might catch a weekend performance of **traditional temple music** played on bells, gongs and zithers – but the gloom, low ceilings and staircases running off in all directions make it an interesting place to explore.

Changtian Pagoda

If you walk up through the monastery and take any of the tracks heading uphill, in another ten minutes or so you'll come to the short **Changtian Pagoda** perched right on the top of the ridges, decorated with mouldings picked out in pastel colours, with views down over Feixia and the treetops.

ARRIVAL AND DEPARTURE   **QINGYUAN**

By bus Qingyuan's new bus station (汽车总站, qìchē zǒngzhàn) is about 3km south of the river, with regular connections to Guangzhou (Liuhua station), Foshan and Shenzhen until around 8pm. City bus #6 heads from here over the Beijiang Bridge and into the kilometre-wide town centre. A taxi will cost around ¥15.

Destinations Foshan (2hr); Guangzhou (1hr 30min); Shenzhen (2hr 30min); Zhaoqing (5hr).

By train The new train station (清远站, qīngyuǎn zhàn) lies 14km east of Qingyuan, with high-speed connections to Guangzhou South railway station. Taxis and motorcycle-taxis can take you into town for about ¥30, as there's no bus.

Destinations Beijing (2 daily; 13hr); Guangzhou (15 daily; 30min).

ACCOMMODATION

Huayuan 花园宾馆, huāyuán bīnguǎn. 178 Xia Haoji, Qingyuan ☎0763 3337738. Cheap and cheerful hotel, centrally located, whose rooms are decent value. Run by a very agreeable, good-humoured and helpful group of women who don't speak a word of English, but it doesn't seem to matter. **¥80**

Tian Hu Grand 天湖大酒店, tiānhú dàjiǔdiàn. 8 Xianfeng Lu, Qingyuan ☎0763 3820168. Moderately comfortable option, whose impressively marble-floored lobby outshines the actual rooms, which are starting to look a bit old (some even have no a/c). But they're still quite good value, and usually discounted to under half the rack rate. **¥450**

EATING AND DRINKING

Yanjiang Lu and Shanglang Lu are the best bet for eating and nightlife, with both streets strung with various restaurants, canteens, KTVs, bars, music-pubs and even a swish new club. The promenade along the river is also popular with locals playing music, dancing, or singing karaoke (badly) in the open air.

Chaozhou

潮州, cháozhōu

In the far east of Guangdong, on the banks of the Han River, **CHAOZHOU** is one of the province's most culturally significant towns, and a splendid place to visit. In addition to some of the most active and manageable street life in southern China, there are some fine historic **monuments**, excellent shopping for local **handicrafts**, and a nostalgically dated small-town ambience to soak up. Chinese-speakers will find that Chaozhou's Teochew **language** is related to Fujian's *minnan* dialect, different from either Mandarin or Cantonese, though both of these are widely understood.

Brief history

By the time of the Ming dynasty Chaozhou had reached its zenith as a place of culture and refinement; the origins of many of the town's monuments date back to this time. A spate of tragedies followed, however. After an anti-Manchu uprising in 1656, only Chaozhou's monks and their temples were spared the imperial wrath – it's said that the ashes of the 100,000 slaughtered citizens formed several fair-sized hills. The town managed to recover somehow, but was brought down again in the nineteenth century by famine and the Opium Wars. Half a million desperately impoverished locals fled Chaozhou and eastern Guangdong through the port of Shantou, 40km south, many of them **emigrating** to Southeast Asia, where their descendants comprise a large proportion of Chinese communities in Thailand, Malaysia, Singapore and Indonesia.

The old quarter

Chaozhou's **old quarter** may be past its heyday, but it remains a functioning part of town. The biggest menace here is over-enthusiastic pedestrianization and reconstruction along main **Shang Dongping shopping street**; and a boom in souvenir stalls, which has started to displace the original traders. But turn down one of the anonymous alleys running towards Huangcheng Lu and you'll find an engaging warren of narrow streets packed with ageing but well-maintained traditional buildings. Look for old wells, Ming-dynasty stone archways and antique family mansions, protected from the outside world by thick walls and heavy wooden doors, and guarded by mouldings of gods and good-luck symbols. Down in the south of town, **Jiadi Xiang**, a

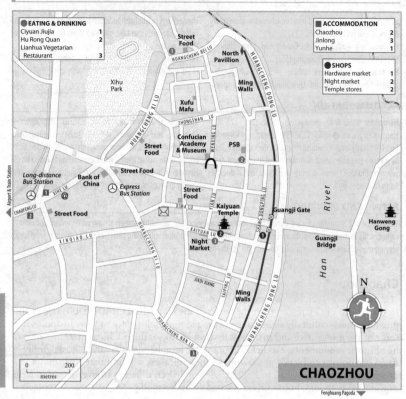

EATING & DRINKING

Ciyuan Jiujia	1
Hu Rong Quan	2
Lianhua Vegetarian Restaurant	3

ACCOMMODATION

Chaozhou	2
Jinlong	3
Yunhe	1

SHOPS

Hardware market	1
Night market	2
Temple stores	2

CHAOZHOU

Fenghuang Pagoda

lane west off Taiping Lu, is an immaculate Qing period piece, its flagstones, ornamental porticoes and murals (including a life-sized rendition of a lion-like *qilin* opposite no. 16) restored for the benefit of residents, not tourists.

Kaiyuan Temple

开元寺, kāiyuán sì • eastern end of Kaiyuan Lu • Daily 6am–6pm • ¥5

If you bother with only one sight in Chaozhou, make it the lively **Kaiyuan Temple**, founded in 738 AD and still a magnet for Buddhist pilgrims – though these days they are outnumbered by tourists. Three sets of solid wooden doors open onto courtyards planted with figs and red-flowered phoenix trees, where a pair of Tang-era **stone pillars**, topped with lotus buds, symbolically support the sky. The various halls are pleasantly proportioned, with brightly coloured lions, fish and dragons along the sweeping, low-tiled roof ridges. Off to the west side is a **Guanyin pavilion** with a dozen or more statues of this popular Bodhisattva in all her forms. Another room on the east side is full of bearded Taoist saints holding a *yin-yang* wheel, while the interior of the **main hall** boasts a very intricate vaulted wooden ceiling and huge brocade banners almost obscuring a golden Buddhist trinity.

Xufu Mafu

许驸马府, xǔfù mǎfǔ • 4 Dongfucheng • Daily 8.30am–5.30pm • ¥20 • ☎ 0768 2250021

Less touristy than Kaiyuan Temple, **Xufu Mafu** is a well-preserved family mansion on an alley running parallel just behind Zhongshan Lu, 100m west of the junction with Wenxing Lu. Dating in part to the Song dynasty, its peaceful wooden interior, darkened by age, is festooned with red lanterns, some rooms containing period furniture (and a couple of waxworks), and the small courtyard garden makes a good place to catch your breath.

Confucian Academy

海阳县儒学宫, hǎiyángxiàn rúxuégōng • Daily 8am–5pm • ¥10 • ☏ 0768 2236199

Wander south down Wenxing Lu and you'll come to both a Ming-style memorial archway and a former **Confucian academy** – now a newly renovated **museum**, full of pre-war photos of town. The gardens outside also make a pleasant place for a stroll and to appreciate the architecture and simple tranquillity of the site, with many tall trees offering cool shade.

The town walls

Daily 8.30am–5.30pm • ticket-office is currently under construction

About 250m east past the temple down Kaiyuan Lu you'll pass the 300-year-old **Matsu Temple** (妈祖庙, māzǔ miào) set below the **old town walls**. Seven metres high and almost as thick, these were only ever breached twice in Chaozhou's history, and more than 1500m still stand in good condition. The walls run from the **North Pavilion** (北亭, běitíng), first constructed during the Song dynasty, and down as far as Huangcheng Nan Lu. There are access steps at several points along the wall, including above the main **Guangji Gate** (广济门, guǎngjì mén), where there's also a guard tower which houses an exhibition on the history of the adjacent Guangji Bridge.

Guangji Bridge

广济桥; guǎngjìqiáo • also known as Xiangzi Bridge • Daily 9am–5pm • ¥50

Piles for the **Guangji Bridge**, a 500m-long span over the Han River, were sunk during the Southern Song Dynasty in the twelfth century, and the wooden floating section of pontoons in the middle (which can be removed to allow the passage of large vessels) was an innovation in bridge-building. Restored in 2009 after years of work, it is an impressive sight, with small pavilions built over each stone pier so that it resembles a street, the line of eighteen boat pontoons floating in the middle, and an iron statue of a cow on the other side to ward off floods. It looks so splendid that it has become a symbol for the city, and is now rated as one of China's four most famous ancient bridges.

8

ARRIVAL AND DEPARTURE

CHAOZHOU

By plane Jieyang Chaoshan Airport (揭阳潮汕机场, jiēyáng cháoshàn jīchǎng) is 24km from the centre of town and has services to most major Chinese cities as well as Bangkok, Seoul, Hong Kong and Singapore. An airport bus (¥12) runs to the *Chaozhou Hotel* and long-distance bus station every hour from 6am till an hour before the last flight. A taxi costs about ¥80 on the meter but you may be charged a stiff surcharge for the driver returning empty.

SHOPPING IN CHAOZHOU

Chaozhou is a great place to buy traditional arts and crafts. For something a bit unusual, the **hardware market**, just inside the Guangji Gate along Shangdong Ping Lu, has razor-sharp cleavers, kitchenware and old-style brass door rings. Temple trinkets, from banners to brass bells, ceramic statues – made at the nearby hamlet of Fengxi – and massive iron incense-burners, are sold at numerous stores in the vicinity of Kaiyuan Temple. It's also a good area to find silk embroideries and ceramic tea sets – in fact Chaozhou considers itself the **ceramics** capital of China, and prices here are low.

For those who enjoy haggling, an impromptu antiques market springs up most mornings along the pavement of Huangcheng Lu outside Xihu Park, and in the evenings a mostly clothing **night market** competes with motorcyclists and cars for road space along Kaiyuan Lu.

Destinations Beijing (4 daily; 3hr); Chengdu (2 daily; 2hr 40min); Guangzhou (4 daily; 1hr).

By train Chaozhou's train station (潮州火车站, cháozhōu huǒchē zhàn) is about 5km northwest; on exiting, walk straight ahead out of the station and, taking your life in your hands, cross the main road to catch city buses #1 or #13 (daily 6.30am–8.30pm; ¥2), which run down to Huangcheng Lu. A taxi costs around ¥15. The station ticket office opens daily 6–11.30am &

1.30–5.30pm, or try the travel agency in the lobby of the *Yunhe Dajiudian*.

Destinations Guangzhou (3 daily; 6hr 30min).

By bus Chaozhou's long-distance bus station is just west of the centre on Chaofeng Lu, with traffic to Guangzhou, Shenzhen and Fujian. Express coaches east and west along the coastal road use a private station on Huangcheng Xi Lu. Destinations Guangzhou (6hr); Shenzhen (5hr); Xiamen (5hr 30min).

GETTING AROUND

By rickshaw Everything in the old town is within walking distance, though motor- and cycle-rickshaws – the only vehicles able to negotiate the older backstreets – are

abundant. Agree a price before you get on; ¥7–10 should cover most journeys within the old town.

ACCOMMODATION

Cheaper places to stay are clustered around the bus station, but few good budget options are willing to take foreigners.

Chaozhou 潮州宾馆, cháozhōu bīnguǎn. Opposite the long-distance bus station ☎0768 2333333, ⓦwww.chaozhouhotel.com. The smartest hotel in town, a four-star with an impressive marble-floored lobby and many English-speaking staff. Large, tastefully decorated and clean rooms with bathrooms. Has a good restaurant, and also a classical teahouse. **¥680**

Jinlong 金龙宾馆, jīnlóng bīnguǎn. Huangcheng Nan Lu ☎0768 2383888, ⓦwww.jinlong-hotel.com. Smart business option at the bottom of the old town,

not quite as swanky as the *Chaozhou* hotel, but they make a good effort. Clean, comfortable and handily placed for reaching the town centre, and its lobby also has a bar. **¥528**

Yunhe 云和大酒店, yúnhé dàjiǔdiàn. 26, Xihe Lu ☎0768 2136128. Don't be fooled by the Doric columns outside the marble lobby with its low-slung and dazzling chandelier: the rooms here are far from five-star, but are comfortable and very good value nonetheless, with a certain kitsch charm. **¥150**

EATING AND DRINKING

Chaozhou's cooking style focuses on light and sweet flavours, with an emphasis on the freshness of ingredients. Seafood is a major feature, while local steamed and roast goose, flavoured here with sour plum, rivals a good Peking duck. Less traditionally, many dishes receive a garnish of fried garlic chips, an idea courtesy of migrants returning from Southeast Asia. There's a good string of restaurants on Huangcheng Xi Lu, overlooking Xihu Park, but wherever you are, and at pretty much any time of the day or night, you will never be far from street stalls doling out hotpots and noodles for just a few yuan.

★ **Ciyuan Jiujia** 瓷苑酒家, cíyuàn jiǔjiā. Huangcheng Xi Lu ☎0768 2253990. Very popular, unpretentious restaurant with superb goose (¥100–200 for a whole bird, or ¥60 for a portion with vinegar and garlic dip), crispy-fried squid, steamed crab, fish ball soup, fried spinach and a selection of dim sum. No English menu, so take a dictionary. Daily 9am–2pm & 4–8pm.

★ **Hu Rong Quan** 胡荣泉, húróng quán. 140 Taiping Lu ☎131 92132573. This bakery, specializing in mooncakes, makes the best spring rolls you'll ever eat, stuffed with spring onions, yellow beans, mushrooms and

a little meat. They also have some tables outside where you can enjoy their wonderful ¥10 wonton soups. Daily 8.30am–11pm.

Lianhua Vegetarian Restaurant 莲华素食府, liánhuá sùshífǔ. At the back of the square opposite Kaiyuan Temple ☎0768 2238033. Meat-free restaurant, where a delicious, enormous six-dish set meal, including sweet-and-sour "ribs" and "kebabs", will set you back about ¥60 for two. There are beggars who hang around the entrance, but they're good-natured and not persistent. Daily 11am–2pm & 5–8.30pm.

DIRECTORY

Banks Branches of the Bank of China (Mon–Fri 8.30–11.30am & 2–5pm) are located next to the *Chaozhou* hotel and on the southern side of Xihe Lu at the junction with Huangcheng Xi Lu. Several ABC branches also have

exchange facilities.

Internet There are a few cheap internet places near the long-distance bus station.

Zhaoqing

肇庆, zhàoqìng

Road, rail and river converge 110km west of Guangzhou at **ZHAOQING**, a smart, modern city founded as a Qin garrison town to plug a gap in the line of a low mountain range. The first Europeans settled here as early as the sixteenth century, when the Jesuit priest **Matteo Ricci** spent six years in Zhaoqing using Taoist and Buddhist parallels to make his Christian teachings palatable. Emperor Wanli eventually invited Ricci to Beijing, where he died in 1610, having published numerous religious tracts. Since the tenth century, however, the Chinese have known Zhaoqing for the limestone hills comprising the adjacent **Seven Star Crags**. Swathed in mists and surrounded by lakes, they lack the scale of Guilin's peaks, but make for an enjoyable wander, as do the surprisingly thick forests at **Dinghu Shan**, just a short local bus ride away from town.

Chongxi Ta and Matteo Ricci Museum

崇禧塔, chóngxǐ tǎ • eastern end of Jiangbin Lu • Wed–Sun 8.30am–4.30pm • ¥20 • ☎ 0758 2262644

Overlooking the river, **Chongxi Ta** is a Ming pagoda which, at 57.5m, is the tallest in the province. The views from the top – which is a lot higher than it looks from the ground – take in cargo boats and the red cliffs across the river surmounted by two more pagodas of similar vintage. Also part of the complex, the **Matteo Ricci Museum** is an example of one of those Chinese museums that have absolutely no genuine artefacts at all, but it is quite informative about the Italian cleric's journey nonetheless, and worth a wander around.

The city walls

Zhaoqing's most interesting quarter surrounds solid sections of the ancient **city walls** on Jianshe Lu, which you can climb and follow around to Chengzong Lu; head north from here along Kangle Zhong Lu and enter a tight knot of early twentieth-century lanes, shops and homes – all typically busy and noisy – along with a brightly tiled **mosque** (清真寺, qīngzhēn sì); there's also a row of plant and bonsai stalls west of the mosque on Jianshe Lu.

Plum Monastery

梅庵, méi'ān • Mei'an Lu • Daily 8.30am–4pm • Free with ID

West of the walls and on the edge of town, the small **Plum Monastery** was established in 996 AD and has close associations with Huineng, the sixth patriarch of Chan

8

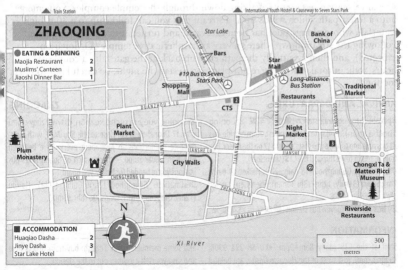

Buddhism. It was he who planted a plum tree here, giving the temple its name, and he is remembered in various paintings and sculptures around the complex. As you get deeper inside, the rumble of the road recedes and you can enjoy its pleasant interior or goggle at the "long-lived tortoise" enclosure.

Seven Stars Park

七星岩公园, qīxīngyán gōngyuán • Daily 7.30am–5.30pm • ¥60 • bus #19 from opposite the bus station, ¥1

Arranged in the shape of the Big Dipper and said to be fallen stars, the seven isolated limestone pinnacles that make up **Seven Stars Park** rise 2km north of town on the far side of **Star Lake** (星湖, xīnghú). The crags are quite modest, named after objects they resemble – **Chanchu** (Toad), **Tianzhu** (Heavenly Pillar), **Shizhang** (Stone Hand) and so on. An interlocking network of arched bridges, pathways, graffiti-embellished caves and willows makes for a pleasantly romantic two-hour stroll.

Dinghu Shan

鼎湖山, dǐnghú shān • Daily 7am–6.30pm • ¥60 • ☎ 07958 2621332, ⓦ dinghushan.net • bus #21 (¥2) every 30min from the stop between HSBC and the main bus station • last bus back to Zhaoqing at 10pm

Twenty kilometres east of Zhaoqing, the thickly forested mountains at **Dinghu Shan** were declared China's first national park way back in 1956. With well-formed paths giving access to a waterfall, temples and plenty of trees, the small area open to the public gets particularly crowded at the weekends, but at other times Dinghu Shan makes an excellent half-day out – particularly in summer, when the mountain is cooler than Zhaoqing. Don't bother with accommodation here though, as rooms are ridiculously expensive.

Around the park

It's best to make an anticlockwise circuit of the park: from the gate, either walk or take an open minibus (¥20) up to the top at **Baoding Park** which overlooks a very pretty lake. After admiring the lake from above, follow the road down to the right where traditional boats can take you across the water to **Butterfly Valley** (¥30) which, unsurprisingly, is full of butterflies.

The road descends from the lake to the large **Qingyun Temple** (清云寺, qīngyún sì), traditionally one of the four most famous in southern China, which is blessed with several vegetarian restaurants. Walking down through the temple complex, you emerge onto a forest path which winds up a stream that you can follow up to a 30m-high **waterfall**, whose plunge pool has been excavated and turned into a swimming hole. Following the stream down, there's a very atmospheric cave temple (¥1 donation expected), and then eventually the path ends up back at the gates. It's a couple of hours' walk in total, but if you're not planning to stay the night, be careful not to linger too long.

ARRIVAL AND DEPARTURE
ZHAOQING

By train Zhaoqing's train station (肇庆火车站, zhàoqìng huǒchē zhàn) lies 4km to the northwest. From outside, bus #1 bus runs into town; a taxi costs about ¥17 on the meter. Buy train tickets in town through the CTS (see below).
Destinations Guangzhou (18 daily; 2hr); Haikou (4 daily; 8hr); Sanya (3 daily; 12hr–13hr 30min); Shenzhen (1 daily; 4hr).
By bus Zaoqing Yueyun bus station (肇庆粤运汽车客站,

zhàoqìng yuèyùn qìchē kèzhàn; ⓦ www.zhqyy.com) is at 17 Duanzhou Si Lu, close to the Star Mall, with long-distance connections to just about everywhere between Guilin and Guangzhou – check which of Guangzhou's bus stations you're headed for before you board.
Destinations Guangzhou (2hr); Guilin (10hr); Haikou (12hr); Qingyuan (5hr); Yangshuo (8hr 30min).

INFORMATION

Staff at the CTS (daily 8am–9pm; ☎ 0758 222 9908, ⓦ zqcts.com), just west of the *Huaqiao Dasha*, are helpful

and some members speak English; buy train tickets here and save yourself a journey out to the station.

ACCOMMODATION

Huaqiao Dasha 华侨大厦, huáqiáo dàshà. 90 Tianning Lu ☎0758 2232650, ⓦzqhd.cn. Not quite as swanky as the *Star Lake*, but this 3-star is cheaper and does have some standard rooms with a lake view out to the Seven Star Crags for ¥60 extra. **¥438**

Jinye Dasha 金叶大厦, jīnyè dàshà. 6 Jianshe Lu ☎0758 222133. Fairly comfortable and just a block from the river, so many of the upper rooms have great views. Not far from the night market, it also has a restaurant and KTV.

Discounts often available. **¥180**

Star Lake Hotel 湖星级酒店, húxīngjí jiǔdiàn. 37 Duanzhou Si Lu ☎0758 2211888, ⓦstarlakehotel-zq .com. Towering over the lake, this is the best hotel in town, with a stylish marble-floored lobby and sumptuous, comfortable rooms that have great views. Boasts three restaurants including a buffet-style Western one on the 29th floor (lunch ¥108, dinner ¥198), which enjoys stunning views out over lake and river. **¥738**

EATING AND DRINKING

Head down side streets off Jianshe Lu to find numerous places selling *zongzi*, sandpots (stews served in earthenware pots) and light Cantonese meals. A string of canteens near the night market at the north end of Wenming Lu (文明路, wénmíng lù) bustles every evening, but for something more refined check out the cluster of Cantonese fish restaurants with river views at the end of Gongnong Lu. Zhaoqing's scanty nightlife revolves around the few bars on Xinghu Xi Lu and riverfront Jiangbin Lu.

Jiaoshi Dinner Bar 教士餐吧, jiàoshì cānba. 19 Xinghu Xi Lu ☎0758 2806666. One of a few bars along this road, serving up a German ambience and beer. Pretty laidback, the owner speaks a little English, it has the obligatory KTV in the back, and a nice view over the lake. Daily 7.30pm–2am.

Maojia Restaurant 毛家饭店, máojiā fàndiàn. 4th Floor, Star Lake Mall, Duanzhou Si Lu ☎0758 2213998, ⓦmaojiahotel.com. Restaurant chain dedicated to Chairman Mao, whose smiling face adorns the walls of this surprisingly stylish modern eatery. Specializes in spicy

Hunanese fare, though the Cantonese food is very good too, especially the barbecued pork. Great value, with mains from ¥30. Daily 10am–10pm.

Muslims' Canteen 清真饭店, qīngzhēn fàndiàn. 2 Jiangbin Lu ☎0758 2557298. For something different try this spacious, airy canteen next to the river, which serves up typical Hui food – lamb skewers (羊肉串, yángròu chuàn), beef noodles (牛肉面, niúròu miàn), flat bread (扁平面包, biǎnpíng miànbāo) et al – at very reasonable prices. The only English in here is on the Coca-Cola signs. Daily 8am–8.30pm.

DIRECTORY

Banks and exchange The main Bank of China is on Duanzhou Lu, opposite Gongnong Lu (Mon–Fri 9am–noon & 2.30–5pm, Sat 10am–4pm).

Post office There's a post office (daily 8am–9pm) on Jianshe Lu.

Shopping Produced for more than a thousand years, Zhaoqing's Duanzhou inkstones are some of the finest in China – you can buy them at stationery and art stores around town, or at the souvenir shops at the Duanzhou Lu/Tianning Lu intersection.

Hainan Island

海南岛, hǎinán dǎo

Rising out of the South China Sea between Guangdong and Vietnam, **Hainan Island** marks the southernmost undisputed limit of Chinese authority, a 300km-broad spread of beaches, mountain scenery and the effects of exploitation. **Haikou**, Hainan's capital, is of importance only as a transit point; the most obvious reason to visit the island is to flop down on the warm, sandy **beaches** near the southern city of **Sanya** – and, as a rest cure after months on the mainland, it's a very good one. To be honest, there's not a whole lot more to the place, though anyone hooked on marine adventure sports can explore, surprisingly perhaps, Hainan's emerging **scuba diving and surfing** potential.

Brief history

Today a province in its own right, Hainan was historically the "Tail of the Dragon", an enigmatic full stop to the Han empire. Chinese settlements were established around the coast in 200 AD, but for millennia the island was seen as being inhabited by

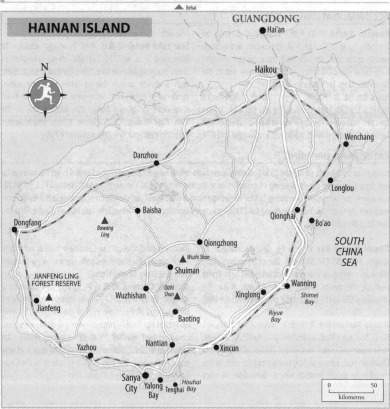

unspeakably backward races, only fit to be a place of exile. So complete was Hainan's isolation that, as recently as the 1930s, ethnic **Li**, who first settled here over two thousand years ago, still lived a hunter-gatherer existence in the interior highlands.

Modern Hainan is no primitive paradise, however. The Japanese occupied the island in 1939, and by the end of the war had executed a full third of Hainan's male population in retaliation for raids on their forces by Chinese guerrillas. Ecological decline began in the 1950s during the Great Leap Forward, and escalated through the 1960s with the **clearing of Hainan's forests** to plant cash crops. Tourism seems to be the sole reliable source of income these days, with the island promoted as China's tropical holiday destination.

Hainan's extremely hot and humid **wet season** lasts from June to October. It's better to visit between February and April, when the climate is generally dry and tropically moderate, and prices reduce considerably.

Haikou

海口, hǎikǒu

Business centre, main port and first stop for newly arrived holidaymakers, **HAIKOU** has all the atmosphere of a typical Southeast Asian city. There's a smattering of French colonial architecture, a few parks and monuments, modern skyscrapers and broad streets choked with traffic and pedestrians. An indication of the ethos driving Haikou is that nobody seems to be a local: officials, businessmen and tourists are all from the mainland, while Li, Miao and Hakka flock from southern Hainan to hawk trinkets, as do the Muslim Hui women selling betel nuts – all drawn by the opportunities that the city represents. More than anything, Haikou is a truly tropical city: humid, laidback, pleasantly shabby and complete with palm-lined streets, something particularly striking if you've just emerged from a miserable northern Chinese winter. It doesn't have a great deal to offer in sights, but you might end up having to stay overnight in transit.

The Old Quarter

Haikou's **old quarter**, boxed in by Bo'ai Bei Lu, Datong Lu and pedestrianized Deshengsha Lu, is the best area to stroll through, with its grid of restored colonial architecture housing stores and businesses. **Jiefang Lu** and **Xinhua Lu** are the main streets here, especially lively in the evening when they're well lit and bursting with people out shopping, eating and socializing; there's also a busy **market** west of Xinhua. Otherwise, **Haikou Park** (海口公园, hǎikǒu gōngyuán) and its lake are small but quite pleasant, particularly in the early morning when the park comes to life with martial-art sessions, dancing and games of badminton.

Five Officials' Temple

五公祠, wǔgōng cí • Daily 8am–6pm • ¥20 • ☎ 0898 65353047 • bus #202

A few kilometres southeast of the centre, **Five Officials' Temple** is a brightly decorated complex built in 1889 to honour Li Deyu, Li Gang, Li Guang, Hu Chuan and Zhao Ding, Tang men of letters who were banished here after criticizing their government.

8

Another hall in the grounds commemorates Hainan's most famous exile, the Sichuanese governor-poet **Su Dongpo**, who lived in the island's northwest between 1097 and 1100 and died on his way back to the imperial court the following year.

Hainan Provincial Museum

海南省博物馆, hǎinánshěng bówùguǎn • 68 Guoxing Lu • Tues–Sun 9am–5pm • Free • ☎ 0898 65238880 • buses #29, #33, #34, #43 or #45

Despite a large, modern and imposing exterior, **Hainan Provincial Museum** manages to be much smaller on the inside than it appears from without. Still, it's free and there are three very interesting and informative exhibitions on the second floor about the history and culture of Hainan, as well as one about the tribal minorities, that are well worth an hour's browsing.

Holiday Beach

假日海滩, jiàrì hǎitān • bus #37 heading west from the clock tower on Changti Dadao, near Renmin Dadao bridge • also served by buses #24 or #40 • taxi around ¥50

If touring Haikou's meagre historical sites seems a bit too serious, Haikou boasts its own stretch of golden sand in the form of 6km-long **Holiday Beach** to the west of the city. While a good place to laze, the beach also has plenty of activities with windsurfers, kayaks and jet skis all for hire. It can get a bit crowded close to town, but keep heading west and the crowds thin out.

8

ARRIVAL AND DEPARTURE	**HAIKOU**

Aside from flying in, you can buy tickets for ferry-bus-train combinations between Haikou and various cities on the mainland.

BY PLANE

Buy tickets at China Travel Air Service, inside the *Hainan Overseas Chinese Hotel* (☎ 0898 66781735), agents for a vast array of domestic and international carriers. Airline tickets can also be reserved through most hotels.

Haikou airport (海口美兰国际机场, hǎikǒu měilán guójì jīchǎng) is 25km southeast of town; shuttle buses (every 30min; 5.30am–9pm; ¥15) run between here and the *Civil Aviation* hotel on Haixiu Dong Lu. A taxi takes around 30min to the town centre (¥50–60 on the meter).

Destinations Beijing (8 daily; 3hr 35min); Changsha (6 daily; 1hr 50min); Chengdu (1 daily; 2hr 15min); Guangzhou (9 daily; 1hr); Guilin (2 daily; 1hr 20min); Hong Kong (2 daily; 1hr 20min); Kunming (5 daily; 2hr 15min); Nanjing (2 daily; 2hr 25min); Shanghai (9 daily; 2hr 40min); Shenzhen (7 daily; 1hr); Wuhan (5 daily; 2hr); Xiamen (3 daily; 1hr 50min); Xi'an (2 daily; 2hr 40min); Zhuhai (2 daily; 50min).

BY TRAIN

Book all tickets, including for trains departing from the mainland port of Zhanjiang, at the CTS office in the *Hainan Overseas Chinese Hotel* on Datong Lu (Mon–Sat 9am–5.30pm; ☎ 0898 66754379), or at the friendly *Hainan Magical Deer Agency* at 22 Renmin Lu (Mon–Sun 9am–6pm; ☎ 0898 31567001, ⊕ www.sl800.com).

Haikou train station lies about 25km east of the centre

and mostly handles services to the mainland, when they put the entire train onto a boat. It's connected to the centre by buses #28 or #40 (¥3; 50min), while taxis (¥60) are a little faster.

Destinations Beijing (1 daily; 32hr); Guangzhou (3 daily; 10hr 30min–12hr); Sanya (6 daily; 2hr 30min); Shanghai (1 daily; 34hr).

Haikou East train station is about 7km south of the centre and is the main terminus of Hainan's high-speed, east-coast rail line.

Destinations Qionghai/Bo'ao (28 daily; 45min–1hr 16min); Sanya (22 daily; 1hr 24min–2hr), Wenchang (30–55min).

BY BUS

The South Bus Station (海口汽车南站, hǎikǒu qìchē nánzhàn) handles mainland traffic – you'll find standard and luxury buses to destinations as far afield as Chongqing, Nanning, Shenzhen and Guangzhou, and tickets include ferry costs – as well as coaches to Sanya, Tongshi, Wuzhishan and Wenchang. The station is a ¥20 taxi ride from the centre, or take bus #20.

Other stations Smaller destinations on the east and west coasts are served respectively by the East Station (海口汽车东站, hǎikǒu qìchē dōngzhàn), 2km down Haifu Dadao (bus #11 or #44), and the West Station (海口汽车西站, hǎikǒu qìchē xīzhàn), 5km out on Haixiu Xi Lu (bus #17 or #30).

Destinations Chongqing (28hr); Guangzhou (12hr); Guilin (12hr); Lingshui (3hr); Qionghai (2hr 30min); Sanya (3–5hr); Shenzhen (15hr); Tongshi (4hr); Wanning (3hr); Wenchang (1hr); Wuzhishan (3–4hr); Zhanjiang (5hr).

BY FERRY

Most hotels and travel agencies in town can make ferry bookings, with a day's warning. Using them is a good idea, since services change frequently and both ports are a way out of the centre. There's usually no trouble getting a seat, though rough seas can suspend services.

The New Port (新港, xīngǎng; ☎ 0898 69693315) is north of Changti Dadao on Xingang Lu; the ticket office opens daily 9am–4pm and bus #6 runs to the centre. The terminal for ordinary and fast ferries (¥30/90) to Hai'an at

Guangdong's southernmost tip, from where you catch a bus for the 150km run to Zhanjiang city (湛江, zhànjiāng), whose long-distance bus and train stations cover southern China.

Destinations Hai'an (9 daily; 1hr–1hr 30min).

Xiuying Wharf (秀英港, xiùyīng gǎng; ☎ 0898 68653680) Binhai Dadao, 5km west of the city on the #7 bus route to the centre. Its ticket office has unpredictable opening hours, so it's best to talk to a travel agent. Ferries from here service Guangzhou (berth ¥160–280) and Beihai in Guangxi province (seat ¥80, berth ¥110–220), from where there are buses and trains to Nanning, the provincial capital.

Destinations Beihai (1 daily; 12hr); Guangzhou (3 weekly; 24hr).

INFORMATION

There's a general lack of tourist information in Haikou, with most agencies only geared to getting you to Sanya as fast as possible.

Maps Detailed maps of the island, including even minor sights marked in English, are sold by hawkers and kiosks (¥7–10).

Tourist services Online you can try ⓦ en.visithainan.gov .cn, or call the multilingual, toll-free Hainan tourism hotline (☎ 8008 88686).

8

GETTING AROUND

By taxi Taxis are so absurdly plentiful that you have only to pause on the street for one to pull up instantly. The safest bet is to insist on the meter, which starts at ¥10 for a ride;

it's also possible to negotiate fares in advance, however, and, if done well, you may pay only two-thirds of the meter rate (check with your hotel how much trips should cost).

ACCOMMODATION

There's plenty of central accommodation in Haikou, much of it conveniently located around Haikou Park. Room rates are always flexible; in summer, ensure that air conditioning is part of the bargain. Most hotels handle transport bookings and have their own restaurants.

★ **Banana Hostel** 巴那那青年旅舍, bānànà qīngnián lǚshè. On east side of Renmin Ave, just north of the junction with Sandong Lu, in the north of town ☎ 0898 66286780, ⓦ haikouhostel.com. This IYHF establishment is the only accommodation in town geared towards budget travellers. Spacious, clean rooms are supplemented with a small bar serving cold beer, and fantastic pizzas, as well as internet access, and staff who are an absolute mine of information. Hidden down an alley, by a black and red restaurant, it's slightly hard to find – call them if you get lost. Dorm beds ¥50, rooms ¥130
Haikou Downtown 海口东堂, hǎikǒu dōngtáng. 38 Datong Lu ☎ 0898 66796999, ⓦ www.hnahotel .com. Luxury, international-standard business affair with all the trimmings – including an outdoor pool – and an

almost economical price considering the standard of the rooms and service. ¥439
Hainan Overseas Chinese Hotel 海南华侨大厦, hǎinán huáqiáo dàshà. 17 Datong Lu ☎ 0898 66773288. Located right next to the old quarter, this three-star business centre built in the early 1990s is beginning to look a bit threadbare, but the rooms are comfortable enough and it offers good discounts. ¥230
Hainan Jiazheng Overseas 海南嘉正海外国际大酒店, hǎinán jiāzhèng hǎiwài guójì dàjiǔdiàn. 11 Wuzhishan Lu ☎ 0898 66796999. Fairly decent three-star venture, with tubs in each room taking advantage of a hot spring located 800m below the hotel, and wooden floors give them a homely feel. Good value with discounts often available. ¥186

EATING, DRINKING AND NIGHTLIFE

Perhaps because Haikou is essentially a mainland Chinese colony, food here is not as exotic as you'd hope. The highest concentration of restaurants is in the old quarter along Jiefang Lu, where grilled chicken wings, kebabs and other snacks proliferate. A couple of palm-shaded cafés on the northern side of Haikou Park serve light snacks, fruit platters and endless teapots and make a good place to watch the world go by. Your best bet for nightlife is the Western-style Binjiang Hai'an Bar Street (滨江海岸酒吧街, bīnjiāng hǎi'àn jiǔbā jiē), just north of the river and easiest reached by taxi.

Coffee Time 咖啡时间, kāfēi shíjiān. 20 Jiefang Lu ☎ 0898 66241506. Chinese interpretation of a Western restaurant with wicker chairs and film posters on the wall, this place serves up reasonably priced Western, Thai, Japanese, Vietnamese and Korean food at ¥18–53 for mains (including steak). Daily 11am–midnight.

Hainan Restaurant 琼菜坊, qióngcàifāng. 17 Datong Lu, close to the Hainan Overseas Chinese Hotel ☎ 0898 66522933. As advertised by the name – lots of Hainan speciality foods and heavy on the seafood. No English menu but plenty of pictures to point at. Mains will set you back ¥30–50. Daily 11.30am–10.30pm.

H Bar 河吧, hébā. 3F Binjiang Haian Bar Street ☎ 0898 66253415. Probably the most foreigner-friendly place in the complex, with Western residents often frequenting at the weekend, and Wednesdays when they have a ladies' night. Live guitar music most days, and BBQ snacks served. Daily 7.30pm–2am.

Hunan Ren 湖南人, húnán rén. 16 Nanbao Lu ☎ 0898 66756030. Smart, ethnic-looking place with wooden beams and bamboo railings, it serves up fiery traditional Hunanese dishes at reasonable prices, with mains mostly ¥20–60. One of the better options in the town centre. Daily 10am–10pm.

Lao Xinjiang Fandian 老新疆饭店, lǎoxīnjiāng fàndiàn. 23 Wuzhishan Lu ☎ 0898 65375027. Muslim restaurant selling hearty Uyghur fare – beef noodles, mutton and heavily seasoned lamb, and chicken kebabs that you can pick from a photo menu. Mains ¥35 upwards. Daily 9am–9pm.

Tong Shan Tang Vegetarian 同善堂全素餐厅, tóngshàntāng quánsù cāntīng. 33 Haidian Sandong Lu, on north side of the road, 200m east of the junction with Heping Lu ☎ 1868 9881210. This Buddhist gem has fake-meat versions of many Chinese dishes. A little hard to find since it looks like a shop and the restaurant is on the second floor, but worth the effort – look for the Buddhas in the window. Daily 8am–8pm.

DIRECTORY

Banks and exchange There are numerous branches of the Bank of China, including opposite the *Huaqiao* hotel on Datong Lu (Mon–Sat 8.30am–5.30pm).

Hospital Hainan People's Hospital, Yangzao Lu, just west off Longhua Lu ☎ 0898 6226666.

Mail The main post office, with parcel post service, is on Jiefang Lu (Mon–Sat 8am–6pm).

PSB The Foreign Affairs Department (Mon–Sat 9am–noon & 3–5.30pm; ☎ 0898 68530977) is at the beginning of Jinlong Lu, the continuation of the southern end of Longhua Lu; catch bus #21 from Renmin Dadao. Be warned that they can be ridiculously heavy-handed to those applying for visa extensions – go elsewhere unless it's an emergency.

Shopping Department stores along Haixiu Dong Lu sell indigenous products such as coconut coffee, coconut powder, coconut wafers, coconut tea, palm sugar and betel nut; clothing sections also stock Hainan shirts, which differ from their Hawaiian counterparts in their use of dragons instead of palm trees on bright backgrounds. Whole shark skins – like sandpaper – dried jellyfish and other maritime curiosities in the shops along Jiefang Lu are also worth a look.

The East Coast

If you can resist heading straight to Sanya, it's worthwhile spending a couple of days hopping down along Hainan's **east coast** – home to some of the few surfable beaches in China, plus some relatively uncrowded sand, at **Qishuiwan** and **Shimei Bay**. This stretch of coast is easily accessible from the main towns, all of which are served by express buses and have stops on the **high-speed rail-line** to Sanya – minibuses or taxis can get you between the stations and the coast. Be warned that unless a resort is maintaining the local beach, it will be none too clean, so finding your own undiscovered strip of tropical paradise is unlikely.

Longlou

龙楼, lónglóu • bus #9 from Wenchang 45min, ¥7 • Longlou–Qishuiwan taxi ¥15 • Longlou–Gusong village taxi ¥40

Accessed via train and bus stations at **Wenchang** (文昌, wénchāng), **LONGLOU** is a small market town of no real significance except that it makes a handy base for visiting nearby beaches. There's decent sand at **Qishuiwan**, (淇水湾泳滩, qíshuǐwān yǒngtān); but the highlight is the eye-wateringly picturesque **Gusong** fishing-village (古松村, gǔsōng cūn), well worth a visit to snap a few photos of the lighthouse on the rocks, and maybe dine in one of the relatively inexpensive and basic seafood restaurants here. Only time will tell if Gusong will survive the ecological damage being inflicted upon it by the construction of a tourist ecological park next door.

Bo'ao

博鳌, bó'áo · city bus #2 (¥7) from Qionghai town · taxi from Qionghai's bus or train station ¥40–45, or ¥10 sharing

BO'AO, about 50km south of Wenchang near Qionghai town (琼海, qíonghǎi), is famous for the Bo'ao Business Forum for Asia held here every spring, so its beaches and water are clean, it has a good tourist infrastructure, and hassles are at a minimum. The beach can be reached on foot and is safe for swimming – just avoid the currents around the mouths of three rivers that arrive into the sea, which can be dangerous. The beach behind the Confucian temple is pretty and quiet.

Shimei Bay

石梅湾, shíměi wān · taxi from Wanning ¥60–80

Shimei Bay, accessed via **Wanning** town (万宁, wànníng), has to rate as one of the best beaches on Hainan, maintained as it is by two huge and exclusive resorts. The best bit of the beach is accessed through the *Le Méridien* hotel, and they even have a bar slap-bang on the sand where ice-cold, imported bottled beers are just ¥30. Shimei is only accessible by taxi, so it's advisable to get your driver's number and arrange for them to pick you up, or hope one of the resorts can help you get back to Wanning.

Riyue Bay

日月湾, riyuè wān · local buses between Wanning and Sanya might stop on the highway outside Riyue if requested; ask when you get on · taxi from Wanning or Lingshui ¥100

Some 6km east of Shimei and exposed to waves from the Pacific, **Riyue Bay** is popular with Hainan's embryonic surfing community (see below). Even if you're not catching waves, this is an idyllic spot where new hotels are only just getting a foothold, and you can almost imagine you're on the hippy trail.

8

ACCOMMODATION
EAST COAST

Djombo 琼博旅馆 qíóngbó lǚguǎn. Wenhua Jie, Bo'ao ☎ 0898 62778082. If you don't fancy stumping up for one of the fancy resorts or hotels, this reasonable cheapie is on a recently gentrified street in the centre of town. Rooms are basic, but clean enough, and there are another couple of similar places on the same street. No English spoken, and make sure they register you with the police. **¥80**

SURFING HAINAN

Hainan has some of the best surfing beaches in China, and there are two easily accessible surf resorts on the east coast with foreign co-owners. Riyue Bay, 19km outside Wanning about halfway down the east coast, is home to the **Riyue Bay Surfing Club** who rent boards for ¥100/day; or you can get 2hr lessons in English for ¥400 (ⓦsurfinghainan.com, or call Brendan 9am–6pm on ☎ 135 19800103). Closer to Sanya, and with warmer water, Houhai Bay is where you'll find the **Karma Surf Hostel and School** who have similar rates and surf from a number of different beaches depending on the season (ⓦsurfhostelkarma.com, or call Francesco on ☎ 136 97559284).

Northeastern and eastern swells bring waves of around 1–2m most of the year, though during typhoon season (June–Sept), waves will be more like 3–5m and sometimes up to 6m. Riyue Bay is a northeast open bay and probably better during the winter months, when it gets up to 5m waves, and is hence the setting for the ISA Hainan International Surfing Festival each January, and the smaller ASB Hainan Classic competition in November (ⓦhainaninternationalsurfingfestival.com). If you know your surfing, Houhai would be the Huntington Beach, and Riyue more like the Hawaiian North Shore. More detailed information is available at ⓦchinasurfreport.com.

Longlou Jiudian 龙楼酒店, lónglóu jiǔdiàn. Just uphill from the bus station, Longlou ☎ 0898 63586888. The town's sole accommodation, with a rack rate that can be knocked down to less than half. The rooms are decent for the price and it's best to get one overlooking the coconut grove behind the hotel rather than on the road. **¥150**

Riyue Bay Surfing Club 日月湾冲浪俱乐部, riyuèwān chōnglàng jùlèbù. Riyue Bay ☎ 135 19800103. Very basic dorm rooms on-site, along with a restaurant where you can eat local Chinese fare for under ¥40. They also arrange good rates on private rooms at nearby hotels. Beds **¥50**

Sanya

三亚, sānyà

Some 320km across the island from Haikou on Hainan's southern coast, **SANYA** is, sooner or later, the destination of every visitor to the island. Sanya City itself is a rather pleasant, once-scruffy fishing port, surrounded by concrete high-rise holiday resorts, that has twice hosted the Miss World contest, but what pulls in the crowds – a huge number of whom are Russian – are surrounding beaches at **Dadonghai** and **Yalong**. Chinese tourists also flock to overcrowded and overpriced scenic spots such as **Tianya Haijiao**, all of which are of little interest to foreigners.

It must be said that though the beaches here are good, a trip to Sanya can involve a few irritations, especially for those on a budget: at peak times – from October to February and especially Chinese New Year – room rates soar and the usual tourist hassles intensify. Off-season, however, beaches are uncrowded and the atmosphere is pretty mellow.

Sanya City

Despite the area's resort image, **Sanya City** doesn't have anything particular to see: recent investment has given the downtown area the appearance of any other mildly

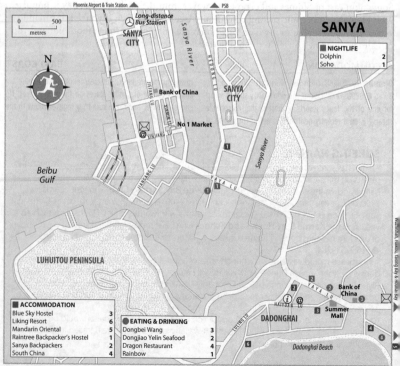

SANYA

NIGHTLIFE
Dolphin   2
Soho   1

ACCOMMODATION
Blue Sky Hostel   3
Liking Resort   6
Mandarin Oriental   5
Raintree Backpacker's Hostel   1
Sanya Backpackers   2
South China   4

EATING & DRINKING
Dongbei Wang   3
Dongjiao Yelin Seafood   2
Dragon Restaurant   4
Rainbow   1

prosperous Chinese city, and its proximity to the beaches is only betrayed by the presence of matching-short-and-shirt-wearing holidaying mainlanders. Sanya's real charm, however, is its laidback atmosphere: the **No. 1 Market** (第一市场, dìyī shìchǎng), centred around Xinjian Jie running east off Jiefang Lu, is a mass of small backstreets and markets, and an interesting place to wander aimlessly night or day. You can sit in a pavement restaurant, sip on a beer or coconut and munch on inexpensive barbecued delights while watching passing street-life, without any hassles whatsoever.

Dadonghai beach

大东海, dàdōnghǎi · bus #2 or #8 to the Summer Mall

Some four kilometres south of the centre, often crowded and seasonally blistering hot, 3km-long **Dadonghai** has pretty well everything you could ask for in a tropical beach: palm trees, white sands and warm, blue water. Beachside bars and kiosks renting out beach umbrellas, jet skis, catamarans and rubber rings complete the scene. Hugely popular with holidaying Russians, almost every shop along the strip has both Chinese and Cyrillic script, and this is one of the few places in China where, as a foreigner, you are likely to be addressed in Russian rather than English. While it's all very relaxed for China, don't mellow too much, as unattended valuables will vanish, and women going topless, or any nudity, could lead to arrests.

Yalong Bay

亚龙湾, yàlóng wān · bus #15 from Dadonghai (¥4; 30min) to the giant stone totem pole from where you can walk through to the beach · taxi ¥60 on the meter

Lying some 22km east of Sanya by road, and a world away in terms of sophistication, the beach at **Yalong Bay** is nicer than Dadonghai's, being better-maintained and with cleaner and clearer water, its golden sands overlooked by a backdrop of expensive hotels and resorts.

Houhai Bay

后海湾, hòu hǎiwān · from Dadonghai, take bus #28 or #29 to the end of the line (40min), then follow the signs to the Wuzhizhou Island ferry, and it's just to the south of the pier

Some 32km from Sanya, lovely little **Houhai Bay** is uncrowded, quiet, stunningly pretty, and without a resort in sight. The beach backs onto the village of **Tenghai**, with just a couple of surf hostels overlooking it. The sands aren't exactly golden, but there's a nice ambience, some great surfing (see p.519) and it's one of the least exploited spots in Hainan.

ARRIVAL AND DEPARTURE   SANYA

By plane Sanya Phoenix International Airport (三亚凤凰国际机场, sānyà fènghuáng guójì jīchǎng; ☎ 0898 88289390, ⓦ www.sanyaairport.com) is about 15km to the northwest, from where you'll need to catch a taxi for ¥50–60, or bus #8 (¥5) into the city. Most hotels have airline agents on hand, or either of the helpful visitor information offices can book domestic flights.
Destinations Beijing (7 daily; 3hr 50min); Guangzhou (11 daily; 1hr 20min); Hong Kong (2 daily; 1hr 45min); Shanghai (10 daily; 2hr 55min); Shenzhen (4 daily; 1hr 20min).
By bus Sanya's main long-distance bus station

(三亚汽车站, sānyà qìchēzhàn) is in the city at the northern end of Jiefang Lu, and handles normal and luxury buses to Haikou, and services to just about everywhere else on the island. For mainland destinations, change at Haikou.
Destinations Dongfang (3hr); Haikou (3–5hr); Lingshui (2hr); Qionghai (4hr 30min); Tongshi (2hr); Wanning (3hr); Wenchang (4hr); Yazhou (1hr).
By train The train station lies just north of the bus station and is accessible to the centre with bus #4 or around ¥25 in a taxi.
Destinations Beijing West (1 daily; 36hr); Haikou East (20 daily; 2hr); Guangzhou (1 daily; 14hr 20min).

GETTING AROUND

By bus Public buses #2 and #8 run regularly between the long-distance bus station in Sanya City and

Dadonghai; bus #15 runs every 15min from Sanya to Yalong Bay, via the Summer Mall at Dadonghai, as do

buses #28 or #29 to Houhai Bay.
By taxi There's the usual overload of taxi cabs. Flag fall is ¥8, with every extra kilometre ¥2, and many drivers insist on a minium ¥10 fare.

By bicycle Sanya is a great place to cycle around and experience the laidback backstreets away from the beach, with hostels renting them for around ¥30 a day.

INFORMATION

Visitor information centres Sanya is blessed with two useful, English-speaking information centres (daily 9am–9pm; ⊕ 0898 38812301), one at the airport, and the other opposite the *Seascape Garden Hotel* near the crossroads of Luling Lu and Yuya Lu. They are a mine of information, as well as being able to book tours and provide free internet access.
Tour agents Any of the hotels or hostels, even those

without their own travel desks, will arrange scuba diving, climbing, coral island or fishing trips and, if not able to actually book air tickets themselves, will be more than happy to point you in the direction of one of the many agencies in the town that can.
Websites Useful websites include ⓦ whatsonsanya.com, ⓦ sanyaweb.com and ⓦ english.sanya.gov.cn.

ACCOMMODATION

Sanya's accommodation is constantly developing, with increasing options across the board. The city itself can be an interesting place to stay, but most visitors head towards either mostly cheap-and-cheerful Dadonghai or more exclusive – and considerably pricier – Yalong Bay.

SANYA CITY

★ **Raintree Backpacker's Hostel** 雨树背包客旅舍, yǔshù bēibāokè lǚshè. 4F Shan Shui Yun Tian Building, 46 Hedong Lu ⊕ 0898 38898877, ⊜ justintiller@gmail.com. If the beaches are a bit hectic, this quiet, clean, family-run hostel is just 10min by bike from Dadonghai. Nice rooms, some with balconies overlooking the river, bikes for rent, and what the family lack, in English ability, they make up for in helpfulness. Dorm bed ¥50, doubles ¥180

DADONGHAI

Blue Sky Hostel 蓝天国际青年旅舍, lántiān guójì qīngnián lǚshè. Lanhai Xiang, Haiyun Lu ⊕ 1387 6791920, ⊜ sy.youthhostel@gmail.com. This newly

refurbished spot is backpacker central: free wi-fi, plus laundry facilities and English-speaking staff who can arrange anything from dive trips to hiking in the rainforest. Dorm beds ¥50, doubles ¥200
Liking Resort 丽景海湾酒店, lìjǐng hǎiwān jiǔdiàn. Dadonghai Beach ⊕ 0898 88228666, ⓦ sanyaliking .com. More charcterful than its contemporaries, this low-rise place is popular with Russian tour groups, and looks like something from 1950s Vegas. It's slap-bang on the beach and the more expensive rooms have vast terraces. ¥672
Mandarin Oriental 文华东方酒店, wénhuá dōngfāng jiǔdiàn. 12 Yuhai Lu ⊕ 0898 88209999, ⓦ mandarinoriental.com. Tranquil, stylish and luxurious hotel complex with its own private bay 1km or so east of

---

SCUBA DIVING SANYA

Low visibility and only moderate maximum depths don't make Hainan the most exciting location for scuba diving, but it can be good fun and there's always the novelty of having dived in China. Don't bother with Dadonghai; the best areas near Sanya are just east at **Yalong Bay** (clear water and best for its coral growth, and a variety of fish); **Tianya Haijiao**, over to the far west of Sanya Bay (good for molluscs); and – best of all – **Wuzhizhou Island**, in Lingshui Bay around 30km east of Sanya (coral, fish, molluscs and crystal-clear water). Bookings can be made through virtually any hotel (the hostels are the best), but touts, who are more amenable to bargaining, often patrol the beachfront at Dadonghai and Yalong Bay.

Yalong Bay is the least expensive, and boat dives around the waters of the bay for certified divers run at ¥580–680 for one tank, with additional tanks ¥200. Without certification, you can do a controlled 30-minute "resort" dive for ¥300–400. Snorkelling trips cost around ¥200 for a couple of hours.

Trips to Tianya Haijao (diving around West Island) and Wuzhizhou Island are both about fifty percent more expensive than Yalong Bay, and require you to pay an "island landing fee" of ¥148 on top of diving costs. You can dive at Wuzhizhou for considerably less, however, by booking in nearby Houhai Bay (see p.521), whose operators dive on the same sites but don't "land".

the main beach. Easily the best in town, with all expected facilities and a superb outdoor French fish restaurant. ¥2500

Sanya Backpackers 三亚背包客, sānyà bēibāokè. Luming Community, Haihua Lu ☎0898 88213963, ⓦsanyabackpackers.com. Clean and modern new hostel in low-rise villa with clean rooms and small outside bar; they specialize in PADI scuba courses and also rent surfboards. Not actually on Huihua Lu, but behind the *Sanya Mountain Hotel*. Dorm beds ¥75, rooms ¥240

South China 南中国大酒店, nánzhōngguó dàjiǔdiàn. Dadonghai Beach ☎0898 88219888, ⓦsouthchinahotel.com. Comfortable beachfront resort with four-star facilities, including a very nice outdoor swimming pool surrounded by palm trees, a gym, and Western and Chinese restaurants. Sea- or garden-views available. ¥1480

YALONG BAY

Cactus Resort 仙人掌度假酒店, xiānrénzhǎng

dùjià jiǔdiàn. Longtang Lu ☎0898 88568866, ⓦcactusresort.com. Set back from the beach and almost in the jungle, this is more peaceful than most of the big hotels in Yalong and is just a 5min stroll from the sea. Lovely swimming pool, all expected five-star facilities, and non-guests can also enjoy the "fish massage" at the spa here for just ¥68. ¥1188

HOUHAI

Karma Surf Hostel 卡玛冲浪客栈, kǎmǎ chōnglàng kèzhàn. ☎0898 88759379, ⓦsurfhostelkarma.com. Very cool surfing school and hostel a street back from this good surfing beach (see p.519), and one of the owners is Italian. Basic but comfortable and clean rooms and dorms as well as a great rooftop restaurant-bar overlooking the bay and serving reasonably priced international and Chinese food, including authentic Italian pizza and wines. Dorm beds ¥50, doubles ¥220

EATING AND DRINKING

Like accommodation, eating here can be an expensive business (though the excellent seafood is reasonably priced): don't eat anywhere – especially cheaper spots – without getting solid confirmation of prices, or you could end up being asked to pay vastly over the odds. The stretch of Haiyu Lu between the turn-off to the *Blue Sky* hostel and the junction with Haiyun Lu is home to Dadonghai's best-value and most varied selection of food, including Japanese, Italian and generic Western restaurants, plus a string of small Chinese seafood canteens which spill out onto the street at night. For the cheapest eats, head to the area around the No.1 Market in Sanya City, where it's easy to get a good feed for under ¥10 – the best-value seafood restaurants are also here, around the fish market. Imported alcohol and various foodstuffs are available at *Corner's Deli* on the 5th floor of Summer Mall.

Dongbei Wang 东北王, dōngběi wáng. 2F, 135 Yuya Lu, Dadonghai ☎0898 88212585. Lively, enjoyable Manchurian restaurant, with an illustrated Russian menu. Portions are huge (one is enough for two people) and the service good. The fried whole fish with pine nuts is a treat, as is cold shredded beef with aniseed. ¥60 will feed two. Daily 11am–11pm.

Dongjiao Yelin Seafood 东郊椰林海鲜城, dōngjiāoyēlín hǎixiānchéng. 109 Yayu Lu, Dadonghai ☎0898 88210999. A warehouse of a restaurant, offering a glut of seafood and Hainanese dishes in an opulent setting. Seafood is seasonally priced and about ¥400 per platter, though the other mains are ¥46– 220. Daily 11am–11pm.

Dragon Restaurant 龙餐厅, lóng cāntīng) Just

above the beach near the South China hotel, Dadonghai ☎0898 88219875. A surprisingly romantic place to eat in the evening: select seafood from the live tanks and say how you want it cooked (prawns go for ¥187/kg), order a couple of beers, then kick back at outdoor tables under the coconut trees. Non-seafood mains start at ¥32. Daily 11am–11pm.

Rainbow 云博西餐酒吧, yúnbó xīcān jiǔbā. On the waterfront of the wharf just off Gangmen Lu, on the island between Dadonghai and Sanya ☎0898 88606063, ⓦrainbowbargrill.com. Pretty good Western favourites such as burgers, pasta and pizza (from ¥50), to eat inside the humdrum sports-bar interior – or preferably in the tranquil annexe next to the river. Great barbecued food after 9.30pm. Daily 5pm–2am.

NIGHTLIFE

As far as Sanya's nightlife is concerned, KTVs and Chinese-style nightclubs abound, although there are a few smaller, more authentic Western bars around.

Dolphin 海豚酒吧, hǎitún jiǔbā. 99 Yayu Lu, Dadonghai ☎0898 88215700, ⓦdolphinbar.cn. Estranged sibling of the less central *Rainbow*, this place

offers the same Western sports bar experience and identical menu, but is smaller, livelier, closer to Dadonghai and more popular with foreigners. Mixed drinks tend to be quite

8

THE SOUTH CHINA SEA ISLANDS

Chinese maps of China always show a looped extension of the southern borders reaching 1500km down through the South China Sea to within spitting distance of Borneo, enclosing a host of reefs and minute islands. These sit over what might be major **oil and gas reserves**, and are consequently claimed by every nation in the region – China, Malaysia, the Philippines, Taiwan and Vietnam have all put in their bids, based on historical or geographic associations.

Occupied by Japan during the 1940s but unclaimed after World War II, the **Spratly and Paracel islands** are perhaps the most contentious groups. Vietnam and China both declared ownership of the Paracels in the 1970s, and 70 Vietnamese soldiers were killed when the Chinese seized the islands in 1974, coming to blows again in 1988 when the Chinese navy sank two Vietnamese gunboats. Then, in 1995, the Philippines stepped in, destroying Chinese territorial markers erected over the most westerly reefs in the Spratly group and capturing a nearby Chinese trawler. Ongoing minor brawls encouraged the nations of the region – including China – to hammer out a landmark agreement in November 2002, which basically allows access for all, while territorial disputes are settled one by one. However, neither China nor Vietnam has kept to the letter of the agreement, and indeed in July of the same year, China established Sansha City on the Paracels to oversee its territory in the South China Sea.

In 2012, the International Court of Justice ruling on the "Nicaragua v Colombia" case (about islands in the Caribbean) cast doubt on whether many of the tiny South China Sea Islands would generate an Exclusive Economic Zone around them under international law. This greatly reduces their economic significance, but not their use as a focus of nationalistic fervour – a difficult issue where China and Japan are concerned.

8

weak, however. Daily 11am–2am.

Soho 苏荷酒吧, sūhé jiǔbā. Yuya Lu ☎0898 88706677, ⓦwww.sohobar.com.cn. Shanghai-style dance bar which is busy all year round, with Shanghai prices, chandeliers, and showy Chinese singers performing before foreign DJs round off the night. Popular with both locals and foreigners, it gets pretty crowded. Daily 9pm–2am.

DIRECTORY

Banks and exchange The main Bank of China is on Jiefang Lu, Sanya City (Mon–Fri 9am–5pm), with another branch opposite the bus station (same hours) as well as a Dadonghai branch (same hours).

Internet Both visitor information centres have computers with free internet access.

Mail There are post offices on Xinjiang Lu, Sanya, and on Yula Lu in Dadonghai (daily 7.30am–6pm).

PSB For visa issues, the Foreign Affairs Department is in the north of the city, just over the bridge on Fenghuang Lu (Mon–Sat 9am–noon & 3–5.30pm; ☎898 88869015).

If extending your visa, make sure you have registered with the police every day of your stay as they're real sticklers for the rules here, and quite unsympathetic.

Shopping Sanya is a good place to pick up pearls, white, pink, yellow or black. The best buys are from local hawkers on Dadonghai beach, who sell strings of "rejects" for ¥40 or less with hard bargaining. Most of these pearls are perfectly genuine, just not of good enough colour, shape or size for commercial jewellery. If in doubt, scratch the surface – flaking indicates a thinly coated plastic bead.

Jianfeng Ling Forest Reserve

尖峰岭森林自然保护区, jiānfēnglǐng sēnlín zìrán bǎohùqū • Daily 8.30am–6.30pm • ¥50

Jianfeng Ling Forest Reserve encloses a tiny pocket of mountain rainforest 115km northwest of Sanya, left untouched following a logging ban in 1992, when a UNESCO survey found 400 types of butterfly and 1700 plant species up here. It's a very peaceful spot, and much cooler than the coast, making it a great relief from frying on the beach.

From the main-road township of **JIANFENG** (尖峰, jiānfēng), it's 18km uphill to the park gates at **Tianchi** (天池, tiānchí), where the road reaches the forest's edge at a couple of tranquil lakes – both have up-market resorts. From here a boardwalk leads off uphill for an hour-long circuit walk taking in some massive trees, vines, orchids, ferns, birds, butterflies and beautiful views from the 1056m ridge. There are also boardwalks around both lakes, which make for a most congenial sunset stroll.

By bus and rickshaw From Sanya, tell your bus driver that you're going to Jianfeng Ling, and you'll get dropped at a small main-road bus depot, where you catch a motor-rickshaw for the few kilometres to Jianfeng township. From here, hire another rickshaw for the last 18km up to Tianchi (¥60).

ACCOMMODATION

In addition to the following, there's a slightly down-at-the-heels resort in the park up by the forest boardwalk, which you can book at the park entrance.

Hainan Tianchi Blossom Hotel 海南天池桃花园酒店, hǎinán tiānchí táohuāyuán jiǔdiàn. Tianchi ☎ 0898 31856888. Right next to the biggest lake, this resort has some lovely rooms in the main building, but the deluxe ones are worth the extra as they are in chalets (with patios), actually on the water. **¥680**

Wuzhishan

五指山市, wǔzhǐshān shì

Lacking heavy traffic or industry, pocket-sized **Wuzhishan town** – also known as **Tongshi** (通什, tōngshí) – is a pleasantly unpolluted spot two hours north of Sanya, surrounded by pretty countryside. Set at the base of low hills, the tiny centre sits on the southern bank of a horseshoe bend of the Nansheng River and mostly consists of the handful of streets around its market area where there's a chance to see Hainan's dark-dressed **minorities** – Miao, and the occasional older Li women with tattoos. It's all pretty relaxed, and wander out of town (especially north; take the first right over the bridge down Shangzhuang Lu) and you'll soon find yourself in vivid green fields and increasingly poor villages, ultimately built of mud and straw and surrounded by split bamboo pickets to keep livestock in.

The Nationality Museum

民族博物馆, mínzú bówùguǎn • Daily 9am–5.30pm • Free with passport

Past the ostentatious green-tiled university (turn right at the crossroads), the **Nationality Museum** affords views across town to the aptly named **Nipple Mountain**, 5km away to

8

LI AND MIAO

Hainan's million-strong **Li** population take their name from the big topknot (*li*) which men once wore. They probably arrived on Hainan from Guangxi about 200 BC, when they occupied the coast and displaced the aboriginal inhabitants before themselves being driven into the highlands by later Chinese migrations. The Li built villages with distinctive tunnel-shaped houses, evolved their own shamanistic religion, and used poisoned arrows to bring down game. Li women were known for their **weaving** skills, and the fact that, until very recently, many got their faces heavily **tattooed** with geometric patterns – apparently to make them undesirable to raiding parties of slavers from the coast, or rival **clans**. The latter have never coexisted very well, quarrelling to this day over territorial boundaries, and only united in their dislike of the Han Chinese – there were fourteen major rebellions against their presence on the island during the Qing era alone.

Though traditional life has all but vanished over the last half-century, there are still a few special events to watch out for. Best is the **San Yue San festival** (held on the third day of the third lunar month), the most auspicious time of the year in which to choose a partner, while in more remote corners of the highlands, **funerals** are traditionally celebrated with gunfire and three days of hard drinking by male participants.

Touted as Hainan's second "native minority" by the tourist literature, the **Miao** are comparatively recent arrivals, forcibly recruited from Guizhou province as mercenaries to put down a Li uprising during the Ming dynasty. When the money ran out, the Miao stopped fighting and settled in the western highlands, where they formed a fifty-thousand-strong community in the remotest of valleys.

the west, while the collection itself is excellent. Historical exhibits include prehistoric stone tools and a bronze drum decorated with sun and frog motifs, similar to those associated with Guangxi's Zhuang; Ming manuscripts about island life; Qing wine vessels with octopus and frog mouldings; and details of the various modern conflicts culminating in the last pocket of Guomindang resistance being overcome in 1950. Artefacts and photos illustrate Hainan's cultural heritage, too – Li looms and textiles, traditional weapons and housing, speckled pottery from Dongfang and pictures of major festivals.

ARRIVAL AND DEPARTURE

WUZHISHAN TOWN

By bus The bus station is north of the river on Huayu Bei Lu, from where you can head to Haikou, Sanya and Wuzhi Shan.

ACCOMMODATION

Aside from the option below, there are a few basic places opposite the bus station asking under ¥100 for a double, and a few mid-range and swankier places along the river.

Hainan Wuzhishan Resort Hotel 海南五指山旅游山庄, hǎinán wǔzhǐshān lǚyóu shānzhuāng. 38 Shangzhuang Lu ☎0898 86623188, ⓦwzsresort.net. Resort in the far northeastern edge of town (2km from the bus station), whose characterful rooms have balconies looking out to the hills. There's a swimming pool to cool down in after a hike – the prettiest countryside is up the river from here – and also has a decent mid-price Chinese restaurant, though unfortunately a noisy KTV too. **¥380**

EATING AND DRINKING

Social life in Wuzhishan town revolves around drinking tea and eating outside while playing cards, majong or dominoes till late in the night. Henan Lu, by the riverside, is strung with a line of earthy outdoor restaurants and teashops where you can point at various produce on display which they'll cook up while you relax. For a proper sit-down meal, all the pricier hotels have reasonable restaurants charging under ¥50 a head, and Haiyu Bei Lu has a few more salubrious establishments springing up.

Xiangwei Yuan 湘味园, xiāngwèi yuán. 68 Haiyu Bei Lu ☎0898 86631180. For something a little different, this stylish little Hunanese joint, with ethnic wooden furniture, specializes in fiery dry-pot casserole dishes at ¥50–70, and one is enough for two people - otherwise there's a colourful photo menu. Very popular, and if it's full, there's another branch just around the corner. Daily 11am–9.30pm.

DIRECTORY

Banks There are a few ICBC branches in town with ATMs that accept foreign cards, including on Jiefang Lu, and near the bus station on Haiyu Bei Lu.

Internet There are a couple of internet cafés around the bus station and more around the market.

Wuzhi Shan Nature Reserve

五指山国家级自然保护区, wǔzhǐshān guójiājí zìrán bǎohùqū • Daily 9am–6pm • ¥50 • ☎0898 86550075, ⓦhnwuzhishan.com

Several Li myths explain the formation of **Wuzhi Shan** (Five-Finger Mountain), whose very pointy 1867m-high summit rises 30km northeast of Wuzhishan town at Hainan's apex. In one tale, the mountain's five peaks are the fossilized fingers of a dying clan chieftain, while another holds that they represent the Li's five most powerful gods. Either way, the mountain was once a holy site drawing thousands of people to animist festivals.

Today, Wuzhi Shan is a nature reserve, with a very luxurious resort 1km or so inside the gate, from where a paved path leads off into the rainforest. At the first junction, the left path will lead you on a gentle thirty-minute stroll up a stream to a very lovely waterfall, while the right path eventually gets to the peak of Whuzi Shan itself: it's an 11km hike, quite tough, and takes around three hours going up (two coming down), so take plenty of water and wear appropriate footwear. Although it's often clouded over, the summit offers contorted pines, begonias and, if you're lucky, absolutely stunning views.

ARRIVAL AND DEPARTURE	WUZHI SHAN NATURE RESERVE

By bus An irregular bus (¥9) leaves from opposite the bus station in Wuzhishan town to Shuiman village (水满乡, shuǐmǎn xiāng); from here walk or catch a motor rickshaw (¥10) the final 4km to the gates. Last bus back to Wuzhishan town departs Shuiman village at 6pm.

ACCOMMODATION

Shuiman Yuan 水满园, shuǐmǎn yuán. Shuiman village ☎ 0898 86666530. Just 4km from the Wuzhi Shan Nature Reserve and close to the bus stop for Wuzhishan town, this lovely little resort has spacious, quiet rooms overlooking either the jungle or Wuzishan mountain itself. Best option if you can't afford the newly opened 5-star *Wuzhishan Yatai Rainforest Resort* actually inside the park. __¥340__

8

Hong Kong and Macau

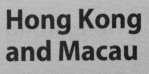

EVENING VIEW FROM THE PEAK, HONG KONG

9

Hong Kong and Macau

The handover of Asia's last two European colonies, Hong Kong in 1997 and Macau in 1999, opened new eras for both. Despite a visible colonial heritage, the dominant Chinese character underlying these two SARs, or "Special Administrative Regions of China" is obvious: after all, Hong Kong and Macau's population is 97 percent Chinese, the main language is Cantonese, and there have always been close ties – if tinged with distrust – with their cousins north of the border. It is hard to overstate the importance that the handovers had for the Chinese government, in sealing the end of centuries of colonial intrusion with the return of the last pieces of foreign-occupied soil to the motherland. Hong Kong and Macau's population widely supported the transfer of power – if only to see how much leeway they could garner under the new administration. Both entities now find themselves in the unique position of being capitalist enclaves subject to a communist state, under the relatively liberal "One Country, Two Systems" policy coined by the late Chinese leader Deng Xiaoping.

First under colonial and now mainland Chinese rule, Hong Kong and Macau's citizens have never had a say in their futures, so they have concentrated their efforts on other things – notably, **making money**. With its emphasis on economics and consumerism, **Hong Kong** offers the greatest variety and concentration of **shops and shopping** on earth, along with a colossal range of **cuisines**, and vistas of sea and island, green mountains and futuristic cityscapes. The excellent **infrastructure**, including the efficient public transit system, the helpful tourist offices and all the other facilities of a genuinely international city make this an extremely soft entry into the Chinese world.

While Hong Kong is a place to do business, **Macau** has leapt ahead in recent years as a haven for **gambling**, its thirty-odd casinos making the enclave a veritable Las Vegas of the East. The wealth has funded a modern cityscape, but evidence of its colonial past persists in extensive quarters of antique, Mediterranean-style architecture, along with

Highlights

❶ Star Ferry The crossing from Tsim Sha Tsui to Hong Kong Island is the cheapest harbour tour on earth – and one of the most spectacular. **See p.537**

❷ Harbour view from the Peak At dusk, watch the city's dazzling lights brighten across Hong Kong, the harbour and Kowloon. **See p.543**

❸ Sai Kung Peninsula Get away from the crowds and concrete, amid beautiful seascapes, beaches and wild countryside in this often overlooked corner of Hong Kong. **See p.555**

❹ Ngong Ping 360 Amazing vistas of Lantau's coast, mountains and Big Buddha on this cable-car ride from Tung Chung to Po Lin Monastery. **See p.559**

❺ Dim sum Tuck in to an authentic *dim sum* lunch alongside enthusiastic families – try the *har gau* (prawn dumplings) and barbecue pork buns. **See p.568**

❻ Old Macau Seek out forts, beautiful Portuguese churches and former Chinese mansions among Macau's narrow alleyways and cobbled civic squares. **See p.578**

❼ Coffee, tarts and port Thanks to Macau's Portuguese heritage, most cafés and restaurants serve ink-black coffee, delicious custard tarts and port wine – almost unknown elsewhere in China. **See p.588**

HIGHLIGHTS ARE MARKED ON THE MAP ON P.532

9

Portuguese wine and Macanese cooking, a fusion of colonial and Chinese styles.

Visitors will spend more **money** here than elsewhere in China, though public transport and food are good value – even if accommodation is always pricey for what you get. Travellers on a tight **budget** who stay in dormitories can just about get by on HK$450 a day, though at the other end of the market in hotels, restaurants and shops, prices quickly rise to international levels.

Hong Kong

香港, xiāng gǎng

HONG KONG – more fully known as the Hong Kong SAR – wears a lot of hats: it remains one of the world's largest financial hubs; its modern face hides a surprisingly traditional culture; and it's also an experiment in governance with which the mainland authorities hope to win over a recalcitrant Taiwan. While Hong Kong's famous addiction to money and brand names tends to mask the fact that most people work long hours and live in tiny apartments, the city is bursting with energy and the population of seven million is sophisticated and well informed compared to their mainland cousins, the result of a relatively free press. The urban panorama of skyscrapered Hong Kong Island, seen across the harbour from Kowloon, is stunning, and you'll find a surprisingly undeveloped countryside within easy commuter range of the hectic centre and its perennial, massive engineering projects.

Orientation

Hong Kong comprises 1100 square kilometres of the south China coastline and a number of islands east of the Pearl River Delta. The principal urban area is spread along the north shore of **Hong Kong Island**, which offers traces of the **old colony** – from English place names to anachronistic double-decker trams trundling along the shore – and also superb **modern cityscapes** of towering buildings teetering up impossible slopes, along with whole districts dedicated to selling Traditional Chinese Medicine and herbs. The south of the island offers several decent **beaches**, a huge **amusement park**, and even **hiking** opportunities.

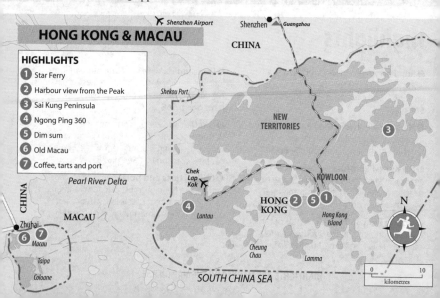

HONG KONG & MACAU

HIGHLIGHTS

1. Star Ferry
2. Harbour view from the Peak
3. Sai Kung Peninsula
4. Ngong Ping 360
5. Dim sum
6. Old Macau
7. Coffee, tarts and port

9

> **THE HONG KONG DOLLAR**
>
> Hong Kong has its own currency, the **Hong Kong dollar**, which is pegged at around $8 to the US dollar and so is currently worth a little less than the Chinese yuan. Yuan cannot officially be used in Hong Kong, though a few stores will take them. In this chapter, the symbol "$" refers to Hong Kong dollars throughout, unless stated.

Immediately north across Victoria Harbour from Hong Kong Island, the **Kowloon Peninsula** – and especially its tip, **Tsim Sha Tsui** – is Hong Kong's principal tourist trap, boasting a glut of accommodation, shops and markets offering an incredible variety of goods. North of Tsim Sha Tsui, Kowloon merges with the **New Territories**, a varied area of **New Towns** and older villages, secluded beaches and undeveloped country parks. In addition, the **Outlying Islands** – particularly **Lamma** and **Lantau** – are worth a visit for their seafood restaurants and relatively laidback pace of life.

Brief history

While the Chinese justifiably argue that Hong Kong was always Chinese territory, its development only began with the **arrival of the British** in 1842, following the first **Opium War** (see p.918). Further gunboat diplomacy eighteen years later secured Britain the Kowloon Peninsula too, and in 1898 Britain obtained a 99-year lease on an additional one thousand square kilometres of land north of Kowloon, the New Territories. Up until World War II, the territory prospered as frequent turmoil in mainland China drove money and **refugees** south into the apparently safe confines of the British colony. This confidence proved misplaced in 1941 when **Japanese forces** seized Hong Kong along with the rest of eastern China, though after Japan's defeat in 1945, Britain swiftly reclaimed the colony. As the mainland fell to the Communists in 1949, a new wave of refugees swelled Hong Kong's population threefold to 2.5 million, causing a housing crisis that set in motion themes still current in the SAR: **land reclamation**, the need for efficient infrastructure, and a tendency to save space by building upwards.

Approaching the handover

In the last twenty years of British rule, the spectre of **1997**, when Britain's lease on the New Territories expired, loomed large. Negotiations on the future of the colony led in 1984 to the **Sino-British Joint Declaration**, paving the way for Britain to hand back sovereignty of the territory in return for Hong Kong maintaining its capitalist system for fifty years. However, fears grew that repression and the erosion of freedoms would follow the handover. The constitutional framework provided by the **Basic Law** of 1988, in theory, answered some of those fears, illustrating how the "One Country, Two Systems" policy would work. But the following year's **crackdown in Tian'anmen Square** only seemed to confirm the most pessimistic views of what might happen following the handover, especially to members of Hong Kong's embryonic **democracy movement**. When **Chris Patten** arrived in 1992 to become the last governor, he cynically broadened the voting franchise for the **Legislative Council** (**Legco**) from around 200,000 to some 2.7 million people, infuriating Beijing and ensuring that the road to the handover would be a rough ride.

> **HONG KONG PHONE NUMBERS**
>
> **Hong Kong phone numbers** have no area codes. From outside the territory, dial the normal international access code + ❶852 (the "country" code) + the number. However, **from Macau** you need only dial ❶01 + the number. To call Hong Kong from mainland China, dial ❶00 + 852 + the number.

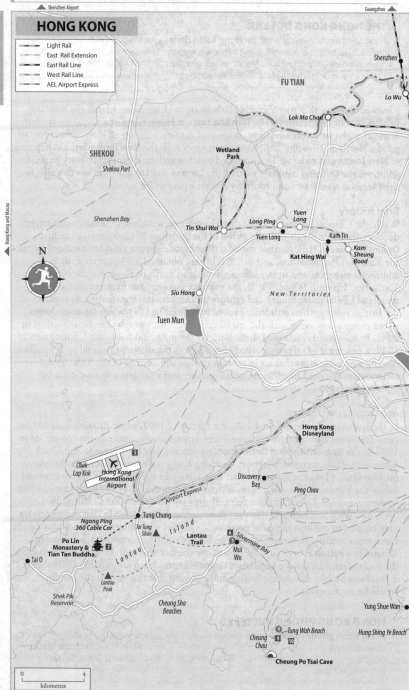

HONG KONG

	Light Rail
	East Rail Extension
	East Rail Line
	West Rail Line
	AEL Airport Express

Shenzhen Airport

Guangzhou

Shenzhen

Lo Wu

FU TIAN

Lok Ma Chau

SHEKOU

Shekou Port

Shenzhen Bay

Wetland Park

Long Ping

Yuen Long

Tin Shui Wai

Yuen Long

Kam Tin

Kam Sheung Road

Kat Hing Wai

Siu Hong

New Territories

Tuen Mun

N

Hong Kong Disneyland

Chek Lap Kok

Hong Kong International Airport

Discovery Bay

Peng Chau

Airport Express

Tung Chung

Ngong Ping 360 Cable Car

Tai Tung Shan

Lantau Trail

Silvermine Bay

Mui Wo

Po Lin Monastery & Tian Tan Buddha

Lantau

Island

Tai O

Lantau Peak

Shek Pik Reservoir

Cheung Sha Beaches

Yung Shue Wan

Tung Wah Beach

Hung Shing Ye Beach

Cheung Chau

Cheung Po Tsai Cave

0 — 4
kilometres

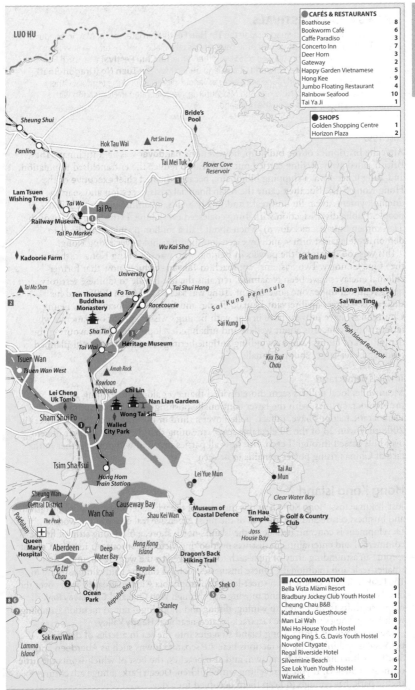

> ## HONG KONG'S FESTIVALS
>
> Festivals specific to Hong Kong include the **Tin Hau Festival**, in late April or May, in honour of the Goddess of the Sea. Large seaborne celebrations take place, most notably at Joss House Bay on the Sai Kung Peninsula (see p.555). Another is the **Tai Chiu Festival** (known in English as the Bun Festival), held on Cheung Chau Island during May. The **Tuen Ng (Dragon-Boat) Festival** takes place in early June, with races in various places around the territory. Other Chinese festivals, such as New Year and Mid-Autumn, are celebrated in Hong Kong with as much, if not more, gusto as on the mainland.

Post-1997

After the histrionics of the build-up, however, the **handover** was an anticlimax. The British sailed away, Beijing carried out its threat to reduce the enfranchised population, and Tung Chee-hwa, a shipping billionaire, became the **first chief executive** of the Hong Kong SAR. But then came the **Asian financial crisis**, recession and soaring unemployment, avian flu outbreaks and finally SARS, a baffling virus that killed 299 people. Public dissatisfaction with Tung coalesced every June 4 (the anniversary of the Tian'anmen Square crackdown), when about half a million people turned out to **demonstrate** against him – and, by extension, Beijing's hold over Hong Kong.

This was too much for the powers in Beijing, who wanted Hong Kong to showcase the "One Country, Two Systems" approach to **Taiwan** – which, now that former colonial enclaves have been reclaimed, remains the last hurdle to Chinese territory being reunited under one government. Tung was sacked in March 2005, and his successors – career civil servant Donald Tsang, and the current incumbent, Leung Chun-ying – have proved more in line with Beijing's wishes, pliant bureaucrats who ignore public concerns about welfare and urban redevelopment, while favouring the demolition of Hong Kong's dwindling antique heritage to make way for ill-planned roads and ever-larger shopping malls.

Towards democracy?

Meanwhile, local politics seem more divided than ever along pro-Beijing and pro-democracy lines, with the latter continually pushing for **universal suffrage**. Democratic factions have, in fact, polled over a third of the vote since the handover (in 2008 they won 23 of the 30 electable seats), meaning that they hold a power of veto over bills passed through Legco. But how all parties involved will pull together in the face of China's rising power remains to be seen.

Hong Kong Island

Just 15km across, **Hong Kong Island** is the heart of the whole territory, its administrative and business centre and site of some of the most expensive real estate in the world. Development is concentrated along the island's north shore, a 6km-long strip of financial, commercial and entertainment districts overlooking **Victoria Harbour**. At its core, **Central** sprouts an astounding array of high-tech towers, edged to the west by **Sheung Wan**'s smaller-scale and traditional Chinese businesses. Behind this the land climbs steeply to **The Peak**, a superb escape from street-level claustrophobia with unequalled views over the city. Back along the harbour and moving east through **Wan Chai** and **Causeway Bay**, the emphasis shifts from finance to wining, dining and shopping – not to mention gambling, with Hong Kong's main horse racetrack located nearby at **Happy Valley**.

The south side of Hong Kong Island straggles into the sea in a series of dangling peninsulas and inlets. The attractions here are separate towns such as **Aberdeen** and **Stanley**, with a flavour of their own, and also beaches, the best of which fronts the little outpost of **Shek O**. If you're travelling with children, **Ocean Park**, a huge adventure theme park, has enough to keep them occupied for a day.

Transport around the island is easy, with the MTR, buses and trams covering the north shore. An MTR line to the south coast is in the early stages of construction, but buses here are plentiful too, and nowhere is more than an hour from Central.

Central

Central takes in the densely crowded heart of Hong Kong's financial district, and extends for a few hundred metres in all directions from Central MTR Station. The waterfront area here is currently in redevelopment limbo, with parks and congestion-relieving expressways under construction, but the **Star Ferry Terminal** remains one of Hong Kong Island's major arrival points. Central's main west–east roads are Connaught Road, Des Voeux Road (with its tramlines) and Queen's Road, with a mesh of smaller streets heading south and uphill.

Hong Kong Maritime Museum

Pier 8, next to the Star Ferry Terminal • Mon–Fri 9.30am–5.30pm, Sat & Sun 10am–7pm • $30 • ⓦ hkmaritimemuseum.org • MTR Hong Kong, Exit A2

Hong Kong's **Maritime Museum** exhibits an engrossing, well-planned collection of Hong Kong's historical seafaring relics, from shipwreck porcelain to cannon and original scroll paintings depicting the nineteenth-century war against piracy. There are also scores of carefully made wooden models of ships and, from the upstairs, superlative harbour views (with free telescopes) over to the ICC tower and eastwards through the harbour. The museum is barely signposted; it's on the next pier east from Central's Star Ferry terminal.

The International Finance Centre (IFC)

Corner of Connaught Rd and Finance St • ⓦ ifc.com.hk • MTR Central, Exit A

At the core of Central's web of elevated walkways, the **International Finance Centre** (**IFC**) houses a **mall** and the Airport Express terminus, while above it rears the 88-storey, 420m-high **IFC2** tower, once Hong Kong's tallest building. This is so beautifully proportioned that it's not until you see the top brushing the clouds that you realize the tower stands half as high again as anything else in the area. Sadly, you can't ride the lift up for views, though there's a virtual 360-degree version on the IFC website.

Exchange Square

MTR Central, Exit A

Inland from the IFC, **Exchange Square** is surrounded by three pastel-pink marble and glass towers housing Hong Kong's Stock Exchange, designed by Swiss architect Remo Riva. The square itself, full of sandwich-guzzling office staff at lunchtime, is decorated with bronze statuary by Elizabeth Frink and Henry Moore. The square's street-level **bus station** is useful for reaching many of the island's outlying sights.

Lan Kwai Fong

MTR Central, Exit D2

South of Queen's Road, the land begins to slope seriously upwards, making walking laborious in hot weather. The whole district, with its original focus around the

---

THE STAR FERRY

One of the most enjoyable things to do in Hong Kong is to spend ten minutes riding the humble **Star Ferry** between Tsim Sha Tsui in Kowloon and the pier in front of the IFC2 Tower on Hong Kong Island (daily 6.30am–11.30pm; upper deck $2.50, lower deck $2; ⓦ www .starferry.com.hk). The views of the island are superb, particularly at dusk when the lights begin to twinkle through the humidity and the spray. You'll also get a feel for the frenetic pace of life on Hong Kong's waterways, with ferries, junks, hydrofoils and larger ships looming up from all directions.

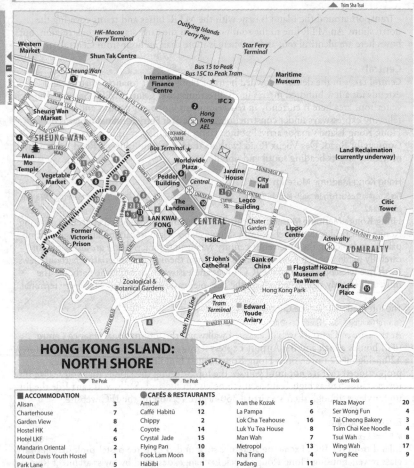

HONG KONG ISLAND: NORTH SHORE

ACCOMMODATION		CAFÉS & RESTAURANTS					
Alisan	3	Amical	19	Ivan the Kozak	5	Plaza Mayor	20
Charterhouse	7	Caffé Habitù	12	La Pampa	6	Ser Wong Fun	4
Garden View	8	Chippy	2	Lok Cha Teahouse	16	Tai Cheong Bakery	3
Hostel HK	4	Coyote	14	Luk Yu Tea House	8	Tsim Chai Kee Noodle	4
Hotel LKF	6	Crystal Jade	15	Man Wah	7	Tsui Wah	8
Mandarin Oriental	2	Flying Pan	10	Metropol	13	Wing Wah	17
Mount Davis Youth Hostel	1	Fook Lam Moon	18	Nha Trang	4	Yung Kee	9
Park Lane	5	Habibi	1	Padang	11		

L-shaped lane of **Lan Kwai Fong**, forms a lively mass of pubs, clubs, bars and restaurants and now spreads south over Hollywood Road and west as far as Peel Street. The line-up of popular venues changes almost every other month, but they make good places to mingle with Western expats and local yuppies.

The Hong Kong and Shanghai Bank (HSBC)

MTR Central, Exit K

Sitting between Queen's Road Central and Des Voeux Road, the **Hong Kong and Shanghai Bank (HSBC)** dates from 1985; designed by Sir Norman Foster, it reputedly cost over US$1 billion. The whole building is supported off the ground so that it's possible to walk right underneath – a necessity stipulated by the *feng shui* belief that the centre of power on the island, Government House, which lies directly to the north, should be accessible in a straight line from the main point of arrival on the island, the Star Ferry. From underneath, the building's insides are transparent, and you can look up into its heart through the glass atrium. The two bronze **lions** out the front, named Stephen and Stitt after former HSBC directors, date to the 1930s and bear shrapnel scars from World War II.

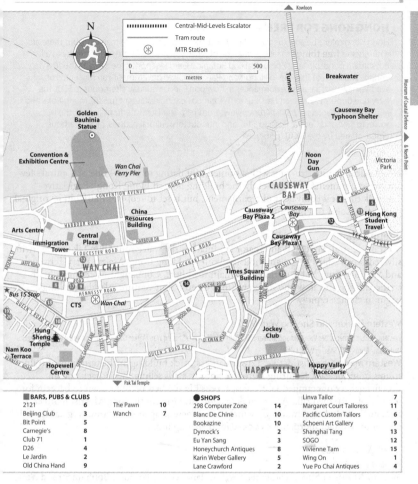

BARS, PUBS & CLUBS				SHOPS		Linva Tailor	7
2121	6	The Pawn	10	298 Computer Zone	14	Margaret Court Tailoress	11
Beijing Club	3	Wanch	7	Blanc De Chine	10	Pacific Custom Tailors	6
Bit Point	5			Bookazine	10	Schoeni Art Gallery	9
Carnegie's	8			Dymock's	2	Shanghai Tang	13
Club 71	1			Eu Yan Sang	3	SOGO	12
D26	4			Honeychurch Antiques	8	Vivienne Tam	15
Le Jardin	2			Karin Weber Gallery	5	Wing On	1
Old China Hand	9			Lane Crawford	2	Yue Po Chai Antiques	4

The Bank of China (BOC)

Mon–Fri 10am–5pm • Free (bring passport) • MTR Central, Exit K

Immediately east of the HSBC, the 300m-high, blue-glass and steel **Bank of China (BOC)** was designed by a team led by the renowned I.M. Pei. Like its nearby neighbour, the HSBC, the Bank of China was also designed using *feng shui*, though here the intentions are entirely aggressive: the bank's threatening, knife-like tower can be seen as a lightning conductor, drawing good luck down from the sky before any can reach its shorter rival next door; its sharp corners also "cut" towards the HSBC. There are exceptional **views** from the 43rd floor, which take in the IFC2, the old Bank of China, Government House, the former Legco Building and the Catholic cathedral.

Statue Square and Legco

MTR Central, Exit K

Immediately north of the HSBC building, **Statue Square** is an oddly empty space. Its main point of interest is the former **Legco Building** on its eastern side, a hefty

HONG KONG FOR FREE

Hong Kong might be an expensive place compared with the Chinese mainland, but there are a number of **free things** to take advantage of while you're here. These include entry to all downtown parks, plus the Zoological and Botanical Gardens (p.542); the Edward Youde Aviary and the Museum of Teaware in Hong Kong Park (p.543); all government-run museums on Wednesdays; martial-arts performances in Kowloon Park on Sunday afternoons (p.550); the ferry ride through Aberdeen Harbour to the *Jumbo* floating restaurant (p.546); Mong Kok's bird and goldfish markets (p.551); harbour views from Tsim Sha Tsui waterfront (p.549); the BOC tower (p.539) and Central Plaza (p.544); and introductory cultural courses, plus a harbour cruise, offered by the HKTB (p.564).

Neoclassical granite structure with a domed roof dating to 1912 – one of Central's few antique monuments. Until recently the building housed Hong Kong's Legislative Council, the local equivalent of a parliament, but is set to reopen in 2019 in its original role as the Court of Final Appeal.

Sheung Wan

West of Central, **Sheung Wan**'s major landmark is the waterfront **Shun Tak Centre**, twin silvered boxes edged in red and housing both the Hong Kong–Macau Ferry Terminal and Sheung Wang MTR station. The main road here, Connaught, is crammed with traffic and the area looks no different from Central, but venture inland and things begin to change rapidly.

Western Market and Sheung Wan Market

Western Market Corner of Des Voeux Rd and Morrison St • Daily 10am–7pm • Sheung Wan Market Corner Morrison and Wing Lok streets • Daily 6am–8pm • MTR Sheung Wan, Exit B

Western Market is a distinctive, Edwardian-era brick building at the terminus of tram routes from the east, featuring a ground floor of stalls selling tourist tack and an upstairs gallery of cramped fabric shops, possibly the best place in town to bargain for lengths of patterned silk. As a complete contrast, head south along Morrison Street to **Sheung Wan Market**, a multistorey maze of Chinese shoppers after fresh vegetables, fish and meat, with an inexpensive **cooked food** area up top.

Dried goods shops

MTR Sheung Wan, Exit B

West of Morrison Street, you enter a web of lanes centred around **Bonham Strand West**, **Queen's Road West** and **Wing Lok Street** whose shops specialize in dried foods and traditional Chinese medicine products such as birds' nests, ginseng, assorted marine creatures, deer antlers, edible fungus and aromatic fruits. There's a fine line between food and medicine in China, but the best way of telling the difference here is seeing what is displayed in tiny red-and-gold gift packages (rare medicines), and what is shifted by the sackful (usually food).

Ladder Street

MTR Sheung Wan, Exit A2

Southwest off Queen's Road Central, **Ladder Street** appears as a set of steep, broad stone steps heading uphill. This is one of many such stairways scattered between here and Central, a relic of the nineteenth-century sedan-chair carriers, who used them to get their loads up the hillsides. Ladder Street extends all the way south to Caine Road, but just a short way up on the right is **Upper Lascar Row**, commonly known as **Cat Street**, a wall-to-wall stretch of curio stalls loaded with coins, ornaments, jewellery, Chairman Mao badges and chops.

9

Man Mo Temple

Corner of Ladder St and Hollywood Rd • Daily 8am–6pm • Free • MTR Sheung Wan, Exit A2

The blocky granite **Man Mo Temple** is one of the oldest in Hong Kong, dating to the 1840s and originally founded as a charitable institution. Just inside the entrance is a hanging board with the four characters for "Omnipotent Divine Grace" written by the emperor Guangxu; the central atrium beyond is hung with great spiral incense coils suspended from the ceiling, filling the interior with eye-watering, aromatic smoke. The temple's name derives from the words for "culture" (*man* in Cantonese) and "martial" (*mo*): the first is embodied by Man Cheong, the deity of literature (he's the red-robed figure holding a writing brush on the right side of the altar); the second by the Three Kingdoms general Guan Yu (the statue opposite Man Cheong in green with a halberd), later deified as patron of the police, pawn shops and underworld gangs.

Soho and Hollywood Road

Soho – the district between Hollywood and Caine roads – is developing into an extension of Lan Kwai Fong, though the emphasis here is towards eating rather than clubs and bars, and the clientele is almost entirely Western. **Hollywood Road** itself is of interest for the slew of antique shops and fine art galleries running all the way east to the Mid-Levels Escalator, with goods and prices ranging from the touristy to the serious-art-collector-only brackets. Two places to note in passing – derelict at the time of writing though earmarked for redevelopment – are the Art Deco frontage of the former **Central Police Station** at 10 Hollywood Rd, within sight of the Mid-Levels Escalator; and the high stone walls of decommissioned **Victoria Prison**, immediately behind, built in 1862.

The Zoological and Botanical Gardens

Main entrance corner of Garden Rd and Upper Albert Rd • Daily 6am–7pm • Free • bus #3B from Connaught Road, outside Exchange Square

Hong Kong's **Zoological and Botanical Gardens** opened in 1864 and currently house a large collection of exotic birds – including rare cranes and pheasants – along with a small number of monkeys. The stone memorial arch and lions at the main gateway commemorate the Chinese soldiers who died defending Hong Kong from the Japanese during World War II; once inside there's a pleasantly shaded mix of shrubs and trees to wander around and admire the views over Central. The gardens' two sections are connected by a walkway underneath Albany Street.

Hong Kong Park

Main entrances off Queen's Rd and Cotton Tree Drive • Daily 6.30am–11pm; Edward Youde Aviary daily 10am–5pm • Free • MTR Admiralty, Exit C1

Hong Kong Park is a beautiful spot, landscaped in tiers up a steep hillside and full of greenery, lotus ponds and waterfalls; it's a favourite location for **wedding photographs** and there's even a registry office here. The highlight of the park is the **Edward Youde Aviary**, where raised walkways lead you through a re-created rainforest canopy inside a

---

THE MID-LEVELS ESCALATOR

Head east along Queen's Road from the Central MTR – or follow walkways from the IFC – and you'll reach the covered **Mid-Levels Escalator**, which rises in sections 800m up the hill as far as Conduit Road and the trendy **Mid-Levels** residential area. During the morning (6–10am), when people are setting out to work, the escalators run downwards only; from 10.20am to midnight they run up. Places to get off and explore include the restaurant district between Wellington Street and Lyndhurst Terrace; the narrow lanes west of the escalator between Queen's Road and Hollywood Road, full of crowded produce markets and small shops specializing in domestic goods; Hollywood Road itself, lined with antique shops (see p.572); and the restaurant, bar and café district of Soho, laid out along Elgin and Staunton streets.

giant meshed enclosure, with rare and colourful birds swooping about, nesting and breeding; a separate enclosure houses various endangered species of hornbill – fantastic black- and white-banded birds with oversized curved beaks.

Flagstaff House Museum of Tea Ware

Hong Kong Park • Mon & Wed–Sun 10am–5pm • Free • MTR Admiralty, Exit C1

Near Hong Kong Park's Queen's Road entrance, the **Flagstaff House Museum of Tea Ware** is an elegant colonial structure built in the 1840s, and houses three thousand Chinese artefacts related to tea making. You can sample quality brews – and buy good-value tea and reproduction antique teaware – next door at the pricey but pleasant *Lock Cha Teahouse* (daily 10am–10pm), which also serves *dim sum* snacks.

The Peak

The Peak – formerly Victoria Peak – rises 552m over Central and the Harbour, providing the few urban elite who are astronomically wealthy enough to own houses up here with the only perspective that really matters in Hong Kong: downwards. Reasons to come up here include not just the superb vistas and forest walks, but also the unnerving ascent – either leaning back at an extreme angle on the **Peak Tram**, or careering around corners at the top of a double-decker bus.

The Peak Tower and Galleria

Mon–Fri 10am–11pm, Sat & Sun 8am–11pm • Sky Terrace observation tower $35

All transport up the Peak terminates around 390m above sea level at the ugly, wok-shaped **Peak Tower**, featuring cafés and a branch of Madame Tussauds, with wax models ranging from basketball superstar Yao Ming to Barack Obama. The attached Sky Terrace observation tower offers views, but there are perfectly decent – and free – ones from a small stone terrace 100m to the east of the tower, and also from the roof of the adjacent **Peak Galleria**. Wherever you get them from, vistas are stupendous, down over the island's intensely crowded north shore (incredibly, you're still lower than the tops of the IFC2 and ICC towers), across the busy harbour to a lower-rise, unspectacular Kowloon and the green peaks of the New Territories – a cityscape which is no less spectacular when lit up at night.

The Peak Circuit Walk

While it's not worth ascending to the very top of the Peak – which is capped by security fencing and radio masts – it is worth strolling around the level, partially forested **Peak Circuit walk** via Lugard and Harlech roads, an easy hour-long return walk from the Peak Tower which provides something like a 360-degree view of the entire island.

ASCENDING AND DESCENDING THE PEAK

The most popular way to arrive at or depart from the Peak is aboard the **Peak Tram** (daily 7am–midnight; $28 one-way, $40 return; ⓦthepeak.com.hk), actually a funicular railway whose incredibly steep track climbs the 386 vertical metres to the Peak Tower in about eight minutes. The tram's lower terminus is on Garden Road, reached aboard bus #15C from outside the Outlying Islands Ferry Pier (daily 10am–11.40pm; approximately every 30min; $3.50).

For an equally fun ride, sit upstairs at the front of **bus #15** (daily 6.15am–midnight; $9.80) as it tackles low branches and hairpin bends on the half-hour ascent from the Outlying Islands Ferry Pier – you can also pick it up at Exchange Square bus station or along Queen's Road East.

An excellent way to descend the Peak – or, if you're a hardened jogger, to ascend it – is on foot via the **Old Peak Road**, a concrete track whose unsigned beginning is a little hard to find around the side of the Peak Tower. An extremely steep, twenty-minute hike lands you among high-rise residences southwest of the Zoological and Botanical Gardens, which you can reach by continuing down the road for a further fifteen minutes.

9

Wan Chai

Wan Chai MTR Station is on Hennessy Road, while trams use Johnston Road, one block south; both are within walking distance of the sights. There's also a Star Ferry service (see p.537) between the Tsim Sha Tsui ferry terminal and the Wan Chai ferry pier, just east of the Convention and Exhibition Centre

East of Central, **Wan Chai** is a nondescript district of broad, busy main roads and more towers, though these mainly house commercial, rather than financial, institutions. Back in the 1950s, **Wan Chai** was a thriving red-light district, famed as the setting for Richard Mason's novel *The World of Suzy Wong*, and there's still a vaguely sleazy feel to its core of **bars and clubs**. The main arteries here are parallel **Hennessy Road**, **Lockhart Road** – both lined with shops, restaurants and businesses – and the waterfront expressway, **Gloucester Road**.

The Convention and Exhibition Centre

Convention Avenue • MTR Wan Chai, Exit A1

Wan Chai's most striking building is the **Hong Kong Convention and Exhibition Centre**, whose curved-roof CEC Extension juts out into the harbour and plausibly resembles a manta ray. This is where the British formally handed Hong Kong back to the Chinese in June 1997, and as such is a huge draw for mainland tourists, who pose beside the **Forever Blooming Golden Bauhinia statue** behind. The adjacent flagpoles fly the red- and gold-spangled banner of the People's Republic, and the five-petalled bauhinia emblem of the Hong Kong SAR.

Central Plaza

Gloucester Rd • public viewing area Mon–Fri 8am–8pm • Free • MTR Wan Chai, Exit A1

Immediately south of the Convention Centre soars the 78-storey **Central Plaza**. Triangular in cross section and topped by a tall spire, it has been dubbed "The Big Syringe" by locals; the tower's glowing cladding changes colour every fifteen minutes from 6pm to 6am. For splendid **360-degree views** over the city, catch the lift to the public viewing area on the 46th floor.

Queen's Road East

MTR Admiralty, Exit J

Up against the Peak's foothills, **Queen's Road East** features a concentration of furniture stores, many dealing in traditional Chinese designs. Partway along and built into a roadside grotto, the tiny **Hung Sheng Temple** is dedicated to a deified Tang-dynasty official skilled in foretelling the weather; nearby Ship Street dead-ends at **Nam Koo Terrace**, a decaying old mansion that is reputedly the most haunted spot in Hong Kong. Farther east off Queen's Road East is a slew of backstreet **markets**, jamming narrow Tai Yuen Street and Tai Wong Street West.

Pak Tai Temple

Stone Nullah Lane • Daily 8am–5pm • Free • MTR Admiralty, Exit J

Off the eastern end of Queen's Road East, the **Pak Tai Temple** is a solid, granite-block building with a roof decorated with a procession of lively, glazed pottery figurines depicting scenes from Chinese legends. The temple is fairly plain inside, with a mighty bronze statue of Pak Tai, the flood-quelling deity of the north, stamping down on the evil forms of a turtle and snake.

Bowen Road and Lovers' Rock

Bus #15 to the Peak from Outer Islands Ferry Pier via Exchange Square and Queen's Road East, or a steep walk up Wan Chai Gap Road from behind Pak Tai Temple

Up on the steep, forested slopes above Queen's Road East, **Bowen Road** is actually a pedestrian track, popular with joggers. As well as providing a surprisingly shaded, rural walk, with the sounds of the city drifting up from below, Bowen Road also gives access to **Lovers' Rock**, a huge stone boulder pointing rudely skywards through the canopy, draped in festive red ribbons. The rock becomes a pilgrimage site during the annual Maidens' Festival during the seventh lunar month (usually in August).

Causeway Bay

Causeway Bay's MTR station is on Hennessy Rd, which, along with its extension, Yee Wo St, is also covered by trams

East of the Aberdeen expressway, Causeway Bay forms a knot of lively, seething streets packed with restaurants, accommodation and shopping plazas. You might also visit midweek for the horse races in Happy Valley, or for relief from urban claustrophobia in nearby Victoria Park.

The Noon Day Gun

Take the tunnel underneath Victoria Park Rd from the car park next to the *Excelsior Hotel* • MTR Causeway Bay, Exit D1

Causeway Bay's sole tourist sight is the waterfront **Noon Day Gun** – immortalized in Noël Coward's song *Mad Dogs and Englishmen*. This small naval cannon is still fired off with a loud report every day at noon, a tradition dating back to the early days of the colony (though the exact reasons for the practice remain obscure); at other times, the gun is covered up and there's nothing to see.

Victoria Park

Open 24hr • MTR Causeway Bay, Exit E

The eastern part of Causeway Bay is dominated by **Victoria Park**, an extensive, open space containing shady paths, swimming pools and other sports facilities. The park has become the location for the annual candlelit vigil held on June 4 to commemorate the victims of Tian'anmen Square, and also hosts Hong Kong's largest Chinese New Year fairs. Come early in the morning and you'll see dozens of people practising *tai ji*.

Happy Valley Racecourse

Races every Wed evening, approximately 7–11pm, Sept–June • Entry from $10 • ⓦ happyvalleyracecourse.com • tram to Happy Valley or MTR Causeway Bay Exit A

Occupying a former malarial swamp, **Happy Valley Racecourse** provides Hong Kong with the only legal outlet for gambling, and as such is indescribably popular every Wednesday evening during the September–June racing season. Trackside in the public enclosure you can mix with a beery expat crowd and pump the staff to make sense of the intricate accumulator bets that Hong Kong specializes in; alternatively, join the hard-bitten Chinese punters up in the stands, for all the cigarette smoke and Cantonese cursing you can handle.

The Museum of Coastal Defence

Tung Hei Rd • Mon–Wed & Fri–Sun 10am–5pm • $10 • ⓦ www.hkcoastaldefence.museum • Island Line MTR to Shau Kei Wan; take Exit B1 and follow the signs for 10min via Shau Kei Wan St East and Tung Hei Rd

Around 6km east of Causeway Bay, the splendid **Museum of Coastal Defence** is located inside the 1887 Lei Yue Mui Fort, which itself is built into a hill overlooking the eastern end of the harbour. There are great views from the seawards-facing gun emplacements, while the former barracks and ammunition rooms are filled with an exhaustive collection of artefacts, mannequins and photographs covering the history of Hong Kong's naval militias from the Ming dynasty to the handover.

Aberdeen

Bus #70 from Exchange Square in Central; bus #73 from Repulse Bay, Deep Water Bay and Stanley; bus #48 from Ocean Park

Down on the south coast, **ABERDEEN** is the largest separate town on Hong Kong Island, with a population of more than sixty thousand living in garishly coloured tower blocks around the sheltered **harbour**. Aberdeen is a **fishing port**, its fleet of family-run trawlers providing around a third of Hong Kong's seafood catch – there's a busy early-morning

9

ABERDEEN HARBOUR CRUISES

Approach Aberdeen Harbour and you'll be grabbed by women touting for a **sampan tour** (around $50/person for a 30min ride, irrespective of the number of travellers). The trip offers photogenic views of houseboats complete with dogs, drying laundry and outdoor kitchens, as well as luxury yachts, boat yards and **floating restaurants**, which are especially spectacular when lit up at night.

Cheapskates can, in fact, enjoy a ten-minute **free harbour trip** by catching a ferry to the garishly decorated three-floor *Jumbo Restaurant* (Mon–Sat 11am–11.30pm, Sun 7am–11.30pm; see p.570) from a signed dock with a red gateway near the fish market; there's no pressure to actually have a meal here if you just want to look around. You'll also pass through the harbour if you use the **Aberdeen–Lamma ferry** (see p.556).

cooperative **fish market** at the harbour daily. You can appreciate the fleet's size during the fishing **moratorium** (June & July), when the harbour is packed to capacity with freshly scrubbed vessels; the harbour is also the venue for the annual **Dragon-Boat Festival**, one of the biggest in Hong Kong, held on the fifth day of the fifth lunar month (usually in June).

Ocean Park

Daily 10am–7.30pm • $280, children aged 3–11 $140, children under 3 free • ⓦ oceanpark.com.hk • bus #260 to the main eastern entrance from Exchange Square station via Admiralty MTR (9am–6.30pm; approximately every 15min); bus #629 from Admiralty MTR, or #48 from Aberdeen, to the western entrance; bus #73 from Stanley stops on the highway outside

Ocean Park, a gigantic theme and adventure park, covers an entire peninsula to the east of Aberdeen. The price of the ticket is all-inclusive, and once you're inside, all rides and shows are free. You could easily spend the best part of a day here, and at weekends in summer you may find yourself frustrated by queues at the popular attractions, so make sure you arrive early in order to enjoy yourself at a relaxed pace. Pick of the sights include four **giant pandas** in their own 2000-square-metre complex; scary rides such as the Dragon roller coaster and Abyss Turbo Drop; the **Ocean Theatre**, where trained dolphins and sea lions perform; plus the **Atoll Reef**, a huge coral-reef aquarium that contains more than five thousand fish.

Stanley

Bus #6, #6A or #260 from Central; bus #73 from Aberdeen or Repulse Bay; green minibus #40 from Times Square in Causeway Bay

Straddling the neck of Hong Kong's most southerly peninsula, **STANLEY** was already settled by fishermen and pirates when the British took Hong Kong Island in 1842. Today this small residential town feels uncomfortably overcrowded with expats and tourists, the former filling the seafront restaurants at Sunday lunchtime, the latter gravitating towards **Stanley Market**, a couple of covered lanes selling a mishmash of souvenirs including clothes, embroideries, prints, paintings and trinkets. Stanley also hosts Hong Kong's largest **dragon-boat races**, held on the fifth day of the fifth month of the lunar calendar.

Murray House and Blake Pier

Just back from the shore, Stanley Plaza faces one of Hong Kong's oldest colonial buildings, two-storey **Murray House**, which was dismantled and removed from its original 1840 site in Central to make way for the Bank of China. Today, its elegant stone colonnades house a handful of bars and restaurants; opposite, the reconstructed **Blake Pier**, its iron pillars and corrugated roof dating to 1900, extends Stanley's heritage architecture right to the seafront.

The Tin Hau Temple

Across the square from Murray House is a **Tin Hau Temple**, built in 1767. Tin Hau is the southern Chinese protective deity of fishermen, and her temples can be found

HIKING THE DRAGON'S BACK

One of the easiest coastal hikes in Hong Kong, the **Dragon's Back** takes just a couple of hours to complete, and at weekends you'll find plenty of other people along the trail.

Catch **bus #9** from Shau Kei Wan MTR station and get off at **To Tei Wan Tsuen**, where there's a roadside parking bay and a billboard showing a map of the route, then follow the track up onto the ridgetop Dragon's Back itself. The ridge runs north, via views of Stanley and beautiful seascapes, before eventually descending to **Big Wave Bay**, where there are beaches and snack stalls, and a final 2km walk along a vehicle track south to Shek O.

throughout Southeast Asia. This temple, besides generously devoting a good deal of space to statues of other gods, is worth a look for the blackened and barely recognizable **tiger skin** spread-eagled on one wall, the remains of an animal bagged near here in 1942 – the last ever shot in Hong Kong.

Shek O

Bus #9 from Shau Kei Wan MTR; bus #309 (Sun only; hourly 2.10–6.10pm) from Exchange Square in Central; bus #14 or #314 from Stanley to the Shek O junction (ask the driver to set you down), then bus #9 or minibus #16 to Shek O

In the far southeast of the island, **Shek O** is Hong Kong's most remote settlement, with an almost Mediterranean flavour in its stone houses, narrow lanes and seafront location. There's a strong surf beating on the wide, white **beach**, which has a shady area of vine trellises at one end for barbecues and, during the week, is more or less deserted. Come for sunbathing and lunch at one of the cheap local restaurants. The surrounding headlands are also popular for **hiking**, especially the fearsome-sounding but straightforward, two-hour-long **Dragon's Back** trail (see box above).

You can't miss the beach – it's just 50m from the bus stop, beyond a small roundabout. Nearby shops such as the Tung Lok Beachside Store sell beachwear, inflatable floats, plastic buckets and so on, and have storage lockers. Most of the other businesses in the village are fairly inexpensive restaurants.

Kowloon

A 4km-long strip of the mainland ceded to Britain in perpetuity in 1860 to add to their offshore island, **Kowloon** was accordingly developed with gusto and confidence. The skyline here has never matched Hong Kong Island's, thanks to Kowloon being in the flight path of the old airport at Kai Tak, though things could be changing: 2010 saw the completion of Hong Kong's tallest building, the 484m-high **International Commerce Centre** (ICC), atop Union Square and the Airport Express terminal in West Kowloon. With rocketing rents and dwindling space along Hong Kong Island's north shore, perhaps ICC marks a shift in venue for the SAR's next wave of cutting-edge, harbourside architecture.

Initially, it's hard to see how such an intensely commercial and crowded place as Kowloon could possibly appeal to travellers. One reason is the staggering **view** across the harbour to Hong Kong Island's skyscrapers; another is the sheer density of **shopping** opportunities here – from high-end jewellery to cutting-edge electronic goods and outright tourist tack – especially in the couple of square kilometres at the tip of the peninsula that make up **Tsim Sha Tsui**. To the north, **Yau Ma Tei** and **Mong Kok** are less touristy – though even more crowded – districts teeming with soaring tenements and local **markets**, some of which sell modern daily necessities, others with a distinctly traditional Chinese twist.

These days, it's not so clear-cut where Kowloon really ends. The original "border" with the New Territories to the north was **Boundary Street**, though now Kowloon district runs on for a further 3km or so, as the commercial emphasis shifts towards towering **residential estates** clustered around shopping plazas, parks and other

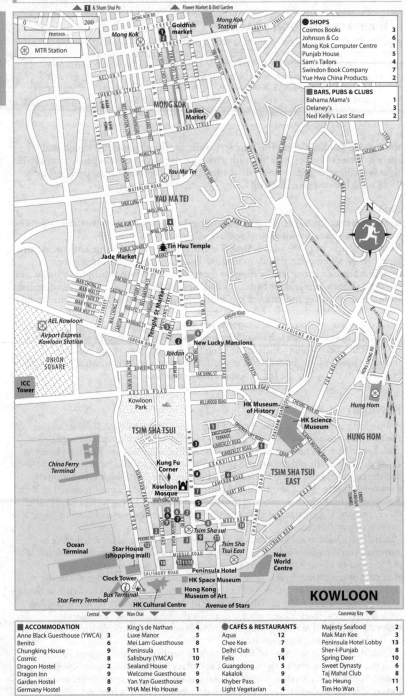

& Sham Shui Po · Flower Market & Bird Garden

MONG KOK ROAD
FIFE STREET
Mong Kok
ARGYLE STREET
Goldfish market
Mong Kok Station
ARGYLE STREET

NELSON ST.

SHANTUNG STREET

MONG KOK

Ladies Market

DUNDAS STREET

HAMILTON ST.

PITT STREET

Yau Ma Tei

WATERLOO ROAD

SHEK LUNG ST.

YAU MA TEI

MAN LING LA.

TUNG KUN ST.

WING SING LA.

PUBLIC SQUARE ST.

Tin Hau Temple

Jade Market

MARKET ST.

KANSU STREET

MAN CHONG ST.
PAK HOI ST.
MAN WAI ST.
SAIGON ST.
MAN YUEN ST.
MAN MING ST.
MAN WUI ST.
NINGPO ST.
NANKING ST.

AEL Kowloon
Airport Express Kowloon Station

Temple St Market

JORDAN ROAD

UNION SQUARE

ICC Tower

New Lucky Mansions

BOWRING STREET

Jordan

TAK SHING ST.

GASCOIGNE ROAD

AUSTIN ROAD

AUSTIN ROAD

Kowloon Park

HILLWOOD ROAD

HK Museum of History

HK Science Museum

Hung Hom

HUNG HOM

China Ferry Terminal

TSIM SHA TSUI

KNUTSFORD TERRACE
OBSERVATORY ROAD
KIMBERLEY ROAD
KIMBERLEY ROAD

GRANVILLE ROAD

TSIM SHA TSUI EAST

Kung Fu Corner

CAMERON ROAD
HART AVE.

Kowloon Mosque

HAIPHONG ROAD

MODY ROAD

Tsim Sha Tsui

Ocean Terminal

Star House (shopping mall)

PEKING ROAD

Tsim Sha Tsui East

New World Centre

MIDDLE ROAD

Peninsula Hotel

SALISBURY ROAD

Clock Tower

HK Space Museum

Bus Terminal

Hong Kong Museum of Art

Star Ferry Terminal

HK Cultural Centre

Avenue of Stars

KOWLOON

Central · Wan Chai · Causeway Bay

0 — 200 metres

⊛ MTR Station

● **SHOPS**

Cosmos Books	3
Johnson & Co	6
Mong Kok Computer Centre	1
Punjab House	5
Sam's Tailors	4
Swindon Book Company	7
Yue Hwa China Products	2

■ **BARS, PUBS & CLUBS**

Bahama Mama's	1
Delaney's	3
Ned Kelly's Last Stand	2

■ **ACCOMMODATION**

Anne Black Guesthouse (YWCA)	3	King's de Nathan	4	
Benito	6	Luxe Manor	5	
Chungking House	9	Mei Lam Guesthouse	8	
Cosmic	8	Peninsula	11	
Dragon Hostel	2	Salisbury (YMCA)	10	
Dragon Inn	9	Sealand House	7	
Garden Hostel	8	Welcome Guesthouse	9	
Germany Hostel	9	Yan Yan Guesthouse	9	
		YHA Mei Ho House	1	

● **CAFÉS & RESTAURANTS**

Aqua	12	Majesty Seafood	2
Chee Kee	7	Mak Man Kee	3
Delhi Club	8	Peninsula Hotel Lobby	13
Felix	14	Sher-I-Punjab	8
Guangdong	5	Spring Deer	10
Kakalok	9	Sweet Dynasty	6
Khyber Pass	8	Taj Mahal Club	8
Light Vegetarian	4	Tao Heung	11
		Tim Ho Wan	1

amenities. A scattering of sights here includes one of Hong Kong's busiest temples, the **Wong Tai Sin**, and its prettiest, the **Chi Lin Nunnery** with its Tang-style architecture and beautiful attached garden.

Tsim Sha Tsui

The tourist heart of Hong Kong, **Tsim Sha Tsui** is an easy place to find your way around. The prime arrival point, the **Star Ferry Terminal**, is right on the southwestern tip of the peninsula. East from here are a number of harbourside museums and galleries – not to mention outstanding views of Hong Kong Island. Hong Kong's most famous street, **Nathan Road**, runs north up through the middle of Tsim Sha Tsui, the lanes either side busy around the clock with shoppers. In among all this brash commercial activity, **Kowloon Park** offers a bit of space to rest, surrounded by ornamental paving and shrubberies.

The Cultural Centre

Salisbury Rd, 50m east of the Star Ferry Terminal • box office daily 9am–9pm • Ⓦ www.lcsd.gov.hk • MTR East Tsim Sha Tsui, Exit J4

A drab, brown-tiled building, the **Hong Kong Cultural Centre** is notable for its astonishing lack of windows over one of the most picturesque urban landscapes in the world; inside are concert halls, theatres and galleries. Adjacent is the **Clock Tower**, the only remaining piece of the Kowloon Railway Station, from where you could once take a train all the way back to Europe, via Mongolia and Russia.

Museum of Art

10 Salisbury Rd • Mon–Wed & Fri 10am–6pm, Sat & Sun 10am–7pm • $10 • Ⓦ hk.art.museum • MTR East Tsim Sha Tsui, Exit J4

Hong Kong's **Museum of Art** houses six galleries of mostly classical Chinese painting, artefacts and calligraphy, enhanced by regular touring exhibitions. Probably the most interesting sections are the first-floor **Chinese Antiquities Gallery**, featuring an ever-changing collection of gold, jade and bronzes; the **Antiquities Gallery** on the third floor, especially strong on pottery; and the **Historical Pictures Gallery**, also on the third floor, which traces the early days of the colony through local artists, both Western and Chinese.

The Space Museum

10 Salisbury Rd • Mon & Wed–Fri 1–9pm, Sat & Sun 10am–9pm • $10, planetarium shows $24–32, concessions $16 •
Ⓦ hk.space.museum • MTR East Tsim Sha Tsui, Exit J4

The Chinese have a genuinely long history of astronomical observations – they were the first to record Halley's Comet in 240 BC, and the later emperors set up accurate observatories with the help of Jesuit priests – and this museum traces the entire history with hands-on displays and videos. There's also a **Space Theatre** planetarium here, which presents OMNIMAX shows for an additional fee.

Avenue of Stars

MTR East Tsim Sha Tsui, Exit J3

For **harbour views**, head down to the promenade that runs for around 500m east from the Clock Tower; it's especially good at night, when Central's skyscrapers flash and pulse to a synthesized beat during the **Symphony of Lights** (daily 8pm; free). The eastern end of the promenade becomes the **Avenue of Stars**, a tribute to Hong Kong's film industry (the third largest in the world after India and the US). Along with actors' handprints pressed into the concrete, there's a large statue of martial-arts star **Bruce Lee**, the man who brought the local industry – and Chinese kung fu – to world attention in the 1970s.

The Peninsula Hotel

Salisbury Rd • ☎ 2920 2888, Ⓦ peninsula.com • MTR Tsim Sha Tsui Exit E

The **Peninsula Hotel** is one of the SAR's great surviving pieces of colonial architecture. Built in the 1920s facing the now-demolished Kowloon Railway Station, the hotel

9

offered a shot of elegance to Hong Kong's weary new arrivals who had just spent weeks rattling down across Europe, Russia and China by rail. Even if you don't stay here – it's one of the most expensive hotels in Hong Kong – echoes of former splendour linger in the elegant lobby, where **afternoon tea** (2–6pm; $190 per head) is still served daily to the sounds of a string quartet performing on the balcony above.

Nathan Road

MTR Tsim Sha Tsui, Exit A1–E

Running north through the heart of Kowloon, **Nathan Road** is by no means a beautiful street, but nonetheless houses a concentrated collection of electronics shops, tailors, jewellery stores and fashion boutiques, somewhere to experience the commercial spirit that really drives Hong Kong. Actually shopping here is not always such a good idea, however – for more details, see "Shopping", p.572.

There's a multicultural flavour provided by the hulking, dubious block of **Chungking Mansions**, the centre of Hong Kong's budget accommodation (see p.566), the lower floors of which form an atmospheric shopping arcade where immigrants from the Indian subcontinent rub elbows with Western tourists, businessmen from central and southeastern Asia and African entrepreneurs.

Kowloon Park

Main entrance at the corner of Haiphong Rd and Nathan Rd • Daily 5am–midnight • Free • MTR Tsim Sha Tsui, Exit A1

West of Nathan Road, half of Tsim Sha Tsui is occupied by **Kowloon Park**, invisible from Nathan Road but marked at its southeastern corner by the white-domed **Kowloon Mosque**, which caters to the area's substantial Muslim population. The park itself provides a welcome, green respite from the rest of Tsim Sha Tsui, with a few huge trees, a swimming pool, aviary and bird ponds (featuring colourful flamingos), a sculpture walk and the **Kung Fu Corner** (up behind the mosque), where experts in various martial arts demonstrate every Sunday between 2.30pm and 4.30pm.

Hong Kong Museum of History

Chatham Rd South • Mon & Wed–Fri 10am–6pm, Sat & Sun 10am–7pm • $10 • ⓦ hk.history.museum • MTR Tsim Sha Tsui, Exit B2

The **Hong Kong Museum of History** features "the Hong Kong Story", a permanent display about the SAR's life and times which utilizes videos, light shows, interactive software and life-sized reconstructions. Pick of the exhibits is a somehow poignant diorama of Stone Age foragers on an as-yet undeveloped seashore; a reconstructed old-style Tanka junk, complete with fishing nets and living quarters; and an entire street, including shops and temple buildings, which you can explore.

Hong Kong Science Museum

Science Museum Rd • Mon & Wed–Fri 10am–7pm, Sat & Sun 10am–9pm • $25 • ⓦ hk.science.museum • MTR Tsim Sha Tsui, Exit B2

Adjacent to the History Museum, the **Hong Kong Science Museum** comprises four floors full of things to prod, poke and pull apart, and is a handy place to bring children for a couple of hours on a rainy day. By far the best feature is the huge "Energy Machine", which features wooden balls racing around the entire museum on a complex giant maze of tracks, buckets, pulleys, drums and gongs – ask at the front desk for performance times.

Temple Street Night Market

Temple St • Daily 6–11pm • MTR Jordan, Exit A

Every evening, **Temple Street Night Market** becomes one of Hong Kong's biggest tourist draws, crammed with stalls selling souvenir T-shirts, leatherwear, games and the sort of trinkets that you never knew you needed until you see them. The most established section sits between Nanking Road and Kansu Street, but push on north past a square housing the local **Tin Hau Temple**, and you'll find yet more stalls selling new antiques, sex toys and electronics. Just before the temple is a crowd of fortune-tellers (some of whom, mysteriously, use live budgerigars in their routines), and a couple of outdoor karaoke tents where locals compete in screaming out folk songs from the 1950s.

The Jade Market
Kansu St • Daily 9am–6pm • MTR Yau Ma Tei, Exit C

Set right underneath a busy overpass, the **Jade Market** features several hundred stalls under a canvas awning; it looks temporary but has been here for decades. Being so hard, jade is believed to prevent decay and many southern Chinese wear pendants or bangles made from the stone as protection against old age. The finest dark green variety comes from Burma; other sources include white jade from Hetian (Khotan) in Xinjiang province (see p.845). You'd have to really know your precious stones to find a bargain, but the market is still a fun place to browse.

The Ladies' and Goldfish markets
Tung Choi St • Daily 10am until evening • MTR Mong Kok, Exit D2

East of Nathan Road as it cuts through the frenetically crowded heart of **Mong Kok** district, the lower end of Tung Choi Street hosts a **Ladies' Market**, flogging piles of cheap clothes, jewellery, toys and bags. Parallel streets are thick with shops specializing in computers, cameras and mobile phones, a more reliable place to buy these things than Tsim Sha Tsui. Push on north over Argyle Street and Tung Choi Street transforms into a **Goldfish Market** lined with shops stocking aquaria, corals, exotic fish and even some dubiously exotic breeds of snake, lizard and turtle.

The Flower Market and Bird Garden
MTR Prince Edward, Exit B1

North of Mong Kok, over Prince Edward Road, it's a short walk east to the **Flower Market** on Flower Market Road (daily from 10am). This is best on Sundays and in the run-up to Chinese New Year, when people come to buy narcissi, orange trees and plum blossom to decorate their apartments in order to bring good luck. Running at an angle from here up to Boundary Street, the **Bird Garden** (daily 7am–8pm) displays hundreds of birds for sale, along with intricately designed bamboo cages to house them in; local men bring their own songbirds here for an airing too.

North of Boundary Street

The 3km-deep area between Boundary Street and the steep Kowloon Hills – beyond which lie the New Territories – offers a mix of temples, more bargain shopping, some surprisingly ancient history and two unusual parks. With the exception of Kowloon Walled City Park, for which you'll need a bus, all are within twenty minutes of downtown Kowloon by MTR.

Sham Shui Po
MTR Sham Shui Po

SHAM SHUI PO lies just 1km northwest of the Boundary Road/Nathan Road intersection. The district is jammed with **wholesale garment outlets**, which line central Cheung Sha Wan Road for a couple of blocks either side of the MTR station. While not the height of fashion, if you're prepared to dig around there are some very good deals to be had. Parallel **Ap Liu Street** has an interesting **flea market** every day from about noon until 7pm; don't expect to find anything remotely valuable, but it's a fun, untouristy place to browse.

Lei Cheng Uk Han Tomb Museum
41 Tonkin St • Mon–Wed & Fri–Sun 10am–6pm • Free • MTR Cheung Sha Wan, Exit A3 and follow signs along Tonkin St

One MTR stop on from Sham Shui Po, **Lei Cheng Uk Han Tomb Museum** is constructed over a 2000-year-old Han-dynasty tomb, which looks like a large brick oven and was

9

uncovered in 1957. The tomb yielded a few bits of pottery but no evidence that it was ever used for a burial; its value lies in the fact that it proves a long Han Chinese presence in the area. There's an informative video and you can peer through a glass window into the tomb chamber itself.

Kowloon Walled City Park

Tung Tau Tsuen Rd, Kowloon City • Daily 6.30am–6pm • Free • bus #1 from the Tsim Sha Tsui Star Ferry Pier or Nathan Road

Kowloon Walled City Park is the site of a Qing-dynasty fortified garrison post whose soldiers refused to cede sovereignty to Britain when it took over the New Territories in 1898. For nearly a century it remained a self-governing enclave of criminals and vagrants, off-limits to the authorities until they negotiated its closure and demolition in 1994. It's now an attractive spread of lawns, trees and traditional buildings, which include the "city's" reconstructed *yamen* (courthouse building).

Wong Tai Sin Temple

Lung Cheung Rd, Wong Tai Sin • Daily 7am–5.30pm • Free • MTR Wong Tai Si, Exit B2

The **Wong Tai Sin Temple** is a thriving complex dedicated to the mythical Yellow Immortal that's packed with more worshippers than any other in Hong Kong. Big, bright and colourful, it provides a good look at popular Chinese religion: vigorous kneeling, incense burning and the noisy rattling of joss sticks in canisters, as well as the presentation of food and drink to the deities. Large numbers of **fortune-tellers**, some of whom speak English, have stands to the right of the entrance and charge around $20 for palm-reading, about half that for a face-reading.

Chi Lin Nunnery and Nan Lian Gardens

Fun Tak Rd, Diamond Hill • MTR Diamond Hill, Exit C2 and follow the signs

The modern **Chi Lin Nunnery** (daily 9am–4pm; free) is an elegant, dark wooden temple built without nails in the Tang style, just about the only example of this type of architecture in all China. Opposite and connected by a walkway, the tranquil and beautiful **Nan Lian Gardens** (daily 7am–9pm; free) continue the Tang theme in an exquisite reconstruction of a contemporary garden; there are contorted pine trees, artfully shaped hillocks, ornamental ponds populated by carp, wooden halls and brightly painted bridges and pavilions.

The New Territories

Many people visit Hong Kong without ever leaving the built-up downtown areas, though the **New Territories**, a 30km-deep swath between Kowloon and the Guangdong border, comes complete with beautiful coastlines, antique villages and craggy mountains. A whole series of designated **country parks** includes the unspoilt **Sai Kung Peninsula** to the east, offering excellent walking trails and secluded beaches, with less demanding nature fixes available at the **Hong Kong Wetland Park** or **Kadoorie Farm**.

HIKING PAT SIN LENG

One of the best day-hikes in Hong Kong – for views at any rate – follows the serrated heights of **Pat Sin Leng**, the Eight Immortals' Ridge. It's an exposed trail, so pack a hat, water and sunscreen, and wear shoes with a decent grip.

Start by catching the MTR to Fan Ling, from where green minibus #52B (daily 6am–8.20pm) runs to the insubstantial hamlet of **Hok Tau Wai**. Follow the road past a small cemetery to Hok Tau Reservoir, from where the trail climbs loose scree to the grassy ridgetop, which you then simply follow east. Around halfway along, **Wong Leng** is the 639m apex, a good place to stop for the views and lunch. From here the trail continually climbs and descends the short, sharp, scrubby summits, before finally descending steeply to Tai Mei Tuk village and buses back to Tai Po.

Elsewhere there's architectural and cultural heritage to soak up around otherwise modern **New Towns**, satellite settlements built from scratch in the last forty years to absorb the overflow from Hong Kong's burgeoning population.

Travelling around the New Territories is straightforward, with the MTR extending right to the Chinese border, and frequent buses and minibuses available where needed.

Tai Mo Shan

MTR Tsuen Wan West, Exit D, then turn left and walk 150m to the station where bus #51 departs (daily 5.40am–10.50pm, $7.60); tell the driver where you're going

Hong Kong's 957m apex, **Tai Mo Shan**, is nearly twice the height of the Peak on Hong Kong Island; people come up here on winter mornings hoping to see frost. The two-hour walk up the west face from the roadside Tai Mo Shan Visitor Centre at the base of the mountain to the summit is steep but not difficult, following a sealed road most of the way past the **Sze Lok Yuen Youth Hostel** (see p.567). Views from the top encompass Hong Kong Island, the Sai Kung Peninsula and Shenzhen's wall of skyscrapers, magnificent on a clear day. It's very exposed, however – bring a hat, water and sunscreen.

Kam Tin and Kat Hing Wai

MTR KamSheung Road, Exit B and follow signposts; bus #64 from Tai Po (daily 5.40am–12.10am) via Kadoorie Farm and the Wishing Trees

Northwest of Tai Mo Shan, **KAM TIN** is the site of **Kat Hing Wai**, one of Hong Kong's last inhabited **walled settlements**. Dating back to the late seventeenth century when a clan named Tang settled here, the village ($3 donation to enter) still comprises thick, 6m-high walls and guard towers. Note the gates, too – confiscated by the British in the late nineteenth century, they were eventually found in Ireland and returned. Inside the walls, there's a wide lane running down the middle of the village, with tiny alleys leading off it. Old Hakka ladies in traditional hats pester visitors with cameras for more donations, and most of the buildings are modern, but the atmosphere is as different from downtown Hong Kong as you can imagine.

Hong Kong Wetland Park

Mon & Wed–Sun 10am–5pm • $30 • ⓦ wetlandpark.com • MTR Tin Shui Wai, Exit E3 to the Light Rail platform, then train #706 to Wetland Park

Hong Kong Wetland Park covers 150 acres of saltwater marsh up along the Chinese border, part of a larger system of lagoons that draws wintering wildfowl between November and February, and a host of migrating birds from August to October. The park itself is carefully landscaped to be just as attractive to human visitors, with paths, bridges, bird hides and an excellent visitor centre, and makes a great half-day out. Highlights include the mangrove boardwalk, where you can watch mudskippers and fiddler crabs scooting over the mud; huge lotus ponds (look for the occasional swimming snake); and the visitor centre's aquarium stocked with gharial crocodiles and fish. There's a branch of *Café de Coral* here, serving inexpensive lunches and drinks.

Sha Tin

MTR Sha Tin

The booming New Town of **Sha Tin**, which spreads along either side of the Shing Mun River, is best known to Hong Kongers as the site of the territory's second **racecourse**. It's probably the most liveable New Town, with water out front and towering green mountains to the east, though it's a rather anonymous experience wandering the vast maze of air-conditioned shopping malls that fill the centre.

Hong Kong Heritage Museum

Man Lam Rd • Mon & Wed–Fri 10am–6pm, Sat & Sun 10am–7pm • $10 • ⓦ www.heritagemuseum.gov.hk • MTR Sha Tin and follow signposts

Exhibits at the **Hong Kong Heritage Museum** are similar to those at the Hong Kong Museum of History (see p.550), and if you've seen those, there's little need to come

9

here. That said, the Cantonese Opera Heritage Hall is full of flamboyant costumes; the Gallery of Chinese Art features fine ceramics and jade; and the New Territories Heritage Hall provides a thorough rundown of the regional ethnic groups and history.

Ten Thousand Buddhas Monastery

Daily 9am–5pm • Free • MTR Sha Tin; exit station down ramp, follow the road around to the left and take the first road right, past the government offices, to the end, where you'll find a sign and footpath for the monastery

Sha Tin's eccentric **Ten Thousand Buddhas Monastery** dates only to the 1960s, but is one of the most interesting temples in the New Territories. The steep stairway from town is flanked by five hundred life-sized statues of Buddhist saints, and lands you at a courtyard filled by a garish collection of concrete sculptures, all brightly painted. The main hall, after which the monastery is named, houses some 13,000 miniature statues of Buddha arranged on shelves around the walls. Check out the outlying waterfall too, with its placid statue of Guanyin and views down to the valley below, where gilded statues of warrior monks are arranged on the hillside as if planning a raid on Sha Tin. Lunch is available at a basic **vegetarian restaurant**.

Tai Po

MTR Tai Po Market

TAI PO is one of the New Territories' longest-established towns, with an older centre surrounded by new housing estates. Follow signs through town for fifteen minutes to the **Man Mo Temple** on Fu Shin Street; the temple is attractive, but the main action is in the busy market packing out surrounding lanes. Uphill from here at the end of On Fu Road, the **Hong Kong Railway Museum** (Mon & Wed–Sun 10am–6pm; free) occupies Tai Po's old Chinese-style station, built in 1913; model trains and photographs cover the construction of the original Kowloon-to-Canton Railway, with some old coaches and engines out back.

Lam Tsuen Wishing Trees

Lam Kan Rd • bus #64K (daily 5.40am–12.10am) from Tai Po Market MTR

About 5km southwest of Tai Po, the **Lam Tsuen Wishing Trees** are two old figs standing by the roadside. People used to write wishes on red slips of paper tied to oranges and hurl them into the tree, until the branches broke off under their accumulated weight; the slips are now posted on nearby boards in order to protect the trees. There's also a pretty Tin Hau Temple here, dating back to 1736, and an astounding toilet block, full of orchids and piped music.

Kadoorie Farm

Lam Kan Rd • Daily 9.30am–5pm; it closes for even minor holidays, so check website for opening hours • $20 • Ⓦ kfbg.org.hk • Bus #64K (daily 5.40am–12.10am) from Tai Po Market MTR

Out on the road between the Wishing Trees and Kam Tin (see p.553), **Kadoorie Farm** is an organic farm and wildlife sanctuary, terraced up the steep rear slopes of Tai Mo Shan. It's a good place for children and zoologists, offering walks, guided tours and close views of orphaned birds, wild boar, leopard cats and muntjac deer – probably your only chance to see such elusive creatures in Hong Kong.

Plover Cove Country Park

Visitors' Centre Sat & Sun 9.30am–4.30pm • ☎ 2498 9326, Ⓦ afcd.gov.hk • MTR Tai Po Market, then bus #75K (daily 5.30am–11.35pm) to Tai Mei Tuk

The coastline east from Tai Po fringes **Plover Cove Country Park**, which surrounds the massive Plover Cove Reservoir. Easy access means it gets very busy at weekends and holidays.

The bus from Tai Po Market MTR station terminates at the small village and service centre of **TAI MEI TUK**. There are a few low-key restaurants here, the *Bradbury Jockey*

Club Youth Hostel (see p.566) and, just up the road, the **Country Park Visitors' Centre**. You can pick up maps and information here for the long, exposed but straightforward day-hike around the **Plover Cove Reservoir Trail**; or it's about an hour's walk along the road, past barbecue sites overlooking the reservoir, to **Bride's Pool**, an attractively wooded picnic and camping site beside a shallow stream and waterfalls.

Clear Water Bay

MTR Diamond Hill, then bus #91 (daily 6am–10.25pm; 40min)

Down at Hong Kong's southeastern extremity, **Clear Water Bay** is a rural area with a couple of popular **beaches** and an important temple. For the beaches, get off at either the Tai Au Mun stop or the Clear Water Bay bus terminus, though you need to bring everything you'll need for a day out as there are no nearby shops or facilities at either.

Joss House Bay

MTR Diamond Hill, then bus #91 (daily 6am–10.25pm; 40min) to the Clear Water Bay terminus, then green minibus #16 (daily 6.30am–8.30pm; 10min) to the end of the road outside the members-only Clear Water Bay Golf and Country Club; from the car park, follow signposts and steps for 500m down to the Tin Hau temple

Minibuses from the Clear Water Bay bus terminus run 5km southeast to **Joss House Bay** and the wonderfully located **Tin Hau Temple**. As one of Hong Kong's few Tin Hau temples actually still commanding the sea, it's of immense significance: on the 23rd day of the third lunar month each year (Tin Hau's birthday) a colossal seaborne celebration takes place on fishing boats in the bay. A nearby **stone inscription**, dated to the Song dynasty and recording a visit by a government official, is the oldest such carving in Hong Kong.

The Sai Kung Peninsula

Hong Kong's easternmost projection, the rugged **Sai Kung Peninsula** is a mass of jagged headlands, spiky peaks, vivid blue seascapes and tiny offshore islands. Most of the area is enclosed within **country parks**, with a range of picnic spots and walking trails around the coast and out to Hong Kong's finest beaches.

Sai Kung Town

MTR Diamond Hill, then bus #92 (daily 6am–11.45pm)

Sai Kung's access point is little **SAI KUNG TOWN**. Moderately developed and with a large expat population, it's also a fishing port, the promenade packed with pricey seafood restaurants and fishermen offering their wares. Shops sell swimming gear, sunscreen and bright inflatable floats, and there's a fruit market and supermarket if you're putting your own lunch together. The harbour is full of cruisers, small fishing boats and ad hoc ferries whose owners will offer rides out to various islands, the nearest and most popular of which is **Kiu Tsui Chau** (or Sharp Island), boasting a beach and a short hike to its highest point.

Tai Long Wan

MTR Diamond Hill, then bus #92 to Sai Kung Town (daily 6am–11.45pm), then minibus #29R to Sai Wan Ting (Mon–Sat 9.15am, 11.30am & 3.30pm; Sun 11 services 8.30am–4.30pm) from outside *McDonald's* on Chan Man St; taxi from Sai Kung Town to Sai Wan Ting about $95

If you're after a fantastic beach, head 10km northeast of Sai Kung Town to **Sai Wan Ting**, a pavilion at the end of a road. From here it's a ninety-minute walk, via beachside restaurant shacks at Sai Wan and Ham Ting Wan villages, to **Tai Long Wan**, a huge, empty stretch of golden sand. Take great care in the water, as there can be strong undercurrents. From here, follow trails inland again past a couple more villages and the track up Sharp Peak, to the main road at **Pak Tam Au**, from where you can catch bus #94 (daily 6.30am–9.35pm) back to Sai Kung Town.

9

The Outlying Islands

Hong Kong's 260-odd **Outlying Islands** offer a mix of seascape, low-key fishing villages and rural calm, with little high-density development. The islands of **Lamma** and **Cheung Chau** are fairly small and easy to day-trip around, while **Lantau** has a far greater range of sights and might even demand a couple of visits. You could also make use of local **accommodation** (see p.567) to base yourself on any one of the three, or just hop over for an evening out at one of the many **fish restaurants**. The main point of departure is the **Outlying Islands Ferry Pier** in Central; Lamma can also be reached by ferry from Aberdeen, while the **MTR** extends along Lantau's north coast.

Lamma

Lying just to the southwest of Aberdeen, Y-shaped **Lamma** is the third-largest island in the SAR – though at only around 7km in length, it's still pleasantly compact. Most of the 5000-strong population live in west-coast **Yung Shue Wan**, and the rest of the island is covered in open, hilly country, with an easy hour-long trail out past a couple of beaches to **Sok Kwu Wan**, a tiny knot of seafood restaurants on the upper east coast – walk from one to the other, enjoy a meal, and then catch a ferry back to Hong Kong Island.

Yung Shue Wan

YUNG SHUE WAN is a pretty tree-shaded village where the boats from Central and Aberdeen dock, with a large expat population, some low-key modern buildings, and very little to do other than seek out either accommodation or somewhere to eat (see p.567 & p.571). For the **trail to Sok Kwu Wan**, follow the easy-to-find cement path that branches away from the shore past the apartment buildings on the outskirts of the village.

Hung Shing Ye Beach

About fifteen minutes along the path from Yung Shue Wan, you'll arrive at **Hung Shing Ye Beach**, a nice place if you stick to its northern half; stray a few metres to the south, though, and you'll find your horizon rapidly being filled by Lamma's all-too-obvious

---

ISLAND FERRIES

The following is a selection of the most useful island ferry services – full timetables can be picked up at the Outlying Islands Ferry Pier in Central. **Lamma ferries** are operated by HKKF (Ⓦ hkkf.com.hk), while those to **Cheung Chau** and **Lantau** are run by First Ferry (Ⓦ www.nwff .com.hk). Prices quoted below rise by a third on Saturdays and Sundays.

TO YUNG SHUE WAN, LAMMA ISLAND
From Outlying Islands Ferry Pier At least hourly departures 6.30am–12.30am (40min; $14.50).
From Aberdeen Pier (on the waterfront near the fish market) 10 departures daily 6.30am–8.15pm (25min; $15.60).

TO SOK KWU WAN, LAMMA ISLAND
From Outlying Islands Ferry Pier 11 departures daily 7.20am–10.30pm (35min; $19.80).

TO CHEUNG CHAU ISLAND
From Outlying Islands Ferry Pier 24hr departures, every 30min 6.15am–11.45pm, then three services 11.45pm–6.15am (ordinary ferry 1hr, $12.60; fast ferry 30min, $16.80).

TO MUI WO (SILVERMINE BAY), LANTAU ISLAND
From Outlying Islands Ferry Pier At least hourly departures 5.55am–11.30pm (ordinary ferry 1hr, $14.50; fast ferry 40min, $28.40).

TAI LONG WAN BEACH, SAI KUNG PENINSULA (P.555) >

9

power station. There are beachside showers and plenty of sand, and the *Concerto Inn* (see p.571) is a decent place to dine.

Sok Kwu Wan

Some forty minutes along the path from Hung Shing Ye, **SOK KWU WAN** comprises a row of **seafood restaurants** built out over the water. The food and the atmosphere are good, and the restaurants are often full of large parties enjoying lavish and noisy meals; some places operate **private boat services** for customers. Make sure you don't miss the last scheduled ferry back, because there's nowhere to stay here – your only other option would be to hire a sampan back.

Cheung Chau

Hourglass-shaped **Cheung Chau** covers just 2.5 square kilometres but is the most crowded of all the outer islands, with a population of 23,000. Historically, the island is notorious as an eighteenth-century base for **pirates** who enjoyed waylaying the ships that ran between Guangzhou and Macau. Today, it still gives the impression of being an economically independent little unit, the main streets busy with shops, markets and seafood restaurants. If you can, visit during the extraordinary **Tai Chiu (Bun) Festival** in April/May, when the island fills to critical mass with raucous martial-arts displays, dragon dances, and a competition to climb vast conical towers made of steamed buns.

Cheung Chau township

Ferries dock at **Cheung Chau township**, comprising a harbourside promenade and a few narrow streets filling the island's centre. The main sight here is the 200-year-old **Pak Tai Temple** on Pak She Praya Road; Pak Tai protects against floods and is something of a patron deity for the island's fishermen. Though the building is the standard heavy granite affair, the roofline is embellished with a pair of brightly coloured ceramic dragons, and the temple also owns an iron sword said to date from the Song dynasty, reputedly fished out of the sea.

Tung Wan Beach

Through the town and across the island's narrow waist, scenic but crowded **Tung Wan Beach** is a 700m-long strip of sand, with various places to rent windsurfing gear, have a snack or just laze on the sand. At the south end of the beach, *Warwick Hotel* is the most upmarket place to stay on the island, though there are also plenty of more modest guesthouses (see p.567).

The south of the island

Turn right from the ferry and it's a half-hour walk to Cheung Chau's **southern headland**. You can circumnavigate this via a bit of scrabbling up and down rocks and through bays; there's also a nice picnic pavilion with sea views, and the **Cheung Po Tsai Cave**, named after Cheung Chau's most famous pirate, who used to hide here in the nineteenth century – it's tightly set into the base of some large granite boulders, and you'll need a torch.

Lantau

Mountainous **Lantau** is twice as big as Hong Kong Island but far less developed, despite the proximity of the International Airport just off the north coast. More than half of the island is a designated **country park**, with trails linking monasteries, old fishing villages and secluded beaches. There are some major sights here, however, notably **Hong Kong Disneyland** on the northeast coast; the western fishing village of **Tai O**; and **Po Lin Monastery**, with its mighty Big Buddha and wonderful **Ngong Ping 360** cable-car ride. Roads and buses link everything – and the MTR extends along Lantau's north coast – so getting around isn't difficult.

Mui Wo

Ferry from Central; bus #1 from Tai O, bus #2 from Po Lin Monastery

MUI WO is just a clutch of restaurants and residential buildings grouped about the **ferry pier**, in front of which is a **bus stop** with departures around the rest of the island – though as most of these only run every hour or so, don't be in too much of a hurry. There's also a nice **beach** with a sprinkling of low-key hotels 500m to the north (see p.567), set in an attractive, curving sandy bay.

The south coast

Bus #1 or #2 from Mui Wo, bus #1 from Tai O, bus #2 from Po Lin Monastery

The road west from Mui Wo passes along the southern shore, which is where Lantau's best beaches are located. **Cheung Sha Upper and Lower beaches** are the nicest: long, empty stretches of sand backed by a fringe of trees, with a couple of café-restaurants near the bus stops all pass by. Beyond here, the road heads inland past the **Shek Pik Reservoir** – look north here and you'll glimpse the Big Buddha sitting up on the ridge.

Tai O

Bus #1 from Mui Wo, bus #11 from Tung Chung, bus #21 from Po Lin

Right at Lantau's far northwestern corner, the fishing village of **TAI O** is home to two thousand people. It's an interesting place to wander, with old lanes, shrines, at least two elderly temples and a quarter full of tin-roofed **stilt-houses** built over the mud flats. The main street is lined with stalls selling dried and live seafood – the smell here is from locally made fermented prawn paste – and there's also a tiny **museum** (9am–5pm; free), displaying everyday artefacts such as washboards, vases, a threshing machine and a cutlass.

Po Lin Monastery

Daily 10am–6pm • Free • bus #2 from Mui Wo, bus #21 from Tai O, bus #23 from Tung Chung; Ngong Ping 360 Cable Car from Tung Chung (see box below)

Located high up on the Ngong Ping Plateau, the **Po Lin Monastery** is the largest temple in Hong Kong, currently undergoing further expansion. The complex is overshadowed by the adjacent bronze **Tian Tan Buddha**, a 34m-high sculpture that depicts the Buddha sitting cross-legged in a lotus flower – climb the steps to his feet for views over the temple. Po Lin's **vegetarian restaurant** serves set meals (daily 11.30am–5pm; meal tickets from $60), with an attached cheaper canteen.

Lantau Peak and Sunset Peak

Rearing over Po Lin, 934m-high **Lantau Peak** – more properly known as Fung Wong Shan – is a popular place to watch the sunrise (you can stay the night before at the nearby *S.G. Davis Youth Hostel*; see p.567). The steep, 2km trail from Po Lin to the summit takes about an hour to complete, and on a clear day views reach as far as Macau. You can pick up a trail here and continue 5km (2hr 30min) east to the slightly lower **Tai Tung Shan**, or "Sunset Peak", for a full day out.

Tung Chung

MTR Tung Chung; bus #11 from Mui Wo, bus #23 from Po Lin Monastery; bus #S1 from the airport

TUNG CHUNG is a burgeoning New Town near the airport. There's an antique stone fort

---

NGONG PING 360 CABLE CAR

The 5.7km ride between Po Lin Monastery and Tung Chung aboard the **Ngong Ping 360 Cable Car** (Mon–Fri 10am–6pm, Sat & Sun 10am–6.30pm; 25min; $94 one-way, $135 return; ⓦnp360.com.hk) provides fantastic panoramas of Lantau's steep north coast. Airport buses run from Tung Chung, making Lantau the perfect place to spend a last afternoon in Hong Kong before catching an evening flight out.

9

about 2km west along the coast, but the only real reason to come here is for transport, all of which is tightly grouped together: there's the MTR; the Ngong Ping 360 Cable Car to Po Lin Monastery (see box, p.559); and a host of **buses**.

Hong Kong Disneyland

Daily 10am–9pm • $450 • ⊛ hongkongdisneyland.com • MTR Disneyland Resort

Up on Lantau's northeastern side, **Hong Kong Disneyland** is a tame place compared with their ten other franchises, but still makes a fun day out for children. It's split into five zones: **Main Street USA**, a re-created early twentieth-century mid-American shopping street (though the goods on sale are distinctly Chinese); **Adventureland**, home to Tarzan's treehouse and a jungle river cruise; **Tomorrowland**, where excellent rides include a blacked-out roller coaster; **Fantasyland**, populated by a host of Disney characters, and whose best feature is the PhilharMagic 4D film show; and **Mystic Point**, with a sinister forest and haunted mansion.

ARRIVAL AND DEPARTURE   HONG KONG

BY PLANE

HONG KONG INTERNATIONAL AIRPORT

The airport (⊛ hongkongairport.com) is at Chek Lap Kok, off the north coast of Lantau Island. Hong Kong is a major international gateway for flights both within Asia and beyond; you can also fly to every provincial capital and many major cities on the mainland, but you'll save a lot of money (and not lose much time) by picking up a flight over the border in Shenzhen – see box below.
Airport tourist office Buffer Halls A and B, Arrivals Level, Terminal 1 (daily 8am–9pm).

TRANSPORT INTO TOWN

Airport Express rail service (AEL) The fastest way into town is from inside the terminal aboard the Airport Express rail service (AEL); trains depart every 8min 5.50am–1am to Kowloon (19min; $90 single) and Central on Hong Kong Island (23min; $100). If you're not travelling alone, note that multiple AEL ticket purchases save a lot of money: two singles between the airport and Hong Kong cost $180, while three singles are just $190. Once in town at either the Kowloon or Hong Kong AEL stations, you'll find taxi ranks and free hotel shuttle buses (coloured blue and marked with a "K"), which, even if you're not staying at one of the hotels they serve, can deliver to within a short walk of most accommodation.
Tung Chung MTR Station A more complicated but cheaper rail option is to catch bus #S1 from the airport to

Tung Chung MTR Station ($3.50), and then take the Tung Chung Line into town along a parallel route to the AEL (around $25). It's slower, with more stops, but cheaper and you can change trains at Lai King Station, and get on the Tsuen Wan Line via Mong Kok, Jordan and Tsim Sha Tsui – useful for reaching Kowloon's accommodation.
Airbuses An even cheaper, slower option (expect an hour or more to reach Tsim Sha Tsui) is to take one of the dozen Airbus routes into town from outside the ground floor of the terminal. The airport customer-service counters can tell you which to catch and sell you tickets (you'll need exact change on the buses). Routes have round-the-clock service, and there's plenty of room for luggage.
Taxis Taxis into the city are metered and reliable (see p.562 for more). You might want to get the arrival hall tourist office to write down the name of your destination in Chinese characters for the driver, though they should know the names of the big hotels in English. It costs roughly $300 to get to Tsim Sha Tsui, about $350 for Hong Kong Island (and so is cheaper than the AEL for a group). There may be extra charges for luggage and for tunnel tolls – on some tunnel trips the passenger pays the return charge, too.
Rush-hour traffic can slow down journey times considerably, particularly if you're using one of the cross-harbour tunnels to Hong Kong Island.

IN-TOWN CHECK-IN

Leaving by air Many international airlines allow you to

FLYING FROM SHENZHEN

Though you can **fly** from Hong Kong to all major Chinese cities, airfares from Hong Kong are vastly more expensive than on the mainland, and you'll save a lot of money **flying from Shenzhen airport**, easily reached by bus in just two hours from downtown Hong Kong – any travel agent can book you a ticket ($100). The bus drops you at the border, you walk 500m to the other side via Hong Kong and Chinese customs, and then pick up another bus to the airport. Buses run every fifteen minutes, so don't worry if you get stuck in a passport queue along the way.

TRAVEL AGENTS

Hong Kong is full of budget travel agents, all able to organize international flights as well as train tickets, tours, flights and visas to mainland China. CTS, 138 Hennessy Rd, Wan Chai (☎2559 2991, ⓦctshk.com), and 27–33 Nathan Rd (entrance on Peking Rd; ☎2315 7171), are especially good for China visas and direct buses to Shenzhen airport. Alternatives include Hong Kong Student Travel Ltd, Hang Lung Centre, Yee Wo St, Causeway Bay (ⓦen.hkst.com); and Shoestring Travel Ltd, Flat A, 4F, Alpha House, 27–33 Nathan Rd, Tsim Tsa Shui (☎2723 2306, ⓦshoestringtravel.com.hk).

check-in for your flight, including checking through your in-hold luggage, up to 24hr in advance downtown at the Hong Kong and Kowloon AEL stations. This is useful if you have a late flight and don't want to drag your luggage around for the rest of the day after checking out of your hotel, and also means you don't have to join the often lengthy check-in queues at the airport. However, you must purchase an AEL ticket in order to access the stations' check-in areas, tying you to using the AEL rather than travelling to the airport by other means.

BY TRAIN

HUNG HOM RAILWAY STATION

The train station (ⓦmtr.com.hk) in eastern Tsim Sha Tsui handles Express trains from China, plus the East Rail MTR line to the pedestrian border crossings from Shenzhen to Lo Wu or Lok Ma Chau.

Transport into town At Hung Hom, signposted walkways lead to a city bus terminal and taxi rank; there's also the MTR from here to Tsim Sha Tsui East Station, which exits into Middle Road (see map, p.548).

Tickets Express tickets are available from Hung Hom Station or online (ⓦwww.it3.mtr.com.hk/b2c) – though you have to collect them in Hong Kong.

Destinations Beijing West (1 on alternate days; 23hr; soft/ hard sleeper $935/600); Guangzhou East (12 daily; 2hr;

$190); Shanghai (1 on alternate days; 19hr; soft/hard sleeper $840/550).

BY BUS

There's no long-distance bus station in Hong Kong, but CTS, 138 Hennessy Rd, Wan Chai (☎2559 2991, ⓦctsbus.hkcts .com), and other companies run direct services from downtown Hong Kong to Guangzhou (3hr 30min; $90) and Shenzhen or Shenzhen airport (1hr 40min; $100).

BY FERRY

Hong Kong has two ferry terminals handling traffic to Macau. Traffic gets very busy at the weekends and holidays, when you'll need to buy tickets in advance; note that you need a passport, but not a special visa, to travel to Macau.

HONG KONG–MACAU FERRY TERMINAL

Located inside the Shun Tak Centre in Sheung Wan, Hong Kong Island (MTR Sheung Wan, exit D), this terminal handles departures to Macau ($147), arriving at either Macau's main Jetfoil Terminal, or the Taipa Temporary Terminal – make sure you know where you're headed before buying a ticket. Ferries are operated by Turbojet (ⓦwww.turbojet.com.hk).

Destinations Macau (every 15min 7am–midnight and then hourly; 55min).

HONG KONG AND CHINA VISAS

Currently, nationals of the US, Canada, South Africa, Australia and New Zealand receive a three-month tourist **visa** on arrival in Hong Kong; British nationals can stay for six months. For present information, contact your local HKTB office or check ⓦwww.immd.gov.hk.

BUYING CHINESE VISAS IN HONG KONG

To enter China you need a **visa**. If you haven't picked one up from a Chinese consulate or embassy at home, it's quickest to obtain one through a **travel agency** (see box above) or through your accommodation, many of which offer the service; agents can also arrange hotel accommodation and onward journeys into China. **Visa fees** vary between $200 and $600 or above, according to your nationality, whether you want a single-entry or double-entry, one-month or three-month visa, and whether you want fast (same-day) processing, or can wait two to three days. **Beware**: visas issued in Hong Kong are only **extendable once** on the mainland; and some multi-entry visas require you to **leave China** every thirty days even if valid, for instance, for a six-month period. It's also possible that you will be refused a further three-month visa in Hong Kong if you've been in China recently.

9

HONG KONG–CHINA FERRY TERMINAL

Located on Canton Road in Tsim Sha Tsui, Kowloon (nearest MTR Tsim Sha Tsui), this terminal operates ferries to Macau's Jetfoil Terminal (ⓦwww.turbojet.com.hk; $147).
Destinations Macau (every 30min 6.40am–10.30pm; 55min).

ON FOOT

There are two pedestrian crossings between Hong Kong and Shenzhen: Lok Ma Chau and (more popular) Lo Wu, both on the East Rail MTR line to Hung Hom. The crossings are open between 6am and 11pm, and border formalities are usually very straightforward.

GETTING AROUND

Hong Kong's public transport system is efficient, extensive and inexpensive – though best avoided during the weekday rush hours (7–9am and 5–7pm). All signs are supposed to be written in English and Chinese, although the English signs are sometimes so discreet as to be invisible.

BY MTR

Hong Kong's trains are all operated by MTR (ⓦmtr.com.hk), whose interconnected network covers: Hong Kong Island's north shore and Kowloon; the Airport Express line; the Tung Chung line between Central and Lantau; and two routes extending through the New Territories to the Shenzhen border. Lines on Hong Kong Island are currently being extended west along the north shore to Kennedy Town, and south across the island to Aberdeen. The LRT (Light Rail Transit) traverses the northwestern New Territories, though tourists rarely use it except to reach the Hong Kong Wetland Park (see p.553). Services run between about 6am and 1am and you buy single-journey tickets ($4–11) from easy-to-use dispensing machines at the stations, or use an Octopus Card. Clear, colour-coded maps can be found at all stations and on tourist maps handed out by the HKTB.

BY BUS

Hong Kong's double-decker buses are comfortable and air-conditioned, and are essential for reaching the south of Hong Kong Island and parts of the New Territories. You swipe your card or pay as you board (exact change is required); the fare is posted up on the timetables at bus stops, and ranges from $1.20 to $45. Useful bus terminals include Exchange Square in Central; outside the Ferry Terminal in Central; and outside the Star Ferry Terminal in Tsim Sha Tsui, Kowloon – though there is talk of shifting this one elsewhere. Check routes on ⓦnwstbus.com.hk.

BY MINIBUS

As well as the big buses, there are also red- or green-striped minibuses, which have set stops but can also be hailed (not on double yellow lines). They cost a little more than regular buses, and you pay the driver the exact amount or swipe your Octopus card as you enter. They only take sixteen seated passengers, so won't stop, or will refuse you entry, if full. Drivers are unlikely to speak English.

BY TAXI

Hong Kong's taxis come in three colours: red on Hong Kong Island and Kowloon (with a flag fall of $20 for the first 2km), green in the New Territories ($16.50) and blue on Lantau ($15). They're usually easy to find and can be hailed in the street, though if they're scarce – likely during rainstorms and at rush hours – look for them outside hotels. Note that there is a toll to be paid (around $5–15) on any trips through the cross-harbour tunnel between Kowloon and Hong Kong, and drivers often double this – as they are allowed to do – on the grounds that they have to get back again. Few taxi drivers speak English, so be prepared to show the name of your destination written down in Chinese. If you get stuck, gesture to the driver to call his dispatch centre on the two-way radio; someone there will speak English. It is obligatory for passengers to wear seat belts.

BY TRAM

Trams have been rattling along Hong Kong Island's north shore since 1904 and remain as popular as ever with locals and tourists alike, especially for the night-time view from the upstairs deck. The trams run between Kennedy Town in the west and Shau Kei Wan in the east, via Central, Wan Chai and Causeway Bay (some going via Happy Valley;

OCTOPUS CARDS

If you plan to travel around a good deal, get hold of an **Octopus Card** (ⓦoctopus.com.hk), a rechargeable stored-value ticket that can be used for travel on all MTR services, most buses and most ferries. The card itself costs $50 and you add value to it by feeding it and your money into machines in the MTR; the Senior version for over 65s provides discounted fares. The fare is electronically deducted each time you use the card by swiping it over yellow sensor pads at station turnstiles or, on a bus, beside the driver. Octopus cards can also be used in many retail outlets, including Park'n'shop supermarkets, *Maxim's* restaurants and 7-11 stores.

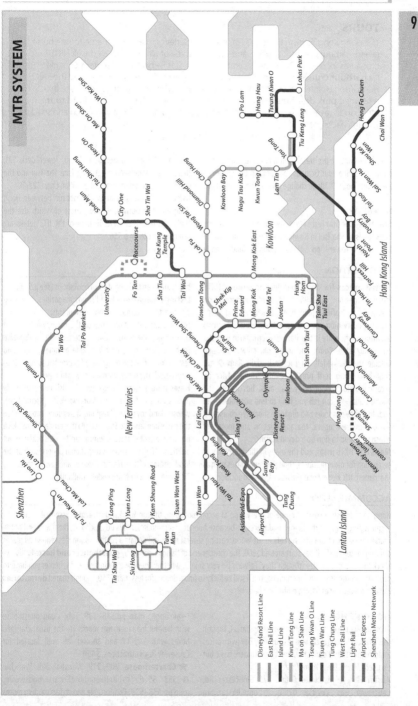

MTR SYSTEM

Disneyland Resort Line
East Rail Line
Island Line
Kwun Tong Line
Ma on Shan Line
Tseung Kwan O Line
Tsuen Wan Line
Tung Chung Line
West Rail Line
Light Rail
Airport Express
Shenzhen Metro Network

Shenzhen

New Territories

Kowloon

Hong Kong Island

Lantau Island

TOURS

The Hong Kong Tourism Board (HKTB) operates a series of interesting theme tours – horse racing, harbour cruises, city sights and the like – some of which are free; consult HKTB's brochures for details. Other tour operators include Star Ferry (ⓦ www.starferry.com.hk) for **harbour cruises**; Gray Line (ⓦ www.grayline.com.hk) for coach tours around the SAR; Hong Kong Dolphinwatch (ⓦ hkdolphinwatch.com), who run boat trips out to see the renowned **pink dolphins**; and the highly recommended Urban Discovery **food tour** (ⓦ urbandiscovery.asia), where you spend an evening sampling local street food and snacks in Jordan's backstreets.

check the front of the tram). You board the tram at the back, and swipe your Octopus Card or drop the money in the driver's box ($2.30; no change given) when you get off.

BY FERRY

Star Ferry The Star Ferry (ⓦ www.starferry.com.hk) runs between Tsim Sha Tsui in Kowloon and the pier in front of the IFC2 Tower on Hong Kong Island (daily

6.30am–11.30pm; upper deck $2.50, lower deck $2); there's a separate service between Tsim Sha Tsui and the Convention and Exhibition Centre in Wan Chai ($2.50).

Other ferries A large array of boats run between Hong Kong and the Outlying Islands, most of which use the Outlying Islands Ferry Pier in front of the IFC; details are given in the box on p.556.

INFORMATION

Tourist offices The Hong Kong Tourism Board or HKTB (daily 9am–6pm; ☎ 2508 1234, ⓦ discoverhongkong .com) issues leaflets, pamphlets, brochures and maps covering everything you can do in Hong Kong. Their two downtown offices are in the Star Ferry Terminal in Tsim Sha Tsui (daily 8am–8pm); and in an old railway carriage outside the Peak Mall, on the Peak (daily 8am–9pm). English-speaking staff provide sound, useful advice on accommodation, shopping, restaurants, bus routes and hiking trails – or can tell you how to find out yourself. In addition, they run tours and organize short free courses on *tai ji*, Cantonese opera, tea appreciation and more, for which you need to sign up a day in advance.

Maps Free HKTB maps, and the maps in this book, should be enough for most purposes, though street atlases such as the paperback *Hong Kong Guidebook*, which includes all

bus routes, can be bought from bookshops (see p.573).

Listings magazines Free listings magazines, providing up-to-date information on restaurants, bars, clubs, concerts and exhibitions, include the trendy *HK Magazine* (ⓦ hk-magazine.com) and acerbic *BC Magazine* (ⓦ bcmagazine.net), both available in hotels, cafés and restaurants. *Time Out Hong Kong* (ⓦ timeout.com.hk; $18) offers much the same, with more weighty reviews.

Newspapers Hong Kong's two English-language daily papers are the *South China Morning Post* (ⓦ scmp.com), whose bland coverage of regional news does its best to toe the party line, and the *Standard* (ⓦ thestandard.com.hk), a business-oriented freebie which can be outspoken about politicians' failings. Other international papers, such as the local edition of the *Herald Tribune*, and journals such as *Time* and *Newsweek*, are widely available.

ACCOMMODATION

Hong Kong boasts a colossal range of every type of accommodation, though **booking ahead** is essential – either to secure a better rate at the higher-end places, or because budget accommodation fills up quickly. At the upper end of the market are some of the best **hotels** in the world, costing several thousand dollars a night, though less renowned places offering motel-like facilities start around $800. The cheaper end of things is served by **guesthouses and hostels**: always check these rooms for size (though they'll always be very small), whether they have a window, and whether you have to pay extra for the use of air conditioning. You'll still be lucky to find a double for less than $350, though shared **dormitories** can come in as low as $150 a night for a bed.

HONG KONG ISLAND

Accommodation on the island is mostly upmarket, though there's a small budget enclave in Causeway Bay (with prices a tad higher than Kowloon's), and the secluded, basic but excellent *Mount Davis Youth Hostel*.

Alisan Flat A, 5F, Hoito Court, 275 Gloucester Rd, Causeway Bay ☎ 2838 0762, ⓦ home.hkstar.com

/~alisangh; map pp.538–539. Tidy, clean guesthouse with helpful management; rooms are the usual cramped boxes with a/c, TV and shower, all well located for Causeway Bay's attractions. **$450**

★ **Charterhouse** 209–219 Wanchai Rd, Wanchai ☎ 2833 5566, ⓦ hongkonghotel.charterhouse.com; map pp.538–539. Comfortable and stylish modern rooms

YOUTH HOSTELS AND CAMPING

The **Hong Kong Youth Hostels Association** (ⓦyha.org.hk) operates seven self-catering hostels – mostly a long way from the centre – offering dormitory accommodation for IYHF members from $90.

You can **camp for free** at the forty campsites run by the Agriculture, Fisheries and Conservation Department (ⓦafcd.gov.hk; click on "Country and Marine Parks"), all in relatively remote sites. Facilities are basic – pit latrines and tank water that must be boiled – and you'll need to be self-sufficient. Pitches are available on a first-come, first-served basis, so get in early at weekends and holidays.

with a boutique-hotel feel, not large but well designed to make use of space. Close to Happy Valley and Causeway Bay shopping, and overall excellent value, especially if you catch one of their online booking discounts. **$1190**

Garden View (YWCA) 1 MacDonnell Rd, Mid-Levels ☎2877 3737, ⓦywca.org.hk; map pp.538–539. This comfortable YWCA-run hotel is off Garden Rd, south of the Zoological and Botanical Gardens; minibus #1A from outside the Star Ferry Terminal and Central MTR runs past. Prices change considerably depending on demand, but their cheaper rates are a very good deal. **$1950**

★ **Hostel HK** 3F, Paterson Building, 47 Paterson St ☎2392 6868, ⓦhostel.hk; map pp.538–539. The lack of a sign makes this tricky to find, but the friendly atmosphere and above-average rooms – plus free laundry – make it worth the effort. Dorm beds **$150**, doubles **$350**

Hotel LKF 33 Wyndham St, Lan Kwai Fong, Central ☎3518 9688, ⓦwww.hotel-lkf.com.hk; map pp.538–539. Boutique design, but generously sized rooms, make this pricey, slick operation a stylish place to stay in the heart of Hong Kong's business and shopping district. **$2500**

★ **Mandarin Oriental** 5 Connaught Rd, Central ☎2522 0111, ⓦmandarinoriental.com; map pp.538–539. Unassumingly set in a plain concrete box, this is one of the best hotels in the world, with unmatched service. The hotel lobby is also a great place to people-watch, as anyone who's anyone in Hong Kong eats or drinks here. **$4500**

Mount Davis Youth Hostel Mount Davis ☎2817 5715, ⓦyha.org.hk; map pp.538–539. Perched on the top of a mountain above Kennedy Town, this self-catering retreat has superb, peaceful views over the harbour. Getting here, however, is a major expedition, unless you catch the infrequent shuttle bus from the ground floor of the Shun Tak Centre (Hong Kong–Macau Ferry Terminal) – phone the hostel for times. Otherwise, catch bus #5 from Admiralty or minibus #3A from the Outlying Islands Ferry Pier in Central and get off near the junction of Victoria Rd and Mount Davis Path; walk back 100m from the bus stop and you'll see Mount Davis Path branching off up the hill – the hostel is a 35min walk. If you have much luggage, get off the bus in Kennedy Town and catch a taxi from there (around $50 plus $5 per item of luggage). Dorms **$190**, doubles/family rooms **$420**

Park Lane 310 Gloucester Rd, Causeway Bay ☎2293 8888, ⓦparklane.com.hk; map pp.538–539. Located right across from Victoria Park, this plush business hotel is conveniently sited for the shopping and eating delights of Causeway Bay, and has good-value rooms considering their size and comfortable modern furnishings. **$2000**

KOWLOON

Most of the following accommodation is located in Tsim Sha Tsui, though there are also useful options in Jordan and Yau Ma Tei – all near Nathan Road's MTR stations. Places listed represent a fraction of the total on offer, and it is always worth having a look at several options.

Anne Black Guesthouse (YWCA) 5 Man Fuk Rd, Yau Ma Tei ☎2713 9211, ⓦywca.org.hk; map p.548. Not far from the Yau Ma Tei MTR, this YWCA pension is surprisingly smart, light and airy, with a choice of either shared or en-suite bathrooms. Check the website for discounts. **$1100**

Benito 7–7B Cameron Rd, Tsim Sha Tsui ☎3653 0388, ⓦhotelbenito.com; map p.548. Bright, clean and modern boutique hotel close to everything that matters in Tsim Sha Tsui. Cheaper rooms are only fractionally larger than in a guesthouse, however. **$1400**

★ **Dragon Hostel** 7F, Sincere House, 83 Argyle St, Mongkok ☎2395 0577, ⓦdragonhostel.com; map p.548. Hard to find – the street entrance is a bland doorway just around the corner in Fa Yuen Street – but helpful management and clean, if extremely plain, single, double and triple rooms (most with their own bathroom) make this place stand out. Double with bathroom **$400**

King's de Nathan 473–473A Nathan Rd, Yau Ma Tei, immediately south of the Yau Ma Tei MTR ☎2780 1281, ⓦwww.kingsdenathan.com; map p.548. Probably the cheapest "real" hotel in town, with modern furnishings and reasonably sized rooms for the price. **$750**

Luxe Manor 39 Kimberley Rd, Tsim Sha Tsui ☎3763 8888, ⓦtheluxemanor.com; map p.548. Another boutique option, with stylish, strikingly themed rooms which will either appeal or appal. Their *Aspasia* restaurant draws the chic and almost-famous to dine. **$1500**

9

★ **Peninsula** Salisbury Rd, Tsim Sha Tsui ☎ 2920 2888, ⓦ peninsula.com; map p.548. One of the classiest hotels in the world, which has been overlooking the harbour and Hong Kong Island for eighty years. Check the website for package rates. $3600

★ **Salisbury (YMCA)** 41 Salisbury Rd, Tsim Sha Tsui ☎ 2268 7888, ⓦ www.ymcahk.org.hk; map p.548. Superb location next door to the *Peninsula Hotel* and with views over the harbour and Hong Kong Island; facilities include indoor pools, a fitness centre and squash court. For the price – which includes a huge buffet breakfast – the doubles are unbeatable value; relatively expensive four-bed dorms with attached shower are also available. Dorms $260, doubles $1430

★ **Sealand House** Block D, 8F, Majestic House, 80 Nathan Rd, Tsim Sha Tsui ☎ 2368 9522, ⓦ sealandhouse .com.hk; map p.548. Located inside a residential block across from Kowloon Mosque, this is the cleanest, roomiest and friendliest of the upper-price-range guesthouses, with a choice of shared or en-suite facilities. $500

YHA Mei Ho House 41 Berwick Street, Sham Shui Po ☎ 2788 1638, ⓦ yha.org.hk; map p.548. Brand-new hostel inside a historic 1950s estate, within easy walking distance of Sham Shui Po MTR and so by far the most accessible Hong Kong youth hostel. Not yet open at the time of writing; check online for details. Around $350

CHUNGKING MANSIONS

Set at the southern end of Nathan Road, Chungking Mansions is an ugly monster of a building, its lower three floors forming a warren of tiny shops and Central Asian restaurants, the upper sixteen storeys crammed with budget guesthouses. While the Mansions has a reputation for sleaze and poor maintenance, recent attention from the health and safety departments have wrought great changes: the guesthouses are generally well-run, if cramped and sometimes windowless. The building is divided into five blocks, lettered A to E, each served by two tiny lifts that are subject to long queues.

Chungking House Block A, 4F and 5F ☎ 2739 1600, ⓦ chungkinghouse.com; map p.548. Long-running place, now recently renovated with clean, decent-sized rooms spread over two floors; cheaper ones are not such a good deal though. Singles $220, doubles $300

Dragon Inn Block B, 3F ☎ 2367 7071, ⓦ www .dragoninn.info; map p.548. No-nonsense but efficient manager and bright rooms (within the Mansions' limits, at any rate) make this a good choice – they also offer a discount on stays of a week or more. Singles $180, doubles $360

★ **Germany Hostel** Block D, 6F ☎ 9832 4807, ⓦ germanyhostelhk.com; map p.548. A real gem of a place: clean, exceptionally friendly and they've taken trouble to make the admittedly small, windowless rooms

as welcoming and bright as possible. Dorms $155, doubles $326

Welcome Guesthouse Block A, 7F ☎ 2721 7793, ⓦ guesthousehk.net; map p.548. A good choice, offering a/c doubles with and without shower. Nice clean rooms, luggage storage, laundry service and China visas available. Singles $180, doubles $300

Yan Yan Guesthouse Block E, 8F ☎ 2366 8930; map p.548. Helpful staff renting out doubles with all facilities; you could sleep three in some – at a squeeze – making them good value. Don't confuse it with the poor *New China Yan Yan* guesthouse in Block D. $250

MIRADOR MANSIONS

This is another block at 54–64 Nathan Rd, on the east side, in between Carnarvon Rd and Mody Rd, right next to the Tsim Sha Tsui MTR station. Dotted about, in among the residential apartments, are large numbers of guesthouses. Mirador Mansions is cleaner and brighter than Chungking Mansions, and queues for the lifts are smaller.

Cosmic 12F ☎ 2369 6669, ⓦ cosmicguesthouse.com; map p.548. Recently refurbished and modernized – almost stylish, in fact – this place feels a cut above the average guesthouse, and even the cheapest rooms are en suite. Singles $180, doubles $330

★ **Garden Hostel** Flat F4, 3F ☎ 2311 1183, ⓦ gardenhostel.com.hk; map p.548. A friendly travellers' hangout, with washing machines, lockers and a patio garden. A *wing chun* martial-arts school is also based here, and you can arrange lessons with them. Mixed and women-only dorms; beds get cheaper if you pay by the week. Beware other hostels using the same name – this is the real one. Dorms $80, doubles $200

Mei Lam Guesthouse Flat D1, 5F ☎ 2721 5278; map p.548. Helpful, English-speaking owner and very presentable singles and doubles, all spick-and-span, with full facilities. Worth the higher-than-usual prices. Singles $180, doubles $330

THE NEW TERRITORIES

Bradbury Jockey Club Youth Hostel 66 Tai Mei Tuk Rd, Tai Mei Tuk, Tai Po ☎ 2662 5123, ⓦ yha.org.hk; map pp.534–535. Not too hard to reach: ride the East Rail Line train to Tai Po, then bus #75K to Tai Mei Tuk. From the bus stop, walk towards the Plover Cove Reservoir and the hostel is a few minutes ahead on the left. Lots of boating, walking and cycling opportunities. Dorms $125, doubles $350

Regal Riverside Hotel 34–36 Tai Chung Kiu Rd, Sha Tin ☎ 2649 7878, ⓦ regalhotel.com; map pp.534–535. The New Territories' best hotel – though there's not a lot of competition – right in the centre of Sha Tin. This comfortable place often appears in holiday packages; there's a fine Asian lunch buffet served here and a free shuttle bus to Tsim Sha Tsui, too. $1600

Sze Lok Yuen Youth Hostel Tai Mo Shan, Tsuen Wan ☎ 2488 8188, ⓦ yha.org.hk; map pp.534–535. Bus #51 from Tsuen Wan to Tai Mo Shan (tell the driver where you're going), then a 40min walk uphill. Just off the main track up Tai Mo Shan, with plenty of hikes, views, sunrises and sunsets. Dorms $95

OUTLYING ISLANDS

LAMMA
Kathmandu Guesthouse Yung Shue Wan, Lamma ☎ 2982 0028; map pp.534–535. Above Bubbles Laundry in Yung Shue Wan town, this hostel-like place has been going forever and offers dorm beds as well as doubles at some of the lowest rates on the island. Don't expect any luxuries. Beds $110, doubles $200

Man Lai Wah Yung Shue Wan, Lamma ☎ 2982 0220, ⓔ ericiris@netvigator.com; map pp.534–535. Right ahead from the ferry pier on the left, this great low-key place has small, double-bed flats with balconies and harbour views, even if the furnishings aren't brand new. $420

CHEUNG CHAU
Bella Vista Miami Resort Tung Wan Beach, Cheung Chau ☎ 2981 7299, ⓦ miamicheungchau.com.hk; map pp.534–535. A huge number of rooms located in a residential block; the cheaper options are best avoided while the better rooms are worth the price, so check the online photos before booking. $550

★ **Cheung Chau B&B** Tung Wan Beach, Cheung Chau ☎ 2986 9990, ⓦ bbcheungchau.com.hk; map pp.534–535. Set just back from the beach along the access road from the village, this is a genuine, modern B&B with a

welcoming atmosphere and excellent furnishings. $650

Warwick Tung Wan Beach, Cheung Chau ☎ 2981 0081, ⓦ www.warwickhotel.com.hk; map pp.534–535. Overlooking the beach, this is the most upmarket and expensive of Cheung Chau's accommodation, with a swimming pool and restaurant. Rooms have balconies, private baths and cable TV; good-value weekly rates are available. $1200

LANTAU
★ **Ngong Ping S.G. Davis Youth Hostel** Ngong Ping, Lantau ☎ 2985 5610, ⓦ yha.org.hk; map pp.534–535. From the Ngong Ping bus terminal (p.559) follow the paved footpath and signposts south, away from the Tian Tan Buddha and past the public toilets; it's a 10min walk. Basic dorms and tent pitches at the base of Lantau Peak, and you can eat at the nearby Po Lin Monastery. It's cold on winter nights, though – bring a sleeping bag. Dorms $110, camping $45

Novotel Citygate 51 Man Tung Rd, Tung Chung, Lantau ☎ 3602 8888, ⓦ novotel.com; map pp.534–535. Right next to the Tung Chung MTR and Ngong Ping 360 station, just 5min from the airport. Rates are a bargain compared to the downtown areas and the website often advertises inexpensive last-minute deals. $1200

Silvermine Beach 648 Silvermine Bay, Mui Wo, Lantau ☎ 2984 8295, ⓦ silvermineresort.com; map pp.534–535. Located right on the beachfront, a few minutes' walk from the Mui Wo Ferry Pier. The rooms are comfortable and quiet, with excellent-value long-term packages available. The restaurant spilling out onto the terraces offers popular barbecues and Thai grub. $1400

EATING

Thanks to its cosmopolitan heritage and the importance attached to food in Chinese culture, Hong Kong boasts a superb range of **restaurants**. The most prominent cooking style is local **Cantonese**, though you can also find places specializing in Chaozhou, Hakka, Beijing, Sichuanese and Shanghai food. International options include Western **fast-food chains**, curry houses, sushi bars, hotel lunchtime buffets, pizzerias and restaurants offering Southeast Asian, vegetarian and South American cuisine. The places listed below are a fraction of the total, with an emphasis on the less expensive end of the market; Chinese characters are given where there is no English sign. For up-to-date reviews, pick up copies of the **free weeklies** *HK Magazine* (ⓦ hk-magazine.com) and *BC Magazine* (ⓦ bcmagazine.net), or check ⓦ womguide.com and ⓦ openrice.com.

WESTERN BREAKFASTS AND SNACKS
For Western breakfasts of coffee, muffins and fry-ups try the places listed below, or café chains such as *Delifrance* and the ubiquitous *Pacific Coffee*. Bigger hotels also frequently offer fixed-price buffets with vast quantities of food. Most offer free wi-fi for customers.

Amical 1 Sun St, Wan Chai, Hong Kong Island ☎ 5489 5330; map pp.538–539. Coffee for aficionados, with beans sourced from around the world for their flavour and strength. The setting is informal – only a single small room with not much decor – but there's a comfortable feeling of

privacy too: it's a hard place to find and so is seldom crowded. Mon–Wed & Fri–Sun 10am–7pm.

Caffé Habitū 77–79 Gloucester Rd, Wan Chai, Hong Kong Island ⓦ caffehabitu.com; map pp.538–539. Small local chain with a handful of downtown outlets striving to be an international player, but retaining a little more panache and style for the time being. Mon–Sat 8am–9pm, Sun 10am–7pm.

Flying Pan 9 Old Bailey St, Soho, Central, Hong Kong Island ⓦ the-flying-pan.com; map pp.538–539. Blow-out portions of toast, bacon, mushrooms, beans and eggs

> ## MEDICINAL TEA
>
> All through downtown Hong Kong you'll see open-fronted shops with large brass urns set out on a counter, offering cups or bowls full of dark brown **medicinal tea** at around $5 a drink. The Cantonese name for this is *lo cha* or "cool tea", because in traditional Chinese medicine, tea is considered "cooling" to the body. The teas are made from various ingredients and claim various benefits, but are usually extremely bitter – ones to try include *ng fa cha* (five-flower tea) and *yat sei mei* (twenty-four-flavour tea).

cooked however you want them, and served with juice and a hot beverage of your choice. Their coffee isn't so great; otherwise a satisfying place to start the day. Open 24hr.

Tai Cheong Bakery 35 Lyndhurst Terrace, Central, Hong Kong Island ☎ 2544 3475; map pp.538–539. A favourite with Chris Patten, Britain's last Governor of Hong Kong, this tiny establishment has been going since 1954 and is famous for its Hong Kong-style egg tarts (not grilled like Macau's version; $6) and flaky *char siu* pastries ($9). Daily 7.30am–9pm.

DIM SUM

Dim sum (also known as *yum cha*) is the classic Cantonese way to start the day – a selection of little dumplings and dishes eaten with tea. Many restaurants serve *dim sum* from early in the morning until mid-afternoon, when they switch over to more extensive menus, but the following places are particularly well known for their *dim sum*. It's an inexpensive way to eat if you stay away from more famous establishments – perhaps $50 per person on average – but get in early at the weekends when whole families pack out restaurants.

Lok Cha Teahouse K.S. Lo Gallery, Hong Kong Park, Hong Kong Island ☎ 2801 7177, ⊕ lockcha.com; map pp.538–539. Vegetarian *dim sum* served in an elegant teahouse, full of wooden screens and furniture. Atmospheric but expensive: from $40/person for the tea, $20/*dim sum* serving. Bookings advised, especially at weekends. Daily 10am–10pm.

Luk Yu Tea House (陸羽茶室) 24–26 Stanley St, just west of D'Aguilar St, Hong Kong Island ☎ 2523 5464; map pp.538–539. A snapshot from the 1930s, with old wooden furniture and ceiling fans, this self-consciously traditional *dim sum* restaurant is good but overrated, and the quality barely justifies the tourist-inflated prices. Upwards of $100/person. Daily 7am–10pm.

Majesty Seafood 3F, Prudential Centre, 216–228 Nathan Rd, Jordan, Kowloon ☎ 2723 2399; map pp.538–539. First-rate beef balls, leek dumplings, *cha siu* puffs and egg custard tarts at this popular local venue. Bring a fleece for the severe air conditioning. Daily 8am–10pm.

★ **Metropol** 4F, United Centre, 95 Queensway, Hong Kong Island ☎ 2865 1988; map pp.538–539. Huge place that still uses trolleys to wheel the *dim sum* selection around

– a dying sight in Hong Kong. Try the flaky *cha siu* pastries and crunchy prawn dumplings. Daily 8am–midnight.

Tai Ya Ji (大日子酒家) 9 Heung Sze Wui St, Tai Po, New Territories ☎ 2656 2668; map pp.534–535. Great lunchtime destination after seeing Tai Po's sights; staff don't speak much English, but they'll help with the order card. Like many *yum cha* institutions, expect bright lights and a mammoth banqueting hall experience. Under $100 a head. Daily 8am–10pm.

★ **Tao Heung** 3 Minden Row, Tsim Sha Tsui, Kowloon ☎ 8300 8084; map p.548. Good choice for an early morning *dim sum* session. Service can be chaotic but beef balls and *har gau* prawn dumplings are crisp, crunchy and tasty; the stuffed rice rolls are excellent too. Daily 7.30am–1am.

RESTAURANTS

The whole of downtown Hong Kong is thick with restaurants, and nowhere is a meal more than a few paces away. Cantonese places are ubiquitous, with the highest concentration of foreign cuisines in Central, Soho, Wan Chai and Tsim Sha Tsui. The scene is, however, notoriously fickle, with places continually opening and withering away. Outside the centre, there are several popular Western-oriented restaurants along Hong Kong Island's south coast, while the Outlying Islands are famous for their seafood restaurants. Restaurant opening hours are from around 11am to 3pm, and 6pm to late, though cheaper Chinese places open all day, winding down around 9pm. Service is traditionally bad in Hong Kong, with staff typically offhand to the point of rudeness, but this has more to do with their insane workload than personal animosity. Don't worry too much about tipping: expensive restaurants add on a ten percent service charge anyway, while in cheaper places it's customary just to leave the small change.

CENTRAL

Chippy 51A Wellington St, entrance down the steps on Pottinger St ☎ 2523 1618; map pp.538–539. The last authentic British fish 'n' chip shop in Hong Kong, with a tiny sit-down counter serving great fries, though the fish is sometimes a bit mushy. A large plate of battered cod and chips costs $130. Daily 10am–midnight.

★ **Habibi** 112–114 Wellington St ☎ 2544 3886; map pp.538–539. Great Egyptian place with a main restaurant (featuring weekend belly dancing) and a cheaper café.

CHA CHAAN TENGS

The cheapest meals are found at local **cha chaan tengs** – literally "tea canteens" – and on the upper floor of indoor produce markets (also known as "wet markets"), where you can get a single-plate meal – *wuntun* noodle soup, or rice with roast pork – for around $40. City-wide versions of these places include *Fairwood*, *Café de Coral* and the above-average *Tsui Wah*, whose main branch is at 15–19 Wellington St in Central, and which serves great fishball soup and Hoinam chicken (cooked in stock and served with rice).

Food is filling, tasty and not too expensive – you can gorge yourself for $160. Mon–Fri 11am–4pm & 5pm–late, Sat 5pm–late; café daily 11am–midnight.

Man Wah 25F, Mandarin Oriental, 5 Connaught Rd ☏ 2522 0111; map pp.538–539. Subtle and accomplished southern Chinese food at connoisseurs' high prices, perhaps worth it if you want one, definitively excellent Cantonese meal – though the view sometimes out-performs the menu. Daily noon–3pm & 6.30–11pm.

★ **Nha Trang** 88–90 Wellington St ☏ 2581 9992; map pp.538–539. The original of this now city-wide Vietnamese chain, whose crisp, clean and sharp flavours make a nice break from more muggy Chinese fare. The grilled prawn and pomelo salad, rice-skin rolls and lemongrass beef are excellent, and two can eat very well for $300. Daily noon–4.30pm & 6–11pm.

Ser Wong Fun (蛇王飯) 30 Cochrane St ☏ 2543 1032; map pp.538–539. Cantonese diner whose reputation rests on its snake soup – something of a Hong Kong speciality – though it also does plenty of other straightforward dishes at low prices. Daily 11am–11.30pm.

★ **Tsim Chai Kee Noodle** (沾仔記) 98 Wellington St ☏ 2850 6471; map pp.538–539. Easily located by the small Chinese sign and lunchtime queue tailing downhill; what makes it worth the wait and being jammed into the packed interior are the *wuntun* – jokingly known here as "ping-pong *wuntun*" because of their huge size – served in soup for $21. Daily 8am–5pm.

★ **Yung Kee** 32–40 Wellington St ☏ 2522 1624; map pp.538–539. An enormous place with bright lights, scurrying staff and seating for a thousand, this is one of Hong Kong's institutions. Their roast goose and pigeon are superb, and the *dim sum* is also good. Moderately expensive – expect $350 a head – but highly recommended. Daily 11am–11.30pm.

SOHO

Ivan the Kozak 46–48 Cochrane St ☏ 2851 1193; map pp.538–539. The portions of chicken kiev, lamb stew, cabbage and potatoes are good value and tasty, but the highlight is donning a fur coat and walking into the huge freezer for a shot of vodka and a photo. About $300/person. Mon–Fri noon–midnight, Sat & Sun 5.30pm–midnight.

La Pampa 32 Staunton St ☏ 2868 6959; map pp.538–539. Argentinian restaurant that does what it does

– barbecued steak, mainly – exceedingly well. You order by weight, it's grilled just how you want it, and served with nominal quantities of vegetables. Count on at least $350/person. Mon–Fri noon–2.30pm & 6–11pm, Sat & Sun 6–11pm.

WAN CHAI AND CAUSEWAY BAY

Coyote 114–120 Lockhart Rd, Wan Chai ☏ 2861 2221; map pp.538–539. Lively Tex-Mex bar and grill that's full of tequila-quaffing patrons digging into plates of barbecued ribs, nachos and spicy pizzas. Around $180/person for a group. Daily noon–2am.

Crystal Jade Basement 2, Times Square, Causeway Bay ☏ 2506 0080; map pp.538–539. Known for its huge bowls of lamian noodles – topped with a variety of meats and sauces – and *xiaolongbao* dumplings, though it also does excellent Shanghai-style cold snacks. Decor is stylish dark wood but cramped, and prices a touch high, but the food is tasty and filling. Around $150 a head. Daily 11am–11pm.

Fook Lam Moon 35–45 Johnston Rd, Wan Chai ☏ 2866 0663; map pp.538–539. Very expensive Cantonese institution with astounding roast suckling pig, crispy-skinned chicken, abalone and bird's-nest soup. Service is not good, however – unless you're famous in Hong Kong. Around $1000 a head. Daily 11.30am–3pm & 6–11pm.

Padang JP Plaza, 22–36 Patterson St, Causeway Bay ☏ 2881 5075; map pp.538–539. A bit overpriced, but very authentic-tasting Indonesian grilled fish, mutton soup and noodle dishes. The highlights, however, are the cakes and durian-flavoured dessert selection. Expect around $100/head. Daily 11am–11pm.

★ **Plaza Mayor** 9 Moon Street, Wan Chai ☏ 2866 6644, ⊕ plazamayor.hk; map pp.538–539. Top-notch Spanish tapas – the garlic shrimps and meatballs are both excellent – best washed down with a bottle of tempranillo from their extensive wine cellar. Good service too, attentive but not overwhelming. Booking essential; expect $250 a head. Tues–Sun 11am–11pm.

Wing Wah (永華麵家) 89 Hennessy Rd at Luard Rd, Wan Chai ☏ 2527 7476; map pp.538–539. Known for its *wuntun*, this locally famous noodle house also serves mostly inexpensive and unusual medicinal soups, beef tendon noodles and shrimp paste on pomelo skins. Daily 11am–1am.

9

CURRY HOUSES IN CHUNGKING MANSIONS

It's an ugly building, but Chungking Mansions on Nathan Road, Tsim Sha Tsui, is where you'll find some of Hong Kong's best-value curry houses, where a filling meal will cost around $100 per head. Establishments include:

Delhi Club 3F, Block C ☎ 2368 1682. A Nepali curry house *par excellence*, once you ignore the spartan surroundings and slap-down service. Daily noon–3.30pm & 6–11.30pm.

Khyber Pass 7F, Block E ☎ 2721 2786. Consistently good Indian, Pakistani, Bangladeshi and Malay dishes; all *halal* and one of the best in Chungking Mansions. Daily noon–3pm & 6–11.30pm.

Sher-I-Punjab 3F, Block B ☎ 2312 0366. Friendly service in clean surroundings, if slightly more expensive than some of its neighbours. Daily noon–3pm & 6–11.30pm.

★ **Taj Mahal Club** 3F, Block B ☎ 2722 5454. Excellent North Indian food, and good value if you avoid the relatively expensive drinks. Daily noon–3.30pm & 6–11.30pm.

SOUTH COAST HONG KONG

Boathouse 86–88 Stanley Main St, Stanley ☎ 2813 4467; map pp.534–535. Popular expat hangout, with waterfront views from the balcony of this stylish "Mediterranean" building. Food concentrates on fresh, unpretentiously cooked seafood with mains upwards of $180. Booking advised. Mon–Fri 11.30am–10.30pm, Sat & Sun 11am–10.30pm.

Happy Garden Vietnamese Between the main bus stop and the seafront, Shek O ☎ 2809 4165; map pp.534–535. One of several laidback places with outdoor tables, luridly coloured drinks and excellent food – try the morning glory with *blechan* beef, or huge Thai fish cakes. Mains around $80. Daily noon–10pm.

Jumbo Floating Restaurant Aberdeen Harbour ☎ 2553 9111, ⓦ jumbokingdom.com; map pp.534–535. A Hong Kong institution, with several restaurants on three garishly decorated floors. While touristy and expensive – the set meal (which includes lobster) costs around $800 per head – as a one-off trip it can also be a lot of fun. Mon–Sat 11am–11.30pm, Sun 9am–11.30pm.

TSIM SHA TSUI

Aqua 29F & Penthouse, 1 Peking Rd ☎ 3427 2288; map p.548. Dark wooden floors and superlative harbour views through angled windows are the setting for consuming an unexpectedly successful blend of Italian and Japanese dishes. The atmosphere is informal, and the prices around $500 per head. Reservations essential. Daily noon–2.30pm & 6–11.30pm.

Chee Kee 37 Lock Rd ☎ 2368 2528; map p.548. Bright Chinese diner serving unpretentious, good-quality *wuntun* and noodle soups, fried pork steak, crispy prawn rolls and fishballs. About $40/dish. Daily 11am–11pm.

Felix 28F, Peninsula Hotel ☎ 2315 3188; map p.548. The incredible views of Hong Kong Island (not least from the gents' glass-walled urinals) warrant a visit to this Philippe Starck-designed restaurant. The Eurasian menu averages over $650/person, but you can just come for one of their famous martinis

at the bar – a great perch for watching a summer storm or the 8pm "Symphony of Lights" across the harbour. Restaurant daily 6–10.30pm; bar daily 5pm–1.30am.

Guangdong 43 Hankou Rd ☎ 2735 5151; map p.548. Slightly tourist-inflated prices and cramped seating even for Hong Kong at this fast-and-furious *cha chaan teng*, but the food – especially their barbecued pork or goose – is tasty and they've got a bilingual menu. Single-plate meals cost around $50. Daily 7am–1am.

Kakalok Corner of Ashley Rd and Ichang St ☎ 2376 1198; map p.548. A fast-food counter with the sole distinction of serving the cheapest fried noodles, rice and fish 'n' chips in Hong Kong. No seats, but Kowloon Park is 100m away. Daily 11am–late.

★ **Peninsula Hotel Lobby** Peninsula Hotel ☎ 2366 6251; map p.548. The set tea, served in the lobby and accompanied by a string quartet, comes to around $190/person – a good way to get a glimpse of a more elegant, civilized and relaxed Hong Kong. Dress is smart-casual; no plastic or nylon footwear, no sportswear and no sleeveless shirts for men. Daily 2–6pm.

Spring Deer 42 Mody Rd ☎ 2366 4012; map p.548. Faded Beijing restaurant that must have been grand when they last redecorated in the 1960s. The food – especially the steamed lamb and Beijing duck – is worth it, though; expect to pay around $250/head. Daily noon–2pm & 6–11.30pm.

Sweet Dynasty Pacific Centre, 28 Hankow Rd ☎ 2199 7799; map p.548. Tasty but expensive noodles and rice dishes; best to stick to the Southeast Asian-style desserts, featuring sago, tofu, mango, lotus seeds and red beans – the pomelo pudding in coconut milk is exceptional. Mon–Thurs 10am–midnight, Fri 10am–11pm, Sat & Sun 7.30am–midnight.

JORDAN AND MONG KOK

Light Vegetarian 13 Jordan Rd ☎ 2384 2833; map p.548. Comprehensive Chinese vegetarian menu, including taro fish, "bird's nest" basket filled with fried vegetables, pumpkin soup served in the shell, vegetarian duck and a big *dim sum* selection. Dishes from $45. Daily 11am–11pm.

★ **Mak Man Kee** (麥文記麵家) 51 Parkes St, Jordan ☎ 2736 5561, ⓦ makmankee.com; map p.548. You'd never guess from the anonymous white tiles and cramped interior, but this famous, long-running family business is held by many to serve the best *wuntun* noodles in town, a bowlful of which costs just $30. Daily noon–12.30am.

Tim Ho Wan (添好運) Shop 8, 2–20 Kwong Wa St, Mong Kok ☎ 2332 2896; map p.548. Crowds queue round the block to eat at this apparently insignificant place, hungry for its Michelin-star-rated lotus-leaf steamed rice, *cha siu* pastries, persimmon cakes and *fun gwor* dumplings. No bookings. Around $50/person. Daily 8am–10pm.

LEI YUE MUN

Gateway (南大門) The last restaurant at Lei Yue Mun village, 750m from Yau Tong MTR, Exit A2, about 3km east of Tsim Sha Tsui ☎ 2727 5628, ⓦ gatewaycuisine .com; map pp.534–535. If you want to blow some money on an excellent Cantonese seafood meal with atmospheric harbour views, you won't get better than this: try the sautéed tiger prawns, steamed scallops, razor shells with black beans and steamed reef trout. Good wine cellar too. A seven-dish meal costs around $350/person in a group. Daily 11am–11pm.

OUTLYING ISLANDS

CHEUNG CHAU

★ **Hong Kee** Turn left off the ferry and it's one of a row of stalls 100m along ☎ 2981 9916; map pp.534–535. No-frills alfresco seafood place, on the harbourside promenade, serving a range of stir-fries – somewhere to order a plate of chilli prawns and a beer, and watch the sun go down. Around $75/person. Open evenings daily.

LAMMA

Bookworm Café 79 Main St, Yung Shue Wan ☎ 2982 4838; map pp.534–535. This organic vegetarian Western restaurant is slightly too worthy, but their burgers and various healthy fruit/veg juices are excellent. There's also a secondhand book exchange and free wi-fi. About $100/head. Daily 10am–9pm.

Concerto Inn Hung Shing Ye Beach, just uphill off the main path ☎ 2982 1668, ⓦ concertoinn.com.hk; map pp.534–535. The food – an Asian-European fusion, with a heavy seafood emphasis – is hit-and-miss in quality, but this is a lovely place to sit on the outdoor terrace and have an ice-cold sundowner after a few hours on the beach. Daily 8am–10pm.

Rainbow Seafood Sok Kwu Wan ☎ 2982 8100, ⓦ rainbowrest.com.hk; map pp.534–535. Built on piles right over the water, this huge open-plan affair seats 800 people and serves consistently good fish, crab, scallop and prawn dishes (beware the small portions of lobster, though). Book ahead unless you want a half-hour wait. Daily 10am–11pm.

LANTAU

★ **Caffe Paradiso** 3 Ngan Wan Rd, Mui Wo ☎ 2984 0498; map pp.534–535. Tiny café with excellent coffee and snacks, run by a laidback expat. It's hidden away in the streets beside the bus stop, to the left as you exit the ferry. Mon–Fri 7.30am–4pm, Sat 7.30am–5pm, Sun 8.30am–7pm.

Deer Horn Mui Wo Centre, 3 Ngan Wan Rd, Mui Wo ☎ 3484 3095; map pp.534–535. Run by a Nepalese couple and serving some pretty authentic-sounding dishes – including yak cheese fritters. Around $180/head. Mon & Wed–Sun noon–late.

NIGHTLIFE

The most concentrated collection of bars is in the **Lan Kwai Fong** area on Hong Kong Island, perennially popular for late-night carousing, with drinkers spilling out onto the street. Other locations include the long-established, slightly sleazy expat scene around **Wan Chai**, and a scattering of options aimed at travellers in **Tsim Sha Tsui**. Some venues charge a $50–500 entrance fee on certain nights (generally Fri & Sat), though almost everywhere also offers daily **happy hours** at some point between 3pm and 9pm – worth catching, as drinks are otherwise pricey. For event details, consult free *HK Magazine* (ⓦ hk-magazine.com) and *BC Magazine* (ⓦ bcmagazine.net). The **gay scene**, while hardly prominent, is at least more active than in other Chinese cities; check *Time Out Hong Kong* (ⓦ timeout.com.hk) for listings.

CENTRAL

2121 G/F, The Plaza, 21 D'Aguilar St, Lan Kwai Fong ☎ 2804 6669; map pp.538–539. Smart, laidback nook among Lan Kwai Fong's clamour, good for an after-work or pre-dinner drink and with indoor seats allowing you to people-watch the crowds outside. Daily 4pm–1am.

Beijing Club Wellington Place, 2–8 Wellington St, Central ☎ 2810 9983; map pp.538–539. Huge industrial bar and dance venue on three floors (plus gold-plated

bathrooms and an outdoor terrace), one of which is for VIPs only. Mon–Sat 10.30pm–2am.

Bit Point 31 D'Aguilar St, Lan Kwai Fong ☎ 2523 7436; map pp.538–539. German-themed bar, concentrating on meals until around 10pm, after which the bar starts selling industrial quantities of lager and schnapps as the jukebox blares. Mon–Sat noon–1am, Sun 4pm–1am.

Club 71 67 Hollywood Rd, Central ☎ 2858 7071; map pp.538–539. Away from Lan Kwai Fong's rowdy mess of

9

bars, this tiny bohemian place still gets busy, but happy-hour prices are reasonable and there's a front-of-house terrace. It's hard to find; look for 69 Hollywood Rd and take the small lane around to the back. Daily 5pm–late.

D26 26 D'Aguilar St, Lan Kwai Fong ☎2877 1610; map pp.538–539. Small, low-key bar; a good place for a warm-up drink or if you actually want a conversation with your companions. Daily noon–1am.

Le Jardin Wing Wah Lane ☎2526 2717; map pp.538–539. Almost impossible to find unless you already know it's there – go right to the end of Wing Wah Lane and take the steps up to the hidden entrance – this comfortable bar has a covered terrace and is usually quieter than alternatives in nearby Lan Kwai Fong. Mon–Fri 4.30pm–late, Sat 5pm–late.

WAN CHAI

Carnegie's 53–55 Lockhart Rd ☎2866 6289; map pp.538–539. Noise level means conversation here is only possible by flash cards, and once it's packed, hordes of punters, keen to party the night away, fight for dancing space on the bar. Regular live music. Mon–Thurs 11am–late, Sat noon–late, Sun 5pm–late.

Old China Hand 104 Lockhart Rd ☎2865 4378; map pp.538–539. Great pub food and a histrionic atmosphere in this dark, barfly hangout, full of embittered, seedy expats acting the part. Mon–Sat 24hr, Sun 9am–2am.

The Pawn 62 Johnston Rd ☎2866 3444; map pp.538–539. Smart pub in a restored old pawnbroker's building dating from 1888, with the facade and some old wooden fixtures still in place, plus a balcony overlooking the busy road, and a rooftop garden. Extensive list of imported spirits, beers and wine, with pub-style fish 'n' chips, ploughman's lunch and English breakfasts ($100–200). Daily 11.30am–11pm.

Wanch 54 Jaffe Rd ☎2861 1621; map pp.538–539. A Hong Kong institution, this tiny bar has live music – usually folk and rock – every night. It also serves cheap chunky cheeseburgers and sandwiches. Mon–Sat 11am–2am, Sun noon–2am.

TSIM SHA TSUI

Bahama Mama's 4–5 Knutsford Terrace, just north of Kimberly Rd ☎2368 2121; map p.548. A good atmosphere, with a vibrant mix of nationalities, and plenty of space for pavement drinking. There's a beach-bar theme and outdoor terrace that prompts party-crowd antics. On club nights, there's a great range of mixed music. Mon–Thurs 5pm–3am, Fri & Sat 5pm–4am, Sun 6pm–2am.

Delaney's Basement, Mary Building, 71–77 Peking Rd ☎2301 3980; map p.548. Friendly and comfortably familiar Irish pub with draught beers, including Guinness; features Irish folk music most nights. Enormous all-day breakfasts also available. Daily 8am–2am.

Ned Kelly's Last Stand 11A Ashley Rd ☎2376 0562; map p.548. Very popular, long-running venue, featuring a nightly performance from an excellent ragtime jazz band. Daily noon–1.45am.

SHOPPING

Many visitors come to Hong Kong to go **shopping**, drawn by the incredible range of goods packed into such a small area. While some things are good value for money – particularly **clothes**, **silk**, **jewellery**, **Chinese arts and crafts**, and some **computer accessories** – it's essential to research online prices for identical goods before buying, and to shop around. The farther you are from touristy Tsim Sha Tsui, the better value shopping becomes, and the less likely that you'll be **ripped off** by some scam. Shops **open** daily; in downtown areas and shopping malls, 10am to 7pm or later is the norm.

ANTIQUES, ARTS AND CRAFTS

Chinese collectors value their heritage, which means that Hong Kong is one of the most expensive places in the world to buy antiques; there are also huge numbers of fakes floating around. But if you know your stuff the range and quality are excellent. Hollywood Road (see p.542) is at the centre of the trade, and Upper Lascar Row is a fun place to browse for lower-end reproductions and souvenirs. Hong Kong is also a reasonable place to pick up modern arts and crafts, with a couple of big chain stores dealing in Chinese products – prices are cheaper on the mainland, however. Some more general stores include:

Eu Yan Sang Ground Floor, 152–156 Queen's Rd, Central ☎2544 3308, ⟨w⟩euyansang.com; map pp.538–539. One of the most famous medicine shops in town, founded in 1879, and now with branches right across Southeast Asia. A source of teas, herbs and Chinese medicines.

★**Honeychurch Antiques** 29 Hollywood Rd, Central ☎2543 2433, ⟨w⟩honeychurch.com; map pp.538–539. Long-running, intimate and foreign-owned gallery with a range of genuine Chinese, Japanese and Tibetan curios and antiques; prices are relatively low for Hong Kong and the shop is well worth a browse.

Karin Weber Gallery 20 Aberdeen St, Central ☎2544 5004, ⟨w⟩karinwebergallery.com; map pp.538–539. Specializes in contemporary paintings from the mainland and Southeast Asia, plus antique Chinese furniture.

Schoeni Art Gallery 21–31 Old Bailey St, Central ☎2869 8802, ⟨w⟩schoeni.com.hk; map pp.538–539. Agents for modern Chinese artists such as Chen Yu, who combines Chinese images with Renaissance-era scenery.

Yue Hwa China Products 301–309 Nathan Rd, Jordan ⟨w⟩yuehwa.com; map p.548. Chinese medicines, clothing, sportswear, tea, books, spirits and every

A NICE SUIT, SIR?

Tailor-made clothes are a speciality of the Hong Kong tourist trade, and wherever you go in Tsim Sha Tsui you'll be accosted by Indian tailors offering this service. Sales pitches are hardcore and prices are relatively low, but not rock bottom; a man's cashmere suit, with a couple of shirts and ties, will cost upwards of $1500, more likely twice this. Don't commit yourself without knowing exactly what's included. Expect at least two or three fittings over several days if you want a good result. You'll need to pay about fifty percent of the price as a deposit.

Johnson & Co 44 Hankow Rd, Kowloon; map p.548. Long-established business that was once a favourite of military and naval customers. Excellent jewellers too.

Linva Tailor 38 Cochrane St, Central; map pp.538–539. Well-established ladies' tailor, popular with locals who want *cheongsams* for parties. They work a lot with embroidery.

Margaret Court Tailoress 8F, Winner Building, 27 D'Aguilar St, Lan Kwai Fong, Central; map pp.538–539. A solid reputation for good work and lots of local Western female clients, although it doesn't come cheaply. A shirt costs around $500 plus fabric.

Pacific Custom Tailors 19 des Voeux Road, Central; map pp.538–539. Upmarket, elegantly tailored suits with prices to match.

Punjab House 5F, Suite C, Golden Crown Court, 66–70 Nathan Rd, Tsim Sha Tsui ⓦpunjabhouse .com.hk; map p.548. Former favourite of the British Forces and Fire Fighters; good-quality male and female formal wear.

Sam's Tailors 94 Nathan Rd, Tsim Sha Tsui ⓦsamstailor.biz; map p.548. Probably the best-known tailor in Hong Kong, Sam is famous as much for his talent for self-publicity as for his clothes.

conceivable tourist knick-knack produced on the mainland, all in one place and with prices that are often subject to negotiation.

Yue Po Chai Antiques 132–136 Hollywood Rd, on the corner of Ladder St and Hollywood Rd, Central ☎2540 4374; map pp.538–539. Across from the Man Mo Temple, this place is crowded with dusty glass cabinets stuffed with porcelain – both real and reproduction (though this isn't necessarily made clear). They'll haggle a little over prices.

BOOKSHOPS

Bookazine F/3 Prince's Building, Chater Road, Central ⓦbookazine.com.hk; map pp.538–539. Excellent English-language bookshop with a good range of popular fiction and local interest; it also hosts regular literary events and book signings.

Cosmos Books 30 Johnston Rd, Wan Chai; 96 Nathan Rd, Tsim Sha Tsui ⓦcosmosbooks.com.hk; map pp.538–539. Offers an excellent range of both English- and Chinese-language books on all topics, from cookbooks to guides, novels, martial art manuals and bestsellers.

Dymock's In many locations including the IFC Mall, Central ⓦdymocks.com.hk; map pp.538–539. Another good English-language bookshop, perhaps best for its range of local interest titles, including coffee-table tomes with gorgeous photography.

Swindon Book Company 13–15 Lock Rd, Tsim Sha Tsui ⓦswindonbook.com; map p.548. Hong Kong's oldest English-language bookshop, with a solid range of works on Hong Kong and China – including academic and out-of-print titles that you won't see elsewhere.

CLOTHES

Clothes are good value in Hong Kong, particularly local casual-wear brand names such as Gordiano and Baleno, which have branches all over the city. Big-name designer clothes are often more expensive than back home because of the cachet attached to foreign upmarket brands, but sales are worth checking out. For markets dealing in inexpensive clothes, try the Temple Street Night Market (p.550), Ladies' Market (p.551) and stalls in lanes off Ap Liu Street in Sham Shui Po (p.551). If you just want to browse, good places to start include Granville Road in Tsim Sha Tsui, the Pedder Building on Pedder Street in Central and, just round the corner, Wyndham and D'Aguilar streets. Other places to check out include:

Blanc De Chine Shop 123, Prince's Building, Central; map pp.538–539. Elegant designs loosely based on traditional Chinese clothes, mostly in silk or cashmere, at high prices. Also sells stylish jewellery to match.

Horizon Plaza Lee Nam Rd, Ap Lei Chau Island, Aberdeen (entrance around side on Li Wing St); bus #95 from Aberdeen or #671 from Causeway Road, near Victoria Park; taxi rank outside; map pp.534–535. Twenty-eight floors of discount outlets – including Joyce, Lane Crawford and Armani – where designer boutiques send last season's (or last month's) stuff that didn't sell, with savings of up to eighty percent. The lobby has a comprehensive directory, and there's a café or two on site.

Shanghai Tang 1 Duddel St, Central; map pp.538–539. A must-visit store, which specializes in stylish new versions of traditional Chinese styles like the *cheongsam*

9

split-sided dress, often in vibrant colours. They can also make to order. Expensive, even during sales.

Vivienne Tam Shop 209, Pacific Place, 88 Queensway, Admiralty, and elsewhere; map pp.538–539. Funky shirts and dresses in David-Hockney-meets-Vivienne-Westwood style, often featuring Chairman Mao and other icons of the East.

ELECTRONIC GOODS

With the advent of internet shopping, prices in Hong Kong for electronic goods such as cameras, MP3 players, mobile phones and computers are no longer the bargain they once were – added to which is the difficulty of getting any sort of warranty, and the possibility of being ripped off. If you do decide to buy, make sure you know exactly what you want, and the price you'd pay for it at home and online. The best time to buy is when new models of products are about to be launched, as shops try to ditch their old stock before it becomes unsaleable to fashion-conscious locals. Chain stores such as Fortress (ⓦfortress.com.hk/en/home) are reliable places to get a base price, though you'll do better at the three warehouse-sized computer centres listed below. For secondhand mobile phones and household appliances, try Ap Liu Street in Sham Shui Po, Kowloon (exit A2 from Sham Shui Po MTR).

298 Computer Zone 298 Hennessy Rd, Wan Chai; map pp.538–539. A disconcerting maze of shops crammed into three levels, with a well-concealed entrance despite the huge sign. Discounted computers and accessories, ranging from dodgy Chinese stuff to top-notch brands.

Golden Shopping Centre 156 Fuk Wa St, Sham Shui Po, Kowloon; Sham Shui Po MTR, exit D2; map pp.534–535. Another claustrophobic warren of tiny stalls selling all sorts of cheap computer components and accessories. You might also find pirated software here, though most people download it online nowadays.

Mong Kok Computer Centre Corner of Nelson St and Fa Yuen St, Mong Kok; map p.548. Yet more discounted electronics, mostly mobile phone-oriented.

JEWELLERY

Hong Kongers love jewellery, and the city sports literally thousands of jewellers. Some offer pieces that look remarkably like famous international jewellery houses' designs, but at much lower prices. The Hong Kong Tourist Board (see p.564) can point you in the direction of reputable stores, but retailers with outlets city-wide include Chow Tai Fook (ⓦchowtaifook.com) and Chow Sang Sang (ⓦchowsangsang.com).

MALLS AND DEPARTMENT STORES

In summer, the air conditioning in Hong Kong's numerous, glossy shopping malls makes as good a reason as any to visit, and most have nice cafés to boot. Some of the best include Times Square (Causeway Bay MTR), IFC Mall (inside the IFC; Central MTR), Lee Gardens (Causeway Bay MTR) and Festival Walk (Kowloon Tong MTR). Department store chains include:

Lane Crawford IFC Mall, Central (and other branches); map pp.538–539. Hong Kong's oldest Western-style department store.

SOGO East Point Centre, 555 Hennessy Rd, Causeway Bay; map pp.538–539. The Japanese contingent. Immaculately presented goods inside one of the largest department stores in Hong Kong.

Wing On 26 Des Voeux Rd, Central (and other branches); map pp.538–539. A long-established store, with branches throughout Hong Kong SAR. Standard, day-to-day goods rather than luxuries.

DIRECTORY

Banks and exchange Banks are generally open Mon–Fri 9am–4.30pm, Sat 9am–12.30pm; almost all have ATMs capable of accepting foreign cards. Banks handling foreign exchange levy commissions on travellers' cheques. Licensed moneychangers, who open all hours including Sun, don't charge commission but usually give poor rates, so shop around and always establish the exact amount you will receive before handing any money over.

Embassies and consulates Australia, 23F, Harbour Centre, 25 Harbour Rd, Wan Chai ☎2827 8881; Canada, 14F, 1 Exchange Square, Central ☎3719 4700; China, 7F, Lower Block, China Resources Building, 26 Harbour Rd, Wan Chai ☎3413 2424; India, 16F, United Centre, 95 Queensway, Admiralty ☎3970 9900; Ireland, Suite 1408, Two Pacific Place, 88 Queensway, Wan Chai ☎2527 4897; Japan, 46F, One Exchange Square, Central ☎2522 1184; Korea, 5F, Far East Finance Centre, 16 Harcourt Rd, Central ☎2529 4141; Malaysia, 24F, Malaysia Building, 50 Gloucester Rd, Wan Chai ☎2821 0800; New Zealand, 6501 Central Plaza, 18 Harbour Rd, Wan Chai ☎2525 5044; Philippines, 14F, United Centre, 95 Queensway, Admiralty ☎2823 8501; Singapore, 901–2 Tower 1, Admiralty Centre, Admiralty ☎2527 2212; South Africa, 2706 Great Eagle Centre, 23 Harbour Rd, Wan Chai ☎2577 3279; Thailand, 8F, Fairmont House, 8 Cotton Tree Drive, Central ☎2521 6481; UK, 1 Supreme Court Rd, Admiralty ☎2901 3000; US, 26 Garden Rd, Central ☎2523 9011; Vietnam, 15F, Great Smart Tower, 230 Wan Chai Rd, Wan Chai ☎2591 4517.

Emergencies For emergency services, call ☎999.

Hospitals Government hospitals have 24hr casualty wards, where treatment is free. These include the Princess Margaret Hospital, Lai King Hill Rd, Lai Chi Kok, Kowloon ☎2990 1111; and the Queen Mary Hospital, Pokfulam Rd, Hong Kong Island ☎2855 3838. For an ambulance, dial ☎999.

FROM TOP PORTUGUESE CUSTARD TARTS, MACAU (P.588); SÃO PAULO, MACAU (P.579) >

澳門馳名葡撻

LIVING LUXURY GAMBLING WITH MACAU
要生活揮霍到澳門搏一搏

9

Internet Some accommodation and café chains offer free wi-fi for their customers. Hong Kong Central Library, opposite Victoria Park in Causeway Bay, Hong Kong Island (Mon, Tues & Thurs–Sun 10am–9pm, Wed 1–9pm), has free internet, though you have to wait for a terminal to become available, plus free wi-fi. There are also net bars in the lower two floors of Chungking Mansions, charging around $20/hour.

Laundry There are many laundries in Hong Kong where you pay by dry weight of clothes ($10–20/kilo) and then pick them up an hour or two later; ask at your accommodation for the nearest.

Left luggage There's an office in the departure lounge at the airport (daily 6.30am–1am), and at the Central and Kowloon stations for the Airport Express. There are also coin-operated lockers in the Hong Kong China Ferry Terminal in Tsim Sha Tsui. Costs are $20–80 depending on size of locker and time used. You can also negotiate to leave luggage at your guesthouse or hotel, but ensure you're happy with general security first. If you're flying out late from Hong Kong and need to get rid of your bags for the day, consider using the In-town Check-in (see p.560).

Mail Hong Kong's general post office is at 2 Connaught Place, Central (Mon–Sat 8am–6pm, Sun 9am–2pm; Poste Restante collection Mon–Sat 8am–6pm), facing Jardine House. The Kowloon main post office is at 10 Middle Rd, Tsim Sha Tsui.

Police Crime hotline and taxi complaints ☎ 2527 7177. For general police enquiries, call ☎ 2860 2000.

Sport Every Easter, Hong Kong is host to an international Rugby Sevens tournament (information from Hong Kong Rugby Football Union; ⓦ hkrugby.com). The following activities are also available in the territory: for excellent tuition in many styles of martial arts, contact CS Tang (ⓦ cstang.www3.50megs.com); for windsurfing rentals and instruction, try the Windsurf Centre on Kwun Yam Wan Beach, Cheung Chau Island; for tennis courts, contact the Hong Kong Tennis Association (ⓦ www.tennishk.org), whose website lists clubs, facilities and events. The Hong Kong Marathon takes place in Feb (ⓦ hkmarathon.com).

Telephones For directory enquiries in English, call ☎ 1081. All local calls from landlines are free; payphones cost $1 for five minutes. Mobile SIM cards and prepaid discount cards for international calls are sold from stalls and small shops inside the Pedder Building on Queen's Rd in Central, and in Chungking Mansions in Tsim Sha Tsui.

Macau

澳门, aòmén

Sixty kilometres west across the Pearl River Delta from Hong Kong lies the former Portuguese enclave of **MACAU**. Occupying a peninsula and a couple of islands of just thirty square kilometres in extent, Macau's atmosphere has been unmistakably shaped by a colonial past – predating Hong Kong's by nearly three hundred years – which has left old fortresses, Baroque churches, faded mansions, cobbled public squares, unusual food and Portuguese place names in its wake. But what draws in millions of big-spending tourists from Hong Kong, the mainland and neighbouring countries are Macau's **casinos**, the only place in China where they have been legalized. Their combined income – reportedly over five billion US dollars annually – now exceeds that of Las Vegas, and has funded a **construction boom** for themed resorts, roads and large-scale land reclamation.

Macau comprises several distinct parts. The largest and most densely settled area is the **peninsula**, bordering the Chinese mainland to the north, where the original city was located and where most of the historic sights and facilities remain. Off to the southeast and linked to the peninsula by bridges are **Taipa** and **Coloane**, once separate islands but now joined by a low-lying area of reclaimed land known as **Cotai**, which is being developed as a new entertainment strip. It's all very compact, and it's possible to get around much of Macau on foot, with public transport available for longer stretches. A day-trip from Hong Kong is possible (tens of thousands do it every weekend), though you really need a couple of nights to do the place justice.

MACAU CURRENCY

The Macau currency is the **pataca** (abbreviated to "MOP$" in this book; also written as "M$" and "ptca"), which is worth fractionally less than the HK dollar. HK dollars (but not yuan) are freely accepted as currency in Macau, and a lot of visitors from Hong Kong don't bother changing money at all.

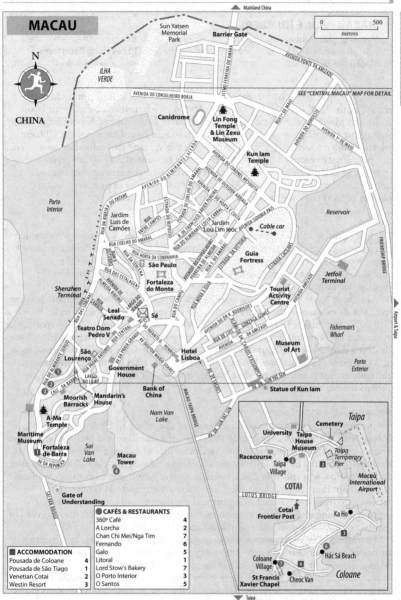

MACAU

N

CHINA

Mainland China

Barrier Gate

Sun Yatsen Memorial Park

ISTMO FERREIRA DO AMARAL

AVENIDA PONTE DA AMIZADE

ILHA VERDE

0   500
metres

AVENIDA DO CONSELHEIRO BORJA

SEE "CENTRAL MACAU" MAP FOR DETAIL

Porto Interior

Canidrome

Lin Fong Temple & Lin Zexu Museum

RUA 1º DE MAIO

AVENIDA DO NORDESTE

AVENIDA 1º DE MAIO

Kun Iam Temple

AVENIDA DO COLONEL MESQUITA

AVENIDA DO DOUTOR ARRAGA

RUA DA RIBEIRA DO PATANE

AVENIDA DO ALMIRANTE LACERDA

Jardim Luis de Camões

ENTRE CAMPOS

RUA DO REPOUSO

RUA DE FRANCISCO XAVIER PEREIRA

AVENIDA COELHO DO AMARAL

R. DE FRANCISCO XAVIER PEREIRA

AVENIDA DE OUDOVIA PAIS

Jardim Lou Lim Ieoc

Cable car

Reservoir

Shenzhen Terminal

RUA DAS ESTALAGENS

AVENIDA DE ALMEIDA RIBEIRO

RUA HORTA DA CONPANHIA

São Paulo

Fortaleza do Monte

Leal Senado

Sé

Teatro Dom Pedro V

São Lourenço

Guia Fortress

Jetfoil Terminal

FRIENDSHIP BRIDGE

Tourist Activity Centre

AVENIDA AMIZADE

Fisherman's Wharf

Airport & Taipa

Hotel Lisboa

Museum of Art

Porto Exterior

Government House

Bank of China

Nam Van Lake

Statue of Kun Iam

MACAU-TAIPA BRIDGE

AV. DR. SUN YAT SEN

Moorish Barracks

Mandarin's House

A-Ma Temple

Maritime Museum

Fortaleza de Barra

Sai Van Lake

Macau Tower

AV DA REPUBLICA

SKY BRIDGE

Gate of Understanding

CAFÉS & RESTAURANTS
360º Café	4
A Lorcha	2
Chan Chi Mei/Nga Tim	7
Fernando	6
Galo	5
Litoral	1
Lord Stow's Bakery	7
O Porto Interior	3
O Santos	5

ACCOMMODATION
Pousada de Coloane	4
Pousada de São Tiago	1
Venetian Cotai	2
Westin Resort	3

University

Taipa House Museum

Cemetery

Taipa

Racecourse

Taipa Village

Taipa Temporary Pier

Macau International Airport

COTAI

LOTUS BRIDGE

Cotai Frontier Post

Ka Ho

Coloane Village

St Francis Xavier Chapel

Cheoc Van

Hác Sá Beach

Coloane

Taipa

Brief history

For more than a thousand years, all **trade** between China and the West was indirectly carried out overland along the Silk Road through Central Asia. But from the fifteenth century onwards, seafaring European nations started making exploratory voyages around the globe, establishing garrisoned ports along the way and so creating new maritime trade routes over which they had direct control. In 1557 – having already gained toeholds in India (Goa) and the Malay Peninsula (Malacca) – the **Portuguese**

9

persuaded Chinese officials to rent them a strategically well-placed peninsula at the mouth of the Pearl River Delta, known as **Macao**. With their trade links with Japan, India and Malaya, the Portuguese found themselves in the profitable position of being sole agents for merchants across a whole swath of East Asia. Given that the Chinese were forbidden from going abroad to trade themselves, and that other foreigners were not permitted to enter Chinese ports, their trade blossomed and Macau grew immensely wealthy. With the traders came **Christianity**, and among the luxurious homes and churches built during Macau's brief half-century of prosperity was the basilica of **São Paulo**, the facade of which can still be seen today.

Decline

By the beginning of the seventeenth century, however, Macau's fortunes were waning alongside Portugal's decline as a maritime power, and following the British seizure of Hong Kong in 1841, Macau's status as a backwater was sealed. Despite the introduction of **licensed gambling** in 1847, as a means of securing some kind of income, virtually all trade was lost to Hong Kong.

As in Hong Kong, the twentieth century saw wave after wave of **immigrants** pouring into Macau to escape strife on the mainland – the territory's population today stands at 540,000 – but, unlike in Hong Kong, this growth was not accompanied by spectacular economic development. Indeed, when the Portuguese attempted to hand Macau back to China during the 1960s and 1970s, they were rebuffed: the gambling, prostitution and organized crime that was Macau's lifeblood would only be an embarrassment to the Communist government if they had left it alone, yet cleaning it up would have proved too big a financial drain.

Return to China and recovery

By the time China finally accepted the return of the colony in 1999 – as the **Macau Special Administrative Region** (MSAR) – the mainland had become both richer and more ideologically flexible. A pre-handover spree of violence by Triad gangs was dealt with, then the monopoly on casino licences – previously held by local billionaire **Dr Stanley Ho** – was ended in 2002, opening up this lucrative market to international competition. Response has been swift, and there are currently **34 casinos** in the territory; tourism has boomed alongside and the once-torpid economy is boiling – though an unforeseen embarrassment is that mainland officials have been accused of gambling away billions of yuan of public funds during holidays in the SAR.

Meanwhile, Macau's **government** operates along the "One Country, Two Systems" principle, with very little dissent. The reality is that, even more than Hong Kong, Macau desperately needs the mainland for its continuing existence, as it has no resources of its own. To this end, some giant infrastructure projects – including a bridge to Hong Kong – are in the pipeline, as the SAR seeks to tie its economy closer to that of the booming Pearl River Delta area.

Macau peninsula

Sights on the **Macau peninsula** comprise the best of the narrow lanes, colonial buildings and cobbled squares that make Macau so much more charismatically historic than Hong Kong – though there is, of course, a strikingly modern district too, along Avenida da Amizade, where a string of casinos jostles for your attention. Everything is technically close enough to walk between, though it's likely you'll resort to buses or taxis to reach more distant attractions up along the Chinese border.

Largo do Senado

Macau's older core centres around **Largo do Senado**, a large, cobbled pedestrianized square north off Avenida Almeida Ribeiro and surrounded by unmistakeably European-influenced buildings, with their stucco mouldings, colonnades and shuttered windows. There's an excellent **market** held daily in the lanes immediately west of the square, good for cheap clothes.

Leal Senado

Largo do Senado • Mon–Sat 1–7pm; public library closed Sat • Free

At Largo do Senado's southern side – across Avenida Ribeira – stands the **Leal Senado**, generally considered the finest Portuguese building in the city. The interior courtyard sports walls decorated with wonderful blue-and-white Portuguese tiles, while up the staircase from the courtyard is the richly decorated **senate chamber**, still used by the municipal government of Macau. In the late sixteenth century, the entire citizenry of the colony would gather here to debate issues of importance; the senate's title *leal* (loyal) was earned by Macao refusing to recognize the Spanish king's rule over Portugal. Adjacent to the chamber is the wood-carved **public library**, which includes a vast collection of China-themed books, some in English, dating back to the sixteenth century.

Sé

Largo de Sé • irregular hours – enquire at entrance; Bishop's House daily 10am–5.30pm • Free

East off Largo do Senado, two small lanes slope uphill to a cobbled square and the uninspiring concrete facade of the **Sé**, Macau's sixteenth-century cathedral, with an interior that impresses in scale, rather than ornamentation. The adjacent **Bishop's House** makes up for this austerity, filled with over-the-top Baroque statuary and religious artefacts in silver and gold.

Casa de Lou Kau

Travessa de Sé • Tues–Sun 9am–7pm • Free

Just east off Largo do Senado, **Casa de Lou Kou** (the Lou Family Mansion) is the house of the wealthy nineteenth-century merchant who sponsored the Lou Lim Ieoc garden (see p.582). The building, a two-storey grey-brick structure with internal galleries around a central atrium, has been perfectly restored. The open roof lets in light and air but keeps out the heat.

São Domingos

Largo do Senado • irregular hours – enquire at entrance • Free

At Largo do Senado's northern end, the honey-and-cream-coloured, seventeenth-century Baroque church, **São Domingos**, is adjoined by Macau's **Religious Museum**, containing a treasury of sacred art under a timbered roof. On May 13 the church is the starting point for a major procession in honour of Our Lady of Fatima.

São Paulo

Rua de São Paulo

North from Largo do Senado, you'll find the streets flanked by *pastellarias* (biscuit shops) and stores selling reproduction antique furniture. At the top of Rua de São Paulo, a broad stone staircase rises to the former site of the church of **São Paulo**, built in 1602 and hailed as the greatest Christian monument in East Asia before being destroyed by fire in 1835. Only the massive stone **facade** has survived, standing at the head of the stairs like a theatre backdrop and lavishly carved in a riot of Christian

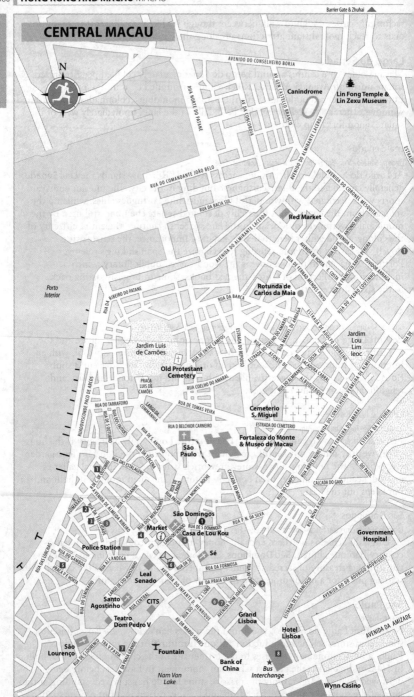

Barrier Gate & Zhuhai

CENTRAL MACAU

N

Porto
Interior

AVENIDO DO CONSELHEIRO BORJA

RUA NORTE DO PATANE

AV. DA CONCORDIA

AV. GEN CASTELO BRANCO

Canindrome

Lin Fong Temple &
Lin Zexu Museum

AVENIDO DO ALMIRANTE LACERDA

AVENIDA DO CORONEL MESQUITA

RUA DO COMANDANTE JOÃO BELO

RUA DA BACIA SUL

Red Market

RUA DE FERNÃO MENDES PINTO

AVENIDA DE HORTA E. COSTA

ANTONIO MOLE

RUA DO PE

AVENIDA DO

RUA DE FRANCISCO XAVIER PEREIRA

OUVIDOR ARRIAGA

RUA DE PEDRO COUTINHO

AVENIDA DO ALMIRANTE LACERDA

Rotunda de
Carlos da Maia

RUA DA BARCA

RUA DA RIBEIRO DO PATANE

RUA DE ENTRE CAMPOS

Jardim Luis
de Camões

Old Protestant
Cemetery

PRAÇA
LUIS DE
CAMÕES

RUA DO CAMPO DO AMARAL

ESTRADA DO REPOUSO

RUA MANUEL DE ARRIAGA

ESTRADA DE ADOLFO LOUREIRO

ESTRADA DO CELHO DO AMARAL

RUA AFONSO DE

RUA DO ALMIRANTE

RUA SACADURA CABRAL

COSTA CABRAL

Jardim
Lou
Lim
Ieoc

RUA DA

RUA DE TOMAS VEIRA

RUA COELHO DO AMARAL

Cemeterio
S. Miguel

RUA D BELCHIOR CARNEIRO

ESTRADA DO CEMETERIO

ALBUQUERQUE

AVENIDA DO CONSELHEIRO FERREIRA DE ALMEIDA

RUADOCONDE PAÇO DE ARGOS

RUA DO TARRAFEIRO

PRAÇA DA
COMMUNHIA

RUA DOS PRAZERES

LARGO DA

RUA DE S. ANTONIO

RUA DA TERCENA

São
Paulo

Fortaleza do Monte
& Museo de Macau

RUA DO CAMPO

RUA FERREIRA DO AMARAL

ESTRADA DA VITTORIA

RUA DAS ESTALAGENS

CALÇADA DO MONTE

RUA ABRIL NUNES

CALCADA DO GAIO

RUA C.COUTINHO

GUIMARÃES

RUA DE FELICIDADE

RUA DE ALMEIDA RIBEIRO

RUA PALHA

RUA MONTE CARONE

RUA DE SABADO

RUA DOS MERCADORES

RUA C.PESSANHA

São Domingos

RUA DE S DOMINGOS

RUA P. N. DA SILVA

RUA NOVA À SUÀ

Government
Hospital

Market

LARGO DO SENADO

Casa de Lou Kou

RUA DAS LORCHAS

RUA DO GAMBOA

Police Station

RUA DA S ANDEGA

PRAÇA P.F.HORTA

Sé

RUA DA SÉ

Leal
Senado

AVENIDA DO INFANTE D. HENRIQUE

RUA DA FORMOSA

RUA DO COMPO

ESTRADA DE S. FRANCISCO

RUA DE S. LOURENÇO

LARGO DE CID AGOSTINHO

Santo
Agostinho

RUA CENTRAL

CITS

AV DA PRAIA GRANDE

R.T LOIRO

AVENIDA DOM JOAO IV

Grand
Lisboa

AVENIDA DO DR RODRIGO RODRIGUES

Teatro
Dom Pedro V

RUA DO PRAIA GRANDE

AV DR MARIO SOARES

Hotel
Lisboa

AVENIDA DA AMIZADE

São
Lourenço

TRA V P X V LA

Fountain

Nam Van
Lake

Bank of
China

Bus
Interchange

Wynn Casino

Largo Do Lilau

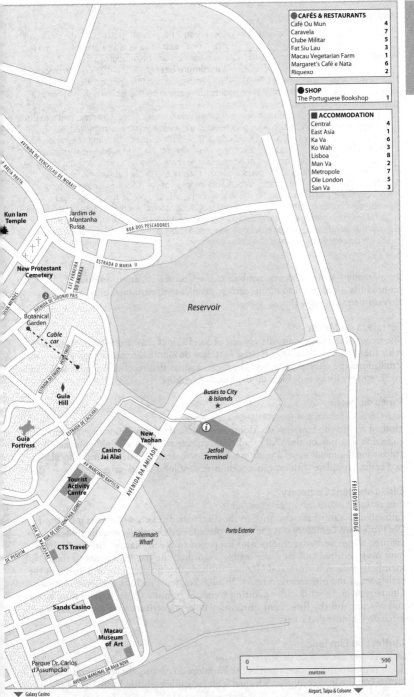

CAFÉS & RESTAURANTS

Café Ou Mun	4
Caravela	7
Clube Militar	5
Fat Siu Lau	3
Macau Vegetarian Farm	1
Margaret's Café e Nata	6
Riquexo	2

SHOP

The Portuguese Bookshop	1

ACCOMMODATION

Central	4
East Asia	1
Ka Va	6
Ko Wah	3
Lisboa	8
Man Va	2
Metropole	7
Ole London	5
San Va	3

9

> ## MACAU CASINOS
>
> Macau's 34 **casinos** (with several more under construction) are all open around the clock and have no clothing restrictions, though you must be at least 18 years of age, are not allowed to bring in cameras, and often have to show your passport and go through a security check at the door. Once inside, many games have a **minimum bet** of MOP$10–100. For information on how to play the various games, ask MGTO for a leaflet; signs in tiny print at the entrances to the casinos politely suggest that punters should engage in betting for fun only, and not as a means of making money.
>
> Each casino has its own atmosphere and (almost exclusively Chinese) clientele, and a **casino crawl** will provide a wide scope for people-watching, even if you're not interested in gambling. The *Casino Jai Alai* on Avenida do Dr Rodrigo Rodrigues is dark and verging on sleazy, with the feel of a hardcore den; the gold-windowed *Sands* on Avenida da Amizade has a Las Vegas slickness and colossal, open interior; the *Wynn* offers a sophisticated and elegant atmosphere; while the *Galaxy* – despite a smart exterior and bright lighting – is another low-end deal specializing in tacky carpets and an ocean of slot machines (known here as "hungry tigers"). Save time, too, for a look around the old *Hotel Lisboa*, the orange- and white-tiled building at the junction of Avenida da Amizade and Avenida Infante D. Henrique, still Macau's best-known casino despite being upstaged by its own new incarnation over the road, the *Grand Lisboa*, whose soaring, gold-topped tower proves that casino mogul Stanley Ho has no peer when it comes to ostentation.

iconography – there are doves, symbols of the Crucifixion, angels, statues of Jesuit saints – and political motifs such as peonies (representing China) and chrysanthemums (Japan).

Fortaleza do Monte

The tree-covered slope immediately east of São Paulo is crowned by another colonial relic, the seventeenth-century fortress **Fortaleza do Monte**. For some great views, take a stroll round the old ramparts, past the huge cannons that repelled a Dutch attack in 1622, when a lucky shot blew up the Dutch magazine.

Museo de Macau

Fortaleza do Monte • Tues–Sun 10am–6pm • MOP$15 • ⓦ macaumuseum.gov.mo

Housed within the Fortaleza do Monte, the **Museo de Macau** holds an excellent collection focusing on the SAR's traditions, culture and habits. Highlights include video shows, a mock-up of a traditional Macanese street and depictions of local arts and crafts, complete with evocative soundtracks of local sellers' cries.

Old Protestant Cemetery

Entrance off Bai Gechao Qiandi • Daily 8.30am–5.30pm • Free

Immediately east of the entrance to the nicely shaded **Luís de Camões garden**, the **Old Protestant Cemetery** was the burial place for all the non-Catholic traders, visitors, sailors and adventurers who happened to die in Macau. The gravestones have been restored and are quite legible, recording the last testaments to these mainly British, American and German individuals who died far from home in the early part of the nineteenth century. Famous residents include the artist **George Chinnery**, who spent decades painting scenes of colonial life in India, Hong Kong and Macau; and the Protestant missionary **Robert Morrison**, who produced an early English–Chinese dictionary.

Jardim Lou Lim Ieoc

Avenida do Conselheiro Ferreira de Almeida • Daily 6am–9pm • Free

A few hundred metres northwest of the Fortaleza do Monte, the scenic and calming **Jardim Lou Lim Ieoc** comprises a formal Chinese garden crowded with bamboos, pavilions, rocks and ancient trees arranged around a large pond. Financed during the nineteenth century by the wealthy Chinese merchant Lou Kou, it was modelled on Suzhou's classical gardens (see p.320) and typically manages to appear much more extensive than it really is. The galleries along the eastern side of the garden host occasional amateur operatics and contain a **tea museum**, with Chinese-only captions.

Guia Hill

Main entrance on Avenida de Sidonio Pais • Daily 7am–8.30pm • Free, cable car to summit MOP$1

Guia Hill is Macau's highest and steepest natural vantage point, despite rising only a few hundred metres above sea level. From the main entrance, the path winds through a small botanical garden up the hill; the whole hilltop is one breezy park, planted with trees and shrubs, with outstanding views of the SAR and neighbouring parts of China. At the summit stands the seventeenth-century **Guia Fortress**, the dominant feature of which is a whitewashed lighthouse, added in 1865 and reputed to be the oldest anywhere on the Chinese coast. The adjacent **Guia chapel** contains recently uncovered Christian frescoes featuring Chinese characters and dragons.

Avenida da Amizade

East of Guia Hill, the main thoroughfare is **Avenida da Amizade**, which runs parallel with the waterfront from the Jetfoil Terminal through a burgeoning **casino district**. Casinos aside, the most obvious attraction is the **Tourist Activity Centre** (Mon & Wed–Sun 10am–6pm), set back slightly on Rua de Luis Gonzaga Gomes, housing the entertaining **Wine Museum** (MOP$15) and the **Grand Prix Museum** (free), which features a scale mock-up of Macau's race circuit, plus a handful of Formula 1 cars.

Museum of Art

Avenida da Amizade • Tues–Sun 9am–7pm • MOP$15 • Ⓦ artmuseum.gov.mo

The waterfront **Macau Museum of Art** houses exhibitions of Chinese calligraphy, China trade paintings, Shiwan ceramics and historical documents. Down on the waterfront behind the museum, a 20m-high **bronze statue of Kun Iam** stands in front of views of the amazing, ribbon-like and hunchbacked **Taipa Bridge** and **Friendship Bridge**, both crossing to Taipa.

The Kun Iam Temple

Avenida do Coronel Mesquita • Daily 7am–6pm • Free • bus #12 from the *Hotel Lisboa*

Macau's major **Kun Iam Temple** is a 400-year-old complex dedicated to the Goddess of Mercy. Though a popular and busy sight, there's something a little decrepit about the temple's grubby granite halls and peeling frescoes. Historically, the temple marks the site of the **first Sino-American treaty**, signed in a rear courtyard in 1844, at which the Americans (in exchange for substantial trade rights similar to those recently forced by Britain) agreed to stop importing opium into China – a trade the British continued for another seventy years.

The Red Market and Three Lamps District

The **Red Market**, an Art Deco affair designed in 1936 by local architect Jio Alberto Basto, lies near the intersection of Avenida de Horta e Costa and Avenida do Almirante Lacerda. Arranged over three levels, the market is a very down-to-earth venue for buying slabs of meat and frozen seafood for the dinner table, along with live chickens, pigeons, ducks, fish, frogs and turtles.

Just south across Avenida de Horta e Costa, a warren of lanes chock-full of budget clothing stalls leads down to the blue-tiled Rotunda de Carlos da Maia, a roundabout marking the centre of the pedestrianized **Three Lamps District** or Sam Jan Dang. The whole area is a great place to browse and watch people bargaining for daily necessities.

9

To the border
Bus #3 or #10 from Avenida Almeida Ribeiro or the *Hotel Lisboa*

North of the Red Market, Avenida do Almirante Lacerda passes Macau's **Canidrome** – Southeast Asia's only greyhound track, with races every Monday, Thursday, Saturday and Sunday from 7.45pm – and the **Lin Fung Temple**, whose main point of interest is its accompanying **Lin Zexu Museum** (Tues–Sun 9am–5pm; MOP$10), a monument to the man who destroyed British opium stocks in Guangzhou and so precipitated the first Opium War (see p.918). Another 700m north is the Porto do Cerco, or **Barrier Gate**, the nineteenth-century stuccoed archway marking the border with China. These days the old gate itself is redundant – people use the modern customs and immigration complex (daily 7am–midnight) to one side.

The Barra
The small but hilly tongue of land south of Largo do Senado is known as **the Barra** – a tight web of lanes, with colonial mansions and their gardens looming up round every corner. The best way to begin an exploration is to walk south along **Rua Central** past the peppermint-coloured **Teatro Dom Pedro V**, built in 1873 and now serving as the members-only *Clube Macao*. Opposite is the early nineteenth-century church of **Santo Agostinho**, its pastel walls decorated with delicate piped icing. Further down on Rua de São Lourenço, the square-towered **São Lourenço** is a wonderfully tropical nineteenth-century church, with a mildewed exterior framed by palms and fig trees.

Largo do Lilau
At the Barra's heart, **Largo do Lilau** is a tiny, pretty square with a shady fig tree and **spring**, whose waters are said to impart longevity. This is the site of Macau's original residential area, and almost all the buildings here are over a century old. The showcase sight is the recently restored **Mandarin's House**, just off to one side at 10 Traversa da Silva (Mon, Tues & Thurs–Sun 10am–6pm; free), a heavy-walled traditional Chinese mansion built around 1869, though it's all a little bare inside.

Calçada da Barra
South of Largo do Lilau, Rua Central mutates into **Calçada da Barra**, which runs down to the A-Ma Temple (see below). Of the many elderly buildings here, you can't miss the strikingly crenellated, yellow-and-white **Moorish Barracks**, built in 1874 to house a Goan regiment and now home to the Port Office; you can enter during office hours to admire the startling array of antique weaponry in the small lobby.

The A-Ma Temple
Rua do Almirante Sérgio • Daily dawn–dusk • Free

Founded around 1370, the **A-Ma Temple** is dedicated to a girl whose spirit would appear to sailors in distress and guide them to land. When the Portuguese arrived during the 1550s, they unintentionally named the entire territory after her, "Macau" being a corruption of *a ma kok*, the name of the headland where the temple is set. The complex comprises a series of small halls and pavilions, jumbled about among granite boulders, some of which are carved with nautical motifs and symbols relating to the A-Ma story. The busiest time to visit is during the **A-Ma Festival**, held on the 23rd day of the third moon (April or May).

The Maritime Museum
Rua do Almirante Sérgio • Mon & Wed–Sun 10am–6pm • MOP$10

Macau's **Maritime Museum**, directly opposite the A-Ma Temple, is excellently presented, covering old explorers, seafaring techniques, equipment, models and boats. The whole collection is made accessible by abundant explanatory notes and video displays in English.

Avenida da Republica

The peninsula's southwestern extremity is accessed along tree-lined **Avenida da Republica**, the old seafront promenade. Today, its views take in **Sai Van Lake** and the 338m-high **Macau Tower** (daily 10am–9pm; various charges, up to MOP$70, depending on level of observation deck). At night, the waterfront promenade also offers Macau's version of Hong Kong's multicoloured harbourside skyline – except, of course, that here the financial institutions are casinos instead of banks.

Taipa, Cotai and Coloane

Macau's two islands, **Taipa** and **Coloane**, were originally dots of land supporting a few small fishing villages; now, joined by the rapidly developing strip of reclaimed land, **Cotai**, they look set to become part of a new entertainment district. Despite the development, both islands retain quiet pockets of colonial architecture where you can just about imagine yourself in some European village, while Coloane also has a fine beach.

Taipa

Taipa, site of Macau International Airport, racecourse, sports stadium, university and residential "suburbs", at first seems too developed to warrant a special stop. However, tiny **Taipa Village,** with its old colonial promenade and covered **Feira do Carmo** market square, makes a pleasant place for an extended lunch (see p.589).

Cotai

Formerly a spread of mud flats, reeds and sea between Taipa and Coloane islands, **Cotai** has now been landfilled and built upon to accommodate a burgeoning entertainment district. Foremost of the developments is the extraordinary **Venetian**, a full-scale reproduction of Venice's St Mark's Square housing the world's largest casino resort, with 850 gaming tables, 4100 slot machines and its own permanent Cirque du Soleil troupe. This is only the first of several similar projects, with **Macau Studio City** – combining a further resort and casino complex with film-production facilities – also set to open in the near future.

Coloane

Coloane, Macau's most southeasterly extremity, comprises nine square kilometres of hills, further colonial fragments and some decent **beaches**, making it a pleasant place to spend a few hours.

Coloane Village

All Coloane buses stop at quiet **Coloane Village**, overlooking mainland China just across the water; here, *Lord Stow's Bakery* (see p.588), at the sea end of the central square, offers irresistible **natas**, Portuguese egg tarts. To the north of the village are a few junk-building sheds, while the street leading south from the village roundabout, one block back from the shore, contains the unexpected yellow-and-white **St Francis Xavier Chapel**, where a relic of the saint's arm bone is venerated, as well as a couple of shops selling dried marine products.

TAIPA AND COLOANE BUSES

From Avenida Almeida Ribeiro on the peninsula, buses #11 and #33 go to Taipa Village; buses #21, #21A, #26 and #26A stop outside the *Hyatt Regency* on Taipa before going on to Coloane.

9

Hác Sá beach

Tree-lined **Hác Sá beach** is without doubt the best in Macau, despite the black colour of its volcanic sand. It has cafés, bars, showers and toilets and some fine restaurants nearby (see p.589), as well as a **sports and swimming pool complex** (Mon–Fri 9am–9pm, Sat & Sun 9am–midnight; MOP$15) which gets pretty crowded at weekends. Otherwise, try the **Parque Natural da Barragem de Hác Sá** (Tues–Fri 2–7pm, Sat & Sun 10am–7pm; MOP$10–40 for boat rental); a short hop from Hác Sá beach, this features barbecue pits, a kids' playground and maze, boating on a small reservoir, and various short trails in the hills.

ARRIVAL AND DEPARTURE
MACAU

BY PLANE

Macau International Airport Macau's airport is on Taipa. From the airport, buses #21 and #26 run to Avenida Almeida Ribeiro, or catch #AP1 to the Jetfoil Terminal.

Destinations Macau has air links to Taiwan, Bangkok, Kuala Lumpur, Manila, Seoul and Singapore, as well as an expanding range of Chinese cities including Beijing, Shanghai, Guangzhou, Xiamen and Kunming.

Hong Kong–Macau helicopter Sky Shuttle runs a helicopter service to Macau (ⓦ www.skyshuttlehk.com; MOP$3900) from the Hong Kong–Macau Ferry Terminal in Central (every 30min 9am–11pm; 15min).

BY FERRY

Macau currently has three ferry ports; two on the peninsula and one at Taipa. During the week you seldom need to book tickets in advance, though weekend and holiday traffic can become very busy. Allow at least half an hour to clear customs before departure; you need a passport, but no special visa, to travel between Macau and Hong Kong.

Jetfoil Terminal The main Jetfoil Terminal sits at the northern end of Avenida da Amizade. Ferries (ⓦ www .turbojet.com.hk; MOP$147) run to Hong Kong's two jetfoil terminals around the clock. Tickets can be bought on the second floor of the terminal or from discount booths on the ground floor. Exit the Jetfoil Terminal and there's a taxi rank and bus stop immediately outside; buses #3, #3A and #10A will get you into town.

Destinations China Ferry Terminal, Canton Road, Tsim Sha Tsui (every 30min 6.40am–10.30pm; 55min); Shun Tak

Centre, Sheung Wan, Hong Kong Island (every 15min 7am–midnight and then hourly; 55min).

Taipa Temporary Pier Next to the airport at Taipa; a permanent terminal is being built alongside. At the time of writing there's a ticket office, taxis and buses into town from a stop outside (MT1 or MT2 across the bridge to the Grand Lisboa; or any of the free casino buses), and a handful of daily departures to the Shun Tak Centre on Hong Kong Island (ⓦ turbojet.com.hk; $148).

Destinations Shun Tak Centre, Sheung Wan, Hong Kong Island (5 daily; 50min).

Porto Interior (Inner Harbour) Ferries to Shenzhen's Port, Shekou (ⓦ szgky.com; ¥190), use this easily missed terminal, about halfway down Rua Das Lorchas on Macau's western side.

Destinations Shekou (10 daily 9.45am–10.30pm; 1hr 20min).

BY BUS

Macau has no bus station, but CTS, based at the Jetfoil Terminal on Avenida da Amizade (ⓣ 2832 2950), run daily services between Macau and Hong Kong, Guangzhou or Zhaoqing in Guangdong province for MOP$50–120.

ON FOOT

The land border between Macau and Zhuhai in the Pearl River Delta is open daily 7am–midnight. Arriving in Macau you'll find yourself at the Porto do Cerco (Barrier Gate; see p.584); from here, take bus #AP1 to the Jetfoil Terminal, or #2, #3A, #5 or #18 to Avenida Almeida Ribeiro.

GETTING AROUND

BY BUS

Macau's comprehensive public bus network operates approximately from 7am to 11pm daily. Fares are a flat

MOP$3.20 on the peninsula, MOP$4.20 to Taipa, and MOP$5 to Coloane, except Hác Sá beach, which is MOP$6.40; you need the exact fare, as change is not

---

MACAU ENTRY REGULATIONS

Visa regulations currently state that citizens of Britain, Ireland and most European countries can stay 90 days on arrival; citizens of Australia, New Zealand, Canada, South Africa, the US and several others can stay 30 days on arrival – check ⓦ www.macautourism.gov.mo for the latest.

9

given. Important interchanges include the Jetfoil Terminal; outside the *Hotel Lisboa*; Avenida Almeida Ribeiro; Barra (near the A-Ma Temple); and the Porto do Cerco.

INFORMATION

Tourist offices The Macau Government Tourist Office, or MGTO (tourist hotline ☎ 2833 3000, ⓦ macautourism.gov .mo) provides helpful leaflets on Macau's fortresses, museums, parks, churches, self-guided walks and outlying islands as well as a good city map. The main office (daily 9am–6pm) is at Largo do Senado 9, with additional counters (all same hours) at the airport, the ferry terminals and the Zhuhai border crossing at Porto do Cerco. In Hong Kong, the Macau Government Tourist Office is at the Macau

BY TAXI
Taxis have a flag fall of MOP$15. The one-way fare, including surcharges, from downtown to Coloane's Hác Sá beach (the longest trip you can possibly make) costs about MOP$90.

Ferry Terminal, Shun Tak Centre, Sheung Wan, Hong Kong Island (☎ 2857 2287).
Travel agents Beng Seng Travel, 310–312 Shun Tak Centre, 200 Connaught Rd, Hong Kong (☎ 2540 3838). can organize discounted ferry tickets and accommodation in Macau; CTS, Jetfoil Terminal, Avenida da Amizade, Macau (daily 9am–8pm; ☎ 2832 2950, ⓦ www.ctshk.com), can book all flights, buses and accommodation, and visas for mainland China.

ACCOMMODATION

Accommodation is good value in Macau: the money that would get you a dingy box in Hong Kong here provides a clean room with private shower and a window. Still, there are fewer real budget options, and at weekends, holidays and during the Macau Grand Prix (third weekend in November) **prices** can more than double from those given below. Online deals and agents in Hong Kong such as CTS offer good-value transport and accommodation packages. The densest concentration and variety of hotels is found on the peninsula – especially in the vicinity of Avenida de Almirante Ribeiro – though Taipa, Cotai and Coloane also sport several upmarket resorts. Note that **addresses** in Macau are written with the number after the name of the street.

MACAU PENINSULA

Central Avenida de Almeida Ribeiro 26–28 ☎ 2837 3888; map pp.580–581. Hundreds of budget rooms on seven floors in this elderly, occasionally disturbingly dingy block just around the corner from the Largo do Senado. Bearable for a night or two if you're on a budget, but insist on seeing the room before paying. MOP$260

East Asia Rua da Madeira 1 ☎ 2892 2433; map pp.580–581. One of Macau's oldest hotels – a little shabby and basic, but comfortable enough, with friendly staff and good views from some of the upstairs windows. MOP$350

Ka Va Calcada de Sao Joao 5 ☎ 2832 3063; map pp.580–581. On the left as you head uphill from Rua da Sé to the Sé church. A good budget choice if you stick to the tidy rear rooms, though those facing the street are windowless and prone to damp. MOP$500

Ko Wah Rua da Felicidade 71 ☎ 2893 0755; map pp.580–581. Inexpensive hostel in one of Macau's most interesting quarters. Ride the lift from the cupboard-sized lobby to the second floor, where the rooms range from fairly modern to quite old; all are clean and en suite. MOP$350

Lisboa Avenida de Lisboa 2–4 ☎ 2837 7666, HK reservations ☎ 800 969130, ⓦ hotelisboa.com; map pp.580–581. Once the most ostentatious building in Macau – but now overshadowed by the ludicrous *Grand Lisboa* opposite – tiled in orange and white and housing a casino, a shopping arcade and numerous restaurants. MOP$930

★ **Man Va** Travessa da Caldeira 30 ☎ 2838 8655; map pp.580–581. Clean and well-designed rooms with

spacious bathrooms, spotless carpets and helpful management, though there's no English spoken. Top value. MOP$350

Metropole Avenida Praia Grande 493–501 ☎ 2838 8166, ⓦ macautshotel.com; map pp.580–581. A few hundred metres west of the *Lisboa*; well located and smartly fitted out, and you should find good deals on most discount booking websites. MOP$830

Ole London Praça Ponte e Horta 4–6 ☎ 2893 7761; map pp.580–581. Smart little boutique hotel with modern rooms and broadband available. The cheapest rooms are windowless; it's best to pay a little extra for one looking out onto the square outside. MOP$800

Pousada de São Tiago Fortaleza de Barra, Avenida da República ☎ 2837 8111, ⓦ saotiago.com.mo; map pp.580–581. Constructed from a seventeenth-century fortress on the southern tip of the peninsula, with walled stairways lined by gushing streams, huge stone archways and twelve luxurious suites. There's nothing else like this in all of China. MOP$2600

★ **San Va** Rua da Felicidade 67 ☎ 8210 0193, ⓦ sanvahotel.com; map pp.580–581. The best budget deal in town, with no-frills but spotless rooms in an atmospheric early-1900s building featuring wooden shutters and balconies over Rua da Felicidade. Friendly management. MOP$190

COTAI AND COLOANE

★ **Pousada de Coloane** Praia de Cheoc Van, Coloane ☎ 2888 2143, ⓦ hotelpcoloane.com.mo; map p.577.

9

Great scenery, if a somewhat remote location, situated by Cheoc Van beach on Coloane's far south shore. All rooms have balconies overlooking the beach, there's a swimming pool and an Italian restaurant. If you want a relaxing holiday experience, this is the place for it. MOP$1400

Venetian Cotai ☎ 2882 8877, ⊛ venetianmacao.com; map p.577. A 3000-room resort, convention centre and casino complex, all packed into a full-scale replica of St Mark's Square in Venice (including canals with gondolas) – the convention space here alone is greater than the total available in Hong Kong. Rooms are well-serviced, modern and an excellent deal for the price. MOP$1700

Westin Resort Estrada de Hác Sá, Coloane ☎ 2887 1111, ⊛ starwoodhotels.com; map p.577. At the far end of Hác Sá's fine beach, this resort is good for a quiet day or two, midweek, although it fills up with Hong Kong families at the weekend. Three restaurants and excellent sports facilities, including an eighteen-hole golf course, two pools and a jacuzzi. Often does good weekend special offers. MOP$1300

EATING, DRINKING AND NIGHTLIFE

Places specializing in Macanese food are plentiful, as are **Cantonese restaurants**, which often serve dim sum for breakfast and lunch, though you'll find wine on the menus even here. **Prices** for the typically generous portions are low compared to Hong Kong, with bills even in smart venues rarely exceeding MOP$250 per person, though watch out for little extras such as water, bread and so forth, which can really add to the cost of a meal. A bottle of house red will set you back around MOP$120 in a restaurant. Macau's **nightlife** is surprisingly flat, if you don't count the casinos. Drinking is done in restaurants or in the handful of bars in the "Macau Lan Kwai Fong", located along the waterfront facing the Porto Exterior, and offering live music and street-side tables.

CAFÉS

★ **Café Ou Mun** Travessa de Sao Domingos 12, off Largo do Senado ☎ 2837 2207; map pp.580–581. Fantastic breads, cakes and coffee, and light meals. Very popular at lunchtime. Mon 11am–7pm, Tues–Sun 9am–10pm.

Caravela Patio Commandante Mata e Oliveira 7, off Avenida Dom João IV ☎ 2871 3080; map pp.580–581. Down an alley near the Grand Lisboa, this smart place serves top coffee, cakes and light meals through the day, and has a host of Portuguese expat regulars – who can get snotty about visitors taking "their" chairs. Daily 10am–6pm.

★ **Lord Stow's Bakery** Coloane Village Square ☎ 2888 2534; map p.577. The best baked custard tarts in Macau, said to be made to a secret recipe without animal fat. Buy takeaways from the bakery, or sit down for coffee and a light meal at their café around the corner. Daily 7am–10pm.

Margaret's Café e Nata Rua Comandante Mata e Oliveira ☎ 2871 0032; map pp.580–581. Surrounded by gloomy apartment blocks, this is an excellent café with outdoor benches and first-rate sandwiches and baked custard tarts. Daily 10am–6pm.

RESTAURANTS

MACAU PENINSULA

360° Café Level 60, Macau Tower ☎ 8988 8622; map p.577. One of Macau's classiest places to dine, serving Indian, Macanese and plain grilled seafood in a revolving restaurant with unparalleled views. One way not to bankrupt yourself is to opt for the set buffets (MOP$168 for lunch, MOP$248 for supper). Daily 11.30am–3pm & 7–10.30pm.

A Lorcha Rua da Almirante Sérgio 289 ☎ 2831 3193; map p.577. Genuine and excellent Spanish, Macanese and Portuguese food; the seafood rice and beer clams are both outstanding. Around MOP$200/head. Wed–Sun 12.30–3.30pm & 7–11.30pm.

Clube Militar Avenida da Praia Grande 975 ☎ 2871 4000; map pp.580–581. Smart, old-world dining room with polished wooden floors and silver service inside a private club, though the restaurant is open to the public. Stay off the à la carte menu and opt instead for the set-price lunchtime buffet, which is fantastic value at MOP$150 and includes a choice of soups, starters, mains and desserts. Daily noon–3pm & 7–11pm.

MACANESE FOOD

Macanese cuisine fuses Chinese with Portuguese elements, further overlaid with tastes from Portugal's Indian and African colonies. Fresh bread, wine and coffee all feature, as well as an array of dishes ranging from caldo verde (vegetable soup) to bacalhau (dried salted cod). Macau's most interesting Portuguese colonial dish is probably **African chicken**, a concoction of Goan and East African influences, comprising chicken grilled with peppers and spices. Other things worth trying include Portuguese baked custard tarts (natas), served in many cafés; almond biscuits, formed in a wooden mould and baked in a charcoal oven, which can be bought by weight in many pastellarias, such as Koi Kei, around São Paulo and Rua da Felicidade; and sheets of pressed roast meat, also sold in pastellarias.

9

Fat Siu Lau Rua da Felicidade 64 ☎ 2857 3580; map pp.580–581. A very popular, traditional old restaurant whose speciality is marinated roast pigeon, though they also do a great crab curry. Around MOP$200/head. Daily noon–11pm.

Litoral Rua da Almirante Sérgio 261-A ☎ 2896 7878, ⓦ restaurante-litoral.com; map p.577. Reputedly the best place for Macanese food in Macau, with excellent charcoal-grilled African chicken, feijoada and stewed chicken rice. Their serradura is the business, too. Portions are huge and two could easily share one main and a salad. Around $350 a head with wine. Daily noon–3pm & 6–10.30pm.

Macau Vegetarian Farm (田耕閣素緣食) Opposite the Kun Iam Temple, Avenida do Coronel Mesquita 11 ☎ 2875 2824; map pp.580–581. Warehouse-sized restaurant offering good-quality Chinese vegetarian cuisine at MOP$30–50 a dish; no English translations, but lots of photos of the food on menus. Daily 11am–3pm & 5.30–10pm.

★ **O Porto Interior** Rua da Almirante Sérgio 259-B ☎ 2896 7770; map p.577. Just by the A-Ma Temple, this restaurant features antique Chinese screens, superb old Macanese cuisine such as African chicken or grilled sardines, plus a splendid wine cellar. Around MOP$250/head. Daily 11.30am–10pm.

Riquexo Avenida de Sidónio Pais 69-B ☎ 2856 5655; map pp.580–581. Self-service Portuguese canteen with no frills at all, though the food is hearty, and nearby office workers flock here for lunch. The menu changes daily but is likely to include feijoada, curry chicken,

grilled lamb and bacalhau – at MOP$28–55 a serving. Mon–Fri 11am–6pm.

TAIPA

Galo In the square at Rua da Cunha 45, Taipa Village ☎ 2882 7423; map p.577. Cute, blue-shuttered place with low prices and a family-run feel. The crab is good, and the emphasis is on providing a plateful of hearty flavours, rather than cuisine. About MOP$180/head. Mon–Fri 10.30am–3.30pm & 5.30–10.30pm, Sat & Sun 10.30am–10.30pm.

O Santos Rua da Cunha, Taipa Village ☎ 2882 7508; map p.577. Huge helpings of seafood rice, pork and bean stew, rabbit, roast suckling pig and other Portuguese mainstays, from MOP$85. Wed–Sun noon–3pm & 6.30–10.30pm.

COLOANE

Chan Chi Mei/Nga Tim Next to the St Francis Xavier Chapel, Coloane Village ☎ 2888 2086; map p.577. A friendly Chinese place with outdoor tables under a colonnade, ideal for lunch or an evening drink; the best dishes on the menu are crab or pork knuckle. Most mains under MOP$70. Daily noon–1am.

Fernando Hác Sá beach, not far from the bus stop ☎ 2888 2531; map p.577. A casual, cheerful atmosphere and great Portuguese food make this place a favourite with expats. You might need a taxi to get home, though. Advance booking recommended, and a necessity at weekends. About MOP$200/head. Daily except May 1, noon–9.30pm.

DIRECTORY

Banks and exchange Most banks have branches around the junction of Avenida Almeida Ribeiro and Avenida Praia Grande, where you'll also find plenty of attached ATMs. Banks generally open Mon–Fri from 9am until 4pm or 4.30pm, but close by lunchtime on Sat. There are also licensed moneychangers that exchange travellers' cheques (and that open seven days a week), including a 24hr one in the basement of the *Hotel Lisboa*, and one near the bottom of the steps leading up to São Paulo.

Bookshop The Portuguese Bookshop, Rua de São Domingos 18–22 (near São Domingos church), has a small English-language section with books on Macau's history, cuisine and buildings.

Festivals The normal Chinese holidays are celebrated in Macau, plus some Catholic festivals introduced from Portugal, such as the annual Procession of Our Lady of

Fatima from São Domingos church (May 13).

Hospital There's a 24hr emergency department at the Centro Hospitalar Conde São Januário, Calçada Visconde São Januário (☎ 2831 3731); English is spoken.

Mail Macau's main post office is on the east side of Largo do Senado (Mon–Fri 9am–6pm, Sat 9am–1pm); poste restante is delivered here. Small red booths all over the territory also dispense stamps from machines.

Police The main police station is on Avenida do Dr Rodrigo Rodrigues (☎ 2857 3333). For emergencies, call ☎ 999.

Telephones Local calls are free from private phones and cost MOP$1 from payphones. Cardphones work with CTM cards, issued by the Macau State Telecommunication Company, and on sale in hotels or at the back of the main post office (open 24hr), where you can also make direct calls.

Guangxi
and
Guizhou

DONG DRUM TOWER, ZHAOXING VILLAGE

Guangxi and Guizhou

The subtropical southwestern provinces of Guangxi and Guizhou are defined by limestone: local rivers are coloured a vivid blue-green by it; everywhere you look are weathered karst hills worn into poetic collections of tall, sharp peaks; and underground is a network of extensive caverns, some flooded, others large enough to fit a cathedral inside. Though something of a tourist phenomenon today, historically this rugged topography has proved an immense barrier to communications and, being porous, created some of China's least arable land, with agriculture often confined to the small alluvial plains in between peaks. So poor that it wasn't worth the trouble of invading, for a long while the region was pretty well ignored by mainstream China, and evolved into a stronghold for ethnic groups. But a period of social stability during the early Qing dynasty caused a population explosion in eastern China and an expansion westwards by the Han.

Some of the ethnic minorities kept their nominal identity but more or less integrated with the Chinese, while others resisted assimilation by occupying isolated highlands; but the new settlers put pressure on available resources, creating a hotbed of resentment against the government. This finally exploded in central Guangxi's **Taiping Uprising** of 1850 (see p.312), marking the start of a century of devastating civil conflict. Even today local economies remain underdeveloped and few of the cities – including **Nanning** and **Guiyang**, the provincial capitals – have much to offer except transport to more interesting locations.

Despite its bleak history, the region offers a huge range of diversions. The landscape is epitomized by the tall karst towers surrounding the city of **Guilin** in northeastern Guangxi, familiar to Chinese and Westerners alike through centuries of eulogistic art. Equally impressive are cave systems at **Longgong** and **Zhijin** in western Guizhou, while there's also the chance of close contact with ethnic groups, particularly the **Miao**, **Dong** and **Zhuang**, whose wooden villages, exuberant festivals, and traces of a prehistoric past are all worth indulging. It's also one of the few places in the country where you can be fairly sure of encountering rare wildlife: notably cranes at **Caohai** in Guizhou's far west.

Improving transport infrastructure means that **travel** across the region is fairly straightforward – though rural dialects are sometimes incomprehensible. **Weather** is fairly localized, though you should expect hot, wet summers and surprisingly cold winters, especially up in the hills.

CORMORANT FISHING ON THE LI RIVER

Highlights

❶ Li River Cruise between Guilin and Yangshuo through a forest of tall, weirdly contorted karst peaks. **See p.601**

❷ Dong villages Communities of wooden houses, bridges and drum towers pepper remote rural highlands along the Guangxi–Guizhou border. **See p.612**

❸ Hua Shan Another boat trip to see a whole cliffside of mysterious rock art flanking Guangxi's Zuo River. **See p.619**

❹ Sisters' Meal Festival Exuberant showpiece of Miao culture, featuring three days of dancing, bull fighting and dragon-boat racing. **See p.630**

❺ Zhijin Caves The largest, most spectacular of China's subterranean limestone caverns, full of creatively named rock formations. **See p.638**

❻ Caohai Spend a day punting around this beautiful lake, a haven for ducks and rare black-necked cranes. **See p.639**

HIGHLIGHTS ARE MARKED ON THE MAP ON PP.594–595

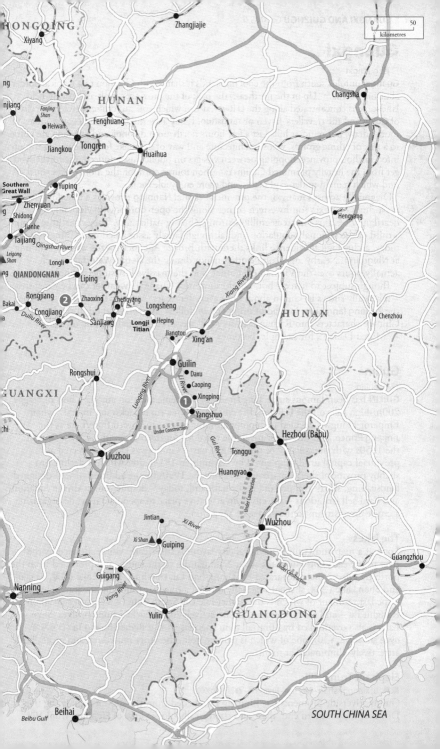

Guangxi

广西, guǎngxī

Guangxi unfolds south from the cool highlands it shares with Guizhou to a tropical border abutting Vietnam. Up in the northeast, the pick of the province's peak-and-paddy-field landscape is concentrated along the **Li River**, down which you can cruise between the city of **Guilin** and the travellers' haven of **Yangshuo**. Easily accessible, this has become a massive tourist draw, but remoter hills just a few hours north around **Longji** and **Sanjiang** are home to a mix of ethnic groups, whose architecture and way of life make for a fascinating trip up into Guizhou province, hopping between villages on public buses. Indeed, the further you get from the heavily promoted Guilin-Yangshuo tourist corridor, the more places you'll find which remain under-exploited – and more enjoyable for it.

Diagonally across Guangxi, the provincial capital **Nanning** provides a base for exploring Guangxi's southwestern corner along the **open border with Vietnam**, heartland of China's thirteen-million-strong Zhuang nationality. They constitute about a third of the regional population and, although largely assimilated into Chinese life today, archeological evidence links them with Bronze Age **rock friezes** west of Nanning at **Ningming**. Nearby are a couple other major draws: the **Detian Waterfall**, which actually pours over the Vietnamese border, and the massive limestone sinkholes at **Leye**.

Though subject to fiercely hot, humid summers, Guangxi's **weather** can be deceptive – it actually snows in Guilin about once every ten years. Another thing of note is that the **Zhuang language**, instead of using *pinyin*, follows its own method of rendering Chinese characters into Roman text, so you'll see some unusual spelling on signs – "Minzu Dadao", for example, becomes "Minzuzdadau".

Guilin

桂林, guìlín

GUILIN has been famous since Tang times for its scenic location among a host of craggy, 200m-high hills on the **Li River**. The city rose from a rural backwater in 1372 when Emperor Hongwu decided to appoint a minor relative to govern from here as the **Jinjiang Prince**, and this quasi-royal line ruled for fourteen generations, dying out in the 1650s with the collapse of the Ming dynasty. Guilin was later resurrected as provincial capital until supplanted by Nanning in 1914, after which it declined to a shabby provincial shell. Smartened up since the 1990s by the addition of well-designed landscaping, shady avenues and rocky parkland, today – despite tourist-driven inflation and hard-sell irritations – the city is an attractive place to spend a day while organizing a cruise downstream to the village of Yangshuo.

The lakes

Look at a map and Guilin's medieval city layout is still clearly visible, defined by the river to the east, Gui Hu to the west, Nanhuan Lu to the south, and protected from the north by Diecai Shan. Separated by Zhongshan Lu, tree-lined **Rong Lake** (榕湖, rónghú) and **Shan Lake** (衫湖, shānhú) originally formed a moat surrounding the inner city walls – the last remnant of which is the tunnel-like **Old South Gate** (古南门, gǔ nánmén) on Ronghu Lu – and are now crossed by attractively hunchbacked stone bridges. Shan Lake is also overlooked by 40m-tall twin pagodas named **Riyue Shuang Ta** (日月双塔, rìyuè shuāngtǎ; ¥30), one of which is painted gold, the other muted red and green, both attractively illuminated at night.

Elephant Trunk Hill

象鼻山, xiàngbí shān • Daily 7am–10pm • ¥75 • ☎ 773 2803000

Guilin's riverside promenade is Binjiang Lu, shaded from the summer sun by fig trees. Down at the southern end, these also strategically block views of **Elephant Trunk Hill**,

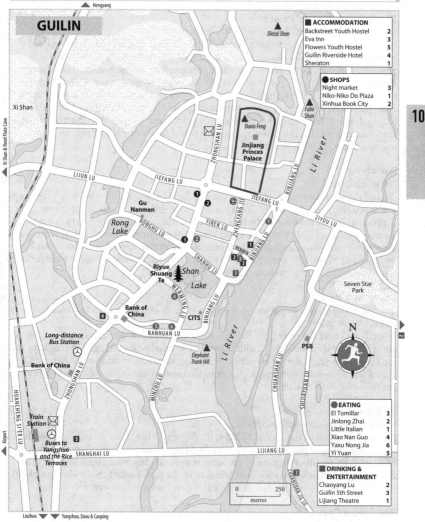

GUILIN

▲ Hengyang

Diecai Shan

Xi Shan

Xi Shan & Reed Flute Cave

Fubo Shan

Duxiu Feng

Jinjiang Princes Palace

Li River

ZHONGSHAN LU

LIJUN LU

JIEFANG LU

JIEFANG LU

BINJIANG LU

ZIYOU LU

Gu Nanmen

Rong Lake

RONGHU LU

YIREN LU

ZHENGYANG JIE

SHANHU LU

RENMIN LU

BINJIANG LU

Riyue Shuang Ta

Shan Lake

WEIMING LU

Seven Star Park

Bank of China

BINJIANG LU

CITS

Long-distance Bus Station

NANHUAN LU

Li River

PSB

Bank of China

MINZHU LU

Elephant Trunk Hill

CHUANSHAN LU

SHIJIAYUAN LU

N

HUANCHENG SI ER LU

Airport

Train Station

Buses to Yangshuo and the Rice Terraces

SHANGHAI LU

LIJIANG LU

CHANGSHAN JIE LU

Liuzhou ▼ ▼ Yangshuo, Daxu & Caoping

0   250
metres

■ ACCOMMODATION
Backstreet Youth Hostel	2
Eva Inn	3
Flowers Youth Hostel	5
Guilin Riverside Hotel	4
Sheraton	1

● SHOPS
Night market	3
Niko-Niko Do Plaza	1
Xinhua Book City	2

10

● EATING
El Tomillar	3
Jinlong Zhai	2
Little Italian	1
Xiao Nan Guo	4
Yaxu Nong Jia	6
Yi Yuan	5

■ DRINKING & ENTERTAINMENT
Chaoyang Lu	2
Guilin 5th Street	3
Lijiang Theatre	1

said to be the fossilized body of a sick imperial baggage elephant who was cared for by locals. For once the name is not poetically obscure; the jutting cliff with an arched hole at the base really does resemble an elephant taking a drink from the river. There's an easy walk to a podgy pagoda on top, and, at river level, you can have your photo taken holding a parasol while you sit next to a cormorant on a brightly coloured bamboo raft.

Fubo Shan

伏波山, fúbō shān • Daily 7am–7pm • ¥30 • ☏ 0773 2803000

Two kilometres upstream from Elephant Trunk Hill, at the north end of Binjiang Lu, **Fubo Shan** is a complementary peak, whose grottoes are carved with worn Tang- and Song-dynasty Buddha images. At the base is the "Sword-testing Stone", a stalactite hanging within 10cm of the ground, which indeed appears to have been hacked through. Steps to Fubo's summit (200m) provide smog-free views of Guilin's low rooftops.

10

The Jinjiang Princes' Palace

靖江王府, jìngjiāng wángfǔ · Daily 8.30am–5pm · ¥70 · ☎ 0773 2803149

North off Jiefang Lu, the **Jinjiang Princes' Palace** is where Guilin's Ming rulers lived between 1372 and 1650. Resembling a miniature Forbidden City in plan (and predating Beijing's by 34 years), it is still surrounded by 5m-high stone walls, though the original buildings were destroyed at the end of the Ming dynasty, and those here today date from the late Qing and house Guangxi's Teachers' Training College. Some older fragments remain, notably a **stone slab** by the entrance embellished with clouds but no dragons, indicating the residence of a prince, not an emperor. The **museum** has abundant historical curios, modern portraits of the fourteen Jinjiang princes, and remains from one of their **tombs**.

Duxiu Feng

独秀峰, dúxiù fēng

Behind the museum – and protecting the buildings from the "unlucky" north direction – is **Duxiu Feng**, another small, sharp pinnacle with 306 steep steps to the summit. Legend has it that the **cave** at the base of the hill was opened up by the tenth prince, thereby breaking Duxiu Feng's luck and seeding the dynasty's downfall. Get someone to point out the bland, eight-hundred-year-old **inscription** carved on Duxiu's side by the governor Wang Zhenggong, which is apparently responsible for the city's fame and translates as "Guilin's Scenery is the Best Under Heaven".

Seven Star Park

七星公园, qīxīng gōngyuán · Daily 7am–7pm · ¥50 · cavern ¥60 · bus #11 via Zhongshan Lu and Jiefang Lu stops outside · 20min walk from the city centre

Directly east over the river from the city, Guilin's most extensive limestone formations are at **Seven Star Park**. With a handful of small wooded peaks arranged in the shape of the Great Bear (Big Dipper) constellation, a large cavern lit with coloured lights and even a few semi-wild monkeys, it's a sort of Guangxi in miniature, and makes a fun excursion on a sunny day.

Xi Shan

西山, xīshān · ¥75 · bus #3 or #4 from Zhongshan Lu

Around 2km west of the centre, **Xi Shan**, the Western Hills, is an area of long Buddhist associations, whose peaks are named after Buddhist deities. **Xiqinglin Temple** here is filled with hundreds of exquisitely executed statues ranging from 10cm to more than 2m in height. There's also a regional **museum** in the park (daily 8.30am–5.30pm; ¥20), which is a massive collection of ethnic clothing and revolutionary gear.

Reed Flute Cave

芦笛岩, lúdí yán · Daily 8am–5.30pm · ¥90 · bus #3 from Zhongshan Lu

Some 6km north of Xi Shan, **Reed Flute Cave** is a huge warren eaten into the south side of Guangming Shan which once provided a refuge from banditry and Japanese bombs. The caverns are not huge, but there are some interesting formations and a small underground lake, which makes for some nice reflections. You're meant to follow one of the tours (some in English) that run every twenty minutes, but you can always linger inside and pick up a later group if you want to spend more time.

ARRIVAL AND DEPARTURE GUILIN

Details for arranging Li River cruises to Yangshuo are covered on p.601.

BY PLANE
Liangjiang International Airport (桂林两江国际机场, guìlín liǎngjiāng guójì jīchǎng) is 30km west of

the city, connected to the train station by airport bus (every 30min 6.30am–9pm; ¥20) and taxi to downtown (around ¥100). Guilin is linked to cities across the mainland, as well as to Hong Kong, Korea and Malaysia. Buy tickets at the CITS or hotel tour desks; Air China have an office at 15 Binjiang Lu, near the *Sheraton* (daily 9am–6pm; ☎ 0773 2866567).

Destinations Beijing (5 daily; 3hr); Chengdu (1 daily; 1hr 40min); Guangzhou (5 daily; 1hr); Guiyang (1 daily; 50min); Hong Kong (2 daily; 1hr); Kunming (3 daily; 1hr 20min); Shanghai (8 daily; 2hr 15min); Shenzhen (3 daily; 1hr 10min); Xi'an (5 daily; 1hr 45min).

BY TRAIN

Guilin train station (桂林火车站, guìlín huǒchē zhàn) is set at the back of a large square off Zhongshan Lu, with direct services to Nanning, Shanghai, Xi'an, Beijing, Guangzhou, Chongqing and Kunming. If you book a few days in advance you should get what you want; queues are not too bad at the station ticket office (daily 7.30–11.30am, 12.30–2.30pm, 3–7pm, & 7.30–9.30pm), though the ticket desk in the Binjiang Lu CITS office (daily 9am–12.30pm & 1.30–6pm) usually has no queues at all.

Destinations Beijing (4 daily; 23–28hr); Changsha (9 daily; 7hr 26min–11hr 42min); Guangzhou (2 daily; 12hr); Guiyang (1 daily; 13hr 33min); Kunming (3 daily; 18hr 40min–23hr); Nanning (16 daily; 5hr 34min–6hr 31min); Shanghai (4 daily; 20–24hr); Shenzhen (1 daily; 13hr 30min).

BY BUS

Guilin long-distance bus station (桂林汽车客运枢纽, guìlín qìchē kèyùn shūniǔ) is 200m north of the train station on Zhongshan Lu. Bear in mind you're likely to get a much better seat here than if picking through services up at Yangshuo.

Destinations Guangzhou (12hr); Hengyang (12hr); Heping (2hr); Nanning (6hr); Sanjiang (4hr); Yangshuo (1hr 15min).

Yangshuo buses Express buses to Yangshuo (1hr 30min; ¥18) arrive and depart from the train station forecourt every few minutes through the day; watch out for bag-slashers and pickpockets who target tourists.

Rice terrace minibuses Minibuses to either Ping An or Dazhai (2hr; ¥60) leave from the train station forecourt (there's a sign), whenever they have at least four passengers, until after 9pm.

GETTING AROUND

By bus Bus fares are a maximum of ¥2.
By taxi Taxis cost ¥7 to hire, with a ¥1 fuel surcharge added to all fares.

INFORMATION

Tour agents Your hotel or the main CITS at 11 Binjiang Lu (☎ 0773 2866789, ⓦ guilincits.com) can sort out river cruises, book onward transport, flights, and organize day-trips to Longji Titian rice terraces (departing daily 8am; ¥350).
Maps The useful *Tour and Communication Map of Guilin* (¥5–10) is sold at most hotels and bookshops.

ACCOMMODATION

Guilin's hotels are mostly mid-range and upmarket, with the choice of youth hostels if you're after a budget bed. Competition is pretty stiff and year-round discounted rates of fifty percent are not unusual. The nicest location is along the river, with lakeside options the next best thing. Everywhere has a booking desk for cruises and local tours.

Backstreet Youth Hostel 后街国际青年旅馆, hòujiē guójì qīngnián lǚguǎn. 3 Renmin Lu, near the Sheraton ☎ 0773 2819936, ⓔ guilinhostel@hotmail.com. Excellent location in the centre of town and close to the river, with café, internet and plain, comfortable doubles and triples – the one drawback being the persistent hawkers swarming outside. Staff speak very good English. Dorms ¥45, rooms ¥145
Eva Inn 四季春天酒店, sìjì chūntiān jiǔdiàn. 66 Binjiang Lu, close to the Sheraton ☎ 0773 2830666, ⓦ evainn.com. Pleasant boutique-style place with smart, modern rooms and decent service despite the pokiness of the lobby. Most notable for being the least expensive of the riverside hotels with a water view, especially from its stylish rooftop café. ¥360
★ **Flowers Youth Hostel** 花满国际青年旅馆, huāmǎnguójì qīngnián lǚguǎn. 6 Shangzhi Gang, Block 2, Zhongshan Lu ☎ 0773 3839625, ⓦ yhaguilin .com. A great option, hidden away behind the bright

yellow *Home Inn* directly opposite the train station: walk through a dreary alley to the back of the hotel from where it's signposted up a flight of stairs. Warm, clean and friendly place, with a bar, café, internet, dorms and doubles, as well as good-value tours. Dorms ¥40, rooms ¥110
★ **Guilin Riverside** 桂林九龙别墅酒店, guìlín jiǔlóng biéshù jiǔdiàn. 5 Zhu Mu Xiang, Nanmen Qiao ☎ 0773 2580215, ⓦ www.guilin-hostel.com. A real gem, hidden down a quiet lane right in the town centre and set up like a European B&B. Very friendly and organized, so usually full. Rooms are clean and comfortable, and many have balconies with water views. ¥220
Sheraton 大宇大饭店, dàyǔ dàfàndiàn. 15 Binjiang Lu ☎ 0773 2825588, ⓦ sheraton.com/guilin. One of the nicest hotels in town, with the best rooms overlooking the river and across to Seven Star Park, though you pay about fifty percent extra for the privilege. Also has a nice coffee shop serving a ¥130 buffet breakfast. ¥2000

10

EATING

Guilin's restaurants are famous for serving rare game meats, and many places display live caged pheasants, cane rats, turtles, fish and snakes outside. Less confrontational options include Western, Italian and Thai restaurants on pedestrianized Zhengyang Jie, with standard Chinese fare available along Nanhuan Lu, Wenming Lu and Yiren Lu. For cheap stir-fries and one-dish meals, try the canteens around the long-distance bus station.

El Tomillar 66 Bingjian Lu ☎0773 2888255. Next to the *Backstreet Youth Hostel*, this rates as one of the better foreign restaurants in Guilin, with the Chinese owner having lived for more than five years in Spain and usually mistaken for a Spaniard. Great tapas and good paella with friendly service in a Spanish ambience. Serves a small, but very good, selection of wines from la Rioja, which are probably the best in town for the price of ¥35/glass. Mains ¥35 upwards. Daily 11am–midnight.

Jinlong Zhai 金龙寨, jīnlóng zhài. 4F, corner of Zhongshan Lu and the adjacent plaza ☎0773 2825533, ⊛jinlongzhai.com. Famous Guangxi chain specializing in local country dishes, such as roast fowl and fatty pork slices with taro – the roast duck is especially recommended. Additionally, they do Sichuanese staples, and kebabs barbecued at your table. Mains ¥30–50. Daily 9am–2.30am.

Little Italian Up past the Sheraton at 18 Binjiang Lu ☎0773 3111068. Small, friendly café (one of several nearby) with several choices of very good coffee, ginger and lemon tea, and various reasonable pizzas and pastadishes, with several good-value meal deals. Also has free wi-fi and internet access. Daily 10am–11.30pm.

★**Xiao Nan Guo** 小南国菜馆, xiǎonánguó càiguǎn. 3 Wenming Lu ☎0773 2855518. Big, bright, cheerful and very popular local-style restaurant, without your menu choices languishing in sight. There's no English menu, but it does have mouthwatering pictures in the menu which look as good as the dishes actually taste. The *chashao* (roast pork) is excellent, as are the freshwater fish dishes, with mains from ¥18. Daily 9.30am–2pm & 5–10.30pm.

Yaxu Nong Jia 雅叙农家菜馆, yǎxù nóngjiā càiguǎn. 21-2 Nanhuan Lu ☎0773 2835028. One of several smart, "country-style" restaurants along this street, with staff dressed in peasant garb and live fish outside awaiting your delectation. Good and earthy, with mains ¥12–23 and the fresh fish ¥28–58 per *jin* (500g). Daily 9am–2am.

Yi Yuan 怡园饭店, yíyuán fàndiàn. 17-3 Nanhuan Lu ☎0773 2820470. Sichuanese food served in comfortable and friendly, English-speaking staff (and English menu) make this a nice place to dine. Try the sizzling beef, green beans with garlic, sugared walnuts, or garlic pork. Mains ¥28–48. Daily 9am–10pm.

DRINKING AND ENTERTAINMENT

There's a knot of tourist-oriented, characterless and pricey pubs along pedestrianized Zhengyang Jie, and a couple of expensive clubs nearby, which play good, very loud music – okay places to go with a crowd, if not alone. For the local scene, try along Chaoyang Lu (朝阳路, chāoyáng lù) in the Guanxi Normal University area, or across the river at Chuanshan Jie Lu (船山结庐, chuánshān jiélú), just south of Lijiang Lu (about 4km from the centre), where the lively bars host a young, hip Chinese crowd, many of whom speak English.

Guilin 5th Street 第五街, dìwǔ jiē. 5–6 Chuanshan Jie Lu ☎0773 5883555. Much more fun than the tourist bars, with DJs playing good music at a reasonable volume, a bijou dancefloor, nice decor, and a young relaxed crowd out to have fun. Imported beers around ¥30 a bottle, and small outdoor terrace. Daily 7pm–2am (or later).

Lijiang Theatre 漓江剧院, líjiāng jùyuàn. 38 Binjiang Lu ☎0773 2851280. Nightly performances at 8pm of *Fantastic Guilin*, a contemporary take on local ethnic dances, incorporating ballet, acrobatics and amazing visuals for your enjoyment. Seats ¥150–220 depending on where you sit. Bring warm clothing in winter.

DIRECTORY

Banks and exchange The most useful branches of the Bank of China lie between the bus and train stations on Zhongshan Lu, and on the corner of Zhongshan Lu and Nanhuan Lu.

Bookshop Xinhua Book City (新华书城, xīnhuá shūchéng) is south across from the Niko-Niko Do Plaza. Books in English – mostly translated Chinese classics – are on floor three. Daily 9am–8pm.

Internet Several internet bars along Zhongshan Lu, and

at the top end of pedestrianized Shazheng Yang Lu, charge ¥3/hour.

Mail The most convenient post office (daily 8am–7pm) is just north of the train station on Zhongshan Nan Lu.

PSB The visa extension department (Mon–Fri 8.30am–noon & 3–6pm; ☎0773 5829930) is at 16 Shijiayuan Lu.

Shopping Zhongshan Lu is lined with well-stocked department stores, the best of which is the Niko-Niko Do Plaza on the corner with Jiefang Lu. For local flavour, try osmanthus tea (*guicha*) or osmanthus wine (*guijiu*), both of can be pleasant. For souvenirs – mostly outright tack and ethnicky textiles – try your bargaining skills at the shops and stalls on Binjiang Lu and Zhengyang Jie, or the nightly street market spreading for about a block either side of Shanhu Bridge along Zhongshan Lu.

The Li River

漓江, lí jiāng

The **Li River** meanders south for 85km from Guilin through the finest scenery that this part of the country can provide, the shallow green water flanked by a procession of jutting karst peaks shaped by the elements into a host of bizarre forms, every one of them with a name and associated legend. In between are pretty rural scenes of grazing water buffalo, farmers working their fields in conical hats, locals poling themselves along on half-submerged bamboo rafts, and a couple of small villages with a scattering of old architecture; the densest concentration of peaks is grouped around the middle reaches between the villages of **Caoping** and **Xingping**.

A **cruise** through all this is, for some, the highlight of their trip to China, with the scenery at its best between May and September, when the landscape is at its lushest and the river runs deepest – a serious consideration, as the water can be so shallow in winter that vessels can't complete their journey. At the far end, the village of **Yangshuo** sits surrounded by more exquisite countryside, making it an attractive place to kick back for a couple of days, though subject to severe tourist overload during the peak summer season.

Daxu to Wangfu Shi

Aside from a few minor peaks, the first place of interest on the Li is around 25km along at the dishevelled west bank town of **DAXU** (大圩, dàxū), which features a long, cobbled street, a few old wooden buildings, and a Ming-dynasty arched bridge. After this it's all rather flat until a grouping of peaks around **Wangfu Shi** (望夫石, wàngfū shí), an east bank outcrop said to be a wife who turned to stone while waiting for her travelling husband to return home.

CRUISING THE LI RIVER

The most popular Li River cruises take about four hours, cover the best stretches of scenery between Yangdi and Xingping and can be organized through the CITS or accommodation in Guilin (see p000). The cheapest fares – around ¥350 – are on **Chinese cruise boats** from Daxu wharf (大圩码头, dàxū mǎtóu) and get you transport to the wharf, a filling meal, return bus from Yangshuo, and a shouty Chinese guide. **Foreign cruise boats** (¥400–780 depending on where you book) depart further downstream at Zhujiang wharf (竹江码头, zhújiāng mǎtóu) and are pretty much the same except they shout at you in English. The cruise boats are air-conditioned and have comfortable seating inside, but the upper observation-decks are usually open.

However, the best way to experience the river and feel part of the landscape is on a covered **bamboo raft** (¥150–180) through the pick of the scenery between **Yangdi wharf** (杨堤码头, yángdī mǎtóu) and Xingping. You get a bus to the wharf and the cruise, but have to feed yourself – bring a packed lunch or they usually stop at a riverside restaurant where a meal costs around ¥30. The same bus then meets you at Xingping, after a short detour to see the ¥20 Scenery (20元背景图, èrshí yuán bēijǐngtú), and will then take you on a 2hr tour of a few sights around Yangshou, before returning to Guilin. There's no room on the raft for luggage, but you can leave it on the bus. Operators in Yangshuo also offer a similar version of this trip, but it's more expensive.

Pickups for both kinds of trip are from hotels in town at around 8am, and they get you back to Guilin at about 6pm with around three to four hours on the river. During peak season (July–October) the river gets crowded, but be aware that in winter the river often runs too low for the cruise vessels to make it down as far as Xingping, let alone Yangshuo, though you get charged the same amount and won't be told this beforehand.

10

Caoping

草坪, cǎopíng • bus from Guilin or Yangshuo

CAOPING, around 40km from Guilin, is marked by **Crown Cave** (冠岩, guànyán; ¥65 including transport inside the cave), a tiara-shaped rise whose naturally hollowed interior forms a 12km-long cavern, garishly lit and complete with a monorail and loudspeaker commentaries – access is from the village where a jeep (¥35) will take you to the cave's entrance, and an elevator takes you 30m down into the cavern. Caoping is only accessible by bus (cruise boats don't pull in here) and the village itself is very pretty in itself, with basic accommodation available.

Yangdi to Yellow Cloth Shoal

South of Caoping is the east bank settlement of **Yangdi** (杨堤, yángdī) and then you're into the best of the scenery, the hills suddenly tightly packed around the river. Pick of the peaks are **Eight Immortals Crossing the River** (八仙过江, bāxiān guòjiāng), and **Nine Horses Fresco Hill** (九马画山, jiǔmǎ huàshān), a 100m-high cliff on whose weathered face you can pick out some horsey patterns – first identified by ex-premier Jiang Zemin. Look into the water past here for **Yellow Cloth Shoal** (黄布滩, huángbù tān), a flat, submerged rock at one of the shallowest spots on the river.

Xingping

兴坪, xīngpíng

XINGPING, 70km downstream from Guilin and around 15km from Yangshuo, is a small market town on the west bank of the river. Mountains hem everything in and Xingping is somewhere you can enjoy doing very little, either hanging out along **Lao Jie** (老街, lǎojiē), an old lane back from the dock, or watching locals buying everything from fruit to carry poles, medicinal herbs and bamboo chairs at the **market**, held on calendar dates ending in a 3, 6 or 9. Tourism is in its infancy here, but a **rail station** is due to open nearby in 2015 and developers are moving in. For now it's a quiet version of Yangshuo – if you are willing to forego any nightlife, it's a pleasant place to experience the Li River landscape.

ARRIVAL AND DEPARTURE

XINGPING

By bus and minibus Xingping's bus station is 200m east of the river, with shuttle buses to and from Yangshuo's bus station throughout the day (every 15min; ¥8), with the last bus back at 7.20pm. After this, more expensive minibuses are available, leaving when full, or costing ¥100.

By boat Bamboo rafts are available by the dock for trips downstream to Yucun (¥100) and Yangshuo (¥260), or upstream to Nine Horses Fresco Hill (¥160) and the Yangdi (¥220).

ACCOMMODATION AND EATING

All the following serve good food, with *Kelly's Guesthouse* serving decent Western-Chinese fare, as do many cafés along the same street. *This Old Place* does some great pizzas from the wood oven in its lobby restaurant, or for more regular and cheaper Chinese food, try the many restaurants and canteens along Rongtan Lu towards the bus station.

Kelly's Guesthouse 凯利客栈, kǎilì bīnguǎn. 12 Lao Jie ☏ 187 78305445, ✉ dasu126@msn.com. The most interesting rooms in town, with guests having futons on the stripped-pine floors of their rooms, which also have

> #### XINGPING HIKES
>
> For a fairly stiff hike from Xingping, ask for directions to the ninety-minute trail over the hills to the tiny, photogenic riverside village of **Yucun** (鱼村, yúcūn), though a far easier path leads upstream from the docks for the twenty-minute walk to the **¥20 Scenery** (20元背景图, èrshí yuán bèijǐngtú) – the landscape on the back of a twenty yuan note. For panoramic views, you can take a thirty-minute hike along the well-marked path up to the pavilion on top of Laowozai Hill (老挝哉山, lǎowōzāi shān).

enormous windows and great views – no rooftop terrace unfortunately. Patrons also enjoy free use of their bikes and internet access. **¥120**

This Old Place YHA 兴坪老地方国际青年旅舍, xīngpíng lǎodì fāng guójì qīngnián lǚshè. 50m from the dock at 5 Rongtan Lu ☎ 0773 8702887, ⓦ topxingping.com. Well-run hostel with clean, modern rooms, and dorms, with a comfortable and sociable rooftop terrace from which you can watch the sunset over the river. They can also arrange tours,

activities, rent bikes, and speak excellent English. Rooms **¥120**; dorms **¥35**

Xingping Our Inn 宝熊庄, bǎoxióng zhuāng. A ferry ride across the river from Xingping at Dahebei village ☎ 136 59638096, ⓦ www.ourinnxp.com. Idyllic location with very large, very comfortable rooms, stunning views and a pretty garden. There are no tourist facilities in the village, but they do serve locally-sourced regional food in their restaurant – check the website for details on how to get there. The owner is a keen climber. **¥150**

Yangshuo

阳朔, yángshuò

Nestled 70km south of Guilin in the thick of China's most spectacular karst scenery, **YANGSHUO** rose to prominence during the mid-1980s, when tourists on Li River cruises realized that the village made a great place to settle down and get on intimate terms with the river and its peaks. Yangshuo has grown considerably since then and, despite retaining an outdated reputation as a mellow haven among Western travellers, has become a rowdy draw for domestic tourists, with the majority of its bars, restaurants and shops catering to their tastes. It remains,

YANGSHUO

Ferry Dock & Secret Beach ▲

Moon Hill, Xingping & Yulong River ▼

Guilin & Yangshuo Traditional Taichi School

ACCOMMODATION	
11 Hostel	5
Backstreet Hostel	3
Magnolia	1
River View	2
Showbiz Inn	5
Wuzhou Hotel	6
Yahngshuo Park Resort	4

EATING	
Cloud 9	7
Ganga Impression	3
Kelly's	4
Lanzhou Lamian Guan	8
Le Vôtre	6
Lucy's Place	5
Pure Lotus Vegetarian	2
Riverview	1

DRINKING & NIGHTLIFE	
DMZ Bar	2
Mojo	1

10

> ### PETTY CRIME
> Be warned that petty crime is on the rise in Yangshou. Be wary of your possessions while swimming, and of your wallet and bags when getting on or off buses. Increasingly, bags are snatched from tourists' bicycles by motorcycling thieves, so don't keep your stuff loose in the basket.

however, an easy place to spend a few days: hills surround everything, village lanes swarm with activity, and there are restaurants and accommodation everywhere. You can rent a bike and spend a day zipping between hamlets, hike around or go **rock climbing** on nearby peaks, or study cooking or martial arts. Just note that during Yangshuo's **peak-season tourism** (July–October) accommodation is scarce and many attractions will be overcrowded.

Some Peaks

Squeezed between the highway and the river, **Green Lotus Peak** (碧莲峰, bìlián fēng) is the largest in the immediate area – there's a track to the top off the highway east of the post office, but it involves some scrambling. An easier path (leading to better views) ascends **Pantao Shan** (蟠桃山, pāntáo shān) from behind the market.

Produce Market

农贸市场, nóngmào shìchǎng

Yangshuo's **produce market**, just across the road and west from the bus station on Pantao Lu, is an interesting place to hang out, especially on market days (held on dates ending in a 3, 6 or 9). There's a good selection of game, fruit, nuts and mushrooms displayed on the stalls here as well as the street outside – look out for rats and pheasants, fresh straw and needle mushrooms, and spiky water caltrops. The back of the market, where the fowl are dispatched, is not for the squeamish.

West Street

西街, xījiē

Flagstoned, vehicle-free **West Street** is Yangshuo's main tourist drag, stretching down to the water past restaurants, bars, accommodation and shops selling a vast array of souvenirs and named after the Westerners who frequented it rather than its geographical location. Trends change here continually, with the current emphasis towards ethnic textiles, traditional paintings, fans, and a few "new antiques". There's very little that you can't purchase elsewhere in the country for far less, even after bargaining; if you do decide to buy, check everything carefully before parting with your cash. In summer, shops stay open late and at night the street is clogged with crowds as they shop and orbit between the many restaurants and thumping dance-bars.

ARRIVAL AND DEPARTURE — YANGSHUO

Agents at accommodation and all around town can book long-distance bus tickets along with flights, taxis to Guilin airport (¥240, or a shared vehicle at ¥80/person) and train tickets from Guilin.

By bus Yangshuo's bus station (阳朔汽车站, yángshuò qìchē zhàn) is a scruffy depot at the junction of the highway and Diecui Jie. Buses up the expressway to Guilin's train station (¥20) depart all day long, as do local services to Xingping (¥7) and other villages. Although you can buy long-distance and sleeper bus tickets here, note that services to Nanning, Guangzhou and elsewhere originate in Guilin, so, if you're planning to take one, go to Guilin first or put up with the worst berths – over the back wheel – as

the bus will be full by the time it gets to Yangshuo to pick you up.

Destinations Guangzhou (8hr); Guilin (1hr 30min); Nanning (6hr); Shenzhen (11hr).

Tour boats The docks are a few hundred metres upstream from Yangshuo, where arriving tourists face a 200m-long gauntlet of souvenir stalls on their way into the village. Note that boats returning upstream to Guilin do not carry passengers.

CORMORANT FISHING

When you've had enough scenery for one day, do something unusual and spend an evening watching **cormorant fishing** (book through your hotel; ¥50–70 per person for 90min). This involves heading out on a bamboo raft or small boat at dusk, in a small flotilla of other tourist craft, closely following a tiny wooden fishing boat from which a group of cormorants fish for their owner. Despite being turned into a tourist activity at Yangshuo, people still make their living from this age-old practice across the region, raising young birds to dive into the water and swim back to the boat with full beaks. The birds are prevented from swallowing by ties around their necks, but it's usual practice for the fisherman to slacken these off and let them eat every seventh fish – apparently, the cormorants refuse to work otherwise.

10

INFORMATION

Tourist information can be found at accommodation – who all have tour desks – or foreigner-oriented cafés, most of which are located around central Guihua Lu. In addition, touts are everywhere, though they're relatively low-pressure and easy enough to brush off if you're not interested.

Maps *The Yangshuo Tour Guide* map of the town, river and surrounding area is available at most hotels and many shops (¥5–10) and shows bus and cycling routes.

ACCOMMODATION

Yangshuo's accommodation ranges from basic dorm beds to comfy doubles: balconies, folksy furnishings and wooden floors are nice touches, though locations within a couple of hundred metres of West Street's nightclubs may not be. During peak season (including the first two weeks of October), and even weekends, prices rise astronomically and it's hard to find anywhere in the centre for under ¥300. Conversely, stiff competition means rates can halve during the winter, when you'll want to check the availability of heating and hot water, while in summer air conditioning is a must.

★ **11 Hostel** 阳朔11青年客栈, yángshuò shíyī qīngnián kèzhàn. 11 Lianfeng Xiang ☎0773 6912228, ✉yangshuo11hostel@QQ.com. Clean, comfortable hostel tucked down an alley just metres from the river which is well managed and also excellent for information about and booking of tours, transportation, and activities. The rooftop terrace (with free washing machines) is relatively peaceful as there's no bar. Dorm beds ¥40, women-only dorm beds ¥50, doubles ¥130

Backstreet Hostel 桂花街国际青年旅馆, guìhuājiē guójì qīngnián lǚguǎn. 60 Guihua Xiang ☎0773 8814077, ✉947927871@qq.com. Sister hostel to the one in Guilin, down a quiet lane, with good dorms and doubles, a little worn round the edges but it's the least expensive hostel in the centre of town. No rooftop, bar or views. Dorm beds ¥35, women-only dorm bed ¥40, double rooms ¥100

Magnolia 白玉兰酒店, báiyùlán jiǔdiàn. 1 Diecui Lu ☎0773 8819288. Smart, good-value, mid-range place close to the downtown action, but far enough away to give you some sleep, with arty minimalist decor set off by pleasing pot plants. Rooms are large, very clean, and most have balconies. ¥400

★ **River View** 望江楼酒店, wàngjiānglóu jiǔdiàn. 11–15 Binjiang Lu ☎0773 8822688, ⊛riverview.com .cn. Nice, quiet hotel with large older rooms in the "hotel" side and smaller but more modern rooms on the "hostel" side – the location is great with the pricier rooms having balconies that overlook the river across the road. Also has a good café/restaurant with tables in the street. ¥300

Showbiz Inn 秀界国际青年旅舍, xiùjiè guójì qīngnián lǚshè. 7 Lianfeng Xiang ☎0773 8883123. Pretty similar to the *11 Hostel* next door, slightly cheaper though less well run. Great views from their rooftop bar and the whole place has a nice lived-in feeling with lots of travellers having left graffiti. Dorm beds ¥35, rooms ¥120

Wuzhou Hotel 五洲酒店, wǔzhōu jiǔdiàn. 26 Pantao Lu ☎0773 8828391. If you arrive without a reservation in high season and all the budget places are full, this is the nicest, cheapest option within walking distance of the bus station that's likely to have vacancies. The rooms are clean enough, and the family who run it are very friendly, though they don't speak English. ¥180

Yahngshuo Park Resort 阳朔公园度假酒店, yángshuò gōngyuán dùjià jiǔdiàn. At the northern end of Yangshuo Park, a 10min walk west of Xi Jie ☎0773 6919888. This characterless mid-range option is quiet, has good facilities and the rooms are comfortable, clean and with nice bathrooms. Perhaps the only place in central Yangshuo where you're sure of a peaceful night's sleep, with a nocturnal soundtrack of insects rather than the thump of dance music and drunken foreigners yelling in the street. ¥558

BEER FISH

Several mid-price Chinese restaurants at the southern end of Xie Lu, as well as on the north end of Guihua Lu (the best are up the alley, after it crosses Diecui Lu) serve the spicy local speciality **beer fish** (啤酒鱼, píjiǔ yú), which costs ¥35–80 per 500g – the most expensive and having the least bones being the *maogu* fish (毛骨鱼, máogǔ yú).

EATING

Yangshuo's numerous restaurants and cafés are split between those by the canals between Xi Jie and Guihua Lu, which mainly cater to Chinese tourists seeking exotic foreign food (Indian, German, Spanish, and even British pub grub), and those along Chengzhong Lu and Guihua Lu, which serve backpacker staples and Chinese and Western fare to a foreign crowd. Everywhere opens early for Western breakfasts, and keeps going well into the night. For inexpensive Chinese canteens and food stalls, try the area around the bus station.

★ **Cloud 9** Upstairs at the corner of Chengzhong Lu and Xi Jie ☎0773 8813686. Seasonal country-style food, juicy and flavourful; locals recommend any one of their slow-simmered medicinal soups (which sell out early), rural specialities such as braised and steamed pork with taro, or Sichuanese classics like crispy-skinned chicken. Around ¥40 upwards per person. Daily 9am–11pm.

Ganga Impression 恒河, hénghé. Block B, Yangguang 100 (just north of Guihua Lu) ☎0773 8811456. Not so fancy-looking, but probably the most authentic-tasting north Indian food in southern China outside of Guangzhou. Very tasty curries and tandoor breads, with real basmati rice as well as *lassi* and Indian desserts, it's reasonably priced and with good service. Mains ¥28–55, and most recommended is the lunchtime *thali* meal for ¥65. Daily 11am–10.30pm.

Kelly's 43 Guihua Lu ☎0773 8813233. Friendly foreigners' café/restaurant, with Western food alongside good home-style Sichuan cooking – try their fiery hot boiled beef slices or famous apple crumble. A nice, bright environment, with art on the walls and a non-smoking, air-conditioned room upstairs. Also good are the breakfasts for ¥20–38 (ask for English-style eggs), and Kelly speaks great English. Daily 7.30am–11pm.

Lanzhou Lamian Guan 兰州拉面馆, lánzhōu lāmiàn guǎn. 61 Pantao Lu, opposite the bus station ☎136 47865006. This Muslim-run joint does hearty bowls of *lanzhou* noodle soup (spiced to your desired heat), and you can watch the noodles being made by the chap twirling the dough around at the front of the shop. Also has a few rice and dry noodle dishes, all for ¥10–20. Daily 8am–midnight.

Le Vôtre 乐德法式餐厅, lèdé fàshì cāntīng. 81 Xi Jie ☎0773 8828040. Yangshuo's fanciest dining, inside a Ming-era building complete with period furnishings or in the courtyard outside. Food is French – snails, pâté, onion soup, steak *au poivre*, chocolate mousse – or Chinese seafood. Also, excellent coffee and croissants for breakfast. In the evenings, it makes a great place to drink, serving two surprisingly good micro-brewed beers, with live guitar music. At least ¥50/person. Daily 11am–1am.

Lucy's Place 露茜餐吧, lùxī cānba. 5 Guihua Lu ☎139 77351663. Foreigner-friendly establishment, similar to others nearby, with the usual mix of Chinese and Western meals, plus Lucy is a good source of tourist information. Has a slightly grungy rustic-feel with farm-implements and tourist graffiti covering the walls. Mains from ¥15, up to ¥60 for the steak. Daily 7am–11pm.

★ **Pure Lotus Vegetarian** 暗香疏影素菜馆, ànxiāng shūyǐng sùcàiguǎn. 7 Diecui Lu ☎0773 8819079. Attractive place inside the *Magnolia Hotel* with attractive food which is not too expensive and worth a slight splurge. The almond rolls, braised vegetable balls, steamed pumpkin, and "steak" with XO brandy sauce are all good. From ¥18–48 a dish. Daily 10.30am–10.30pm.

Riverview 江景餐厅, jiāngjǐng cāntīng. 1 Binjiang Lu ☎0773 8813497. Overlooking the river at the end of Diecui Lu. The café-style food and Chinese staples here are fine, but its romantic position as Yangshuo's only waterfront restaurant is the real attraction, with the outdoor patio and a couple of the inside tables having river views. Two can eat well for ¥80. Daily 9am–11pm.

DRINKING AND NIGHTLIFE

For drinking, almost all the backpacker-style restaurants along Guihua Lu have bars and there are also a load of fairly similar loud bars along Xian Qian Lu, though the best places to hang out are the places listed below, or the rooftop bars at the hostels near the river, such as the *Showbiz Inn* or the nearby and more raucous *Monkey Janes*. West Street is strung with almost identical clubs, all of which play similar generic pounding techno for the mainly Chinese crowds. It's hard to recommend one over the others, and they generally stay open till around 2am during high season.

THE LIU SAN JIE SHOW

Yangshuo's most spectacular after-dark event is **Liu San Jie**, an open-air song, dance and light spectacular put together by renowned film director Zhang Yimou. Featuring a cast of 600 local cormorant fishermen, minority women, singing children and the like, the whole affair lasts an hour, costs ¥198–680 depending on your seat and takes place about 2km downstream from town – book through your accommodation.

DMZ Bar 41, Guihua Lu ☏ 186 29313719, ⓦ thedmzbar .com. Foreigner-run, and the smallest bar in Yangshou, this friendly and slightly grungy place is a regular hangout for both tourists and old China-hands. Easiest to find by following the signs from Xie Jie for the *London Tavern* and *Tapas Bar* which are both next door. Daily noon–midnight or later.

Mojo 莫祚, mòzuò. 6F rooftop of the Alshan Hotel, 18 Xie Lu ☏ 137 37721427. This rooftop place is funky and a little beat-up, but popular with local and foreign residents. It also has an open-air dancefloor that overlooks the river, which gets going at weekends and features a good mix of blues and hip-hop (occasionally live), as well as dance-tunes. Daily 7pm–3am or later.

10

DIRECTORY

Bank There's a Bank of China on Xi Jie with a 24hr automated foreign-bill exchanger and ATMs, with other ATMs around town.

Books Many cafés and hostels offer book exchanges, the best being at *Café Too* on Chengzhong Lu, and the *DMZ Bar* sells English-language comics and books.

Internet Free at many cafés and restaurants if you have a meal too, and at most accommodation. There are many internet cafés around town, but they require a Chinese ID.

Laundry Most hostels have washing machines, either for free or ¥10, or there are several laundries around town including a super-fast 1hr-service at *Speed Queen* by the Jin Long Supermarket on Chengzhong Lu (¥15/kg).

Medical For acupuncture or Chinese massage, contact Dr Lily Li at 46 Guihua Lu (☏ 130 77632299, ⓦ dr-lily-li .com). Therapeutic massages cost ¥90/hr, and – if pain is any indication of quality – might be the best you'll ever have. Relaxation massage (¥70–130/hr) or foot massages (¥70/hr) are also available.

Post Office On Pantao Lu, by the junction with Xie Lu (daily 8am–9pm).

Around Yangshuo

Pick of the countryside around Yangshuo is the scenery west along the Yulong River, and the unmissable Moon Hill. Markets, which rotate through the villages on specific dates, make good excuses to drop into otherwise torpid communities; the one at Xingping (see p.602) is particularly good. All can be reached from Yangshuo on local transport, cycling or hiking, either on your own or with guides. There is also a handful of self-contained, quiet places to stay in the area.

The Yulong River

玉龙河, yùlóng hé

Paralleling the highway to Guilin west of Yangshuo, the **Yulong River** offers a 12km walk or cycle between small hamlets, with a couple of old stone bridges and at least two older-style villages with antique buildings. The road from Yangshuo leaves the highway near the bus station – you might have to ask for directions to **Chaoyang** (朝阳, cháoyáng), the first large settlement along the way – and follows the east side of the Yulong via **Xia Tangzhai** (下堂寨, xiàtáng zhài), the old villages of **Huang Tu** (黄土, huángtǔ) and **Gu Cheng** (古城, gǔchéng), before rejoining the highway at **Baisha** (白沙, báishā), whose market runs on dates ending in a 1, 4 or 7 and from where you can either cycle or catch a bus back to Yangshuo.

Moon Hill

月亮山, yuèliàng shān • Daily 8am–7pm • ¥15 • minibus from Yangshuo bus station to Gaotian (高田, gāotián), and ask the driver to put you off at the right spot; return by flagging down passing traffic • taxi ¥50 after bargaining

Moon Hill lies on the highway 8km from town, named after a large crescent-shaped

10

TOURS AND ACTIVITIES AT YANGSHUO

Thanks to its spectacular natural location, Yangshuo has well-established guides for any number of organized activities. **Freelance guides** work Yangshuo's streets and cafés; all claim to have unique, untouristed places to take you for lunch with a farming family and offer insights into village life. Some have been doing this for years, including the English-speaking, cheery and helpful "Wendy" Li Yunzhao (☎1319 7638186, ✉liyunzhaowendy@yahoo.com). Expect to pay about ¥50–75 per person per day depending on the size of the group.

COOKERY

For cookery classes, contact English-speaking Linda at *Cloud 9* restaurant (☎135 07838851; a 3hr class costs ¥120). For the more serious, the **Yangshuo Cooking School** (☎137 88437286, ⊛yangshuocookingschool.com) runs one- to four-day courses, including a vegetarian one.

BICYCLE RENTAL AND TOURS

Accommodation or operators at the western end of Yangshuo's West Street **rent bicycles** for ¥20–30 a day, depending on whether you want an ordinary rattletrap or an off-roader with decent springs: ¥300 or your ID may be asked for as a deposit. The excellent **Bike Asia** (⊛bikeasia.com) is based in town too, at 8 Guihua Lu – they rent out the best bikes for ¥70 a day including maps, helmets and repair kits, with high-end mountain bikes costing more at ¥150. They also run guided bike-tours in English around Yangshuo of around 30–40km which cost ¥150 and leave daily at 9am.

ALONG THE LI RIVER

Accommodation can arrange **bamboo raft trips** between Xingping and Yangdi (2hr; ¥200) and full-day **kayak trips** (¥200); or in hot weather you can simply buy a **rubber tube** from shops along Diecui Jie and head down to the water for a splash – but leave it until the last ferries have departed upstream around 4pm. The now badly named **Secret Beach**, a couple of kilometres upstream, down a small track, is the nicest place for a swim. For those brave (or foolish) enough, another great experience is to jump off the 9m-high **Yulong Bridge** (玉龙桥, yùlóng qiáo), which is 15km northwest of the town, and a 2km stroll from Baisha Town (白沙镇, báishā zhèn).

MARTIAL ARTS

Yangshuo has become a martial arts hangout, with the long-established **Budi Zhen school** founded by the incredible, ancient Mr Gao and now run by his twin sons. Visit their training hall (步地真功夫馆, bùdì zhēngōngfu guǎn) off West Street (☎1397 7350377, ✉budizhen.info @gmail.com), to study a whole range of martial disciplines at around ¥80 a lesson. For **tai ji** try the **Yangshuo Traditional Taichi School** (阳朔传统太极学校, yángshuò chuántǒng tàijí xuéxiào), housed in a Qing-dynasty farmhouse at Jima village close to the Yulong River (☎152 9592 0102, ⊛traditionaltaichischool.com). They teach courses up to instructor-level and also offer accommodation and food, with lessons costing ¥70 per hour and up, though for long-term students discounts are available.

ROCK CLIMBING

Yangshuo is a popular **rock-climbing centre** with over four hundred mostly short but very tough graded climbs on local peaks ranging from 5.6 to 5.13. New climbs are being pioneered all the time and the *Yangshuo Climbing Guide* available from climb-shops will show you most of them, along with detailed climbing info too. For experienced climbers, equipment-rental is around ¥180 a day for two, with one-day beginners' courses starting at ¥450 a day per person. **Insight Adventures**, at 53 Xianqian Jie (☎0773 8811033, ⊛insight-adventures.com) are the most established operator, and although slightly pricier than most, have foreign guides and a good safety record. The *Karst Cafe* on Xianqian Jie is the spot to go to socialize with other climbers and get the latest info.

hole that pierces the peak. It takes an easy thirty minutes to ascend stone steps through bamboo and brambles to the summit where fairytale views take in the whole of the Li River valley, fields cut into uneven chequers by rice and vegetable plots, and Tolkienesque peaks framed through the hole. In summer, be sure to take water, or you'll have to pay through the nose to the avaricious little old ladies who stalk the area with drinks.

ACCOMMODATION AND EATING   **AROUND YANGSHUO**

For transport information to these places, contact the hotels directly.

Giggling Tree Guesthouse 咯咯树宾馆, gēgē shù bīnguǎn. Aishanmen village, about 5km south of Yangshuo along the Yulong River ☎ 136 67866154, ⓦ gigglingtree.com. Converted stone farmhouse buildings now forming an attractive Dutch-owned hotel and restaurant, with courtyard, tiled roofs and a beautiful mountain backdrop. Rooms are very large, beautifully furnished and have lovely wooden floors and ceilings. Dorm bed ¥75, doubles ¥220

★ **Snow Lion** 雪狮岭度假饭店, xuěshīlǐng dùjià fàndiàn. Mushan village, about 2.5km south of Yangshuo ☎ 0773 8826689, ⓦ yangshuosnowlion resort.com. Fantastic food and scenery coupled with comfortable and airy rooms make this a great place for a break, and all rooms have their own balconies. Located 150m from the village and owned by the same people who own *Cloud 9* in town. ¥328

Longji Titian

龙脊梯田, lóngjǐ tītián • ¥80 • ☎ 0773 7583088 • ⓦ txljw.com

Around 90km north of Guilin, **Longji Titian** – literally "Dragon's Spine Terraces" – is a range of steep-sided and closely packed hills, whose slopes have been carved out over centuries of farming to resemble the literal form of a contour map. Most of the people up here are **Zhuang**, but there are also communities of **Yao**, some of whom still hunt for a living. The Yao women also have a custom to never cut their hair, and you will see them with it piled up on top of their head like a turban, though if you want a photo, it'll cost you ¥10. Tourism is well established, with the wooden villages of **Ping An** and **Dazhai** acting as comfortable bases for viewing the terraces or hiking around the hilltops. Day-trips are offered by agents in Guilin (see p.599), but you'll get more by staying for a couple of nights, and it's easy to reach here on local buses.

Ping An

平安, píngān

PING AN is a small Zhuang village of wooden homes and cobbled paths squeezed into a steep fold between the terraces, whose seven hundred or so inhabitants all share the surname Liao. You get dropped off in a car park and walk up 500m of stone steps to the village, where you're faced with a glut of **accommodation**, all offering cosy rooms with or without en suite in "traditional-style" three-storey houses – look for something with a view. Ping An is the focus of Chinese package tours, though these visitors tend not to wander very far from the village centre and generally all leave by 3pm. Walks around Ping An include short climbs to lookouts at **Seven Stars** (七星, qīxīng) and **Nine Dragons and Five Tigers** (九龙五虎, jiǔlóng wǔhǔ), either of which give superlative views of the rice terraces.

Dazhai

大寨, dàzhài • cable car daily 8.30am–7pm, ¥70 one-way, ¥120 return

DAZHAI is a larger but slightly less touristy version of Ping An, reached along a separate road. The relatively few package tourists who visit are funnelled off up the cable car to

---

PING AN TO DAZHAI HIKE

Though there is no direct vehicle road, it's possible to **hike** between Ping An and Dazhai in around four hours, via the attractive village of **Zhongliu** (中六, zhōngliù), where there is very basic food but no accommodation. Yao women along the way will offer their services as guides (around ¥50), though with basic maps from accommodation, they're not really necessary.

10

the viewing point at **Jinfo Ding** (金佛顶, jīnfó dǐng), and the village is consequently more peaceful than Ping An. Further up the hillside are hamlets such as **Tiantou** (田头, tiántóu), just over 1km and twenty minutes' walk up steps – quite a hike with a heavy pack, though the tough old ladies at Dazhai will offer their services as porters for ¥20–40. Once up on the ridgetops, there are further walks to fabulous views at **Xi Shan** (西山, xīshān), or over to Ping An via Zhongliu village (see p.609).

ARRIVAL AND DEPARTURE
LONGJI TITIAN

By bus Longji Titian is accessed from the hamlet of Heping (和平, hépíng), on the Guilin–Sanjiang highway. At Heping, you purchase your entrance ticket and find minibuses uphill to Ping An or Dazhai which depart when full (¥10). Leaving, if you can't find direct transport to Guilin or Sanjiang, first catch a minibus 12km north to the town of Longsheng (龙胜, lóngshèng), which has better connections.

By minibus Minibuses depart Guilin's train station square through the day, whenever they have at least four passengers, going all the way to either Dazhai or Ping An (¥60).

By tour Day tours from Guilin cost around ¥300–350/ person and include return transport, entry and an English-speaking guide with around 5hr on site.

ACCOMMODATION AND EATING

All accommodation serves food – Western staples and some good Chinese meals, including rice or chicken grilled in bamboo tubes (竹筒鸡, zhútǒng jī). Do try the local rice-wine too, which is sweet, fizzy, has rice floating in it and about the same alcohol content as a strong beer.

PING AN

Longji International Youth Hostel 龙脊国际青年旅舍, lóngjǐ guójì qīngnián lǚshě. ☎ 0773 7583265. The only hostel in the centre of the village (and not as busy as those in Dazhai), with clean rooms in a nice wooden building with all the normal hostel facilities such as wi-fi and laundry. Serves good Western (though better Chinese) food in its restaurant. Dorm beds ¥30, double room ¥60

Ping An Jiudian 平安酒店, píngān jiǔdiàn. ☎ 0773 7583198. A 15min walk up the hill from the village, it has two buildings, with the more expensive one having really nice, comfortable rooms with views, though the economical ones aren't bad either. Economical rooms ¥180, standard doubles ¥358

DAZHAI

Dayao Zhai Tavern 大姚县翟酒店, dàyáoxiàn zhái jiǔdiàn. ☎ 0773 7585699. At the north of the village and to the right of the stream, this is typical of the accommodation here, but is quieter, being on the edge. Comfortable, clean rooms, in a traditional building, and for ¥30 extra you get a/c and a computer in your room. Very good restaurant downstairs. ¥90

Dragon's Den Hostel 龙穴青年旅舍, lóngxué qīngnián lǚshě. Tiantou hamlet ☎ 0773 7585780, ⓦ dragonsdenhostel.com. Above Dazhai at Tiantou, among the best of the scenery, with fantastic views and clean rooms and dorms in a traditional wooden building. Rooms have a/c and wi-fi, and you pay ¥10 extra for a room with a view. Dorm beds ¥35, double rooms ¥110

Sanjiang
三江, sānjiāng

Some 80km west of Longsheng near the Guizhou border, **SANJIANG** is a small, dishevelled service town on the Rongshui River. Most of the people here are **Dong**, renowned for their wooden houses, towers and bridges which dot the countryside hereabouts, most notably at **Chengyang** village to the north. Sanjiang's own unmissable **drum tower** rises 47m over the river; this one is modern, but similar towers were traditionally used as lookout posts in times of war, or social areas in times of peace. While there is no real reason to stop at Sanjiang except in transit to **Zhaoxing** (see p.612), you might get stuck here between connections – though Chengyang is a better place to stay the night.

Chengyang
程阳, chéngyáng • ¥60 • free traditional music and dance show daily at 10.30am and 4.20pm

CHENGYANG, 18km north of Sanjiang on the Linxi River, is an attractive Dong village reached over a covered **wind-and-rain bridge**, an all-wooden affair built in

1916. The village forms a collection of warped, two- and three-storey traditional wooden houses surrounding a square-sided drum tower, and makes a pleasantly rural place to spend a day, walking out to smaller hamlets with similar congregations of dark wood and cobbles, many with their own, less elaborate bridges and towers. Look for creaky black **water wheels** made from plaited bamboo, somehow managing to supply irrigation canals despite dribbling out most of their water in the process. For views over the whole region, return to Chengyang's main-road entrance and make the short climb to two pavilions on the ridge above, offering vistas of dark, gloomy villages nestled among vivid green fields.

ARRIVAL AND DEPARTURE
SANJIANG

BY TRAIN
Sanjiang train station (三江火车站, sānjiāng huǒchē zhàn) is about 10km northwest of town on the Huaihua–Liuzhou rail line, with services to Mayang in Hunan (for Fenghuang, see p.437). Minibuses (¥5) meet arrivals and land them in central Sanjiang, from where you'll have to catch a bus to Chengyang.

Destinations Chongqing (1 daily; 3hr 16min); Zunyi (1 daily; 5hr 34min).

BY BUS
Chengyang There is no bus station at Chengyang, and you will be dropped at the village ticket office. Returning, stand on the main road and flag down traffic; the last bus to Sanjiang passes by around 5pm, though there are also very crowded and badly driven minibuses to Saniang's Hexi bus station (¥6).

Sanjiang Hedong bus station (河东汽车站, hédōng qìchē zhàn) lies east of the river in the newer part of Sanjiang, with connections south as far as Guilin and north to Zhaoxing and Congjiang.

Sanjiang Hexi bus station (河西汽车站, héxī qìchē zhàn), in the older part of Sanjiang, serves local destinations, including Chengyang and Zhaoxing.

Destinations Chengyang (40min); Guilin (4hr); Longsheng (2hr); Zhaoxing (4hr).

ACCOMMODATION AND EATING

SANJIANG
There are plenty of cheap, basic places to stay near both bus stations, but none takes foreigners. Noodle and hotpot stalls surround the Hedong bus station, while the *Sanjiang Hotel* has a proper sit-down restaurant, and makes a good place to wait for buses.

Sanjiang Hotel 三江酒店, sānjiāng jiǔdiàn. 2 Chinhua Lu ☎ 0772 8626888. Fairly nice mid-range hotel around a 5min walk from the long-distance bus station – turn right, then left after 150m up the main road and it's just on the left. Rooms are clean and well equipped, and rooms often heavily discounted. ¥368

CHENGYANG
Dong Village Hotel 董村酒店, dǒngcūn jiǔdiàn. 50m left as you cross the larger of the two bridges ☎ 0772 8582421. Best of Chengyang's several family-run, folksy guesthouses. The clean and rustic rooms have a/c (vital in the summer), and there's a communal balcony with rocking chairs to admire the view from. The kitchen serves home-cooked food – certainly better than the appalling Western dishes available at Chengyang's restaurants – though it closes after dark. ¥80

Into Guizhou: Sanjiang to Kaili

The road west of Sanjiang enters Guizhou and cuts through Dong territory and up to the Miao stronghold of **Kaili**, a 300km-long run of traditional villages, steeply terraced hillsides, vivid blue rivers and winding roads. Daily buses run from Sanjiang to **Zhaoxing** – itself a highlight – from where you can town-hop on to Kaili. Two days is a likely minimum for the trip, and it's not one that you'll get much out of by rushing in any case.

10

Zhaoxing

肇兴, zhàoxīng

ZHAOXING, around four hours by bus from Sanjiang, is an extremely attractive single-street Dong town set in a small valley, with a generous smattering of old wooden buildings including five square-based **drum towers**, each differently styled and built by separate clans. Accompanying wind-and-rain bridges and theatre stages are decorated with fragments of mirrors and mouldings of actors and animals. Houses are hung with strings of drying radishes for sour hotpots, and the back lanes resound to the noise of freshly dyed cloth being pounded with wooden mallets to give it a shiny patina.

Tang An and Shage

Rice terraces and muddy tracks around Zhaoxing provide fine country walks, the best of which is 7km uphill through paddy fields to **Tang An** (堂安, tángān), another photogenic collection of wooden buildings. To escape any last trappings of government-sponsored gentrification, carry on up through Tang An a further 2km to the smaller hamlet of **Shage** (傻哥, shǎgē), which is more authentic and also has lovely views.

ARRIVAL AND DEPARTURE

ZHAOXING

By bus There's no bus station at Zhaoxing; buses running between Sanjiang and Congjiang or elsewhere drop off and collect along the main street. As no services originate at Zhaoxing, and buses are often already full by the time they pass through, you might need to ask at your accommodation about how to use minibuses to hop in stages towards your next port of call. The following times will be reduced with the opening of new highways in the near future.

Destinations Congjiang (2hr); Rongjiang (5hr); Sanjiang (4hr).

INFORMATION

Tourist office Zhaoxing's tourist office is opposite the main street meat market (daily 8.30am–5.30pm; ☏0855 6130800), supplying hand-drawn maps of the local area (¥10) which also describe Dong culture and traditions.

ACCOMMODATION AND EATING

There is plenty of inexpensive accommodation in Zhaoxing, though better views and a more peaceful environment – if extremely basic rooms – are available up at Tang An for under ¥50. For food, the main road is lined by open-fronted stir-fry restaurants, but given the amount of dust stirred up by passing traffic you might opt for an indoor venue.

Dong Village 侗乡涉外旅馆, dòngxiāng shèwài lǚguǎn. On the street parallel to Zhaoxing's main street ☏0855 6130188. Nice wooden building and typical of the guesthouses in the village, with clean and comfortable, if slightly basic rooms. Also serves inexpensive local-style rice food and the owner is quite a good cook. **¥80**

Zhaoxing Binguan 肇兴宾馆, zhàoxīng bīnguǎn. Just uphill from Zhaoxing's tourist office ☏0855 6130899. Costlier than the in-town hotels but much more scenic, with staff dressed in local costume, and very comfortable, clean rooms in a large wooden building. Also has a good Chinese restaurant and a balcony overlooking the rooftops of the village. **¥240**

Congjiang and Basha

CONGJIANG (从江, cóngjiāng) is a not too unattractive logging town on the Duliu River some two hours west from Zhaoxing. The reason to stop here in transit to Kaili is to make a side-trip to **BASHA** (岜沙, bāshā), a Miao hill village 8km southwest whose inhabitants grow a long topknot and wear traditional clothes and heavy metal jewellery as a matter of course, not just for festivals. Unusually, the men also carry home-made flint-lock guns, with even the children carrying toy ones. Basha is really a loose grouping of five separate wooden villages on a forested ridge, with cobbled lanes and paths off across the fields to explore; there are several places to stay here too.

ARRIVAL AND DEPARTURE — CONGJIANG AND BASHA

By bus Congjiang's bus station is on main street Jiangdong Nan Lu, with two buses to Zhaoxing daily, and more frequent departures to Rongjiang and Kaili.

Destinations Kaili (5hr); Rongjiang (2hr 30min); Zhaoxing (5hr).

GETTING AROUND

Minibus and motorbike Turn left out of Congjiang's bus station, walk 100m to the bridge, cross it and you'll find freelance minibuses and motorbikes to Basha (¥5 on either way) hanging around on the left-hand corner.

ACCOMMODATION AND EATING

CONGJIANG

There's plenty of poor-value accommodation near Congjiang's bus station, though the nearby stir-fry places serve excellent inexpensive meals, including the local version of sour fish soup (酸汤鱼, suāntāngyú), where they fry the fish first.

Kaitai Holiday Hotel 开泰假日酒店, kāitài jiàrì jiǔdiàn. Directly across the bridge on Xincheng Lu ☎ 0855 6929999. By far the best option in town: the carpets might be a little threadbare but the rooms are comfortable and clean, and half of them have river views. It also boasts a small bar in the lobby with imported liquors. **¥188**

BASHA

Gufeng Zhai Qingnian Luguan 古风寨青年旅馆, gǔfēngzhài qīngnián lǚguǎn. ☎ 0855 6925053, ⓦ gz135.cn/gfz. The pick of Basha's accommodation, this is a lovely, quiet and clean wooden hostel with outstanding views from the lounge, and a small terraced garden. Beds are comfortable, bathrooms are clean, and there's even wi-fi, though no a/c. Serves basic meals for ¥25. **¥100**

Rongjiang and Zengchong

RONGJIANG (榕江, róngjiāng) is a comparatively large, modern town two hours northwest of Congjiang across the mountains, and has a frenetic Sunday **market** where you can watch villagers bargaining the last Mao out of a deal. As at Congjiang, you're in Rongjiang to get out – this time 30km east to the isolated Dong village of **ZENGCHONG** (增冲, zēngchōng), which sports a four-hundred-year-old drum tower. Zengchong makes no concessions to the few tourists who drop in – it's an authentically poor, muddy, rickety place with a couple of tiny stores, where Chinese-speakers might negotiate a home stay for the night for around ¥20–30.

ARRIVAL AND DEPARTURE — RONGJIANG AND ZENGCHONG

By bus Rongjiang's bus station is on the east side of town, with several daily services to both Congjiang (3hr) and Kaili (3hr 30min).

GETTING AROUND

By bus Reaching Zengchong takes two steps; first catch one of the hourly buses to Wangdong (往洞, wǎngdòng) and then walk or hitch for the final 6km – the last bus leaves Rongjiang at 5.20pm.

ACCOMMODATION

There are plenty of decent, inexpensive places to stay near Rongjiang's bus station, but none is authorized to take foreigners.

Shengding Hotel 盛鼎大酒店, shèngdǐng dàjiǔdiàn. ☎ 0855 6653669. About a 5min walk north of the bus station, you can see it behind and east of the main road on a slight hill. The only obvious option for foreign tourists, this is at least fairly modern, has large, clean rooms and is well run, if pricey. **¥388**

10

Nanning

南宁, nánníng

Way down in southern Guangxi, fairly close to China's open border with Vietnam, **NANNING** was just a medium-sized market town when European traders opened a river route from neighbouring Guangdong in the early twentieth century, starting a period of rapid growth that saw the city supplanting Guilin as the provincial capital. The city has capitalized on recent trade agreements with Vietnam, and today Nanning is a bright, easy-going place with a mild boom-town atmosphere and a mix of leafy boulevards, modern architecture and a handful of narrow, colonial-era streets. There's good shopping, decent food, a **museum** strong on regional archeology, and both international and domestic transport connections.

The Provincial Museum

省博物馆, shěng bówùguǎn • Tues–Sun 9am–5pm • Free • ☎ 0771 2847055, ⓦ gxmuseum.com • bus #6 from Chaoyang Lu

Nanning's well-presented **Provincial Museum** on Gucheng Lu provides an insight into the **Baiyue culture**, which flourished in southern Guangxi from prehistoric times until the early Han dynasty. The pick of the exhibits are **bronze storage drums** embossed with stylized images of rowers and birds which, according to a Ming historian, became a symbol of power: "Those who possess bronze drums are chieftains, and the masses obey them; those who have two or three drums can style themselves king". Drums were

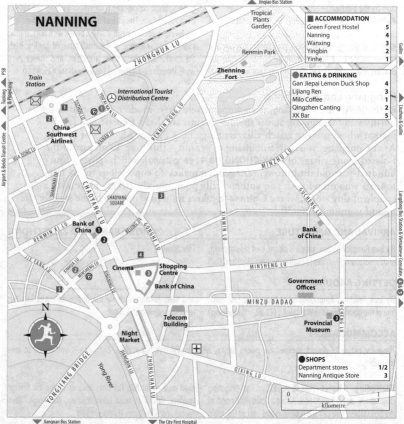

NANNING

ACCOMMODATION	
Green Forest Hostel	5
Nanning	4
Wanxing	3
Yingbin	2
Yinhe	1

EATING & DRINKING	
Gan Jiepai Lemon Duck Shop	4
Lijiang Ren	3
Milo Coffee	1
Qingzhen Canting	2
XK Bar	5

SHOPS	
Department stores	1/2
Nanning Antique Store	3

cast locally right up until the late Qing dynasty; their ceremonial use survives among several ethnic groups in China, Southeast Asia and Indonesia.

ARRIVAL AND DEPARTURE   **NANNING**

The easiest way of organizing onward travel from Nanning is to go to the Nanning International Tourist Distribution Centre (南宁国际旅游集散中心, nánníng guójì lǚyóu jísàn zhōngxīn), just five minutes' walk from the train station at 5 You'an Nan Lu (daily 9am–6pm; ☎0771 2102362, ⊛yunde.net). They can book domestic and international flights, buses to Vietnam and destinations served by the Longdong bus station, train tickets (excluding Hanoi), as well as tours and car rental. Online, the government website (⊛english.nanning.gov.cn) carries timetables, as well as other transport information.

10

BY PLANE
Nanning airport (南宁吴圩机场, nánníng wúxū jīchǎng) is 32km southwest of Nanning, with flights across China, though not to Vietnam at present. Airport buses (hourly; 45min; ¥15) run to near the *Yinhe* hotel; or the more frequent #301 bus will take you to the centre for just ¥3. Taxis run exactly the same route for around ¥100, or ¥25 per person.

Destinations Beijing (9 daily; 3hr 10min); Chengdu (4 daily; 3hr); Chongqing (5 daily; 1hr 20min); Guangzhou (8 daily; 1hr 5min); Guiyang (2 daily; 1hr); Hong Kong (2 daily; 1hr 40min); Kunming (6 daily; 1hr 20min); Shanghai (6 daily; 2hr 15min); Shenzhen (7 daily; 1hr 20min); Xi'an (6 daily; 2hr).

BY TRAIN
Nanning train station (南宁火车站, nánníng huǒchē zhàn) sits at the top of Chaoyang Lu, with daily services to Guilin and the rest of the country, as well as Vietnam. Ticket windows here open 7am–7pm; or use the less crowded International Tourist Distribution Centre.

Destinations Beihai (2 daily; 3hr); Beijing (2 daily; 28hr); Chengdu (1 daily; 32hr 30min); Chongqing (1 daily; 21hr 20min); Guangzhou (6 daily; 11hr 48min–14hr 48min); Guilin (16 daily; 4hr 52min–6hr 24min); Hanoi (1 daily; 12hr); Kunming (7 daily; 12–13hr); Pingxiang (3 daily; 3hr 30min–6hr); Tuolong/Ningming (2 daily; 3hr 15min–4hr 34min).

BY BUS
Beida Transit Centre (北大客运中心, běidà kèyùn zhōngxīn), 2km from the train station at 26 Beida Bei Lu, is of most use for traffic to Daxin (for Detian Waterfall), Baise (for Leye) and Kunming. It's on the #31 bus route.
Jiangnan station (江南汽车站, jiāngnán qìchēzhàn) is 7km south of Chaoyang Lu on the #31 bus;

CROSSING INTO VIETNAM
You need a **visa** for Vietnam, issued by the Vietnamese Consulate, 27F Yahang Wealth Center, 55 Jinhu Rd (Mon–Fri 8.30am–noon & 2.30–6pm; ☎0771 5510562). A 30-day visa costs ¥380 for 2-day processing, ¥480 for one, and ¥650 for same day (drop off in morning and collect after 5pm). There is no photo-booth at the consulate so remember to bring a recent passport-size photo with you. Most hotels, and the Nanning International Tourist Distribution Centre, can also obtain visas for you with little or no mark-up.

Buses to Hanoi (8hr; ¥148), Haiphon (8hr; ¥158) and Yalong Bay (8hr; ¥168) depart from the International Tourist Distribution Centre on You'an Nan Lu (see above); you can also catch Hanoi buses from Langdong bus station.

The direct **train to Hanoi** currently leaves at 6.45pm (8hr; sleeper ¥200–350) and it stops for ages both sides of the border for passport checks and customs inspections, so be aware they might not turn the lights off till around 1am – eye shades are a good idea. Buy tickets at the station at ticket window #16.

If you'd rather make a more sedate journey to Vietnam to see some of the beautiful landscape down this way such as at Hua Shan (see p.619), then you can cross the border at **Pingxiang** by foot. There are two daily trains which head from Nanning to Pingxiang via Ningming (for Hua Shan), as well as more frequent buses. From Pingxiang, minibuses shuttle to the border at the **Friendship Pass** (中国和越南边境友谊之路, zhōngguó hé yuènán biānjìng yǒuyì zhīlù), or there are two direct afternoon buses to Hanoi (5–6hr; ¥70) from Pingxiang's bus station. If you are going to visit northern Vietnam, south of the border is **Dong Dang** where there are buses 5km south to **Lang Son**, which is a transport hub.

Finally, be **warned** that when crossing the border you should keep this book buried deep in your bags – customs officials have been confiscating them because the maps colour Taiwan in differently, which is taken to imply support for the island's separatist cause.

10

allow 40min. Destinations cover the southwestern border area such as Ningming and Pingxiang, as well as Guilin, and inter-provincial buses to Haikou, Guangzhou and Shenzhen. Tickets and timetables can be obtained from a booth on Zhonghua Lu, about 500m west of the train station on the corner with Huaqiang Lu, or from the International Tourist Distribution Centre.

Langdong station (琅东客运站, lángdōng kèyùn zhàn), 10km east of the centre on Minzu Dadao – a #6 bus

will get you to Chaoyang Lu in 50min. Nanning's biggest bus station, with departures for Vietnam, as well as cities all across China including frequent services to Guilin and Guiyang. Buy tickets from booths at the corner of Chaoyang Lu and Hua Dong Lu (daily 6.40am–9.30pm) or at the International Tourist Distribution Centre; they also have timetables in English.

Destinations Beihai (3hr 30min); Guangzhou (18hr); Guilin (6hr); Ningming (4hr); Pingxiang (5hr); Yangshuo (6hr).

GETTING AROUND

By bus Bus maps, which are pretty good for navigation too, are available from the otherwise useless tourist office next to the train station or from the main bus stations. Bus #6 is very useful, running as it does from the train station, down Chaoyang Lu, and then along Minzu Dadao.

By taxi In the city itself, a taxi costs ¥7 to hire for the first couple of kilometres, with a ¥1 fuel surcharge added to all trips.
By three-wheeler rickshaws These cost about the same as a taxi, but are far more adept at slipping through the traffic, quite often via the pavement.

ACCOMMODATION

There's abundant good-value, central accommodation in Nanning for all budgets. Unusually for China, the train station area is by no means seedy or unpleasant.

Green Forest Hostel 绿色森林旅馆, lǜsè sēnlín lǚguǎn. 3 Jiefang Lu ☎0771 2813977. Centrally located hostel just 2km from the train station, with good, clean dorms as well as doubles and triples. Also has a stylish communal area with a café serving international food. They speak English and can help with information and Vietnam visas. Wi-fi throughout. Dorm beds **¥60**, doubles **¥130**
Nanning 南宁饭店, nánníng fàndiàn. 38 Minsheng Lu ☎0771 2103888. Smart, upmarket business venue, right across from the city's newest shopping plaza. Has all the facilities you'd expect, including currency exchange. Can often be discounted by almost half. **¥920**
★ **Wanxing** 万兴酒店, wànxīng jiǔdiàn. 47 Minzhu Lu ☎0771 2381000, ⓦnnwxhotel.com. Behemothic, budget business hotel with two buildings, a block apart. The newer and far better wing is at this address, and you

can't miss it. Bright doubles, free internet, and usually heavily discounted. **¥438**
Yingbin 迎宾饭店, yíngbīn fàndiàn. 71 Chaoyang Lu ☎0771 2116029, ⓔyingbin.hotel@yahoo.com. Unpretentious budget option more or less opposite the train station, taking up almost a whole block above fast-food canteens. Clean throughout, but some rooms are basic with hard beds – have a look at a few. **¥130**
Yinhe 银河宾馆, yínhé bīnguǎn. 84–86 Chaoyang Lu ☎0771 2116688. Two buildings 50m apart; the northernmost budget wing, though slightly institutional, has spick-and-span doubles, while the main hotel has more comfortable rooms with computers (as does the budget wing for ¥30 more), though the carpets are showing wear. Budget wing **¥200**, main hotel **¥380**

EATING AND DRINKING

The best place for inexpensive buns, dumplings, noodles, grilled chicken wings, steamed packets of lotus leaf-wrapped *zongzi* and basic stir-fries are along the eastern end of Hua Dong Lu or at the night market on Zhongshan Lu – though be careful of pickpockets with long tweezers. Western fast-food chains are grouped in the modern plaza development north of the corner of Chaoyang Lu and Minzu Dadao.

Gan Jiepai Lemon Duck Shop 甘界牌柠檬鸭店, gānjièpái níngméngyā diàn. 12-2 Yuanhu Nan Lu ☎0771 5855585. Popular place specializing in local cuisine and featuring the zingy stir-fry lemon duck of its name. Well-presented dishes, good portions and a comfortable environment make this an enjoyable place to eat. This branch is just off Minzu Dado, with another further south at 16-2 Qingshan Lu. Around ¥40 per person. Daily 11am–11pm.
Lijiang Ren 漓江人, líjiāng rén. 2F Gelan Yuntian

Plaza, Chaoyang Lu ☎0771 2843805. Yunnanese chain situated up the wooden stairs on the southwest corner of the building offering chilli-rich stews and stir-fries in comfortable period surroundings. Mains come in at around ¥25–80 for large portions. Daily 9.30am–10pm.
Milo Coffee 米罗咖啡, mǐluó kāfēi. 7 You Ai Lu ☎0771 2428908. Situated a few minutes' walk from the train station, this place isn't especially cheap, but good if you're hankering after coffee, waffles and

TO HAINAN ISLAND

As an alternative route to Hainan Island, there are ferries running from Guangxi's sole seaport at Beihai (北海, **běihǎi**), some 200km southeast of Nanning, connected by train (2 daily) and bus (every 30min). There are two daily sailings to Haikou in Hainan from the Beihai International Port (北海国际客运港, **běihǎi guójì kèyùngǎng**), departing at 6pm and 6.30pm (☎0779 3904011; 10hr; seats ¥130, basic private cabins ¥280/person). Note that toilets are shared, and hot water urns and a snack shop are the only sources of refreshment.

10

light Western-style meals. In addition, its very comfortable sofas and good a/c make it an ideal place to nurse a drink if you've got to wait for a train. Daily 9am–2am.

Qingzhen Canting 清真餐厅, qīngzhēn cāntīng. 25 Xinhua Lu ☎135 58483838. Inexpensive Muslim restaurant on the first two floors of the pale green mosque. Spicy noodle soups are served for under ¥8 on the ground floor with more sophisticated dishes such as lemon duck or a pretty good South Asian-style mutton curry upstairs at ¥30–80. Daily 6.30am–8pm; second floor till 10pm.

XK Bar 中西吧, zhōngxī ba. 13-8 Yuanhu Road Xiyili ☎135 57118234. Intimate Sino-British-owned bar tucked down a backstreet off Minzu Dado about 1km east of the museum. Has a nice mix of local and expat clientele and serves inexpensive sausage (or pie) and mash, fish'n'chips and some German beers. The English owner can point you in the direction of the rest of the expat scene. Daily 7.30pm–after 2am.

DIRECTORY

Banks and exchange The main Bank of China (foreign exchange Mon–Fri 8–11.30am & 2.30–5.30pm) is on Gucheng Lu; other branches around town have ATMs and might change money.

Hospital The City First Hospital (市第一医院, shì dìyī yīyuàn) is southeast of the centre at 89 Qi Xing Lu and is probably the best in the region.

Internet Net bars all over town charge ¥3/hr.

Mail The most central post office is on Suzhou Lu (daily 8am–7pm).

PSB The visa department (Mon–Thurs 9am–4.30pm, Fri 9am–noon; ☎0771 2891264) is 1.5km north of the train station, at 4 Xiuling Lu. Catch bus #14, #31, #71, #72, #84 or #85 and get off after the hospital – it's about 100m south of the East Gate of Guangxi University.

Shopping Nanning is a great place to shop for clothes, either at the department stores full of good-quality, low-price attire along Chaoyang Lu (including a Walmart) or at the brand-label stores along Xingning Lu, such as Giordano, Baleno Meters/Bonwe and Yishion. The Nanning Antique Store, next to the Provincial Museum, has a touristy and expensive selection of teapots, chops, paintings and jade, set across two floors.

Detian Waterfall

德天瀑布, détiān pùbù · Daily 6am–6.30pm · ¥80 · ☎0771 5595608

Perched right on the Vietnamese border 150km west of Nanning, **Detian waterfall** is worth the trip not just for the falls – best in full flood during the summer rains – but also because it draws you into the Zhuang heartlands: a world of dark karst hills, grubby towns, water buffalo wallowing in green paddy fields, and farmers in broad-sleeved pyjamas and conical hats.

At the falls

The **village** down the hill from the park entrance is more or less just a bus station surrounded by hotels, gift shops and restaurants; but the falls themselves form a delightful set of cataracts broader than their 30m height and framed by limestone peaks and fields. Paths lead down to the base past a series of pools and bamboo groves; at the bottom you can hire a **bamboo raft** and be punted over to straddle the mid-river borderline. The best part, however, is to follow the road along the top to its end in a field, where you'll find a **stone post** (known as Stone 53) proclaiming the Sino-Vietnamese frontier in French and Chinese, along with a bizarre **border market** – a clutch of trestle tables laden with Vietnamese sweets, cigarettes and stamps in the middle of nowhere.

ARRIVAL AND DEPARTURE

DETIAN WATERFALL

By bus During the summer at least, there's one direct bus daily to Detian from Nanning's Langdong bus station at 8.30am (5hr; ¥50). Otherwise, catch a bus from the Beida Transit Centre to Daxin (大新, dàxīn; 3hr; ¥40), from where there are hourly minibuses direct to Detian (3hr; ¥35).

ACCOMMODATION AND EATING

There are fairly cheap places to eat in the main square of the village where you can fill up for under ¥30, or the *Detian Shanzhuang* has more formal (and expensive) dining.

Detian Binguan 德天宾馆, détiān bīnguǎn. ☎ 0771 5595608. This place offers clean, comfortable rooms just off and above the main square and bus station with many other less expensive options opposite. Also has wi-fi, and you can use the receipt to get your ticket to the falls validated for an extra day at the entrance. **¥120**

Detian Shanzhuang 德天山莊大酒店, détiān shānzhuāng dàjiǔdiàn. ☎ 0771 3773570. Perched on a slope above the falls with stunning views of the cascade and across the river into Vietnam. Rooms are nothing special, but then you're paying for the location. Also has a mid-price restaurant, but few other facilities. **¥500**

Leye

乐业, lèyè

LEYE sits some 400km northwest of Nanning near the Guizhou border. There's nothing much to the town itself – just a 2km-long main street and a dozen adjacent lanes strung along a valley – but it's set right on the edge of rugged landscape of huge limestone sinkholes. The area is so remote that the largest of these, **Dashiwei Tiankeng**, was only explored for the first time during the 1980s and tourism is still developing – if you like to get away from the crowds, this is where to head.

Dashiwei Tiankeng

大石围天坑, dàshí wéitiānkēng • Daily 8am–5pm • ¥98 includes a Chinese-speaking tour guide and transport around the park in a golf buggy • ☎ 0776 2844288, ⓦ dswtk.com • bus from opposite the post office on Tangle Lu in Leye every 30min from 8am–5pm, ¥5 • motor-rickshaw from the bus stop ¥15–20

The extraordinary landscapes at **Dashiwei Tiankeng** are 15km northwest of Leye. From the **park gates**, you join a tour and, after stopping off at a few minor sinkholes, you arrive at Dashiwei itself, which looks like – and probably is – a 1400m-high mountain which has collapsed in on itself, leaving a deep crater ringed by the jagged remnants of peaks. It takes a couple of hours to walk around the rim via interconnected stone staircases, with superlative vertigo-inducing views into the central sinkhole from the west ridge; sadly, you can't climb down inside. With some limestone caves thrown in on the return trip to the park gates, it's easy to spend four or five hours on site.

ARRIVAL AND DEPARTURE

LEYE

Baise (百色, bǎisè), a large rail town on the Youjiang River 265km northwest of Nanning and 100km southwest of Leye, is the jumping-off point for reaching the area.

BY TRAIN

By train Baise train station (百色火车站, bǎisè huǒchēzhàn) is off Zhanqian Dadao, at the top of Jinzhan Dadao, over at the eastern end of town on the Nanning–Kunming line. On arrival, bus #2 or a ¥30 taxi-ride can take you the 6km westwards to the Beida Transit Centre.

Destinations Kunming (6 daily; 9–10hr); Nanning (9 daily; 2hr 44min–3hr 48min).

BY BUS

Baise Beida Transit Centre (北大客运中心, běidà kèyùn zhōngxīn) is just north of Baise's city centre, with regular departures until 4pm to Nanning (3hr; ¥80) and Leye (4hr; ¥30).

Leye Bus Passenger Transport Station (乐业巴士客运站, lèyè bāshì kèyùn zhàn) is a couple of kilometres west of Leye's centre – catch a rickshaw for ¥10 to anywhere in town. Buses return to Baise until 5.30pm.

ACCOMMODATION AND EATING

BAISE

Jindu Dajiudian 金都大酒店, jīndú dàjiǔdiàn. Next to Baise Beida bus station ☎0776 2881180. The victim of patchy maintenance, but you can beat the rate down with some persistence and it makes a convenient place to stay in Baise. Also has an excellent restaurant on the second floor – more or less the only mid-price place in the vicinity. ¥228

LEYE

There are stir-fry stalls and noodle restaurants around Leye's central crossroads-cum-market, as well as on Xingle Lu, a strip of hotels, inexpensive restaurants and KTVs of varying quality. More upmarket hotels and bad Western restaurants line the posh shopping street of Sanle Nan Lu.

Jundu Hotel 君度酒店, jūndù jiǔdiàn. Xingle Lu

☎0776 2550189. This respectable mid-range place 200m north from the junction with Sanle Nan Lu is happy to take foreigners, has clean, comfortable rooms, wi-fi, and an attached restaurant serving decent food. Many other lessrespectable options on the same street. ¥218

DASHIWEI TIANKENG PARK AREA

Xiuxian 休闲度假农家乐, xiūxián dùjià nóngjiālè. Inside the park area at Meijia village (梅家山庄, méijiā shānzhuāng), ☎0776 2555671. Small, inexpensive and very friendly resort with clean rooms, firm beds and a mid-priced restaurant serving hearty local food. The turn-off there is about 2km south of Dashiwei Tiankeng and signposted for Chaundong Tiankeng. Chuandong is a cathedral-sized cave where no tourists go, but there is a path there through the lower part of the village – ask for directions. ¥50

10

Hua Shan

花山, huāshān • ¥80

If you fancy seeing more of the countryside between Nanning and Vietnam, **Hua Shan** is well worth the slight effort. Set in a beautifully isolated spot where tall karst peaks flank the **Zuo River**, waterfront cliffs at Hua Shan are daubed with **rock art** associated with prehistoric local culture. You can only get here by boat, and it's a placid journey up the Zuo, with buffalo wallowing in the shallows, people fishing from bamboo rafts and tending family plots, and the banks thick with spindly-branched, red-flowering kapok trees. The boat docks by the paintings, where steps lead to viewing platforms to see them close up. Nobody has worked out a definitive interpretation of the 1900 figures, but they include drummers and dancers, dogs and cattle, a dragon-boat race, men with arms bent upwards, a "king" with a sword, and just two women, long-haired and pregnant. Interesting as the paintings are, as with many of the best travels, the journey there is more rewarding than the destination.

ARRIVAL AND DEPARTURE
HUA SHAN

The access point for Hua Shan is Ningming (宁明, níngmíng).

By train Ningming station (宁明站, níngmíng zhàn) is right on the river, with two daily departures each to Nanning and the Vietnam border at Pingxiang.

By bus Ningming's bus station is 5km distant from the train station and river in the town itself. Regular buses run to Nanning until 7.50pm (2hr), and to Pingxiang until 6.20pm (1hr).

GETTING AROUND

There are two ways to get from Ningming to the site entrance and ticket office at Hua Shan village, 10km downstream from the rock art itself.

By rickshaw and boat You can take a rickshaw (¥40; 30min) along a very bumpy 9km road from Ningming to Hua Shan village, where you buy a ticket for one of three daily boat departures upstream (10am, 2pm and 4pm), though often you can tag along on package groups at other times. The trip from the ticket office takes two hours there and back, including 30min at the site.

By sampan Sampan owners at Tuolong Bridge Dock (驮龙桥码头, tuólóngqiáo mǎtóu), under the bridge 200m south of the train station, ask about ¥200 per person for the run upstream to Hua Shan village to buy a ticket, then continue to the rock art. Allow at least four or five hours for the return trip, including time on site.

10

ACCOMMODATION AND EATING

NINGMING

Ningming is a cheaply built-up concrete town. Good street food is available along Dehua Lu where, as probably the only foreigner in town, you'll be the focus of good-natured attention.

Jin Yuan Hotel 金圆旅馆, jīnyuán lǚdiàn. Near the bridge on Jiangbin Nan Lu, about 3km south of the train station, and 3km east of the bus station – ¥10 in a rickshaw from either ☎0771 8622189. Good rooms for the price which are clean and very homely

– and some even overlook the river. Also has free wi-fi. **¥108**

HUA SHAN VILLAGE

Hua Shan Resort 华山度假村, huáshān dùjiàcūn. ☎137 68596977. Huge, clean rooms with balconies looking out upon jungles and cliffs on the edge of the village make this a great place to stay, and only slightly more expensive than the cheapest hotels in Ningming. Has an overpriced but decent restaurant opposite, and very flexible room rates. **¥180**

Guizhou

贵州, guìzhōu

A traditional saying describes **Guizhou** as a land where there are "no three days without rain, no three fields without a mountain, and no three coins in any pocket". This is sadly accurate: Guizhou records the highest rainfall in China and has a poverty ensured by more than eighty percent of its land being covered in untillable mountains or leached limestone soils.

Still, ethnic identity and romantic landscapes have become marketable commodities in China, and Guizhou is beginning to capitalize on its two major assets. The province's most visible minority groups are the many branches of **Miao**, concentrated in the southeast around **Kaili**; and the **Bouyei**, who are based around the provincial capital, **Guiyang**, and the westerly town of **Anshun**. The Miao in particular indulge in a huge number of festivals, some of which attract tens of thousands of participants and are worth any effort to experience. As for **scenery**, there are spectacular **limestone caverns** at Longgong and Zhijin, both accessed from Anshun; impressive **waterfalls** at Huangguoshu – again near Anshun; and everywhere terraced hills, dotted with small villages. Naturalists will want to clock up rare **black-necked cranes**, which winter along the northwestern border with Yunnan at **Caohai Lake**; and at least have a stab at seeing the reclusive **golden monkey**, which lives in the cloud forests atop Guizhou's single holy mountain, northeasterly **Fanjing Shan**.

While Guizhou's often shambolic towns are definitely not a high point of a trip to the region, the one place worth a visit in its own right is **Zhenyuan**, over on the eastern side of the province, which features some antique buildings and temples squeezed along a beautiful stretch of river.

Brief history

Chinese influence was established here around 100 BC, but it wasn't until the government began settling Han migrants in the province during the seventeenth century that the local **ethnic groups** began to fight back, resistance culminating in the **Miao Uprising** of 1854–73, which rivalled the contemporary Taiping insurrection in terms of chaos and bloodshed. Sixty years later the region still hadn't recovered: Red Army soldiers passing through Guizhou in the 1930s found people working naked in the fields and an economy based on opium, and it's only in the last decades that Guizhou's population has exceeded numbers prior to the uprising. Today it's mining – coal and limestone – and tourism which keep Guizhou's economy afloat.

Guiyang

贵阳, guìyáng

GUIYANG lies in a valley basin, encircled by a range of hills that hems in the city and concentrates its traffic pollution. Established as a capital during the Ming

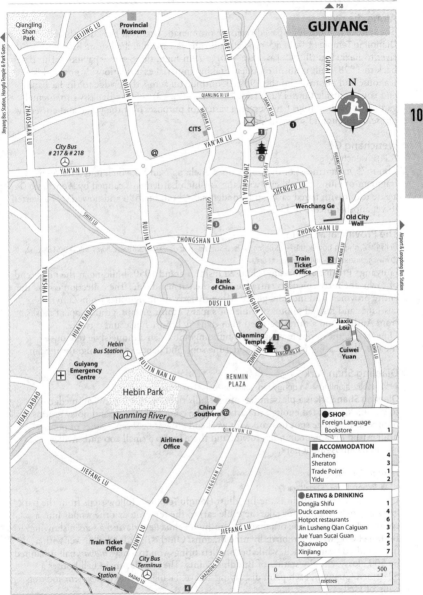

dynasty, modern Guiyang is a patchwork of elderly apartment blocks rubbing shoulders with glossy new high-rises and department stores, all intercut by a web of wide roads and flyovers. The effect may be downmarket and provincial, but Guiyang is a friendly place, whose unexpected few antique buildings and a surprisingly wild park lend a bit of character. With a spare half day, it's worth making an easy side-trip to the old garrison town of **Qingyan**, whose cobbled lanes and merchants' guildhalls provide a relief from Guiyang's crowded streets.

10

Along the river

The start of a 500m-long paved riverside promenade begins at the rather bland
Qianming Temple (黔明寺, qiánmíng sì) and runs east to an arched stone bridge across the
river to **Jiaxiu Lou** (甲秀楼, jiǎxiù lóu; ¥10), a 29m-high, three-storey pavilion. This dates
back to 1598, built to inspire students taking imperial examinations; it now holds a
teahouse and photos from the 1930s. Continue on across the bridge to the far bank,
and you're outside **Cuiwei Yuan** (粹惟园, cuìwéi yuán; ¥2), a Qing-dynasty ornamental
garden whose buildings have served a variety of purposes over the years, and currently
house tearooms and souvenir shops.

Wenchang Ge

文昌阁, wénchāng gé
About 750m northeast of the centre up Wenchang Nan Lu, you'll find a restored
fragment of Guiyang's old city wall, the 7m-high battlements capped by **Wenchang Ge**,
a gate tower with flared eaves and wooden halls, built in 1596 and nowadays converted
to yet another breezy teahouse.

The Provincial Museum

省博物馆, shěng bówùguǎn · 168 Beijing Lu · Tues–Sun 9am–5pm · Free · song and dance show ¥180 · ☎ 0851 6822232,
Ⓦ www.gzmuseum.com · northbound bus #1 or #2
Guiyang's **Provincial Museum** is housed inside a grand 1950s building at the north end
of town; the inconspicuous entrance is on the left-hand side. The collection covers the
entire province, and includes glazed Ming-dynasty tomb figurines from Zunyi,
costumes and festival photos of Guizhou's many ethnic groups, ground opera masks
from Anshun and a third-life-sized Han-dynasty bronze horse and carriage.
Downstairs, the opposite wing of the building houses an antique-style **teahouse
theatre**, showcasing Miao, Dong and Tujia song and dance routines nightly at 8pm.

Qianling Shan Park

黔灵山公园, qiánlíngshān gōngyuán · Daily 6am–6pm · ¥5 · northbound bus #1 or #2
Qianling Shan Park is a pleasant handful of hills right on the northwestern edge of
town, thickly forested enough to harbour some colourful birdlife and noisy groups of
monkeys. It's a nice spot to stroll with weekend crowds between a series of ponds,
bridges and ornamental undergrowth, and there is also a small **zoo** and smaller
children's **amusement park**.

Hongfu Temple

弘福寺, hóngfú sì · ¥2 · cable car ¥20
Qianling Shan's highlight is the Buddhist **Hongfu Temple** — follow steps from the park
gates for forty minutes (or take the cable car) to the top. You exit the woods into a
courtyard containing the ornamental, 4m-high **Fahua Pagoda** and a screen showing
Buddha being washed at birth by nine dragons. On the right is a bell tower with a
five-hundred-year-old bell, while bearing left brings you to a new *luohan* hall inhabited
by 500 glossy, chunky statues of Buddhist saints. The temple's main hall houses a
32-armed Guanyin, each palm displaying an eye, facing a rather benevolent-looking
King of Hell.

ARRIVAL AND DEPARTURE
GUIYANG

BY PLANE

Domestic and international tickets can most easily be
bought at the English-speaking CITS on Hequan Lu (see
p.624).
Longdongbao airport (龙洞国际机场, lóngdòng

guójì jīchǎng) lies 15km southeast of town; the airport
bus (every 30min 8.30am–7pm; ¥10) runs to the train
station, or a taxi to the centre costs ¥60.
Destinations Beijing (11 daily; 3hr); Chengdu (11 daily;
1hr); Guangzhou (24 daily; 1hr 30min); Guilin (2 daily;

10

45min); Kunming (10 daily; 1hr 10min); Nanning (3 daily; 1hr); Shanghai (13 daily; 2hr); Shenzhen (12 daily; 1hr 30min).

Yuping (23 daily; 6hr); Zhenyuan (17 daily; 5hr); Zunyi (16 daily; 3hr).

BY TRAIN

Buying tickets at the station is easy, or pay a ¥5 mark-up at the advance-purchase offices (8.30am–noon & 1–4pm) outside the station and downtown on Fushui Lu; see the map on p.621 for locations.

Guiyang train station (贵阳火车站, guìyáng huǒchē zhàn) is 1km south of the centre at the end of Zunyi Lu. In the large square outside you'll find taxis, and a city bus terminus ahead to the east: #1, which goes along Zunyi Lu and Zhonghua Lu, turning west along Beijing Lu and back to the train station down Ruijin Lu; and bus #2, which does the same route in reverse, are the two best routes for getting you close to the hotels.

Destinations Anshun (26 daily; 1hr 10min–1hr 43min); Beijing (4 daily; 30hr); Changsha (5 daily; 14hr); Chengdu (7 daily; 11–22hr); Chongqing (10 daily; 8–11hr); Guangzhou (5 daily; 21hr); Guilin (1 daily; 15hr); Huaihua (23 daily; 7hr); Kaili (23 daily; 2hr 20min–3hr); Kunming (13 daily; 10–15hr); Liupanshui/Shuicheng (21 daily; 4hr); Shanghai (5 daily; 30hr).

BY BUS

Coming from either long-distance bus station, touts will pick up passengers for share-taxis going to the centre for around ¥10, saving you time and stress.

Jinyang bus station (金阳客车站, jīnyáng kèchēzhàn) is a colossal depot about 15km west of the city, handling departures to more or less everywhere west and south of the province and cities within (except Zunyi); from here, catch bus #219 to the train station or #217 or #218 to Yan'an Lu, which takes about 1hr. Taxis charge about ¥60.

Longdong Bao (East) bus station (龙洞公共汽车站, lóngdòng gōnggòng qìchē zhàn) is a new bus station near the airport and handles all provincial and national buses heading east and north of Guiyang. Take a #240 bus to the train station; a taxi is again about ¥60, and takes 40min to an hour.

Destinations Anshun (1hr 30min); Huangguoshu (3hr); Kaili (3hr); Kunming (19hr); Nanning (18hr); Rongjiang (8hr); Zunyi (2hr).

GETTING AROUND

Getting around Guiyang can be a pain due to the horrendous traffic. Walking is usually quicker for shorter journeys, especially at rush-hour.

By bus The bus system is straightforward, although buses are usually quite crowded and slow.

By taxi Taxis are plentiful, starting at ¥8 on the meter with

a ¥1 fuel surcharge added to all journeys. It's near impossible to get one at 4–4.30pm when the shifts change, however.

INFORMATION

Travel agents CITS are at 7F, Longquan Dasha, 1 Hequan Lu, near the corner with Yan'an Lu ☎ 0851 6901575 (daily 9am–6pm). The 25-storey yellow tower is easy to find, but the entrance is not, especially as there is no CITS sign outside – you have to cut down the first alley on the left

north of the junction, then turn left at the police post to a lift lobby at the back. The helpful staff speak English, French and German, and are a mine of information about the province, as well as being the easiest place to book flights, hotels and tours. Ask for Arnaud Xie or Otti Zhang.

ACCOMMODATION

Guiyang's accommodation is mostly mid-range, and the few budget options for under ¥100, along Dadao Lu by the train station, are a bit grotty and usually fill quickly.

Jincheng 金城酒店, jīnchéng jiǔdiàn. 3 Dadao Lu ☎ 0851 5764111. Almost opposite the *Home Inn* sign, this mid-range place is one of the nicest near the train station for the price, with it's homely, slightly shabby rooms having comfortable beds and computers. ¥336

Sheraton 喜来登贵航酒店, xǐláidēng guìháng jiǔdiàn. 49 Zhonghua Nan Lu ☎ 0851 5888280, ⓦ sheraton.com/guiyang. Amazing marble construction featuring a bar on the 37th floor and an Italian restaurant on the 38th that offer great views at a price. Rooms are as

luxurious and comfortable as you'd expect, and it also has a gym, pavement café outside, and an indoor swimming pool. ¥855

★ **Trade Point** 柏顿宾馆, bódùn bīnguǎn. 18 Yan'an Dong Lu ☎ 0851 5827888, ⓦ trade-pointhotel .com. Sharp, four-star option in a central location with local and Cantonese, and Western restaurants (the latter does a great buffet breakfast 7–10.30am for ¥82 per person) and all executive trimmings – including broadband and a good coffee shop in the lobby. ¥595

Yidu 逸都酒店, yìdū jiǔdiàn. 9 Zhiye Lu (off Wenchang Nan Lu) ☎0851 8649777. Mid-range hotel which allows single travellers to pay by the bed, rather than for a whole room. Rooms are comfortable and those not overlooking the main road are quiet. Rates usually discounted. Beds **¥70**, doubles **¥358**

EATING AND DRINKING

With its predilection for dog meat, chillies and sour soups, Guizhou's cuisine comes under the western Chinese cooking umbrella, though there's a wide variety of food available in town. Snack stalls are scattered through the centre; the block on Fushui Lu north of Zhongshan Lu has several long-established, inexpensive duck canteens, serving it crisp-fried in the local style (ask them to hold the pepper if you don't want a numb mouth). One local speciality is thin crêpes – called "silk dolls" (丝娃娃, sīwáwa) – which you fill from a selection of pickled and fresh vegetables to resemble an uncooked spring roll. The best places to try them lie just outside Qianling Shan Park. Hotpots are a Guizhou institution, with tables centred round a bubbling pot of slightly sour, spicy stock, in which you cook your own food – the best are along Qingyun Lu and serve freshwater fish, fried in a hotpot at your table. For Western food, there are dozens of cafés serving coffee and set meals of steak or burgers. The main drag for nightlife is along Xingguan Lu, which is dotted with Chinese-style drinking venues.

Dongjia Shifu 侗家食府, dóngjiā shífǔ. 242 Beijing Lu ☎0851 6507186, ⊛djsf.com.cn. Dong minority theme restaurant with staff dressed in colourful garb and a tree in the middle of the restaurant. Haute cuisine meets bush tucker, with turtle and various insects impeccably presented on fine china. Otherwise, the noodles and sour soups are good and the place has some character. Mains around ¥40–60, but enough for two. Daily 7am–9pm.

Jin Lusheng Qian Caiguan 金芦笙黔菜馆, jīn lúshēng qián càiguǎn. 18 Gongyuan Lu ☎0851 5821388. Another ethnic theme restaurant, this time Miao. Downstairs is an inexpensive canteen with mostly noodle soups; head upstairs for more formal settings and a proper picture-menu with pricey mains around ¥45, with what looks like a pyramid of pig particularly popular. Daily 8am–9pm.

★ **Jue Yuan Sucai Guan** 觉园素菜馆, juéyuán sùcàiguǎn. 49 Fushui Bei Lu ☎0851 5841957. Vegetarian restaurant attached to a small Buddhist temple.

Along with fairly inexpensive stir-fries, they also do elegant "Lion's Head" stewed rissoles, "Eight Treasure Duck" (stuffed with sweet bean paste and sticky rice), "Lotus Fish" and Guizhou-style chicken – despite the names, all are made from meat substitutes. Photo menu and large portions. Dishes ¥30–80. Daily 8am–8pm.

Qiaowaipo 巧外婆, qiǎowàipó. 6 Yangming Lu ☎0851 5860288. Guizhou country cooking – lots of chillies, sour soups and pork stews – nicely served in a smart, modern establishment with possible views of the river. Even a portion of the excellent fried rice is enough for two. Mains ¥20–60. Daily 11am–10pm.

Xinjiang 新疆维吾尔天山餐厅, xīnjiāng wéiwú'ěr tiānshān cāntīng. Zunyi Lu, set back off the street north of Jiefang Lu ☎138 85196882. Lively, slightly seedy place offering Muslim grills, stews and noodles, from just a few yuan up to around ¥35. Best are the inexpensive lamb kebabs and fresh bread, cooked at the outside breadoven and barbecue. Daily 11am–10pm.

DIRECTORY

Banks and exchange The main Bank of China (Mon–Fri 9–11.30am & 1.30–5pm) with a foreign exchange is just west of Zhonghua Lu on Dusi Lu.

Bookshop The Foreign Language Bookshop, on Yan'an Lu, is well stocked with classics, an eclectic range of children's books, maps of the city and province, and Chinese guidebooks on Guizhou.

Internet Two convenient places charging ¥3/hr are on

Yan'an Lu, just east of Ruijin Lu; and opposite China Southern on Zunyi Lu – one is a gaming centre so look for the MMORPG characters in the window.

Mail The main post office (daily 9am–6pm) is on the Huabei Lu/Yan'an Lu intersection.

PSB The visa department is in the north of the city at 5 Daying Lu (Mon–Fri 9am–noon & 1.30–5pm; ☎0851 7987284), on the bus #26 route.

CANINE CUISINE

Dog meat is widely appreciated not only in southwestern China, but also in culturally connected countries across Southeast Asia, with the meat considered to be warming in cold weather and an aid to male virility. For some Westerners, eating dog can be akin to cannibalism; others are discouraged by the way restaurants display bisected hindquarters in the window, or soaking in a bucket of water on the floor. If you're worried about being served dog by accident, 我不吃狗肉, wǒ bùchī gǒuròu, means "I don't eat dog".

10

10

Qingyan

青岩, qīngyán • ¥80 • Daily 8.30am–6.30pm

The remains of a Ming-dynasty fortified town 36km south of Guiyang at **QINGYAN** makes for an interesting few hours' excursion. On arrival, don't despair at the shabby bus station area, but turn left and left again then cross the road to the ticket office and entrance to the **old town** (古镇, gǔzhèn), which was founded in 1373 as a military outpost during the first major Han incursions into the region. The best area is at the southern end, where a flagstoned street lined with low wooden shops – most of them now given over to tourism concerns – leads to the **Baisui memorial arch** (百岁坊, bǎisuì fāng), decorated with crouching lions, and out through the town wall into the fields via the solid stone south gate.

ARRIVAL AND DEPARTURE   QINGYAN

By bus Bus #210 from Guiyang's Hebin bus station (河滨 客运站, hébīn kèyùnzhàn) on Ruijin Lu runs to Qingyan (1hr 30min–2hr; ¥5) via Huaxi (花溪, huāxī), where most of Guizhou's universities are, so the traffic is quite bad and rush hour is best avoided. Transport back to Guiyang runs until late afternoon.

ACCOMMODATION AND EATING

There are plenty of places to snack as you wander Qingyan's lanes – deep-fried balls of tofu are a local speciality – and even some accommodation.

Guzhen Kezhan 古镇客栈, gǔzhèn kèzhàn. 38 Dong Jie Lu ✆ 0851 3200031. An atmospheric hotel housed in an old guildhall next to the market, which can get noisy, so the rooms at the back are better. Still, it's clean and characterful, with high ceilings and all mod cons, such as wi-fi. **¥160**

Zunyi

遵义, zūnyì

Some 170km north of Guiyang, **ZUNYI** is surrounded by heavy industry, but the city centre contains a pleasant older quarter and hilly parkland. It was here that the Communist army arrived on their **Long March** in January 1935, in disarray after months on the run and having suffered two defeats in their attempts to join up with sympathetic forces in Hunan. Having captured the city by surprise, the leadership convened the **Zunyi Conference**, at which Mao Zedong supplanted Russian Comintern advisors as political head of the Communist Party. The Russians had modelled their strategies on urban-based uprisings, but Mao felt that China's revolution could only succeed by mobilizing the peasantry, and that the Communist forces should base themselves in the countryside to do this. His opinions carried the day, marking the Communists' first step towards Beijing. (For more on the Long March, see p.450.)

The Zunyi Conference Site

遵义会议址, zūnyì huìyìzhǐ • Daily 8.30am–5.30pm • Free but passport required • bus #1, #3 or #4 from the train station via Beijing Lu

The **Zunyi Conference Site** occupies a block of the **old town** and adjacent lanes, with several 1930s grey-brick buildings restored and turned into museums. These include the grand **Zunyi Conference Museum** (遵义会议博物馆, zūnyì huìyì bówùguǎn) on Ziyin Lu, stocked with old photos, maps, heroic sculptures and a few period weapons captioned in Chinese; and the **Site of the Red Army Political Department** (红军总政治部

ZUNYI ORIENTATION

Zunyi is awkwardly laid out around triangular **Fenghuang Shan** (凤凰山, fènghuáng shān), with the old town and revolutionary sites 3km from arrival points on Fenghuang Shan's southwestern slopes.

旧址, hóngjūn zǒngzhèngzhì bùjiùzhǐ) in the grounds of a French Catholic church behind, built in 1866 in an interesting compromise between Chinese and European Gothic styles. Strangely, the original Conference Hall is not even signposted – it's the locked, two-storey brick building on the right as you enter the Zunyi Conference Museum grounds. Just up the lane from here, 500m-long **Red Army Street** (红军街, hóngjūn jiē) has, ironically, been turned into the inevitable pedestrianized "old street", full of souvenirs and local snack stalls.

ARRIVAL AND DEPARTURE   ZUNYI   **10**

Zunyi's bus and train stations are within 100m of each other at the grimy eastern side of town.

By train The train sation sits off the eastern end of Beijing Lu, with services through the day to Guiyang and Chongqing. Destinations Chongqing (11 daily; 7hr); Guiyang (16 daily; 3hr).

By bus There are buses to Guiyang between 7am and 7pm (2hr 30min; ¥59) and three morning buses to Chishui (¥60; 6hr).
Destinations Chishui (6hr); Guiyang (2hr 30min).

ACCOMMODATION AND EATING

Frankly, Zunyi isn't a great place to stay, and frequent transport onwards means that you might not have to. Inexpensive accommodation surrounds the stations, where hostel staff pounce on passing foreigners. The area also has abundant places to get a bowl of noodles or plate of dumplings.

Keyunzhan Binguan 客运站宾馆, kèyùnzhàn bīnguǎn. Right beside the bus station ☎0852 8460000. Basic, echoing concrete building offering bare comforts, but good enough if you get stuck in town for the night – though rooms at the front collect traffic noise wafting up from the street. **¥85**

7 Days Inn 7天连锁酒店, qītiān liánsuǒ jiǔdiàn. 36 Beijing Lu, 250m west of the station area ☎0852 8702888. Not quite up to the chain's usual standards – it looks as if it was built in a hurry and on a tight budget – but much more pleasant than anything else in the neighbourhood. **¥185**

Chishui

赤水, chìshuǐ

CHISHUI is a fairly large riverside town on the Sichuanese border, among a forested spread of red sandstone formations: *chishui* means "red water", and during the summer rains the river runs a vivid ochre colour. A substantial fragment of the old city walls stands down by the river, but the town is basically just a stepping stone out to bamboos and waterfalls at Sidonggou.

Sidonggou

四洞沟, sìdòng gōu • Daily 8am–5pm • Sept–June ¥15, July–Aug ¥25 • minibus from Renmin Lu to park gates ¥7

Some 15km from town, **Sidong Gou** comprises verdant pockets of bamboos, 3m-high *spinulosa* tree ferns, gingers, orchids and moss-covered rocks flanking a narrow gully. Six kilometres of flagstoned paths follow either side of a small, bright-red river, up through thick bamboo forests past four big **waterfalls** – including one split by a large boulder – and several water curtains to walk behind, to the trail's end at 30m-high **Bailong Falls** (白龙瀑布, báilóng pùbù).

ARRIVAL AND DEPARTURE   CHISHUI

By bus Chishui's Keyun bus station (科韵汽车站, kēyùn qìchēzhàn) is uphill from the river on Renmin Lu. From Guiyang, you'll need to change buses in the industrial town of Zunyi, which is pretty straightforward. To head into

Sichuan, cross the river to tiny Jiuzhi (九支, jiǔzhī) and pick up one of the frequent minibuses to Luzhou (3hr; ¥20), for connections to Yibin (see p.742).

ACCOMMODATION AND EATING

Stalls and cheap diners down along the river wall are the best places to eat, and there are also a few places to stay, though most suffer from damp.

Chishui Dajiudian 赤水大酒店, chìshuǐ dàjiǔdiàn.
106 Renmin Xi Lu ⊕ 0852 2821334. Situated right next
to the bridge that crosses the river into Sichuan, this place
has some reasonable, fairly clean rooms which were
renovated not long ago. The deluxe rooms have river
views. **¥160**

Southeastern Guizhou

Southeastern Guizhou forms a landscape of high hills cut by rivers and dotted with
dark wooden houses with buffaloes plodding around rice terraces. Women working in
the fields have babies strapped to their backs under brightly quilted pads, and their
long braided hair is coiled into buns secured by silver hairpins and fluorescent plastic
combs. They are **Miao**, and their villages around the district capital, **Kaili**, are noted for
their exuberant festivals, which though increasingly touristed have managed to retain
their cultural integrity. Beyond Kaili, there's a scenic route southeast to the
mountainous border with Guangxi province, where **Dong** hamlets sport their unique
drum towers and bridges (see p.612). Kaili is connected by good road and rail links to
Guiyang and neighbouring Hunan, with buses and minibuses providing regular
services elsewhere.

Kaili

凯里, kǎilǐ

KAILI, 170km east of Guiyang, is a moderately industrialized, easy-going focus for
China's 7.5 million Miao ethnic minority, though there's little to see in town. The most
interesting **market area** is along the eastern end of Ximen Jie, a narrow street packed
with village-like stalls selling vegetables, trinkets, meat and even livestock. Dage Xiang
heads uphill from here to **Dage Park** (大阁公园, dàgé gōngyuán), a paved area with a
granite **pagoda** where old men gather to smoke and decorate the trees with their caged
songbirds. The whole area at the top of Dage Xiang comes alive at night, when
barbecue stalls with tables are set up, creating a very convivial atmosphere.

Minority Culture Museum

贵州省凯里博物馆, guìzhōu shěng kǎilǐ bówùguǎn · Zhaoshan Lu · Daily 9am–5pm · Free with passport
The town's only other diversion is the excellent **Minority Culture Museum** at the south
end of Zhaoshan Lu, with three floors of bright festival garments and silver jewellery,
photographs of many of the more famous festivals, and a potted history of the region
– most displays have captions in English.

ARRIVAL AND DEPARTURE

KAILI

BY TRAIN

In the north of town, on the Hunan–Guiyang line. Catch
buses #1 or #2 to the centre; a taxi or motorbike costs ¥10–
15. In town, tickets can be purchased at the Railway
Booking Office, by the bridge at the north end of Dongmen
Jie.

Destinations Changsha (5 daily; 10hr 13min–15hr
30min); Guiyang (23 daily; 2hr 20min–3hr); Huaihua (25
daily; 4hr); Yuping (19 daily; 2hr 30min); Zhenyuan (14
daily; 1hr 30min).

BY BUS

Journey times below will be greatly reduced by the

imminent opening of new highways through the region.
Long-distance bus station (长途客运站, chángtú
kèyùnzhàn) is just on the edge of the town centre on
Wenhua Bei Lu, and is the main station for most
destinations.

Shiyusi bus station (市晕死总线站, shìyū sī
zōngxiàn zhàn), just west of the centre on Shiyu Lu,
serves buses heading northeast to Huangping, via Matang
and Chong An.

Destinations Guiyang (2hr 30min); Rongjiang (4hr);
Zhenyuan (4hr); Huangping (1hr 30min); Matang (20min);
Chong An (1hr).

INFORMATION AND TOURS

Travel agents Kaili's CITS is just left inside the
gates at the *Yingpanpo* hotel (Mon–Sat 8.30am–6pm

⊕ 0855 8222506, ⊛ minority-tour.com). They have
information about village festivals and market days, useful

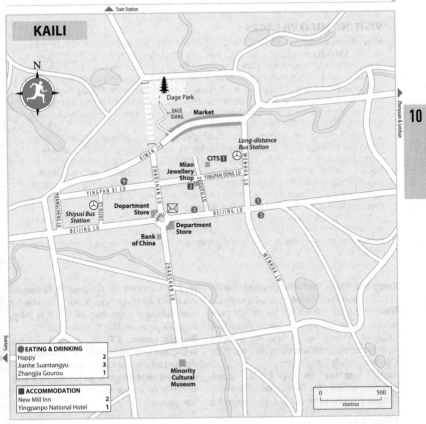

EATING & DRINKING

Happy	2
Jianhe Suantangyu	3
Zhangjia Gourou	1

ACCOMMODATION

New Mill Inn	2
Yingpanpo National Hotel	1

bilingual maps of Kaili and its environs, and guiding services in English starting at ¥400 per day. Ask for Wu Zeng Ou who is very knowledgeable about the region – especially the Dong areas – and speaks excellent English.

Private guides For an extremely helpful and reliable Miao guide contact Li Maoqing (☏ 01398 5298315, ✉ leemqing@hotmail.com, ⊕ tribaltours.net); he charges similar rates to the CITS and also speaks good English.

ACCOMMODATION

The bus and train stations both sit among basic lodgings charging ¥100 or even less, though not all are foreigner-friendly.

New Mill Inn 新磨坊连锁酒店, xīnmòfāng liánsuǒ jiǔdiàn. 26 Yingpan Dong Lu ☏ 0855 2100188. Actually hidden just off Yingpan Donglu, this is the nicest of Kaili's less expensive options. Rooms are very clean with surprisingly comfortable beds, and wooden floors. Staff don't speak any English but do their best to help you out. **¥120**

Yingpanpo National Hotel 营盘坡民族宾馆, yíngpánpō mínzú bīnguǎn. Take Zhoufu Lu round the back of 53 Yingpan Dong Lu, just past the tennis court ☏0855 3827779. Old but well-maintained establishment, offering friendly service, very comfortable rooms which boast clean bathrooms and beds you can sink into. Nice and quiet, it's also centrally located, and within walking distance of both the main bus station and the old town. **¥350**

EATING

Bun and noodle stalls surround the bus station on Wenhua Lu, though the best munching can be done at night either along the night food street running west off Dage Xiang or around the pagoda in the old town, where you can eat various inexpensive barbecued foods on sticks at plastic outside tables.

10

VISITING MIAO VILLAGES

Miao villages around Kaili are best visited on market days or during one of the many annual festivals. **Markets** operate on a five-day cycle, with the busiest at Chong An and Shidong; most festivals take place in early spring, early summer or late autumn and attract thousands of people for buffalo fights, dances, performances of *lusheng* (a long-piped bamboo instrument) and horse or boat races. The biggest event of the year is the springtime **Sisters' Meal**, the traditional time for girls to choose a partner: don't miss it if you're in the region. Just note that Chinese information sometimes confuses lunar and Gregorian dates – "9 February", for instance, might mean "the ninth day of the second lunar month".

If there's nothing special going on, head south of Kaili to the picturesque villages of Langde Shang and Xijiang, though easy access means plenty of other visitors. Kaili's CITS can suggest less touristic alternatives, where it's possible to end up sharing lunch at a farmer's home (usually sour fish or chicken hotpot) and being given impromptu festival performances by young women in their best silver and embroidered jackets – you'll have to pay, of course, but it's worth the price. Beware the hospitable Miao custom of encouraging guests to indulge in their very drinkable but potent **sticky rice wine**.

Most villages are connected by at least daily bus services from Kaili, and also make possible stopovers on the way out of the region. Return transport can leave quite early, however, so be prepared to stay the night or hitch back if you leave things too late. There are no banks in any of the villages.

Happy 开心, kāixīn. North off Beijing Dong Lu ✆ 189 08552949. Hidden behind barbecue stalls, this is a popular Taiwanese-style café selling bubble tea and light meals, including *siwawa* (see p.625) as well as various fairly inexpensive and tasty fried-rice dishes. Has an English menu and friendly service with mains and drinks in the ¥12–20 range. Daily 11am–11.30pm.

Jianhe Suantang yu 剑河酸汤鱼, jiànhé suāntāngyú. 83 Beijing Dong Lu ✆ 136 38084327. Best place in town to try the local speciality sour soup fish

(酸汤鱼, suān tāng yú). Chose your fish, sit down and they'll kill it and bring it to you to cook on the table in a wonderfully tangy hotpot. Prices are ¥60–80/*jin* (500g), around ¥50 per person. Daily 11.30am–11pm.

Zhangjia Gourou 张家狗肉, zhāngjiā gǒuròu. Beijing Dong Lu ✆ 159 85524353. The most popular dog restaurant in town – they cook it up in a spicy soup here, though you might struggle to get past the doggy hind-quarters in the window. About ¥40–50 a person. Daily 9am–9pm.

DIRECTORY

Banks and exchange The main Bank of China and ATM is on Zhaoshan Lu (foreign exchange Mon–Fri 8.30–11am & 2–5pm) – the last branch until you reach Guilin in Guangxi

province, if you're heading that way.
Post office Right in the centre of town on Beijing Dong Lu at the main crossroads.

Northwest of Kaili

Some interesting places northwest of Kaili can be tied together into a long day-trip, or used as a stage in a roundabout journey to Zhenyuan (see p.633).

Matang

麻塘, mátáng

MATANG, a village about 20km west of Kaili, is inhabited by **Geyi**, a group who, despite similarities with the Miao, insist on their individuality. Buses heading to Longchang drop you off by a pink gateway on the main road, from where it's a twenty-minute walk to the village, an attractive place with many wooden buildings. Big groups get a welcome dance and there are always people selling embroideries and **batik**, a Geyi speciality.

Chong An

重安, chóngān

Past Matang and about 35km from Kaili, **CHONG AN** is a dishevelled riverside town with a few old wood-and-stone buildings and a superb **market** held every fifth day,

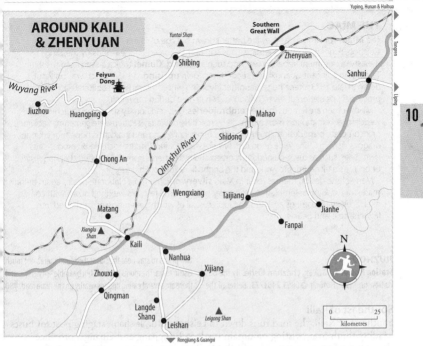

where you'll be battered by diminutive Miao grandmothers as they shop or bring in clothes (everything from traditional pleated skirts to jeans) for dyeing in boiling vats of indigo. There's also a **suspension bridge** here, with chains smelted from locally mined iron, built in 1874 on the orders of Zhou Dawu, a Qing general who had been fighting the Miao.

Jiuzhou

旧洲, jiùzhōu
Some 20km north of Chong An, **HUANGPING** (黄平, huángpíng) is an anonymous small town, from where minibuses run high up into the hills to **JIUZHOU**. Jiuzhou is a surprise: a substantial market town whose main street is lined with old buildings, some dating back three hundred years. Remains of a southern-style **Tianhou Temple** (天后宫, tiānhòu gōng), a European **Catholic church** and a merchants' **guildhall** all point to a formerly cosmopolitan population, unexpected given the remote location. There's another big market here every four days; check dates with Kaili's CITS.

GETTING AROUND NORTHWEST OF KAILI

By bus and minibus Buses and minibuses shuttle along the main road between Kaili and Huangping all through the day, taking about an hour and a half and stopping at both Matang and Chong An. From Huangping, there are slightly less regular minibuses to Jiuzhou, though be aware the road is quite atrocious – one of the reasons the town feels relatively untouched by tourism. There are also buses between Huangping and Shibing (施秉, shībǐng), 30km to the northeast, which itself has services to Zhenyuan until late afternoon.

ACCOMMODATION

CHONG AN

Wangjiang Lou 望江楼, wàngjiāng lóu. ☎0855 2351999. Right in the middle of the village, this has clean, neat rooms with a/c, though only squat toilets. A step up from the other more basic accommodation nearby, and there's also a reasonable restaurant on the second floor. **¥120**

10

THE MIAO

The **Miao** – or Hmong, as they are better known outside of China – are spread through Guizhou, Yunnan, Sichuan, Vietnam, Laos and Burma. Forced off their lands by the Qing-dynasty government, rebels in Guizhou such as **Zhang Xiumei** took a lesson from the Taipings in adjacent Guangxi and seeded their own **uprising** in 1854, which was only put down in late 1873 after a huge slaughter involving whole towns being obliterated: out of a provincial population of seven million, over half died during the revolt.

Miao women are famous for their **embroideries**: girls traditionally spent years stitching their wedding jackets, though most are made by machine nowadays. Patterns are sometimes abstract, or incorporate plant designs, butterflies (the bringer of spring and indicating hoped-for change), dragons, fish – a China-wide good luck symbol – and buffalo motifs. Each region produces its own styles, such as the sequined, curly green and red patterns from the southerly Leishan district, Chong'an's dark geometric work, and the bright, fiery lions of Shidong.

Many of the design themes recur in Miao **silverwork**, the most elaborate pieces again being made for wedding assemblages. Women appear at some festivals weighed down with coil necklaces, spiral earrings and huge headpieces, all of which are embossed or shaped into flowers, bells and beasts.

JIUZHOU

Station Hostel 车站旅社, chēzhàn lǚshè. By the bus station on Majia Hutong ☎ 0855 2483773. Better of the two places to stay near the bus station, and there's not much else in town. The rooms are basic but bearable – if noisy – and there are several eating options nearby on the main road. **¥80**

Southeast of Kaili

Southeast of Kaili, the road runs down to **Leishan** (雷山, léishān), staging post for buses heading south over twisting mountain roads to Rongjiang and Guangxi province through the Dong regions (see p.612). On the way to Leishan, either Langde Shang or Xijiang villages offer picturesque places to get off the bus and explore.

Langde Shang

郎德上, lángdé shàng

LANGDE SHANG, about 40km from Kaili, was a rebel base during the Miao Uprising and remains a tremendously photogenic collection of wooden houses, cobbles, fields and chickens set on a terraced hillside capped in pine trees, a 2km walk from the main road. Plenty of silverwork is thrust at you as you wander, but get past this and the atmosphere is pretty genuine – locals might offer home-stay accommodation for the night for as little as ¥20.

Xijiang

西江, xījiāng • ¥120

XIJIANG is an incredible collection of closely packed wooden houses built on stone foundations, all ranged up the side of two adjacent hills about 90km southeast of Kaili. The fact that there's a hefty entry fee hints at the commercialization here, and on market days you can barely move for tourists – in fact the majority of houses are now small hotels. However, there's real pleasure in exploring the narrow, stepped lanes that lead through the village and onto the terraced fields above, where you could hike around for hours among tremendous views. There are traditional Miao singing and dancing performances in the main square daily at 11.30am and 5pm.

GETTING AROUND   SOUTHEAST OF KAILI

By bus and minibus Langde Shang is just off the main Kaili–Leishan road, served by shuttles between the two (every 30min, 8am–5pm). Xijiang is on its own loop road, with services to Kaili five times a day until early afternoon (1hr; ¥10), and to Leishan every 30min (6.30am–5.30pm; 1hr 30min).

ACCOMMODATION

Xijiang Yue Hotel 西江月酒店, xijiāngyuè jiǔdiàn. Xijiang village ☎0855 3348678. Located on the main square by the river (look for four red lanterns outside), this hotel's neat, clean rooms are well equipped. Their restaurant has a lovely outdoor terrace, most pleasant in the evenings when you can see the lanterns twinkling across the village. **¥200**

Shidong

施洞, shīdòng

SHIDONG is a single-street town on the banks of the **Qingshui River**, 60km northeast from Kaili. There's a great market here, one of the best in the region, held on the riverside shingle, where jostling farmers sort though the selection of livestock, clothing, foodstuffs and modern silverwork and textiles. Shidong also hosts the second and third days of the Miao Sisters' Meal festival, featuring bullfights (head-to-head combat between rival buffaloes), dragon-boat races, communal dancing and mass consumption of rice wine. The colourful dragon boats can be viewed in a boathouse next to the main road.

ARRIVAL AND DEPARTURE **SHIDONG**

By bus Buses leave from Kaili's long-distance bus station direct to Shidong every hour and a half until 5pm, and take 3hr.

ACCOMMODATION

Yingbin Zhaodaisuo 迎宾招待所, yíngbīn zhāodàisuǒ. ☎0855 5359174. Right next to the post office on the main street, this place offers extremely basic accommodation with shared bathrooms and no a/c. There's another similar place, *Luoping Zhaodaisuo*, on the other side of the post office. Note that rates increase tenfold during festivals. **¥30**

Zhenyuan

镇远, zhènyuan

ZHENYUAN town – occupying a straight, constricted valley 100km northeast of Kaili on the **Wuyang River** – sprang up in the Ming dynasty to guard the trade route through to central China. Quite aside from a couple of genuinely old structures to check out, Zhenyuan is probably the only town in the whole province that could be described as attractive: the aquamarine river runs westwards, with tall, antique-style houses piled together along both banks, all lit at night by lanterns.

The old town

古城, gǔchéng

Zhenyuan's old town sits north of the river along Xinzhong Jie, comprising a kilometre of wood and stone buildings, built in the Qing style and backed up against stony cliffs. Part-way along, the town museum (镇远博物馆, zhènyuǎn bówùguǎn; daily 7.30am–5pm; ¥10) is more interesting perhaps as an unrestored example of Qing architecture than for the exhibition of old photos. Past here, the road turns north with the river and you'll reach a multiple-arch, solid stone **Ming-dynasty bridge** (祝圣桥, zhùshèng qiáo) over the river to sixteenth-century **Qinglong Dong** (青龙洞, qīnglóng dòng; 7.30am–6pm; ¥60), whose separate Taoist, Buddhist and Confucian halls appear to grow out of a cliff face, all dripping wet and hung with vines.

The Southern Great Wall

南长城, nán chángchéng • ¥30 • Daily 7am–6pm

By the western end of the old bridge you'll find a small set of steps (and ticket office), which lead through back lanes, via forest and a small temple, to a fragment of the thirteenth-century **Southern Great Wall**. The wall, which runs eastwards to Fenghuang in Hunan (see p.437), is almost totally demolished, standing only 3m at its highest point, but there are superb views northeast into Hunan from the ridge – especially beautiful at night when the lights from towns and villages across the landscape seem to reflect the stars.

ARRIVAL AND DEPARTURE | ZHENYUAN

The train and bus stations are next to each other about 3km west of town on the south side of the river – a taxi to the old town is ¥7.

By train Zhenyuan station (镇远站, zhènyuǎn zhàn) is on the Hunan–Kaili–Guiyang line. There's no train booking office in town, so best book tickets when you arrive, as the ticket office at the station isn't very big.

Destinations Guiyang (18 daily; 3hr 33min–5hr); Huaihua (25 daily; 2hr 30min); Kaili (14 daily; 1hr 30min); Yuping (16 daily; 1hr).

By bus There are half a dozen buses daily southwest via Shidong to Kaili, and also east to Yuping (for Fanjing Shan) and Tongren (铜仁, tóngrén) for connections to Fenghuang in Hunan.

ACCOMMODATION AND EATING

The old town is lined with accommodation and attractive restaurants, though food isn't memorable; in summer, it's more fun to head over the new bridge to the opposite bank and enjoy simple hotpots at alfresco tables with the rest of town.

One Meter Sunshine Inn 一米阳光客栈, yīmǐ yángguāng kèzhàn. Next to the river by the Ming Dynasty bridge ☏ 0855 5723996. One of the few places that has an English sign, this small inn is fantastically placed and its inexpensive rooms are clean enough (if a little basic), with balconies looking over the river at its most picturesque point. **¥120**

Yongfurong Kezhan 永福荣客栈, yǒngfúróng kèzhàn. 200m down Xinzhong Jie from the bridge ☏ 0855 5730888, ⓦ yongfurong.net. This well-run place has comfortable and very chic ethnic-style rooms which are clean and have modern bathrooms and river views. Its café also overlooks the river and its restaurant serves pretty good mid-price food. **¥288**

Fanjing Shan

梵净山, fànjìng shān • ¥110 • minibus from Heiwan to steps ¥20 • cable car ¥90 one-way, ¥160 return

Hidden away in Guizhou's remote northeastern corner, not far from the Hunan border, **Fanjing Shan** is an ancient religious site, the name translating as "Mountain of the Pure Buddhist Land". With its upper reaches covered in wild cloud forests, it's also home to endangered **golden monkeys** (金丝猴, jīnsī hóu), though with the entire population numbering only 400 adults, you'll be lucky to see them. Recent development has tamed the formerly epic ascent, especially if you use the modern cable car, but despite an influx of tourists, Fanjing Shan remains one of Guizhou's highlights – though visit on a weekday if you can, when there are fewer people about.

Heiwan

Fanjing Shan's park gates are at **HEIWAN** (黑湾, hēiwān), a couple of streets that funnel visitors from the grubby bus station past restaurants and stalls of overpriced tourist tat to a large square. Here there are the park gates, a ticket office, a car park and a drinks stand – a good place to stock up on liquids as prices inside the park are expensive. Take something warm for the top – it snows in winter – but don't bring up more than a day-pack.

To the summit

From Heiwan, minibuses cover the twenty-minute, 9km run to the foot of Fanjing Shan. Here, you can catch a **cable car** to just below summit area in twenty-five minutes, though this still leaves a good forty-minute walk to Fanjing Shan's 2572m-high summit.

For the fit and healthy only, there are also more than eight thousand **steps** up the mountain, which follow steep ridges with no regard for gradient – allow three to four hours to ascend and at least two to come down. Steps are numbered with red paint and carved inscriptions, and refreshment shacks provide sustenance until step 4500 and then there's nothing until the top. The forest – hung with vines and old man's beard and with a dwarf bamboo understorey – is vibrantly green and stiflingly humid in summer.

The summit area

Give yourself as much time as you can to explore along the stone and boardwalked **paths**, which lead through woodland and rhododendron thickets until you reach the summit area itself at **Zhenguo Temple** (镇国寺, zhènguó sì), a largish place surrounded by three enormous slate stacks which offer some of the most epic sights in the region. Each stack has small temples crowning them as well as others perched on spurs or hidden in crevices.

Golden Summit

金顶, jīndǐng

The tallest stack, **Golden Summit**, is especially mystic-looking, often wreathed in mist, and the steep climb up to the temple at the top takes you up narrow steps carved into fissures in the rock, with chains on the side to help haul yourself up. The views from the top are truly stupendous, and worth every bit of effort and expense the journey here might have taken.

ARRIVAL AND DEPARTURE   **FANJING SHAN**

By train and bus Fanjing Shan is best reached via Yuping (玉屏, yùpíng), a stop on the Kaili–Zhenyuan–Hunan rail line, where you'll find buses through the day to Jiangkou (江口, jiāngkǒu; 2hr). Here you change again for further frequent departures (1hr) to the park gates at Heiwan. There are also direct buses to Heiwan from the city of Tongren (铜仁, tóngrén; 1hr 30min), which is quicker if you're coming from Hunan.

ACCOMMODATION AND EATING

At Heiwan, the road leading from the bus station to the gates is lined with many hotel-cum-restaurants which all charge the same rate for identical clean, neat rooms for around ¥150. There is no accommodation in the park itself, although there are a couple of basic but pricy canteens serving instant noodles near the summit.

Western Guizhou

Extending for 350km between Guiyang and the border with Yunnan province, **Western Guizhou** is a desperately poor region of beautiful mountainous country and depressingly functional mining towns. **Anshun** is a transit hub for visiting **Bouyei villages**, the tourist magnets of **Longgong Caves** and **Huangguoshu Falls** and the remoter, more spectacular **Zhijin Caves**.

All routes west from Anshun ultimately lead to Yunnan's capital, Kunming (see p.647), whether you travel by bus along one of the three highways or – more comfortably – take the train. The landscape here forms a tumultuous barrier of jagged peaks and deep valleys, rising to a high plateau where wintering birdlife can be spied on at **Caohai** – being poled around this shallow lake on a sunny day is one of Guizhou's highlights.

Anshun

安顺, ānshùn

Some 100km west of Guiyang, **ANSHUN** was established as a garrisoned outpost in Ming times to keep an eye on the empire's unruly fringes. Today it's a fairly large, healthy but rough-around-the-edges market town, whose modern facade vanishes the moment you leave the main roads and find yourself among muddy alleys running between tumbledown shacks and wobbly wooden houses on the town's outskirts.

10

THE BOUYEI

The limestone countryside around Anshun is homeland to China's 2.5 million **Bouyei**, whose villages are built of split stone and roofed in large, irregularly laid slate tiles. Bouyei specialities include blue-and-white **batik work** and **ground opera** (地戏, dìxì) in which performers wear brightly painted wooden masks; though native to the region and overlaid with animistic rituals, the current forms are said to have been imported along with Han troops in the Ming dynasty, and are based on Chinese tales such as *The Three Kingdoms*. The Spring Festival period is a good time to see a performance, held in many villages around Anshun, including Shitou Zhai and Tianlong.

The town centre

Anshun's central crossroads is overlooked to the northwest by a hillock topped by a short Ming-dynasty **pagoda** (白塔, báitǎ), with a park around the base containing some representative, restored antique buildings, including a long stone **church** with a Chinese-style bell tower. The other point of interest is the **Confucian temple** (文化庙, wénhuà miào; ¥10), built in 1394, hidden away in the northeastern backstreets (just north of the river on Ruilin Lu) which, while somewhat neglected, has some superbly carved dragon pillars, rivalling those at Qufu's Confucius Mansion (p.293). There is also a traditional arts centre opposite the gates, selling local crafts.

ARRIVAL AND DEPARTURE

ANSHUN

BY TRAIN

Anshun train station (安顺火车站, ānshùn huǒchē zhàn), on the Guiyang–Kunming line, is 1km south of town at the end of Zhonghua Nan Lu; catch bus #1 or #2 past the main bus station to Xin Dashizi and the west bus station.

Destinations Guiyang (26 daily; 1hr 9min–2hr 15min); Kunming (14 daily; 7hr 15min–9hr); Liupanshui/ Shuicheng (24 daily; 2hr–3hr 30min).

BY BUS

Main bus station (客车南站, kèchē nánzhàn) is

about 500m south of the town centre on Zhonghua Nan Lu; it handles traffic to Guiyang, Zhenning, Huangguoshu and Kunming.

West bus station (客车西站, kèchē xīzhàn), 200m west of the centre on Ta Shan Xi Lu, has frequent departures to Zhenning, Tianlong, Guiyang, Huangguoshu and Longgong.

Beimen bus station (北门客车站, běimén kèchēzhàn) is 1km north of the centre on Zhonghua Bei Lu, and has buses to Zhijin.

Destinations Guiyang (2hr); Huangguoshu (1hr); Liupanshui (3hr); Longgong (1hr).

ACCOMMODATION

Between the bus and train stations, Zhonghua Nan Lu is awash with inexpensive hotels where small, noisy rooms are available for under ¥100.

Tielu Jiudian 铁路酒店, tiělù jiǔdiàn. West side of the train station square ☏0853 3290555. Immediately left out of the train station, this place has pretty comfortable, tidy carpeted rooms for the price, although without wi-fi. Set back from the road, it's also quiet. **¥268**

Magical Fuyun Hotel 参芪富蕴酒店, cānqí fùyùn jiǔdiàn. 18 Gui Huangguoshu Jie ☏0853 3290000. Best-value of the mid-range places around the the main bus station and refurbished not long ago, the rooms are modern, comfy and clean. Also has a travel agents and a decent restaurant. **¥658**

EATING

There are some excellent and inexpensive noodle stands in front of the train station where you can eat for under ¥10. Otherwise the crossroads by the night market at Dong Jie, and Guofu Jie and its surrounding streets, become crammed after dark with stalls and tents selling noodles and lamb kebabs.

Magical Fuyun Restaurant 参芪富蕴餐厅, cānqí fùyùn cāntīng. 18 Gui Huangguoshu Jie ☏0853 3290000. Western food and comfy sofas right by the main bus station make it a great spot to get your bearings. Done

out with wrought-iron chandeliers and flowing drapes, it serves a range of steaks, pizzas and pasta from around ¥45, as well as overpriced coffee and reasonably priced cocktails. Daily 9.30am–11.30pm.

Tianlong

天龙屯, tiānlóng tún • Daily 8.30am–6pm • ¥35 • ⓦ tp600.com

Some 30km east of Anshun off the Guiyang highway, **TIANLONG** is an old stone settlement founded as a garrison town in the Ming dynasty whose inhabitants, though dressing in embroidered coloured smocks like the **Bouyei**, insist they are in fact descendants of the original Han settlers. Tour groups come for the free ground opera shows at the **Dixi Performance Hall** (地戏堂, dìxì táng); otherwise a couple of twisting stone alleys and a nineteenth-century **church-school** built by French priests will keep you busy for an hour or so.

Wulong Temple

伍龙寺, wǔlóng sì • ¥20

Some 3km east of Tianlong, sheer-sided **Tiantai Shan** (天台山, tiāntái shān) is crowned by fortress-like **Wulong Temple**, founded by the traitorous Ming general **Wu Sangui**, who defected to the Manchu cause in 1644 and was rewarded by being made overlord of all Guizhou. The top hall contains a rather fine carved wooden Buddha.

ARRIVAL AND DEPARTURE   TIANLONG

By bus and minibus Tianlong doesn't have its own bus station, so buses tend to drop off at suitable points along the Anshun–Guiyang highway, where waiting minibuses to the village charge ¥5. Heading on, catch minibuses back to Anshun or east to Pingba (平坝, píngbà, for connecting traffic to Guiyang).
Destinations Anshun (30min; ¥8) Pingba (20min; ¥6).

Shitou Zhai

石头寨, shítóu zhài • ¥40

Six-hundred-year-old **SHITOU ZHAI** lies 30km southwest of Anshun off the Huangguoshu road. The village – whose name translates as "Stone Head Stockade" – comprises forty or so stone houses grouped around a rocky hillock, all surrounded by vegetable plots. At the gates, **Bouyei** women, wearing traditional dark-blue embroidered dresses, act as guides. You will be offered batik jackets for sale, and might witness the whole process, from drawing the designs in wax, to dyeing in indigo and boiling the wax away to leave a white pattern. You can easily walk out to similar, more tranquil surrounding villages, none of which charges admission.

ARRIVAL AND DEPARTURE   SHITOU ZHAI

By bus There's no direct traffic to Shitou Zhai, which lies off the old Anshun–Huangguoshu highway; tell the driver, and buses will drop you at the junction, leaving a 2km walk along a quiet road to the village gates. To move on, return to the main road and flag down passing traffic.

Longgong Caves

龙宫洞, lónggōng dòng • Daily 9am–6pm • ¥120 • ☎ 0853 5864898

The huge, partially flooded cavern complex comprising **Longgong Caves** lies 28km from Anshun's west bus station; you could be dropped at either entrance, which are

10

about 5km apart. From the nearer, western gate, you begin by being ferried down a river between willows and bamboo to a small knot of houses; walk through the arch, bear left, and it's 250m up some steps to **Guanyin Dong** (观音洞, guānyīn dòng), a broad cave filled with Buddhist statues. A seemingly minor path continues around the entrance but this is the one you want: it leads through a short cavern lit by coloured lights, then out around a hillside to **Jiujiu Tun** – site of an old guard post – and **Yulong Dong** (玉龙洞, yùlóng dòng), a large and spectacular cave system through which a guide will lead you (for free). Out the other side, a small river enters **Long Gong** (Dragon's Palace) itself, a two-stage boat ride through tall, flooded caverns picked out with florid lighting, exiting the caves into a broad pool at Longgong's eastern entrance.

ARRIVAL AND DEPARTURE
LONGGONG CAVES

By minibus Minibuses run through the day between Longgong's two entrances and Anshun's west bus station (hourly; 30min; ¥10); and there are regular minibuses from Longgong to Huangguoshu (1hr; ¥20). The last bus from the caves departs around 5pm.

Huangguoshu Falls

黄果树瀑布, huángguǒshù pùbù • ¥180

Clogged with sightseers during holidays and weekends, and safely skipped if you've ever seen a large waterfall before, **Huangguoshu Falls** lie 64km from Anshun along the Anshun–Yunnan highway. You get dropped off at little Huangguoshu township and walk down to the entrance; at 67m this may not quite rank as China's highest cataract, but in full flood the thunder rolls way off into the distance. A staircase descends past plagues of souvenir stalls to the blue-green river below the falls; the most imposing view of Huangguoshu is off to the left where the full weight of its 81m span drops into the **Rhino Pool** – prepare yourself for a good soaking from the spray. Be sure not to miss the **Water Curtain Cave** either, whose six windows allow viewing the water from behind which produces vivid rainbows.

ARRIVAL AND DEPARTURE
HUANGGUOSHU FALLS

By bus Minibuses connect Huangguoshu with Longgong Caves, Anshun (daily 7am–7pm; 1hr) and Guiyang (daily 10am–5pm; 2hr). If you're Yunnan-bound, first catch a minibus 7km west to the small town of Guanling (关岭, guānlíng) and look for connections there.

Zhijin Caves

织金洞, zhíjīn dòng • Daily 8.30am–5.30pm • ¥140

About 100km from Anshun or 150km from Guiyang – there's direct traffic from either – the dismal country town of **ZHIJIN** (织金, zhíjīn) sits among some gorgeous limestone pinnacles, beneath which are the astounding **Zhijin Caves**, some 25km northeast. Minibuses from Zhijin to the caves leave you at the **visitors' centre** where you have to hook up with one of the guided tours that run whenever they have ten people. The caves are immensely impressive and absolutely worth the money; tours with Chinese commentary last up to two hours and wind through untold numbers of caverns, the largest of which is 240m long, 170m wide and 60m high.

ARRIVAL AND DEPARTURE
ZHIJIN CAVES

By bus Zhijin town's bus station (织金汽车站, zhíjīn qìchē zhàn) handles traffic to Anshun and Guiyang. It's just about possible to get here, tour the caves and get out without staying the night, but you'll need to arrive early on, with the first bus leaving Anshun at 7am and the last bus departing Zhijin at 5.30pm.
Destinations Anshun (every 30min; 4hr; ¥35); Guiyang (hourly; 6hr; ¥60)

GETTING AROUND

By minibus From Zhijin's bus station, catch a taxi (¥5–10) to the Yuping local bus station (玉屏汽车站, yùpíng qìchē zhàn), from where minibuses to the caves (40min;

¥10) depart when full until mid-afternoon.
By taxi If minibuses to the caves don't fill, you'll need a taxi (around ¥200, including waiting time).

ACCOMMODATION

Hongzhou International Hotel 宏洲国际大酒店, hóngzhōu guójì dàjiŭdiàn. 151 Jinbei Dadao, about 4km north from the bus station ☏0857 7758888. Best bet if you don't fancy any of the three cheap options around

the main bus station, this place has very nice clean, modern rooms with a nice atmosphere. You'll need a cab from the station. **¥350**

Weining and Caohai

WEINING (威宁, wēiníng) – a small, run-down shell of a place populated by a friendly mix of Muslim Hui, Yi and Dahua Miao – sits above the clouds on a 2000m-high plateau in Guizhou's far northwestern corner. Immediately south of the town, 5km-wide **Caohai** (草海, cǎohǎi), the "Grass Lake", forms the core of a regional nature reserve. Caohai is a twitcher's paradise: wintering wildfowl shelter here in huge numbers, with over 170 different species spotted annually – including 400 rare **black-necked cranes** (黑颈鹤, hēijǐng hè).

On the lake

Boats ¥120 per hour for 2–3 people • rickshaw from town ¥10, or it's a 30min walk

At the lakeshore you'll be approached by touts wanting to take you out on a **boat trip** to find the birds; prices are posted, so don't pay more. Chinese tourists head first for a meal at the hamlet of **Longjia** (龙家, lóngjiā) on the far shore, famed for its food. On a sunny day, Caohai's overall tranquillity is a complete break with daily life in China; wintering cranes often hang out in the shallows near the shore and are not too hard to catch on camera. Be sure to bring your boots as it gets quite muddy.

ARRIVAL AND DEPARTURE

CAOHAI

By train Weining train station (威宁火车站, wēiníng huǒchē zhàn) is a few kilometres (¥10 by taxi) outside town. It's a minor branch with only 9 trains a day, most at awkward times late at night. The nearest main station, on the direct Guiyang–Anshun–Kunming line, is 100km south of Weining at Liupanshui (六盘水, liùpánshuǐ).
Destinations from Liupanshui Anshun (24 daily; 2–3hr); Guiyang (25 daily; 3hr 40min–4hr 30min); Kunming (17

daily; 4hr 30min–6hr); Weining (9 daily; 1hr 12min–1hr 53min).
By bus The bus station is right in the centre of Weining, with services to Anshun, Guiyang, Liupanshui and into Yunnan. Buses are the most convenient way to get to and from Liupanshui.
Destinations Anshun (5hr); Guiyang (7hr); Liupanshui (3hr).

ACCOMMODATION AND EATING

The *Heijing He* is the only proper hotel in Weining which takes foreigners, though many of the cheaper hostels around the bus station are happy to take you. The restaurants outside the *Heijing He* do inexpensive stir-fries and hotpots, and street-stalls selling chilli-dusted potato kebabs are everywhere in winter.

Heijing He 黑颈鹤大酒店, hēijǐnghè dàjiŭdiàn. Opposite the Power Authority building on Jianshe Dong Lu, near Dico's ☏0857 6229306. Exit the bus

station, turn right, and you'll find Weining's only comfy hotel for foreigners, which has small but decent rooms, though the service leaves a lot to be desired. **¥180**

Yunnan

PLOUGHING RICE TERRACES, YUANYANG

Yunnan

云南, yúnnán

Yunnan has always stood apart from the rest of China, set high on the empire's barbarous southwestern frontiers, and shielded from the rest of the nation by the unruly, mountainous neighbours of Sichuan and Guizhou. Within this single province, and dwelling among a stew of border markets, mountains, jungles, lakes, temples, modern political intrigue and remains of vanished kingdoms are 28 recognized ethnic groups, the greatest number in any province. Providing almost half the population and a prime reason to visit Yunnan in themselves, the indigenous list includes Dai and Bai, Wa, Lahu, Hani, Jingpo, Nu, Naxi and Lisu plus a host shared with other provinces (such as the Yi; see p.739) or adjoining nations. Each minority has its own spoken language, cuisine, distinctive form of dress for women, festivals and belief system, and with enough time you should be able to flesh out the superficial image of these groups laid on for the tourist industry.

In recent years tourism has boomed out of all proportion to Yunnan's remote image, bringing batallions of tour buses, souvenir stalls and loudspeaker-toting guides from far and near; the upside is improved resources geared to their needs, including backpacker cafés and companies offering cycling and trekking trips, ensuring that Yunnan is one of the easiest regions to explore in China.

The northeast of the province is home to the attractive capital, **Kunming**, whose mild climate earned Yunnan its name, meaning literally "south of the clouds". A scattering of local sights – including the brilliant green, near-vertically terraced valleys at **Yuanyang** – extends southeast from the city towards the border with **Vietnam**. Northwest of Kunming, the Yunnan plateau rises to serrated, snowbound peaks, extending to **Tibet** and surrounding the ancient historic towns of **Dali** and **Lijiang**; there's one of China's great hikes here too, through **Tiger Leaping Gorge**. The **Far West**, laid out along the ghost of old trade routes, has less of specific interest but allows gentle probing along the **Burmese border**. Yunnan's deep south comprises a further isolated stretch of the same frontier, which reaches down to the tropical forests and paddy fields of **Xishuangbanna**, a botanical, zoological and ethnic cornucopia abutting Burma and **Laos** – about as far from Han China as it's possible to be.

Getting around can be time-consuming, thanks to Yunnan's sheer scale, but the state of country **buses and roads** is often surprisingly good; new expressways are springing

SAN TA PAGODAS, DALI

Highlights

❶ Kunming's bars Check out the laidback nightlife in one of China's most relaxed cities. **See p.654**

❷ Yuanyang Base yourself in this attractive town and visit nearby minority villages set in a landscape spectacularly sliced up by rice terraces. **See p.659**

❸ Dali An old town with an enjoyable, relaxed travellers' quarter, offering café society and lush scenery. **See p.663**

❹ Cycling around Lijiang Take yourself out of the touristy town centre and cycle around the well-preserved villages at the heart of the Naxi Kingdom. **See p.672**

❺ Lugu Lake Tranquil lakeside resort with matriarchal villages on a backroads route into Sichuan. **See p.679**

❻ Tiger Leaping Gorge Relax for a few days on the ridge of this dramatic gorge, trekking between farmstead homestays. **See p.680**

❼ Meili Xue Shan Dramatic jagged scenery along the northwestern border with Tibet. **See p.689**

❽ Jungle trekking, Xishuangbanna Explore a region populated by many different ethnic groups, each with their own distinctive dress and customs. **See p.698**

HIGHLIGHTS ARE MARKED ON THE MAP ON PP.644–645

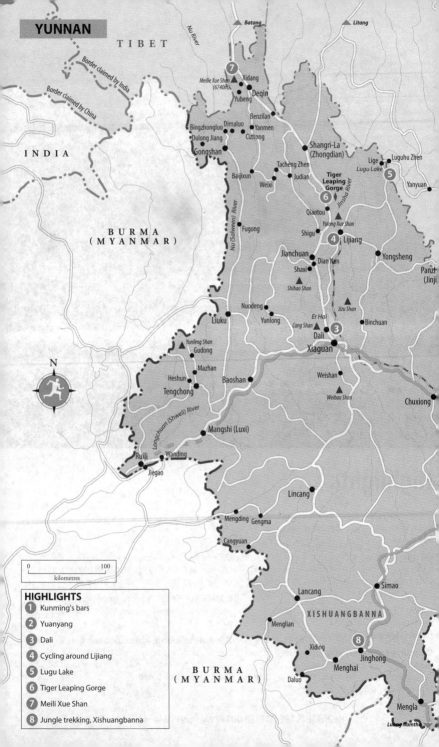

up at a regular rate and it's an undeniable achievement that some of the lesser routes exist at all. Yunnan's fairly limited **rail network** is due for expansion too, with recently completed services to Dali and Lijiang making these popular destinations more accessible than ever.

The **weather** is generally moderate throughout the year, though northern Yunnan has cold winters and heavy snow up around the Tibetan border, while the south is always warm, with a torrential wet season in summer.

Brief history

According to the Han historian Sima Qian, the Chinese warrior prince Zhuang Qiao founded the pastoral **Dian Kingdom** in eastern Yunnan during the third century BC. The Dian were a slave society, who vividly recorded their daily life and ceremonies involving human sacrifice in sometimes gruesome **bronze models**, which have been unearthed from their tombs. In 109 AD the kingdom was acknowledged by China: the emperor Wu, hoping to control the Southern Silk Road through to India, sent its ruler military aid and a golden seal. However, the collapse of the Han empire in 204 AD was followed by the dissolution of Dian into private statelets.

The Dali and Nanzhao kingdoms

In the eighth century, an aspiring Yunnanese prince named **Piluoge**, favouring Dali for its location near trade routes beteen central and southeastern Asia, invited all his rivals to dinner in the town, then set fire to the tent with them inside. Subsequently he established the **Nanzhao Kingdom** in Dali, which later expanded to include much of modern Burma, Thailand and Vietnam. In 937, the Bai warlord **Duan Siping** toppled the Nanzhao and set up a smaller **Dali Kingdom**, which survived until **Kublai Khan** and his Mongol hordes descended in 1252.

The Muslim Uprising

Directly controlled by China for the first time, Yunnan served for a while as a remote dumping ground for political troublemakers, thereby escaping the population

---

YUNNANESE FOOD

Yunnanese food splits broadly into three cooking styles. In the **north**, the cold, pastoral lifestyle produces dried meats and – very unusually for China – **dairy products**, fused with a Muslim cuisine, a vestige of the thirteenth-century Mongolian invasion. Typical dishes include wind-cured ham (火腿, huǒtuǐ), sweetened, steamed and served with slices of bread; dried cheese or yoghurt wafers (乳扇, rǔshān or 乳饼, rǔbǐng); the local version of crisp-skinned duck (烧鸭, shāoyā), flavoured with Sichuan peppercorns – you'll see drum-shaped duck ovens outside many restaurants – and a tasty fish claypot (沙锅鱼, shāguō yú).

Eastern Yunnan produces the most recognizably "Chinese" food. From here comes chicken flavoured with medicinal herbs and stewed inside a specially shaped earthenware steamer (气锅鸡, qìguōjī), and perhaps the province's most celebrated dish, **crossing-the-bridge noodles** (过桥米线, guòqiáo mǐxiàn), a sort of individualized hotpot eaten as a cheap snack; you pay by the size of the bowl. The curious name comes from a tale of a Qing scholar who retired every day to a lakeside pavilion to compose poetry. His wife, an understanding soul, used to cook him lunch, but the food always cooled as she carried it from their home over the bridge to where he studied – until she hit on the idea of keeping the heat in with a layer of oil on top of his soup.

Not surprisingly, Yunnan's **south** is strongly influenced by Burmese, Lao and Thai cooking methods, particularly in the use of such un-Chinese ingredients as lime juice, coconut, palm sugar, cloves and turmeric. Here you'll find a vast range of soups and stews, roughly recognizable as **curries**, displayed in aluminium pots outside fast-turnover restaurants, and oddities such as purple rice-flour pancakes sold at street markets. The south is also famous in China for producing good **coffee** and red pu'er, Yunnan's best **tea**.

explosions, wars and migrations that plagued central China. However, the Mongol invasion had introduced a large Muslim population to the province, who, angered by their deteriorating status under the Chinese, staged the **Muslim Uprising** in 1856. Under the warlord **Du Wenxiu**, the rebellion laid waste to Kunming and founded an Islamic state in Dali before the Qing armies ended it with the wholesale massacre of Yunnan's Muslims in 1873, leaving a wasted Yunnan to local bandits and private armies for the following half-century.

Modern times

Strangely, it was the **Japanese invasion** of China during the 1930s that sparked a resurgence of Yunnan's fortunes. Blockaded into southwestern China, the **Guomindang government** initiated great programmes of rail-and-road building through the region, though it's only recently that Yunnan has finally benefited from its forced association with the rest of the country. Never agriculturally rich – only a tenth of the land is considered arable – the province looks to mineral resources, tourism and its potential as a future conduit between China and the much discussed, but as yet unformed, trading bloc of **Vietnam**, **Laos**, **Thailand** and **Burma**. Should these countries ever form an unrestricted economic alliance, the amount of trade passing through Yunnan would be immense, and highways, rail and air services have already been planned for the day the borders open freely.

11

Kunming

昆明, kūnmíng

Basking 2000m above sea level in the fertile heart of the Yunnan plateau, **KUNMING** does its best to live up to its traditional nickname, the City of Eternal Spring. Until recently it was considered a savage frontier settlement; the authorities only began to realize the city's promise when people exiled here during the Cultural Revolution refused offers to return home to eastern China, preferring Kunming's climate and more relaxed life. Today, its citizens remain mellow enough to mix typically Chinese garrulousness with introspective pleasures, such as quietly greeting the day with a stiff hit of Yunnanese tobacco from fat, brass-bound bamboo pipes.

The city's potential as a hub for both domestic tourism and cross-border trade has seen Kunming develop rapidly in recent years. With its sprouting malls and streets bustling with shoppers from every corner of the country – not to mention some interesting markets and an excellent museum – Kunming is no longer the sleepy outpost of old, but the growing tourist infrastructure, together with a student and expat-fuelled nightlife, ensures the city is an enjoyable stop-off. Which is just as well, as virtually every traveller coming through Yunnan will end up here at some point.

Brief history

Historically the domain of Yunnan's earliest inhabitants and first civilization, Kunming long profited from its position on the caravan roads through to Burma, India and Asia. It was visited in the thirteenth century by Marco Polo, who found the locals of **Yachi Fu** (Duck Pond Town) using cowries for cash and enjoying their meat raw. The city suffered widespread destruction as a result of the 1856 Muslim rebellion and events of forty years later, when an uprising against working conditions on the **Kunming–Haiphong rail line** saw 300,000 labourers executed after France shipped in weapons to suppress the revolt.

In the 1930s, **war with Japan** brought a flock of wealthy east-coast refugees to the city, whose money helped establish Kunming as an industrial and manufacturing base for the wartime government in Chongqing. The allies provided essential support for this, importing materials along the Burma Road from British-held Burma and, when that was lost to the Japanese, with the help of the US-piloted **Flying Tigers**, who escorted

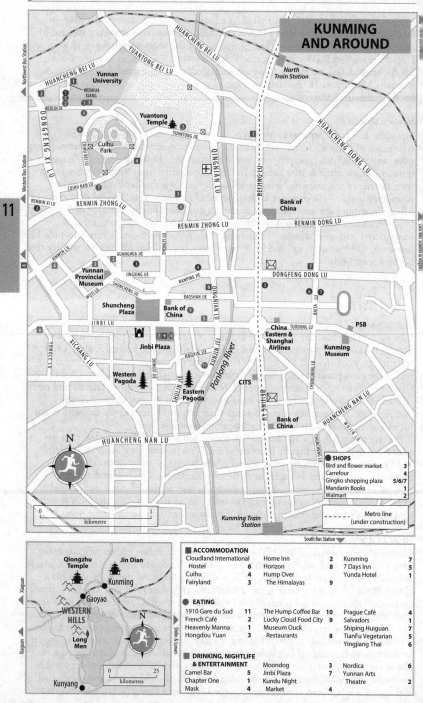

KUNMING AND AROUND

11

SHOPS

Bird and flower market	3
Carrefour	4
Gingko shopping plaza	5/6/7
Mandarin Books	1
Walmart	2

Metro line
(under construction)

Western Hills inset map labels:
Qiongzhu Temple, Jin Dian, Kunming, Gaoyao, WESTERN HILLS, Long Men, Kunyang, Xiaguan, Shilin & Lunan

ACCOMMODATION

Cloudland International Hostel	6	Home Inn	2	Kunming	7
Cuihu	4	Horizon	8	7 Days Inn	5
Fairyland	3	Hump Over		Yunda Hotel	1
		The Himalayas	9		

EATING

1910 Gare du Sud	11	The Hump Coffee Bar	10	Prague Café	4
French Café	2	Lucky Cloud Food City	9	Salvadors	1
Heavenly Manna		Museum Ouck		Shiping Huiguan	7
Hongdou Yuan	3	Restaurants	8	TianFu Vegetarian	5
				Yingjiang Thai	6

DRINKING, NIGHTLIFE & ENTERTAINMENT

Camel Bar	5	Moondog	3	Nordica	6
Chapter One	1	Jinbi Plaza	7	Yunnan Arts Theatre	2
Mask	4	Kundu Night Market	4		

supply planes over the Himalayas from British bases in India. The city consolidated its position as a supply depot during the Vietnam War and subsequent border clashes and today is profiting from snowballing tourism and foreign investment. Neighbouring nations such as Thailand trace their ancestries back to Yunnan and have proved particularly willing to channel funds into the city, which has become ever more accessible as a result.

Bird and Flower Market

花鸟市场, huāniǎo shìchǎng • Daily 8am–8pm

Running west off central Zhengyi Jie, Jingxing Jie leads into one of the more offbeat corners of the city. Once a huge **bird and flower market**, the area has now been rebranded as "Old Street" (老街, lǎojiē) and features rather less in the way of birds and flowers and rather more in the way of standard cheap tat. That said, some birds – as well as lizards, pigs, snakes and cute bunny rabbits – remain, and look beyond the "jade" bangles, blindingly powerful torches and overly-embroidered handbags on display and you'll find one of the few areas where Kunming's original wooden buildings remain standing. Their increasing decrepitude suggests they won't be here for much longer, but for the moment cutting down the back alleys here can give a real glimpse back in time, just metres from the city's most modern shopping streets.

Yunnan Provincial Museum

云南省博物馆, yúnnánshěng bówùguǎn • Daily 9am–5pm • Free except special exhibitions

About 500m west of the centre along Dongfeng Xi Lu, the **Yunnan Provincial Museum** gives an insight into Yunnan's early Dian Kingdom. Best are the **bronzes** on the second floor, dating back more than two thousand years to the Warring States Period and excavated from tombs south of Kunming. The largest pieces include an ornamental plate of a tiger attacking an ox and a coffin in the shape of a bamboo house, but lids from storage drums used to hold cowries are the most impressive, decorated with dioramas of figurines fighting, sacrificing oxen and men and, rather more peacefully, posing with their families and farmyard animals outside their homes.

Cuihu Park

翠湖公园, cuìhú gōngyuán • Daily dawn–10pm • Free

Cuihu Park is predominantly lake, a good place to join thousands of others exercising, singing, feeding wintering flocks of black-headed gulls, or just milling between the plum and magnolia gardens and over the maze of bridges. Main **entrances** are at the south, north and east of the park, and encircling Cuihu Lu is lined with restaurants and bars, which spill into adjacent **Wenlin Jie**, the best place in the city to look for a drink and a feed (see p.654). Immediately north of the park, the **Yunnan University** campus offers a glimpse of old Kunming, its partially overgrown 1920s exterior reached via a wide flight of stone steps.

Yuantong Temple

圆通寺, yuántōng sì • Yuantong Jie • Daily 9am–5.30pm • ¥6

East from Cuihu Park, the Qing-vintage **Yuantong Temple** has undergone major renovations to emerge as Kunming's brightest Buddhist temple. A bridge over the central pond crosses through an octagonal pavilion dedicated to a multi-armed Guanyin and white marble Sakyamuni, to the threshold of the main hall, where two huge central pillars wrapped in colourful, manga-esque **dragons** support the ornate wooden ceiling. Faded frescoes on the back wall were painted in the thirteenth century, while the rear annexe houses a graceful gilded bronze Buddha flanked by peacocks, donated by the Thai government.

Kunming City Museum

昆明市博物馆, kūnmíngshì bówùguǎn · Daily 9.30am–5pm · Free

Besides more bronze drums and some dinosaur skeletons, the highlight of the **Kunming City Museum**, east of Beijing Lu along Tuodong Lu, is the **Dali Sutra Pillar**. In its own room on the ground floor, it's a 6.5m-high, pagoda-like Song-dynasty sculpture, in pink sandstone; an octagonal base supports seven tiers covered in Buddha images, statues of fierce guardian gods standing on subjugated demons, and a mix of Tibetan and Chinese script, part of which is the Dharani Mantra. The rest is a dedication, identifying the pillar as having been raised by the Dali regent, **Yuan Douguang**, in memory of his general Gao Ming. The whole thing is topped by a ring of Buddhas carrying a ball – the universe – above them, and the pillar is full of the energy that later seeped out of the mainstream of Chinese sculpture.

Two pagodas

Two large Tang-dynasty pagodas, each a solid thirteen storeys of whitewashed brick crowned with four jolly iron cockerels, rise a short walk south of the city centre. The **Eastern Pagoda** (东寺塔, dōngsì tǎ) on Shulin Jie sits in a little ornamental garden, while the **Western Pagoda** (西寺塔, xīsì tǎ) is a few minutes' walk away at the back of a flagstoned square on Dongsi Jie. You can't enter either, but the sight of these 1300-year-old towers surrounded by modern office blocks is striking.

ARRIVAL AND DEPARTURE

KUNMING

BY PLANE

For air tickets, China Eastern and Shanghai Airlines share the airline office on Tuodong Lu (☎0871 63164270 or 63138562; ☷ travelsky.com). Agents around town all offer the same fares.

Kunming Changshui International Airport (昆明长水国际机场, kūnmíng chángshuǐ guójì jīchǎng), known locally as New Kunming Airport (昆明新机场, kūnmíng xīnjīchǎng), lies 25km northeast of the city centre. As well as domestic services, there are international flights to Bangkok, Hong Kong, Kuala Lumpur, Phnom Penh, Singapore, Taipei, Vientiane and Yangon. Outside the airport, shuttle buses (¥20) head into town every 20–30min: #1 terminates at the *Xiyi Hotel* on Dongfeng Xi Lu, just west of Cuihu Park; while #2 services the southeast of the centre, calling at the *Telecom International Hotel* near the junction of Huancheng Nan Lu and Chungcheng Lu, and Kunming Train Station. A taxi into town can take up to an hour and costs around ¥100. Metro line #6 (every 25min, ¥5) runs from the airport, but at time of writing only as far as the East Bus Station, still 10km from the city centre.

Destinations Baoshan (4 daily; 1hr); Beijing (daily; 3hr 30min); Changsha (12 daily; 1hr 50min); Chengdu (16 daily; 1hr 25min); Chongqing (many daily; 1hr 15min); Dali (4 daily; 45min); Guangzhou (18 daily; 2hr); Guilin (2 daily; 1hr 30min); Guiyang (6 daily; 1hr 10min); Hong Kong (4 daily; 2hr 45min); Jinghong (many daily; 55min); Lhasa (3 daily; 2hr 10min); Lijiang (18 daily; 1hr); Mangshi (11 daily; 1hr); Nanning (6 daily; 1hr); Shanghai (many daily; 3hr); Shenzhen (12 daily; 2hr); Xi'an (13 daily; 2hr).

BY TRAIN

Kunming train station (昆明火车站, kūnmíng huǒchē zhàn) is at the southern end of Beijing Lu; the building is two-tiered, with the ticket windows downstairs (daily 5am–11pm) and departures upstairs. Useful buses from here include #23 up Beijing Lu past the all but defunct North train station; and #59, which heads up Qingnian Lu to within striking distance of Yuantong Temple and Cuihu Park. If you're immediately heading onwards, there's also bus #C71 to the South bus station and buses #C72 or #80 to the Western bus station. Note that trains to Xiaguan (for Dali) and Lijiang are quicker than making the same journey by bus.

Destinations Beijing (2 daily; 36–48hr); Chengdu (6 daily; 18–24hr); Chongqing (3 daily; 20–24hr); Guangzhou (4 daily; 24–27hr); Guilin (1 daily; 22hr); Guiyang (13 daily; 8–11hr); Lijiang (5 daily; 9–10hr); Nanning (6 daily; 11–14hr); Shanghai (3 daily; 34–42hr); Shenzhen (1 daily; 30hr); Xiaguan (6 daily; 8hr); Xi'an (1 daily; 35hr); Xichang (5 daily; 9hr).

BY BUS

Kunming's many bus stations are scattered around the city perimeter, generally at the point of the compass relevant to the destination. They are all a long way out: allow plenty of transit time, even in a cab, especially during rush hours (about 7–9am and 5–7pm). Agents in town might be willing to buy tickets for a fee, otherwise you'll have to get out to the stations yourself.

Western bus station (西部汽车客运站, xībù qìchē kèyùnzhàn), also known as **Majie bus station** (马街客运站, mǎjiē kèyùn zhàn), is 10km out towards the Western Hills. It deals with traffic to Xiaguan, Lijiang, Deqin, Shangri-La, Tengchong and Ruili. On arrival, catch bus #82 to the western end of Nanping Jie or bus #C72 to Kunming train station; a taxi is ¥30.

South bus station (南部汽车客运站, nánbù qìchē kèyùnzhàn) is 15km southeast of the centre, with departures to Xishuangbanna, Jianshui, Yuanyang and Luang Prabang in Laos among others. Take bus #C71 to Kunming train station, or a taxi for ¥45.

East bus station (东部汽车客运站, dōngbù qìchē kèyùnzhàn), 10km out, is for services to Shilin and points east, plus Hekou on the Vietnam border. Bus #60 runs to Kunming train station via Bailong Lu; a taxi costs ¥30. Metro line #6 runs northeast from the station to the airport.

North bus station (北部汽车客运站, běibù qìchē kèyùnzhàn). Unless arriving from Panzhihua in Sichuan, you're unlikely to find yourself here; bus #23 heads through town via both train stations.

Destinations Baoshan (8hr); Hekou (7hr); Fugong (16hr); Jianshui (3hr); Jinghong (10hr); Lijiang (10hr); Liuku (11hr); Ruili (13hr); Shilin (3hr); Wanding (12hr); Weishan (7hr); Xiaguan (5hr); Yuanyang (5hr).

GETTING AROUND

By bus You might resort to city buses (¥1–2) to reach some of the further-flung sights, but they're slow and not that useful around the centre.

By metro Limited sections of the still-under-construction metro are operational but at time of writing only cover areas well outside the city centre. The comprehensive six-line network is due for completion in 2018.

By taxi Taxis ply all the main streets in central Kunming, charging a minimum ¥8 for the first three kilometres and ¥1.60 for each additional kilometre during the day. At night a minimum ¥9.80 charge applies.

By bicycle Bicycles can be rented from the *Hump* or *Cloudland* hostels for ¥30 per day.

LEAVING CHINA

Kunming is a springboard for travel into Thailand, Laos, Vietnam and Burma, all of which maintain consulates in town.

For **Thailand**, there are flights to Bangkok from Kunming: Thai Airways are in the *Jinjiang Hotel*, 98 Beijing Lu (☏0871 63548655, ⊚thaiairways.com.cn; Mon–Fri 9am–5.30pm). Depending on the security situation, it may also be possible to catch a ferry from Jinghong in Xishuangbanna (see p.702). Many nationalities can stay visa-free in Thailand for 30 days if arriving at an airport, or 15 days arriving by land; if you need longer, head to Kunming's consulate for a visa.

You can fly to **Laos**, and there's also a direct bus from Kunming's South bus station to Luang Prabang (daily 7am; 30hr; ¥300). For **Vietnam** either fly, or catch a bus to Hekou (p.660) and cross the border on foot. Laos visas might again be available at the border depending on nationality; for Vietnam you'll need to get one in advance.

For **Burma**, arrange both visas and obligatory tour package in Kunming before either flying direct to Yangon or crossing the border on foot near Ruili (see p.696).

KUNMING'S CONSULATES

The Guandu Consular District (外国领馆区, wàiguó lǐngguǎnqū), home to an increasing number of consulates, is around 15km southeast of the city centre and can be reached by taxi for around ¥30.

Cambodia Royal Consulate General, 4th Floor, *Kunming Guanfang Hotel*, 172 Xinying Lu ☏0871 63317320.

Laos Consulate General, 6800 Caiyun Bei Lu, Foreign Consular Zone, Guandu District (next to the *Empark Hotel*) ☏0871 67334522.

Myanmar (Burma) Consulate General, 99 Yingbin Lu, Foreign Consular Zone, Guandu District. Office hours: Mon–Fri 9am–noon, 1–2pm. Closed the last day of every month.

Thailand Royal Consulate General, South Building, *Kunming Hotel*, 52 Dongfeng Dong Lu ☏0871 63168916.

Vietnam Consulate General, Suite 507, Hongda Mansion, 155 Beijing Lu ☏0871 63522669.

11

11

INFORMATION

Travel agents Travel agents abound in Kunming, with virtually every hotel able to organize visas and private tours around the city, and to Shilin, Dali, Lijiang and Xishuangbanna, and to obtain tickets for onwards travel. Expect to pay commissions of at least ¥20 for bus or train ticket reservations, though plane tickets shouldn't attract a mark-up. CITS (☎0871 63157499; Mon–Sat 9am–6pm) are at 328 Beijing Lu, but are mostly concerned with organizing package tours. The best bet for travel and tourist advice without the hard sell is at one of the city's youth hostels; staff at the *Hump* and *Cloudland* are generally helpful and informative.

ACCOMMODATION

Cloudland International Hostel 大脚氏国际青年旅舍, dàjiǎoshì guójì qīngnián lǚshè. 23 Zhuantang Lu ☎0871 64103777. Hard to find, in a street at right-angles to Xichang Lu, northwest of its junction with Xinwen Lu, *Cloudland* has rooms in tiers around a courtyard, a good café, and hiking info for Tiger Leaping Gorge and Meili Xue Shan. Can be noisy, depending on who is staying. Dorm ¥35, room ¥150

★ **Cuihu** 翠湖宾馆, cuìhú bīnguǎn. 6 Cuihu Nan Lu ☎0871 65158888, ⓦgreenlakehotel.com. The place to stay in Kunming. Long-established, luxurious, and good value in pleasant surroundings by Cuihu Park, with a fancy lobby, impeccably polite staff and an excellent restaurant. Airport transfers can be arranged; all major credit cards are accepted. ¥1000

Fairyland 四季酒店鼓楼店, sìjì jiǔdiàn gǔlóu diàn. 716 Beijing Lu ☎0871 6285777, ⓦyssjhotel.com. Budget business hotel, not in the smartest part of town but not far from Yuantong Temple and Cuihu Park either; cheaper rooms are tiny, but pay a bit more and you get a modern, comfortable place to stay. Bus #23 stops nearby. ¥250

Home Inn 如家酒店, rújiā jiǔdiàn. 492 Dongfeng Xi Lu ☎0871 65387888, ⓦhomeinns.com. Handily, if noisily, located not far from the university area and Green Lake, what this chain hotel lacks in charm it mostly makes up for in cleanliness. Free wi-fi and en-suite rooms throughout. ¥200

Horizon 天恒大酒店, tiānhéng dàjiǔdiàn. 432 Qingnian Lu ☎0871 63186666, ⓦwww.horizonhotel .net. An overblown, multi-starred place with a mountain of marble in the lobby and an overflow of cafés and restaurants; rooms are clean and comfortable enough, but also a little dated and drab. ¥600

★ **Hump Over The Himalayas** 驼峰客栈, tuófēng kèzhàn. Jinbi Lu ☎0871 63640359, ⓦthehumphostel .com. Three hundred police once raided this place to close it down, but despite this wild reputation, today it's clean, organized and secure. Rooms are no-frills, though a comfy lounge-bar and rooftop terrace compensate. The only downside is noise from surrounding nightclubs, but they'll give you earplugs if you ask. Dorm ¥35, room ¥175

Kunming 昆明饭店, kūnmíng fàndiàn. 52 Dongfeng Dong Lu ☎0871 63162063. Another big, upmarket hotel with an ageing, gaudy lobby, reasonable service, decent rooms and a restaurant specializing in dishes from Chaozhou in Guangdong province. ¥780

7 Days Inn 七天连锁酒店, qītiān liánsuǒ jiǔdiàn. 10 Huashan Dong Lu ☎0871 63166877. Just one of a dozen indistinguishable branches this characterless but clean and convenient franchise has opened in the city. All rooms are en suite and come with wi-fi access, and this branch is well placed close to Yuantong Temple and the city centre. ¥150

Yunda Hotel 云大宾馆, yúndà bīnguǎn. Wenhua Xiang ☎0871 65034181. At the university's west gate, the hotel itself is not up to much but is in one of the most enjoyable parts of town. Try and get a room in the main building rather than in the musty annex across the road which is actually a dormitory for overseas students. Prices can be negotiated. ¥200

EATING

Kunming is stacked with good places to eat, from street stalls and Western cafés to smart restaurants offering local cuisine. Back lanes off Jinbi Lu hold some great cheap places where you can battle with the locals over grilled cheese, hotpots, fried snacks rolled in chilli powder, loaves of excellent meat-stuffed soda bread, and rich duck and chicken casseroles. There's a string of inexpensive Muslim duck restaurants on Huashan Nan Lu, southeast of Cuihu Park, but by far the best place to look for a feed is around Cuihu Park itself: Indian, Chinese, Korean, Japanese, Thai and Western food can all be found here, as can a decent cup of coffee.

★ **1910 Gare du Sud** 火车南站, huǒchē nánzhàn. 8 Houxin Jie, accessed from Chongshan Lu, near its junction with Xunjin Lu ☎0871 63169486. Traditional Yunnan fare served in a former French colonial train station; there's a large balcony and courtyard and photos of colonial Kunming throughout. A popular place with trendy middle-class locals but nowhere near as expensive as you'd think, and two can eat very well for ¥100. Daily 11.30am–10pm.

French Café 兰白红咖啡, lánbáihóng kāfēi. 70

Wenlin Jie ☎0871 65382391. There's a large French contingent in Kunming, drawn perhaps by the colonial connection; this café, with its pastries and baguettes, must make them feel at home. Sandwiches from ¥25, with larger mains around ¥40. Daily 9am–midnight.

Heavenly Manna 吗哪, manǎ. 74 Wenhua Xiang ☎0871 65369399. Home-style Yunnanese dishes: inexpensive, varied, interesting and very spicy indeed. Setting is crowded, with no-frills low wooden tables and chairs; watch out for the low ceiling with protruding pipes upstairs. Mains ¥15–40. Daily 11am–9.30pm.

Hongdou Yuan 红豆园餐厅, hóngdòuyuán cāntīng. 142 Wenlin Jie ☎0871 5392020. Branch of popular Sichuanese-Yunnanese chain, with an easy-to-follow photo menu. Not everything is spicy; they do excellent crisp-skinned duck with cut buns, cold-sliced pork, stewed spare ribs and rice-coated pork slices. The fish looks good too. Mains ¥25–45. Daily 9am–9pm.

★ **The Hump Coffee Bar** 驼峰咖啡吧, tuófēng kāfēi ba. Jinbi Lu, underneath the Hump hostel ☎0871 63646229. Managed by long-time Yunnan wheeler-dealer, Burmese Moe, *The Hump* offers an excellent range of curries, many of them vegetarian, for ¥30. Add snacks, including fried cheese and chips, for around ¥15, free wi-fi, and decent coffee, and you have a very pleasant place to chill. Daily 9am–10pm.

★ **Lucky Cloud Food City** 祥云美食城, xiángyún měishíchéng. Junction of Xiangyun Jie and Nanqiang Jie. Calling this place a food court does it a massive disservice but that's basically what it is, only for street food. There's seating for 500 and dozens of cubbyhole serveries whacking out everything from kebabs to iced fruits, and from noodles to fried eel. Prices range from ¥2 for a single kebab to ¥20 for pork and rice. There are pricier, more civilized hotpot and barbecue restaurants with outdoor seating at the southeast corner. Daily 11am–9.30pm.

Prague Café 布拉格咖啡馆, bùlāgē kāfēi guǎn. 40 Wenlin Jie ☎0871 65332764. This offshoot of a successful Lijiang enterprise offers very strong coffee and a decent breakfast, as well as internet access and a book exchange. One of the better cafés in this locality, it's a good place to while away an afternoon. Mains ¥20–40. Daily 9am–midnight.

Salvadors 沙尔瓦多咖啡馆, shāěrwǎduō kāfēiguǎn. 76 Wenhua Xiang ☎0871 65363525, ⓦsalvadors.cn. Expat-run and populated, and somewhere to get information and conversation from jaded, in-the-know foreign residents. Well-stocked bar with pavement taking overflow, plus coffee and pub-style menu. Mains ¥20–50. Daily 9am–10pm.

Shiping Huiguan 石屏会馆, shípíng huìguǎn. 24 Zhonghe Xiang, Cuihu Nan Lu ☎0871 63627444. Tucked back off the street behind an ornamental archway and heavy stone wall, this elegantly restored courtyard restaurant is a great place to sample Yunnanese cuisine. It tends to get booked out by tour groups and wedding parties, so reservations are essential. Ranges from ¥20 for fried greens to ¥100 for steaming plates of meat. Daily 11am–10pm.

TianFu Vegetarian 添福素心, tiānfú sùxīn. 26 Yuantong Jie, at the front gate of Yuantong Temple ☎1388 8772263. Awaiting reopening after upmarket refurbishment at time of writing; expect an impressive array of meat-like tofu dishes from ¥40. Daily 10am–9.30pm.

Yingjiang Thai 盈江傣味园, yíngjiāng dǎiwèiyuán. 66 Cuihu Bei Lu ☎0871 65337889. Strongly Sinocized Thai food, though favourites like sweet pineapple rice, grilled fish, sour bamboo shoots and *laab* (spicy mince salad) are all pretty good. Count on ¥35 per person. Daily 11am–10pm.

DRINKING, NIGHTLIFE AND ENTERTAINMENT

Kunming is a great place to go out, with plenty of friendly, reasonably priced bars and clubs patronized by a good mix of locals and foreigners; the most Western-friendly are in the Wenlin Jie area. Check GoKunming (ⓦgokunming.com) for the latest hotspots, entertainment and cultural events.

Camel Bar 骆驼酒吧, luòtuó jiǔbā. 310 Jinbi Lu ☎0871 63195841, ⓦcamelbarkm.com. Not far from *The Hump*, this place is a bit more polished than most in the city, appealing to middle-class Chinese rather than just students. There's a pricier menu to match, with drinks from ¥18 and main dishes, including pizza and burgers, starting at ¥35. It gets lively with dancing at weekends, but during the day is a good place to relax over a coffee. Daily 9am–1am.

Chapter One 联系, liánxì. 146 Wenlin Jie ☎0871 6365635, ⓦchapteronekunming.com. Good pub atmosphere, cheap happy-hour drinks (5–8pm) and a decent range of inexpensive, mostly Western food served all day. Expect to pay upwards of ¥20 for a main. Daily 11am–midnight.

Jinbi Plaza 金碧广场, jīnbì guǎngchǎng. Jinbi Lu. A complex (or, after a few drinks, a maze) of interlinked clubs such as *The Hump* – stumble out of one and you fall straight into another.

Kundu Night Market 昆都夜市, kūndū yèshì. Off Xinwen Lu. If you can't live without cheesy techno and flashing lights, head to this clutch of bars and clubs with late-night restaurants, nail bars and tattoo parlours in between. Everywhere's free to get in, but drinks cost at least ¥30. Daily 6pm–late.

Mask 脸谱酒吧, liǎnpǔ jiǔbā. 14 Kundu Nightmarket ☎0871 66438358. Popular expat party spot on the square in the heart of the Kundu. Marginally more restrained than its neighbours, *Mask*'s big selling point is regular live music, including a jam session on Mon. Daily 6pm–late.

Moondog 月亮狗, yuèliàng gǒu. 138-5 Wacang Nan Lu ☎1588 7146080. Despite the name, and being perilously close to the Kundu Night Market area, this is actually a relaxed bar with friendly staff, and a surprising selection of Scotch whiskies. Daily 6pm–late.

★ **Nordica** 诺地卡, nuòdìkǎ. 101 Xiba Lu ☎0871 64114692, ⓦ tcgnordica.com. Gigs, club nights and talks take place frequently at this Scandinavian-run converted

factory complex of galleries, cafés and studio spaces. Daily 11am–10pm.

Yunnan Arts Theatre 云南艺术剧院, yúnnán yìshù jùyuàn. Dongfeng Xi Lu ☎0871 63109365. Large-scale, energetic dance shows, based (loosely) on authentic ethnic folk cutlure, play out every night. Tickets at ¥130–480 can be bought during the day from the box office outside the theatre, or from any travel agency in town.

SHOPPING

Nanping Jie and Zhengyi Lu are full of ordinary clothing and shoe stores; the bird market area is where to find jolly souvenirs.

Bookshops Kunming's best English-language bookshop is Mandarin Books at 52 Wenhua Xiang, near the university. It has many imported novels, obscure academic texts, guidebooks and much that is published in English in China, all of it fairly pricey. Many of the cafés and bars along Wenlin Jie have cases of mostly fairly trashy secondhand novels for sale.

Department stores Kunming's most upmarket stores are the three Gingko Shopping Plazas strung across Beijing Lu

and Baita Lu, crammed with luxury brands.

Supermarkets Both the huge Carrefour supermarket on Nanping Jie, or similarly enormous Walmart, south off Renmin Xi Lu, just west of the junction with Dongfeng Xi Lu, have imported Western food, plus Yunnan ham sold in slices, chunks and entire hocks.

Tea Yunnan's famous *pu'er* tea, usually compressed into attractive "bricks" stamped with good-luck symbols, is sold almost everywhere.

DIRECTORY

Banks and exchange The main branch of the Bank of China (Mon–Fri 9am–5.30pm) is at the corner of Beijing Lu and Renmin Dong Lu. There are smaller branches and ATMs all through the centre.

Cinema The best in town, showing some films in English, is the Beijing-run Broadway Cinema, inside the Shuncheng Plaza between Shuncheng Jie and Jinbi Lu. There's an IMAX screen here too.

Hospital English-speaking, Western-trained medics can be found at the Kunming International Clinic (昆明福华国际门诊, kūnmíng fúhuá guójì ménzhěn; ☎0871 64119100) at 32 Xiyuan Nan Lu, on the second floor of Yunnan Kidney Hospital.

Internet Most accommodation and foreigner-friendly cafés have terminals and/or free wi-fi.

Mail The GPO is towards Kunming train station at 231 Beijing Lu (daily 8am–7pm).

Massage There are several genuine massage studios staffed by blind masseurs around town, charging around ¥40/hr, including a string of shops at the end of Yuantong Jie near Cuihu Park.

PSB "Public Security Bureau Visas and Permits Office" – the visa extension office, in other words – is opposite Kunming City Museum at 118 Tuodong Lu (☎0871 63017878; Mon–Fri 9–11.30am & 1–5pm). They speak good English but are slow with visa extensions; expect five days.

Around Kunming

Despite the recent construction of some half-baked attractions, the key sights around Kunming have been pulling in visitors for centuries. Don't miss the extraordinary sculptures at westerly **Qiongzhu Temple**, or the view over Dian Chi lake from the Dragon Gate, high up in the **Western Hills**. Further afield, the spectacular **Stone Forest** makes an enjoyable day-trip if you can accept the fairground atmosphere and the crowds dutifully tagging behind their cosmetically perfect tour guides.

Jin Dian Park

金殿公园, jīndiàn gōngyuán • Daily 7am–7pm • ¥20 • bus #71 from Beijing Lu, north of Dongfeng Guangchang

Around 10km northeast of the city, steps at **Jin Dian Park**, also known as the Golden Temple, head up through woodland to a cluster of pleasantly worn Qing-dynasty halls housing weapons used in 1671 by the rebel Ming general Wu Sangui – the man who deliberately let the Manchu armies through the Great Wall, and then later revolted against China's new overlords. Behind the halls is Jin Dian itself, a **gilded bronze temple** built as a replica of the one atop Wudang Shan in Hubei (see p.425). The woods here are full of fragrant camellias and weekend picnickers, and a tower on the hilltop encloses a large Ming bell from Kunming's demolished southern gates.

Avoid taking the cable car from the back of the park to the **1999 Horticultural Expo Site** – a monster scam at ¥100 for a walk through vast, drab squares of low-maintainance flower beds. The Chinese do excellent gardens, but this isn't one of them.

Qiongzhu Temple

筇竹寺, qióngzhú sì • Daily 8.30am–6pm • ¥10 • taxi around ¥100 return including waiting time • bus #82 from the western end of Nanping Jie or bus #C72 from Kunming train station to the West bus station, and then bus #C61 (7am–7pm) to the temple – check with the driver because not all #C61 buses come here

Up in the hills 10km west of Kunming and tedious to reach on public transport, tranquil **Qiongzhu Temple** features a fantastic array of over-the-top Buddhist sculptures. Late in the nineteenth century, the eminent Sichuanese sculptor **Li Guangxiu** and his five assistants were engaged to embellish Qiongzhu's main halls with five hundred clay statues of *arhats*, which they accomplished with inspired gusto, spending ten years creating the comical and grotesquely distorted crew of monks, goblins, scribes, emperors and beggars that crowd the interior: some sit rapt with holy contemplation, others smirk, roar with hysterical mirth or snarl grimly as they ride a foaming sea alive with sea monsters. Unfortunately it all proved too absurd for Li's conservative contemporaries and this was his final commission. There's also a good, if pricey, **vegetarian restaurant** here, which is open at lunchtime.

The Western Hills

西山, xīshān • Daily 8.30am–6pm • Park entry ¥20, Long Men area ¥30 • bus #54 from Renmin Zhong Lu to its terminal at Mian Shan car park (眠山车场, miánshān chēchǎng), and from there bus #6 to the park gates

The well-wooded **Western Hills**, 16km outside Kunming, are an easy place to spend a day out of doors – if again a little awkward to reach – with cable cars and pleasant walking trails ascending a 2500m-high ridge for superb vistas over **Dian Chi**, the broad lake southwest of town.

In the hills

From the park gates at Gaoyao (高峣, gāoyáo) it's over an hour's walk to the main sights, but take time to visit the atmospheric **Huating Temple** (华亭寺, huátíng sì) and **Taihua Temple** (太华寺, tàihuá sì), the latter reached along a warped, flagstoned path through old-growth forest. Past here you come to two **cable car stations**: one crosses back towards town (¥40), the other climbs to the Dragon Gate area (¥25). You can walk up too: just carry straight on along the road and it's about twenty minutes to the Dragon Gate ticket office. Then it's up narrow flights of stone steps, past a group of minor temples, and into a series of chambers and narrow tunnels which exit at **Dragon Gate** (龙门, lóngmén) itself, a narrow balcony and ornamented grotto on a sheer cliff overlooking the lake. It took the eighteenth-century monk **Wu Laiqing** and his successors more than seventy years to excavate the tunnels, which continue up to where another flight of steps climbs to further lookouts.

The Stone Forest

石林景区, shílín jǐngqū • Daily 8.30am–6pm • ¥175 • day-trips are run by every tour desk in Kunming • public buses from the East bus station ¥35 • make sure you get one to the scenic area and not to Shilin town

Yunnan's renowned **Stone Forest** comprises an exposed bed of limestone spires weathered and split into intriguing clusters, 90km east of Kunming. It takes about an hour to cover the main circuit through the pinnacles to **Sword Peak Pond**, an ornamental pool surrounded by particularly sharp ridges, which you can climb along a narrow track leading right up across the top of the forest. This is the most frequented part of the park, with large red characters incised into famous rocks, and ethnic **Sani**, a Yi subgroup, in unnaturally clean dresses strategically placed for photographers. This area can be intimidatingly crammed with Chinese tour groups, but the paths that head out towards the perimeter are much quieter, leading to smaller, separate stone groupings in the fields beyond where you could spend the whole day without seeing another visitor.

Southeastern Yunnan

The region southeast of Kunming is a nicely unpackaged corner of the province, and there are good reasons, besides the **Vietnamese border crossing** at Hekou, to head down this way. Amiable, old-fashioned **Jianshui** boasts a complement of Qing architecture, and an unusual attraction in nearby caves, while **Yuanyang** is the base for exploring the cultures and impressive terraced landscapes of the Hong He Valley. Jianshui and Yuanyang can be tied together in a trip to the border, or each are directly accessible by bus from Kunming.

11

Jianshui

建水, jiànshuǐ

JIANSHUI, a country town 200km south of Kunming, has been an administrative centre for over a thousand years. There's a good feel to the place, buoyed by plenty of **old architecture** and a very casual approach to tourism, making for a pleasant overnight stop. While you're here, visit **Yanzi Dong**, an impressive limestone cavern out in the countryside nearby.

The old town

On arrival, head straight for Jianshui's scruffy **old town**, a web of lanes entered through the huge red gateway of **Chaoyang Lou** (朝阳楼, cháoyáng lóu), the Ming-dynasty eastern gate tower. Past here, cobbled Lin'an Lu runs through the old town, lined with wooden-fronted shops, but cutting down along parallel Guilin Jie leads into a completely unrestored quarter, past blocks of mud-brick mansions and a stack of ancient **wells**, many of which are clearly still used by locals.

Zhu Family Gardens

朱家花园, zhūjiā huāyuán • Hanlin Jie • Daily 9am–10pm • ¥60

Right in the centre of the old town, the traditionally arranged **Zhu Family Gardens** are a Chinese box of interlocking halls and courtyards, brightly painted and in good condition. The gardens were laid out in the 1880s, when the Zhus were at their height of wealth; they later fell from grace and the gardens only escaped complete destruction during the 1960s because the family had fought both the Manchus in 1911 and the Nationalist armies twenty years later. Pick of the small pavilions is the open-sided **Hua Ting**, an elegant timber and stone hall facing a small pond.

Confucian Academy

文庙, wénmiào • Lin'an Lu • Daily 8am–6.30pm • ¥60

West along Lin'an Lu is the main entrance to Jianshui's venerable **Confucian Academy**. Once in past the large lily pond out front, there are ornamental stone gateways and halls containing statues of the Great Sage and his more gifted followers, with worried parents bringing their offspring here to kowtow to this patron of learning before school exams in the summer. Although what survives here is in good condition, it's clear the academy has suffered very badly over the years.

11

Yanzi Dong

燕子洞, yànzi dòng • ¥80 • Buses leave Jianshui bus station when full approximately 7am–3pm (¥10) • last bus back 6pm • minibus or taxi from Jianshui about ¥200 return, including waiting time

Yanzi Dong, the Swallows' Caves, lie about 30km from Jianshui in the forested Lu River valley. For the last few centuries people have come to see the tens of thousands of **swiftlets** who nest here – the noise of wheeling birds is deafening during the early summer – but even without the birds the caves are an enjoyable Chinese-style tourist attraction, featuring a dragon-boat ride, a few coloured lights, some spectacular rock formations, and an **underground restaurant** selling bird's-nest cakes (an expensive delicacy for the Chinese). If you can, catch the **Bird Nest Festival** on August 8, the only day of the year that collecting the then-vacant nests is allowed – a very profitable and dangerous task for local Yi men, who scale the 60m-high cliffs as crowds look on.

ARRIVAL AND DEPARTURE   JIANSHUI

By bus Jianshui's bus station is on Yinghui Lu in the bland modern town, 1km northeast of the old town; catch bus #1, #12, or #13 to the Chaoyang Lou, or a taxi (¥4) to Lin'an Lu-Hanlin Jie intersection in the old town. There are regular departures to Kunming, and less frequent services to Hekou

and Yuanyang – the latter a long trip on a direct, scenic but rough road south.

Destinations Hekou (4hr); Jinghong (10hr); Kunming (4hr); Yuanyang (3hr).

ACCOMMODATION

Hongmantian Kezhan 红满天客栈, hóngmǎntiān kèzhàn. Hanlin Jie ☎0873 3183818. Opposite the *Lin'an*, this place has a wildly decorated facade in a pseudo-antique style; rooms are large, but overall it lacks the appealing atmosphere of its neighbour. **¥180**

Huaqing Hotel 话请酒店, huàqǐng jiǔdiàn. 5 Hanlin Jie ☎0873 7666166. Popular with tour groups, this place has good standard, perfectly clean rooms and an adjoining café. There's no lift, so rooms on the fourth floor can easily be bargained down to a great deal. **¥120**

★ **Lin'an Inn** 临安客栈, línān kèzhàn. 32 Hanlin Jie ☎0873 7655866. Just north of the Zhu Gardens, this friendly courtyard-style hotel has large, clean, airy rooms which are excellent value, and some enormous beds. They also rent bikes for ¥30 per day. **¥170**

Zhu Family Gardens 朱家花园, zhūjiā huāyuán. 16 Hanlin Jie ☎0873 7667109. This has to be the pick of Jianshui's places to stay, at least for atmosphere, with its rooms full of imitation Qing furniture and a genuine sense of history. That all comes at a price, though. **¥480**

EATING

★ **Xiangman Lou** 香满楼, xiāngmǎn lóu. 65 Hanlin Jie ☎0873 7655655. This wooden building in the heart of the old town is the best place to eat in Jianshui. There's an extensive menu including the local speciality *qiguo*, a casserole whose inverted funnel design

simultaneously poaches meat and creates a soup, as well as regional mushroom dishes and a decent selection for vegetarians. Expect to pay around ¥40 per person for a full meal. Daily 11am–9.30pm.

DIRECTORY

Banks and exchange There are Construction Bank and ICBC ATMs taking foreign cards on Lin'an Lu.

The Hong He Valley

Hong He, the Red River, starts life near Xiaguan in Yunnan's northwest and runs southeast across the province, entering Vietnam at Hekou and flowing through Hanoi before emptying its russet-coloured waters, laden with volcanic soil, into the Gulf of Tonkin. For much of its journey the river is straight, channelled by high mountain ranges into a series of fertile, steep-sided valleys. These have been **terraced** by resident **Hani**, whose mushroom-shaped adobe-and-thatch houses pepper the hills around **Yuanyang**. In spring and autumn thick mists blanket the area, muting the violent contrast between red soil and brilliant green paddy fields. Though the best time to see them is between March and May, when the paddies are full of water, they are spectacular at any time.

Yuanyang

元阳, yuányáng

The access point for viewing the rice terraces is **Yuanyang**, a district 80km south of Jianshui and 300km from Kunming. The name covers two settlements: the riverside township of **Nansha** (元阳南沙, yuányáng nánshā), terminus for Jianshui buses; and, where you actually want to base yourself, **XINJIE** (元阳新街镇, yuányáng xīnjiēzhèn), 30km uphill at the top of a high ridge. Xinjie is a small, untidy brick-and-concrete town which becomes a hive of activity on **market days** (every five days), when brightly dresssed Hani, Miao, Yi and Yao women pour in from surrounding villages.

Around Xinjie

Xinjie sits surrounded by pretty villages and deeply terraced hillsides, some within walking distance or a short drive on local transport; one easy walk is a loop, via various hamlets, to the Hani village of **Jinzhuzhai** and **Longshuba**, a Yi settlement, which nestle quietly amid trees, giant bamboo and paddy fields. Try and catch at least one village **market**, where fruit and veg, daily necessities, wild honey, buffaloes and chickens are sold, and watch men discreetly gambling in the background. Markets run between villages on a rota, and activity peaks around noon.

Rice terraces

There are several places from where you can view the famous **terraces**, each with an entry fee. A roadside viewing platform 18km northwest of town at **Mengping** (勐平, měngpíng; ¥30) gives you the chance to be mobbed by Yi women selling postcards; **sunset** is the best time to visit. The southwestern road (¥100 covers all sights along it) will get you to viewpoints at **Bada** (坝达, bàdá; 16km from Xinjie) and the recently renovated farm village of **Duoyishu** (多依树, duōyīshù; 27km), famed for its sunrises, where there's a range of basic accommodation.

ARRIVAL AND DEPARTURE

BY BUS

There are long-distance stations at both Nansha and Xinjie. **Nansha** Nansha's bus station is at river level, right at the junction of the road up to Xinjie, and handles traffic to Jianshui (¥33).

HONG HE VALLEY

Xinjie Just off the main square. There are three direct buses daily to Kunming's South bus station (¥128), and a couple to Hekou.

Destinations Hekou (3hr); Jianshui (3hr); Kunming (7hr).

INFORMATION

Information For the latest on where to go, how to get there and how much to pay, visit the World Vision-sponsored Window of Yuanyang (元阳之窗, yuányáng zhīchuāng, ☏0873 5623627, ⓦwindowofyuanyang .com), 100m or so down the street past the Agricultural Bank of China, below the *Yunti Hotel* (see below). They can organize minibus rental and tour guides, and have simple but useful hiking maps of the local area.

GETTING AROUND

By minibus Minibuses shuttle between Nansha and Xinjie bus stations throughout the day (¥10; 1hr). Private minibuses ply popular routes from village to village for a few yuan per person (they display their destinations in their front windows). If you're pushed for time you'll probably need to hire a minibus at Xinjie; ¥250 for the vehicle should cover a day's exploration and get you around most of the sights.

ACCOMMODATION

Accommodation in Xinjie is plentiful; there are also several basic guesthouses among the terraces at Duoyishu village.

XINJIE

Chen Family Guesthouse 陈家旅社, chénjiā lǚshè. Immediately out of the bus station and left ☏0873 5622343. This guesthouse with basic tiled rooms (and Snoopy curtains) has some of the best views in town from its terrace. En-suite rooms come with hot showers and a squat toilet. Dorm ¥25, room ¥50

Yunti 云梯大酒店, yúntī dàjiǔdiàn. Across the road

11

from the main square ☎0873 5624858, ⓦyunti-hotel .cn. Of the two *Yunti* hotels in Xinjie, this has the better rooms but lesser views. Newly refurbished, large and clean, this is the most comfortable place in town, with a good restaurant too. **¥200**

Yunti Sunshine 云梯顺捷酒店, yúntī shùnjié jiǔdiàn. In the main square ☎0873 5621588, ⓦyunti -hotel.cn. Boasting wonderful views, the rooms here have an unfinished quality to them, but are perfectly comfortable. You also have a grandstand spot for morning aerobics in the square – which kicks off at 7am sharp, accompanied by blasting techno. Bring earplugs. **¥130**

DUOYISHU

Sunny Guesthouse 阳光客栈, yángguāng kèzhàn.

☎1598 7371311. Down at the bottom of the village, the friendly *Sunny* is hard to find but run by fluent English-speakers, so give them a call before you arrive and they'll come and find you. Somewhere between a guesthouse and a hostel, rooms are basic but have fantastic views down the valley. Dorm **¥40**, room **¥130**

Yuanyang International Youth Hostel 元阳国际青 年旅舍, yuányáng guójì qīngnián lǔshè ☎136 9498158. At the top of the village, down a flight of steps from the main road, the modern building is functional but hardly pretty, much like this hostel's rooms. There's an excellent terrace for watching the sunrise though, and the bar downstairs also turns out a good selection of evening meals. Dorm **¥45**, room **¥100**

EATING

Liu Jun Fandian 六军饭店, liùjūn fàndiàn. West side of the town square, Xinjie. There are simple restaurants dotted all over Xinjie, particularly along the road from the square to the bus station, but this is the best. In two units either side of a pharmacy, both served by the same kitchen, take your pick from a large fridge stuffed full of ingredients. Check the prices when you order, but most dishes are around ¥25 per plateful. Daily 9am–9.30pm.

DIRECTORY

Banks and exchange There's an Agricultural Bank ATM along Xinjie's pedestrianized shopping street off the square which claims to take foreign cards, but don't count on it.

Hekou and the border

河口, hékǒu

HEKOU, 360km southeast of Kunming, is only worth a special visit if you're in transit between China and Vietnam – the border post is a few minutes' walk from the bus station. On the other side, **Lao Cai** has a huge game market, a few despondent hotels, and a train station 3km south that offers two services daily for the ten-hour run to Hanoi. Most travellers take a bus or motorbike-taxi (US$5) to the hill resort town of **Sa Pa**.

ARRIVAL AND DEPARTURE   HEKOU

By bus Arriving from Vietnam, head 50m up the main road and the bus station is on the left. Here you can catch fast buses to Kunming's East bus station (8hr; ¥139), or ordinary buses to Yuanyang and Jianshui.
Destinations Jianshui (5hr); Kunming (8hr).

DIRECTORY

Banks and exchange To change money, walk up the main street from the border, turn right after 200m, and you'll arrive at the Bank of China (daily 8am–5.30pm; foreign exchange closed Sun).

Northwestern Yunnan

Vigorously uplifted during the last fifty million years as the Indian subcontinent buckled up against China, **northwestern Yunnan** is a geologically unsettled region of subtropical forests, thin pasture, alpine lakes and shattered peaks painted crisply in blue, white and grey. **Xiaguan** is the regional hub, springboard for the route north via a string of old towns, once staging posts on the *chama dao*, the "Tea-Horse Road" **trade routes** between China and Tibet, along which goods were transported on horseback. The lakeshore town of **Dali** is the first, home to the Bai nationality and backed by a long mountain range;

ROUTES THROUGH THE NORTHWEST

Xiaguan, just a stone's throw from Dali, is just five hours from Kunming by bus, and from here there are at least regular, if not always speedy, services through the rest of the region. **Trains** link Kunming to Xiaguan and Lijiang, with talk of an extension to Shangri-La; and you can also **fly** to Lijiang and Shangri-La. There are overland routes **into Sichuan** from Lijiang and Shangri-La too; but at the time of writing the **Tibet road** from Deqin, which follows the dramatic upper reaches of the Lancang River to Markam, then turns west towards Lhasa, was closed to foreigners. Ask agencies in Dali, Lijiang and Shangri-La about the latest situation.

but picturesque **Lijiang**, a few hours up the road at the base of Yulong Xue Shan, pulls in the biggest crowds as the former capital of the **Naxi** kingdom. Hikers can organize themselves here for a two-day trek through **Tiger Leaping Gorge**, where a youthful Yangzi River cuts through the deepest chasm on Earth. Nearby is **Lugu Lake**, lakeside home to the matrilineal **Mosuo**, while north again is the Tibetan monastery town of **Shangri-La**. By now you're barely in Yunnan, and a day's further travel will carry you up to **Deqin**, where a spectacular string of peaks marks the Tibetan borderlands.

If possible, it's probably best to head up this way in autumn: winters are extremely cold, and while early spring is often sunny, summers – though fairly mild – can also be very wet, leading to landslides. Also be aware that the border regions around Shangri-La and Deqin might be **closed off** during March, historically a time of political unrest in Tibet – see p.857.

Xiaguan

下关, xiàguān

Some 380km west of Kunming underneath a string of mountain-top wind turbines, **XIAGUAN** – also confusingly known as **Dali city** (大理市, dàlǐ shì) – is a sprawling transport hub on the southern shore of Er Hai Lake. With Dali so close – less than an hour's ride up the lakeshore – you won't need to spend the night here, but you'll almost certainly pass through Xiaguan at some stage, if only to top up your **China visa** at the local, highly amenable, PSB office. In addition, both the holy mountain of **Jizu Shan** and **Weishan**, a small, largely unspoiled market town to the south, are just about manageable as day-trips from the town's bus stations.

ARRIVAL AND DEPARTURE   XIAGUAN

Xiaguan is where most long-distance "Dali" transport actually terminates; Dali itself is less than an hour distant from the city on frequent public transport. Though it's possible to get tickets at the respective train and bus stations in Xiaguan, booking in Dali at a small mark-up (¥20) saves a lot of hassle, and for buses often includes a complementary shuttle to the station. A taxi from bus or train stations in Xiaguan to Dali takes around 40min and costs ¥60.

BY PLANE

Dali airport (大理机场, dàlǐ jīchǎng) is 15km east of Xiaguan, for which you'll need a taxi (flat rate of ¥100 to Dali old town).

Destinations Guangzhou (1 daily; 3hr 30min); Jinghong (2 daily; 1hr); Kunming (3 daily; 45min).

BY TRAIN

Xiaguan train station (下关火车站, xiàguān huǒchēzhàn) is in the east of town on Weishan Lu; city bus #8 to old Dali town stops right outside. Buy tickets on the first floor.

Destinations Kunming (5 daily; 8hr); Lijiang (4 daily; 2hr).

BY BUS

Dali bus station (大理汽车客运站, dàlǐ qìchē kèyùn zhàn). Diagonally across Weishan Lu from the train station, this bus station is of most use for Kunming. Catch city bus #8 from outside the train station to old Dali town.

North bus station (客运北站, kèyùn běizhàn), 3km north of the centre on the Dali highway. Further buses to Kunming and regular departures for Lijiang and Shangri-La (Zhongdian) – the #8 and #4 buses stop right outside.

South bus station (客运南站, kèyùn nánzhàn) Nanjian Lu. Only needed for buses to Weishan. It's at the terminus of the #2 bus route from the North bus station.

Xingcheng express bus station (兴盛高快客运站, xīngshèng gāokuài kèyùnzhàn), Xingcheng Lu. Express coaches to Kunming and points west, such as Baoshan and Tengchong. For old Dali town, turn right out of the bus station, walk to the main intersection, then turn right again and it's 150m to the #8 bus stop.

Destinations Baoshan (3hr); Binchuan (2hr); Dali (30min); Jinghong (18hr); Kunming (4hr); Lijiang (3hr 30min); Liushui (6hr); Mangshi (4hr); Ruili (6hr); Shangri-La (7hr); Shaxi (4hr); Tengchong (6hr); Weishan (1hr 30min).

GETTING AROUND

By bus Xiaguan has a good city bus network, several of which run from arrival points, through town and north to Dali. Fare in town is ¥1.5, with most buses running 7am–8pm.

By taxi Taxis can be found throughout town, but congregate at bus and train stations. Flag fall is ¥6, then ¥1.6 per additional km.

DIRECTORY

PSB Xiaguan's helpful PSB (Mon–Fri 9–11.30am & 2–5pm; ☏0872 2142149) is located north of town on the Xiaguan–Dali highway, on the bus #8 route: get off at the Century Middle School stop (世纪中学, shìjì zhōngxué), and the PSB is the building in front of you with a radio tower on the roof.

Jizu Shan

鸡足山, jīzú shān · ¥60

The holy mountain of **Jizu Shan** lies about 90km northeast of Xiaguan, and is associated with Buddhism's Chan (Zen) sect; Tibetans also consider it a place of pilgrimage. There are a handful of temples here, but perhaps the best thing about a visit is the scenery, especially views from the mountain's summit. On the trek up, you can ponder various unlikely explanations for Jizu Shan's odd name – it means "Chickenfoot Mountain".

On the mountain

The vehicle road ends halfway up the mountain, in woodland between the simple **Shizhong Temple** (石钟寺, shízhōng sì) and larger **Wanshou Nunnery** (万寿庵, wànshòu ān). There's a knot of cheap restaurants off to one side here, whose owners also offer **beds**. Follow the road up to a sharp kink, then take the unsigned path alongside the **horse pen** up the mountain. It's 3.5km on foot from here to the top, following steps through the forest and onto heathland; 1km along, there's also a **cable car** (¥40 one-way) to just below the summit. Walking, give yourself at least two hours to complete the ascent, which ends where the ninth-century **Lengyan Pagoda** (楞严塔, lèngyán tǎ) and accompanying **Jinding Temple** (金顶寺, jīndǐng sì) – identical to Kunming's Jin Dian (see p.655) – rise splendidly against the skyline.

ARRIVAL AND DEPARTURE   JIZU SHAN

By bus and minibus To reach Jizu Shan, catch one of the frequent buses from Xiaguan's Dali bus station to Binchuan (宾川, bīnchuān; 2hr; ¥25), then a minibus from the back of the station to Jizu Shan (¥13; 1hr 30min) – these leave when full, and run from around 8am until 4pm. Minibuses from the mountain to Binchuan run approximately 8am–3pm.

ACCOMMODATION

Jizu Shan Hotel 鸡足山宾馆, jīzúshān bīnguǎn. On the main mountain road, 300m below Zhusheng Temple ☏0872 7350478. Very basic hostel-style accommodation, but good enough for a single night. You may want to bring your own sleeping bag – it can be cold and damp and the hot water is intermittent. **¥80**

Weishan

巍山, wēishān

WEISHAN, a charismatic old town 50km south of Xiaguan, is now largely forgotten, but as the cradle of the Nanzhao kingdom and a prosperous former stop on the tea-horse trade routes, it has a distinguished past. Today it's a supply town for the local Bai, Muslim and – especially – **Yi** population, but its history, still evident in some impressive ancient buildings, makes it worth a visit.

The old town

Head east from Weishan's bus station, and you'll soon be walking the cobbled lanes of the **old town**; there are few street signs, but the only thing you need to find anyway is **Gongchen Lou** (拱辰楼, gǒngchén lóu), a huge old gate tower marking the centre of town. Climb it (¥2) and you'll see Weishan's pedestrianized main street, lined with old wooden shops, running 500m south to smaller **Xinggong Lou** (星拱楼, xīnggǒng lóu), once a bell tower. Weishan's back lanes are full of markets and wobbly adobe houses, but the town's biggest appeal is the fact that nothing is geared to tourism, and people are just getting on with their lives – the barber shop on the east side of the square around Gongchen Lou, and seemingly unchanged for the last 100 years, is a particular treat.

ARRIVAL AND DEPARTURE   WEISHAN

By bus Weishan's bus station is at the western edge of town, with departures to Xiaguan's South bus station every 15min until 5.30pm (¥13).

Destinations Kunming (3 daily; 6hr); Xiaguan (1hr 30min).

ACCOMMODATION AND EATING

For food, head to Xiaochi Jie (小吃街, xiǎochī jiē) or "Snack Street", the first lane running east, south of Gongchen Lou, which is lined with inexpensive restaurants.

Gucheng Kezhan 古城客栈, gǔchéng kèzhàn. 59 Dongxin Jie ☎0872 6122341. Just east from Gongchen Lou, the *Gucheng* has basic en-suite rooms tucked around a small, old courtyard. The rooms aren't great but the family that runs the place are friendly. **¥80**

Mengshe Stagehouse 蒙舍驿站, mēngshě yìzhàn. 9 Nan Jie, 50m past Xinggong Lou ☎0872 6123338. This reconstructed old inn has a lovely wooden facade and Bai-style wall murals, though once past this welcomingly authentic rustic frontage, the rooms at the back are a little concrete and bland. **¥80**

Weishan Binguan 巍山宾馆, wēishān bīnguǎn. 52 Dongxin Jie ☎0872 6122655. Virtually next door to the *Gucheng*, this larger operation is more of a standard Chinese hotel really – hard beds, large en-suite rooms, a/c and bathtubs – and seems oversized for the town. **¥140**

Dali

大理, dàlǐ

A thirty-minute local bus ride north of Xiaguan, **DALI** draws swarms of holidaying middle-class urban Chinese seeking an "old China" experience, while foreign backpackers drift through a Westerner-friendly theme park of beer gardens and hippified cafés. It's not hard to see why people flock here: despite the tourist overkill along the main streets, Dali is pretty, interesting and relaxed, full of old houses and an indigenous **Bai** population rubbing shoulders with local Yi and Muslims. To the east lies the great lake, **Er Hai**, while the invitingly green valleys and clouded peaks of the **Cang Shan range** rear up behind town, the perfect setting for a few days' walking or relaxation. Some visitors, seduced by China's closest approximation to bohemia (and the local weed), forget to leave, and plenty of resident Westerners run businesses here.

Brief history

There's much more to Dali than its modern profile. Between the eighth and thirteenth centuries, the town was at the centre of the Nanzhao and Dali kingdoms, which at one

> ### DALI'S FESTIVALS
>
> If you can, visit Dali during the **Spring Fair**, held from the fifteenth day of the third lunar month (April or May). The event spans five hectic days of horse trading, wrestling, racing, dancing and singing, attracting thousands of people from all over the region to camp at the fairground just west of town. You'll probably have to follow suit, as beds in Dali will be in short supply. In addition, an impressive but frankly scary **Yi torch festival** is held on the 24th day of the sixth lunar month – flaming torches are paraded at night, and people even throw gunpowder at each other.

11

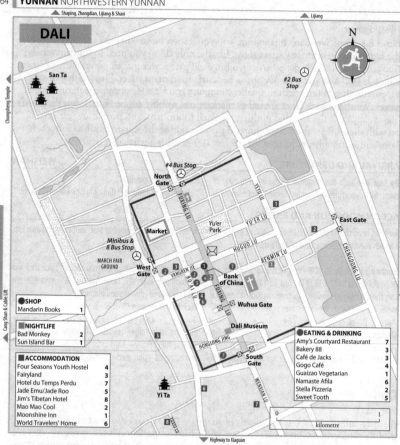

DALI

Shaping, Zhongdian, Lijiang & Shaxi

Lijiang

N

Chongsheng Temple

San Ta

#2 Bus Stop

Er Hai

#4 Bus Stop

North Gate

FUXING LU

YENU LU

East Gate

Market

Yu'er Park

YU'ER LU

CHENGDONG LU

Minibus & 8 Bus Stop

HUGUO LU

RENMIN LU

MARCH FAIR GROUND

West Gate

YANGREN JIE

Bank of China

Xiaguan

BO'AI LU

FUXING LU

Wuhua Gate

Cang Shan & Cable Lift

Dali Museum

HONGLONG JING

South Gate

WENXIAN LU

Yi Ta

Highway to Xiaguan

●**SHOP**
Mandarin Books — 1

■**NIGHTLIFE**
Bad Monkey — 2
Sun Island Bar — 1

■**ACCOMMODATION**
Four Seasons Youth Hostel — 4
Fairyland — 3
Hotel du Temps Perdu — 7
Jade Emu/Jade Roo — 5
Jim's Tibetan Hotel — 8
Mao Mao Cool — 2
Moonshine Inn — 1
World Travelers' Home — 6

●**EATING & DRINKING**
Amy's Courtyard Restaurant — 7
Bakery 88 — 3
Café de Jacks — 3
Gogo Café — 4
Guaizao Vegetarian — 1
Namaste Afila — 6
Stella Pizzeria — 2
Sweet Tooth — 5

0   1
kilometre

point expanded into Burma, Sichuan and Thailand; while in the mid-nineteenth century it briefly became capital of the Islamic state declared by **Du Wenxiu**, who led a Muslim rebellion against Chinese rule. But the revolt failed and the Yunnan governor, Cen Yuying, unleashed a merciless slaughter of Dali's unarmed civilian population; the town was utterly devastated, never to recover its former political position.

The South Gate

南门, nánmén · ¥20

Get your bearings on top of Dali's old **South Gate**, where you can study Xiaguan, the lake, town and mountains from the comfort of a teahouse. Dali's antique **pagodas** stand as landmarks above the roof lines, solitary Yi Ta due west, and the trinity of San Ta a few kilometres north. From here the town's original, grid-like street plan, and the line of its old walls, are still apparent, despite encroachment from highways and Xiaguan's ever-spreading suburbs.

The central streets

Fuxing Lu, choked with tour groups and souvenir stalls selling ethnic silverware and embroideries, runs north through the town: about 150m along, the heavy stone **Wuhua Gate** (五华楼, wǔhuá lóu) is a modern construction, similar in style to the South Gate. Past here, Fuxing Lu is crossed by **Renmin Lu** and **Yangren Jie** ("Foreigners' Street") which – along with parallel **Bo'ai Lu** – are where to find most of Dali's Westerner-friendly bars, cafés, masseurs, tour agents and trinket and clothing stalls. Escape the middle-aged Bai ladies hissing "ganja, ganja" at you by detouring east down Renmin Lu to the splendid blue, multi-tiered Bai-style **Catholic church** (天主教堂, tiānzhǔ jiàotáng) in an alley off to the south.

Dali Museum
大理博物馆, dàlǐ bówùguǎn • Daily 8.30am–5pm • Free

Down on Fuxing Lu near the South Gate, **Dali Museum** takes the form of a small Chinese palace with guardian stone lions and cannons in the courtyard. It was built for the Qing governor and appropriated as Du Wenxiu's "Forbidden City" during the Muslim insurrection. Historic relics include a strange bronze model of two circling dragons, jaws clenched around what might be a tree; a few Buddhist figurines from the Nanzhao period; and some lively statues of an orchestra and serving maids from a Ming noblewoman's tomb – a nice addition to the usual cases of snarling gods and warrior busts.

The north of town

Dali's north end is far less touristy than the south, and it's worth just wandering the cobbled residential back lanes. **Yu'er Park** (玉洱公园, yù'ěr gōngyuán; daily 6am–8pm; free) is a pleasant, if small, patch of trees; and Dali's northwesterly **produce market** is worth a look too, especially when crowds of hawkers, farmers and shoppers descend for the weekly market. Finally, the **North Gate** (北门, běimén) can again be climbed for views; Zhonghe Lu to the east is lined with little **marble factories**, turning out the grey-streaked sculptures for which Dali is famous.

San Ta

三塔, sāntǎ • Daily 8am–7pm • ¥121, or ¥190 including Chongsheng temple • bus #19 from outside the South Gate on Wenxian Lu

The ostentatious Three Pagodas, or **San Ta**, were built around 850: the 69m-tall, square-based **Qianxun tower** is a century older than the two smaller octagonal pagodas behind. As the structures are sealed, the stiff entrance fee gives access only to souvenir stalls around their base, so you're probably just as well looking at them from outside the gate – though if you have bought the full ticket you can visit the huge and completely forgettable **Chongsheng Temple** (崇圣寺, chóngshèng sì) behind, built from scratch in 2005.

ARRIVAL AND DEPARTURE   DALI

By bus Dali doesn't have its own bus station: arriving from the north will see you dropped off on the highway outside the east gate, from where you can either walk into town or catch bus #2 up Yu'er Lu. From the south, your bus will terminate at Xiaguan and you'll need to catch city bus #4 or #8, or grab a cab (¥60) into Dali old town. Leaving, book long-distance bus

tickets through agents in town – who will also tell you where to pick buses up – or head down to the relevant stations in Xiaguan and sort things out yourself.
Destinations Kunming (5hr 30min); Lijiang (3hr 30min); Shangri-La (6hr); Shaping (1hr); Shaxi (3hr 30min); Xiaguan (30min); Xizhou (30min); Zhoucheng (45min).

INFORMATION

Travel agents Agents in Dali – such as Michael's Travel (on Bo'ai Lu) – can organize tickets onwards plus Er Hai boat trips (¥100/person), visits to a Bai home (¥50/person) and discounted tickets for the Cang Shan cableways.
Tour operators There are a number of specialist tour operators based in Dali to help you get the most out of your

trip: these include Climb Dali (☎0872 2501920, ⓦclimbdali.com), with offices at 20 Renmin Lu and the *Boulder Bar* at 393 Renmin Lu; and Amiwa (☎158 21994181, ⓦamiwa-trek.com), a trekking company with Bai guides. Agents in Dali can also organize train and plane tickets from Xiaguan.

GETTING AROUND

By bus City buses shuttle between Dali and Xiaguan through the day: bus #8 runs from outside the

West Gate, turns east along Yu'er Lu and then heads south along Chengdong Lu; bus #4 from the North Gate runs down Bao'ai Lu and onto the highway. Both cost ¥2.

By taxi Taxis endlessly ply the streets of Dali, so finding one is no problem – basic charges will be ¥50–60 into Xiaguan and ¥100 for the airport. Nowhere within Dali itself should cost more than ¥10.

ACCOMMODATION

Dali has plenty of good-value places to stay, both inside and outside the old city walls, though rates can double during local festivals. If you're really looking to avoid the tourist hordes, there's more remote accommodation in the Cang Shan range and at Xizhou (see p.669).

Fairyland 连锁酒店, liánsuǒ jiǔdiàn. 31 Yangren Jie, west off Bo'ai Lu ⊕ 1898 7080802. Probably the smartest place in town for the price, though not especially cheap, with modern hotel rooms inside an attractive, restored old Bai courtyard house. **¥249**

Four Seasons Youth Hostel 春夏秋冬青年舍, chūnxiàqiūdōng qīngnián lǚshè. 46 Bo'ai Lu (entrance on Renmin Lu) ⊕ 0872 2671668. Modern courtyard setting with pool table, free internet, aimiably clueless staff and obligatory bar. Dorms are functional while private en-suite rooms with a/c are very well furnished. Dorms **¥45**, rooms **¥160**

★**Hotel du Temps Perdu** 风清大理客栈, fēngqīng dàlǐ kèzhàn. 81 Wenxian Lu, 200m south of the South Gate ⊕ 1398 8414203, ⊜ hoteldutemps perdu@gmail.com. Comfortable modern rooms are arranged around a central atrium and decked out in Chinese furnishings, with a good restaurant and helpful, friendly staff. They put out tables and chairs among plants in the courtyard and serve free tea and nibbles. **¥180**

Jade Emu/Jade Roo 金玉缘中澳国际青年舍, jīnyùyuán zhōngào guójì qīngnián lǚshè. West Gate Village, across the western highway from town ⊕ 0872 2677311, ⊛ jade-emu.com. Large, clean, institution-like hostel complex with a touch too much concrete around the place, though the exterior is nicely done out in Bai-style decorations. Dorms **¥30**, rooms **¥130**

Jim's Tibetan Hotel 吉姆藏式酒店, jímǔ zāngshì jiǔdiàn. 4 Luyuan Xiang ⊕ 0872 2677824, ⊛ jims -tibetan-hotel.com. Likeable Jim has been a Dali fixture for decades, and this colourful modern take on a traditional Tibetan home – with a rooftop terrace and multiple floors facing out into a rose garden – is a quiet, spacious option well geared to travellers' needs. There's an excellent restaurant and fair-value trips out of town. **¥300**

★**Mao Mao Cool** 猫猫果儿客栈, māomāo guǒér kèzhàn. 419 Renmin Lu ⊕ 0872 2474653. Very stylish, open-plan modern atrium building with goldfish pond; rooms have wooden floors and are just a bit too comfortable to be minimalist. Quiet location might be a plus. Café and small library too; excellent value. **¥120**

★**Moonshine Inn** 苍岳别院, cāngyuè biéyuàn. 16 Yu'er Xiang, Yu'er Lu ⊕ 0872 2671319, ⊛ moon360 .net. Beautifully constructed old-style three-storey courtyard guesthouse run by a Bai lady and her German husband. Rooms are priced according to floor: the ones on the top, with access to a roof terrace, are the nicest and priciest. Note that all the loos are squat style. It's 50m down a narrow alley off Yu'er Lu; look for the sign painted on the wall. **¥170**

World Travelers' Home 旅友驿站, lǚyǒu yìzhàn. 3 Luyu Lu ⊕ 0872 2680288. Friendly, quiet, Chinese-style hotel with good-value basic doubles with a/c and larger – though slightly stuffy – rooms with wooden four-poster beds. Sound hiking info. **¥100**

EATING AND DRINKING

Chinese restaurants outside the south gate and around the intersections of Fuxing Lu with Renmin Lu and Huguo Lu offer steamers of dumplings and Bai specialities such as fish or tofu casseroles, snails and stir-fried mountain vegetables and fungi. On the whole, food at these places isn't great, though the home-made plum wine (梅酒, méijiǔ) is worth a try. Similar Muslim canteens display grilled kebabs and fresh bread, and are a sounder bet. For cafés and bars serving a mix of Western and Chinese staples, head to Renmin Lu's western end, along with adjacent Yangren Jie and Bo'ai Lu. Food aside, they make good places to meet other foreigners and swap news, use the internet and get in touch with the latest martial-art, language or painting courses.

Amy's Courtyard Restaurant 庭院餐厅 tíngyuàn cāntīng. 2 Bo'ai Lu, just past the gate. One of the better places to try Bai fish head (or tofu) casseroles, cold cucumber salad and deep-fried goat's cheese with sugar. Around ¥30 per person for a good feed. Daily 11am–9pm.

Bakery 88 88号西点店, bāshíbā hào xīdiǎndiàn. 52 Yangren Jie Zhong Xin, Bo'ai Lu ⊕ 0872 2679129.

German-managed café with superb European cakes and breads to eat in or take away. The breakfast bagels and *baba ganoush* can make a nice break from the usual Chinese/Western options – sandwiches from ¥30. Daily 9am–9pm.

★**Café de Jacks** 樱花园西餐厅, yīnghuāyuán xīcāntīng. 82 Bo'ai Lu ⊕ 0872 2671572. Comfortable place to spend an afternoon over a coffee (¥15) and chocolate cake (¥20), or dig into their selection of curries, pizzas – from ¥30 – and Bai dishes. The open fire makes it cosy on winter evenings. Daily 9.30am–10.30pm.

Gogo Café. 51 Renmin Lu ☏0872 2672506. Popular for spaghetti, pizzas and large breakfasts – all from ¥30, as well as fruit juices and good coffee. They also have a book exchange, free internet and can burn CDs. Like most restaurant-bars in the street, they stick tables outside during the summer. Daily 9am–11pm.

Guaizao Western Vegetarian 拐枣国际素食咖啡馆, guǎizǎo guójì sùshí kāfēiguǎn. 176 Renmin Lu. Vegetarian restaurant doing proper hippy food – like tofu curry and lentil bakes – rather than the fake meat of most Chinese vegetarian places. Nice setting with a small garden at the back, terrace in front and free wi-fi. Mains from ¥25. Daily 10am–9.30pm.

★ **Namaste Afila** 亚菲拉印度菜, yàfēilā yìndùcài. 80 Bo'ai Lu ☏0872 8868865. Tucked into a small Moorish mud-brick-and-tiled courtyard, *Namaste* serves a wide selection of excellent, mostly vegetarian, Indian samosas, curries and thalis. There's a huge fireplace indoors for cooler weather. Stuff yourself for ¥50. Daily 11.30am–10pm.

Stella Pizzeria 新星比萨房, xīnxīng bǐsà fáng. 21 Huguo Lu ☏0872 2679251. The wood-fired clay oven here delivers the best pizzas in town, and the laidback decor, with seating on different mezzanine levels as well as outside, is appealing too. Daily 9am–10.30pm.

Sweet Tooth 甜点屋, tiándiǎn wū. 52 Bo'ai Lu ☏1581 2178779. A polished and pristine Western-style café, run by staff who are deaf-mute, with great cheesecake and breakfast pancakes from ¥20. Daily 9am–8pm.

NIGHTLIFE

★ **Bad Monkey** 坏猴子酒吧, huàihóuzi jiǔbā. 59 Renmin Lu ⌨badmonkeybar.com. Run by a pair of English wide boys, *Bad Monkey* is the black hole around which the rest of Dali's nightlife has revolved for more than a decade. Hosting nightly live music and serving cocktails, beer, fish and chips, and shepherd's pie, this place even has its own microbrewery, and is packed out virtually every night. Drinks from ¥25, main meals ¥35. Daily 8.30am–1am.

Sun Island Bar 日岛酒吧, rìdǎo jiǔbā. 324 Renmin Lu. One of several smaller speakeasies down towards the east gate, ideal for falling in and out of and with far more character than the row of new places along nearby Honglong Jing bar street. Daily 4pm–1am.

DIRECTORY

Banks and exchange The Bank of China (foreign exchange daily 8am–7pm) is on Fuxing Lu, where you'll also find the only ATMs in town.

Bookshop Mandarin Books, 285 Fuxing Lu (☏0872 2679014). Branch of Kunming's excellent English-language bookshop, with a wide range of special- and local-interest titles; not cheap, however.

Internet There's a 24hr internet café (¥3/hr) at the top of Renmin Lu, near Bo'ai Lu, though most accommodation and cafés have terminals and/or free wi-fi.

Mail The post office (daily 8am–9pm) is on Fuxing Lu, at Hugou Lu. Expect to have all parcels sent from here checked minutely for drugs.

Martial arts training Contact Wuwei Temple (see p.669).

Around Dali

Lying either side of Dali, **Er Hai Lake** and the **Cang Shan Range** can keep you busy for a few days, though the lake itself is probably of less interest than the villages dotting its shore. Some of these also host **markets**, full of activity and characters, where you can watch all manner of goods being traded and pick up locally made tie-dyed cloth.

Cang Shan

苍山, cāngshān • ¥30

Cang Shan, the Green Mountains, are just that: a 50km-long range peaking between 2000m and 4000m, cloaked in thick forest, cloud and – often well into spring – snow. Ascending the heights is easy thanks to two **cableways**, linked by a walking trail, or you can hike up.

Once in the mountains, a well-made, level, 13km-long **hiking track** connects the two upper cableway stations at Gantong Temple and Zhonghe Temple, allowing an easy 4hr walk through thick forest between the two. Along the way are some fantastic lookouts and, in summer, plenty of squirrels, birds and butterflies. Whatever the conditions are when you start out, take along food, water and weatherpoof gear, as things can change very quickly, often for the worse, up on top.

11

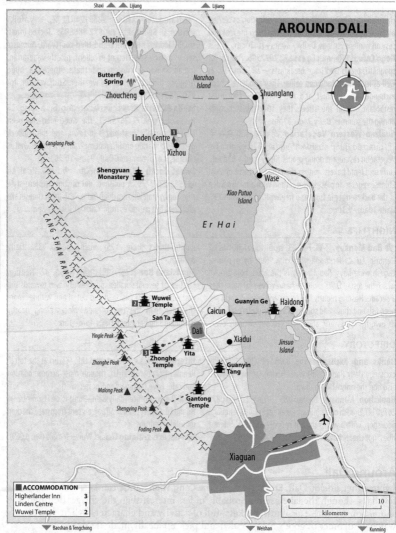

AROUND DALI

Shaxi | Lijiang | Lijiang

Shaping

Butterfly Spring

Zhoucheng

Nanzhao Island

Shuanglang

Canglang Peak

Linden Centre ①

Xizhou

Shengyuan Monastery

Wase

Xiao Putuo Island

Er Hai

Wuwei Temple ②

San Ta

Guanyin Ge | Haidong

Caicun

CANG SHAN RANGE

Dali

Xiadui

Jinsuo Island

Yingle Peak

Zhonghe Temple ③ | Yita

Zhonghe Peak

Guanyin Tang

Malong Peak

Shengying Peak

Foding Peak

Gantong Temple

Xiaguan

N

Binchuan & Jizu Shan

Kunming

■ ACCOMMODATION	
Higherlander Inn	3
Linden Centre	1
Wuwei Temple	2

0 — 10
kilometres

Baoshan & Tengchong | Weishan | Kunming

ARRIVAL AND DEPARTURE

CANG SHAN

BY CABLE CAR

Gantong Temple (感通寺索道, gǎntōngsì suǒdào; ¥50 one-way, ¥80 return). Take bus #4 heading south down the highway for 5km to the Guanyin Tang temple complex (观音堂, guānyīn táng), from where you can catch a cab (¥10) uphill to the Gantong Temple terminus. The ascent from here in modern, enclosed gondolas offers a fantastic 25min journey over the treetops, with unsurpassed views of the lake, town and peaks.

Zhonghe Temple Cableway (中和寺索道, zhōnghésì suǒdào; ¥35 one-way, ¥50 return). Cab from town to the lower terminus ¥10. This is more like a ski lift, ferrying you up the mountain in open-sided chairs; at the top is small Zhonghe Temple itself, with more views and access to the *Higherland Inn* (see opposite). It doesn't run on windy days, or if they don't think enough people are going to show – in which case, you can hike up here in about two hours.

INFORMATION

Hiking tours *Higherland Inn* (see below) run multi-day treks of Cang Shan's upper reaches; they can also provide advice, route information and limited camping equipment if you want to explore on your own.

ACCOMMODATION

Higherland Inn 高地宾馆, gāodì bīnguǎn. Zhonghe Temple upper terminus ☎ 0872 2661599, ⓦ higherlandinn.com. A self-contained and well-equipped hostel near Zhonghe Temple; you need to book at least three days in advance, and can only get here via the cableway (see opposite) or on foot. Dorms ¥30, rooms ¥80

Wuwei Temple 无为寺, wúwéi sì. The temple is up in the hills 8km north of Dali – a cab to the gates costs ¥30. A Buddhist temple whose monks teach martial arts. This is not an ordinary hotel, but a working monastery with strict rules for kung fu students: no meat, smoking or alcohol; separate dorms for men and women; and five hours' training a day, six days a week. Accommodation, food and training/week ¥300

Er Hai and villages

洱海, ěrhǎi

Er Hai stretches 40km along the flat valley basin east of Dali, its shore fringed with Bai villages. At present, only tourist boats venture out on the lake; for a more authentic experience you'll want to head to the villages, especially on market days – there's transport from both Dali and Xiaguan.

Xizhou

西洲镇, xīzhōu zhèn

Some 20km north from Dali, **XIZHOU** has a daily morning market and substantial numbers of Bai mansions in its backstreets, most in a run-down state; signs in English guide you to them. You can spend an enjoyable morning wandering around with a camera, before winding up at the **Linden Centre**, a 1940s mansion beautifully restored by an American art collector and now a cultural centre and very suave hotel, its rooms a mix of traditional and modern furnishings – drop in for a tour.

Zhoucheng

周城, zhōuchéng

At the top of Er Hai's western shore, **ZHOUCHENG** is a small strip along the highway with a low-key afternoon market, best known for its dark blue tie-dyed cloth. The adjacent **Butterfly Spring** (蝴蝶泉, húdié quán; ¥80) is an electric-blue pond haunted by clouds of butterflies when an overhanging acacia flowers in early summer. You can also catch a ferry across the lake to Shuanglang from here.

Shaping and the eastern lakeshore

Overlooking the very top of the lake around 30km from Dali, **SHAPING** (沙坪, shāpíng) is worth a visit for its **Monday market**, when what seems like the entire regional population crowds on to the small hill behind town to trade.

Public transport dries up beyond Shaping as the road cuts around to Er Hai's east shore; there's a great Tuesday market at **SHUANGLANG** (双廊, shuāngláng) and another on dates ending in 5 or 0 at **WASE** (挖色, wāsè), about 15km south. From Wase, there are buses through the day to Xiaguan's Dali bus station.

ARRIVAL AND DEPARTURE

ER HAI

By bus Regular buses depart from outside Dali's west gate for Xizhou (30min; ¥7), Zhoucheng (40min; ¥9) and Shaping (50min; ¥12), all along Er Hai's western side; moving on from these places, stand by the roadside and flag down passing traffic. There's also a regular bus service through the day between Xiaguan and Wase, on the east side of the lake.

By bicycle Agents in town rent out bikes, but be aware that roads on both sides of the lake are fairly narrow, considering the number of fast-moving trucks and buses on them at any one time.

By boat The only cruises available at present are on tourist ferries (¥150 return) from the dock at Cai Cun (才村, cáicūn), on the lakeshore east of Dali at the end of bus #2 route from Bo'ai Lu. These cross to the east shore at Guanyin

Ge, a flashy viewing pavilion, then return. You can also catch a ferry from Zhoucheng's Taoyuan dock (桃源码头, táoyuán mǎtóu) to Shuanglang (1hr; around ¥40); prices and schedules are by negotiation.

ACCOMMODATION

Linden Centre 喜林苑, xǐlín yuàn. Xizhou village ☎0872 2452988, ⌨linden-centre.com. A meticulously and luxuriously renovated Bai mansion filled with antiques and fine art, which describes itself as a living museum. Whether or not the commendable, if ever-so-slightly pretentious, concept of cultural exchange behind the centre appeals, this is an undeniably beautiful place to stay. **¥1000**

Shaxi

沙系, shāxī · ¥30

SHAXI, 90km northwest of Dali, is a tiny rustic relic of the once busy **tea-horse trade route** between China and Tibet. Listed as an endangered site by the World Monuments Fund, much of the old town has been sympathetically restored and, although it now feels a little sterile, its architectural delights remain largely intact: **Xingjiao Temple** (兴教寺, xīngjiāo sì) was founded in 1415 and overlooks cobbled **Sifang** (四方, sìfāng), the main square; and there are stacks of muddy alleyways, old bridges and wood and stone mansions to admire in Shaxi's handful of back lanes. It's all very small and quiet, however; the best time to come is for the **Friday market**, when Yi and Bai villagers descend from the remote hills roundabout.

Shibao Shan

石宝山, shíbǎo shān · ¥50 · taxi from Shaxi ¥150 return, including waiting time

Shibao Shan forms a high, forested sandstone ridge scattered with small temples, a three-hour hike or a forty-minute taxi ride from Shaxi. The main sight here is the **Shizhong Temple** (石钟寺, shízhōng sì), a series of galleries of Tang-dynasty Buddhist figures carved into an overhang, with wooden awnings protecting the more exposed images. Some of the carvings depict Nanzhao kings, others show Buddha, Guanyin and other saints; many show a strong Indian influence. At the end is a carving of, as the sign tactfully phrases it, "female reproductive organs", and a further niche – generally closed off from view – decorated with graphically sexual frescoes.

ARRIVAL AND DEPARTURE

SHAXI

By bus and minibus Shaxi lies southwest of the Dali–Lijiang highway town of Jianchuan (剑川, jiànchuān), where any traffic heading between Dali and Lijiang can drop you off. From Jianchuan, minibuses to Shaxi (¥8) run when full. There's no bus station at Shaxi; minibuses congregate from about 8am onwards on the road above the old town and, again, leave when full.

ACCOMMODATION AND EATING

Despite its diminutive size, Shaxi has plenty of accommodation, all of it in converted old mansions. Being more than four hours from the nearest tourist centres of Dali and Lijiang, and with some pleasant walks in the surrounding countryside, it's worth staying at least one night. There are plenty of places to eat too, with stir-fry kitchens along the road in the new town and tourist cafés in the old.

★ **Horse Pen 46** 马围客栈, mǎwéi kèzhàn. Sifang, the old town square ☎0872 4722299, ⌨horsepen46.com. A great location, with English-speaking owners, good hiking information and a cosy bar/communal area. Rooms are perfunctory but comfortable, and the not-too-restored old building is very atmospheric. Dorm **¥30**, room **¥80**

★ **Laomadian Lodge** 沙系老马店, shāxī lǎomǎdiàn. Sideng Jie ☎0872 4722666, ✉laomadian@gmail.com. Close to the Sifang, Laomadian is in a class of its own, beautifully restored, with genuinely luxurious en suites, and a superb restaurant. **¥380**

Tea and Horse Caravan Trail Inn 古茶马客栈, gǔchámǎ kèzhàn. 83 Lao Deng Jie ☎0872 4721051, ⌨shaxitrip.com. Clean, if bare, modern rooms in a vintage courtyard complex deep inside the lanes of the old town. Dorm **¥50**, room **¥120**

OPPOSITE KUNMING BARS

Lijiang

丽江, lìjiāng

LIJIANG, capital of the **Naxi Kingdom**, nestles 150km north of Dali at foot of the inspiringly spiky and ice-bound massif of **Yulong Xue Shan**, the Jade Dragon Snow Mountain. Surrounded by green fields and pine forests, the town's winding cobbled lanes form a centuries-old maze, flanked by clean streams, weeping willows and rustic stone bridges. It is also, however, China's biggest **tourist black spot**, in many ways little more than a cultural theme park, and the template against which all "old towns" in China are being remodelled. Hordes of visitors pack out the streets, while the Naxi family homes that line them have been converted into rank after rank of guesthouses and souvenir shops, mostly run by Han Chinese posing in ethnic costumes. Despite this, it's easy to spend a couple of days in Lijiang, especially if you've been out in the wilds and need a good feed and a hot shower. Fairground atmosphere aside, there's also some genuine culture lurking around the town's fringes, and plenty of potential **excursions** into the countryside.

Dayan old town

大研古城, dàyán gǔchéng

It's not easy to navigate Dayan's crowded backstreets, and you will inevitably get lost, but as there are few specific sights this hardly matters. Dong Dajie and adjacent lanes follow streams south to **Sifang** (四方, sìfāng), formerly the main marketplace, a broad cobbled square sided with the inevitable souvenir shops selling silver jewellery, hand-woven cloth, *pu'er* tea and bright baubles. It's fun at dusk, when Naxi women gather for surprisingly authentic-feeling group dances, in which everyone is welcome to join. Heading south again takes you right into Dayan's maze, and eventually you'll find where Sifang's **market** has relocated; an acre of dried goods, fresh herbs, vegetables and fruit, jerked meat, pickles and Lijiang's famous copper and brass utensils. Clothing stalls towards the bottom of the market sell the handmade fleece jackets worn by Naxi women.

Mu Palace and Lion Hill

South of Sifang, the **Mu Palace** (木府, mùfǔ; daily 8.30am–5.30pm; ¥60) was home of the influential Mu family, the Qing-dynasty rulers of Lijiang, though they fell into decline during the nineteenth century. What was left of the mansion was destroyed during the terrible **earthquake** which flattened half the town in 1995, but the grounds – containing some ornamental pavilions and flower gardens – have been restored. You can walk through them and up onto pretty **Lion Hill** (狮子山, shīzi shān; ¥15), site of some ancient cypress trees and the **Wangu Tower** (万古楼, wàngǔ lóu), where you can look down over Dayan's sea of grey-tiled roofs.

Black Dragon Pool Park

黑龙潭公园, hēilóngtán gōngyuán • Daily 7am–9pm • Free with "Old Town Maintenance Fee" ticket

Up on Lijiang's northern outskirts, **Black Dragon Pool Park** is a beautiful place to stroll. The sizeable, pale green pool here is known as **Yuquan** (Jade Spring) and, with the peaks of Yulong Xue Shan rising behind, the elegant mid-pool **Deyue Pavilion** is

---

LIJIANG ORIENTATION

There are two parts to Lijiang: the **old town of Dayan** with all the quaint architecture, markets and pedestrianized streets; and the **new town**, a bland place of wide roads and low-rise boxes, which surrounds Dayan, mostly to the south and west. The old town's layout is indescribable, but at its core is the central market square, **Sifang**, and **Dong Dajie**, the road north from here to a wide, open area at the old town's border known as **Gucheng Kou** (古城口, gǔchéng kǒu). Beyond lies the new town and the crossroads at **Fuhui Lu** and **Xin Dajie**, the latter running 1km north to **Black Dragon Pool Park**.

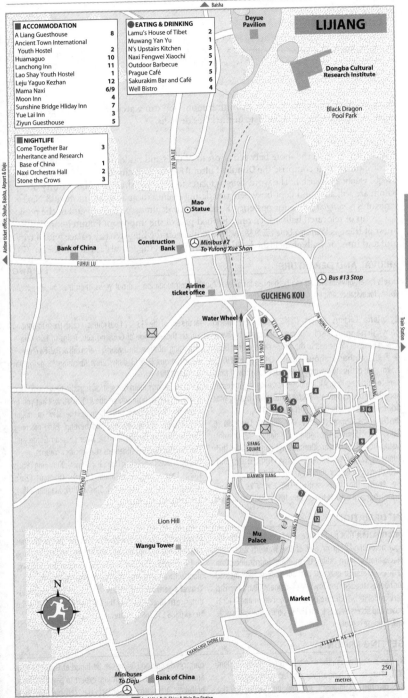

Baisha

Deyue Pavilion

LIJIANG

ACCOMMODATION
A Liang Guesthouse	8
Ancient Town International Youth Hostel	2
Huamaguo	10
Lanchong Inn	11
Lao Shay Youth Hostel	1
Leju Yaguo Kezhan	12
Mama Naxi	6/9
Moon Inn	4
Sunshine Bridge Hliday Inn	7
Yue Lai Inn	3
Ziyun Guesthouse	5

EATING & DRINKING
Lamu's House of Tibet	2
Muwang Yan Yu	1
N's Upstairs Kitchen	3
Naxi Fengwei Xiaochi	5
Outdoor Barbecue	7
Prague Café	5
Sakurakim Bar and Café	6
Well Bistro	4

NIGHTLIFE
Come Together Bar	3
Inheritance and Research Base of China	1
Naxi Orchestra Hall	2
Stone the Crows	3

Dongba Cultural Research Institute

Black Dragon Pool Park

11

Mao ⊙ Statue

Airline ticket office, Shuhe, Baisha, Airport & Daju

Bank of China

Construction Bank

Minibus #7 To Yulong Xue Shan

FUHUI LU

Bus #13 Stop

Airline ticket office

GUCHENG KOU

Train Station

Water Wheel

XINYI JIE

DONG DAJIE

XIN HUA

JIN HONG LU

WEIZHI XIANG

HUILI JIE

MISHI XIANG

MENHUA JIE

SIFANG SQUARE

XIANWEN XIANG

LINYING XIANG

GUANG YI JIE

N

MINGZHU LU

Lion Hill

Wangu Tower

Mu Palace

Market

XIANG HE LU

CHANGSHUI ZHONG LU

Minibuses To Daju

Bank of China

0   250
metres

Lashi Hai, Dali, Shigu & Main Bus Station

11

> ## LIJIANG FEES
>
> While there is no charge to enter Lijiang itself, you do have to buy an "Old Town Maintenance Fee" **ticket** (¥80; valid for a month, available from most hotels and tourist sites) before you can visit specific sights in and around the town – though you still have to pay additional entry fees for these sights, where they exist.

outrageously photogenic. In the early afternoon, you can watch traditionally garbed musicians performing Naxi music in the lakeside halls.

Around the pool

A path runs around the shore between a spread of trees and buildings, passing the cluster of compounds that comprise the **Dongba Cultural Research Institute** (东巴文化研究室, dōngbā wénhuà yánjiūshì). The word *dongba* relates to the Naxi shamans, about thirty of whom are still alive and kept busy here translating twenty thousand rolls of the old Naxi scriptures – *dongba jing* – for posterity. Further around, almost at the top end of the pool, is a group of relocated halls which once formed part of the important **Fuguo Temple**. The finest of these is **Wufeng Lou** (五凤楼, wǔfèng lóu), a grand Ming-dynasty palace with a triple roof and interior walls embellished with reproductions of the murals at Baisha (see p.677).

ARRIVAL AND DEPARTURE
LIJIANG

Tickets for all onwards travel can be booked for a fee through accommodation – if not yours, then the *Lao Shay Youth Hostel*, for instance – or tour agents around town.

By plane Lijiang's airport (丽江三义机场, lìjiāng sānyì jīchǎng) is 20km southwest along the highway. Airport buses (¥15) deliver to the airline ticket office (民航售票处, mínháng shòupiàochù ☎0888 5399 999), 1.5km west of the old town on Fushui Lu – take bus #1 from here to Gucheng Kou. Airline buses for each flight depart from the Fushui Lu office – ask for times when buying your ticket. Taxis to or from the airport charge ¥100.
Destinations Beijing (4 daily; 3hr 30min); Chengdu (8 daily; 1hr 15min); Chongqing (5 daily; 1hr 20min); Guangzhou (3 daily; 2hr 30min); Jinghong (6 daily; 1hr); Kunming (21 daily; 50min); Shanghai (3 daily; 5hr); Shenzhen (1 daily; 2hr 20min); Xi'an (2 daily; 2hr).
By train The train station (丽江火车站, lìjiāng huǒchēzhàn) is out in the country 10km southeast of town

at the end of the #13 or #4 bus routes – catch these to Jinhong Lu, on the east side of Gucheng Kou. Trains to Kunming – departing mostly in the evening – also call at Dali en route.
Destinations Dali (3 daily; 2hr); Kunming (5 daily; 9hr 30min–12hr).
By bus Lijiang's main bus station is in the new town, 1km south of Dayan, from where bus #11 or #8 will get you to Gucheng Kou. Buses run through the day to major destinations in the province and beyond. Early-morning services depart for Baishui Tai, Tiger Leaping Gorge and Qiaotou; for other destinations see specific accounts.
Destinations Daju (3hr); Dali (3hr 30min); Kunming (9hr); Lugu Lake (8hr); Panzhihua (10hr); Qiaotou (2hr); Shangri-La (4hr); Shaxi (3hr); Shigu (2hr); Xiaguan (4hr); Xishuangbanna (23hr).

INFORMATION

Information Your best source of information is probably your accommodation or one of the Western cafés; the places around town calling themselves "Tourist Reception Centres" or similar only sell packaged tours. Look instead for booths labelled "Old Town Management Board Tourism Service Point", which give neutral information about local buses and access details for outlying sights, though usually only Chinese is spoken.

Maps of Lijiang are sold everywhere; bilingual ones printed on brown card and called "Exploring Dali, Lijiang and Shangrila" (¥6) have a detailed layout of the old town, along with an area map of all northwestern Yunnan.
Travel agents For ambitious schedules – including long-distance trekking – contact The Yak Traveller, at 188 Minzhu Lu (☎0888 5102666, ☻theyaktraveller.com).

GETTING AROUND

By bus Buses through the new town run 7.30am–6.30pm (¥1), of use for reaching arrival and departure points.
By minibus Minibuses for touring sights in the

countryside around Lijiang can be found at Gucheng Kou around Xin Dajie in the morning; expect to pay ¥150 for a half-day. Alternatively, contact the reliable, Chinese-

THE NAXI

The Naxi are descended from Tibetan nomads who settled the Lijiang region before the tenth century, bringing with them a shamanistic religion known as **Dongba**. A blend of Tibetan Bon, animism and Taoist tendencies, Dongba's scriptures are written in the only hieroglyphic writing system still in use, with 1400 pictograms. The Naxi deity **Sanduo** is a warrior god depicted dressed in white, riding a white horse and wielding a white spear. Murals depicting him and other deities still decorate temples around Lijiang, and are a good excuse to explore nearby villages.

Strong **matriarchal** influences permeate Naxi society, particularly in the language. For example, nouns become weightier when the word female is added, so a female stone is a boulder, a male stone a pebble. Inheritance passes through the female line to the eldest daughter. Women do most of the work, and own most of the businesses; accordingly, the Naxi women's costume of caps, shawls and aprons is sturdy and practical, while retaining its symbolic meaning; the upper blue segment of the shawl represents night, a lower sheepskin band represents daylight, and two circles around the shoulder depict the eyes of a frog deity. Naxi men often appear under-employed, though they have a reputation as good gardeners and musicians. You'll likely see a few falconers too. *Forgotten Kingdom*, by Peter Goullart, available at bookshops in town, is an entertaining account of Lijiang and the Naxi during the 1930s.

11

speaking Ms Mu Chou (mobile ☏ 1390 8883404).
By taxi Plentiful on the streets around the old town, charging a fixed minimum ¥6 for the first 3km, and ¥1.6 for each additional km.

By bicycle If your accommodation can't find you one to rent, try *N's Kitchen* (see p.676) who charge ¥10–30 per day, plus your passport or deposit.

ACCOMMODATION

Lijiang's abundant accommodation is mostly in Naxi-style wooden houses with two or three storeys arranged around a small central courtyard. Though these places look like family-run homestays, many of Lijiang's Naxi have sold up to Han entrepreneurs and moved on. Doubles are usually en suite, but older places might only have shared facilities. Rooms on the ground floor are less private and sometimes cheaper. Though addresses are listed, they probably won't be much help – see the map on p.673 for locations.

A Liang Guesthouse 阿亮客栈, āliàng kèzhàn. 110 Wenzhi Xiang ☏ 0888 5129923. Shanghai-run operation in converted old Naxi house; upstairs rooms are large, airy and with good views, though fairly plain considering the building's traditional facade. Location in a quiet part of town is a bonus. **¥160**

Ancient Town International Youth Hostel 古城国际青年旅舍, gǔchéng guójì qīngnián lǚshè. 44 Mishi Alley, Xinyi Jie ☏ 0888 5105403. One of two YHA-affiliated places in town, set inside another old courtyard home; rooms are bare but clean, and there's a large atrium area for socializing. Decent travel info too. Dorm **¥35**, room **¥138**

Huamaguo 花吗国客栈, huāmaguó kèzhàn. Xingren Shangduan, by the big stone bridge ☏ 0888 5129099. The best of the newer old-style guesthouses, thanks to a superb location right beside the main willow-fringed canal, which you can appreciate from a pleasant courtyard or the pricier rooms. **¥260**

Lanchong Inn 懒虫小住客栈, lǎnchóng xiǎozhù kèzhàn. 6 Xingwen Gang, Qiyi Jie ☏ 1588 7075519, ⓦ lanchonginn.taobao.com. Laidback place run by young, friendly staff, popular with young middle-class Chinese backpackers; usual antique style and beautiful

mosaic courtyard. It's close to Sifang and the Mu Palace but the lane itself is fairly quiet. All rooms en suite **¥120**

Lao Shay Youth Hostel 老谢车马店, lǎoxiè chēmǎdiàn. 25 Jishan Xiang, Xinyi Jie ☏ 0888 5116118, ⓦ laoshay.com. Located at the heart of the old town, with all the information you could ever need about the area; there's a wide range of rooms, though it's a little pricier than its competitors. Dorms **¥45**, rooms **¥138**

★ **Leju Yaguo Kezhan** 乐居雅国客栈, lèjū yǎguó kèzhàn. 13 Xingwen Xiang, Qiyi Jie ☏ 0888 8882266. A real beauty, friendly and with a courtyard garden full of flowers. Rooms are excellent: smart and modern, and worth the slightly higher-than-average price. **¥200**

★ **Mama Naxi** 78 Wenhua Jie ☏ 0888 5100700 & 70 Wenhua Jie ☏ 0888 5107713. The most popular backpacker guesthouse, thanks largely to its welcoming management. All rooms, including three-bed dorms, are arranged around a courtyard. The second, larger, branch has an excellent restaurant offering communal meals cooked by the garrulous owner. Dorms **¥40**, rooms **¥150**

Moon Inn 新月阁客栈, xīnyuègé kèzhàn. 34 Xingren Xiang, Wuyi Jie ☏ 0888 5153699, ⓔ ericlijiang@163.com. Down a little alley running north by the little stone bridge, this place has a large, quiet courtyard with chairs for lounging, and well-sized rooms. Popular with independent foreign travellers after some mid-range comforts. **¥200**

Sunshine Bridge Holiday Inn 民居水景客栈, mínjū shuǐjǐng kèzhàn. 19 Xingren Duan, Wuyi Jie, just by the small stone bridge ☏ 0888 5112080. Right on a stream, but tucked off the main drag. Very private, with a charming flower garden and great place to sit out for breakfast. **¥200**

Yue Lai Inn 悦来客栈, yuèlái kèzhàn. 54 Mishi Xiang,

left at the top of the street past Well Bistro ☏ 1310 8888100. Excellent-value, modern mid-range take on the Naxi courtyard theme, with cobbled courtyard and pleasant, though fairly small, doubles. Don't take the room at the top of the stairs; they leave the safety light on all night. **¥120**

Ziyun Guesthouse 子云客栈, zǐyún kèzhàn. Around the back of the Naxi Orchestra Hall, off Xinyi Jie ☏ 1398 8892697. What makes this place memorable is that the staff are genuinely friendly, the rooms are tidy and simple, and prices are low. **¥120**

EATING AND DRINKING

Local dishes include *baba*, a stodgy deep-fried flour patty stuffed with meat or cheese and honey; roast and steamed pork; Yunnan ham; chicken steamed in special *qiguo* casseroles; crossing-the-bridge noodles; chicken steamed with local herbs; grilled fish; and wild plants such as fern tips. Mongolian-style hotpots, cooked at the table in a distinctive copper funnel-pot, are a staple of Naxi home cooking. Foreigner-oriented cafés in the vicinity of Sifang all have wi-fi, book exchanges, mellow music and set-price Western breakfasts. Keep an eye open in the markets for the best walnuts in Yunnan, and bright orange persimmons growing on big, leafless trees around town – these have to be eaten very ripe and are an acquired taste.

★ **Lamu's House of Tibet** 西藏屋西餐厅, xīzàngwū xīcāntīng. 56 Xinyi Jie ☏ 0888 115776. Tasty Western and Chinese staples, including filling breakfasts for around ¥30. One of the best places in town to pick up local cycling maps and the latest trekking information for Tiger Leaping Gorge. Daily 7am–10pm.

Muwang Yan Yu 木王盐语, mùwáng yányǔ. 1 Xinyi Jie ☏ 0888 8887336. One of several local stream-side restaurants serving Naxi-inspired food; camphor-smoked duck, medicinal herb soups, vegetable hotpots and roast meats, plus some Cantonese dishes. Not cheap – expect ¥100/person – but the setting and good service make it perhaps worth a splash. Daily 11am–10pm.

N's Upstairs Kitchen 二楼小厨, èrlóu xiǎochú. 17 Jishan Xiang ☏ 0888 5120060. Set on Maicao Chang (卖草场, màicǎo chǎng), the "Grass Market Square" where caravan owners would buy food for their horses, N's has, quite honestly, the best burgers you'll get in China (¥45), great breakfasts, coffee at ¥10 a cup, and heaps of hiking and biking information, along with bike rental. Daily 8.30am–10pm.

Naxi Fengwei Xiaochi 纳西风味小吃, nàxī fēngwèi xiǎochī. Tucked just off the street past the Prague Café. Small, inexpensive courtyard canteen with the run of Yunnan staples and snacks from ¥15. Steer clear of the yak stew, though – too much stew and

precious little yak. Daily 11am–10pm.

★ **Outdoor Barbecue** 烤肉区, kǎoròu qū. Junction of Guangyi Jie and Qiyi Jie. An area with dozens of barbecue stalls selling everything from chicken skewers to insect larva kebabs, which gets absolutely rammed around dinner time. Just point and choose, expect to pay ¥5 per skewer, or three for ¥10. Daily 11am–11pm.

Prague Café 布拉格咖啡馆, bùlāgē kāfēi guǎn. 80 Mishi Xiang, off Xinyi Jie ☏ 0888 5123757. Scores highly for its location, excellent coffee and light meals such as sandwiches and pasta from ¥35. Also a great range of cakes, including cheese and blueberry, from ¥20. Daily 8.30am–10pm.

Sakurakim Bar and Café 樱花屋金酒吧, yīnghuāwū jīnjiǔbā. On Sifang ☏ 1376 9006900, ⊕ sakura.yn.cn. A behemoth of the Lijiang nightlife scene, there are about five places here, all under the Sakura umbrella and all offering reasonably priced beers and coffees, and Japanese, Korean and local food from ¥35 per meal. It's fine for lunch but gets very, very noisy in the evening when the nightclub fires up. Daily 9am–1am.

Well Bistro 井卓餐馆, jǐngzhuō cānguǎn. 32 Mishi Xiang, Xinyi Jie ☏ 0888 5186431. This cosy place wins universal approval for its pasta, apple cake and chocolate brownies, drinks from ¥20 and meals from ¥40. Daily 11am–10pm.

NIGHTLIFE

Parallel and west of Dong Dajie, narrow Xinhua Jie and Jiuba Jie ("Bar Street") are lined with barn-sized nightclubs, all sporting identical heavy wooden furniture, smoke machines, green-and-blue spots and dancers in fake-ethnic garb doing fake ethnic moves to high-decibel pop.

Come Together Bar 云集酒吧, yúnjí jiǔbā. 130 Wenzhi Xiang, at the junction with Wuyi Lu. Laidback place serving imported European beers at ¥30, but the real

highlight is the view from the terrace, looking out over the rooftops of the old town. Daily 6pm–1am.

Stone the Crows 乌鸦酒吧, wūyā jiǔbā. 134 Wenzhi

NAXI MUSIC AND DANCING

The **Naxi Orchestra** is an established part of Lijiang's tourist scene. Using antique instruments, the orchestra performs Song-dynasty tunes derived from Taoist scriptures, a tradition said to have arrived in Lijiang with Kublai Khan, who donated half his court orchestra to the town after the Naxi chieftain helped his army cross the Yangzi. The orchestra regrouped after the Cultural Revolution, though the deaths of many older musicians have reduced its repertoire. To counter this, the orchestra's scope has been broadened by including traditional folk singing in their performances.

The orchestra plays nightly in Lijiang in the well-marked hall on Dong Dajie (8pm; ¥120–160; some agents offer discounted tickets). The music is haunting, but introductory commentaries overlong; try to catch the orchestra practising in the afternoon in Black Dragon Pool Park, for free.

Also on Dong Dajie, another hall, called the "Inheritance and Research Base of China", hosts a song and dance troupe who put on spirited nightly performances to a small audience (8–9.30pm; ¥80). Expect to be dragged on stage at the end. Similar audience participation is encouraged in the nightly dances that start around 7pm in Sifang Square.

11

Xiang, Wuyi Jie. Just down hill from *Come Together*, this place has been stoking the embers of Lijiang's sputtering foreign party crowd for years. Western music, Western drinks and overwhelmingly Western chat in an enjoyably ramshackle setting. Drinks from ¥20 and there's a pool table. Daily 6pm–1am.

DIRECTORY

Bank The Bank of China, along with several ATMs, is on Changshui Zhong Lu, just south of the old town.

Internet All the foreigner-oriented cafés have internet access, and most have wi-fi.

Mail The post office (daily 8am–8pm) is in the old town, on Dong Dajie.

Massage There's a hard-fingered blind masseur (¥50/hr)

on Guangyi Jie: head down Dong Dajie into Sifang, and Guangyi Jie is ahead and slightly to the left; the masseur is 75m along, up a staircase on the left-hand side. Perfect for strained muscles after the Tiger Leaping Gorge trek.

PSB For those wanting to extend their visa, the PSB office is south of the old town on Taihe Lu (☎0888 5132310) – ask your accommodation for directions.

Around Lijiang

Rich pickings surround Lijiang, with a stock of pleasant countryside, temples and villages on the lower slopes of **Yulong Xue Shan**, which rises about 18km north. Several of the following sights are within **bicycle range**; there's also transport to all of them from Lijiang.

Lashi Hai

拉市海, lāshì hǎi · ¥30 · boating and horseriding about ¥90 · shared taxis ¥10 per person each way

Lashi Hai is a seasonal wetlands area 10km west of Lijiang, with the pleasant, near-deserted Tibetan Buddhist **Zhiyun Temple** (指云寺, zhǐyún sì; ¥15) on the far shore. The lake is best visited in winter, when hosts of migratory wildfowl pour in. Horseriding here trammels part of the old tea-horse route (or so the locals say), and it's also a popular spot for people to come and take wedding pictures, so keep a watch out for radiant meringue-clad brides and their bashful, heavily made-up, husbands-to-be.

Baisha

白沙, báishā · bus #11 from Lijiang old town to the "Jinjia Shichang" stop (金甲市场, jīnjiǎ shìchǎng), then a shared minibus to Baisha for ¥5–10

BAISHA, a small village about 10km north of Lijiang, is known for two things: the **Dabaoji Gong** temple complex (大宝积宫, dàbǎojī gōng; ¥30, plus the Lijiang Maintenance Fee ticket) with some fifteenth-century **murals** – admittedly in sad condition; and **Doctor He**, a traditional Chinese physician whose knowledge of local medicinal herbs is second to none. Baisha comprises little more than a single main street and there's no trouble at all locating the sights (Doctor He's surgery is amply signed in several languages); the village is also a staging post on the way to Yuhu or Wenhai (see below).

ACCOMMODATION AND EATING   BAISHA

Country Road Café 乡村路咖啡, xiāngcūn lù kāfēi. Just north from the village centre ☎ 15288 497325. Café-restaurant supplying light meals for around ¥20, biking and hiking information, plus kung fu demonstrations. The owner Rosey can also help arrange basic homestay accommodation.

Yulong

玉龙, yùlóng

YULONG, 3km north of Baisha, is worth a quick pause to look at the small, Tibetan **Yufeng Temple** (玉峰寺, yùfēng sì; ¥25, plus the Lijiang Maintenance Fee ticket), set among pine forest. It's not of great interest in itself, but the pair of ancient, intertwined **camellia trees** in the top terrace produce huge magenta flowers in spring, when the courtyard with its mosaic floor is a nice spot for peaceful contemplation.

Yuhu

玉湖村, yùhú cūn

Four kilometres beyond Yulong, the tiny Naxi settlement of **YUHU** is where the eccentric Austrian-American botanist-anthropologist **Joseph Rock** based himself from 1921 to 1949, and where he wrote articles on the Naxi that appeared in *National Geographic* magazine. His old wooden **house** (洛克故居, luòkè gùjū; ¥15), now a simple museum to his memory with a few period photos, is on the main street and is visited daily by busloads of foreigners. Yuhu is otherwise little disturbed by tourism and, set in grassland on the slopes of Yulong Xue Shan, is an attractive place to stop over and do some hiking – again, Wenhai (see below) makes a good target.

ACCOMMODATION AND EATING   YUHU

Nguluko Guest House 雪嵩客栈, xuěsōng kèzhàn. ☎ 0888 5131616 or 1398 8838431, ✉ lilyhe9@gmail .com. Provides simple but clean accommodation, with meals and shared facilities in a rustic, Naxi courtyard building. Staff can also help arrange hiking and horseriding tours. ¥100

Yulong Xue Shan

玉龙雪山, yùlóng xuěshān • ¥105 (plus sight of Lijiang Old Town Maintenance Fee ticket) • chairlift fees • reach chairlift stations on minibus #7 (¥15, 1hr) from the northeastern corner of the Xin Dajie/Fuhui Lu intersection in Lijiang

With a summit at 5596m, **Yulong Xue Shan** can't be climbed without proper equipment, but you can take in alpine meadows, glaciers and the peaks via three separate **chairlifts**.

On the mountain

Yunsha Ping (云杉坪, yúnshān píng; chairlift ¥77) is a 3205m plateau with boardwalks leading out to grassland and fir trees, and views of the mountain's peaks rising above. Similar **Maoniu Ping** (牦牛坪, máoniú píng; ¥82) is higher at 3600m, with a temple; while the cable car at **Ganhaizi** (干海子, gànhǎizǐ; ¥182 one-way) is an impressive 3km long and climbs to 4506m, where a short trail leads to a windswept viewing point over the

> ### WENHAI
>
> As an alternative to the cable cars for exploring Yulong Xueshan, **WENHAI** (文海, wénhǎi) is a beautiful lakeside village in the mountain's foothills that's a three-hour trek from Baisha or Yuhu. **Xintuo Ecotourism** (☎ 1398 8826672, ✉ ecotourism.com.cn) charge ¥1000 for a three-day, two-night return trek to Wenhai from Lijiang, including all transport, guides, accommodation and food; contact them in advance about accommodation if you plan to visit independently.

TO SICHUAN VIA PANZHIHUA

From Lijiang, the quickest route into Sichuan begins by catching a bus 200km east to heavily industrialized **PANZHIHUA** (攀枝花, pānzhīhuā; 10hr; ¥80), a stop on the Kunming–Chengdu **rail line**. Buses set down right outside the train station: try and get on one of the evening trains, as Panzhihua is no place to stay for long. The train ride to Chengdu goes via Xichang and Emei Shan (see p.735), and takes a further 10–14 hours. The train station is a good 10km out of town, but for overnight accommodation the *Juxing Hotel* (聚兴酒店, jùxīng jiǔdiàn; ¥100) is directly opposite, and there's a daybreak bus back to Lijiang.

Yulong Glacier. Ganhaizi is by far the most spectacular spot, and despite the altitude can get very crowded.

Shigu

石鼓, shígǔ • minibuses to Shigu (¥10) run whenever full from Lijiang's bus station

Seventy kilometres west of Lijiang on the banks of the Yangzi River, **SHIGU** (Stone Drum) is a small place named after a tablet raised here in the sixteenth century by one of Lijiang's Mu clan to mark a particularly bloody victory over an invading army – whether a Tibetan or Chinese force depends on who is telling the story. The river makes its first major **bend** here, deflected sharply to the northeast towards Tiger Leaping Gorge, having flowed uninterrupted in a 1000km arc from its source away on the Tibet/Qinghai border; there are viewpoints along the waterfront.

11

Lugu Lake

泸沽湖, lúgū hú • ¥100

Some 200km north of Lijiang, **Lugu Lake** is shallow and attractive, surrounded by mountains and bisected by the Sichuan border. The people up here are **Mosuo**, who maintain matrilineal traditions such as *axia* marriage, where a woman takes several husbands. Women run the households and children are brought up by their mothers – men have no descendants or property rights. Glibly marketed as a "Girl Kingdom" free-for-all to single Chinese men – who inevitably head back home disappointed – tourism has become well established in recent years, but the lake remains a pleasant place to kick back and do nothing much for a couple of days, before making the tiring bus journey to Xichang in southern Sichuan.

The lake

At more than 2500m above sea level, and surrounded by forested mountains, Lugu Lake's 10km-long, hourglass-shaped surface is a wonderfully tranquil setting – particularly if you have just escaped the seething crowds of Lijiang. Arriving from the south there are settlements dotted along the shore leading up to, and past, the Sichuan border. There's not a vast amount to do here beyond strolling in the villages and surrounding hills, and taking the odd boat trip to one of the lake's five islands, but it is all wonderfully relaxing, calm and, above all, peaceful. Wherever you end up, minibuses shuttle between villages, **wooden canoes** can be hired out for trips across the lake, and accommodation can provide just about everything you'll need.

The villages

The largest village, where buses from Lijiang drop tourists, is **LUOSHUI** (落水, luòshuǐ) on the west shore, with cobbled streets, a central square, some gift shops, guesthouses and a few basic facilities. It's quaint enough, but most people don't stay long, opting instead to head northwest to tiny **LIGE** (里格, lǐgé), set on an attractive bay. Lige mostly comprises guesthouses and restaurants these days, but remains a quiet and enjoyable place to rest up for a few nights. Venture further beyond Lige and you're into Sichuan, where **LUGUHU ZHEN** (泸沽湖镇, lúgūhú zhèn) is the main town and **Wuzhiluo** (五指落, wǔzhǐluò) – a nearby string of houses along the shore – the nicest spot to settle down.

ARRIVAL AND DEPARTURE
LUGU LAKE

By plane Lugu Lake airport (泸沽湖机场, lúgūhú jīchǎng), about two hours south of the lake at Ninglang, is due to open at some point in 2014; initial flights are scheduled to Kunming and Guangzhou.

By bus Lugu Lake is on a back road between Lijiang and Xichang in southern Sichuan province (see p.738), with daily

connections to both. Buses from Lijiang (6hr) stop at Luoshi and Lige on the northwest side of the lake; those from Xichang terminate at Lugu Zhen on the eastern shore. Leaving, you'll need to book your seat through accommodation the day before.

ACCOMMODATION AND EATING

Village restaurants lay on evening barbecues of grilled lake fish and whole suckling pigs, while *Lao Shay* and *Wind's* hostels serve pretty decent Chinese and Western staples – though come prepared for laidback service.

LIGE
Lao Shay Youth Hostel 老谢车马店, lǎoxiè chēmǎdiàn. ☎0888 5881555, ⦿laoshay.com. Sister to the hostel in Lijiang, whose comfortable dorms and pricey doubles (some without windows) are similarly decked out in Naxi-style decor. Dorms ¥45, rooms ¥238

Husi Teahouse Hostel 湖思茶屋, húsī cháwū. ☎0888 5825071, ⦿husihostel.com. Right on the lake shore, the restaurant area has fantastic views across the water, as do some rooms on the upper floors. En suites are

a definite step up in quality from the dorms or those with shared bathrooms. Dorms ¥45, rooms ¥100

WUZHILUO
Wind's Guesthouse 湖畔青年旅舍, húpàn qīngnián lǚshè. ☎0888 5824284, ⦿windguesthouse.com. Fulfils all the usual backpacker needs – dorms, café, information – and located on a rather under-visited side of the lake. With plenty of advance notice, can arrange 10-day horse-treks to Yading in Sichuan (see p.769). Beds ¥35, rooms ¥88

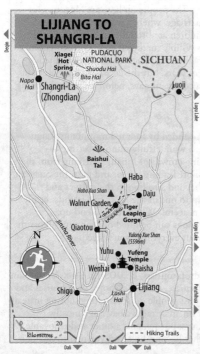

LIJIANG TO SHANGRI-LA

Deqin
Xiagei Hot Spring
PUDACUO NATIONAL PARK
Shuodu Hai
SICHUAN
Napa Hai
Shangri-La (Zhongdian)
Bita Hai
Luoji
Lugu Lake
Baishui Tai
Haba
Haba Xua Shan
Daju
Walnut Garden
Tiger Leaping Gorge
Jinsha River
Qiaotou
Yulong Xue Shan (5596m)
Lugu Lake
Yuhu
Yufeng Temple
Wenhai
Baisha
Shigu
Lashi Hai
Lijiang
Panzhihua

N

0   20
kilometres
– – Hiking Trails
Dali   Dali   Dali

Tiger Leaping Gorge
虎跳峡, hǔtiào xiá • ¥65

Around 100km north of Lijiang, just east of the highway to Shangri-La, the Yangzi River channels violently through **Tiger Leaping Gorge**, the 3000m-deep rift between Haba Xue Shan to the north and Yulong Xue Shan to the south. The **hiking trail** through the gorge is one of the most accessible and satisfying in China, with dramatic scenery and – despite the 2500m-plus altitude – relatively straight-forward walking.

Qiaotou to Walnut Garden
Buses from Lijiang deliver to main-road **QIAOTOU** (桥头, qiáotóu), also known as **Hutiaoxia Zhen** (虎跳峡镇, hǔtiàoxiá zhèn), a knot of cafés and shops at the western entrance to the gorge. Once across the bridge the vehicle road heads downhill, but past the **school** hikers need to start heading uphill – you'll be followed by **horse teams** offering to carry your bags. From here the going is steady until you reach the *Naxi Family Guesthouse* at the start of the steep, twisting **Twenty-four Bends**. At the top of

HIKING TIGER LEAPING GORGE

To hike Tiger Leaping Gorge, you'll need to be fit, carrying full weatherproof gear, a torch and a first-aid pack, and to be stocked up with snacks and a water bottle. Solid boots are a plus but, as long as your shoes have a firm grip, not essential. **Weather** can be warm enough in summer to hike in a T-shirt, but don't count on it; winters are cold. **Accommodation** along the way is in guesthouses, so you won't need a tent. **Two days** is the minimum time needed for a hike; give yourself an extra day to make the most of the scenery.

Originally there were two trails through the gorge, but the former **Lower Path** has been surfaced to handle tour buses, and isn't suitable for hiking anymore – though it's useful if you're looking for a quick ride out at the end of your trek. The remaining **Upper Path** is the route described below. End points are at westerly **Qiaotou**, on the Lijiang to Shangri-La road, and easterly **Daju**, a small township on a back route to Lijiang. Most people hike from Qiaotou to the midpoint around **Walnut Garden** – which covers the best of the scenery – and then catch transport back to Qiaotou and thence on to Lijiang or Shangri-La; the advantage here is that you can leave heavy bags at Qiaotou. Alternatively, you can continue on from Walnut Garden to Daju, or – with a guide – north to Baishui Tai (see p.686). Before you arrive, try to pick up the home-made **maps** that float around cafés in Lijiang and Shangri-La.

There seem to be almost continual roadworks going on in the gorge, connected with ongoing construction of a **hydro dam** across the river and regular seasonal **landslides**, a potentially lethal hazard; do not hike in bad weather or during the June–September rainy season. There have been a couple of knifepoint **muggings** of solo travellers in past years, so try not to walk alone. For current information, check ⓦ www.tigerleapinggorge.com, maintained by *Sean's Guesthouse* in Walnut Garden.

11

this you're about five hours into the hike at 2670m, near the *Tea Horse Guesthouse* and gifted with superb views.

From here the track levels out a bit before descending, via the *Halfway Guesthouse* at **Bendiwan village** (本地湾村, běndìwān cūn) and some waterfalls, to the vehicle road at *Tina's Guesthouse*. You've now been walking for around nine hours, with a further thirty-minute level track to **WALNUT GARDEN** (核桃园, hétáo yuán) and more accommodation.

Walnut Garden to Daju

One option from Walnut Garden is simply to arrange a ride with minibuses **back to Qiaotou** along the vehicle road. Alternatively, it's a couple of hours eastwards, partly along the road, to the **New Ferry** over the Yangzi River. How much you'll pay depends on the whim of the ferryman, but don't expect to get off lightly – ¥40 or more per person is normal. From here, you've another hour's walk to the vehicle roadhead at **Xiahu Tiao** (下虎跳, xiàhǔ tiào), and then a final 7km to **DAJU** (大具, dàjù), where buses head south to Lijiang until about 1.30pm.

Walnut Garden to Baishui Tai

Accommodation at Walnut Garden can arrange a **guide** for the popular two-day trek, via an overnight stop in pretty **HABA village** (哈巴村, hābācūn), to **Baishui Tai**, which has charmless guesthouses and a bus on to Shangri-La (see p.686). You might prefer to tackle this trek southwards from Baishui Tai as an alternative route into Tiger Leaping Gorge – in this direction, it heads downhill much of the time.

ARRIVAL AND DEPARTURE   **TIGER LEAPING GORGE**

By bus Qiaotou, at the western end of Tiger Leaping Gorge, sits on the highway between Lijiang and Shangri-La and is served through the day by buses from both. Daju, at the eastern end of the gorge, has a couple of services daily to a depot in Lijiang at the corner of Changshui Lu and Minzhu Lu, just outside the old town's southwestern edge.

ACCOMMODATION

Haba Snow Mountain Guesthouse 哈巴雪山客栈, hābā xuěshān kèzhàn. Haba village, between Walnut Garden and Baishui Tai ☏ 0887 8866596. Recently refurbished and now the proud host of clean rooms and steaming hot showers; the enthusiastic owner will also cook up basic meals – just point out the ingredients you fancy in her kitchen. Dorm ¥35, room ¥88

Naxi Family Guesthouse 纳西雅阁, nàxī yǎgé. Changshen Village ☏ 0887 8806928. Pleasant rooms with great views around a traditional courtyard and friendly staff make this an enjoyable stopoff if you're taking things at a relaxed pace. Dorm ¥35, room ¥70

Sean's Spring Guesthouse 山泉客栈, shānquán kèzhàn. Walnut Garden ☏ 1575 8456256, ⓦ tigerleapinggorge.com. A pleasantly low-key, friendly place with good meals, beer, warm beds and the eponymous, Tibetan, owner. Dorm ¥35, room ¥70

Tea Horse Guesthouse 茶马客栈, chámǎ kèzhàn. Yongsheng Village ☏ 1398 8717292. One of several places at roughly the half-way point. Aside from the fantastic views shared by most accommodation, *Tea Horse* also offers massages to ease aching limbs, often a clincher in the decision-making process. Dorm ¥30, room ¥120

Tina's Guesthouse 中峡国际青年旅舍, zhōngxiá guójì qīngnián lǚshè. Jiantang village ☏ 0887 8202258 or 1398 8750111. Large and pretty ugly compared to most of the guesthouses along the gorge, Tina's is still a comfortable place to stay, has excellent facilities, and the views from inside are as good as anywhere else. Dorms ¥30, rooms ¥120

Shangri-La

香格里拉, xiānggélǐlā · 中甸, zhōngdiàn

SHANGRI-LA, also known as **Zhongdian** – or **Gyalthang** in Tibetan – sits on a high plateau at the borderland between Yunnan, Sichuan and Tibet. When this former logging town was hit by a 1998 ban on deforestation, the provincial government renamed it Shangri-La after the Buddhist paradise of James Hilton's 1930s novel, *Lost Horizon*, to try to stimulate a tourist boom. They also spent a fortune turning the dismally poor Tibetan settlement here into a fairly convincing "old town", complete with obligatory traditional houses, cobbled streets, religous monuments, cafés, guesthouses and bars; there are also less contrived attractions in the **monastery** just north of town and excellent possibilities for local hiking and horseriding. Shangri-La's altitude is over 3000m, so take it easy if you've arrived from the lowlands, and be aware that's it's very chilly between October and March.

The old town

古城, gǔchéng

Down at the southern outskirts of Shangri-La, the old town is good for a couple of hours' wander, though there are no essential sights; streets are unsigned and weave off in all directions, but as the whole place is only a few hundred metres across you can't get seriously lost. The alleyways are lined with sturdy two-storey wooden Tibetan homes, all built with a great deal of skill and care; they look as though they'll stand for centuries, which you can't say about most contemporary Chinese buildings. Overlooking the old town, **Turtle Hill** is topped by a small temple and huge **golden prayer wheel**, apparently the largest in the world.

The new town

Despite a backdrop of scruffy concrete-and-tile buildings, there's also a bit of interest in the **new town**. Changzheng Dadao is lined with shops aimed at Tibetan customers, where you can buy everything from electric blenders for churning butter tea, to carpets, horse saddles, copperware and fur-lined jackets and boots. The **farmers' market**

THE 2014 FIRE

In January 2014, a massive **fire** swept through Shangrila-La's old town, destroying over 200 of the wooden, Tibetan-style buildings. At the time of writing it was impossible to know how much, if any, of the town has survived, but damage has certainly been severe and extensive. For the latest information, it's best to contact one of the tour agents listed on p.888.

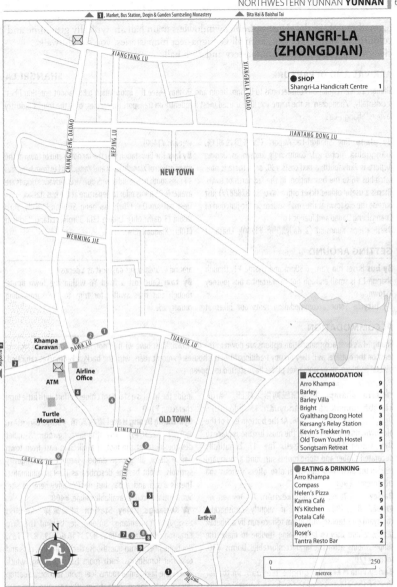

SHANGRI-LA (ZHONGDIAN)

● **SHOP**
Shangri-La Handicraft Centre 1

■ **ACCOMMODATION**
Arro Khampa	9
Barley	4
Barley Villa	7
Bright	6
Gyalthang Dzong Hotel	3
Kersang's Relay Station	8
Kevin's Trekker Inn	2
Old Town Youth Hostel	5
Songtsam Retreat	1

● **EATING & DRINKING**
Arro Khampa	8
Compass	5
Helen's Pizza	1
Karma Café	9
N's Kitchen	4
Potala Café	3
Raven	7
Rose's	6
Tantra Resto Bar	2

(建塘农市场, jiàntáng nóng shìchǎng), about a block north of the post office, has more of the same along with big blocks of yak butter and other foodstuffs.

Ganden Sumtseling Monastery

松赞林寺, sōngzànlín sì • ¥115 • northbound bus #3 from Changzheng Dadao

Shangri-La's star attraction is the splendid **Ganden Sumtseling Monastery**, just north of the new town. Destroyed during the 1960s but later reactivated, it now houses four hundred Tibetan monks. Among butter sculptures and a forest of pillars, the freshly painted murals in the claustrophobic, windowless main hall are typically gruesome and colourful. Don't forget that, as in all Gelugpa-sect monasteries, you should walk clockwise around both the monastery and each hall.

ARRIVAL AND DEPARTURE   SHANGRI-LA

Shangri-La has regular bus connections to Lijiang, Deqin and Sichuan – see the information p.865 about entering Tibet. Incidentally, "Zhongdian" is the name you'll hear used most frequently on transport timetables; only the tourist industry favours "Shangri-La".

By plane Tiny Shangri-La Airport (香格里拉机场, xiānggélǐlā jīchǎng), confusingly known as Deqing Airport, is 7km south; a taxi costs ¥30, or, if there is one, catch bus #6 to the bus station, in the far north of town. There's a useful airline ticket office (☎ 0887 8288877) just outside the old town at the small square on the junction of Changzheng Dadao and Tuanjie Lu.
Destinations Kunming (2 daily; 1hr; ¥1180); Lhasa (2 weekly; ¥1480).

By bus The bus station is at the far north end of town at the intersection of Xiangbala Lu and Kangding Lu; from here, bus #1 runs south to the old town's outskirts. Advance tickets are available 36 hours prior to departure at the bus station.
Destinations Dali (7hr); Daocheng, Sichuan (1 daily; 5hr); Deqin (3 daily; 6hr); Lijiang (3hr 30min); Litang, Sichuan (10hr); Xiaguan (6hr).

GETTING AROUND

By bus Buses run 7am–6.30pm and charge ¥1, though Shangri-La is small enough not to warrant a bus journey in town.
By bicycle Some accommodation rents out bikes at around ¥20/day, plus passport as a deposit.
By taxi Cabs cost a fixed ¥6 within the town limits, though this rises swiftly for trips to the surrounding countryside.

ACCOMMODATION

Shangri-La's best accommodation options are down in the old town. Most have wi-fi (if not, head to cafés) and look, at least on the outside, as if they occupy traditional Tibetan houses. In recent years, with the backpacker market saturated, several boutique, more upmarket places have started to appear.

★ **Arro Khampa** 阿若康巴南索达庄园, āruò kāngbā nánsuǒdá zhuāngyuán. 15 Jinlong Jie, Donglan Lu ☎ 0887 8881006. At the bottom end of the old town, this new venture is the most luxurious place to stay within Shangri-La itself. The 17 beautifully decorated timber and stone rooms surround a courtyard restaurant area, and the hotel also offers various spa treatments. **¥900**

Barley 青稞客栈, qīngkè kèzhàn. 76 Beimen Jie ☎ 0887 8232100. Colourful, if slightly ramshackle, courtyard guesthouse with warm terrace run by a Tibetan family, where they've taken some trouble to make the simple rooms attractive and comfortable. Dorms **¥30**, rooms **¥120**

Barley Villa 青稞别院, qīngkè biéyuàn. On the far side of the old town near Tancheng Square ☎ 0887 8290688. This beautifully refurbished Tibetan-style farm house around a bright open courtyard is a world away from their hostel. The large rooms are expensive, but those in the mid-range are a bit of a bargain. Doubles **¥280**, large rooms **¥800**

Bright 鲁生追康客栈, lǔshēngzhuīkāng kèzhàn. 13 Dianlaka, next to the Raven ☎ 0887 8288687. If you're after a straightforward, roomy en-suite double, this is your best bet – though, despite a "Tibetan" exterior,

inside the hotel is a standard Chinese effort with little local character. **¥100**

Gyalthang Dzong Hotel 建格宾馆, jiàngé bīnguǎn. ☎ 0887 8223646, ⊛ gyalthangdzong.com. A quiet designer hotel at the foot of a hill 3km east from town whose decor, all orange drapes, lacquer and longevity symbols, might best be described as Tibetan minimalist. There's a spa and a bar, but no TVs anywhere on site. Substantial discounts available online. **¥400**

★ **Kersang's Relay Station** 恪桑藏驿, késāng zàngyì. 1 Yamenlang, Jinlong Jie, behind the Arro Khampa restaurant ☎ 0887 8223118 or 1398 8797785. Boutique Tibetan-run guesthouse decked in pine, rugs and colourful furnishings. Each room has a balcony, which makes the fairly small rooms feel more spacious. Rooftop terrace with views over town. Owner also arranges motorbike rental and tours. Dorm **¥50**, room **¥180**

Kevin's Trekker Inn 龙门客栈, lóngmén kèzhàn. Just outside the old town at 138 Dawa Lu ☎ 0887 8228178, ⊛ kevintrekkerinn.com. Modern concrete buildings around a large courtyard; the big lounge area, cheerful rooms and the manager's trekking and touring info make this an excellent choice. Dorms **¥30**, rooms **¥120**

Old Town Youth Hostel 独克宗国际青年旅馆, dúkèzōng guójì qīngnián lǚguǎn. 4 Zoubarui,

Jinlong Jie ☎0887 8227505. Straightforward, snug wood-panelled rooms, with a very helpful manager; the building itself is nothing special, however. Dorms ¥30, rooms ¥80

Songtsam Retreat 松赞林卡酒店, sōngzànlínkǎ jiǔdiàn. ☎0887 8285566, 🌐songtsam.com. The very upmarket wing of the Ganden Sumtseling Monastery's accommodation; a tasteful, atmospheric – not to mention luxurious – place to stay, with views over the monastery building. ¥760

EATING AND DRINKING

As with accommodation, the old town has the pick of the eating opportunities; the cafés also have free wi-fi for customers. For cheap staples, there are many Muslim places in the New Town serving noodles and dumplings. As there's no street lighting, mind those cobbles on the way home.

Arro Khampa 阿若康巴餐厅, āruò kāngbā cāntīng. 27 Jinlong Jie, south of the Old Town Youth Hostel ☎1338 8873878. This smart French-Tibetan outfit wears its Gallic heart on its sleeve, with a signature Tibetan *raclette* – local *charcuterie* smothered in melted cheese. The special will set you back ¥188 per person and needs to be ordered before 5pm, but elsewhere on the menu you can eat for around ¥60. Daily 9am–10pm.

Compass 舒灯库乐, shūdēng kùlè. 3 Chilang Gang, just off the main square in the old town ☎0887 8223638. Unashamedly Western food – pizza, burgers, spaghetti, sandwiches – served up in a sympathetic mock-Tibetan interior. Mains around ¥40. Tues–Sun 8.30am–10pm.

Helen's Pizza 比萨屋, bǐsàwū. Dawa Lu, on the corner with Heping Lu ☎0887 8224456. Helen whips up what are certainly the best pizzas and *calzone* in town – yours for only ¥38 – perhaps because they use imported olive oil, not yak butter. There are other Italian/Western options on the menu, but pizza is what they do best. Daily 9am–10pm.

★ **Karma Café** 卡玛咖非, kǎmǎ kāfēi. 6 Lunhuolang, Jinlong Jie ☎0887 8224768. Virtually impossible to find, and accessed via a narrow lane running up the east side of the *Arro Khampa* hotel, you could easily walk past this place without even realizing. It's worth the effort of tracking down, though; decrepit from the outside, inside it's a beautifully restored old house serving outstanding yak steak and mashed potatoes for a bargain ¥48. Tibetan snacks and a set meal (¥60/person) will leave you bursting. Great place for quiet coffee too. Daily 10.30am–10pm.

N's Kitchen 依若木廊厨房, yīruò mùláng chúfáng. 33 Beimen Jie ☎0887 8233870. This bright, modern and clean place is popular for Western breakfasts and great coffee, though at around ¥30 a plateful, it's just a little bit more expensive than its competitors. You can also rent bikes, pick up cycling maps and arrange tours. Daily 8am–10pm.

Potala Café 布达拉咖啡, bùdálā kāfēi. Dawa Lu, corner of Changzhen Dadao ☎0887 8228278. This upstairs Tibetan teahouse serves up big, cheap portions of Western, Tibetan and Chinese food for ¥20–50, and hot chocolate made with the real thing, not powder. The ambience is pleasant, attracting a mix of Chinese tourists, grizzly locals and foreigners. Daily 9am–10pm.

★ **Raven** 乌鸦酒吧, wūyā jiǔbā. 19 Dianlaka ☎0887 8289239. Friendly and atmospheric foreign-owned bar with pool table, beer from ¥20 and a huge stock of spirits; the best place to get the lowdown on the local scene. Daily 4pm–late.

Rose's 加瑟米朵, jiāsèmǐ duǒ. 15 Cuolang Jie ☎1398 8768377. A pretty little teahouse serving drinks (¥15) and light meals (¥25) in pleasant café surroundings, although it is marred in the evening by noise from the nightclub opposite. Daily 9am–10pm.

★ **Tantra Resto Bar** 唐得拉餐吧, tángdélā cān bā. Dawa Lu ☎0887 8881213. Another result of international fusion, with Indian, Tibetan and Chilean influence all perfectly brought to the boil. As well as serving probably the best curry in town for ¥38, you'll also find South American favourites, including *empanadas*, and the ever-convivial Ricky behind the bar. Daily 9am–10.30pm.

SHOPPING

Handicrafts One business employing Tibetans and preserving local crafts is the Shangri-La Handicraft Centre at 1 Jinlong Jie (☎0887 8227742, 🌐ymhfshangrila.com), a cultural centre aimed particularly at supporting women in the local community. They're open Tues–Sun 10am–6pm.

DIRECTORY

Banks There's a Construction Bank, with a foreign-friendly ATM, at the mouth of the old town, plus several more banks up along Changzheng Dadao in the new town.

Post office There's a small post office at the mouth of the old town, though the main branch is 1km north along Changzhang Dado in the new town.

Around Shangri-La

There is limitless **trekking** around Shangri-La, and a number of specialist agents can help you out with routes and guides. If you're planning anything major though, contact them well before you're in town – they'll need time to organize things. Cafés and hotels also provide information and can book you on **trips out** from Shangri-La, including the popular three-day hike via Baishui to **Tiger Leaping Gorge** (see p.680).

Napa Lake

纳帕海, nàpà hǎi · ¥40

Shallow **Napa Lake**, 7km north of town, is a seasonal wetlands which attracts rare black-necked cranes in winter. Through the summer it's more of a pasture for yaks, thick with grass and flowers; there's a **Botanic Gardens** (¥20) and café just outside, where at certain times of the year you can see blue poppies and orchids. Pick up a **cycling map** for Napa from *N's Kitchen* (see p.685) in Shangri-La.

Xiagei Hot Springs

下给温泉, xiàgěi wēnquán · ¥30 · rafting on the river with any tour agency in town ¥200 for an afternoon

Ten kilometres east of town, the **Xiagei Hot Springs** are attractively situated beside a river and below a cave. Eschew the claustrophobic private rooms and swim in the small public pool; a shop on site sells swimming trunks (¥20). There's also a walking trail, and rafting trips available on the river.

Pudacuo National Park

普达措国家公园, pǔdácuò guójiā gōngyuán · ¥190, including bus inside the park · boat ride ¥30 · horse rental ¥50–80

Pudacuo National Park covers a huge area some 25km east of Shangri-La past Xiagei, with **two alpine lakes** within day-trip range. The first, **Shuodu Lake** (属都海, shǔdōu hǎi), is a renowned beauty spot that attracts plenty of tour buses. However, day-trippers don't seem to get much further than the restaurant and the huge shop in the car park that sells traditional medicines such as ginseng and dried ants. Turn right and follow the lakeshore for a pleasant, easy walk through old forest. Horses can carry you all the way around the lake, which will take about two hours, or you can walk it in four.

Bita Lake

碧塔海, bitǎ hǎi · boats a negotiable ¥30/person

The less visited of Pudacuo's two sections, attractive **Bita Lake** is set at an altitude of 3500m and surrounded by lush meadows and unspoilt forest. The best way to explore the place is to ask to be dropped at either of its two entrances, south or west, and then be picked up at the other. Most visitors arrive at the south entrance, from where it's an easy walk down to the lake. Take a rowing boat across to the ferry quay, and you can then walk for around two hours along a well-marked trail to the west entrance.

Baishui Tai

白水台, báishuǐ tái · ¥30

Around 60km southeast of Shangri-La on the north side of Haba Xue Shan from Tiger Leaping Gorge, **Baishui Tai** is a large, milky-white series of limestone terraces, built up over thousands of years as lime-rich water cascaded down a hillside. Plenty of less prosaic legends account for their formation too, and this is one of the holy sites of the Naxi. Wooden ladders allow in-depth exploration of the tiers, which glow orange at sunset. The village at the foot of the site, **Sanba** (三坝, sānbà), is busy transforming itself into a tourist town of guesthouses, all of which offer basic and fairly unattractive rooms.

Until recently Baishu Tai was quite remote, but now a back road from Qiaotao, at the mouth of Tiger Leaping Gorge (see p.680), links it to Shangri-La; you can also **hike** from here to Walnut Garden in two days via Haba village (p.681).

FROM TOP LIGE, LUGU LAKE (P.679); CYCLING IN LIJIANG (P.672) >

REACHING SIGHTS AROUND SHANGRI-LA

You can cycle from Shangri-La to a couple of the closer sights, but anywhere further will require a **vehicle** – either rented through Turtle Mountain (see below), or by heading down to the little square on Tuanjie Lu, at the edge of the old town, where minibus drivers will approach you and offer their services. The likely rate is ¥150–300 per day, depending on destination and bargaining skills.

TOUR AGENTS

Haiwei Trails above the bar at the *Raven* (☎0887 8289245 or 1398 8756540, ⓦ haiweitrails .com). Plenty of imaginative treks and mountain-biking across northwestern Yunnan.
★ **Khampa Caravan** Dawa Lu (☎0887 8288648, ⓦ khampacaravan.com). Long-established agency who offer everything from easy day hikes and sorting out Tibet logistics, to multiday treks to Lijiang or into Sichuan; one of their specialities is the demanding fourteen-day kora circuit around Meili Xue Shan (opposite). All their guides are local Tibetans, fluent in English.
Turtle Mountain off Beimen Jie at 32 Gun Ma Lang (☎0877 8233308 ⓦ turtlemountaingear .com). Another excellent option whose American owner, long resident in Shangri-La, has solid hiking and exploring information. They also stock a range of camping supplies and rent ski gear, snowboards, motorbikes (with breakdown support) and jeeps.

11

Deqin

德钦, déqīn

DEQIN lies around 120km north of Shangri-La across some permanently snowy ranges, only 80km from the Tibetan border at Yunnan's northwestern extremes. The town itself, a charmlessly ramshackle, tile-hung outpost, is no great shakes, but there are exciting opportunities for hiking around nearby **Meili Xue Shan**, whose thirteen peaks are of great religious significance to Tibetans.

Feilai Temple

飞来寺, fēilái sì · observation platform ¥60 · taxi from Deqin about ¥30 each way

Unless you miss all transport out, it's better to skip Deqin town altogether in favour of heading another 15km north to the Meili Xue Shan viewing point just below **Feilai Temple** – a name which now refers not only to the temple complex itself but also to the growing cluster of hostels, guesthouses and restaurants along the main road below. There used to be sublime vistas of the mountain from here, but, in a demonstration of extreme greed, the local authorities have built a **wall**, forcing tourists to pay to use an observation platform.

ARRIVAL AND DEPARTURE   DEQIN

By bus Deqin's bus station (7am–7pm) is on the main street towards the north end of town.

Destinations Kunming (19hr); Lijiang (11hr); Shangri-La (8hr).

GETTING AROUND

Minibus Minivans cruise Deqin's main street looking for passengers, and set off only once full. The trip to Feilai Temple is ¥5 per person.
Taxi You'll see a few, often informal, taxis along Deqin's

single main street and you're likely to be approached by drivers hawking for business. The 10km run up to Feilai Temple should cost around ¥30.

ACCOMMODATION AND EATING

DEQIN
Dragon Cloud Guesthouse 龙行客栈, lóngxíng kèzhàn. 94 Beimen Jie, 1km or so south of the bus station ☎0887 8289250, ⓦ dragoncloud.cn. Traditional-style wooden-framed Tibetan building with a contemporary/Western coffee shop attached, plus clean,

basic rooms with shower and toilet. <u>¥140</u>
FEILAI TEMPLE
As a well-established tourist stop, there is no shortage of places to stay or eat at Feilai Temple, though prices are relatively high.
Feilai Si Youth Hostel 飞来寺国际青年旅舍, fēiláisì

guójì qīngnián lǚshě. North side of the main road, up a small turn-off just before the ninety-degree bend leading up to the temple ☎0887-8416133 or 1338 8875 956. A pretty Tibetan-style building with decorations inside and out; some English spoken. Rooms, dorms particularly, can be a bit grubby. Wi-fi throughout and hot water evenings and mornings. Dorm ¥80, room ¥230

Meili Guesthouse 梅里客栈, méilǐ kèzhàn. South side of the main road, just before the ninety-degree bend leading up to the temple ☎0887 8416998 or 1398 8755717. As well as basic comfortable rooms, this straightforward guesthouse has internet access and, best of all, hot water around the clock. Dorm ¥40, room ¥240

Meili Xue Shan

梅里雪山, méilǐ xuěshān • three different tickets covering a number of sites ¥150–230

Sacred to Tibetan Buddhists as home to the protective warrior god Kawagarpo, as well as attracting tourists drawn by its natural beauty, the **Meili Xue Shan** range is also visited by tens of thousands of pilgrims each year. While the arduous two-week **kora circuit** of the mountain conducted by the faithful is not for everyone, there are also some less demanding hikes – still with spectacular views – to be had.

Entry to the park area is from **Xidang**, while most visitors stay in **Yubang** as a base for hiking local trails. Any visit to the area should be taken seriously, despite the relatively well-worn paths: always carry food, water, a torch and first-aid kit. Full weatherproof gear and good hiking shoes are a necessity.

Xidang

西当, xīdāng

From the Feilai Temple viewing point, it's a ninety-minute drive to the Meili Xue Shan **reserve entrance** at pretty **XIDANG** village, which sits high above the Lancang Jiang (Mekong River). There's accommodation here and a three-hour ascent on foot along a reasonable road to the **Mingyong glacier** (明永冰川, míngyōng bīngchuān), one of the world's lowest at 2700m, and advancing relatively quickly at 500m per year. You'll find a fair few souvenir shops and guesthouses at the glacier viewing point.

About 3km past Xidang village on the path to Yubeng, **Xidang Hot Springs** (温泉, wēnquán) sound better than they are – instead of invitingly steaming outdoor pools, the water is piped into people's houses where you pay to take a shower.

Yubeng

雨崩, yùbēng • ¥85

From Xidang's hot springs, a **hiking trail** heads west to the hamlet of **Yubeng**, though bear in mind that it should not be attempted alone or unprepared. The route kicks off with a gruelling four-hour ascent to 3800m-high **Nazongla Pass**, followed by ninety minutes down a well-marked trail to **UPPER YUBENG** (雨崩上村, yùbēng shàngcūn), a Tibetan settlement of considerable charm.

Lower Yubeng

雨崩下村, yùbēng xiàcūn

Though plenty of visitors stay with families in Upper Yubeng, it's worth persevering to the even prettier **LOWER YUBENG** – take the trail to the left as you come into Upper Yubeng and walk for thirty minutes, over a stream and then a bridge. The most popular trip from Lower Yubeng is the straightforward two-hour walk to the dramatic **Yubeng Shenpu** (雨崩神瀑, yùbēng shénpù), a sacred waterfall, with bears, snow leopards and the highly endangered Yunnan golden monkey said to be lurking in the nearby forests.

ARRIVAL AND DEPARTURE   MEILI XUE SHAN

By taxi or minibus The run between Feilai Temple and the Meili Xue Shan entrance at Xidang costs about ¥150 for a cab or ¥15 per person in a minibus, which depart once full.

THE KAWA KARPO KORA

Meili Xue Shan's highest peak, unclimbed **Kawa Karpo** (6740m), is holy to Tibetans, who trek around its base every year to complete the **Kawa Karpo kora**, or pilgrimage circuit, three circumnavigations of which are said to guarantee a beneficial reincarnation. The circuit takes fourteen days or so, beginning in Deqin and ending in the village of Meili. If you plan to attempt it, be aware that the route **crosses the Tibetan border** and you need permits, as the police keep an eye on this area; you also definitely need a **guide** – you're above 4000m most of the time and people have died attempting the trek solo. Travel agencies in Shangri-La can make all arrangements for you.

ACCOMMODATION

UPPER YUBENG
Family homestays at Upper Yubeng charge about ¥10/ night, plus ¥10 for a meal.

LOWER YUBENG
Aqinbu's Mystic Waterfall Lodge 神瀑客栈,

shénbào kèzhàn. Lower Yubeng ✆0887 8411082. At the end of Lower Yubeng, this farmhouse-style hostel, with the brilliant green, cloud-swept mountains rearing up behind, makes a handy base for further treks, on which the helpful owner can advise. Dorm **¥25**, rooms **¥100**

The far west

Southwest of Xiaguan, **Yunnan's far west** bumps up against the **Burmese border**, an increasingly tropical area of mountain forests and broad valleys planted with rice and sugar cane, all cut by the deep watershed gorges of Southeast Asia's mighty **Mekong** and **Salween rivers** (in Chinese, the Lancang Jiang and Nu Jiang, respectively). Settlements have large populations of **ethnic minorities**, and mainstream China has never had a great presence in the region; indeed, at times it's still often unclear whether rules and regulations originate in Beijing or with the nearest officer in charge.

The far west's main artery, the underused G56 Expressway, roughly follows the route of the old **Burma Road**, built during World War II as a supply line between British-held Burma and Kunming, from where goods were shipped to China's wartime capital, Chongqing. Something of the road's original purpose survives today, with towns along the way, especially **Ruili**, right on the Burmese frontier, still clearly benefiting from the cross-border traffic. With the exception of geologically unsettled **Tengchong**, however, sights are few and – unless you're heading into Burma – the main point of visiting is simply to experience a fairly untouristed, if not actually remote, corner of the country, not least along the upper reaches of the **Nu Jiang Valley**.

Transport through the far west is by bus, though you can also fly to Tengchong and the district capital Mangshi, just a couple of hours by road from Ruili. Some minor scuffles along the Burmese border in recent years, plus the area's perennial drug-trafficking problems, mean you'll encounter **military checkpoints** in the region, where you have to show passports and wait while vehicles are checked for contraband. The **weather** is subtropically humid, especially during the wet season between May and October, when landslides frequently cut smaller roads.

The Nu Jiang valley

Far over near China's border with Burma, the **Nu Jiang**, or **Salween River**, enters Yunnan from Tibet and flows south for over 500km through the province. To the east towers the Gaoligong mountain range, a huge rock wall that has kept this area an isolated backwater: the only connection with the rest of the province is the road from

TOURS TO THE NU JIANG VALLEY

Tourism to the Nu Jiang Valley is in its infancy, with regional agencies offering **guided treks** – currently the best way to explore the area. While tours organized from Dali and Lijiang are likely to access the river valley via Xiaguan, agencies in Shangri-La may be able to organize a trek west towards the far north of the area, depending on the time of year. Be wary trekking in winter and spring, however, when high rainfall makes landslides common.

Xiaguan via **Liuku** to the head of the valley at **Bingzhongluo**, from where hardy trekkers can hike over the mountains to Deqin.

There are some fascinating attractions in this, Yunnan's last true wilderness and part of the UNESCO **Three Parallel Rivers** World Heritage Site. The Nu Jiang itself is narrow, fast, full of rapids and crisscrossed by precarious rope bridges, and the settlements clinging to the gorge's sides are highly picturesque. Most of the population are Tibetan, Lisu or Dulong, and there are a surprising number of Catholics, the result of French missionary work during the nineteenth century.

The far north of the Nu valley, being effectively a dead end, is also very poor, and degrees of malnutrition and alcoholism can be seen among the local minorities. Though tourism promises to be a lucrative new source of income, as yet there are fairly few facilities. Certainly it is not a good idea to venture too far alone, and a local guide is always advised for any ambitious walk.

Liuku

六库, liùkù

Buses from Kunming, Tengchong, Xiaguan or Baoshan can get you to **LIUKU** – also known as **Lushui** (泸水县, lúshuǐ xiàn) – the capital of Nu Jiang prefecture. This rapidly expanding, modern town straddles both sides of the Nu Jiang, its streets lined with the usual clothing, shoe and mobile phone emporiums; there's little to see aside from nightly dancing down by the river and an eight-storey pagoda on a ridge north of town, and most people only stop overnight on the way up to Bingzhongluo. Around December 20, however, the Lisu hold the **Kuoshijie festival**, at which, besides singing and dancing, you'll see local men showing off by climbing poles barefoot using swords as steps.

ARRIVAL AND DEPARTURE   LIUKU

By bus Liuku's bus station (7am–7pm) is on the east side of the river, 2km south of the town centre. A taxi into town from the bus station is a flat ¥15.

Destinations Baoshan (4hr); Bingzhongluo (9hr); Fugong (4hr); Gongshan (8hr); Kunming (12hr); Tengchong (5hr); Xiaguan (5hr).

ACCOMMODATION AND EATING

For food, try the covered night market area along the east bank of the river between Zhenxing Lu and the road bridge. As well as barbecues and Sichuan restaurants, there are also a couple of waterfront bars.

Jindou Binguan 金都宾馆, jīndōu bīnguǎn. 282 Chuancheng Lu @0886 3629555. Useful budget option in the middle of town, whose serviceable tile-clad doubles come with en-suite showers and squat toilets. **¥80**

Shengshi Hongbang Hotel 晟世红邦大酒店, shèngshì hóngbāng dàjiǔdiàn. Corner of Renmin Lu and Xiangyang Dong Lu @0886 8887888. The most upmarket place in town at time of writing, featuring clean en-suite rooms with a/c and internet. Wi-fi is available in the lobby. **¥200**

DIRECTORY

Banks The Bank of China, with 24-hour ATM, is near the bus station, uphill at the junction with the main road. There are also several banks with ATMs on central Renmin Lu.

Post office On Dukou Lu, at the north end of Renmin Lu (daily 9am–5pm).

Fugong

福贡, fúgòng

Heading north from Liuku, the river becomes increasingly hemmed in by a gorge and begins to reveal its fierce character, with scenic Lisu villages clinging to the steep hillsides. So it's a shame that **FUGONG**, a township of bleak concrete vistas 123km along, is such a dump, though things perk up with the **market** held every fifth day, well attended by local Lisu, Dulong and Nu villagers.

ARRIVAL AND DEPARTURE   FUGONG

By bus Fugong's bus station (7am–7pm) is in the centre of town, just off the main street.

Destinations Bingzhongluo (5hr); Gongshan (4hr); Kunming (16hr); Liuku (4hr).

ACCOMMODATION

Fugong Binguan 福熙宾馆, fúxī bīnguǎn. Next door to the bus station ☎0886 3411442. You'd only really stop in Fugong if you arrived too late to leave again.

Conveniently next door to the bus station, this place has clean enough doubles with attached bathrooms for an overnight stay ahead of an early escape. ¥60

Gongshan

贡山, gòngshān

The two-street town of **GONGSHAN** is around a four-hours bus ride north of Fugong. You'll likely see plenty of **Dulong** people here, the smallest ethnic minority in Yunnan with a current population of just 6000. Older women have tattooed faces, supposedly for beautification, though the practice seems to have started as a way to dissuade Tibetan slave-traders from kidnapping them. There's plenty of bustle and construction at Gongshan, though little to divert visitors longer than it takes to catch the next bus to Bingzhongluo.

ARRIVAL AND DEPARTURE   GONGSHAN

By bus Gongshan's bus station (7am–7pm) is on the main street through town. Departures for Bingzhongluo (¥12) leave from across the street.

Destinations Bingzhongluo (90min); Fugong (4hr); Liuku (8hr).

ACCOMMODATION

Gongshan Tongbao 贡山通宝大酒店, gòngshān tōngbǎo dàjiǔdiàn. ☎0886 3513339. Directly across from the bus station, the *Tongbao* is nothing extraordinary,

but besides being handily located it has decent rooms with their own shower, toilet, and 24-hour hot water. ¥100

Bingzhongluo

丙中洛, bǐngzhōngluò · ¥100

A bumpy ninety-minute ride north of Gongshan through dramatic gorge scenery brings you to **BINGZHONGLUO**, the village at the end of the road. It's a scruffy little place, but the setting is stunning, and it's a great base for hiking – there are a couple of hostels in town which can fix you up with basic maps, as well as guiding services for more taxing routes.

ARRIVAL AND DEPARTURE   BINGZHONGLUO

Bingzhongluo's bus station is halfway down the village's main street, although most buses don't actually use it, preferring to crawl the main drag picking people up between runs. There are only a couple of long-distance departures each day, but hourly shuttles to Gongshan where you can pick up connections for further afield.
Destinations Fugong (5hr); Gongshan (2hr); Liuku (9hr).

INFORMATION

Trekking Treks on foot or horseback can be arranged through Aluo at the *International Youth Hostel*

(☎1398 8672792) or through the *Guodaofang Hostel* (☎1350 8868076). Both charge around ¥250 per person

> ## TREKKING FROM DIMALUO
>
> From Dimaluo it's possible to trek to neighbouring valleys and avoid having to catch the bus all the way back down to Liuku. You'll need a guide, though: expect to pay around ¥250 per day, including very basic food and accommodation.
>
> One popular option begins with a stiff, two-day hike across the Nushan range to **Cizhong** (茨中, cízhōng), a village with another stone church in the parallel Lancang River valley; the locals even make their own red wine for Communion, though Christianity has been laid on top of much older, animist beliefs. There is an irregular, fair-weather bus service south from Cizhong to **Weixi** (维西, wéixī; 6–10hr), from where you can catch a bus to Lijiang via Shigu (see p.679).

per day and it can be worth hiring a porter too, for another ¥100 per day. Check before you leave whether you need to bring your own food, or if it will be supplied en route.

ACCOMMODATION

Bingzhongluo International Youth Hostel 丙中洛国际青年旅舍, bǐngzhōngluò guójì qīngnián lǚshè.. Follow along the main street and take the first turning off to the right, downhill, after the bus station ☎0886 3581168 or 1890 8861299. Friendly place with clean rooms, hard beds, communal dining and shared bathrooms. The manager, Aluo, runs a guesthouse in Dimaluo and can provide guiding services. Dorm **¥30**, room **¥80**

Gudaofang Hostel 古道坊客栈, gǔdàofāng kèzhàn. On the main street, near the turning for the youth hostel ☎0886 3581181 or 1350 8868076. Rooms are upstairs; those at the back have a fantastic view over the valley, and mattresses are a step up from the *IYH*'s efforts. There's also a pleasant café on the ground floor and an attached ethnic gift shop. Dorm **¥40**, room **¥100**

Yudong 玉洞宾馆, yùdòng bīnguǎn. Opposite the bus station ☎0886 3581285 or 1398 8689887. No surprises here at this Chinese-syle effort, just standard, clean, en-suite rooms with wi-fi. Again, go for one at the back to wake up to amazing vistas. **¥100**

Dimaluo

迪麻洛, dímáluò

From Bingzhongluo, a popular ramble – simple enough to do alone – is to **DIMALUO**, a community of Catholic Tibetans. Board a bus heading south and get off at the footbridge that leads to **Pengdang** (捧当, pěngdāng), then cross the river and walk south until you reach a bridge and a dirt track, which you follow north to the village. The walk takes about two hours. At Dimaluo, there's accommodation – run by Bingzhongluo's youth hostel – and an intriguing **Catholic church** built in Tibetan style.

Tengchong

腾冲, téngchōng

Some 250km west of Xiaguan, **TENGCHONG** was once an important administrative post, though now isolated and well off the new highway. The town's scruffy old core is surrounded by modern main roads and apartments, though earthquakes have left Tengchong largely bereft of historic monuments or tall buildings. The old stone **gate tower** (文星楼, wénxīng lóu) survives at the eastern end of central Fengshan Lu; there's a big – though rather too organized – **jade market** (玉泉园, yùquán yuán) at the northern edge of town; and a museum at the **Anti-Japanese War Memorial Hall** (滇西抗日纪念馆, diānxī kàngrì jìniànguǎn), which includes copious photos and a memorial to the US-organized "Flying Tigers" (see p.748).

Laifeng Shan Park

来风山公园, láifēngshān gōngyuán • Free

Just west of the centre, Tengchong's main attraction is **Laifeng Shan Park**, several square kilometres of hilly green woodland. Paths ascend through the forest to Laifeng Temple, a monastery-turned-museum, and a resurrected, thirteen-storey pagoda – looking much like a lighthouse ringed in multiple balconies – which will guide you to the park from Tengchong.

Heshun

和顺, héshùn • ¥80 including all buildings • bus #6 from town ¥1 • taxi ¥20

Five kilometres west of Tengchong, **HESHUN** is an attractive old village with several hundred stone houses packed together in a narrow maze of streets. Once a quiet retreat for overseas Chinese, this is now a fully fledged tourist attraction, including a barrage of new-built Qing-style shops and a couple of **museums**, though many exhibits have been moved to the Anti-Japanese War Memorial Hall in Tengchong. Head away from the busy main gate, however, and you could still spend half a day exploring Heshun with a camera.

Hot Sea

热海, rèhǎi • ¥60 entry • bathing pools ¥268 • bus #2 from town ¥1 • taxi ¥15

Geological shuffles over the last fifty million years have opened up the "Hot Sea", 11km southwest of Tengchong along the Ruili road, where the scalding **Liuhuang** and **Dagungguo** pools steam and bubble away, contained by incongruously neat stone paving and ornamental borders. Situated in a wooded valley, it's a pleasant enough spot for a stroll, but not really that much of a visual spectacle; its only really worth visiting if you're willing to splash out on a soak.

ARRIVAL AND DEPARTURE   TENGCHONG

BY BUS

Main bus station (旅游客运站, lǚyóu kèyùnzhàn), 1km south of the centre down Rehai Lu. Kunming and Xiaguan traffic, plus buses to Liuku in the Nu Jiang valley (see p.691).

Tengchong bus station (腾冲客运站, téngchōng kèyùnzhàn), east of the centre on Dongfang Lu, with frequent departures to Ruili 7am–3pm.
Destinations Kunming (10hr); Liuku (6hr); Ruili (4hr); Xiaguan (6hr).

INFORMATION

Maps Large maps of Tengchong and Heshun are available free from most hotel receptions.

GETTING AROUND

By taxi A taxi to anywhere within Tengchong's small centre costs ¥6.

ACCOMMODATION AND EATING

While Tengchong itself sports dozens of ordinary hotels, Heshun is where to find guesthouses and hostels. For food, evening stalls selling charcoal-grilled chicken and fish pop up along Guanghua Lu and Dong Jie, while there is a string of decent eateries on Dongfang Lu, south of its junction with Feicui Lu.

TENGCHONG

Home Inn 如家酒店, rújiā jiǔdiàn. Dongfang Lu ☎0875 5144999, ⓦhomeinns.com. Unsurprising branch of this nationwide budget hotel chain, with all the usual cut-price comforts. Rooms are tiny but spotless, and the staff are helpful. **¥139**

Yudu Dajiudian 玉都大酒店, yùdū dàjiǔdiàn. 15 Binhe Xiaoqu, Tengyue Lu ☎0875 5138666, ⓦtcyuduhotel.com. This modern affair, near the jade market, is one of Tenchong's plusher venues but pretty good value; rooms come with some elbow room, modern glass-walled showers and wi-fi. **¥280**

Zhongda Jiudian 中大酒店, zhōngdà jiǔdiàn. 222 Dongfang Lu ☎0875 5195888. A hotel in a bus station that you might actually choose to stay in. Smart, clean and extremely convenient if arriving late in the day by bus from Ruili. **¥220**

HESHUN

Heshun Youth Hostel 和顺青年旅舍, héshùn qīngnián lǚshè. A good 1km walk from the main gate. ☎0875 5158398. Nice-looking courtyard compound with wooden buildings, though facilities are a bit basic – beds are hard and there's no bar or

11

restaurant – but it does have a washing machine. Dorms ¥30, rooms ¥128

Zongbingfu Kezhan 总兵府客栈, zǒngbīngfǔ kèzhàn. ☎0875 5150288. Smart place with some genuine character, whose period rooms – all with modern furnishings – are housed in an old courtyard building. Call ahead and get someone to meet you at the main gate and guide you there. ¥480

DIRECTORY

Bank There's a Bank of China with ATM at the Laifeng Shan Park end of Fengshan Lu.

Post office The post office is at the Laifeng Shan Park end of Fengshan Lu.

Ruili
瑞丽, ruìlì

Once the capital of the Mengmao Dai Kingdom, the frontier town of **RUILI** revels in the possibilities of its proximity to Burma, 5km south over the Shweli River: so porous is the border between Jiegao in China and **Mu Se** on the Burmese side that locals quip, "Feed a chicken in China and you get an egg in Burma". Burmese, Pakistani and Bangladeshi nationals wander around in sarongs and thongs, clocks are often set to Rangoon time (90 minutes behind Beijing), and markets display foreign goods. Many Chinese in town are tourists, attracted by the chance to pick up cut-price trinkets, though recent massive growth means thousands are now here for work. The town's **markets** are fascinating; many foreign traders speak good English and make interesting company. Additionally, the surrounding countryside, studded with Dai villages and temples, is only a bike ride away.

The jade and gem market
瑞丽珠宝街, ruìlì zhūbǎo jiē

By day Ruili's broad pavements and drab construction pin it down as a typical Chinese town; fortunately, its **markets** and people are anything but typical. The **jade and gem market**, in the north of town along Bianmao Jie, has a "Disneyland Burma" look, but there is serious business being done. Dealers come to stock up on ruinously expensive wafers of deep green jade; unless you really know your stuff it's safer just to watch the huddles of pensive merchants, or negotiate souvenir prices for coloured pieces of

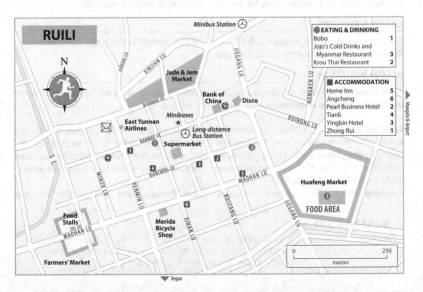

sparkling Russian glass "jewels", chunks of polished substandard jade and heavy brass rings.

Huafeng market

华丰市场, huáfēng shìchǎng

Dai and Jingpo haunt Ruili's huge **Huafeng market** on Jiegang Lu. **Burmese stallholders** here can sell you everything from haberdashery and precious stones to birds, cigars, Mandalay rum and Western-brand toiletries; Dai girls powder their faces with yellow talc, young men insistently offer jewellery from their shoulder bags. It really comes alive at night when the stalls in a southeastern covered area start serving spicy Burmese barbecue and chilled Myanmar beer.

Farmers' market

综合农贸市场, zōnghé nónghè shìchǎng

For a rough-and-ready shopping experience, try the morning **farmers' market** at the western end of Maohan Lu, where you'll find not only meat (the live animal section, including dogs for consumption, is not for the faint-hearted), fish, fruit and vegetables, but also locally made wood and cane furniture as well as shoes, clothes and even roadside jewellers selling "gold" rings and bracelets. If you manage to keep your appetite, this is also a good place to pick up a bowl of spicy noodles from stalls in the heart of the market's covered area.

ARRIVAL AND DEPARTURE

RUILI

By plane The nearest airport is 100km northeast at Mangshi (芒市, mángshi), also known as Luxi (潞西, lùxī). Getting to and from Mangshi's airport costs ¥35 in a minibus or ¥50 per person in a taxi. East Yunnan Airlines in Ruili, at 15 Renmin Lu (📞 0692 4155700 or 4111111), usually offers discounted fares.

Destinations from Mangshi Guangzhou (1 daily; 4hr 40min); Kunming (11 daily; 50min).

By bus The long-distance station on Nanmao Jie has at least daily services to everywhere along the highway between here and Kunming; there's also at least one departure daily for the lengthy ride down to Jinghong in Xishuangbanna.

By minibus Minibuses to Mangshi depart from the minibus station opposite the north end of Jiegang Lu, while vans to closer sights go from just outside the bus station on Nanmao Jie – keep repeating the name of your destination and you'll be shepherded to the correct vehicle.

Destinations Jinghong (30hr); Kunming (13hr); Mangshi (2hr); Tengchong (4hr); Xiaguan (6hr).

GETTING AROUND

Ruili's centre is small enough to get around on foot.
By bike Bikes can be rented from the Merida bicycle shop (美利达, měilìdá) on Biancheng Lu for ¥50 per day.

ACCOMMODATION

Ruili is littered with basic hotels and there's a good choice of rooms right in the town centre, though there are no real budget bargains. You need air conditioning in summer.

Home Inn 如家酒店, rújiā jiǔdiàn. 11 Lecheng Jie 📞 0692 3031333, 🌐 homeinns.com. The newcomer keeping the others honest. Basic and clean, and looks like all the others in the chain. Stay here if you want to meet middle-class students from Beijing. **¥180**
Jingcheng 景成大酒店, jǐngchéng dàjiǔdiàn.

Maohan Lu 📞 0692 4159666, 🌐 jcdjd.cn. About the only place with real pretentions towards luxury in town, this starred pile has decent rooms, a swimming pool, tennis court and gym, all enclosed inside Ruili's tallest building. **¥500**
Pearl Business Hotel 明珠商务酒店, míngzhū

RUILI TO BURMA

At present it is not possible for foreigners to cross on foot from Ruili into Burma without having previously arranged to be met by an official tour guide at the border. You'll need to have set everything up – including visas – before leaving Kunming (see p.651).

shāngwù jiŭdiàn. Biancheng Lu ☎0692 6636222. Easy to find thanks to neon lights outside and a video games arcade on the ground floor. The lobby of this new, and currently smart, hotel is on the third floor. **¥150**

Tianli 天丽宾馆, tiānlì bīnguǎn. Biancheng Lu ☎0692 4155000. Yet another of Ruili's simple, clean options whose spacious tiled doubles with bathrooms and a/c are good value, if absolutely ordinary and functional. **¥120**

Yingbin Hotel 迎宾楼大酒店, yíngbīnlóu

dàjiŭdiàn. Behind the bus station at 83 Biancheng Lu ☎0692 4129969. Recently renovated, smart rooms all come with an ADSL internet connection, the more expensive ones with a computer as well. **¥148**

Zhong Rui 钟瑞宾馆, zhōngruì bīnguǎn. 1 Nanmao Jie ☎0692 4100556. Old-style business hotel that's starting to look rather grubby. Rooms come with internet connections and ash trays in the bathroom. It is cheap, though. **¥100**

EATING AND DRINKING

Food is all-important to domestic tourists, and Ruili certainly doesn't fall down here. As well as clear influence from Burma, the town's dining also features flavours from further afield including Thailand, as well as China's own cuisine brought by internal migrants. For conventional Chinese food, head to the string of restaurants on Ruijiang Lu beside the long-distance bus station, or for a rustic early lunch try noodles in the farmers' market.

Bobo 步步冷饮店, bùbù lěngyǐndiàn. Xinan Lu. Sited on a covered rooftop, this relaxed café boasts a vast array of drinks and Southeast Asian-style desserts (coconut milk, sago and mango), and a much shorter food list. The menu is in English, though little is spoken, and they also have wi-fi. Drinks ¥5–10, food ¥15–25. Daily 9am–9pm.

Jojo's Cold Drinks and Myanmar Restaurant Huafeng Market. One of the big treats in Ruili is heading to Huafeng after sundown, especially at weekends, to gorge on spicy barbecued skewers. The covered area at the bottom end has

seating for several hundred diners; look for the green sign for Jojo's. The food is laid out on show so ordering is as simple as pointing, and you can wash it down with Myanmar beer or any number of fresh juices. ¥15–40. Daily 8pm–late.

Krou Thai Restaurant 可傣饭店, kědǎi fàndiàn. Biancheng Lu. Not the only Thai restaurant in town, but probably the best, with a selection of spicy soups, *laab*, and rice dishes, and they'll do vegetarian versions to order. The picture menu has some English translations. Mains ¥20–40. Daily 11am–10pm.

DIRECTORY

Banks and exchange Bank of China is on Nanmao Jie; foreign exchange Mon–Fri 9–11.30am & 2.30–4.30pm.

Internet There are plenty of internet cafés scattered around town (¥3/hr). Most hotels have cable internet

connections in rooms and wi-fi available in the lobby. The *Bobo* café also has wi-fi.

Maps Large double-sided maps of Ruili and attractions in the surrounding area can be bought from hotel receptions (¥10).

Around Ruili

Villages and Buddhist monuments dot the plains around Ruili, though most of the destinations below are only of mild interest in themselves, really just excuses to get out into the attractive countryside. For more about the Dai, see the Xishuangbanna section (p.698).

Jiegao and the border

姐告, jiěgào · taxi from town ¥5

The quickest trip is virtually inside town. Hail a shared red taxi and it's five minutes to **Jiegao**, a huge bubble-shaped duty-free trading estate on Ruili's southern outskirts, surrounded on all sides by Burma. There are three official crossings – for people, cars and trucks – and multiple unofficial ones, set amid a vast grid of shops selling everything from pneumatic drills to washing-up bowls.

Jiele Jin Ta

姐勒金塔, jiělè jīntǎ · taxi from town ¥10

About 5km east of Ruili along the Wanding road is the two-hundred-year-old **Jiele Jin Ta**, a group of seventeen portly Dai pagodas painted gold and said to house several of Buddha's bones. In some open-air **hot springs** nearby, it's said that you can wash away various ailments.

West to Jiexiang town

minibus from Ruili ¥15

West of Ruili, it's 5km to a small bridge near the region's largest Buddhist monastery, the nicely decorated **Hansha Temple** (喊沙寺, hǎnshā sì). Ten kilometres further on, the town of **JIEXIANG** (姐相, jiěxiàng) boasts the splendid Tang-era **Leizhuang Nunnery** (雷奘相佛寺, léizàngxiàng fósì), whose complex is dominated by a huge central pagoda and four corner towers, all in white. Another fine temple with typical Dai touches, such as "fiery" wooden eave decorations, **Denghannong Temple** (等喊弄寺, děnghǎnnòng sì) is further west again. The current halls only date from the Qing dynasty, but Buddha is said to have stopped here once to preach.

Xishuangbanna

西双版纳, xīshuāngbǎnnà

A tropical spread of rainforests, plantations and paddy fields nestled 750km southwest of Kunming along the Burmese and Laotian borders, **Xishuangbanna** has little in common with the rest of provincial China. Foremost of the region's many ethnic groups are the **Dai**, northern cousins to the Thais, whose distinctive temples, bulbous pagodas and saffron-robed clergy are a common sight down on the plains, particularly around **Jinghong**, Xishuangbanna's increasingly touristed capital. The region's remaining 19,000 square kilometres of hills, farms and forest are split between the administrative townships of **Mengla** in the east and **Menghai** in the west, peppered with villages of Hani, Bulang, Jinuo, Wa and Lahu. Cultural tourism aside, there are plenty of hiking trails and China's **open border with Laos** to explore.

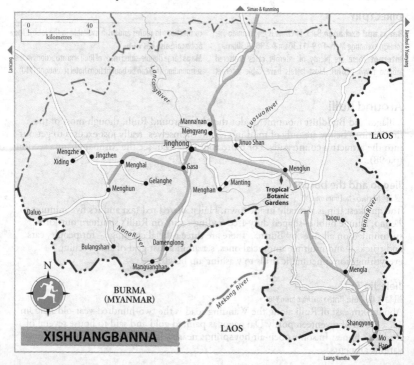

Xishuangbanna's emphatically tropical **weather** divides into a dry stretch between November and May, when warm days, cool nights and dense morning mists are the norm; and the June–October **wet season**, featuring high heat and torrential daily rains. The busiest time of the year here is mid-April, when thousands of tourists flood to Jinghong for the Dai **Water-splashing Festival**; hotels and flights will be booked solid for a week beforehand. **Getting around** Xishuangbanna is easy enough, with well-maintained roads connecting Jinghong to outlying districts.

Brief history

Historically, there was already a Dai state in Xishuangbanna two thousand years ago, important enough to send ambassadors to the Han court in 69 AD; it was subsequently incorporated into the Nanzhao and Dali kingdoms. A brief period of full independence ended with the Mongols' thirteenth-century conquest of Yunnan and the area's division into **twelve rice-growing districts** or *sipsawng pa na*, rendered as "Xishuangbanna" in Chinese. A fairly "hands-off" approach to Chinese rule ended in the 1950s, since when more contentious aspects of religion have been banned, extensive deforestation has occurred, and recent mass planting of **rubber** as a cash crop has drastically altered the landscape. Many minority people feel that the government would really like them to behave like Han Chinese, except in regards to dress – since colourful traditional clothing attracts tourists – and it's certainly true that Xishuangbanna is a rather anaemic version of what lies across the border in Laos.

11

Jinghong

景洪, jǐnghóng

JINGHONG, Xishuangbanna's fast-developing capital, sits on the southwestern bank of the **Lancang River** (澜沧江, láncāng jiāng), which later winds downstream through Laos and Thailand as the Mekong. Ever since the Dai warlord Bazhen drove the Bulang and Hani tribes off these fertile central flatlands, and founded the independent kingdom of Cheli in 1180, Jinghong has been maintained as an administrative centre. There was a moment of excitement in the late nineteenth century when a battalion of British soldiers marched in during a foray from Burma, but they soon decided that Jinghong was too remote to be worth defending.

Today the towering gaudiness of Jinghong's newly acquired high-rises and strip malls, bedecked with faux-ethnic fibreglass mouldings – not to mention parties of domestic

---

THE DAI

Although the **Dai** once spread as far north as the Yangzi Valley, they were driven south by the Mongol expansion in the thirteenth century. These days, they are found not only in southwest China but also throughout Thailand, Laos and Vietnam. Reputed as skilful farmers, they have always flourished in fertile river basins, growing rice, sugar cane, rubber trees and bananas. Accordingly, **Dai cuisine** is characterized by sweet flavours not found elsewhere in China – you'll encounter rice steamed inside bamboo or pineapple, for instance. Oddities such as fried moss and ant eggs appear on special occasions.

Dai women wear a sarong or long skirt, a bodice and a jacket, and keep their hair tied up and fixed with a comb, and often decorated with flowers. Married women wear silver wristbands. Dai men sport plenty of **tattoos**, usually across their chests and circling their wrists. Their homes are raised on stilts, with the livestock kept underneath. Some of the most distinctive and ornate Dai architecture is well decoration, as the Dai regard water as sacred. They're Buddhists, but like their compatriots in Southeast Asia follow the Thervada, or Lesser Wheel, school, rather than the Mahayana school favoured throughout the rest of China. When visiting Dai temples, it's important to **remove your shoes**, as the Dai consider feet to be the most unclean part of the body.

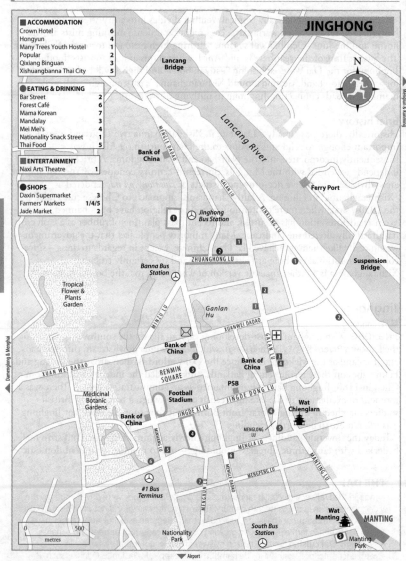

JINGHONG

■ ACCOMMODATION
Crown Hotel	6
Hongyun	4
Many Trees Youth Hostel	1
Popular	2
Qixiang Binguan	3
Xishuangbanna Thai City	5

● EATING & DRINKING
Bar Street	2
Forest Café	6
Mama Korean	7
Mandalay	3
Mei Mei's	4
Nationality Snack Street	1
Thai Food	5

■ ENTERTAINMENT
Naxi Arts Theatre	1

● SHOPS
Daxin Supermarket	3
Farmers' Markets	1/4/5
Jade Market	2

tourists rushing about – is a stark contrast to the laidback, easy style of Dai women in their bright sarongs and straw hats who meander the gently shimmering, palm-lined streets. For the most part, the city is an undemanding place to spend a couple of days, and once you've tried the local food and poked around the temples, there's plenty of transport into the rest of Xishuangbanna.

The streets

The pick of Jinghong's many **markets** is Zhuanghong Lu's 500m of Burmese jade and jewellery shops, plus a few stalls selling ethnic-style textiles and trinkets. There are also big farmers' markets (农贺市场, nónghè shìchǎng), packed with Dai women picking over piles of tropical fruit and veg, opposite the bus station on Mengle Dadao, west of the centre on Mengla Lu, and west of Manting Park on Menghai Lu.

Riverside **Binjiang Lu** is a great place to stroll in the evening, when the bars, snack stalls and night market lining the river fire up and where you can watch locals flying kites and bringing their cars, trucks and buses to the water's edge to give them a good clean.

Tropical Flower and Plants Garden

热带花卉园, rèdài huāhuìyuán • Daily 7.30am–6.30pm • ¥40

Jinghong's **Tropical Flower and Plants Garden**, 500m west of the centre down Xuanwei Dadao, holds palms, fruit trees and brightly flowering shrubs and vines, nicely arranged around a lake. The different sections – aerial flower subgarden, bougainvillea subgarden, and so on – host afternoon performances of Dai dancing for tour groups.

Medicinal Botanic Gardens

药用植物园, yàoyòng zhíwùyuán • Daily 9am–6pm • ¥104

Across the road from the Tropical Flower garden, the **Medicinal Botanic Gardens** consist of quiet groves scattered among the shaded gloom of closely planted rainforest trees. They lead to a large **Traditional Medicine Clinic**, whose friendly staff may invite you in for a cup of tea and impromptu *qi gong* demonstration.

Manting

曼听, màntīng

A kilometre southeast of the centre via Manting Lu, **Manting** was once a separate village, now absorbed into Jinghong's lazy spread. Near the end of the road, **Wat Manting** (曼听佛寺, màntīng fósì) is Jinghong's main Buddhist monastery and the largest in all Xishuangbanna. Check out the very Dai gold trim, the guardian creatures at the gates, the glossy *jinghua* murals adorning the temple walls and a giant ceremonial canoe in the monastery grounds. Traditionally, all Dai boys spend three years at temples like Wat Manting getting a grounding in Buddhism and learning to read and write.

Manting Park

曼听公园, màntīng gōngyuán • Daily 7.30am–5.30pm • ¥40 • evening shows 7.40–9.40pm, ¥260–480

Next to Wat Manting is the more secular **Manting Park**, where the royal slaves were formerly kept. A giant gold statue of former premier Zhou Enlai welcomes visitors, tour groups are treated to water-splashing displays every afternoon, and there's also a

---

NEW YEAR FESTIVITIES

Dai New Year celebrations, once set by the unpredictable Dai calendar, are now held **April 13–16** annually. The first day sees a **dragon-boat race** on the river, held in honour of a good-natured dragon spirit who helped a local hero outwit an evil king. On the second day everybody in Jinghong gets a good soaking as **water-splashing** hysteria grips the town, and basinfuls are enthusiastically hurled over friends and strangers alike to wash away bad luck. Manting Park also hosts cockfighting and dancing all day. The finale includes **Diu Bao** (Throwing Pouches) games, where prospective couples fling small, triangular beanbags at each other to indicate their affection, and there's a mammoth **firework display**, when hundreds of bamboo tubes stuffed with gunpowder and good-luck gifts are rocketed out over the river. Nightly carousing and dancing – during which generous quantities of *lajiu*, the local firewater, are consumed – take place in the parks and public spaces. Look out for the **Peacock dance**, a fluid performance said to imitate the movements of the bird, bringer of good fortune in Dai lore, and the **Elephant-drum dance**, named after the instrument used to thump out the rhythm.

large pen bursting with **peacocks**, which you can feed. Corners of the park are very pleasant, with paths crossing over one of the Lancang River's tiny tributaries to full-scale copies of Jingzhen's Bajiao Ting (see p.706) and a portly, Dai-style pagoda. The park hosts nightly shows featuring Dai dancing and mass water-splashings.

ARRIVAL AND DEPARTURE   JINGHONG

Remember to confirm visa requirements for Laos and Thailand before booking transport – the nearest consulates are in Kunming (see box, p.651).

BY PLANE

Daily flights link Jinghong with Kunming, Xiaguan/Dali, Lijiang and a few cities elsewhere in China. There's also talk of Lao Air starting a service between Jinghong and Luang Prabang, while China Eastern fly once a week to Bangkok in Thailand. Buy onward tickets for all flights from agents around town who chalk up daily deals on blackboards outside.

Xishuangbanna airport (西双版纳嘎洒机场, xīshuāngbǎnnà gāsǎ jīchǎng) lies about 10km southwest of the city; catch bus #1 to its terminus at the western extension of Mengla Lu, or it's a 10min, ¥25 taxi ride into the centre along an expressway.

Destinations Beijing (1 daily; 5hr); Chengdu (1 daily; 2hr); Dali (2 daily; 50min); Kunming (30 daily; 55min); Lijiang (5 daily; 1hr); Shanghai (1 daily; 5hr).

BY BUS

Note that you can reach Jinghong direct from Kunming's south bus station, Xiaguan, Tengchong, Ruili and Luang Namtha in Laos (the latter costing US$12; 8hr). Coming from Yuanyang in southeast Yunnan, aim first for Jianshui (see p.657) and change buses there. In Jinghong, buy bus tickets at the relevant stations – and watch out for pickpockets.

Banna bus station (版纳客运服务站, bǎnnà kèyùn fúwùzhàn), right in the centre on Minzu Lu, is where to find most traffic heading to outlying villages around Xishuangbanna.

Jinghong bus station (景洪客运站, jǐnghóng kèyùn zhàn), on the northern arm of Mengle Dadao, handles almost all long-distance traffic, including those from Luang Namtha in Laos.

South bus station (客运南站, kèyùn nánzhàn), a kilometre south of town, deals in traffic around Xishuangbanna, and a few Kunming services; catch bus #3 or a cab to the centre.

Destinations Damenglong (1hr 30min); Jianshui (12hr); Kunming (10hr); Menghai (1hr); Menghun (1hr 20min); Menglun (2hr); Ruili (30hr); Xiaguan (16hr).

BY FERRY

Mekong ferries used to operate between Jinghong and Chiang Saen in northern Thailand, but were suspended in 2011 after the drug-related killing of 13 Chinese sailors.

Jinghong ferry port (景洪港, jǐnghóng kèyùnzhàn) is across the river via the main suspension bridge – bus #5 from the nearby main road will get you into the town centre. The port ticket office (daily 8am–5.30pm, ☏ 0691 2211899) is where to check on the latest situation regarding boats to Thailand (¥800).

Destinations Chiang Saen, Thailand (2 weekly; 7hr).

INFORMATION

Cruises Nightly pleasure cruises, taking in the lights of Jinghong, depart on two-hour trips from the ferry port from 7pm (¥200). Most boats feature their own entertainment in the form of cabaret floor shows. Tickets are available from most travel agencies in town, or from the ferry port.

Trekking agents Guided treks offered by Jinghong's tourist cafés explore remoter villages, waterfalls and forest, with the chance of encountering wildlife. Most trips include an overnight stay with a local host family and cost around ¥300 per person per day, though prices fall as the number of people in your group goes up. The most experienced guide is Sarah at the *Forest Café* (☏ 0691 8985122, ⦿ forest-cafe.org), though Summer at *Mei Mei's Café* (☏ 0691 2161221, ✉ zhanyanlan@hotmail.com) is also a mine of information and will happily provide a map and instructions for you to head off on your own. A recommended independent tour guide is Zhao Yao (English name "Joe"; ☏ 1376 9146987).

GETTING AROUND

By bus City buses operate 7am–7pm (¥1), though nowhere in Jinghong is more than a 20min walk away. Bus #5 runs east–west across the town centre and #4 north–south.

By bicycle *Many Trees* hostel rents bike at ¥30 per day for exploring town and Xishuangbanna's lowlands – though country roads are steep, twisting and long, and heavy traffic along the narrow roads, particularly south along the river toward Menghan, can make this a dangerous option.

By taxi Cabs charge ¥7 for anywhere in town.

ACCOMMODATION

All but the smallest lodgings have restaurants, and most offer either wi-fi, wired internet connection, or even computers in the room for an extra ¥20 or so. You'll need air conditioning in summer.

Crown Hotel 皇冠大酒店, huángguān dàjiǔdiàn. 70 Mengle Dadao ☎0691 2199888, Ⓦnewtgh.com. One of a number of upmarket places grouped around the Mengle/Mengla roads intersection, all aimed at wealthy Chinese tourists. Unmemorable, but clean and comfortable, and you can get big discounts on older rooms at the back. The same company also operates a genuine five-star hotel south of town towards the airport. **¥248**

Hongyun 鸿云酒店, hóngyún jiǔdiàn. 12 Galan Nan Lu ☎0691 2165777. Older place, now showing its age, with carpeted, quite spacious en suites with a/c and squat toilets. Upper rooms just about have views of the river. **¥160**

Many Trees Youth Hostel 曼丽撸国际青年旅舍, mànlìcuì guójì qīngnián lǚshè. 5 Manyun Xiang, down a lane opposite the gymnasium on Galan Lu ☎0691 2126210. Veteran, basic and haphazardly brightened up Chinese hostel, but a/c rooms are a fair deal for the money, and they've got a rooftop washing machine. Dorm **¥40**, room **¥108**

Popular 假日时尚酒店, jiàrì shíshàng jiǔdiàn. 104 Galan Zhong Lu ☎0691 2139001. A decent, newish place with clean and tidy en-suite doubles with a/c; the only drawback is that there's no lift. **¥120**

Qixiang Binguan 气象宾馆, qìxiàng bīnguǎn. 10 Galan Nan Lu ☎0691 2130188. Run by the Weather Bureau, this place's small tiled rooms with a/c are a budget bargain, though there are only squat toilets throughout. **¥80**

Xishuangbanna Thai City 西双版纳傣都大酒店, xīshāngbǎnnà dǎidū dàjiǔdiàn. 26 Minghang Lu ☎0691 2137888. This three-star establishment was once as upmarket as Jinghong got, and it's still of a decent standard – and good value – full of clean, furnished rooms. **¥240**

EATING AND DRINKING

Jinghong is the best place in Xishuangbanna to try authentic Dai cooking, either in restaurants or on the street. Formal menus often feature meat or fish courses flavoured with sour bamboo shoots or lemongrass, while oddities include fried moss, and pineapple rice for dessert – the fruit is hollowed out, stuffed with pineapple chunks and sweet glutinous rice, and steamed. Tourist cafés are comparatively expensive places to eat, but aside from their Western/Dai menus they also hand out local information, rent bikes and arrange tours. In the evening the night market along the river, south of the suspension bridge, is packed with open-air barbecues.

Forest Café. 23 Mengla Lu ☎0691 8985122, Ⓦforest-cafe.org. Owner-manager Sarah has an encyclopedic knowledge of local treks, and both she and her brother Stone can knock out a fantastic cup of Yunnan coffee or pu'er tea (¥15), but there's precious little in the way of food available. Daily 9am–7pm.

Mama Korean 韩国小吃店, hánguó xiǎochīdiàn. 13 Menghun Lu ☎1597 4955043. A little way out of the town centre, this place does excellent-value soups, rice bowls and sushi rolls – try the kimchi fried rice for ¥20, which comes with a starter of soup and pickles. Daily 11am–9pm.

Mandalay 耶待纳美餐厅, yēdàinàměi cāntīng. Above the Dico's on Renmin Square ☎0691 2141640. A vast canteen serving up cheap and plentiful Dai and Chinese dishes, and they also have a decent stab at pizza. It's best to stick to the Dai side of the menu though – the fish with lemongrass is fantastic. Expect to pay around ¥25 per person. Daily 11am–10pm.

★ **Mei Mei's** 美美咖啡, měiměi kāfēi. 107 Menglong Lu ☎0691 2161221, Ⓦmeimei-cafe.com. One of a clutch of similar cafés along this newish development serving great breakfast pancakes and other Western staples from ¥25, as well as a smattering of Chinese and Yunnanese specialities. It's also a good place to pick up info on local treks, as is their website. Daily 9am–10pm.

Nationality Snack Street 民族食尚街, mínzú shíshàng jiē. Binjiang Lu. A line of large, wooden restaurant-bars with loud – sometimes live – music on the promenade above the riverside, decked out in coloured fairy lights. It's a nice idea, but the establishments are all much the same and a drink costs at least ¥30. Daily from 5pm.

Thai Food 泰国风味, tàiguó fēngwèi. 193 Manting Lu, opposite Meimei's Café ☎0691 2161758. Terrific food, great value and always busy, this outdoor eatery is a Jinghong institution. It's not the fanciest place in town, but it is one of the best, with a massive choice of spicy Thai dishes and low prices – mains from ¥15. Daily 11am–9pm.

ENTERTAINMENT

Naxi Arts Theatre 蒙巴拉纳西艺术宫, měngbālā nàxī yìshùgōng. Galan Zhong Lu. Hugely popular with Chinese tour groups, during the high season they put on two shows a night here, but if you come early they usually do a half-hour warm-up in the square outside the theatre from about 7pm which you can watch for free. Tickets for the full performance cost ¥190.

11

SHOPPING

Markets For fresh fruit, including mangoes, coconuts, bananas, mangosteens and durian, head to either of the big produce markets on Mengle Dadao or Mengla Lu.

Supermarket Jinghong's best supermarket is the Daxin Mart, underneath Renmin Square on Mengle Dadao; aside from daily necessities, you can buy cheese and small packets of Yunnan ham.

DIRECTORY

Banks and exchange The main Bank of China (daily 8am–11.30am & 3–5.30pm) with ATM is at 29 Minhang Lu, at the junction with Jingde Lu. There are ATMs all around the centre.

Hospital The Provincial Hospital is at the lower end of Galan Lu.

Internet There are plenty of internet cafés along Manting Lu; foreigner cafés and some hotels have wi-fi.

Laundry *Many Trees Youth Hostel* charges ¥10 a load, while some of the foreigner cafés also offer laundry services.

Mail and telephones The GPO (daily 8am–8pm) is on the corner of Xuanwei Dadao and Mengle Dadao.

Massage Taiji Blind Massage (太极宣人按摩中心, tàijí xuānrén ànmó zhōngxīn) is just north of the Jingde Dong Lu/Mengle Dadao intersection, on the east side of the road. Go through the arch marked "Blind Massage" then immediately turn left up the staircase to the second floor. Full body ¥40, feet ¥50.

PSB 13 Jingde Lu (Mon–Fri 8–11.30am & 3–5.30pm; ☎0691 2130366) – look for the yellow English sign.

Northern and eastern Xishuangbanna

Aside from ethnic villages to the north of Jinghong, heading east through Xishuangbanna allows access to the excellent **botanic gardens** at Menglun, beyond which lies the open **border with Laos**. All traffic out this way departs from Jinghong's Banna bus station.

Huayao villages

MENGYANG (勐养, měngyǎng), 30km north of Jinghong, is a market and transport stop surrounded by a host of **Huayao** villages. The **Huayao** ("Flower Belt") form one of three Dai subgroups, though they differ greatly from the lowland "Water Dai", who scorn them for their over-elaborate costumes – Huayao women wear turbans draped with thin silver chains – and the fact that they are not Buddhists. Though you'll see plenty of Huayao at Mengyang, the village considered most typical is about 10km further north along the main road at **MANNA'NAN** (曼那因, mànnànān).

Jinuo Shan

基诺山, jīnuò shān

Some 18km east of Mengyang, **JINUO SHAN** is home to the independently minded **Jinuo**. Jinuo women wear a distinctive white-peaked hood, while both sexes pierce their ears and sport tattoos. The **Jinuo Folk Culture Village** (基诺山民族山寨, jīnuòshān mīnzú shānzhài; ¥50) here is a bit touristy, but at any rate can give you a glimpse of Xishuangbanna's smallest ethnic group.

Menghan

勐罕, měnghǎn

MENGHAN, 30km southeast of Jinghong, is the main settlement of the fertile "Olive-shaped Flatland", as its alternative name, **Ganlanba** (橄榄坝, gǎnlǎnbà), translates. This is one of Xishuangbanna's three major agricultural areas, won by force of arms over the centuries and now vitally important to the Dai (the other two are west at Damenglong and Menghai). Immediately west of town, the **Xishuangbanna Dai Garden** (傣园, dǎiyuán; ¥100) offers a sanitized version of minority life and daily water-splashing festivals to visiting tour groups. You can stay here too, inside "Dai Family Homes" – or at any rate, a tourist industry vision of them – which also provide meals.

Menghan itself is pleasantly surrounded by paddy fields and low hills, with plenty of day walks and cycle rides – accommodation will be able to help you rent a bike. One popular trip is to take a bike across the Mekong on the local ferry, and then head left for Dai villages.

Manting
曼听, màntīng

A couple of kilometres east of Menghan at **MANTING**, the excellent **Manting Buddhist Temple** (曼听佛寺, màntīng fósì) and **Dadu Pagoda** (大独塔, dàdú tǎ) are fine reconstructions of twelfth-century buildings destroyed during the 1960s. Paths lead further east from Manting along and across the river to more pagodas and villages, somewhere to spend a couple of days of easy exploration.

ACCOMMODATION   MENGHAN

Huaxin Binguan 华鑫宾馆, huáxīn bīnguǎn. 179 Xiandao, Menghan ☎ 0691 2411258. Up on the north side of the main road, this basic but clean place is a decent deal, and there's a tasty local restaurant directly across the street. ¥60

Xishuangbanna Sha La Hotel 沙拉酒店, shālā

jiǔdiàn. 68 Xiandao, Menghan ☎ 0691 2494168. Ugly, multi-storey three-star affair up the road from the *Huaxin*. En-suite twins and doubles are clean, comfortable and come equipped with the standard dark-wood furnishings, but lack any semblance of character. ¥300

Menglun
勐仑, měnglún

MENGLUN, about 40km east of Menghan, comprises a dusty grid of streets overlooking the broad flow of the Luosuo River. Take the side street downhill through the all-day market, and within a couple of minutes you'll find yourself by a large pedestrian suspension bridge crossing to Menglun's superb **Tropical Botanic Gardens** (热带植物园, rèdài zhíwùyuán; daily 7.30am–6.30pm; ¥80). These were carved out of the jungle in 1959, and are now divided up into shaded palm and bamboo groves, clusters of giant fig trees, lily ponds, vines and shrubs. There are plenty of birds and butterflies flitting about too – in all, an enjoyable mix of parkland and forgotten, overgrown corners. Look for Chinese visitors serenading the undistinguished-looking "Singing Plant", which is supposed to nod in time to music.

ARRIVAL AND DEPARTURE   MENGLUN

By bus There's no bus station at Menglun, so vehicles pull up wherever convenient on the main road, usually among the restaurants and stores on the eastern side of town. To

catch onward transport, head to the main road and flag down passing traffic.

ACCOMMODATION

Chunlin Binguan 春林宾馆, chūnlín bīnguǎn. Right by the main gate of the tropical gardens ☎ 0691

8715681. Basic, clean and tidy en suites with a/c at a budget price. ¥80

INTO LAOS

Beyond Menglun, the main road runs southeast for 130km, via Mengla (勐腊, měnglà), to the **Lao border**, just beyond Mo Han township (边贸站, biānmào zhàn). Assuming you've already obtained a visa from the Laotian consulate in Kunming (see p.651), the border crossing itself should be uncomplicated, though note that it closes mid-afternoon. On the far side lies the Laotian village of **Ban Boten**, where yuan are accepted, but there's nowhere to stay or change currency for Laotian kip. The nearest banks and beds are a ¥10 truck ride away at the town of **Luang Namtha**, from where you can hitch out to the early-morning markets at Muong Sing to see local people in full tribal regalia. There's transport from Luang Namtha to **Nung Kie** via Muong Tai, and thence by boat down the Mekong to **Luang Phabang** (though you can also come the whole way from the border by road).

Tropical Plant Gardens Hotel 热带植物园宾馆, rèdài zhíwùyuán bīnguǎn. ☏ 0691 8716852. Within the park itself, this government-run guesthouse has a tremendous location but, partly because of this, suffers from both damp and trespassing insects. If these don't scare you off, it's a fair place to stay and has a pool, though you'll want to scoop the bugs out before taking the plunge. **¥250**

Western Xishuangbanna

Western Xishuangbanna, which butts up against the (closed) Burmese border, is a little bit less explored than the east – many treks out of Jinghong's cafés come here – and has a couple of good markets. Most traffic out this way departs from Jinghong's Banna bus station, though Damenglong is reached from the South bus station.

Damenglong
大勐龙, dàměnglóng

DAMENGLONG – also known as **Menglong** – is a scruffy, busy crossroads town 55km southwest of Jinghong, with a big, all-day **Sunday market**. The disappointingly shoddy **Black Pagoda** (黑塔, 黑塔, hēitǎ) is just south of the central crossroads and shouldn't be confused with the **North Pagoda** (北塔, běi tǎ; ¥5), 2km north of town above the village of **Manfeilong** (曼飞龙, mànfēilóng). A long flight of stairs ascends to the North Pagoda, which is adorned with fragments of evil-repelling mirrors and silver paint, and is worshipped for the two **footprints** left by Sakyamuni in an alcove at the base. It is also known as the Bamboo Shoot Pagoda (笋塔, sǔntǎ; ¥10), after its nine-spired design, which resembles an emerging cluster of bamboo tips.

ACCOMMODATION AND EATING
DAMENGLONG

Eating options are street stalls or the Sichuanese place east from the crossroads, heading towards the highway.

Jintai Binguan 金泰宾馆, jīntài bīnguǎn. ☏ 0691 2740334. There's not a huge amount of choice in Damenglong, but this friendly and clean-ish, eggshell-blue building down a backstreet towards the market is one of the better choices. **¥60**

Menghai
勐海, měnghǎi

Western Xishuangbanna's principal town, **MENGHAI** is centrally placed on the highland plains 55km from Jinghong. A relatively organized assemblage of 1km-long high street and back lanes, the town is little more than a stop on the way towards outlying Dai and Hani settlements, but has an important history. Menghai was once a **Hani** (Aini) settlement until, as elsewhere, the Hani were defeated in battle by the Dai and withdrew into the surrounding hills. They remain there today as Xishuangbanna's second-largest ethnic group and long-time cultivators of **pu'er tea**, the local red, slightly musty brew that's esteemed from Hong Kong to Tibet for its fat-reducing and generally invigorating properties.

ARRIVAL AND DEPARTURE
MENGHAI

By bus Menghai's bus station – with buses to Jinghong and other centres, and minibuses to outlying villages – is at the eastern end of town.

The Mengzhe road
Minibuses heading west from Menghai can drop you 20km along at the bizarre **Jingzhen Octagonal Pavilion** (景真八角亭, jǐngzhēn bājiǎo tíng; ¥20), built in the eighteenth century to quell an angry horde of wasps. This, and **Manlei Buddhist Temple** (曼磊佛寺, mànlěi fósì; ¥20), a further 10km on past **MENGZHE** (勐遮, měngzhē), are inferior copies of older buildings, but have important collections of Buddhist manuscripts written on fan-palm fibre.

Xiding

西定, xīdìng

From Mengzhe, it's worth heading 15km southwest to the Hani village of **XIDING**, whose busy **Thursday market** is one of the best in the region. You'll need to get here on Wednesday, and sleep over in one of Xiding's rudimentary guesthouses, as the market kicks off at dawn.

Menghun

勐混, měnghún

Some 25km southwest of Menghai is **MENGHUN**, whose excellent **Sunday market** starts at daybreak and continues until noon. Akha women arrive under their elaborate silver-beaded headdresses, Bulang wear heavy earrings and oversized black turbans, and remote hill-dwellers come in plain dress, carrying ancient rifles. Most common of all are the Dai, who buy rolls of home-made paper and sarongs. Take a look around Menghun itself, too, as there's a dilapidated nineteenth-century **monastery** with a pavilion built in the style of Jingzhen's octagonal effort, and a **pagoda** hidden in the bamboo groves on the hills behind town.

11

ACCOMMODATION   MENGHUN

Dai Hotel 傣家宾馆, dǎijiā bīnguǎn. On the main road, just north of the village centre and signed in English from near the post office. Though very basic, this clean establishment is almost certainly your best bet for a night in Menghun, though there are several other options to inspect nearby. ¥60

Daluo and the Burmese border

At the end of the road 50km west of Menghun, and served by two daily buses from Menghai, **DALUO** (打落镇, dǎluò zhèn) is set just in from the Burmese border. Here there's a multi-trunked, giant **fig tree** whose descending mass of aerial roots forms a "forest", and a daily **border trade market**, timed for the arrival of Chinese package tours between 11am and 1pm. Chinese nationals can also get a two-hour visa for Burma, ostensibly to shop for jade; in fact, many are really going over to catch transvestite stage shows held for their benefit.

Sichuan and Chongqing

CUBS AT THE PANDA BREEDING RESEARCH BASE, CHENGDU

Sichuan and Chongqing

Ringed by mountains that, according to the Tang poet Li Bai, made the journey here "harder than the road to heaven", Sichuan (四川, sìchuān) and Chongqing (重庆, chóngqìng) stretch for more than 1000km across China's southwest. Administratively divided in 1997, when Chongqing was carved off the eastern end of Sichuan province, the region has long played the renegade, differing from the rest of China in everything from food to politics and inaccessible enough both to ignore central authority and to provide sanctuary for those fleeing it. Recent divisions aside, Sichuan and Chongqing share a common history, and the area splits more convincingly into very different geographic halves. The more gentle of the two lies east, where peaks surround one of the country's most densely settled areas, the fertile Red Basin, whose subtropical climate and rich soil conspire to produce endless green fields turning out three harvests a year.

12

This bounty has created an air of easy affluence in **Chengdu**, Sichuan's relaxed capital, and the southern river towns such as **Zigong**. Elsewhere, visitors have the opportunity to join pilgrims on **Emei Shan** in a hike up the holy mountain's forested slopes, or to **cruise down the Yangzi** from Chongqing, industrial powerhouse and jumping-off point for one of the world's great river journeys. You'll also find that the influence of Buddhism has literally become part of the landscape, most notably at **Leshan**, where a giant Buddha sculpted into riverside cliffs provides one of the most evocative images of China; and farther east at **Dazu**, whose wooded hillsides conceal a marvellous procession of stone carvings.

In contrast, **western Sichuan** is dominated by densely buckled ranges overflowing from the heights of Tibet: a wild, thinly populated land of snowcapped peaks, where yaks roam the tree line and roads negotiate hair-raising gradients as they cross ridges or follow deep river valleys. The west's appeal is its Tibetan heritage – clearly visible in the many important monasteries – and raw, rugged alpine scenery. Travelling north towards Gansu takes you through ethnic Hui and Qiang heartlands past the vivid blue lakes and medieval battlements at **Songpan** and **Jiuzhaigou**, with the tranquil village of **Langmusi** the most remote of targets, right on the provincial border. Due west of Chengdu, the real wilds begin beyond **Kangding**, with the monastery towns of **Dêgê** and **Litang** the pick of destinations – not forgetting an exciting back-road **route to Yunnan**.

RECLINING BUDDHA, DAZU

Highlights

❶ Teahouses A central feature of Sichuanese social life. **See p.718**

❷ Giant Panda Breeding Research Base, Chengdu One of the few zoos in China where the animals are clearly happy, healthy and well cared for. **See p.720**

❸ Huanglongxi Crowded but enjoyably touristy village of Qing-dynasty shops and temples. **See p.726**

❹ The Big Buddha, Leshan You will never forget the first time you see this gargantuan riverside statue looming above you. **See p.733**

❺ Emei Shan A tough climb is rewarded with gorgeous scenery and monasteries that make

atmospheric places to stay. **See p.735**

❻ Dazu China's most exquisite collection of Buddhist rock art, illustrating religious parables and cartoon-like scenes from daily life. **See p.743**

❼ Cruising the Yangzi Relax as your boat glides past the magnificent scenery of the towering Three Gorges. **See p.753**

❽ Horse-trekking, Songpan Get really out into the wild and give your feet – though not your seat – a rest. **See p.756**

❾ Litang Gritty Tibetan monastery town in the heart of Sichuan's wild west, where monks and cowboys tear around on motorbikes. **See p.767**

HIGHLIGHTS ARE MARKED ON THE MAP ON PP.712–713

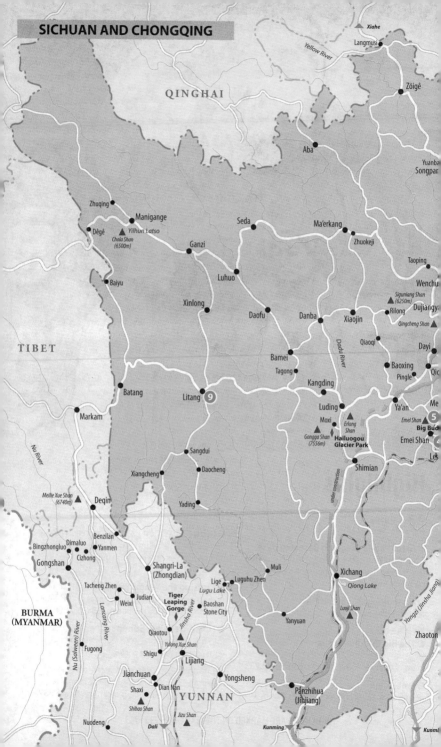

SICHUANESE COOKING

Dominating the southwestern China cooking school, **Sichuanese cooking** is noted for its heavy use of **chilli**, which locals explain as a result of climate – according to Traditional Chinese Medicine, chillies dispel "wet" illnesses caused by Sichuan's seasonally damp or humid weather. But chillies don't simply blast the tastebuds, they stimulate them as well, and flavours here are far more complex than they might appear at the initial, eye-watering, mouthful.

Sichuan cuisine's defining taste is described as **mala** – "numb and hot" – created by the potent mix of chillies and **huajiao** (Sichuan pepper), with its soapy perfume and mouth-tingling afterbuzz. One classic *mala* dish is *mapo doufu*, bean curd and minced pork; others include "strange-flavoured chicken" (dressed with sesame paste, soy sauce, sugar and green onions mixed in with the chillies and *huajiao*), and the innocently named "boiled beef slices", which actually packs more chillies per spoonful than almost any other Sichuanese dish.

Other more general dishes include **hot and sour soup**, flavoured with pepper and vinegar; **double-cooked pork**, where a piece of fatty meat is boiled, sliced thinly and then stir-fried with green chillies; **fish-flavoured pork** (whose "seafood" sauce is made from vinegar, soy sauce, sugar, ginger and sesame oil); **gongbao chicken**, the local version of stir-fried chicken and peanuts; and **smoked duck**, a chilli-free cold dish, aromatic and juicy. There's also a great number of Sichuanese **snacks** – *xiaochi* – which some restaurants specialize in: green beans with ginger, pork with puréed garlic, cucumber with chilli-oil and sesame seeds, *dandan mian* ("carry-pole" noodles, named for the way in which street vendors used to carry them around), tiger-skin peppers, scorched then fried with salt and dark vinegar, pork steamed in ground rice (served in the bamboo steamer), and a huge variety of sweet and savoury dumplings.

One Chongqing speciality now found all over China is **huoguo** (hotpot), a social dish eaten everywhere from streetside canteens to specialist restaurants. You get plates or skewers of meat, boiled eggs or vegetables, cooked – by you at the table – in a bubbling pot of stock liberally laced with chillies and cardamom pods. You then season the cooked food in oil spiced with MSG, salt and chilli powder. The effect is powerful, and during a cold winter you may well find that hotpots fast become your favourite food.

Travelling around Sichuan is fairly straightforward, but those heading westwards need to prepare for unpredictably long and uncomfortable journeys. The most useful **rail routes** are the high-speed Chengdu–Chongqing link, and the Xi'an–Kunming line, which runs southwest from Chengdu via Emei Shan and Xichang. Expect hot, humid summers and cold winters, with the north and west frequently buried under snow for three months of the year.

Brief history

In prehistoric times, what is now eastern Sichuan and Chongqing was divided into the eastern **Ba** and western **Shu kingdoms**, slave societies with highly developed metalworking skills and bizarre aesthetics. Agricultural innovations at the end of the third century BC opened up eastern Sichuan to intensive farming, and when the Qin armies stormed through, they found an economic base that financed their unification of China in 221 BC – as did Genghis Khan's forces almost 1500 years later. In between, the area became the Three Kingdoms state of **Shu** – a name by which Sichuan is still sometimes known – and later twice provided refuge for deposed emperors.

Otherwise too distant to play a central role in China's history, the region leapt to prominence in 1911, when government interference in local rail industries sparked the nationwide rebellions that toppled the Qing empire. The next four decades saw rival warlords fighting for control, though some stability came when the **Nationalist government** made Chongqing their capital after the Japanese invaded China in 1937. The province suffered badly during the Cultural Revolution – Jung Chang's autobiography, *Wild Swans*, gives a first-hand account of the vicious arbitrariness of the times in Sichuan. Typically, it was the first province to reject Maoist ideals, when the

Sichuan governor, Zhao Ziyang, allowed farmers to sell produce on the free market, spearheading the reforms of his fellow native Sichuanese, **Deng Xiaoping**. So effective were these reforms that by the 1990s Sichuan was competing vigorously with the east-coast economy, a situation for which Chongqing – the already heavily industrialized gateway river port between Sichuan and eastern China – claimed a large part of the credit; Chongqing's economic weight secured separate administrative status for the city and its surrounds. Meanwhile, development continues across the region, bringing all the problems of runaway growth: appalling industrial pollution, ecological devastation and an unbelievable scale of urban reconstruction.

Chengdu

成都, chéngdū

Set on the western side of the Red Basin, **CHENGDU** is a determinedly modern city, full of construction sites, high-rise department stores and residential blocks. But it's also a cheerful place: seasonal floral displays and ubiquitous **ginkgo trees** lend colour to its many excellent parks, and the population is also nicely laidback, enjoying its **teahouse culture** at every opportunity and unfazed by this being interpreted as laziness by other Chinese.

Chengdu was styled Brocade City in Han times, when the urban elite were buried in elegantly decorated tombs, and its silk travelled west along the caravan routes as far as imperial Rome. A refuge for the eighth-century Tang emperor Xuan Zong after his army mutinied over his infatuation with the beautiful concubine Yang Guifei, the city later became a **printing** centre, producing the world's first paper money. Sacked by the Mongols in 1271, Chengdu recovered soon enough to impress Marco Polo with its busy artisans and handsome bridges, since when it has survived similar cycles of war and restoration to become a major industrial, educational and business centre. There are some **downsides** – the city's traffic congestion and pollution can be atrocious – but on the whole it's not hard to spend a couple of days here touring historical monuments, spiking your tastebuds on one of China's most outstanding cuisines, and getting close-up views of locally bred **pandas**.

12

Renmin Park

人民公园, rénmín gōngyuán • Free except during floral exhibitions • metro to People's Park

Just west of central **Tianfu Square** (天府广场, tiānfǔ guǎngchǎng), a huge space with dancing fountains, a subterranean metro stop and a white statue of Mao Zedong, **Renmin Park** comprises a few acres of trees, paved paths, ponds and ornamental gardens with seasonally varying displays. Near the north entrance there's an ever-busy **teahouse** shaded by wisteria (marked by a large bronze teapot at the gate) and the tall **Monument to the Martyrs**, an obelisk commemorating the 1911 rail disputes that marked the beginning of the end for the Qing empire – hence the unusual motifs of trains and spanners. Otherwise, the park is just a good place to stroll: look for vendors with little burners and a slab of marble along the paths who execute skilful designs of Chinese zodiac animals in **toffee**; there's also a **canteen** next to the teahouse serving Sichuanese snacks.

> ## TOURIST BUS ROUTES
>
> Two useful **tourist buses** leave from outside the *Traffic* hotel on Linjiang Lu between about 8am and 6pm: **bus #901** (¥3) travels via Chunxi Lu, Wuhou Ci, Renmin Park, Qingyang Gong, Dufu Caotang and terminates at the Jinsha Museum; while **bus #902** (¥2) heads northeast to the Giant Panda Breeding Research Base.

CHENGDU

DRINKING, NIGHTLIFE & ENTERTAINMENT

Café Paname	10
Carol's By The River	4
Jah Bar	2
Jinjiang Theatre	3
Jin Li Theatre	5
Lan Kwai Fong	8
Little Bar	7
Little Bar II	9
Shamrock	1
Shufeng Yayun Theatre	1
Underground Bar	6

SHOPS

Camping stores	6
Carrefour	1
Sichuan Antique Store	3
Songxian Qiao curio market	2
Southwest Book Centre	5
Tianfu Bookstore	4

▲ Wuguiqiao Bus Station

Jin River

East Gate

Wangjiang Lou Park

Sichuan University

South Gate

North Gate

BAR STREET AREA

Global Doctor

US Consulate

Xinnanmen Bus Station

Tourist Bus Terminus

Rail Ticket Booth

Airport Bus Stop

Tianfu Square

PSB

China Eastern Airlines

Renmin Park

Rail Ticket Booth

Jinjiang Bridge

Wuhou Ci

Baihuatan Park

Du Fu's Thatched Cottage

Renmin Nan Lu

Renmin Nan Lu

12

► Shuangliu Airport & South Train Station

● EATING

Bookworm	8
Chen Mapo Doufu	2
Langqin Pozhang	6
Long Chaoshou	5
Manting Fang	9
Muslim Restaurant	4
Shizi Lou Hotpot	3
Tandoor	7
Vegetarian Lifestyle	1

■ ACCOMMODATION

Chengdu Airport Express	11
Chouxi Central	7
Dragon Town	4
Holiday Inn Express	5
Home Inn	6
Jinjiang	8
Loft	3
Mix	2
Sim's	1
Sofitel Wanda	9
Traffic	10
Traffic Inn	10

Kuan Xiangzi

宽巷子, kuān xiàngzi

After an uprising in 1789, a Manchu garrison was stationed in Chengdu and built themselves a miniature version of Beijing's *hutongs* in the area north of Renmin Park along **Kuan Xiangzi** and two adjacent lanes. The old streets and grey-brick houses here have been renovated and turned into an "antique" entertainment district, full of snack stalls, restaurants, and crowds orbiting between them – all especially busy at night, when competing coloured lights are added to the mix.

Wenshu Temple

文殊院, wénshū yuàn • east off Renmin Zhong Lu • Daily 8am–5pm • ¥5 • metro to Wenshu Monastery

Wenshu Temple, a bustling, atmospheric Chan (Zen) establishment dedicated to the Buddhist incarnation of Wisdom, sits 1.5km north of Tianfu Square. The elegant, single-storey halls are filled with motifs of **lions** – the symbol of Wenshu – such as the mural in the fourth hall, though this looks more like a shaggy, red-haired dog. If you bear east (right) immediately on entering the temple you'll encounter a narrow, eleven-storey **pagoda**. According to some, the gold-leafed object visible in the base includes the skull of **Xuanzang**, hero of *Journey to the West* (see p.830), though other temples in China also claim to own his mortal remains. At time of writing, the temple area was undergoing extensive renovation: hopefully, once completed, the former open-air **teahouse** area, along with a fine **vegetarian restaurant** – both previously good enough reasons on their own to visit Wenshu – will remain.

Wenshu Fang

文殊坊, wénshū fāng • metro to Wenshu Monastery

Just east of Wenshu Temple, the **Wenshu Fang** district is another reconstructed antique quarter of stone streets and brick and timber buildings, including a couple of temples. Though it's all very touristy, with shops selling fair-quality (if pricey) souvenirs, it's also quite atmospheric and there are some good places to **eat** local snacks – though check prices first.

Qingyang Gong

青羊宫, qīngyáng gōng • Daily 8am–5pm • ¥10 • tourist bus #901, or bus #58 from north side of Renmin Park • Chengdu University of TCM metro stop

Sited about 2km west of Renmin Park, **Qingyang Gong**, or the Green Goat Temple, is dedicated to Taoism's mythical proponent, Laozi. According to legend, Laozi lost interest in teaching and headed west into the sunset, first baffling posterity by saying that he could be found at the green goat market once his philosophy was understood

---

TEAHOUSES

Teahouses hold much the same place in Sichuanese life as a local bar or pub does in the West; some are formal establishments with illuminated signs; others are just a humble spread of bamboo or plastic chairs in the corner of a park, a temple or indeed any available public space. Whatever the establishment, just sit down to have a waiter come over and ask you what sort of tea you'd like – the standard jasmine-scented variety costs around ¥5 a cup, up to ¥40 or more for a really fine brew. Most are served in the three-piece Sichuanese *gaiwancha*, a squat, handleless cup with lid and saucer. **Refills** are unlimited – either the waiter will give you a top-up on passing your table, or you'll be left with a flask of boiling water. In a country where it's usually difficult to find somewhere to relax in public, teahouses are very welcome: idlers can spend the whole day chatting, playing mahjong, reading or just staring into space, without anyone interrupting – except cruising masseurs and ear-wax removers.

– hence the temple's unusual name. Straight ahead from the entrance, the Bagua Pavilion is an eight-sided hall with supporting posts wreathed in golden dragons, which houses a statue of Laozi astride his buffalo. His tale is again reflected at the main **Three Purities Hall**, where two **bronze goats** have been worn smooth by the caresses of luck-seekers. The bizarre right-hand "goat" is actually the simultaneous incarnation of all twelve zodiacal animals.

Sichuan Museum

四川博物馆, sìchuān bówùguǎn • Qingyang Shang Jie • Tues–Sun 9am–5pm • Free with ID • tourist bus #58 from north side of Renmin Park

The **Sichuan Museum**, about 700m west of Qingyang Gong, provides a thorough – if unimaginatively presented – look at the province's recorded history. Spread over three floors, there is Han-dynasty pottery, antique bronzeware, ethnic embroideries and artefacts (including a collection of what are politely termed "double-bodied" statuettes from Tibet), shadow puppets and even examples of Chengdu's once-famous silk brocade. It's easy to spend an hour here, but save time for the livelier **Songxian Qiao curio market** (送仙桥古玩艺术城, sòngxiānqiáo gǔwán yìshù chéng) across the road.

Du Fu's Thatched Cottage

杜甫草堂, dùfǔ cǎotáng • Daily 8am–6pm • ¥60 • tourist bus #901, or #58 from north side of Renmin Park

Vehicles jamming the car park at **Du Fu's Thatched Cottage**, 500m west of Sichuan Museum, attest to the respect the Chinese hold for the Tang-dynasty poet. Du Fu's works record the upheavals of his sad and difficult life with compassion and humour, and are considered, along with the more romantic imagery of his contemporary Li Bai (see p.729), to represent the archetype for Chinese poetry.

Three centuries after his death in 770, a pleasant park was founded at the site of Du Fu's cottage, and around 1800 it was expanded to its current layout of artfully arranged gardens, bamboo groves, pools, bridges and whitewashed halls. Besides antique and modern statues of Du Fu – depicted as sadly emaciated – there's a small museum illustrating his life.

Wuhou Ci

武侯祠, wǔhóu cí • Wuhouci Dajie • Daily 8am–6pm • ¥60 • tourist bus #901, or bus #1 from Renmin Nan Lu

Southwest of the centre, **Wuhou Ci** is a memorial hall nominally dedicated to **Zhuge Liang**, the strategist of Three Kingdoms fame. However, as his emperor **Liu Bei** is also buried here, the whole site is really a big shrine to the Three Kingdoms era (see p.393). To the left of the entrance, the **Three Kingdoms Culture Exhibition Hall** has contemporary sculptures, lacquered furniture, painted bricks showing daily life, and a few martial relics such as arrowheads and copper cavalry figurines. Elsewhere, halls and colonnaded galleries house brightly painted statues of the epic's heroes, notably a white-faced Liu Bei flanked by his oath-brothers Guan Yu and Zhang Fei; and Zhuge Liang (holding his feather fan) and his son and grandson. Over in the complex's northwestern corner, **Liu Bei's tomb** is a walled mound covered in trees and guarded by stone figures.

Jin Li

锦里, jǐn lǐ • bus #1 from Renmin Nan Lu runs past, as does tourist bus #901

Immediately east of Wuhou Ci, **Jin Li** is yet another of Chengdu's new "old" streets: this one is more of an alley, about 300m long, and jammed with wooden-fronted shops selling souvenirs and snacks. The street winds up at an open-air **theatre**, where performances of Sichuanese opera are held nightly (see p.725).

12

The Tibetan quarter

Bus #1 from Renmin Nan Lu, or tourist bus #901 to Wuhou Ci

The district south of Wuhou Ci forms Chengdu's **Tibetan quarter**, full of shops stocked to their roofs with heavy clothes, boots, amber and turquoise jewellery, knives and prayer wheels, conches and other temple accessories – not to mention heavy-duty blenders capable of whipping up a gallon of butter tea in one go. Move beyond the periphery, and this is not just for the tourists; customers are Tibetan monks, cowboys, and Khampa women with braided hair, looking decidedly tall and robust next to the local Chinese.

Yong Ling

永陵博物馆, yǒnglíng bówùguǎn • Yongling Lu • Daily 8.30am–5pm • ¥30 • bus #48 from Xinnanmen station

Northwest of the centre, **Yong Ling** is the tomb of **Wang Jian**, a member of the Imperial Guard who broke away from the disintegrating Tang dynasty in 907 AD and set himself up here as emperor of Shu. After Wang Jian's death in 918, his "fatuous and self-indulgent son" Wang Yan was unable to hold onto the kingdom, which the Tang empire reclaimed in 925. Tomb robbers stripped the site centuries before it was excavated during the 1940s, but the brick-lined chambers retain Wang Jian's stone **sarcophagus platform**, richly carved with musicians and twelve very Central Asian-looking bodyguards.

Jinsha Museum

金沙遗址博物馆, jīnshā yízhǐ bówùguǎn • Daily 8am–6pm • ¥80 • terminus of the #901 tourist bus route • bus #5 from Renmin Park

Around 5km west from the centre, the **Jinsha Museum** sits over the remains of one of western China's major prehistoric settlements, and the fascinating collection, housed in two halls set among gardens, leaves plenty of questions unanswered. The Chengdu region was already settled as early as 2700 BC, though its first cultural flowering came a thousand years later at Sanxingdui (see p.726), which itself went into a decline as the settlement at Jinsha blossomed from 1200 to 600 BC.

The exhibition

Covering five square kilometres in total, Jinsha has yielded house remains, tools and artefacts of all descriptions, thousands of graves, and scores of sacrificial pits filled with ornaments and animal bones, all dating back to the Shang dynasty. The **first hall** is built right over these pits, which were dug a couple of metres deep into the grey soil in a regular grid pattern; the glass-sided building is well lit, and wooden boardwalks allow a close look. The **second hall** houses dioramas of the site, plus the pick of the finds, including some beautifully coloured, transluscent jades, small statues of tigers and kneeling slaves with bound hands, and a thin, serrated gold disc interpreted as depicting *rishen*, the Sun God.

The Giant Panda Breeding Research Base

大熊猫繁育研究基地, dàxióngmāo fányù yánjiū jīdì • Daily 8am–6pm • ¥58 • hostel minibus tours ¥98 • tourist bus #902 can take 2hr through Chengdu's traffic; it's quicker to ride the metro to North Railway Station and then catch a cab (¥35; 15min)

Some 8km northeast of central Chengdu, the excellent **Giant Panda Breeding Research Base** offers close-up views of both giant and arboreal red pandas. Perhaps uniquely for China, this zoo is a genuinely pleasant place to visit, well laid out with a decent amount of information in English, and even spacious enclosures for the animals, who are fed truckloads of fresh bamboo by concerned staff. If you feel flush, several hostels and travel agencies offer the chance to be a "volunteer keeper" for the day (¥700) – basically a worthy-sounding way of paying to hand-feed a few of the inhabitants. Try to get here early, as the pandas slump into a stupor around 10am after munching their way through piles of bamboo.

PANDAS

Two animals share the name panda: the **giant panda**, black-eyed symbol of endangered species worldwide; and the unrelated, raccoon-like **red panda**, to which the Nepalese name "panda" was originally applied in the West. The Chinese call the giant panda *da xiongmao*, meaning "big bear-cat".

News of giant pandas first reached Europe in the nineteenth century through the French zoologist and traveller **Père Armand David**, who came across a skin in China in 1869. They are decidedly odd creatures, bearlike, endowed with a carnivore's teeth and a digestive tract poorly adapted to their largely vegetarian diet. Though once widespread in southwestern China, they've probably never been very common, and today their endangered status is a result of human encroachment combined with the vagaries of their preferred food – **fountain bamboo** – which periodically flowers and dies off over huge areas, leaving the animals to make do with lesser shrubs and carrion, or starve. Half of Sichuan's panda habitat was lost to logging between 1974 and 1989, which, coupled with the results of a bamboo flowering during the 1980s, reduced the total wild population to just over a thousand animals, scattered through **reserves** in Sichuan, Yunnan and Guizhou.

ARRIVAL AND DEPARTURE   CHENGDU

Most accommodation can make train and plane bookings, though expect to pay a ¥40 booking fee per person for the former.

BY PLANE

China Eastern and Shanghai Airlines have a joint office at 6 Xiyu Jie (☏028 61102018, ⊛ishanghang.com), though other agents around town should be able to book flights at no mark-up.

Shuangliu airport (双流机场, shuāngliú jīchǎng) is 16km southwest of town, connected by several airport buses (7am–8pm; approximately every 30min; ¥10), with #300 and #303 running to the centre of town. Heading back to the airport, #300 can be picked up along Renmin Nan Lu, just south of Tianfu Square, while the #303 departs every 20min from the Civil Aviation Office on Renmin Nan Lu, just north of the junction with Binjiang Lu. A taxi either way would cost around ¥50. A new airport is under construction some 60km outside Chengdu; 2017 seems a likely completion date.

Destinations Beijing (30 daily; 2hr 30min); Changsha (6 daily; 1hr 45min); Guangzhou (20 daily; 2hr 15min); Guilin (3 daily; 1hr 20min); Guiyang (8 daily; 1hr); Hong Kong (5 daily; 2hr 30min); Jiuzhaigou (17 daily; 50min); Kangding (daily; 55min); Kunming (14 daily; 90min); Lanzhou (3 daily; 1hr 20min); Lhasa (15 daily; 2hr); Shanghai (20 daily; 2hr 30min); Shenzhen (19 daily; 2hr); Ürümqi (11 daily; 3hr 30min); Wuhan (7 daily; 1hr 30min).

BY TRAIN

Chengdu is halfway along the Xi'an–Kunming rail line, and also connected to routes into Guizhou and central China through easterly Chongqing. You can reach Chongqing itself in just two hours aboard a D-class train, via the high-speed rail link. It's easiest to buy train tickets at Chengbei bus station (ticket window #9) or from various booths

around town, which open 8am–8pm and charge a ¥5 fee per ticket: there's one at the north gate of Renmin Park; one halfway down Renmin Nan Lu; and another on Renmin Zhong Lu near the Wenshu Yuan. Bus #16 and the metro run the length of Renmin Lu between the two stations.

North train station (成都火车站, chéngdū huǒchēzhàn). Chengdu's main station is 4km north of the city centre. A city bus terminus and metro station is just west off the station square, from where you should be able to find transport to within striking distance of your accommodation.

South train station (火车南站, huǒchē nánzhàn). This small station, 4km south of the centre, services all stops along the Chengdu–Kunming line, including Xichang and Panzhihua.

Destinations Beijing (4 daily; 27–30hr); Chongqing (23 daily; 2–10hr); Dujiangyan (13 daily; 30min); Emei (8 daily; 2–6hr); Guangyuan (23 daily; 4–6hr); Guangzhou (4 daily; 30–40hr); Guiyang (7 daily; 12–21hr); Jiangyou (20 daily; 2hr 30min); Kunming (6 daily; 18–23hr); Lhasa (1 daily; 44hr); Panzhihua (8 daily; 13hr); Qingcheng Shan (12 daily; 50min); Shanghai (6 daily; 20–38hr); Wuhan (30 daily; 16–23hr); Xi'an (10 daily; 12–18hr); Xichang (11 daily; 10hr).

BY BUS

Chengdu's many long-distance bus stations are mostly scattered around the city perimeter.

Beimen (北门汽车站, běimén qìchēzhàn) is 1km northeast of the centre on the first ring road, near the junction with Jeifang Lu. It can be reached via metro line #1 and bus #802 from the north train station. Departures to Langzhong, Zigong and northeastern Sichuan.

12

TO TIBET

While road routes **into Tibet** remain off-limits to foreigners at time of writing, rail and air links remain open and regular, and you'll find plenty of agencies here organizing tours. Flights to Lhasa cost about ¥1600; train tickets are ¥700 hard sleeper, or ¥1000 soft sleeper, and can be hard to get hold of, so allow a few days. Before buying any tickets, you'll have to show a **permit for Tibet** (an extra ¥400). Most likely you'll have to secure the permit through a travel agent as, at the time of writing, it was not possible to visit Tibet independently; you had to be part of an organized tour – see the box on p.864.

Chadianzi (茶店子客运站, chádiànzi kèyùn zhàn) 8km northwest of the city centre on the third ring road; bus #82 goes from here to Wuhouci Dajie and Binjiang Lu (opposite the *Traffic* hotel). Chadianzi is the main station for Western Sichuan, including Xiaojin, Songpan, Danba, Kangding, Jiuzhaigou and Zöige; most services depart first thing in the morning, when you might need a taxi to get here in time (¥35).

Wuguiqiao (五桂桥中心站, wǔguìqiáo zhōngxīnzhàn), 3km east of the city centre, reachable on bus #81 from People's Park. Transport east, including to Chongqing, Yibin, Zigong and Dazu.

Xinnanmen (新南门汽车站, xīnnánmén qìchēzhàn), centrally located next to the *Traffic* hotel and most easily reached from the *Jinjiang Hotel* metro stop.

Southern Sichuan (Emei Shan and Leshan), as well as some western destinations – including Jiuzhaigou, Kangding and Ganzi.

Zhaojue Temple Station (照觉寺汽车站, zhàojuésì qìchēzhàn) 5km northeast of the centre; bus #64 from the east side of Tianfu Square. Services to Jiangyou, Jianmen Guan and Guangyuan in northeastern Sichuan.

Destinations Chongqing (6hr); Daocheng (2 days); Dazu (4hr); Dujiangyan (2hr); Emei Shan (2hr 30min); Ganzi (2 days); Guanghan (1hr); Guangyuan (4hr); Huanglongxi (1hr); Jiangyou (2hr); Jiuzhaigou (10–12hr); Kangding (8hr); Langzhong (4hr 30min); Leshan (2hr 30min); Songpan (8hr); Xichang (8hr); Yibin (8hr); Ya'an (2hr); Zigong (6hr); Zöigê (14hr).

GETTING AROUND

Chengdu's roads are approaching gridlock, so give yourself enough time to get around.

By bus Buses run from about 6am until after dark, and charge ¥2; there are also some useful tourist buses linking major sights, leaving from outside *Traffic* hotel (see p.715).

By metro Chengdu's first metro line opened in 2010, running north–south through the city, with line #2 running northwest–southeast following in 2012. Lines #3 (running northeast–southwest) and #4 (east–west) are due to open by the end of 2015. Useful stops include the train stations, *Jianjiang Hotel*, Tianfu Square and Chunxi Lu. Trains run 7am–11.30pm and cost ¥2–4.

By taxi Cabs are everywhere – though it can be hard to find a free one – and cost ¥8 to hire.

By bike Motorbikes are illegal in the downtown area, so bicycles (and electric mopeds) remain popular, with cycle lanes and guarded parking throughout the city – see p.39 for details on rentals. All hostels rent bikes for around ¥30/day, plus a ¥500 deposit.

INFORMATION

Guides The best independent guide in Chengdu is Tray Lee (℡01390 8035353, ✉lee@rt98.com – he's not good at answering emails, though), who can often be found in Renmin Park. He speaks excellent English and has been guiding foreigners around the province for twenty years. Another good option, especially for wildlife and ethnic adventure tours of Sichuan, Tibet and Qinghai, is Pepper Mountain (✆peppermountains.com), run by a long-time resident Westerner.

Information For local news, events and the latest bars and restaurants, check expat-run online magazine Go Chengdoo (✆gochengdoo.com) or its rival More Chengdu (✆morechengdu.com). The *Bookworm* (see p.724) is another good source of local information.

Travel agents and tours Hostels and other accommodation all offer part- and multi-day tour packages of the city and surrounds – you don't have to be staying to make bookings. Tours include two-hour Sichuan opera trips (¥120); three hours at Chengdu's Giant Panda Breeding Research Base (¥98 including entry); a day-trip to Qingcheng Shan (¥120); four days at Jiuzhaigou and Huanglong (around ¥850). Hostels also arrange five-seater minibuses with a driver for the day to tour local sights (plus Leshan or Emei Shan) at ¥300–700 depending on distance. Most can also book you on Yangzi ferry trips through the Three Gorges (see p.753). Tibet packages should come in around ¥3000 for flights, or ¥1800 for the train.

ACCOMMODATION

Chengdu has a great number of places to stay, with a choice for every budget; the following are all central. Everywhere can make transport bookings, and hostels also offer internet access, bike rental, travellers' noticeboards and good-value tours (see opposite).

HOSTELS

Dragon Town 龙城宽巷子青年旅馆, lóngchéng kuānxiàngzǐ qīngnián lǚguǎn. 26 Kuan Xiangzi ⓣ0288 6648408, ⓦdragontown.com.cn. Set in one of Chengdu's old-style streets and either quaint or a bit tacky, depending on your point of view. *Dragon Town* mostly seems to act as overflow for when the *Loft*, run by the same people, is full, but is comfortable enough in its own right. Dorms **¥60**, rooms **¥240**

★ **Loft** 四号虎工厂青年旅馆, sìhào hǔgōngchǎng qīngnián lǚguǎn. 4 Xiaotong Xiang, Zhong Tongren Lu ⓣ0288 6265770, ⓦwww.lofthostel.com. A very sharp operation in slickly converted 1980s warehouse, with a smart café and great second-floor venue offering pool table, video lounge and bar. Always busy so you may need to book ahead, even if rooms are a little expensive for what you get. Dorms **¥60**, rooms **¥220**

Mix 驴友记国际青年旅舍, lǘyǒujì guójì qīngnián lǚshě. 23 Xinghui Xi Lu ⓣ0288 3222271, ⓦmixhostel.com. Nasty tiled building on the outside but cosy and homely place once you're through the door. Close to the metro and in a fairly quiet residential district. Shared bathrooms only, hence the low price. Dorms **¥45**, rooms **¥100**

★ **Sim's** 观华青年旅舍, guānhuá qīngnián lǚshè. North Section 4, 211 Yihuan Lu ⓣ0288 3355322, ⓦchengduhostels.com. A very friendly, roomy place though the location is disappointing, on a drab, busy stretch of the ring road. But bus connections aren't bad and, although reception staff can be a bit caught up in their internetting, the travel information and trips on offer are second to none. Dorm beds **¥55**, rooms **¥100**

Traffic Inn 交通饭店, jiāotōng fàndiàn. Behind the Traffic hotel at 6 Linjiang Lu, near Xinnanmen bus station ⓣ0288 5450470, ⓦtrafficinnhostel.com. Simple, clean doubles and twins with or without bathroom, plus dorms (in the main hotel building). The *Highfly Café* here serves tasty Western and Chinese staples. Dorms **¥50**, rooms **¥150**

HOTELS

Chengdu Airport Express 成都空港商务酒店, chéngdū kōnggǎng shāngwù jiǔdiàn. ⓣ0288 5208899, ⓦwww.cdairport.com. Just a few hundred metres from the main terminal, call the hotel and they will send a free shuttle bus to pick you up. Not only is this place hugely convenient, its also smart, clean and excellent value. **¥300**

Chouxi Central 春熙里酒店, chūnxīlǐ jiǔdiàn. 18 Liansheng Xiang ⓣ0288 6663666. Difficult to find, but head through the out-of-place ceremonial archway on the walkway between Chunxi Lu and Hongxing Lu and reception is in the entrance hall of the residential block. Very central, and rooms with and without private bathrooms are reasonable for those on a budget. **¥130**

Holiday inn Express 鼓楼快捷假日酒店, gǔlóu kuàijié jiàrì jiǔdiàn. 72 Daqiang Xi Jie ⓣ0288 6785666, ⓦhiexpress.com.cn. Comfortable, modern and efficient – what you'd expect from this budget international chain. Newly refurbished rooms offer excellent value, but prices rise considerably if there's a conference in town. **¥470**

Home Inn 如家酒店, rújiā jiǔdiàn. 9 Shaocheng Lu ⓣ0288 6253111. Across from the north entrance to Renmin Park, this branch offers the dependable comforts associated with this chain, plus a decent canteen on the ground floor – prices are a little on the high side and if you're staying more than three nights it's worth getting a membership card which gives you a small discount. **¥250**

★ **Jinjiang** 锦江宾馆, jǐnjiāng bīnguǎn. 80 Renmin Nan Lu ⓣ0288 5506666, ⓦjjhotel.com. Chengdu's original tourist hotel, now revamped with some panache to make the international grade and featuring smart rooms, bilingual staff, conference and business facilities, and a host of restaurants. At weekends, rooms in the new building can be got at a slight discount online. **¥1600**

Sofitel Wanda 索菲特万达大饭店, suǒfēitè wàndá dàfàndiàn. 15 Binjiang Zhong Lu ⓣ0286 6669999, ⓦsofitel.com. Hard not to be impressed by the acres of marble in the lobby, even if some of the palms are looking a bit past their best. Restaurants, bars and a swimming pool are part of the package. **¥978**

Traffic 交通饭店, jiāotōng fàndiàn. 77 Linjiang Lu, near Xinnanmen bus station ⓣ0288 5451017. Well-maintained stand-by, though rooms, with TV and shared or private bathroom, are looking increasingly dated. The attached *Traffic Inn* (see above) is their backpackers' wing. **¥200**

EATING

The best places to try local snacks are the canteen in Renmin Park and Jin Li "old" street. Inexpensive hotpot places are legion, and your accommodation can point you to the nearest. Sichuanese food tastes especially good with beer – try locally brewed "Snow".

12

★ **Bookworm** 老书虫, lǎo shūchóng. 2–7 Yujie Dong Lu, off Renmin Nan Lu ☎0288 5520177, ⓦchengdubookworm.com. Comfy expat haunt serving coffee, pizzas, sandwiches, burgers, pasta and desserts, with well-stocked library and bar, which also hosts regular events. Mains ¥30–120. Daily 9am–1am.

★ **Chen Mapo Doufu** 陈麻婆豆腐, chén mápó dòufu. 197 Xi Yulong Jie ☎0288 6743889. Founded in 1862, this is the home of Grandma Chen's bean curd, where ¥30 buys a large bowl of tofu glowing with minced meat, chilli oil and *huajiao* sauce. They also do a good range of Sichuanese favourites. Daily 11am–3pm and 5–10pm.

Langqin Pozhang 朗钦颇丈, lǎngqīn pōzhàng. Floor 3, 246 Wuhouci Da Jie, ☎0288 5561027. Directly across from *Holly's Hostel*, this is the pick of several Tibetan eateries in the area. Though lacking the spit-and-sawdust atmosphere of some of its neighbours, the food is top notch, with spicy potato and yoghurt balls a particular treat. Around ¥40/person. Daily 10am–10pm.

Long Chaoshou 龙抄手饭店, lóng chāoshǒu fàndiàn. At the crossroads of pedestrian alleys, just east of Chunxi Lu. A big, busy dumpling house renowned for its *chaoshou*, Sichuanese *wuntun*, and other local snacks, a limited English menu gives just a fraction of what is on offer. Eat in the downstairs canteen; the upper floors have the same food and terrible table service at ten times the price. Around ¥20/person. Daily 9am–9pm.

★ **Manting Fang** 满庭芳, mǎntíng fāng. Erhuan Lu, at Yulin Lu ☎0288 5193111. Classic Sichuanese dishes served in smart surroundings; try the mouthwatering chicken, rice-coated spare ribs, dry-fried beans, tiger-skin chillies and *mapo tofu*. Fine flavours prove that Sichuanese cuisine can be about more than just chillies and oil. Count on ¥80/person in a group. Daily 11am–10pm.

Muslim Restaurant 皇城寺大饭店, huángchéngsì dà fàndiàn. At the mosque on Xitu Jie. Catering to Chengdu's large Muslim population, this serves everything from *lamian* soup to meat-and-potato stew and upmarket Sichuanese dishes. Uyghurs stand outside grilling kebabs and bread, if you fancy a take-away. ¥20/person. Daily 8.30am–9.30pm.

Shizi Lou Hotpot 狮子楼火锅琴台店, shīzilóu huǒguō qíntái diàn. 101 Qintai Lu, a "Chinatown" street between Renmin Park and Qingyang Gong ☎028 86158988. Eat hotpot surrounded by smart gold-and-red glitz, served by simpering waitstaff. Choose white stock, red stock or a divided pot with both, then pay per plate of morsels to cook: ¥15–30 for straightforward veg and meat, up to several hundred yuan for rare fungi and game. Figure on around ¥70–¥100/person. Daily 11am–10pm.

Tandoor 天都里印度餐厅, tiāndūlǐ yìndù cāntīng. 34 Renmin Nan Lu, behind Sunjoy Inn ☎0288 5551958, ⓦtandoorchina.cn. Indian dining for the well-heeled; comparatively expensive in the evening, but at lunch there are set-meal bargains available. All the standards and a decent spread of vegetarian options. ¥70/person. Daily 11am–10pm.

Vegetarian Lifestyle 枣子树铂金店, zǎozìshù bójīn diàn. 4F Bojincheng Building, 27 Qinglong Jie, just west of the main Bank of China ☎0288 6282848. Local branch of *Jujube Tree* Shanghai chain, serving excellent, imaginative vegetarian Chinese dishes in a minimalist-smart setting at about ¥45/person. Daily 11am–10pm.

DRINKING, NIGHTLIFE AND ENTERTAINMENT

Chengdu's nightlife venues open and close rapidly, so check the latest at ⓦgochengdoo.com or ⓦmorechengdu.com. Don't overlook the *Bookworm's* (see above) Friday-night jazz sessions either. The liveliest bar and club district centres around the Jiuyan bridge, just north of the Sichuan University Campus; for somewhere a bit more polished, the Lan Kwai Fong development across the river behind the *Shangrila* hotel is packed full of restaurants, bars and clubs.

Café Paname 巴黎咖啡, bālí kāfēi. 143 Kehua Bei Lu, second floor balcony of a restaurant complex ☎1398 2133619, ⓦcafepaname.com. A popular expat watering hole with half-litres of beer for ¥20, a pool table, DJs on Friday and ever-popular fussball. Daily 5pm–2am.

Carol's By The River 卡罗西餐吧, kǎluó xīcānbā. Hongmen Jie-Linjiang Xi Lu ☎0288 5585529. Open-fronted sports bar with a pool table, draught beer from ¥20 and regular live music throughout the week. Daily 3pm–1am.

Jah Bar 家吧, jiābā. Next door to Carol's, Hongmen Jie/Linjiang Xi Lu ☎1368 9051773. Very relaxed reggae-centric spot with couches by the river. If you're lucky you may catch one of their irregular live music events. Daily 5pm–late.

Lan Kwai Fong 兰桂坊, lánguìfáng. Shuijin Jie ⓦlkfchengdu.com. The first Mainland development from the operators of Hong Kong's renowned entertainment district to officially carry the LKF moniker, this 18-building complex houses a host of restaurants, bars and the city's most up-scale nightclubs, including *Mango* and the *D+ Lounge*. Daily 10am–2am.

Little Bar 小酒吧玉林店, xiǎojiǔbā yùlín diàn. 55 Yulin Xi Lu, ☎0288 5568552. Small, vaguely bohemian place with a good range of inexpensive beers and spirits – previously famed for live music which has now moved to it's new sister venue (see below). Somewhere to chill out or hold a conversation rather than party. Daily 6pm–2am.

Little Bar II 小酒吧芳沁街店, xiǎojiǔbā fāngqìnjiē. 87 Fangqin Lu, ☎0288 5158790. Bigger brother to the

SICHUAN OPERA

Sichuan opera – **chuanxi** – is a rustic variant on Beijing's, based on everyday events and local legends. Most pieces are performed in Sichuanese, a rhythmic dialect well suited to theatre, which allows for humour and clever wordplay to shine through. As well as the usual bright costumes, stylized action and glass-cracking vocals, *chuanxi* has two specialities: **fire-breathing** and **rapid face-changing**, where the performers – apparently simply by turning around or waving their arms across their faces – completely change their make-up.

Today, *chuanxi* has gone into a decline as a form of popular entertainment, though there are several places around town to catch tourist-oriented **variety shows** featuring short opera scenes, fire-breathing and face-changing, comedy skits, puppetry, shadow-lantern play and storytelling. These are pretty enjoyable and you might even catch occasional full-length operas. Venues include **Shufeng Yayun** (蜀风雅韵, shǔfēng yǎyùn) in the Cultural Park (enter off Qintai Lu); the Ming-style open-air stage at the end of **Jin Li**, near Wuhou Ci; and the downtown **Jinjiang Theatre** (锦江川戏馆, jǐnjiāng chuānxìguǎn) in a lane north of Shangdong Jie. Seats cost ¥120–220, depending on the venue and row.

original, this is Chengdu's premier rock venue with live bands every Fri and Sat evening, when there is a ¥30–100 cover charge. Be warned: punk is alive and well, and living in Chengdu. Daily 6pm–2am.

Shamrock 三叶草西餐酒吧, sānyècǎo xīcān jiǔbā. 15, Section 4, Renmin Nan Lu ☎ 0288 5236158, ⓦ shamrockinchengdu.com. This place has been going forever but is trying to move with the times, now offering swing and salsa dancing during the week, and the

tried-and-tested DJ and drinks offer combo on Fridays and Sat. Daily 10am–late.

Underground Bar 隧道酒吧, suìdào jiǔbā. 6 Taipingnanxi Jie ☎ 0288 5294142, ⓦ underground chengdu.com. Hidden down a tunnel, behind a cigar shop, this British pub, owned and run by Mancunian landlord Gary, is an oasis of calm amid the raucous Jiuyan bridge bar district. More than 50 beers on offer and decent Western bar food. Daily 5pm–2.30am.

SHOPPING

Bookshops The Southwest Book Centre opposite the south end of Chunxi Lu, and the Tianfu Bookstore at the southwest corner of Tianfu Square, stock maps, guidebooks in Chinese, and English-language novels.

Camping supplies If you're heading to Tibet, western Sichuan or elsewhere in China's wilds, try the clutch of outdoor stores selling good-quality gear at competitive prices on Yihuan Lu, just west of the intersection with Renmin Nan Lu.

Clothing For clothing, head to Chunxi Lu, where all the

Chinese designer brands (and a few Western ones) have stores.

Souvenirs The Songxian Qiao curio market near Sichuan Museum is good for "Maomorabilia", wooden screens and all sorts of old-looking knick-knacks. For genuine antique snuff bottles, jewellery, birdcages and porcelain, try the Sichuan Antique Store, corner of Dongchenggen Lu and Renmin Xi Lu.

Supermarkets There are around half-a-dozen branches of Carrefour dotted around central Chengdu, including a large store at the junction of Dongcheng Lu and Qinglong Jie.

DIRECTORY

Banks and exchange The main Bank of China (Mon–Fri 8.30am–5.30pm) is up on Renmin Zhong Lu. Many other branches and banks around town have ATMs accepting foreign cards.

Consulates France, 30F, Times Plaza, 2 Zongfu Lu, ☎ 0286 6666060; Germany, 25F, Western tower, 19 Renmin Nan Lu, Section 4, ☎ 0288 5280800; US, 4 Lingshiguan Lu, Renmin Nan Lu, ☎ 0288 5583992, ⓦ chengdu.usembassy-china.org.cn.

Hospitals and medical centres For English-speaking doctors and international standard medical treatment, try Parkway Health, Chengdu No.1 People's Hospital, 18 Wanxiang Bei Lu, Fanxiang Dadao, out of town in the South High Tech Zone (☎ 0288 5317899 ⓦ www.parkwayhealth

.cn); or Global Doctors, 62 Kehua Beilu, 2F Lippo Tower (☎ 1398 2256966, ⓦ www.globaldoctor.com.au).

Internet Hostels and the motels all have internet access; there's also a huge net bar above Xinnanmen bus station – enter from the river side, not the station.

Left luggage Accommodation will look after excess gear while you're off in the wilds for around ¥3/item/day.

Mail Chengdu's main post office (8am–6pm) is in a 1920s grey brick building on the corner of Shuwa Bei Yi Jie and Xinglong Jie, with an Express Mail centre opposite.

PSB The branch dealing with visa extensions and foreigners' problems is bang in the middle of town in Tianfu Square, directly behind the Mao statue; 3F, 2 Renmin Xi Lu, ☎ 028 86407067 (Mon–Fri 9am–noon & 1–5pm).

Around Chengdu

Chengdu's surrounding attractions all make worthy day-trips from the capital, and most can be used as first stops on longer routes. Just to the northeast, the **Sanxingdui Museum** is stuffed with prehistoric bronzes, while unpretentious Qing architecture graces the picturesque market town of **Huanglongxi** southwest of Chengdu. Northwest, **Dujiangyan** sports a still-functional two-thousand-year-old irrigation scheme surrounded by wooded parkland, and nearby forested **Qingcheng Shan** is peppered with Taoist shrines.

Sanxingdui Museum

三星堆博物馆, sānxīngduī bówùguǎn • at Guanghan town (广汉, guǎnghàn) • Daily 8.30am–5pm • ¥80 • city bus #1 or #45 from Renmin Nan Lu to Chengdu's Zhaojue Temple bus station, then bus to Guanghan, from where local bus #6 (¥1) runs 8km out to the museum

In 1986, an archeological team, investigating what appeared to be a Shang-dynasty town 25km northeast of Chengdu, made an extraordinary discovery: a set of rectangular **sacrificial pits** containing a colossal trove of jade, ivory, gold and **bronze** artefacts, all of which had been deliberately broken up before burial. Subsequent excavation revealed a settlement that from 2700 BC is believed to have been a major centre for the shadowy Ba-Shu culture, until it was upstaged by Jinsha (see p.720) and abandoned around 800 BC.

All this is covered at the excellent **Sanxingdui Museum**, with two main halls and English captions. The thousands of artefacts on display are both startling and nightmarish, the products of a very alien view of the world: a 2m-high bronze figure with a hook nose and oversized, grasping hands standing atop four elephants; metre-wide masks with obscene grins and eyes popping out on stalks; a 4m-high "spirit tree" entwined by a dragon with knives and human hands instead of limbs; and finely detailed bronzes, jade tools and pottery pieces.

Huanglongxi

黄龙溪古城, huánglóngxī gǔchéng • buses (¥8) from Xinnanmen station half-hourly 6.30am–6pm

HUANGLONGXI, 40km south of Chengdu, is a riverside village with a half-dozen **Qing-dynasty streets**, all narrow, flagstoned and sided in rickety wooden shops. Tourism aside – visitor numbers are frankly overwhelming at weekends or during holidays – it's a pretty place to wander around for an hour and then have lunch or a cup of tea at one of the many riverside restaurants; it's also popular with old ladies coming to pray for grandchildren to Guanyin, to whom all the village's **temples** are dedicated.

From the old village gate, take the left-hand lane, which is almost narrow enough to touch either side as you walk down the middle. You soon reach the 500m-long main street; turn left for two tiny **nunneries** (one on the left, the other at the end of the street beside a beribboned banyan tree), both containing brightly painted statues of Guanyin, Puxian and Wenshu. At the opposite end of town, larger **Gulong Temple** (古龙寺, gǔlóng sì; ¥5) is in a wobbly state of repair: one of the halls features a dog-headed guillotine for executing criminals, while another contains an unusually three-dimensional, fifty-armed Guanyin statue.

Dujiangyan

都江堰, dūjiāngyàn • high-speed train from Chengdu's North train station (30min; ¥15) or Qingcheng Shan, then bus #4 to the Lidui park gate (20min; ¥2)

DUJIANGYAN is a large town 60km northwest of Chengdu, where in 256 BC the provincial governor, **Li Bing**, set up the **Dujiangyan Irrigation Scheme** to harness the notoriously capricious Min River. Li used a central dam and artificial islands to split the Min into an inner flow for irrigation and an outer channel for flood control, and

> ## DUJIANGYAN AND QINGCHEN SHAN BY TRAIN
>
> **High-speed trains** to Dujiangyan and Qingcheng Shan depart Chengdu's North train station (13 daily; 7.15am–8.15pm); if you start out early enough, the two can be combined in a single day-trip. The last train back to Chengdu departs Dujiangyan at 9.15pm.

the scheme has been maintained ever since, the present system of dams, reservoirs and pumping stations irrigating 32,000 square kilometres – even though the project's flood-control aspects became redundant when the **Zipingpu Dam**, 9km upstream, began operation in 2006.

Lidui Park

离堆公园, líduī gōngyuán • Daily 8am–6pm • ¥90

The scheme's **entrance** is at **Lidui Park**, which encloses the original heart of the project. An ancient, 3m-high stone statue of Li Bing graces **Fulong Guan** (伏龙观, fúlóng guān), a 1600-year-old temple flanked with vertical nanmu trees, which sits right at the tip of the first channel. From here the path crosses to the midstream artificial islands, before arriving at the **Anlan Suspension Bridge**, which spans the width of the river. Crossing to the east side brings you to steps ascending to **Erwang Miao** (二王庙, èrwáng miào), an ornate Taoist hall dedicated to Li Bing and his son, where temple volunteers provide lunch (¥7.5). Look out here for a Qing-era mural showing a bird's-eye view of the whole scheme. Heading back in a loop, follow signs for the wooded **Songmao Road**, a fragment of the ancient route from Dujiangyan to Songpan, which passes through two stone gateways and the old **Town God's Temple** at the park exit on Xingfu Lu, about 500m east of the main entrance.

Qingcheng Shan

青城山, qīngchéng shān • ¥90 • high-speed train from Chengdu's North train station (50min; ¥20) or Dujiangyan • bus from Lidui Park in Dujiangyan

Covered in verdant forest and amazingly fresh after Chengdu's smog, **Qingcheng Shan** is a smaller, easier version of Emei Shan. The mountain's many **Taoist shrines** are all set in courtyards with open-fronted halls, at the back of which are ornate, glassed-in cases containing painted statues of saints. Most have restaurants, and though the food isn't great, the mountain's tea is worth trying.

The return walk from Qingcheng Shan's main gates to the 1200m summit takes around three hours, following stone steps through the forest; there's also a **cable car** (¥50 return). Pick of the shrines are **Ci Hang Dian**, dedicated to Ci Hang, the Taoist version of Guanyin; **Tianshi Dong**, a complex surrounding a small cave where the Taoist hermit Zhang Ling lived before his death at the age of 122; and **Shangqing Gong** (上清宫, shàngqīng gōng), whose attractions include gateway calligraphy by the Guomindang leader Chiang Kai-shek. At the top is a six-storey **tower** containing a 12m-high golden statue of Laozi and his buffalo, with views from the balconies of back-sloping ridges and lower temples poking out of the forest.

Northeastern Sichuan

The fertile valleys of **northeastern Sichuan** wind through hilly, heavily farmed countryside, terminating around 400km from Chengdu at severe escarpments marking the border with Shaanxi. Originally, the sole way through these ranges was provided by **Shudao**, the "Road to Sichuan" linking Chengdu with the former imperial capital Xi'an, along which culture and personalities flowed over the centuries. The region contains the hometowns of the great poet **Li Bai** and the country's only empress; it was the escape route down which the Tang emperor Xuan Zong fled the An Lushan rebellion of 756 AD (see p.915); while

Shudao itself breaks out of the region through a sheer cleft in the ranges known as **Jianmenguan**, the Sword Pass. Shudao can also serve as the first stage in a journey to Jiuzhaigou (see p.758); given the seemingly permanent roadworks under way on the Chengdu–Songpan highway (see p.756), it's sometimes the only viable route.

Well east from Shudao, a large grid of old streets at the pleasant riverside town of **Langzhong** is one of the few places in Sichuan where you can still see substantial areas of archaic architecture – a welcome refuge from the country's frenzied demolition of its past.

Jiangyou

江油, jiāngyóu

JIANGYOU is a pleasantly leafy town on the north bank of the Fu River some 170km from Chengdu, within sight of the steep line of hills slanting northeast towards the Shaanxi border. It's famed as the hometown of the Tang poet Li Bai, but what really justifies a visit is a side trip to quirky **Doutuan Shan**, whose monks perform some bizarre acrobatic stunts. Largely destroyed in the terrible 2008 earthquake, Doutuan's temples have now been restored to their former glory.

Li Bai's Former Home

李白故居, lǐbái gùjū • 8am–5pm • ¥50 • bus #9 from a depot on Taiping Lu, near Jiangyou's bus station

Li Bai was born in a period when China's arts, stimulated by unparalleled contact with the outside world, reached their height. He became China's most highly regarded romantic poet, his works masterpieces of Taoist, dream-like imagery, often clearly influenced by his notorious **drunkenness** – he drowned in the Yangzi in 762 AD, allegedly while trying to grasp the moon's reflection in the water. **Li Bai's Former Home** sits on a hill above **Qinglian** township (青莲, qīnglián), some 10km south of Jiangyou; rebuilt many times, the quiet Ming-era halls and courtyards are filled with statues and paintings illustrating his life, and a shrine to his ancestor, the Han-dynasty general Li Xin.

Doutuan Shan

窦团山, dòutuán shān • ¥67 • buses (¥18 return) depart 7am–6pm from a depot 150m west of Jiangyou's south bus station on Taiping Lu • minibus or taxi ¥100 one-way

Doutuan Shan is a little twin-peaked ridge 26km northwest of Jiangyou, famed for its martial arts and covered in historic temples. Extensive sympathetic **reconstruction** in the wake of the 2008 earthquake is now complete, and though the whole site is something of a tourist trap, with monks offering to tell your fortune for a fee, it's definitely worth watching the famed wire-walking performances (¥10) between sheer pinnacles, now carried out with safety harnesses attached. It all makes for a fun day out, and the views over the surrounding countryside are fantastic.

ARRIVAL AND DEPARTURE
JIANGYOU

By train Jiangyou's train station (江油火车站, jiāngyóu huǒchē zhàn) is on the Chengdu–Xi'an line some 5km east of Jiangyou, from where city bus #2 will carry you via the centre to the bus station on Taiping Lu. Destinations Chengdu (20 daily; 2hr); Guangyuan (20 daily; 2hr 30min–3hr 30min); Xi'an (7 daily; 13hr).

By bus Jiangyou's south bus station (南汽车站, nán qìchēzhàn) – the town's major depot – is just south of the centre on Taiping Lu. Destinations Chengdu (3hr); Doutuan Shan (1hr); Guangyuan (2hr 30min); Jianmenguan (1hr 30min).

ACCOMMODATION

Jindu Binguan 金都宾馆, jīndū bīnguǎn. Taiping Lu, over the road from the *Jinxin* ☎0816 3258133. Budget rival for its neighbour across the street but actually not all that much cheaper. Small, basic rooms with a/c, 24hr hot water and breakfast included. **¥120**

Jinxin Binguan 金鑫宾馆, jīnxīn bīnguǎn. Taiping Lu, next to the bus station ☎0816 3277222. This modern hotel has wi-fi access in the lobby, clean en-suite rooms with a/c, TV and wired internet, plus a great restaurant. Convenient and excellent value. **¥148**

12

DIRECTORY

Banks and exchange The main Bank of China and ATM is in the centre of town on the Jiefang Lu/Jinlun Lu crossroads.

Jianmenguan

剑门关, jiànménguān • ¥100 • bus from Guangyuan (¥10) • buses from Jiangyou drop 14km short on the Jiangyou–Guangyuan expressway; walk down a sliproad for 1km to waiting minibuses (¥40 for the vehicle)

Jianmenguan, the "Sword Pass" 100km from Jiangyou and 50km from Guangyuan, commands a strategic position along Shudao as the only break in a line of 72 imposing peaks. The pass itself is marked by a heavy stone **gateway** and watchtower, around which progress is slowed by the number of restaurants. A **cable car** (¥40) heads up to a viewing area and tea terrace, or you can get here from the gateway by following Shudao's original route – a very narrow, steep and slippery stone path along the base of the cliffs – for a couple of kilometres. Recent building work, both in recovery from the 2008 earthquake and to simply develop tourism, detracts from historic associations, but the location is impressive nonetheless, and you'll certainly still be able to appreciate the sentiment behind Li Bai's poem, *Hard is the Road to Shu*.

Guangyuan

广元, guǎngyuán

GUANGYUAN, on the Jialing River halfway between Chengdu and Xi'an, is the last town before Shaanxi and seems to have picked up its neighbour's penchant for industrial sprawl. An unattractive manufacturing town, and home to a plutonium production plant, Guangyuan's main attraction is as a jumping-off point for **Jiuzhaigou** buses, but it is also the birthplace of China's only acknowledged empress, the Tang-dynasty ruler **Wu Zetian** (see p.215).

Huangze Temple

皇泽寺, huángzé sì • ¥50

About 2km south along the river from the train station, Tang-dynasty rock sculptures at **Huangze Temple** give a positive spin on Wu Zetian's reign after centuries of censure as a result of her perceived challenge to Confucian values (mostly just by being a woman in a position of authority). Carvings here include portraits of Wu Zetian and an elegant, Indian-influenced sculpture of Guanyin. It's generally a quiet spot, but is packed each September 1 when families come to celebrate "Daughters' Day".

ARRIVAL AND DEPARTURE
GUANGYUAN

By train The train station (广元火车站, guǎngyuán huǒchē zhàn) sits at the back of a huge square, about 1.5km northwest from the centre over the Jialing River.

Destinations Chengdu (24 daily; 5hr); Xi'an (10 daily; 8–11hr).

By bus The main bus station (客运中心, kèyùn zhōngxīn) is next to the train station in the northwest of

town; there are dawn departures for the 348km run to Jiuzhaigou, and services through the day to Xi'an and Langzhong. The Nanhe bus station (南河汽车站, nánhé qìchēzhàn), for travel to Chengdu, is at the southern end of town, just over the river on Shumen Nan Lu.

Destinations Chengdu (4hr); Jiangyou (2hr 30min); Jianmenguan (1hr); Jiuzhaigou (1 daily; 8hr); Langzhong (4hr); Xi'an (8hr).

GETTING AROUND

By bus Bus #6 runs from the train and main bus stations, down central Shumen Bei Lu.

By taxi A taxi anywhere shouldn't cost more than ¥7.

ACCOMMODATION AND EATING

The train station is surrounded by hostels charging ¥30 a bed. For meals, hotpot stalls and restaurants fill the town's backstreets. More substantial options are available near the Nanhe bus station at the Shumen Bei Lu-Lizhou Lu crossroads.

Zhongyuan 中源宾馆, zhōngyuán bīnguǎn. 32 Lizhou Xi Lu ☎0839 8867777. Near the Nanhe bus station, this is a smart, straightforward and comfortable place with small but well-furnished en suites equipped with a/c, TV and ADSL sockets. **¥198**

DIRECTORY

Banks and exchange The most convenient Bank of China with an ATM is at the corner of pedestrianized Shichang Jie and Bei Jie in the older part of town, west off Shumen Bei Lu.

Langzhong

阆中, làngzhōng

About 225km northeast of Chengdu, **LANGZHONG** occupies a broad thumb of land around which the Jialing River loops on three sides. The town once played a pivotal role in provincial history, even becoming the **Sichuanese capital** for seventeen years at the start of the Qing. Notable people associated with Langzhong include the Three Kingdoms general **Zhang Fei**, who is buried here, and Luo Xiahong, the Han-dynasty inventor of the Chinese calendar and armillary sphere – a spherical framework of interconnecting hoops mapping the movement of celestial bodies. About a quarter of Langzhong comprises a protected **old town**, Sichuan's largest collection of antique architecture, whose streets, houses and temples provide a fascinating wander. A very few small industries, elderly canteens and teahouses survive alongside the countless touristy shops selling souvenirs, locally produced Baoning vinegar and preserved Zhangfei beef.

12

The old town

古城, gǔchéng · Free, but combined tickets for sights available from ¥120

Langzhong's **old town** covers about a square kilometre southwest of the centre. Orient yourself near the river at **Huaguang Lou** (华光楼, huáguāng lóu; ¥15), a three-storey, 36m-high Tang-style gate tower on Dadong Jie, last reconstructed in 1867. From the top, there are views south over the river, north to the modern town, and down over the grey-tiled roofs and atriums of Langzhong's classical buildings.

Gongyuan

贡院, gòngyuàn · ¥45

An unusual target in the north of the old town is the seventeenth-century **Gongyuan**, one of only a very few surviving imperial examination halls in China. Single-storey cells surround a long courtyard where prospective candidates lived and elaborated on their knowledge of the Confucian classics, on which the exams were based and according to which the country was governed.

Zhang Fei Temple

张飞庙, zhāngfēi miào · Xi Jie · ¥50

Langzhong's most popular sight is the **Zhang Fei Temple**, a shrine to the ferocious Three Kingdoms general who was murdered in 221 AD by his own troops while campaigning at Langzhong. Four courtyards of Ming halls, full of painted statuary and interlocking roof brackets, lead through to the grassy mound of his **tomb**, in front of which a finally

---

SIHEYUAN

Many of Langzhong's *siheyuan*, or **courtyard houses**, are open to the public (approx 9am–6pm; ¥4–8) and house museums or accommodation. There's no need to see more than a couple to get the idea of a central hall divided up by wooden screens opening into a courtyard, decorated with potted flower gardens. You can poke around inside both the ancient *Du Jia* hotel and *Water Wharf Inn* for free.

Dafo Si and Scholars' Cave & Main Bus Station

triumphant Zhang Fei sits between two demons who are holding his cringing assassins **Zhang Da** and **Fan Qiang** by the hair.

Across the river

Taxi from the centre about ¥7

As well as the old town, it's worth heading east across the river below a prominent Ming-dynasty pagoda to **Scholars' Cave** (状元洞, zhuàngyuán dòng; ¥40), a peaceful grotto laid with ponds and willows where two students, both later court officials, studied in their youth. Behind here, **Dafo Temple** (大佛寺, dàfó sì; ¥40) protects a 10m-high Buddha, which was carved into a rockface in Tang times and has survived more or less intact, along with thousands of smaller carvings and reliefs.

ARRIVAL AND DEPARTURE
LANGZHONG

By bus Langzhong's main bus station (阆中客运中心, làngzhōng kèyùn zhōngxīn) is 5km southeast on the highway, where you'll arrive from Chengdu; catch city bus #89 (¥2) from the forecourt into town, or a taxi (¥7). The Baba Si bus station (巴巴寺汽车站, bābāsì qìchēzhàn), in the north of town on Zhang Fei Dadao, handles traffic to Guangyuan.

Destinations Chengdu (3hr 30min); Chongqing (4hr); Guangyuan (4hr).

ACCOMMODATION

Head to the old town for accommodation, where many places offer rooms inside antique buildings. As well as formal hotels, you can also stay in any one of the family hostels scattered about, though you'll need some Chinese, if only to find them – look for flags with the characters for accommodation (住宿, zhùsù) or guesthouse (客栈, kèzhàn).

★ **Dujia Kezhan** 杜家客栈, dùjiā kèzhàn. 63 Xiaxin Jie ☎0817 6221102, ⊕www.djkz.com.cn. In the south of the old town, this place was founded during the Tang dynasty and is, incredibly, still in business – though these days rooms come with toilets and a/c. Staff are helpful, rooms atmospheric and there's also a very good restaurant. **¥178**

Lee's Courtyard 李家大院, lǐjiā dàyuàn. 47 Wumiao Jie ☎0817 6236500, ⓦwww.lzljdy.com. Up towards the Zhang Fei Temple, this is a superior vintage courtyard affair with newly refurbished luxurious rooms, and an excellent restaurant to match. **¥410**

Tianyi Youth Hostel 天一青年旅舍, tiānyī qīngnián lǚshě. 100 Da Dong Jie ☎0817 6225501. Next door to the Feng Shui Museum, this is the only real budget

accommodation within the old town. Housed in a beautiful old building, the rooms are excellent, it's clean, and some staff speak English. Dorm beds **¥80**

Water Wharf Hotel 水码头客栈, shuǐmǎtóu kèzhàn. 61 Xiaxin Jie ☎0817 6233333, ⓦwww .hxsmtkz.com. Virtually next door to the *Dujia*, this is a similarly labyrinthine old courtyard building. Though claims to be a museum are a slight overstatement, there are some nice old pictures on the wall and it's worth having a look in even if you're not staying. En-suite rooms are a little cramped, but clean. **¥160**

EATING

Decent restaurants are scarce in the old town; there is a string of hole-in-the-wall places on Yanshikou, running north from Nei Dong Jie, selling noodles for a few yuan per bowl, but for a proper feed head further into the new town, along Dongtang Jing Jie.

Shun Wei 顺味餐馆, shùnwèi cānguǎn. 1 Dongtang Jing Jie ☎0817 6236833. A rip-roaring Sichuan eatery that's full of noise and deeply ingrained with the smell of

baijiu; the atmosphere's great, it's packed at weekends, and the food is fiery, delicious and excellent value – expect around ¥30 per person. Daily 11am–10pm.

Southern Sichuan

12

Southwest of Chengdu, fast-flowing rivers converge at **Leshan**, where more than a thousand years ago sculptors created a **giant Buddha** overlooking the waters, one of the world's most imposing religious monuments. An hour away, **Emei Shan** rises to more than 3000m, its forested slopes rich in scenery and temples. As Sichuan's most famous sights, the Buddha and Emei Shan have become tourist black holes thanks to easy access – don't go near either during holidays, when crowds are so awful that the army is sometimes called in to sort out the chaos – but at other times they are well worth the effort.

If you're on your way down south to Yunnan, you might also want to break your journey at **Xichang**, a Yi minority town with a backroad route to **Lugu Lake**, right on the Yunnanese border. Emei and Dafo are best reached on buses, but it's easier to get to Xichang via the Chengdu–Emei Shan–Kunming rail line.

Leshan

乐山, lèshān

Set beside the wide convergence of the Qingyi, Min and Dadu rivers, 180km from Chengdu and 50km from Emei Shan, **LESHAN** is a dull, spread-out market town with a modern northern fringe and older riverside core, a transit point for visiting the Big Buddha, carved deep into a niche in the facing cliffs.

The Big Buddha

大佛, dàfó • Daily April–Sept 7.30am–6.30pm, Oct–March 8am–5.30pm • ¥90

Impassive and gargantuan, the **Big Buddha** peers out from under half-lidded eyes, oblivious to the swarms of sightseers trying to photograph his bulk. In 713 AD the monk **Haitong** came up with the idea of carving the Buddha into the riverside's red sandstone cliffs, using the rubble produced to fill in dangerous shoals below. The project took ninety years to complete and, once construction started, temples sprang up on the hills above the Buddha. At 71m tall, this is the world's largest Buddhist sculpture – his ears are 7m long, his eyes 10m wide, and around six people at once can

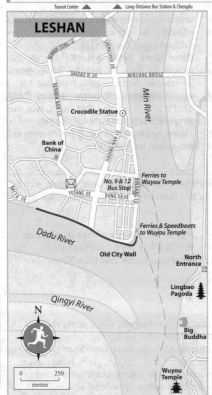

Transit Centre ▲ ▲ Long-Distance Bus Station & Chengdu

LESHAN

RENMIN DONG LU

SHENGSHUI JIE

DAQIAO XI JIE

MINJIANG BRIDGE

RENMIN NAN LU

Min River

Crocodile Statue

Bank of China

JIADING NAN LU

BINJIANG LU

Ferries to Wuyou Temple

No. 9 & 12 Bus Stop

YUTANG JIE

DONG DAJIE

BAI TA JIE

Ferries & Speedboats to Wuyou Temple

Dadu River

Old City Wall

North Entrance

Lingbao Pagoda

Qingyi River

N

Big Buddha

Wuyou Temple

0   250
metres

12

stand on his big toenail – though statistics can't convey the initial sight of this squat icon, comfortably seated with his hands on his knees, looming over you.

Around the Buddha

The easiest route in is via the **north entrance** (大佛北门, dàfó běimén), from where you walk up to the crowded terrace around the Buddha's ears; there's an insane-looking statue of Haitong here, and the one-way **staircase of nine turns** down to the Buddha's toes, after which you return to the top via the 500m-long **cliff road** cut into the rocks. From here you can press on to Maohao Mu, a set of Han-dynasty tombs, and then, via a covered bridge to **Wuyou Temple** (乌优寺, wūyōu sì), a warm pink-walled monastery – don't miss the grotesque gallery of saints in the Luohan Hall. Downhill from here, **ferries** can cart you back to the dock in Leshan town, via superb views of Dafo from the water. You could, of course, start by ferry from Leshan too; either way, give yourself at least a couple of hours in the park to see everything – on weekends and public holidays, and pretty much any day during August, queuing to descend the stairs past Buddha can take an hour in itself.

ARRIVAL AND DEPARTURE   LESHAN

By bus Leshan has at least three large bus stations, but you're most likely to arrive at the transit centre (乐山客运中心站, lèshān kèyùn zhōngxīnzhàn zhàn) on Baichang Xi Lu, several kilometres northwest of the sights; buses #9 and #12 run from here to

the ferry terminals on Binjiang Lu, while #3 or #13 will get you to Dafo's north entrance.
Destinations Chengdu (2hr 30min); Chongqing (5hr); Dazu (3hr); Emei (45min); Xichang (8hr); Yibin (5hr); Zigong (2hr 30min).

GETTING AROUND

By ferry You can catch a ferry from the dock on Binjiang Lu in town, over the river to the jetty below Wuyou Temple (¥70), giving you a great view of the Buddha from

the water.
By taxi A taxi from arrival points to the ferry or the north gate shouldn't cost more than ¥12.

ACCOMMODATION

Don't plan to stay at Leshan; the hotel situation is terrible and you're better off day-tripping from Chengdu or combining with a trip to Emei Shan and staying the night there.

EATING

Its not really worth heading into Leshan proper just to eat, and fortunately there is a string of Sichuanese and Muslim restaurants by the north gate of the Buddha Scenic Area. The local Xiba tofu is reckoned to be some of the best in the country, thanks to the region's high-quality water. Expect around ¥50 per person.

Emei Shan

峨眉山, éméi shān · ticket ¥185, valid for three days · trails open daily 7am–6pm

Some 160km southwest of Chengdu, **Emei Shan**'s thickly forested peaks and dozens of **temples**, all linked by exhausting flights of stone steps, have been pulling in pilgrims (and tourists) ever since the sixth-century visit of **Bodhisattva Puxian** and his six-tusked elephant, images of whom you'll see everywhere. Religion aside, the pristine natural environment is a major draw, and changes markedly through the year – lush, green and wet in the summer; brilliant with reds and yellows in autumn; white, clear and very cold in winter.

You can see something of the mountain in a single day, but three would allow you to experience more of the forests, spend a night or two in a temple, and perhaps assault Emei's sumit. It's only worth climbing this high if the weather's good, however: for a richer bag of views, temples, streams and vegetation, you won't be disappointed with the lower paths.

Baoguo

报国, bàoguó · mountain ticket not needed to visit the town and nearby temples

The mountain's trailhead is at **BAOGUO**, basically one straight kilometre of hotels and restaurants, apparently constructed from a mix of concrete and neon, running up past an ornamental **waterfall** to a gilded pavilion. Immediately left here is **Lingxiu Hot Springs** (灵秀温泉, língxiù wēnquán; daily 2pm–midnight; ¥168), a modern, professionally run spa and a great spot to unkink trail-weary muscles following your descent.

Two temples

Two of the liveliest temples on the mountain lie just outside Baoguo: turn right at the waterfall and follow paths for 250m to **Baoguo Temple** (报国寺, bàoguó sì; daily 7am–7pm; ¥8), a large and serene complex where you can opt to spend the night, featuring flagstoned courtyards decorated with potted magnolias and cycads, and high-roofed Ming-style halls. Alternatively, bear left up the road past the waterfall and it's about 1km to ancient ginkgo trees outside the charming **Fuhu Temple** (伏虎寺, fúhǔ sì; daily 6.30am–8pm; ¥6). Emei's largest temple and once associated with Taoism, today it's a Guanyin nunnery, whose bronze sixteenth-century **Huayan Pagoda** is engraved with 4700 Buddha images.

The long route

Following the long route, it's 5km from Fuhu Temple to **Chunyang Nunnery** (纯阳殿, chúnyáng diàn), founded in honour of the Taoist Immortal Lü Dongbin, spookily surrounded by mossy pine trees. A further 5km lands you at **Qingyin Ge** (清音阁, qīngyīn gé), a pavilion built deep in the forest where two streams converge and tumble through a small gorge down **Niuxin Shi** (牛心石, niú xīnshí), the ox-heart rock. It's a charming spot with a small **temple** to spend the night in, though being also just a short walk from the Wuxianggang bus stop, it can get busy with guests.

Qingyin Ge to Xixiang Chi

Qingyin Ge is just 3km from Wannian Temple (see p.736), but to continue the long route, follow the path up past the left side of Qingyin; this takes you along a river bed and past a **monkey-watching area**, before starting to climb steeply through a series of gorges. About 6km further on, **Hongchun Ping** (洪椿坪, hóngchūn píng;) is an eighteenth-century temple named after surrounding *hongchun* (toona) trees, and is about as far as you'd make it on the first day.

From here it's a very tough 15km of seemingly unending narrow stairs to **Xianfeng Temple** (仙峰寺, xiānfēng sì), a strangely unfriendly place, though well forested with pine and dove trees and planted with camellia and rhododendrons. The following 12.5km are slightly easier, heading partly downhill to a dragon-headed bridge, then up again to

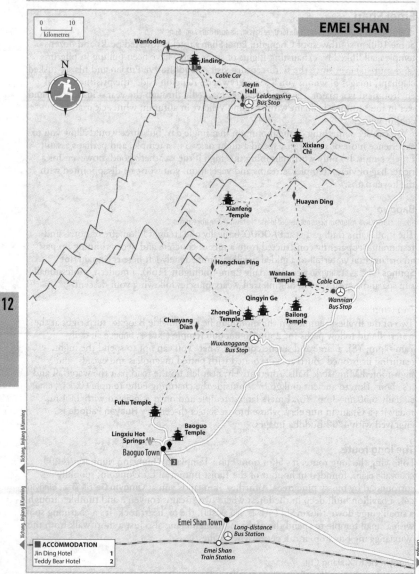

EMEI SHAN

■ ACCOMMODATION	
Jin Ding Hotel	1
Teddy Bear Hotel	2

where the trail joins the north route near Xixiang Chi (see opposite), around 43km from Fuhu Temple and two-thirds of the way to the summit.

The short route

Most people start their ascent by catching a bus from Baoguo to the Wannian Temple bus stop at the start of Emei's short route. From here a 3km path or cable car (¥50) leads to **Wannian Temple** (万年寺, wànnián sì; daily 7.30am–7pm; ¥6), where a squat brick pavilion out back, built in 1601, houses a life-sized enamelled bronze **sculpture of**

ASCENDING EMEI SHAN

An ascent of Emei Shan can be tackled via two main routes from Baoguo: the 60km, three-day **long route**; and the 40km, two-day **short route**. Most people knock 15km or so off these by catching **buses** from Baoguo to alternative starting points near Qingyin Ge (Wuxianggang bus stop) or Wannian Temple; leaving early enough, you could make it to the top in one day from either of these up the short route, descending the next day – though your legs will be like jelly afterwards. If you're really pushed for time, you could get up and down in a single day by catching a **minibus** between Baoguo Temple and Jieyin Hall (Leidongping bus stop), located a **cable-car ride** (¥120 return) from the summit, but this way you'll miss out on what makes Emei Shan such a special place.

Bring a torch in case you unexpectedly find yourself on a path after dark. **Footwear** needs to have a firm grip; in winter, when stone steps become dangerously icy, straw sandals and even iron cleats (sold for a few yuan and tied onto your soles) are an absolute necessity. Don't forget **warm clothing** for the top, which is around 15°C cooler than the plains and so liable to be below freezing between October and April; lower paths are very humid during the summer. You'll also want some protection against the near certainty of rain. A walking stick is handy for easing the pressure on thigh muscles during descent – a range is sold along the way – or for fending off aggressive monkeys (the macaques here have been known to go for people, particularly when food is present). Store any heavy gear at the bottom of the mountain, or in Chengdu if you're contemplating a round trip.

If you need a **guide**, an excellent choice is Patrick Yang (☏0137 08131210, 🌐emeiguides .com), who speaks good English and often takes tour groups up Emei Shan. He also arranges local "culture tours" for about ¥100 per person, touring a kung-fu school, noodle factory and kindergarten, with lunch in a farmer's house.

12

Puxian, riding a gilt lotus flower astride his great six-tusked white elephant – note the gold spots on the elephant's knees, which people rub for good luck.

From Wannian, a steady 14km hike through bamboo and pine groves should see you to where the two routes converge just south of **Xixiang Chi** (洗象池, xǐxiàng chí). This eighteenth-century monastery sits on a ridge where Puxian's elephant stopped for a wash, and on cloudy days – being more or less open to the elements and prowled by monkeys – it's amazingly atmospheric, though somewhat run-down and frigid in winter. It's a popular place to rest up, however, so get in early to be sure of a bed.

On to the summit

Beyond Xixiang Chi the path gets easier, but you'll encounter gangs of aggressive **monkeys**; keep a good grip on your bags. The path continues for 9km past some ancient, gnarled rhododendrons to **Jieyin Hall** (接引殿, jiēyǐn diàn) where the 50km-long road from Baoguo, which has snaked its way round the back of the mountain, ends at **Leidongping bus stop** (雷洞坪车站, léidòngpíng chēzhàn) and a cable car to the summit (¥65 up, ¥55 down). The area is thick with minibus tour parties fired up for their one-day crack at the peak, and is also where to find buses back to Baoguo. Hotels around Jieyin and at the summit are expensive and badly kept, and you shouldn't plan to stay here unless you are set on seeing the sunrise at all costs.

Jinding

金顶, jīndǐng

Whether you take the cable car or spend the next couple of hours hoofing it, 3077m-high **Jinding**, the Golden Summit, is most people's final stop. There are two temples: the friendly **Woyun Nunnery** (卧云庵, wòyún ān) and the oversized **Huazang Temple** (华藏寺, huázàng sì), crowned by a massive gilded statue of a multifaced Puxian on four elephants. In the afternoon, the sea of clouds below the peak sometimes catches rainbow-like rings known as **Buddha's Halo**, which surround and move with your shadow, while in clear conditions you can even make out Gongga Shan (see p.763), 150km to the west.

ARRIVAL AND DEPARTURE

EMEI SHAN

Access to the region is largely via Emei Shan town (峨眉山市, éméi shān shì), a transit hub 150km southwest of Chengdu and 7km short of the mountain.

BY TRAIN

Emei Shan town is on the Chengdu–Kunming line, and is also the closest station to Leshan. The *Teddy Bear Hotel* can book train tickets from Emei, though for a heavy fee.

Emei Shan train station (峨眉山火车站, éméi shān huǒchē zhàn) is 3.5km from Emei Shan town; catch blue city bus #1 to the terminus in town, then green bus #5 to the mountain trailhead at Baoguo.

Destinations Chengdu (7 daily; 2–4hr); Kunming (4 daily; 17hr); Panzhihua (7 daily; 11hr); Xichang (9 daily; 8hr).

BY BUS

Emei Shan bus station (峨眉山气车站, éméi shān qìchēzhàn), the largest in the region and where to find most long-distance transport, is close to the train station 3.5km from Emei Shan town; catch blue city bus #1 to the terminus, then green bus #5 to the mountain trailhead at Baoguo.

Baguo bus station (报国气车站, bàoguó qìchēzhàn), a decent sized depot in the middle of Baoguo, has long-distance transport to Chengdu and Leshan until 6pm.

Destinations Chengdu (2hr 30min); Leshan (45min); Xichang (8hr).

GETTING AROUND

By bus Baoguo bus station is where to catch transport up the mountain (every 30min; 6am–5pm) to Wuxianggang (for Qingyin Ge; ¥50 return); Wannian Temple (¥50 return); and Leidongping (for Jieyin Hall and the summit; ¥90 return).

12

ACCOMMODATION AND EATING

There are some hotels on the mountain, but it can't be stressed enough that temples offer far more interesting lodgings; all charge from ¥15 for a basic dorm bed to more than ¥150 for a double room with air conditioning and toilet. It's a good idea to reach your intended temple accommodation by 3pm; popular places such as Xixiang Chi can fill up early on. Food on the mountain tends to be overpriced and ordinary; stir-fries and noodle soups are available either at roadside stalls or vegetarian temple restaurants.

Jin Ding Hotel 金顶酒店, jīndǐng jiǔdiàn. At the summit of the mountain, immediately outside the cable-car station ⓣ0833 5098088, ⓦemsjdjd.com. The few new rooms are smart but this place is still outrageously expensive for what you get. The only remotely reasonable option, if you're desperate to see the sunrise, is the four-bed room. Despite the prices, the hotel still books out so you will need to make a reservation. Four-bed room **¥680**, standard doubles **¥980**

Teddy Bear Hotel 玩具熊酒店, wánjùxióng jiǔdiàn. In a side street just downhill from Baoguo bus station ⓣ0833 5590135, ⓦteddybear.com.cn. A useful base at the bottom of the mountain with stuffy dorms, good doubles, internet and a restaurant. Management can be a bit pushy. Dorms **¥30**, rooms **¥80**

Xichang

西昌, xīchāng

XICHANG, seven hours south from Emei Shan by train, is a surprisingly bustling place, focus for southwestern China's five-million-strong **Yi** minority – whose **torch festival** in August is one of the largest ethnic events in all Sichuan. Xichang is also a **satellite launching site** for China's Long March space programme, and a staging post for a couple of backroads trips into Yunnan, if the straightforward train ride to Kunming doesn't appeal.

The old town

Xichang's partially walled **old town** is just northeast of the centre, a fifteen-minute walk north from central Yuechang Plaza. The old quarter's streets form a cross, of which the southern extension, **Nan Jie**, is the most interesting, running 150m through a busy market and past rickety wooden teahouses to the heavy stone **south gate** and attached battlements.

Liang Shan

凉山, liángshān • Bus #106

The area around Xichang, known as **Liang Shan**, the Cool Mountains, is the heartland of the Yi community. Until the 1950s, the Yi here lived pretty much any way they wanted to, owning slaves, raiding the lowlands and conducting clan warfare. Some 5km south from town by bus, **Qionghai Lake** (邛海湖, qiónghǎi hú) is where the **Museum of Liangshan Yi Slave Society** (凉山彝族奴隶社会博物馆, liángshān yízúnúlì shèhuì bówùguǎn) exhibits Yi festival clothing and household items, and books written in the Yi script – you'll also see this on official signs around town.

ARRIVAL AND DEPARTURE   XICHANG

BY TRAIN

There's a train ticket office on Chang'an Dong Lu, just west of central Shengli Lu, but be warned that Xichang is a tough place from which to get reserved berths – or even hard seats. **Xichang train station** (西昌火车站, xīchāng huǒchē zhàn) is on the city's western outskirts, from where bus #6 will get you to main street Chang'an Dong Lu. Destinations Chengdu (11 daily; 9–11hr); Emei (8 daily; 6–8hr); Kunming (5 daily; 8–10hr); Panzhihua (12 daily; 3–6hr).

BY BUS

Bus tickets are easily available at the stations; note that aside from obvious destinations there are services to Lugu Lake in Yunnan, and to Kangding in western Sichuan (see p.761).

Western bus station (汽车西站, qìchē xīzhàn) is west of the centre, on the #6 bus route, handling traffic to Chengdu, Emei and Kangding.

South bus station (汽车南站, qìchē nánzhàn), on Sanchakou Lu and the #14 bus route, handles buses travelling the expressway to Panzhihua – where you can catch transport to Lijiang in Yunnan (p.672) – and the rough road west to Lugu Lake, on the Yunnanese border (p.679). Destinations Chengdu (8hr); Kangding (8hr); Kunming (24hr); Lugu Lake (8hr); Panzhihua (3hr).

ACCOMMODATION AND EATING

Inexpensive restaurants are scattered throughout the old town.

Hotel Pretty 美丽华大酒店, měilì huá dàjiǔdiàn. 79 Sancha Xi Lu ☏ 0834 2237777. Down near the main Bank of China, this place provides clean, modern budget en-suite rooms and is nowhere near as tacky as the name suggests, though they have squeezed a surprising amount of fake marble into the petite lobby. ¥230
Jinsha 金沙宾馆, jīnshā bīnguǎn. 67 Chang'an Zhong Lu ☏ 0834 3228169. An older, cheaper place, showing its age with some worn carpets but conveniently central. Road noise can be an issue for rooms at the front, and try and avoid quarters with deep-seated cigarette odour. ¥150
Ziwei 紫葳酒店, zǐwēi jiǔdiàn. 56 Chang'an Dong Lu ☏ 0834 3286888. Modern hotel in the middle of town, well presented, with the usual trimmings, but just a cut above the normal Chinese business hotel. Smart and clean with wi-fi and a/c throughout. ¥318

DIRECTORY

Banks and exchange Xichang's Bank of China and ATM is south over the bridge on Sancha Xi Lu, an extension of central Chang'an Dong Lu.

Southeastern Sichuan

Surrounding the fertile confluence of the Yangzi and Min rivers 250km from Chengdu, where Sichuan, Yunnan and Guizhou provinces meet, southeastern Sichuan has some intriguing attractions. The town of **Zigong** is a treat, with some well-preserved architecture, dinosaurs and salt mines, especially worth checking out during its Spring Festival lantern displays. Some 80km farther south, **Yibin** offers access to the aptly named **Shunan Bamboo Sea**; and, further eastwards towards Chongqing, you shouldn't miss the carved gallery of comic-book-like Buddhist rock art at **Dazu**.

Zigong

自贡, zìgòng

ZIGONG, a thriving industrial centre, has long been an important source of **salt**, tapped for thousands of years from artesian basins below the city. In the fourth century, the Sichuanese were sinking 300m-deep boreholes here using bamboo-fibre cables attached to massive stone bits; by the 1600s, bamboo buckets were drawing brine from wells bored almost 1km beneath Zigong, centuries before European technology (which borrowed Chinese techniques) could reach this deep. **Natural gas**, a by-product of drilling, was used from the second century to boil brine in evaporation tanks, and now also powers Zigong's buses and taxis.

Xiqin Guildhall

西亲会馆, xīqīn huìguǎn · Jiefang Lu · Daily 8.30am–5pm · ¥22

The splendid **Xiqin Guildhall**, built in the Qing dynasty by merchants from Shaanxi, is now an absorbing salt museum. Photos and relics, with plenty of English captions, chart Zigong's mining history, from pictorial Han-dynasty tomb bricks showing salt panning, to the bamboo piping, frightening metal drills and wooden derricks used until the 1980s. All this is overshadowed by the building itself, whose curled roof corners, flagstone-and-beam halls and gilded woodwork date to 1872.

Other guildhalls

Of Zigong's many other scattered period buildings, the most notable are **Wangye Miao** (王爷庙, wángyé miào), a former guildhall-temple which sits high over the river on Binjiang Lu; and **Huanhou Gong** (桓侯宫, huánhóu gōng), a guildhall for pork butchers – or rather their patron, the Three Kingdoms' general Zhang Fei (see p.393) – whose beautifully carved stone gateway overlooks the junction of Jiefang Lu and Zhonghua Lu. Both are now highly atmospheric teahouses.

Shenhai Salt Well

燊海井, shēnhǎi jǐng · Daily 9am–5pm · ¥20 · bus #3 from the riverside "Shawan" bus stop on Binjiang Lu

About 3km northeast from the city centre is **Shenhai Well**, which in 1835 reached a fraction over 1000m, the deepest ever drilled using traditional methods. Operational until 1966, the 20m-high wooden tripod minehead still overlooks the site, where you can inspect bamboo-fibre cables and the tiny well shaft itself, corked, reeking of gas, and barely 20cm across. Eight shallow vats in the building behind are evaporation pans, where the muddy brine is purified by mixing in tofu and skimming off the resultant scum as it rises, leaving a thick crust of pure salt when the liquid has been boiled off.

Zigong dinosaur museum

恐龙博物馆, kǒnglóng bówùguǎn · Daily 8.30am–5pm · ¥42 · bus #3 from the riverside "Shawan" bus stop on Binjiang Lu via Shenhai Salt Well

Right on the city's northeastern outskirts, about 45 minutes from the centre by bus, Zigong's **dinosaur museum** is built over the site of excavations carried out during the 1980s. Near-perfect skeletal remains of dozens of Jurassic fish, amphibians and dinosaurs – including monumental thigh bones, and Sichuan's own **Yangchuanosaurus**, a toothy, lightweight velociraptor – have been left partially excavated *in situ*, while others have been fully assembled for easy viewing, posed dramatically against painted backgrounds.

ARRIVAL AND DEPARTURE   ZIGONG

By train Zigong is on a side-spur of the Guangzhou–Chengdu rail line, with the train station 1.5km east of the river on Jiaotong Lu, from where bus #34 heads to the central "Shawan" bus stop.

By bus Zigong's long-distance bus station (自贡客运中心, zìgòng kèyùn zhōngxīn) is about 2km south of town on Dangui Dajie; turn right out of the station and it's 100m to the city bus stop. Bus #33 travels via the central

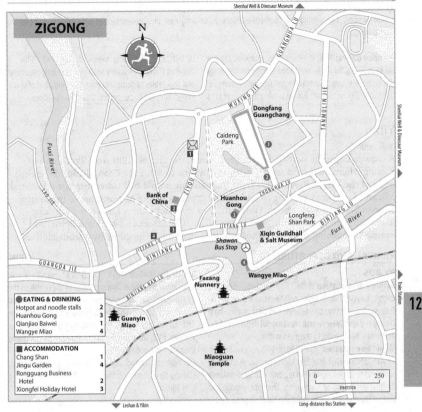

"Shawan" bus stop, continuing to the bottom of Ziyou Lu; taxis charge about ¥7.

Destinations Chengdu (3hr); Chongqing (4hr); Dazu (2hr); Emei (2hr); Leshan (2hr 30min); Yibin (1hr 30min).

By taxi If you're heading to the Shunan Bamboo Sea (see p.742), a new expressway means that you can get there from Zigong in just two hours in a cab – contact the *Xiongfei Holiday Hotel* about hiring one for the day.

ACCOMMODATION

Chang Shan 长闪远景宾馆, chángshān yuǎnjǐng bīnguǎn. 133 Ziyou Lu ☎ 0813 5390666. Cheap basic hotel in the centre of town. Tile-clad rooms come with a/c and en suite with a squat toilet, shower and 24hr hot water. **¥90**

Ronngguang Business Hotel 荣光商务酒店, rónggguāng shāngwù jiǔdiàn. 25 Ziyou Lu ☎ 0813 2117777. Has some well-maintained rooms, but also some tatty, damp, and smelly ones – all at the same price – so have a look at a few first before you check in. **¥140**

Jingu Garden 雄飞锦绣花园酒店, xióngfēi jǐnxiù huāyuán jiǔdiàn. Jiari Guangcheng ☎ 0813 2118266.

Budget sister of luxury *Xiongfei* just up the road, but rooms here are still up to a good standard. Carpets are a little worn and it's worth checking to make sure your room doesn't smell too smoky. **¥198**

Xiongfei Holiday Hotel 雄飞假日酒店, xióngfēi jiàrì jiǔdiàn. 193 Jiefang Lu ☎ 0813 2118888. The only slice of luxury you're likely to find in Zigong is this four-star pile in the town centre. It's part of a failing shopping centre complex so doesn't look great from the outside, but en-suite rooms come with bath tub, a/c, TV and a sit-down toilet. Good value. **¥269**

EATING

Zigong has an extraordinary density of teahouses, even for Sichuan; the most atmospheric are Wangye Miao and Huanhou Gong, with their century-old wood and stonework. For eating, street food is the order of the day, with dumpling and noodle vendors surrounding the southern entrance to Caideng Park in a pedestrianized area known as Dongfang Guangchang.

Qianjiao Baiwei 千椒百味, qiānjiāo bǎiwèi. Xinmin Jie ☎0813 5579999. If street food is not your thing, try this hotpot restaurant up near the junction with Wuxing Lu. Upholding Zigong's reputation for serving the hottest food in Sichuan – the name means "A Thousand Chillies, a Hundred Flavours" – simply order dishes of uncooked meat and vegetables to dump into your steaming bowl of broth. Expect around ¥80 per person. Daily 11am–10pm.

Yibin

宜宾, yíbīn

A crowded, grubby port with a modern veneer, the city of **YIBIN** sits 50km south of Zigong where the Jinsha and Min rivers combine to form the **Chang Jiang**, the main body of the Yangzi River. Aside from **Daguan Lou**, an old bell tower just east off central Minzhu Lu, there's nothing to do here in between organizing transport to the nearby **Shunan Bamboo Sea**, though Yibin produces three substances known for wreaking havoc: enriched plutonium; Wuliangye *bai jiu*, China's second-favourite spirit; and *ranmian*, "burning noodles", whose chilli content has stripped many a stomach lining.

ARRIVAL AND DEPARTURE

BY BUS

Beimen bus station (北门汽车客运站, běimén qìchē kèyùnzhàn), 250m northwest of the centre off Zhenwu Lu. Mostly short-range regional traffic from Zigong and elsewhere; worth checking out departures here first before hauling out to the main station.

Main bus station (川高客运中心, chuāngāo kèyùn zhōngxīn) is a few kilometres north of town, covering the largest number of regional and long-distance destinations including Chongqing, Chengdu, Zigong and Luzhou (for connections to Chishui in Guizhou province).

South bus station (南岸汽车客运站, nánàn qìchē kèyùn zhàn), about 2km southeast of the centre on the #4 city bus route. Scheduled buses to the Shunan Bamboo Sea, though service is patchy and usually it's quicker to aim first for Changning (长宁, chángníng; last bus at 7.30pm; ¥10), from where you can organize transport into the park – see opposite.

Destinations Changning (1hr 30min); Chengdu (4hr); Chongqing (3hr 30min); Dazu (4hr); Luzhou (3hr); Zigong (1hr 30min).

ACCOMMODATION AND EATING

Jiudu Fandian 酒都饭店, jiǔdū fàndiàn. 50 Zhuanshu Jie ☎0831 8188888. If only every Chinese business hotel was up to the standard of this imposing place out east towards the river. Trim rooms, decent carpets and an excellent restaurant. **¥318**

Ranmian Fandian 燃面饭店, ránmiàn fàndiàn. Next to the crossroads at 19 Renmin Lu ☎0831 8228047. Typical of the town's canteens, a tidy place where a bowl of cold *ranmian* noodles dressed in chopped nuts, coriander, vinegar and chillies costs just ¥4. Lots of other snacks too. Daily 8am–9pm.

Tianhe 天和宾馆, tiānhé bīnguǎn. Zhuanshu Jie ☎0831 5166333. A big step down from the *Jiudu* opposite, but then this place is half the price. Rooms are basic and bare but mostly clean. **¥150**

DIRECTORY

Banks and exchange The Bank of China (with ATM) is at the southern end of central Nan Jie.

The Shunan Bamboo Sea

蜀南竹海国家公园, shǔnán zhúhǎi guójiā gōngyuán • ¥112

Some 75km southeast of Yibin, the extraordinary **Shunan Bamboo Sea** covers more than forty square kilometres of mountain slopes with feathery green tufts, and makes for a refreshing few days' rural escape. It's a relatively **expensive** one, however, as you'll need to charter a taxi for the day to see much. The two settlements inside the park, **Wanling** (万岭, wànlǐng), 1.5km inside the main West Gate entrance, and **Wanli** (万里, wànlǐ), 20km inside, are tiny but have plenty of places to stay.

12

Around the park

Shunan is a beautiful spot, if a bit spooky given the graceful 10m-high stems endlessly repeating into the distance. There's pleasure in just being driven around, but make sure you have at least one walk along any of the numerous paths – the trail paralleling the cable car just outside Wanling is steep but superb, taking in a couple of waterfalls – and get a look down over the forest to see the bowed tips of bamboo ripple in waves as breezes sweep the slopes. The surreal atmosphere is enhanced by the park being a favourite film location for martial-arts movies and TV series, so don't be too surprised if you encounter Song-dynasty warriors galloping along the roads.

ARRIVAL AND DEPARTURE   SHUNAN BAMBOO SEA

By bus Although there's an erratic direct Yibin–Shunan bus service, the main transport hub is Changning (长宁, chángníng), a small town 15km short of Shunan's West Gate, which has a bus station and minibuses into the park. Destinations from Changning Chengdu (10hr); Chongqing (6hr); Yibin (2hr).

GETTING AROUND

By public minibus In theory, public minibuses shuttle between Changning, the West Gate, Wanling and Wanli through the day; you stand by the road and wave them down. In practice, service is patchy, tourists tend to be outrageously overcharged, and while useful for reaching accommodation they don't service the park sights.
By taxi The only way to comfortably see much of the Bamboo Sea is to hire a cab for the day; you can do this through accommodation and should expect to pay ¥150–250 depending on where you want to go.

ACCOMMODATION AND EATING

Accommodation is available inside the park with the cheapest charging about ¥50 a bed, though most are mid-range. Food in the park is universally good and not too expensive, with lots of fresh bamboo shoots and mushrooms.

Feicui Binguan 翡翠宾馆, fěicuì bīnguǎn. Wanling ☎ 0831 4970000. Very well located right in the middle of the park, this two-star effort is a decent, if ordinary, option with en suites, hot water and a/c. **¥120**

Dazu

大足, dàzú

About 200km east of Chengdu and 100km west of Chongqing, sleepy **Dazu town** is the base for viewing some fifty thousand Tang- and Song-dynasty **Buddhist cliff sculptures**, which are carved into caves and overhangs in the surrounding lush green hills – most notably at **Baoding Shan**. What makes these carvings so special is not their scale – they cover very small areas compared with better-known sites at Luoyang or Dunhuang – but their quality, state of preservation, and variety of subject and style. Some are small, others huge, many are brightly painted and form comic-strip-like narratives, their characters portraying religious, moral and historical tales. While most are set fairly deeply into rockfaces or are protected by galleries, all can be viewed in natural light, and are connected by walkways and paths.

Baoding Shan

宝顶山, bǎodǐng shān • Daily 8.30am–5pm • ¥120 • bus from Dazu town every 30min 8am–4pm, ¥5

The carvings at **Baoding Shan**, 16km to the northeast of Dazu town, are exciting, comic and realistic by turns. The project was the life work of the monk **Zhao Zhifeng**, who raised the money and designed and oversaw the carving between 1179 and 1245, explaining the unusually cohesive nature of the ten thousand images depicted here.

The sculptures

The bus drops you among a knot of souvenir stalls, with a path bearing right for a kilometre to the main site, **Dafowan**, whose 31 niches are naturally incorporated into the inner side of a broad, horseshoe-shaped gully. As every centimetre is carved with

12

scenes illustrating Buddhist and Confucian moral tales, intercut with asides on daily life, you could spend a couple of hours walking the circuit here, though it's only around 700m long. Don't miss the fearsome 6m-high sculpture of a demon holding the segmented **Wheel of Predestination** (look for the faint relief near his ankles of a cat stalking a mouse); or the Dabei Pavilion, housing a magnificent gilded **Guanyin**, whose 1007 arms flicker out behind her like flames.

Further around, a 20m-long **Reclining Buddha** features some realistic portraits of important donors, while the **Eighteen Layers of Hell** is a chamber-of-horrors scene interspersed with amusing cameos such as the Hen Wife and the Drunkard and his Mother. The final panel, illustrating the **Life of Liu Benzun**, a Tang-dynasty ascetic from Leshan, is a complete break from the rest, with the hermit surrounded by multifaced Tantric figures, showing a very Indian influence.

ARRIVAL AND DEPARTURE

DAZU

By bus Dazu has two bus stations. The old station (老站, lǎozhàn) on Longzhong Lu handles Chongqing traffic, while the new station (新站, xīnzhàn), on Nanhuan Lu 1km distant in the south of town, is where to catch services to Chengdu.

Destinations Chengdu (4hr 30min); Chongqing (2hr 30min); Leshan (3hr); Yibin (4hr); Zigong (2hr).

ACCOMMODATION

Dazu 大足宾馆, dàzú bīnguǎn. Corner of Longzhong Lu and Longgang Lu ☎ 0234 3721888. Proudly boasting three stars, this place is either packed with tour groups or empty – in which case you can bargain for a discount. Under renovation at time of writing so phone ahead to check work is complete. ¥180

Jinye 金叶宾馆, jīnyè bīnguǎn. Longzhong Lu ☎ 0234 3775566. This cosy place next to Dazu's tobacco factory is showing its age, and unlikely to be anyone's first choice, but a handy alternative if the *Dazu* is full. ¥138

EATING

For food, cheap noodle and stir-fry places are everywhere, with a string of inexpensive restaurants – including hotpot, noodle and fried chicken options – on Dazu's central pedestrian street (步行街, bùxíng jiē), running south off Beihuan Lu, just west of its junction with Shuangta Lu.

Chongqing

重庆, chóngqìng

Based around a hilly, comma-shaped peninsula at the junction of the Yangzi and Jialing rivers, **CHONGQING** is southwestern China's dynamo, its largest city both in scale and population. Formerly part of Sichuan province and now the heavily industrialized core of **Chongqing Municipality**, which stretches 300km east to the Hubei border, the city is also a busy port, whose location 2400km upstream from Shanghai at the gateway between eastern and southwestern China has given Chongqing an enviable commercial acumen. While it's not such a bad spot to spend a day or two while arranging **Yangzi River cruises**, in many other respects the Mountain City (as locals refer to it) has little appeal. Overcrowded and fast-paced, the city is plagued by oppressive pollution, winter fogs and summer humidity. Nor is there much to illustrate Chongqing's history – as China's wartime capital, it was heavily bombed by the Japanese – though the nearby village of **Ciqi Kou** retains a glimmer of Qing times.

Brief history

Chongqing has a long tradition as a place of defiance against hostile powers, despite being ceded as a nineteenth-century **treaty port** to Britain and Japan. From 1242, Song forces held Mongol invaders at bay for 36 years at nearby Hechuan, during the longest continuous campaign on Chinese soil, and it was to Chongqing that the Guomindang government withdrew in 1937, having been driven out of Nanjing by the Japanese.

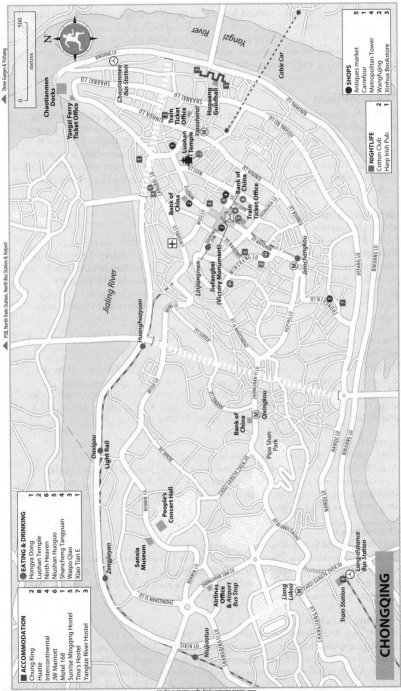

CHONGQING

ACCOMMODATION	
Chung King	2
Huatie	8
Intercontinental	4
JW Marriott	6
Motel 168	1
Sunrise Mingqing Hostel	5
Tina's Hostel	7
Yangtze River Hostel	3

EATING & DRINKING	
Hongya Dong	1
Luohan Temple	2
Ninth Heaven	6
Niushan Huoguo	5
Shancheng Tangyuan	4
Waipo Qiao	3
Xiao Tian E	1

NIGHTLIFE	
Cotton Club	2
Harp Irish Pub	1

SHOPS	
Antiques market	5
Carrefour	4
Metropolitan Tower	2
Wangfujing	2
Xinhua Bookstore	3

12

The US military also had a toehold here under **General Stilwell**, who worked alongside the Nationalists until falling out with Chiang Kai-shek in 1944. Though still showing a few wartime scars, since the 1990s Chongqing has boomed; now over two million people rub elbows on the peninsula, with five times that number in the ever-expanding mantle of suburbs and industrial developments spreading away from the river.

The peninsula

During its Qing-dynasty heyday, almost all of Chongqing city was packed into the walled **peninsula**, forming an enormously rich port with abundant temples, pagodas and public buildings. Not much of these times survive, largely thanks to Japanese saturation bombing during World War II, and the peninsula as a whole is shambolic – most development seems to be targeting Chongqing's newer, ever-expanding western suburbs – though it's being modernized to resemble a miniature Hong Kong, complete with skyscrapers, hills and a profit-hungry populace.

Jiefangbei district

解放碑, jiěfàngbēi · Xiaoshenzi metro station

Isolated by a broad, paved pedestrian square and glassy modern tower blocks, **Jiefangbei**, the Victory Monument – actually a clocktower – marks the peninsula's social and commercial heart. Northeast along Minzu Lu, **Luohan Temple** (罗汉寺, luóhàn sì; daily 8am–6pm; ¥10) is named for its **luohan hall**, a maze of 524 life-sized, grotesque statues of Buddhist saints. The excellent vegetarian restaurant is open at lunchtime, and if you explain you're coming to eat you won't need to buy an entry ticket for the temple.

The cable car

长江索道, chángjiāng suǒdào · ¥5

Around the corner from the temple, a **cable-car station** on Xinhua Lu, just by the Xiaoshenzi metro station exit, carries passengers over the Yangzi to southern Chongqing. Views on the five-minute trip take in river traffic, rampant redevelopment along the southern shore of the peninsula, trucks collecting landfill in low-season mud, and distant hills – merely faint grey silhouettes behind the haze.

Hongya Dong

洪崖洞传统风貌区, hóngyádòng chuántǒng fēngmào qū

Along Cangbai Lu, west of the new suspension bridge, **Hongya Dong** is a multilevel entertainment area with antique flourishes built into the cliffside facing the river; food stalls and a popular expat-run Irish bar are probably its biggest attraction, though there are plenty of souvenir shops too.

Chaotianmen

朝天门码头, cháotiānmén mǎtóu · Chaotianmen metro station

To spy on more waterfront activity, head down to **Chaotianmen docks**, a five-minute walk downhill from the Luohan Temple along Xinhua Lu. The paved **viewing area** on the high bank overlooking the tip of the peninsula makes a great perch to look down on Yangzi ferries and barges moored along the river.

Huguang Guildhall

湖广会馆, húguǎng huìguǎn · Daily 9am–6pm · ¥30 · Xiaoshenzi metro station

The **Huguang Guildhall**, uphill in the backstreets off Binjiang Lu, was built in 1759 as a hotel and meeting point for merchants from Jiangxi, Hunan and Hubei. Surrounded by a high, warm yellow wall, the complex comprises a dozen or more halls, atriums,

12

ornate gateways and florid roof designs, now converted into a museum of Qing-dynasty trade. Cross the road in front and walk down to the river, and you pass through a surviving fragment of Chongqing's **old city wall**, via a heavy stone gateway and staircase.

Peoples' Concert Hall

人民大礼堂, rénmín dàlǐtáng • Daily 8am–6pm • ¥10 • Zengjiayan metro station

The mighty **Peoples' Concert Hall**, at the western end of the peninsula on Renmin Lu, was built in the 1950s along the lines of Beijing's Temple of Heaven, and accommodates four thousand opera-goers in the circular, green-tiled rotunda. It's certainly a striking (and large) building sited as it is at the head of People's Square, but, unless you are lucky enough to catch a concert here, paying to go inside is not an absolute necessity.

Sanxia Museum

三峡博物馆, sānxiá bówùguǎn • Daily 9am–5pm, last entry 4pm • Free • Zengjiayan metro station

Facing the People's Concert Hall, the **Sanxia Museum** commemorates Chongqing's regional history over four floors. Picks here include the Three Gorges Hall, with beautifully arranged dioramas of gorge scenery and a range of archeological finds; the Ba-Yu Hall, which covers everything from pre-human fossils to a marvellous array of Eastern Han tomb bricks; and the Li Chunli Hall, a donated collection of exquisite antique porcelain and paintings.

12

West along the Jialing River

Two worthwhile sights lie west of Chongqing's peninsula along a 12km strip of the Jialing River: the wartime US command centre at the **Stilwell Museum**, and antique streets at the one-time port town of **Ciqi Kou**. Both can be tied into a single trip using the light rail and city buses, but give yourself enough time – it can take well over an hour to get to Ciqi Kou from the centre.

The Stilwell Museum

史迪威将军博物馆, shǐdíwēi jiāngjūn bówùguǎ • Jialingxin Lu • Daily 9am–5pm • ¥15 • metro to Fotuguan station (佛图关站, fótúguān zhàn), then walk 250m downhill to the museum

The **Stilwell Museum** occupies the former home of General Joseph Stilwell, Chief Commander of the US forces' China, Burma and India operations from 1942 until 1944. Stilwell had served as a military attaché in China during the 1930s, and during the war had to coordinate the recapture of Burma and the re-establishment of overland supply lines into China from India. He was also caught up in keeping the shaky Nationalist-Communist alliance together, and his insistence that equal consideration be given to both the Guomindang and CCP caused him to fall out with Chiang Kai-shek. The modernist 1930s building has been decked out in period furniture, with informative photo displays charting Stilwell's career.

Flying Tigers Museum

飞虎队展览馆, fēihǔduì zhǎnlǎnguǎn • March–Oct only • donation • metro to Fotuguan station (佛图关站, fótúguān zhàn), then walk 250m downhill to the museum

Directly opposite the Stilwell Museum, the little **Flying Tigers Museum** is dedicated to the "American Volunteer Group of the Chinese Air Force", better known as the Flying Tigers, which formed under General Chennault in 1941 to protect supply flights over the "hump" of the Himalayas between Burma and China. There are maps and photos of pilots and their P-40 Tomahawk fighter planes painted with tigers' eyes and teeth, and the rear of the building has been turned into a pricey gallery selling contemporary Chinese paintings.

Ciqi Kou

磁器口, cíqì kǒu • bus #808 from the train-bus station, via the road below the Stilwell museum, or buses #215, #262 or #265 from Chaotianmen bus station

Though well within the modern city's boundaries, **CIQI KOU**, a former porcelain production centre and port, incredibly retains a handful of flagstoned, one-hundred-year-old streets and wooden buildings. At weekends and holidays the place reaches critical mass with visitors; try to come midweek. Near the entrance, **Zhongjia Yuan** (¥4) is an old courtyard house, worth a quick browse for its antique furniture, clothing and carvings in each room. Then you're into Ciqi Kou's crowded alleys and lanes, thronged with touristy crafts shops (selling embroideries and romantic paintings of Ciqi Kou), old-style teahouses featuring traditional music recitals, snack stalls and small restaurants. On sunny days, many people head down to the river, where there's a beach of sorts and thousands of deckchairs.

ARRIVAL AND DEPARTURE
CHONGQING

BY PLANE

Chongqing Jiangbei International airport (重庆江北飞机场, chóngqìng jiāngběi fēijīchǎng) is 20km northeast of Chongqing, connected to the city by metro (¥7), shuttle bus (¥15) and taxi (40min, ¥50).

Destinations Beijing (23 daily; 2hr 30min); Guangzhou (17 daily; 2hr); Guilin (3 daily; 1hr 15min); Guiyang (2 daily; 1hr 45min); Hong Kong (3 daily; 2hr 10min); Kunming (14 daily; 1hr 10min); Lhasa (12 daily; 2hr 20min); Shanghai (many daily; 2hr 15min); Shenzhen (12 daily; 2hr); Xi'an (7 daily; 1hr); Yichang (1 daily; 1hr).

BY TRAIN

You can buy train tickets for a ¥5 mark-up at the Yangzi Ferry Terminal, and also through several booths around town.

Chongqing train station (重庆火车站, chóngqìng huǒchēzhàn), located on the south side of the peninsula, has useful links through to Kunming, Guiyang, Xi'an, Beijing, Shanghai and beyond. Bus #503, #120 or #68 will get you to Chaotianmen at the peninsula's tip.

North train station (重庆火车北站, chóngqìng huǒchē běizhàn), 5km north of the peninsula, is the terminal for express trains to Chengdu (2hr; ¥100), by far the quickest way to get there. From here catch bus #141 to Chaotianmen bus station or hop on the metro towards Jiefangbei.

Destinations Beijing (5 daily; 24–31hr); Chengdu (23 daily; 2–10hr); Guangzhou (8 daily; 20–30hr); Guiyang (11 daily; 9–11hr); Shanghai (3 daily; 27–40hr); Wuhan (16 daily; 14–18hr); Xi'an (7 daily; 10–12hr).

BY BUS

Main long-distance bus station (重庆长途汽车站, chóngqìng chángtú qìchēzhàn) is on a complex traffic flow near river level at the western end of the peninsula. There are services from here to Chengdu, Langzhong, Leshan, Emei Shan, Dazu, Zigong, Yibin, Changning (for the Shunan Bamboo Sea) and beyond; it's a frenetic place but buying tickets is easy enough.

North bus station (重庆北汽车站, chóngqìng běiqìchēzhàn), next to the North train station, 5km from the city centre on the metro to Jiefangbei or bus #141 to Chaotianmen. You'll need to come here for express coach connections to the Yangzi hydrofoil to Yichang, which actually departs upstream from Fengjie (see p.754).

Destinations Changning (5hr); Chengdu (4hr); Dazu (3hr); Emei Shan (8hr); Langzhong (5hr); Leshan (7hr); Yibin (3hr 30min); Zigong (1hr 30min).

BY FERRY

Buy tickets for Yangzi ferries and the hydrofoil either through an agent – such as accommodation in Xi'an, Chengdu or Chongqing – or at the Chaotianmen ferry terminal ticket office (daily 8am–5pm) at the peninsula's eastern tip. At time of writing the area was undergoing major renovation, but the office itself was still in operation. The main tourist season, when you might have trouble getting tickets for next-day departures, is May through to October.

Public ferries As a guide, ferry fares from Chongqing to Yichang cost approximately ¥650 per person for a double with bathroom, ¥490 for a bed in a quad, down to ¥150 for a bunk in a sixteen-berth dorm. When booking, be clear that you want a stopping boat, which will take around three days – the commuter boats which also ply the route plough through in just 40hr.

Luxury cruisers cost upwards of ¥3000 per person and need to be booked through a reputable agent, preferably overseas, though you can also try out tour desks at upmarket hotels in Chongqing.

Destinations Wanzhou (daily; 12hr); Yichang (daily; 40–72hr).

Hydrofoil to Yichang (5hr; ¥250). The hydrofoil port is now a hardly convenient five-hour bus ride downstream from Chongqing at Fengjie, though the combined 10hr bus-and-hydrofoil journey to Yichang, plus waiting time, is still significantly faster than the 40hr cruise. Buses to Fengjie (¥165) depart from Chongqing's North bus station.

12

GETTING AROUND

By bus City buses (¥1–2) are comprehensive if slow, and, with the growth of the metro, only necessary if venturing beyond central Chongqing.

By metro Chongqing's nippy metro network covers virtually all the sights in the city centre, with lines running along the north side of the peninsula and through the middle. Trains run every 6min 7am–7pm and cost up to ¥7

a ride, depending on distance; finding stations can be tricky, though.

By taxi Taxis cost ¥7 to hire and, while drivers aren't too unscrupulous, it won't hurt to be seen studying a map along the way.

By bicycle Chongqing's gradients and horrendous road interchanges mean that nobody uses bicycles.

ACCOMMODATION

Given that the ferry is the main reason to come to Chongqing, it makes sense to stay near the dock up in the peninsula's eastern end around Jiefangbei and Chaotianmen.

Chung King 重庆饭店, chóngqìng fàndiàn. 41–43 Xinhua Lu ⊕ 0236 3916666, ⊛ www.chungkinghotel .cn. Renovated Art Deco building, rooms are the standard urban Chinese model, comfy enough but starting to age. Tours groups often end up here. **¥429**

Huatie 华铁宾馆, huátiě bīnguǎn. Between the main bus and train stations ⊕ 0236 1603518. This is a well-run budget hotel managed by the railways, but the area is grubby and it's only recommended for an emergency overnight stay. **¥120**

Intercontinental 重庆洲际酒店, chóngqìng zhōujì jiǔdiàn. 101 Minzu Lu ⊕ 0238 9066888, ⊛ intercontinental.com. Business hotel with good-sized extremely well turned-out rooms, coolly professional service, and a lobby café with piano and cream cakes. **¥941**

JW Marriott JW万豪酒店, JW wànjiā jiǔdiàn. 77 Qingnian Lu ⊕ 0236 3888888, ⊛ jwmarriottchongqing .com. Close to the centre and rooms are genuinely luxurious, though the immediate streets are a little grotty. Nightclub complex over the road, and city views from the staeakhouse on the 39th floor. **¥900**

Motel 168 莫泰连锁旅店, mòtài liánsuǒ lǚdiàn. 52 Cangbai Lu ⊕ 0236 3849999, ⊛ motel168.com. The usual friendly deal with spacious rooms at lowish rates, though rooms are subterranean and only the pricier ones have windows. If the 168 doesn't grab you, there's also a

slitlightly pricier Home Inn in the same building. **¥190**

Sunrise Mingqing Hostel 尚悦明清客楼, shàngyuè míngqíng kèlóu. 23 Xiahongxue Xiang ⊕ 0236 3931 579, ⊛ srising.com. Hidden on the west side of the Huguang Guildhall, this atmospheric, 200-year-old courtyard building may be facing demolition, though having survived this long it has to be hoped it can stay up a bit longer. Rooms are clean, if a little dark, and staff can help with the usual tours and travel advice. Dorms **¥40**, rooms **¥180**

Tina's Hostel 重庆老街客栈青年旅舍, chóngqìng lǎojiē kèzhàn qīngnián lǚshè. 149 Zhongxing Lu ⊕ 0238 6219188, ⊛ cqhostel.com. This place isn't easy to find, tucked down an alley near the antiques market, and it's in an area facing imminent demolition. Having said this, the hostel itself is in a nicely converted old building, the owner and staff are helpful and speak good English, and the food is above average. Call ahead to check. Dorms **¥40**, rooms **¥100**

Yangtze River Hostel 玺院国际青年旅舍, xǐyuàn guójì qīngnián lǚshè. 80 Changbin Lu ⊕ 0236 3104208, ⊛ chongqinghostels.com. Faux-antique building on the main waterfront road just downhill from the guildhall. Has a bar and all the usual facilities, rooms are on the small side but comfortable enough and the location is good. Staff are helpful with information and tours. Dorms **¥40**, rooms **¥140**

EATING AND DRINKING

Chongqing's centre is alive with canteens and food stalls, and at meal times already busy side streets and markets become obstacle courses of plastic chairs, low tables and wok-wielding cooks. Local tastes lean towards snacks; a local speciality is the use of puréed raw garlic as a dressing, which only the Sichuanese could get away with. Hotpot is believed to have originated here, with the basic ingredients arriving on plates, not skewers, so the pots are divided up into compartments to prevent everyone's portions getting mixed up. For a wide range of light meals and snacks, head to Hongya Dong on Cangbai Lu (see p.746); café chains such as *Shangdao* are your best bet for non-Sichuanese fare. Chongqing Beer is the local brew, served in squat, brown-glass bottles.

Luohan Temple 罗汉寺饭店, luóhànsì fàndiàn. Minzu Lu ⊕ 0236 3717779. A comfy vegetarian temple restaurant serving everything from humble *douhua* (soft tofu served with a chilli relish) to imitation spareribs and suckling pig. The menu has pictures, and some staff speak English. You

can eat well here for ¥40/person. Daily 9am–8pm.

Ninth Heaven 九重天饭店, jiǔchóngtiān fàndiàn. 29F, Yudu Hotel, 168 Bayi Lu ⊕ 023 63830383. The Sichuanese food here is competent and tasty, if a little expensive – try the "rabbit threads" in cut buns and mountain mushrooms with cold bamboo shoots – but the bonus is that the restaurant revolves, with the city looking its best after dark. Count on ¥100/person. Daily 11am–10pm.

Niushan Huoguo 牛山火锅, niúshān huǒguō. 248 Wuyi Lu. Seemingly the last of the fast-and-furious hotpot shacks that once lined this street, where you bump elbows with your fellow diners while dipping skewers into boiling hot, chilli-laced oil. Inexpensive and unconcerned about hygiene. Expect to pay ¥40 per person. Daily 11am–10pm.

Shancheng Tangyuan 山城汤圆, shānchéng tāngyuán. 175 Bayi Lu. Recently expanded to fill two holes in the wall on both sides of Bayi Lu, these tiny establishments are famed city-wide for their glutinous rice dumplings at ¥5/serving. Daily 9am–8pm.

★ **Waipo Qiao** 外婆桥, wàipó qiáo. 7F Metropolitan Tower, 68 Zourong Lu ☎0236 3835988. On top of one of the city's swishest shopping malls, this excellent restaurant has three separate rooms, an inexpensive one for snacks, one for hotpot (with the ingredients floated past you in little boats) and a smart one for proper dining. They're all good and have bilingual photo menus. ¥30–150/person. Daily 11am–10pm.

Xiao Tian E 小天鹅火锅城, xiǎo tiāné huǒguō chéng. Level 4, Hongya Dong, Cangbai Lu ☎023 63788811. Rated as one of the best hotpot restaurants in Chongqing, choose from an seemingly unending list of meat, vegetables, river food and tofu and cook your selection boil in a vat of fiery broth. ¥100/person. Daily 11am–10pm.

NIGHTLIFE

Chongqing's nightlife has grown along with its affluence, and drinking holes and nightclubs have spread throughout the town centre. As with elsewhere, places often open and close pretty quickly, so for the latest listings and what's-on visit Ⓦ cscene.com or Ⓦ cqexpat.com.

Cotton Club 棉花酒乐吧, huājiǔ lèba. In the entertainment complex opposite the JW Marriott hotel ☎023 63810028. A reliable nightspot which has been going for years. Drinks are a pricey ¥30 and up, but there's a house band recognized as the best in the city. Daily 7pm–3am.

Harp Irish Pub 9F Hongya Dong, Cangbai Lu ☎0236 3038655, Ⓦharpcq.com. A standard, but popular, Irish bar with friendly clientele, drinks from ¥20 and decent Western bar food. They also have a rooftop area on the 11th Floor which shows big-screen sports including English Premier League. Daily 4pm–late.

SHOPPING

Antiques and curios For a good browse through four floors of wooden screens, stone basins, Mao-era mementos, comics, pottery and ceramics, try the antiques market (收藏品市场, shōuzángpǐn shìchǎng), inside what looks like an abandoned 1960s department store at 75 Zhongxin Lu.

Bookshop The huge Xinhua Bookstore just west of Jiefangbei on Zourong Lu has Chinese-language maps and

guides on the first floor, and a small stock of English-language titles on the fourth floor.

Shopping malls The Metropolitan Tower at 68 Zourong Lu has smart international boutiques on the lower floors, an ice-rink on the 6th, and restaurants throughout; nearby Wangfujing has more of the same, plus a cinema. For all manner of food – including a few Western imports – head to Carrefour, just off Minzu Lu near Luohan Temple.

DIRECTORY

Banks and exchange The main Bank of China is in the centre of the peninsula on Zhongshan Yi Lu, though the Jiefangbei area is full of branches and ATMs.

Consulates Britain, Suite 28, Metropolitan Tower, 68 Zourong Lu (☎0236 3691500); Cambodia, 10F, China Life Insurance Building, 2 Kuaizi Lu (☎0236 3113666); Canada, Suite 1705, Metropolitan Tower, Wuyi Lu (☎0236 3738007); Denmark, Suite 3101, Daduhui Building, Jiefangbei (☎0236 3726600).

Internet Free terminals at the hostels, plus most

accommodation has wi-fi or ADSL sockets in rooms.

Mail There's a post office (daily 8.30am–9.30pm) in Jiefangbei behind all the mobile-phone sellers at 5 Minquan Lu.

PSB A long way north of the centre at 555 Huanglong Lu, Yubei District (☎0236 3961916), and its reputation for granting visa extensions is not good – best go elsewhere if possible.

Medical Global Doctor International Clinic, Room 701 Business Tower, Hilton Chongqing, 139 Zhongshan San Lu (☎0238 9038837, Ⓦglobaldoctor.com.au).

Wulong

武隆, wǔlóng

Some 250km southeast of Chongqing along the Guizhou border, **Wulong** is a national park enclosing a massive, rugged area of limestone sinkholes, caves and river systems.

The place to aim for at present is **Natural Three Bridges** (天生三桥, tiānshēng sān qiáo; daily 9am–6.30pm; entry, including transport inside the park, ¥95), about 50 minutes away. Once inside the park, buses drop you off at a two-hour circuit walk through a system of colossal, collapsed tunnels and caves; the Tang-style buildings at the bottom of one sinkhole are sets from Zhang Yimou's period bodice-ripper *Curse of the Golden Flower*.

ARRIVAL AND DEPARTURE   WULONG

The access point for Wulong national park is little Wulong town (武隆县, wǔlóng xiàn).

By train Wulong town is on the Chongqing–Huai Hua rail line with regular services to and from Chongqing.

Destinations Chongqing (12 daily; 2hr 30min).

By bus Wulong's bus station is on Baiyang Lu. Buses to Chongqing run 6am–6pm every half-hour.

Destinations Chongqing (2hr).

GETTING AROUND

By bus and minibus Minibuses from Wulong town (¥20) run north into the national park headquarters through the day; buses from the park headquarters carry you to various locations inside.

ACCOMMODATION

Aside from the following, touts around the bus and train stations can lead you to cheaper places.

Hongfu Fandian 宏福饭店, hóngfú fàndiàn. Wulong town, on the corner of main street Wuxian Lu and Baiyang Lu ☎0236 4501666. Modern, impressively ugly edifice offering clean, sparsely furnished en-suite rooms with a/c. Despite its aesthetic shortcomings, the rooms inside are a decent size, if a bit gloomy. **¥250**

The Yangzi River: Chongqing to Yichang

Rising in the mountains above Tibet, the **Yangzi** links together seven provinces as it sweeps 6400km across the country to spill its muddy waters into the East China Sea, making it the third-longest flow in the world. Appropriately, one of the Yangzi's Chinese names is **Chang Jiang**, the Long River, though above Yibin it's generally known as **Jinsha Jiang** (River of Golden Sands).

Although people have travelled along the Yangzi since recorded history, it was not, until recently, an easy route to follow. The river's most dangerous stretch was the 200km-long **Three Gorges** (三峡, sānxiá) where the waters were squeezed between vertical limestone cliffs over fierce rapids: well into the twentieth century, nobody could negotiate this stretch of river alone; boats had to be hauled literally bit by bit through the rapids by teams of **trackers**, in a journey that could take several weeks, if the boat made it at all.

All this is very much academic today, however, as the **Three Gorges Dam** above Yichang (see p.417) has raised water levels through the gorges by up to 175m, effectively turning the Chongqing–Yichang stretch into a huge lake and allowing **public ferries** and **cruise boats** easy access to the scenery. While rising waters have

CRUISING THE YANGZI

Chongqing is the departure point for the two-day cruise downriver through the **Three Gorges** to Yichang. There are two main **cruise options**, both of which run year-round: relatively inexpensive public ferries, which stop along the way to pick up passengers; and upmarket cruise ships, which only stop at tour sites. For **prices** from Chongqing to Yichang, along with practical information on buying both ferry and cruise-ship tickets, see p.749.

Public ferries are crowded and noisy, with berths starting at **first class** – a small and functional double cabin with bathroom – and descending in varying permutations through triples and quads with shared toilets, to a bed in sixteen-person cabins. **Timing** is important: try to avoid leaving Chongqing between 10am and noon, as you'll hit the first gorge too early and the third too late to see much. Not all ferries pull in at all ports, and schedules can change en route to compensate for delays, so it's possible that you'll miss some key sights. At each stop, departure times are announced in Chinese. **Meals** (buy tickets from the mid-deck office) are cheap, basic and only available for a short time at 7am, 10am and 6pm, though there's plenty available onshore at stops. Bring snacks and, in winter, **warm clothing**. Many tourists complain of unhelpful or plain useless tour guides, and of being harassed by ferry staff to buy expensive on-board tickets for observation decks when access is, in fact, free or much cheaper than advertised.

Alternatively, you could travel in style on a **cruise ship**. These vessels verge on five-star luxury, with comfortable cabins, glassed-in observation decks, games rooms and real restaurants. They're usually booked out by tour parties during peak season, though at other times you can often wrangle discounts and get a berth at short notice.

12

submerged some of the landscape – not to mention entire towns – many settlements and historical sites have been relocated in the interests of preservation and much of the scenery retains its grandeur.

Chongqing to Wanzhou

The cruise's initial 250km, before the first of the Three Gorges begins at Baidicheng, takes in hilly farmland along the riverbanks, with the first likely stop 172km from Chongqing at south-bank **FENGDU** (丰都, fēngdū), the "Ghost City". On the opposite side of the Yangzi, **Ming Shan Park** (名山公园, míngshān gōngyuán; ¥80) is a hillside covered in monuments to Tianzi, King of the Dead; the main temple here, **Tianzi Dian** (天子殿, tiānzǐ diàn), is crammed full of colourful demon statues and stern-faced judges of hell.

Shibaozhai

石宝寨, shíbǎozhài • ¥50

A further 70km along the Yangzi from Fengdu, **Shibaozhai** is a 220m-high rocky buttress a few kilometres downstream from Zhongxian county town. Grafted onto its side – and protected from new water levels by an embankment – is the twelve-storey, bright-red **Lanruo Dian** (兰若殿, lánruò diàn; ¥50), a pagoda built in 1819. The temple above dates to 1750, famed for a hole in its granary wall through which poured just enough rice to feed the monks; greedily, they tried to enlarge it, and the frugal supply stopped forever.

Wanzhou

万州, wànzhōu

Ferries might pull in overnight 330km from Chongqing at the halfway point of **WANZHOU**, now a large, modern city clinging to the hills above the river. Almost half the old settlement, and the entirety of its port, were submerged as waters rose behind the dam downstream. Being a virtually brand-new city, there's not a huge amount to see, but it's worth getting off the boat to have a wander up its steep streets, sample its restaurants, and see how people are adapting to their post-dam lives.

The Three Gorges

The **Three Gorges** themselves begin 450km from Chongqing 18km past **FENGJIE** (奉节, fēngjié) at **Baidi Cheng** (白帝城, báidì chéng), a fortified island strategically located right at the mouth of the first gorge. Baidi Cheng is closely associated with events of the *Romance of the Three Kingdoms* (see p.393); it was here in 265 AD that **Liu Bei** died after failing to avenge his sworn brother Guan Yu in the war against Wu. These events are recalled at the **Baidi temple** (白帝庙, báidì miào; ¥70), where there's a waxworks tableau of Liu Bei on his deathbed, and paths up to lookout points into the narrow, vertical-sided Qutang gorge.

Qutang Gorge

瞿塘峡, qútáng xiá

Beyond Baidicheng, the river pours through a narrow slash in the cliffs and into **Qutang Gorge**, the shortest at just 8km long, but also the narrowest and fiercest, its once-angry waters described by the Song poet Su Dongpo as "a thousand seas in one cup". The vertical cliffs, rising to a sharp peak on the north bank, are still impressive despite the new water levels.

Little Three Gorges

小三峡, xiǎo sānxiá • cruise from Wushan in a modern, glass-topped canal boat ¥250

On the far side of Qutang, **WUSHAN** (巫山, wūshān) marks a half-day detour north up the Daning River through the **Little Three Gorges**. This 33km excursion offers narrower, tighter and steeper scenery than along the Yangzi, particularly through the awesome **Longmen Gorge**.

Wu Gorge

巫峡, wūxiá

Wushan also sits at the mouth of 45km-long **Wu Gorge**, where the goddess **Yao Ji** and her eleven sisters quelled some unruly river dragons and then turned themselves into mountains, thoughtfully positioned to help guide ships downriver.

Zigui and Xiling Gorge

Out the other side of Wu Gorge and in Hubei province, **ZIGUI** (秭归, zǐguī) was the birthplace of the poet **Qu Yuan**, whose suicide a couple of millennia ago is commemorated throughout China by dragon-boat races. Zigui is also where 76km-long **Xiling Gorge** (西陵峡, xīlíng xiá) begins. The Xiling stretch was once the most dangerous: Westerners passing through in the nineteenth century described the shoals as forming weirs across the river, the boat fended away from threatening rocks by trackers armed with iron-shod bamboo poles, as it rocked through into the sunless, narrow chasm. Nowadays vessels cruise through with ease, sailing on to a number of smaller gorges, some with splendid names – Sword and Book, Ox Liver and Horse Lung – suggested by the rock formations.

The Three Gorges Dam and Yichang

At the eastern end of the gorges, cruises terminate at the monstrous **Three Gorges Dam** (三峡坝, sānxiá bà), from where there are minibus tours of the dam site and buses onwards to Yichang, 30km downstream – for more on which, see p.420.

Western Sichuan

Sichuan's western half, sprawling towards Gansu, Yunnan and Tibet, is in every respect an exciting place to travel. The countryside couldn't be farther from the Chengdu plains, with the western highlands forming some of China's most imposing scenery – broad grasslands grazed by yaks and horses, ravens tumbling over snowbound gullies and passes, and unforgettable views of mountain ranges rising up against crisp blue skies.

How you explore western Sichuan will depend on your long-term travel plans. If you're heading north out of the province **to Gansu**, you first want to aim for the walled town of **Songpan**, horse-trekking centre and base for excursions to the nearby scenic reserves of **Huanglong** and **Jiuzhaigou**. Beyond Songpan, the road continues north via the monastery town of **Langmusi**, and so over into Gansu province.

Sichuan's immense **far west** is accessed from the administrative capital **Kangding** – itself worth a stopover for easy access to the nearby scenery, or as a springboard north to pretty **Danba**. Alternatively, you can either weave northwest to Tibet via the monastery towns of **Ganzi** and **Dêgê**, with a faith-inducing mountain pass and Dêgê's Scripture Printing Hall as the pick of the sights along the way; or head due west to the high-altitude monastic seat of **Litang**, from where you can continue down into Yunnan.

Brief history

Though larger towns throughout the west have to a certain extent been settled by Han and Hui (Muslims) – the latter spread between their major populations in adjoining provinces – historically the region was not part of Sichuan at all but was known as **Kham**, a set of small states which spilled into the fringes of Qinghai and Yunnan. The Tibetans who live here, the **Khampas**, speak their own dialect, and see themselves as distinct from Tibetans further west – it wasn't until the seventeenth century, during the aggressive rule of the Fifth Dalai Lama, that monasteries here were forcibly converted to the dominant Gelugpa sect and the people brought under Lhasa's thumb. The Khampas retain their tough, independent reputation today, and culturally the region remains emphatically Tibetan, containing not only some of the country's most important lamaseries, but also an overwhelmingly Tibetan population – indeed, statistically a far greater percentage than in Tibet proper. For details on Tibetan food, language and religious thought, see the relevant sections at the start of Chapter 14.

12

GETTING AROUND WESTERN SICHUAN

Travel in western Sichuan requires stamina: journey times between towns are long, roads twist interminably, breakdowns are far from uncommon, and landslides, ice or heavy snow can block roads for days at a time. At time of writing a major road-building programme was under way, affecting almost all main routes through the region. When completed, these new highways, featuring a seemingly endless alternation of enormous bridges and lengthy tunnels, will massively reduce journey times; until then, expect long delays as smaller back routes, often limited to taking traffic in a single direction at a time, take the strain.

Almost all of western Sichuan rises above 2500m – one pass exceeds 5000m – and you'll probably experience the effects of altitude (see p.53). You'll need to carry enough **cash** to see you through, as there are no cash machines taking international cards, or banks capable of dealing with travellers' cheques, beyond Kangding. **Horse-trekking** is a popular pastime in the region, too, with well-established operations at Songpan, Tagong and Langmusi, and plenty of ad hoc opportunities elsewhere. As for the **seasons**, the area looks fantastic from spring through to autumn – though warm, weatherproof clothing is essential whatever the time of year. Note that much of the region is **closed to foreigners through March**, anniversary of various uprisings in Tibet – Songpan and Jiuzhaigou will probably be open, but travel north to Gansu, or to Kangding and far western Sichuan, will be impossible.

DOG WARNING

Western Sichuan's wild, open countryside makes for good hiking, but you need to beware of **dogs**. Some of these are just the scrawny mongrels that roam around all Tibetan settlements, including monasteries; carry a pocketful of stones and a good stick, and you should be fine. Guard dogs, however, you need to keep well clear of: you don't want an encounter with a Tibetan mastiff. These are kept chained up as a rule, but don't go near isolated houses or, especially, nomad tents without calling out so that people know you're there and will check that their dogs are secure.

Songpan

松潘, sōngpān

SONGPAN, 320km north of Chengdu, was founded in Qing times as a garrison town straddling both the Min River and the main road to Gansu. Strategically, it guards the neck of a valley, built up against a stony ridge to the west and surrounded on the remaining three sides by 8m-high stone **walls**. These have been partially restored, and you can walk between the north and east gates and above the south gate. Though increasingly touristed, Songpan's **shops**, stocked with handmade woollen blankets, fur-lined jackets, ornate knives, saddles, stirrups, bridles and all sorts of jewellery, cater to local Tibetans and **Qiang**, another mountain-dwelling minority. In spring, Songpan – along with every town in western Sichuan – becomes a marketplace for bizarre **caterpillar fungus** (虫草, chóngcǎo); for more on this strange trade, see p.791.

Inside the walls

Songpan itself forms a small, easily navigated rectangle: the main road, partially pedestrianized, runs for about 750m from the **north gate** (北门, běimén) straight down to the **south gate** (南门, nánmén) – both mighty stone constructions topped with brightly painted wooden pavilions. Around two-thirds of the way down, covered **Gusong Bridge** (古松桥, gǔsōng qiáo) has a roof embellished with painted dragon, bear and flower carvings. Side roads head off to the **east gate** (东大门, dōng dàmén) – another monumental construction – and west into a small grid of market lanes surrounding the town's main **mosque** (古清真寺, gǔ qīngzhēn sì), an antique wooden affair painted in subdued yellows and greens, catering to the substantial Muslim population (there's another mosque north of town). Just outside the south gate is a **second gateway**, with what would originally have been a walled courtyard between the two, where caravans were inspected for dangerous goods before entering the city proper.

12

ARRIVAL AND DEPARTURE | **SONGPAN**

In 2008, the area between Chengdu and Songpan was hit by a terrible force-eight earthquake, which destroyed most of the regional infrastructure. At the time of writing, the direct Chengdu–Songpan road remained in an atrocious state, taking anything between twelve and thirty-six hours to negotiate, and buses were making a very roundabout eleven-hour journey via Pingwu (平武, píngwǔ) to Jiuzhaigou and then Songpan. Note that a rail line to Songpan is also under construction, though completion dates are unknown. Check in Chengdu about the current situation before booking bus tickets.

By plane Jiuhuang airport (九黄机场, jiǔhuáng jīchǎng) is 30km to the northeast of Songpan, with transport waiting for Songpan, Huanglong and Jiuzhaigou. Tickets can be bought at travel agencies and hotels in Songpan, or online, though fares are extortionate; it costs ¥1200 to Chengdu, for example.
Destinations Beijing (2 daily; 2hr 30min); Chengdu (19

daily; 1hr); Chongqing (8 daily; 1hr); Guangzhou (1 daily; 2hr 30min); Xi'an (5 daily; 1hr).
By bus Songpan's bus station is about 250m outside the north gate. For Langmusi, either catch a Xiahe-bound bus and ask to be dropped off on the main road nearby, or catch the 10am Zöigê bus, and with luck you'll just make the 2pm Zöigê–Langmusi service.

HORSE-TREKKING AT SONGPAN

The reason to stop in Songpan is to spend a few days **horse-trekking** through the surrounding hills, which harbour hot springs and waterfalls, grassland plateaus and permanently icy mountains. Shunjiang Horse Treks (☏0837 17231161 or 0139 09043513), on the main road between the bus station and the north gate, charge ¥220 a person per day, including everything except entry fees to reserves. Accommodation is in tents, and the guides are generally attentive, though may not speak much English. Prepare for extreme cold and tasteless food; some groups have bought and slaughtered a goat (¥400) to bolster rations. Note that the friendly veneer of the company's staff disappears rapidly if they're presented with a complaint, so be sure to agree beforehand on exactly what your money is buying.

Destinations Chengdu (8–12hr); Huanglong (2hr); Jiuzhaigou (2hr); Langmusi (4–6hr); Zöigê (4hr).

By minibus *Emma's Kitchen* can organize shared taxis to various destinations, including Huanglong and Langmusi.

ACCOMMODATION

Songpan's water – hot or otherwise – flows at unpredictable times, ditto electricity, so use it when available. Room rates can double July to September, when domestic tourism peaks.

★ **Guyun Kezhan** 古韵客栈, gǔyùn kèzhàn. Opposite the bus station ☎ 0837 17231368. This Muslim homestay has very nicely done traditional wooden galleries around a central atrium. Clean, cosy – some might say small – rooms, 24-hr hot water and wi-fi. Dorm ¥30, room ¥100

Jiaotong Binguan 交通宾馆, jiāotōng bīnguǎn. Attached to the bus station ☎ 0837 17231818. A serviceable, convenient place, but also basic and doesn't boast the 24hr hot water of other options in town. Dorm ¥25, room ¥50

Shunjiang Guesthouse 顺江旅游客栈, shùnjiāng lǚyóu kèzhàn. Shunjinag Bei Lu ☎ 0837 17231064. Between the bus station and the north gate, and next door to the horse-trekking agency, this is another simple, sparsely furnished guesthouse, but there is 24hr hot water and beds come with electric blankets. Dorm ¥25, room ¥80

EATING AND DRINKING

Songpan's places to eat revolve around the numerous noodle joints between the north gate and the bus station; *maoniurou gan* (yak jerky) is sold in shops around town; you should also try sweet *qingke jiu*, local barley beer.

★ **Emma's Kitchen**. South of the bus station, on the main road ☎ 0837 7231088, ✉ emmachina@hotmail .com. Foreigners' café, serving tasty burgers and barley soup, among other options – expect to pay around ¥25 for mains. Emma is also a good source of tour and transport information, can book onward tickets, and runs a laundry service. Daily 8am–11pm.

Xingyue Lou 星月楼, xīngyuè lóu. 150m inside the north gate along the main road south through Songpan. A large but fairly rough-around-the-edges Muslim restaurant, serving delicious crisp-roast duck and noodle soup. It's good value too, around ¥30 for duck and ¥15 for noodles. Daily 8am–10pm.

DIRECTORY

Banks The Agricultural Bank of China, about 100m inside the north gate, has an ATM accepting credit cards.

Massage There's a blind masseur next door to *Emma's* if you're stiff after a tour in the saddle.

Huanglong

黄龙, huánglóng • Daily 9am–4pm • April–Oct ¥200, Nov–March ¥60 • optional cable car ¥80

Huanglong, a 4km-long glacial valley, lies at an altitude of 3000m in the mountains 60km northeast of Songpan. Limestone-rich waters flowing down the valley have left yellow calcified deposits between hundreds of shallow blue ponds, and their scaly appearance gives Huanglong – "Yellow Dragon" – its name. The reserve here is fairly small and can be walked around in a few hours (though the altitude can easily wear you out); note that public transport in and out is limited and you'll want to make sure you know when the last bus is leaving and time your visit accordingly.

Around the reserve

An 8km circuit track on well-made boardwalks over the fragile formations ascends east up the valley from the main-road **park gates**, through surprisingly thick deciduous woodland, pine forest and, finally, rhododendron thickets. Pick of the scenery includes the broad **Golden Flying Waterfall** and the kilometre-long calcified slope **Golden Sand on Earth**, where the shallow flow tinkles over innumerable ridges and pockmarks. Around 3km along, the small **Middle Temple** (中寺, zhōngsì) was once an important centre for **Bon**, Tibet's original religion; today, it seems inactive – even if signs do ask you to circuit to the right in the Bon manner.

Huanglong Ancient Temple

黄龙古寺, huánglóng gǔsì

At the head of the valley, **Huanglong Ancient Temple** is a Qing building, featuring an atrium and two small Taoist halls, dedicated to the local guardian deity. Behind here, a 300m-long valley bowl is filled with multi-hued blue pools, contrasting brilliantly with the drab olive vegetation; the best views are from a small platform on the slopes above.

ARRIVAL AND DEPARTURE   HUANGLONG

By bus In theory, buses travelling directly between Songpan and Pingwu can drop you off en route (¥36), though in reality this road is seldom used and there is, at best, only one bus a day in each direction. There is also one scheduled bus daily each way between Jiuzhaigou and Huanglong.
By minibus taxi Eight-seater minibuses for day-trips to Huanglong can be rented in Songpan for ¥300–400.

ACCOMMODATION

Hualong 华龙山庄, huálóng shānzhuāng. At the park gates ☏ 0837 7249025, ⌨ www.hlszhotel.com. Huanglong's only accommodation is this upmarket four-star establishment. Rooms are excellent and well furnished, there is a choice of restaurants, a gym, karaoke facilities and a spa, all of which go some way to justifying the price tag. **¥700**

Jiuzhaigou

九寨沟 jiǔzhàigōu • Daily 7am–7pm • April–Nov ¥220/day, Nov–March ¥80 • unlimited bus use around the park ¥90

Around 100km northeast of Songpan, the perpetually snow-clad Min Shan range encloses **Jiuzhaigou** – "Nine Stockades Valley" – named after it was settled by Tibetans several hundred years ago. The reserve forms a Y-shaped series of valleys clothed in thick alpine forests and strung with hundreds of impossibly toned **blue lakes** – said to be the scattered shards of a mirror belonging to the Tibetan goddess Semo. Jiuzhaigou's landscape looks spectacular in the autumn when the gold and red leaves contrast brilliantly with the water, or at the onset of winter in early December, when everything is dusted by snow.

Despite its remote location, Jiuzhaigou is the target of **intense tourism** – packages are offered by every travel agent in Sichuan – so don't come here expecting a quiet commune with nature, as the park clocks up over a million visitors annually. The best you can do is to get in when the gates open at 7am and try to stay one step ahead of the hordes.

Into the reserve

The entrance is at **JIUZHAIGOU KOU** (九寨沟口, jiǔzhàigōu kǒu), a kilometre-wide blob of services either side of the park gates. It's 14km from here to the centre of the reserve around Nuorilang, a journey that passes a marshy complex of pools at the foot of imposing Dêgê Shan that forms the **Shuzheng lakes** (树正海, shùzhèng hǎi), the largest group in the reserve and cut part-way along by the 20m **Shuzheng Falls**.

Nuorilang

诺日朗, nuòrìlǎng

Nuorilang is a tourist village where you can don Tibetan garb and pose on horseback for photos; there's also a **visitors' centre** with set lunches; and Jiuzhaigou's most famous cascades, the **Nuorilang Falls** (诺日朗瀑布, nuòrìlǎng pùbù). They look best from the road, framed by trees as water forks down over the strange, yellow crystalline rockfaces.

To the Primeval Forest and Five-coloured Lake

The road forks east and west at Nuorilang, with both forks around 18km long. The **eastern branch** first passes Pearl Beach Falls (珠滩瀑布, zhūtān pùbù), where a whole hillside has calcified into an ankle-deep cascade similar to Huanglong, but the main attraction here is the **Primeval Forest** (原始森林, yuánshǐ sēnlín), a dense and very

---

JIUZHAIGOU ECO-TOURS

If you're fairly fit and want to escape Jiuzhaigou's tourist overload, it's possible to organize **three-day treks** through the otherwise inaccessible Zharu Valley with Jiuzhaigou's eco-tourism department (¥1580, including entry fees, guides, food and all camping gear; ☎0837 7739753, ⓦjiuzhai.com); the route circuits 4500m-high Zhayi Zhaga mountain.

---

atmospheric belt of ancient conifers right at the end of the road. There's less to see along the **western branch** from Nuorilang, but don't miss the stunning **Five-coloured Lake** (五彩池, wǔcǎi chí), which, for sheer intensity, if not scale, is unequalled in the park.

ARRIVAL AND DEPARTURE JIUZHAIGOU

Via Jiuzhaigou town Jiuzhaigou town, 40km east of the reserve entrance at Jiuzhaigou Kou, has a large long-distance bus station where some traffic travelling via Pingwu might terminate. Shared taxis shuttle back and forth between Jiuzhaigou town and the park gates all day long, charging ¥10 per person.

Via Jiuzhaigou Kou Jiuzhaigou Kou's bus station (九寨沟口汽车站, jiǔzhàigōukǒu qìchēzhàn) lies

just east of the park entrance; all its services depart between 7am and 8am and you need to buy tickets from the booth here at least a day in advance. Aside from long-distance routes, there is also one bus daily each way between Jiuzhaigou and Huanglong.

Destinations Chengdu (2 daily; 9–13hr); Guangyuan (1 daily; 8hr); Lanzhou (1 daily; 11hr); Songpan (2 daily; 2hr 30min).

GETTING AROUND

Some people plan to save on the bus fare by hiking everywhere, but given the distances involved – over 30km from the gates to either end of the "Y" – this isn't a realistic option.

12

By bus Buses run around the park all through the day; ticket holders have unrestricted use of them. The best plan is to head to the more distant sights and work your way back towards the entrance, as services begin to thin out after 3pm.

On foot Most tourists get off the bus en masse at sights, pose for photos, and move on. However, there's quite a network of under-used, erosion-resistant boardwalks around each stop, which will soon take you away from the crowds.

ACCOMMODATION

Note that there is no official accommodation inside the park, though some people have stayed there – illegally – with Tibetan families.

Grass Roots Hostel 草根人家, cǎogēn rénjiā. 250m west of the park gates ☎0837 7764922. Mirror image of the nearby *Ziyou*, with each acting as overflow for the other. Basic plain rooms, 24hr hot water and resident Chinese backpackers. Dorm **¥35**, room **¥80**

MCA MCA国际乡村客栈, MCA guójì xiāngcūn kèzhàn. Behind the bus station, east of the park ☎0837 7739818. Nicely situated beside a stream and slightly away from the crowds at the gate, slightly smarter and pricier than other budget options. Dorm **¥80**, room **¥150**

Sheraton 喜来登国际大酒店, xǐláidēng guójì dàjiǔdiàn. On the main road just north of the park gates. ☎0837 7739988, ⓦstarwoodhotels.com. Characterless luxury accommodation in an enormous faux Tibetan complex, complete with a giant stupa outside.

Certainly the best quality rooms in the area, but also the most expensive by far. **¥2000**

★ **Zhuo Ma's** 卓玛, zhuōmǎ. 13km west of the park ☎01356 8783012, ⓦwww.zhuomajiuzhaigou.hostel .com. Best option in the whole area is this, a Tibetan homestay in a beautiful traditional family home, run by the welcoming Zhuo Ma. Call ahead and she'll pick you up from the park gates. Price includes meals. Per person **¥180**

Ziyou Youth Hostel 自游国际青年旅舍, zìyóu guójì qīngnián lǚshě. Just outside the park gates ☎0837 7764617. Simple dorms and private rooms, popular with Chinese student backpackers on their holidays, so can get busy in peak season. Also has 24hr hot water. Dorm **¥35**, room **¥80**

EATING

For lunch a set meal is available at the Nuorilang visitor centre for around ¥60–80; alternatively, there are plenty of other options scattered around outside the gates.

★ **Abuluzi** 阿布穋孜风情藏餐吧, ābùluzī fēngqíng zàngcānba. East of the park gates, by the MCA and Sheraton ☎ 1399 0421118. Run by Zhou Ma's brother, this traditional Tibetan restaurant serves generous portions of genuine local food served in comfortable and friendly surroundings. They also offer cooking classes. Expect around ¥35 for mains. Daily 11am–10pm.

The Aba Grasslands

Songpan sits just east of the vast, marshy **Aba grasslands**, which sprawl over the Sichuan, Gansu and Qinghai borders. Resting at around 3500m and draining into the headwaters of the Yellow River, the grasslands are home to nomadic herders and birdlife – including black-necked cranes and golden eagles – and form a corridor between Sichuan and Gansu province. Buses from Songpan run north to the grassland town of **Zöigê** and over the border, with Tibetan monasteries at **Langmusi** offering a prime reason to stop off along the way.

Zöigê

若尔盖, ruò'ěrgài

Around 150km northwest of Songpan at the grasslands' northernmost edge, **ZÖIGÊ** is a tidy collection of markets and shops along Shuguang Lu and parallel Shangye Jie. The town's low-key **Daza monastery** (达扎寺, dázā sì) is worth a visit – not least for the small hall here whose galleried porch is hung with badly stuffed yaks, deer and blood-spattered wolves – but most people only spend time in Zöigê because they've missed the bus out.

12

ARRIVAL AND DEPARTURE ZÖIGÊ

By bus The bus station (若尔盖汽车站, ruò'ěrgài qìchēzhàn) on Shuguang Lu has dawn departures for Songpan, Jiuzhaigou, Chengdu, and Hezuo (in Gansu); there's also one morning and one afternoon bus (around 2pm) to Langmusi.

ACCOMMODATION AND EATING

For food, there are plenty of places to grab a simple meal, or you can just hang out at the *A-Lang* teahouse across from the post office on Shangye Jie.

Ruoergai 若尔盖大酒店, ruò'ěrgài dàjiǔdiàn. Shangye Jie ☎ 0837 2291998. The town's most upmarket option, a short, squat building painted on the outside to look like something traditionally Tibetan. Inside, rooms are good quality, clean and nicely furnished with reproduction traditional furniture. **¥480**

Zangle 藏乐宾馆, zànglè bīnguǎn. Shangye Jie ☎ 0837 2298685 or 1899 0405006. A clean, basic, concrete block, the building is hardly pretty and staff perfunctory, but en suites have a ready and plentiful supply of hot water, as well as a/c, and prices are bargainable. **¥150**

Langmusi

郎木寺, lángmùsì

Just off the Songpan–Hezuo highway, 90km from Zöigê, you'll find the scruffy, single-street village of **LANGMUSI**, whose surrounding forests, mountain scenery and lamaseries give an easy taster of Tibet.

Langmusi's two small eighteenth-century **lamaseries** (¥30) sit at the western end of the village. Walk up the main street and bear right over a bridge, and the road leads uphill to **Saizu Gompa**, whose main hall's walls are covered in pictures of meditating Buddhas and where you might see monks debating in the courtyard outside. For **Gaerdi Gompa**, bear left along the main road and then aim for the temple buildings in the back lanes; this is the larger complex with several sizeable, tin-roofed halls, but seems almost totally deserted.

ARRIVAL AND DEPARTURE LANGMUSI

By bus If you can't find direct transport to Langmusi, buses travelling the Songpan–Gansu highway might agree to drop you off at the intersection with the Langmusi road, where jeeps wait to take you the 3km to the village itself (¥2–5). There's no

---

TREKKING AT LANGMUSI

There's immense **hiking** potential up to ridges and peaks above Langmusi, but make sure you're equipped for dogs (see p.755) and changeable weather. To arrange longer guided hikes or **horse-trekking**, contact Langmusi Tibetan Horse Trekking (☏ 1389 3991541, ⊛ langmusi .net), near the bus stop, a very organized operation whose one- to four-day trips take in nomad camps and mountain scenery – the website has current schedules and costs, currently around ¥220 per person per day.

---

bus station at Langmusi; buses deliver and collect from along the single main street. Leaving, vehicles assemble at dawn; ask at your accommodation the night before for times.

Destinations Zöigê (2 daily; 2hr).
By minibus Leisha's can help charter minibuses to Jiuzhaigou and elsewhere (about ¥800 for a five-seater).

ACCOMMODATION

Langmusi 郎木寺宾馆, lángmùsì bīnguǎn. Just south of the main crossroads ☏ 0941 6671555. Probably the smartest place in town, this concrete place doesn't look much from the outside, but rooms are well presented, have 24hr hot water, and there's a roof-top terrace and a very helpful manager. You need to bargain doubles down. **¥480**
Nomad's Youth Hostel 旅朋青年旅舍, lǚpéng qīngnián lǚshè. On the main street ☏ 0941 6671460. Standard Chinese youth hostel, popular with domestic students who are used to dormitory living – for those who aren't, the rooms here can feel cramped and in need of a clean. But staff are friendly enough and can help with treks and onward travel. Dorm **¥30**, room **¥80**

EATING

For food, there are several simple Muslim and Chinese restaurants along the main street, though foreigners tend to gravitate towards Leisha's.

Leisha's 丽莎饭馆, lìshā fànguǎn. On the main road through town. This traveller-style café has been serving apple pie and yak burgers to contented clientele for years, but as well as the Westernized dishes they also do an excellent range of Chinese, Tibetan and Muslim cuisine, all from around ¥30. Daily 8.30am–9.30pm.

DIRECTORY

Internet There's a net bar opposite the Langmusi hotel, full of young, network-gaming monks.

Kangding

康定, kāngdìng

KANGDING, 250km from Chengdu at the gateway to Sichuan's far west, is a crowded, expanding collection of artless modern white-tiled blocks packed along the fast-flowing **Zheduo River**. Visually this is a very Chinese town, but the deep gorge that Kangding is set in is overlooked by chortens and the frosted peaks of **Daxue Shan** (the Great Snowy Mountains), and, whatever the maps might say, this is where Tibet really begins.

The town is the capital of huge **Ganzi prefecture** and bus schedules mean that a stopover here is likely, but with a couple of temples to check out and huge, communal evening dancing in the central square, it's not the worst of fates. In addition, Kangding is a stepping stone for day-trips to the **Hailuogou Glacier Park**, which descends **Gongga Shan**, western China's highest peak.

Some monasteries

Kangding's most central monastery is the little **Anjue Temple** (安觉寺, ānjué sì), just off Yanhe Xi Lu; it was built in 1654 at the prompting of the Fifth Dalai Lama. Following the main road southwest out of town brings you to the short stone arch of the **Princess Wencheng Bridge** (文成公主桥, wénchéng gōngzhǔ qiáo); on the other side, a path runs uphill to **Nanfu Temple** (南甫寺, nánfǔ sì), built in 1639. Check out the murals of Buddha in all his incarnations here – with their typically Tibetan iconography of skulls,

12

demons and fierce expressions, they paint a far less forgiving picture of Buddhism than the mainstream Chinese brand.

The markets and Paoma Shan

Kangding's **markets** – mostly selling clothing and household knick-knacks of all descriptions – surround the old town **spring** (水井子, shuǐjǐngzi) and a **mosque** off Yanhe Dong Lu. A lane opposite the mosque heads up to the entrance of pine-clad **Paoma Shan** (跑马山, pǎomǎ shān; ¥50), the mountain southeast of town, which hosts a **horse-race festival** in the middle of the fourth lunar month. It's a half-hour walk up stone steps to lookouts and the Roman-theatre-style racetrack, or you can catch a **cable car** (¥30 return) from near the Princess Wencheng Bridge.

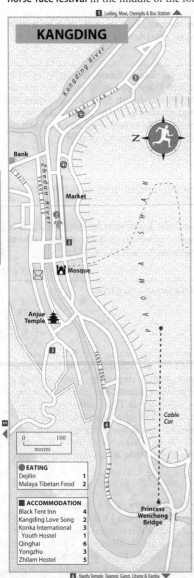

ARRIVAL AND DEPARTURE KANGDING

By bus Kangding's bus station (康定汽车站, kāngdìng qìchē zhàn) is 1km from town towards Chengdu, a ¥7 cab ride or 20min walk to anywhere central.

Destinations Chengdu (6–8hr); Danba (4hr); Daocheng (14hr); Daofu (9hr); Dêgê (2 days); Ganzi (12hr); Litang (9hr); Manigange (15hr); Tagong (3hr); Xichang (8hr).

By minibus and taxi Minibuses touting for Danba, Tagong and Chengdu, and taxis to Luding, cruise the streets outside the main bus station.

ACCOMMODATION

Black Tent Inn 安觉寺黑包客栈, ānjuésì hēibāo kèzhàn. Junction of Yanhe Dong Lu and Xiangyang Jie ☎ 1580 8366530. Friendly, helpful, family-run place west of the centre and next to the Anjue Temple. Good atmosphere, but its charm struggles to distract from what is very basic accommodation. Beds **¥25**

Kangding Love Song 康定情歌大酒店, kāngdìng qínggē dàjiǔdiàn. 156 Dong Lu ☎ 0836 2813333. Probably the best (and certainly the most expensive) hotel in town, this place sports an air of slightly worn luxury but is still regularly booked out in advance by tour groups. **¥460**

Konka International Youth Hostel 贡嘎国际青年旅舍, gònggā guójì qīngnián lǚshě. Qingge Da Dao ☎ 0836 2817788. Conveniently located on the third floor of a block a minute's walk west of the bus station, this place is aimed at Chinese students and is correspondingly basic. It fills up quickly, but the hotel on the floor below can take overflow and is arguably better value. Beds **¥35**, rooms **¥150**

Qinghai 康定清海假日酒店, kāngdìng qīnghǎi jiàrì jiǔdiàn. Lucheng Nan Lu ☎ 0836 6992222. New hotel at the west end of town, opposite the fruit and vegetable market. Reception staff not the most helpful, but until the usual wear and tear takes its toll rooms are clean and en-suite showers hot and powerful. **¥280**

Yongzhu 拥珠驿栈, yōngzhū yìzhàn. On an alley running uphill from Guangming Lu ☎ 0836 2832381 or 1598 3738188. Basic but central hotel, clean and run by a cheery proprietor who speaks no English but is always delighted to welcome Western faces through the door. Beds **¥40**, rooms **¥120**

★ **Zhilam Hostel** 汇道客栈, huìdào kèzhàn. ☏ 0836 2831100, ⓦ zhilamhostel.com. A tiring 10min

hike uphill from town, this foreign-owned venture is far and away the best place to stay, with Tibetan-style decor, a good café and excellent travel advice. Book ahead, however – it's often full. Beds **¥35**, rooms **¥260**

EATING

From the bus station to the town centre, Xinshi Qian Jie hosts heaps of cheap Sichuan restaurants, while for a Western food-fix the *Zhilam Hostel* can serve up a passable pizza.

Dejilin 德吉林藏餐, déjílín zàngcān. Xinshi Qian Jie. A down-to-earth Tibetan place with murals, butter tea, meat dumplings, yak stew, communal bench tables and windswept rural clientele. It's well worth a visit, but, if they're full, try the similar *Tagong Tibetan Restaurant* next door. Around ¥15 per person. Daily 8am–9pm.

Malaya Tibetan Food 玛拉亚藏餐, mǎlāyà zàngcān. Yan He Dong Lu ☏ 0836 2877111. On the sixth floor above *Dico's*, you won't find any rugged yak herders in this superior establishment, but the food is still authentic Tibetan. There's a wider choice than at *Dejilin*, more sophisticated ambience, and markedly less staring. Around ¥30 per person. Daily 11am–10pm.

Luding

泸定, lúdìng • taxi from Kangding ¥20

An hour east of Kangding, at the junction of the roads to Chengdu and Hailuogou Glacier, the market town of **LUDING** is worth a ten-minute stop to check out the attractive old **Luding Suspension Bridge** (泸定桥, lúdìng qiáo; ¥15) over the Dadu River. It was here that 22 Communist soldiers climbed hand-over-hand across the chains and took Guomindang emplacements on the west bank during the Long March in 1935, an event greatly played up in the propaganda of the Long March.

Hailuogou Glacier Park

海螺沟冰川公园, hǎiluógōu bīngchuān gōngyuán • ¥75 • park bus ¥80

Hailuogou Glacier Park encloses an alpine backdrop of deep valleys forested in pine and rhododendron, with the four glaciers in question descending **Gongga Shan** (贡嘎山, gònggā shān), known as Minya Konka in Tibetan. At 7556m, this is western China's highest point – a stunning sight on the rare mornings when the near-constant cloud cover and haze of wind-driven snow above the peak suddenly clear. Warm, weatherproof **clothing** is advisable whatever time of year you visit.

Moxi and the camps

The **park entrance** is 100km from Kangding at **MOXI** (磨西, móxī) a group of hotels, restaurants and souvenir stalls centred around a crossroads where buses cluster. A road runs 25km from the gates here to the main glacier, via three **camps** along the way at the 8-, 15- and 22-kilometre marks. There are **hot springs** (¥65) on hand at the first two, while Camp 2, near where the thicker pine forests begin, is the nicest spot to stay.

The glacier

It's 3.5km from Camp 3 to the glacier, from where you can reach a **viewing platform** by cable car (¥150 return) or by simply hiking up along a small path; allow two hours. From the platform, the glacier is revealed as a tongue of blue-white ice scattered with boulders and streaked in crevasses edged in black gravel, with – if you're lucky – Gongga Shan's peak rising in the distance.

ARRIVAL AND DEPARTURE | HAILUOGOU GLACIER PARK

By taxi Shared taxis between Moxi and Kangding, via Luding, charge ¥35 per person. If you don't have a full van-load you'll need to negotiate or wait for additional passengers.

12

ACCOMMODATION

Hailuogou No 2 Camp Hot Spring Resort 海螺沟二号营地, hǎiluógōu èrhào yíngdì. Inside the park near Buzi village ☏ 0836 3266171. This is a well-put-together place, with much-vaunted "European style" rooms, which basically means pine furniture and a sit-down toilet. Very comfortable and cosy, and considering the location it's a fair deal, though at busy times prices can rise to ludicrous levels. **¥450**

Mingzhu Huayuan 明珠花园酒店, míngzhū huāyuán jiǔdiàn. Near the park gates, Moxi ☏ 0836 3266166. Top-notch accommodation for wealthy Chinese tourists, very conveniently situated. Traditional-style modern building with marble lobby, furnishings inside are all beige, cream and gold. Good quality, and it should be for the price. **¥580**

Milan Youth Hostel 米兰青年旅舍, mǐlán qīngnián lǚshè. Southeast of the church, Moxi ☏ 0836 3266518. Friendly place with a mix of four-bed doms, each with their own toilet and shower, and en-suite twins and doubles. Popular with domestic backpackers. Dorm **¥40**, room **¥20**

Hamu Hostel 哈姆青年旅舍, hāmǔ qīngnián lǚshè. 150m northeast of the main gate, Moxi ☏ 1528 1572918. Another basic hostel, this time with eight-bed dorms and shared bathrooms. Gets very busy at peak times, but pleasant otherwise. Dorm **¥40**, room **¥148**

Danba

丹巴, dānbā

Around 120km north of Kangding, **DANBA** is a 2km-long service town for surrounding Tibetan hamlets. These feature distinctive stone towers (碉楼, diāolóu), used in former times as watchtowers and safe havens from attack. Some reach up to 35m high and are hundreds of years old – the use of stone for construction in the area has been dated back to 1700 BC.

Jiaju

甲居, jiǎjū • ¥30

The most accessible hamlet is **Jiaju**, just 7km up into the hills above Danba town. Jiaju occupies a relatively flat terrace on an otherwise steep mountainside, all dotted with traditional stone houses surrounded by their fields and farm animals. Well-formed paths link clusters of buildings, which you can spend a couple of hours exploring – bring a camera.

ARRIVAL AND DEPARTURE

DANBA

By bus Danba's bus station is at the west end of the town; buy tickets here the day before if possible.

Destinations Ganzi (1 daily; 9hr); Kangding (1 daily; 5hr).

By minibus Minibuses to Bamei (for connections to Tagong) leave when full from a depot at Danba's eastern side near the Caihong bridge (彩虹桥, cǎihóng qiáo). Kangding minibuses depart through the day from the bus station.

GETTING AROUND

By minibus Accommodation should be able to arrange a shared minibus to Jiaju for ¥80 return, including waiting time.

ACCOMMODATION AND EATING

The restaurant opposite the *Zaxi* does a fantastic spicy potato and spare-rib stew (土豆排骨, tǔdòu páigǔ).

Jiaju Homestays There are numerous private homestays at Jiaju, though you can't really arrange these in advance. It's well worth the experience, however; facilities are extremely basic but rates include a huge evening meal. Per person **¥50**

Zaxi Zhoukang Hostel 扎西桌康游客之家, zāxī zhuōkāng yóukè zhījiā. Near the Caihong Bridge, Danba ☏ 0836 3521806. Spotless rooms and friendly staff make this a good option – as do 24hr hot water and wi-fi. Management can also help organize trips out to villages, though very little English is spoken. Dorm **¥25**, room **¥80**

Tagong

塔公, tǎgōng

Some 110km northwest of Kangding, the single-street Tibetan township of **TAGONG** is a popular stop for **horse trekking** opportunities on the surrounding grasslands. Tagong itself is oriented around the modest **Tagong Temple** (塔公寺, tǎgōng sì; ¥10), built to honour Princess Wencheng but now busy with monks chatting on their mobile phones during morning prayers. The seventeenth-century main hall houses a sculpture of Sakyamuni as a youth, said to have been brought here by the princess in Tang times. Behind the monastery is **Fotalin**, an overgrown and under-tended forest of a hundred 3m-high stupas, each built in memory of a monk.

The golden stupa

¥10

Just 500m along the main road past Tagong Temple is the spectacular **golden stupa**, fully 20m tall and backed by snowy peaks, surrounded by a colonnade of prayer wheels – though according to the monks, this recent construction is less of a religious site than an excuse to collect tourist revenue.

The Tagong grasslands

Spreading out from behind the golden stupa, the **Tagong grasslands** occupy a string of flat-bottomed valleys on a 3700m-high plateau, all surrounded by magnificent snowy peaks. Hiking and riding possibilities are legion: **Shedra Gompa**'s monastery and Buddhist college is only a couple of kilometres away; **Shamalong** village is two hours along a track from the stupa, and **Ani Gompa** is a valley nunnery with a sky-burial site some two hours' hike cross-country. Get full directions for these routes from *Sally's* or the *Khampa Café* – and beware of dogs.

ARRIVAL AND DEPARTURE

TAGONG

By bus There's no bus station at Tagong, so buses drop off along the Kangding–Ganzi highway, which forms the town's main street. Leaving, you can stand on the road and flag down passing traffic – accommodation can advise on likely times – or there should be a steady supply of minibuses from Kangding looking for passengers (¥50). **Destinations** Bamei (1hr); Danba (3hr); Ganzi (8hr); Kangding (2hr).

INFORMATION

Tour guides For horse treks, bike, motorbike and camping gear rental, contact long-established Chyoger Treks at the *Khampa Café and Arts Centre* (☎ 1368 4493301, ⊚ definitelynomadic.com).

ACCOMMODATION

The pick of Tagong's accommodation options are all in the town square in front of the temple.

★ **Jya Drolma & Gayla's Guesthouse** 甲志玛大姐家, jiǎzhìmǎ dàjiějiā. Facing the temple, it's the building behind you in the left corner of the square ☎ 0836 2866056. The hospitality and traditional Tibetan home here are almost worth the trip in themselves, though the combination of altitude and steep stairs could leave you out of breath. Beds ¥30, room ¥60

Khampa Café and Arts Centre On your left as you

VISITING MONASTERIES

Among the draws of many towns in western Sichuan are their Tibetan Buddhist **monasteries**, most of which belong to the yellow-hat Gelugpa sect. Monasteries form huge medieval-looking complexes sprawling over hillsides, with a central core of large, red-walled, gold-roofed **temples** surrounded by a maze of smaller buildings housing monks and staff. Monasteries are **free** to enter, except where noted in the text; if there are no signs to the contrary, assume that **photography** is forbidden inside temples. Monks are generally friendly, encouraging you to explore, steering you firmly away from closed areas, and sometimes offering **food and accommodation** – though don't take these for granted. Most importantly, remember to orbit **clockwise** around both individual temples and the complex as a whole (the only exception to this rule being at the region's few Bon temples).

face the temple ☏ 1368 4493301, ⓦ definitelynomadic
.com. The roof terrace here is the best place to hang out in
Tagong, while the basic but clean doubles are the most
sought-after in town. ¥100

Snowland Hostel 雪域旅社, xuěyù lǔshè. Directly

next to the Khampa Café ☏ 0836 2866098. *Snowlands* is
one of Tagong's original hostels and is still going strong.
Rooms are spartan but have their own bathrooms. They
also hand out good travel advice, as does the connected
Sally's café. Beds ¥30, rooms ¥60

EATING

Sally's Kham Restaurant Ground floor of the
Snowland   Guesthouse   ☏ 1399   0454752,
ⓔ tagongsally@yahoo.com. A foreigners' hangout with

Tibetan, Chinese and Western staples and plenty of helpful
information. Meals around ¥20 per person. Often closed
Nov–March; otherwise daily 8am–9pm.

Ganzi
甘孜, gānzī

GANZI sits at 3500m in a broad, flat-bottomed river valley some 300km northwest
of Kangding, with the long, serrated Que'er Shan range rising to the south.
The dusty, noisy town owes its importance to the adjacent **Kandze monastery**,
founded by the Mongols after they invaded in 1642 and once the largest
Gelugpa monastery in the Kham region. A bit empty today, it nevertheless
remains an important cultural centre, especially for the teaching of religious
dances and musical instruments.

Ganzi town itself acts as a transport and social focus, with blue trucks rumbling
through at all hours, wild crowds cruising the streets, and markets throughout the back
lanes; the kilometre-long main road is lined with shops selling knives, rugs, silverware,
all sorts of jewellery, saddles, religious accessories, copper and tin kitchenware.

Kandze monastery
甘孜寺庙, gānzī sìmiào • ¥15

The **Kandze monastery** is 2km north of town – follow Jiefang Lu uphill from the bus
station – and for such an obvious complex the entrance is not easy to find, being
hidden behind mud-brick homes among medieval backstreets. The recently renovated
buildings are splendid, and just wandering around fills in time, though there's little
specific to seek out aside from the **main hall** – covered in gold, murals and prayer flags,
and with an incredible view of the valley and town from its roof. The large adobe walls
below the monastery are remains of the Mazur and Khangsar **forts**, built by the
Mongols after they took the region.

ARRIVAL AND DEPARTURE   GANZI

By bus Ganzi's bus station is central, on the crossroads of
east–west Chuanzang Lu and Jiefang Lu. Staff here are
helpful enough with information but you might have to
buy tickets on the bus. If you're aiming for Litang and want
to avoid going all the way back to Kangding, there's a
morning bus south to Xinlong (新龙, xīnlóng), from
where minibuses run to Litang if they get enough people

(¥60–80 each, or about ¥300 for the whole van). Check first
in Ganzi with the Xinlong bus driver that the Xinlong–
Litang stretch is open, as it's barely more than a walking
track in places, subject to wash-outs and landslides.
Destinations Chengdu (2 days); Dêgê (8hr); Kangding
(12hr); Xinlong (3hr).

ACCOMMODATION AND EATING

Almost every other business in town is a restaurant, though don't expect much beyond noodles and dumplings.

Golden Yak 金牦牛宾馆, jīnmáoniú bīnguǎn.
Inside the bus station compound ☏ 0836 7525288.
Convenient and relatively comfy, this place has simple
dorms and doubles and is the best of the lower-budget
options. Dorm ¥40, room ¥100

Hotel   Himalaya   喜马拉雅宾馆,   xǐmǎlāyǎ
bīnguǎn. Dong Da Jie ☏ 0836 7521878. The pick of
Ganzi's fairly down-to-earth accommodation, with clean
doubles, en suites with sit-down toilets, and hot water.
¥150

Dêgê

德格, dégé

Eight hours from Ganzi via the crossroads town of **Manigange** (马尼干戈, mǎnígàngē) and the scary, 5500m-high Chola Shan mountain pass, **DÊGÊ** initially appears to be no more than a small cluster of ageing concrete buildings squeezed into a narrow gorge. Dêgê was, however, once the most powerful Kham state, and the only one to resist the seventeenth-century Mongol invasion – hence the absence of Gelugpa-sect monasteries in the region.

Gongchen Gompa

簧庆寺庙, gàngqìng sìmiào

At the top of Dêgê's main street is **Gongchen Gompa**, encircled by peregrinating pilgrims busy thumbing rosaries, whose red-walled buildings form one of three hubs of Tibetan culture (the other two are Lhasa, and Xiahe in Gansu). The first building encountered is the **Bakong Scripture Printing Hall** (印经院, yìnjīng yuàn; ¥25; cameras forbidden): built in 1729, the four-storey hall houses 290,000 **woodblocks** of Tibetan texts, stored in racks on the second floor like books in a library, and covering everything from scriptures to scientific treatises – some seventy percent of all Tibetan literary works. You can watch the **printing process** on the third floor: though all done by hand, the printers work at a furious pace, and it's not unusual to watch ten of them turning out a hundred pages a minute.

ARRIVAL AND DEPARTURE   DÊGÊ

12

By bus Dêgê's vestigial bus stop is on the main road, just where the single street crosses a stream and rises uphill to the monastery. Leaving, you'll need to buy Ganzi or Kangding tickets a day in advance; the roadside bus-ticket booth opens at 7am and again at 2.30pm.

Destinations Ganzi (daily; 8hr); Kangding (daily; 24hr).

ACCOMMODATION AND EATING

The road to the monastery is lined with shops, a supermarket and dozens of stir-fry restaurants.

Dêgê Binguan 雀儿山宾馆, què'érshān bīnguǎn. Zheng Jie ☏0836 8222167. The primary source of beds, try to go for one of their newer rooms; they're still overpriced, but a little less so than the older ones. The comfortable tearoom here, however, is a treat after the journey. **¥280**

Litang

理塘, lǐtáng

LITANG, 300km west of Kangding, is a lively, gruff place with a large Tibetan population and an obvious Han presence in its businesses, army barracks, and expanding spread of concrete-and-tile architecture. Wild West comparisons are inevitable: you'll have to get used to sharing the pavement with livestock, and watching monks and dreadlocked Khampa toughs tearing around the windy, dusty streets on motorbikes. Litang is also inescapably **high** – at 4014m above sea level, it actually beats Lhasa by over 300m – so don't be surprised if you find even gentle slopes strangely exhausting. As usual, the main distraction here is people-watching: the shops are packed with Tibetans bargaining for temple accessories, solar-power systems for tents and practical paraphernalia for daily use, while Muslim smiths are busy in workshops along the main street, turning out the town's renowned knives and jewellery.

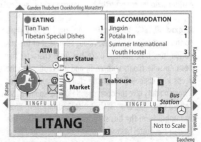

LITANG'S HORSE FESTIVAL

Litang's week-long **horse festival** kicks off each year in late July/early August on the plains outside town. Horsemen from all over Kham descend to compete, decking their stocky steeds in bells and brightly decorated bridles and saddles. As well as the four daily **races**, the festival features amazing demonstrations of horsemanship, including acrobatics, plucking silk scarves off the ground, and shooting (guns and bows) – all performed at full tilt. In between, you'll see plenty of **dancing**, both religious (the dancers wearing grotesque wooden masks) and for fun, with both men and women gorgeously dressed in heavily embroidered long-sleeved smocks. The exact date varies each year: contact the *Potala Inn* or *Summer Youth Hostel* before you arrive, for confirmation.

Ganden Thubchen Choekhorling monastery

理塘寺庙, lǐtáng sìmiào • taxi ¥3

A fifteen-minute walk north of town, Litang's **Ganden Thubchen Choekhorling monastery**, founded in 1580 at the behest of the Third Dalai Lama, has been undergoing several years of steady renovation (including the installation of plate-glass frontages on the main temples) and is today populated by over a thousand monks. The complex is entirely encircled by a wall, the four main halls (two of them brand new) gleaming among an adobe township of monks' quarters. At the entrance is a large stupa and pile of brightly painted mani stones left by pilgrims for good luck, whose inscriptions have been carved to resemble yaks.

The upper temple

The **upper temple** (Tsengyi Zhatsang) is the most interesting, its portico flanked by aggressively postured statues of guardians of the four directions, along with a typical, finely executed mural of a three-eyed demon wearing tiger skins and skulls, holding the Wheel of Transmigration. Side gates in the wall allow you to hike up onto the hills behind the monastery, sharing the flower-filled pasture with yaks, or join pilgrims circuiting the walls to the **sky-burial ground** to the right of the main gates.

ARRIVAL AND DEPARTURE

LITANG

Aside from routes back to Kangding, the road south of Litang runs right down to Zhongdian in Yunnan, and you might want to detour along the way to take in Yading – see opposite.

By bus Litang's bus station is at the eastern end of town on main street Xingfu Lu. While there is a daily early-morning service to Kangding leaving from here, most buses are through services and only able to pick you up if other passengers have got off.
Destinations Daocheng (5hr); Kangding (9hr); Shangri-La (12hr).

By minibus Minibus-taxis to Daocheng, Xinlong (for Ganzi) and anywhere else they can get enough customers for hang around opposite the bus station. Alternatively, the *Potala Inn* or *Summer Youth Hostel* may be able to help organize a vehicle. Prices yo-yo significantly depending on the hugely variable road conditions and consequent journey times.

ACCOMMODATION

A string of dorms opposite the bus station might appeal on arrival, but are grotty to the point of squalor and best avoided.

Jingxin 晶鑫宾馆, jīngxīn bīnguǎn. 306 Xingfu Dong Lux ☎ 0836 5323989. About 50m west of the bus station, this tidy, modern place has little character but clean en-suite rooms with wi-fi, and a receptionist who sleeps in a cupboard under the stairs – if you can't see anyone on duty give the door a gentle knock. Rooms **¥150**
Potala Inn 布达拉大酒店, bùdálā dàjiǔdiàn. West and uphill from the bus station ☎ 0836 8322533. This Tibetan-run hostel has rooms which are in need of a bit of

attention, but there's a decent café-bar and excellent travel advice and tours, though they sometimes refuse to book trips unless you're staying here. Dorm **¥30**, rooms **¥180**
Summer International Youth Hostel 夏天国际青年旅舍, xiàtiān guójì qīngnián lǚshè. Aimin Jie ☎ 1801 5791574. Newly opened hostel, with the cleanest rooms in town and a friendly bar area with a pool table. Young Chinese reception staff are enthusiastic, but lack the local travel info and contacts of the *Potala Inn*. Dorm **¥40**, rooms **¥140**

EATING

Stir-fry restaurants, some of which have English menus and all serving much the same food, line Xingfu Lu.

Tian Tian 天天饮食, tiāntiān yīnshí. 108 Xingfu Dong Lu, a 10min walk west of the bus station ☎ 1354 1467941. Food here is not fantastic, though the breakfast pancakes are good comfort food; the main reason to come is to browse the walls which are pasted with all manner of local travel information and guide contacts. Main dishes ¥20. Daily 8am–9pm.

Tibetan Special Dishes 藏人家特餐, zàngrénjiā tècān. Xingfu Dong Lu. Just west of the junction for the *Summer Youth Hostel*, this place has the best Tibetan food in town and boasts an English menu to boot – the potato *momos* (dumplings) are a particular treat. Main dishes ¥20. Daily 8am–9pm.

Daocheng

稻城, dàochéng

DAOCHENG (or Dabpa) is a small, touristy T-intersection of low buildings and shops some 150km south of Litang; the main reason to come here is to catch onwards transport to Yading or Yunnan. Some 5km north of town is a collection of **hot springs** (茹布查卡温泉, rúbùchákǎ wēnquán) set among a tiny village at the head of a valley, where bathhouses ask ¥3 for a soak. From the springs, you can cross the valley and hike along a ridge back into town – tiring, given the 3500m altitude.

ARRIVAL AND DEPARTURE　　　　　　　　　　　DAOCHENG

By bus Daocheng's bus station is just off the main street, with several daily departures, all things being equal – but they often aren't. Come to the ticket office around 2pm the day before you need to

leave and be prepared to fight for a place in the queue.
By minibus Minibuses outside the bus station tout for customers heading to Yading or Litang.
Destinations Litang (5hr); Shangri-La in Yunnan (8–12hr).

ACCOMMODATION AND EATING

Plateau Inn 高原客栈, gāoyuán kèzhàn. 78 Gongga Lu, just north of the bus station ☎ 0836 5721555 or 1388 0854911, ✪ www.inoat.com. The accommodation here is basic to say the least, but the location – in a renovated old Tibetan house – is wonderful. There is hot water, though, and a café serving excellent coffee. Dorm ¥30, room ¥50

Seaburay 喜波热, xǐbōrè. Follow English signs from the bus station ☎ 0836 5728668. The overwhelming hospitality dished out here will severely test your ability to consume vast amounts of *tsampa*, dumplings and butter tea. Rooms and toilets are basic, and you shower at the public bathhouse or, more enjoyably, at the hot springs. Dorm ¥30

Yading

亚丁, yàdīng • ¥150

Around 76km south of Daocheng, **Yading** is a beautiful reserve of alpine meadows, lakes and 6000m peaks. The entry point is **Yading village** (亚丁村, yǎdīng cūn), where there's basic accommodation and you can organize trips into the rest of the reserve. Some sights can be reached by local bus, but ideally you'll be prepared to hike or travel on horseback. While most visitors are simply drawn by the immense natural beauty of the place, for Tibetans, the three 6000m peaks the reserve is focused around represent the Buddhas of wisdom, power and compassion; coming here and not completing the *kora* (pilgrim circuit) of the tallest mountain, **Chenresig**, would be a serious missed opportunity.

ARRIVAL AND DEPARTURE　　　　　　　　　　　YADING

By minibus Everybody with a vehicle in Daocheng will offer to take you to Yading village (about ¥50 a person); the

trip takes around 2hr 30min.

ACCOMMODATION

There is limited guesthouse accommodation near the park entrance at Yading village; ask at Daocheng before coming out here.

12

The Northwest

MOGAO CAVES

13

The Northwest

Gansu, Qinghai and Xinjiang spread across the Chinese northwest in a dizzying agglomeration of desert, grassland, raging rivers and colossal mountains. Despite the region's impressive size, which alone would form the eighth-largest country in the world, it contains just four percent of China's population – a baffling statistic considering the staggering ethnic variety found here. Lowland Xinjiang is home to the Uyghur, a predominantly Muslim people who speak a language closer to Turkish than Chinese. In Xinjiang's mountains live communities of Kazakh, Kyrgyz and Tajik, making for the curious existence of occasional blond-haired, blue-eyed holders of Chinese passports. Qinghai forms the northern edge of the Tibetan Plateau; with transport to Lhasa often restricted, the province is popular with travellers looking for an accessible window into Tibetan culture. In Gansu, there are large communities of Mongolians – also keen adherents of Tibetan Buddhism – and Hui Muslims, as well as lesser-known groups such as Bao'an and Salar.

The Chinese of old considered that these *saiwairen* – peoples from beyond the pale – threatened the safety of the Empire itself; today, the relatively unrestricted use of **local languages and religions** in these areas could be taken as a sign of China's desire to restore goodwill and nurture patriotism in the minority peoples. However, the degree of actual autonomy in the "autonomous" regions is strictly controlled, and relations between Han China and these more remote corners of the People's Republic remain fractious in places, most notably Xinjiang.

Tourism across the Northwest focuses on the **Silk Road**, a series of historic towns and ruins running from Xi'an in Shaanxi, through Ningxia, Gansu and Xinjiang, and into Central Asia. The Northwest also offers opportunities to enjoy China's last great wildernesses – the grasslands, mountains, lakes and deserts of the interior – far from the teeming population centres of the east. **Gansu**, the historical periphery of ancient China,

Highlights

❶ Labrang Monastery The most imposing Lamaist monastery outside of Tibet, set in a beautiful mountain valley. **See p.788**

❷ Qinghai Lake China's largest lake is a magnet for birdwatchers and waterfowl, including rare black-necked cranes. **See p.798**

❸ Jiayuguan Fort Stronghold at the western end of the Great Wall, symbolically marking the limit of China proper. **See p.806**

❹ Mogao Caves Huge collection of Buddhist grottoes and sculptures, carved into a desert gorge a millennium ago. **See p.811**

❺ Turpan Relax under grape trellises or investigate Muslim Uyghur culture and ancient Silk Road relics, such as the intriguing ruins of Jiaohe. **See p.828**

❻ Kashgar's Sunday markets Join crowds haggling for goats, carpets, knives and spices in China's most westerly and wild city. **See p.840**

HIGHLIGHTS ARE MARKED ON THE MAP ON P.774

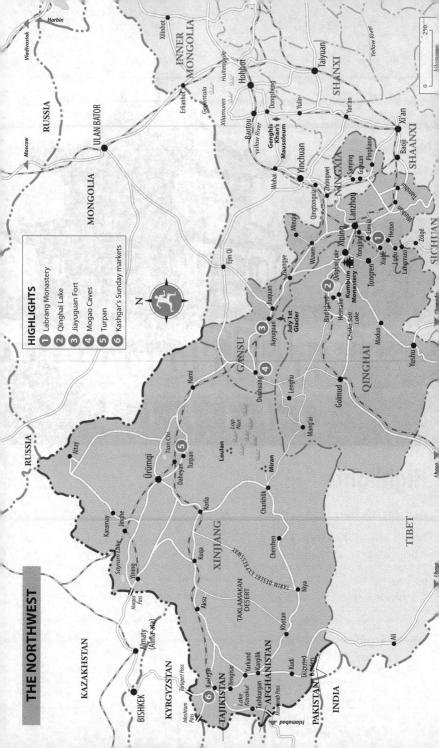

is a rugged region of high peaks and desert, spliced from east to west by the **Hexi Corridor**, historically the only road from China to the West, still marked along its length by the Great Wall – terminating magnificently at the fortress of **Jiayuguan** – and a string of Silk Road towns culminating in **Dunhuang**, with its fabulous Buddhist cave art.

Qinghai, the remote borderland plateau between Tibet and China proper, has monasteries, mountains, the colossal **Qinghai Lake** and a **route to Tibet** via the highest railway in the world. Qinghai is also the source of China's greatest rivers: the Yellow, Yangzi and Mekong rivers all originate in the mountains here.

Guarding China's westernmost passes is **Xinjiang**, where China ends and Central Asia – once known as Chinese Turkestan – begins; a vast, isolated region of searing deserts and snowy mountains, formerly the most arduous section of the Silk Road. Here Turkic Uyghurs outnumber Han Chinese, mosques trade places with temples and lamb kebabs replace steamed dumplings. Highlights include the desert town of **Turpan** and, in the far west, fabled **Kashgar**, a city that until recent decades few Westerners had ever reached.

THE SILK ROAD

The Khunjerab and Torugart passes that link China with Central Asia were, a thousand years ago, on well-trodden trade routes between eastern China and the Mediterranean. Starting from Chang'an (Xi'an), the **Silk Road** curved northwest through Gansu to the Yumen Pass, where it split. Travellers could follow one of two routes across the deserts to Kashgar: the **southern route** ran through Dunhuang, Miran, Niya, Khotan and Yarkand; the **northern route** through Hami, Turpan, Kuqa and Aksu. Beyond Kashgar, merchants traded their goods with middlemen who carried them south to Kashmir and Bactria, or north to Ferghana and Samarkand. Then, laden with Western goods, the Chinese merchants would turn around for the 3000km journey home. **Oases** along the route prospered as caravanserai, becoming wealthy in their own right. When Chinese domination periodically declined, many of these cities turned into self-sufficient statelets, or **khanates**.

The foundations of this **road to the West**, which was to become one of the most important arteries of **trade and culture** in world history, were laid over two millennia ago. In 139 BC, the imperial court at Chang'an dispatched a man called **Zhang Qian** to investigate the world to the west and to seek possible allies in the struggle against nomadic marauders from the north. Zhang set out with a party of a hundred men; thirteen years later he returned, with only one member of his original expedition – and no alliances. Nevertheless, the news he brought of the lands to the west set Emperor Wu Di and his court aflame. Further **expeditions** purchased horses for military purposes, and from these beginnings trade developed.

By 100 BC a dozen immense caravans were heading into the desert each year. From China emerged **silk** – of course – along with jade, porcelain, peaches, roses, cast iron, gunpowder and paper; the West sent back cucumbers, figs, sesame, walnuts, grapes (and wine-making), wool, ivory and **religion** – including Nestorian Christianity and **Buddhism**. The first Buddhist missionaries appeared in China in the first century AD, and by the fourth century Buddhism had become the official religion of much of northern China. Along the Silk Road, monasteries, stupas and grottoes proliferated, often sponsored by wealthy traders. The remains of this early flowering of **Buddhist art** are among the great attractions of the Northwest for modern-day travellers. History has taken its toll – zealous Muslims, Western archeologists, Red Guards and the forces of nature have all played a destructive part – but some sites have survived intact, above all the cave art at **Mogao** outside Dunhuang.

The Silk Road flourished for centuries, reaching its zenith under the Tang dynasty (618–907 AD) and bringing immense wealth to the Chinese nobility and merchants. But it remained a dangerous, expensive and slow route, taking at least five months from Chang'an to Kashgar, whole caravans occasionally disappearing into the deserts or in the high mountain passes.

There was a final flowering of trade in the thirteenth century, when the whole Silk Road came temporarily under Mongol rule. But with the arrival of sericulture in Europe and the opening of sea routes between China and the West, the Silk Road had had its day. The road and its cities were slowly abandoned to the wind and the blowing sands.

13

Travel can be hard going, with **enormous distances** and an unforgiving **climate**. **Winter** is particularly severe, with average temperatures as low as -30°C in Qinghai and Xinjiang. Conversely, in **summer**, Turpan is China's hottest city, with temperatures exceeding 40°C. Despite the rugged terrain and the great expanses, however, facilities for visitors have developed considerably in recent years. The rail network has been expanded, roads improved, and new airports constructed. Finally there is the possibility of **travel** between China and its Central Asian neighbours – Kazakhstan, Kyrgyzstan and Pakistan are all connected by road or rail from Xinjiang.

Gansu and Qinghai

The gigantic, naturally splendid provinces of **Gansu** (甘肃, gānsù) and **Qinghai** (青海, qīnghǎi) sit side by side, far west of Beijing and the Chinese seaboard. Together they form an incredibly diverse expanse, from **colossal mountains** in the south to vast tracts of **desert** in the northwest. On a map, these provinces appear to be at the very centre of China, but this is only true in a geographical sense. Traditionally, the Chinese have regarded Gansu, the "closer" of the pair, as marking the outer limit of Chinese cultural influence.

Gansu's population is relatively small – just 26 million – if comprising an extraordinary ethnic mix, including Hui, Kazakhs, Mongols and Tibetans. The province's remarkable geography encompasses stretches of the great **Yellow River**, its waters dense with silt, and the **Hexi Corridor**, a 1000km passage sandwiched between the Tibetan and the Gobi Desert that narrows to a 16km-wide bottleneck at its skinniest point. Silk Road caravans trudged through the corridor, the Great Wall was built through it and even today Gansu's main rail lines and highways are funnelled along it. Here too you'll find some of the region's most spectacular historic sites: the **Mogao Caves** at **Dunhuang** house the finest examples of Buddhist art in all China; there's the country's largest reclining Buddha at **Zhangye**; plus more rock art at **Bingling Caves**, near Lanzhou, and **Maiji Shan**, near **Tianshui**. The Great Wall snakes across Gansu to its end at the great Ming fortress at **Jiayuguan**, and in Gansu's mountainous southwest is the fascinating **Labrang Monastery** and the Tibetan town of **Xiahe**.

A huge, empty landscape with a population of less than 6 million, Qinghai is in many respects a part of Tibet, covering the northern section of the **Tibetan Plateau**, with a strong **minority presence** – as well as Tibetans and Hui, there are Salar, Tu, Mongol and Kazakh people all living here. Qinghai's unspoilt natural wilderness incorporates the enormous **Qinghai Lake**, which offers opportunities for hiking and birdwatching. Only the eastern part of the province around **Xining** has a long-established Han presence, though the splendid **Kumbum Monastery**, one of the four great Tibetan lamaseries, is located just outside the city.

Brief history

China made its first serious effort to expand into the western deserts, primarily as a means to ensure control over the Silk Road trade, during the Han dynasty (206 BC–220 AD). Prefectures were established even though Gansu did not officially become a Chinese province for another millennium; during several periods, however, Chinese control extended well beyond here and into Xinjiang. Nevertheless, right into the nineteenth century the primarily Muslim inhabitants of this region were considered little better than barbarians, and the great revolts of 1862–77 were ruthlessly quashed.

Given that agriculture is barely sustainable in arid Gansu, since 1949 the central government has tried to develop heavy industry in the province. The exploitation of mineral deposits, including oil and coal, had a tentative beginning, followed by Mao's paranoid "Third Line" policy in the 1960s, when factories were built in remote areas to save them from possible Soviet attack.

Geographically and culturally part of the **Tibetan Plateau**, Qinghai has for centuries been a frontier zone, contested between the Han Chinese, Tibetans and Muslims who dwelt in its pastures and thin snatches of agricultural land. Significant Han migration didn't occur until the late nineteenth century, when it was encouraged by the Qing dynasty. However, effective Han political control was not established until 1949 when the Communists defeated **Ma Bufang**, a Hui warlord who had controlled the area since 1931. The area is still perceived by the Han Chinese as a frontier land for pioneers and prospectors, and, on a more sinister note, a dumping ground for criminals and political opponents to the regime, with hundreds of thousands held in Qinghai **prison and labour camps**.

Eastern Gansu

West of the border with Shaanxi, the first significant Silk Road city is **Tianshui**, with the spectacular **Maiji Shan** complex just a few kilometres to the southeast. Maiji Shan – literally "Haystack Mountain", a name derived from its shape – is set amid beautiful wooded hills, and easily accessed from Tianshui, which is about halfway along the Lanzhou–Xi'an rail line. You will probably need to spend at least one night at Tianshui, the nearest transport hub to the caves, though the town is of limited interest. A little to the west of Tianshui, toward Lanzhou, are some more fascinating Silk Road relics, near the town of **Wuhan**.

Tianshui
天水, tiānshuǐ

The area around **TIANSHUI** was first settled back in Neolithic times, though today the city is a long industrial strip with two distinct centres, known as **Qincheng** (also called Qinzhou) in the west and **Beidao** (also known as Maiji – not to be confused with Maiji Shan) 20km to the east. Tianshui's only notable sights are in Qincheng, but where you stay will probably be determined by whether you arrive at the Beidao train station or the Qincheng bus station. If your only interest is a trip to Maiji Shan, you should stay in Beidao, from where all the Maiji Shan buses depart, though this is the grottier of the two ends of town.

Fuxi Miao & City Museum
伏羲庙, fúxī miào • Fuxi Lu Pedestrian Street • Tues–Sun; summer 8am–6pm, winter 9am–5.30pm • ¥30 • ☎ 0938 8227304, Chinese-only website ⓦ www.fuximiao.com • bus #21 from Qincheng Bus Station or bus #26 from Long-Distance Bus Station (both ¥1)

Qincheng's premier sight is **Fuxi Miao**, a Ming-dynasty complex commemorating the mythological Fuxi, who is credited with introducing the Chinese to fishing, hunting and animal husbandry – there is a statue of him, looking startled and clad in leaves, in the main hall. The temple is notable for its beautiful cypress trees; there is a thousand-year-old tree in the first courtyard.

13

To the rear of the same complex is the **Tianshui City Museum**, home to a small but varied collection that includes lively Tang statues and a 2000-year-old bronze money tree, created to ensure a wealthy afterlife for its owner. Sadly, Fuxi Miao's excellent English captions disappear once in the museum.

Nanzhaizi Folk Museum

南宅子, nán zháizi • Minzhu Lu • Daily, summer 8am–6pm, winter 8.30am–5.30pm • Free • ☎ 0938 8229253 • bus #23 (¥1) from the Long-Distance Bus Station

Central Qincheng's **Nanzhaizi Folk Museum** is housed in a sprawling Ming-dynasty mansion that formerly belonged to a high-ranking imperial official. Half of the complex's courtyards have been furnished as they would have been when in use, while the remaining courtyards are given over to exhibits of local handicrafts. Of particular interest are occasional performances at the small shadow puppet theatre, and the family vault (used as an air-raid shelter in the 1970s) – take a torch.

Yuquan Guan

玉泉观, yùquán guàn • off Chengji Dadao • Daily 8am–6pm • ¥20 • bus #24 (¥1) from the Long-Distance Bus Station runs past a path to the entrance

Yuquan Guan, a 700-year-old Taoist temple complex, is about ten minutes' walk northwest of Qincheng's main square. Pavilions dot an attractive hillside park and offer good views over the city. If you work up a thirst climbing up the hill, head for the Jade Spring in the park's northeast corner – locals drink the spring water, claiming that it aids digestion.

ARRIVAL AND DEPARTURE TIANSHUI

By train Tianshui's train station (天水火车站, tiānshuǐ huǒchēzhàn) is in Beidao on Longchang Lu. The ticket office at the station is open 24hr; tickets are also available from a ticket office (9am–noon and 1–5pm) in the Hengtong Dasha, 150m west of the Bank of China on Minzhu Lu. Hard-seat tickets are easy to buy for the same day, while sleeper tickets will need to be purchased in advance. The #6 bus shuttles between the train and long-distance bus stations (6am–10pm; 30min; ¥3).
Destinations Jiayuguan (9 daily; 15hr); Lanzhou (regular; 4hr 30min); Ürümqi (11 daily; 29hr); Wuwei

(14 daily; 7hr–10hr); Xi'an (regular; 5hr); Zhangye (14 daily; 11hr).
By bus Qincheng's long-distance bus station (秦城长途汽车站, qínchéng chángtú qìchēzhàn) is on Xinhua Lu. Tickets are only available from the station ticket hall (6am–10pm). The station services destinations across southern Gansu, Ningxia and Shaanxi. Bus route #6 from Beidao's train station stops out front (6am–10pm; 30min; ¥3).
Destinations Guyuan (1 daily; 10hr); Lanzhou (regular; 6hr); Linxia (1 daily; 8hr); Pingliang (9 daily; 5hr); Wushan (regular; 2hr); Xi'an (12 daily; 7hr); Yinchuan (3 daily; 12hr).

GETTING AROUND

By bus Buses are the cheapest way to get around town, but slow – there are often long gaps between services. There is a city bus depot on Dazhong Zhong Lu, 200m south of the central square. Services cost ¥1, except those between Qincheng and Beidao (¥3) and the bus to Maiji

Shan (¥5).
By taxi Taxis are plentiful. Flag fall is ¥5; between Qincheng or Beidao it will cost ¥40, or ¥10 if you share with others – to do the latter, stand by a stop for the #1 or #6 buses and look interested and a cab ought to stop and help.

INFORMATION

Travel agents CITS (☎ 0938 8287337) is on the northwest corner of the Hezuo Lu/Minzhu Lu intersection in Qincheng. English-speaking staff here can organize tours to Maiji

Shan for ¥200 (car-only) or ¥400 with an English-speaking guide – tickets not included.

ACCOMMODATION

There's adequate accommodation in both Beidao and Qincheng, but as there's little to detain you in town after a visit to Maiji Shan, you might consider getting a late train out.

BEIDAO

Garden 花园酒店, huāyuán jiǔdiàn. 1 Longchang Lu

– opposite the train station ☎ 0938 2651111. Easily the glitziest hotel in the train station area, the *Garden* offers pleasant – if smoky – rooms with baroque flourishes, as well as an in-house sauna and karaoke lounge. **¥208**

Maiji 麦积大酒店, màijī dàjiǔdiàn. West side of the train station plaza ☎ 0938 4920000. Beidao's oldest hotel, Maiji is gently dilapidated and offers elderly furnished rooms, wi-fi and friendly staff. Conveniently located for buses to Maiji Shan and the train station. **¥136**

U House 悦居精品酒店, yuèjū jīngpǐn jiǔdiàn. 1 Longchang Dong Lu ☎ 0938 2888811. Incredibly brightly lit "boutique" hotel near the train station plaza with enthusiastic staff, low rates and clean, modern rooms. **¥138**

QINCHENG

Golden Sun 阳光饭店, yángguāng fàndiàn. On pedestrianized Zhonghua Lu ☎ 0938 8277777. The most upmarket option in town, with a bar, a Western restaurant, wi-fi throughout the hotel and English-speaking staff. A taxi from the nearby bus station costs ¥5. Breakfast included. **¥448**

★ **Tianjia** 天嘉商务酒店, tiānjiā shāngwù jiǔdiàn. Xinhua Lu, East side of the long-distance bus station building ☎ 0938 8319333. Newly opened, this is one of the region's nicest bus station hotels, with a sunny teahouse on the fifth floor. Clean, modern rooms, all with 24hr hot water and broadband internet access. **¥128**

Tianshui 天水大酒店, tiānshuǐ dàjiǔdiàn. 1 Dazhong Zhong Lu ☎ 0938 8289999. A basic hotel on the south side of Qincheng's central square – not far from Nanzhaizi. The hotel's slightly grotty doubles are spacious, if spartan. **¥138**

EATING

Tianshui's local specialities include *shaguo*, a soup of glass noodles and vegetables or meat served sizzling in an earthenware pot, or *guagua*, a snack of boiled buckwheat starch served with chilli oil, sesame sauce and garlic. *KFC* has reached Tianshui – there's a branch on the southeast side of the central square.

Shaguo Laodian 砂锅老店, shāguō lǎodiàn. Qingnian Nan Lu, Qincheng ☎ 0938 8296831. This popular restaurant is a great place to try *shaguo* and their Chinese-only menu has some interesting variations; try the quail egg (鹌鹑蛋, ānchún dàn) version for ¥10. Standard fried dishes also available for around ¥25. Daily 11am–9pm.

Shangbu Lu Pedestrian Street 商埠路步行街, shāngbù lù bùxíngjiē. Shangbu Lu, Beidao. This busy street in Beidao is home to most of the area's restaurants – a mix of steamy Sichuanese restaurants and Muslim barbecue joints – that really comes alive in the evenings. None has an English menu, so head to the busier restaurants, point and expect to pay under ¥20 for a dish.

DIRECTORY

Banks and exchange Beidao's Bank of China (Mon–Fri 8.30am–5pm) is at the end of the street running south from the train station but can exchange cash only; to exchange travellers' cheques, you will need to visit the head office in Qincheng on Minzhu Lu (Mon–Fri 8.30am–6pm). There are ATMs that accept international cards in both locations.

Post office Beidao's post office (daily 8.30am–5.30pm) is just southwest of the train station. Qincheng's post office (daily 8.30am–5pm) is in an obscure alleyway in the northeast corner of the central square – look for the Suning shop and the alley is on the right.

Maiji Shan

麦积山, màijī shān • Daily 8am–6pm • ¥70 or ¥85 including the 2km bus ride up the mountain, with an additional fee (¥500–600 per cave) for access to the most interesting caves • ☎ 0938 2731407

The trip to **Maiji Shan's** Buddhist grottoes is the highlight of eastern Gansu. As is often the case with similar sites in China, the natural setting is spectacular: although the whole area is hilly, the sheer, sandstone cliffs of Maiji Shan, rising out of the forest, make this one hill a complete anomaly. The centrepiece of the statuary, a **16m-high Buddha** (complete with birds nesting in one of its nostrils), is visible from far away, flanked by two bodhisattvas high up on the cliff. The combination of rickety walkways across the cliff face and the beautiful scenery opposite adds charm to the site.

The caves

The cliffs were split apart by an earthquake in the eighth century, leaving a total of 194 surviving **caves**, dating from the northern Wei (the earliest inscription is dated 502 AD) right through to the Qing. The wall paintings are fading due to rain erosion, but the statues are worth visiting. The caves on the western cliff are particularly well preserved, and date mainly from the fourth to the sixth century AD. You are free to

13

explore on your own, climbing higher and higher up the narrow stairways. The caves are all locked, though, and you often find yourself peering into half-lit caverns through wire grilles; for the non-specialist the view is probably adequate – the artwork and statuary generally show up clearly.

ARRIVAL AND DEPARTURE

MAIJI SHAN

By bus Bus #32 (¥5; 45min–1hr) runs to Maiji Shan from outside Tianshui's train station; the last bus returns to Tianshui at 6.30pm.

Water Curtain Caves

水帘洞, shuǐlián dòng • Daily 8am–6pm, occasionally shut after wet weather • ¥30 with an additional ¥10 for a bus up the final 1km to the caves

Accessible along a dry riverbed some 30km north of **WUSHAN** (武山, wǔshān) – itself a small town between Tianshui and Lanzhou – the **Water Curtain Caves** contain a number of important relics, including the **Lashao Temple** (拉稍寺, lāshāo sì), as well as a Thousand Buddha Cave. This extraordinary area is all the better preserved for being so inaccessible – the temple, set into a natural cave in a sandstone cliff, is not visible from the ground. Digging at the grottoes began during the Sixteen States period (304–439 AD). There is a 40m-high relief of Sakyamuni on the mountain cliff, flanked by bodhisattvas, his feet surrounded by wild animals, including lions, deer and elephants, imagery derived from the Hinayana branch of Buddhism, and very rarely found in northern Chinese religious art.

ARRIVAL AND DEPARTURE

WATER CURTAIN CAVES

By bus, train and taxi Buses and trains between Lanzhou and Tianshui pass through Wushan, from where you can get bus #1 to Luomen – the caves are a ¥30 taxi ride from here.

Kongtong Shan

崆峒山, kōngtóng shān • Daily April–Oct 7am–8pm, Nov–March 8am–7pm • ¥120 April–Oct, ¥60 Nov–March • shuttle bus ¥32 each way • cable car ¥50 each way • ☎ 0933 8510202, ⓦ ktsly.com

Kongtong Shan lies 15 km west of the small city of Pingliang (平凉, píngliáng), 200km northeast of Tianshui. Buses from Pingliang deliver visitors to the entrance at the bottom of the mountain, from where you then walk, take a cable car or catch a shuttle bus to the top – there's a steep but pretty footpath that leads 4km straight up the mountain from the ticket office. On arrival you're rewarded with spectacular views over an azure lake, the ribbed landscape dotted with Taoist temples. Maps of the mountain are available from kiosks at the top, and you're free to hike off in any direction – head up for the best buildings, or down toward the lake for the best scenery – allow at least half a day to see it all.

ARRIVAL AND DEPARTURE

KONGTONG SHAN

The access point for Kongtong Shan is Pingliang, where all long-distance transport terminates.

By train Pingliang's train station (平凉火车站, píngliáng huǒchēzhàn) is 2km northeast of the town centre on the Baoji–Baotou line, and handles only a dozen or so services per day including midnight trains to Yinchuan and Xi'an. Hard-seat tickets are easy to buy, sleepers less so – tickets are available from the train station, or from a ticket booth at #54 Hongqi Jie, just southeast of the Pingliang Hotel. Bus #1 runs from the train station, past the east bus station and the *Pingliang Hotel* to the west bus station.
Destinations Baoji (4 daily; 4hr); Lanzhou (1 daily; 12hr); Xi'an (4 daily; 6hr); Yinchuan (4 daily; 8hr).

By bus Pingliang has two bus stations. The west bus station (西车站, xīchēzhàn), just beyond the western end of Xi Dajie, is the busier, with buses to Kongtong Shan and long-distance services to destinations including Beijing, Ürümqi, Yinchuan and Lanzhou. The east bus station (东车站, dōngchēzhàn) is just over 1km southwest of the train station on Jiefang Lu and has hourly buses to Xi'an (¥98) and Lanzhou (¥107), as well as to Guyuan and Tianshui – the last services to either destination depart at 2pm.
Destinations Guyuan (3 daily; 2hr); Lanzhou (hourly; 5hr); Tianshui (hourly; 5hr); Xi'an (hourly; 5hr).

GETTING AROUND

Once at Pingliang, you need to catch local transport to Kongtong Shan.

By bus Bus #13 (¥1) runs from Pingliang's west bus station to Kongtong Shan; allow up to an hour for the journey.

By taxi A cab to the mountain entrance from Pingliang costs about ¥30.

ACCOMMODATION AND EATING

The most interesting option is to spend the night on Kongtong Shan, although Pingliang may be the more comfortable choice. Once on Kongtong Shan, eating options are limited to *Juxian Zhai* (a vegetarian restaurant popular with tour groups), monks' canteens or instant noodles.

KONGTONG SHAN

Kongtong Shanzhuang 崆峒山庄, kōngtóng shānzhuāng. Kongtong Shan Main Village ☎ 0933 8510102. Draughty rooms set around a pleasant courtyard; this hotel is owned by the people who run the vegetarian restaurant next door. The only rooms with en-suite bathrooms are the suites; otherwise you'll need to use the grotty communal washrooms. Closed Nov–April. Doubles **¥200**, suites **¥350**

Taihe Gong 太和宫, tàihé gōng. Offspring Temple, Kongtong Shan ☎ 1529 4031090. The most atmospheric – if the least comfortable – place to stay on Kongtong

Shan, the welcoming monks at Taihe Gong have a few simple twin-bed rooms available. Head to the highest point on the mountain – signed as "Offspring Temple" (子孙宫, zǐsūn gōng) but known locally as "Taihe Gong". Meals included. **¥50**

PINGLIANG

Pingliang 平凉宾馆, píngliáng bīnguǎn. 86 Xi Dajie ☎ 0933 8253361, ✉ plbgzb@163.com. The only hotel where foreigners are allowed to stay in Pingliang itself, this is fortunately a very pleasant option with comfortable doubles and broadband internet. Breakfast included. **¥260**

Lanzhou

兰州, lánzhōu

Squeezed 1600m up into a narrow valley along the Yellow River, and stretching out for nearly 30km east to west, gritty **LANZHOU** sits at the head of the Hexi Corridor (see p.802), which means that almost everyone heading to Xinjiang from eastern China will pass through at some point. Many travellers break their journey here, but most head on before too long, thanks in no small part to Lanzhou's awful air quality: the colossal assortment of factories and petroleum processing plants around the city, coupled with

13

its location – hemmed in by large mountains – once earned it the unfortunate title of "World's Most Polluted City". Today, atrocious traffic means that the pollution shows little sign of abating.

However, the city itself is slowly becoming more attractive, especially with the tarting up of the **Yellow River**'s north bank. There are also a number of good day-trip possibilities, including the **Bingling Caves**, and Lanzhou forms the start or finish line for the fascinating **Xiahe loop** (see p.787). Lastly, this is the best place in China to slurp down a bowl of **Lanzhou beef noodles** – a dish now available all around the country.

Brief history

On the map, Lanzhou appears to lie very much in the middle of China, though this is misleading. Culturally and politically it remains remote, despite being both the Gansu provincial capital and the largest industrial centre in the Northwest. At the head of the Hexi Corridor, it was a vital stronghold along the Silk Road and was the principal crossing point of the mighty Yellow River. For centuries it has been a transportation hub, first for caravans, then shallow-draft boats and now rail lines. Not until the city became a base for imperial military operations against the Tungan Muslim rebels in the 1870s, however, did it become a large population centre as well. Now the city has nearly three million people, the vast majority of them Han Chinese.

The Yellow River

Running right past the city centre, Lanzhou's greatest sight is the **Yellow River**, already wide despite still being 1500km from its mouth in Shandong. In summer, the water is a rich, muddy-brown colour, a legacy of the huge quantity of silt it picks up upstream – in some years the river runs dry, leaving boats stranded on sandbanks.

Nanbinhe Lu, on the south bank, has a paved promenade from where you can watch the river slide by, with large *Journey to the West* statues featuring Xuanzang, Monkey, Pigsy, Sandy and the horse (see p.956); across the road, **Baiyun Guan** (白云观, báiyún guàn; daily 8am–8pm) is a small but cute Taoist temple that provides some respite from the hubbub. **Zhongshan Bridge** (中山桥, zhōngshān qiáo), 500m east of Baiyun Guan, was the first permanent bridge across the Yellow River, constructed between 1907 and 1909 using parts shipped from Germany.

The Waterwheel Park

水车园, shuǐchē yuán • Daily 8am–6pm • ¥30

Lanzhou's **Waterwheel Park** sits beside Huanghe Bridge, east of Zhongshan Bridge. The first waterwheels were constructed during the Ming dynasty to irrigate the city's fields, and by the 1950s the city had over two hundred waterwheels on its riverbanks – a scene that the park tries to re-create.

Baita Shan Park

白塔山公园, báitǎ shān gōngyuán • Daily 6am–6pm • Free • cable car from south bank daily 8.30am–6pm, ¥35 one-way, ¥45 return

Baita Shan Park is ranged up a steep hillside on the north bank of the Yellow River, with great views down over the water and cityscape from stone terraces that span the Park's leafy heights. The Baita (White Pagoda), a 17m-tall pale brick pagoda, was raised in 1228 to honour a Tibetan monk who died here en route to pay his respects to Genghis Khan.

RAFTS AND SPEEDBOATS

To go **boating** on Yellow River, head for the south bank around Huanghe Bridge and Zhongshan Bridge – ride across the river on a traditional, inflated sheepskin raft (¥30/15min), or take a short scenic trip on a motorboat (¥20/10min; two-person minimum).

Lanzhou City Museum

兰州市博物馆, lánzhōu shì bówùguǎn • 240 Qingyang Lu • Daily summer 8.30am–6pm, winter 9am–5.30pm • Free •
Ⓦ www.lzmuseum.org • bus #1, between Lanzhou's main train station and Lanzhou West Station, passes the museum

Undergoing renovation at the time of writing, **Lanzhou City Museum** is housed in a former Buddhist temple built in 1629, complete with its own stupa. The complex's location is rather poignant; with dusty high-rises looming above it, it looks as alien as a spaceship. The permanent collection includes some amazing photos of old Lanzhou from the late nineteenth century, ancient pottery drums and a comprehensive collection of Buddhist statuary.

Gansu Provincial Museum

甘肃省博物馆, gānsù shěng bówùguǎn • 3 Xijin Xi Lu • Tues–Sun 9am–5pm, last admission 4pm • Free • ☎ 0931 2339712,
Ⓦ www.gansumuseum.com • bus #1 or #6 from the main train station or Xiguan Shizi

The one sight worth visiting in western Lanzhou, the **Gansu Provincial Museum** occupies a boxy Stalinist edifice on the area's main artery, Xijin Lu. It has an interesting collection including some remarkable **ceramics** dating from the Neolithic age, as well as a huge collection of **wooden tablets and carvings** from the Han dynasty – priceless sources for studying the politics, culture and economy of the period. However, the bronze **Flying Horse of Wuwei**, two thousand years old and still with its accompanying procession of horses and chariots, is the highlight – note the stylish chariots for top officials with round seats and sunshades. The 14cm-tall horse, depicted with one front hoof stepping on the back of a flying swallow, was discovered in a Han-dynasty tomb in Wuwei in 1969. Most of the exhibits are well labelled in English.

Wuquan and Lanshan parks

Daily 6am–6pm • ¥6 each • bus #8 to its terminus at Wuquan Park gates from anywhere along Jiuquan Lu in the town centre

In the hills bordering the south of the city, **Wuquan Park** (五泉公园, wǔquán gōngyuán) is a nice place to wander with the locals on weekends, full of Qing pavilions, convoluted stairways twirling up the mountainside, teahouses and ponds. One of the oldest buildings, the **Jingang Palace**, contains a 5m-high bronze Buddha – though first cast in 1370, it was restored after being smashed into pieces in the late 1940s. From Wuquan

13

Park, **Lanshan Park** (兰山公园, lánshān gōngyuán) can be reached by chairlift (¥20) – it's about twenty minutes to the very top, from where you'll have superb views of the city, a full 600m below.

ARRIVAL AND DEPARTURE

BY AIR

Lanzhou Zhongchuan airport (兰州中川飞机场, lánzhōu fēijīchǎng) lies about 70km north of the city, a 1hr 30min journey along a purpose-built expressway. Airport buses (¥30, hourly between 6am–7pm) run to and from the main airlines office on Dong Gang Xi Lu (daily 8am–8pm; ☎ 0931 8166058), which also sells flight tickets.
Destinations Beijing (11 daily; 2hr 30min); Chengdu (4 daily; 1hr 30min); Chongqing (3 daily; 1hr 30min); Dunhuang (3 daily; 1hr 40min); Guangzhou (2 daily; 3hr); Jiayuguan (daily; 1hr 10min); Kunming (5 daily; 2hr); Shanghai (8 daily; 2hr 30min); Ürümqi (6 daily; 2hr 30min); Xi'an (9 daily; 1hr).

BY TRAIN

Lanzhou train station (兰州火车站, lánzhōu huǒchēzhàn). As the main rail hub of northwest China, Lanzhou train station is very well served. The ease of buying tickets depends on your route – it's easier for services that start from Lanzhou rather than those that pass through. If you can't face the queues in the main ticket hall (open 24hr), try one of the ticket offices around town: outside the *Lanzhou Hotel* (daily 8.30am–noon & 1–4pm) on the east side of town; and at 127 Dunhuang Lu (daily 9am–noon & 2–6pm) in the west. Aside from the main station in the southeast corner of the city, an enormous new station is being built in the western side of the city, expected to open in 2016. Bus #1 runs from the main train station plaza, past Xiguan Shizi to the western side of the city, while #6 runs from the station north up Tianshui Lu, to the east bus station and on to Xiao Xihu in the west.

Destinations Beijing (6 daily; 17hr–26hr 30min); Chengdu (5 daily; 22hr); Daheyan (12 daily; 18hr 30min); Guangzhou (3 daily; 29hr 30min–37hr); Guyuan (daily; 10hr); Hohhot (2 daily; 21hr); Jiayuguan (regular; 7–10hr); Lhasa (6 daily; 27hr); Shanghai (5 daily; 22–28hr); Tianshui (regular; 5hr); Ürümqi (12 daily; 26hr); Wuwei (regular; 5hr); Xi'an (regular; 7hr 30min–12hr); Xining (regular; 3hr 45min); Yinchuan (3 daily; 9hr 30min); Zhangye (regular; 5–9hr); Zhongwei (7 daily; 6hr).

BY BUS

Main bus station (兰州客运中心, lánzhōu kèyùn zhōngxīn). 200m east of the main train station on Huochezhan Dong Lu, this serves major long-distance destinations including Pingliang, Tianshui, Xi'an, Xining and through the Hexi Corridor.

East bus station (汽车东站, qìchē dōngzhàn) About 1km north of the main train station on Pingliang Lu, buses to Guyuan, plus some services through the Hexi Corridor, to Xining and eastern Gansu, use this station.

South bus station (汽车南站, qìchē nánzhàn) Langongping Lu. All traffic to southwest Gansu – including Xiahe and Hezuo – uses this station. City bus #111 outside can take you to Xiguan Shizi and the east bus station.

West bus station (汽车西站, qìchē xīzhàn). 1km east of the Provincial Museum on Xijin Lu, the West Station is only useful for its frequent service to Liujiaxia, for the Bingling Caves. City bus #1 runs past the front.
Destinations Guyuan (2 daily; 5hr); Hezuo (4hr); Liujiaxia (2hr); Pingliang (5hr); Tianshui (4hr); Wuwei (5hr); Xiahe (4 daily; 5hr); Xining (3hr); Zhangye (10hr).

GETTING AROUND

By bus All buses charge a flat fare of ¥1, no change given, and run from 6am–9pm. Useful services include the #1 and #6 buses, which go from the train station to more central parts of town and on to the west side of the city, and #111, which runs between the east and south bus stations.
By taxi Cabs are not easy to hail in Lanzhou, especially during rush hour. Drivers often pick up additional passengers en

route, so you may end up sharing your taxi with others. Fares start at ¥7 for the first 3km – most drivers use the meter, although you may need to bargain for longer journeys.
By motorbike taxi Not for the faint of heart, one of the best ways to beat Lanzhou's horrible traffic is by taking a motorbike taxi. Expect to bargain hard and pay roughly the same as a regular taxi.

INFORMATION

Travel agents The *Lanzhou* hotel's Western Travel Service (daily 8am–noon & 2.30–6pm; ☎ 0931 8820529, ✉ 751043462@qq.com), with English-speaking staff,

comes highly recommended for organizing tours to Bingling Caves and booking train tickets, though they'll need 36hr notice and charge ¥30 commission.

ACCOMMODATION

Budget accommodation in Lanzhou is thin on the ground – places where foreign travellers can stay are strictly controlled, so you can expect to be turned away from smaller hotels.

Crowne Plaza 皇冠假日酒店, huángguàn jiàrì jiǔdiàn. 1 Beibinhe Dong Lu ☎0931 8711111, ⓦcrowneplaza.cn; map p.781. Lanzhou's newest luxury option, this outpost of the international chain in east Lanzhou is particularly nice, with enthusiastic, English-speaking staff, a big swimming pool, a great breakfast buffet and non-smoking rooms. Located next to a conference centre on the quiet north bank of the Yellow River. **¥1018**

Friendship 友好宾馆, yǒuhǎo bīnguǎn. 32 Langongping Lu ☎0931 2740555; map p.783. A good-value option, clean, quiet and with 24hr hot water. Convenient for the south bus station if you have an early bus to Xiahe and a 15min walk from the Provincial Museum, this is one of the few foreigner-friendly hotels in western Lanzhou. **¥150**

Hualian 华联宾馆, huálián bīnguǎn. 1 Tianshui Lu ☎0931 4992102, ⓦlzhlbg.com; map p.781. As you emerge from the train station, you can't miss this tinted-windowed monster. The lobby seems pretty plush for the price, though the rooms don't quite match up and can smell of drains. Still, it's good value, conveniently located and there's an on-site travel service. **¥188**

Legend 飞天大酒店, fēitiān dàjiǔdiàn. 529 Tianshui Lu, ☎0931 8532888, ⓦwww.lanzhoulegendhotel.com; map p.781. One of the most appealing hotels in town, with international-standard rooms, three restaurants, a quiet bar and friendly staff – much better value for money than the similarly priced but old-fashioned Lanzhou Hotel across the road. Rates include breakfast. **¥552**

New Victory 新胜利宾馆, xīnshènglì bīnguǎn. 285 Qingyang Lu ☎0931 8465221; map p.781. Between the eastern and western halves of the city, handily placed for the downtown eating areas, with large, if unexceptional, rooms. Public areas of this formerly state-owned hotel feel a little tired. The #1 and #111 buses stop nearby. Rates include breakfast. **¥288**

EATING AND DRINKING

Lanzhou, famed around China for its beef noodles (牛肉面, niúròumiàn) and delicious summer fruits, has plenty of good places to eat. You can try the noodles even if you're not staying: the train station plaza is lined with such restaurants. Otherwise, Nongmin Xiang, north of *Lanzhou Fandian* off Tianshui Lu, is a good place to find inexpensive Chinese restaurants, as is Tianping Jie which runs west off Tianshui Lu about 600m north of the train station. The south bank of the Yellow River has a few overpriced "floating" fish restaurants, and lastly there are a few branches of *KFC*, including one at the entrance to the Ya'ou Department Store at Xiguan Shizi and another on Dongfanghong Square.

★ **Boton Coffee** 伯顿餐厅, bódùn cāntīng. Tianshui Lu ☎0931 8878686, map p.781. The elegant Western-style interior of this café-cum-restaurant is a wonderful respite from the gritty city outside. Well-dressed waitresses float around delivering coffee (¥28 a pot) and snacks such as delicious pancakes, or larger meals like pizza or steak (around ¥60). Daily 9am–midnight.

Dehua 德华餐厅, déhuá cāntīng. Langongping Lu ☎0931 2164481, map p.783. A popular Muslim restaurant just 200m east of the *Friendship* hotel. The crowds here are filling up on *mianpian* noodles – cheap, and filling at ¥15 for a huge plateful. Order from their picture menu and expect to pay ¥20–30 per dish. 24hr.

Huifeng Lou 惠丰楼, huìfēng lóu. 100m west of the Lanzhou Hotel on Donggang Xi Lu ☎0931 8820815, map p.781. A busy, mid-range, Muslim place serving local delicacies. Try their *cuipi baozi* (crispy-bottomed dumplings, stuffed with lamb, ¥5 each) or *suancai fentiao* (noodles flavoured with pickled vegetables, chillies and aniseed, ¥18). Daily 11.30am–2pm and 4.30–9pm.

Yunfeng Shouzhua 云峰手抓, yúnfēng shǒuzhuā. 5/F Guangxing Building, Qingyang Road, opposite a branch of Home Inn ☎0931 2168888, map p.781. This popular Muslim restaurant is an excellent place to try *shouzhua yangrou*, mutton served with chilli and raw garlic (¥88). The cheaper standard dishes on their hilarious English menu are good too – try the garlic beef. Daily 10am–2pm and 5–9pm.

SHOPPING

Army surplus gear Good things to buy in Lanzhou include army surplus clothes: winter coats, waistcoats, hats and boots are all locally produced, tough and cheap. They're made at the 3512 Leather and Garment factory at the west end of Yanchang Lu, north of the river, the largest factory of its kind in China. You can even visit and buy direct (bus #7 from the train station; get off at Caochang Jie).

DIRECTORY

Banks and exchange The main Bank of China (daily 8.30am–6pm) is on Tianshui Lu, just south of the *Lanzhou Legend*; foreign exchange is on the second floor. Other branches are scattered all over town with ATMs accepting foreign cards.

Internet There's a little café in the middle of the train

13

station plaza with free wi-fi, although you'll need to buy a drink to use it – look for the *Coca Cola* sign outside. *Boton Coffee* also has wi-fi.

Mail and telephones The main Post and Telecommunications Office (daily 8.30am–7pm) stands at the junction of Pingliang Lu and Minzhu Dong Lu. There's also a post office on Qingyang Lu, and you can make collect calls at the China Telecom Building on the corner of Qingyang Lu and Jinchang Lu.

PSB Visas can be extended upstairs at Lanzhou's Exit & Entry Administration Centre on Wudu Lu, a couple of hundred metres west of Jiuquan Lu – look for the yellow sign (Mon–Fri 8.30–11.30am, 2.30–5.30pm).

The Bingling Caves

炳灵寺石窟, bǐnglíngsì shíkū · Daily from April–Oct, 8.30am–6.30pm · ¥50 · ☎ 0930 8879070

The excursion from Lanzhou to the Buddhist **Bingling Caves**, carved into a canyon on the Yellow River, provides an introduction to both the monumental **religious art** that filtered along the Silk Road, and also to the Yellow River itself. The caves are among the earliest significant Buddhist monuments in China – started in the Western Jin and extended by the Northern Wei, the Tang, Song, Yuan and Ming. Though the earliest wall paintings here have been virtually washed away, a considerable number of exquisite carvings survive, mostly in good condition, with some impressive restoration work in progress.

The caves

Water levels rose 20m after the dam was completed, and buried the lower level of caves in mud – fortunately the best sculptures were saved and have been transplanted to caves higher up. Cut into the western escarpment of **Dasi Gou** (Big Temple Gully), the remaining 183 caves stretch for 200m amid stunning scenery. The centrepiece is a huge 27m-high **seated Buddha** (cave 172), carved under the Tang and currently swathed in scaffolding for restoration. The majority of the caves, some little more than hollows in the rock face, are protected behind wooden doors that are opened each morning. The oldest and largest cave, number 169, is tucked away at the top of dizzying network of stairs and ramps – if you want to see it you will need to shell out an additional ¥300 at the entrance for a guide with the key. If you have time, it's also possible to climb to the **Upper Temple**, a further 45-minute hike up the gully, home to a small, quiet community of Tibetan lamas, who live in huts against the cliff and tend a small, modern temple.

ARRIVAL AND DEPARTURE BINGLING CAVES

By bus and boat Frequent buses (¥12) depart Lanzhou's west bus station from 7am to Liujiaxia Dam near Yongjing (永靖, yǒngjìng), 75km southwest of Lanzhou. At the bus stop there's an arch with a Chinese-only map; here, you can pick up a speedboat for a return trip (1hr each way; ¥100/person or ¥400/boat). On the way back you may need to stay the night in Yongjing, if the last public bus back to Lanzhou (around 5pm) leaves without you.

By tour Day-trips from Lanzhou are offered by the Western Travel Service (see p.784). An all-inclusive price (car, speedboat, entry ticket and insurance) usually comes to ¥550 per person for a group of four; or ¥350 per person if you're happy to tag along with a Chinese group and use the slow boat (3hr one-way).

REACHING THE BINGLING CAVES

The caves can only be reached by boat, and only then between April and early October when water levels are sufficiently high. From Lanzhou, the first stage of the expedition is a two-hour bus ride to the massive **Liujiaxia Hydroelectric Dam**, a spectacular sight poised above the reservoir. At the dam you board a speedboat, which takes a further hour to reach the caves and offers excellent views of fishermen busy at work and peasants cultivating wheat, sunflowers and rice on the dark, steep banks. Towards the end of the trip, the boat enters a dramatic **gorge**, where the river froths and churns between jagged hills that have been eroded into bizarre shapes by the wind and water.

THE OLD ROAD TO XIAHE

Though direct buses and a highway connect Lanzhou to Xiahe, you'll get a better feel for the region by hopping slowly between towns along the more scenic **old road**, which travels via Yongjing and Liujiaxia (the jumping-off points for Bingling Caves), and then traverses **Dongxiang Autonomous County**. Such is the beauty of this trip that you may find yourself wanting to stop off at one of the ridge towns en route, whose populations are almost entirely Muslim: you'll see very few men who aren't wearing skullcaps. Women wear a square veil of fine lace, black if they are married and green if they are not. The largest ridge town goes by a few different names, but is generally referred to as **Dongxiang** (东乡, dōngxiāng) and makes for a fascinating stay, with its bustling, regular livestock market.

In the mountains around Dongxiang, the Islamic and Tibetan Buddhist worlds begin to overlap and villages are interspersed with ancient communities of some of China's lesser-known ethnicities. The **Dongxiang people**, numbering nearly two hundred thousand, are Muslims of Mongol origin and descended from troops garrisoned in Linxia under Genghis Khan in the thirteenth century. These days, to outsiders at least, they are indistinguishable from the Hui except at certain celebrations when old Mongol customs re-emerge. The **Bao'an**, who number barely eight thousand, are similar to the Dongxiang in that they, too, are of Mongolian origins – while their language is written in Chinese, it contains a high percentage of Mongolian words. The **Salar** are a Turkic-speaking people whose origins lie, it's thought, in Samarkand in Central Asia; they live primarily in Xunhua County in neighbouring Qinghai province.

Regular buses ply the 25km route between Dongxiang and **Linxia** (临夏, línxià), a strongly Muslim town, full of mosques. Linxia's Hui are inveterate traders and their enterprises, together with burgeoning local industry, have seen factories and tower blocks sprouting up on the outskirts. The town is rather ugly; nevertheless, it's an interesting enough place to spend a few hours should you get stuck between buses. The main **Nanguan Mosque** (南关清真寺, nánguān qīngzhēn sì) is immediately south of the square at the intersection of central Tuanjie Lu and Jiefang Lu. From Linxia, there are regular buses on to Xiahe.

The Xiahe loop

The verdant, mountainous area south of Lanzhou, bordering Qinghai to the west and Sichuan to the south, is one of enormous scenic beauty, relatively untouched by the scars of industry and overpopulation. The people who live in the so-called **Xiahe loop** are diverse in culture and ethnicity, including a very strong **Hui** and **Tibetan** presence. Xiahe, in particular, is a delightful place to visit, site of the major **Labrang Monastery**, one of the largest Lamaist institutions in China, which attracts monks and pilgrims from across the Tibetan Plateau. From Xiahe, you can loop back to Lanzhou via **Tongren** – itself home to a large Tibetan population – and Xining, both in **Qinghai** province, or follow an adventurous route south into **Sichuan** province.

Note that towns throughout the loop are small affairs with few ATMs or exchange facilities – it's best to take enough **cash** to cover the entire trip.

Xiahe

夏河, xiàhé

A tiny, rural town tucked away 3000m up in the remote hills of southern Gansu, right on the edge of the Tibetan Plateau, **XIAHE** is unforgettable: the town's **Labrang Monastery** is one of the six major centres of the Gelugpa, or Yellow Hat Sect (of the others, four are in Tibet and one, Kumbum Monastery, is just outside the Qinghai capital, Xining; see p.797). Tibetans come here on pilgrimage in traditional dress (equipped with mittens, kneepads and even leather aprons to cushion themselves during their prostrations), and the constant flow of monks in bright purple, yellow and red, alongside semi-nomadic herdsmen wrapped in sheepskins, makes for an endlessly fascinating scene.

Xiahe also offers visitors the chance to spend some time in open countryside, set as it is in a sunny, fresh valley surrounded by green hills. There are a number of superb

13

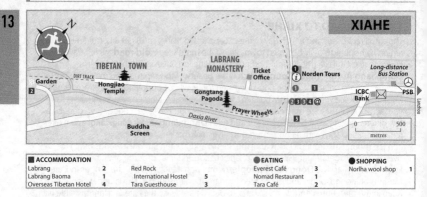

■ ACCOMMODATION			● EATING		● SHOPPING	
Labrang	2	Red Rock	Everest Café	3	Norlha wool shop	1
Labrang Baoma	1	International Hostel 5	Nomad Restaurant	1		
Overseas Tibetan Hotel	4	Tara Guesthouse 3	Tara Café	2		

walks around town, including the **Upper Kora**, a pilgrim trail snaking through the peaks north of the monastery.

Brief history

Labrang monastery was founded in 1709 by E'ang Zongzhe, a Living Buddha latterly recognized as the first **Jiamuyang**, born in Xiahe in 1648. Upon the death of each Jiamuyang, a new one is born, supposedly representing the reincarnation of the previous incumbent – the present Jiamuyang being the sixth incarnation.

Although Labrang may seem a peaceful haven today, ferocious battles took place here in the 1920s between Muslim warlords and Tibetans, with atrocities committed by both sides. The Cultural Revolution brought further disaster: persecution for the monks and the virtual destruction of the monastery. It was not until 1980 that it reopened, and although it is flourishing once again, it is nevertheless a smaller place than before. There are now around nine hundred registered lamas and two thousand unofficial monks, about half their former number.

Labrang Monastery

拉卜楞寺, lābǔlèng sì

Phenomenally beautiful and surrounded by mountains on all sides, **Labrang Monastery** sits just west of Xiahe's centre. There's no wall separating the town from the monastery – the two communities just merge together and the main road goes right through the middle of both. The signs that you're entering the monastery are the long lines of

---

XIAHE ORIENTATION

Xiahe is essentially built along a single street that stretches 3–4km along the north bank of the Daxia River, from the bus station in the east, through Labrang Monastery to the old Tibetan town and, finally, the **Labrang Hotel** in the west.

The **eastern end** of town, predominantly Hui- and Han-populated, is the commercial and administrative centre, with a couple of banks, a post office and plenty of shops and markets. The shops round here make interesting browsing, with religious objects for sale, including hand-printed sutras, prayer wheels, bells and jewellery. There's also riding equipment – saddles and bridles – for the nomads from the nearby grasslands who come striding into town, spurs jangling.

Beyond the monastery, at the **western end** of town, is the Tibetan town. The road eventually becomes a bumpy dirt track with homes built of mud and wood, and pigs and cows ambling around. There is one more religious building up here, the **Hongjiao Temple**, or Temple of the Red Hat sect, whose monks, clad in red robes with a large white band, live in the shadow of their wealthier and more numerous Yellow Hat brethren.

VISITING LABRANG MONASTERY

While there is nothing to stop you from wandering around the monastery complex by yourself – be sensitive, use your discretion, and move clockwise – given the bewildering wealth of architecture, art and statuary, it's a good idea to take a **guided tour** at some stage. This can be arranged at the ticket office – take the only sizeable turn off the north side of the road within the monastery area (on the right if coming from the station). The hour-long tours (roughly at 10.15am and 3.15pm; ¥40) include entrance to five buildings and are led by English-speaking monks.

Labrang Monastery is the site of some spectacular festivals that, as with Chinese festivals, take place according to the lunar calendar. The largest is the **Monlam Festival**, three days after the Tibetan New Year (late Feb or early March). The opening of the festival is marked by the unfurling of a huge *thangka* on the south side of the Daxia River. Processions, dances and the lighting of butter lamps take place on subsequent days.

---

roofed **prayer wheels** stretching out either side of the road, tracing a near-complete circle around the monastery. To the south side, along the north bank of the river, you can follow the prayer wheels to the other end of the monastery. It's mesmerizing to walk clockwise alongside the pilgrims, who turn each prayer wheel they pass.

The majority of the important **monastery buildings** are north of the main road. The buildings include six colleges, prayer halls, sutra printing workshops and mud-brick dormitories for the monks. At the colleges monks study towards degrees in astronomy, esoteric Buddhism, law, medicine and theology (higher and lower). There are also schools for dance, music and painting. The **Gongtang Pagoda** (贡唐宝塔, gòngtáng bǎotǎ; daily 7am–11pm; ¥20), first built in 1805, is the only major monastery building south of the main road – on the prayer wheel circuit – and is worth climbing for spectacular views over the shining golden roofs of the monastery.

ARRIVAL AND DEPARTURE XIAHE

By bus Xiahe's bus station (夏河客运站, xiàhé kèyùn zhàn) is at the eastern end of town, and served by frequent buses from Linxia and Hezuo; there are also a few services each day to Lanzhou and Xining, and one early-morning departure for Tongren in Qinghai. For the route to Sichuan, take one of the two daily buses to Luqu and continue from there. It's best to purchase tickets a day in advance for all destinations except Linxia and Hezuo. The ticket office is open daily 6.30am–5pm.

Destinations Hezuo (2hr); Lanzhou (4hr); Linxia (2hr); Tongren (4hr); Xining (6hr).

GETTING AROUND

By bicycle You can rent bikes from *Norden Tours* or the *Overseas Tibetan and Labrang Baoma* hotels for ¥10/hour or ¥50/day.

By taxi Shared taxis shuttle up and down Xiahe's main street. A trip anywhere in the town ought to cost ¥5.

INFORMATION

Agencies A few agencies can arrange local tours and onward travel, including *Norden Tours* (☎ 1398 3919170, ✉ sonamdolma3@yahoo.com), which operates from a café just northeast of the *Nomad Restaurant* on the eastern edge of the prayer wheel circuit; and ★ OT Travels (☎ 0941 7122642, ✉ amdolosang@hotmail.com), which runs out of the *Overseas Tibetan Hotel*.

ACCOMMODATION

The east end of town has plenty of comfy, Chinese-style hotels. However, it's more fun to try one of the charismatic Tibetan-owned guesthouses farther up the road, which attract a mixed clientele of pilgrims and budget travellers.

Labrang 拉卜楞宾馆, lābǔlèng bīnguǎn. In the fields to the west of the town ☎ 0941 7121849. It's 4km from the bus station and nearly 1km from the edge of town, a ¥10 taxi ride from the station. Accommodation ranges from grotty twin rooms to standard Chinese-style hotel rooms, and rather damp, "Tibetan-style" cabins. Ring ahead if possible. Basic twins <u>¥180</u>, doubles <u>¥280</u>, cabins <u>¥360</u>

13

Labrang Baoma 拉卜楞宝马宾馆, lābǔlèng bǎomǎ bīnguǎn. In a courtyard off Renmin Xi Jie, 100m northwest of the prayer wheel circuit ☎0941 7121078, ⓦlabranghotel.com. Very popular hotel sporting traditionally decorated rooms, wi-fi, a small restaurant and 24hr hot water. Good discounts available outside the peak summer season. **¥220**

Overseas Tibetan Hotel 华侨饭店, huáqiáo fàndiàn. ☎0941 7122642, ⓦoverseastibetanhotel .com. A clean, well-maintained building offering private rooms pleasantly decorated in a vaguely Tibetan style, as well as a couple of nice dorms with communal bathrooms. Well staffed with English-speaking employees, plus a wide range of services. Dorm beds **¥50**, doubles **¥300**

★ **Red Rock International Hostel** 红石国际青年旅馆, hóngshí guójì qīngnián lǚshè. In a courtyard

next to the river, just south of town ☎0941 7123698, ⓔlabranghongshi@yahoo.com.cn. Away from the hubbub of the main road, this hostel centres on its lobby: with its alpine feel and wi-fi access, it makes a good place to meet fellow travellers (although most guests are Chinese and staff do not speak English). The communal showers are poor, but rooms are nicely decorated. Dorm beds **¥40**, doubles **¥120**

Tara Guesthouse 才让卓玛旅舍, cáiràng zhuómǎ lǚshè. On the south side of Renmin Xi Jie, just east of the prayer wheel circuit ☎0941 7121274. The young Tibetan owners are a little odd (some say in a good way, others aren't so impressed) and the rooms can be shabby, but this is perfect for those on a tight budget. The 11pm curfew shouldn't matter too much – this is Xiahe, after all. Dorm beds **¥20**, doubles **¥50**

EATING

As with accommodation, Chinese restaurants are concentrated in the east end of town, Tibetan restaurants in the west. Locals head for the cheap Tibetan canteens offering *momos* (dumplings filled with yak meat or mutton) and *thugkpa* (noodle soup) that dot Renmin Xi Jie, but few have menus, making ordering your meal a challenge.

Everest Café 华侨餐厅, huáqiáo cāntīng. Inside the Overseas Tibetan hotel on Renmin Xi Jie ☎0941 7122642. A quiet restaurant with friendly English-speaking staff, an extensive menu of Western, Chinese and Tibetan dishes and a decent set breakfast (¥30). Daily 8am–10pm.

Nomad Restaurant 牧民齐全饭庄, mùmín qíquán fànzhuāng. 3/F, Opposite Tara Café on Renmin Xi Jie ☎0941 7121897. A reliable restaurant with rooftop views and an English menu. They serve good breakfasts, tasty

Western, Chinese and Tibetan food and delicious sweet tea (¥6). Daily 8am–10pm.

Tara Café 才让卓玛旅舍, cáiràng zhuómǎ lǚshè. On the south side of Renmin Xi Jie, inside the Tara Guesthouse ☎0941 7121274. This Tibetan-style teahouse is popular with travellers and Tibetans alike, who flock here for Chinese standards, noodle soup and *momos*. They also serve a simple buffet breakfast each morning (¥15). Daily 8am–10pm.

SHOPPING

Yak wool products In addition to the shops in the eastern side of town, check out the Norlha shop next to

Norden Tours' office. Their beautiful but pricey yak wool products are made by a nomads' cooperative near Hezuo.

DIRECTORY

Banks and exchange There is no Bank of China in Xiahe, but the *Overseas Tibetan Hotel* can exchange cash (euros and US dollars only), and some get lucky with the ATM at the Industrial & Commercial Bank of China (ICBC) next to the post office.

Internet Most hotels and backpacker cafés have wi-fi.

PSB Visas can be renewed with relative ease in a courtyard just west of the bus station, on the same side of the road. Open Mon–Fri 8.30am–noon and 2.30–6pm.

Mail and telephones The main post office (Mon–Fri 8am–6pm) stands 100m west of the bus station on Renmin Xi Jie.

Hezuo

合作, hézuò

About 70km southeast of Xiahe on the road to Langmusi and the Sichuan border, **HEZUO** is a trading post for Tibetan nomads, and you'll see some fairly wild-looking types in town. If you're here in summer, don't miss Hezuo's **Caterpillar Fungus Market** (虫草批发市场, chóngcǎo pīfā shìchǎng; free), an ad hoc street market for this odd herbal remedy (see opposite) that gathers daily in the early summer on the western side of the junction of Panxuan Lu and the G213 main road.

13

Amdo Milarepa Pavilion

米拉日巴佛楼阁, mǐlārìbāfó lóugé • Daily 9am–4.30pm • ¥20

Hezuo's main attraction is the **Amdo Milarepa Pavilion**, in the north of the city. You'll see it as you drive into town from Xiahe – indeed, you can hardly miss the nine-storey structure. From the town, walk north until you reach the main road to Lanzhou and Xiahe, then head east until you reach the pavilion and monastery on the left. The exterior of the tower may look stern and robust, but the interior is dazzling, each room gaudy with paintings and sculpture. Provided you take your shoes off at the door, you are free to ascend eight of nine floors – from the roof you gaze out at hills dotted with prayer flags.

ARRIVAL AND DEPARTURE HEZUO

By bus Hezuo's north bus station (合作汽车北站, hézuò qìchē běizhàn) serves Lanzhou, Xiahe and Xining, and is located at the northern end of Nianqin Street, one block west of Hezuo's main road. The ticket office is open 6am–6pm, and houses a booth selling train tickets (although the nearest train station is in Lanzhou). All buses heading south into Sichuan depart from the south bus station (合作汽车南站, hézuò qìchē nán zhàn) 1km south of the centre on Lazikou Lu; your first target in this direction is 80km south at Luqu (碌曲, lùqǔ), halfway to Langmusi (see p.760).

Destinations Lanzhou (4hr); Linxia (2hr); Luqu (2hr); Xining (6hr).

ACCOMMODATION

Foreigner-friendly, budget accommodation is sparse in Hezuo – attempt to check in at any of the cheaper places in the town centre and you'll be pointed towards one of the smart, new hotels shooting up across town.

Gele Hotel 格乐宾馆, gélè bīnguǎn. 200m west of the Amdo Milarepa Pavilion ☏0941 8231118. This Tibetan hotel has a collection of slightly ragged rooms, friendly but chaotic service and 24hr hot water. Broadband is available in the more expensive rooms. **¥140**

Kaibin Hotel 凯宾大酒店, kǎibīn dàjiǔdiàn. Panxuan Lu ☏0941 8226888. This centrally located hotel near the caterpillar fungus market is better value than some of Hezuo's other upmarket options, with adequate standard rooms and broadband internet. **¥219**

Yinxing Hotel 银星宾馆, yínxīng bīnguǎn. 8 Xishan Po, 200m north of the north bus station ☏0941 8237777. A Muslim-run hotel in a convenient location for the north bus station and monastery, with pleasant enough rooms, 24hr hot water and broadband internet. **¥138**

CHONGCAO – HIMALAYAN VIAGRA

Over the past three decades, the impoverished edges of the Tibetan Plateau have remained stubbornly resistant to the economic development that has transformed the rest of China. However, this is finally changing, thanks to an unlikely commodity.

The caterpillars of the ghost moth live underground in high-altitude regions (between 3000–5000m elevation). While feeding on roots, the subterranean larva is attacked by a parasitic fungus, **Cordyceps sinensis**, which kills the caterpillar and erupts from its forehead in a stalk-like growth. When hand-collected and dried by nomads, the bizarre-looking fungus – half caterpillar, half stalk and known as **chongcao** ("insect grass") in Chinese, or *yertse kumbu* ("winter insect, summer grass") in Tibetan – has long been used in traditional Tibetan and Chinese medicine, where it is reputed to act as an aphrodisiac and improve a range of conditions from asthma to cancer.

As China's middle class has grown, demand for **caterpillar fungus** has increased and prices have soared. The profits from this booming trade – prices can reach well over US$100 per gram, more expensive than gold – have started to improve the livelihoods of people across the Himalayan region. The practice of harvesting the fungus before it has released its spores has decimated the harvest elsewhere on the plateau, pushing prices ever higher in the places where the fungus is still relatively plentiful, as it is in the Tibetan fringes of Gansu, Qinghai and Sichuan, encouraging locals to cash in while the boom lasts.

EATING

Hezuo's restaurants are mostly cheap Muslim canteens.

Gangnuo'er Restaurant 岗诺尔美食府, gǎngnuò'ěr měishífǔ. Next to the Gele Hotel, just west of the Amdo Milarepa Pavilion. A popular place for Tibetan wedding banquets, come here to try Tibetan dishes, like sizzling yak meat with onions, and *tsampa* – barley meal with yak butter. Daily 11am–9pm.

Muslim Restaurant 清真餐厅, qīngzhēn cāntīng. On the northeast side of the Caterpillar Fungus Market junction. Spot this inexpensive canteen by the picture menu covering one wall. It's equally popular with Muslims and Tibetans, who come here to fill up on enormous plates of noodles. Daily 8am–8pm.

DIRECTORY

Banks The Agricultural Bank (Mon–Fri 8.30am–5.30pm), just south of the caterpillar fungus market junction on the east side of the main road, is the only place in town that will change foreign currency and has an ATM that accepts international cards.

Tongren

同仁, tóngrén

Just across the Qinghai border from Gansu, and approximately 170km south of Xining, is the autonomous Tibetan region of **Tongren**, its centre a small but growing city of the same name. Known as Repkong in Tibetan, this makes an excellent base for nearby sights, including **Wutun Temple**, the source of Tibet's famed **thangka** paintings.

Wutun

吾屯, wútún • public minibus from Tongren ¥2 • taxi ¥10

The superbly detailed pieces of Buddhist art known as *thangka* started life 8km northeast of Tongren in the incredibly scenic village of **Wutun**. They continue to be produced to this day in a number of artists' houses surrounding **Wutun Temple**. Some travellers choose to walk the whole way here from Tongren but, however you arrive, the village's dirt lanes are well worth a wander – this is the Tibet people pay hundreds of dollars to see: an impoverished but happy collection of earth buildings with not a streetlight or mobile phone store in sight.

Wutun Temple

吾屯寺, wútún sì • Daily 9am–5pm

Wutun's temple complex is split into upper (上, shàng) and lower (下, xià) sections that are about ten minutes from each other on foot. **Wutun Lower Temple** (¥30) is the larger and showier of the two, although this isn't saying much – both are pleasantly quiet. Keep an eye out for the beautiful old *thangka* outside the Maitreya Hall. During the Cultural Revolution these panels survived by being reversed and covered with newspaper and political slogans. Small *thangka* can usually be acquired for around ¥300 from the monastery shop, while full-size versions – which take well over a month to make – will set you back ten times that amount.

When visiting the **upper temple** (free) you'll need to find a monk to open the halls for you. Of particular interest here is a narrow chapel at the rear of the main prayer hall containing an enormous rolled-up *thangka* that the monks display on festival days and thousands of miniature bronze statues of the Gelugpa sect's revered founder, Tsongkhapa.

Longwu Monastery

隆务寺, lóngwù sì • Daily 9am–5pm • ¥50

In Tongren itself is the Yuan-dynasty Tibetan lamasery **Longwu Monastery**. Locally known as Gonchen Gompa, the temple buildings have recently been spruced up – keep an eye out for the monastery kitchens. There's an official tourist trail leading around the complex, but it's better to follow the fascinating flow of worshippers around the busiest chapels. The temple is an easy walk from Zhongshan Lu in the centre of Tongren – turn left at the T-junction at the top end of the road, and it'll appear on your left after 1km or so.

ARRIVAL AND DEPARTURE   TONGREN

By bus Buses arrive at a small station (黄南汽车站, huángnán qìchēzhàn) in the centre of town, just downhill from Zhongshan Lu; there are plenty of services heading to Xining, but the single departure to Xiahe leaves at 8am sharp every morning.

Destinations Xiahe (4hr); Xining (3hr).
By taxi Shared taxis (¥50 per person) drive between Tongren and a stop on Bayi Lu in Xining. Handy if you're travelling in a group and in a hurry, but solo travellers may find themselves waiting for ages until the car fills up.

ACCOMMODATION

Regong 热贡宾馆, règòng bīnguǎn. 1 Dongge'er Lu ☏0973 8727088. While it's not the most central of Tongren's hotels – located on the opposite side of the Longwu River to the main town – this is one of the best, with clean rooms, 24hr hot water and only slightly grotty bathrooms. Room rates include breakfast. **¥240**

Yongqing 永庆宾馆, yǒngqìng bīnguǎn. Dehalong Zhong Lu ☏0973 8798888. On the corner of Zhongshan Lu just uphill from the bus station, this basic hotel is convenient both for Longwu Temple and onward transport. Rooms are on the small side and can be noisy, so get one facing away from the street if possible. **¥120**

EATING

Qingyalou 清雅楼, qīngyǎlóu. 69 Zhongshan Lu ☏0973 8726997. This Muslim hotpot restaurant is one of the many places to eat around the centre of town

– *qiangguo yu*, a fish dish, is their speciality. Look for "Restaurant" in large white letters on the sign outside. Daily 11am–9.30pm.

Xining

西宁, xīníng

Qinghai's unassuming provincial capital, **XINING** contains few tourist sights and is usually regarded simply as a base from which to explore the nearby Tibetan **Kumbum Monastery**, start a trip around Qinghai or head off on the superb **Xiahe loop** (see p.787). Nevertheless, Xining is an interesting place in its own right. Set in an attractive location, enclosed on all sides by mountains, the city has a cosy, reassuring feel. At a height of 2260m, on the outermost edge of the Tibetan Plateau, Xining experiences pleasantly cool weather in summer and bitter cold in winter.

Brief history

Today a largely Han Chinese city, Xining is still home to a few **minority nationalities**, in particular Hui and Tibetans. Settled during the Han dynasty and having served as a stopover on a minor branch of the Silk Road, Xining has a long history, and has been a regional trading centre since at least the sixteenth century. It became the provincial capital when Qinghai was elevated to proper provincial status in 1928. Today, connected by train to Lanzhou and other Chinese cities, Xining is a firmly established part of the network of Han China.

Dongguan Great Mosque

东关清真大寺, dōngguān qīngzhēn dàsì • Dongguan Dajie • Mon–Thurs, Sat & Sun 8am–8pm, Fri 8–10am & 2–8pm • ¥25
• buses #1 & #2 run past the mosque from the Central Square and Ximen

Xining's major site is the **Dongguan Great Mosque**. Originally built in 1378, it encloses a large public square where worshippers can congregate – as many as 20,000 gather here for Friday prayers (during which time the Mosque is closed to visitors). The architecture is a synthesis of Arabic and Chinese styles, its exterior adorned with the old Chinese favourite – white tile. Fortunately the beautiful main prayer hall has escaped this treatment. The Tibetan prayer wheels on the roof were gifts from the monks of Labrang Monastery (p.788).

13

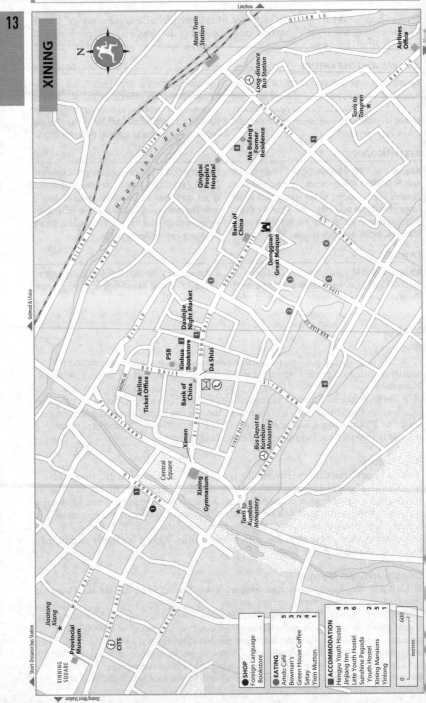

XINING

N

Lanzhou

QILIAN LU

Main Train Station

Airlines Office

BAYI LU

Long-distance Bus Station

Taxis to Tongren

Ma Bufang's Former Residence

JIANGUO LU

Huangshui River

QILIAN LU

Qinghai People's Hospital

Bank of China

DONGGUAN DAJIE

Dongguan Great Mosque

GONGHE LU

QILIAN NAN LU

BINHE NAN LU

QILIN LU

TIYU LU

Daxinjie Night Market

DONG DAJIE

PSB

Xinhua Bookstore

Da Shizi

BEI DAJIE

Airline Ticket Office

Bank of China

XI DAJIE

Ximen

JIABU DAJIE

NAN DAJIE

NAN XIAO JIE

Bus Depot to Kumbum Monastery

KUNLUN ZHONG LU

Central Square

HUANGHE LU

Xining Gymnasium

Taxis to Kumbum Monastery

DATONG JIE

CHANGJIANG LU

Golmud & Lhasa

Short-Distance bus Station

Jiaotong Xiang

Provincial Museum

XINING SQUARE

WU SI DAJIE

KEGUAN DAJIE

KUNTUN LU

Xining West Station

CITS

SHOP

Foreign Language Bookstore 1

EATING
Amdo Café   5
Bowman's   3
Green House Coffee   2
Satay   4
Yixin Mutton   1

ACCOMMODATION
Hengyu Youth Hostel   4
Jinjiang Inn   3
Lete Youth Hostel   6
Sunshine Pagoda   2
Xining Mansions   5
Yinlong   1

0   600
metres

13

Qinghai Provincial Museum

省博物馆, shěng bówùguǎn • Xiguan Dajie • Tues–Sun, summer 9am–4.30pm, winter 9.30am–4pm • Free • bus #9 runs to Jiaotong Xiang on Wusi Dajie via Xining Mansions and the Central Square

The provincial **museum** lies on the southeast side of Xinning Square (新宁广场, xīnníng guǎngchǎng), in the west of the city. The most interesting permanent exhibition displays artefacts that illustrate Qinghai's history, ranging from prehistoric rhinoceros skulls to a copy of a beautiful Qing-dynasty drum mounted on a stone elephant – the original is housed in Qutan Temple, (see p.798), with English captions. Ignore signs pointing you to the carpet-weaving exhibition around the side of the building – it's a showroom.

Ma Bufang's Former Residence

马步芳公馆, mǎbùfāng gōngguǎn • 13 Weimin Xiang • Daily 8.30am–6.30pm • ¥30 • bus #26 runs to the nearby provincial hospital from the eastern side of the Central Square via Dongguan Mosque

Ma Bufang, one of the most prominent members of the Ma family of warlords, who ruled Qinghai, Gansu and Ningxia in the first half of the twentieth century, built this luxurious house in 1942 while Governor of Qinghai. Having fought the communists through the 1930s, Ma was chased out of China in 1949 and finally wound up in Saudia Arabia as the Taiwanese ambassador. Today his former home – recently restored after decades of use as a vegetable market – is a fascinating example of how upper-class families lived during the Republican era, the walls of its many rooms faced with jade tiles and filled with imported luxuries.

ARRIVAL AND DEPARTURE · XINING

By air Xining's airport (西宁曹家堡机场, xīníng cáojiābǎo jīchǎng) is 30km east of town; a bus (¥21) delivers to the airline offices (daily 8.30am–noon & 2–5.30pm; ☎0971 8133333) on Bayi Lu, 1500m southeast of the train station. Buses from the city to the airport depart about two hours before each flight, taxis cost around ¥100. Flight tickets are available from booths and hotels across town, and at the central post office.
Destinations Beijing (9 daily; 2hr 10min); Chengdu (3 daily; 1hr 30min); Guangzhou (5 daily; 3hr 30min); Shanghai (4 daily; 3hr); Ürümqi (2 daily; 2hr 30min); Xi'an (regular; 1hr 30min).

By train At the time of writing, Xining's main train station (西宁火车站, xīníng huǒchēzhàn) was closed for expansion, with all services on the Lanzhou–Lhasa line temporarily redirected via Xining West Station (火车西站, huǒchē xīzhàn). While it's easy to buy sleeper tickets for services originating in Xining, you may have difficulty getting on trains from elsewhere. Tickets are available upstairs at the main post office, as well as from ticket offices at 70 Wusi Dajie and the *Tiedao Hotel* at 14 Jianguo Lu. Special Bus #2 runs from the main station to the west station via the Central Square and Ximen.
Destinations Beijing (3 daily; 25hr); Golmud (11 daily; 9hr 30min); Lanzhou (regular; 3hr); Lhasa (9 daily; 24hr); Shanghai (2 daily; 25–31hr 30min); Xi'an (10 daily; 12hr 45min).

By bus Xining's long-distance bus station (西宁汽车站, xīníng qìchēzhàn) is 1.5km east of the centre, near the main train station. Tickets are only available from the station itself and same-day tickets are easy to buy. Buses to Ledu (for Qutan Temple) leave from the short-distance bus station north of Xinning Square.
Destinations Golmud (16hr); Lanzhou (4hr); Ledu (1hr 30min); Linxia (6hr); Tongren (4hr); Zhangye (7hr).

INFORMATION

Travel agents For buying train or plane tickets, and for organizing trips to Qinghai Lake (see p.798), call the English-speaking staff at CITS (14/F, Tower B, 49 Xiguan Dajie, ☎0971 6133844). For more interesting trips to remote parts of Qinghai and into Tibet, Tibetan Connections (ⓦ tibetanconnections.com), which operates from the *Lete Youth Hostel*, is the best option. Their friendly and knowledgeable staff can help organize Tibet entry permits (which you will need if you plan to continue to Lhasa), as well as wildlife-watching trips and horse trekking.

ACCOMMODATION

The amount of accommodation in Xining is increasing as tourism in Qinghai becomes more established, and the city now boasts a couple of superb hostels.

13

★**Hengyu Youth Hostel** 恒裕国际青年旅舍, héngyù guójì qīngnián lǚshè. 13 Weimin Xiang ☎0971 5223399, ✉yhaqhhy@163.com. A great hostel in a quiet location next to Ma Bufang's Former Residence. Clean dorms and double rooms open onto a sunny courtyard with wi-fi, bike rental and travel advice available. Dorms ¥40, rooms ¥138

Jinjiang Inn 锦江之星, jǐnjiāng zhī xīng. 30 Dong Dajie ☎0971 4928333, 🌐jinjianginns.com. A convenient branch of this reliable chain, rooms are clean and bright, if a little impersonal. The entrance is inside a courtyard off Dong Dajie – look for the large red-and-white neon sign above the courtyard entrance. ¥239

★**Lete Youth Hostel** 理体青年旅舍, lǐtǐ qīngnián lǚshè. Jiancai Xiang ☎0971 8202080 🌐letehostel.com. One of the best hostels in western China: its sixteenth-floor location makes for superb city views, beds are comfy and the on-site bar/restaurant is a great place to eat or drink. It's a little hard to find, though, on the top of a nondescript tower block. Dorms ¥40, rooms ¥120

Sunshine Pagoda Youth Hostel 塔顶阳光国际青年旅舍, tǎdǐng yángguāng guójì qīngnián lǚshè. Wenhua Jie ☎0971 8215571, 🌐tdyg-inn.com. Another good hostel, particularly popular with Chinese backpackers, this is more central than either of the above, although the rooms are getting a little shabby. Dorms ¥45, rooms ¥120

Xining Mansions 西宁大厦, xīníng dàshà. On the corner of Dongguan Dajie and Jianguo Lu ☎0971 8164999. Once upon a time, this was Xining's swankiest hotel – today it's fallen down the rankings, but still offers plush, if slightly cramped, rooms at reasonable rates. Helpful staff here speak adequate English, and rates include breakfast and broadband. ¥360

Yinlong 西宁银龙酒店, xīníng yínlóng jiǔdiàn. 38 Huanghe Lu, northwest side of the Central Square ☎0971 6166666 🌐ylhotel.net. Xining's poshest hotel, the *Yinlong* offers seven different restaurants (including a good Western buffet), a spa and a gym. The luxurious rooms are pricey, but if you're heading west it might be the last 5-star hotel for a while. Includes breakfast. ¥1128

EATING

There's an abundance of food on offer in multi-ethnic Xining. Local staples include kebabs, bowls of spicy noodles, mutton hotpots and *zasui* soup, made with ox and sheep entrails, and there is also a good selection of international cuisine around town.

Amdo Café 安多咖啡, ānduō kāfēi. 19 Ledu Lu ☎0971 8213217. This cute café – with a sister branch in Langmusi – sells handmade souvenirs and handicrafts, as well as serving up good coffee, cake and wi-fi. Mon–Sat 9am–8pm.

Bowman's 佰曼斯特, bǎimànsītè. Qingzhen Xiang, directly south of the Beixiaojie bus stop ☎0971 8185445. This ice-cream shop, tucked away in a small street near the Dongguan Mosque, serves up delicious ice cream in a range of flavours for ¥10 a scoop. Daily 10am–9pm.

Green House Coffee 古林坊, gǔlín fāng. Xiadu Dadao, near Guojicun ☎0971 8209376. This pleasant café is the best of several along Xiadu Dadao, and is popular with both locals and expats. Expect excellent coffee (¥28 a cup), tasty snacks and a lot of passive smoking if you sit upstairs. They also

sell ingeniously packaged "backpacker's coffee" if you need a quality brew on the road. Daily 8am–9.30pm.

Satay 泰国风味餐厅, tàiguó fēngwèi cāntīng. Xiadu Dadao, near Guojicun ☎0971 8278989. Quite possibly the only Thai restaurant in Qinghai, *Satay* serves a range of good Thai standards and Western dishes. Try their *pad thai* (¥30), or barbecue beef (¥35). Daily 11am–9pm.

Yixin Mutton 益鑫羊肉手抓馆, yìxīn yángròu shǒuzhuāguǎn. Baiyu Xiang ☎0971 8179336. One of Xining's top Muslim restaurants, bustling *Yixin* is renowned for its tender yellow-stewed mutton (*huangmen yangrou*, ¥86) and deep-fried potato slices (¥16). No English on the menu or on the signs outside – spot it by the gold characters on a green background. Daily 9am–9.30pm.

DIRECTORY

Banks and exchange The main Bank of China is in a huge building on Dongguan Dajie; it is only this branch that will change travellers' cheques (Mon–Fri, 8.30am–5.30pm). ATMs accepting international cards can be found here, and across town.

Bookshop The Foreign Language bookshop, west of Ertong Park on Huanghe Lu, has a surprisingly good

selection of English-language classics and Chinese works in translation (daily 8.30am–6pm).

Mail and telephones The main post office (Mon–Sat 8.30am–6pm) is on the southwest corner of Da Shizi. Send parcels from the EMS office on the ground floor (entrance on Nan Dajie); buy stamps and train/plane tickets from the first floor (entrance facing the crossroads).

Kumbum

塔尔寺, tǎ'ěr sì • Daily, summer 8.30am–5pm, winter 9am–4.30pm • ¥80 includes access to nine temples • English audio-guides ¥30 from the visitor centre

13

Twenty-five kilometres southeast of Xining, **Kumbum** is one of the most important monasteries outside Tibet. Set in the cleft of a valley, the **walled complex** is an imposing sight, an active place of worship for over six hundred monks as well as the constant succession of pilgrims from Tibet, Qinghai and Mongolia, who present a startling picture with their rugged features, huge embroidered coats and chunky jewellery. There are plenty of tourists too (not to mention a hulking great **military base** right next door), but Kumbum remains a good introduction to Tibetan culture.

The monastery dates from 1560, when building began in honour of **Tsongkhapa**, founder of the Gelugpa Sect of Tibetan Buddhism, who was born on the Kumbum Monastery estates. Legend tells how, at Tsongkhapa's birth, drops of blood fell from his umbilical cord causing a tree with a thousand leaves to spring up; on each leaf was the face of the Buddha (the trunk is now preserved in one of the stupas). During his lifetime, Tsongkhapa's significance was subsequently borne out: his two major disciples were to become the greatest living Buddhas, the Dalai and Panchen Lamas.

The great halls

The most attractive of the temples is perhaps the **Great Hall of Meditation** (大经堂, dàjīngtáng), an enormous, very dimly lit prayer hall, colonnaded by dozens of carpeted pillars and hung with long silk tapestries. Immediately adjacent to this is the **Great Hall of the Golden Roof** (大金瓦殿, dàjīnwǎ diàn), with its gilded tiles, red-billed choughs nesting under the eaves, wall paintings of scenes from the Buddha's life and a brilliant silver stupa containing a statue of Tsongkhapa. The grooves worn into the wooden floor in front of the temple have been made by the hands of prostrating monks and pilgrims. Built in 1560, this hall was built on the site of the pipal tree that grew with its Buddha imprints. You will still see pilgrims studying fallen leaves here, apparently searching for the face of the Buddha.

Other temples

Other noteworthy temples include the **Lesser Temple of the Golden Roof** (护法殿, hùfǎ diàn) and the **Hall of Butter Sculpture** (酥油花馆, sūyóuhuā guǎn). The former is dedicated to animals, thought to manifest characteristics of certain deities – from the central courtyard you can see stuffed goats, cows and bears on the balcony, wrapped in scarves and flags. The Hall of Butter Sculpture contains a display of colourful painted yak-butter tableaux, depicting Tibetan and Buddhist legends. After touring the temples, you can climb the steep steps visible on one side of the monastery to get a general view over the temples and hills behind.

ARRIVAL AND DEPARTURE   **KUMBUM**

Private tour buses start rolling up at the monastery around 10am, after which the place gets crowded.

By bus or minibus Transport for Kumbum (¥5) departs Xining from a depot on Xiguan Dajie near the roundabout for Kunlun Bridge. These run frequently from around 7.20am until late afternoon; on arrival, you may be dropped at the bus station 1km short of the monastery, or taken right up to the complex itself. From the bus station,

---

> **KUMBUM'S FESTIVALS**
>
> During the year, four major **festivals** are held at Kumbum, each fixed according to the lunar calendar. In January or February, at the end of the Chinese New Year festivities, there's a large ceremony centred on the lighting of yak-butter lamps. In April or May is the festival of Bathing Buddha, during which a giant *thangka* is unfurled on a hillside facing the monastery. In July or August the birthday of Tsongkhapa is celebrated, and in September or October there's one more festival commemorating the nirvana of Sakyamuni.

13

walk uphill past the trinket stalls and rug-sellers until you pass through a gate and see a row of eight stupas at the monastery entrance. Returning to Xining, exit the monastery and grab a cab, or hang around on the street by

the bus station until the bus arrives.

By taxi Shared taxis to the monastery from the roundabout on Kunlun Zhong Lu in Xining cost ¥10, or ¥40 for the cab all to yourself.

ACCOMMODATION

Most visitors just come up to Kumbum for a few hours, but it is also possible to stay the night and appreciate the monastery in more peace.

Sipo Hotel 寺坡宾馆, sìpō bīnguǎn. Jinta Lu ☎ 0971 2237184. This compact and cheap little local hostel is not easy to find – it's an anonymous doorway on the road between the town and temple, opposite the only junction. Once you find it, the friendly Muslim owners ought to make you feel at home – the basic rooms are spotless and pleasant, although the shared bathrooms are a bit grim. **¥60**

Tsongka Hotel 宗喀宾馆, zōngkā bīnguǎn. Opposite Kumbum Monastery main entrance ☎ 0971 2236761. In a great location close to the monastery and with friendly staff, there are Chinese-style and Tibetan-style rooms available here – it's worth paying for the more attractive Tibetan rooms. No internet available. Chinese doubles **¥260**, Tibetan doubles **¥280**

Qutan Temple

瞿昙寺, qútán sì • Daily, summer 8.30am–6pm, winter 9am–5pm • ¥50

Qutan Temple, 65km to the east of Xining in Ledu County, is much less frequented by tourists than Kumbum – reason enough to hunt it down – plus it's a beautiful monastery in its own right. Built in 1387, this was once among the most important Buddhist centres in China and remains impressive, with plenty of original Ming-dynasty temple halls and a fascinating corridor around the edge of the main courtyard lined with exceptional murals illustrating the life of Sakyamuni. Inside, you'll find more paintings, and a beautiful 3m-high Qing-dynasty drum in the shape of a kneeling elephant, which is used today to call the monks to prayer. Qutan owes its survival to generations of politically flexible abbots – reflected in the monastery's enormous stone *stelae*, which were presented to the monastery by various Ming and Qing emperors.

ARRIVAL AND DEPARTURE   QUTAN TEMPLE

By train, bus and taxi Access to Qutan Temple is via Ledu (乐都, lèdū), which can be reached by train (6 daily, 1.5hr, ¥12.50) or bus from Xining – hourly fast buses (¥20, 1hr) leave from the short-distance bus station near Xining Square, while more frequent slow buses (¥12.50, 2hr) leave from the southeast corner of the Kunlun Bridge

intersection. The last bus back to Xining leaves at 6pm. Between Ledu and Qutan you can take a minibus (¥7 one-way) for the 22km-long ride to Qutan Temple – these leave from a courtyard behind the *Dazhong Hotel* near the bus station. A return taxi fare should cost about ¥80.

West of Xining

West of Xining, Qinghai for the most part comprises a great emptiness. The 3000m plateau is too high to support agriculture, and the only people who traditionally have managed to eke out a living here have been nomadic yak-herders. The real highlight of the area is the huge and virtually unspoilt **Qinghai Lake**, whose saline waters are home to thousands of birds. A few hours beyond, **Chaka Salt Lake** is an interesting stop for those wishing to break the long journey to **Golmud**, the only town of note for hundreds of kilometres, and a place to catch trains to Lhasa as well as onward transport to Dunhuang and southern Xinjiang.

Qinghai Lake

青海湖, qīnghǎi hú

Situated in an extraordinarily remote location – 150km west of Xining, at 3100m above sea level on the Tibetan Plateau – **Qinghai Lake** is the largest in China, occupying

13

an area of over 4000 square kilometres. Its cold and briny waters nevertheless teem with fish (mainly the endemic **naked carp**) and are populated by nesting migratory birds, particularly at **Bird Island**, which, along with several manmade scenic spots, has become the lake's main tourist attraction.

If you don't have time to stop here, you can admire the view while travelling between Golmud and Xining; it's worth scheduling your journey to pass by during daylight hours. The train spends hours running along the northern shore; by bus you'll skirt the southern shore instead.

Be aware that access for foreigners to certain parts of the lakeshore is restricted, particularly around the "nuclear town" of **Xihai** on the northeast edge of the lake, where China's first nuclear weapons were developed.

Bird Island

鸟岛, niǎodǎo • Daily 7am–6pm • ¥100 • optional tour bus ¥25

Bird Island is in fact a peninsula, on the far western side of Qinghai Lake. A variety of migratory birds spend time here – gulls, cormorants, bar-headed geese and rare **black-necked cranes**. The main **birdwatching season** is from April to June, although the cranes stop by in February and March. Sadly, bird numbers have been dropping as visitor numbers increase, and the site has been identified as a potential nexus in the spread of bird flu. While noisy cormorants still squabble on top of **Cormorant Rock**, Bird Island's future is looking increasingly uncertain.

ARRIVAL AND DEPARTURE   QINGHAI LAKE

The easiest way to reach Qinghai Lake is on a tour from Xining. Although it's possible to visit independently on public transport, you may end up hitchhiking or stranded en route for a night.

By bus, taxi and hitching From Xining's long-distance bus station, take any westbound service for Dulan (都兰, dūlán) or Wulan (乌兰, wūlán). Either route passes along the lake's southern shore, and will be able to drop you off – the grubby little Tibetan town of Heimahe (黑马和, hēimǎhé), about four hours out of Xining, is a convenient place to aim for, with shops, restaurants and a comfortable hotel. From here you'll need to hitch a lift to Bird Island – walk to the western end of town and flag down vehicles heading around the lake. Alternatively, take the 7.30am bus from Xining around the southern side of the lake to Niaodao Zhen (鸟岛镇niǎodǎo zhèn), where pricey accommodation is available, and then hitch or take a taxi (¥25) for the last 10km or so out to Bird Island.

By tour Xining's travel services (see p.795) charge in the region of ¥600 per car for a return day-trip to Qinghai Lake's main scenic spots, including Bird Island. It's a very long day out, leaving at 7am and returning at 10pm, but travelling this way will give you maximum flexibility to enjoy the lake scenery – go where you want and stop where you like.

ACCOMMODATION

Camping If you have a tent, and really want a wilderness experience in China, Qinghai Lake may be the place to get it, although frigid winter temperatures mean that the summer months – particularly July, when swaths of yellow rapeseed cover the lakeshore – are the best time to camp. Even during the summer months it's wise to bring warm clothing and enough drinking water if you're planning to stop over.

Heimahe 黑马河商务宾馆, hēimǎhé shāngwù bīnguǎn. Heimahe ☎0974 8519377. Cheerful budget hotel with a nod to local aesthetics in the Tibetan-style coloured trim around the windows. Rooms are basic but comfortable enough, and the en suites have sit-down toilets. **¥120**

Niaodao 鸟岛宾馆, niǎodǎo bīnguǎn. Niaodao Zhen ☎0970 8655012. Bizarre, mock-Palladian facade fronts for this huge hotel in the middle of nowhere; inside, it's a standard Chinese effort with clean and tidy en suites but very little beyond a modicum of comfort, despite the steep price. Good restaurant, however. **¥480**

Chaka Salt Lake

茶卡盐湖, chákǎ yánhú • Daily 8am–8pm • ¥50

Eighty kilometres beyond Qinghai Lake is **Chaka Salt Lake**, which has recently become something of a tourist attraction for its dazzling expanse of gleaming white salt crystals, which are visible from far away. At the site, you can ride a small train across the lake

(¥35), take a short ride on the lake's salt-excavating ship (¥45), and cart off a hunk of the stuff with you afterwards.

ARRIVAL AND DEPARTURE   CHAKA SALT LAKE

By bus Buses heading to Dulan and Wulan from Xining's long-distance bus station pass through the small town of Chaka Zhen (茶卡镇, chákǎ zhèn), near the lake – the earliest bus leaves at 8am. To return to Xining, flag down local buses to Heimahe, from where there are more frequent buses back to Xining. To continue westwards from the lake to Golmud is tricky, as there are no direct buses – you'll need to take the daily bus to Dulan, and stay overnight before catching an early bus to Golmud.

ACCOMMODATION

Qingyan 青盐宾馆, qīngyán bīnguǎn. North side of the G109 highway ☎0977 8240254. The only hotel in Chaka that accepts foreigners, this is a decent option in the centre of town, opposite Chaka's compact square. Rooms in the new building are the best, but slightly more expensive than the older rooms at the rear of the hotel. Breakfast included. Older rooms **¥220**, newer rooms **¥280**

Golmud

格尔木, gé'ěrmù

Nearly 3000m up on the Tibetan Plateau, **GOLMUD** is an incredibly isolated city, even by northwest China's standards. The airport provides a link to Xining, but otherwise it lies at least nine hours away overland from the nearest sizeable population centre in Lhasa. In spite of this, Golmud is still the second-largest city in Qinghai, with 130,000 residents – mainly Han Chinese employed at the local potash plants.

Geographically, Golmud is located between the massive **Kunlun Mountains** to the south, and the **Cai Erhan Salt Lake** to the north. The Kunlun Mountains are a major source of jade, and Golmud has a fascinating **open-air jade market** (昆仑玉批发市场, kūnlún yù pīfā shìchǎng; daily during summer) near the junction of Jiangyuan Zhong Lu and Bayi Lu, where huge lumps of stone change hands for millions of yuan.

Golmud's main attraction is as somewhere to catch the train to Lhasa, as buying tickets here is easy. There are also bus routes north to Dunhuang (see p.808) or west to Charkhlik in Xinjiang (see p.848).

ARRIVAL AND DEPARTURE   GOLMUD

By air Golmud's airport (格尔木机场, gé'ěrmù jīchǎng) is 15km west of downtown Golmud. Taxis cost around ¥30; at present there is no airport bus service.
Destinations Xi'an (3 daily; 2hr); Xining (1 daily; 1hr).

By train Golmud's train station (格尔木火车站, gé'ěrmù huǒchēzhàn) is to the south of the city centre. A taxi to anywhere in town costs ¥5. The station ticket office is open 24hr a day with tickets to Lhasa relatively easy to buy. Tickets to other destinations need to be purchased a few days in advance. The Golmud–Lhasa section of the Qinghai–Tibet railway is the world's longest and highest track, peaking at over 5000m. Note that Lhasa-bound travellers need to arrange Tibet entry permits ahead of time through a tour operator in Xining or Lhasa and have them before boarding the train.
Destinations Lhasa (8 daily; 14hr); Xining (11 daily; 9hr 15min).

By bus The long-distance bus station shares the square with the train station, and the ticket office is open 7am–7pm. Again, a taxi into town costs ¥5.
Destinations Charkhlik (14hr); Dunhuang (10hr); Korla (24hr); Xining (14hr).

INFORMATION

Travel agents CITS, 60 Bayi Zhong Lu ☎0979 8496150. Erratically staffed, this office can supply permits, tours and tickets to Tibet, along with local tours to Cai Erhan Salt Lake.

ACCOMMODATION

Golmud Mansion 格尔木大厦, gé'ěrmù dàshà. 33 Yingbin Lu ☎0979 8450876. Conveniently located for the bus and train stations on the eastern side of the train station plaza, rooms here are aged but clean and there's a life-sized Mao statue welcoming you into the foyer. Broadband available. **¥180**
Salt Lake Hotel 盐湖大酒店, yánhú dàjiǔdiàn. 26 Huanghe Zhong Lu ☎0979 8436000. A 10min walk

13

YUSHU: AFTER THE QUAKE

It was all looking so promising for **Yushu** (玉树, yùshù), an **autonomous Tibetan prefecture** perched 4000m above sea level at the far south of Qinghai province. The source of the famed Yellow River, this remote, mountainous and extremely picturesque area had started to become a magnet for adventurous travellers seeking a Tibetan experience without having to pay through the nose for a sanitized, pre-packaged tour to Lhasa.

Then came the events of April 14, 2010, when a 7.1-magnitude **earthquake** hit Yushu. The main tremor – and its devastating aftershocks – destroyed 85 percent of the houses in Gyegu, the county seat, and killed some 2700 people, a fair chunk of the tiny local population. The national authorities were quick to respond, having learned from the far deadlier Wenchuan earthquake that struck Sichuan in 2008. Yushu had few medical facilities, which meant that everything had to be flown in and that those buried under the rubble had to be dug out, often by hand, in freezing conditions.

The area is slowly getting back on its feet, but is likely to remain off the travel radar for a while to come. The *Lete Youth Hostel* in Xining (see p.796) made admirable fundraising efforts after the earthquake, and is as good a place as any to get up-to-date information about the area.

north of the train station plaza, this upmarket option has comfy rooms with broadband and breakfast included – there's even an in-house bowling alley. The most luxurious rooms are in the "executive wing" next door. Doubles ¥398, executive wing ¥680

EATING

Guxiangwei 故乡味, gùxiāngwèi. Huanghe Xi Lu, opposite the Salt Lake Hotel ☎0979 8432827. This restaurant serves up tasty Chinese standards, with an emphasis on Hunanese and Sichuanese dishes. Vegetables from ¥20, meat from ¥40 – try the pumpkin with jujubes or *jiachang chaoji* – homestyle fried chicken. Daily 11am–9.30pm.

Ma Yihei 马义黑, mǎ yìhēi. Opposite the police station on Zhanqian Er Lu ☎1399 7398605. Take the second road on the left as you walk north from the station and you will find *Ma Yihei*, one of Golmud's most popular Muslim restaurants, serving up immense (and inexpensive) piles of excellent roast lamb every day. There's no English or picture menu, so be prepared to mime. Daily 11am–4am.

DIRECTORY

Banks and exchange The main Bank of China (Mon–Fri 9am–5.30pm), at the junction of Kunlun Lu and Chaidamu Lu, has ATMs accepting international cards, and you can exchange cash and travellers' cheques here.

PSB 300m east of the junction between Jiangyuan Lu and Chaidamu Lu (Mon–Fri 8.30am–noon & 2.30–6pm) – look for the huge, white complex with a red/gold badge on top.

The Hexi Corridor

For reasons of simple geography, travellers entering or leaving China from the west have always been channelled through the narrow strip of land that stretches 1000km northwest of Lanzhou. With the Qilian Mountains soaring up to the south, and a merciless combination of waterless desert and bone-dry mountains to the north, the road known as the **Hexi Corridor** offers the only feasible route through the physical obstacles that crowd in west of Lanzhou.

Historically, whoever controlled the corridor could operate a stranglehold on the fabulous riches of the Silk Road trade. The Chinese took an interest early on, and early Great Wall-building efforts were taking place along the Hexi Corridor under Emperor Qin Shi Huang in the third century BC. Subsequently, the powerful Han dynasty incorporated the region into their empire, though the central government's influence remained far from constant for centuries, as Tibetans, Uyghurs and Mongols vied for control. Not until the Mongol conquests of the thirteenth century did the corridor finally become a settled part of the Chinese empire, with the Ming consolidating the old wall and building its magnificent last fort at **Jiayuguan**.

Two cities along the corridor, **Wuwei** and **Zhangye**, offer convenient places to break the long journey between Lanzhou and the extraordinary Buddhist sculptures at **Dunhuang**, and have their own share of historic sights.

Wuwei

武威, wǔwēi

Halfway between Lanzhou and Zhangye is the small city of **WUWEI**. Gansu's most famous historic relic, the Han-dynasty **Flying Horse of Wuwei**, was discovered here in 1969 underneath Leitai Temple, just north of the town; it's now housed in Lanzhou's Provincial Museum (see p.783). The symbol of the horse, depicted in full gallop and stepping on the back of a swallow, can be seen everywhere in Wuwei.

WUWEI

■ ACCOMMODATION		● EATING	
Tianma	2	Wanglaosan	
Wuwei	1	Niuroumian	1

Leitai Han Culture Museum

雷台汉文化博物馆, léitái hàn wénhuà bówùguǎn • Daily 9am–5pm • Temple & Museum free, tomb ¥45 • ☎ 0935 2215852 • bus #2 or #6 from the southeast corner of Wenhua Square

One kilometre north of Wuwei's central Wenhua Square, **Leitai Han Culture Museum** contains a number of sights. **Leitai Temple** is a pleasant Taoist complex built high up on impressive mud ramparts, and a small **museum** displays Han-dynasty finds from around Wuwei, including a beautiful green-glazed pottery temple that was unearthed during construction of a nearby housing development. The main attraction, however, is the famous **Han-dynasty tomb** where the Flying Horse statue was discovered, which lies beneath the temple through a separate entrance. There's not much to see – just a series of very low passageways – but the 2000-year-old brickwork is still in perfect condition and amazingly modern in appearance. Ironically, the bronze Flying Horse, now a prized relic, remained in the tomb long after accompanying items of gold and silver had been stolen.

ARRIVAL AND DEPARTURE

WUWEI

By train Wuwei's train station (武威火车站, wǔwēi huǒchēzhàn) is 3km south of town, at the junction of lines between Ürümqi, Lanzhou and Beijing. It costs ¥6 by taxi or ¥1 on bus routes #6 and #10 to reach the town. It's easy to buy hard-seat tickets at the station – fine for short hops to Lanzhou or Zhangye – but sleepers are best arranged through a travel agent such as CITS (☎ 0935 2267239), immediately outside the *Tianma*, despite their ¥30 commission. There is also a train ticket booth at 26 Nanguan Xi Lu, a few hundred metres east of the main bus station, open daily 8am–noon and 2–6pm.

Destinations Daheyan (regular; 15–21hr); Jiayuguan

(regular; 4hr 30min–10hr 30min); Lanzhou (regular; 3hr–5hr 30min); Zhangye (regular; 2hr 30min–6hr).

By bus The main bus station (武威客运中心, wǔwēi kèyùn zhōngxīn) lies on Nanguan Xi Lu, and handles traffic across Gansu and beyond. At the time of writing, staff here abide by a regulation long abandoned elsewhere in Gansu that requires foreign passengers to hold a PICC insurance certificate in order to buy tickets. The Wuwei PICC office is at 58 Xi Dajie, open Mon–Fri 8.30am–noon and 2.30–6pm.

Destinations Dunhuang (14hr 30min); Lanzhou (4hr); Xining (7hr); Zhangye (4hr).

ACCOMMODATION

As is the case across Gansu, in Wuwei foreign passport holders must stay in designated hotels, with no real budget accommodation available at present.

Tianma 天马宾馆, tiānmǎ bīnguǎn. Xi Xiaoshizi ☎ 0935 2212355, ✉ tianmabinguan@sina.com. This

stalwart of Wuwei's hotel scene has recently been refurbished and has bright, pleasant rooms to suit a range

13

of budgets. It frequently hosts large official meetings – call ahead to ensure they're not booked up. Buffet breakfast included. **¥200**

Wuwei 武威大酒店, wǔwēi dàjiǔdiàn. Beiguan Dong

Lu ☎ 0935 2218888. Halfway between Wenhua Square and Leitai Han Culture Museum, rooms here don't quite match up to its smart lobby. Rates are often discounted, but foreigners are expected to pay full whack. **¥288**

EATING

Restaurants are thin on the ground around central Wenhua Square (apart from a *Dico's* on the southwest corner) – it's better to head south along Nan Dajie, which offers a range of restaurants including Sichuanese and the usual cheap noodle places.

Wanglaosan Niuroumian 王老三牛肉面, wánglǎosān niúròumiàn. Nanguan Xi Lu. This popular Muslim restaurant does a fantastic *chaomian* (¥8)

that serves up more or less like a huge spaghetti Bolognese, along with other cheap and filling noodle-based dishes. Daily 6am–9pm.

DIRECTORY

Banks and exchange The Bank of China with international ATMs is just east of the *Tianma* (Mon–Fri 8.30am–5.30pm).

Mail The post office is on the east side of Wenhua Square

(daily 9am–5pm).

PSB Wuwei's PSB office, which deals with visa extensions, is inside a courtyard at 98 Dong Dajie (Mon–Fri 8.30am–noon and 2.30–6pm). Look for a small English sign outside.

Zhangye

张掖, zhāngyè

About 500km northwest of Lanzhou and 200km southeast of Jiayuguan, on the edge of the Loess plateau, medium-sized **ZHANGYE** has long been an important stopover for travellers on the Silk Road. Indeed, Marco Polo spent a whole year here. During the Ming period, Zhangye was a garrison post for soldiers guarding the **Great Wall**, and the road from Wuwei to Zhangye remains a good place from which to view the Wall, visible for a large part of the way as a crumbling line of mud ramparts, a fascinating contrast to the restored sections elsewhere. Initially it runs to the north of the road, until, quite dramatically, the road cuts right through a hole in the brickwork and continues on the other side.

Although Zhangye is not especially attractive, there are a number of places that should fill at least a day of sightseeing. A **Drum Tower**, built in 1507, marks the old centre, but today the heart of the town is **Zhongxin Square**, the air above which fills with impressive strings of kites on fine summer evenings.

Dafo Temple

大佛寺, dàfó sì • Daily summer 8am–6pm, winter 8.30am–5.30pm • ¥41 • English audio-guide ¥10

South of Zhongxin Square, on the eastern side of a small plaza, the central smoke-grimed hall at **Dafo Temple** houses a 34m-long **reclining Buddha**, easily China's largest, whose calm expression and gentle form make a powerful impression. Immediately behind the Buddha are ten disciples and grotesque-looking *luohan* (saintly warriors) standing around in the gloom. Built in 1098 and restored in 1770, the temple buildings also house a few small, well-presented exhibits on Buddhist relics in the region.

In the same grounds, the **Tu Ta** (土塔, tǔtǎ; same ticket) is a former Buddhist monastery, its dun-coloured stupa contrasting rather pleasingly with its neighbour. To the side of the Tu Ta is the Qing-dynasty **Shanxi Guildhall** that formerly provided lodging and entertainment for travelling merchants from Shanxi. Today, its decorative halls house reconstructions of a stage, meeting rooms and a small shrine.

The Wooden Pagoda

木塔, mùtǎ • Daily summer 7.30am–6.30pm, winter 8.30am–5.30pm • ¥5

Rearing on the west side of Zhongxin Square, the 31m-tall **Wooden Pagoda** was built in the sixth century, before being burned down and then restored in 1925 … in brick. The octagonal tower is now home to a number of jackdaws, and from the top you can see the snowcapped Qilian Mountain rising up to the south.

ZHANGYE

Map labels:
Ganquan Park
Marco Polo Statue
Rail Office
Food Street
MINGQING JIE
BEI DAJIE
West Bus Station
Bank of China
Daode Guan
XI DAJIE
DONG DAJIE
Drum Tower
XIANFU JIE
East Bus Station
Train Station
QINGNIAN XI JIE
QINGNIAN DONG JIE
NAN DAJIE
Wooden Pagoda
ZHONGXIN SQUARE
Shanxi Guildhall
Dafo Temple
Tu Ta
Xilai Temple
South Bus Station
HUANCHENG NAN LU
0 — 300 metres

● EATING
Ji Xiang Cun ... 1

■ ACCOMMODATION
Honghao ... 1
Huachen International ... 2

ARRIVAL AND DEPARTURE

ZHANGYE

By train Zhangye's train station (张掖火车站, zhāngyè huǒchēzhàn) is 7km away to the northeast. Bus #1 (¥1) runs from the train station to the south bus station via the drum tower; a taxi costs ¥15. You can buy train tickets at the rail office off Mingqing Jie; look for the Marco Polo statue – the office is to its southwest (Mon–Fri 8am–noon and 1–6pm).

Destinations Daheyan (regular; 13–21hr); Jiayuguan (regular; 3hr); Lanzhou (regular; 5hr 30min–9hr); Wuwei (regular; 2hr 30min–6hr).

By bus Zhangye has three bus stations. The west station (西站, xīzhàn) is the busiest, with frequent services to all major destinations in Lanzhou and eastern Qinghai. The quieter south station (南站, nánzhàn) and east station (东站, dōngzhàn) operate buses to destinations in the south and east respectively, as well as the odd long-distance route.

Destinations Dunhuang (10hr); Jiayuguan (5hr); Lanzhou (10hr); Wuwei (6hr).

ACCOMMODATION

Honghao 泓昊宾馆, hónghào bīnguǎn. 141 Xianfu Jie ☎ 0936 8252222. Close to Zhongxin Square, good-value rooms are neat and spacious, with tiny en-suite bathrooms and broadband. Rate includes breakfast. **¥158**

Huachen International 华晨国际大酒店, huáchén guójì dàjiǔdiàn. 20 Dongda Jie ☎ 0936 8257777, ⊛ www.zyhchotel.com. The most upmarket place in town; staff speak good English and rooms are very comfortable, plus there's a conference centre and swimming pool. Breakfast included. **¥580**

EATING

The northern end of Xianfu Jie leads onto Mingqing Jie – a mock Ming-dynasty food street with more restaurants than you can shake a chopstick at, serving noodle soups, kebabs, hotpots and the like.

13

Ji Xiang Cun 冀乡村春饼屋, jìxiāngcūn chūnbǐng wū. Mingqing Jie ☎0936 8221958. This restaurant specializes in thin and crispy savoury pancakes, which you roll up and dip into a plum sauce (¥6), with homestyle fried dishes starting from ¥20. Daily 11am–2.30pm & 4.30–9.30pm.

DIRECTORY

Banks and exchange The main Bank of China (daily 8.30am–6pm) is at 386 Dong Dajie. Head here to cash travellers' cheques – there are ATMs accepting international cards here and around town.

Mail The post office is on Xi Dajie, just west of the drum tower (Mon–Fri 8am–6pm).

PSB Zhangye's PSB is on Huancheng Nan Lu, southwest of Xilai Temple.

Jiayuguan

嘉峪关, jiāyùguān

One more cup of wine for our remaining happiness. There will be chilling parting dreams tonight.

Ninth-century poet on a leave-taking at Jiayuguan

To some Chinese, the very name **JIAYUGUAN** is synonymous with sorrow and ghastly remoteness. The last **fortress** of the Great Wall was built here by the Ming in 1372, over 5000km from the wall's easternmost point at Shanhaiguan, from which time the town made its living by supplying the needs of the fortress garrison. This was literally the final defence of the empire, the spot where China ended and beyond which lay a terrifying wilderness. Everything that travelled between the deserts of Central Asia and China's central plain – goods, traders and armies – had to go through this pass. The desolation of the landscape only adds to the melancholy: being forced to leave China altogether was a citizen's worst nightmare, and it was here that disgraced officials and condemned or fleeing criminals had to make their final, bitter farewells. The perfectly restored fort, just west of nondescript **Jiayuguan town**, is one of the highlights of northwest China, with a number of additional Wall-related sights scattered in the desert nearby.

The fort

城楼, chénglóu • Daily 8.30am–5.30pm • ¥120, including entry to the First Beacon Tower, Overhanging Wall, Underground Gallery and Heishan rock carvings • bus #4 (¥1) runs from the train station past the Jiayuguan hotel to the fort • taxi from town ¥15

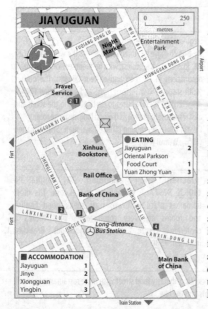

Jiayuguan's **fort** is the most important sight in the Hexi Corridor. Its location, between the permanently snowcapped Qilian Mountains to the south and the black humps of the Mazong (Horse's Mane) Mountains to the north, could not be more dramatic – or more strategically valuable. As you climb the walls and survey the bleached and shimmering desert beyond, it's still possible to evoke the foreboding felt by earlier visitors to Jiayuguan.

Some kind of fort may have occupied this site as early as the Han dynasty, but the surviving building is a Ming construction, completed in 1372. Sometimes referred to as the "Impregnable Defile under Heaven", it is comprised of outer and inner walls, the former more than 700m in circumference and about 10m high. At the east and west ends of the inner wall stand symbolic gates, the Guanghua Men (Gate of Enlightenment) and the Rouyuan Men

DESERT SIGHTS AROUND JIAYUGUAN

Several other attractions around Jiayuguan could be combined with a trip to the fort. 6km south of town are the ruins of the **First Beacon Tower** (第一墩, dìyīdūn; ¥21). Built on the Great Wall in the sixteenth century, the long-abandoned tower lies crumbling on a cliff top overlooking the Taolai River at the foot of the Qilian Mountains.

The **Overhanging Wall** (悬壁长城, xuánbì chángchéng; ¥21), 8km northwest of the fort, is a section of the Great Wall connecting the fort to the Mazong range, originally built in the sixteenth century and recently restored. The ramparts afford excellent views of the surrounding land; it was more atmospheric before they built a crass tourist village nearby, but is still worth a visit to gaze out west and imagine what it was like when this place represented the end of China's civilized world.

The desert also harbours a couple of unusual collections of ancient Chinese art. One is the **Underground Gallery** (新城魏晋墓, xīnchéng wèijìnmù; ¥31), 20km northeast of Jiayuguan. Actually a burial site from the Wei and Jin periods, more than eighteen hundred years ago, the brick-built graves contain vivid paintings of contemporary life on each brick.

A kilometer beyond the fort are the **Heishan rock carvings** (黑山岩画, hēishān yánhuà). These look more like classic "cave man" art: a hundred or so pictures of hunting, horseriding and dancing dating from the Warring States Period (476–221 BC), are etched into the cliffs of the Heishan range. Visiting the First Beacon Tower and the two art sites in conjunction with a tour of the fort and Overhanging Wall takes a full day. Hiring a taxi to get you around will cost ¥200–250.

Finally, one stupendous but rather inaccessible natural sight is the **July 1st Glacier** (七一冰川, qīyī bīngchuān; ¥51), located 4300m up in the Qilian Mountains some 120km from Jiayuguan – remarkably close considering how toasty Jiayuguan is in summer. A day-trip by taxi costs around ¥600. Travel agents (see p.808) in town provide tours with an English guide for ¥700. It's a long day, involving a three-hour drive, followed by five hours climbing up and down, and three hours driving back. The do-it-yourself option is to take a train to **Jingtieshan** (京铁山, jīngtiěshān) then a taxi – around ¥140 return.

(Gate of Conciliation), respectively. Inside each are sloping walkways that lead to the top of the wall, enabling soldiers on horseback to climb up and patrol the turrets. In between the Gate of Enlightenment and the outer wall stand a pavilion, a temple and an open-air theatre once used to entertain troops. Few of the buildings are permanent, leaving a haunting vacuum at the heart of the fort.

The Great Wall Museum

长城博物馆, chángchéng bówùguǎn • Daily 9am–5pm • Free

Right beside the fort entrance, the **Great Wall Museum** reviews the history of the Wall from the Han to the last frenzied spurt of construction under the Ming. The highlights are photos and scale models of the Great Wall taken from points across northern China, places that for the most part lie well away from tourist itineraries. In front of the museum is a gnarled old Euphrates poplar hung with red ribbons. This is the sole survivor of a Qing-dynasty greening project organized by Zuo Zongtang, a Chinese general posted to the area in the 1870s to put down the Tungan Muslim revolt.

ARRIVAL AND DEPARTURE · JIAYUGUAN

By air Jiayuguan's airport (嘉峪关机场, jiāyùguān jīchǎng) is 10km north of town. At the time of writing there was no airport bus; a taxi should cost ¥30, but you're essentially at the mercy of the drivers.

Destinations Lanzhou (daily; 70min); Xi'an (daily; 2hr).

By train Jiayuguan's train station (嘉峪关火车站, jiāyùguān huǒchēzhàn) is in the far southwest of the city and linked by bus #1 and #4 (¥1) to the centre. All trains running between Ürümqi and eastern China stop here. Tickets are often hard to come by and you will almost certainly need to buy tickets in advance. There is a ticket office at 28 Xinhua Zhong Lu, just north of the junction with Jingtie Lu (Mon–Fri 8am–noon and 1–4pm; Sat–Sun 8am–noon and 1–3.30pm).

Destinations Daheyan (14 daily; 13hr); Lanzhou (12 daily; 19hr 30min); Tianshui (14 daily; 14hr 30min); Ürümqi (12 daily; 15hr); Wuwei (regular; 6hr); Zhangye (regular; 3hr).

By bus The long-distance bus station (客运中心, kèyùn zhōngxīn) is conveniently located on Lanxin Xi Lu, 1km south of the central roundabout.

Destinations Dunhuang (6hr); Zhangye (5hr).

13

INFORMATION

Travel agents Both the *Jiayuguan* and *Xiongguan* hotel travel desks can supply plane tickets for a small commission and organize local tours.

ACCOMMODATION

Jiayuguan 嘉峪关宾馆, jiāyùguān bīnguǎn. 1 Xinhua Bei Lu ☏0937 6226983, ⊛www .jiayuguanhotel.com. The poshest hotel in town, on the central roundabout with ticket booking service and a fancy restaurant on-site. Rooms are very pleasant, with nice sofas and computers as standard. Includes breakfast. **¥380**

Jinye 金叶宾馆, jīnyè bīnguǎn. 12 Lanxin Xi Lu – diagonally opposite the bus station ☏0937 6201333 ✉jinyehotel@126.com. Despite its cramped rooms and tiny bathrooms, this decent, clean hotel is a good-value option – and the location is convenient too. **¥120**

Xiongguan 雄关宾馆, xióngguān bīnguǎn. 31 Xinhua Zhong Lu ☏0937 6201116. Slightly overpriced and with dubious plumbing, this hotel is easy to find and has helpful staff, as well as a handy travel service on the third floor. Pay an additional ¥20 for a room with a/c. **¥130**

Yingbin 迎宾商务宾馆, yíngbīn shāngwù bīnguǎn. 6 Shengli Lu ☏0937 6211777. The small but nicely furnished rooms come with breakfast and broadband included – there's also a fancy teahouse with wi-fi on the second floor. **¥200**

EATING

Jiayuguan is a migrant town, and nowhere is this more obvious than when it comes to food. There's little in the way of local cuisine, but instead you'll have a chance to try dishes from across the country. The night market north of the *Jiayuguan* hotel on the road to the Entertainment Park has the highest concentration of eateries in the city, although hygiene standards can be dubious – try one of the restaurants below for a sit-down meal.

Jiayuguan 嘉峪关餐厅, jiāyùguān cāntīng. Inside Jiayuguan Hotel ☏0937 6235397. A typical hotel restaurant, specialities here include expensive but tasty Cantonese and Sichuanese dishes – expect to pay ¥50 plus per dish. Daily 11am–1.30pm & 4.30–8.30pm.

Oriental Parkson Food Court 东方百盛, dōngfāng bǎishèng. Xinhua Bei Lu. Jiayuguan's fanciest department store, Oriental Parkson, has a *KFC* at ground level – if you make it past that, join hordes of local schoolchildren and head up to the top-floor food court, which has a range of interesting snacks and simple meals starting from around ¥10. Daily 9am–9pm.

Yuan Zhong Yuan 苑中苑酒店, yuànzhōngyuàn jiǔdiàn jiǔdiàn. Opposite the bus station ☏0937 6232699. This restaurant pulls in the crowds with a good-value selection of Chinese standards and efficient service – it even has an English menu. Daily 10.30am–10pm.

DIRECTORY

Banks and exchange To cash travellers' cheques, you'll need to go to the main Bank of China office on Xinhua Zhong Lu. For ATMs or to exchange cash, use this branch or the smaller branch further north on the same road (both Mon–Fri 9am–5pm).

Dunhuang

敦煌, dūnhuáng

An oasis town surrounded by inhospitable desert, **DUNHUANG** has been a backpacker favourite for decades, with two main claims to fame. Colossal **sand dunes** – among the world's largest, reaching hundreds of metres in height – rise along its southern flank, while the nearby **Mogao Caves** boast a veritable encyclopedia of Chinese artwork on their walls. The town has become something of a desert resort for visiting these imposing sights, though there's little to actually see in Dunhuang itself bar the well-presented **City Museum** (敦煌市博物馆, dūnhuángshì bówùguǎn; April–Dec Tues–Sun 8.30am–6.30pm; free) on Mingshan Lu, which houses a small collection of scrolls, pottery and statues that survived the twentieth-century depredations of foreign archeologists.

ARRIVAL AND DEPARTURE

DUNHUANG

By air Dunhuang's airport (敦煌机场, dūnhuáng jīchǎng) is 12km east of town; buy tickets at the airline office (daily 8am–10pm; ☏0937 8800000) on Yangguan Zhong Lu. A minibus (¥8) runs between

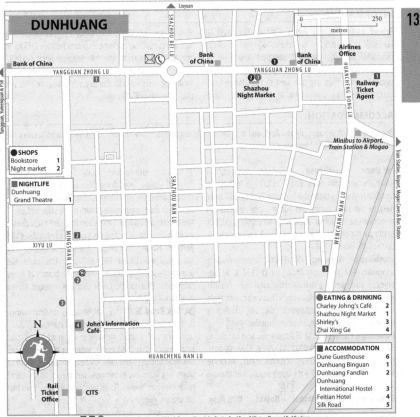

SHOPS
Bookstore — 1
Night market — 2

NIGHTLIFE
Dunhuang
Grand Theatre — 1

EATING & DRINKING
Charley Johng's Café — 2
Shazhou Night Market — 1
Shirley's — 3
Zhai Xing Ge — 4

ACCOMMODATION
Dune Guesthouse — 6
Dunhuang Binguan — 1
Dunhuang Fandian — 2
Dunhuang
 International Hostel — 3
Feitian Hotel — 4
Silk Road — 5

the airport and the *Silk Road Hotel*, otherwise it's around ¥30 in a cab.

Destinations Beijing (daily; 3hr); Lanzhou (3 daily; 1hr 30min); Ürümqi (2 daily; 1hr 30min); Xi'an (5 daily; 2hr 30min).

By rail Dunhuang station (敦煌火车站, dūnhuáng huǒchēzhàn) is inconveniently located 12km from town, next to the airport. The airport minibus (¥8) from the *Silk Road Hotel* stops at the train station en route. Dunhuang sits on a branch of the Ürümqi–Xi'an line; traffic from the east is reliable, but direct services from Ürümqi have been unreliable for years. The nearest alternative station is Liuyuan (柳园, liǔyuán), about 120km to the north – take a bus (¥20) or shared taxi (from ¥100/car). Train tickets

for either station can be booked from the booths on Mingshan Lu or Yangguan Zhong Lu (or a travel agency, for a fee).

Destinations Jiayuguan (4 daily; 5hr 15min); Lanzhou (3 daily; 16hr); Xi'an (daily; 24hr).

By bus The bus station is 1km east of the town centre on Sanwei Lu. While the availability of trains and the poor state of roads around Dunhuang make bus travel in and out of the town unappealing, the buses are still useful – particularly if you're heading to Qinghai or Xinjiang.

Destinations Golmud (10hr); Hami (5hr); Jiayuguan (5hr); Lanzhou (17hr); Turpan (12hr); (Wuwei (15hr); Zhangye (13hr).

GETTING AROUND

By bus Private minibuses to Mogao Caves, the airport and the train station depart from outside the *Silk Road Hotel* (all ¥8). Bus #3 (¥1) runs from the post office roundabout to Crescent Moon Lake.

By taxi There are probably more cabs in Dunhuang than

all other vehicles put together – ¥5 should cover the ride to almost anywhere central, while ¥15 will get you to the sand dunes.

By bike You can rent bikes from *Charley Johng's Café* or *John's Information Café* for ¥5/hr.

13

INFORMATION

Travel agents Charley Johng's Café on Mingshan Lu (☎1389 3763029, ✉dhzhzh@163.com) comes recommended for organizing transport and tours – especially an overnight camel trip into the dunes (¥460/person), and a multi-day trek west to two Han-dynasty gate towers long-abandoned in the desert. John's Information Café in the Feitian hotel (🌐johncafe.net) is also worth checking out but gets poorer reviews. CITS are in the building next to the International Hotel (☎0937 8829273) on Mingshan Lu – an English-speaking guide from here costs ¥200 for the day, while a car will set you back upwards of ¥500/day.

ACCOMMODATION

Prices rise in peak season (July and Aug), and are considerably discounted in low season, though you'll need to check the availability of heating and hot water.

★ **Dune Guesthouse** 月泉山庄, yuèquán shānzhuāng. Mingsha Shan ☎1389 3763029. A fantastic hostel way to the south of town (¥15 by cab), right next to the sand dunes and run by local information merchant Charley Johng. The dorms are pretty good, but better are the private cabins, set in a small apricot orchard. Dorms <u>¥40</u>, cabins <u>¥120</u>

Dunhuang Binguan 敦煌宾馆, dūnhuáng bīnguǎn. 151 Yangguan Zhong Lu ☎0937 8859268, Chinese-only website 🌐dunhuanghotel.com. Popular with tour groups, this enormous hotel has very comfortable rooms and several restaurants on site, including Dunhuang's only Japanese. Breakfast included. <u>¥468</u>

Dunhuang Fandian 敦煌饭店, dūnhuáng fàndiàn. 373 Mingshan Bei Lu ☎0937 8852999, Chinese-only website 🌐dhfd.cn. The cheapest rooms in this mid-range hotel are small and smoky – it's worth paying a little more to stay in one of the nicer ones. <u>¥188</u>

Dunhuang International Hostel 敦煌国际 青年旅舍, dūnhuáng guójì qīngnián lǚshě. Zhongzi Gongsi, Wenchang Nan Lu ☎0937 8833121, ✉dunhuangyha@gmail.com. This bright, plant-filled hostel has great common areas with comfy sofas and a pool table. Dorm rooms have lockers and there are a few double rooms with en-suite bathrooms. Dorms <u>¥55</u>, doubles <u>¥180</u>

Feitian Hotel 飞天宾馆, fēitiān bīnguǎn. 551 Mingshan Bei Lu ☎0937 8852318. This place has acceptable, if dingy, doubles, wi-fi and a branch of John's Information Café outside. Credit cards are accepted. Closed in winter. <u>¥160</u>

★ **Silk Road** 敦煌山庄, dūnhuáng shānzhuāng. Dunyue Lu ☎0937 8882088, 🌐www.dunhuangresort .com. Part of a small nationwide chain of hotels that employ local styles and motifs, which in this case means Silk Road antiques and rugs. It's near the dunes, south of town – a little lonely perhaps, but there's an excellent restaurant (see below). Room rates drop by more than half off-season. <u>¥860</u>

EATING AND DRINKING

In addition to the omnipresent kebabs and noodles, Dunhuang has some exotic local specialities – think braised camel feet and donkey meat noodles. There is a good selection of Western food available in town, from backpacker staples, like Shirley's and Charley Johng's, to the upmarket Zhai Xing Ge.

Charley Johng's Café 风味餐厅, fēngwèi cāntīng. 21 Mingshan Lu ☎0937 88333039. Run by the ubiquitous Charley Johng, this little café offers excellent pancakes and banana fritters, as well as more expensive Chinese dishes. The café organizes tours (see information, above), rents bikes and offers a laundry service. Daily 8am–10pm.

Shazhou Night Market 沙州夜市场, shāzhōu yèshìchǎng. Yangguan Zhong Lu. Unquestionably the most atmospheric place to eat in Dunhuang, diners recline on deckchairs in this covered market while waitresses fetch food and beer from the surrounding stalls at no extra cost. Daily 4–10pm.

Shirley's 敦煌风味餐厅, dūnhuáng fēngwèi cāntīng. Mingshan Lu, opposite the Feitian ☎0937 8837943. One of the most popular cafés in this stretch of eateries, Shirley's is popular for its apple pie, coffee and ginger tea; their Chinese food isn't bad either. Wi-fi and computers available for customers. Daily 8am–11.30pm.

Zhai Xing Ge 摘星阁, zhāixīng gé. Inside the Silk Road Hotel ☎0937 8882088. This rooftop restaurant has stunning views of the sand dunes; ¥30 seems a small price to pay for a coffee or light meal while admiring the sunset. The restaurant serves Western food – expect to pay ¥50 for a pizza, ¥128 for a full steak dinner. Daily 8am–8.30pm.

NIGHTLIFE

Theatre The Dunhuang Grand Theatre (敦煌大剧院, dūnhuáng dàjùyuàn) puts on 90min dance and acrobatic performances (nightly May–Sept; ¥200).

SHOPPING

Night market Shazhou night market sells souvenirs – coins, jade articles, Tibetan bells and horns, leather shadow puppets, scroll paintings and Chinese chops – with no real pressure to buy.

DIRECTORY

Banks and exchange Both Bank of China branches (Mon–Fri 8am–5.30pm), one at either end of Yangguan Zhong Lu, have ATMs. To change travellers' cheques, you'll need to head to the larger branch near the Shazhou night market.

The Mogao Caves

莫高窟, mògāo kū • Daily 8.30am–5.30pm, last entry at 4pm, but closed during wet weather • May–Sept ¥180, Oct–April ¥100, includes English-speaking guide • minibus from Dunhuang ¥8 • Taxi one-way ¥50, or over ¥100 return

The **Mogao Caves**, carved out of a stretch of wild desert cliffs 25km southeast of Dunhuang, are one of China's greatest archeological sites – it is from here that Buddhism and Buddhist art radiated across the Chinese empire. Work started on the caves in 366AD, and continued up until the fourteenth century. The earliest artwork shows considerable artistic influence from Central Asia, India and Persia, though you can see how these foreign styles waned over time, as the iconography slowly adapted to Chinese aesthetics.

Of the original thousand plus caves, over six hundred survive in recognizable form, but many are off-limits, either no longer considered to be of significant interest or containing murals that the Chinese consider too sexually explicit for visitors. Of the thirty caves open to the public, you are likely to manage only around fifteen in a single visit. Some grasp of the caves' history is essential to appreciate them properly, but restorations and replacements in the modern era have complicated the picture, and many of the statues, in particular, are not original. The caves are all clearly labelled with numbers above the doors but the interiors are unlit to preserve the murals; bring a flashlight if you have one. Photography at the caves is prohibited.

Research and exhibition centre

石窟文物研究陈列中心, shíkū wénwù yánjiū chénliè zhōngxīn • Daily 9am–5pm

The **Research and Exhibition Centre**, the giant modern building opposite the car park, provides a history of Mogao in English, photos of off-limits caves and reproductions of some of the plundered frescoes now in Europe. There are full replicas of eight caves, the big advantage here being that the lights are on, the colours are fresh and you can study the murals up close. The most impressive is a statue of the one-thousand-hand and one-thousand-eye Bodhisattva Guanyin – the original piece is no longer on view, due to its deteriorating condition. Upstairs are a few surviving silk scrolls and manuscripts, and there's a film about the caves.

The Northern Wei caves

The earliest caves were hewn in the fourth and fifth centuries AD during the **Northern Wei** (386–581). The Wei caves are relatively small in size, and are often supported in the centre by a large column – a feature imported from India. A statue of the Buddha is usually central, surrounded in tiers on the walls by a **mass of tiny Buddhas** brilliantly painted in black, white, blue, red and green. The statues are actually made of terracotta: the rock inside the caves was too soft for detailed carving, so craftsmen would first carve a rough outline of the figure, then build it up with clay.

The style of the murals in these caves shows a great deal of **foreign influence. Cave 101**, decorated towards the end of the fifth century, provides a good example: the Buddha, flanked by Bodhisattvas, is essentially a Western figure and recognizably Christ-like.

Though originally designed as a focus of devotional contemplation, the murals soon move towards a wider subject matter, their narrative sequences arranged in long horizontal strips. **Cave 135** (early sixth century) illustrates a *jataka* story – concerning a

13

THE MOGAO CAVE TREASURES

Before the arrival of Buddhism from India, Chinese religious activities had been performed in wooden buildings. Cave temples were introduced to China from India, where they were developed in response to poverty, heat and scarce building materials.

The emergence of the **Mogao** cave complex dominated early Chinese Buddhism, as pilgrims, monks and scholars passing along the Silk Road settled here to translate sutras. Merchants stopped too, endowing temples to ensure the success of their caravans and to benefit their souls. Huge numbers of **artists and craftsmen** were employed at Dunhuang, often lying on high scaffoldings in the dim light of oil lamps. The workers were paid a pittance – one document discovered at the site is a bill of indenture signed by a sculptor for the sale of his son.

The monastic community reached its peak under the Tang, with more than a thousand cave temples. Later, as ocean-going trading links supplanted the Silk Road, Mogao became increasingly provincial, until eventually the caves were **sealed and abandoned** in the fourteenth century.

In 1900 a wandering Taoist priest, **Wang Yuanlu**, stumbled upon Mogao and decided to make it his life's work to restore the site, excavating caves full of sand, touching up the murals, and even building a guesthouse, which he financed through alms. His efforts might have continued in obscurity save for his discovery of a bricked-up chamber (cave 17), which revealed an enormous collection of **manuscripts**, **sutras** and **silk and paper paintings** – some 1000 years old and virtually undamaged. The Dunhuang authorities, having first appropriated a fair amount, had the cave resealed and so it remained until the arrival of Central Asian explorer **Aurel Stein** in 1907. Stein, a Hungarian working for the British Indian Survey, had heard rumours of the caves and persuaded Wang to reopen the chamber. This is how Stein later described what he saw:

Heaped up in layers, but without any order, there appeared in the dim light of the priest's little lamp a solid mass of manuscript bundles rising to a height of nearly 10 feet and filling, as subsequent measurement showed, close on 500 cubic feet – an unparalleled archeological scoop.

This was no exaggeration. Among other manuscripts, Stein found original sutras brought from India by the Tang monk and traveller **Xuanzang** (see p.830), Buddhist texts in many languages (even ones unknown to the scholar) and dozens of original Tang-dynasty paintings on silk and paper – all crushed but untouched by damp.

Donating the equivalent of £130 to Wang's restoration fund, Stein left Mogao with some seven thousand manuscripts and five hundred paintings. Later the same year a Frenchman, Paul Pelliot, negotiated a similar deal, shipping thousands more scrolls back to Paris. And so, virtually overnight, the British Museum and the Louvre had acquired the core of their Chinese manuscript and painting collections.

Today the Chinese are pressing for the **return** of all paintings and manuscripts in foreign collections. It is hard to dispute the legitimacy of these claims, though had the treasures not been removed, more would almost certainly have been lost in the chaotic years of the twentieth century. Fortunately, despite the massive loss in terms of manuscripts and scrolls, the artwork at the caves themselves is still fabulously preserved.

former life of Buddha – in which he gave his own body to feed a starving tigress, unable to succour her cubs.

The Sui Caves

Sixth-century China had been wracked by civil war for decades, but with the founding of the short-lived but dynamic **Sui dynasty** in 581 came a boom in Buddhist art. In the four decades up to the emergence of the Tang, more than seventy caves were carved at Mogao.

Structurally, the Sui caves dispense with the central column, while artistically they replace the bold, slightly crude Wei brushwork with intricate, flowing lines and an increasingly extravagant use of colour that includes gilding and washes of silver. Sui period statuary also shows change, with the figures stiff and dressed in Chinese robes, with short legs, long bodies (indicating power and divinity) and big, square heads – cave 427 contains some good examples.

The Tang caves

The caves at Mogao reached their artistic zenith during the **Tang dynasty** (618–906). The classic Tang cave has a square floor, tapering roof and a niche set into the back wall. The statuary includes **warriors** – a new theme – and huge depictions of the **Buddha**, including a 34m-high seated example in **cave 96**, dressed in the traditional dragon robe of the emperor – possibly designed deliberately to remind pilgrims of the Tang empress Wu Zetian. In **cave 148** there's yet another huge Buddha, this time reclining and surrounded by acolytes.

Tang murals range from hugely scaled scenes from the sutras – now contained within one composition rather than the earlier cartoon-strip convention – to vivid paintings of individuals. One of the most popular and spectacular themes was that of the *Visit of the Bodhisattva Manjusri to Vimalakirti*. **Cave 1** contains perhaps the utmost expression of this story. Vimalakirti, on the left, is attended by a great host of heavenly beings, eager to hear the discourse of the ailing old king. The most developed Tang mural in the caves is **cave 139A**'s depiction of the *Western Paradise of the Amitabha Buddha*, a supremely confident painting, showing the souls of the reborn rising from lotus flowers, while heavenly scenes surround the Buddha above.

Later caves

Later work, executed during the **Five Dynasties**, **Song and Western Xia** (906–1227), shows little real progression from the Tang. Much, in any case, is simply restoration or repainting of existing murals. Song work is perhaps the most interesting, tending toward a heavy richness of colour, and with many of its figures displaying the features of minority races.

Toward the end of the Mongol **Yuan dynasty** (1260–1368), before Mogao was abandoned, the standard niche in the caves' back wall gave way to a central altar, creating more surface space for murals. Tibetan-style Lamaist and Tantric figures were introduced, and occult diagrams and mandalas became fashionable. The most interesting Yuan art is in **cave 465**, set apart from the main body of grottoes. You could ask the guides if they will open this up for you, though they will probably only do so for a huge fee. The cave's murals include Tantric figures in the ultimate state of enlightenment, graphically represented by the state of sexual union.

Crescent Moon Lake and the Singing Sand Dune

Daily 5.30am–9pm, closed in wet weather • May–October ¥120, November–April ¥60 • optional bus ride to lake ¥20 or camel ride ¥100 • bus #3 from Mingshan Lu in Dunhuang ¥1 • taxi ¥10–15

A few kilometres to the south of Dunhuang is the much-touted **Crescent Moon Lake** (月牙泉, yuèyá quán) and **Singing Sand Dune** (鸣沙山, míngshā shān), set amid the most impressive sand-dune scenery in China, with mounds 200–300m high. The sands hum in windy weather, hence the name. The Crescent Moon Lake is not much to look at, but is curious for its permanence – despite being surrounded by shifting sands, it was first recorded some two thousand years ago. A number of activities, including tobogganing (¥10) and paragliding (¥200), are on offer from the top of the main dune; paragliding is particularly fun. Climbing the dune in the first place, however, is incredibly hot, exhausting work; you can pay to ride up on a camel or to use the wooden steps. Note that, in the summer, the only sensible time to come is either before 8.30am or after 5pm.

13 Xinjiang

新疆, xīnjiāng

Xinjiang is an extraordinary region more than 3000km from any coast which, despite all the upheavals since the collapse of the Silk Road trade, still comprises the same oasis settlements strung out along the ancient routes, many producing the silk and cotton for which they were famed in Roman times (see box, p.847). Geographically, Xinjiang – literally "New Territories", and more fully the **Xinjiang Uyghur autonomous region** – occupies an area slightly greater than Western Europe, and yet its population is just 22 million. With ethnic minorities comprising almost sixty percent of the total population, Xinjiang is perhaps the least "Chinese" part of the People's Republic.

The **Tian Shan** range bisects Xinjiang from east to west. South of this dividing line is **Nanjiang** (southern Xinjiang), a predominantly Uyghur region that encompasses the **Tarim Basin** and the scorching Taklamakan Desert, its sands covering countless forgotten cities and another buried treasure – **oil**. China estimates that three times the proven US oil reserves are under the Taklamakan alone. The cooler forests and steppes north of the Tian Shan, in **Beijiang** (northern Xinjiang) are home to populations of Kazakhs and Mongols living a partially nomadic existence. Beijiang's climate is warm in summer, and virtually Siberian from October through to March.

Regional **highlights** include the mountain pastures outside Ürümqi, where you can hike in rare solitude and stay beside **Heaven Lake** with Kazakhs in their yurts; but it is the old **Silk Road** that will attract most travellers, predominantly the oasis towns of **Turpan** and **Kashgar**. It is possible to follow either the Northern Silk Road from Turpan to Kashgar via Kuqa, or the virtually forgotten southern route via Khotan. There's also the possibility of continuing the Silk Road journey out beyond the borders of China itself, via the relatively well-established **Karakoram Highway** into Pakistan, or over less well-known routes into Kazakhstan or Kyrgyzstan (see p.818).

Brief history

While Xinjiang's past has been coloured by such great personalities as Tamerlane, Genghis Khan, Attila the Hun and Alexander the Great, the region's fortunes have waxed and waned throughout its history. Likewise, China's influence has been far from constant. The area first passed under Han control in the second century BC, under Emperor Wu Di, but it was not until the **Tang dynasty** (650–850 AD) that this control amounted to more than a vague military presence. Xinjiang enjoyed something of a golden age under the Tang, with the culture and Buddhist art of the **Silk Road** oases at their zenith.

From Tang dynasty to twentieth century

The ninth century saw the gradual rise of the **Uyghurs**, and their conversion to **Islam**. Subsequent centuries saw the **Mongol conquests** under Genghis Khan and Tamerlane. Both brought havoc and slaughter in their wake, though the brief period of Mongol rule (1271–1368) hugely facilitated Silk Road trade – for the first and only time in history, east and west Asia were under a single government.

After the fall of the Mongols, Xinjiang began to split into oasis kingdoms and **khanates** and suffered a succession of religious and factional wars. Nonetheless, the Qing **reassertion** of Chinese domination in the eighteenth century was fiercely contested. A century later, in 1864, full-scale **Muslim rebellion** broke out, led by the ruler of Kashgaria, **Yakub Beg**. Ultimately the revolt failed and by the beginning of the twentieth century, Xinjiang was a Chinese backwater controlled by a succession of warlords who acted virtually independently of the central government.

Since 1949, the Chinese government has made strenuous attempts to stabilize the region by **settling Han Chinese** from the east. The Uyghur proportion of Xinjiang's population slipped from ninety percent in 1949 to below fifty percent in the 1980s, and is still on the way down, despite the minorities' exemption from the One Child Policy.

THE UYGHUR

The **Uyghur** are the easternmost branch of the extended family of **Turkic peoples** who inhabit most of Central Asia. Around ten million Uyghurs live in Xinjiang with another 300,000 in Kazakhstan. Despite centuries of domination by China and some racial mingling along the way, the Uyghur remain culturally distinct from the Han Chinese, and many Uyghurs look decidedly un-Chinese – stockily built, bearded, with brown hair and round eyes. Although originally Buddhists, Uyghurs have been **Muslim** for at least a thousand years and Islam remains the focus of their identity in the face of relentless Han penetration.

For the most part Uyghurs are unable to speak fluent Chinese, and have difficulty finding well-paid work – their prospects for self-improvement within China are generally bleak. Many Han Chinese look down on Uyghurs as unsophisticated ruffians, and are wary of their supposedly short tempers and love of knives. Perhaps as a consequence of this, at times Uyghurs seem to extend their mistrust of Han Chinese to all foreigners, tourists included. Nevertheless, gestures such as trying a few words of their language or drinking tea with them will help to break down the barriers, and invitations to Uyghur homes frequently follow.

TRAVELLERS' UYGHUR

The **Uyghur language** is essentially an Eastern Turkish dialect (spoken Uyghur can be understood by Uzbek-, Kazakh- and Kyrgyz-speakers). There are several dialects, of which the Central Uyghur (spoken from Ürümqi to Kashgar) is the most popular and hence given here, including commonly used alternatives. Unlike Chinese, Uyghur is not a tonal language. It involves eight vowels and 24 consonants and uses a modified Arabic script. The only pronunciations you are likely to have difficulties with are **gh** and **kh**, but you can get away by rendering them as **g** and **k** with a light **h** at the end. **X** is pronounced "ksh", while **q** is a "ch" sound.

Hello	*Yahximusiz*	Sunday	*Yekxembe*
Goodbye/Cheers	*Hosh*	Monday	*Doxembe*
Thank you	*Rhamat sizge*	Tuesday	*Sixembe*
Please/Sorry	*Kequrung*	Wednesday	*Qarxembe*
Yes	*He'e*	Thursday	*Peyxembe*
No	*Yakh*	Friday	*Jume*
Very	*Bek*	Saturday	*Xembe*
What is your name?	*Ismingiz nime?*		
My name is…	*Mening ismim…*	**NUMBERS**	
How much is it?	*Bahasi khange?*	1	*bir*
OK	*Bolidu*	2	*ikki*
Good	*Yahxi*	3	*uq*
Where is the…?	*…nede?*	4	*tort*
toilet	*Hajethana*	5	*bash*
hospital	*Duhturhana*	6	*alte*
temple	*Buthana*	7	*yet'te*
tomb	*Khebre*	8	*sekkiz*
I don't have	*Yenimda yeterlik*	9	*tokh'khuz*
enough money	*pul yokh*	10	*on*
Please stop here	*Bu yerde tohtang*	11	*on bir*
This is delicious	*Temlik/lezzetlik*	12	*on ikki* etc
Cold	*Soghukh*	20	*yigrime*
Hot	*Issikh*	30	*ottuz*
Thirsty	*Ussitidighan*	40	*khirkh*
Hungry	*Ag khusakh*	50	*ellik*
When?	*Vakhitta?*	60	*atmix*
Now	*Emdi/hazir*	70	*yetmix*
Today	*Bugun*	80	*seksen*
Yesterday	*Tunogun*	90	*tokhsen*
Tomorrow	*Ete*	100	*yuz*

XINJIANG TIME

For travellers, the classic illustration of Xinjiang's remoteness from the rest of the country is in the fact that all parts of China set their clocks to Beijing time. The absurdity of this is at its most acute in Xinjiang, 3000–4000km from the capital – which means that in Kashgar, in the far west of the region, the summer sun rises at 9am or 10am and sets around midnight. Locally, unofficial **"Xinjiang time"** (新疆时间, xīnjiāng shíjiān), two hours behind Beijing time, is used more frequently the further west you travel; when buying bus, train or plane tickets, you should be absolutely clear about which time is being used. In general, Uyghurs are more likely to use Xinjiang time, while Han Chinese prefer Beijing time. All times given in this section use Beijing time.

Modern Xinjiang

Today, the Chinese government remains nervous about Xinjiang, especially given its enormous **economic potential**. **Uyghur dissent** reached a peak in July 2009, when Ürümqi witnessed Xinjiang's worst-ever clashes between its Uyghur and Han populations in recent times. Official sources put the number of dead at just under 200, the majority of them Han; Uyghur groups claim that the overall figure was much higher, and that hundreds of their own people's deaths had been covered up. Security was tightened across the region, and hundreds of Uyghur men were arrested in huge sweeps of the main cities; an unknown number have since been executed.

With numerous minor incidents since 2009 tourist numbers have, understandably, taken a tumble. Visitors will notice a heavy security presence across Xinjiang but especially around the strongly Uyghur regions surrounding Khotan and Kashgar.

Ürümqi

乌鲁木齐, wūlǔmùqí

Well connected by road, rail and plane to the rest of China, as well as a smattering of cities abroad, **ÜRÜMQI** forms the introduction to Xinjiang for many. But the city is hardly representative of the region: the vast majority of the city's two million-strong population are Han Chinese, and while you'll get to see Uyghur people and eat a bit of their food, you'll have a far more authentic experience elsewhere even in Turpan, just a few hours away by bus, (see p.828). Ürümqi means "Beautiful Pastures", yet the name hardly applies these days: this is a political, industrial and economic capital, and there are few reasons to stay in town for more than a few days unless you're applying for Kazakh or Kyrgyz **visas**.

That said, for travellers arriving from Central Asia, Ürümqi will be the first truly Chinese city on your route – modern Han culture can be just as interesting as that of the Uyghurs. If you're heading the other way, there are also lively bazaars and food markets, and a vibrant nightlife, its businesspeople, gold- and oil-miners lending the city a certain pioneering feel.

Brief history

Under the name of **Dihua**, Ürümqi became the capital of Xinjiang in the late nineteenth century. During the first half of the twentieth century, the city was a battleground for feuding warlords – in 1916 Governor Yang Zengxin invited all his personal enemies to a dinner party here and had them beheaded one by one during the course of the banquet. Later, shortly before the outbreak of World War II, **Soviet troops** entered the city to help quell a Muslim rebellion; they stayed until 1960. Ürümqi began to emerge from its extreme backwardness only with the completion of the Lanzhou–Ürümqi **rail line** in 1963. More than anything, this helped to integrate the city, economically and psychologically, into the People's Republic. And with the opening of the Ürümqi–Almaty rail line in 1991, the final link in the long-heralded direct route from China through Central Asia to Europe was complete.

13

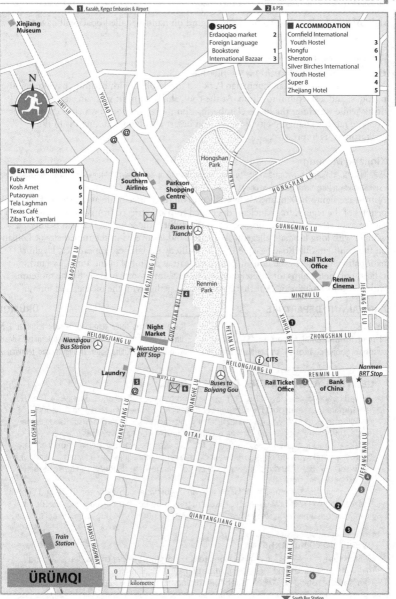

Xinjiang Museum

● **SHOPS**
Erdaoqiao market	**2**
Foreign Language	
Bookstore	**1**
International Bazaar	**3**

■ **ACCOMMODATION**
Cornfield International	
Youth Hostel	**3**
Hongfu	**6**
Sheraton	**1**
Silver Birches International	
Youth Hostel	**2**
Super 8	**4**
Zhejiang Hotel	**5**

● **EATING & DRINKING**
Fubar	**1**
Kosh Amet	**6**
Putaoyuan	**5**
Tela Laghman	**4**
Texas Café	**2**
Ziba Turk Tamlari	**3**

Hongshan Park

China Southern Airlines

Parkson Shopping Centre

Buses to Tianchi

Renmin Park

Rail Ticket Office

Renmin Cinema

Night Market

Nianzigou Bus Station

Nianzigou BRT Stop

Laundry

Buses to Baiyang Gou

CITS

Rail Ticket Office

Bank of China

Nanmen BRT Stop

Train Station

ÜRÜMQI

0   1
kilometre

South Bus Station

Renmin Park

人民公园, rénmín gōngyuán • Daily 8am–10.15pm • Free

Visitors to Ürümqi are likely to gravitate toward the east of the city near **Renmin Park**. Almost every Chinese city boasts something similar, but Ürümqi's version is particularly pleasant, with a boating pond and a funfair, as well as scores of locals doing anything from practising on musical instruments to group *tai ji*. Those travelling with children may be unwilling to unleash their progeny on the most rickety rides, but the

13

sight of kids finger-painting or racing around on hand-pedalled boats will have you wishing you were younger.

Hongshan Park

红山公园, hóngshān gōngyuán • Daily 7am–11pm • Free

North of Guangming Lu, **Hongshan Park** is a lovely place with boating, pavilions and pagodas, and a steep hill to climb. At the cool, shady summit you can sit and have a drink while watching the locals clambering about over the rocks; on clear days the view over the rapidly changing city skyline, with desert and snowy mountains in the background, is impressive.

Xinjiang Museum

新疆博物馆, xīnjiāng bówùguǎn • Xibei Lu • Tues–Sun, summer 10am–6pm, winter 10.30am–6pm • last tickets 4.30pm • Free
• 5 mins' walk from Ming Yuan BRT station on Line 1

A must-see sight, the **Xinjiang Museum** focuses on the lives, culture and history of the peoples of the region, from ancient, desiccated **corpses** retrieved from desert burial sites to dioramas of ethnic minority homes. The star exhibit is the so-called "Loulan Beauty", a woman with long fair hair, allegedly 3800 years old, recovered in the ruined city of Loulan on the Southern Silk Road (see p.843). Of distinctly un-Chinese appearance, Uyghur nationalists have taken the Loulan Beauty to heart as a symbol of the antiquity (and validity) of their claims for sovereignty; a counterclaim of sorts is made by the museum, with an exhibit making it clear that Xinjiang is "together with the motherland forever".

ARRIVAL AND DEPARTURE ÜRÜMQI

BY AIR
Diwopu International Airport (地窝堡国际机场, diwōbǎo guójì jīchǎng) is 15km northwest of the city.

The airport has three terminals; elderly terminal 1 is currently being refurbished and expanded, terminal 3 deals exclusively with China Southern flights, and terminal 2

CENTRAL ASIAN TRAVEL CONNECTIONS

Ürümqi has become a travel hub for those heading between China and Central Asia. The lovely new terminal at the **airport** handles an ever-increasing number of international flights, including services to Azerbaijan, Kazakhstan, Kyrgyzstan, Iran, Pakistan, Tajikistan and Siberian Russia. Third-party nationals will, in many of these cases, need to have **visas** in advance – check with your local embassy for details. The two visas that you can get in Ürümqi are for Kazakhstan and Kyrgyzstan (see p.839), although many nationalities can now get a Kyrgyz visa on arrival and visa situations are always subject to change – check ahead and arrive at the embassy as early as possible.

Ürümqi has also become a popular pit stop on the **bicycle** route between China and Central Asia – at certain times of the year, cyclists seem to outnumber "normal" backpackers. The city's hostels are great places to swap useful information with other cycle nuts, either in person or through guestbooks.

OVERLAND TO KAZAKHSTAN

Ürümqi has a couple of land **connections to Kazakhstan**. Sleeper **trains** depart around midnight on Saturday and Monday for **Almaty** (阿拉木图, ālāmùtú), and at the same time on Thursdays for Astana (阿斯塔娜, āsītǎnà). Returning trains leave Almaty around midnight on Saturdays and Mondays, and Astana on Tuesday afternoons. In Ürümqi, tickets (¥1100 to Almaty, ¥1300 to Astana) can be bought from the ticket office inside the *Ya'ou Hotel* next to the main train station (daily, 10am–1pm & 3.30–7.30pm). The journey to Almaty takes around thirty hours, eight of which are spent at the border changing the carriages' wheels to fit Kazakh rails.

The bus journey to Almaty is around ten hours shorter – services run from Ürümqi's long-distance bus station most days of the week – again, the schedule is continually changing; tickets cost around ¥400. These services pass through Yining (see p.824), and it's possible to head there first on local transport to break the journey.

mops up all other departures. You can get into town on the airport bus (¥10), which delivers to various airline offices, terminating at the *Ya'ou Hotel* near the train station. The budget option is to take bus #51 (¥1), which runs between Nianzigou and Hongshan Park BRT stations and the airport. A taxi will set you back around ¥40. To purchase flight tickets, the best prices are available online or from one of Ürümqi's numerous independent ticket offices. As a last resort, try the China Southern office at 576 Youhao Nan Lu, although their prices are often higher than elsewhere. Besides the domestic services listed below, there are international flights linking Ürümqi with Almaty, Astana, Bishkek, Dushanbe, Islamabad, Moscow, Novosibirsk, Osh, Seoul and Tehran.

Destinations Beijing (regular; 3hr 30min); Chengdu (11 daily; 3hr 15min); Chongqing (8 daily; 3hr 30min); Dunhuang (2 daily; 1hr 15min); Guangzhou (6 daily; 4hr 50min); Kashgar (regular; 1hr 45min); Khotan (7 daily; 1hr 45min); Korla (10 daily; 1hr); Lanzhou (8 daily; 2hr 30min); Shanghai (13 daily; 4hr 20min); Xi'an (regular; 3hr 5min); Xining (2 daily; 2hr 10min); Yinchuan (5 daily; 2hr 25min); Yining (13 daily; 1hr).

BY TRAIN

Ürümqi train station (乌鲁木齐火车站, wūlǔmùqí huǒchēzhàn) lies in the southwest of the city, with services arriving from as far afield as Beijing and Shanghai in the east, and Kashgar in the west, not to mention Almaty and Astana in Kazakhstan (see p.839). Long distances make trains the most comfortable option if arriving or departing from anywhere bar Turpan or Korla – sadly everyone else seems to feel the same, and you will need to book sleeper

tickets well in advance or be ready to travel hard-seat. The station is easy to reach – it's at the southern end of BRT #1 and served by several bus routes (including #2, #10, #16, #20). Crowds and tight security in the station itself mean that it is often better to purchase tickets from one of the ticket booths around town (all daily 9.30am–9pm) – the ones at 176 Renmin Lu and 245 Jianshe Lu are the most centrally located.

Destinations Almaty (Kazakhstan; weekly; 34hr); Astana (Kazakhstan; weekly; 40hr); Beijing (2 daily; 34–40hr); Chengdu (2 daily; 50hr); Daheyan (regular; 2hr); Jiayuguan (15 daily; 15hr); Kashgar (3 daily; 26–32hr); Korla (5 daily; 13hr); Lanzhou (10 daily; 26hr); Shanghai (1 daily; 45hr); Tianshui (10 daily; 30hr); Xi'an (8 daily; 34hr).

BY BUS

Nianzigou bus station (碾子沟客运中心, niǎnzigōu kèyùn zhōngxīn). 500m west of the Nianzigou BRT station, this bus station deals with traffic to northern Xinjiang, including Saryam Lake, Yining and Altai, as well as regular buses to Korla and occasional departures for Hami and into Gansu. The ticket office is open daily 7am–9pm.

South bus station (南郊客运站, nánjiāo kèyùnzhàn), 2km south of the centre at the southern end of Xinhua Nan Lu, serving destinations south of Ürümqi, including Turpan, Korla, Kuqa, Khotan and Kashgar. Bus routes #1 and #7 stop here and a taxi ought to cost around ¥10. The ticket office opens daily 7am–9pm.

Destinations Almaty (Kazakhstan; 24hr); Kashgar (24hr); Khotan (20hr); Korla (6hr); Kuqa (10hr); Turpan (2hr 30min); Yining (12hr).

GETTING AROUND

By BRT (Bus Rapid Transit) Ürümqi's traffic can be awful, especially during rush hour – just one reason to learn to love the BRT (¥1). These special bus services escape the worst of the traffic by shooting up and down dedicated lanes in the middle of the busiest roads. Line #1 is particularly useful, running from the train station north up Changjiang Lu to Hongshan Park and on towards the museum. Line #3 runs between Erdaoqiao Market and Nanmen.

By bus City buses serve more destinations than the BRT. Buses #1 and #102 both run from Youhao Lu to the south bus station via Erdaoqiao. Bus #8 runs between the train station and Xinhua Bei Lu via Nianzigou BRT stop.

By taxi Cabs cost ¥6 for the first three kilometres – it can be difficult to find one during rush hour, but enterprising locals might stop and offer lifts for around 50 percent above the taxi fare.

INFORMATION

Travel agencies Ürümqi's helpful, English-speaking CITS office is at 16/F, 33 Renmin Lu (☎0991 2821426, ⓦwww

.xinjiangtour.com). The youth hostels can also provide up-to-date travel advice.

ACCOMMODATION

Cornfield International Youth Hostel 麦田国际青年旅舍, màitián guójì qīngnián lǚshè. Youhao Nan Lu ☎0991 4591488, ⓦxjmaitian.net. Passable hostel with good beds, tiny communal bathrooms and indifferent staff – it's occasionally hard to tell who, if anyone, is on duty. Also known as the *Maitian*. Dorm beds ¥45, rooms ¥150

Hongfu 鸿福大饭店, hōngfú dàjiǔdiàn. 160 Wuyi Lu ☎0991 5881588, ⓔreservations@hongfuhotel.com. Get away from the chains at this swanky, upper-class hotel, with a small on-site shopping centre and several excellent restaurants. Rooms are very pretty, with curved floor-to-ceiling windows, thick carpets and enormous beds. ¥788

13

Sheraton 喜来登酒店, xǐláidēng jiǔdiàn. 669 Youhao Bei Lu ☏0991 6999999, ⊛sheraton.com. Excellent, modern hotel providing all the comfort you'd expect from this chain. Food, service standards and room quality are as good as you'll get in Xinjiang, and some rooms have tremendous mountain views. The only downside is a slightly out-of-the-way location on the airport road. ¥1500

Silver Birches International Youth Hostel 白桦林国际青年旅舍, báihuálín guójì qīngnián lǚshè. 186 Nanhu Nan Lu ☏0991 4881428, ⊛yhaxinjiang. com. Like the *Cornfield*, this gets patchy reviews, mostly due to the pervasive smell of drains, but this

out-of-the-way hostel has pleasant common areas and friendly staff. Dorm beds from ¥50, rooms ¥120

★ **Super 8** 速8酒店, sùbā jiǔdiàn. 140 Gongyuan Bei Jie ☏0991 5590666, ⊛super8.com.cn. A particularly nice outpost of this Chinese chain, *Super 8* offers individually decorated rooms and suites including breakfast and broadband internet. An additional ¥10 gets you a larger room overlooking Renmin Park. ¥288

Zhejiang Hotel 浙江大酒店, zhèjiāng dàjiǔdiàn. 196 Changjiang Lu ☏0991 5617888. This newly opened hotel is good value with comfortable beds, marble-covered bathrooms and helpful staff. Room rates include broadband internet and breakfast. ¥298

EATING AND DRINKING

Ürümqi has a good variety of places to eat, whether you're after Uyghur specialities or Cantonese favourites, with a couple of exceptional food night markets. For drinking, start at the *Fubar*, find some new friends and progress from there.

★ **Fubar** 福吧, fúbā. 40 Gongyuan Bei Jie ☏0991 5844498. Almost every traveller who passes through Ürümqi seems to end up here, and with good reason: it's a veritable oasis of travel information, wi-fi, beers, spirits and Western food, including great pizzas. Brave souls can try their signature "Stinger" cocktail, made with a scorpion tail and a sinful amount of alcohol. Daily 11am–2am.

Kosh Amet 库西阿买提大盘鸡, kùxī āmǎití dàpánjī. Lingguan Xiang, 200m west of the Yan'an Lu BRT station. Kosh Amet specializes in a Hui dish, *dapanji* – "big plate of chicken" – simply decide if you want a medium dish (*zhongpanji*, ¥50) or a big one (¥85) and join the crowds of diners who flock here from the mosque on nearby Shengli Lu. Spot it by the English sign for "Chicken Food". Daily 11am–midnight.

Putaoyuan 葡萄园, pútáo yuán. Jiefang Nan Lu, just north of the International Bazaar. A wonderful place to rest on hot days, this is less a restaurant and more an open-air food court. Join Uyghur families in the shade of the grape vines for cold noodles, fried pastries and a delicious concoction of yogurt and rose syrup mixed with crushed ice. Daily in summer, 10am–2am.

Tela Laghman 特拉快餐, tèlā kuàicān. Longquan Jie. There's no menu at this popular restaurant, but then there's only one thing on the menu; laghman (hand-pulled noodles fried with diced mutton, tomatoes and peppers). Join crowds of local diners and slurp up some of the tastiest noodles (¥17) in the city. No English sign – spot it by its dark wood interior. Daily 11am–8pm.

Texas Café 德克萨斯西餐厅, dékèsàsī xīcāntīng. Mashi Xiang, off Renmin Lu, ☏0991 2810025, ⊛texascafe.weebly.com. Enjoy good Tex-Mex food at this attractive restaurant/café, tucked away down an alley on the south side of Renmin Lu – the alley is opposite the Agricultural Bank of China at 203 Renmin Lu. With a leafy little patio at the back and a lending library of English books, it's a great place to relax with a drink. Mon & Wed–Sun 1–10.30pm.

Ziba Turk Tamlari 滋巴土耳其风味餐厅, zība tǔ'ěrqí fēngwèi cāntīng. Jiefang Nan Lu ☏0991 2810899. This glitzy restaurant serves up Turkish classics from great kebabs (¥40) to enormous slabs of baklava (¥20) and thick, thick coffee. At its best in the evenings when there's a floor show. Daily 11am–11pm.

SHOPPING

Bookshops The Foreign Language Bookstore (daily 10am–8pm) at 14 Xinhua Bei Lu has English novels and a few Chinese classics In English on the third floor. English maps of Ürümqi can be found on the first floor.

Markets The Erdaoqiao market, on Jiefang Nan Lu, sells knives, handmade musical instruments, jade, carpets,

clothes and various ornate handicrafts (be prepared to bargain prices down to about one third of the initial cost). The less atmospheric International Bazaar complex opposite sells similar items at cheaper prices, though a string of music shops here sell CDs of traditional Uyghur music (see p.844).

DIRECTORY

Banks and exchange The main Bank of China is at the junction of Renmin Lu and Jiefang Lu (Mon–Fri 10am–6.30pm); it's the only branch where you can change travellers' cheques but its ATMs only accept credit cards.

Any China Construction bank will take cards with Cirrus; try the one opposite the *Hongfu Hotel*.

Embassies Kazakhstan, 216 Kunming Lu (☏0991 3815796; Mon–Thurs 10am–1pm); Kyrgyzstan, 58 Hetian

UYGHUR FOOD

Uyghur food, unsurprisingly, has far more of a Central Asian than a Chinese flavour. The most basic staple – which often seems to be the only food available – is **laghman**, known in Chinese as *lamian*, literally "pulled noodles". Watching these being made to order is greatly entertaining: the cook grabs both ends of a roll of elastic dough and pulls it into a long ribbon by stretching his arms apart; he then slaps it down onto a floured counter, and brings his hands together to join the ends of the dough, so forming two ribbons. These are slapped again, pulled again, the cook once more rejoins his hands to make four ribbons; and the process is repeated, doubling the number of ribbons each time, until a mass of thin, metre-long noodles is strung between the cook's hands. The "handles" of surplus dough are torn off either end, and the noodles dropped into boiling water to cook for a couple of minutes. The speed at which a skilled cook transforms the raw dough into a bowlful of noodles, banging, pulling, and managing to keep all the strands separate, is incredible.

In Xinjiang, *laghman* is served with a stew of mutton, tomatoes, chilli and other vegetables; rather different from the more soupy version sold elsewhere in China. For the same spicy sauce but without the noodles, try *tohogish* (known in Chinese as *dapan* ji), a chicken served chopped up in its entirety, head, feet and all; or *jerkob*, a beef stew - both are served in smarter restaurants. Coriander leaf is used as a garnish on everything.

In summer, apart from *laghman*, street vendors also offer endless cold noodle soup dishes, usually very spicy. Rice is rare in Xinjiang, though it does appear in the saffron-coloured **pilau**, comprising fried rice and hunks of mutton. More familiar to foreigners are the skewers of grilled mutton **kebabs**, dusted with chilli and cumin powder – buy several of them at once, as one skewer does not make much more than a mouthful. They are often eaten with delicious glasses of ice-cold **yoghurt** (known in Chinese as *suannai*), which are available everywhere in Xinjiang. Tea often comes flavoured with cinnamon, cardamom and rose hips.

Oven-baked **breads** are also popular in markets: you'll see bakers apparently plunging their hands into live furnaces, to stick balls of dough on to the brick-lined walls; these are then withdrawn minutes later as bagel-like bread rolls, and *naan* flat breads, or sometimes *permuda* (known in Chinese as *kaobao*), tasty baked dough packets of mutton and onions, which can also be fried – as *samsa* – rather than baked. The steamed version, *manta*, recalls Chinese dumplings or *mantou*.

A couple of other specialities are worth trying: *madang* is nougat thick with walnuts, raisins, and dried fruit, sold by pedlars who carve the amount you want (or usually, more than you want – it's sold by weight) off massive slabs of the stuff. More refreshing is that characteristic Central Asian fruit, the **pomegranate**, known as *shiliu* in Chinese; they're about the size of an apple, with leathery yellow and red skin, and packed with hundreds of juicy, ruby-red seeds. You can find them whole at markets, or buy the juice off street vendors – look for the piles of skins and the juicing machines, which resemble a large, spiky torture implement.

Lu (☎0991 5189980; closed Wed, call to check opening hours). Note that service at both of these embassies ranges from offhand to wretched – try not to make any firm travel plans until you have your visa in hand. Several nationalities can now get visas on arrival in Kyrgyzstan – check current requirements before travelling.

Mail and telephones The main post office (daily 10am–7pm) is west of the northern end of Renmin Park. For long-distance phone calls you can buy and use phone cards from the lobbies of upmarket hotels, post offices or *Fubar*.

Tian Chi

天池, tiānchí • Daily in summer 8.30am–8.30pm • ¥100 • bus between the ticket office and the lake ¥70

Tian Chi means "Heaven Lake", and this natural haven 100km east of Ürümqi – the starting point of Vikram Seth's book *From Heaven Lake* – almost lives up to its name, especially for travellers who have spent a long time in the deserts of northwest China. At the cool, refreshing height of 2000m, the lake is surrounded by grassy meadows, steep, dense pine forests and jagged snow-covered peaks, including the mighty **Bogda Feng**, which soars to over 6000m. The nicest feature of the area is that you can wander at will; there are no restrictions on accommodation (most people stay in yurts, with the

13

> ### KAZAKHS AT HEAVEN LAKE
>
> The **Kazakhs** at Heaven Lake have recently seen massive changes to their livelihoods. Originally, they led a semi-nomadic herding existence in these hills, selling lambs in spring if the winter spared them – a hard, unpredictable business. However, in 2011 livestock grazing inside scenic areas was banned across Xinjiang, and overnight their traditional way of life disappeared. While this sea change has challenged the herders to adapt centuries-old habits, the natural environment has undeniably benefited, and the meadows of wild flowers around the lake have now returned to their former glory.
>
> Today tourism has largely replaced herding as the chief source of local revenue, with the Kazakhs providing food and accommodation for visitors to Heaven Lake, as well as working and performing in the "Kazakh Village" that you'll pass through en route to the lake. The sheep may have gone, but some traditions are still adhered to: visit in May – considered the most beautiful time – and you may get to try the alcoholic *kumiss*, fermented mare's milk, a rare delicacy.

semi-nomadic Kazakh population), and there is virtually limitless hiking. You need only to watch the **weather** – bitterly cold in winter, the lake is really only accessible during the summer months, May to September.

At the lake

Tian Chi is Xinjiang's premier tourist destination, and attracts thousands of visitors every day in the summer, most plumping for day-trips by coach; independent travellers have to fit in where they can, with the buses stopping en route for various manufactured "attractions".

The upside of the tour groups is that, once at the lake, the majority of people seldom stray beyond the cluster of scenic spots on the north shore. If you're prepared to hike beyond this, or to stay overnight, then you ought to be able to experience the beauty of the lake in near solitude. There is a wide range of **trails** in the lake area, from a 3km path that leads steeply downhill past a pretty waterfall to the visitor centre (from where you can catch a bus back to the ticket office), to a 9km climb up "Horse Tooth Mountain" (马牙山, mǎyá shān). It takes five hours or so to hike around the lake itself. All trails are well signed from the lakeshore.

ARRIVAL AND DEPARTURE — TIAN CHI

By public transport Take a bus to Fukang (阜康, fùkāng) from Ürümqi's Nianzigou bus station, and take a taxi from there to the Tian Chi ticket office (¥40).

By tour bus Booths around the northern entrance of Renmin Park in Ürümqi run good-value buses to the Tian Chi ticket office each morning (¥50 return). You can sign up for their day-trip package for an additional fee (typically including entry to the park, a boat ride and lunch at the Kazakh Village), or simply do your own thing until the allotted departure time. If you stay overnight, you'll need to pay another ¥50 or make your own way back.

By taxi A taxi from Ürümqi ought to cost around ¥280 for the return journey and a few hours' waiting time.

ACCOMMODATION AND EATING

Drinks and snacks are available from kiosks inside the park, but for proper food, you will need to depend on the Kazakhs or be prepared for self-catering.

Yurts To find a yurt to stay in, head around the lake anticlockwise after arriving at the main viewpoint and walk uphill at the first junction – accommodation is clustered along the road. The price per bed varies, depending on how many meals are included and the conditions inside the yurts. Beds ¥50–80

Nanshan

南山, nánshān • Daily in summer 8.30am–8.30pm • ¥15

South of Ürümqi spreads the **Nanshan** area of the Tian Shan range: these thickly forested hills, dotted with waterfalls, lakes and glaciers, are the traditional summering place for the region's Kazakh and Uyghur herders. Nanshan's most accessible part is **Xi Baiyang Gou** (西白杨沟, xi báiyáng gōu), easily reached by public bus from Ürümqi, with a pretty waterfall (5km gently uphill from the entrance) and horseriding opportunities – it's also a popular spot with couples taking wedding photographs. Further afield are several similar scenic spots, the most interesting of which is **Tianshan Glacier No. 1** (天山一号冰川, tiānshān yīhào bīngchuān), the source of the Ürümqi River and the world's closest glacier to a major population centre, just 125km south of the city.

ARRIVAL AND DEPARTURE   **NANSHAN**

By bus and tour bus The tour operators outside the north gate of Renmin Park organize tours to Xi Baiyang Gou and elsewhere in NanShan, although it's easy enough to get to Xi Baiyang Gou by bus (9.30am–4.30pm; 4 daily; ¥14.50) from the depot hidden in a lane off Heilongjiang Lu.

ACCOMMODATION AND EATING

There are a few simple restaurants at Xi Baiyang Gou, concentrated near the car park where the bus stops.

Yurts Xi Baiyang Gou is the best place to stay overnight in the Nan Shan area, with plenty of yurts by the roadside near the car park – haggling is expected, and be sure to check whether the price includes meals. Per person **¥80**

The Ili Valley

The pretty **Ili Valley** is centred on the city of **Yining**, just 60km east of the border with Kazakhstan and 600km northwest of Ürümqi. Being well off the principal Silk Road routes, not many people make the detour to get here, but it's a worthwhile trip: Ili is one of the three so-called **Kazakh Autonomous Prefectures** within Xinjiang (the other two are Karamay and Altai), which form a block along the northwest frontier. Despite the name, the Uyghurs are the more dominant minority group in the city, and there have been occasional protests against Beijing's rule. Today, however, after years of Han migration, the "frontier" character of Yining is fast disappearing.

The **climate** in the valley is cool and fresh even at the height of summer (and very chilly sometimes – make sure you have warm clothes whatever the time of year), and the views of the Tian Shan – from all routes into Yining, but especially if you're coming up from Kuqa to the south – are fabulous. The road climbs out of the harsh, rocky landscape of the northern Taklamakan, before entering pure alpine scenery with marching pine forests and azure skies, before drifting into vast grasslands ringed by snowy peaks. Another draw, north of Yining, is beautiful **Sayram Lake**, where you can find accommodation in Kazakh yurts.

Brief history

The **history** of the Ili Valley is one of intermittent Chinese control. During the Han dynasty, the area was occupied by the **Wusun**, ancestors of today's Kazakhs, who kept diplomatic relations with the Han court and introduced them to the region's tough Ferghana horses. By the eighth century, however, Ili's value as a staging post on the Silk Road had become too great a temptation, and the Tang dynasty invaded the area. Throughout the thirteenth and fourteenth centuries, the area was controlled first by Genghis Khan and then Tamerlane. This tug of war has gone on ever since, with the Qing seizing the area in the eighteenth century, only for the Russians to march in, in 1871, under the cover of protecting the territory against Yakub Beg's rebellion (see p.814). There remained a significant Russian presence in one form or another until 1949, and traces of this can still be seen in the architecture of Yining.

13

Yining

伊宁, yīníng

Known to the Uyghurs as Ghulja, booming **YINING** is growing quickly, with older buildings rapidly being replaced by shiny office blocks and fancy shops. While still a small city by Chinese standards, with around 500,000 inhabitants, Yining is developing into an urban sprawl – outside of the eastern and southern districts it is not a rewarding place to walk around. The centre of town isn't readily obvious – most of the action seems to be in the area between **Jiefang Lu**, and **Qingnian Park** in the southeast of the city. The main Uyghur areas are south and east of Qingnian Park, and it is these areas that are most rewarding to walk through and poke around, peppered as they are with mosques, street markets and traditional adobe buildings.

ARRIVAL AND DEPARTURE

YINING

By air Yining's little airport (伊宁机场, yīníng jīchǎng) is located 7km north of town. It's served by bus route #8 (¥1), or a taxi will set you back ¥15. Yining's airline office (📞 0999 8044000) is in the *Yilite* hotel.

Destinations Altay (1 daily; 1hr); Kanas (1 daily; 1hr 15min); Ürümqi (12 daily; 1hr).

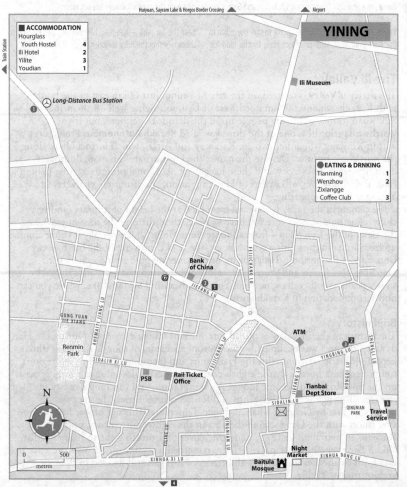

Huiyuan, Sayram Lake & Horgos Border Crossing ▲   ▲ Airport

YINING

■ ACCOMMODATION
Hourglass Youth Hostel	4
Ili Hotel	2
Yilite	3
Youdian	1

Train Station

Ⓜ Long-Distance Bus Station

Ili Museum

● EATING & DRNKING
Tianming	1
Wenzhou	2
Zixiangge Coffee Club	3

Bank of China

@

JIEFANG LU

FEIJICHANG LU

GONG YUAN JIE XIANG

AHEMAITI JIANG LU

Renmin Park

SIDALIN XI LU

FEIJICHANG LU

ATM

YINGBING LU

SHENGLI LU

HONGQI LU

PSB

Rail Ticket Office

JIEFANG LU

Tianbai Dept Store

SIDALIN LU

QINGNIAN PARK

Travel Service

QINGNIAN LU

Night Market

XINHUA XI LU

XINHUA DONG LU

Baitula Mosque

N

0   500
metres

▼ 4

By rail Yining was connected to the rest of China by rail in 2010; the station is 6km northwest of the city centre. Bus routes #4 and #401 run out there from Sidalin Lu. Tickets can be purchased from the office at 89 Sidalin Xi Jie (Mon–Fri 9.30am–5.30pm) – you'll need to buy sleeper tickets at least two days before you travel, as everything gets booked up quickly. Note that trains from Ürümqi to Kazakhstan go via Alashankou, 300km away from Yining, and not via Horgos.
Destinations Ürümqi (5 daily; 11hr 45min).

By bus The bus station is in the northwest of the city, well concealed on Jiefang Lu – bus #1 comes out here from the Xinhua Bookshop on Sidalin Lu. Buses from the station serve destinations across Xinjiang, as well as daily buses to Almaty in Kazakhstan (12hr; US$30; get your visa in Ürümqi). The road south to Kuqa has been closed for years following a tunnel collapse in the middle of the route, but was about to reopen at the time of writing.
Destinations Almaty (Kazakhstan; 12hr); Ürümqi (12hr).

ACCOMMODATION

Accommodation in Yining is tightly restricted – unless a hotel has a permit to host foreign guests, you'll be turned away at the door.

Hourglass Youth Hostel 小时光青年旅舍, xiǎoshíguāng qīngnián lǔshè. 158 Yilihe Lu ☏ 0999 8330977. A lovely, new hostel with nice dorms and a sunny common area upstairs. Laundry, wi-fi and bike rental available – the only downside is the out-of-the-way location, down an obscure alley well south of town. Dorm beds ¥35, rooms ¥120
Ili Hotel 伊犁宾馆, yīlí bīnguǎn. 8 Yingbin Lu ☏ 0999 8023126. An old-fashioned place set in huge leafy grounds, with a number of buildings offering varying degrees of comfort and different prices – no. 4 has respectable, if small, doubles with bath. Bus #9 from

People's Park stops right outside. Rates include breakfast and broadband. ¥288
★ **Yilite** 伊力特大酒店, yīlìtè dàjiǔdiàn. Northeast corner of Qingnian Park ☏ 0999 7829666. A range of smart, sizeable rooms at reasonable prices at this straightforward place, with friendly staff. Breakfast and broadband included. ¥198
Youdian 邮电宾馆, yóudiàn bīnguǎn. Jiefang Lu ☏ 0999 8223844. Mid-range doubles in a standard Chinese-style hotel, slightly aged and not great value, but the location is convenient for the bus station. ¥238

EATING AND DRINKING

Street food is particularly good in Yining, although some of the best markets have fallen victim to the city's modernisation. One of the liveliest surviving street eating spots is outside the Baitula Mosque on Jiefang Nan Lu – *naan*, kebabs, iced yogurt and excellent, locally made *kurut* (hard, dry little cheeses) are on sale here each evening.

Tianming 天明餐厅, tiānmíng cāntīng. Opposite the bus station, under the Baodi Hotel ☏ 0999 8131987. This basement restaurant is where Yining's bus drivers come to eat – good fried dishes are served over rice and noodles – a whole *dapanji* will set you back ¥60, but noodles start at a more reasonable ¥15. Daily 10am–midnight.
Wenzhou 温州酒店 wēnzhōu jiǔdiàn. Inside the Wenzhou Hotel on Jiefang Lu ☏ 0999 8217888. On the first floor of the *Wenzhou Hotel*, this restaurant looks much

fancier than it really is. Good Sichuanese and Hunanese standards are served up for very reasonable prices (¥20 a dish) – order from the enormous picture menu covering one wall. Daily 11am–10pm.
Zixiangge Coffee Club 紫香阁, zǐxiānggé. Inside the grounds of the Ili Hotel ☏ 0999 8039388. This rather swish coffee house also serves up decent pizza (¥48) and pricey steaks. It's not cheap, but is a pleasant place to sit and drink of an evening. Mon 2pm–4am, Tues–Sun 11am–4am.

Huiyuan

惠远, huìyuǎn • combined trip from Yining about ¥350 by taxi or through travel agency

HUIYUAN, 30km west of Yining, is a small but historic town with a three-storey **drum tower** (鼓楼, gǔlóu; ¥10) dating from the nineteenth century. Another 20km north of here is the pretty Persian-style tomb of fourteenth-century Muslim leader **Telug Timur** (吐虎鲁克铁木尔墓, tǔhǔ lǔkè tiěmù'ěr mù; ¥10), located just outside the small town of **Qingshuihe** (清水河, qīngshuǐhé). You can climb a staircase to the upper floor and even onto the roof to see the view.

Sayram Lake

赛里木湖, sàilǐmù hú • buses between Yining and Ürümqi can drop you off, or take a local bus to Bole (博乐, bólè) and get off at the lake, shared taxi from Yining ¥150 • ¥60 for access to western shore

About 120km north of Yining on the road to Ürümqi, **Sayram Lake** occupies a fantastic

13

location between mountains and grassy banks. Over 20km across, more than 2000m above sea level and decidedly chilly for most of the year, Sayram is a great place to escape the urban hustle. Tourism here is still at a pioneering stage – although it's becoming very popular with domestic visitors – with accommodation and food provided by Kazakhs or Mongols and their **yurts**. The road follows the southeast shore, and it is here that tourist facilities are concentrated. An entry fee is payable for access to the quieter western shore – it's not yet possible to drive right around the lake. Every year on July 13–15, thousands of nomads congregate here for traditional games and entertainment.

Horgos border crossing

霍尔斯口岸, huòguǒsī kǒu'àn • bus from Yining Bus Station ¥20 • shared taxi ¥30

About 100km west of Yining is the Horgos **border crossing into Kazakhstan**. While it's not a major destination in itself (unless you're Kazakhstan-bound), the little border town of **Horgos** is an interesting place to look around, home to a thoroughly bizarre shopping mall full of imported goods – from Russian chocolate and cigarettes to stuffed wolves.

The Northern Silk Road

Tracing a vague southern parallel to the **Tian Shan** range, the road from Dunhuang in western Gansu to Turpan covers some of the harshest terrain in all of China – little water ever reaches this area of scorching depressions, which was dreaded by the Silk Road traders as one of the most hazardous sections of the entire cross-Asia trip.

The first major city you'll hit on crossing from Gansu is **Hami**, though most visitors skip this and head straight to **Turpan**, famed for its grapes and intense summer heat – despite which it can be one of the most relaxing and enjoyable places in all China. The route then skirts along the Tarim Basin to the wealthy but dull town of **Korla**, but it is **Kuqa**, just beyond, which is more deserving of a stopover, thanks to its traditional feel and the Silk Road relics in the surrounding deserts. There's then a long journey to Kashgar, via Aksu – the scene of a major terrorist bombing in 2010.

The **road** is in fairly good condition all the way, though given the vast distances involved, it makes more sense to travel by **train**. Note that east of Turpan (itself rather far from its attendant station) there are only a couple of services per day in either direction.

Hami

哈密, hāmì

The small town of **HAMI** is often overlooked, located as it is between better-known Dunhuang and Turpan. While it's not northwest China's most thrilling destination, the town itself is pleasant and relaxed, with plenty of good food, a clutch of interesting sights and arguably the most famous **melons** in the world.

Brief history

Known to the Uyghurs as Kumul, Hami's fertile oasis was tussled over for centuries, as Chinese and Turkic rulers invaded in search of ways to keep their armies fed and watered – the region was already famous for its fruit and wine by the Han dynasty. Hami has hosted two of China's most famous travellers: the monk Xuanzang (see p.830), who stopped here in 644 to recover after a near fatal crossing of the Taklamakan Desert on his way back to Chang'an; and Marco Polo, resting on his way to the court of Kublai Khan. Much to his delight, Polo discovered a particularly hospitable local custom, where a host would share his wife with guests for the duration of their stay.

Between the seventeenth century and 1930, Hami was nominally ruled by the Muslim **Hami kings**, a family of local chiefs elevated to the rank of kings by a grateful Qing emperor after they helped put down a local rebellion. Their initial allegiance to the Qing dynasty eventually dissolved when they were swept up in the Muslim rebellions that swept across Xinjiang in the nineteenth and early twentieth centuries.

13

Tombs of the Hami Kings

哈密回王墓, hāmì huíwáng mù • Daily, summer 9am–8pm, winter 10am–7pm • ¥40 • bus #10 from Dashizi stops outside, ¥1

Next to the bus station in the south of town are the **Tombs of the Hami Kings**, a group of attractive mausoleums built in different styles (one still clad in its original blue tiles), set in a leafy park. Particularly attractive is the **Id Kah Mosque** inside the complex, with Quranic verses painted on the walls, swallows nesting in the rafters and 108 red pillars holding up the roof. The building was built by the first Hami King in the early eighteenth century and expanded by his successors.

Museum of Muqam

哈密木卡姆传承中心, hāmì mùkǎmǔ chuánchéng zhōngxīn • Daily, summer 9.00am–1pm & 4–7pm • museum ¥15, or ¥40 including performance • bus #10 from Dashizi (¥1) stops outside

Across the road from the tombs, the run-of-the-mill Hami Museum is best skipped in favour of the adjacent **Museum of Muqam**. This newly developed complex (for more on this Uyghur musical style, see box on p.844). This newly developed complex displays a wide range of traditional instruments, both antique and new, and there are regular thirty-minute performances of music and dancing – this might be your only opportunity to see *muqam* performed live.

ARRIVAL AND DEPARTURE
HAMI

By train At the time of writing Hami's main train station was undergoing expansion and all passenger services had moved to the temporary south train station (哈密南火车站 hāmì nán huǒchēzhàn), 8km southeast of the city centre – a taxi out here ought to cost ¥15. Hami is on the main Lanzhou–Ürümqi line, and is well served by trains. Tickets are available from the station ticket office (daily 7.30am–9pm) or from the ticket booth inside the China Mobile store at 15 Zhongshan Bei Li (daily 8.30am–9pm). It is only possible to buy tickets for same-day travel at the station – better to buy sleeper tickets in advance in town.

Destinations Daheyan (regular; 4hr 15min–7hr 30min); Jiayuguan (regular; 6hr 30min–10hr 30min); Korla (2 daily; 15hr 15min); Lanzhou (13 daily; 14hr 30min–24hr); Ürümqi (regular; 6hr 15min–9hr 45min).

By bus Hami's bus station (哈密南郊客运站 hāmì nánjiāo kèyùnzhàn) is 2km southwest of Dashizi on Zhongshan Bei Lu; bus #10 (¥1) runs along this route. The ticket office is open daily 8am–8pm, and tickets are easy to get hold of.

Destinations Dunhuang (7hr); Turpan (7hr); Ürümqi (10hr).

ACCOMMODATION

Hami Hotel 哈密宾馆, hāmì bīnguǎn. 4 Yingbin Lu ☏ 0902 2233140. A stalwart of Hami's tourism industry, this was the first hotel in town. Rooms range from shabby, elderly rooms in building 1 to fancy modern doubles with wi-fi in building 6. Rates include a buffet breakfast. Older doubles **¥200**, newer doubles **¥558**

EATING AND DRINKING

Hami's lively restaurant scene is focussed on Zhongshan Bei Lu between Xiaoshizi and Dashizi (i.e. the junctions with Wenhua Lu and Jiefang Lu). Each evening stalls selling fragrant lamb kebabs, *pilau* and chilled *kvass* (a sweet, lightly fermented beverage) set up along the street.

Avzal In the middle of Dashizi at the southern end of Zhongshan Bei Lu. This pavement café near the night market makes a brilliant place to people-watch. Come here to enjoy their creamy ice cream and a frosty glass of home-made *kvass* (¥5) – owner Shukrat has been brewing his own here for the past seventeen years. Daily noon–midnight.

Shandong Jiaozi 山东饺子馆, shāndōng jiǎoziguǎn. On the southeast corner of Xiaoshizi. Serving up traditional northern Chinese dishes and specializing in dumplings, fill up here on pork and cabbage dumplings (¥0.7 each – around 15 makes a meal), washed down with a bowl of broth, served here instead of tea. Daily 9.30am–11pm.

DIRECTORY

Banks and exchange There's a branch of Bank of China at 11 Zhongshan Bei Lu (Mon–Fri, 9am–12.40pm & 4–7pm); the ATMs accept credit cards and you can exchange cash.

Mail The post office is at the northern end of Zhongshan Bei Lu (Mon–Fri, 9.30am–7.30pm), on the same side as the Bank of China.

13

Turpan

吐鲁番, tǔlǔfān

The small oasis town of **TURPAN** is an absolute must-see if you're in Xinjiang. A former Silk Road outpost, it has long been a favourite with adventurous travellers. The town is surrounded by a number of fascinating historical sites – from **ruined cities** to **Buddhist caves**, testimony to its historical importance as a Silk Road stopover.

Turpan is located in a depression 80m below sea level, which accounts for its extreme climate – above 40°C in summer and well below freezing in winter. In summer the **dry heat** is so soporific that, despite the preponderance of places to explore, you may be hard-pushed to do anything but sleep or sip cool drinks under shady grapevines with the locals – this laidback vibe is another reason behind Turpan's enduring popularity.

Surprisingly, despite its bone-dry surroundings, Turpan is an agricultural centre of note, famed across China for its **grapes**. Today, virtually every household in the town has a hand in the business, both in cultivating the vine, and in drying the grapes at the end of the season (a **Grape Festival** is held at the end of August).

Note that if you come out of season (Nov–March), Turpan is cold and uninspiring, with the vines cut back and most businesses closed – although the sights remain interesting, and at these times are almost devoid of other tourists.

Brief history

Turpan is a largely **Uyghur-populated** area and, in Chinese terms, an obscure backwater, but it has not always been so. As early as the Han dynasty, the oasis was a crucial point along the Northern Silk Road, and the cities of **Jiaohe**, and later **Gaochang** (both of whose ruins can be visited from Turpan), were important and wealthy centres of power. On his way to India, Xuanzang spent more time than he had planned here, when the king virtually kidnapped him in order to have him preach to his subjects. This same king later turned his hand to robbing Silk Road traffic, and had his kingdom annexed by China in 640 as a result. From the ninth to the thirteenth century, a rich intellectual and artistic culture developed in Gaochang and it was not until the fourteenth century that the Uyghurs of the Turpan region converted to Islam.

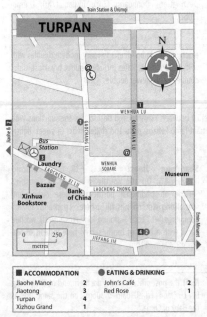

The town centre

Turpan's downtown doesn't amount to much, with most of the services near the bus station on Laocheng Lu; pedestrianized Qingnian Lu is protected from the baking summer sun by vine trellises. There is a **museum** on Laocheng Dong Lu (吐鲁番博物馆, tǔlǔfān bówùguǎn; daily 10.30am–6.30pm; free), with a smallish collection of dinosaur fossils, silk fragments, tools, manuscripts and preserved corpses recovered from the nearby Silk Road sites. Other than this, the **bazaars** off Laocheng Lu, almost opposite the bus station, are worth a casual look, though they are not comparable to anything in Kashgar. You'll find knives, clothes, hats and boots on sale, while the most distinctively local products include delicious sweet raisins, as well as walnuts and almonds.

■ **ACCOMMODATION**

Jiaohe Manor	2
Jiaotong	3
Turpan	4
Xizhou Grand	1

● **EATING & DRINKING**

John's Café	2
Red Rose	1

DONKEY CART RIDES

One of the nicest ways to spend an evening after the heat of the day has passed is to **hire a donkey cart** and take a tour of the countryside south of town, a world of dusty tracks, vineyards, wheat fields, shady poplars, running streams and incredibly friendly people. You are unlikely to encounter many more tranquil rural settings than this. Donkey-cart drivers gather outside the *Turpan* hotel; two or three people will pay around ¥15 each for a tour lasting an hour or more.

ARRIVAL AND DEPARTURE

TURPAN

By train Turpan's train station is actually located 55km away at Daheyan (大河沿, dàhéyán), at least an hour from town by bus (summer 8am–11pm, winter 9am–8pm; ¥10). If you arrive after the buses have stopped, you can take advantage of Daheyan's cheap hotels, or put on your bargaining hat and seek out a taxi. Advance train tickets can be purchased in Turpan from the booth at 405 Laocheng Lu (daily, 9.30am–7pm).

Destinations Jiayuguan (regular; 14hr); Korla (7 daily;

10hr 45min); Lanzhou (13 daily; 19hr–26hr 30min); Ürümqi (regular; 2hr 30min).

By bus Turpan's bus station is on Laocheng Lu, with buses every 20min to Ürümqi, as well as less regular services to major destinations in Xinjiang and Dunhuang in Gansu. The ticket office is open daily 6.30am–8.30pm, and it's best to buy tickets a day in advance.

Destinations Dunhuang (12hr); Hami (6hr); Khotan (20hr); Korla (10hr); Ürümqi (3hr).

GETTING AROUND

By bicycle and car *John's Information Cafe* rents bikes for ¥5/hr, and can arrange a car and driver for ¥300/day.

INFORMATION

Travel agents Both CITS, on the first floor of the *Jiaotong Hotel* (☎0995 8535809), and *John's Information Café* (☖johncafe.net) at the *Turpan* hotel, can help out with transport bookings for around ¥20 commission (including flights out of Ürümqi), as well as local tours. Friendly, English-speaking driver and guide Tahir Tomur (☎1502 6261388), a local agent for Kashgar's Old Road Tours (see p.841), is also able to arrange tours to local sights.

ACCOMMODATION

Turpan has a good range of accommodation and most places have air conditioning – just make sure that yours is working when you check in.

Jiaohe Manor 交河庄园酒店, jiāohé zhuāngyuán jiǔdiàn. 9 Jiaohe Dado, 2km west of the centre of town ☎0995 7685999. Built in the style of an old fort, this venture lies right in the heart of the old Uyghur district and all its vineyards. Rooms are as neat as you would expect for this price, with big reductions out of season. Includes breakfast. **¥300**

Jiaotong 交通宾馆, jiāotōng bīnguǎn. 230 Laocheng Xi Lu, at the bus station ☎0995 6258666. Recently nicely refurbished, this bus station hotel offers comfortable and decently priced rooms, including breakfast and broadband internet. **¥208**

★ **Turpan** 吐鲁番宾馆, tǔlǔfān bīnguǎn. Qingnian Nan Lu ☎0995 8568888. This hotel basically mops up almost all foreign visitors, and for good reason: rooms are cheap and perfectly adequate, they've got dorm beds (although their subterranean rooms are a little ragged and smelly), and there's a shady branch of *John's Café* out back. Dorms **¥50**, rooms **¥240**

Xizhou Grand 西州大酒店, xīzhōu dàjiǔdiàn. 882 Qingnian Lu ☎0995 8554000. The plushest place in the town centre, with an unmistakeable, bulging brown front. Very comfortable, with clean rooms, good beds and pleasant staff. **¥280**

EATING AND DRINKING

The most atmospheric places to eat are the vine-covered restaurants lining pedestrianized Qingnian Lu, as there's little in the way of street eats in Turpan. Make sure to try some of Turpan's delicious fruit, particularly the grapes, if you're here in season.

John's Café At the rear of the Turpan Hotel ☖johncafe .net. This backpacker favourite run by a friendly couple is set in a vine-covered courtyard, and makes a lovely place to escape the afternoon heat. Food is average, with the Chinese dishes of a higher standard than the Western ones.

Daily 7.30am–11pm.

Red Rose 红玫瑰美食, hóng méiguī měishí. 551 Gaochang Road ☎0995 8522999. The underground dining room of this Uyghur restaurant is packed at lunchtimes, quieter in the evenings. Enjoy a cup of rose-scented tea on the house, and slurp up some of the best *laghman* (¥18) in town. Other dishes are good, but can be on the expensive side. Daily 10.30am–10pm.

DIRECTORY

Banks and exchange There's a Bank of China (Mon–Fri; 9.30am–12.30pm & 4.30–7pm) with ATMs accepting credit cards on Laocheng Xi Lu – you can change travellers' cheques here as well.

Laundry There's a laundry (佳力干洗店, jiālì gānxǐ diàn jiāohé) near the bazaar on Laocheng Xi Lu, which does a next-day service and charges per item.
Post office Laocheng Xi Lu (Mon–Fri 9.30am–8pm).

Around Turpan

Nearly all visitors to Turpan end up taking the customary **tour** of the historical and natural sights outside town. These are quite fun, as much for the chance to get out into the desert as for the sights in themselves, which usually include the two ancient cities of **Jiaohe** and **Gaochang**, the **Emin Minaret**, the **Karez irrigation site**, the **Bezeklik Caves** and **Astana Graves**. Only Jiaohe is indisputably worth the cost – and, in fact, you can get good views of Gaochang and the Emin Minaret without actually entering the sites. Entry fees are typically not included in tour packages.

The Emin Minaret is within **cycling** distance, and if you're a healthy sort then Jiaohe will be too. For sights further afield, you'll have to arrange a **car** or **minibus**, with prices

---

XUANZANG AND THE JOURNEY TO THE WEST

Goods were not the only things to travel along the Silk Road; it was along this route that **Buddhism** first arrived in China at some point in the first century AD. Cities on the Silk Road became bastions of the religion (hence their abandonment and desecration following the introduction of Islam after 1000), and from early on, Chinese pilgrims visited India and brought back a varied bag of Buddhist teachings. The most famous was the Tang-dynasty monk **Xuanzang**, who undertook a seventeen-year pilgrimage from the then capital, Chang'an (Xi'an), to India.

Born in 602, Xuanzang was schooled in Mahayana Buddhism but became confused by its contradictory texts, and in 629 decided to visit India and study Buddhism at its source. He went without official permission, narrowly avoiding arrest in western Gansu; Turpan's king detained him for a month to hear him preach but eventually provided a large retinue, money and passports for safe passage through other kingdoms. Xuanzang crossed the Tian Shan into modern Kyrgyzstan, where his religious knowledge greatly impressed the Khan of the Western Turks, before he continued, via the great central Asian city of **Samarkand**, through modern-day Afghanistan, over the Hindu Kush and into **India**, arriving about a year after he set out.

Xuanzang spent fifteen years in India visiting holy sites, studying Buddhism in its major and esoteric forms, lecturing, and debating with famous teachers. If he hoped to find ultimate clarity he was probably disappointed, as the interpretation of Buddhist lore in India was even more varied than in China. However, he amassed a vast collection of Buddhist statues, relics and **texts**, and in 644 decided that it was his responsibility to return to China with this trove of knowledge. The journey back via Kashgar took Xuanzang another year, not counting eight months spent at Khotan, waiting for imperial permission to re-enter China, but he arrived at Chang'an in 645 to find tens of thousands of spectators crowding the roads: the emperor became his patron, and he spent the last twenty years of his life translating part of his collection of Buddhist texts.

Xuanzang wrote an autobiography, but highly coloured accounts of his travels also passed into folklore, becoming the subject of plays and the sixteenth-century novel *Journey to the West*. In it, Xuanzang is depicted as terminally naïve, hopelessly dismayed by the various disasters that beset him. Fortunately, he's aided by the Bodhisattva of Compassion, **Guanyin**, who sends him spirits to protect him in his quest: the vague character of **Sandy**; the greedy and lecherous **Pigsy**; and **Sun Wu Kong**, the brilliant Monkey King. A good abridgement in English is Arthur Waley's *Monkey* (see on p.956).

13

dependent upon exactly what you wish to see. Be aware that, however you travel, you'll be in blistering heat for the whole of the day, so sun cream, a hat, water bottle and sunglasses are essential.

The Emin Minaret

苏公塔, sūgōng tǎ · Daily dawn to dusk · ¥30

You can walk to the eighteenth-century **Emin Minaret**, 2km southeast of Turpan, by following Jiefang Jie east out of town for about thirty minutes. The minaret is built in a very simple style – slightly bulging and potbellied – and erected from sun-dried bricks arranged in differing patterns. The tower tapers its way 40m skyward to a rounded tip, adjoining a mosque with a splendidly intricate latticework ceiling. You can see the complex without entering the site; entry allows an ascent of the tower to gain good views over the green oasis in the foreground and the distant snowy Tian Shan beyond.

Jiaohe

交河, jiāohé · Daily dawn to dusk · ¥40 · bilingual booklet "The Ruins of Jiaohe" (¥10) for sale on site

About 11km west of Turpan, and occupying a spectacular defensive setting on top of a 2km-long, steep-sided plateau carved out by the two halves of a forking river, the ruined city of **Jiaohe** is just about within cycling range on a hot day. Although for large parts of its history Jiaohe was under the control of Gaochang (see opposite), it became the regional administrative centre during the eighth century.

What sets Jiaohe apart from all other ruined cities along the Silk Road is that although most of the buildings comprise little more than crumbling, windswept mud walls, so many survive, and of such a variety – gates, temples, public buildings, graveyards and ordinary dwellings – that Jiaohe's **street plan** is still evident; there's a real feeling of how great this city must have been. A **Buddhist monastery** marked the town centre, and its foundations – 50m on each side – can still be seen. Another feature is the presence of ancient **wells** still containing water. Make sure you walk to the far end of the site, where the base of a former **tower**, dated to around 360 AD, overlooks the river.

Karez

坎儿井, kǎn'ér jǐng · Daily dawn to dusk · ¥40

Minibus drivers returning from Jiaohe usually drop you off at a dolled-up **Karez irrigation site**, an intrinsically interesting place unfortunately turned into an ethnic theme park, complete with regular Uyghur dance shows, presumably to justify the entry fee. Karez irrigation taps natural underground channels carrying water from the source – in this case glaciers at the base of the Tian Shan – to the point of use. Strategically dug wells then bring water to small surface channels that run around the streets of the town. From modern Xinjiang as far as Iran, many ancient Silk Road cities relied on this system, and Karez systems are still in use throughout Xinjiang – there are plenty of opportunities to see them for free on the way to Kashgar.

The Bezeklik Caves

柏孜克里克石窟, bózīkèlǐkè shíkū · Daily dawn to dusk · ¥30 · camel rides from here along the Flaming Mountains ¥80

The **Bezeklik Caves**, in a valley among the Flaming Mountains some 50km northeast of

---

THE FLAMING MOUNTAINS

Along the way to the Bezeklik Caves and other destinations northeast of Turpan, you'll pass the **Flaming Mountains**, made famous in the sixteenth-century Chinese novel *Journey to the West* (see p.956). It's not hard to see why the novel depicts these sandstone mountains as walls of flame, the red sandstone hillsides lined and creviced as though flickering with flame in the heat haze. The plains below are dotted with dozens of small "nodding donkey" **oil wells**, all tapping into Xinjiang's vast reserves.

Turpan, are disappointing, offering mere fragments of the former wealth of Buddhist cave art here, dating back to 640 AD. The location is nonetheless striking, with stark orange dunes behind and a deep river gorge fringed in green below, but most of the murals were cut out and removed to Berlin by Albert Von Le Coq at the beginning of the twentieth century, and the remainder painstakingly defaced by Red Guards during the 1960s. (The Allied bombing of Berlin in World War II subsequently destroyed a number of the murals removed by Le Coq.)

Astana Graves

阿斯塔娜古墓区, āsītǎnà gǔmùqū • Daily dawn to dusk • ¥20

South of the Bezeklik Caves, the **Astana Graves** mark the burial site of the imperial dead of Gaochang from the Tang dynasty. Unfortunately, the graves have had most of their interesting contents removed to museums in Ürümqi and Turpan, and little remains beyond a couple of preserved corpses and some murals.

Gaochang

高昌, gāochāng • Daily dawn to dusk • ¥40 • donkey cart around site ¥20/person

Adjacent to the Astana Graves, the ruins of **Gaochang** are impressive for their huge scale, despite having suffered from the ravages of both Western archeologists and the local population, who for centuries have been carting off bits of the city's 10m-high adobe walls to use as soil for their fields. Walk or take a donkey cart to the centre of the site, which is marked by a large square building, the remains of a monastery. Its outer walls are covered in niches, in each of which a Buddha was originally seated; just a few bare, broken traces of these Buddhas remain, along with their painted haloes. If you have time you can strike off on your own and listen to the hot wind whistling through the mud-brick walls.

Grape Valley

葡萄沟, pútáo gōu • Daily dawn to dusk • ¥60

Some 13km north of Turpan at the western end of the Flaming Mountains, **Grape Valley** makes a pleasant refuge in the middle of a stark desert, covered in shady trellises bulging with fruit (which you have to pay for if you want to eat). It's best between mid-July and September – at other times, in fact, the scenery here is not much different from that of downtown Turpan – and your ticket includes a Uyghur dance performance.

Aiding Lake

艾丁湖, àidīng hú • ¥10 • return 2hr taxi trip along a rough road about ¥180

About 50km south of Turpan, the bleak but dramatic **Aiding Lake** is located in a natural depression 154m below sea level, making this the second-lowest lake in the world after the Dead Sea. You won't actually see any water here except in spring – the rest of the year the lake is a flat plain of dried mineral deposits. The land around the lake is crusted with salt and dotted with bright yellow-green pools of saturated water that feels like oil on the skin. Locals rub it over themselves enthusiastically, claiming that it's good for you. The area around the lake is very muddy; don't take your best shoes.

Korla

库尔勒, kù'ěrlè

There's been a settlement at **KORLA** since the Tang dynasty, and today the city is capital of the **Bayangol Mongol Autonomous Prefecture**, a vast region that encompasses the arid eastern side of the Taklamakan as well as better-watered areas around the city itself. Despite all this, Mongols are not much in evidence, and Korla functions mostly as a base for companies tapping into the Taklamakan's **oil reserves**. It's inescapable as a transport nexus: the rail line and roads from Ürümqi and Turpan converge here; the

13

Northern Silk Road heads due west; and the Southern Silk Road snakes south to Charkhlik. The town is also a terminus for buses shortcutting the Southern Silk Road by crossing diagonally southwest across the Taklamakan to Niya and Khotan.

ARRIVAL AND DEPARTURE
KORLA

By train Korla's east train station (库尔勒火车东站, jiālì gānxǐdiàn) is 5km east of town – about ¥10 by taxi from the bus station or ¥1 on bus #26 from the bus station on Beishan Lu. The ticket office opposite the station is open daily 8.30am–11pm, and there's another ticket booth (daily 9.30am–7pm) in the Tangming Building at 37 Jiaotong Lu in the centre of town.

Destinations Daheyan (6 daily; 9hr–12hr 30min); Kashgar (3 daily; 14hr–17hr 45min); Kuqa (5 daily; 5hr); Ürümqi (4 daily; 15hr).

By bus Korla's main bus station (州客运中心, zhōu kèyùn zhōngxīn) is on Beishan Lu. There are two stations inside the complex; one for coaches and one for shared taxis – you may well be approached by drivers looking for passengers to fill up their cars to nearby destinations – it's best to use the coaches for anywhere further afield.

Destinations Charkhlik (8hr); Golmud (20hr); Kashgar (18hr); Khotan (13hr); Kuqa (4hr); Turpan (6hr); Ürümqi (6hr).

ACCOMMODATION

Although Korla has an excellent bus station hotel, there are no foreigner-friendly options around the train station – you'll need to stay in the town centre.

Communication Hotel 交通宾馆, jiāotōng bīnguǎn. Beishan Lu, inside the bus station ☏ 0996 2078876. One of Xinjiang's better bus station hotels, this hotel has cramped but very clean rooms and friendly staff, as well as broadband. **¥120**

Kangcheng Jianguo 康城建国国际酒店,

kāngchéng jiànguó guójì jiǔdiàn. 618 Jiaotong Dong Lu ☏ 0996 2275076, ⊛ kcjghotel.com. This rather fancy hotel has large, plush rooms, several in-house restaurants and even a cigar lounge, with occasional discounts. Breakfast included. **¥690**

EATING AND DRINKING

There's little in the way of local cuisine in Korla, although you'll find any number of small restaurants selling dumplings from Hangzhou, snacks from Chengdu and noodles from Shanxi – testament to the city's many migrants. Both the train station and bus station are surrounded with grotty little canteens – for something more substantial, head down to Jiaotong Lu, the main road through downtown Korla, where the proper restaurants are concentrated. There's a *KFC* and *Dico's* at the Tianbai Shopping Centre on Jiaotong Dong Lu.

Kuqa
库车, kùchē

Roughly halfway on the 1500km journey from Ürümqi to Kashgar, **KUQA** was once a cosmopolitan town full of Silk Road traders and travellers. It was described as the "land of jewels" in Xuanzang's journal, and the fourth-century linguist and scholar **Kumarajiva**, one of the most famous of all Chinese Buddhists, came from here. Having travelled to Kashmir for his education, he later returned to China as a teacher and translator of Buddhist documents from Sanskrit into Chinese. It was in large measure thanks to him that Buddhism came to be so widely understood in China, and by the early Tang, Kuqa was a major centre for the religion, with giant monasteries and its own Indo-European language. With the arrival of Islam in the ninth century, however, this era drew to a close, and today only a few traces of Kuqa's ancient history remain. There's little evidence of past wealth today – the small city is dusty and poor – but there is at least a substantial and intrinsically interesting Uyghur old town.

The New City

The **New City**, largely Han-populated, contains all the facilities you'll need and a few sights of marginal interest. One is the remains of the ruined city of **Qiuci** (龟兹古城, qiūcí gǔchéng gǔchéng); the overgrown rammed-earth walls lie on the edge of the new town, 1km west of Wenhua Square along Wenhua Xi Lu. The **Tomb of Molena Ashidinhan**

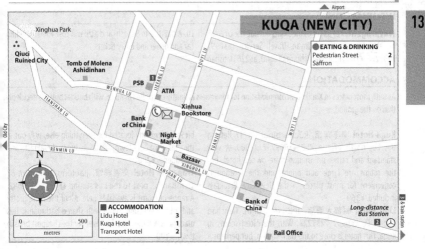

(莫拉纳俄仕丁坟, mòlānà'é shídīng fén), also on Wenhua Xi Lu, is a simple wooden shrine built in 1867 in honour of an Arab missionary who visited here in the fourteenth century. There's also a daily **bazaar** along pedestrianized Xinghua Lu, which houses Xinjiang's second-largest **goldsmiths' quarters** after Kashgar.

The Old City

古城, gǔchéng · bus route #1 from the bus station along Renmin Lu to the bridge across the river into the Old City

The largely Uyghur **Old City** is peppered with mosques and bazaars and has a Central Asian atmosphere. Right by the bridge over the Kuqa River, the **bazaar** is the main venue for the highly enjoyable **Sunday market**. Here, the Uyghur population are out in force, buying and selling leather jackets, carpets, knives, wooden boxes, goats and donkeys; livestock are traded on the riverbanks below.

Beyond the bridge, you can soon lose yourself in the labyrinth of narrow streets and adobe houses. Right in the heart of this, approximately fifteen minutes northwest of the bridge, is the **Kuqa Mosque** (清真大寺, qīngzhēn dàsì; ¥15; daily 9.30am–8pm), built in 1923. Neat and compact, with an attractive green-tiled dome, this mosque is of wholly arabesque design, displaying none of the Chinese characteristics of mosques in more eastern parts of the country. Beyond the mosque, on Linji Lu, the town **museum** (库车博物馆, kùchē bówùguǎn; daily 9.30am–7.30pm; free) houses interesting collections of archeological relics. Also on Linji Lu, you can see fragments of the original **town wall**.

ARRIVAL AND DEPARTURE   KUQA

By air Kuqa's new airport (库车机场, kùchē jīchǎng) is 20km from the new town. A taxi will set you back ¥30, while the airport bus (¥10) runs between the *International Hotel* at 337 Tianshan Lu and the airport terminal. Plane tickets can be purchased from the Kuqa Yinyan Travel Service (see p.836).
Destinations Ürümqi (4 daily; 1hr).

By train The train station (库车火车站, kùchē huǒchēzhàn) is 5km southeast of the New City (¥10 in a taxi or ¥1 in the #6 and #8 buses from Tianshan Lu). Tickets can be purchased from the advance ticket booth in town (59 Wuyi Nan Lu, 9.30am–1pm & 3–7pm), from the station itself (6am–5.30pm & 6–8pm).

Destinations Kashgar (3 daily; 12hr 30min); Ürümqi (3 daily; 16–20hr).

By bus Kuqa's bus station (库车客运中心, kùchē kèyùn zhōngxīn) is in the far southeast of the New City. Given the distances involved, you'd be mad to want to take a bus any further than Aksu to the west or Korla to the east, though the reopening of the tough road to Yining brings that city within reach –the occasional buses in that direction stop overnight in Xinyuan. To travel west to Kashgar, you'll need to head to Aksu first.
Destinations Aksu (3hr 30min); Khotan (9hr); Korla (4hr); Ürümqi (9hr); Yining (24hr).

13

INFORMATION

Travel agents For a tour of the sights outside the city, call on the friendly Kuqa Yinyan Travel Service (☎0997 7233228, ✉qiuci_lingyan@hotmail.com), at 226 Tianshan Lu. A day-trip to Subashi and Kizil will cost ¥500 including car and driver and entry tickets.

ACCOMMODATION

As with most places in Xinjiang, accommodation for foreigners is tightly controlled in Kuqa, with budget options decidedly thin on the ground.

Kuqa Hotel 库车宾馆, kùchē bīnguǎn. 17 Jiefang Bei Lu, north of the PSB ☎0997 7123500. A very standard and rather uninspiring state-owned hotel, but the rooms are large and bright and the location is convenient for most places in the New City. Breakfast included. ¥360

Lidu Hotel 丽都大酒店, lìdū dàjiǔdiàn. Tianshan Zhong Lu ☎0997 7233222. With the nicest rooms in Kuqa, this hotel is close to the train station, but perhaps a bit inconveniently located for everything else, way out in the far east of town. Rate includes breakfast and broadband. ¥288

Transport Hotel 交通宾馆, jiāotōng bīnguǎn. 87 Tianshan Lu, next to the bus station ☎0997 7122682. A range of rooms is available here. All of them are grotty and a bit depressing, some with shared bathrooms. This place does win the prize, however, for the cheapest beds in town. ¥100

EATING AND DRINKING

In addition to the places below, there are numerous food stands around the Youyi Lu-Xinghua Lu intersection where you can tuck into delicious baked *kaobao*, *samsa*, bowls of *laghman* and Uyghur tea with great rough sticks and leaves floating in the cup. One thing definitely worth trying is the giant *naan* bread, served, unlike elsewhere in Xinjiang, thin and crispy and covered with onion, sesame and carrot.

Pedestrian Street 步行街, bùxíngjiē. The eastern end of Xinghua Lu. The epicentre of Kuqa's restaurant scene, Pedestrian Street is a bustling strip of Chinese and Muslim restaurants. Busiest on summer evenings, this is a fun place to sit out, drink beer and eat a wide range of different regional cuisines – plus most places here are excellent value. Daily noon–late.

Saffron 再帕尔美食, zàipàěr měishí. Behind the Ihlas supermarket, just east of the southern end of Jiefang Lu in the New City ☎0997 7133088. Decorated in classic Xinjiang style – lots of dark wood and atmosphere – this place serves Uyghur dishes, including a delicious *pilau* with pomegranate (¥18) and a variety of vegetable and meat dishes. No Chinese or English spoken, but thankfully there's a picture menu. Daily 9am–10pm.

DIRECTORY

Banks and exchange The Bank of China (Mon–Fri 10am–1.30pm & 4–6.30pm) is on Renmin Lu with ATMs that accept credit cards.

Post office On Wenhua Lu (Mon–Fri 10am–6.30pm).

Kizil Thousand Buddha Caves

克孜尔千佛洞, kèzī'ěr qiānfódòng • Daily during daylight • ¥55 • ¥400 by taxi or tour from Kuqa

Around 75km northwest of Kuqa, the **Kizil Thousand Buddha Caves** were once a Central Asian treasure-trove, a mixture of Hellenistic, Indian and Persian styles with not even a suggestion of Chinese influence. Sadly, the caves suffered the ravages of the German archeologist and art thief **Albert Von Le Coq** who, at the beginning of the twentieth century, cut out and carried away many of the best frescoes. However, it is still an intriguing place to visit and even older than the more extensive Mogao Caves in Gansu. Your ticket covers eight caves but you can pay extra to be guided round others, including no. 38, the "cave of musicians" – which has Bodhisattvas playing musical instruments on the ceiling.

Subashi

苏巴什佛寺遗址, sūbāshí fósì yízhǐ • Daily during daylight • ¥25 • ¥100 by taxi or tour from Kuqa

Twenty-five kilometres north of Kuqa along a good paved road, the **Subashi Ancient Buddhist Complex**, abandoned in the twelfth century, comprises fairly extensive ruins from east to west, intercepted by a river. Today only the more interesting western parts of the ruins are open to visitors – these contain various pagodas and temples, and the remains of some wall paintings. The entire site looks very atmospheric with the bald, pink and black mountain ranges rising up behind. Along the way there, look for the **irrigation channels** carrying runoff from the mountains to villages.

Kashgar

喀什, kāshí

The remoteness of Uyghur-dominated **KASHGAR** is palpable. Set astride overland routes to Pakistan and Kyrgyzstan, the city is over 4000km from Beijing, with the last thousand kilometres from Ürümqi for the most part uninhabitable desert: indeed, part of the excitement of Kashgar lies in the experience of reaching it. The distinctively Central Asian air to the old city's mosques and markets makes it a visible bastion of old **Chinese Turkestan** – the muezzin's call booms out across the city, and each evening the desert air is scented and blurred by the smoke of roasting lamb.

Increasingly, however, this is a bastion under siege. Han Chinese have relocated here in their thousands, and much of the old town has been ripped up and rebuilt – just a few small areas of the original buildings have been preserved as tourist attractions. The locals are understandably angry: Kashgar is the focal point of **tensions** between the Han and Uyghur peoples, as made painfully clear by the city's ubiquitous **security personnel** – both in uniform and undercover.

Nonetheless, the city remains well worth a visit; its population remains overwhelmingly Muslim, a fact you can hardly fail to notice with the great **Id Kah Mosque** dominating the central square, the Uyghur bazaars and teashops and, above all, the faces of the Turkic people around you. If you can choose a time to be here, aim for the Uyghur Corban **festival** at the end of the Muslim month of Ramadan, which involves activities such as dancing and goat-tussling. Whatever time of year you visit, don't miss Kashgar's **Sunday market**, for which half of Central Asia seems to converge on the city.

Brief history

Kashgar's **strategic position** has determined its history and, although a Chinese military governor was stationed here as early as the Tang dynasty, the region was only ever loosely under imperial control. By the early twentieth century, Kashgar had become a nexus between Chinese, Soviet and British **spheres of influence**, with both foreign powers maintaining consulates here: the British with an eye to their interests across the frontier in India; the Soviets with the intention of absorbing Xinjiang into their Central Asian orbit – the tangled conspiracies of this period are brilliantly evoked in Peter Fleming's *News from Tartary* (see p.953). At the time of Fleming's visit in 1935, Kashgar was effectively run by the Soviets; Kashgar swung back under Chinese control during World War II, and with the break in Sino-Soviet relations in the early 1960s, the Soviet border (and influence) firmly closed.

The old town

Despite the fact that most of the buildings have been reconstructed since 2009, Kashgar's **old town**, north of Renmin Lu, remains the city's focal point for foreign travellers. The main attractions here are the ordinary streets, the bazaars, the restaurants, the teahouses and the people in them. Roads radiate out from **Id Kah Square**, marked by a clock tower and huge mosque, with the main markets in neighbouring lanes; while you're in the area, keep an eye open for a couple of substantial fragments of Kashgar's **old city walls**, most easily viewed south of Seman Lu and west off Yunmulaxia Lu. And don't miss out on the **old consulates** either: the British had theirs behind the *Royal Qinibagh* hotel, while the Russian headquarters survive as a fun restaurant in the courtyard behind the *Seman* hotel.

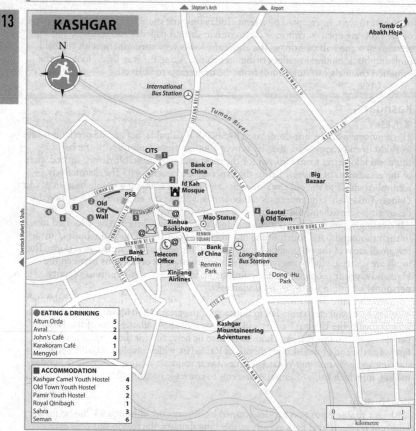

One small area of original buildings in the east of the old town, now known as **Gaotai** (高台民居, gāotái mínjū), charges an **entrance fee** of ¥30 – although you may be able to wander around without paying up.

Id Kah Mosque

艾提尕尔清真寺, àitígǎ'ěr qīngzhēnsì • Sat–Thurs 9am–4pm, Fri 9am–1pm • ¥20

Kashgar's main historical sight is the **Id Kah Mosque**, occupying the western side of Id Kah Square. Originally built in 1442, it has been restored many times, most recently in 1999. It is one of the biggest mosques, and almost certainly the most active, in the country. Although visitors are allowed in, tourists are sometimes shooed away by zealous worshippers – note that visitors of either sex should have their arms and legs fully covered when entering this (or any other) mosque. While admission is curtailed on Fridays, the main Muslim prayer day, it's still worth a look as some ten thousand people crowd the mosque and square; the quietest time, when your presence will cause least disturbance, is probably early to mid-morning on any other day. Inside are pleasant poplar-lined courtyards and rose gardens where worshippers assemble.

The hat, clothes and crockery markets

A small road east of Id Kah Square, parallel to Jiefang Lu, is good for Central Asian **hats**. As well as the green-and-white square-shaped variety so beloved of old Uyghur

TO KYRGYZSTAN AND PAKISTAN

The **international bus station** handles traffic to Sust in Pakistan, as well as two different routes into Kyrgyzstan. Note that you're charged **excess baggage** rates for every kilo over 20kg on international buses.

THE ROAD TO KYRGYZSTAN

The 720km-long road due north from Kashgar via the Torugart Pass to **Bishkek** in **Kyrgyzstan** has been open to Westerners since the 1990s, though this trip is complicated by the fact that foreign travellers are not allowed through the border in either direction on public transport, and must be delivered and met by official guides. While, in theory, the border crossing is open Mon–Fri, 10am–5pm, in practice you need to cross before noon and be prepared for sudden closure of the border post for national holidays, bad weather (the pass lies at 3750m and snow is frequent even in summer) and random political reasons. You'll have to organize the trip though an agent in Kashgar or Bishkek and expect to pay upward of US$200 per car from Kashgar to the border, and US$150 per car for onward transport to Bishkek.

An alternative, and easier, option is to head across the southern **Irkeshtam Pass**, 210km west of Kashgar, by bus (currently Mon and Thurs; US$50), heading on to the southern Kyrgyz city of Osh on a rough road. This route has become popular with **cyclists**; although there are five major 2400m-plus climbs before the border, there are petrol stations about every 40km for water, and towns or villages no more than 65km apart. Note that Osh was the scene of inter-ethnic riots in 2010; check the current situation before heading this way.

Whichever way you take to Kyrgyzstan, check and double-check the **visa requirements** in advance before you rely on getting a visa on arrival; in China, you can do this at the Kyrgyz embassy in Beijing or the consulate in Ürümqi (see p.820).

THE ROAD TO PAKISTAN

The fabled **Karakoram Highway** (see p.848 heads from Xinjiang to Pakistan over the **Khunjerab Pass**. It would be a shame to do this all in one go (see p.848 for places to stop en route), but there are direct buses – in theory every day, in practice whenever there are enough people – from Kashgar to the Pakistani city of **Sust** (¥290). It may make more sense to go to Tashkurgan and take the bus from there, as there are occasional buses from Tashkurgan to Sust and all the Kashgar buses stop in Tashkurgan anyway. Despite the gradient (the pass tops out at 4693m), this route is popular with **bikers** and **cyclists**. Note that the border is only open from May 1 until October (the exact closure date varies), and third-party nationals will need to have organized their **visa** in advance, something usually only possible in their home country.

men, there are prayer caps, skullcaps, furry winter hats and plain workmen's caps. Following this lane south, turn right, where a large, semi-underground market occupies the space between the square and hat lane. Here you will find a large selection of **clothes**, carpets and **crockery**, as well as Uyghur nuts, sweets and spice stands, and the occasional blacksmith hammering at his trade. Further south down hat lane, you will come to a **woodcraft** area.

The gold, knife and music markets

Running parallel to the north side of Id Kah Square you'll find Kashgar's **gold** market inside a covered arcade, along with some jewellers' workshops. Around the north edge of the square you can find shops selling high-quality ornate **knives**, produced in Yengisar. The lane directly south of Id Kah Mosque, heading due west, sells a mixture of hats, jewellery, and large **chests** inlaid with brightly coloured tin (purpose-built for carrying gifts for brides-to-be). Further west, running south towards the main post office, you'll find an interesting street of workshops along with some stalls selling handmade **musical instruments**. The two-stringed *dutah* is the most common. The *tanber* is similar but has an even longer stem and a round bowl shaped like half a gourd, while the *rawap* has five strings and a snakeskin drum.

KASHGAR'S SUNDAY MARKETS

Like many aspects of life in Kashgar, the famous **Yekshenbe Bazaar** (Sunday Market) is evolving. While it's still one of Kashgar's top sights, and a fascinating place to people-watch, it has lost some of its former chaotic charm. The first change was the departure of the **livestock market** or Ulagh Bazaar (牛羊市场, niúyáng shìchǎng) in 2007, which, due to the chaos it caused in the city centre each Sunday, was relocated 10km northwest to Pamir Dadao, a ¥30 cab ride from downtown. Happily, should you make it out here, you'll still find a colourful bunch of traders haggling over cattle and the occasional camel, while sheep turn a blind eye to the food stalls on the periphery.

The second wave of change saw the rest of the market rehoused in a permanent structure just northeast of Dong Hu Park, now simply called the "big bazaar" (大巴扎, dà bāzhā or also 中西亚巴扎, zhōngxīyà bāzhā). Some stalls open every day, but it really gets going on a Sunday, when side markets spring up in the surrounding streets. Knives, hats, pots, carpets, pans, fresh fruit and vegetables, clothes and boots and every kind of domestic and agricultural appliance – often handmade in wood and tin – are available, and some produce, such as Iranian saffron, has come a very long way to be sold here. The market goes on all day and into the early evening, and food and drink are widely available around the site.

To get to the main bazaar take bus #20 from Renmin Square; or from the Id Kah Mosque you can take a fascinating thirty-minute walk through the old city with its lanes full of traders, coppersmiths and blacksmiths. A taxi from the centre of town costs around ¥8.

While they may not be as impressive as Kashgar's, it might be worth heading out to one of the smaller markets in the region – the small town of Shufu (疏附, shūfù), 17km southwest of Kashgar, is a good candidate. Today, these have a more authentic feel about them, and you're almost guaranteed to be the only one with a camera.

Tomb of Abakh Hoja

阿巴克霍加麻扎, abākè huòjiā mázhā or 香妃墓, xiāngfēi mù • Daily 9.30am–8pm • ¥30 • bus #20 from Renmin Square • 30 dusty minutes by bike

The most impressive of all Kashgar's tombs is the **Tomb of Abakh Hoja**, 5km northeast of the centre. A large, mosque-like building of blue and white tiles with a green dome and tiled minarets, it was constructed in the seventeenth century and is the resting place for a large number of people – the most famous being Abakh Hoja and his granddaughter Ikparhan, who is known in Chinese as **Xiang Fei**, "Fragrant Concubine". Having led the Uyghurs in revolt against Beijing, she was subsequently captured and married to the Qing emperor Qianlong, and later ordered to commit suicide by the emperor's jealous mother. In both commemorating a local heroine and stirring anti-Qing feeling for the cruelty she suffered, the story serves the convenient dual purpose of pleasing both the Uyghurs and the Han Chinese.

On the same site is a small **exhibition of historic relics** (¥10), the highlight of which is an Iron Age mummy recovered from the nearby desert, still dressed in felt hat and fur-lined jacket, woollen trousers, leather boots and belt with herbs and knife attached.

Moor Pagodas

莫尔佛塔, mò'ěr fótǎ • ¥30 • Return taxi around ¥100

Accessible only by car, the **Moor Pagodas** are part of the **ancient city of Hanoi** down a rough road about 30km east of Kashgar. The pagodas have been worn to rough stumps about a dozen metres high, but the remains of ruined Buddhist temples make quite a dramatic scene in what is a virtual desert.

Shipton's Arch

天洞, tiāndòng • 4wd and driver through tour agency around ¥800

One unusual attraction outside Kashgar is **Shipton's Arch**, just over two hours' drive to the west; at a height of around 400m (just topping the Empire State Building), this may be the tallest **natural rock arch** in the world. Though discovered in the 1940s by

TOURS AROUND KASHGAR

One of the most convincing reasons to visit Kashgar is, a little paradoxically, the opportunity to get out of town. Distances can be huge, public transport non-existent and the weather unrelenting, so it's usually best to go through a **tour operator**. Among the tours on offer – other than those to places nearby – are **mountaineering expeditions**, trips to **Tibet**, day- to week-long **camel treks** across the Taklamakan desert, and visits to remote villages of minority peoples.

TOUR OPERATORS

CITS ☎ 0998 2980473, ⓦ www.kscits.com.cn. This Chinese tourist staple has a branch inside the *Royal Qinibagh*. Staff are friendly and speak English.

Elvis Ablimit ☎ 1389 9136195, ⓔ elvisablimit @yahoo.com. A long-time freelance operator organizing trips around Kashgar, his English is good and he knows the area well, but at heart he remains – as he started out – an expert in Kashgar's carpet markets.

Kashgar Mountaineering Adventures ☎ 0998 2821832, ⓦ ksalpine.com. Inside the Kashgar Gymnasium on Jiefang Nan Lu, the helpful,

English-speaking staff here can organize a range of adventure activities including climbing and rafting trips. Contact them well in advance if you plan something ambitious, as most activities require some equipment and paperwork preparations.

★ **Old Road Tours** ☎ 1389 9132103, ⓦ oldroadtours .com. Formerly Abdul Wahab Tours, this local company is run by six friendly brothers and marshalled by Abdul himself, a real fountain of local knowledge. They can organize any trip imaginable, big or small, and in a number of languages including French, German and Russian.

former British consul to Kashgar, Eric Shipton, its remoteness meant that it was only accurately surveyed in 2000. Visiting the site involves a thirty-minute hike from the road and scaling a series of fixed ladders.

ARRIVAL AND DEPARTURE
KASHGAR

By plane Kashgar airport (喀什机场, kāshí jīchǎng) is 10km north of town; bus #2 (¥2) drives between the airport and People's Square. A taxi should cost ¥20, though drivers will ask for more. For tickets, China Southern are at 152 Seman Lu (daily May–Oct 9am–8pm, Nov–April 10am–7.30pm; ☎ 0998 2985118), although you'll find cheaper prices online.
Destinations Ürümqi (hourly; 1hr 30min).

By train Kashgar train station (喀什火车站, kāshí huǒchēzhàn) is 7km east of town, where minibuses and taxis, as well as bus #28 to the Id Kah Mosque, await new arrivals. Tickets can be purchased from the station itself, or from the ticket booth inside the bus station on Tiannan Lu (daily 9.30am–7pm) – buy as far in advance as possible if you want a sleeper to Ürümqi.
Destinations Korla (2 daily; 13hr 40min & 17hr); Kuqa (2 daily; 9hr 20min & 11hr 45min); Ürümqi (2 daily; 25hr & 32hr).

By bus The main long-distance bus station (天南路客运站, tiānnánlù kèyùnzhàn; daily 8am–9.30pm) is just east of the centre on Tiannan Lu, handling connections from southern Xinjiang, including Yarkand and Khotan. Tickets are available for same-day travel until 5pm, when they start selling tickets for the next day.

The international bus station (喀什国际客运站, kāshí guójì kèyùnzhàn; daily 8.30am–8.30pm), north of the city on Jiefang Bei Lu and the #2 bus route, is the terminus for buses to and from Ürümqi, Kuqa, Korla and Tashkurgan, and for all international traffic (see box, p.839). Be prepared to wait a few days until the bus fills up if you're travelling to Sust; services to Osh in Kyrgyzstan are more straightforward.
Destinations Khotan (11hr); Korla (17hr); Kuqa (12hr); Lake Karakul (3hr); Sust (36hr); Tashkurgan (4hr); Yarkand (2hr 30min); Kargilik (4hr).

GETTING AROUND

By taxi Cabs are cheap, ubiquitous and easy to hail, with the starting price a reasonable ¥5. Expect to agree a price in advance and haggle for trips to more distant destinations.

By bicycle Kashgar's youth hostels all have bicycles to rent for around ¥5/hr.

ACCOMMODATION

Thanks to Kashgar's rising popularity with Chinese backpackers, the city now has several excellent youth hostels, plus a few more luxurious options.

13

★ **Kashgar Camel Youth Hostel** 喀什骆驼青年旅舍, kāshí luòtuó qīngnián lǚshè. 148 Tuman Lu ☎ 0998 2832609. This new hostel, not far from the big bazaar, has pretty dorms and double rooms covered with murals by a local artist, and pleasant common areas. Dorms ¥40, rooms ¥200

★ **Old Town Youth Hostel** 老城青年旅舍, lǎochéng qīngnián lǚshè. 233 Wusitangboyi Lu ☎ 0998 2823262, ⦿ pamirinn.com. At the edge of the old town along Wustangboyi Lu, this hostel has decent rooms, helpful staff and a courtyard that's great for meeting other travellers. Dorms ¥40, rooms ¥150

Pamir Youth Hostel 帕米尔青年旅舍, pàmǐ'ěr qīngnián lǚshè. Level 3, Id Kah Bazaar ☎ 0998 2823376, ⦿ pamirhostel.com. This hostel, in a great but tricky-to-find location, upstairs on the north side of the Id Kah Mosque, has airless dorms but a fantastic rooftop café – come here to smoke shisha and listen to the call to prayer. Dorms ¥40, rooms ¥140

Royal Qinibagh 其尼瓦克皇家大酒店, qíníwǎkè huángjiā dàjiǔdiàn. 144 Seman Lu ☎ 0998 2982103. One of Kashgar's older hotels, this has recently been given a massive facelift – its new tower can be seen from across the old city. Rooms are now firmly at the upper end of the market, with bathtubs, soft beds and marble everywhere. ¥588

Sahra 色哈乐宾馆, sèhālè bīnguǎn. Seman Lu opposite the *Seman* ☎ 0998 2581122. A budget option with 24-hour hot water, a roof and beds. Popular with Pakistani traders, though it won't be to everyone's taste. ¥80

Seman 色满宾馆, sèmǎn bīnguǎn. Seman Lu ☎ 0998 2582129. This rambling, nicely aged hotel is a popular choice; its cheap rooms augmented by *John's Café* nearby, the old Russian embassy out back, and some useful tour agencies in the lobby. Book ahead if you plan to stay in their cheapest doubles – these often get filled up. ¥100

EATING AND DRINKING

Kashgar has a slew of excellent places to eat. Uyghur restaurants are concentrated around Id Kah Square. Street vendors sell pilau, kebabs and cold spicy noodles; *laghman* is available almost everywhere.

★ **Altun Orda** 金奥尔达饮食, jīnàoěrdá yǐnshí. Seman Lu ☎ 0998 2583555. This Uyghur establishment is perhaps the classiest restaurant in town, though there are some simple ¥10–20 dishes hidden away among the more expensive items on the picture menu. The ¥88 "tower kebab" is especially recommended, as is the walnut ice cream. Daily 10am–midnight.

★ **Avral** 阿吾拉乐奶油冰淇淋, awúlālè nǎiyóu bīngqílín. Seman Lu, just west of the Bank of China. If there's even one sweet tooth in your mouth, be sure to head to this inconspicuous café. The owners blew US$1000 on a special Arabic ice-cream machine, and the results are rather dreamy: ¥8 will buy you a little bowlful of heaven. The menu is in Uyghur and Chinese only, but all bowls are based on their signature sweet cream ice cream – particularly good served with the home-made cherry syrup. Daily 11am–11pm.

John's Café Inside the Seman Hotel complex ☎ 0998 2581186. The original branch of this backpacker-friendly chain doles out Sino-Western food, coffees, juices and beer. A great place to relax over a book or catch up on e-mails using their wi-fi. Daily 8am–midnight.

Karakoram Café K咖啡厅, K kāfēi tīng. 87 Seman Lu, opposite the Royal Qinibagh Hotel, ☎ 0998 2822655. A great café serving up good coffee (¥28), breakfasts and sandwiches, this place is convenient for the old town. They also run some simple tours and show the film "Kite Runner" occasionally in the evenings. Free wi-fi. Mon, Tues & Thurs–Sun 8am–9pm.

★ **Mengyol** 明邀乐饮食, míngyāolè yǐnshí. South side of Id Kah Square ☎ 0998 2844000. Climb up to this fourth-floor venue overlooking the mosque to feast on Uyghur dumplings, pilau or meat dishes. Try to time your visit for sunset, when you'll hear the muezzin – sit mosque-side if at all possible. Daily 10am–midnight.

DIRECTORY

Banks and exchange The main Bank of China, in the northeast corner of Renmin Square (Mon–Fri; summer 9.30am–1.30pm & 4–7pm; winter 10am–2pm & 3.30–6.30pm), can change foreign currency (both cash and travellers' cheques). Their ATMs accept foreign cards.

Bookshops Xinhua Bookshop is at 32 Jiefang Bei Lu, on the east side of the road and just north of the intersection with Renmin Lu. The *Karakoram Café* and *John's* both have small collections of English books to lend.

Mail The main post office is at 40 Renmin Xi Lu, a short walk west of Jiefang Lu (Mon–Sat; summer 9.30am–8pm, winter 10am–7.30pm).

PSB The visa office on Yunmulaxia Lu (Mon–Fri 10.30am–1.30pm & 4–8pm, but closed Wed & Fri afternoons), close to the end of Wusitangboyi Lu, theoretically issues visa extensions, but in practice it's very difficult to get anything done here – head to Ürümqi if at all possible.

The Southern Silk Road

The **Southern Silk Road** splits off from the northern route at Kashgar, skirting the southern rim of the **Taklamakan** and curving north at **Charkhlik** on the desert's eastern edge before re-joining the northern route near Dunhuang in Gansu (see p.808). In modern times this path has fallen into obscurity, with punishing distances, forlorn and dusty towns, and sparse transport connections. However, this is actually the older and historically more important of the two branches. The most famous Silk Road travellers used it, as well as Marco Polo, and, in the 1930s, the British journalist Peter Fleming. The ancient settlements along the way were desert oases, kept alive by streams flowing down from the snowy peaks of the Kunlun Shan, which border the southern edge of this route.

Following the southern Silk Road opens up the possibility of travelling overland from Kashgar to Turpan one way, and returning another, thus circumnavigating the entire Taklamakan Desert. The road from Kashgar runs for 1400km to the town of Charkhlik, from where it's still a fair way either back to Turpan, or on to Golmud in Qinghai (see p.801). The ancient city of **Khotan** is the pick of places to get off the bus and explore; it's also linked to Korla via the splendid 522km-long **Tarim Desert Expressway**, one of the longest desert roads in the world.

Yengisar

英吉沙, yīngjí shā

A mere 70km from Kashgar, the town of **YENGISAR** has for centuries been supplying the Uyghur people with handcrafted knives. Most of the knives on sale in Xinjiang these days are mass-produced, but at the **Anarguli Knife Factory** (阿娜尔古丽小刀厂, anà'ěrgǔlì xiǎodāochǎng) 1km south of Yengisar on the G315 national road, a few craftsmen still ply their old skills, inlaying handles with horn or silver alloy. Some of the more decorative examples take nearly a fortnight to forge.

Yarkand

莎车, shāchē

The town of **YARKAND**, 130km southwest of Yengisar, has been a strategically important staging post for at least the last thousand years; now that Kashgar is becoming ever more developed and sanitized, this may be the best place to soak up the character of Muslim Xinjiang and old-time Central Asia. The best thing to do here is simply wander the northeastern backstreets, a warren of muddy lanes lined with willows and crowded by donkey carts, artisans' quarters, bazaars and traditional adobe homes with wooden-framed balconies. Sundays are the best time to visit Yarkand, when a huge rustic **market** along the same lines as the more famous one in Kashgar is held in the main bazaar behind the fort – though this area has plenty of interest most days.

The old town

You'll find the town's major sights lie close together on a road running north off Laocheng Lu: the recently restored **old fort** is opposite Yarkand's **Altunluq mosque** (阿勒屯清真寺, ālètún qīngzhēnsì) and **Amannisahan tomb** (阿曼尼莎汗纪念陵, āmànísháhàn jìniànlíng; ¥15). The mosque is off limits to non-Muslims, but the tomb, built for Amannisahan, the wife of a sixteenth-century khan, is a beautiful white- and blue-tiled affair; Amannisahan was also the most influential contributor to *muqam* music (see box, p.844).

The adjacent **cemetery** contains the mausoleums of several of Yarkand's former rulers, including Amannisahan's husband, and is crowded with more ordinary cylindrical Muslim tombs and ancient trees.

ARRIVAL AND DEPARTURE — YARKAND

By bus The bus station (莎车客运站, shāchē kèyùnzhàn) is south of the centre off Xincheng Lu, with frequent departures through the day to Kashgar, Kargilik, Khotan and Yengisar.

13

UYGHUR MUSIC – MUQAM

Song and dance is at the core of Uyghur cultural identity and is commonly presented at all social gatherings. The most established form of Uyghur music, **muqam**, has developed since the sixth century into a unique collection of songs and instrumentals, quite separate from Arabic and Persian influence. A *muqam* must open with a flowing rhythm that complies with strict modal constraints, followed by a suite of pieces that tie into this opening. In the late sixteenth century scholars and folk musicians gathered to collate this music into a definitive collection of twelve *muqams*. The entire collection takes 24 hours to play and involves around fifteen traditional instruments such as the plucked mandolin-like *rawap*, metal-stringed *dutah* and large *dumbak* drums. Sadly, few people can play *muqam* nowadays, but recordings are popular and sold on CD and DVD throughout Xinjiang.

ACCOMMODATION

Shache Hotel 莎车宾馆, shāchē bīnguǎn. 10min walk west along Xincheng Lu from the central crossroads ☏0998 8512365. A decent hotel that accepts foreigners – which is fortunate, as almost nowhere else in Yarkand does. **¥360**

EATING

Meraj Restaurant 米热吉快餐, mǐrèjí kuàicān. 16 Xincheng Lu. Extremely popular with locals, *Meraj* serves stuffed naan bread and all kinds of noodle dishes; but the delicacy here is pigeon meat. Daily 9am–midnight.

Yurtum Restaurant 尤土木, yóutǔmù. Overlooking the Altunluq Mosque. This Uyghur restaurant's location is brilliant – take a table upstairs overlooking the square outside the mosque and fortify yourself with their incredibly strong coffee and tasty pilau. Daily 10am–midnight.

DIRECTORY

Services The Bank of China (with ATMs accepting credit cards), post office and China Telecom are all clustered around the central Qini'aibage Lu–Laocheng/Xincheng Lu intersection, known locally as Dashizi.

Kargilik
叶诚, yèchéng

Sixty kilometres south of Yarkand, **KARGILIK** is a long, straggling town, stretching along the highway. Every Wednesday there's a fantastic **market** about 1km towards Khotan; far more earthy and colourful than the Kashgar Sunday market, it's well worth your time.

The road divides at Kargilik, with one fork running southwest into **Tibet**; this used to be a prime target for hardy travellers attempting to sneak to Ali in the back of a truck, but, quite aside from the appalling rigours of the trip, heavy-handed security these days makes that inadvisable – you'll have to arrange a tour through an agent in Lhasa (see p.865).

ACCOMMODATION

Jiaotong Hotel 交通宾馆, jiāotōng bīnguǎn. Beside the bus station ☏0998 7285540. With its dingy-but-clean doubles, the accommodation might be a bit unappealing, but this bus station hotel is convenient for transport links and surrounded by busy restaurants. **¥100**

Yudu Hotel 玉都大酒店, yùdū dàjiǔdiàn. 1 Kahe Lu ☏0998 7222888. A perfectly comfortable, if unexciting, option close to downtown Kargilik, just a short taxi ride from the bus station. Rooms have broadband internet. **¥168**

Khotan
和田, hétián

Five hundred kilometres southeast of Kashgar, predominantly Uyghur **KHOTAN** has for centuries enjoyed countrywide fame for its **carpets**, **silk** and **white jade**. A bleak and dusty grid of wide streets, the town is pretty ordinary, but the people are hospitable, and there are rare opportunities to see traditional weaving and silk production.

The town centre

Khotan centres on **Tuanjie Square**, from where the city is partitioned by Beijing Lu (running east–west) and Ta'naiyi Lu (north–south). The giant sculpture in the middle of the square shows Chairman Mao shaking hands with an elderly Uyghur man, an actual person who went to Beijing to congratulate the Communist party on its victory in the 1950s – the symbol still serves its function, though the hostility of the local Uyghurs towards Han Chinese is no secret. The square comes alive on summer evenings, when an impromptu funfair and night market sets up on the southeast corner.

Jade Dragon Kashgar River

玉龙喀什河, yùlóng kāshíhé

About 4km to the east of town, following Beijing Dong Lu, is the **Jade Dragon Kashgar River**, which still yields the odd stone for casual searchers. The river flows through a wide, stony plain; it's easy to get down here and forage, but you'll need to find one of the locals – who rake for stones with garden forks – to show you what you are looking for or you may end up with a pocketful of pretty but worthless quartz. Jade-hunting peaks in spring and autumn, when the water level is at its lowest.

The carpet factory

地毯厂, dìtǎn chǎng • 22 Ahegong Lu • Daily 10am–1pm & 3–7pm

Khotan's **carpet factory** stands just across the river to the left, worth a visit in particular if you are interested in buying. Prices here, and in the shop in town, are very cheap. The atmosphere in the factory workshop is friendly, with the workers, mostly young women, exchanging banter as they weave with incredible dexterity. They encourage visitors to take pictures, and ask to be sent copies.

Melikawat

米力克瓦特古城, mǐlìkèwǎtè gǔchéng • ¥20 • taxi from town about ¥100 • make sure your driver knows the way

Silk Road specialists should visit the ruined city of **Melikawat**, out in the desert 30km to the south of Khotan beside the Jade Dragon Kashgar River. This city, formerly an important Buddhist centre on the Silk Road, was abandoned well over a thousand years ago, and the arrival of Islam in the region did nothing to aid its preservation. The site is

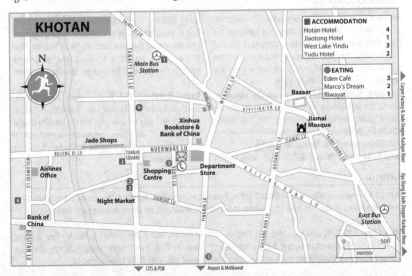

13

KHOTAN'S BAZAAR

Khotan's fascinating **bazaar** takes place every Sunday, although there's some action here every day. Silk, carpets, leather jackets, fruit and spices are all on sale, with innumerable blacksmiths, tinsmiths, goldsmiths and carpenters hard at work among the stalls. The bazaar stretches across the northeast part of town; the easiest way to reach it is to head east along Aiyitika'er Lu, off Wenhua Lu near the centre. Follow the stalls south toward Jiamai Lu, along which you can see the pretty Jiamai mosque.

a fragmentary collection of crumbling walls set among the dunes and tamarisk bushes, thousands of wind-polished potshards littering the ground – you might find odd bits of glass or wood poking out of the ruins.

ARRIVAL AND DEPARTURE
KHOTAN

By plane Khotan's airport (和田机场, hétián jīchǎng) lies 10km southwest of town; reach the centre by taxi (¥25) – there's no airport bus. Buy flight tickets in the airline office at 14 Wulumuqi Lu (daily 9.30am–9pm; 📞0903 2518999) a few minutes north of the *Hetian Binguan*.
Destinations Ürümqi (7 daily; 1hr 45min).
By bus The main bus station (和田客运中心, hétián kèyùn zhōngxīn) is north of the city on Taibei Xi Lu; taxis from here charge ¥5 to anywhere in the city centre. There

are daily services to Korla and Ürümqi across the Taklamakan Desert, and to all destinations west of Khotan. To anywhere east of Khotan along the Southern Silk Road, as well as to Jiya Xiang, you'll need to use the East Bus Station (东车站, dōng chēzhàn) on Taibei Dong Lu.
Destinations Kashgar (8hr); Korla (15hr); Niya (5hr); Cherchen (12hr); Ürümqi (20hr); Yarkand (5hr).
By taxi At both bus stations there are official shared taxis running along some long-distance bus routes, although the prices are roughly double that of regular tickets.

INFORMATION

Travel agents All hotels have travel services for booking plane and bus tickets and arranging tours. Local excursions with a guide, taking in the carpet and silk factories, should set you back ¥50–100, and it's possible to organize lengthier jeep or camel trips around the region, using routes not necessarily covered by public transport. Expect

to pay ¥300 per day for a jeep, ¥100 for a camel; camping gear is around ¥50 per person, and a guide will cost ¥100 a day. If your accommodation can't help, try Khotan's helpful, English-speaking CITS (📞0903 2516090), inconveniently located at 49 Tunken Lu, in the south of the city.

ACCOMMODATION

Hotan 和田宾馆, hétián bīnguǎn. 57 Wulumuqi Nan Lu 📞0903 2023456. An old-school option on the edge of the town centre, this hotel has a tranquil feel, and is decorated with some local touches. Pleasant rooms come with bathtubs and breakfast included, and you can pay extra for a room with broadband. **¥220**

Jiaotong Hotel 交通宾馆, jiāotōng bīnguǎn. Beside the bus station 📞0903 2032700. Despite the decent, clean bedrooms overlooking the bus station parking lot, the bathrooms here are nasty – stay elsewhere if you have a horror of dodgy plumbing. **¥160**

West Lake Yindu 西湖银都国际酒店, xīhú yíndū

guójì jiǔdiàn. 111 Ta'naiyi Nan Lu 📞0903 2521365. One of the most luxurious options in Khotan, the beds here are among the most comfortable in Xinjiang. Your fellow guests are likely to be a mix of Chinese businessmen and wealthy Uyghurs. Breakfast included. **¥418**

Yudu Hotel 玉都大酒店, yùdū dàjiǔdiàn. Southwest corner of Tuanjie Square 📞0903 2023456. The staff here may be unhelpful, but the location is right in the heart of the action, making this a good central option. Rooms are a bit ordinary, but include breakfast and broadband. **¥198**

EATING

There's a wide range of street eats in Khotan, although development work in the city centre means that locations keep changing – failing all else, check out the southern end of Tuanjie Square, and the streets running south from here.

Eden Café 一甸咖啡, yīdiàn kāfēi. 360 Yingbin Lu 📞0903 2518888. A smart restaurant, full of middle-class Uyghur families enjoying leisurely meals and a combination

of Uyghur, Turkish and Western dishes. Try their delicious mint tea (¥36) and, if you're seriously hungry, the huge mixed grill (¥98). Daily 1pm–midnight.

SILKY SECRETS IN KHOTAN

One of Khotan's best assets is the chance to see the whole process of silk production, from grub to garment.

To see the nurturing of the **silkworms** – only possible in summer – you'll need to explore **Jiya Xiang** (吉亚乡, jíyà xiāng), northeast of the city, a tiny Uyghur settlement specializing in **atalas silk**, made in small, family-run workshops; get here by minibus (9am–9pm; ¥2.5) from the east bus station on Taibei Dong Lu. If you are able to explain your purpose to people (a drawing of a silkworm might do the trick), they will take you to see silkworms munching away on rattan trays of fresh, cleaned mulberry leaves in cool, dark sheds. Eventually each worm should spin itself a cocoon of pure silk; each cocoon comprises a single strand about 1km in length. The hatching and rearing of silkworms is unreliable work, and for most farmers it's a sideline.

At the small **workshops** near Jiya you will also be able to see the rest of the silk-making process – about 5km down the Jiya road **Atlas Silk** (daily 9.30am–8pm) is a good place to aim for. Inside, you'll be able to see the initial unpicking of the cocoons, the twisting together of the strands to form a thread (ten strands for each silk thread), the winding of the thread onto reels and finally the weaving and dyeing. There are also a few shops along the road where you can pick up a vivid scarf or shirt of atalas silk as a souvenir.

Marco's Dream 马克驿站, mǎkè yìzhàn. Tucked away in a residential courtyard, just north of the Xihu Hotel – look for signs to "Marco" ☎0903 2027515. This café serves a range of Western and Asian dishes, from Malaysian chicken rice to sticky toffee pudding. The owners speak English and are knowledgeable about the region. Daily 1.30–9.30pm.

Riwayat 生态餐厅, shēngtài cāntīng. 39–43 Youyi Lu ☎0903 2032230. A fun restaurant, somewhat bizarrely decked out like a tropical jungle, complete with a papier-mâché crocodile. The food is much less eccentric than the decor – kebabs, *pilau* and some fried dishes. Daily 11am–11.30pm.

DIRECTORY

Banks and exchange The main Bank of China (9.50am–12.30pm & 4.20–7.20pm) is on Wulumuqi Nan Lu – this is the place to come to exchange travellers' cheques, and the ATMs here accept international cards, as do the ATMs at the branch on Nuerwake Lu.

Post office (Mon–Fri 9.30am–8pm) is on Nuerwake Lu. **PSB** For visa-related issues, head to the PSB on Tunken Lu (Mon–Fri; 9.20am–1.30pm & 4–8pm), although this is not a good place to apply for an extension – head to Ürümqi instead.

Niya

民丰, mínfēng

On the way to **NIYA**, 300km east of Khotan, you'll pass through some of the most vividly empty landscapes you will ever see, a formless expanse of sky and desert merging at a vague, dusty yellow horizon. The modern town is 100km south of **Niya Ancient City**, first discovered by Aurel Stein in 1901; ongoing excavations have uncovered the remains of pagodas, orchards, and over a hundred dwellings beneath the desert sands. The most important artefacts have been removed to museums in Ürümqi, although there is still a small **museum** (尼雅文物馆, níyǎ wénwùguǎn) in the town.

Cherchen

且末, qiěmò

CHERCHEN, 300km east of Niya, is another small, surprisingly modern town, famed for the frequency of its sandstorms (especially in April). There is a group of 2600-year-old **tombs** about 5km to the southeast at **Zagunluk** (扎滚鲁克古墓群, zhāgǔnlùkè gǔmùqún; daily 8am–8pm; ¥30). While only one tomb is open to view, it's been carefully reconstructed, and the taxi ride (¥30) out here through attractive villages is interesting as well. Closer to town, is the **Tohlaklek Manor** (地主庄园, dìzhǔ zhuāngyuán; daily 9.30am–1.30pm & 4–7.30pm; ¥20), a former landlord's house

13

FROM KHOTAN TO KORLA

The cities of Khotan and Korla – respectively on the Northern and Southern silk routes – can be linked in three different ways. The most painless option is to take the new **cross-desert highway** from Khotan to **Aksu** (阿克苏; ākèsū) on the Northern Silk Route, from where you'll at least have the option of continuing on by train; the 440km journey across the desert takes just five or six hours, since there's precious little chance of a traffic jam. There's another such highway several hundred kilometres to the east of Khotan, its southern terminus the town of **Niya**; this is longer at 522km, and will save you a little time if you're heading directly to Korla, Turpan or Ürümqi. Both roads cross the **Taklamakan desert**, and will give you a close-up of why the Uyghurs call this the "Sea of Death". Unfortunately, most buses travelling in either direction make the crossing at night, so you don't get a view of the impressive irrigation grid that provides water for shrubs to protect the road from the ever-shifting desert sands.

For a dustier, more interesting trip to Korla, you'll want to catch a bus east from Khotan, continuing on the Southern Silk Road.

built in 1911. There's not much inside, but it's a good example of local architecture all the same.

Charkhlik

若羌, ruòqiāng

CHARKHLIK, 360km east of Cherchen, is a small, busy place, notable for being the jumping-off point for treks by camel or jeep out to two little-known ruined cities of Silk Road vintage, Miran and Loulan (see box opposite). It's also one final long push across the desert from Charkhlik to **Korla** (see p.833), or, for a hardy few, a tough bus trip across the Qaidam Basin to **Golmud** (see p.801) in Qinghai province, through a corner of China that few foreigners ever see.

ARRIVAL AND DEPARTURE
CHARKHLIK

By bus The main bus station (若羌客运中心, ruòqiāng kèyùn zhōngxīn) is on Shengli Lu, just north of Charkhlik's centre. The ticket office is open daily 8.30am–6.30pm, and tickets are easy to buy. Destinations Cherchen (4hr); Golmud (14hr); Korla (7hr).

ACCOMMODATION AND EATING

Longdu Business Hotel 龙都商务宾馆, lóngdū shāngwù bīnguǎn. On the corner of Shengli Lu and Jianshe Lu ☏ 0996 7010111. This is the only place close to the bus station that takes foreigners, although the staff might be a bit rusty at the registration process. Rooms are adequate and very large, but beds are rock hard. ¥138

Shudu Restaurant 蜀都食府, shǔdū shìfǔ. 388 Jianshe Le ☏ 0996 7105467. A reasonably priced Sichuanese place with friendly staff and a picture menu of their chilli-laden fare. Daily 11am–10pm.

The Karakoram Highway

For millennia the 4700m-high **Khunjerab Pass**, 400km south of Kashgar, has been the nexus between the Chinese world and the Indian subcontinent. Today, the entire 1300km route from Kashgar over the mountains to Rawalpindi in northern Pakistan is known as the **Karakoram Highway** (中巴公路, zhōngbā gōnglù) and, while not without its perils, it's hard to think of a more exciting route out of China.

The journey takes a minimum of four days, though the pass is open only from the beginning of May until the end of October, and can close without notice in bad weather. Travellers have to spend a night on the Chinese side, either in Tashkurgan or camping out by the wintry but beautiful **Lake Karakul**. You'll also need to have already arranged Pakistan visas in your home country unless you live in China, in which case you can apply through the Pakistani Embassy in Beijing.

LOST CITIES: MIRAN AND LOULAN

Two remote, ruined cities make intriguing targets from Charkhlik, if you have time and plenty of cash. **Miran** (米兰古城, mǐlán gǔchéng) – subject of Christa Paula's book *Voyage to Miran* – is relatively accessible, approximately 75km northeast of Charkhlik; a far more ambitious trip would be to **Loulan** (楼兰古城, lóulán gǔchéng), 250km from town on the western edge of Lop Nor. Loulan's very existence had been completely forgotten until the Swedish explorer Sven Hedin rediscovered the site, which had been buried in sand, in the early twentieth century; it wasn't until the 1980s that the first Chinese archeological surveys were undertaken, during which distinctively un-Chinese mummified remains, including the "Loulan Beauty", were found (see p.818).

There's a **Loulan Museum** (10.30am–12.30pm & 4.30–6.30pm) in Charkhlik, but the most interesting remains have already been removed to Ürümqi. In order to visit the sites themselves, you'll need to make an application to the local department of cultural heritage whose office is in Charkhlik's Loulan Museum. The fees and permits required will depend upon the trip you have in mind, but can run to thousands of dollars for official expeditions, and non-specialists may simply be refused entry.

Lake Karakul

喀拉库勒湖, kālākùlē hú

Southwest of Kashgar, the road soon leaves the valley, with its mud-brick buildings and irrigated wheat and rice plantations, behind. Climbing through river gorges strewn with giant boulders, it creeps into a land of treeless, bare dunes of sand and gravel, interspersed with pastures scattered with grazing yaks and camels. The sudden appearance of **Lake Karakul** by the roadside, some 200km out of Kashgar, is dramatic. Right under the feet of the Pamir Mountains and the magnificent 7546m Mount Muztagata, whose vast snowy flanks have been split open by colossal glaciers, the waters of the lake are luminous blue.

While there's a small **official scenic spot** (喀拉库勒湖观景台, kālākùlē hú guānjǐng tái, ¥50) on the west side of the lake, there's really no need to come here in particular, unless you're desperate for somewhere to stay (see below).

ARRIVAL AND DEPARTURE
LAKE KARAKUL

By bus and taxi From the Kashgar international bus station there are two buses daily May–Oct, leaving at 10am and 4pm (¥50). Buy tickets in advance if you plan to travel to the lake on a Monday – an exodus of foreigners from Kashgar after the Sunday market can make tickets scarce. It's also possible to take a shared taxi (¥120) from a spot on Xiyu Dadao (ask for the 老塔县办事处, lǎotǎxiàn bànshìchù). From Tashkurgan you can take the Kashgar bus and get off at the lake. Leaving the lake requires slightly more ingenuity – in either direction you will need to flag down the passing buses or taxis, which may involve standing assertively in the middle of the road. Fortunately hitchhiking is relatively common along this stretch, and ought to be straightforward. Taxis back to Kashgar cost a minimum of ¥100 per person.

GETTING AROUND

The opportunities for hiking over the surrounding green pasture are extensive. While the hike around the lake takes around half a day, for anything more ambitious be sure to take a tent and warm clothing; at 3800m, the weather can be extremely cold even in summer, with snow showers occurring well into June. Whatever your plans, make sure to take plenty of food and water, as there's little available at the lake. Tour agencies in Kashgar (see box, p.841) can help to organize more ambitious treks around Mount Muztagata and beyond.

ACCOMMODATION

Hikers will almost certainly encounter amenable Kyrgyz yurt dwellers on their way around the lake – especially along the west side of the lake along the road. There is some food available at the scenic spot, but otherwise you'll need to eat with the herders or bring your own food.

13

★ **Apudi's** 400m north of the scenic spot ☎ 1377 9617293. While this small house looks unprepossessing from outside, it's very cosy inside and Apudi and his wife are welcoming and experienced at dealing with hikers stricken by altitude sickness. Dinner included. Beds ¥50

Official Yurt Camp Inside the scenic spot. The only formal accommodation around the lake, this is aimed at tour groups, and has regular rooms in addition to unappealing concrete yurts. Yurts ¥90, rooms ¥180

Tashkurgan

塔什库尔干, tǎshí kù'ěrgān or 塔县, tǎ xiàn

The last town before the border, **TASHKURGAN** lies 280km southeast of Kashgar, and about 220km north of the Pakistani town of **Sust** (苏斯特, sūsītè). Its primary importance for travellers is as a staging post between the two settlements, and all travellers passing through, in either direction, must stay the night here. It's a tiny place, comprising a couple of tree-lined streets, with a bus station and a sprinkling of hotels.

The native population is mainly **Tajik**, whose customs differ markedly from both Uyghur and Chinese – keep an eye out for the elaborate way they greet each other on the street – as well as intrepid Pakistanis setting up shop.

Stone City

石头城, shítou chéng • Daily 9.30am–8pm • ¥30

Few visitors bother to stop at Tashkurgan longer than necessary, but worth a look, especially at sunset, is the six-hundred-year-old, crumbling, mud-brick **Stone City**, which found fame as a location in the film adaptation of **The Kite Runner**. If you clamber to the top, the scenes of snowy mountains running parallel on both flanks, and woods and wetland dotted around, are more than picturesque. To reach it, walk east from the bus station right to the end of town then strike off a few hundred metres to the left. Beyond this, on the southeast edge of town, is an area of **grassland** used by Tajik herders in the summer months.

ARRIVAL AND DEPARTURE

By bus Tashkurgan's tiny bus station (汽车站, qìchē zhàn) is right in the middle of town. There are morning buses to Kashgar as well as an unreliable daily service to Sust in Pakistan. If you plan to get off at Lake Karakul (see p.849) en route to Kashgar, you may be asked to pay the full Kashgar fare anyway.

By truck The alternative to catching buses is to hitch a ride on a truck; these often cruise around town in the evening looking for prospective customers to Kashgar (or Karakul) for the day after. You'll pay, but it will be cheaper than travelling by bus.

ACCOMMODATION

Crowne Inn 皇冠大酒店, huángguàn dàjiǔdiàn. 23 Pamir Lu, on the southern edge of town ☎ 0998 3422888. A modern, bright hotel with a slightly out-of-the-way location, this Singaporean-owned establishment is very comfortable, but seems out of kilter with its surroundings. Includes buffet breakfast. ¥550

Jiaotong Hotel 交通宾馆, jiāotōng bīnguǎn. 385 Tashkurgan Lu, next to the bus station ☎ 0998 3421192. This convenient option in the middle of town is clean and simple, with equally basic bathrooms. 24hr hot water and broadband in every room. Open May–Oct only. ¥150

K2 Youth Hostel 凯途国际青年旅社, kǎi tú guójì qīngnián lǚshè. Hongqilafu Lu, at the northern end of town ☎ 0998 3492266. A surprisingly good hostel to find in such a remote place, with a sunny common area and enormous windows looking out at the mountains. Dorms are huge, as are the private rooms, and the only grumble is the total lack of heating or insulation – lucky it's only open in summer. Dorms ¥45, rooms ¥120

EATING

In addition to the food available inside hotels – both *K2* and *Crowne Inn* offer a selection of Chinese and Western dishes – the following options are worth considering.

Bashu Renjia 巴蜀人家, bashǔ rénjiā. Tashkurgan Lu, opposite the bus station ☎ 1510 9051813. This smoky Sichuanese restaurant is very popular with Tashkurgan's Han Chinese residents, serving up reasonably priced and highly spiced dishes (¥20–30). Daily 11am–10pm.

Shanhua 山花快餐, shānhuā kuàicān. Tashkurgan Lu, next to the Traffic Hotel ☎ 1516 0869270. For something other than Chinese food, try this nice garden restaurant near the bus station dolling out local-style kebabs and *pilau* from early until late. Daily 9am–midnight.

DIRECTORY

Banks and exchange An Agricultural Bank of China (Mon–Fri 9.30am–1.30pm & 4.30–7.30pm) lies 300m to the south of the bus station. Cash (and sometimes travellers' cheques) can be changed here at official exchange rates, but the ATMs only accept Chinese cards.

If arriving from Pakistan, you can easily change your rupees with the locally resident Pakistanis if the banks are closed.

Post office The post office is just southeast of the bus station, open Mon–Fri 10am–1.30pm & 3–6.30pm.

The Khunjerab Pass
红其拉甫口岸, hóngqí lāfū kǒu'àn

Khunjerab means "River of Blood" in the Tajik language – which may refer to the rusty colour of local rivers, or to the long tradition of banditry in these areas. The trip across the border at the **Khunjerab Pass** is not a totally risk-free affair – people are killed almost every year by falling rocks on the highway, and you should be aware that if your bus departs in rainy weather, you can almost certainly expect mud slides.

Through the pass

From Tashkurgan, the road climbs into a vast, bright plain, grazed by yaks and camels, with the mountains, clad in snow mantles hundreds of metres thick, pressing in all around. Emerging onto the **top of the pass** at 4693m, you're greeted by a clear, silent, windswept space of frozen streams, protruding glaciers and glimpses of green pasture under the sunshine. The only creature that lives here is the chubby ginger Himalayan marmot, easily spotted from the bus. At these heights many travellers experience some form of **altitude sickness** (see p.53). The journey between Tashkurgan and the small town of **Sust**, where Pakistani customs and immigration take place, takes about seven hours. Travellers in both directions have to spend a night here, and accommodation is plentiful. From Sust there are direct daily buses to Gilgit, from where frequent buses cover the sixteen-hour route to **Rawalpindi** and **Islamabad**.

TASHKURGAN TO PAKISTAN

Bring **warm clothing** and plenty of **snacks and water** on your Karakoram journey. Travellers heading to Pakistan do not need to buy onward bus tickets – the ticket from Kashgar covers the whole route right through to Sust – but Western tourists should be aware that they'll need to have arranged a Pakistani **visa** beforehand in their home country (though it's worth checking the current state of play at their Beijing embassy; ⊛ pakembassy.cn). Stamp in hand, the entry and exit formalities are dealt with a few hundred metres south from the bank, and are straightforward to the point of being lax. Note that **cyclists** are not allowed to ride their bikes through the pass, but have to bus it between Tashkurgan and Sust. As for **Sust**, there's plenty of accommodation to go around, as well as places in which to change *yuan* for rupees.

Tibet

THE FRIENDSHIP HIGHWAY

Tibet

西藏, xīzàng

Tibet (Bod to Tibetans), the "Roof of the World", has exerted a magnetic pull over travellers for centuries. The scenery is awe-inspiring, the religious devotion overwhelming, and the Tibetan people welcoming and wonderful. Below the surface, however, it is all too apparent that Tibet's past has been tragic, its present painful and the future bleak: today Tibet is a subjugated colony of China. While foreign visitors are perhaps more worldly than to expect a romantic Shangri-La, there is no doubt that many are shocked by the heavy military presence and authoritarian restrictions, both reinforced following pre-Olympic protests in 2007–08 and an ongoing campaign of self-immolations. The growing presence of Chinese immigrants and snap-happy tourists, construction of apartments and factories alongside traditional Tibetan rural homes and monasteries, and a programme of resettling nomads en masse to permanent new towns, are further causes of disquiet, but don't stay away: many people, the Dalai Lama included, believe travellers should visit Tibet to learn all they can of the country.

One of the most isolated parts of the world, the massive **Tibetan plateau** sits at an average height of 4500m above sea level, guarded on all sides by towering **mountain ranges.** To the south, the Himalayas separate Tibet from India, Nepal and Bhutan; to the west lie the peaks of the Karakoram and Pakistan; while to the north the Kunlun range forms a barrier to Xinjiang. Eastwards, dividing Tibet from Sichuan and Yunnan, a further series of ranges stretches for a thousand kilometres. Some of Asia's greatest **rivers** are born up on the plateau, including the Yangzi, Mekong, Yellow, Salween, Indus and Brahmaputra.

Any trip to Tibet faces **obstacles**. Following the centuries of self-imposed isolation which ended with Tibet being forcibly annexed by China in 1950, Tibet has become increasingly accessible, with approaches eased by plane links, paved roads and the Qinghai–Lhasa railway. Each new route has accelerated heavy, government-sponsored migration into the region, and although it is impossible to know how many Han Chinese actually live here it is likely that, at least in urban areas, they now outnumber ethnic Tibetans and have become economically dominant.

There are, of course, two sides to every story. The pre-Chinese Tibetan administration was a xenophobic religious dictatorship that tolerated slavery; when the Chinese

PILGRIMS AT THE JOKHANG, LHASA

Highlights

❶ The Jokhang, Lhasa Shrouded in juniper smoke and surrounded by prostrating pilgrims, it's hard not to be affected by this, one of the world's most venerated sites. **See p.872**

❷ Samye Remote walled town encapsulating Tibet's first Buddhist monastery. **See p.885**

❸ Namtso Lake A dream image of Tibet lies bright as a jewel beneath muscular peaks. **See p.891**

❹ The Friendship Highway This undulating road connecting Lhasa and Nepal cuts through some of the region's best and certainly most accessible sights. **See p.900**

❺ Mount Everest Base Camp Breathe deep and gaze up at the jagged, snow-blown peak of the world's highest mountain. **See p.904**

❻ Mount Kailash The world's holiest mountain, its very remoteness an intrinsic part of its appeal. **See p.907**

HIGHLIGHTS ARE MARKED ON THE MAP ON P.856

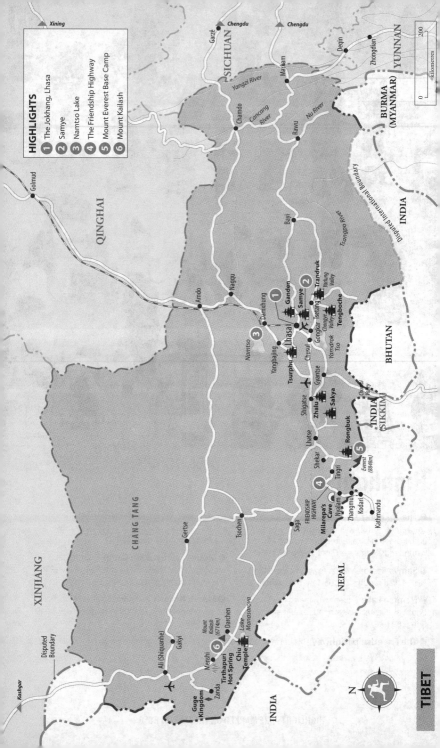

arrived, the monied and the ruling classes escaped to India, leaving behind an uneducated working class. China has spent billions bringing modern infrastructure to the region, giving Tibetan people the chance to make a better life for themselves and, ironically, strengthen their culture. Meanwhile, the Chinese migrating into Tibet are not demons. Most are people simply trying to make a life for themselves and their families, with little understanding of the implications of their presence. As with Taiwan and Xinjiang, all Chinese are taught almost from birth that Tibet is an "inalienable part of China", and to suggest otherwise is heresy.

As part of their Beijing Olympic bid, the Chinese government promised increased freedom for Tibetans, but a confluence of events – the unfurling of a Tibetan flag at Everest Base Camp by some American students in 2007, mass protests and rioting by Tibetans in spring 2008 – ended those dreams. Since 2008 an ongoing campaign in Tibet, Sichuan and even across the border in Nepal, has seen scores of Tibetan protesters set themselves ablaze. Extremely **strict travel regulations** are in place, and temporary bans on all foreign travellers from visiting the region are regularly imposed (see p.862). Any visit to Tibet will be **expensive**, with transport and accommodation options for foreigners limited, on the whole, to the higher end of the market, though Tibetan organizations abroad ask visitors to try, wherever possible, to buy from Tibetans and to hire Tibetan guides. At all times, you should avoid putting Tibetans – and yourself – at risk by bringing up **politically sensitive issues**: you can go home, Tibetans have to live here. The Chinese authorities monitor internet activity here more strictly than in the rest of the Republic so, again, avoid sensitive topics and mentioning people by name in your emails.

Where to go

Today's **Tibetan Autonomous Region** (TAR), while still a massive 1.2 million square kilometres, is but a shadow of the former "Greater Tibet" carved up by China in the 1950s, when the Amdo and Kham regions were absorbed into Qinghai, Sichuan, Gansu and Yunnan provinces. The current TAR comprises only the former West and Central regions of Greater Tibet, and is itself divisible into four distinct geographical areas. The northern and largest portion is the almost uninhabited **Chang Tang**, a rocky desert at an average altitude of 4000m, where winter temperatures can fall to - 44°C. South of this is the **mountainous grazing area**, inhabited by wide-ranging nomads tending herds of yaks, sheep and goats. **Eastern Tibet**, occupying around a quarter of the TAR, is heavily forested. The relatively temperate **southern valleys**, sandwiched between the nomad areas and the Himalayas along the southern border, is the most hospitable and populated area, and where most visitors spend the majority of their time.

Tourist-friendly Lhasa, **Shigatse** and **Gyantse** offer the most accessible monasteries and temples – the Jokhang, Tashilunpo and Kumbum, respectively. The **Potala Palace** in Lhasa remains an enduring image of Tibet in the Western mind and should on no account be missed. Farther afield, the **Yarlung** and **Chongye** valleys to the southeast boast temples and ancient monuments, with a visit to the ancient walled monastery of **Samye** easily combined with these. The route along the "Friendship Highway" between Zhangmu on the Nepalese border and Lhasa is well established, with stops at the Mongolian-style monastery at **Sakya** and **Everest Base Camp** along the way. Further west lie the sacred peak of **Mount Kailash**, its nearby, and similarly holy, neighbour **Lake Manasarovar**, and the mysterious cave dwellings of the **Guge Kingdom**, burrowed into the walls of an enormous, crumbling canyon.

Brief history

According to legend, the **earliest Tibetans** came from the union of the ogress, Sinmo, and a monkey, reincarnation of the god Chenresi, on the mountain of Gangpo Ri near Tsetang. Ethnographers, however, think it more likely that Tibetans are descended

14

TIBETAN BUDDHISM

Tibetan Buddhism is divided into several schools that have different philosophical emphases rather than fundamental differences. The **Nyingma**, the Old Order, traces its origins back to Guru Rinpoche, Padmasambhava, who brought Buddhism to Tibet. The **Kagyupa**, **Sakya** and **Kadampa** all developed during the eleventh-century revival of Buddhism, while the now-dominant **Gelugpa** (Virtuous School) was founded by Tsongkhapa (1357–1419) and numbers the Dalai Lama and Panchen Lama among its adherents. Virtually all monasteries and temples are aligned to one or other of the schools, but, apart from an abundance of statues of revered lamas of that particular school, you'll spot little difference between the temples. Tibetan people are pretty eclectic and will worship in temples that they feel are particularly sacred and seek blessings from lamas they feel are endowed with special powers, regardless of which school they belong to.

VISITING TEMPLES

There is little ceremony attached to **visiting temples**, which are generally welcoming places. Most are open in the mornings (9am–noon), when pilgrims do the rounds, and again after lunch (around 2pm or 3pm, until 5pm). Smaller places may well be locked, but ask for the caretaker and the chances are you'll be let in. There is no need to remove your shoes, but you should always circulate in a **clockwise** direction, and shouldn't eat, drink or smoke inside. Ask before taking photographs, which isn't always allowed, and if it is, you may be charged for the privilege. **Entrance fees** collected from tourists are often claimed by local authorities, so if you want to give to the institution itself, leave an offering on an altar or pay the photography charge.

The range of **offerings** Tibetans make to their gods is enormous: juniper smoke sent skyward in incense burners, prayer flags erected on rooftops and mountains, tiny papers printed with religious images (*lungda*) and cast to the wind on bridges and passes, white scarves (*katag*) presented to statues and lamas, butter to keep lamps burning on altars, repetitious mantras invoking the gods and the spinning of prayer wheels that have printed prayers rolled up inside are all part of religious observance. The idea of each is to gain merit in this life and hence affect karma. If you want to take part, watch what other people do and copy them; nobody is at all precious about religion in Tibet. Giving **alms to beggars** is another way of gaining merit, and most large Tibetan temples have a horde of beggars who survive on charity from pilgrims. Whether or not you give money is up to you, but if you do it's wise to give a few small denomination notes or so, the same amount as Tibetans.

GODS AND GODDESSES

Tibetan Buddhism has an overwhelming number of **gods and goddesses**, and each deity in turn has different manifestations or forms. For example, there are 21 forms of the favourite goddess Tara, and even the most straightforward image has both a Sanskrit and Tibetan name. Below are some of the most common you will encounter:

from the nomadic Qiang, who roamed eastern Central Asia several thousand years ago. The first Tibetan king, Nyatri Tsenpo, who legend has it came to earth via a magical "sky-cord", was the first of 27 kings who ruled in the pre-Buddhist era when the indigenous, shamanistic **Bon religion** held sway. Each of the **early kings** held power over a small area, the geographical isolation of Tibet making outside contact difficult. While pens, ink, silk, jewels and probably tea reached Tibet from China in the seventh century, for many centuries Tibet looked to India for religious teaching.

Arrival of Buddhism

It was in the time of **King Songtsen Gampo**, born in 617 AD, that expansion began. Songtsen Gampo's twenty-year rule saw the unification of the country and the aggressive spread of his empire from northern India to China. China and Nepal each offered Songtsen Gampo a wife: in 632, he married Princess Bhrikuti (also known as

Amitayus (Tsepame) and **Vijaya** (Namgyelma), often placed with White Tara to form the Three Gods of Longevity.

Avalokiteshvara (Chenresi in Tibetan, Guanyin in Chinese temples), patron god of Tibet, with many forms, most noticeably with eleven faces and a thousand arms.

Maitreya (Jampa), the Buddha of the Future.

Manjusri (Jampelyang), the God of Wisdom.

Padmasambhava, with eight manifestations, most apparent as Guru Rinpoche. You may see him with his consorts, Yeshe Tsogyel and Mandarava.

Sakyamuni, Buddha of the Present.

Tara (Dolma), Goddess of Compassion. Green Tara is associated with protection and White Tara with long life.

FESTIVALS

Festival dates are calculated using the Tibetan lunar calendar and as a result correspond to different dates on the Western calendar each year. There is a list of festival dates in the Western calendar at Ⓦ kalachakranet.org/ta_tibetan_calendar.html.

February/March

Driving out of evil spirits. Twenty-ninth day of the twelfth lunar month, the last day of the year.

Losar, Tibetan New Year. First day of the first lunar month.

Monlam, Great Prayer Festival, Lhasa. Eighth day of the first lunar month.

Butter Lamp Festival, on the final day of Monlam. Fifteenth day of the first lunar month.

May/June

Birth of Buddha. Seventh day of the fourth lunar month.

Saga Dawa (Buddha's Enlightenment). Fifteenth day of the fourth lunar month.

Gyantse Horse Festival. Fifteenth day of the fourth lunar month.

July

Tashilunpo Festival, Shigatse. Fifteenth day of the fifth lunar month.

July/August

Buddha's First Sermon. Fourth day of the sixth lunar month.

Drepung Festival. Thirtieth day of the sixth lunar month.

August/September

Shotun (Yoghurt Festival), Lhasa. First to the seventh day of the seventh lunar month.

Bathing Festival, Lhasa. Twenty-seventh day of the seventh lunar month.

September

Damxhung Horse Festival. Thirtieth day of the seventh lunar month.

September/October

Harvest Festival. First to the seventh day of the eighth lunar month.

November

Lhabab (Buddha's descent from heaven). Twenty-second day of the ninth lunar month.

November/December

Palden Lhamo Festival, Lhasa. Fifteenth day of the tenth lunar month.

Tritsun) of Nepal, and in 641 Princess Wencheng arrived from the Tang court, sent by her father, Emperor Taizong. They both brought their **Buddhist faith** and magnificent statues of the Buddha, which are now the centrepieces of Ramoche temple and the Jokhang in Lhasa. Songtsen Gampo himself embraced Buddhism and established temples throughout the country, although the indigenous Bon faith remained the religion of the ordinary people. Following his death in 650, his descendants strengthened the kingdom politically, and in 763 Tibetan armies even took the Chinese capital Chang'an (modern Xi'an).

In 838, having assassinated his brother, **Langdarma** came to the throne. A fervent supporter of the by-then marginalized Bon faith, he set about annihilating Buddhism. Temples and monasteries were destroyed, monks fled, and Tibet broke up into a number of small principalities. A century later, the arrival of **Atisha** (982–1054), the most famous Indian scholar of his time, sparked a Buddhist revival involving monastery construction, the translation of scriptures into Tibetan and the establishment of several of the schools of Tibetan Buddhism. Politically, the country was divided, with the various independent principalities having little contact with China.

Mongol period

Absorbed in domestic events, the Tibetans were largely unaware of the Muslim surge across India in the twelfth and thirteenth centuries, which destroyed the great Buddhist centres of teaching. Meanwhile, to the north and east, Mongol leader **Genghis Khan** was beginning his assault on China. In 1207, he sent envoys to Tibet demanding submission, which was given without a fight, and the territory was largely ignored until his grandson, Godan Khan, sent raiding parties to explore the country. Hearing from his troops about the spirituality of the Tibetan lamas, Godan invited the head of the Sakya order, Sakya Pandita, to his court. In exchange for peace, Sakya Pandita again offered Tibetan submission and was created regent of Tibet at the Mongolian court, effectively making the Sakya lamas rulers of the country. This lasted through the generations, with Godan's son **Kublai Khan** deeply impressed by Sakya Pandita's nephew, Phagpa.

When the Chinese Ming dynasty overcame the Mongols in the fourteenth century, Tibet began a long period of independence, which ended in 1642 with the Mongols intervening directly in support of the Fifth Dalai Lama, Lobsang Gyatso (1617–82), of the **Gelugpa order**. Often referred to as "**the Great Fifth**", he united the country under Gelugpa rule and within fifteen years established authority from Kham to Kailash – the first time that one religious and political leader had ruled the country. He invited scholars to Tibet, expanded religious institutions and began work on the Potala Palace.

Regency period

One disadvantage of the **reincarnation system** of succession (in which a newborn child is identified as a new manifestation of the dead lama) is that an unstable regency period of fifteen or twenty years inevitably follows the death of a Lama while his latest incarnation grows up. For two centuries after the death of the Fifth Dalai Lama in 1682 the most influential figures in Tibet were these regents, and the representatives of China's Manchu rulers, whose influence – despite Tibet's official continuing status as a Chinese protectorate until 1912 – waned to the extent that Tibet became, to all intents and purposes, self-governing.

British invasion

During the **nineteenth century**, Tibet became increasingly isolationist, fearing Russian plans to expand their empire south and British plans to expand theirs north. But Indian and Tibetan traders continued to do business along the borders: in 1904, British patience with this one-sided arrangement ran out, and a force under Colonel Francis Younghusband was dispatched to extract favourable trading terms.

Younghusband advanced into the country, slaughtering Tibet's poorly armed peasant soldiers – largely reliant on invulnerability charms for protection – along the way. Having cut their way through to Lhasa (where they were expecting, but failed, to find evidence of Russian influence), the British faced disappointment, one accompanying journalist writing:

If one approached within a league of Lhasa, saw the glittering domes of the Potala and turned back without entering the precincts one might still imagine an enchanted city. It was in fact an unsanitary slum. In the pitted streets pools of rainwater and piles of refuse were everywhere: the houses were mean and filthy, the stench pervasive. Pigs and ravens competed for nameless delicacies in open sewers.

The invaders forced a treaty on the Tibetans which the Dalai Lama – who had fled their advance – did not ratify, and which was rejected too by China's representative.

Britain then washed its hands of the whole affair, principally because of the public outcry against the first battle of the campaign, in which 700 Tibetans were machine-gunned as they walked away from the battlefield.

Chinese Invasion

The **Thirteenth Dalai Lama**, Tubten Gyatso (1876–1933), realized that Tibet's political position needed urgent clarification. But he had a difficult rule, fleeing into exile twice, and was much occupied with border fighting against the Chinese and tensions with conservatives inside the country. Following his death, the **Fourteenth Dalai Lama** was identified in Amdo in 1938 and was still a young man when world events began to close in on Tibet. The British left India in 1947, withdrawing their representative from Lhasa. In 1950, the Chinese government declared their intention "to liberate the oppressed and exploited Tibetans and reunite them with the great motherland". The venture, however, probably had more to do with pre-empting growing Indian and Russian influence in the region, than with any high-minded ideals of emancipation. In October 1950, the People's Liberation Army took the Kham region of eastern Tibet before proceeding to Lhasa the following year. Under considerable duress, Tibet signed a seventeen-point treaty in 1951, allowing for the "peaceful integration of Tibet" into China.

Early Communist era

Initially, the Chinese offered goodwill and modernization. Tibet had made little headway into the twentieth century; there were few roads, no electricity or lay education, and glass windows, steel girders and concrete were all recent introductions. While some Tibetans viewed modernization as necessary, the opposition was stiff, with the religious hierarchy seeing changes within the country as a threat to their own power. In March 1959, underground resistance to Chinese rule flared into a public confrontation. Refugees from eastern Tibet fled to Lhasa complaining of the brutality of Chinese rule, including the sexual humiliation of monks and nuns, arbitrary executions and even crucifixions. In Lhasa, the Chinese invited the Dalai Lama to a theatrical performance at the Chinese military HQ. It was popularly perceived as a ploy to kidnap him, and huge numbers of Tibetans mounted demonstrations and surrounded the Norbulingka where the Dalai Lama was staying. On the night of March 17, the Dalai Lama and his entourage fled into **exile** in India where they have since been joined by tens of thousands of refugees.

Crushing of the rebellion

The **uprising in Lhasa** was ferociously suppressed within a couple of days, the Tibetan rebels massively out-gunned by Chinese troops. Recriminations and further consolidation of Chinese power, however, were to continue: between March 1959 and September 1960 the Chinese killed an estimated 87,000 people. All pretence of goodwill vanished, and a huge military force moved in, with a Chinese bureaucracy replacing Tibetan institutions. Temples and monasteries were destroyed, and Chinese **agricultural policies** proved particularly disastrous. During the years of the Great Leap Forward (1959–60), it is estimated that ten percent of Tibetans starved – harrowing accounts tell of parents mixing their own blood with hot water and *tsampa* to feed their children.

Cultural Revolution and aftermath

In September 1965, the U-Tsang and western areas of Tibet officially became the **Xizang Autonomous Region** of the People's Republic of China, but more significant was the **Cultural Revolution** (1966–76), during which mass eradication of religious monuments and practices took place. In 1959, there were 2700 monasteries and temples in Tibet; by 1978, there were just eight. Liberalization followed Mao's death in

14

1976, leading to a period of relative openness and peace in the early 1980s when monasteries were rebuilt, religion revived and tourism introduced. However, by the end of the decade, martial law was again in place – thanks to Hu Jintao, later China's president – following riots in Lhasa in 1988–89. In the early 1990s, foreigners were allowed back into the region, and as the decade progressed it appeared the Chinese government was loosening their heavy-handed authoritarian approach to Tibet, and were keen to exploit Tibet's potential for international tourism.

Olympic recriminations

All this fell apart during the build-up to the 2008 Beijing Olympics: pre-Games riots and protests in Tibet, Sichuan, Gansu and Qinghai focused international attention on underlying tensions in Tibet; the Chinese government, embarrassed and angry, re-sealed borders and introduced all-but martial law. Since then, thousands have been arrested and any open dissent – or even discussion – has been almost entirely stifled, arguably resulting in an ongoing campaign of **self-immolation** by Tibetan monks which began in 2009.

A Chinese future

The **Tibetan Government in Exile**, meanwhile, based at Dharamsala in northern India, represents some 130,000 refugees. Its leader, the Dalai Lama – known to the Tibetans as Gyalwa Rinpoche and regarded as the earthly incarnation of the god Chenresi – has never faltered from advocating a peaceful solution for Tibet, a stance that led to his being awarded the 1989 Nobel Peace Prize. The Chinese government, however, has consistently denounced the Dalai Lama as being responsible for dissent, branding him "a devil with the face of a human but the heart of a beast". His increasing age and frailty, the certainty of his death and the challenge of finding a successor pose serious questions for both China and the Tibetan authorities in exile.

In the meantime, several thousand Tibetans every year make the month-long trek to India, an arduous and dangerous journey over the mountains. Pilgrims have been picked off by Chinese snipers as they crossed the Himalayas, though increasingly those who escape stay only for a few years before heading back home. For the Tibetans who remain, life in Tibet is harsh. Per capita annual income in rural areas is pitiful and the rate of adult literacy has been describe by the UN as "horrendous". It is estimated that China subsidized the TAR between 1952 and 1998 to the tune of ¥40 billion – yet Tibetans are among the poorest people in China, with some of the lowest life expectancies. As Tibet provides the Chinese with land for their exploding population along with a wealth of natural resources, the influx of more educated and better-skilled Chinese settlers, with considerable financial resources, threatens to swamp the Tibetan population, culture and economy.

ARRIVAL AND DEPARTURE TIBET

Travel restrictions for Tibet have been in place since 2008, and there seems no sign of a thaw for the time being. No independent travel by foreign visitors is allowed; you must be booked on a fixed-itinerary guided tour, though you can

14

TRAVELLERS' TIBETAN

Although most tour guides are now conversant in several languages, including English, most Tibetans speak only their native tongue, with a smattering of Mandarin. A few words of Tibetan from a foreigner will always be greeted enthusiastically, and the further off the beaten track you get, the more useful they'll be.

Tibetan belongs to the small Tibeto-Burmese group of languages and has no similarity at all to Mandarin. Tibetan script was developed in the seventh century and has thirty consonants and five vowels, which are placed either beside, above or below other letters when written down. There are obvious inaccuracies when trying to render this into the Roman alphabet, and the situation is further complicated by the many dialects across the region; the Lhasa dialect is used in the vocabulary below. Word order is back-to-front relative to English, and verbs are placed at the ends of sentences – "this noodle soup is delicious" becomes "tukpa dee shimbo doo", literally "noodle soup this delicious is". The only sound you are likely to have trouble with is "**ng**" at the beginning of words – it is pronounced as in "sa**ng**".

BASIC PHRASES

Hello	*tashi delay*
Goodbye, to someone staying	*kalay shu*
Goodbye, to someone going	*kalay pay*
Thank you	*tuk too jay*
Sorry	*gonda*
Please	*coochee*
How are you?	*kusu debo yinbay?* or *kam sangbo dugay?*
I'm…	*nga…*
Fine	*debo yin*
Cold	*kya*
Hungry	*throko-doe*
Thirsty	*ka gom*
Tired	*galay ka*
I don't understand	*nga ha ko ma-song*
What is your name?	*kayranggi mingla karay ray?*
My name is…	*ngeye mingla…sa*
Where are you from?	*kayrang kanay ray?*
I'm from…	*nga…nay yin*
Britain	*Injee*
Australia	*Otaleeya*
America	*Amerika*
How old are you?	*kayrang lo katsay ray?*
I'm…	*nga lo…yin*
Where are you going?	*kaba drogee yin?*
I'm going to…	*nga…la drogee yin*
Where is the…?	*…kaba doo?*
hospital	*menkang*
monastery	*gompa*
temple/chapel	*lhakhang*
restaurant	*sakang*
convent	*ani gompa*
caretaker	*konyer*
Is there…?	*…doo gay?*
hot water	*chu tsa-bo*
a candle	*yangla*
I don't have…	*nga…mindoo*
Is this OK/can I do this?	*deegee rebay?*
It's (not) OK	*deegee (ma)ray*
(Not) Good	*yaggo (min)doo*

This is delicious	*dee shimbo doo*
Do you want…?	*kayrang…gobay?*
I want tea	*nga cha go*
I don't want this	*dee me-go*
What is this/that?	*dee/day karray ray?*
How much is this?	*gong kadso ray?*
When?	*kadoo?*
Now	*danta*
Today	*dering*
Yesterday	*kezang*
Tomorrow	*sangnyee*
Monday	*sa dowa*
Tuesday	*sa mingma*
Wednesday	*sa lagba*
Thursday	*sa purbur*
Friday	*sa pasang*
Saturday	*sa pemba*
Sunday	*sa nima*

NUMBERS

1	*chee*
2	*nyee*
3	*soom*
4	*zhee*
5	*nga*
6	*droo*
7	*doon*
8	*gyay*
9	*goo*
10	*chew*
11	*chew chee*
12	*chew nyee*
20	*nyi shoo*
21	*nyi shoo chee* etc
30	*soom chew*
40	*shib chew*
50	*ngab chew*
60	*drook chew*
70	*doon chew*
80	*gyay chew*
90	*goop chew*
100	*gya*
200	*nyee gya*
1000	*dong*

tailor this yourself (remembering, of course, that some areas of Tibet are permanently off-limits). You cannot change your route during the trip, and you are not allowed to stay on after the tour ends. The situation does ebb and flow: travellers have occasionally made it through to Tibet on their own (usually in winter, when the security forces let their guard down a bit), while you're unlikely to be allowed into Tibet at all in March, always a time of unrest. Contact one of the more established agencies (see p.866) to arrange tours and to get the latest on the situation. Despite this, basic public transport information is included in some of the accounts through the chapter, in the hopes that independent travel may one day again be possible. However, all foreigners would be advised against attempting these routes without first establishing whether they are permitted to do so.

14

BY PLANE

From China Planes operate between Lhasa and Chengdu (¥1300), Beijing (¥2500), Shangri-La (¥1200) and Kunming (¥1700) – prices quoted are economy one-way. The easiest option is to fly from Chengdu, where plenty of tour operators offer tickets, tours and permits.

From Nepal It is also possible to fly in to Lhasa from Kathmandu in Nepal, but you will need to ensure you have a Chinese visa and Tibet Travel Permit before attempting the journey. As permits can now be emailed for you to print out, you are not limited to booking your tour in Nepal, and, as long as you can arrange payment, any of the China or Tibet-based agencies will be able to meet you off the plane in Lhasa.

BY TRAIN

The largest threat to the Tibetan way of life – and the biggest promise of modernization, and therefore rising living standards – comes from the Qinghai–Lhasa railway line. This extrordinary feat of engineering opened in 2006 at a cost of US$4 billion; more than 1200km of new track was laid by 11,000 migrant workers, much of it at an altitude of over 4000m and on permafrost, with more than 30km of tunnels. Passengers hoping to be protected from the effects of altitude by the much-vaunted "pressurized carriages" will be disappointed – with toilet windows left open and some passengers experiencing altitude sickness, the carriages are not all they're cracked up to be. The journey itself,

---

TIBET TRAVEL PERMITS

In order to enter Tibet – in fact, even to buy a plane or train ticket to Lhasa – foreign travellers must have a **Tibet Travel Permit**. Issued by the TAR authorities, this lists a full travel itinerary and provides evidence of having booked a car, driver and guide for every day you are in the region. Available through registered travel agencies only, the permit should be included as part of your travel package by whichever agency you book with. Though the permit officially carries no cost, agencies arranging permits will charge a significant **handling fee** for the service, covering the huge amount of paperwork and "other costs" involved.

Be aware that until the permit is issued, which often occurs only a day or two before your tour will be due to start, you will not be able to independently book flights or trains into the region. The agency you have booked your tour through, safe in the knowledge of your full itinerary and in possession of a fair-sized deposit, is likely willing to make reservations on your behalf, or you can wait to book travel yourself at the last minute; either way, don't expect discounted tickets. While it may be tempting to try to sidestep the regulations, all foreign travellers coming from inside China will have their permits checked at point of purchase, on departure, and on arrival; hotels will not let foreigners stay unless accompanied at check-in by an official tour guide with a valid permit, and they are required to be shown again when visiting the Potala Palace and other tourist sights. Add the regular checkpoints along roads outside Lhasa and it would take a serious, concerted effort, and a massive slice of luck, for a permitless traveller to get very far.

Once in Tibet, **further permits** are needed for specific areas. Travel along the Friendship Highway to Everest, and to Mount Kailash, requires permits that are most often secured from the Public Security Bureau in Shigatse, costing around ¥150. Getting these permits is the responsibility of your tour guide and costs will have been included in the overall agency fee, so its not something you should have to worry about. That said, it's best to politely double check that they are being taken care of. Anyone caught without permits or overstaying their alloted time faces fines and deportation from the region. The agency that applies for the permit on your behalf may also face stiff penalties, so your guides will also be anxious for you to stick to the leaving dates set out on the permit. Bear in mind that regulations have shifted fairly regularly in the past, so it's best to check up on the latest requirements before booking.

however, provides fantastic vistas of the plateau, with herds of yaks and fascinating glimpses of human life that exists – against the odds – in this thinly-oxygenated environment.

Buying tickets Tickets to Lhasa go on sale ten days before departure, and demand is high, particularly during the summer when sleeper tickets are incredibly hard to come by. Mysteriously, travel agencies don't seem to have the same problems and can usually supply any tickets you need, but with a mark-up of several hundred percent. Hard-seat tickets are easier to secure yourself, but with a forty-hour journey time between Beijing and Lhasa this is not for the faint of heart (or tender of bottom).

Departure points There are numerous departure points to Lhasa: Beijing (¥763); Chengdu (¥709); Chongqing (¥751); Golmud (¥375); Guangzhou (¥919); Lanzhou (¥550); Shanghai (¥841); and Xining (¥511). Prices quoted are for a single in a hard-sleeper berth.

OVERLAND

From China Aside from the train, regulations bar foreigners from independent travel overland into Tibet, for instance on bicycle, foot or public buses from adjoining provinces. Private tours to Lhasa from places like Chengdu, Shangri-La in Yunnan, or Kashgar in Xinjiang are theoretically possible but expensive, require considerable organizing and inevitably involve spending days on end cooped up in a jeep.

From Nepal Kathmandu to Lhasa is a popular route and in this instance, if you don't want a guided tour all the way from Kathmandu, you can travel up to the Nepal-Tibet border by bus and cross into Tibet on foot, provided you've arranged for a tour guide to collect you on the Tibet side. To get a Chinese visa in Nepal and secure the necessary Tibet Travel Permit, you will need to be booked on an organized tour. This can be done through travel companies in Kathmandu, or you may be able to find a Tibet-based agency who, after finishing one tour from Lhasa to Zhangmu, are keen to pick a group up at the border and run the tour in the opposite direction on their way home. Visas issued in Kathmandu are often only valid for three weeks, so if you plan on crossing from Nepal into Tibet, it's worth getting your Chinese visa elsewhere. Expect to pay around US$800 for an organized seven-day overland trip to Lhasa, or around US$400 for a three-day trip – but make sure you are clear on exactly what is and isn't included in terms of accommodation, food and entry tickets. One agency that will group individual travellers together is Nature Trail Trekking at Durbar Marg in Kathmandu (☎977 14701925, ⊕ allnepal.com). The best advice is to spend some time in Kathmandu to get a feel for the current situation and check out your options. Beware of your guides offering money-changing services, citing a dearth of options in Tibet. This is untrue, and once you're in Tibet you'll find plenty places to change cash at more competitive rates.

GETTING AROUND

By jeep One side effect of the current travel regulations is that getting around in-country is easy – you just get in your allotted 4WD and go wherever your guide and driver take you. The vehicles provided are generally ageing Toyota Landcruisers or similar, though larger groups sticking to the well-surfaced Friendship Highway may be given people carriers or even minibuses. As you can't view vehicles before you book, it can be worth putting any requirements you may have – such as seatbelts – in writing and get them agreed by the your travel agency before you arrive, which will provide leverage for getting the vehicle swapped if it isn't up to standard. During travel outside Lhasa your vehicle will stay with you at all times, and while in Lhasa will ferry you to sites listed on your itinerary too far to walk to – for extra travel within Lhasa, you'll need to take a taxi or agree an additional fee with your driver.

By bus and minibus The public transport system in Tibet, such as it is, consists of large buses and smaller, nippier minibuses. In-town use of public transport by foreigners is generally tolerated, though only in Lhasa might it be actually necessary. Intercity travel by bus is not permitted, and even if you can find someone willing to sell you a ticket and a driver happy to take you, you are unlikely to make

your destination without running into a checkpoint of some kind, where you will be fined and ordered to leave Tibet. Nevertheless, basic public transport information is included through the chapter for reference, though foreigners would be advised against attempting these routes without first establishing whether they are currently allowed to do so.

By bicycle Long-distance cycling is not technically illegal, but even cyclists have to hire a guide, jeep and driver while they are on the road. Authorities (and the tour agency) will do their best to make sure you stay in hotels, even if you come equipped with camping and warm-weather gear. To be fair, having a backup team can prove helpful: though most of the traditional route from Kathmandu to Lhasa is level and the road in decent condition, dogs and weather can be a hazard, and there are five 5000m-high passes to contend with. The route is covered by a few cycle tour companies, such as the UK-based Exodus (☎0845 527 1391, ⊕www.exodus .co.uk) and Nepal Mountain Bike Tours in Kathmandu (☎977 14701701, ⊕bikehimalayas.com), or you can negotiate with any of the Lhasa-based tour companies on prices for your required chaperone.

14

ARRANGING TOURS

With independent travel in Tibet currently impossible for foreign tourists, the only option is to book a **guided tour** – including a private vehicle, driver and guide – through an agency before you arrive. Despite the huge number of travel agencies in Chengdu, Xining, Golmud and Lhasa, all claiming to offer a unique service, most operate through CITS or FIT in Lhasa, hiring drivers and tour guides who are registered with the Lhasa authorities and work as freelancers. That you are forced to book from outside the region, preventing you from meeting the tour guide or seeing the vehicle before signing up, means it pays to be circumspect – try to get a recommendation from a fellow traveller if possible, and go through your itinerary with a fine-tooth comb working out exactly what is covered and what you will have to pay extra for. Getting a group of four or five together to fill a **jeep** will ensure the per-person cost is as low as it can be, though if you are on your own or in a couple, most agencies will be able to match you up with a group which has spaces that need filling.

Despite the requirement to book a tour, regulations do not stipulate that **accommodation** reservations are made in advance. As a result, not all tour agencies include accommodation in their prices – clarify whether accommodation is included and, if so, where. You may be able to bring down the price of your tour, or ensure you're not bedding down in the worst place in every town, by negotiating where you stay.

The **most popular tour** follows the Friendship Highway up to the Nepalese border, and includes three days in Lhasa and five on the road taking in Gyantse, Shigatse and Everest Base Camp. It costs around ¥7000 per person including accommodation. However, as you have to book a driver, guide and vehicle anyway, there is no reason to simply stick to the tours offered – you can draw up your own itinerary and negotiate costs with the agency. Expect to pay around ¥1300 per day to hire a Land Cruiser. For driver and guide fees it is best to haggle prices as low as you can with the agency and tip heavily at the end of the tour to ensure the money goes where you want it to.

ESTABLISHED AGENCIES

In the event of a misunderstanding, you may wish to complain to the Tour Service Inspection Office of Lhasa's Tibet Tourism Bureau, 208 Luobulingka Lu (☎0891 6333476 or 6334193).
Budget Tibet Tour ⊛budgettibettour.com
CITS ⊛tibettravel.org
Khampa Caravan ⊛khampacaravan.com
Tibet Culture Tour ⊛tibetculturetour.com
Tibetan Expeditions ☎0086 (0)1351 8984 224 ⊛tibetanexpeditions.com
Tibet Nakqu International Travel Service ☎0086 891 6328851, ✉namgyal_tenzin @hotmail.com
Wind Horse ⊛windhorsetour.com

ACCOMMODATION

Hotels The widest choice of accommodation is found in the main tourist centres of Lhasa, Shigatse, Gyantse, Tsetang and Zhangmu, where tourist-class hotels provide comfortable rooms with attached bathrooms and at least some hours of hot water.

Guesthouses In most Tibetan towns, simple guesthouses offer accommodation to foreigners, pilgrims and truck drivers. You can expect a basic dormitory experience, with bedding (of variable cleanliness) provided. The communal toilets are often pit latrines and there are few washing facilities, although most places have bowls and washstands. Hot water in vacuum flasks, for drinks and washing, can be found everywhere.

Camping and homestays If you are trekking, you can camp, although many trekkers find accommodation in village houses or with nomadic yak-herders. You should not expect them to feed you, and should pay ¥20 or so per night.

CLOTHING

Despite the plateau's altitude and the perennially snowcapped mountains, not everywhere in Tibet is constantly beset by ice and freezing temperatures. In summer, Lhasa and the valleys across the region reach temperatures well above 20°C. During the day T-shirt and shorts are perfectly adequate, though a hat and serious sun cream are advisable to fend off the UV rays (be aware that long trousers are required for entry into most temples, and hats should be removed once inside). Summer evenings and night-times can be chilly, and a jumper is the minimum requirement. Everest Base Camp can fall below zero even in the summer – thermals, winter jacket, gloves and woolly hat are all recommended whatever the time of year. All hotels, including the guesthouse tents at Everest, supply their own bedding, but bringing your own sleeping bag is not a bad idea for hygiene as well as thermal considerations, especially if you're planning on hostelling. Don't worry if you don't want to lug your full winter wardrobe around until you get to Tibet; there is a good supply of cheap anoraks, winter jackets and general hiking and camping gear in Lhasa, most of it reasonable-quality fakes imported from Nepal.

EATING AND DRINKING

The traditional Tibetan diet – constrained by what little will grow at over 4000m – consists in large part of butter tea, a unique mixture of yak butter, tea and salt, all churned into a blend that many Westerners find undrinkable, but which Tibetans consume in huge quantities. Into this is stirred *tsampa*, roasted barley flour, to make dough with the consistency of raw pastry and a not unpleasant nutty flavour. Yak meat, yoghurt and cheese (often dried into bite-sized cubes to preserve it), and sometimes a soup of a few vegetables, supplement this. *Thukpa* (pronounced "tukpa") is a noodle soup with a few bits and pieces of whatever is available thrown in. If you're lucky, you'll find *momos*, tiny steamed or fried dough parcels containing meat, vegetables or cheese (a *thri momo* is a solid dough parcel without a filling). In Lhasa and most stops along the Friendship Highway restaurants have Nepali cooking staff churning out very decent curries and dhals, but indifferent approximations of Tibetan and Chinese cuisine. The local brew, *Lhasa Beer*, is widely available – and very drinkable.

HEALTH

Altitude sickness Almost every visitor is affected by altitude sickness, as most of Tibet is over 3000m, with plenty of passes over 5000m. For your first two or three days, rest as much as possible and drink plenty of water. You can buy oxygen canisters in most hotel receptions (¥20), though whether they're much use is debatable. A few painkillers should help to relieve any aches and pains and headaches, but more serious problems can develop; see Basics, p.53, for more details.

Giardiasis A small but significant number of travellers to Tibet also suffer from giardiasis, an unpleasant and debilitating intestinal complaint. The treatment is Tinadozol or Flagyl, neither or which is reliably available in Lhasa; bring a course along with you if you're planning an ambitious or lengthy trip. They can both be purchased cheaply and easily in big cities within China.

Rabies Travellers to Tibet should seriously consider rabies immunization before they travel. The dogs can be aggressive, bites are relatively common and, if you get bitten, Kathmandu is the nearest place stocking rabies serum.

WHEN TO VISIT

Bad times to visit Chinese authorities are much pricklier around festival times (see p.859) and the week before and after certain historically significant dates, when they may stop issuing permits for foreigners. Dates to bear in mind include March 5 and 10 (the anniversaries of uprisings in 1959, 1988, 1989 and 2008), July 6 (the Dalai Lama's birthday), September 27 and October 1 (the anniversaries of protests in 1987), and December 10 (International Human Rights Day, and the anniversary of the Dalai Lama's Nobel Peace Prize). On a different note, August is especially popular with domestic tour groups, which might again make it a month to avoid if possible.

Weather The best time to visit Tibet is from April to October, outside the coldest months. June to September is the wettest period, when blocked roads and swollen rivers can make travel difficult, but the countryside will be at its greenest. Health considerations should be taken seriously at any time of the year, and even in relatively balmy Lhasa, temperatures fall below freezing on a regular basis. In winter, as long as you come fully prepared for the cold (most hotels have no heating) and possible delays due to snow-covered passes, the lack of tourists and the preoccupation of the security forces with staying warm can make for a pleasant trip.

Lhasa

拉萨, lāsà

Situated in a wide, mountain-fringed valley at 3700m on the north bank of the Kyichu River, **LHASA** (Ground of the Gods) is a sprawling modern city with a population of around 200,000. An important settlement for well over a thousand years, it was not until the seventeenth century, with the installation of the Fifth Dalai Lama as ruler by

14

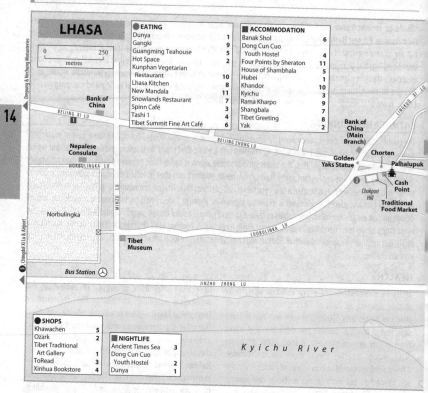

LHASA

| 0 | 250 |
| metres |

EATING
Dunya	1
Gangki	9
Guangming Teahouse	5
Hot Space	2
Kunphan Vegetarian Restaurant	10
Lhasa Kitchen	8
New Mandala	11
Snowlands Restaurant	7
Spinn Café	3
Tashi 1	4
Tibet Summit Fine Art Café	6

ACCOMMODATION
Banak Shol	6
Dong Cun Cuo Youth Hostel	4
Four Points by Sheraton	11
House of Shambhala	5
Hubei	1
Khandor	10
Kyichu	3
Rama Kharpo	9
Shangbala	7
Tibet Greeting	8
Yak	2

SHOPS
Khawachen	5
Ozark	2
Tibet Traditional Art Gallery	1
ToRead	3
Xinhua Bookstore	4

NIGHTLIFE
Ancient Times Sea	3
Dong Cun Cuo Youth Hostel	2
Dunya	1

Mongolian emperor Gushri Khan, that Lhasa became the seat of government. It continues now as the capital of the TAR, but with its wide boulevards, shopping centres, and the concrete-and-glass high rises spreading south and west along the valley, China has well and truly left its architectural stamp upon the city. Despite the passing of sixty years, Lhasa is still palpably under imposed rule; the armed soldiers may have taken a lower profile, with much of the security work now falling to large numbers of police and plain-clothes officers on street corners and rooftops, but the air of occupation remains.

There are enough sights in and around Lhasa to keep visitors occupied for at least a week (even if most tours cram them into a couple of days): the **Potala Palace**, **Jokhang** and the **Barkhor** district are not to be missed, and at least one trip to an outlying monastery is a must. It's also worth taking time to see some of the smaller, less showy temples and simply to absorb the atmosphere of the "Forbidden City", which large numbers of explorers died in vain efforts to reach just over a hundred years ago.

The Potala Palace

布达拉宫, bùdálāgōng · Daily 8.30am–6pm, last entry 3.30pm · Nov–April ¥100, May–Oct ¥200 · bus #8 from Beijing Dong Lu passes the front gate · taxi from the city ¥10

Perched 130m above Lhasa atop Marpo Ri (Red Mountain), and named after India's Riwo Potala – holy mountain of the god Chenresi – the **Potala Palace** is dazzling inside and out, an enduring landmark of the city. As you revel in the views from the roof, gaze at the glittering array of gold and jewels and wend your way from chapel to chapel,

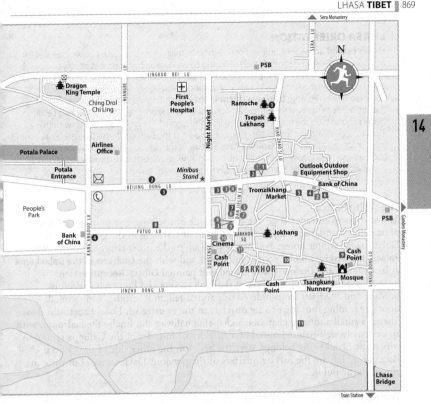

14

you'll rub shoulders with excited, awestruck pilgrims from all over ethnic Tibet, making offerings at each of the altars. But be aware that, beyond the areas approved for tourists and pilgrims, the Potala is a shadow of its former self: most of the rooms are off limits, part of a UNESCO World Heritage grant was spent on a CCTV system and the caretaker monks are not allowed to wear their robes.

Though close enough to town to reach on foot, don't tackle the Potala on your first day at altitude – the palace is a long climb, and even the Tibetans huff and puff on the way up; you'll enjoy it more once you've acclimatized. Morning is certainly the best time to visit, when the place bustles with pilgrims. **Photography** is banned inside, and neither, bizarrely, are you supposed to take pictures of the fabulous views from the roof. Snapping away in the palace's courtyards is tolerated, however.

Brief history

Rising thirteen storeys and consisting of over a thousand rooms, the Potala took some 8500 builders and craftsmen over fifty years to complete. The main mass of the Potala is the **White Palace** (Potrang Karpo), while the building rising from its centre is the **Red Palace** (Potrang Marpo). Though founded back in the seventh century, today's White Palace (1645–48) was built during the reign of the Fifth Dalai Lama, who took up residence in 1649; the Red Palace, begun at the same time, was completed in 1693. Built for several purposes, the Potala served as administrative centre, seat of government, monastery, fortress and the home of all the Dalai Lamas from the Fifth to the Fourteenth, although from the end of the eighteenth century, when the Norbulingka was built as the Summer Palace, they stayed here only in winter.

14

The White Palace

The tour-goup entrance is on the western side of the huge compound, and after a permit check and bag X-ray you'll find yourself standing in the grounds of the Dalai Lama's winter home. Follow the path up to the inner courtyard of the **White Palace**, flanked by monks' rooms and stores and with the **Quarters of the Dalai Lama** at its eastern end. The opulently carved and painted **Official Reception Hall** beyond is dominated by the bulk of the high throne and hung with fabulous brocade and *thangkas* (embroidered or painted religious scrolls), with a small doorway leading into the private quarters of the Fourteenth Dalai Lama next door. There's a small audience chamber, a chapel, a hallway and finally the bedroom, with an extremely well-painted mural of Tsongkhapa, founder of the Gelugpa school to which the Dalai Lama belongs, over the bed. On the other side of the Official Reception Hall are the private quarters of the previous Dalai Lamas, but these are closed to the public.

The Red Palace

Stairs lead from the inner courtyard up straight to the roof of the **Red Palace**, for fabulous views across Lhasa. You can then descend a floor at a time, moving clockwise all the way. The first room on the **upper floor** is the **Maitreya Chapel**, its huge number of fabulously ornate statues setting the tone for the remainder of the chapels. It's dominated by a seated statue of Maitreya, made at the time of the Eighth Dalai Lama and said to contain the brain of Atisha, the eleventh-century Indian scholar responsible for a Buddhist revival in Tibet (see p.859). On the far left of the Dalai Lama's throne is a statue of the Fifth Dalai Lama, commissioned soon after his death and supposedly containing some of his hair.

Upper floor tombs of the Dalai Lamas

The **tombs** of the Thirteenth and the Eighth Dalai Lamas are near the Meitreya Chapel on the upper floor. The Potala is the final resting place of the Fifth to Thirteenth Dalai Lamas, except for the Sixth, who died on his way to China and is said to be buried near Qinghai Hu in Qinghai province. Although the tombs vary in size, all are jewel-encrusted golden chortens (traditional multi-tiered Tibetan Buddhist monuments that usually contain sacred objects), supporting tier upon tier of fantastic engravings; encased deep within are the bodies, preserved in dry salt.

Lokeshvera Chapel and Practice Chamber

Considered the oldest and holiest shrines in the Potala, the **Lokeshvara Chapel**, on the upper floor, and the **Practice Chamber of the Dharma King**, directly below on the upper middle floor, date back to Songtsen Gampo's original construction, and are the focus of all Potala pilgrims. It's easy to miss the Practice Chamber, entered from a small corridor

> **POTALA TICKETS**
>
> **Potala tickets** have to be bought one or two days in advance. Foreign tourists must be accompanied by a guide, but as a visit will certainly be part of any tour to Tibet, your travel agency should be supplying tickets as part of the package. A major downside of this is that registered tour groups are – ludicrously, given the scale of the complex – limited to just one hour inside. Some visitors have reported being able to buy their own time-unlimited tickets the day before, but with only 2300 tickets issued per day – and 1600 of these reserved for tour groups – you'll need to get to the ticket office early and be prepared for disappointment.

from the balcony. King Songtsen Gampo supposedly meditated in this dark, dingy room now dominated by statues of the king and his ministers, Tonmi Sambhota and Gawa. At the base of the main pillar is a stove, apparently used by Songtsen Gampo himself.

The other floors

Although you pass through the **lower middle floor**, the chapels here are all closed and the remainder of the open rooms are on the lower floor leading off the large, many-columned Assembly Hall. The highlight down here is the grand **Chapel of the Dalai Lamas' Tombs**, containing the awesome golden chorten of the Fifth Dalai Lama, which is three storeys high and made from 3700kg of gold. To the left and right are smaller chortens with the remains of the Tenth and Twelfth Dalai Lamas, and the chortens on either side of these main ones are believed to contain relics of Buddha himself. Visitors leave by a door behind the altar in the **Chapel of the Holy Born**, from where the path winds down the west side of the hill to the western gate.

Peoples' Park

人民公园 rénmín gōngyuán • Beijing Dong Lu • Daily 5.30am–11pm • Free

Opposite the front of the Potala Palace palace, **People's Park** is a mini Tian'anmen Square, built in an effort to reinforce China's claim to the region; there is a Chinese flag and a monument celebrating Tibet's "liberation". Each night in summer Chinese tourists congregate to perform traditional Tibetan circle dances to the strains of nationalistic Chinese pop songs – it's quite a sight, but not a patch on the floodlit palace opposite.

Palhalupuk Temple

鲁普岩寺, lǔpǔyán sì • ¥20

From just east of the public toilets at the chorten to the west of the Potala Palace, a path leads a couple of hundred metres past some busy stone carvers to the fabulously atmospheric but under-visited **Palhalupuk Temple**, built around an ancient cave. You'll spot the less interesting ochre-and-maroon **Neten Temple** on the cliff first; Palhalupuk is the smaller, white building below. Entered from an ante-chapel, the cave, about five square metres, was King Songtsen Gampo's retreat in the seventh century and is lined with rock carvings, many of which date from that time. The most important altar is in front of the huge rock pillar that supports the roof, the main image being of Sakyamuni, flanked by his chief disciples. At the far right-hand corner stands a jewel- and *katag*-bedecked statue of Pelden Lhamo, the fierce protective deity of Tibet, on a tiny altar. The back wall has been left untouched, and it's said that the jewels of Songtsen Gampo's Nepalese wife, Princess Bhrikuti, are hidden behind.

14

Ching Drol Chi Ling Park

宗角禄康公园 zōngjiǎo lùkāng gōngyuán • Free • bus #8 from Beijing Dong Lu

Around the north side of the Potala Palace is **Ching Drol Chi Ling** park, which has fine views of the north facade of the Potala and sports a large area of trees plus two boating lakes (formed by the removal of earth during the construction of the palace).

Dragon King Temple

禄康, lùkāng • Daily 8am–5pm • ¥10

On an island in the westernmost of the two lakes is the small, pleasant **Dragon King Temple**, built by the Sixth Dalai Lama. Legend tells that the king of the **nagas**, subterranean creatures who resemble dragons, allowed earth to be excavated for the Potala's construction only as long as this chapel was built in their honour. The temple is famed for the very old and detailed murals on the middle and top floors, but you'll need a torch if you want to study them in detail – the protective wire in front doesn't help. The top-floor pictures, showing the stages of human life, the journey of the soul after death, and various legends, are somewhat esoteric, but the middle-floor murals, depicting the construction of the great monasteries of Sera and Drepung among others, are far more comprehensible.

The Jokhang

大昭寺, dàzhāo sì • Daily 8am–6pm • ¥85 • Bus #7 from the southwest of town or #8 from the Potala Palace will drop you at Beijing Dong Lu

The **Jokhang** – sometimes called Tshuglakhang (Cathedral), and the holiest temple in the Tibetan Buddhist world – can be unprepossessing from afar, but get closer and you'll be swept up by the anticipation of the pilgrims and the almost palpable air of veneration. It stands 1km east of the Potala Palace, in the centre of the only remaining Tibetan enclave in the city, the **Barkhor** area, a maze of cobbled alleyways between Beijing Dong Lu and Jinzhu Dong Lu. Inside, you're in for one of the most unforgettable experiences in Tibet. Devout pilgrims turn left to move clockwise and enter each chapel in turn to pray and make offerings, though they don't hang around; stand still to admire anything and you'll be trampled in the rush. As with all temples in Tibet, it's often difficult to know exactly what you are looking at. Some of the statues are original, others were damaged during the Cultural Revolution and have been restored either slightly or extensively, and others are replicas; in any event, all are held in deep reverence by the pilgrims. The best time to visit is in the morning, when most pilgrims do the rounds.

SUPPRESSING DEMONS

King Songtsen Gampo built the Jokhang in the seventh century to house the **dowry** brought by his Nepalese bride, Princess Bhrikuti, including the statue known as the Akshobhya Buddha. This later changed places with the Jowo Sakyamuni statue from Princess Wencheng's dowry, which was initially installed in Ramoche temple (see p.874), and which is now regarded as Tibet's most sacred object. The **site** of the temple was decided by Princess Wencheng after consulting astrological charts, and confirmed by the king following a vision while meditating. However, construction was fraught with problems. Another vision revealed to the king and his queens that beneath the land of Tibet lay a huge, sleeping **demoness** with her head in the east, feet to the west and heart beneath Lhasa. Only by building monasteries at suitable points to pin her to the earth could construction of the Jokhang succeed. The king embarked on a scheme to construct twelve demon-suppressing temples: four around Lhasa, which included Trandruk (see p.888), to pin her at hips and shoulders; a set of four farther away, to pin elbows and knees; and four even more distant, to pin her hands and feet. When these were finished, construction of the Jokhang began.

Barkhor Square

八角街广场, bājiǎojiē guǎngchǎng

The **main entrance** to the Jokhang is from **Barkhor Square**, which is to the west of the temple. Two bulbous incense burners in front of the temple send out juniper smoke as an offering to the gods, and the two walled enclosures here contain three ancient engraved pillars. The tallest is inscribed with the Tibetan–Chinese agreement of 821 AD and reads: "Tibet and China shall abide by the frontiers of which they are now in occupation. All to the east is the country of Great China; and all to the west is, without question, the country of Great Tibet. Henceforth on neither side shall there be waging of war or seizing of territory".

14

The lower chapels

In front of the huge temple doors, a constant crowd of pilgrims prostrate themselves – you can hear the clack of the wooden protectors on their hands and the hiss as the wood moves along the flagstones when they lie flat on the ground. Head round the southern side to the visitors' entrance to enter the main courtyard, where ceremonies and their preparations take place. Rows of tiny butter lamps burn on shelves along the far wall, and it's a bustling scene as monks make butter statues and dough offerings and tend the lamps. Through a corridor in the north wall, with small chapels to left and right – many of whose wooden door frames and columns are original, carved by Nepalese craftsmen – you pass into the inner area of the temple. The central section, **Kyilkhor Thil**, houses statues galore, six of them considered particularly important. The most dramatic are the 6m-high Padmasambhava on the left, which dates from 1955, and the half-seated figure of Maitreya, the Buddha of the Future, to the right.

Chapel of Jowo Sakyamuni

It's easy to feel overwhelmed, but if you manage only one chapel it should be the **Chapel of Jowo Sakyamuni** in the middle of the eastern, back wall of the temple. The 1.5m-high Sakyamuni is depicted at twelve years of age, with a sublimely beautiful golden face; draped in heavy brocade and jewels, this is the most deeply venerated statue in Tibet. Although the Jokhang was originally built to house the statue, it first stood in the temple of Ramoche until rumours of a Tang invasion late in the seventh century led to its removal to a hiding place in the Jokhang. During the reign of Trisong Detsen, the Bon opponents of Buddhism buried the statue, but it was found and sent out of Lhasa for safety; it was again buried during King Langdarma's attempt to annihilate Buddhism, but eventually returned to the Jokhang. Although there is a rumour that the original was destroyed in the eighteenth century by Mongol invaders, the statue is widely regarded as the original. Monks here keep the butter lamps topped up while the pilgrims move around the altar, bowing their heads to Jowo Sakyamuni's right leg and then his left.

The upper floor and roof

By the time you reach the **upper floor**, you'll probably be punch-drunk; fortunately perhaps, there is less to detain you up here, although most of the chapels are now open after restoration. Of most interest is the **Chapel of Songtsen Gampo**, directly above the main entrance in the west wall and featuring a large statue of the king flanked by his two queens. Continue up the stairs in the southwest corner of the chapel to one fierce and one peaceful image of **Pelden Lhamo**, who is regarded as the protective deity of Tibet and is particularly popular with pilgrims.

From the temple **roof**, the views over Barkhor Square, into the temple courtyard and as far as the Potala Palace in the distance, are wonderful, and the golden statues even more impressive.

14

The Barkhor

八角街, bājiǎojiē

Traditionally, pilgrims to Lhasa circled the city on two clockwise routes: an outer circuit called the Lingkhor, now vanished under two-lane highways and rebuilding, and the shorter **Barkhor circuit** through the alleyways a short distance from the Jokhang walls. This maze of picturesque streets, a world away from the rest of Lhasa, is now largely a market selling all manner of goods – saddles and stirrups, Chinese army gear, *thangkas*, jewellery, blankets, DVDs, carpets, tin trunks and pictures of lamas, and many, many other things. The pilgrims are an amazing sight: statuesque Khampa men with their traditional knives and red-braided hair, decorated with huge chunks of turquoise; Amdo women dripping jewels with their hair in 108 plaits; and old ladies spinning their tiny prayer wheels and intoning mantras. The Barkhor circuit is most atmospheric in the early hours of the morning, before the sun has risen, when a feeling of devotion is prevalent, and the constant mumble of prayer and shuffle of prostrations emanate from the shadows.

Tromzikhang market

The whole Barkhor area is worth exploring – with its huge wooden doors set in long, white walls and leading into hidden courtyards – but try not to miss **Tromzikhang market** to the north of the Jokhang; take the main alleyway into the Barkhor that leads off Beijing Dong Lu just east of Ramoche Lu and it's just down on your left. The two-storey modern building is a bit soulless, but nowhere else in the world can you see (or smell) so much yak butter in one place.

Sela Daguo Xiang

色拉达果巷, sèlā dáguǒ xiàng

Rubbing up against the Jokhang's back wall, though easily missed among the throng, are a further three temples hidden along **Sela Daguo Xiang**, a narrow and fantastically preserved alleyway. The first temple, closest to the Barkhor, houses a single giant prayer wheel – you'll hear the ringing of its bell before you see it – eagerly turned by a devoted scrum.

Ani Tsangkung Nunnery

仓姑寺, cānggū sì · Daily 8am–5pm · ¥30

It's well worth seeking out the **Ani Tsangkung Nunnery** to the southeast of the Jokhang; you'll probably need to ask the way. With over a hundred nuns in residence, several of whom speak good English, there is a lively but devout atmosphere, especially around prayer time at 11am. A fabulous Chenresi in a glass case dominates the main chapel. From the back of the chapel, facing the main door, you can head right, round the outside, to visit the long, narrow room containing King Songtsen Gampo's meditation chamber in a pit at the end. Supposedly, his meditation altered the course of the Kyichu River when it looked likely to flood the construction of the Jokhang.

Ramoche

小昭寺, xiǎozhāo sì · Xiao Zhaosi Lu, between Beijing Dong Lu and Linkuo Bei Lu · Daily 9am–4.30pm · ¥30 · photos up to ¥50/chapel

The three-storey, robust **Ramoche temple** is small but intriguing, and second only in importance to the Jokhang. A short walk north of the Barkhor, it was built in the seventh century by Songtsen Gampo's Chinese wife, Princess Wencheng, to house the Jowo Sakyamuni statue that she brought to Tibet. The statue later ended up in the Jokhang and was replaced by the Akshobhya Buddha, a representation of Sakyamuni at the age of eight, a version of which sits here today. This much-revered statue was

NAMTSO LAKE (P.891) >

broken in two during the Cultural Revolution, with one part taken to China and the other later discovered on a factory scrapheap in Tibet. The statue in position today in the main shrine, at the rear of the temple, is likely to be a copy.

Tsepak Lhakhang

Daily 9am–4.30pm • Free

To the south of Ramoche, call in on the tiny **Tsepak Lakhang**. The entrance is just beside a huge incense burner, and, once inside, you pass along an alley lined with a row of prayer wheels. There are two small chapels in this hugely popular temple, and the 55 friendly monks in residence chant their daily prayers around noon. You can walk the brief circuit around the walls of Tsepak Lakhang, where the murals have been newly painted.

Norbulingka

罗布林卡, luóbùlínkǎ • Daily 9am–6.30pm • ¥60 • bus #7 from Beijing Dong Lu • taxi from the city ¥10

Situated in the west of town, the **Norbulingka** (Jewel Park), the Summer Palace of the Dalai Lama, is not in the top league of Lhasa sights, but is worth a look during the festivals of the Worship of the Buddha (July) or during Shotun, the Yoghurt Festival (Aug/Sept), when crowds flock here for picnics and to see masked dances and traditional opera. The park has been used as a recreation area by the Dalai Lama since the time of the Seventh incarnation.

Palace of the Eighth Dalai Lama

The first palace to be built on the Norbulingka site was the **Palace of the Seventh Dalai Lama**, constructed in the mid-eighteenth century. However, it is his successor's work, the palace of the Eighth Dalai Lama, that is most famed for its splendour and which became the official summer residence to which all Dalai Lamas moved, with due ceremony, on the eighteenth day of the third lunar month.

The New Summer Palace

The **New Summer Palace** was built in 1956 by the Fourteenth Dalai Lama; it was from here that he fled Lhasa in 1959. Visitors pass through the audience chamber, via an anteroom, to the meditation chamber, on to his bedroom and then into the reception hall dominated by a fabulously carved golden throne, before passing through to the quarters of the Dalai Lama's mother. Western plumbing and a radio sit beside fabulous *thangkas* and religious murals. It's all very sad and amazingly atmospheric, the forlorn rooms bringing home the reality of exile.

The Tibet Museum

西藏博物馆, xīzàng bówùguǎn • Tues–Sun 10am–6pm • ¥35 • bus #7 from Beijing Dong Lu • taxi from the city ¥10

Opposite the Norbulingka, the **Tibet Museum** offers curiosities to anyone who's had enough of religious iconography; there are some fascinating *thangkas* illustrating theories from Tibetan medicine, as well as stuffed Tibetan wildlife, Neolithic tools and the like. Its primary purpose, however, is propaganda emphasizing China's claim to the region, so it's best to take the captions with a pinch of salt.

ARRIVAL AND DEPARTURE

LHASA

By plane Gongkhar airport (贡嘎机场, gònggā jīchǎng) is a hefty 93km to the southwest of the city. Airport buses (¥25) run to the airline office on Niangre Lu in less than two hours, though foreigners coming on tours should be met by guides with transport – a direct car or taxi will take around an hour.

Destinations Ali (2 weekly; 1hr 30min); Beijing (1 daily; 4hr 30min); Chengdu (1 daily; 2hr); Chongqing (1 daily;

2hr); Kathmandu (March–Oct 2 weekly; 1hr); Kunming (1 daily; 2hr 20min); Shangri-La (1 daily; 1hr 40min).

By train Lhasa train station (拉萨火车站, lāsà huǒchē zhàn) is an enormous building about 3km south from the centre. Bus #7 runs to the city for ¥2; a taxi costs ¥10 from the station to Lhasa, but ¥20 in the opposite direction. Tickets out of Lhasa are generally easy to secure, and can be bought at the Tibet Tourism Office on Luobulingka Lu, at the station itself, or from any of the travel agencies or hotels. At time of writing construction of a Lhasa to Shigatse rail line was well under way and likely for completion around 2015.

Destinations Beijing (1 daily; 47hr); Changsha (every other day; 48hr); Chengdu (every other day; 43hr); Chongqing (1 daily; 43hr); Golmud (4 daily; 13hr); Guangzhou (every other day; 58hr); Lanzhou (3 daily; 24–27hr); Shanghai (1 daily; 48hr); Xi'an (2 daily; 34hr); Xining (4 daily; 24 hr).

By bus The main bus station (拉萨气车站, lāsà qìchēzhàn) is west of the centre at the junction of Jinzhu Zhong Lu and Minzu Lu. A taxi costs ¥10. All travel by foreigners on public transport outside of Lhasa is forbidden at present.

GETTING AROUND

As the main sights are all walkable from the old town and tour operators provide airport and rail station pick-up, as well as transport to outlying monasteries on tour itineraries, there is generally no need to take public or other transport within Lhasa. Possible exceptions include trips to the Norbulingka and Tibet Museum, which are a little out of the centre.

By bus Numbered buses run fixed routes around the city and its environs. From the old town the most useful buses are #7 and #8 which run to the train station and Potala Palace respectively (daily 7am–10pm; ¥2 flat fare).

By taxi Cabs have a ¥10 basic rate that should cover most destinations in town.

By cycle-rickshaw You'll have to haggle to use these, but central destinations will cost around ¥5.

By bicycle Bikes can be rented from the *Dong Cun Cuo Youth Hostel* on Beijing Lu at ¥40 per day, plus a ¥500 deposit. However, within Lhasa cycling is both unnecessary and unpleasant, the busy roads full of speeding vehicles and crazily ridden rickshaws, all combined with the effects of altitude. Attempting to cycle beyond the city limits could put you at serious risk of deportation, leaving your agency and guide facing a fine and possible blacklisting.

INFORMATION

Maps English maps can be purchased at hotels and news-stands for around ¥10. For an alternative view of the city, the *On This Spot Lhasa Map*, published by the International Campaign for Tibet and including the notorious Drapchi Prison, security facilities and army bases, can be found outside China – needless to say, you shouldn't bring it with you.

ACCOMMODATION

Whether you require budget or luxury accommodation, the old town area around the Barkhor is the place to stay. Mid-range hotels are springing up west of the centre, and with the sustained cranking up of investment in China, Western brands have started to re-enter the market (*Holiday Inn* withdrew in 1997 under pressure from rights groups), but however comfortable, they simply cannot compete with the charm of the labyrinthine old town.

Banak Shol 八朗学旅馆, bālǎngxué lǚguǎn. Beijing Dong Lu ☎0891 6323829. Handily located on the north edge of the Barkhor, this place offers two kinds of room – one in a cheaper, shabby Chinese business style, the other a renovated Tibetan version with colourful furniture and walls, for which it's well worth paying the extra. Chinese rooms **¥200**, Tibetan rooms **¥260**

Dong Cun Cuo Youth Hostel 正昌东措国际青年旅馆, zhèngchāng dōngcuò guójì qīngnián lǚguǎn. 10 Beijing Dong Lu ☎0891 6273388, ⓦwww.yhachina .com. Hugely popular with Chinese students, this well-located, spacious establishment with six-bed dorms is clean and efficiently run. En-suite private rooms don't have a/c but there is wi-fi throughout and the courtyard behind is home to a clutch of popular bars, a restaurant and a couple of craft shops. Dorm beds **¥50**, rooms **¥260**

Four Points by Sheraton 福朋喜来登酒店, fúpéng xīláidēng jiǔdiàn. 10 Bolinka Lu ☎0891 6348888, ⓦstarwoodhotels.com. One of the first Western-backed hotels to re-enter the Tibetan market, this is reliably clean and up to standard presentation-wise, but don't expect service to be quite up there with international standards just yet. **¥1200**

House of Shambhala 香巴拉宫, xiāngbālā gōng. 7 Jiri Erxiang ☎0891 6326533, ⓦshambhalaserai.com. Newly built in traditional Tibetan style, this wonderfully decorated boutique hotel offers chic suites and a great – if expensive – rooftop restaurant in the heart of the Barkhor district, just a couple of minutes' walk from the Jokhang. **¥480**

Hubei 湖北宾馆, húběi bīnguǎn. Beijing Xi Lu ☎0891 6820999. Chinese, business-oriented hotel, friendly, well run and offering better value than any of its nearby competitors. Big discounts off-season. **¥400**

★ **Khandor** 西藏康卓渡假村, xīzàng kāngzhuó

14

14

dùjiàcūn. 31 Lubu Yi Xiang, Barkhor ☎ 0891 6378444. Fantastically located on a quiet alley just south of the Jokhang, the nondescript frontage belies its traditional-style interior with rooms running off a brightly decorated atrium. Popular with tour groups, it fills up quickly in peak season. Breakfast included. **¥370**

★ **Kyichu** 拉萨吉曲饭店, lāsà jíqū fàndiàn. 149 Beijing Dong Lu ☎ 0891 6331541, ⊛ kyichuhotel.com. Centrally located, good value, with friendly Tibetan staff, this is one of the best mid-range choices, with practical, large and not over-decorated rooms in two buildings around a pleasant, grassy courtyard restaurant. **¥400**

Rama Kharpo 热玛嘎布宾馆, rèmǎgābù bīnguǎn. Ongto Shingka Lam ☎ 0891 6346963 or 1365 9505918. Close to the Muslim quarter, just around the corner from the mosque, this friendly, family-run guesthouse is a little hard to find but worth the effort. It's basic but clean, and much calmer than some of the crammed hostels along Beijing Lu. Dorm beds **¥50**, rooms **¥240**

Shangbala 香巴拉酒店, xiāngbālā jiǔdiàn. 1

Danjelin Lu, ☎ 0891 6323888. Behind the row of shops and restaurants leading from Beijing Dong Lu into the Barkhor, this place is ugly from the outside but smart inside and popular with superior foreign tour groups. Also boasts a decent but expensive Chinese restaurant on the ground floor. **¥480**

Tibet Greeting 西藏迎宾馆, xīzàng yínbīnguǎn. 3 Yutuo Lu, ☎ 0891 6355555. Built by the central government in 1965, the hotel's architecture possesses all the charm you would expect from the regime of the time – it's worth popping by just to take in the imposing soviet-style frontage. Grand, but with fraying carpets, and no a/c or wi-fi, rooms are overpriced and it's only worth staying if you can get a large discount. **¥880**

Yak 亚宾馆, yà bīnguǎn. 100 Beijing Dong Lu ☎ 0891 6323496, ⊛ chinayak.com. Rooms here are a bit hit or miss, but get a good one with a tub and a/c and it's decent value, especially given the central location. Very popular with international tour groups. **¥300**

EATING

Besides the vast number of restaurants in Lhasa, there are noodle places near Tromzikhang market, and bakeries outside the mosque in Barkhor selling *naan* breads. For trekking food try one of the supermarkets at the west end of Linkuo Bei Lu – thanks to Lhasa's large military presence army rations of tinned beef and high-calorie energy bars crop up on many shelves. There is also a traditional food market – complete with live produce, fruit, vegetables, tins and an impressive array of spices – just west of the chorten by the Potala Palace. For a more civilized picnic, both the *Dunya* and *New Mandala* turn out excellent lunchboxes.

Dunya. 100 Beijing Dong Lu ☎ 0891 6333374, ⊛ www .dunyarestaurant.com. Dutch-run and very civilized, but not particularly Tibetan. A diverse range of specials, good Western, Indian and Nepali food, and even half-decent Australian wine. Expect to pay around ¥60 a head for a main meal. A choice of breakfasts are also available for ¥40, while the bar upstairs has a good selection of drinks and a terrace looking out towards the old town. Daily 8am–11pm.

Gangki 刚吉餐厅, gāngjí cāntīng. Corner of Danjielin Lu and Barkhor Square, ☎ 0891 6328263. This rooftop place is good value and has great views of the Jokhang. Very popular with Tibetans and often extremely busy. Main dishes cost from ¥15; Tibetan tea and *tsampa* are also available. No toilets. Daily 11am–10pm.

Guangming Teahouse 光明港琼甜茶馆, guāngmínggǎng qióngtián cháguǎn. Dongjielin Lu. Spit-and-sawdust tea house close to the Barkhor entrance, always packed with Lhasans quaffing tea and playing cards. It can be tricky finding a seat but as long as you're not precious about personal space they'll cram you in somewhere. Tea from ¥5 and noodle soup from ¥10. Daily 8am–10pm.

Hot Space 麻辣空间, málà kōngjiān. Luobulinka Lu-Beijing Dong Lu, ☎ 0891 6831818. An enormous modern hotpot restaurant just west of the chorten. Hardly traditional, but their spicy broth is guaranteed to warm you

up if the Tibetan chill is biting. Expect around ¥80 per person. Daily 11.30am–11pm.

Kunphan Vegetarian Restaurant 素食餐厅, sùshí cāntīng. 34 Yutuo Lu ☎ 0891 6339808. A little surplus to requirements as most places offer a few veggie options, but at least here there is an entire meat-free menu to peruse. Sadly it's mostly versions of Chinese dishes rather than Tibetan cuisine, but the momo-like dumplings are close enough. Around ¥40 per person. Daily 11.30am–10pm.

Lhasa Kitchen 拉萨厨房, lāsà chúfáng. Danjielin Lu ☎ 0891 6848855. Friendly English-speaking service, but can be temper-stretchingly slow when busy. The food is good though, particularly the Nepali options, and there is a good range of Tibetan cuisine: soup with *shaphali* (meat and vegetable patties) followed by *deysee* (rice, raisins and yoghurt), for example. Mains around ¥35. Daily 8am–10pm.

New Mandala 新满斋餐厅, xīnmǎnzhāi cāntīng. On the southwest corner of Barkhor Square ☎ 0891 6329645. This two-level affair specializes in Nepali and Indian cuisine. The main draw is the rooftop seating area with a great view of the Jokhang and attendant plain-clothes officers on the building opposite. The *saag aloo* is excellent, as is the ginger tea. Around ¥40 per person. Daily 11am–10pm.

Snowlands Restaurant 雪域餐厅, xuěyù cāntīng. Danjielin Lu ☎ 0891 6337323. Tour group-friendly, long-established eatery with bland curries and standard Western and Tibetan dishes for around ¥40. Very busy at lunchtime with Chinese tourists, and orders can go astray. Daily 11.30am–10.30pm.

Spinn Café 风转, fēngzhuǎn. Qingu Xiang, Beijing Donglu ☎0891 6361163, ⓦcafespinn.com. Run by two cycling-mad expats – Kong from Hong Kong and Oat from Thailand – this is a relaxed spot for a decent cup of coffee (¥20), though there is virtually nothing available in the way of food. The owners are a fount of knowledge and their website is regularly updated with the latest travel situation. Daily 10am–10pm.

Tashi 1 Corner of Beijing Dong Lu and Danjielin Lu. A mainstay for budget travellers in Lhasa with mains from their limited Tibetan menu starting at ¥15. Their special is the *bobbi* – a kind of Tibetan tortilla – which comes with a delicious garlic and yoghurt sauce. Daily 11.30am–10pm.

Tibet Summit Fine Art Café 顶蜂美艺术咖啡店, dǐngfēngměi yìshù kāfēidiàn.. 1 Danjielin Lu ☎0891 6913884, ⓦthetibetsummitcafe.com. American-owned venture aiming to promote the arts in Tibet by serving up what are arguably the best cakes and coffee in the city, amidst overpriced works by local artists. Expect to pay ¥40 for a drink and something to eat. Daily 9am–10pm.

DRINKING AND ENTERTAINMENT

While Lhasa is world-renowned for its wealth of religious cultural heritage sights, it is not well known for the quality of its night life. And rightly so. Maybe it's the altitude that makes people too tired to go out, the lack of disposable income among Tibetans or the strict security, but after-dark entertainment is limited to shopping or hanging out in Chinese-style bars. Sadly, there's not much chance to see traditional Tibetan music, dance or opera, unless you're here during a festival, though occasional shows are put on for tourists; ask in your hotel or at a travel agency. It can also make for a pleasant post-prandial stroll heading up towards People's Park where you'll find fountains, ad hoc group dancing and stunning floodlit views of the Potala Palace.

Ancient Times Sea 古海酒吧, gǔhǎi jiǔbā. 6 Danjielin Xiang. Down a little alley off Danjielin Lu, this cosy little place is one of a clutch of similar bars along the same street. More like a tiny restaurant that only serves booze than a bar, the esoteric decor and unavoidable intimacy make it a decent spot to whet your whistle. And if you get bored you can always move to the next place along. Beers from ¥15. Daily 5.30–10pm.

Dong Cun Cuo Youth Hostel 正昌东措国际青年旅馆, zhèngchāng dōngcuò guójì qīngnián lǚguǎn.

10 Beijing Dong Lu. Yes it's a youth hostel, but in behind is a courtyard boasting three bars, live music and, in summer, a large scrum of Chinese students up for the craic. Beers from ¥15. Daily 5.30–10pm.

Dunya 100 Beijing Dong Lu ☎0891 6333374 ⓦwww .dunyarestaurant.com. Upstairs from the restaurant, this Dutch-run bar is a favourite for Westerners in search of a familiar tipple and pub ambience. A good selection of drinks, friendly owner, an excellent terrace for people-watching over sundowners, and beers from ¥20. Daily 5.30–10pm.

SHOPPING

Shopping is a major tourist activity in Lhasa. The main area for browsing is the Barkhor and the street market stretching west from here along Yutuo Lu; shops here are generally more expensive than vendors outside, and during peak tourist season (July–September) market traders hawk their wares until well after 10pm – generally they're not too aggressive with their sales technique. A string of gift shops on Danjielin Lu sells jewellery, handmade paper and the like – the gift shop next door to the *Lhasa Kitchen* has a particularly good range of handmade scarfs, clothes and soft toys, but is expensive. The search for postcards can be frustrating, and sets on offer at the main sights are generally pricey; those at the post office and the Xinhua Bookstores are the best value, though there are some pricier "post-card cafés" where you can buy and write postcards over a coffee on Beijing Dong Lu near the *Dong Cun Cuo Youth Hostel*.

Books Tibet is pretty much the worst place you could possibly go to find books about Tibet, with much that would be considered essential reading in the West well entrenched on China's banned list. However, coffee-table books featuring sumptuous photos of the sites around Lhasa and beyond are plentiful and much easier to find here than back home. As well as at the sites themselves – the Potala Palace has books of photos which are not available anywhere else – the Xinhua Bookstore at the corner of Yutuo Lu and Kang'angduo Lu has a good selection, though prices are high – expect to pay upwards of ¥200.

Carpets Khawachen, 102 Jinzhu Xi Lu (Mon–Sat 9am–6.30pm; ☎0891 6865226, ⓦinnerasiarugs.com). This government-affiliated and US-financed organization offers the best selection of rugs in Lhasa and the chance to watch them being produced; they can also arrange to ship the merchandise home for you. Available in muted, traditional designs, plus some with a modern slant, the carpets range in size and price – from tens of dollars to well over a thousand.

Clothes There are plenty of tailors in town, both Chinese and Tibetan, who can make traditional Tibetan or Western

14

14

TREKKING TIBET

For the experienced hiker, Tibet offers plenty of enticing **trekking routes** – though you will currently need to negotiate for a guide and a travel agency to endorse your travel permit and accompany you for the entire duration of the trek. The popular Ganden–Samye trek (see box, p.884) has the advantages that both the start and finish points are relatively accessible from Lhasa and that it takes only three to four days. Also worth considering are treks to the cave hermitage of **Drak Yerpa** from Lhasa (allow a full day and be prepared to camp), and the five-day trek from Tingri to **Everest Base Camp** via Rongbuk. More challenging options include: the sixteen-day mammoth trek to the **Kangshung** face of Everest, exploring the valleys east of the mountain (the trip to second base camp and beyond on the mountain itself should only be tackled by experienced climbers); the 24-day circumnavigation of **Namtso Lake**, including the arduous exploration of the Shang Valley to the southwest; and the great thirty-day circuit from Lhatse to **Lake Dangra** up on the Chang Tang plateau.

Spring (April–June) and autumn (Sept–Nov) are the best **seasons** in which to trek, though cold-weather threats such as hypothermia and frostbite should be taken seriously even in these months. While trekking is possible at any time in the valleys, high altitudes become virtually impossible in the winter; anyone contemplating trekking at this time should be sure to check information about the terrain and likely conditions. During the wettest months (June–Sept), rivers are in flood, and crossing them can be difficult, even impossible. Once you start trekking, you get off the beaten track extremely quickly, and there is no infrastructure to support trekkers and no rescue service; you therefore need to be fit, acclimatized, self-reliant and prepared to do some research before you go. There are two essential books: *Tibet Handbook: a Pilgrimage Guide* by Victor Chan (Moon), and *Trekking in Tibet* by Gary McCue (Cordee), which is especially good for shorter day-treks that anyone can do without all the gear.

clothes; look on Beijing Dong Lu west of the *Yak Hotel*. A huge range of materials is available, from light, summer-weight stuff, to heavier, warmer textiles. Prices depend on the material, but light jackets start at around ¥100, while skirts, trousers or a floor-length Tibetan woman's dress (*chuba*) cost ¥80 and up. Many places have samples made up and you can simply shop around until you find the style and material you want. From first measuring to collecting the finished item usually takes 24 hours.

Thangkas Tibetan *thangkas* (religious scrolls) would appear to be obvious souvenirs, but many are of poor quality – best to spend some time browsing before you buy. The better-quality, higher-priced ones have a hand-painted central image, with finely drawn and highly detailed backgrounds. Asking prices are high – bargain hard. The best place to start looking is the Tibet Traditional Art Gallery, next door to the Ramoche, which stocks an excellent range – expect prices to start at ¥3000.

Trekking gear Plenty of places sell shoes, boots, fleeces and jackets of dubious lineage near the junction of Dongjielin Lu and Beijing Dong Lu, but for hiking gear you may need to actually rely on, head west along Beijing Dong Lu to the Ozark store at 21 Beijing Zhong Lu, next to the *Yun Long Hotel*. Here you'll find genuine coats, rucksacks, footwear and sleeping bags, but at prices very similar to, or even higher than, those at home. Across the road, the *ToRead* chainstore stocks Jack Wolfskin clothing among other brands.

DIRECTORY

Banks and exchange Lhasa's main Bank of China is on Linkuo Bei Lu, north of the Golden Yaks Statue (Mon–Fri 9am–1pm & 3.30–6pm). The branch on Beijing Dong Lu is conveniently located close to the Banak Shol (Mon–Fri 9.30am–6pm, Sat & Sun 11am–3pm); around the old town you'll find ATM kiosks which take foreign bank cards, including opposite the Mosque and on the corner of Dosengge Lu and the street leading into the Barkhor.

Consulates The Nepalese Consulate, 13 Norbulingka Lu (Mon–Fri 10am–noon; ☎0891 6815744), has a next-day visa service, for which you'll need to submit one passport photograph. At the time of writing you could get single-entry visas at Kodari (at the Zhagmu border, see p.905), but payment there had to be in US dollars.

Hospital First People's Hospital, 18 Linkuo Bei Lu (Mon–Fri 10am–12.30pm & 4–6pm; emergencies only ☎0891 6371571 or ☎6371265). It's better to go in the morning when more staff are available, and you'll need to take a Chinese translator.

Internet Most hotels provide wi-fi or internet connections, but cybercafés are not hard to find in Lhasa. The most convenient are next to the *Dong Cun Cuo Youth*

Hostel, in the _Shangrila_ bar, and in the _Bank Shol_, all on Beijing Dong Lu.

Mail The main post office is on Beijing Dong Lu, just east of the Potala Palace (daily 9am–8pm).

Pharmacies Most are along Yutuo Lu around the junction with Dosengge Lu. There is a pharmacy specializing in Tibetan medicine on the north side of Barkhor Square. Again, you'll need a translator.

PSB 14 Linkuo Bei Lu (Mon–Fri 9.30am–1pm & 3.30–7pm, ☎0891 6248012). While PSB offices should be the place to go for facts about closed and open areas, the information is rarely reliable and frequently inconsistent from one office to the next. Unless there are circumstances which make this impossible, it is always best to approach the PSB through your guide or travel agency.

14

Around Lhasa

Just outside Lhasa, the major monasteries of **Sera**, **Drepung**, **Nechung** and **Ganden** are easily accessible from the city as half-day or day-trips. Indeed, Sera and Drepung have virtually been gobbled up in the urban sprawl that now characterizes Lhasa, while the trip to Ganden or to **Samye** – the latter slightly further out to the southeast – is a good chance to get out into the countryside. Morning visits to any of them are likely to be in the company of parties of devout pilgrims who'll scurry around the temples making their offerings before heading on to the next target. Follow on behind them and you'll visit all the main buildings; don't worry too much if you aren't sure what you are looking at – most of the pilgrims haven't a clue either. The monasteries are generally peaceful and atmospheric places where nobody minds you ambling at will, and sooner or later you're bound to come across some monks who want to practise their English.

LIFE IN THE GREAT MONASTERIES

Fifty years ago, there were still six great, functioning **Gelugpa monasteries**: Sera, Drepung and Ganden near Lhasa, plus Tashilunpo in Shigatse (see p.896), Labrang (see p.789) and Kumbum (see p.797). They each operated on a similar system to cope with the huge numbers of monks who were drawn to these major institutions from all over Tibet. In their heyday, Sera and Ganden had five thousand residents each and Drepung (possibly the largest monastery the world has ever known) had between eight and ten thousand.

Each monastery was divided into colleges, **dratsang**, which differed from each other in the type of studies undertaken. Each college was under the management of an abbot (_khenpo_), and a monk responsible for discipline (_ge-kor_). Attached to each college were a number of houses or _khangsten_, where the monks lived during their time at the monastery. Usually, these houses catered for students from different geographical regions, and admission to the monastery was controlled by the heads of the houses to whom aspirant monks would apply. Each college had its own assembly hall and chapels, but there was also a main assembly hall where the entire community could gather.

Not every member of the community spent their time in scholarly pursuits. Communities the size of these took huge amounts of organization, and the largest monasteries also maintained large estates worked by serfs. About half the monks might be engaged in academic study while the other half worked at administration, the supervision of the estate work and the day-to-day running of what was essentially a small town.

The most obvious feature of these **monasteries today** is their emptiness; hundreds of monks now rattle around in massive compounds built for thousands. Such has been the fate of religious establishments under the Chinese and the flow of lamas into exile that there are now questions about the quality of the Buddhist education available at the monasteries inside Tibet. Monks and nuns need to be vetted and receive Chinese-government approval before they can join a monastery or convent, and although there are persistent rumours of tourists being informed on by monks, it's also apparent that both monks and nuns have been, and continue to be, at the forefront of open political opposition to the Chinese inside Tibet.

14

Sera Monastery

色拉寺, sèlā sì · Mon–Sat 9am–4pm · ¥50 · taxi ¥10–15

Sera Monastery, 4km north of central Lhasa, will be included on most tour itineraries. Established in 1419 by Sakya Yeshe, one of the main disciples of Tsongkhapa, founder of the Gelugpa order, Sera is situated below a hermitage where the great man spent many years in retreat. Spared during the Cultural Revolution, the buildings are in good repair, although there is always a fair amount of ongoing building work. Pilgrims proceed on a clockwise circuit, visiting the three main **colleges** – Sera Me, Sera Ngag-Pa and Sera Je – and the main assembly hall, Tsokchen. All are constructed with chapels leading off a central hall and more chapels on an upper floor. They're great places to linger and watch the pilgrims rushing about their devotions.

Tsokchen

If you just want to catch the flavour of Sera's most dramatic buildings, head straight up the hill from the main entrance. After a couple of hundred metres, you'll reach the **Tsokchen**, Sera's largest building, built in 1710. The hall is supported by over a hundred columns, and it's here, between statues of the Fifth and Thirteenth Dalai Lamas, that you'll find the main statue of Sakya Yeshe, the founder of the monastery. The Sakya Yeshe statue is a reproduction of the original one in Sera Ngag-Pa college. When there were plans to move the original to the Tsokchen, the story goes that the statue itself said that it wished to stay in the college, so a copy was made.

The debating courtyard

At the top of the path uphill from the entrance, the walled and shady **debating courtyard** is definitely worth a visit at 3.30pm, when the monks assemble in small animated groups to practise their highly stylized debating skills, involving much posturing, clapping and stamping. They're used to visitors – indeed, it's hard not to feel the whole circus is put on for tourists – and there's no problem about taking photographs.

Sera Je college

To the left of the courtyard, the college of **Sera Je** is the best to visit if you manage only one. Its spacious assembly hall is hung with fine *thangkas*, but the focus for pilgrims here is the Hayagriva Chapel (Hayagriva or Tamdrin, "the Horse-Headed One", is the protective deity of Sera), reached via an entrance in the left-hand wall.

Choding Khang

If you're feeling energetic, take the path up the hillside, from behind the Tsokchen (follow the telegraph wires) to **Choding Khang** (Tsongkhapa's Hermitage), which is a reconstruction of the original – his meditation cave is a bit farther up. There are splendid views over Lhasa from here.

Drepung monastery

哲蚌寺, zhébàng sì · Daily 9am–6pm · chapels closed noon–3pm · ¥50 · taxi ¥15–20

Just 8km west of Lhasa, **Drepung Monastery** was founded in 1416 by Jamyang Choje, a leading disciple of Tsongkhapa. Once the largest monastery in the world, it was an immediate success, and a year after opening there were already two thousand monks in residence, and ten thousand by the time of the Fifth Dalai Lama (1617–82). Although it has been sacked three times – in 1618 by the king of Tsang, in 1635 by the Mongols, and in the early eighteenth century by the Dzungars – there was relatively little damage during the Cultural Revolution.

Drepung is a huge place, and it's easy to attempt to see everything and get overloaded. One thing to make sure to do is to go up on to the **roofs** – the views across the Kyichu

Valley are splendid – and you should make sure you spend a bit of time just wandering the alleyways, through courtyards, and past ancient doorways.

The Ganden Palace

The easiest way to find your way around is to follow the clockwise pilgrim circuit. This leads left from the entrance up to the grand and imposing **Ganden Palace**, built in 1530 by the Second Dalai Lama, and home to the Dalai Lamas until the Fifth incarnation moved to the Potala Palace. The private quarters of the Dalai Lama are behind the balcony at the top right-hand side of the building, but there's little to see inside.

14

The Tsokchen

The **Tsokchen**, the main assembly hall, is entered via a small door on the left-hand side, facing the building. Its roof supported by over 180 solid wooden columns, the hall is the highlight of Drepung, a space of awesome size and scale. The *thangkas* and brocade hangings add to the ambience, with dust motes highlighted by the rays of the sun slanting down from the high windows. At the rear is the **Buddha of the Three Ages Chapel**, the most impressive in Drepung, with statues crammed together in such profusion the mind reels. The central figures are Sakyamuni with his two main disciples, Shariputra and Maudgalyayana. The main steps of the Tsokchen, looking across the huge courtyard in front of the building, are a good place to sit and admire the view and watch the comings and goings of the other visitors.

The upper storeys

There are two upper storeys, both definitely worth a visit. On the next floor up, the **Maitreya Chapel** contains the head and shoulders of a massive statue of Maitreya at a young age, commissioned by Tsongkhapa himself, while the **Tara Chapel** contains a version of the Kanjur, sacred Buddhist scriptures, dating from the time of the Fifth Dalai Lama. In the middle of the volumes, which are loose leaves stored between wooden planks and wrapped in brocade, sits a statue of the incarnation of Prajnaparamita, the Mother of Buddhas; the amulet on her lap is said to contain a tooth of Tsongkhapa's. Of the three chapels on the top floor, the highlight is the stunning statue of the head of Maitreya, boasting exquisite gold ornamentation.

Outlying buildings

Behind the Tsokchen, there's a tiny **Manjusri Temple**, obligatory for the pilgrims who make offerings to the image of the Bodhisattva of Wisdom, carved out of a large rock. The remainder of the circuit is taken up with the **Ngag-Pa College**, to the northwest of the Tsokchen, and **Loseling**, **Gomang** and **Deyang colleges** to the southeast. They all have items of interest – the stuffed goat at the entrance to the Protector Chapel on the upper storey of Loseling, the cosy Deyang, and the wonderful array of statues in the central chapel of Gomang – but don't feel too bad if you've had enough by now.

Nechung Monastery

乃琼寺, nǎiqióng sì • Daily 9am–6pm • chapels closed noon–3pm • ¥10 • taxi ¥15–20

Easily combined with a trip to Drepung is the eerie **Nechung Monastery**, less than 1km southeast via a well-trodden path; try to visit on the 8th, 15th or 30th days of the Tibetan lunar month, when the faithful seek special favour.

Nechung was, until 1959, the seat of the **state oracle of Tibet**. By means of complex ritual and chanting, an oracle enters a trance and becomes the mouthpiece of a god, in this case Dorje Drakden, the chief minister of the main spiritual protector of Tibet,

Pehar Gyalpo; no important decisions are made by the Dalai Lama or government without reference to Drakden. The original shrine on the site was built in the twelfth century, and the Fifth Dalai Lama built the temple later. The state oracle fled Tibet in the footsteps of the Dalai Lama in 1959, having questioned Dorje Drakden himself as to what he should do.

The lower halls

Nechung's spookiness begins outside. The beggars are abject, and the villagers seem sullen. Inside you are confronted by a panoply of gore – the doors are decorated with images of flayed human skins and the murals in the courtyard depict torture by devils and people drowning in a sea of blood. In the chapels, unusually subdued supplicants are more likely to offer booze than apples. Bloodshot eyes sunk into the sockets of grinning skulls seem to follow you around.

Upstairs

Upstairs, the main room is the audience chamber, where the Dalai Lama would come to consult the oracle. The inner chapel is dedicated to Tsongkhapa, whose statue is between those of his two main disciples, Gyeltsab Je and Khedrup Je. In the only chapel at roof level is the statue of Padmasambhava that, though it dates from the early 1980s, is gloriously bedecked in old Chinese brocade. It's worth the climb up, if only to escape the air of sinister corruption below.

Ganden Monastery

甘丹寺, gāndān sì • Daily 9am–4pm • ¥45 • foreigners are barred from riding public transport this far out of Lhasa, but the monastery can be reached in a couple of hours in a chartered jeep

Farther than the other main temples, **Ganden Monastery** is 45km east of Lhasa, the final 6km of the journey along a winding track off the Lhasa–Sichuan Highway. It is also the most dramatically situated, high up on the Gokpori Ridge with excellent views over the surrounding countryside.

Founded by Tsongkhapa himself in 1410 on a site associated with King Songtsen Gampo and his queens, the main hall was not completed until 1417, two years before Tsongkhapa died after announcing his disciple, Gyeltsab Je, as the new **Ganden Tripa**, the leader of the Gelugpa order. The appointment is not based on reincarnation but on particular academic qualifications. The Chinese have always particularly targeted Ganden, possibly because it is the main seat of the Dalai Lama's order, and what you see today is all reconstruction.

The Serdung Lhakhang

While it is possible to follow the pilgrims through the various buildings on their circuit, the highlight here is really the imposing **Serdung Lhakhang**, on the left side as you follow the main path north from the car park. This temple contains a huge gold and silver chorten. The original contained the body of Tsongkhapa, who was said to have changed into a 16-year-old youth when he died. The body was embalmed and

---

THE GANDEN–SAMYE TREK

Though popular, the **Ganden–Samye trek** is no less serious or demanding than other treks. The route, which takes four days to complete, crosses the mountains that divide the **Kyichu Valley** from that of the Tsangpo and travels through high mountain passes and alpine pasture to the dry, almost desert-like countryside around Samye. The trek goes by **Hebu** village (three hours south of Ganden and a good place to hire yaks and guides) and involves camping out or sleeping in caves or nomad encampments, long climbs to the Jooker La and Sukhe La passes, and some deep-river wading.

placed in the chorten and, when the Red Guards broke it open during the Cultural Revolution, they supposedly found the body perfectly preserved, with the hair and fingernails still growing. Only a few pieces of skull survived the destruction and they are in the reconstructed chorten.

The Sertrikhang
Up the hill and to the right, the **Sertrikhang** houses the golden throne of Tsongkhapa and all later Ganden Tripas; behind the throne you'll see images of the Tsongkhapa himself flanked by two of his most senior students. The bag on the throne contains the yellow hat of the present Dalai Lama.

The Ganden kora
Be sure to allow time to walk the **Ganden kora**, the path around the monastery. The views are startling, and it takes about an hour to follow round. There is a basic guesthouse at the monastery, used mostly by people heading off on the Ganden–Samye trek (see box opposite).

Samye
桑木耶寺, sāngmùyē sì • Daily 7.30am–6pm • ¥40

A visit to **SAMYE**, on the north bank of the Tsangpo River around 50km southeast of Lhasa, is a highlight of Tibet. A unique monastery and walled village rolled into one, it's situated in wonderful scenery and, however you arrive, the journey is splendid. You can climb the sacred Hepo Ri to the east of the complex for excellent views (1hr); it was here that Padmasambhava is said to have subdued the local spirits and won them over to Buddhism.

Brief history
Tibet's first monastery, Samye was founded in the eighth century during King Trisong Detsen's reign, with the help of the Indian masters Padmasambhava and Shantarakshita, whom he had invited to Tibet to help spread the Buddhist faith. The first Tibetan Buddhist monks were ordained here and are referred to as the "Seven Examined Men". Over the years, Samye has been associated with several of the schools of Tibetan Buddhism – Padmasambhava's involvement in the founding of the monastery makes it important in the Nyingma school, and later it was taken over by the Sakya and Gelugpa traditions. Nowadays, followers of all traditions worship here, and Samye is a popular destination for Tibetan pilgrims, some of whom travel for weeks to reach it.

SAMYE ORIENTATION
The design of the extensive monastery complex, several hundred metres in diameter, is of a giant **mandala**, a representation of the Buddhist universe, styled after the Indian temple of Odantapuri in Bihar. The main temple, the **Utse**, represents Buddha's palace on the summit of Mount Meru, the mythical mountain at the centre of the Buddhist universe. The four continents in the vast ocean around Mount Meru are represented by the *lingshi* temples, a couple of hundred metres away at the cardinal points, each flanked by two smaller temples, *lingtren*, representing islands in the ocean. The *Utse* is surrounded by four giant chortens, each several storeys high, at the corners, and there are *nyima* (sun) and *dawa* (moon) temples to the north and south, respectively. A renovated enclosing wall, topped by 1008 tiny chortens with gates at the cardinal points, flanks the whole complex. This sounds hugely ordered, but the reality is far more confusing and fun. Samye has suffered much damage and restoration over the years; today, you'll find the temples dotted among houses, barns and animal pens, with only a few of the original 108 buildings on the site remaining in their entirety.

The Utse

Daily 9am–12.30pm & 3–5pm • ¥40

A grand, six-storey construction, the Utse needs a couple of hours to be seen thoroughly. Be sure to take a torch as there are some good murals tucked away in shadowy corners.

The first floor

The main assembly hall dominates the first floor, with fine, old mandalas on the high ceiling. On either side of the entrance to the adjoining main chapel are statues of historical figures associated with the monastery. Those on the left include Shantarakshita, Padmasambhava (said to be a good likeness of him), Trisong Detsen and Songtsen Gampo. The impressive main chapel, **Jowo Khang**, is reached through three tall doorways and is home to a Sakyamuni statue showing the Buddha aged 38. To the left of the assembly hall a small temple, **Chenresi Lhakhang**, houses a gorgeous statue of Chenresi with an eye meticulously painted on the palm of each of his thousand hands – if you look at nothing else in Samye, search this out. To the right is the **Gonkhang**, a protector chapel, with all the statues heavily and dramatically draped. Most of the deities here were established as the demons of the Bon religion and were adopted by Buddhism as the fierce protectors – the chapel is an eerie place, imbued with centuries' worth of fear.

The upper storeys

Although the first floor is the most striking, the upper storeys are also worth a look. The **second floor** is an open roof area, where monks and local people carry out the craftwork needed for the temple. The highlight of the **third floor** is the **Quarters of the Dalai Lama**, consisting of a small anteroom, a throne room and a bedroom. A securely barred, glass-fronted case in the bedroom is stuffed full of fantastic relics, including Padmasambhava's hair and walking stick, a Tara statue that is reputed to speak, and the skull of the Indian master Shantarakshita. The Tibetan pilgrims take this room very seriously, and the crush of bodies may mean you can't linger as long as you would like. From the **fourth floor** up, you'll see only recent reconstruction, but the views from the balconies are extensive.

The surrounding buildings

The rest of the buildings in the complex are in varying stages of renovation. Unashamedly modern, the four coloured **chortens** are each slightly different, and visitors love or hate them. There are internal stairs and tiny interior chapels, but generally they are more dramatic from a distance. It's difficult to locate the outer temples accurately, and many are still awaiting renovation – some serve as barns and stables, others show the effects of the Cultural Revolution. The most finely worked murals in Samye are in **Mani Lhakhang**, now a chapel in a house compound in the northwest of the complex, but the occupants are happy for visitors to look around.

ARRIVAL AND DEPARTURE   SAMYE

As with all destinations outside the Lhasa city limits, Samye can only be reached if you are accompanied by your guide in a chartered vehicle, with the excursion listed on your official tour itinerary. The following information on public transport is provided for reference only. From Lhasa you first need to head south to Chusul and then east along the Lhasa–Tsetang road, which runs along the south bank of the Tsangpo and is served by public transport from both ends. Some 33km from Tsetang and 150km from Lhasa you'll need to catch the the Samye ferry across the river. Be aware that the full trip between Lhasa and Samye, including transport either side of the ferry and the ferry crossing itself, can take as much as seven hours.

By bus A bus departs from Barkhor Square to the Samye ferry crossing point (¥40) between 6am and 8am daily. Leaving Samye, a bus departs from the front of the Utse each morning at 8am to connect with the ferry and a Lhasa-bound bus on the other side of the river. In addition, local tractors and trucks run until mid-afternoon, but you may well have to wait at the ferry and on the other side of the river for connections.

By ferry Ferries leave when full and are more frequent in the morning, but run until mid-afternoon. The crossing (¥10) is highly picturesque and takes an hour or more as the boats wind their way among the sandbanks inhabited by Brahmini ducks, grebes and plovers. On the other side, tractors (45min; ¥5) and trucks (30min; ¥3) ply the bumpy 8km to Samye through sand dunes, planted here and there with willows. The small, white-painted chortens carved out of the hillside about halfway along mark the place where King Trisong Detsen met Padmasambhava when he came to Samye in the eighth century.

ACCOMMODATION

Monastery Guesthouse 桑耶寺宾馆, sāngyēsì bīnguǎn. Northeast of the Utse itself ☏ 0891 7836666. Convenient, basic place to stay with rooms that are clean enough and an adjoining restaurant, though you wouldn't want to stay for more than a couple of days. Dorm **¥40**, room **¥180**

EATING

Friendship Snowland Restaurant 友谊雪域餐厅, yǒuyì xuěyù cāntīng. East gate of the Utse ☏ 0136 18932819. Serving a basic range of Chinese and Tibetan dishes, plus Western pancakes, this is a far better option than the lacklustre and more expensive monastery restaurant. Expect to pay around ¥30 for a meal. Daily 8am–8pm.

Southeast from Lhasa

The region around **Tsetang**, southeast of Lhasa and just south of the Tsangpo River, is steeped in ancient history. Legend has it that the first Tibetans originated on the slopes of Gongpo Ri to the east of Tsetang, and that the **Yarlung Valley** (where the country's earliest Buddhist scriptures magically appeared) was where the first king of Tibet descended from the heavens on a sky-cord, to father the original royal dynasty – many members of which are buried in the nearby **Chongye Valley**.

Tsetsang

泽当, zédāng

There is little to recommend an extended stay in **TSETANG**, though the town, located 60km southeast of Lhasa as the crow flies (double this by road), is largely unavoidable as a base for explorations of Lhoka province, which stretches from the Tsangpo down to the Bhutan border. South from Tsetang's main traffic intersection along Naidong Lu, take a left and head east along Bare Jie into the **Tibetan area** of town, a typical jumble of walled compounds swarming with dogs and children.

Ganden Chukorlin

Daily 10am–6pm • ¥45

The first – and largest – monastery you'll encounter in the Tibetan area is **Ganden Chukorlin**, now bright and gleaming from restoration, having been used as a storeroom for many years. It was founded in the mid-eighteenth century on the site of an earlier monastery, and there are good views of the Tibetan quarter from the roof.

Narchu Monastery and Sanarsensky Nunnery

The fourteenth-century **Narchu Monastery** is worth stopping by for the three unusual, brown-painted Sakyamuni statues on the altar. A little farther up the hill, the **Sanarsensky Nunnery** was one of the first of its kind in Tibet. It was founded in the fourteenth century in the Sakya tradition, later becoming a Gelugpa establishment.

Lhamo Lhatso

Tsetang is the base for a trip to **Lhamo Lhatso**, a small sacred lake 115km to the northeast, where it's reputed that visions appearing on the surface of the water contain prophecies. Regents searching for the next incarnations of high lamas come here for clues, and Dalai Lamas have traditionally visited for hints about the future. From the nearest town, Gyatsa, it's a five-hour walk up to the lake, so you'll have to negotiate with your guide whether to camp or make the long return journey in a single day.

14

<table>
<tr><td>

ARRIVAL AND DEPARTURE
</td><td align="right">

TSETANG
</td></tr>
</table>

By jeep Currently the only way for foreign visitors to reach Tsetang is by chartered jeep, and you'll need to have the excursion listed on your trip itinerary. The journey takes 2.5hr from Lhasa.

By bus Tsetang's bus station is about 500m west of the main traffic intersection in town.

By minibus Direct minibuses leave Lhasa's main bus station for Tsetang from 8am onwards.

Destinations Lhasa (frequent; 3hr).

ACCOMMODATION AND EATING

While there are some decent accommodation options in Tsetang, none of them is particularly cheap, or good value, though for a small town the standard is surprisingly high.

Tibet Yulong Holiday Hotel 裕荟假日大酒店, yùlóng jiàrì dàjiǔdiàn. 16 Naidong Lu ☎0893 7832888. The *Yulong* sits across the road from the four-star *Tsetang* like a seedy evil twin on the make. Run-down and in need of a good clean, make sure you see your room before checking in, and seriously consider forking out the extra to stay across the street. **¥300**

Tsetang Hotel 泽当饭店, zédāng fàndiàn. 21 Naidong Lu ☎0893 7825555. The most upmarket place in town; really just a slightly fancy Chinese business hotel, but it does boast an excellent Chinese restaurant and wi-fi in the lobby. **¥480**

The Yarlung Valley

雅鲁鲁流域, yǎlǔlǔ liúyù

Though the 100km-long **Yarlung Valley**, just 40km south of Lhasa, is renowned as the seat of the first Tibetan kings, these days it is the dramatically sited and picturesque **Yumbulakhang**, the first Tibetan palace, which draws visitors to the area.

Trandruk Monastery

昌珠寺, chāngzhū sì · ¥70

The small but significant **Trandruk Monastery**, 7km south of Tsetang, is a grand and imposing structure. One of the earliest Buddhist temples in Tibet, Trandruk was built in the seventh century during the reign of King Songtsen Gampo and is one of the twelve Demon-Suppressing Temples (see p.872) – Trandruk anchors the demoness's left shoulder to the earth. Legend tells how the site chosen for Trandruk was covered by a large lake containing a five-headed dragon. King Songtsen Gampo emerged from a period of meditation with such power that he was able to summon a supernatural falcon to defeat the dragon and drink up all the water of the lake, leaving the earth ready for Trandruk (meaning Falcon-Dragon).

The Pearl Thangka

Damaged during the Bon reaction against Buddhism in the ninth century, and again by Dzungar invaders in the eighteenth century, Tandruk then suffered the loss of many highly prized religious relics and objects following the Chinese invasion. Its remaining glory is the **Pearl Thangka**, an image of King Songtsen Gampo's wife, Princess Wencheng, as the White Tara, created from thousands of tiny pearls meticulously sewn onto a pink background. This is in the central chapel upstairs, which also houses an original statue of Padmasambhava at the age of eight.

Yumbulakhang

雍布拉康, yōngbùlākāng · ¥70

From afar, the fortress temple of **Yumbulakhang**, 12km south of Tsetang, appears dwarfed by the scale of the Yarlung Valley. But once you get close and make the thirty-minute climb up the spur on which it is perched, the drama of the position and the airiness of the site are apparent. Widely regarded as the work of the first king of Tibet, Nyatri Tsenpo, the original Yumbulakhang would have been over two thousand years old and the oldest building in Tibet when it was almost totally destroyed during the Cultural Revolution. The present building is a 1982 reconstruction in two parts, with a small, two-storey chapel and an 11m-high tower.

The chapel

The lower floor of the chapel is dedicated to the early Tibetan kings: Nyatri Tsenpo is to the left and Songtsen Gampo to the right of the central Buddha statue. The delightful and unusual upper-storey chapel, with Chenresi as the central image, is built on a balcony. Some of the modern murals up here show legendary events in Tibetan history; look out on the left for Nyatri Tsenpo and for the Buddhist scriptures descending from heaven.

The tower

The energetic can ascend by ladders almost to the top of the tower where King Nyatri Tsenpo supposedly meditated. The deep, slit windows at knee level mean the views aren't that wonderful, however; for the best scenery, take a walk up to the ridge behind the temple.

The Chongye Valley

From Tsetang it's a bumpy 27km south along unsurfaced roads through the attractive **Chongye Valley** to the village of **CHONGYE** (阱结, jǐngyiē), a sleepy little place but expanding with plenty of new buildings. There are a couple of restaurants and a basic guesthouse here, which you'll need to ask to find. On the way, you'll pass the **Tangboche Monastery**, though the target for most visitors, the **Tombs of the Kings**, is around 1km farther south. The entire valley is an agricultural development area and the patchwork of fields is interspersed with irrigation work.

Tangboche Monastery

On the east side of the valley, about 20km southeast of Tsetang, **Tangboche Monastery** sits at the base of the hill and is somewhat difficult to spot among the village houses. Founded in the eleventh century, it was said to have hosted the great Tsongkhapa, originator of the Gelugpa tradition, three centuries later. Take a torch so you can really appreciate the most interesting features – genuinely old murals, commissioned in 1915 by the Thirteenth Dalai Lama. Look out in particular for Pelden Lhamo on the left as you enter, and, on the right-hand wall, Padmasambhava, Trisong Detsen and Shantarakshita. The artistry and detail of subject and background make an interesting comparison with some of the more modern painting you'll see in Tibet.

Atisha's hermitage

A couple of hundred metres up the hill is the **hermitage** where the scholar **Atisha** spent some time in the eleventh century. It's small, recently renovated and, not surprisingly, dominated by rather lurid images of the Indian master.

The Tombs of the Kings

藏王墓群, zángwáng mùqún · ¥60

One kilometre south of Chongye, the **Tombs of the Kings** are scattered over a vast area on and around the slopes of Mura Ri. Some are huge, up to 200m in length and 30m high. The body of each king was buried along with statues, precious objects and, some sources suggest, live servants. Some of the greatest kings of the Yarlung dynasty were interred here, although there is disagreement over the precise number of tombs – some sources claim it's 21, but far fewer are visible, and there is uncertainty about which tomb belongs to which king.

Songtsen Gampo's tomb

For the best view of the entire area, climb the largest tomb, **Bangso Marpo** (Red Tomb), belonging to **Songtsen Gampo**, just beside the road that heads south along the valley; it's easily identifiable by the chapel on the top. Songtsen Gampo, supposedly embalmed and incarcerated in a silver coffin, was entombed with huge numbers of precious gems, gifts from neighbouring countries (India sent a golden suit of armour), his own jewelled robes and objects of religious significance, all of which were looted long ago. The cosy **chapel** (¥10), originally built in the twelfth century, has central statues of Songtsen Gampo, his wives and principal ministers, Gar and Thonmi Sambhota.

Other tombs

Looking east from this viewpoint, the large tomb straight ahead belongs to Songtsen Gampo's grandson, **Mangsong Mangtsen** (646–76), who became king at the age of four. The tomb some distance to the left is that of **Tri Ralpachan** (805–36); the nearby enclosure contains an ancient pillar that records the events of his reign and is constructed on top of a stone turtle, symbolizing the foundation of the universe. Originally every tomb had one of these pillars on top, but the others have long since disappeared.

Chingwa Tagtse Dzong

The ruins of **Chingwa Tagtse Dzong**, perched high on the mountainside to the west, give an idea of the scale of the fortress and capital of the early Yarlung kings before Songtsen Gampo moved to Lhasa. To the left, the monastery of **Riwo Dechen** is visible, and a rough road means you can drive to within ten minutes' walk of this thriving Gelugpa community of around eighty monks. Originally founded in the fifteenth century, it was later expanded by the Seventh Dalai Lama and restored in the mid-1980s. There are three main chapels, the central one dominated by a large Tsongkhapa figure.

Tsurphu and Namtso

One of the most rewarding and popular trips in Tibet is to **Namtso Lake**, around 230km northwest of Lhasa, taking in **Tsurphu Monastery** on the way. This can be done on a two-night/three-day jaunt from Lhasa by jeep.

Tsurphu Monastery

楚布寺, chǔbù sì • Daily 9am–1pm • ¥45

Some 70km or so northeast of Lhasa, **Tsurphu Monastery**, set at an altitude of 4480m, is the seat of the **Karmapa Lama**, though it's a seat that's pretty cold these days as the

---

BLACK HAT LAMAISM

Founded in the twelfth century by Dusun Khenyapa, the Karmapa order is a branch of the Kagyupa tradition, where members are known as the **Black Hats** after the Second Karmapa was presented with one by Kublai Khan. Most powerful during the fifteenth century, when they were close to the ruling families of the time, they were eventually eclipsed in 1642 when the Fifth Dalai Lama and the "Yellow Hat" Gelugpa order, aided by the Mongol army, gained the ascendancy. The Karmapa were the first order to institute the system of reincarnated lamas, *tulkus*, a tradition later adopted by the Gelugpa school.

present incumbent, Urgyen Trinley Dorge, fled to India in 1999. Identified in 1992 at the age of seven, the questionable standing of the current Panchen Lama makes Urgyen the second-holiest Tibetan after the Dalai Lama; he seems charismatic and able and is regarded by many in exile as a natural successor for the role of leader when the Dalai Lama dies.

Zhiwa Tratsang

The solid **Zhiwa Tratsang** has a splendidly ornate gold roof and houses the main assembly hall, dominated by statues of Sakyamuni and a chorten containing the relics of the Sixteenth Karmapa Lama, who played a major part in establishing the order overseas and died in Chicago in 1981. The murals here depict the successive Karmapa lamas. The festival of **Saga Dawa**, on the fifteenth day of the fourth lunar month, usually in May or June, is especially fine at Tsurphu, as the massive new *thangka*, completed in recent years, is displayed at this time.

The kora circuit

A visit to the monastery can be exhausting, as it's at a considerably higher altitude than Lhasa. In addition, the clockwise path, the **kora**, climbs steeply up the hill behind the monastery from the left of the temple complex and circles around high above and behind the monastery before descending on the right. The views are great and the truly fit can even clamber to the top of the ridge, but you need to allow two to three hours for the walk.

ACCOMMODATION   **TSURPHU**

Monastery guesthouse 楚布寺宾馆, chǔbùsì bīnguǎn. There's little reason to stay at Tsurphu unless you're trekking in the area. There is a basic monastery guesthouse here which offers few amenities beyond a place to lie down – bring your own sleeping bag, food and candles. **¥50**

Damxhung

当雄, dāngxióng

If you're heading up to Namtso from Tsurphu, you'll need to continue on the main highway past the Yangbajing turning for another 80km to **DAMXHUNG**, a bleak truck-stop town at a breath-defying 4360m above sea level. The road is good, and the awesome Nyanchen Tanglha mountain range to the north is dramatically topped by the peak of Nyanchen Tanglha itself (7117m).

ARRIVAL AND DEPARTURE   **DAMXHUNG**

By minibus Minibuses from Lhasa to Namtso, departing just east of the *Yak Hotel* around 7am each morning, travel via Damxhung.
By bicycle If you're cycling or otherwise travelling independently, the turning north to Namtso is about halfway through Damxhung, where a large concrete bridge crosses the river towards the mountains.

ACCOMMODATION AND EATING

Damshung Pema Hotel 当雄县白马宾馆, dāngxióngxiàn báimǎ bīnguǎn. **Dangquhe Dong Lu** ☎ 0891 6112098. Nicely kitted out with Tibetan rugs and furniture, the en-suite rooms in this place west of the town centre are a more than comfortable place to stop over. The dorms with shared squat toilets are less impressive, but still more homely than similar options elsewhere. Dorm **¥40**, room **¥230**

Namtso

纳木错, nàmùcuò • ¥85

Set at 4700m and frozen over from November to May, **Namtso** (Sky Lake) is 70km long and 30km wide, the second-largest saltwater lake in China (only Qinghai Lake is

14

bigger; see p.798). The scenery comes straight from a dream image of Tibet, with snowcapped mountains towering behind the massive lake and yaks grazing on the plains around nomadic herders' tents.

At the lake

From Damxhung, it takes around two hours to pass through the Nyanchen Tanglha mountain range at Lhachen La (5150m) and descend to **Namtso Qu**, the district centre numbering just a couple of houses at the eastern end of the lake. The target of most visitors is **Tashi Dor Monastery** (¥10), considerably farther west (a hefty 42km from Lhachen La), tucked away behind two massive red rocks on a promontory jutting into the lake. At **Tashi Dor**, a small Nyingma monastery is built around a cave, and there's a dirt-floored guesthouse. You can walk around the rock at the end of the promontory and also climb to the top for even more startling views. For true devotees, a circuit of the lake can be attempted, though this takes twenty days and involves camping on the way.

ARRIVAL AND DEPARTURE   NAMTSO

By minibus Minibuses from Lhasa, via Damxhung to Namtso, depart just east of the *Yak Hotel* around 7am each morning (3–4hr; ¥30).

ACCOMMODATION

Yang's Hostel 羊宾馆, yáng bīnguǎn. Near the chapels at Tashi Dor Monastery. This ugly collection of prefabs, similar to those used by Chinese migrant workers on building sites, also has dormitory tents, if you prefer sleeping under canvas to laminated polystyrene. Bedding is provided but you'll probably want to use your own sleeping bag. ¥50

To Everest and the Nepal border

Roads run southwest of Lhasa to **Mount Everest and the Nepal border**, past some of the region's most historically significant **monasteries**: Gyantse, site of a shameful episode in Britain's colonial past; Shigatse, spiritiual seat of the Panchen Lamas; and spectacular Sakya, home to one of the foremost orders of Tibetan Buddhism. Then comes Everest itself, though – given the surprising urbanity of the base camp "village" here – the mountain's rugged splendor is perhaps best appreciated from afar.

Yamdrok Tso

羊卓雍错, yángzhuó yōngcuò
From Chusul Bridge, on the western outskirts of Lhasa, the southern road climbs steeply up to the Kampa La Pass (4794m); at the top, a car park offers stunning views of the turquoise waters of the sacred **Yamdrok Tso**, the third-largest lake in Tibet. It's a good place to take a picture, and there are plenty of Tibetans armed with baby goats, yaks and Tibetan mastiffs – dogs traditionally used by nomads to fend off wolves – who

---

THE OLD SOUTHERN ROAD

The road west from Lhasa divides at the Chusul Bridge and most vehicles follow the paved **Friendship Highway** along the course of the Yarlung Tsangpo to Shigatse. However, there is an alternative route, the longer but extremely picturesque **old southern road** that heads southwest to the shores of Yamdrok Tso, before turning west to Gyantse and then northwest to Shigatse – it is this route that most tour groups follow. Expect around six or seven hours' driving time from Lhasa to Gyantse in a good jeep, but day-trips to Yamdrok Tso from Lhasa are feasible.

will be only too happy to pose with you, for a small fee of ¥10–20. It is said that if the lake ever dries up then Tibet itself will no longer support life – a tale of heightened importance now that Yamdrok Tso, which has no significant inflowing rivers to keep it topped up, is powering a controversial hydroelectric scheme. From the pass, the road descends to Yamtso village before skirting the northern and western shores amid wild scenery dotted with a few tiny hamlets, yaks by the lakeside and small boats on the water.

The western shore

On the western side of the lake, 57km beyond the Kampa La Pass, the dusty village of **Nakartse** (4500m) is the birthplace of the mother of the Great Fifth Dalai Lama. There is basic accommodation in the village, but few tours overnight here, preferring to push on to Gyantse or Shigatse – though most do stop for lunch.

The lake circuit trek

Yamdrok Tso has many picturesque islands and inlets visible from the road, and there's a seven-day **circular trek** from Nakartse exploring the major promontory into the lake. The climb up from Nakartse to the glacier-topped **Karo La Pass** (5045m) is long and dramatic, with towering peaks on either side as the road heads south and then west toward apparently impenetrable rock faces. From the pass, the road descends gradually, via the mineral mines at Chewang, and the stunning reservoir at the **Simila Pass** (4717m) to the broad, fertile and densely farmed **Nyang Chu Valley** leading to Gyantse.

EATING   **YAMDROK TSO**

Tibetan restaurant Nakartse, on the western shore. This pleasant place has tables in a tiny courtyard, hidden away in the middle of the village, where you can eat rice with potato and meat curry (they fish out the meat for vegetarians) under the watchful eyes of local dogs. Jeep drivers usually come here; otherwise, look for the tourist vehicles parked outside.

Gyantse

江孜, jiāngzī

On the eastern banks of the Nyang Chu at the base of a natural amphitheatre of rocky ridges, **GYANTSE** is an attractive, relaxed town, offering the splendid sights of the **Gyantse Kumbum** (pronounced goom-boom) – famous among scholars of Tibetan art throughout the world – and the old Gyantse Dzong. Despite the rapidly expanding Chinese section of town, it has retained a pleasant, laidback air. It lies 263km from Lhasa on the old southern road and 90km southeast of Shigatse.

Brief history

Little is known about the history of any settlement at Gyantse before the fourteenth century, when it emerged as the capital of a small kingdom ruled by a lineage of princes claiming descent from the legendary Tibetan folk hero, **King Gesar of Ling**. Hailing originally from northeast Tibet, they allied themselves to the powerful Sakya

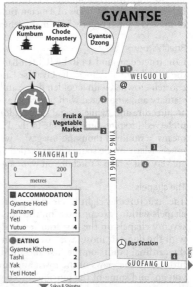

GYANTSE

■ ACCOMMODATION

Gyantse Hotel	3
Jianzang	2
Yeti	1
Yutuo	4

● EATING

Gyantse Kitchen	4
Tashi	2
Yak	3
Yeti Hotel	1

order. Also at this time, Gyantse operated as a staging post in the **wool trade** between Tibet and India, thanks to its position between Lhasa and Shigatse. By the mid-fifteenth century, the Gyantse Dzong, Pelkor Chode Monastery and the Kumbum had been built, although decline followed as other local families increased their influence.

The Younghusband Expedition

Gyantse rose to prominence again in July 1904 when Younghusband's machine-gun-equipped British expedition approached the town via the trade route from Sikkim, killing over half of the 1500 Tibetans sent to stop them. The British later took the Dzong with four casualties while a further three hundred Tibetans were killed. As part of the ensuing agreement between Tibet and Britain, a British Trade Agency was established in Gyantse allowing the route from Calcutta up through Sikkim and on to Gyantse to become increasingly busy.

Gyantse Dzong

江孜古堡, jiāngzī gǔbǎo • Daily 9.30am–6.30pm • ¥30

The original **Gyantse Dzong** dates from the mid-fourteenth century, though the damage caused by the British in 1904 means a lot of what you see is a reconstruction. Having climbed up to the fort, visitors are allowed into the **Meeting Hall**, which houses a waxworks tableau, and the **Anti-British Imperialist Museum**, where weapons, used by the defenders against the British, are on display. Climb higher and you reach the upper and lower chapels of the **Sampal Norbuling Monastery**. A few of the murals in the upper chapel probably date from the early fifteenth century, but most of the other artefacts are modern. The best views are from the top of the tallest tower in the north of the complex. You'll need to climb some very rickety ladders, but the scenery is well worth it.

Gyantse Kumbum

江孜千佛塔, jiāngzī qiānfótǎ • Daily 9am–8pm • ¥60 • photos up to ¥20/chapel

At the northern edge of town, the rather barren monastic compound that now contains the glorious **Gyantse Kumbum** was once home to religious colleges and temples belonging to three schools of Tibetan Buddhism: the Gelugpa, Sakya and Bu (the last of these is a small order whose main centre is at Zhalu; see opposite).

Brief history

Constructed around 1440 by Rabten Kunsang, the Gyantse prince most responsible for the town's fine buildings, the Gyantse Kumbum is a remarkable building, a huge chorten crowned with a golden dome and umbrella, with chapels bristling with statuary and smothered with paintings at each level. It's a style unique to Tibetan architecture and, while several such buildings have survived, Gyantse is the best preserved (despite some damage in the 1960s) and most accessible. The word *kumbum* means "a hundred thousand images" – which is probably an overestimate, but not by much. Many of the statues have needed extensive renovation, and most of the murals are very old – take a torch if you want a good look.

The chapels

The structure has eight levels, decreasing in size as you ascend; most of the chapels within, except those on the uppermost floors, are open. With almost seventy chapels on the first four levels alone, there's plenty to see. The highlights, with the densest, most lavish decoration, include the two-storey chapels at the cardinal points on the first and third levels and the four chapels on the fifth level. The views of the town and surrounding area get better the higher you go, and some of the outside stucco work is especially fine. At the sixth level, you'll emerge onto an open platform, level with the eyes of the chorten that look in each direction.

Pelkor Chode Monastery

In the same compound as Gyantse Kumbum, the **Pelkor Chode Monastery** was built by Rabten Kunsang some twenty years earlier and used for worship by monks from all the surrounding monasteries. Today, the main assembly hall contains two thrones, one for the Dalai Lama and one for the main Sakya Lama. The glitter and gold and the sunlight and flickering butter lamps in the chapels make a fine contrast to the gloom of much of the Kumbum. The main chapel, **Tsangkhang**, is at the back of the assembly hall and has a statue of Sakyamuni flanked by deities amid some impressive wood carvings – look for the two peacocks perched on a beam. The second floor of the monastery contains five chapels, and the top level just one, **Shalyekhang** (Peak of the Celestial Mansion), with some very impressive, 2m-wide mandalas.

14

ARRIVAL AND DEPARTURE   GYANTSE

By bus There is a bus station along Yingxiong Nan Lu, near the junction with Guofang Lu, with regular departures to both Lhasa and Shigatse.

Destinations Lhasa (6hr); Shigatse (2hr).
By private jeep Lhasa (6hr); Shigatse (2hr).

ACCOMMODATION

Gyantse Hotel 江孜饭店, jiāngzī fàndiàn. 2 Shanghai Dong Lu ☎0892 8172222. East of the main crossroads, this cavernous three-star affair lacks character but is comfortable spacious, generally clean and has 24hr hot water and a tub in every bathroom. **¥300**

Jianzang 建藏饭店, jiànzàng fàndiàn. 14 Yingxiong Nan Lu ☎0892 8173720. Built around an old courtyard, this centrally located, family-run place has some nice Tibetan decoration as well as free wi-fi and a laundry service. **¥260**

Yeti 雅迪花园酒店, yàdí huāyuán jiǔdiàn. 11 Weiguo Lu ☎0892 8175555, ⊛yetihoteltibet.com.

Smart new place at the top of town near the Gyantse Dzong. Hotel reception is through the restaurant on the ground floor; friendly staff will usher you through. Rooms are on a par with the *Gyantse Hotel*, but being smaller and more central this has bags more character. **¥300**

Yutuo 玉妥饭店, yùtuǒ fàndiàn. Guofang Bei Lu ☎0892 8175688. A little out of the town centre, and still a bit rough around the edges, this new guesthouse is clean, comfortable and has hot water, although the rooms themselves can get cold and the youthful staff are still finding their feet. **¥180**

EATING

Gyantse Kitchen 江孜橱房, jiāngzī chúfáng. Shanghai Dong Lu ☎0892 8176777. Opposite the *Gyantse Hotel*, this place is popular with tour groups and churns out decent quality, if uninspired, Chinese and Tibetan food. The evening buffet is decent value at ¥40 if you're hungry, but service can be slow. Daily 8.30am–10pm.

Tashi 打西餐厅, dáxī cāntīng. Yingxiong Zhong Lu ☎0892 8172793. An unashamedly Nepalese restaurant and all the better for it. This friendly place knocks out excellent curries as well as the standard momos, pizzas and pancakes. You can get breakfast here, but you should let them know the night before. Around ¥35 per head for a main meal. Daily 8.30am–10.30pm.

Yak 亚美食餐厅, yà měishí cāntīng. Yingxiong Zhong Lu. Opposite *Tashi*, this place is aimed at the dwindling number of foreign visitors, advertising French and Italian efforts on a board out front. Probably the best approximation of Western food in town, but you may well find yourself the only customer. Around ¥35 for mains. Daily 11am–10pm.

Yeti Hotel 雅迪花园酒店, yàdí huāyuán jiǔdiàn. 11 Weiguo Lu ☎0892 8175555, ⊛yetihoteltibet.com. Modern, clean restaurant at the front of this friendly hotel, with an English picture menu for ease of ordering and an enormous list of food available including Chinese, Tibetan and Western options. A bit pricey at around ¥40 for mains; breakfast available. Daily 8am–10pm.

Zhalu Monastery

夏鲁寺, xiàlǔ sì

Zhalu Monastery is around 22km from Shigatse, 75km from Gyantse and 4km south of the village of Tsungdu, between kilometre-markers 18 and 19 on the

14

Gyantse–Shigatse road. Originally built in the eleventh century, Zhalu rose to prominence as the seat of the **Bu tradition** of Tibetan Buddhism founded by Buton Rinchendrub in the fourteenth century. Buton's claim to fame is as the scholar who collected, organized and copied the Tengyur commentaries by hand into a coherent whole, comprising 227 thick volumes, though the originals were destroyed during the Cultural Revolution. There were once about 3500 monks living here, but the tradition never had as many followers as the other schools. It did, however, have a fair degree of influence: **Tsongkhapa**, among others, was inspired by Buton's teachings.

The monastery has a finely colonnaded courtyard decorated with luck symbols, but is most remarkable for the green-glazed tiles that line the roof. Major renovations are ongoing and chapels have been closed and rearranged, but the monks are friendly and the village is a quiet and pleasant place.

Riphuk

For the energetic, it's a one- to two-hour walk up in the hills southwest of Zhalu to the hermitage of **Riphuk**, where Atisha (see p.859) is supposed to have meditated during his journey from Sakya to Samye. Here you'll find a clutch of rebuilt temples and a stupa inside the ruined walls of a complex once home to some 300 monks. Current residents will probably dispense with administering the traditional blessing of three pitchers of cold spring water over the head of visitors. You'll need directions or a guide from Zhalu, as you can't see it from the monastery.

Gyankhor Lhakhang

About 1km north of Zhalu, **Gyankor Lhakhang** dates from 997. Sakya Pandita, who established the relationship between the Mongol Khans and the Sakya hierarchy in the thirteenth century (see p.860), was ordained here as a monk, and the stone bowl over which he shaved his head prior to ordination is in the courtyard. Just inside the entrance is a conch shell, said to date from the time of Buton Rinchendrub and reputedly able to sound without human assistance.

Shigatse

日喀则, rìkāzé

Traditionally the home of the Panchen Lamas – religious and political rivals to the Dalai Lamas – Tibet's second city, **SHIGATSE**, is used by travellers as an overnight stop on the way to or from Lhasa. One day is long enough to see the two main sights, **Tashilunpo Monastery** and **Shigatse Dzong**, but if you're not pressed for time it's worth spending at least an extra night here simply to do everything at a more leisurely pace, take in the market, wander the attractive, tree-lined streets and absorb the buzz provided by the huge numbers of Tibetan pilgrims and foreign visitors. Although most of the city is modern, you'll find the traditional Tibetan houses concentrated in the old town west of the market, where you can explore the narrow alleyways running between high, whitewashed walls.

Tashilunpo Monastery

扎什伦布寺, zhāshílúnbù sì • Mon–Sat 9.30am–7pm • ¥55 • photography ¥150/chapel • ¥1800 to shoot video

Something of a showcase for foreign visitors, the large complex of **Tashilunpo Monastery** is situated on the western side of town just below the Drolma Ridge – the gleaming, golden roofs will lead you in the right direction. Tashilunpo was founded in 1447 by **Gendun Drup**, Tsongkhapa's nephew and disciple, who was later recognized as the First Dalai Lama. It rose to prominence in 1642 when the Fifth Dalai Lama declared that Losang Chokyi Gyeltsen, who was his teacher and the abbot of Tashilunpo, was a manifestation of the Amitabha Buddha and the Fourth reincarnation

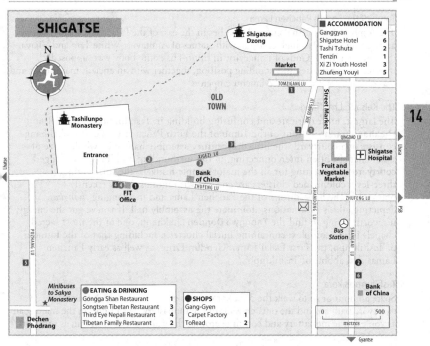

of the **Panchen Lama** (Great Precious Teacher), in what has proved to be an ill-fated lineage (see box, p.898). The Chinese have consistently sought to use the Panchen Lama in opposition to the Dalai Lama, beginning in 1728 when they gave the Fifth Panchen Lama sovereignty over western Tibet.

The monastery has some of the most fabulous chapels outside of Lhasa, and it takes several hours to do it justice.

Jamkhang Chenmo

The **temples** and shrines of most interest in Tashilunpo stand in a long line at the northern end of the compound. From the main gate, head uphill and left to the **Jamkhang Chenmo**. Several storeys high, this was built by the Ninth Panchen Lama in 1914 and is dominated by a 26m gold, brass and copper statue of Maitreya, the Buddha of the Future. Hundreds of small images of Maitreya and Tsongkhapa and his disciples are painted on the walls.

Tomb of the Tenth Panchen Lama

To the east of the Jamkhang Chenmo, the next main building contains the gold and jewel-encrusted **Tomb of the Tenth Panchen Lama**, which was consecrated in 1994 and cost US$8 million. Near the top is a small window cut into a tiny niche, containing his picture.

Palace of the Panchen Lamas

Past the Tenth Panchen Lama's tomb, the **Palace of the Panchen Lamas**, built in the eighteenth century, is closed to the public, but the long building in front houses a series of small, first-floor chapels. The Yulo Drolma Lhakhang, farthest to the right, is worth a look and contains 21 small statues showing each of the 21 manifestations of Tara, the most popular goddess in Tibet.

Tomb of the Fourth Panchen Lama

The **Tomb of the Fourth Panchen Lama** lies to the east of the Palace of Panchen Lamas, and contains an 11m-high chorten, with statues of Amitayus, White Tara and Vijaya, the so-called Three Gods of Longevity, in front. His entire body was supposedly interred in the chorten in a standing position, together with an ancient manuscript and *thangkas* sent by the second Manchu emperor.

The Kelsang Lhakhang

The largest, most intricate and confusing building in Tashilunpothe, the **Kelsang Lhakhang** stands in front of the Tomb of the Fifth Panchen Lama. The Lhakhang consists of a courtyard, the fifteenth-century assembly hall and a whole maze of small chapels, often interconnecting, in the surrounding buildings. The flagged **courtyard** is the setting for all the major temple festivals; the surrounding three-level colonnaded cloisters are covered with murals, many recently renovated. The huge throne of the Panchen Lama and the hanging *thangkas*, depicting all his incarnations, dominate the **assembly hall**. If you've got the energy, it's worth trying to find the **Thongwa Donden Lhakhang**, one of the most sacred chapels in the complex, containing burial chortens, including that of the founder of Tashilunpo, the First Dalai Lama, Gendun Drup, as well as early Panchen Lamas and abbots of Tashilunpo.

Tashilunpo's kora

Spare an hour or so to walk the 3km **kora**, the pilgrim circuit, which follows a clockwise path around the outside walls of the monastery. Turn right on the main road as you exit the monastery and continue around the walls; a stick is useful, as some of

THE PANCHEN LAMA CONTROVERSY

The life of Choekyi Gyaltsen, the **Tenth Panchen Lama** (1938–89), was a tragic one. Identified without approval from Lhasa by the Nationalist authorities in 1949, he fell into Communist hands and was for years China's highest-profile Tibetan collaborator. In 1959, however, his role changed when he openly referred to the Dalai Lama as the true ruler of Tibet. Ordered to denounce the Dalai Lama, Gyaltsen refused and was barred from speaking in public until 1964, when, to an audience of ten thousand people, he again proclaimed support for the exiled leader. He spent the following fourteen years in jail. Released in 1978, Gyaltsen never again criticized the Chinese in public, arguing for the protection of Tibetan culture at all costs, even if it meant abandoning independence. Some saw him as a sellout; others still worship him as a hero. He died in 1989, officially from a heart attack, though rumours of poisoning persist.

The **search for a successor** was always likely to be fraught, with the Dalai Lama and the Chinese government both claiming authority to choose the next incarnation. The search was initially led according to tradition by checking on reports of "unusual" children, and in January 1995 the Dalai Lama identified the Eleventh Panchen Lama but – concerned for the child's safety – delayed a public announcement. The Chinese authorities, meanwhile, decreed selection should take place by drawing of lots from a golden urn.

In May, the Dalai Lama publicly identified his choice, and within days the boy and his family had disappeared. Fifty Communist Party officials moved into Tashilunpo to root out monks loyal to the Dalai Lama and his choice of Panchen Lama. In July, riot police quelled an open revolt by the monks, but by the end of 1995 dissent was suppressed enough for the drawing of lots to take place. The lucky winner, **Gyaincain Norbu**, was enthroned at Tashilunpo and taken to Beijing for publicity appearances, where he has since stayed to complete his studies. Two decades later, the fate of the Dalai Lama's choice and his family remains unknown, though Beijing claims they are free and voluntarily opting to remain anonymous.

As for Gyaincain Norbu, despite Beijing's best efforts, his returns home are lacklustre affairs, and it is overwhelmingly his predecessor, the rotund Choekyi Gyaltsen, who you'll see smiling beatifically down from Tibetan living-room walls.

the dogs are aggressive. The highlight of the walk is the view of the glorious golden roofs from above the top wall. The massive, white-painted wall at the top northeast corner is where the 40m, where the 40m appliquéd *thangka* is displayed annually at the festival on the fifteenth day of the fifth lunar month (usually in July). At this point, instead of returning downhill to the main road, you can follow the track that continues on around the hillside above the Tibetan part of town and leads eventually to the old Shigatse Dzong.

Shigatse Dzong

日喀则宗, rìkāzézōng

Shigatse Dzong was built in the seventeenth century by Karma Phuntso Namgyel when he was king of the Tsang region and held sway over much of the country. It's thought that its design was used as the basis for the later construction of the Potala Palace in Lhasa. The structure was initially ruined by the Dzungars in 1717, and further damage took place in the 1950s. The main reason to climb up is for the fantastic views.

The market

The **market**, opposite the *Tenzin Hotel*, is worth a browse for souvenirs, jewellery, fake antiques and religious objects (if not for its most obvious product, whole dead sheep), and the scale of the place is a bit easier to manage than Lhasa's Barkhor. You'll need to brush up on your bargaining skills and be patient – the stallholders are used to hit-and-run tourists, so the first asking prices can be sky-high.

Gang-Gyen Carpet Factory

刚坚地毯厂, gāngjiān dìtǎn chǎng • Zhufeng Lu • Mon–Fri 9am–12.30pm & 2.30–7pm

Even if you're not interested in rugs it's worth dropping into the **Gang-Gyen Carpet Factory**, a few minutes' walk from the entrance of Tashilunpo. You can see the whole carpet-making process – from the winding of the wool through to the weaving and finishing – and the dexterity of the women working here is mind-boggling. There's also a shop with a good range of traditional and modern designs, but even with prices well below what you'd find in the West there's still nothing on offer for under a couple of hundred dollars. If you do take the plunge, the factory can arrange shipping.

ARRIVAL AND DEPARTURE   SHIGATSE

By bus Shigatse's bus station is in the centre of town on Shanghai Lu, south of its junction with Zhufeng Lu. Buses to Lhasa leave in the morning (8am & 9am). Those to and from Gyantse run until around 4pm.
Destinations Gyantse (frequent; 3hr); Lhasa (1 daily; 8hr);

Lhatse (1 daily; 4hr); Sakya (1 daily; 5hr); Tingri (1 daily; 10hr).
By private jeep Gyantse to Shigatse will take around three hours, while Lhasa to Shigatse takes at least seven. Sakya can be reached in around four hours.

INFORMATION

Tourist permits Shigatse's PSB, on Zhufeng Dong Lu (Mon–Fri 9.30am–1pm & 3.30–7pm, ☎ 0892 8829803), is used to dealing with tour groups and is where permits for

Everest and Mount Kailash are issued – such formalities should be handled by your tour guide.

GETTING AROUND

By taxi Taxis are ¥10 for any destination in town, or it's about a 20min walk from the bus station to the

Tenzin Hotel.

ACCOMMODATION

Ganggyan 刚坚宾馆, gāngjiān bīnguǎn. 77 Zhufeng Xi Lu ☎ 0892 8820777. Run as a business by the

nearby Tashilunpo monastery, the *Ganggyan* has plainly decorated, decent-value en-suite rooms and three-bed

14

THE FRIENDSHIP HIGHWAY

From Shigatse, the **Friendship Highway** is surfaced all the way to Zhangmu on the Nepalese border. The only public buses in this direction are the Shigatse to Sakya, Lhatse and Tingri services. From the broad plain around Shigatse, the road gradually climbs to the pass of Tsuo La (4500m) before the steep descent to the Sakya Bridge and the turn-off to Sakya village. If you have time, a detour off the Friendship Highway to **Sakya** is worthwhile; the valleys are picturesque, the villages retain the rhythm of their rural life and Sakya Monastery is a dramatic sight. Further south, the side-trip to **Mount Everest Base Camp** is a once-in-a-lifetime experience.

dorms, though the latter come without a/c or a toilet – communal bathrooms are at the end of the corridor. Dorms **¥60**, rooms **¥200**

Shigatse Hotel 日喀则饭店, rìkāzé fàndiàn. 12 Shanghai Zhonglu ☎0892 8822525. Tour-group hotel, a bit out of the centre, and rather cavernous if there aren't plenty of people around. There's the choice of taking heavily decorated "Tibetan-style" rooms over the cookie-cutter Chinese options. **¥480**

Tashi Tshuta 扎西曲塔大酒店, zhāxī qūtǎ dàjiǔdiàn. 2 Xuechang Lu ☎0892 8830111. Four-star luxury option, rooms are at least on a par with the *Shigaste*, but this is plum in the middle of town. Hands-down the best place to stay. **¥480**

Tenzin 旦增宾馆, dànzēng bīnguǎn. 8 Tomzigang Lu, opposite the Tibetan market ☎0892 8822018. A long-standing, centrally located budget option. Rooms are unremarkable but clean and have a/c, so it's a good deal, but service doesn't exactly come with a smile. **¥180**

Xi Zi Youth Hostel 日喀则喜孜青年旅舍, rìkāzé qīngnián lǚshè. 10 Xigezi Lu ☎0892 8822298. Sparsely furnished but busy youth hostel right in the middle of Shigatse's premier tourist street. Popular with Chinese students and cyclists, there is wi-fi throughout and en-suite doubles are fair value. Dorm **¥40**, room **¥170**

Zhufeng Youyi 珠峰友谊宾馆, zhūfēng yǒuyì bīnguǎn. Puzhang Lu ☎0892 8663000. Smart and comfortable hotel with clean doubles and helpful desk staff. Not too far from the monastery, but a long walk from just about everything else. **¥180**

EATING AND DRINKING

There's no shortage of restaurants in Shigatse, including several aimed at the stuttering flow of Western tourists. If you're getting a picnic together, visit the fruit and vegetable market south off Qingdao Lu.

Gongga Shan Restaurant 贡嘎山美味藏餐厅, gònggāshān měiwèi zàngcāntīng. Xuechang Lu. Rough-and-ready Tibetan eatery with an English menu featuring yak's heart salad, and pig's trotters and ears, alongside more orthodox dishes from ¥15–30. Daily 10am–9pm.

Songtsen Tibetan Restaurant 松赞西藏餐厅, sōngzàn xīzàng cāntīng. 19 Xigezi Lu ☎0892 8832469. Cosy place turning out a good mix of tourist-friendly Tibetan, Nepali, Western and Chinese favourites. Great location, though not particularly cheap; mains around ¥40. Daily 9am–10pm.

Third Eye Nepali Restaurant 尼泊尔雪莲餐厅, níbóěr xuělián cāntīng. Zhufeng Xi Lu, upstairs next to the Ganggyan Hotel ☎0892 8838898. Very well turned-out Nepali dishes and average Chinese standards, particularly good for vegetarians who can opt for *paneer* curry or a vegetable *thali*. Popular with tour groups; expect ¥50 per head. Daily 11am–10pm.

Tibetan Family Restaurant 丰盛藏式餐厅, fēngshèng zàngshì cāntīng. 62 Xigezi Lu ☎1390 8929222. Friendly and usually full of Tibetan tea-drinkers, this place also has a small balcony for sitting outside and people-watching. The food is also tasty and very reasonably priced, with mains from ¥20. Daily 9am–10pm.

DIRECTORY

Banks and exchange The Bank of China (Mon–Sat 10am–4pm), south of the *Shigatse Hotel*, and on Zhufeng Lu, east of the Gang Gyan, cashes travellers' cheques and gives advances on visa cards. If you're heading west, stock up here on local currency, as there are no more facilities until Zhangmu.

Hospital The Shigatse hospital on Shanghai Lu has a first-aid post (daily 10am–12.30pm & 4–6pm) – take a Chinese translator with you.

Internet There are a couple of internet cafés just south of the post office and also opposite the *Shigatse Hotel*.

Post office Corner of Shandong Lu and Zhufeng Lu (daily 9am–7pm). You can send international letters and faxes, but not parcels, and they don't stock postcards – go to the *Shigatse Hotel* for those.

Trekking Equipment There is a ToRead store on Shanghai Lu, just north of the *Shigatse Hotel*. Clothing sold here should be genuine but won't be cheap.

Sakya

萨迦, sàjiā

The small but rapidly growing village of **SAKYA**, set in the midst of an attractive plain, straddles the small Trum River and is highly significant as the centre of the Sakya school of Tibetan Buddhism. The main reason to visit is to see the remaining monastery, a unique, Mongol-style construction dramatically visible from far away. The village around is now a burgeoning Chinese community, full of ugly concrete, and can be crowded with coach parties in peak season, but while it's not a place to linger, the monastery makes this a more than worthwhile side-trip from the Friendship Highway.

14

The Southern Monastery

萨迦南寺, sàjiānán sì • Mon–Sat 9am–6pm • ¥45 • photography ¥25/chapel

A massive fortress, the **Southern Monastery** was built in the thirteenth century on the orders of **Phagpa**, nephew of Sakya Pandita. The entrance is in its east wall; on the way there, note the unusual decoration of houses in the area – grey, with white and red vertical stripes – which dates back to a time when it denoted their taxable status within the Sakya principality.

The Puntsok Palace

The five main temples in the complex are surrounded by a huge wall with turrets at each corner. On the left of the entrance is the tall, spacious chapel on the second floor of the **Puntsok Palace**, the traditional home of one of the two main Sakya lamas, who now live in the US. It is lined with statues – White Tara is nearest to the door and Sakya Pandita farther along the same wall. The central figure of Kunga Nyingpo, the founder of the Northern Monastery, shows him as an old man. The chortens contain the remains of early Sakya lamas.

As you move clockwise around the courtyard, the next chapel is the **Phurkhang**, with statues of Sakyamuni to the left and Manjusri to the right of Sakya Pandita. The whole temple is stuffed with thousands of small statues and editions of sacred texts with murals on the back wall.

The Great Assembly Hall

Facing the entrance to the courtyard, the **Great Assembly Hall** is an imposing chapel, with walls 3.5m thick. Its roof is supported by forty solid wooden columns, one of

---

SAKYA'S NORTHERN MONASTERY

Originally, there were two monasteries at Sakya: the imposing, Mongol-style structure of the Southern Monastery that visitors come to see today, and a **Northern Monastery** across the river, which was a more typical complex containing 108 chapels. The Northern Monastery was founded in 1073 by Kong Chogyal Pho, a member of the Khon family, whose son, Kunga Nyingpo, did much to establish Sakya as an important religious centre. He married and had four sons; three became monks, but the fourth remained a layman and continued the family line. The Sakya order has remained something of a family affair, and, while the monks take vows of celibacy, their lay brothers ensure the leadership remains with their kin. One of the early leaders was a grandson of Kunga Nyingpo, known as Sakya Pandita. He began the most illustrious era of the order in the thirteenth century when he journeyed to the court of the Mongol emperor, Godan Khan, and established the Sakya lamas as religious advisers to subsequent emperors and effective rulers of Tibet. This state of affairs lasted until the overthrow of the Mongols in 1354.

The Northern Monastery was completely destroyed during the Cultural Revolution and has been largely replaced by housing. Prior to the Chinese occupation, there were around five hundred monks in the two monasteries; there are now about a hundred.

which was said to be a personal gift from Kublai Khan and carried by hand from China; another was supposedly fetched from India on the back of a tiger, a third brought in the horns of a yak and yet another is said to weep the black blood of the naga water spirit that lived in the tree used for the column. The chapel is overwhelmingly full of brocade hangings, fine statues, butter lamps, thrones, murals and holy books. The grandest statues, of Buddha, are against a golden, carved background, and contain the remains of previous Sakya lamas.

14

Silver Chorten Chapel

Next along, the **Silver Chorten Chapel** houses eleven chortens, with more in the chapel behind. Completing the circuit, the **Drolma Lhakhang** is on the second floor of the building to the right of the entrance. This is the residence of the other principal Sakya lama, the **Sakya Trizin**, currently residing in India, where he has established his seat in exile in Rajpur. Be sure to take time to walk around the top of the walls for fine views, both into the monastery and over the surrounding area.

ARRIVAL AND DEPARTURE   SAKYA

Situated 150km southwest of Shigatse, Sakya is an easy side-trip off the Friendship Highway if you've got your own transport; most tours call in here on the way to Everest before overnighting at Lhatse.

By bus Public buses run to Sakya from Shigatse on weekdays, departing again at 11am the next morning; it's a surprisingly slow trip – allow six hours or more each way. If you continue from Sakya to Lhatse, get the bus to drop you at the Friendship Highway turn-off, which it reaches around 1pm. The bus from Shigatse to Lhatse

passes here about 1.30pm, so you shouldn't have to wait for long.

Destinations Lhatse (daily; 1hr); Shigatse (daily; 6hr).

By jeep Everest (7hr); Lhatse (45min); Saga (7hr); Shigatse (3hr).

ACCOMMODATION

Manasarovar Sakya Hotel 神湖萨迦宾馆, shénhú sàjiā bīnguǎn. 1 Kelsang Xi Lu ☎0892 8242222. The main hotel in town and owned by the same people as the *Yak* hotel in Lhasa, so many tour groups end up here. Rooms are clean, but can be cold and there's often not

enough hot water to go round. On the plus side, the adjoining restaurant turns out steaming platefuls of Chinese, Tibetan and Western food (of sorts), though little English is spoken and orders do go astray. **¥200**

Lhatse

拉孜, lāzī

Just 24km west of Sakya Bridge, the truck-stop town of **Lhatse** (4050m) sits alongside the Friendship Highway and has plenty of restaurants and basic accommodation. There's little to detain you, but most bus drivers pull in here, and it's where many tour groups spend the night. Another 6km west from Lhatse, the road divides: the Friendship Highway continues to the left, and the route to the far west of Tibet heads right.

ACCOMMODATION AND EATING   LHATSE

Both of Lhatse's hotels have restaurants, and there are numerous good-value places – Sichuanese, especially – to eat along the main drag.

Shanghai Hotel 上海大酒店, shànghǎi dàjiǔdiàn. ☎0892 8323678. Top billing in town goes to this Chinese-run establishment which dominates the central square. Cavernous and totally lacking character, but with smart, clean rooms it's a sensible choice, though hardly inspiring. **¥350**

Tibetan Farmers' Adventure Hostel 西藏拉孜农民

娱乐旅馆, xīzàng lāzī nóngmín yúlè lǚguǎn. At the western end of town ☎0892 8322858. Proudly proclaims itself "Tibet's first hotel by peasants": enjoy the charm of the ramshackle cells at the front, but do your best to actually stay in one of the new, decidedly unpeasant-like en-suite rooms at the back. Breakfast is included. **¥280**

Approaching Everest

¥180

Approaching Everest along the Friendship Highway from Lhatse, allow about four hours in a good jeep to get up over the Lhakpa La Pass (5220m) to **NEW TINGRI** (新定日, xīndìngrì; also known as **Shekar**). Almost entirely constructed from concrete blocks, it's not the nicest place, but it holds the ticket office for **entry to the Mount Everest area** and represents the last chance to stock up on provisions before the mountain.

There's a checkpoint on the highway about 5km further on where some visitors have reported guards being particularly assiduous in confiscating printed material specifically about Tibet (books on China that include Tibet seem to be fine). Just 7km west of this checkpoint, the small turning to **Rongbuk Monastery** and on up to **Mount Everest Base Camp** is on the south side of the road.

14

Through Pang La Pass

It's a long, windy, spellbinding 90km to Rongbuk and worth every tortured minute of the three-hour drive. The road zigzags steeply up to the **Pang La Pass** (5150m), from where the glory of the Everest region is laid out before you – the earlier you go in the day the better the views, as it clouds over later. There's a lookout spot with a plan to help you identify individual peaks such as Cho Oyu (8153m), Lhotse (8501m) and Makalu (8463m), as well as the mighty **Mount Everest** (8848m; Chomolungma in Tibetan, Zhumulangma in Chinese). From here the road descends into a network of fertile valleys with small villages in a patchwork of fields. You'll gradually start climbing again and pass through **Peruche** (19km from Pang La), **Passum** (10km further) and **Chodzom** (another 12km), before the scenery becomes rockier and starker and you eventually reach Rongbuk Monastery, 22km farther on.

Rongbuk Monastery

绒布寺, róngbù sì • ¥25

Rongbuk Monastery – at 4980m, the highest in the world – was founded in 1902 by the Nyingma Lama, Ngawang Tenzin Norbu, although a hardy community of nuns had used meditation huts on the site for about two hundred years before this. The chapels themselves are of limited interest; Padmasambhava is in pride of place and the new murals are attractive, but the position of the monastery, perched on the side of the Rongbuk Valley leading straight towards the north face of Everest, is stunning. Just to sit outside and watch the play of light on the face of the mountain is the experience of a lifetime.

ACCOMMODATION AND EATING	RONGBUK MONASTERY

Campsite Around 2km past Rongbuk Monastery there's a large horseshoe of tents pitched around what is presumably the world's highest car park. Each of the tents claims the status of a "guesthouse", offering relatively comfortable dormitory accommodation for the single night most people stay. There's a stove in the centre of each, with basic meals a pricey ¥20–30 per dish. In the corner of the car park is a post office from where you can send Everest-stamped postcards. Beds ¥60

Mt Qomolangma View Hotel 珠峰大本营观景台宾馆, zhūfēng dàběnyíng guānjǐngtái bīnguǎn. ☎ 1390 8928499. Pink-tiled, battlemented monstrosity at the end of the valley, 100m or so from Rongbuk. That this eyesore was even built is a scandal – though it does have the best rooms in the vicinity, some with fantastic views towards Everest's north face. No showers or running hot water, and bathrooms and toilets are shared. ¥300

Rongbuk Monastery Hotel 绒布寺饭店, róngbùsì fàndiàn. ☎ 1890 8925152. Traditional-style single-storey building directly opposite the monastery, with basic but clean rooms around a small courtyard-cum-car park. They advertise 24hr hot water, but don't get too excited by the thought: it all comes via a flask rather than pipes and taps, and the toilets are communal long-drops. The highlight is its teahouse/restaurant which has windows facing down the valley – a perfect place to sit and watch the mountain play peek-a-boo, over a tankard of hot, sweet, milky tea. ¥160

14

Everest Base Camp

珠峰大本营, zhūfēng dàběnyíng • bus from Rongbuk ¥20

Everest Base Camp (5150m) is 4km due south from Rongbuk Monastery. There's a bus, but the walk alongside the river through the boulder-strewn landscape and past a small monastery on the cliff is glorious and the route fairly flat. Base camp is often a bit of a surprise, especially during the climbing seasons (March–May, Sept & Oct), when you'll find a colourful and untidy tent city festooned with Calor gas bottles and satellite dishes. At other times of year it's almost completely deserted, save for a perpetual detachment of Chinese troops keeping an eye out for potential "trouble".

Don't be surprised if you suffer with the **altitude** here – breathlessness and headaches are the norm. However well you were acclimatized in Lhasa, base camp is around 1500m higher, so be sensible and don't contemplate a trip here immediately after arrival up on the Tibetan plateau.

Tingri

From the Rongbuk and Mount Everest Base Camp turning on the Friendship Highway, it's a fast 50km south to **TINGRI** (定日, dìngrì; 4342m). The road is good, and you should allow about an hour in a jeep. A convenient stop on the final day's drive to Zhangmu, Tingri has some good restaurants, and excellent views south towards Everest. To get the best of these, climb up to the old fort that stands sentinel over the main part of the village.

ACCOMMODATION AND EATING   TINGRI

Snowland Hotel 定日雪域饭店, dìngrì xuěyù fàndiàn. ☏ 1520 8027313. At the western end of town, *Snowland* is more popular as a restaurant than a place to stay, and don't be surprised if you're rubbing shoulders with plenty of other tour groups. There's an English menu and a good range of Chinese and Western dishes; expect around ¥30 per person. Dorm **¥50**, room **¥100**

To the Nepalese border

The road west of Tingri is good and lined with ruins of buildings destroyed in an eighteenth-century Gurkha incursion from Nepal. The road climbs gradually for 85km to the double-topped **Lalung La Pass** (5050m), from where the views of the Himalayas are breathtaking, especially looking west to the great slab of Shishapangma (8013m). The descent from the pass is steep and startling as the road drops off the edge of the Tibetan plateau and heads down the gorge of the Po Chu River. Vegetation appears, and it becomes noticeably warmer as you near **Nyalam**, around four hours' drive by jeep from Tingri.

Milarepa's Cave

Although difficult to spot if you're coming from the north, **Milarepa's Cave** (10km north of Nyalam) is worth a halt – look out for a white chorten, to the left of the road on the edge of the gorge. Milarepa (1040–1123) was a much-revered Tibetan mystic who led an ascetic, itinerant life in caves and was loved for his religious songs. The **Kagyu** order of Tibetan Buddhism was founded by his followers, and the impressions in the walls and roof are believed to have been made by Milarepa himself. A temple has been built around the cave, the main statue being of Padmasambhava.

Nyalam

Perched on the side of the Matsang Zangpo River gorge, **NYALAM** (3750m) is a small village with several Chinese restaurants and a variety of basic accommodation,

ENTERING NEPAL

The **border posts** (both open daily 9.30am–5pm Chinese time) on the Chinese and Nepalese side, at **Kodari** (1770m), are separated by the short "Friendship Bridge", about 7km further downhill from Zhangmu. It can be extremely busy with tour groups and local traders crossing back and forth so it's best to get here early – baggage checks on leaving and entering Tibet on this route are noted for their rigour, which can add to the time spent queuing. The **Nepalese Immigration** post is a couple of hundred metres over the bridge on the left. You can only get single-entry visas here, and you have to pay in US dollars and produce a passport photograph (see p.865 for details of Nepali visas available in Lhasa). Don't forget to put your watch back (2hr 15min) when you cross into Nepal.

To head to **Kathmandu**, either take the express bus direct to Kathmandu or the cheaper local bus to Barabise, where you change for a connecting service. Alternatively, there are taxis in Kodari, or you can negotiate for space in a tourist bus that has just dropped its group at the border – bargain hard and you'll end up paying Rs400–600 (US$13 or so) per person for the four-hour trip.

14

although there is little to recommend staying the night here rather than continuing to Zhangmu.

Zhangmu

樟木, zhāngmù

The steep descent through the Himalayas continues from Nyalam and the bare mountain scrub gives way to sudden greenery, trees and almost unbelievably beautiful alpine scenery with rivers cascading down both sides of the sheer valley. Here, **ZHANGMU** (2300m), a Chinese-Tibetan-Nepalese hybrid, clings gamely to the mountainside, a collection of guesthouses, restaurants, construction sites, shops, brothels and offices. It's a great place, with a Wild-West-comes-to-Asia atmosphere, although good-quality accommodation is limited.

ACCOMMODATION AND EATING   ZHANGMU

With hot running water and sanitation still something of a novelty in Zhangmu, the best place to stay is whichever guesthouse has been most recently renovated. The *Sherpa* has a good restaurant, though there are plenty of places to choose from, most serving very decent Nepalese curries.

JinXin 金鑫宾馆, jīnxīn bīnguǎn. In the middle of town along the main street ☎0892 8743299. This place has clean, tidy en-suite rooms and is popular with tour groups, but its sterile-feeling tiled rooms lack character. ¥200

Sunny Youth Hostel 阳光客栈, yángguāng kèzhàn. Near the bottom end of town ☎0892 8742299. This is a smart, friendly hostel popular with young Chinese travellers. The twins and doubles are comfortable, the gloomy dorms less so. Dorm ¥35, room ¥160

Tibet Sherpa Hotel 厦尔巴酒店, shàěrbā jiǔdiàn. Again on the main road, downhill on a sharp bend ☎0892 8742098. The *Sherpa* is one of the longest-running hotels in town and also popular with tour groups. Try and get a room at the back, away from the road and looking out over the valley. ¥120

DIRECTORY

Banks and exchange Zhangmu has a Bank of China (Mon–Fri 10am–1pm & 3.30–6.30pm, Sat 10am–2pm) but does not change cash. There's a thriving black market for money changing in town and you will no doubt be endlessly approached with offers, but rates are bad and you shouldn't have any trouble changing Chinese currency once in Nepal.

PSB The PSB is up at the top of town close to the Bank of China (Mon–Fri 10am–1pm & 3.30–6.30pm, Sat 10am–2pm).

Western Tibet

14

Travellers spend huge amounts of time and money plotting and planning trips to **Western Tibet**, with its key sights of Mount Kailash, Lake Manasarovar and the remains of the tenth-century Guge kingdom. However, this is no guarantee of reaching any of these destinations – regulations change frequently and weather can be a factor. Access to Mount Kailash generally isn't a problem – you just need to find a tour agency running the trip. Cost is likely to be the largest obstacle as tours to Kailash take at least two weeks.

Saga

萨嘎, sàgā

From Sakya or Lhatse it's a solid day's journey to the dusty town of **SAGA**. There's a military garrison here and not much else, but Saga, already a well-established stopover for pilgrims from Tibet, is growing quickly with increasing numbers of visitors from China, Nepal, and India heading to Kailash.

ACCOMMODATION   SAGA

Bo Clan Hotel 博扎家族旅馆, bózhā jiāzú lǚguǎn. 1 Deji Lu ☎ 1364 8929988. Basic accommodation in twin rooms around a courtyard – there's no running water or electricity, and toilets are a pit in one corner of the courtyard, but it's perfectly adequate for a one-night stop over. Beds **¥50**

Norbuling Hotel 落福岭宾馆, luòfúlíng bīnguǎn. 8 Lunzhu Lu ☎ 1828 9128885. At the south end of town, along a street running parallel to the highway, this place has en suites with hot showers, 24hr electricity and wi-fi. The rooms themselves would be standard anywhere else in China; here they are luxury. It is expensive, though. **¥420**

Saga Hotel 萨嘎宾馆, sàgā bīnguǎn. At the corner of Deji Lu and Gesang Lu ☎ 0892 8202888. The *Saga* is easily the most impressive-looking hotel in town. Hot running water, flush toilets and electricity make it much sought after by bus-loads of Indian tour groups on their way to Kailash. **¥420**

EATING

Tian Fu Restaurant 天府川菜馆, tiānfú chuāncàiguǎn. Deji Lu, just north of the junction with Gesang Lu ☎ 1398 9021128. This little Sichuan restaurant is far and away the best place to eat in town, churning out fiery *mala tofu* as well as milder standard Chinese fare. Mains ¥25. Daily 11am–10pm.

Darchen

塔钦, tǎqīn

Access to the Mount Kailash and Lake Manasarovar area is via **DARCHEN**, 450km northwest of Saga, where there's accommodation. At time of writing a vast new hotel complex was under construction at the entrance to town and should be open for business by 2015. Modern facilities will be a boon as, with little running water and no mains electricity, the options are currently on the spartan side – though you

---

ROUTES THROUGH WESTERN TIBET

The **southern route**, a well-surfaced highway running parallel to the Himalayas all the way to Western Tibet's main town, **ALI** (also known as Shiquanhe), passes through Saga, and on to Darchen, and makes for a stunningly picturesque journey. From Lhasa to Mount Kailash is around 1400km.

The alternative **northern route** via Tsochen, Gertse and Gakyi is longer: it's over 1700km to Ali, and then another 300km or so southeast to Mount Kailash. It is also less scenic, but less liable to be affected by snow or flooding. Some tours plan to go on one route and return on the other – expect around a week's travelling time on either.

can always visit the Holy Shower and Bathing Centre public baths (¥30) if you're missing hot water.

ACCOMMODATION

DARCHEN

Country Guest House 家乡宾馆, jiāxiāng bīnguǎn. At the southern end of town on the east side of the road ☎ 1363 8970123. Provides bare dormitories around a central car park, a few hours of electricity in the evening and a pit latrine across the yard, though they do hand out flasks of hot water and there's a cosy teahouse in one corner. Dorm **¥60**

Holy Mountain and Land Youth Hostel 神山圣地青 年旅舍, shénshān shèngdì qīngnián lǔshè. A hundred metres up from the Country Guest House on the opposite side of the road ☎ 1363 8972997. Chinese-run and popular with domestic backpackers, this place has comfortable enough twins and doubles with heating, private toilets, and occasional hot water in the shared showers. Dorm **¥60**, room **¥220**

EATING

Lhasa Ocean Family Restaurant 藏餐馆, zàng cānguǎn. Above a supermarket at the top of town ☎ 1890 8977555. This bright, clean place is a tour-group favourite, and rightly so: the food, albeit a selection of standard Chinese, Tibetan and Western (including banana pancakes), is excellent, and the views towards lake Manasarovar wonderful. Mains ¥30. Daily 11am–10pm.

Mount Kailash

冈仁波齐峰, gāngrénbōqí fēng · Joint ticket for Mount Kailash and Lake Manasarovar ¥300

Top of most Western Tibet itineraries is **Mount Kailash** (6714m, Gang Rinpoche to the Tibetans), the sacred mountain at the centre of the universe for Buddhists, Hindus and Jains. The 58km tour around the mountain takes around two and a half days (though Tibetans usually do it in one); you might consider hiring a porter and/or yak (from about ¥120/day each) as it's a tough walk and you need to carry all your gear and at least some food. On the first day you should reach **Drirapuk Monastery**; on the second day you climb over the Dolma La Pass (5636m) to **Zutrulpuk Monastery**; and the third day you arrive back in Darchen.

ACCOMMODATION AND EATING

MOUNT KAILASH

Guesthouses At each stop on the mountain there are basic guesthouses which also turn out simple food for breakfast and in the evenings, but you'll need to bring lunches with you, plus trekking snacks. Beds **¥50**

Lake Manasarovar

玛旁雍错, mǎpáng yōngcuò · Joint ticket for Mount Kailash and Lake Manasarovar ¥300

After the exertions of Mount Kailash, most tours head south 30km to **Lake Manasarovar** (Mapham Tso), the holiest lake in Asia for Hindus and Tibetan Buddhists alike. For the energetic, it's a four-day, 90km trek to get around the lake (or a ¥690, eight-hour bus journey from the new **visitors' centre** on the northern shore), but plenty of travellers and pilgrims relax lakeside for a day or two, with the cluster of guesthouses half an hour south of Darchen along the northwest shore, overlooked by the **Chiu Temple** (极物寺, jíwù sì), a popular haunt.

ACCOMMODATION AND EATING

LAKE MANASAROVAR

Guesthouses Guesthouses near the Chiu Temple offer extremely basic beds and simple meals; have a look around a few before making your choice, though don't expect anything like clean linen, running water or flush toilets. **¥50**

Menshi

门石, ménshí

Truck-stop town **MENSHI**, around 100km west from Mount Kailash, is a common stop-off on the way to and from Guge Kingdom sites near Zanda, a further four hours'

14

drive west. The whole town stretches little more than 200m along the road, but the backstreets are picturesque, the sunsets beautiful and – hundreds of kilometres from the nearest city – the stars breathtaking.

Tirthapuri Hot Springs

扎达布日, zhādá bùrì

The third major pilgrimage site in Western Tibet is **Tirthapuri Hot Springs**, which are closely associated with Padmasambhava; they're situated less than 10km south of Menshi and accessible by road. Pilgrims used to immerse themselves in pools here before visiting the nearby monastery containing Padmasambhava's footprint and the cave that he used, and digging for small, pearl-like stones believed to have healing properties.

ACCOMMODATION   MENSHI

Song Sung River Hotel 象泉河旅馆, xiàngquánhé lǚguǎn. Right on the bend of the only junction in town. Another basic roadhouse of twin rooms around a courtyard/car park. There are shared pit latrines, wash stands and flasks of hot water in each room, and a few hours of electricity after dark. Dorm ¥50

EATING

Sichuan Restaurant 川味饭店, chuānwèi fàndiàn. ☎ 1388 9074388. A minute's walk north from the *Song Sung* on the west side of the road, this place, run by Sichuanese sisters, turns out excellent bowls of noodles and spicy favourites. And they'll open for breakfast if you let them know the night before. Mains ¥30. Daily 10am–10pm.

Zanda and the Guge Kingdom

扎达, zhādá

These days just another arid army town, **ZANDA** (also known as **Tholing**; 托林, tuōlín) was once capital of the **Guge Kingdom**. Today only Tholing Monastery, some chortens, and ruins just outside town remain, but it is still the best place to base yourself to visit the Guge sites.

Guge Kingdom sites

古格王国, gǔgé wángguó · ¥200 including Tsaparang, Piyang, Tholing Monastery and five other sites

The major remains of the tenth-century **Kingdom of Guge** (pronounced to rhyme with "cougar"), where Buddhism survived while being eclipsed in other parts of Tibet, are the monastery of **Tholing** in Zanda; the crumbling ancient capital of **Tsaparang** (古格王国遗址, gǔgé wángguó yízhǐ), 20km to the west; and the cliff-top settlement of **Piyang** (皮央石窟群, píyāng shíkū qún), 30km to the north. The whole area – an incredible two-and-a-half-thousand square kilometres of sand-stone canyons, now protected as **Zanda Earth Forest National Park** – is littered with ancient caves dug out of cliff walls and crumbling ruins, some of which are around 1000 years old. Views from the edge of the park, the vast canyons in the foreground and the Himalayas behind, defy description.

ACCOMMODATION   ZANDA

Tholing Monastery Hotel and Restaurant 托林寺旅馆和食堂, tuōlínsì lǚguǎn hé shítáng. Directly opposite the monastery on the north edge of town ☎ 1398 9973914. Rooms in this beautifully decorated traditional-style Tibetan guesthouse are on the small side, but it does have bags of character. The food-free "restaurant" is actually a relaxing area upstairs to sit and drink tea. No hot running water either; use the public showers half way up on the west side of Hebei Lu. ¥130

EATING

North West Flower Restaurant 西北风味餐馆, xīběi fēngwèi cānguǎn. 10 Hebei Lu ☎ 0897 2622406. Run by a smiley couple from Lanzhou, this unexpectedly varied restaurant turns out huge platefuls of good-value grub, including vegetable dishes (depending on supply). Mains ¥20. Daily 11am–9pm.

Guge Teahouse 古格象谁茶馆, gŭgé xiàngshuí cháguăn. 6 Hebei Lu, near the top of town ☎ 1363 8973364. This place is always busy with local Tibetans, and is a great spot to sit down with a flagon of sweet tea. Meals are mostly bowls of noodles with meat, but you can get eggs for breakfast if you ask. Mains ¥15. Daily 8am–8pm.

14

LAXIWA HYDROELECTRIC DAM, QINGHAI

Contexts

History

As modern archeology gradually confirms ancient records of China's earliest times, it seems that, however far back you go, Chinese history is essentially the saga of the country's autocratic dynasties. Although this generalized view is inevitable in the brief account below, bear in mind that, while the concept of being Chinese has been around for over 2,000 years, the closer you look, the less "China" seems to exist as an entity – right from the start, regionalism played an important role. And while concentrating on the great events, it's easy to forget that life for the ordinary people wavered between periods of stability, when writers, poets and artisans were at their most creative, and dire times of heavy taxation, war and famine. While the Cultural Revolution, ingrained corruption and clampdowns on political dissent may not be a good track record for the People's Republic, it's also true that since the 1980s – only yesterday in China's immense timescale – the quality of life for ordinary citizens has vastly improved.

Prehistory and the Three Dynasties

Chinese legends relate that the creator, **Pan Ku**, was born from the egg of chaos and grew to fill the space between Yin, the earth, and Yang, the heavens. When he died his body became the soil, rivers and rain, and his eyes became the sun and moon, while his parasites transformed into human beings. A pantheon of semi-divine rulers known as the **Five Sovereigns** followed, inventing fire, the calendar, agriculture, silk-breeding and marriage. Later a famous triumvirate included **Yao the Benevolent** who abdicated in favour of **Shu**. Shu toiled in the sun until his skin turned black and then he abdicated in favour of **Yu the Great**, the tamer of floods. Yu was said to be the founder of China's first dynasty, the **Xia**, which was reputed to have lasted 439 years until its last degenerate and corrupt king was overthrown by the **Shang** dynasty. The Shang was in turn succeeded by the **Zhou**, whose written court histories put an end to this legendary era. Together, the Xia, Shang and Zhou are generally known as the **Three Dynasties**.

As far as archeology is concerned, **homo erectus** remains indicate that China was already broadly occupied by human ancestors well before modern mankind began to emerge 200,000 years ago. Excavations of more recent Stone Age sites show that agricultural communities based around the fertile Yellow River and Yangzi basins, such as **Banpo** in Shaanxi and **Homudu** in Zhejiang, were producing pottery and silk by 5000 BC. It was along the Yellow River, too, that solid evidence of the bronze-working Three Dynasties first came to light, with the discovery of a series of large rammed-earth palaces at **Erlitou** near Luoyang, now believed to have been the Xia capital in 2000 BC.

Little is known about the Xia, though their territory apparently encompassed Shaanxi, Henan and Hebei. The events of the subsequent Shang dynasty, however, were

4800 BC	21C–16C BC	16C–11C BC
First evidence of human settlement. Banpo in the Yellow River basin build Bronze Age town of Erlitou in Henan. Yin in Anyang boasts a rich and developed culture	Xia dynasty	Shang dynasty. First extant writing in China

first documented just before the time of Christ by the historian **Sima Qian**. Shang society, based over much the same area as its predecessors and lasting from roughly 1750 BC to 1040 BC, had a king, a class system and a skilled **bronze technology** which permeated beyond the borders into Sichuan, and which produced the splendid vessels found in today's museums. Excavations on the site of Yin, the Shang capital, have found tombs stuffed with weapons, jade ornaments, traces of silk and sacrificial victims – indicating belief in **ancestor worship** and an afterlife. The Shang also practised divination by incising questions onto tortoiseshell or bone and then heating them to study the way in which the material cracked around the words. These **oracle bones** provide China's **earliest written records**, covering topics as diverse as rainfall, dreams and ancestral curses.

Around 1040 BC a northern tribe, the **Zhou**, overthrew the Shang, expanded their kingdom west of the Yellow River into Shaanxi and set up a capital at Xi'an. Adopting many Shang customs, the Zhou also introduced the doctrine of the **Mandate of Heaven**, a belief that heaven grants ruling authority to leaders who are strong and wise, and takes it from those who aren't – a justification of successful rebellion that remains integral to the Chinese political perspective. The Zhou consequently styled themselves "Sons of Heaven" and ruled through a hierarchy of vassal lords, whose growing independence led to the gradual dissolution of the state from around 600 BC.

The decline of the Zhou

Driven to a new capital at Luoyang, later Zhou rulers exercised only a symbolic role; real power was fought over by some two hundred city states and kingdoms during the four hundred years known as the **Spring and Autumn** and the **Warring States** periods. This time of violence was also an era of vitality and change, with the rise of the ethics of **Confucianism** (see p.929) and **Taoism** (see p.930). As the warring states rubbed up against one another, agriculture and irrigation, trade, transport and diplomacy were all galvanized; iron was first smelted for weapons and tools, and great discoveries were made in medicine, astronomy and mathematics. Three hundred years of war and annexation reduced the competitors to seven states, whose territories, collectively known as Zhong Guo, the **Middle Kingdom** (China's present name in Mandarin), had now expanded west into Sichuan, south to Hunan and north to the Mongolian border.

The Qin dynasty (221–207 BC)

The Warring States period came to an end in 221 BC, when the **Qin** armies overran the last opposition and united China as a single centralized state for the first time,

---

HISTORY TODAY: THE THREE DYNASTIES

Hubei Museum Wuhan (see p.412). A collection of relics from the Warring States period.
Luoyang Museum Luoyang (see p.257). Luoyang was one of the largest cities in the world during the Three Dynasties; its wonderful new museum is, accordingly, one of the best places to see treasure from those days.
The Tomb of Confucius Qufu (see p.293). Confucius was born in this small Shandong town, and his burial place sits just to the north in a pleasant, forest-like area.

11C–771 BC	770–476 BC	457–221 BC
Zhou dynasty. Concept of Mandate of Heaven introduced	Spring and Autumn period. Kong Fuzi or Confucius (c. 500 BC) teaches a philosophy of adherence to ritual and propriety	Warring States period. The Great Wall "completed"

HISTORY TODAY: THE QIN

The Terracotta Army Xi'an (see p.212). Standing silently in their thousands, these famed clay warriors rank among China's most important historical sights.

The Tomb of Qin Shi Huang Xi'an (see p.214). The unexcavated mound that the terracotta soldiers were built to protect.

Xianyang Shaanxi (see p.214). 60km west of Xi'an, this was the capital of the Qin, and boasts its own miniature terracotta army.

---

introducing systems of currency and writing that were to last two millennia. The rule of China's first emperor, **Qin Shi Huang**, was absolute and harsh, his advisers favouring the philosophy of **Legalism** – the idea that mankind is inherently bad, and needs to be kept in line by draconian punishments. Ancient literature and historical records were destroyed and peasants were forced off their land to work as labourers on massive construction projects, including his tomb outside Xi'an (guarded by the famous **Terracotta Army**) and an early version of the **Great Wall**. Determined to rule the entire known world, Qin Shi Huang gradually pushed his armies west and southeast beyond the Middle Kingdom. But when he died in 210 BC the provinces rose in revolt, and his heirs proved to lack the authority that had held his empire together.

The Han dynasty (206 BC–220 AD)

In 206 BC the rebel warlord **Liu Bang** took Xi'an and founded the **Han dynasty**. Lasting some four hundred years and larger at its height than contemporary imperial Rome, the Han was China's first great empire, one that experienced a flowering of culture and a major impetus to push out frontiers. In doing so it defined the national identity to such an extent that the main body of China's population still style themselves "**Han Chinese**".

While Liu Bang maintained the Qin model of central government, to prevent others from repeating his own military takeover he handed out large chunks of land to trustworthy relatives. This secured a period of stability, with effective taxation financing a growing civil service and the construction of a huge and cosmopolitan capital, **Chang'an**, at today's Xi'an. Growing revenue also refuelled the expansionist policies of a subsequent ruler, **Wu**. From 135 to 90 BC he extended his lines of defence well into Xinjiang and Yunnan, opening up the **Silk Road** for trade in tea, spices and silk with India, west Asia and Rome. At home Wu stressed the Confucian model for his growing civil service, beginning a two-thousand-year institution of Confucianism in government offices.

By 9 AD, however, the empire's resources and supply lines were overstretched: increased taxation led to unrest, and the ruling house was split by political intrigue. Following fifteen years of civil war, the dynasty re-formed as the **Eastern Han** at a new capital, Luoyang. But the Han had passed their peak, and were unable to stem the civil strife caused by local authorities setting themselves up as semi-independent rulers. Despite everything, Confucianism's ideology of a centralized universal order had crystallized imperial authority; and **Buddhism**, introduced into the country from India, began to enrich life and thought, especially in the fine arts and literature, while itself being absorbed and changed by native beliefs.

221–207 BC	**206 BC–220 AD**
Qin dynasty. Emperor Qin Shi Huang founds first centralized empire. Terracotta Army guard Qin's tomb	Han dynasty. Han emperors bring stability and great advances in trade; leave Han tombs near Xi'an. Confucianism and Buddhism ascendant. Silk Road opens up first trade with Central Asia

HISTORY TODAY: THE HAN

Famen Temple Shaanxi (see p.216). 120km west of Xi'an, this stunning temple houses the legendary finger of the Buddha.
Jingzhou Museum Hubei (see p.416). A superb collection of Western Han tomb remains.
Mao Ling and Qian Ling Shaanxi (see p.215). The resting places of two Han-dynasty emperors, respectively 40km and 80km west of Xi'an.
Shaanxi Museum Xi'an (see p.202). Look for some great Han-dynasty funerary ceramics, most notably a clutch of model houses.

The Three Kingdoms to the Sui (220–581)

Nearly four hundred years separate the collapse of the Han in about 220 AD from the return of unity under the Sui in 589. However, although China was under a single government for only about fifty years of that time, the idea of a unified empire was never forgotten.

From 200 AD the three states of **Wei**, **Wu** and **Shu** struggled for supremacy in a complex war later immortalized in the saga *Romance of the Three Kingdoms*, (see p.393) that ruined central China and encouraged mass migrations southwards. The following centuries saw China's regionalism becoming entrenched: the **Southern Empire** suffered weak and short-lived dynasties, but nevertheless saw prosperity and economic growth, with the capital at **Nanjing** becoming a thriving trading and cultural centre. Meanwhile, with the borders unprotected, the north was invaded in 386 by the **Tobas**, who established the **Northern Wei dynasty**: at their first capital, **Datong**, the Tobas created a wonderful series of Buddhist carvings, but in 534 their empire fell apart.

The period was a dark age of war, violence and genocide, but it was also a richly formative one, and when the dust had settled a very different society had emerged. For much of this time, many areas produced sufficient **food surpluses** to support a rich and leisured ruling class in the cities and the countryside, as well as large armies and burgeoning Buddhist communities. So culture developed, literature flourished, and calligraphy and sculpture – especially Buddhist carvings, all enriched by Indian and Central Asian elements – reached new levels.

The Sui (581–618)

After grabbing power from his regent in 581, general **Yang Jian** unified the fragmented northern states, conquered southern China and founded the **Sui dynasty**. Yang Jian (Emperor **Wen**) was an active ruler who simplified and strengthened the bureaucracy, brought in a new legal code, recentralized civil and military authority and made tax collection more efficient. Near Xi'an his architects designed a new capital, **Da Xing Cheng** (City of Great Prosperity), with an outer wall over 35km round – the largest city in the world at that time.

Following Wen's death in 604, **Yang Di** elbowed his elder brother out to become emperor. Yang encouraged a revival of Confucian learning but is generally remembered for his use of forced labour to complete vast engineering projects: half the total workforce of five million died during the construction of the 2000km **Grand Canal**, built to transport produce from the southern Yangzi to his capital at Xi'an. Yang was assassinated in 618 after popular hatred inspired a military revolt.

220–280	265–420	420–581
Three Kingdoms period; influence of Buddhist India and Central Asia enlivens a Dark Age	Jin dynasty. Northern barbarians absorbed into Chinese culture	Southern dynasties and Northern dynasties: rapid succession of short-lived dynasties brings disunity. Earliest Longmen caves near Luoyang

---

HISTORY TODAY: THE THREE KINGDOMS TO THE SUI

The Longmen Caves Henan (see p.261). Just south of Luoyang, these caves feature some imposingly monumental Buddhist art.

The Mogao Caves Gansu (see p.281). Southeast of Dunhuang, these caves are remote and quite spectacular; the earliest were hewn out during the Northern Wei.

The Yungang Caves Shanxi (see p.243). A series of caves built just before the Longmen ones, containing art that's every bit as beautiful.

Wuhou Ci Chengdu (see p.719). The burial place of Liu Bei, a Three Kingdoms emperor, and a memorial to his chief strategist, Zhuge Liang.

Medieval China (618–1271)

The seventh century marks the beginning of the medieval period of Chinese history. This was the age in which Chinese culture reached its peak, a time of experimentation in literature, art, music and agriculture, and one which unified seemingly incompatible elements.

Tang dynasty

Li Yuan consolidated his new **Tang dynasty** by spending the rest of his eight-year reign eliminating rivals. Under his son **Tai Zong**, Tang China broadened its horizons: the Turkic peoples of the Northwest were crushed, the Tibetans brought to heel and relations established with Byzantium. China kept open house for traders and travellers of all races and creeds, who settled in the mercantile cities of Yangzhou and Guangzhou, bringing with them their religions, especially **Islam**, and influencing the arts, cookery, fashion and entertainment. Chinese goods flowed out to India, Persia, the Near East and many other countries, and China's language and religion gained currency in Japan and Korea. At home, **Buddhism** remained the all-pervading foreign influence, with Chinese pilgrims travelling widely in India. The best known of these, **Xuanzang** (see p.830), set off in 629 and returned after sixteen years in India with a mass of Buddhist sutras, adding greatly to China's storehouse of knowledge.

Within a decade after Tai Zong's death in 649, China's only empress, **Wu Zetian**, had consolidated the Tang empire's direct influence on neighbouring nations. Though widely unpopular, Wu Zetian was a great patron of Buddhism, commissioning the famous Longmen carvings outside Luoyang; she also created a civil service selected on merit rather than birth. Her successor, **Xuan Zong**, began well in 712, but his later infatuation with the beautiful concubine **Yang Guifei** led to the **An Lushan rebellion** of 755, his flight to Sichuan and Yang's ignominious death at the hands of his mutinying army. Xuan Zong's son, **Su Zong**, enlisted the help of Tibetan and Uyghur forces and recaptured Xi'an from the rebels; but though the court was re-established, it had lost its authority, and real power was once again shifting to the provinces.

Five Dynasties and Ten Kingdoms

The following two hundred years saw the country split into regional alliances. From 907 to 960, all the successive **Five Dynasties** were too short-lived to be effective. China's northern defences were permanently weakened, while her economic dependence on the south increased and the dispersal of power brought social changes. The traditional elite

---

581–618	618–907	907–960
Sui dynasty. Centralization and growth under Wen Di. Extension and strengthening of Great Wall; digging of Grand Canal	Tang dynasty. Arts and literature reach their most developed stage. Great Buddha at Leshan completed	Five dynasties. Decline of culture and the northern defences. Cliff sculptures of Dazu

whose fortunes were tied to the dynasty gave way to a military and merchant class who bought land to acquire status, alongside a professional ruling class selected by examination. In the south, the **Ten Kingdoms** (some existing side by side) managed to retain what was left of the Tang civilization, their greater stability and economic prosperity sustaining a relatively high cultural level.

The Song

Eventually, in 960, a disaffected army in the north put a successful general, **Song Tai Zu**, on the throne. His new ruling house, known as the **Northern Song**, made its capital at **Kaifeng** in the Yellow River basin, well placed at the head of the Grand Canal for transport to supply its million people with grain from the south. By skilled politicking rather than military might, the new dynasty re-established civilian primacy. However, northern China was occupied by the **Jin** in 1115, who pushed the imperial court south to **Hangzhou** where, guarded by the Yangzi River, their culture continued to flourish from 1126 as the **Southern Song**. Developments during their 150-year dynasty included gunpowder, the magnetic compass, fine porcelain and moveable type printing. In due course, however, the Song were overrun by their aggressive northern "barbarian" neighbours, who launched the thirteenth-century **Mongol Invasion**.

The Yuan dynasty (1271–1368)

In fact, Mongolian influence had first penetrated China in the eleventh century, when the Song emperors paid tribute to separate Mongolian states to keep their armies from invading. These individual fiefdoms were unified by **Genghis Khan** in 1206 to form an immensely powerful army, which swiftly embarked upon the conquest of northern China. By 1271 the **Yuan dynasty** was on the Chinese throne at Khanbalik – modern **Beijing** – with **Kublai Khan**, Genghis Khan's grandson, at the head of an empire that stretched way beyond the borders of China. The country was thrown open to foreign travellers, traders and missionaries; the Grand Canal was extended; while in Beijing the **Palace of All Tranquillities** was built inside a new city wall, later known as the **Forbidden City**. Descriptions of much of this were brought back to Europe by **Marco Polo**, who recorded his impressions of Yuan lifestyle and treasures after he'd served in the government of Kublai Khan.

HISTORY TODAY: TANG TO SONG

Baoding Shan Dazu (see p.743). A series of delightful carvings, created between 1179 and 1245.

Dafo Leshan (see p.733). Built from 713, and still one of the world's largest Buddhist sculptures after all these years.

Kaifeng Henan (see p.465). Pleasant city which maintains a small array of Song-dynasty sights.

Kaiyuan Temple Quanzhou (see p.465). A gigantic temple founded in 686.

Mausoleums of the Western Xia Ningxia (see p.225). Monuments to the nine kings of the Xi Xia kingdom, just west of Yinchuan.

The Small and Big Goose Pagodas Xi'an (see p.202 & p.203). Two splendid towers just to the south of the walled city.

Suzhou Jiangsu (see p.318). Some of this city's many enchanting gardens date back to the Song.

960–1271	1271–1368	1368–1644
Song dynasties. Consolidation of the lesser kingdoms	Yuan dynasty. Genghis Khan invades. Trade with Europe develops under Kublai Khan. Forbidden City built. Marco Polo visits China 1273–92	Ming dynasty. Imperial investigative fleet under Admiral Zheng He reaches Africa. Later isolationist policies restrict contact with rest of world

The Yuan only retained control over all China until 1368. Their power was ultimately sapped by the combination of becoming too Chinese for their northern brethren to tolerate, and too aloof from the Chinese to assimilate. After northern tribes had rebelled, and famine and disastrous floods brought a series of uprisings in China, a monk-turned-bandit leader from the south, **Zhu Yuanzhang**, seized the throne from the last boy emperor of the Yuan in 1368.

The Ming dynasty (1368–1644)

Taking the name **Hong Wu**, Zhu proclaimed himself the first emperor of the **Ming dynasty**, with Nanjing as his capital. Zhu's extreme despotism culminated in two appalling purges in which thousands of civil servants and literati died, and he initiated a course of **isolationism** from the outside world which lasted throughout the Ming and Qing eras. Nowhere is this more apparent than in the Ming construction of the current Great Wall, a grandiose but futile attempt to stem the invasion of northern tribes into China, built in the fifteenth century as military might and diplomacy began to break down.

Yet the period also produced fine artistic accomplishments, particularly **porcelain** from the imperial kilns at Jingdezhen. Nor were the Ming rulers entirely isolationist. During the reign of **Yongle**, Zhu's 26th son, the imperial navy (commanded by the Muslim eunuch, Admiral **Zheng He**) ranged right across the Indian Ocean as far as the east coast of Africa on a fact-finding mission. But stagnation set in after Yongle's death in 1424, and the maritime missions were cancelled as being incompatible with Confucian values, which held contempt for foreigners. Thus the initiative for world trade and exploration passed into the hands of the Europeans, with the great period of world voyages by Columbus, Magellan and Vasco da Gama. In 1514, **Portuguese** vessels appeared in the Pearl River at Guangzhou (Canton) and Portugal was allowed to colonize nearby **Macau** in 1557. Although all dealings with foreigners were officially despised by the imperial court, trade flourished as Chinese merchants and officials were eager to milk the profits.

In later years, a succession of less able Ming rulers allowed power to slip. By the early seventeenth century, frontier defences had fallen into decay, and the **Manchu tribes** in the north were already across the Great Wall. A series of uprisings against the Ming began in 1627, and when rebel forces led by **Li Zicheng** managed to break into the capital in 1644, the last Ming emperor fled from his palace and hanged himself – an ignoble end to a three-hundred-year-old dynasty.

The Qing dynasty (1644–1911)

The Manchus weren't slow to turn internal dissent to their advantage. Sweeping down on Beijing, they threw out Li Zicheng's army, claimed the capital as their own and founded the **Qing dynasty**. It took a further twenty years to capture the south of the country, but on its capitulation China was once again under foreign rule. The Qing initially did little to assimilate domestic culture, ruling as separate overlords. Manchu became the official language, the Chinese were obliged to wear the Manchu **pigtail**, and intermarriage between a Manchu and a Chinese was strictly forbidden. Under the Qing dynasty the distant areas of Inner and Outer Mongolia, Tibet and Turkestan were fully incorporated into the Chinese empire, uniting the Chinese world to a greater extent than during the Tang period.

1644	Mid- to late 17C	Late 18C
Qing dynasty begins. Manchus gain control over China and extend its boundaries	Potala Palace in Lhasa rebuilt by Fifth Dalai Lama	East India Company monopolizes trade with Britain. Summer Palace in Beijing completed

HISTORY TODAY: THE MING

Ancient Observatory Beijing (see p.88). An underrated sight, this old observatory boasts a clutch of beautiful Ming-dynasty astrological instruments.

Chengde Hebei (see p.148). A wonderful small city, featuring an old imperial retreat, and a series of stunning temples.

The Forbidden City Beijing (see p.70). One of China's most famous tourist sights, this old imperial stomping ground goes back to the Mongol era, but its present structure is essentially Ming.

The Great Wall Beijing (see p.120). Another Chinese icon, the wall also pre-dates the Ming, but it's work from this period that's most visible.

The Imperial Palace Shenyang (see p.164). A miniature Forbidden City, constructed by the Mongols before their takeover of the country.

The Jinjiang Princes' Palace Guilin (see p.598). Another mini-Forbidden City, though actually 34 years older than the one in Beijing.

The Ming Tombs Nanjing (see p.315). The resting place of the first Ming emperor.

The Temple of Heaven Beijing (see p.88). Justly regarded as the epitome of Ming design, the centre of annual agricultural rituals.

Yixian Anhui (see p.403). A collection of antique villages dating back to the Ming.

Three outstanding early Qing emperors brought an infusion of new blood and vigour to government. **Kangxi**, who began his 61-year reign in 1654 at the age of six, assiduously cultivated his image as the Son of Heaven by making royal progresses throughout the country. His fourth son, the emperor **Yungzheng** (1678–1735), ruled over what is considered one of the most efficient and least corrupt administrations ever enjoyed by China. This was inherited by **Qianlong** (1711–99), whose reign saw China's frontiers widely extended and the economy stimulated by peace and prosperity. In 1750 the nation was perhaps at its apex, one of the strongest, wealthiest and most powerful countries in the world.

During the late eighteenth century, however, problems began to increase. Settled society had produced a **population explosion**, causing a land shortage. This in turn saw trouble flaring as migrants from central China tried to settle the remoter western provinces, dispossessing the original inhabitants. Meanwhile, Portuguese traders in Guangzhou had been joined by the British **East India Company**, who were eager to be granted a trade monopoly. Convinced of their own superiority, however, China's immensely rich and powerful rulers had no desire to deal directly with foreigners. When **Lord Macartney** arrived in 1793 to propose a political and trade treaty between Britain and China, he found that the emperor totally rejected any idea of alliance with one who, according to Chinese ideas, was a subordinate.

The Opium Wars

Foiled in their attempts at official negotiations with the Qing court, the East India Company decided to take matters into their own hands and create a clandestine market in China for Western goods. Instead of silver, they began to pay for tea and silk with **opium**, cheaply imported from India. As demand escalated during the early nineteenth century, China's trade surplus became a deficit, as silver drained out of the country to pay for the drug. The emperor intervened in 1840 by ordering the confiscation and

1839–62	**1851–64**	**1899**
Opium Wars. As part of the surrender settlement, Hong Kong is ceded to Britain	Taiping Uprising. Conservative policies of Dowager Empress Cixi allow foreign powers to take control of China's industry	Boxer Rebellion

destruction of over twenty thousand chests of opium – the start of the first **Opium War**. After two years of British gunboats shelling coastal ports, the Chinese were forced to sign the **Treaty of Nanking**, whose humiliating terms included a huge indemnity, the opening up of new ports to foreign trade, and the **cession of Hong Kong**. The war was later reignited and, in 1860, Britain – joined by other Western powers – destroyed Beijing's Summer Palace and forced further concessions on the country.

The Taiping Uprising

The Opium Wars brought anti-Manchu feeling, economic hardship and internal **rebellions**. While serious unrest occurred in Guizhou and Yunnan, the most widespread revolt was the **Taiping Uprising**, which stormed through central China in the 1850s to occupy much of the rich Yangzi Valley. Having captured Nanjing as their "Heavenly Capital", the Taipings began to make military forays towards Beijing, and European powers decided to step in, worried that the Taiping's anti-foreign government might take control of the country. With their support, Qing troops defeated the Taipings in 1864, leaving twenty million people dead and five provinces in ruins.

The late nineteenth century

It was during the Taiping Uprising that the **Empress Dowager Wu Cixi** first took control of the country, ruling from behind various emperors from 1861 until 1908. Certain that reform would weaken the Qings' grasp on power, she pursued a deep conservatism at a time when China needed desperately to overhaul its political and economic structure. Her stance saw increased foreign ownership of industry, rising Christian missionary activity that undermined traditional society, and the disintegration of China's **colonial empire**. France took the former vassal states of Laos, Cambodia and Vietnam in 1883–85; Britain gained Burma; and **Tibet**, which had nominally been under China's control since Tang times, began to assert its independence. Even worse, a failed military foray into Korea in 1894 saw China lose control of **Taiwan** to Japan, while a Russian-built rail line into the northeast effectively gave Russia control of Manchuria.

The Boxer Movement

By the late 1890s, popular anti-foreign feeling crystallized into the **Boxer Rebellion**, a quasi-spiritual martial arts movement that set itself loose to slaughter missionaries and Christian converts. During the summer of 1900 the Boxers took control of Beijing, besieging the foreign legation compound, though they were routed when an international relief force arrived on August 14. In the massacre, looting and confusion which followed, Cixi and the emperor disguised themselves as peasants and fled to Xi'an in a cart, leaving her ministers to negotiate a peace.

Though they clung feebly on for another decade, this was the end of the Qing, and internal movements to dismantle the dynastic system and build a new China proliferated. The most influential of these was the **Tong Meng Hui** society, founded in 1905 in Japan by the exile **Sun Yatsen**, a doctor from a wealthy Guangdong family. Cixi died three years later, and, in 1911, opposition to the construction of railways by foreigners drew events to a head in Wuchang, Hubei province, igniting a popular uprising which finally toppled the dynasty. As two thousand years of dynastic succession ended, Sun Yatsen returned to China to take the lead in the provisional **Republican Government** at Nanjing.

1911	1921	1927
End of imperial China. Sun Yatsen becomes leader of the Republic	Chinese Communist Party founded in Beijing	Chiang Kai-shek orders massacre of Communists in Shanghai. Mao Zedong organizes first peasant-worker army

HISTORY TODAY: THE QING

Pingyao Shanxi (see p.252). Perhaps the most convincing of China's many walled cities, and justifiably popular with international tourists.
The Potala Palace Lhasa (see p.868). The most recognizable symbol of Tibet, and the traditional seat of power for the Dalai Lama.
The Puppet Emperor's Palace Changchun (see p.176). A forlorn full-stop to China's rich dynastic history, this is where the last emperor lived during the Japanese annexation of Manchuria.
The Summer Palace Beijing (see p.95). Though it dates back to the eleventh century, this park-like area is inextricably connected to the follies of the Dowager Empress Cixi.
St Sofia's Cathedral Harbin (see p.184). China's most beautiful Christian place of worship.

From republic to communism

Almost immediately the new republic was in trouble. Though a **parliament** was duly elected in 1913, northern China was controlled by the former leader of the Imperial Army, **Yuan Shikai**. Sun Yatsen, faced with a choice between probable civil war and relinquishing his presidency at the head of the newly formed Nationalist People's Party, the **Guomindang**, stepped down. Yuan promptly dismissed the government, forced Sun into renewed exile, and attempted to establish a new dynasty. But his plans were stalled by his generals, who wanted private fiefdoms of their own, and Yuan's sudden death in 1916 marked the last time in 34 years that China would be united under a single authority. As civil war erupted, Sun Yatsen returned once more, this time to found a southern Guomindang government.

Thus divided, China was unable to stem the increasingly bold territorial incursions made by Japan and other colonial powers as a result of **World War I**. Siding with the Allies, Japan had claimed the German port of Qingdao and all German shipping and industry in the Shandong Peninsula on the outbreak of war, and in 1915 presented China with **Twenty-One Demands**, many of which Yuan Shikai, under threat of a Japanese invasion, was forced to accept. After the war, hopes that the 1919 **Treaty of Versailles** would end Japanese aggression (as well as the unequal treaties and foreign concessions) were dashed when the Western powers, who had already signed secret pacts with Japan, confirmed Japan's rights in China. This ignited the anti-foreign **May 4 Movement**, a series of demonstrations and riots which slowly forced the return of the foreign concession areas to Chinese control.

The rise of the CCP

Against this background, the **Chinese Communist Party** (CCP) was formed in Shanghai in 1921, its leadership including the young **Mao Zedong** and **Zhou Enlai**. Though the CCP initially listened to its Russian advisers and supported the Guomindang in its military campaigns against the northern warlords, this alliance became untenable after Sun Yatsen died in 1925 and his brother-in-law **Chiang Kai-shek** took over the Guomindang. Chiang was a staunch nationalist who had no time for the CCP or its plans to end China's class divisions. In 1927, a general strike organized by left-wing elements in Shanghai was brutally suppressed by Chiang's henchmen: around five thousand striking workers were massacred, including much of the original Communist hierarchy. Those who escaped the purge regrouped in remote areas across the country, principally at **Jinggang Shan** in Jiangxi province, under the leadership of Mao Zedong.

1932	1936–41	1945
Japan invades Manchuria	The Nationalist Guomindang and the People's Liberation Army form the United Front against the Japanese	Surrender of Japan. Civil war between the Guomindang and the People's Liberation Army

Mao Zedong, the Red Army and the Long March

Son of a well-off Hunanese farmer, **Mao** believed social reform lay in the hands of the peasants who still had few rights and no power base. Drawing upon the analyses of Karl Marx, Mao argued that a mass armed rebellion was the only way the old order could be replaced, and organized what was later to be called the **Autumn Harvest Uprising** in Changsha. Moving with other Communist forces to the Hunan-Jiangxi border in 1927, this **Red Army** of peasants, miners and Guomindang deserters achieved unexpected successes against the Nationalist troops sent against them until **Li Lisan**, the overall Communist leader, ordered Mao out of his mountain base to attack the cities. After the ensuing open assaults against the superior Guomindang forces proved disastrous, Chiang Kai-shek mobilized half a million troops, and encircled Jinggang Shan with a ring of concrete block-houses and barbed-wire entanglements.

Forced to choose between fight or flight, in October 1934 Mao organized eighty thousand troops in an epic 9500km retreat which became known as the **Long March**. By the time they reached safety in **Yan'an** in Shaanxi province a year later, the Communists had lost three-quarters of their followers to the rigours of the trip, but had also started their path towards victory: Mao had become undisputed leader of the CCP at the **Zunyi Conference**, severing the Party from its Russian advisers.

Japanese invasion and the United Front

Meanwhile, **Japan** had taken over Chinese Manchuria in 1933 and installed Pu Yi (last emperor of the Qing dynasty) as puppet leader. The Japanese were obviously preparing to invade eastern China, and Mao wrote to Chiang Kai-shek advocating an end to civil war and a **United Front** against the threat. Chiang's response was to move his Manchurian armies, under **Zhang Xueliang**, down to finish off the Reds in Shaanxi. Zhang, however, saw an alliance as the only way to evict the Japanese from his homeland, and so secretly entered into an agreement with the Communists. On December 12, 1936, Chiang was kidnapped by his own troops and forced to sign his assent to the Communist-Nationalist United Front, an alliance to fight the Japanese.

Full-scale war broke out in July 1937 when the Japanese attacked Beijing, and by the end of the year they controlled most of eastern China. With a capital-in-occupation at Nanjing, the Japanese concentrated their efforts on routing the GMD, leaving a vacuum in the north that was filled by the Communists, establishing what amounted to stable government of a hundred million people across the North China Plain.

The outbreak of war in Europe in September 1939 soon had repercussions in China. Nazi Germany stopped supplying the weaponry upon which the GMD relied, while the bombing of Pearl Harbor two years later put an end to all military aid from the United States to Japan. With the country's heavy industry in Japanese hands, China's United Front government, having withdrawn to **Chongqing** in Sichuan province, became dependent on supplies flown over the Himalayas by the Americans and British.

The end of the war and the Communist victory

By the time the two atom bombs ended the Japanese empire and World War II in 1945, the Red Army was close on a million strong, with a widespread following throughout the country. It was not, however, that secure. Predictably enough, the US sided with Chiang Kai-shek and the GMD; more surprisingly, so did the Soviet Union

1949

1957

Communist takeover. Chiang Kai-shek flees to Taiwan. The newly proclaimed People's Republic of China supports North Korea in the Korean War

The Hundred Flowers campaign unsuccessfully attempts liberalization

– Stalin believed that with American aid, the GMD would easily destroy the CCP. All the same, **peace negotiations** between the Nationalist and Communist sides were brokered by the US in Chongqing, where Chiang Kai-shek refused to admit the CCP into government, knowing that its policies were uncontrollable while the Red Army still existed. For their part, it was evident to the CCP that without an army, they were nothing.

In 1948 the Communists' newly named **People's Liberation Army** (PLA) rose against the GMD, decisively trouncing them that winter at the massive battle of **Huai Hai** in Anhui province. With Shanghai about to fall before the PLA in early 1949, Chiang Kai-shek packed the country's entire gold reserves into a plane and took off for **Taiwan** to form the **Republic of China**. Here he was to remain until his death in 1975, forlornly waiting to liberate the mainland with the two million troops and refugees who later joined him. Mopping-up operations against mainland pockets of GMD resistance would continue for several years, but in October 1949 Mao was able to proclaim the formation of the **People's Republic of China** in Beijing. The world's most populous nation was now Communist.

The People's Republic under Mao

With the country laid waste by over a century of economic mismanagement and war, massive problems faced the new republic. By the mid-1950s, however, all industry had been nationalized and output was back at prewar levels, while, for the first time in Chinese history, land was handed over to the peasants as their own. A million former landlords were executed, while others were enrolled in "**criticism and self-criticism**" classes, a traumatic re-education designed to prevent elitism or bourgeois deviancy from contaminating the revolutionary spirit.

With all the difficulties on the home front, the government could well have done without the distraction of the **Korean War**. After Communist North Korea invaded the south in 1950, US forces intervened on behalf of the south and, despite warnings from Zhou Enlai, continued through to Chinese territory. China declared war in June, and sent a million troops to push the Americans back to the 38th parallel and force peace negotiations. As a boost for the morale of the new nation, the campaign could not have been better timed. Meanwhile, China's far western borders were seen to be threatened by an uprising in **Tibet**, and Chinese troops were sent there in 1951, swiftly occupying the entire country and instituting de facto Chinese rule. Eight years later, a failed coup by Tibetan monks against the occupation saw a massive clampdown on religion, and the flight of the **Dalai Lama** and his followers to Nepal.

The Hundred Flowers

By 1956 there were signs that the euphoria driving the country was slowing. Mao – whose principles held that constant struggle was part of existence, and thus that acceptance of the status quo was in itself a bad thing – felt that both government and industry needed to be prodded back into gear. In 1957 he decided to loosen restrictions on public expression, and following the slogan "Let a hundred flowers bloom, and a hundred schools of thought contend", people were encouraged to voice their complaints. The plan backfired: instead of picking on inefficient officials as Mao had hoped, the **Hundred Flowers** campaign resulted in attacks on the Communist system

1958	1964	1966–68
Agricultural and industrial reform in the shape of the commune system and the Great Leap Forward. Widespread famine results	China explodes its first atomic weapon	In the Cultural Revolution, Red Guards purge anti-Maoist elements along with "ideologically unsound" art and architecture

itself. As Mao was never one to take personal criticism lightly, those who had spoken out found themselves victims of an **anti-rightist** campaign, confined to jail or undergoing heavy bouts of "re-education". From this point on, intellectuals as a group were mistrusted and scrutinized.

The Great Leap Forward

Agriculture and industry were next to receive a shake-up. In August 1958 it was announced that all farmland was to be pooled into 24,000 self-governing **communes**, with the aim of turning small-scale farming units into hyper-efficient agricultural areas. Industry was to be fired into activity by the co-option of seasonally employed workers, who would construct heavy industrial plants, dig canals and drain marshes. Propaganda campaigns promised eternal well-being in return for initial austerity; in a single **Great Leap Forward**, China would match British industrial output in ten years.

From the outset, the Great Leap Forward was a disaster. Having been given their land, the peasants now found themselves losing it once more, and were not eager to work in huge units. This, combined with the problem of ill-trained commune management, led to a slump in agricultural and industrial production. In the face of a stream of ridiculous **quotas** supplied by Beijing – one campaign required that all communes must produce steel, regardless of the availability of raw materials – no one had time to tend the fields. The 1959 and 1960 harvests both failed, and millions starved. As if this wasn't enough, a thaw in US–USSR relations in 1960 saw the Soviet Union stopping all aid to China.

With the economy in tatters, the commune policy was abandoned, but the incident had ruined Mao's reputation and set members of the Communist Party Central Committee against his policies. One critic was **Deng Xiaoping**, who had diffused the effects of commune policy by creating a limited free-market economy among the country's traders. Behind this doctrine of material incentives for workers was a large bureaucracy over which Mao held little political sway.

The Cultural Revolution

Mao sought to regain his authority. Using a campaign created by Communist Party Vice-Chairman **Lin Biao**, he began in 1964 to orchestrate the youth of China against his moderate opponents in what became known as the **Great Proletarian Cultural Revolution**. Under Mao's guidance, the movement spread in 1966 to Beijing University, where the students organized themselves into a political militia – the **Red Guard** – and within weeks were moving out onto the streets.

The enemies of the Red Guard were the **Four Olds**: old ideas, old culture, old customs and old habits. Brandishing copies of the *Quotations of Chairman Mao Tsetung* (the famous **Little Red Book**), the Red Guard attacked anything redolent of capitalism, religion or foreign influence. Academics were assaulted, books were burned, temples and ancient monuments desecrated. Shops selling anything remotely Western were destroyed along with the gardens of the "decadent bourgeoisie". As under the commune system, quotas were set, this time for unearthing and turning in the "Rightists", "Revisionists" and "Capitalist Roaders" corrupting Communist society. Officials who failed to fill their quotas were likely to fall victim themselves, as were those who failed to destroy property or denounce others enthusiastically enough. Offenders were paraded through the streets wearing placards carrying humiliating

1971	1972	1976
People's Republic replaces Taiwan at the United Nations	US president Nixon visits Beijing	The Tian'anmen Incident reveals public support for moderate Deng Xiaoping. Mao Zedong dies, and the Gang of Four are arrested shortly afterwards

slogans; tens of thousands were humiliated, beaten to death or driven to suicide. On August 5, 1966, Mao proclaimed that reactionaries had reached the highest levels of the CCP: Deng Xiaoping and his followers were dismissed from their posts and imprisoned, condemned to wait on tables at a Party canteen, or given menial jobs.

Meanwhile, the violence was getting completely out of control, with Red Guard factions attacking foreign embassies and even turning on each other. In August 1967 Mao ordered the arrest of several Red Guard leaders and the surrender of all weapons to the army, but was too late to stop nationwide street fighting, which was halted only after the military stormed the Guard's university strongholds. To clear them out of the way, millions of Red Guards were rounded up and shipped off into the countryside, ostensibly to reinforce the Communist message among the rural community.

Ping-pong diplomacy

The US, its foreign policy determined by business and political interests that stood to gain from the collapse of Communism, had continued to support Chiang Kai-shek's Guomindang in Taiwan during the postwar period, while also stirring up paranoia over the possibility of a Sino-Soviet pact. After China exploded its first **atomic bomb** in 1964, however, the US began to tread a more pragmatic path. In 1970, envoy Henry Kissinger opened communications between the two countries, cultural and sporting links were formed (the latter gave rise to the phrase "**ping-pong diplomacy**"), and in 1971 the People's Republic became the official representative at the UN of the nation called China, displacing Taiwan. The following year US president **Richard Nixon** was walking on the Great Wall and holding talks with Mao, trade restrictions were lifted and China began commerce with the West. The "bamboo curtain" had parted, and the damage caused by the Cultural Revolution began slowly to be repaired.

The Gang of Four

This new attitude of realistic reform derived from the moderate wing of the Communist Party, headed by Premier Zhou Enlai – seen as a voice of reason – and his protégé Deng Xiaoping, now in control of the day-to-day running of the Communist Party Central Committee. Zhou's tact had given him a charmed political existence which for fifty years kept him at Mao's side despite policy disagreements. But with Zhou's death early in 1976, the reform movement immediately succumbed to the **Gang of Four**, who, led by Mao's third wife **Jiang Qing**, had become the radical mouthpiece of an increasingly absent Mao. In early April, at the time of the **Qing Ming** festival commemorating the dead, the Heroes Monument in Beijing's Tian'anmen Square was filled with wreaths in memory of Zhou. On April 5 radicals removed the wreaths and moderate supporters flooded into the square in protest; a riot broke out and hundreds were attacked and arrested. The obvious scapegoat for what became known as the **Tian'anmen Incident**, Deng Xiaoping, was publicly discredited and thrown out of office for a second time.

The death of Mao

In July 1976 the catastrophic **Tangshan earthquake** centred on Hebei province killed half a million people. The Chinese hold that natural disasters always foreshadow great events, and no one was too surprised when Mao himself died on September 9.

1977	1980	1981	1989
Deng Xiaoping rises to become Party Chairman	Beginning of the "open door" policy	Trial of the Gang of Four	Suppression of the democracy movement in Tian'anmen Square

Deprived of their figurehead, and with memories of the Cultural Revolution clear in everyone's mind, Jiang Qing and the other members of the Gang of Four were arrested. Deng returned to the political scene for the third time and was granted a string of positions that included Vice-Chairman of the Communist Party, Vice-Premier and Chief of Staff to the PLA; titles aside, he was now running the country. The move away from Mao's policies was rapid: in 1978 anti-Maoist **dissidents** were allowed to display wall posters in Beijing and elsewhere, and by 1980 Deng and the moderates were secure enough to sanction officially a cautious condemnation of Mao's actions. His ubiquitous portraits and statues began to come down, and his cult was gradually undermined.

"One Party" capitalism

Under **Deng Xiaoping**, China became unrecognizable from the days when the Red Guards enforced ideological purity. Deng's legacy was the "open door" policy, which brought about new social freedoms as well as a huge rise in the trappings of Westernization, especially in the cities. The impetus for such sweeping changes was economic. Deng's statement, "I don't care whether the cat is black or white as long as it catches mice", illustrates the pragmatic approach that he took to the economy, one which has guided policy ever since. Deng **decentralized production**, allowing more rational decision-making based on local conditions, and the production and allocation of goods according to market forces; factories now contracted with each other instead of with the state. In agriculture, the collective economy was replaced, and farming households, after meeting government targets, were allowed to sell their surpluses on the free market. On the coast, **Special Economic Zones** (SEZs) were set up, where foreign investment was encouraged and Western management practices, such as the firing of unsatisfactory workers, were cautiously introduced.

Tian'anmen Square

Economic reform did not precipitate **political reform**, and was really a way of staving it off, with the Party hoping that allowing the populace the right to get rich would halt demands for political rights. However, dissatisfaction with corruption, rising inflation, low wages and the lack of freedom was vividly expressed in the demonstrations in **Tian'anmen Square** in 1989. These started as a mourning service for former Party General Secretary **Hu Yaobang**, who had been too liberal for Deng's liking and was dismissed in 1987; by mid-May there were nearly a million students, workers and even Party cadets around the square, demanding free speech and an end to corruption. On May 20, **martial law** was declared, and by the beginning of June, 350,000 troops were massed around Beijing. In the early hours of June 4 they moved in, crushing barriers with tanks and firing into the crowds, killing hundreds or possibly thousands of the demonstrators. Discussion of the event is still contentious in China – particularly as the issues the students identified have not been dealt with.

China in the twenty-first century

The spectacular **growth** of the Chinese economy was among the great success stories of the twentieth century, and will be one of the most important factors in defining the

1992	1995	1997
Major cabinet reshuffle puts Deng's men in power	Death of Chen Yun, last of the hardline Maoists in the Politburo. Work begins on the Three Gorges Dam	Hong Kong returns to the mainland. Death of Deng Xiaoping

character of the twenty-first. For a quarter of a century, China's GDP has grown at an average rate of 9 percent per year, and it came quickly out of the global recession in 2010, overtaking Japan to become the world's second-largest economy. China is now the world's main producer of coal and steel and, among other things, makes two-thirds of the world's shoes, mobiles and photocopiers. Chinese production and US consumption together form the engines for global growth, and some predict that the Chinese economy will overtake that of the US by 2040. The speed of change has been astonishing: in the 1970s the "three big buys" – consumer goods to which families could realistically aspire – were a bicycle, a watch and a radio; in the 1980s they were a washing machine, a TV and a refrigerator; and the urban Chinese today can aspire to the same material comforts as their Western counterparts. No wonder the country comes across as confident and ambitious.

Under **the curent leadership** – headed since 2012 by **Xi Jinping** – China has continued its course of controlled liberalization. In its pursuit of a "socialist market economy with Chinese characteristics", the state has retreated from whole areas of life. Mechanisms of control such as the household registration and work-unit systems have largely been abandoned. The private sector now accounts for almost half of the economy, and foreign-funded ventures represent more than half the country's exports.

Today, "scientific development" and "harmonious society" are the catchphrases coming from the Politburo technocrats. In practice, that means both heavy-handed

HOW CHINA IS GOVERNED

Since 1949 the Chinese state has been controlled by the **Communist Party**, which brooks no dissent or rival, and which, with 66 million members, is the biggest political party in the world. It has a pyramid structure resting on millions of local organizations, and whose apex is formed by a Politburo of 24 members controlled by a nine-man standing committee. The Party's workings are opaque; personal relations count more than job titles, and a leader's influence rests on the relations he builds with superiors and protégés, with retired party elders often retaining a great deal of influence. Towards the end of his life, for example, Deng Xiaoping was virtually running the country when his only official title was head of a bridge club. The country's head of state is its president, while the head of government is the premier. Politburo members are supposedly chosen by the three thousand delegates of the National People's Congress, officially a parliament though it in fact serves largely as a rubber stamp for Politburo decisions.

The Party owes its success, of course, to the **military**, and links with the PLA remain close, though the army has lost power since Jiang Zemin stripped its huge business empire in the 1990s. There is no PLA representative on the standing committee, but the military has a strong influence on policy issues, particularly over Taiwan and relations with the US, and generally maintains a hard line.

The law in China is a mix of legislation based on Party priorities and new statutes to haul the economy into line with those of major foreign investors. The National People's Congress is responsible for drafting laws covering taxation and human rights, among other subjects. In other areas, the State Council and local governments can legislate. Even after laws have been passed there is no guarantee they will be respected; provincial governments and state-owned enterprises view court decisions as negotiable, and for the Party and the state, the rule of law is not allowed to supersede its own interests.

1999	2001	2003
Macau returns to the mainland. Persecution of Falun Gong	China admitted to the World Trade Organization	China puts a man into space

political control and a genuine effort to deal with social problems. Alarmed at growing income inequality, efforts have been made to shift society away from unbridled capitalism towards a more socially responsible model of development.

Stumbling blocks

Perhaps China's biggest problem is its massive **population** (1.35 billion in 2012), which could put unbearable pressure on resources if it continues to rise – though it is, in fact, predicted to contract from 2030, shortly after being eclipsed by India. Under the **one-child policy**, which began in 1979, couples who have a second child face a cut in wages and restricted access to health care and housing. The policy has been most successful in the cities, where a burgeoning middle class are desiring fewer and fewer children in any case, and does not apply to ethnic minorities, or in swaths of rural China. However, given the heavy preference for male children, female infanticide and the selling of girls as brides are not unusual, while there is a growing trend for kidnapping male children for ransom or, again, sale.

HUMAN RIGHTS

Despite magnificent progress on the economic level, the Chinese state continues to be one of the world's worst regimes for human rights abuses – despite many of those rights being enshrined in its own constitution.

The Communist Party tolerates no dissent, permits no rivals and locks up anyone perceived as a challenge, be they journalists, lawyers, bloggers, whistleblowers, petitioners or followers of religious cults such as Falun Gong. The highest-profile incarcerated dissident is 2010 Nobel Peace Prize winner **Liu Xiaobo**, whose crime was to write "Charter 08", a document calling for political reform; he started an 11-year sentence in 2009. Other activists recently imprisoned include Doctor Gao Yaojie, who exposed how blood collectors were spreading AIDS (she's now living in New York); Zhao Lianhai, who lobbied for compensation for the families whose babies were harmed by tainted baby milk (released, but still under surveillance); and Chen Guangcheng, who campaigned against forced sterilizations (also in New York, after fleeing to Beijing's US embassy in 2012). There are many more, and observers say that the situation for activists has worsened in recent years.

China has no independent judiciary, rule of law or due process, and around half a million people are currently enduring detention without charge or trial. Torture and execution remain commonplace. But the country's most serious human rights abuses are being perpetrated in **Tibet**, where dissent is ruthlessly suppressed and indigenous culture is being swamped by Han migration. In 1995, when the exiled Dalai Lama selected a new Panchen Lama following the death of the previous one, the boy he chose, Gedhun Choekyi Nyima, was arrested, along with his family. None has been seen since, though in 2007 the Chinese government released an update of his life at the time, stating that he was "a perfectly normal Tibetan boy", who "likes Chinese culture and has recently taken up calligraphy." It is common for Tibetans to receive long sentences of hard labour not just for criticizing the regime, but also for singing songs about freedom or owning a picture of the Dalai Lama.

In 2008, a group of Tibetans fleeing to Nepal were fired on by border guards at the Nangpa Pass; they shot a teenage nun, Kelsang Namtso, in the back then left her to die in the snow. What is unusual about this incident is not that it occurred – exiles say that sort of thing happens all the time – but that it was filmed by Western climbers. You can see the footage on YouTube (search for "Murder in the Snow").

2004	2006	2008
SARS epidemic; China's population reaches 1.3 billion	The Three Gorges Dam is finished, and the new railway line to Tibet opens	Beijing hosts the Olympic Games, at which China tops the medals table, cementing China's status as a modern global power

Despite being one of the cornerstones of domestic policy, economic prosperity has not been delivered evenly across the country, with the east-coast cities benefiting most. But the burgeoning economy has delivered one constant: rising **inflation** and living costs, which in turn have seen the **mass migration** of rural workers to seek better-paid jobs in the cities, where most remain unemployed or are hired by the day as labourers. As success is largely dependent on *guanxi* (connections), the potential for **corruption** in all walks of life is enormous – indeed, graft is thought to be slicing at least a percentage point off growth figures. There is also a desperate lack of official **accountability** in China: every year, there are widespread demonstrations against local corruption by industrial workers who are out of work or owed back pay, by villagers protesting at pollution – China now boasts several of the most **polluted cities** in the world – and by homeowners angry at enforced demolitions. Such actions represent possibly the biggest internal threat to the state. The blame, as well as the credit for creating and managing an economic boom, lies squarely with the Communist Party; designed to change society, it seems incapable of adapting to it.

China and the world

China's tactic during her stellar period of economic development has been not to intervene on the world stage. But its explosive expansion is now forcing engagement, and the country is coming under scrutiny as never before. As the world's biggest emitter of greenhouse gases, it is under increasing international pressure to start cleaning up its act. China's skewed **business environment** – lax enforcement of intellectual property and business laws, bullying of foreign companies in favour of local competition, unfair regulatory barriers and an artificially low currency – is now attracting plenty of criticism from its trading partners.

In order to fuel growth, China needs to look elsewhere for raw materials: in Africa, the Pacific and Southeast Asia, China has become the new **resource colonizer**, striking deals with all comers, including nations shunned by the West such as Zimbabwe and Sudan. How China handles its growing influence will determine whether east Asia (and, perhaps, great chunks of Africa too) will remain stable enough to continue to prosper, or tumbles back into conflict and rivalry. China's willingness to bind itself to global rules, such as those of the World Trade Organization, has been a welcome way to assimilate it, but an authoritarian, anti-democratic China will never be easy for its neighbours to live with, and Chinese primacy in the Pacific is contested by both Japan and the US.

CHINA AND JAPAN

China's antipathy towards **Japan** stems from Japan's perceived failure to be properly contrite over its crimes in World War II, ongoing territorial disputes over some insignificant islands, and simple rivalry; every year some trivial issue (most recently regarding the ownership of the contested Diaoyu islands) becomes a flashpoint for anti-Japanese demonstrations. These are awkward for the government: patriotic demonstrations in the last century were often the precursor to pro-democracy unrest, but at the same time the Party would rather not crack down on expressions of nationalism, as such fervour is whipped up by the Party to justify its existence and right to rule.

2012	2013
New generation of leaders under Xi Jinping elected at the National People's Congress	China lands unmanned "Jade Rabbit" rover on the moon. Continued dissent in Xinjiang and Tibetan regions

Chinese beliefs

The resilience of ancient beliefs in China, and the ability of the Chinese people to absorb new streams of thought and eventually to dominate them, has been demonstrated repeatedly over the centuries. That said, any visitor to modern China will find few obvious indications of the traditional beliefs that have underpinned the country's civilization for three thousand years. Certainly, the remains of religious buildings litter the cities and the countryside, yet they appear sadly incongruous amid the furious pace of change all around. The restored temples – now "cultural relics" – are garish and evoke few mysteries. This apparent lack of religion is hardly surprising, however: for decades, the old beliefs have been derided by the authorities as feudal superstition, and the oldest and most firmly rooted of them all, Confucianism, was criticized and repudiated for fifty years. Yet in actual fact, the outward manifestations of the ancient beliefs are not essential: the traditions are expressed more clearly in how the Chinese think and act than in the symbols and rituals of overt worship.

The Three Teachings

The product of the oldest continuous civilization on earth, **Chinese religion** actually comprises a number of disparate and sometimes contradictory elements. At the heart of it lie **three basic philosophies**: Confucianism, Taoism and Buddhism. The way in which a harmonious balance has been created among these three is expressed in the often quoted maxim *san jiao fa yi* – "Three Teachings Flow into One".

Confucianism

China's oldest and greatest philosopher, Kong Zi, known in the West by his Latinized name **Confucius**, was in his lifetime an obscure and unsuccessful scholar. Born in 551 BC, during the Warring States period, he lived in an age of petty kingdoms where life was blighted by constant conflict. Confucius taught the simple message that society could be improved if individuals behaved properly. Harking back to an earlier, mythic

---

SUPERSTITIONS

Though the Chinese are not generally religious in the conventional sense, they are often very **superstitious**. You'll see evidence of this everywhere you go, especially in the form of wordplay. Thus the Chinese expression for "let luck come", *fudao*, happens to sound similar to "upside-down luck"; hence the inverted *fu* character pasted up outside homes and businesses at Spring Festival, encouraging good fortune to arrive on the premises. Other **lucky symbols** include peaches and cranes (for longevity), fish (surplus), mandarin ducks (marital fidelity), dragons (male power), phoenixes (female power) and bats (happiness).

    Colours are also important. Red, the colour of fire, and gold, the colour of money, are auspicious, and used extensively for decorations, packaging, weddings and festive occasions. White traditionally represents death or mourning, though traditional Western wedding dresses are becoming increasingly popular. Yellow is the colour of heaven, hence the yellow roof tiles used on temples; yellow clothing was formerly reserved for the emperor alone.

age of peace and social virtues, he preached adherence to **ritual and propriety** as the supreme answer to the horrifying disorder of the world as he found it. No one paid much attention while he was alive; after his death, however, his writings were collected as the **Analects**, and this book became the most influential and fundamental of Chinese philosophies.

Never a religion in the sense of postulating a higher deity, Confucianism is rather a set of **moral and social values** designed to bring the ways of citizens and governments into harmony with each other. Through proper training in the scholarly classics and rigid adherence to the rules of propriety, including ancestor-worship, the superior man could attain a level of moral righteousness that would, in turn, assure a stable and righteous social order. As a political theory, Confucianism called for the "**wisest sage**", the one whose moral sense was most refined, to be ruler. A good ruler who exemplified the **five Confucian virtues** – benevolence, righteousness, propriety, wisdom and trustworthiness – would bring society naturally to order. As Confucius said:

Just as the ruler genuinely desires the good, the people will be good. The virtue of the ruler may be compared to the wind and that of the common people to the grass. The grass under the force of the wind cannot but bend.

Instead of God, **five hierarchical relationships** are the prerequisites for a well-ordered society; given proper performance of the duties entailed in these, society should be "at ease with itself". The five relationships outline a structure of duty and obedience to authority: ruler to ruled, son to father, younger brother to older, wife to husband, and – the only relationship between equals – friend to friend. In practice, adherence to the unbending hierarchy of these relationships, as well as to the precepts of filial piety, has been used to justify totalitarian rule throughout Chinese history. The supreme virtue of the well-cultivated man and woman was always **obedience**.

During the time of the Han dynasty (206 BC–220 AD), Confucianism became institutionalized as a **system of government** that was to prevail for two thousand years. With it, and with the notion of the scholar-official as the ideal administrator, came the notorious Chinese **bureaucracy**. Men would study half their lives in order to pass examinations on Confucian thought and attain a government commission. Right until the start of the twentieth century, power was wielded through a bureaucracy steeped in the rites and rituals written five hundred years before Christ.

The ideal ruler, of course, never quite emerged (the emperor was not expected to sit the exams), and today, Confucian rituals are no longer practised. However, just as Protestantism is seen as having provided the underpinning to the advance of the West, so Confucianism, with its emphasis on order, harmony and cooperation, has been regarded as providing the ideological foundations for the recent successes of Asian culture.

Taoism

Taoism is the study and pursuit of the ineffable "Way", as outlined in the fundamental text, the **Daodejing** (often written as *Tao Te Ching*) or "The Way of Power". This obscure and mystical text comprises the wise sayings of the semi-mythical hermit **Lao Zi**, a contemporary of Confucius, compiled three centuries after his death.

The *Tao* is never really defined – indeed by its very nature it is undefinable. To the despair of the rationalist, the first lines of the *Daodejing* read:

The Tao that can be told
is not the eternal Tao.
The name that can be named
is not the eternal name.

In essence, however, it might be thought of as the underlying principle and source of all being, the bond that unites man and nature. Its central principle, **Wu Wei**, can crudely be translated as "no action", though it is probably better understood as "no action which runs contrary to the laws of nature". Whereas Confucianism is concerned with repairing social order and social relationships, Taoism is interested in the relationship of the individual with the natural universe.

Taoism's second major text is a book of parables written by one ideal practitioner of the Way, **Zhuang Zi**, another semi-mythical figure. In the famous butterfly parable, Zhuang Zi examines the many faces of reality:

Once upon a time Zhuang Zi dreamed he was a butterfly. A butterfly flying around and enjoying itself. It did not know it was Zhuang Zi again. We do not know whether it was Zhuang Zi dreaming that he was a butterfly, or a butterfly dreaming he was Zhuang Zi.

In its affirmation of the irrational and natural sources of life, Taoism has provided Chinese culture with a balance to the rigid social mores of Confucianism. In traditional China it was said that the perfect lifestyle was to be Confucian during the day – a righteous and firm administrator, upholding the virtues of the gentleman ruler – and a Taoist when relaxing. If Confucianism preaches duty to family and to society, Taoism champions the sublimity of withdrawal and non-committedness. The **art and literature** of China have been greatly enriched by Taoism's notions of contemplation, detachment and freedom from social entanglement, and the Tao has become embedded in the Chinese soul as a doctrine of yielding to the inevitable forces of nature.

Buddhism

The first organized religion to penetrate China, **Buddhism** enjoyed a glorious period of ascendancy under the Tang dynasty (618–907 AD). In the eighth century there were over 300,000 Buddhist monks in China, and this period saw the creation of much of the country's **great religious art** – above all the cave shrines at **Luoyang** (Henan), **Datong** (Shaanxi) and **Dunhuang** (Gansu), where thousands of carvings of the Buddha and paintings of holy figures attest to the powerful influence of Indian art and religion.

Gradually, though, Buddhism was submerged into the native belief system. Most contemporary schools of Indian Buddhism taught that life on earth was essentially one of suffering, an endless cycle in which people were born, grew old and died, only to be born again in other bodies; the goal was to break out of this by attaining nirvana, which could be done by losing all desire for things of the world. This essentially individualistic doctrine was not likely to appeal to the regimented Chinese, however, and so it was the relatively small **Mahayana School** of Buddhism that came to dominate Chinese thinking. The Mahayana taught that perfection for the individual was not possible without perfection for all – and that those who had already attained enlightenment would remain active in the world as **Bodhisattvas**, to help others along the path. In time Bodhisattvas came to be ascribed miraculous powers, and were prayed to in a manner remarkably similar to conventional Confucian ancestor-worship. The mainstream of Chinese Buddhism came to be more about maintaining harmonious relations with Bodhisattvas than about attaining nirvana.

Another entirely new sect of Buddhism also arose in China through contact with Taoism. Known in China as **Chan** (and in Japan as Zen), it offered a less extreme path to enlightenment. For a Chan Buddhist, it was not necessary to become a monk or a recluse in order to achieve nirvana – instead this ultimate state of being could be reached through life in accord with, and in contemplation of, the Way.

In short, the Chinese managed to marry Buddhism to their pre-existing belief structures with very little difficulty. This was facilitated by the general absence of dogma within Buddhist thought. Like the Chinese, the **Tibetans**, too, found themselves able to adapt the new belief system to their old religion, **Bon** (see p.858), rather than

GETTING AROUND A CHINESE TEMPLE

Whether Buddhist or Taoist, Chinese temples share the same broad features. Like cities, they **face south** and are surrounded by walls. Gates are sealed by **heavy doors**, guarded by paintings or statues of warrior deities to chase away evil. Further protection is ensured by a **spirit wall** that blocks direct entry; although easy enough for the living to walk around, this foils spirits, who are unable to turn corners. Once inside, you'll find a succession of **halls** arranged in ornamental courtyards. In case evil influences should manage to get in, the area nearest the entrance contains the least important rooms or buildings, while those of greater significance – living quarters or main temple halls – are set deeper inside the complex.

One way to tell Buddhist and Taoist temples apart is by the colour of the **supporting pillars** – Buddhists use bright red, while Taoists favour black. **Animal carvings** are more popular with Taoists, who use decorative good-luck and longevity symbols such as bats and cranes; some Taoist halls also have distinctive raised octagonal cupolas sporting the black-and-white *yin-yang* symbol.

simply replacing it. Over the centuries, they established their own schools of Buddhism, often referred to as **Lamaism**. The now dominant **Gelugpa** (or Yellow Hat) school, of which the Dalai and Panchen Lamas are members, dates back to the teachings of Tsongkhapa (1357–1419).

Minority faiths and popular beliefs

Though Buddhism was the only foreign religion to leave a substantial mark on China, it was not the only one to enter China via the Silk Road. Both **Islam** and **Christianity** also trickled into the country this way, and to this day a significant minority of Chinese, numbering in the tens of millions, are Muslim. Unlike much of the rest of Asia, however, China did not yield wholesale to the tide of Islam, and thoroughly rejected it as a political doctrine.

When Jesuit missionaries first arrived in China in the sixteenth and seventeenth centuries, they were astounded and dismayed by the Chinese **flexibility of belief**. One frustrated Jesuit put it thus: "In China, the educated believe nothing and the uneducated believe everything". For those versed in the classics of Confucianism, Taoism and Buddhism, the normal belief was a healthy and tolerant scepticism. For the great majority of illiterate peasants, however, **popular religion** offered a plethora of ghosts, spirits, gods and ancestors who ruled over a capricious nature and protected humanity. If Christian missionaries handed out rice, perhaps Christ too deserved a place alongside them. In popular Buddhism the hope was to reach the "Pure Land", a kind of heaven for believers ruled over by a female deity known as the Mother Ruler. Popular Taoism shared this feminine deity, but its concerns were rather with the sorcerers, alchemists and martial-arts aficionados who sought solutions to the riddle of immortality; you may see some of these figures depicted in Taoist temples.

Modern China

During the twentieth century, confronted by the superior military and technical power of the West, the Chinese have striven to break free from the shackles of superstition. Since the imperial examinations were abolished at the start of the twentieth century, Chinese intellectuals have been searching for a modern yet essentially Chinese philosophy. The **Cultural Revolution** can be seen as the culmination of these efforts to repudiate the past. Hundreds of thousands of temples, ancestral halls and religious objects were defaced and destroyed. Monasteries were burnt to the ground, and their monks imprisoned. The classics of literature and philosophy – the "residue of the reactionary feudal past" – were burned. In 1974, towards the end of the Cultural

Revolution, a campaign was launched to "criticize Lin Biao and Confucius", pairing the general with the sage to imply that both were equally reactionary in their opposition to the government.

Yet the very fact that Confucius could still be held up as an object for derision in 1974 reveals the tenacity of traditional beliefs. With the Cultural Revolution now long gone, religion and philosophy are again being accepted as an essential part of the cultural tradition that binds the Chinese people together. Despite a lifetime of commitment to the Marxist revolution, the older generation are comforted and strengthened by their knowledge of the national heritage, while the young are rediscovering the classics, the forbidden fruit of their school days. The welcome result is that Chinese temples of all descriptions are once more prosperous, busy places, teeming with people who have come to ask for grandchildren or simply for money. The atmosphere may not seem devout or religious, but then perhaps it never did.

Traditional Chinese Medicine

As an agricultural society, the Chinese have long been aware of the importance of the balance of natural, elemental forces: too much heat causes drought; too much rain, floods; while the correct measure of both encourages farmers' crops to grow. The ancient Chinese saw heaven, earth and humankind existing as an integral whole, such that if people lived in harmony with heaven and earth, then their collective health would be good. The medical treatise *Huang Di Neijing*, attributed to the semi-mythical Yellow Emperor (2500 BC), mentions the importance of spiritual balance, acupuncture and herbal medicine in treating illnesses, and attests to the venerable age of China's medical beliefs – it may well be a compilation of even earlier texts. Acupuncture was certainly in use by the Han period, as tombs in Hebei dated to 113 BC have yielded acupuncture needles made of gold and silver, as well as illustrations of therapeutic exercises, similar to those still practised today.

The belief in universal balance is known as **Dao** (or Tao) – literally "the Way". As an extension of Daoist principles, life is seen as consisting of opposites – man and woman, sun and moon, right and left, giving and receiving – whereby all things exist as a result of their interaction with their opposites. This is expressed in the black-and-white Daoist diagram which shows two interacting opposites, the **yin** ("female", passive energy) and the **yang** ("male", active energy). At the core of Traditional Chinese Medicine lies the belief that in order for a body to be healthy, its opposites must also be in a state of dynamic balance; there is a constant fluctuation, for example, between the body's heat, depending on its level of activity and the weather, and the amount of water needed to keep the body at the correct temperature. An excess of water in the system creates oedema, too little creates dehydration; too much heat will cause a temperature, and too little cause chills. Chinese medicine therefore views the body as an integrated whole, so that in sickness, the whole body – rather than just the "ill" part of it – requires treatment.

Qi and acupuncture

An underlying feature of Chinese medical philosophy, **qi** (or *chi*) is the energy of life: in the same way that electricity powers a light bulb, *qi*, so the theory goes, enables us to move, see and speak. *Qi* is said to flow along the body's network of **meridians**, or energy pathways, linking the surface tissues to specific internal **organs** that act as *qi* reservoirs; the twelve major meridians are named after the organ to which they are connected. The meridians are further classed as *yin* or *yang* depending on whether they are exposed or protected. In the limbs, for instance, the channels of the outer sides are *yang*, and important for resisting disease, while the channels of the inner sides are *yin*, and more involved with nourishing the body.

Mental and physical tensions, poor diet, anger or depression, even adverse weather, are said to inhibit *qi* flow, causing illness. Needles inserted in the body's **acupuncture points** reinforce or reduce the *qi* flow along a meridian, in turn influencing the activities of the organs. When the *qi* is balanced and flowing smoothly once more, good health is regained; acupuncture is specifically used to combat inflammation, to regenerate damaged tissue and to improve the functional power of internal organs.

That said, despite some acceptance of acupuncture in the West, there remains no good evidence for its efficacy. Studies have found that patients treated by acupuncturists had the same recovery rate as patients poked with needles at random positions. Sceptics argue that the act of sticking needles in the body produces pain-killing endorphins, which, combined with the placebo effect, aids recovery.

Herbal medicine

In the 2200 years since the semi-mythical Xia king **Shennong** compiled his classic work on **medicinal herbs**, a vast amount of experience has been gained to help perfect their clinical use. Approximately seven thousand herbs, derived from roots, leaves, twigs and fruit, are today commonly used in Chinese medicine, with another thousand or so of animal or mineral origin (also classified as "herbs"). Each is first processed by cleaning, soaking, slicing, drying or roasting, or even stir-frying with wine, ginger or vinegar, to influence its effects; the brew is then boiled down and drunk as a tea (typically very bitter and earthy tasting).

Herbs are used to prevent or combat a wide variety of diseases. Some are used to treat the underlying cause of the complaint, others to treat symptoms and help strengthen the body's own immune system, in turn helping it to combat the problem. An everyday example is in the treatment of flu: the herbal formula would include a "cold action" herb to reduce the fever, a herb to induce sweating and thus clear the body-ache, a purgative to clear the virus from the system, and a tonic herb to replenish the immune system. In all treatments, the patient is re-examined regularly, and as the condition improves the herbal formula is changed accordingly.

Just as Western aspirin is derived from willow bark, many Chinese drugs have been developed from herbs. One example is the anti-malarial herb *qinghaosu*, or artemisinin, which has proved effective in treating certain strains of malaria with minimal side effects.

Art

Chinese art objects have had a difficult modern history: in the nineteenth century many were acquired by Westerners; then the greatest collections were taken by the Nationalists to Taiwan, where they are now in the National Palace Museum; many more art objects were destroyed during the Cultural Revolution; and today destruction – or dubious appropriation – of cultural relics continues as a consequence of modern development. Yet an astonishing wealth of treasures remains in China, mostly in local museum collections.

Pottery, bronzes and sculpture

The earliest Chinese objects date back to the Neolithic farmers of the **Yangshao** culture – **pottery** vessels painted with geometric designs. The decoration is from the shoulders of the pots upwards, as what has survived is mostly from graves and was designed to be seen from above when the pots were placed round the dead. From the same period come decorated clay heads, and pendants and ornaments of polished stone or jade – a simplified sitting bird in polished jade is a very early example of the Chinese tradition of animal sculpture. Rather later is the Neolithic **Longshan** pottery – black, thin and fine, wheel-turned and often highly polished, with elegant, sharply defined shapes.

The subsequent era, from around 1500 BC, is dominated by **Shang and Zhou bronze vessels** that were used for preparing and serving food and wine, and for ceremonies and sacrifices. One of the most common shapes is the *ding*, a three- or four-legged vessel that harks back to the Neolithic pots used for cooking over open fires. Casting methods were highly sophisticated, using moulds, while design was firm and assured and decoration often stylized and linear, featuring geometric and animal motifs, as well as grinning masks of humans and fabulous beasts. There are some naturalistic animal forms among the vessels, too – fierce tigers, solid elephants and surly rhinoceroses. Other bronze finds include weapons, decorated horse harnesses and sets of bells used in ritual music.

Later, under the **Zhou**, the style of the bronzes becomes more varied and rich: some animal vessels are fantastically shaped and extravagantly decorated; others are simplified natural forms; others again seem to be depicting not so much a fierce tiger, for example, as utter ferocity itself. You'll also see from the Shang and Zhou small objects – ornaments, ritual pieces and jewellery pendants – bearing highly simplified but vivid forms of tortoises, salamanders and flying birds. Some painted clay funeral figures and a few carved wooden figures also survive from the end of this period.

Although the Shang produced a few small sculpted human figures and animals in marble, **sculptures** and works in stone begin to be found in great quantities in **Han-dynasty** tombs. The decorated bricks and tiles, the bas-reliefs and the terracotta figurines of acrobats, horsemen and ladies-in-waiting placed in the tombs to serve the dead, even the massive stone men and beasts set to guard the Spirit Way leading to the tomb, are all lifelike and reflect concern with everyday activities and material possessions. The scale models of houses with people looking out of the windows and of farmyards with their animals have a spontaneous gaiety and vigour; some of the watchdogs are the most realistic of all.

It was the advent of **Buddhism** that encouraged stone carving on a large scale in the round, using mallet and chisel. **Religious sculpture** was introduced from India; in the fourth-century caves at **Datong** (see p.243), and the earlier caves at **Longmen**, near

Luoyang (see p.261), the Indian influence is most strongly felt in the stylized Buddhas and attendants. Sometimes of huge size, these have an aloof grace and a rhythmic quality in their flowing robes, but also a smooth, bland and static quality. Not until the **Tang** do you get the full flowering of a native Chinese style, where the figures are rounder, with movement, and the positions, expressions and clothes are more natural and realistic. Some of the best examples are to be seen at **Dunhuang** (see p.811) and in the later caves at Longmen. The **Song** continued to carve religious figures, and at **Dazu** in Sichuan (see p.743), you'll find good examples of a decorative style that had broadened its subject matter to include animals, ordinary people and scenes of everyday life; the treatment is down-to-earth, individual, even comic. As the Dazu carvings are well preserved, they can still be seen painted, as they were meant to be. In later years, less statuary was produced until the **Ming** with their taste for massive tomb sculptures. You can see the best of these in **Nanjing** and **Beijing**.

Ceramics

From Neolithic painted pottery onwards, China developed excellent **ceramics**, a pre-eminence recognized even in the English language, which took the word "china" to mean fine-quality ceramic ware. In some of the early wares you can see the influence of shapes derived from bronzes, but soon the rise of regional potteries using different materials, and the development of special types for different uses, led to an enormous variety of shapes, textures and colours. This was really noticeable in the **Tang dynasty**, when an increase in the production of pottery for daily use was stimulated by the spread of tea drinking, and by the restriction of the use of valuable copper and bronze to coinage. The Tang also saw major technical advances; the production of true **porcelain** was finally achieved, and Tang potters became skilled in the delicate art of polychrome glazing. You can see evidence of this in the *san cai* (three-colour) statuettes of horses and camels, jugglers, traders, polo players, grooms and court ladies, which have come in great numbers from imperial tombs, and which reflect in vivid, often humorous, detail and still-brilliant colours so many aspects of the life of the time.

The **Song** dynasty witnessed a refinement of ceramic techniques and of regional specialization. The keynote was simplicity and quiet elegance, in both colour and form. There was a preference for using **single pure colours**, and for incized wares made to resemble damask cloth. In the museums you'll see the famous green celadons, the thin white porcelain *ding* ware and the pale grey-green *ju* ware reserved for imperial use. The Mongol **Yuan** dynasty, in the early fourteenth century, enriched Chinese tradition with outside influences – notably the introduction of **cobalt blue underglaze**, early examples of the blue and white porcelain that was to become so famous.

The **Ming** saw the flowering of great potteries under imperial patronage, especially **Jingdezhen**. Taste moved away from Song simplicity and returned to the liking for the vivid, almost gaudy, colour previously displayed by the Tang – deep **red**, **yellow** and **orange** glazes, with a developing taste for pictorial representation. From the seventeenth century onwards, Chinese export wares flowed in great quantity and variety to the West to satisfy a growing demand for chinoiserie, and the efforts of the Chinese artists to follow what they saw as the tastes and techniques of the West produced a style of its own. The early **Qing** created delicate enamel wares and *famille rose* and *verte*. So precise were the craftsmen that some porcelain includes the instructions for the pattern in the glaze.

Painting and calligraphy

While China's famous ceramics were made by craftsmen who remained anonymous, **painting and calligraphy** pieces were produced by famous scholars, officials and poets. It has been said that the four great treasures of Chinese painting are the brush, ink, inkstone and paper. The earliest **brush** to have been found dates from about 400 BC, and is made out of animal hairs glued to a hollow bamboo tube. **Ink** was made from pine soot, mixed with glue and hardened into a stick that would be rubbed with water on a slate **inkstone**. The first known painting on silk was found in a **Han** tomb; records show that a great deal of such painting was created, but in 190 AD the vast imperial collection was destroyed in a civil war, when soldiers used the silk to make tents and knapsacks. All we know of Han painting comes from decorated tiles, lacquer, painted pottery and a few painted tombs, enough to show a great sense of movement and energy. The British Museum holds a scroll in ink and colour on silk from around 400 AD, attributed to **Gu Kaizhi** and entitled *Admonitions of the Instructress to Court Ladies*, and it's known that the theory of painting was already being discussed by then, as the treatise *The Six Principles of Painting* dates from about 500 AD.

The Sui and Tang

The **Sui-Tang** period, with a powerful stable empire and a brilliant court, was the perfect moment for painting to develop. A great tradition of **figure painting** grew up, especially of court subjects – portraits and pictures of the emperor receiving envoys, and of court ladies, can be seen in Beijing. Although only a few of these survived, the walls of Tang tombs, such as those near Xi'an, are rich in vivid frescoes that provide a realistic portrayal of court life. Wang Wei in the mid-eighth century was an early exponent of monochrome **landscape painting**, but the great flowering of landscape painting came with the **Song dynasty**. An academy was set up under imperial patronage, and different schools of painting emerged which analysed the natural world with great concentration and intensity; their style has set a mark on Chinese landscape painting ever since. There was also lively **figure painting**, as epitomized by a famous horizontal scroll in Beijing that depicts the Qing Ming River Festival. The Southern Song preferred a more intimate style, and such subjects as flowers, birds and still life grew in popularity.

The Yuan

Under the **Mongols**, many officials found themselves unwanted or unwilling to serve the alien Yuan dynasty, and preferred to retire and paint. This produced the "**literati**" **school**, in which many painters harked back to the styles of the tenth century. One great master, **Ni Can**, also devoted himself, among many others, to the ink paintings of bamboo that became important at this time. In this school, of which many examples remain extant, the highest skills of techniques and composition were applied to the simplest of subjects, such as plum flowers. Both ink painting as well as more conventional media continued to be employed by painters during the next three or more centuries. From the **Yuan** onwards, a tremendous quantity of paintings has survived.

The Ming and Qing

The **Ming dynasty** saw a great interest in collecting the works of previous ages, and a willingness by painters to be influenced by tradition. There are plenty of examples of bamboo and plum blossom, and bird and flower paintings being brought to a high decorative pitch, as well as schools of landscape painting firmly rooted in traditional techniques. The arrival of the Manchu **Qing dynasty** did not disrupt the continuity of Chinese painting, but the art became wide open to many influences. It included the Italian **Castiglione** (Lang Shining in Chinese) who specialized in horses, dogs and flowers; the Four Wangs, who reinterpreted Song and Yuan styles in an orthodox manner; and individualists such as the Eight Eccentrics of Yangzhou and certain Buddhist monks who objected to derivative art and sought a more distinctive approach to subject and style.

CONTEMPORARY ART

Contemporary art is flourishing in China. There are hundreds of private galleries and every major city has an arts centre, often an old factory converted into studios and exhibition spaces – 798 in Beijing (see p.98) and 50 Moganshan Lu (see p.369) in Shanghai are the biggest examples, but it's also worth noting Nordica in Kunming (see p.655) and OCT in Shenzhen, among others. Fairs such as the Shanghai Biennale and Guangzhou's triennial have become enormous events. Chinese art is seen as hot by investors, and there's plenty of money sloshing around; it helps that art is less easy to counterfeit than other cultural forms, and, because "meaning" in art can be nebulous, trickier for the government to censor.

However, the first crop of modern Chinese artists, who emerged in the 1990s, worked in obscurity with, it seemed, no prospects of exhibition. They banded together for survival in artists' villages, most famously at the **Yuanmingyuan Artists' Community** outside Beijing. The artists here developed a school of painting that expressed their individualism and their sceptical, often ironic and sometimes jaundiced view of contemporary China; this was, of course, the generation that had seen its dreams of change shot down at Tian'anmen Square. Nurtured by curator **Li Xianting**, as well as sympathetic foreign collectors, they built the foundations of the art scene as it is today. The most famous of these so-called "cynical realists" is **Fang Lijun**, whose paintings of disembodied bald heads against desolate landscapes are now some of the most characteristic images of modern Chinese art. Look out too for **Yue Minjun**'s Goya-esque paintings of the Tian'anmen massacre (though he's equally famous as a sculptor), **Yang Shaobin**'s slickly painted sinister figures, the bitingly satirical caricatures of **Wang Yinsong** and **Song Yonghong**, and pigeonhole-phobic **Wang Xingwei**'s impressively diverse range of paintings.

Artists such as **Wang Guangyi** developed another school of distinctly Chinese contemporary art, "political pop". Here, a mocking twist is given to the iconography of the Cultural Revolution in order to critique a society that has become brashly commercial; Red Guards are shown waving iPods instead of Little Red Books, for example. Of late this has become rather a hackneyed genre, though every artist seems to go through a phase of it, and it's enthusiastically collected in the West.

Although it's hard to pick out trends amid such a ferment of activity, many artists these days are, unsurprisingly, preoccupied with documenting the destruction of the Chinese urban landscape and the gut-wrenching changes that have accompanied modernization. As spaces for viewing art have grown, artists have diversified into new media such as **performance and video**; exciting new faces to look out for include **Cui Xiuwen**, whose videos of women in a toilet at a karaoke bar are shocking and memorable, and **Xu Zhen**, whose video *Rainbow* shows his back turning red from unseen slaps. **Documentary photography** is also popular; among its finest exponents is **Yang Fudong**, notable for his wistful images of city life. **Wu Gaozhong** first drew attention for a performance piece in which he climbed into the belly of a slaughtered cow, but his recent work, involving giant props implanted with boar hair, is more subtle, and has a creepy beauty. And it's always worth looking out for a show curated by *enfant terrible* **Gu Zhenqing**, who has a reputation for gleefully pushing the limits.

Calligraphy

Calligraphy – the word is derived from the Greek for "beautiful writing" – was crystallized into a high art form in China, where the use of the brush saw the development of handwriting of various styles, valued on a par with painting. Of the various different scripts, the **seal script** is the archaic form found on oracle bones; the **lishu** is the clerical style and was used in inscriptions on stone; the **kaishu** is the regular style closest to the modern printed form; and the cursive **cao shu** (grass script) is the most individual handwritten style. Emperors, poets and scholars over centuries have left examples of their calligraphy cut into stone at beauty spots, on mountains and in grottoes, tombs and temples all over China; you can see some early examples in the caves at Longmen (see p.261). At one stage during the Tang dynasty, calligraphy was so highly prized that it was the yardstick for the selection of high officials.

Other arts

Jade and lacquerware have also been constantly in use in China since earliest times. In Chinese eyes, **jade**, in white and shades of green or brown, is the most precious of stones. It was used to make the earliest ritual objects, such as the flat disc **Bi**, symbol of Heaven, which was found in Shang and Zhou graves. Jade was also used as a mark of rank and for ornament, in its most striking form in the jade burial suits to be seen in the country's museums.

Lacquer, made from the sap of a specific tree which dries to a tough, shiny coat, is also found as early as the Zhou. Many layers of the stuff were painted on a wood or cloth base that was then carved and inlaid with gold, silver or tortoiseshell, or often most delicately painted. Numerous examples of painted lacquer boxes and baskets survive from the Han, and, as with jade, the use of this material has continued ever since.

Music

The casual visitor to China could be forgiven for thinking that the only traditional style of music to compete with bland pop is that of the kitsch folk troupes to be heard in hotels and concert halls. But an earthy traditional music still abounds throughout the countryside; it can be heard at weddings, funerals, temple fairs and New Year celebrations – and even downtown in teahouses. A very different, edgier sound can be heard in certain smoky city bars – the new Chinese rock, with its energetic expressions of urban angst.

Traditional music

Chinese musical roots date back millennia – archeological finds include a magnificent set of 65 bronze bells from the fifth century BC – and modern forms can be directly traced to the Tang dynasty. Traditional Han music, like Irish music, is **heterophonic** – the musicians play differently decorated versions of a single melodic line. Percussion plays a major role, both in instrumental ensembles and as accompaniment to opera, narrative-singing, ritual music and dance.

But in the turbulent years after 1911, some intriguing **urban forms** sprang up from the meeting of East and West, such as the wonderfully sleazy Cantonese music of the 1920s and 1930s. As the movie industry developed, people in Shanghai, Guangzhou and Hong Kong threw themselves into the craze for Western-style dance halls, fusing the local traditional music with jazz, and adding saxophone, violin and xylophone to Chinese instruments such as the *gaohu* (high-pitched fiddle) and the *yangqin* (dulcimer). Composers **Lü Wencheng** and **Qiu Hechou** (Yau Hokchau), the violinist **Yin Zizhong** (Yi Tzuchung), and **He Dasha** ("Thicko He"), guitarist and singer of clown roles in Cantonese opera, made many wonderful commercial recordings during this period. While these musicians kept their roots in Cantonese music, the more Westernized (and even more popular) compositions of **Li Jinhui** and his star singer **Zhou Xuan** subsequently earned severe disapproval from Maoist critics as decadent and pornographic.

New "**revolutionary**" music, composed from the 1930s onwards, was generally march-like and optimistic, while in the wake of the Communist victory of 1949, the whole ethos of traditional music was challenged. Anything "feudal" or "superstitious" – which included a lot of traditional folk customs and music – was severely restricted, while Chinese melodies were "cleaned up" with the addition of rudimentary harmonies and bass lines. The Communist anthem "**The East is Red**", which began life as a folksong from the northern Shaanxi province, is symptomatic. Its local colour was ironed out as it was turned into a conventionally harmonized hymn-like tune. It was later adopted as the unofficial anthem of the Cultural Revolution, during which time musical life was driven underground, with only eight model operas and ballets permitted on stage.

The **conservatoire style** of **guoyue** (national music) was an artificial attempt to create a pan-Chinese style for the concert hall, with composed arrangements in a style akin to Western light music. There are still many conservatoire-style chamber groups – typically including *erhu* (fiddle), *dizi* (flute), *pipa* (lute) and *zheng* (zither) – playing evocatively titled pieces, some of which are newly composed. While the plaintive pieces for solo *erhu* by musicians such as **Liu Tianhua** and the blind beggar **Abing** (also a Daoist priest), or atmospheric tweetings on the *dizi*, have been much recorded by *guoyue* virtuosos like **Min Huifen** or **Lu Chunling** respectively, there is much more to

Chinese music than this. Folk music has a life of its own, and tends to follow the Confucian ideals of moderation and harmony, in which showy virtuosity is out of place.

The qin and solo traditions

The genuine solo traditions date back to the scholar-literati of imperial times, and live on in the conservatoires today, in pieces for the *pipa*, *zheng* and *qin*.

The **qin** (also known as *guqin*) is the most exalted of these instruments. A seven-string plucked zither, it is the most delicate and contemplative instrument in the Chinese palette. It's also the most accessible, producing expressive slides and ethereal harmonics. Modern traditions of the **pipa** (lute) and **zheng** (zither) derive from regional styles, transmitted from master to pupil, although "national" repertoires developed during the twentieth century. For the *zheng*, the northern styles of Henan and Shandong, and the southern Chaozhou and Hakka schools, are best known. The *pipa*, on the other hand, has thrived in the Shanghai region. It makes riveting listening, with its contrast between intimate "civil" pieces and the startlingly modern-sounding martial style of traditional pieces such as "Ambush from All Sides" (*shimian maifu*), with its frenetic percussive evocation of the sounds of battle.

The north: blowers and drummers

Classical traditions derived from the elite of imperial times live on today in **folk ensembles**, which are generally found in the north of the country. The most exciting examples are to be heard at **weddings** and **funerals**.

These occasions usually feature raucous **shawm** (a ubiquitous instrument in China, rather like a crude clarinet) and percussion groups called **chuigushou** – "blowers and drummers". While wedding bands naturally tend to use more jolly music, funerals may also feature lively pieces to entertain the guests. The blowers and drummers play not only lengthy and solemn suites but also the latest pop hits and theme tunes from TV and films. They milk the audience by sustaining notes, using circular breathing, playing even while dismantling and reassembling their *shawms*, or by balancing plates on sticks on the end of their instruments while playing.

Mentioned as far back as the tenth century BC, the **sheng** ranks among the oldest Chinese instruments. It comprises a group of bamboo pipes of different lengths bound in a circle and set in a wooden or metal base into which the player blows. Frequently used for ceremonial music, it adds an incisive rhythmic bite. Long and deafening strings of firecrackers are another inescapable part of village ceremony. Some processions are led by a Western-style brass band with a *shawm*-and-percussion group behind, competing in volume, oblivious of key. In northern villages, apart from the blowers and drummers, ritual **shengguan** ensembles are also common, with their exquisite combination of mouth organs and oboes, as well as darting flutes and the shimmering halo of the *yunluo* gong-frame, accompanied by percussion. Apart from this haunting melodic music, they perform some spectacular ritual percussion – the intricate arm movements of the cymbal players almost resemble martial arts.

Around Xi'an, groups performing similar wind and percussion music, misleadingly dubbed **Xi'an Drum Music** (**Xi'an guyue**), are active for temple festivals not only in the villages but also in the towns, especially in the sixth moon, around July. If you remember the tough *shawm* bands and haunting folksong of the film *Yellow Earth*, or the harsh falsetto narrative in *The Story of Qiuju*, go for the real thing among the barren hills of northern Shaanxi. This area is home to fantastic folk singers, local opera (such as the Qinqiang and Meihu styles), puppeteers, *shawm* bands and folk ritual specialists. Even *yangge* dancing, which in the towns is often a geriatric form of conga dancing, has a wild power here, again accompanied by *shawms* and percussion.

The south: silk and bamboo

In southeast China, the best-known instrumental music is that of **sizhu** ("silk and bamboo") ensembles, using flutes (of bamboo) and plucked and bowed strings (until recently of silk). More mellifluous than the outdoor wind bands of the north, these provide perhaps the most accessible Chinese folk music.

The most famous of the many regional styles is that of **Shanghai**, where enthusiasts get together in the afternoons, sit round a table and take it in turns to play a set with Chinese fiddles, flutes and banjos. The most celebrated meeting place is the teahouse in the **Chenghuang Miao** (see p.360), a picturesque two-storey structure on an island in the old quarter, where there are Monday-afternoon gatherings. The contrasting textures of plucked, bowed and blown sounds are part of the attraction of this music, each offering individual decorations to the gradually unfolding melody. Many pieces consist of successive decorations of a theme, beginning with the most ornate and accelerating as the decorations are gradually stripped down to a fast and bare final statement of the theme itself. Above the chinking of tea bowls and subdued chatter of the teahouse, enjoy the gradual unravelling of a piece like "Sanliu", or feel the exhilarating dash to the finish of "Xingjie", with its breathless syncopations.

Amateur *sizhu* clubs can be found throughout the lower Yangzi area, including Nanjing and Hangzhou. Although this music is secular and recreational in its urban form, the *sizhu* instrumentation originated in ritual ensembles and is still so used in the villages and temples of southern Jiangsu. In fact, amateur ritual associations exist all over southern China, as far afield as Yunnan, punctuating their ceremonies with sedate music reminiscent of the Shanghai teahouses, albeit often featuring the *yunluo* gong-frame of northern China.

Another fantastic area for folk music is the coastal region of **southern Fujian**, notably the cities of Quanzhou and Xiamen. Here you can find not only opera, ritual music and puppetry, but the haunting **nanguan ballads**. Popular all along the coast of southern Fujian, as in Taiwan across the strait, *nanguan* features a female singer accompanied by end-blown flute and plucked and bowed lutes. The ancient texts depict the sorrows of love, particularly of women, while the music is mostly stately and the delivery restrained yet anguished.

Still further south, the coastal regions of **Chaozhou** and **Shantou**, and the **Hakka** area (inland around Meixian and Dabu), also boast celebrated string ensembles that feature a high-pitched *erxian* (bowed fiddle) and *zheng* (plucked zither), as well as large and imposing ceremonial percussion bands, sometimes accompanied by shrill flutes.

The temples

All over China, particularly on the great religious mountains such as **Wutai Shan**, **Tai Shan**, **Qingcheng Shan**, **Wudang Shan** and **Putuo Shan**, temples are not just historical monuments but living sites of worship. Morning and evening services are held daily, and larger rituals on special occasions. The priests mainly perform vocal liturgy accompanied by percussion. They intone sung hymns with long melismas, alternating with chanted sections accompanied by the relentless and hypnotic beat of the woodblock.

Melodic instrumental music tends to be added when priests perform rituals outside the temples. These styles are more earthy and accessible even to ears unaccustomed to Chinese music. The Daoist priests from the Xuanmiao Guan in **Suzhou**, for example, perform wonderfully mellifluous pieces for silk-and-bamboo instruments, gutsy blasts on the *shawm*, music for spectacularly long trumpets, and a whole battery of percussion.

Opera and other vocal music

Chinese musical drama became overwhelmingly popular from the Yuan dynasty onwards. Of the several hundred types of regional opera, **Beijing Opera**, a rather late

CHINESE ROCK

Although often connected to the Hong Kong/Taiwanese entertainment industry, China's indigenous **rock** is a different beast, one which has its traditions in passionate and fiery protest, and which still possesses a cultural and political self-awareness. The rock scene was nonexistent in China until the mid-1980s, when foreign students on cultural exchange brought tapes of their favourite rock and pop music (and their own electric guitars) to the Chinese mainland, and shared them with their fellow students. Their music quickly caught the imagination of Chinese university youth and the urban vanguard.

Chinese **protest-rock** really began with singer-trumpeter-guitarist Cui Jian, who was influenced by the Taiwanese singer **Teresa Teng** (known to the Chinese by her original name, Deng Lijun; 1953–95). Teng's singing style can be directly traced to Zhou Xuan and 1930s Shanghai. Probably the most popular Chinese singer of her time, her recordings were circulated in China on the black market from the late 1970s onwards, when such music was officially banned.

A Beijinger born to parents of Korean descent, **Cui Jian** studied the trumpet at an early age, trained as a classical musician and joined the Beijing Symphony Orchestra in 1981. After being introduced to Anglo-American rock in the mid-1980s, however, he forged an independent path and his gritty voice became the primary reference point of Chinese rock. His love song "Nothing To My Name" became an anthem of the democracy movement, evoking a memorable complaint from General Wang Zhen, a veteran of the Long March: "What do you mean, you have nothing to your name? You've got the Communist Party, haven't you?"

Notable **1980s bands** that followed in Cui Jian's wake include Black Panther (*Hei Bao*) and Tang Dynasty, though their long hair and leathers were perhaps more influential than their soft rock. They were followed by Cobra, China's first all-female rock band, folk-rocker Zhang Chu, bad boy He Yong, Compass, Overload, and Breathing, among others. Unsigned, these bands would perform for very little money as part of vaudeville shows, until 1990, when China's first domestic full-scale rock concert took place. Six bands, including Tang Dynasty and Cobra, played at the Beijing Exhibition Centre Arena and were immediately signed by Japanese and Taiwanese labels, who then brought their music to the mainstream. They paved the way for home-grown labels such as Modern Sky, Scream, New Bees Records and Badhead, which now specialize in Chinese rock, hip-hop and alternative music.

The rock scene these days remains healthy, with hundreds of bands, and though it does centre heavily on **Beijing**, the **Shanghai** scene continues to grow apace. For visitors, it's well worth exploring, and surprisingly accessible, as most bands sing at least half of their songs in English. Acts to look out for include Sex Pistols wannabes Joyside; Shanghainese folk punk showmen Top Floor Circus; long-running ska punk outfit Brain Failure; and Joy Divisionistas, the Retros. For dance and electronica you can't beat Queen Sea Big Shark, Car Sick Cars are the indie shoegazers to catch, Beijing low-fi rockers Mr. Graceless are always worth a listen, while Snapline produce a fusion of post-punk and electronica. If you're tired of hearing Western-style music, hunt down the Mongolian folk stylings of Hanggai, or Xiban's quirky mix of Beijing opera, Tibetan mantras and good old rock.

To immerse yourself fully in the scene, visit Beijing's annual three-day **Midi Festival** in July – see Ⓦ www.midifestival.com for current information.

---

hybrid form dating from the eighteenth century, is the most widely known – now heard throughout China, it's the closest thing to a "national" theatre. Many librettos now performed date back to the seventeenth century and describe the intrigues of emperors and gods, as well as love stories and comedy. Northern "clapper operas" (*bangzi xi*), named after the high-pitched woodblock that insistently runs through them, are earthy in flavour – for example, the "Qinqiang" of Shaanxi province. **Sichuan opera** is remarkable for its female chorus. **Ritual masked opera** may be performed in the countryside of Yunnan, Anhui and Guizhou. Chaozhou and Fujian also have beautiful ancient styles of opera: **Pingju** and **Huangmei Xi** are genteel in style, while **Cantonese opera** is funkier. If you're looking for more music and less acrobatics, try to seek out the classical but now rare **Kunqu**, often accompanied by the sweet-toned *qudi* flute. There are also some beautiful **puppet operas**, often performed for ritual events; Quanzhou in Fujian boasts a celebrated marionette troupe, and other likely areas include northern Shaanxi and the Tangshan and Laoting areas of eastern Hebei.

While Chinese opera makes a great visual spectacle, musically it is frankly an acquired taste, resembling to the uninitiated the din of cats fighting in a blazing firework factory. The singing style is tense, guttural and high-pitched, while the music is dominated by the bowed string accompaniment of the *jinghu*, a sort of sawn-off *erhu*. It also features plucked lutes, flutes and – for transitional points – a piercing *shawm*. The action is driven by percussion, with drum and clappers leading an ensemble of gongs and cymbals in an assortment of set patterns. Professional opera troupes exist in the major towns, but rural opera performances, which are given for temple fairs and even weddings, tend to be livelier. Even in Beijing you may come across groups of old folk meeting in parks to go through their favourite Beijing Opera excerpts.

Narrative-singing also features long classical stories. You may find a teahouse full of old people following these story-songs avidly, particularly in Sichuan, where one popular style is accompanied by the *yangqin* (dulcimer). In Beijing, or more often in Tianjin, amateurs sing through traditional *jingyun dagu* ballads, accompanied by drum and *sanxian* banjo. In Suzhou, *pingtan*, also accompanied by a plucked lute, is a beautiful genre.

Film

Film came early to China. The first moving picture was exhibited in 1896 at a "teahouse variety show" in Shanghai, where the country's first cinema was built just twelve years later. By the 1930s, cinema was playing an important role in the cultural life of Shanghai, though the huge number of resident foreigners ensured a largely Western diet of films. Nevertheless, local Chinese films were also being made, mainly by the so-called May Fourth intellectuals (middle-class liberals inspired by the uprising of May 4, 1919), who wanted to modernize China along Western lines. Naturally, Western influence on these films was strong, and they have little to do with the highly stylized, formal world of traditional performance arts such as Beijing Opera or shadow-puppet theatre. Early film showings often employed a "storyteller", who sat near the screen reading out the titles for the benefit of those who could not read.

The Shanghai studios

Of the handful of important **studios** in Shanghai operating in the 1920s and 1930s, the most famous was the **Mingxing**, whose films were left-leaning and anti-imperialist. *Sister Flower* (1933) tells the story of twin sisters separated at birth, one of whom ends up a city girl living in Shanghai, while the other remains a poor villager. Another film from the same year, *Spring Silk Worm*, portrays economic decline and hardship in Zhejiang province, and levels the finger of accusation at Japanese imperialism. Finally, *The Goddess* (1934), from the **Lianhua** studio, depicts the struggle of a prostitute to have her son educated. The improbably glamorous prostitute was played by China's own Garbo, the languorous Ruan Lingyu. Despite the liberal pretensions of these films, it was inevitable – given that audiences comprised a tiny elite – that they would later be derided by the Communists as bourgeois.

When the **Japanese occupied** Shanghai in 1937, "subversive" studios such as the Mingxing and Lianhua were immediately closed, and much of the film-making talent fled into the interior. The experience of war put film-makers in touch with their potential future audiences, the Chinese masses. China's great wartime epic, **Spring River Flows East** (1947–48), was the cinematic result of this experience. The story spans the duration of the anti-Japanese war – and the ensuing civil war – through the lives of a single family torn apart by the conflict. The heroine, living in poverty, contrasts with her husband, who has abandoned his wife for a decadent existence in Shanghai. Traumatized by a decade of war, the Chinese who saw this film appreciated it as an authentic account of the sufferings through which the nation had lived. Over 750,000 people saw the film at its release, a remarkable figure given that the country was still at war.

Communism and the cinema

The story of Chinese film-making under the **Communists** really dates back to 1938, when Mao Zedong and his fellow Long Marchers set up their base in **Yan'an**. No world could have been further removed from the glamour of Shanghai than this dusty, poverty-stricken town, but it was the ideal location for the film-makers of the future

People's Republic to learn their skills. Talent escaping through Japanese lines trickled through in search of employment, among them the actress **Jiang Qing**, later to become Mao's wife and self-appointed empress of Chinese culture. One thing upon which all the leading Communists in Yan'an were agreed was the importance of film as a **centralizing medium**, which could be used to unify the culture of the nation after the war had been won.

The immediate consequence of the Communist victory in 1949 was that the showing of foreign films was curtailed, and the private Shanghai studios wound down. A **Film Guidance committee** was set up to decide upon film output for the entire nation. The first major socialist epic, **Bridge**, appeared in 1949, depicting the mass mobilization of workers rushing enthusiastically to construct a bridge in record time. Although predictably dull in terms of character and plot, the cast still contained a number of prewar Shanghai actors to divert audiences. At the end of the film the entire cast gathers to shout "Long live Chairman Mao!", a scene that was to be re-enacted time and again in the coming years.

A year after *Bridge*, one of the very last non-government Shanghai studio films appeared, **The Life of Wu Xun**, a huge project that had started well before 1949, and, surprisingly, was allowed to run to completion. Its subject was the famous nineteenth-century entrepreneur, Wu Xun, who started out as a beggar and rose to enormous riches, whereupon he set out on his lifetime's ambition to educate the peasantry. Despite the addition of a narrator's voice at the end of the film, pointing out that it was revolution and not education that peasants needed, the film was a disaster for the Shanghai film industry. Mao wrote a damning critique of it for idolizing a "Qing landlord", and a campaign was launched against the legacy of the entire Shanghai film world – studios, actors, critics and audiences alike.

The remains of the May Fourth movement struggled on. The consolation for the old guard was that newer generations of Chinese film-makers had not yet solved the problem of how to portray life in the contemporary era. The 1952 screen adaptation of Lao She's short story *Dragon's Beard Ditch*, for example, was supposed to contrast the miserable pre-1949 life of a poor district of Beijing with the prosperous life that was being lived under the Communists. The only problem, as audiences could immediately see, was that the supposedly miserable pre-1949 scenes actually looked a good deal more heart-warming than the later ones.

Nevertheless, the Communists did achieve some of their original targets during the **1950s**. The promotion of a universal culture and language was one of them. All characters in all films – from Tibetans to Mongolians to Cantonese – were depicted as speaking in flawless **Mandarin Chinese**. Above all, there was an explosion in audiences, from around 47 million tickets sold in 1949, to 600 million in 1956, to over 4 billion in 1959. The latter figure should be understood in the context of the madness surrounding the Great Leap Forward, a time of crazed overproduction in all fields, film included. Film studios sprouted in every town in China, though with a catastrophic loss of quality – a typical studio in Jiangxi province comprised one man, his bicycle and an antique stills camera. The colossal output of that year included uninspiring titles such as *Loving the Factory as One's Home*.

The conspicuous failure of the Great Leap Forward did, however, bring certain short-lived advantages to the film industry. While Mao was forced temporarily into the political sidelines during the late 1950s, the cultural bureaucrats signalled that in addition to "revolutionary realism", a certain degree of "**revolutionary romanticism**" was to be encouraged. Chinese themes and subjects, as opposed to pure Marxism, were looked upon with more favour. A slight blossoming occurred, with improbable films such as *Lin Zexu* (1959), which covered the life of the great Qing-dynasty official who stood up to the British at the time of the Opium Wars. There was even a tentative branching out into comedy, with the film *What's Eating You?* based on the relatively un-socialist antics of a Suzhou waiter. Unusually, the film featured local dialects, as well as a faintly detectable parody of the government's campaign to encourage greater sacrifices by promoting the mythical hero worker Lei Feng.

The Cultural Revolution

Sadly, this bright period came to a swift end in 1966 with the **Cultural Revolution**. No interesting work was made in China for nearly fifteen years – indeed, no film was produced anywhere in the whole country between 1966 and 1970. The few films that did subsequently appear before Mao's death were made under the personal supervision of Jiang Qing, and all were on the revolutionary model, a kind of ballet with flag waving. Attendance at these dreadful films was virtually **compulsory** for people who did not wish to be denounced for a lack of revolutionary zeal. Ironically, Jiang Qing herself was a big fan of Hollywood productions, which she would watch in secret.

Recovery from the trauma of the Cultural Revolution was bound to take time, but the years 1979 and 1980 saw a small crop of films attempting to assess the horror through which the country had just lived. The best known, *The Legend of Tianyun Mountain*, made in Shanghai in 1980, featured two men, one of whom had denounced the other for "Rightism" in 1958. The subsequent story is one of guilt, love, emotions and human relationships, all subjects that had been banned during the Cultural Revolution. Understandably, the film was an enormous popular success, though before audiences had time to get too carried away, a subsequent film, *Unrequited Love* (1981), was officially criticized for blurring too many issues.

Modern cinema

In **1984** the Chinese film industry was suddenly brought to international attention for the first time by the arrival of the so-called "**fifth generation**" of Chinese film-makers. That year, director **Chen Kaige** and his cameraman **Zhang Yimou**, both graduates from the first post-Cultural Revolution class (1982) of the Beijing Film School, made the superb art-house film **Yellow Earth**. The film was not particularly well received in China, either by audiences, who expected something more modern, or by the authorities, who expected something more optimistic. Nevertheless, it set the pattern for a series of increasingly overseas-funded (and overseas-watched) films comprising stunning images of a "traditional" China, irritating the censors at home and delighting audiences abroad.

Chen Kaige's protégé Zhang Yimou was soon stealing a march on his former boss with his first film **Red Sorghum**. This film was not only beautiful, and reassuringly patriotic, but it also introduced the world to heart-throb actress **Gong Li**. Zhang and Gong worked together on a string of hits, including *Judou*, *The Story of Qiu Ju*, *Raise the Red Lantern*, *Shanghai Triad* and *To Live*. None of these could be described as art-house in the way that *Yellow Earth* had been, and the potent mix of Gong Li's sexuality and figure-hugging dresses with exotic, mysterious locations in 1930s China was clearly targeted at Western rather than Chinese audiences.

Zhang Yimou has since been warmly embraced by the authorities, though his films have become worse. His most recent Hollywood-friendly martial-arts spectaculars **Hero** (2002), **The House of Flying Daggers** (2004) and **Curse of the Golden Flower** (2007) are commercial successes, and beautifully shot, but they are shallow and soulless.

Contemporary realism

The best Chinese films of the modern age are those that have turned their back on the frigid perfection on offer from Zhang Yimou and are raw, gritty reflections of Chinese life. Inevitably, the fifth generation was followed by a sixth, which produced **underground movies**, generally shot in black-and-white, depicting what they consider to be the true story of contemporary China – ugly cities, cold flats, broken and depressed people. **Beijing Bastards** (1993) is a good example. Many of the finest modern movies turn a baleful eye on the recent past - see **Lei Feng is Gone** (1997), **In the Heat of the Sun** (1995) and **Devils at the Doorstep** (2000).

Many recent films are simply too controversial for domestic release, but if they garner attention abroad they then become available at home as DVDs – see the box below for a selection to look out for.

MAINLAND MOVIES ON DVD

★ **24 City** (2009). Film by Chollywood bad-boy Jia Zhangke, following three generations of a Chengdu family as their factory closes down, and gives way to a modern apartment complex. Very well received by international critics.

Beijing Bastards (1993). A story of apathetic, fast-living youths, this was one of China's first independently produced films; it stars rock singer and rebel Cui Jian, who is depicted drinking, swearing and playing the guitar.

Beijing Bicycle (2001). Told in a social-realist aesthetic, this is the story of a lad trying to get his stolen bike back – a lot more interesting than it may sound.

★ **Blind Shaft** (2003). Sharply directed by Yang Li, this is about two coal miners who kill colleagues, make it look like an accident, then collect the mine owner's hush money. As well as a telling indictment of runaway capitalism, it's a great piece of film noir.

Cell Phone (2003). Perhaps the most successful work of Feng Xiaogang, one of China's most revered directors, this satirical comedy revolves around two men having affairs.

Devils on the Doorstep (2000). Set during the anti-Japanese war, this black farce concerns a group of peasants who get a couple of hostages dumped on their farm by the local Communists. It was banned in China, having failed to demonize the Japanese.

★ **Farewell My Concubine** (1994). Chen Kaige's superb summation of modern Chinese history, although the main protagonist – a homosexual Chinese opera singer – is hardly typical of modern China.

Ke Ke Xi Li (2004). Chuan Lu's hard-boiled true story about a volunteer gang fighting against ruthless antelope poachers on the high Tibetan plateau. It was filmed using non-professional local actors and has the feel of a western, but is entirely unsentimental.

Lei Feng is Gone (1997). Based on the true story of the man who accidentally killed the iconic hero of Maoist China, the soldier Lei Feng. The potent personal story also works as a metaphor for the state of the nation.

Let the Bullets Fly (2010). A Chinese "Noodle" Western starring Chow Yun-fat and set in 1920s Sichuan; it broke all sorts of box-office records on release.

★ **Raise the Red Lantern** (1991). Beautifully-shot Gong Li vehicle set in the 1920s, and directed by Zhang Yimou. This time she plays the concubine of a wealthy businessman, vying for his affection with her fellow mistresses.

Red Sorghum (1987). Set in a remote wine-producing village of northern China at the time of the Japanese invasion, this film was based on parts of *The Red Sorghum Clan*, a novel which contributed heavily towards writer Mo Yan's 2012 Nobel prize.

Still Life (2007). Extremely controversial Jia Zhangke film about the search for people who have gone missing in the mass displacements caused by the Three Gorges Dam project.

To Live (1994). One of Zhang Yimou's most powerful films, this follows the fortunes of a family from "liberation" to the Great Leap Forward and the Cultural Revolution.

Tuya's Marriage (2006). Wang Quan'an employed non-professional actors and grand scenery to great effect with this story of a Mongolian herdswoman's search for a new husband. Like much good contemporary Chinese art of all genres, its subject is people struggling to cope with vast social change.

The World (2004). Jia Zhangke film set in a world culture theme park in Beijing, where the workers squabble and fail to communicate against a backdrop of tiny replicas of internationally famous monuments.

Xiao Wu (1997). Too controversial for domestic release, this Jia Zhangke film is the intimate portrayal of a pickpocket whose life is falling apart.

Yellow Earth (1984). The story of a soldier who travels north from Yan'an, tasked with rewriting local folk songs with Communist lyrics. Still shots predominate, recalling traditional Chinese scroll painting, with giant landscapes framed by hills and the distant Yellow River.

Hong Kong

The movies that have the least difficulty with the Chinese censors are those produced in **Hong Kong**, the world's fourth-largest movie producer behind India, the US and Nigeria. Its popular appeal is made easier by the content: generally easy-to-digest romances, comedies or high-speed action, with little interest in deeper meanings or the outside world – and certainly not in politics.

World interest in Hong Kong's film industry dates back to 1970s martial-arts legend **Bruce Lee**. Although Lee was better known overseas for the Hollywood-financed *Enter the Dragon* (1973), the success in Hong Kong of his earlier films *Fist of Fury* and *The Big Boss* launched a domestic **kung-fu movie boom**, off the back of which sprang **Jackie Chan** and a much-needed element of slapstick comedy – best seen in Chan's early works, such as *Drunken Master* (1978). As the genre faltered in the 1980s, directors mixed in a supernatural aspect, pioneered by **Tsui Hark** in *Zu: Warriors from the Magic Mountain* (1983) and *Chinese Ghost Story* (1987). The kung-fu genre was later revived by director **Stephen Chow**, whose *Kung Fu Hustle* (2004) sported uniquely surreal humour and visuals, and **Wilson Yip**'s fictionalized biopic of Bruce Lee's teacher, *Ip Man* (2008).

Martial arts remain an inevitable component of Hong Kong's modern **action movies** and **police thrillers**. This genre can largely be attributed to **John Woo**'s influential hits *A Better Tomorrow* (1986) and *Hard Boiled* (1992), which feature Chow Yun Fat shooting his way through relentless scenes of orchestrated violence. Woo's many imitators have mostly succeeded only in making pointless, bloody movies whose plots inevitably conclude with the massacre of the entire cast, though above-average efforts such as *Infernal Affairs* (2002; remade in the US as *The Departed*) at least add a little depth to the heroes' moody characters.

At present, Hong Kong's only director interested in anything but light entertainment is **Wong Karwai**, whose early works such as *Chungking Express* (1994) and *Fallen Angels* (1995) depict Hong Kong as a crowded, disjointed city where people, though forced together, seem unable to communicate. His subsequent films added a European sense of style, which worked in the sensuous *In the Mood for Love* (2000) but overwhelmed the plot in the obscure, self-referential *2046* (2004). His most recent film, *The Grandmaster* (2013) – another martial-arts epic – was a box-office hit but divided the critics.

Books

The last few years have seen a glut of excellent writing coming out of China, from Western commentators' views on current economic and social upheavals, to translated journalism and popular novels, and often eccentric – or jaundiced – expat memoirs. Classics aside, few of the titles below are available in China (though you might get lucky in Hong Kong), so it's best to locate them before your trip.

HISTORY

Patricia Ebrey *Cambridge Illustrated History of China*. An up-to-date, easy-going historical overview, excellently illustrated and clearly written.

Peter Fleming *The Siege at Peking*. An account of the events that led up to June 20, 1900, when the foreign legations in Beijing were attacked by the Boxers and Chinese imperial troops. The 55-day siege marked a watershed in China's relations with the rest of the world.

Paul French *Midnight in Peking*. A real-life murder mystery, revolving around the search for the killer of Pamela Warner, an English girl whose body was found in Beijing, minus its heart and blood, in 1937.

Jacques Gernet *Daily Life in China on the Eve of the Mongol Invasion 1250–1276*. Based on assorted Chinese sources, this is a fascinating survey of southern China under the Song, focusing on the capital, Hangzhou, then the largest and richest city in the world. Gernet also deals with the daily lives of a cross section of society, from peasant to leisured gentry, covering everything from cookery to death.

★ **Larry Gonick** *The Cartoon History of the Universe vols II and III*. A masterwork setting world history in cartoon format, full of verve, great visuals and awful puns, but also accurate – the bibliography shows how much research has gone into this manic project. About the only textbook that attempts to set Chinese history in a world context.

★ **Peter Hopkirk** *Foreign Devils on the Silk Road* and *The Great Game*. *Foreign Devils* is the story of the machinations of the various international booty-hunters who operated in Turkestan and the Gobi Desert during the early twentieth century – essential for an appreciation of China's northwest regions. *The Great Game* is a hugely entertaining account of the nineteenth-century struggle between Britain and Russia for control of Central Asia. In tracing the roots of the Chinese occupations of Tibet and Xinjiang, and also detailing the invariable consequences for foreign powers who meddle with Afghanistan, it's also disturbingly topical.

Ann Paludan *Chronicle of the Chinese Emperors*. Lively stories on the lives of all 157 of those strangest of characters, the Chinese emperors. Well illustrated and a good starting point for getting to grips with Chinese history.

Sima Qian *Historical Records* aka *Records of the Historian*. Written by the Han-dynasty court historian, *Records* is a masterpiece, using contemporary court documents and oral tradition to illuminate key characters – everyone from emperors to famous con men – from early Chinese history. Although long discredited, Sima Qian's accounts have now been partially corroborated by recent archeology.

Edgar Snow *Red Star Over China*. The definitive first-hand account of the early days of Mao and the Communist "bandits", written in 1936 after Snow, an American journalist, wriggled through the Guomindang blockade and spent months at the Red base in Yan'an.

★ **Jonathan Spence** *The Gate of Heavenly Peace*, *The Search for Modern China*. The first of these traces the history of twentieth-century China through the eyes of the men and women caught up in it – writers, revolutionaries, poets and politicians – and is among the best books for getting to grips with China's complex modern history. Though quite hard for a straight-through read, *The Search for Modern China* is authoritative and probably the best overall history of China available.

Susan Whitfield *Life Along the Silk Road*. Using archeological remains and historical sources, Whitfield creates ten fictional characters to illustrate life in northwestern China during its tenth-century Buddhist heyday.

TIBET

John Avedon *In Exile From the Land of Snows*. A detailed and moving account of modern Tibetan history, covering both those who remained in the country and those who fled into exile. Required reading for anyone contemplating a trip.

Edmund Candler *The Unveiling of Lhasa*. China was not the first country to invade Tibet: in 1904, a British military expedition marched on Lhasa, using modern machine guns against the peasant armies sent to stop them. Candler, a journalist embedded with the expedition, paints an honest and ultimately disillusioned picture of the events, which were to open the country up to colonization.

Victor Chan *Tibet Handbook: a Pilgrimage Guide*. A hugely detailed guide to Tibet's pilgrimage sites and treks, and how to reach them. Absolutely essential if you're considering a trek.

Graham Coleman (ed) *A Handbook of Tibetan Culture: a Guide to Tibetan Centres and Resources Throughout the World*. The subtitle says it all; the book exhaustively documents cultural organizations, teaching centres and libraries across the globe that have a Tibetan focus. It also includes biographies of major Tibetan lamas, brief histories of the major schools of Tibetan Buddhism and an illustrated glossary.

Jonanthan Green *Murder in the High Himalaya*. In 2008 a Romanian mountain climber filmed border guards shooting down fleeing Tibetans in cold blood. This sad but gripping telling of the story gives equal weight to both refugees and climbers in one of the few good reads to come out of the tragedy of modern Tibet.

★ **Heinrich Harrer** *Seven Years in Tibet*. A classic account of a remarkable journey to reach Lhasa and of the years there prior to the Chinese invasion, when Harrer was tutor to the Fourteenth Dalai Lama.

Isabel Hilton *The Search for the Panchen Lama*. The whole sorry story of the search for the Eleventh Panchen Lama, and how the Tibetans' choice ended up as the world's youngest political prisoner (see p.898).

Thubten Jigme and Colin Turnbull *Tibet, Its History, Religion and People*. The best account around of the traditional everyday lives of the Tibetan people, co-authored by the brother of the Fourteenth Dalai Lama.

CULTURE AND SOCIETY

★ **Jasper Becker** *The Chinese*. An incisive portrait of modern China at both government and individual level by one of the great Sinologists. Becker draws intriguing parallels between modern rulers and ancient emperors. His latest book, *The City of Heavenly Tranquility*, is an excellent look at Beijing's history, and a condemnation of its rapid destruction.

David Bonavia *The Chinese: a Portrait*. A highly readable introduction to contemporary China, focusing on the human aspects as a balance to the socio-political trends.

Ian Buruma *Bad Elements*. Interviews with dissident exiles abroad tell an (inevitably anti-government) story of modern China.

Gordon Chang *The Coming Collapse of China*. A detailed and well-informed overview of what's wrong with contemporary Chinese society by an influential prophet of doom – though his thesis, that a popular revolution will eventually destroy the Communist Party, is overstretched.

Leslie T. Chang *Factory Girls*. This tells the personal stories of a couple of migrant workers, giving the story of wrenching change and development in modern China a human face. Good for general readers.

Chen Guidi and Wu Chuntao *Will the Boat Sink the Water?*. Modern China was founded to improve the lot of its peasant majority, but the journalist authors show how – and how badly – the country's officials are failing them. Banned in China, it reputedly sold ten million copies on the black market.

Tim Glissold *Mr China*. The eye-opening story of how the author went to China to make a fortune and instead lost US$400 million. A great first-person account of the eccentric Chinese business environment, and a must for anyone thinking of investing there.

Alexandra Harney *The China Price*. This powerful exposé of the true environmental and social costs of manufacturing in China makes a compelling, if uncomfortable, read, especially for anyone thinking of outsourcing production.

★ **Duncan Hewitt** *Getting Rich First*. Written by a long-term foreign resident and journalist, this excellent book moves beyond commonplace Western views of China – all dynastic history, Cultural Revolution and economic boom – with an informed look at the major social themes shaping the nation.

Jen Lin-Liu *Serve the People*. Equal parts travelogue and cook book, which tries to understand the Chinese by heading in through the stomach. Light, witty and entertaining.

Joe Studwell *The China Dream*. Mandatory reading for foreign businesspeople in China, this is a cautionary tale, written in layman's terms, debunking the myth that there's easy money to be made from China's vast markets. A great read for anyone interested in business, economics or human greed.

Robert Temple *The Genius of China*. Condensed from Joseph Needham's epic work *Science and Civilization in China*, this thoroughly illustrated compendium covers hundreds of important Chinese inventions through the ages – though the text does browbeat readers over how little credit the West gives China's creative talent.

Xinran *The Good Women of China*. Tales of the struggles of Chinese women; their stories are heart-warming, though the editor, a Beijing journalist, seems smug and self-obsessed.

Lin Yutang *My Country and My People*. An expatriate Chinese scholar writes for Western audiences in the 1930s about what it means to be Chinese. Obviously dated in parts, but overall remarkably fresh and accessible.

★ **Zhang Xinxin and Sang Ye** *Chinese Lives*. This Studs Terkel-like series of first-person narratives from interviews with a broad range of Chinese people is both readable and informative, full of fascinating details of day-to-day existence that you won't read anywhere else.

TRAVEL WRITING

Mildred Cable with Francesca French *The Gobi Desert*. Cable and French were missionaries with the China Inland Mission in the early part of the twentieth century. *The Gobi Desert* is a poetic description of their life and travels in Gansu and Xinjiang, without the sanctimonious and patronizing tone adopted by some of their contemporary missionaries.

Austin Coates *Myself a Mandarin*. Despite dated views and the changing times, this humorous account of the author's time as a Hong Kong magistrate during the 1950s still rings true.

★ **Rachel DeWoskin** *Foreign Babes in Beijing*. Wry, witty snapshot of 1990s Beijing as a place of untested, unexpected opportunities: the author arrives to manage a PR firm and ends up as a bohemian soap-opera star.

Peter Fleming *One's Company: a Journey to China* and *News from Tartary*. The former is an amusing account of a journey through Russia and Manchuria to China in the 1930s. En route, Peter Fleming (brother of Ian) encounters a wild assortment of Chinese and Japanese officials, and the puppet emperor Henry Pu Yi himself. *News from Tartary* records an epic journey of 5600km across the roof of the world to Kashmir in 1935.

Rob Gifford *China Road: a Journey Into the Future of a Rising Power*. An interesting look into China's future, from the eyes of a traveller on Route 312 – China's own Route 66, which zips from the eastern seaboard to the Gobi Desert.

Peter Hessler *River Town – Two Years on the Yangtze*. One of the best of the mini-genre "how I taught English for a couple of years in China and survived". The book accepts China's positive aspects and avoids cynicism when dealing with social problems and contradictions.

Somerset Maugham *On a Chinese Screen*. Brief, sometimes humorous, and often biting sketches of the European missionaries, diplomats and businessmen whom Maugham encountered in China between 1919 and 1921; worth reading for background detail.

★ **Matthew Polly** *American Shaolin*. A stereotypical weakling, Polly dropped out of a US college to spend two years studying kung fu at the legendary Shaolin temple. Not just the macho romp you'd expect, the book is self-deprecating, funny and steers clear of cultural cringe.

Marco Polo *The Travels*. Said to have inspired Columbus, *The Travels* is a fantastic read, full of amazing details picked up during Polo's 26 years of wandering in Asia between Venice and the court of Kublai Khan. It's not, however, a coherent history, having been ghost-written by a novelist from Marco's notes.

Vikram Seth *From Heaven Lake: Travels through Sinkiang and Tibet*. A student for two years at Nanjing University, Seth set out in 1982 to return home to Delhi via Tibet and Nepal. This account of how he hitched his way through four provinces – Xinjiang, Gansu, Qinghai and Tibet – is in the finest tradition of the early travel books.

Colin Thubron *Behind the Wall*. A thoughtful and superbly poetic description of an extensive journey through China just after it opened up in the early 1980s. The single best piece of travel writing to have come out of modern China.

GUIDES AND REFERENCE BOOKS

Kit Chow and Ione Kramer *All the Tea in China*. Everything you need to know about Chinese teas, from variations in growing and processing techniques to a rundown of fifty of the most famous brews. Good fun and nicely illustrated.

Mackinnon, Showler and Phillipps *A Field Guide to the Birds of China*. By far the best book on the subject, with over 1300 species illustrated (mostly in colour), plus outline text descriptions and distribution maps.

Jessica Rawson *Ancient China: Art and Archaeology*. By an oriental antiquities specialist at the British Museum, this scholarly introduction to Chinese art puts the subject in historical context. Beginning in Neolithic times, the book explores the technology and social organization that shaped its development up to the Han dynasty.

George Schaller *Wildlife of the Tibetan Steppe*. Reference book on the mammals – especially the rare Tibetan antelope – that inhabit the inhospitable Chang Tang region, by a zoologist who spent over thirty years studying China's wildlife.

Karen Smith *Nine Lives: Birth of Avant-Garde Art in New China*. Explores the development of the Chinese contemporary art scene through dense studies of nine of its founders and key players.

Mary Tregear *Chinese Art*. An authoritative, clearly written and well-illustrated summary of the main strands in Chinese art from Neolithic times, through the Bronze Age and up to the twentieth century.

COOKERY

★ **Fuchsia Dunlop** *Sichuan Cookery*. The best available English-language cookbook on Chinese cuisine, from a talented writer who spent three years honing her skills at a Chengdu cookery school. Dishes smell, look and taste exactly as you find them in Sichuan.

⭐ **Hsiang Ju Lin and Tsuifeng Lin** *Chinese Gastronomy*. A classic work, relatively short on recipes but strong on cooking methods and philosophy – essential reading for anyone serious about learning the finer details of Chinese cooking. Wavers in and out of print, sometimes under different titles; look for Lin as the author name.

Kenneth Lo *Chinese Food*. Good general-purpose cookbook covering a wide range of methods and styles, from Westernized dishes to regional specialities.

Wei Chuan Cultural Education Foundation *Vegetarian Cooking* and *Chinese Dim Sum*. Two in a series of excellent, easy-to-follow cookbooks published by the Taiwanese Wei Chuan cooking school; simplified versions of classic dishes that produce good results. Not available in China, but easy enough to find in major bookshops in the West.

RELIGION AND PHILOSOPHY

⭐ *Asiapac* series. These entertaining titles, available in Hong Kong and Beijing, present ancient Chinese philosophy in comic-book format, making it accessible without losing its complexity. Particularly good are the *Book of Zen*, a collection of stories and parables, and the *Sayings of Confucius*.

Kenneth Chen *Buddhism in China*. Very helpful for tracing the origin of Buddhist thought in China, the development of its many different schools and the four-way traffic of influence between India, Tibet, Japan and China.

⭐ **Chuang Tzu** *The Book of Chuang Tzu*. Wonderful Taoist parables, written in antiquity by a philosopher who clearly had a keen sense of humour and a delight in life's very inexplicability.

Confucius *The Analects*. Good modern translation of this classic text, a collection of Confucius's teachings focusing on morality and the state.

Lao Zi *Tao Te Ching*. The collection of mystical thoughts and philosophical speculation that form the basis of Taoist philosophy.

Arthur Waley *Three Ways of Thought in Ancient China*. Translated extracts from the writings of three of the early philosophers – Zhuang Zi, Mencius and Han Feizi. A useful introduction.

BIOGRAPHIES AND AUTOBIOGRAPHIES

Anchee Min *Red Azalea*. Half-autobiography, half-novel, this beautifully written book is an unusually personal and highly romantic account of surviving the Cultural Revolution.

Dalai Lama *Freedom in Exile*. The autobiography of the charismatic, Nobel Prize-winning Fourteenth Dalai Lama.

Jung Chang *Wild Swans*. Enormously popular in the West, this three-generation family saga was banned in China for its honest account of the horrors of life in turbulent twentieth-century China. As well as being a good read, it serves as an excellent introduction to modern Chinese history.

⭐ **Ma Jian** *Red Dust*. Facing arrest for spiritual pollution, writer and artist Ma Jian fled Beijing to travel around China's remotest corners in the 1980s, often in extreme poverty. This picaresque tale of China in the first phase of its opening up is told in lively prose and offers the kind of insights only an alienated insider could garner.

John Man *Genghis Khan*. Lively and readable biography of the illiterate nomad who built the biggest empire the world has ever seen, intercut with Man's travels to Mongolia and China to find his tomb.

Naisingoro Pu Yi *From Emperor to Citizen*. The autobiography of the young boy who was born into the Qing imperial family and chosen by the Japanese to become the puppet emperor of the state of Manchukuo in 1931.

Philip Short *Mao: a Life*. Despite its length, an extremely readable account of Mao and his times – even if the Great Helmsman's ideologies are becoming ever less relevant in contemporary China.

⭐ **Hugh Trevor-Roper** *Hermit of Peking: the Hidden Life of Sir Edmund Backhouse*. Intrigued by Backhouse's thoroughly obscene memoirs, Trevor-Roper used external sources to uncover the facts behind the extraordinarily convoluted life of Edmund Backhouse – Chinese scholar, eccentric recluse and phenomenal liar – who lived in Beijing from the late nineteenth century until his death in 1944.

Marina Warner *The Dragon Empress*. An exploration of the life of Cixi, one of only two female rulers of China, that lays bare the complex personality whose conservatism, passion for power, vanity and greed had such a great impact on the events that culminated in the collapse of the imperial ruling house and the founding of the republic.

LITERATURE

MODERN WRITING

JG Ballard *Empire of the Sun*. This, the best literary evocation of old Shanghai, is a compelling tale of how the gilded life of expat Shanghai collapsed into chaos with the onset of war, based on the author's own experience growing up in a Japanese internment camp. It was made into a pretty decent film by Steven Spielberg.

⭐ **Pearl S. Buck** *The Good Earth*. The best story from a writer who grew up in China during the early twentieth century, *The Good Earth* follows the fortunes of the peasant Wang Lung from his wedding day to his dotage, as he struggles to hold onto his land for his family through a series of social upheavals.

Louis Cha *The Book and the Sword*. Northwestern China

becomes a battleground for secret societies, evil henchmen, Muslim warlords and sword-wielding Taoists as a quest to save a valuable copy of the Quran uncovers a secret that threatens to topple the Qing emperor. Written in the 1950s by China's foremost martial-arts novelist, it has inspired numerous films and TV shows.

Chen Yuanbin *The Story of Qiuju*. A collection of four tales, of which the title story, about a peasant woman pushing for justice after her husband is assaulted by the village chief, was made into a film by award-winning director Zhang Yimou.

Chun Sue *Beijing Doll*. A rambling *roman à clef* about a confused teenage girl who has unsatisfactory sexual encounters with preening rock-and-rollers – it has to be said, if it wasn't China it wouldn't be interesting.

Robert Van Gulik *The Judge Dee Mysteries*. Sherlock Holmes-style detective stories set in the Tang dynasty and starring the wily Judge Dee, who gets tough on crime as detective, judge and jury. Recommended are *The Red Pavilion*, *Murder in Canton* and *The Chinese Nail Murders*. Fun, informative and unusual.

Guo Xiaolu *A Chinese English Dictionary for Lovers*. A Chinese girl's journey of self-discovery when she comes to London, this is a bright, lively book, daringly written in Chinglish.

James Hilton *Lost Horizon*. The classic 1930s novel of longevity in a secret Tibetan valley, which gave the world – and the Chinese tourist industry – the myth of Shangri-La.

Lao She *Rickshaw Boy*. Lao She was driven to suicide during the Cultural Revolution for his belief that all politics were inherently unjust. The story is a haunting account of a young rickshaw-puller in pre-1949 Beijing.

Lu Xun *The True Story of Ah Q*. Widely read in China today, Lu Xun is regarded as the father of modern Chinese writing. Ah Q is one of his best tales, short, allegorical and cynical, about a simpleton who is swept up in the 1911 revolution.

Mian Mian *Candy*. This louche tale of self-destruction, drugs, sex and navel-gazing garnered its colourful Shanghai authoress a reputation as China's foremost literary wild child – it helped, of course, that it was banned.

★ **Mo Yan** *The Red Sorghum Clan*, *The Garlic Ballads*. China's only winner of the Nobel Prize for literature, Mo Yan (whose name, meaning "don't speak", says volumes about how popular he is with the regime) is most famed for *The Garlic Ballads*, a hard-hitting novel of rural life; and *The Red Sorghum Clan*, parts of which were turned into *Red Sorghum*, a Zhang Yimou film (see p.948). Both books were banned in China.

Qian Zhongshu *Fortress Besieged*. Scathing satire, set in the 1930s, about a failed student who uses a fake degree to win a teaching post and a wife. Now highly influential, it was banned for years in both mainland China and Taiwan.

Qiu Xiaolong *When Red Is Black*, *A Loyal Character Dancer*, *A Case of Two Cities*, *The Mao Case*. Procedural detective stories set in Shanghai, featuring the poetry-loving Inspector Chen. Though sometimes Qiu seems more interested in examining society and morals than in weaving a mystery, his stories of corrupt officials, sharp operators and compromised cops are some of the best evocations of modern China in contemporary English-language fiction.

Neal Stephenson *The Diamond Age*. An ambitious, flawed but brilliant science fiction novel set in China, in "Nu-Chusan" – a re-imagining of Shanghai's concession era in the age of nano-technology.

Wang Shuo *Playing for Thrills* and *Please Don't Call Me Human*. Wang Shuo writes in colourful Beijing dialect about the city's wide boys and chancers. *Playing for Thrills* is fairly representative – a mystery story whose boorish narrator spends most of his time drinking, gambling and chasing girls. *Please Don't Call Me Human* is a satire of modern China as a place where greed is everything, as the Party turns a dignified martial artist into a vacuous dancer in order to win an Olympic gold medal.

Wei Hui *Shanghai Baby*. Salacious chick-lit about a Chinese girl who can't decide between her Western lover and her drug-addled Chinese boyfriend (though her real love seems to be for designer labels). Notable for the Chinese authorities' attempts to ban it and for spawning a genre in modern Chinese writing, the urban girl's saucy confessional.

Yiyun Li *A Thousand Years of Good Prayers*; *Gold Boy, Emerald Girl*. Two short stories looking at how China's rapid changes have affected the lives of ordinary folk, from a Beijinger now living in the States.

CLASSICS

Asiapac series. Chinese classics and folk tales entertainingly rendered into cartoon format. Titles include *Journey to the West*, *Tales of Laozhai* and *Chinese Eunuchs*.

Cyril Birch (ed) *Anthology of Chinese Literature*. Two volumes that cover three thousand years of poetry, philosophy, drama, biography and prose fiction, with interesting variations of translation.

Cao Xueqing and Gao E *Dream of Red Mansions/Story of the Stone*. This intricate eighteenth-century tale of manners follows the fortunes of the Jia clan through the emotionally charged adolescent lives of Jia Baoyu and his two girl cousins, Lin Daiyu and Xue Baochai. The full translation fills five paperbacks, but there's also a much simplified English version available in China.

★ **Li Bai and Du Fu** *Li Po and Tu Fu*. Fine translations of China's greatest Tang-dynasty poets, with a detailed introduction that puts them in context. Li Bai was a drunken spiritualist, Du Fu a sharp-eyed realist, and their surprisingly accessible and complementary works form an apex of Chinese literature.

★ **Luo Guanzhong** *Romance of the Three Kingdoms*. Despite being written 1200 years after the events it portrays, this tale vividly evokes the battles, political schemings and myths surrounding China's turbulent Three Kingdoms period. One of the world's great historical novels.

Pu Songling *Strange Tales from a Chinese Studio*. Born during the early Qing dynasty, Pu Songling spent his life amassing these contemporary folk tales, which range from the almost believable to downright weird stories of spirits, ghosts and demons.

Shi Nai'an and Luo Guanzhong *Outlaws of the Marsh* aka *The Water Margin*. A heavy dose of popular legend, as a group of Robin Hood-like outlaws takes on the government in feudal times. Wildly uneven, and hard to read right through, but some amazing characters and set pieces.

Sun Zi *The Art of War*. "Lure them with the prospect of gain, then take them by confusion". This classic on strategy and warfare, told in pithy maxims, is as relevant today as when it was written around 500 BC. A favourite with the modern business community.

★ **Wu Cheng'en** *Journey to the West*. Absurd, lively rendering of the Buddhist monk Xuanzang's pilgrimage to India to collect sacred scriptures, aided by Sandy, Pigsy and the irrepressible Sun Wu Kong, the monkey king. Arthur Waley's version, *Monkey*, retains the spirit of the tale while shortening the hundred-chapter opus to paperback length.

Chinese

As the most widely spoken language on earth, Chinese can hardly be overlooked. Chinese is, strictly speaking, a series of dialects spoken by the dominant ethnic group within China, the Han. Indeed, the term most commonly used by the Chinese themselves to refer to the language is hanyu, meaning "Han-language", though zhongyu, zhongwen and zhongguohua are frequently used as well. However, non-Han peoples such as Uyghurs and Tibetans speak languages which have little or nothing to do with Chinese.

The dialects of *hanyu* are diverse, having about as much in common as, say, German and English. The better-known and most distinct dialects include those spoken around China's coastal fringes, such as **Shanghainese** (*shanghai hua*), **Fujianese** (*minnan hua*) and **Cantonese** (*guangdong hua* or *yueyu*). Cantonese and Fujianese are themselves languages of worldwide significance, being the dialects spoken by the people of Hong Kong and among Overseas Chinese communities, particularly those in Southeast Asia.

What enables Chinese from different parts of the country to converse is **Mandarin Chinese**. Historically based on the language of Han officialdom in the Beijing area, Mandarin has been promoted over the past hundred years or so to be the official, unifying language of the Chinese people. It is known in mainland China as **putonghua** – "common language". As the language of education, government and the media, Mandarin is understood to a greater or lesser extent by the vast majority of Han Chinese, and by many non-Han as well.

Another element tying the various dialects together is the Chinese **script**. No matter how different two dialects may sound when spoken, once they are written down in the form of Chinese characters they become mutually comprehensible again, as the different dialects use the same written characters.

From the point of view of foreigners, the main distinguishing characteristic of Chinese is that it is a **tonal** language: in order to pronounce a word correctly, it is necessary to know not only its sound but also its correct tone. Accuracy in **pronunciation** is particularly important in Chinese, for which an understanding of the **pinyin** phonetic system is vital (see p.958).

Chinese characters

There are tens of thousands of **Chinese characters**, though the vast majority are obsolete – you need about 2500 to read a newspaper, and even educated Chinese are unlikely to know more than ten thousand. The characters themselves originated as **pictograms**, each representing a **concept** rather than a specific pronunciation. Chinese speakers have to memorize the sounds of individual characters, and the meanings attached to them.

THERE'S AN APP FOR THAT

Travellers are increasingly using their mobile phones to counter linguistic difficulties faced during their time in China. One of the most useful apps is the **Waygo Visual Translator**, which allows the steady-handed to scan Chinese characters, which it then translates for you – particularly handy in restaurants with no English-language menu. Better for word-to-word translation is the excellent **Pleco** app, which also has scanning facilities if you're prepared to pay extra fees; the **Dian Hua** app is similar, and nearly as good.

Although to untrained eyes many Chinese characters seem impossibly complex, there is a logic behind their structure which helps in their memorization. Firstly, each character is written using an exact number of brush (or pen) **strokes**: thus the character for "mouth", which forms a square, is always written using only three strokes: first the left side, then the top and right side together, and finally the base. Secondly, characters can (very broadly) be broken up into two components, which often also exist as characters in their own right: a **main** part, which frequently gives a clue as to the pronunciation; and a **radical**, which usually appears on the left side of the character and which vaguely categorizes the meaning. As an example, the character for "mother" (妈, mā) is made up of the character for "horse" (马, mǎ; note the similar sound), combined with the radical "女, nǔ" which means "female". In some cases, the connection between the pictogram and its meaning is obvious – the character for wood (木, mù) resembles a tree. Others require some lateral thinking, or have become so abstract or complex that the meaning is hidden.

Given the time and difficulty involved in learning characters, and the negative impact this has had on the general level of literacy, in 1954 a couple of thousand of the most common characters were **simplified**, making them easier to learn and quicker to write. For example, the traditional version of "dragon" is written 龍, while the simplified version is 龙. The simplified characters were adopted in mainland China and Singapore, but Hong Kong and Taiwan continue to use the older, traditional forms.

Grammar

Chinese **grammar** is relatively simple. There is no need to conjugate verbs, decline nouns or make adjectives agree – being attached to immutable Chinese characters, Chinese words simply cannot have different "endings". Instead, context and fairly rigid rules about word order are relied on to make those distinctions of time, number and gender that Indo-European languages are so concerned with. Instead of cumbersome tenses, the Chinese make use of words such as "yesterday" or "tomorrow"; instead of plural endings they simply state how many things there are, or use quantifier words equivalent to "some" or "many".

For English-speakers, **Chinese word order** follows the familiar subject-verb-object pattern, and you'll find that by simply stringing words together you'll be producing fairly grammatical Chinese. Just note that adjectives, as well as all qualifying and describing phrases, precede nouns.

Pronunciation and pinyin

Back in the 1950s it was hoped eventually to replace Chinese characters with a regular alphabet of Roman letters, and to this end the **pinyin** system was devised. Basically, pinyin is a way of using the Roman alphabet to write out the sounds of Mandarin Chinese, with Mandarin's four tones represented by **accents** above each syllable. Other dialects of Chinese, such as Cantonese – having nine tones – cannot be written in *pinyin*.

The aim of replacing Chinese characters with *pinyin* was abandoned long ago, but in the meantime *pinyin* has one very important function, that of helping foreigners to pronounce Chinese words. However, in *pinyin* the letters do not all have the sounds you would expect, and you'll need to spend an hour or two learning these. You'll often see *pinyin* in China, on street signs and shop displays, but only well-educated locals know the system well. Occasionally, you will come across **other systems** of rendering Mandarin into Roman letters, such as **Wade-Giles**, which writes Mao Zedong as Mao Tse-tung. These forms are no longer used in mainland China, but you may see them in Western books about China.

The Chinese terms in this book have been given both in characters and in *pinyin*; the pronunciation guide below is your first step to making yourself comprehensible. Don't get overly paranoid about your tones: with the help of context, intelligent listeners should be able to work out what you are trying to say. If you're just uttering a single word, however, for example a place name – without a context – you need to hit exactly the right tone, otherwise don't be surprised if nobody understands you.

The tones

There are **four tones** in Mandarin Chinese, and every syllable of every word is characterized by one of them, except for a few syllables which are considered toneless. This emphasis on tones does not make Chinese a particularly musical language – English, for example, uses all of the tones of Chinese and many more. The difference is that English uses tone for effect – exclaiming, questioning, listing, rebuking and so on. In English, to change the tone is to change the mood or the emphasis; in Chinese, to change the tone is to change the word itself.

First or "High" ā ē ī ō ū. In English this level tone is used when mimicking robotic or very boring, flat voices.

Second or "Rising" á é í ó ú. Used in English when asking a question showing surprise, for example "eh?". Try raising your eyebrows when attempting to make a sound with this tone – it never fails.

Third or "Falling-rising" ǎ ě ǐ ǒ ǔ . Used in English when echoing someone's words with a measure of incredulity. For example, "John's dead." "De-ad?!".

Fourth or "Falling" à è ì ò ù. Often used in English when counting in a brusque manner – "One! Two! Three! Four!". Try stamping your foot lightly when attempting to make a sound with this tone.

Toneless A few syllables do not have a tone accent. These are pronounced without emphasis, much like that lovely word "meh".

Note that if there are two consecutive characters with the third tone, the first character is pronounced as though it carries the second tone.

Consonants

Most consonants are pronounced in a similar way to their English equivalents, with the following exceptions:

c as in ha**ts**

g is hard as in **g**od (except when preceded by "n", when it sounds like sa**ng**)

q as in **ch**eese

x has no direct equivalent in English, but you can make the sound by sliding from an "s" sound to a "sh" sound and stopping midway between the two

z as in su**ds**

zh as in fu**dge**

Vowels and diphthongs

As in most languages, the vowel sounds are rather harder to quantify than the consonants. The examples here give a rough description of the sound of each vowel followed by related combination sounds.

a usually somewhere between f**a**r and m**a**n

ai as in **eye**

ao as in c**ow**

e usually as in f**ur**

ei as in g**ay**

en is an unstressed sound as at the end of hyph**en**

eng as in s**ung**

er as in f**ur** (ie with a stressed "r")

i usually as in t**ea**, except in *zi, ci, si, ri, zhi, chi* and *shi*, when it is a short clipped sound like the American military "sir"

ia as in y**ak**

ian as in y**en**

ie as in **yea**h

o as in b**o**re

ou as in sh**ow**

ü as in the German ü (make an "ee" sound and glide slowly into an "oo"; at the mid-point between the two sounds you should hit the ü sound); in *pinyin* it's sometimes written as a V

u usually as in f**oo**l except where u follows j, q, x or y, when it is always pronounced **ü**

ua as in s**ua**ve

uai as in **why**

ue as though contracting "you" and "air" together, **you'air**

ui as in **way**

uo as in w**o**re

Useful words and phrases

Chinese put their **family names first** followed by their given names, the reverse of Western convention. The vast majority of Chinese family names comprise a single character, while given names are either one or two characters long. So Zuo Zongtang has the family name of Zuo, and the given name of Zongtang.

When asked for their name, the Chinese tend to provide either just their family name, or their whole name. In **formal situations**, you might come across the terms "Mr" (*xiansheng*), "Mrs" (*taitai*, though this is being replaced by the more neutral term *airen*) or "Miss" (*xiaojie*), which are attached after the family name: for example, Mr Zuo is *zuo xiansheng*. In more casual encounters, people use familiar terms such as "old" (*lao*) or "young" (*xiao*) attached in front of the family name, though "old" or "young" are more relative terms of status than indications of actual age in this case: Mr Zuo's friend might call him "Lao Zuo", for instance.

BASICS

I	我	wǒ
You (singular)	你	nǐ
He	他	tā
She	她	tā
We	我们	wǒmén
You (plural)	你们	nǐmén
They	他们	tāmén
I want...	我要	wǒ yào...
No, I don't want...	我不要...	wǒ bú yào...
Is it possible...?	可不可以...?	kěbùkěyǐ...?
It is (not) possible	(不)可以	(bù) kěyǐ
Is there any/Have you got any...?	有没有...?	yǒuméi yǒu...?
There is/I have	有	yǒu
There isn't/I haven't	没有	méiyǒu
Please help me	请帮我忙	qǐng bāng wǒ máng
Mr...	...先生	xiānshēng
Mrs...	...太太	tàitài
Miss...	...小姐	xiǎojiě

COMMUNICATING

I don't speak Chinese	我不会说中文	wǒ bú huì shuō zhōngwén
My Chinese is terrible	我的中文很差	wǒ de zhōngwén hěn chà
Can you speak English?	你会说英语吗?	nǐ huì shuō yīngyǔ ma?
Can you get someone who speaks English?	请给我找一个会说 英语的人	qǐng gěiwǒ zhǎoyíge huìshuō yīngyǔ de rén?

Please speak slowly	请说得慢一点	qǐng shuōde mànyìdiǎn
Please say that again	请再说一遍	qǐng zài shuōyíbiàn
I understand	我听得懂	wǒ tīngdedǒng
I don't understand	我听不懂	wǒ tīngbùdǒng
I can't read Chinese characters	我看不懂汉字	wǒ kànbùdong hànzì
What does this mean?	这是什么意思?	zhè shì shénme yìsi?
How do you pronounce this character?	这个字怎么念?	zhègezi zěnme niàn?

GREETINGS AND BASIC COURTESIES

Hello/How do you do?	你好	nǐhǎo!
How are you?	你好吗?	nǐ hǎo ma?
I'm fine	我很好	wǒhěnhǎo
Thank you	谢谢	xièxie
Don't mention it/You're welcome	不客气	búkèqì
Sorry to bother you...	麻烦你	máfan nǐ
Sorry/I apologize	对不起	duìbùqǐ
It's not important/No problem	没关系	méiguānxi
Goodbye	再见	zàijiàn
Chitchat	聊天	liáotiān
What country are you from?	你是哪个国家的?	nǐ shì nǎge guójiā de?
Britain	英国	yīngguó
Ireland	爱尔兰	ài'ěrlán
America	美国	měiguó
Canada	加拿大	jiā'nádà
Australia	澳大利亚	àodàlìyà
New Zealand	新西兰	xīnxīlán
China	中国	zhōngguó
Outside China	外国	wàiguó
What's your name?	你叫什么名字?	nǐ jiào shěnme míngzi?
My name is...	我叫...	wǒ jiào...
Are you married?	你结婚了吗?	nǐ jiéhūnle ma?
I am (not) married	我(没有)结婚(了)	wǒ (méiyǒu) jiéhūn (le)
Have you got (children)?	你有没有孩子?	nǐ yǒu (méiyǒu) háizi?
Do you like...?	你喜不喜欢...?	nǐ xǐbùxǐhuān...?
I (don't) like...	我不喜欢...	wǒ (bù)xǐhuān...
What's your job?	你干什么工作?	nǐ gàn shénme gōngzuò?
I'm a foreign student	我是留学生	wǒ shì liúxuéshēng
I'm a teacher	我是老师	wǒ shì laǒshī
I work in a company	我在一个公司工作	wǒ zài yí ge gōngsī gōngzuò
I don't work	我不工作	wǒ bùgōngzuò
Clean/dirty	干净/脏	gānjìng/zāng
Hot/cold	热/冷	rè/lěng
Fast/slow	快/慢	kuài/màn
Pretty	漂亮	piàoliàng
Interesting	有意思	yǒuyìsi

NUMBERS

Zero	零	líng
One	一	yī
Two	二/两	èr/liǎng*
Three	三	sān
Four	四	sì
Five	五	wǔ
Six	六	liù

Seven	七	qī
Eight	八	bā
Nine	九	jiǔ
Ten	十	shí
Eleven	十一	shíyī
Twelve	十二	shíèr
Twenty	二十	èrshí
Twenty-one	二十一	èrshíyī
One hundred	一百	yībǎi
Two hundred	二百	èrbǎi
One thousand	一千	yīqiān
Ten thousand	一万	yīwàn
One hundred thousand	十万	shíwàn
One million	一百万	yībǎiwàn

*liǎng is used when enumerating, for example "two people" is liǎng ge rén. èr is used when counting.

TIME

Now	现在	xiànzài
Today	今天	jīntiān
(In the) morning	早上	zǎoshàng
(In the) afternoon	下午	xiàwǔ
(In the) evening	晚上	wǎnshàng
Tomorrow	明天	míngtiān
The day after tomorrow	后天	hòutiān
Yesterday	昨天	zuótiān
Week/month/year	星期/月/年	xīngqī/yuè/nián
Monday	星期一	xīngqī yī
Tuesday	星期二	xīngqī èr
Wednesday	星期三	xīngqī sān
Thursday	星期四	xīngqī sì
Friday	星期五	xīngqī wǔ
Saturday	星期六	xīngqī liù
Sunday	星期天	xīngqī tiān
What's the time?	几点了?	jǐdiǎn le?
10 o'clock	十点钟	shídiǎn zhōng
10.20	十点二十	shídiǎn èrshí
10.30	十点半	shídiǎn bàn

TRAVELLING AND GETTING ABOUT TOWN

North	北	běi
South	南	nán
East	东	dōng
West	西	xī
Airport	机场	jīchǎng
Ferry dock	船码头	chuánmǎtóu
Left-luggage office	寄存处	jìcún chù
Ticket office	售票处	shòupiào chù
Ticket	票	piào
Can you buy me a ticket to...?	可不可以给我买到 ...的票?	kěbùkěyǐ gěi wǒ mǎi dào de piào?
I want to go to...	我想到...去	wǒ xiǎng dào qù
I want to leave at (8 o'clock)	我想(八点钟)离开	wǒ xiǎng (bā diǎn zhōng) líkāi
When does it leave?	什么时候出发?	shénme shíhòu chūfā?

When does it arrive?	什么时候到?	shénme shíhòu dào?
How long does it take?	路上得多长时间?	lùshàng děi duōcháng shíjiān?
CITS	中国国际旅行社	zhōngguó guójì lǚxíngshè
Train	火车	huǒchē
(Main) Train station	主要火车站	(zhǔyào) huǒchēzhàn
Bus	公共汽车	gōnggòng qìchē
Bus station	汽车站	qìchēzhàn
Long-distance bus station	长途汽车站	chángtú qìchēzhàn
Express train/bus	特快车	tèkuài chē
Fast train/bus	快车	kuàichē
Ordinary train/bus	普通车	pǔtōngchē
Minibus	小车	xiǎochē
Sleeper bus	卧铺车	wòpùchē
Lower bunk	下铺	xiàpù
Middle bunk	中铺	zhōngpù
Upper bunk	上铺	shàngpù
Hard seat	硬座	yìngzuò
Soft seat	软座	ruǎnzuò
Hard sleeper	硬卧	yìngwò
Soft sleeper	软卧	ruǎnwò
Soft-seat waiting room	软卧候车室	ruǎnwò hòuchēshì
Timetable	时间表	shíjiān biǎo
Upgrade ticket	补票	bǔpiào
Unreserved ticket	无座	wúzuò
Returned ticket window	退票	tuìpiào
Platform	站台	zhàntái

GETTING ABOUT TOWN

Map	地图	dìtú
Where is…?	……在哪里?	zàinǎlǐ?
Go straight on	往前走	wǎng qián zǒu
Turn right	往右拐	wǎng yòu guǎi
Turn left	往左拐	wǎng zuǒ guǎi
Taxi	出租车	chūzū chē
Please use the meter	请打开记价器	qǐng dǎkāi jìjiàqì
Underground/Subway station	地铁站	dìtiě zhàn
Bicycle	自行车	zìxíngchē
I want to rent a bicycle	我想租自行车	wǒ xiǎng zū zìxíngchē
How much is it per hour?	一个小时得多少钱?	yí gè xiǎoshí děi duōshǎo qián?
Bus	公共汽车	gōnggòn gqìchē
Which bus goes to…?	几路车到...去?	jǐlùchē dào…qù?
Number (10) bus	(十)路车	(shí)lùchē
Does this bus go to…?	这车到...去吗?	zhèchē dào…qù ma?
When is the next bus?	下一班车几点开?	Xiàyìbān chē jǐdiǎn kāi?
The first bus	头班车	tóubān chē
The last bus	末班车	mòbān chē
Please tell me where to get off	请告诉我在哪里下车	qǐng gàosù wǒ zài nǎlǐ xià chē
Museum	博物馆	bówùguǎn
Temple	寺院	sìyuàn
Church	教堂	jiàotáng
Mosque	清真寺	qīngzhēn sì
Toilet (men's)	男厕所	nán cèsuǒ
Toilet (women's)	女厕所	nǚ cèsuǒ

ACCOMMODATION

Accommodation	住宿	zhùsù
Hotel (upmarket)	宾馆	bīnguǎn
Hotel (downmarket)	招待所，旅馆	zhāodàisuǒ, lǚguǎn
Hostel	旅社	lǚshè
Foreigners' guesthouse (at a university)	外国专家楼	wàiguó zhuānjiālóu
Is it possible to stay here?	能不能住在这里?	néngbùnéng zhùzài zhèlǐ?
Can I have a look at the room?	能不能看一下房间?	néngbùnéng kànyíxià fángjiān?
I want the cheapest bed you've got	我要你最便宜的床位	wǒ yào nǐ zuìpiányi de chuángwèi
Single room	单人房	dānrénfáng
Twin room	双人房	shuāngrén fáng
Three-bed room	三人房	sānrénfáng
Dormitory	多人房	duōrénfáng
Suite	套房	tàofáng
(Large) bed	(大)床	(dà)chuáng
Passport	护照	hùzhào
Deposit	押金	yājīn
Key	钥匙	yàoshi
I want to change my room	我想换一个房间	wǒ xiǎng huàn yíge fángjiān
Laundry (the action)	洗衣服	xǐyīfú
Laundry (the place)	洗衣店	xǐyīdiàn
Washing powder	洗衣粉	xǐyīfěn

SHOPPING, MONEY AND BANKS, AND THE POLICE

How much is it?	多少钱?	duōshǎo qián?
That's too expensive	太贵了	tàiguìle
Have you got anything cheaper?	有没有便宜一点的?	yǒuméiyǒu piányi yìdiǎn de?
Department store	百货商店	bǎihuò shāngdiàn
Market	市场	shìchǎng
¥1 (RMB)	一块(人民币)	yíkuài (rénmínbì)
US$1	一块美金	yíkuài měijīn
£1	一个英磅	yígè yīngbàng
HK$1	一块港币	yí kuài gǎngbì
Change money	换钱	huànqián
Bank of China	中国银行	zhōngguó yínháng
Travellers' cheques	旅行支票	lǚxíngzhīpiào
PSB	公安局	gōng'ān jú

COMMUNICATIONS

Post office	邮电局	yóudiànjú
Envelope	信封	xìnfēng
Stamp	邮票	yóupiào
Airmail	航空信	hángkōngxìn
Surface mail	平信	píngxìn
Telephone	电话	diànhuà
International telephone call	国际电话	guójì diànhuà
Reverse charges/collect call	对方付钱电话	duìfāng fùqián diànhuà
Fax	传真	chuánzhēn
Telephone card	电话卡	diànhuàkǎ
I want to make a telephone call to (Britain)	我想给(英国)打电话	wǒ xiǎng gěi (yīngguó) dǎ diànhuà

I want to send a fax to (US)	我想给(美国) 发一个传真	wǒ xiǎng gěi (měiguó) fā yíge chuánzhēn
Can I receive a fax here?	能不能在这里 收传真?	néngbùnéng zàizhèlǐ shōu chuánzhēn?
Internet café	网吧	wǎngbā

HEALTH

Hospital	医院	yīyuàn
Pharmacy	药店	yàodiàn
Medicine	药	yào
Chinese medicine	中药	zhōngyào
Diarrhoea	腹泻	fùxiè
Vomit	呕吐	ǒutù
Fever	发烧	fāshāo
I'm ill	我生病了	wǒ shēngbìng le
I've got flu	我感冒了	wǒ gǎnmào le
I'm (not) allergic to	我对…(不)过敏	wǒ duì…(bù) guòmǐn
Antibiotics	抗生素	kàngshēngsù
Condom	避孕套	bìyùntào
Mosquito coil	蚊香	wénxiāng
Mosquito	蚊帐纱	wénzhàngshā

A food and drink glossary

The following lists should help out in deciphering the characters on a Chinese menu – if they're written clearly. If you know what you're after, try sifting through the staples and cooking methods to create your order, or sample one of the everyday or regional suggestions, many of which are available all over the country. Note that some items, such as seafood and *jiaozi*, are ordered by weight.

GENERAL

Restaurant	餐厅	cāntīng
House speciality	拿手好菜	náshǒuhǎocài
How much is that?	多少钱?	duōshǎoqián?
I don't eat (meat)	我不吃(肉)	wǒ bùchī(ròu)
I'm Buddhist/I'm vegetarian	我是佛教徒/我只吃素	wǒshì fójiàotú/wǒ zhǐchī sù
I would like…	我想要…	wǒxiǎngyào…
Local dishes	地方菜	dìfāngcài
Snacks	小吃	xiǎochī
Menu/set menu/English menu	菜单/套餐/英文菜单	càidān/tàocān/yīngwén càidān
Small portion	少量	shǎoliàng
Chopsticks	筷子	kuàizi
Knife and fork	刀叉	dāochā
Spoon	勺子	sháozi
Waiter/waitress	服务员/小姐	fúwùyuán/xiǎojiě
Bill/cheque	买单	mǎidān
Cook these ingredients together	一块儿做	yíkuàir zuò
Not spicy/no chilli please	请不要辣椒	qǐng búyào làjiāo
Only a little spice/chilli	一点辣椒	yìdiǎn làjiāo
500 grams	斤	jīn
1 kilo	公斤	gōngjīn

DRINKS

Beer	啤酒	píjiǔ
Sweet fizzy drink	汽水	qìshuǐ
Coffee	咖啡	kāfēi
Milk	牛奶	niúnǎi
(Mineral) water	(矿泉)水	(kuàngquán) shuǐ
Wine	葡萄酒	pútáojiǔ
Spirits	白酒	báijiǔ
Soya milk	豆浆	dòujiāng
Yoghurt	酸奶	suānnǎi

TEAS

Tea	茶	chá
Black tea	红茶	hóngchá
Chrysanthemum	菊花茶	júhuāchá
Green tea	绿茶	lǜchá
Iron Buddha	铁观音	tiěguānyīn
Jasmine	茉莉花茶	mòlìhuā chá
Pu'er	普洱茶	pǔ'ěr chá

STAPLE FOODS

Aubergine	茄子	qiézi
Bamboo shoots	笋尖	sǔnjiān
Bean sprouts	豆芽	dòuyá
Beans	豆	dòu
Beef	牛肉	niúròu
Bitter gourd	葫芦	húlú
Black bean sauce	黑豆豉	hēidòuchǐ
Bread	面包	miànbāo
Buns (filled)	包子	bāozi
Buns (plain)	馒头	mántou
Carrot	胡萝卜	húluóbo
Cashew nuts	腰果	yāoguǒ
Cauliflower	菜花	càihuā
Chicken	鸡	jī
Chilli	辣椒	làjiāo
Chocolate	巧克力	qiǎokèlì
Coriander (leaves)	香菜	xiāngcài
Crab	蟹	xiè
Cucumber	黄瓜	huángguā
Duck	鸭	yā
Eel	鳝鱼	shànyú
Eggs (fried)	煎鸡蛋	jiānjīdàn
Fish	鱼	yú
Fried dough stick	油条	yóutiáo
Garlic	大蒜	dàsuàn
Ginger	姜	jiāng
Green pepper (capsicum)	青椒	qīngjiāo
Green vegetables	绿叶素菜	lǜyè sùcài
Jiaozi (dumplings, steamed or boiled)	饺子	jiǎozi
Lamb	羊肉	yángròu
Lotus root	莲心	liánxīn
MSG	味精	wèijīng
Mushrooms	磨菇	mógū

Noodles	面条	miàntiáo
Omelette	摊鸡蛋	tānjīdàn
Onions	洋葱	yángcōng
Oyster sauce	蚝油	háoyóu
Pancake	摊饼	tānbǐng
Peanut	花生	huāshēng
Pork	猪肉	zhūròu
Potato (stir-fried)	(炒)土豆	(chǎo) tǔdòu
Prawns	虾	xiā
Preserved egg	皮蛋	pídàn
Rice, boiled	白饭	báifàn
Rice, fried	炒饭	chǎofàn
Rice noodles	河粉	héfěn
Rice porridge (aka "congee")	粥	zhōu
Salt	盐	yán
Sesame oil	芝麻油	zhīma yóu
Sichuan pepper	四川辣椒	sìchuān làjiāo
Snails	蜗牛	wōniú
Snake	蛇肉	shéròu
Soup	汤	tāng
Soy sauce	酱油	jiàngyóu
Squid	鱿鱼	yóuyú
Sugar	糖	táng
Tofu	豆腐	dòufu
Tomato	蕃茄	fānqié
Vinegar	醋	cù
Water chestnuts	马蹄	mǎtí
White radish	白萝卜	báiluóbo
Yam	芋头	yùtóu

COOKING METHODS

Boiled	煮	zhǔ
Casseroled (see also "Claypot")	焙	bèi
Deep-fried	油煎	yóujiān
Fried	炒	chǎo
Poached	白煮	báizhǔ
Red-cooked (stewed in soy sauce)	红烧	hóngshāo
Roast	烤	kǎo
Steamed	蒸	zhēng
Stir-fried	清炒	qīngchǎo

EVERYDAY DISHES

Braised duck with vegetables	炖鸭素菜	dùnyā sùcài
Cabbage rolls (stuffed with meat or vegetables)	卷心菜	juǎnxīn cài
Chicken and sweetcorn soup	玉米鸡丝汤	yùmǐ jīsī tāng
Chicken with bamboo shoots and babycorn	笋尖嫩玉米炒鸡片	sǔnjiān nènyùmǐ chǎojīpiàn
Chicken with cashew nuts	腰果鸡片	yāoguǒ jīpiàn
Claypot/sandpot (casserole)	沙锅	shāguō
Crispy aromatic duck	香酥鸭	xiāngsūyā
Egg flower soup with tomato	蕃茄蛋汤	fānqié dàntāng
Egg-fried rice	蛋炒饭	dànchǎofàn

Fish-ball soup with white radish	萝卜鱼蛋汤	luóbo yúdàn tāng
Fish casserole	焙鱼	bèiyú
Fried shredded pork with garlic and chilli	大蒜辣椒炒肉片	dàsuàn làjiāo chǎoròupiàn
Hotpot	火锅	huǒguō
Kebab	串肉	chuànròu
Noodle soup	汤面	tāngmiàn
Pork and mustard greens	芥末肉片	jièmò ròupiàn
Pork and water chestnut	马蹄猪肉	mǎtí zhūròu
Pork and white radish pie	白萝卜肉馅饼	báiluóbo ròuxiànbīng
Prawn with garlic sauce	大蒜炒虾	dàsuàn chǎoxiā
"Pulled" noodles	拉面	lāmiàn
Roast duck	烤鸭	kǎoyā
Scrambled egg with pork on rice	滑蛋猪肉饭	huádàn zhūròufàn
Sliced pork with yellow bean sauce	黄豆肉片	huángdòu ròupiàn
Squid with green pepper and black beans	豆豉青椒炒鱿鱼	dòuchǐ qīngjiāo chǎoyóuyú
Steamed eel with black beans	豆豉蒸鳝	dòuchǐ zhēngshàn
Steamed rice packets wrapped in lotus leaves	荷叶蒸饭	héyè zhēngfàn
Stewed pork belly with vegetables	回锅肉	huíguōròu
Stir-fried chicken and bamboo shoots	笋尖炒鸡片	sǔnjiān chǎojīpiàn
Stuffed bean-curd soup	豆腐汤	dòufutāng
Stuffed bean curd with aubergine and green pepper	茄子青椒煲	qiézi qīngjiāobāo
Sweet-and-sour spareribs	糖醋排骨	tángcù páigǔ
Sweet bean paste pancakes	赤豆摊饼	chìdòu tānbǐng
White radish soup	白萝卜汤	báiluóbo tāng
Wuntun soup	馄饨汤	húntun tāng

VEGETABLES AND EGGS

Aubergine with chilli and garlic sauce	大蒜辣椒炒茄子	dàsuàn làjiāo chǎoqiézi
Aubergine with sesame sauce	拌茄子片	bànqiézipiàn
Bean curd and spinach soup	菠菜豆腐汤	bōcài dòufu tāng
Bean-curd slivers	豆腐花	dòufuhuā
Bean curd with chestnuts	马蹄豆腐	mǎtí dòufu
Braised mountain fungus	炖香菇	dùnxiānggū
Egg fried with tomatoes	蕃茄炒蛋	fānqié chǎodàn
Fried bean curd with vegetables	豆腐素菜	dòufu sùcài
Fried bean sprouts	炒豆芽	chǎodòuyá
Monks' vegetarian dish (stir-fry of mixed vegetables and fungi)	罗汉斋	luóhànzhāi
Pressed bean curd with cabbage	卷心菜豆腐	juǎnxīncài dòufu
Spicy braised	香茄子条	xiāngqiézitiáo
Stir-fried bamboo shoots	炒冬笋	chǎodōngsǔn
Stir-fried mushrooms	炒鲜菇	chǎoxiān'gū
Vegetable soup	素菜汤	sùcài tāng

NORTHERN DISHES

Aromatic fried lamb	炒羊肉	chǎoyángròu
Beijing (Peking) duck	北京烤鸭	běijīng kǎoyā
Fish with ham and vegetables	火腿素菜鱼片	huǒtuǐ sùcài yúpiàn
Fried prawn balls	炒虾球	chǎoxiāqiú

Lion's head (pork rissoles casseroled with greens)	狮子头	shīzitóu
Mongolian hotpot	蒙古火锅	ménggǔ huǒguō
Red-cooked lamb	红烧羊肉	hóngshāo yángròu

EASTERN DISHES

Beggars' chicken (baked)	叫花鸡	jiàohuājī
Brine duck	盐水鸭	yánshuǐ yā
Crab soup	蟹肉汤	xièròu tāng
Dongpo pork casserole (steamed in wine)	东坡焙肉	dōngpō bèiròu
Drunken prawns	醉虾	zuìxiā
Five flower pork (steamed in lotus leaves)	五花肉	wǔhuāròu
Fried crab with eggs	蟹肉鸡蛋	xièròu jīdàn
Pearl balls (rice-grain-coated, steamed rissoles)	珍珠球	zhēnzhūqiú
Shaoxing chicken	绍兴鸡	shàoxīng jī
Soup dumplings (steamed, containing jellied stock)	汤包	tāngbāo
Steamed sea bass	清蒸鲈鱼	qīngzhēnglúyú
Stuffed green peppers	馅青椒	xiànqīngjiāo
West Lake fish (braised in a sour sauce)	西湖醋鱼	xīhúcùyú
"White-cut" beef (spiced and steamed)	白切牛肉	báiqiē niúròu
Yangzhou fried rice	杨州炒饭	yángzhōu chǎofàn

WESTERN CHINESE DISHES

Boiled beef slices (spicy)	水煮牛肉	shuǐzhǔ niúròu
Carry-pole noodles (with a chilli-vinegar-sesame sauce)	担担面	dàndànmiàn
Crackling-rice with pork	爆米肉片	bàomǐ ròupiàn
Crossing-the-bridge noodles	过桥面	guòqiáomiàn
Deep-fried green beans with garlic	大蒜刀豆	dàsuàn dāodòu
Dong'an chicken (poached in spicy sauce)	东安鸡子	dōng'ān jīzǐ
Doubled-cooked pork	回锅肉	huíguōròu
Dried yoghurt wafers	乳饼	rǔbǐng
Dry-fried pork shreds	油炸肉丝	yóuzhá ròusī
Fish-flavoured aubergine	鱼香茄子	yúxiāng qiézi
Gongbao chicken (with chillies and peanuts)	宫保鸡丁	gōngbǎo jīdīng
Green pepper with spring onion and black bean sauce	豆豉青椒	dòuchǐ qīngjiāo
Hot and sour soup (flavoured with vinegar and white pepper)	酸辣汤	suānlà tāng
Hot-spiced bean curd	麻婆豆腐	mápódòufu
Rice-flour balls, stuffed with sweet paste	汤圆	tāngyuán
Smoked duck	熏鸭	xūnyā
Strange flavoured chicken (with sesame-garlic-chilli)	怪味鸡	guàiwèijī
Stuffed aubergine slices	馅茄子	xiànqiézi

Tangerine chicken	桔子鸡	júzijī
"Tiger-skin" peppers (pan-fried with salt)	虎皮炒椒	hǔpí chǎojiāo
Wind-cured ham	火腿	huǒtuǐ

SOUTHERN CHINESE DISHES

Baked crab with chilli and black beans	辣椒豆豉焙蟹	làjiāo dòuchǐ bèixiè
Barbecued pork ("char siew")	叉烧	chāshāo
Casseroled bean curd stuffed with pork mince	豆腐煲	dòufubǎo
Claypot rice with bean curd stuffed sweet sausage	香肠饭	xiāngchángfàn
Crisp-skinned pork on rice	脆皮肉饭	cuìpíròufàn
Fish-head casserole	焙鱼头	bèiyútóu
Fish steamed with ginger and spring onion	清蒸鱼	qīngzhēngyú
Fried chicken with yam	芋头炒鸡片	yùtóu chǎojīpiàn
Honey-roast pork	叉烧	chāshāo
Kale in oyster sauce	蚝油白菜	háoyóu báicài
Lemon chicken	柠檬鸡	níngméngjī
Litchi (lychee) pork	荔枝肉片	lìzhīròupiàn
Salt-baked chicken	盐鸡	yánjī
White fungus and wolfberry soup (sweet)	枸杞炖银耳	gǒuqǐ dùnyín'ěr

DIM SUM

Dim sum	点心	diǎnxīn
Barbecued pork bun	叉烧包	chāshāo bāo
Crab and prawn dumpling	蟹肉虾饺	xièròu xiājiǎo
Custard tart	蛋挞	dàntà
Doughnut	炸面饼圈	zhá miànbǐngquān
Fried taro and mince dumpling	蕃薯糊饺	fānshǔ hújiǎo
Lotus paste bun	莲蓉糕	liánrónggāo
Moon cake (sweet bean paste in flaky pastry)	月饼	yuèbǐng
Paper-wrapped prawns	纸包虾	zhǐbāoxiā
Pork and prawn dumpling	烧麦	shāomài
Prawn crackers	虾片	xiāpiàn
Prawn dumpling	虾饺	xiājiǎo
Prawn paste on fried toast	芝麻虾	zhīmaxiā
Shanghai fried meat and vegetable dumpling ("potstickers")	锅贴	guōtiē
Spring roll spare ribs and chilli	春卷	chūnjuǎn
Steamed	排骨	páigǔ
Stuffed rice-flour roll	肠粉	chángfěn
Stuffed green peppers with black bean sauce	豆豉馅青椒	dòuchǐ xiànqīngjiāo
Sweet sesame balls	芝麻球	zhīma qiú
Turnip-paste patty	萝卜糕	luóbo gāo

FRUIT

| Fruit | 水果 | shuǐguǒ |
| Apple | 苹果 | píngguǒ |

Banana	香蕉	xiāngjiāo
Durian	榴莲	liúlián
Grape	葡萄	pútáo
Honeydew melon	哈密瓜	hāmì guā
Longan	龙眼	lóngyǎn
Lychee	荔枝	lìzhī
Mandarin orange	橘子	júzi
Mango	芒果	mángguǒ
Orange	橙子	chéngzi
Peach	桃子	táozi
Pear	梨	lí
Persimmon	柿子	shìzi
Plum	李子	lǐzi
Pomegranate	石榴	shíliu
Pomelo	柚子	yòuzi
Watermelon	西瓜	xīguā

Glossary

Arhat Buddhist saint.

Bei North.

Binguan Hotel; generally a large one, for tourists.

Bodhisattva A follower of Buddhism who has attained enlightenment, but has chosen to stay on earth to teach rather than enter nirvana; Buddhist god or goddess.

Boxers The name given to an anti-foreign organization which originated in Shandong in 1898 (see p.919 & p.96).

Chorten Tibetan stupa.

CITS China International Travel Service. Tourist organization primarily interested in selling tours, though they can help with obtaining train tickets.

CTS China Travel Service. Tourist organization similar to CITS.

Concession Part of a town or city ceded to a foreign power in the nineteenth century.

Cultural Revolution Ten-year period beginning in 1966 and characterized by destruction, persecution and fanatical devotion to Mao (see p.923).

Dagoba Another name for a stupa.

Dong East.

Dougong Large, carved wooden brackets, a common feature of temple design.

Fandian Restaurant or hotel.

Feng Peak.

Feng shui A system of geomancy used to determine the positioning of buildings.

Gang of Four Mao's widow and her supporters who were put on trial immediately after Mao's death for their role in the Cultural Revolution, for which they were convenient scapegoats.

Ge Pavilion.

Gong Palace; usually indicates a Taoist temple.

Guan Pass; in temple names, usually denotes a Taoist shrine.

Guanxi Literally "connections": the reciprocal favours inherent in the process of official appointments and transactions.

Guanyin The ubiquitous Buddhist Goddess of Mercy, the most popular Bodhisattva in China.

Gulou Drum tower; traditionally marking the centre of a town.

Guomindang (GMD) The Nationalist Peoples' Party. Under Chiang Kai-shek, the GMD fought Communist forces for 25 years before being defeated and moving to Taiwan in 1949, where it remains a major political party.

Hai Sea; in western China, also lake.

Han Chinese The main body of the Chinese people, as distinct from other ethnic groups such as Uyghur, Miao, Hui or Tibetan.

He River.

Hu Lake.

Hui Muslim minority, mainly based in Gansu and Ningxia. Visually they are often indistinguishable from Han Chinese.

Hutong A narrow alleyway.

I Ching The Book of Changes, an ancient handbook for divination that includes some of the fundamental concepts of Chinese thought, such as the duality *yin* and *yang*.

Inkstones Decoratively carved blocks traditionally used by artists and calligraphers as a palette for mixing ink powder with water.

Jiang River.

Jiao (or **mao**) A tenth of a yuan.

Jiaozi Crescent-shaped, ravioli-like dumpling, usually served fried by the plateful for breakfast.

Jie Street.

Kang A raised wooden platform in a Chinese home, heated by the stove, on which the residents eat and sleep.

Kazakh A minority, mostly nomadic, in Xinjiang.

Lamian "Pulled noodles", a Muslim speciality usually served in a spicy soup.

Legalism In the Chinese context, a belief that humans are intrinsically bad and that strict laws are need to rein in their behaviour.

Ling Tomb.

Little Red Book A selection of "Quotations from Chairman Mao Zedong", produced in 1966 as a philosophical treatise for Red Guards during the Cultural Revolution.

Long March The Communists' 9500km tactical retreat in 1934–35 from Guomindang troops.

Lu Street.

Luohan Buddhist disciple.

Mandala Mystic diagram which forms an important part of Buddhist iconography, especially in Tibet.

Mantou Steamed bread bun (literally "bald head").

Men Gate/door.

Miao Temple, usually Confucian.

Middle Kingdom A literal translation of the Chinese words for China.

Nan South.

PLA The People's Liberation Army.

PSB Public Security Bureau, the branch of China's police force which deals directly with foreigners.

Pagoda Tower with distinctively tapering structure, often associated with pseudo-science of *feng shui*.

Pinyin The official system of transliterating Chinese script into Roman characters.

Putonghua Mandarin Chinese; literally "Common Language".

Qianfodong Literally, "Thousand Buddha Cave", the name given to any Buddhist cave site along the Chinese section of the Silk Road.

Qiao Bridge.

RMB Renminbi. Another name for Chinese currency literally meaning "the people's money".

Red Guards The unruly factional forces unleashed by Mao during the Cultural Revolution to find and destroy brutally any "reactionaries" among the populace.

Renmin The people.

SEZ Special Economic Zone. A region in which state controls on production have been loosened and Western techniques of economic management are experimented with.

Sakyamuni Name given to future incarnation of Buddha.

Shan Mountain.

Shi City or municipality.

Shui Water.

Shuijiao Similar to *jiaozi* but boiled or served in a thin soup.

Si Temple, usually Buddhist.

Siheyuan Traditional courtyard house.

Spirit wall Wall behind the main gateway to a house, designed to thwart evil spirits, which, it was believed, could move only in straight lines.

Spirit Way The straight road leading to a tomb, lined with guardian figures.

Stele Freestanding stone tablet carved with text.

Stupa Multi-tiered tower associated with Buddhist temples that usually contains sacred objects.

Sutra Buddhist texts, often illustrative doctrines arranged in prayer form.

Ta Tower or pagoda.

Tian Heaven or the sky.

Taiping Uprising Peasant rebellion against Qing rule during the mid-nineteenth century.

Uyghur Substantial minority of Turkic people, living mainly in Xinjiang.

Waiguoren Foreigner.

Xi West.

Yuan China's unit of currency. Also a courtyard or garden (and the name of the Mongol dynasty).

Yurt Round, felt tent used by nomads. Also known as *ger*.

Zhan Station.

Zhao Temple; term used mainly in Inner Mongolia.

Zhong Middle; China is referred to as *zhongguo*, the Middle Kingdom.

Zhonglou Bell tower, usually twinned with a Gulou.

Zhou Place or region.

Small print and index

Rough Guide credits

Editors: David Leffman, Claire Saunders
Layout: Anita Singh
Cartography: Animesh Pathak
Picture editor: Tim Draper
Proofreaders: Jan McCann, Xiaosong Que
Managing editor: Keith Drew
Assistant editor: Dipika Dasgupta

Production: Charlotte Cade
Cover design: Sarah Stewart-Richardson, Anita Singh
Photographer: Tim Draper
Editorial assistant: Olivia Rawes
Senior pre-press designer: Dan May
Programme manager: Helen Blount
Publisher: Joanna Kirby

Publishing information

This seventh edition published June 2014 by
Rough Guides Ltd,
80 Strand, London WC2R 0RL
11, Community Centre, Panchsheel Park,
New Delhi 110017, India
Distributed by Penguin Random House
Penguin Books Ltd,
80 Strand, London WC2R 0RL
Penguin Group (USA)
345 Hudson Street, NY 10014, USA
Penguin Group (Australia)
250 Camberwell Road, Camberwell,
Victoria 3124, Australia
Penguin Group (NZ)
67 Apollo Drive, Mairangi Bay, Auckland 1310,
New Zealand
Penguin Group (South Africa)
Block D, Rosebank Office Park, 181 Jan Smuts Avenue,
Parktown North, Gauteng, South Africa 2193
Rough Guides is represented in Canada by Tourmaline
Editions Inc. 662 King Street West, Suite 304, Toronto,
Ontario M5V 1M7
Printed in Malaysia by Vivar Printing Sdn.Bhd.

© Rough Guides, 2014
Maps © Rough Guides
No part of this book may be reproduced in any form
without permission from the publisher except for the
quotation of brief passages in reviews.
992pp includes index
A catalogue record for this book is available from the
British Library
ISBN: 978-1-40934-181-9
The publishers and authors have done their best to
ensure the accuracy and currency of all the information
in **The Rough Guide to China**, however, they can accept
no responsibility for any loss, injury, or inconvenience
sustained by any traveller as a result of information or
advice contained in the guide.
1 3 5 7 9 8 6 4 2

Help us update

We've gone to a lot of effort to ensure that the seventh
edition of **The Rough Guide to China** is accurate and up-
to-date. However, things change – places get "discovered",
opening hours are notoriously fickle, restaurants and
rooms raise prices or lower standards. If you feel we've got
it wrong or left something out, we'd like to know, and if
you can remember the address, the price, the hours, the
phone number, so much the better.

Please send your comments with the subject line
"Rough Guide China Update" to ✉ mail@uk.roughguides
.com. We'll credit all contributions and send a copy of the
next edition (or any other Rough Guide if you prefer) for
the very best emails.

Find more travel information, connect with fellow
travellers and plan your trip on ⓦ roughguides.com

Readers' updates

Thanks to all the readers who have taken the time to write in with comments and suggestions (and apologies if we've
inadvertently omitted or misspelt anyone's name):

Allan Dreyer Andersen; Mark & Lynn Davis; Erin Henshaw;
Jendra Jarnagin; Joanne Opthof; Joan Redemer;

Steinar Saethre.

Acknowledgements

Simon Foster: Thanks to Steven Huang; Judy Wang; Rose Xiaomo; Christine, Tot, Sasha & Molly.

Jo James: In the field, my thanks go to Ablikim in Khotan, Evan and Loja in Xiahe, the Apudis and their teapot at Lake Karakul, Weili and his truck in Kashgar, Wumarjan in Chechen, and the bus drivers of Northwest China. Behind the scenes, many thanks to Olga and David; and to Jerry, with love wherever I am.

David Leffman: Special thanks to Narrell, James Lucas, CS Tang, Olga, Anthony Liu, Osmond Lam, Samuel, Phillip, Pete Spurrier and all who fed, watered, punched and otherwise kept me busy in Hong Kong.

Simon Lewis would like to thank Kat, Mayguli, Zoe, Mark, Chris, Xiao Song, Xiao Shan, Wang Bin and Du.

Mark South: Family South, David L, Simon L, Martin Z, Hsuan-Fen, Sarah, Chih Hsing, Ravia, Nikki, Siobhan, David Niven, Andy Jones, George and all at BRC.

Charles Young: Thanks to Simon, Keith and David at RG, Al, Gina, Geoff and Janice in HK, and Qing Qing in China.

Martin Zatko: I would like to thank Jee Young Lee for being a great travel partner for much of his time in China, and for getting over a baptism of fire (theft of brand-new phone on first day; being attacked by a falling glass case three days later) in an admirable manner. Thanks, too, to Eivind Hestetun Thomassen for all of his help in Beijing: font of knowledge, supplier of snus, occasional taxi service and fun drinking buddy, all in one. Honourable mentions also for the Harmony, Tian Yuan Kui and Jing's Residence teams in Pingyao; Pru Goudie at On The Go Tours for welcome assistance with accommodation; and the excellent chefs, and friendly waitresses, at literally hundreds of restaurants across the land.

The editor would like to thank Keith for guidance, Katie and the cartography team for great maps, Tim Draper for photo selection and Anita for typesetting. Not forgetting a big thank you to all the authors for packing so much research into such a tight bundle, and to Andrew Commins, for his help in Beijing.

Photo credits

All photos © Rough Guides except the following:
(Key: a-above; b-below/bottom; c-centre; f-far; l-left; r-right; t-top)

p.1 Getty Images: Bobi
p.2 123RF.com: 吕 九一
p.4 Corbis: Phil Borges
p.5 Getty Images: Coolbiere (t); Keren Su (b)
p.9 Corbis: Qilai Shen (t). Getty Images: Maremagnum (bl, br)
p.11 Getty Images: Blackstation (t). Corbis: Mark Alberhasky (c); Christian Kober (b)
p.13 Getty Images: Celso Mollo Photography (t)
p.14 123RF.com: Wang Yimin
p.15 Corbis: Keren Su (t). Getty Images: EIGHTFISH (b)
p.16 Corbis: Yi Lu (b)
p.17 Corbis: Imaginechina (t). Alamy: Henry Westheim (b)
p.18 Corbis: Keith Levit (t). Alamy: Victor Paul Borg (b)
p.19 Alamy: DBA Images (t). Corbis: Liu Liqun (c); Keren Su (b)
p.20 Corbis: Franck Guiziou (t); Barbara Walton (c). Getty Images: Shiwei (b)
p.21 Corbis: Keren Su (t); Liu Xu (b)
p.22 Corbis: Wang Miao (tl). Alamy: Hu Zhao (tr)
p.23 Corbis: Diego Azubel (t). Alamy: Henry Westheim (b)
p.24 Corbis: Bruno Morandi (t). Alamy: Robert Preston (b)
p.25 Getty Images: Tom Bonaventure (t). Corbis: Mike Kemp (c). Alamy: FLPA (b)
p.26 Getty Images: Alex Linghorn (t). Corbis: Jose Fuste Raga (b)
p.27 Corbis: Gardel Bertrand (t). 123RF.com: santorini (b)
p.28 Corbis: George Steinmetz (tl). Getty Images: Billy Hustace (tr)
p.30 Getty Images: Image Source
p.63 Corbis: Gavin Hellier
p.77 Corbis: Mike Kemp (t)
p.130 Corbis: Franck Guiziou
p.133 Getty Images: Keren Su
p.147 Getty Images: RedChopsticks (t). Alamy: Henry Westheim (b)
p.156 Getty Images: Keren Su
p.159 Getty Images: Keren Su
p.175 Getty Images: Peter Parks (t). Corbis: Yu Chu Di (b)
p.190 123RF.com: Nastya Tepikina
p.193 Corbis: Li Xin
p.211 Corbis: Michael Runkel
p.249 Alamy: Mike Abrahams (t). 123RF.com: yucelunal (b)

p.276 Getty Images: Keren Su
p.279 Getty Images: Keren Su
p.309 Getty Images: Tim Robberts
p.323 Getty Images: Ian Trower (t). Alamy: Henry Westheim (b)
p.344 Getty Images: Scott E Barbour
p.347 Corbis: Yang Liu
p.367 UrbanEye (t). Alamy: TAO Images (b)
p.388 Corbis: Du Huaju
p.391 Alamy: dbimages
p.409 Corbis: Adam Jones
p.427 Getty Images: Christian Kober (t); Yann Layma (b)
p.452 Getty Images: Jess Yu
p.455 Alamy: Brian Yarvin
p.475 Alamy: dbimages (t, b)
p.505 Corbis: Ryan Pyle (t). Getty Images: Paul Todd (b)
p.557 Alamy: Lyndon Giffard Images
p.575 Corbis: Steven Vidler (t)
p.590 Corbis: Bruno Morandi (b)
p.593 Corbis: Martin Puddy
p.623 Alamy: John Warburton-Lee (t). Corbis: Keren Su (b)
p.640 Corbis: Keren Su
p.643 123RF.com: silverjohn
p.653 Getty Images: Wx Photography (t); Romana Chapman (b)
p.669 Alamy: age fotostock
p.687 Alamy: Henry Westheim (t); John Henshall (b)
p.708 Corbis: Chen dsb
p.711 Getty Images: Christian Kober
p.727 Alamy: Ville Palonen (t); amana images (b)
p.747 Getty Images: Peter Adams
p.770 Getty Images: Fuste Raga
p.773 Getty Images: Frank Lukasseck
p.799 Getty Images: Reinhard Krause (t); George Steinmetz (b)
p.831 Corbis: Christian Kober
p.852 Corbis: Michael Runkel
p.855 Corbis: Kent Kobersteen
p.875 Getty Images: Lan Yin
p.910 Corbis: Hou Deqiang

Front cover Corbis: Joel Santos/Aurora Photos
Back cover Getty Images: Alan Copson (t); Rough Guides: Tim Draper (cl) (cr)

Index

Maps are marked in **grey**

The following abbreviations are used throughout this index:

AH Anhui	**HEB** Hebei	**QH** Qinghai
BJ Beijing	**HEN** Henan	**SAX** Shaanxi
CQ Chongqing	**HN** Hainan	**SC** Sichuan
DB Dongbei	**HUB** Hubei	**SD** Shandong
FJ Fujian	**HUN** Hunan	**SX** Shanxi
GD Guangdong	**IM** Inner Mongolia	**T** Tibet
GS Gansu	**JS** Jiangsu	**XJ** Xinjiang
GX Guangxi	**JX** Jiangxi	**YN** Yunnan
GZ Guizhou	**NX** Ningxia	**ZJ** Zhejiang

N

M

O

Z

Map symbols

The symbols below are used on maps throughout the book

✈ Airport	E Embassy	⋀⋁ Spring/spa	Tower
★ Bus stop	⊠ Gate	Swimming/pool	Museum
Ⓜ Metro station	♦ Place of interest	Border crossing	⌒ Arch
Ⓢ Subway	∴ Ruin	Swamp	Building
Ⓖ Beijing subway	Golf course	Bridge	Church (town maps)
Ⓜ MTR station	⊙ Statue	▲ Mountain peak	Stadium
Ⓐ Bus station/depot	Mosque	Mountain range	Beach
Ⓒ Telephone office	Chinese temple	Mountain pass	Park
@ Internet café/access	Dagoba	Viewpoint	Pine tree
ⓘ Information office	Pagoda	Ski area	Cemetery
✚ Hospital	Gardens	Cave	Cable car
✉ Post office	Waterfall	● Sinkhole	

Listings key

- ■ Accommodation
- ● Eating & drinking
- ■ Bar/club/nightlife
- ● Shop

A ROUGH GUIDE TO
ROUGH GUIDES

Published in 1982, the first Rough Guide – to Greece – was a student scheme that became a publishing phenomenon. Mark Ellingham, a recent graduate in English from Bristol University, had been travelling in Greece the previous summer and couldn't find the right guidebook. With a small group of friends he wrote his own guide, combining a highly contemporary, journalistic style with a thoroughly practical approach to travellers' needs.

The immediate success of the book spawned a series that rapidly covered dozens of destinations. And, in addition to impecunious backpackers, Rough Guides soon acquired a much broader and older readership that relished the guides' wit and inquisitiveness as much as their enthusiastic, critical approach and value-for-money ethos.

These days, Rough Guides feature recommendations from shoestring to luxury and cover more than 200 destinations around the globe. Our ever-growing team of authors and photographers is spread all over the world, particularly in Europe, the US and Australia.

Rough Guides now number around 200 titles, including Pocket city guides, inspirational coffee-table books and comprehensive country and regional titles, plus technology guides from iPods to Android. As well as print books, we publish groundbreaking apps and eBooks for every major digital device.

Visit Ⓦ roughguides.com to see our latest publications.

Rough Guide travel images are available for commercial licensing at Ⓦ roughguidespictures.com.

Discover China

Uncover the beauty and contrast of China with On The Go Tours

A World Of Discovery

As an award-winning adventure tour operator, On The Go Tours specialises in group tours and tailor-made holidays to far-flung destinations around the world. Come discover China with us!

✔ GROUP TOURS
✔ TAILOR-MADE HOLIDAYS
✔ FAMILY ADVENTURES
✔ YANGTZE RIVER CRUISES
✔ LOCAL FESTIVALS & EVENTS

020 7371 1113
ONTHEGOTOURS.COM

AiTO Assured

ABTA The Travel Association